HARLEM RENAISSANCE

A Gale Critical Companion

HARLEM RENAISSANCE

A Gale Critical Companion

Volume 3: Authors I-Z

Foreword by *Trudier Harris-Lopez, Ph.D.*
University of North Carolina at Chapel Hill

Janet Witalec, *Project Editor*

Detroit • New York • San Diego • San Francisco • Cleveland • New Haven, Conn. • Waterville, Maine • London • Munich

Harlem Renaissance, Vol. 3

Project Editor
Janet Witalec

Editorial
Tom Burns, Kathy D. Darrow, Lisa Gellert, Madeline S. Harris, Edna M. Hedblad, Michelle Kazensky, Jelena Krstović, Allison Marion, Ellen McGeagh, Jessica Menzo, Thomas J. Schoenberg, Lawrence J. Trudeau, Russel Whitaker

Research
Nicodemus Ford, Sarah Genik, Tamara C. Nott, Tracie A. Richardson

Permissions
Kim Davis, Susan Rudolph

Imaging and Multimedia
Leitha Etheridge-Sims, Lezlie Light, Christine O'Bryan, Kelly A. Quin

Product Design
Pamela Galbreath, Michael Logusz

Composition and Electronic Capture
Carolyn Roney

Manufacturing
Stacy L. Melson

For more information, contact
The Gale Group, Inc.
27500 Drake Rd.
Farmington Hills, MI 48331-3535
Or you can visit our internet site at
http://www.gale.com

LIBRARY OF CONGRESS CATALOGING-IN-PUBLICATION DATA

The Harlem Renaissance : a Gale critical companion / Janet Witalec, project editor.
p. cm. -- (Gale critical companion collection)
Includes bibliographical references and index.
ISBN 0-7876-6618-1 (set hardcover) -- ISBN 0-7876-6619-X (v. 1) --
ISBN 0-7876-6620-3 (v. 2) -- ISBN 0-7876-6621-1 (v. 3)
1. American literature--African American authors--History and criticism--Handbooks, manuals, etc. 2. American literature--New York (State)--New York--History and criticism--Handbooks, manuals, etc. 3. American literature--20th century--History and criticism--Handbooks, manuals, etc. 4. Harlem (New York, N.Y.)--Intellectual life--20th century--Handbooks, manuals, etc. 5. African Americans--Intellectual life--Handbooks, manuals, etc. 6. African Americans in literature--Handbooks, manuals, etc. 7. Harlem Renaissance--Handbooks, manuals, etc. I. Witalec, Janet, 1965- II. Series.
PS153.N5 H245 2003
810.9'89607307471--dc21

2002010076

Printed in the United States of America
10 9 8 7 6 5 4 3

CONTENTS

VOLUME 2

VOLUME 3

FOREWORD

In 1950, Alain Locke offered several reflective comments on the significance of the Harlem Renaissance. He considered it a movement that never surpassed the "gawky" and "pimply" stage of adolescence, one that had essentially failed in its attempt to achieve universal, objective approaches in its creations. Overall, he concluded that perhaps he and others had "expected too much of the Negro Renaissance" (*Phylon* 11 : 391). Locke, who had been one of the key supporters of and inspirational figures in the lives of several of the writers who came to prominence during that period, was perhaps more critical of what the movement had achieved than his contemporaries during the Renaissance or in the 1950s. He was certainly more disparaging than literary evaluations have proven to be in the past five decades. The period of the1920s has become one of the most written about in African American literary history and one in which numerous scholars specialize. And not undeservedly so. By most standards of measurement, especially ones that might take into consideration a before and after effect, the Harlem Renaissance, or the New Negro Movement as some prefer to call it, is arguably *the* defining moment in African American literary creativity.

That moment occurred because of the confluence of historical and social forces. The devastation the boll weevil wrought on southern crops and the ensuing economic chaos led many Blacks to migrate from the South to northern cities as a part of what became known as the Great Migration, a mass movement that noted artist Jacob Lawrence captures vividly and colorfully in his Migration Series. Economic opportunity the North represented was appealing not only because of the decline in the southern farm economy but because the mythical presentations by relatives of Black people who had migrated north made it equally glamorous. The legendary promise of the North and particularly New York City, as Rudolph Fisher depicts in "The City of Refuge" (1925) and about which Langston Hughes rhapsodizes in several poems as well as his autobiographies, drew Black people from the southern United States, the Caribbean, and Africa. Harlem thus more than tripled its Black population between 1900 and 1930. Word of mouth was powerful, but determined efforts to gather a critical mass of young Black creative artists were also factors in bringing about the literary production known as the Harlem Renaissance. Charles Spurgeon Johnson, who became editor of *Opportunity,* the official organ of the National Urban League, directed his secretary, Ethel Nance, to write to aspiring young writers and artists and encourage their migration to New York. While many responded eagerly, it was only with repeated coaxing that Aaron Douglas, who became the foremost artist of the period, was persuaded to leave his position as an art teacher in Kansas and head to

New York. Of the writers who are now prominently identified with the movement, Hughes came from Kansas and Ohio, Zora Neale Hurston from Florida, Wallace Thurman from Idaho, Claude McKay from Jamaica, Eric Walrond from British Guiana, Jean Toomer from Washington, D.C., Dorothy West from Boston, and Countee Cullen from Kentucky (although he always claimed New York as his point of origin).

From its beginnings, therefore, the Harlem Renaissance was spawned by a mixture of happenstance and deliberate planning. This was the first time in African American literary history that editors and writers saw the possibilities of collaborative creative efforts—or at least creative efforts expended in the midst of others who were also about literary production. Such concerted effort distinguished the 1920s from what had gone before, distinguished the New Negro with a self-directed cultural purpose from the Old Negro who was often driven by circumstance. Awareness of themselves as artists in a variety of media was one of the distinguishing characteristics of the editors, writers, visual artists, and musicians who became the most well-known figures of the Harlem Renaissance and about whom Hughes wrote in his first autobiography, *The Big Sea* (1940), and whom Thurman fictionalized in *Infants of the Spring* (1932).

The movement thus marks the period in African American literary development during which Black writers could *claim* their creativity in ways that were not previously available to them. The tradition of slave—or *freedom*—narratives was the most productive group effort prior to the Harlem Renaissance (the grouping, however, was not something the writers themselves orchestrated); the productivity was frequently cast in a white envelope/Black message mold. Abolitionists and other persons who identified potential writers as well as those who published their works often had their own agendas for what Black narrators could or should put forth in their own so-called individualized works. Black writers did not control the means of production of their words or the editorial prerogatives that sometimes shaped their final form. Black literary dependency on white cultural philanthropy was the order of the day. While it would be rash to suggest that such limitations completely disappeared during the 1920s, it is nonetheless reasonable to argue that persons of African descent had a stronger say in what they published, where, and under what circumstances. Of course we are familiar with the stories of how Carl Van Vechten, guru and midwife extraordinaire of the Renaissance, read, revised, and suggested further revisions to *The Weary Blues* (1926), Hughes's first volume of poetry. And the tales of Mrs. Charlotte Osgood Mason's attempts to interfere in the creativity of Hughes and Hurston are equally well known. More to the point, however, are the instances in which African American writers were mostly in charge of what they produced and the manner of its production.

Two significant outlets for "in charge" production were *Opportunity* magazine and its counterpart, the *Crisis,* the official publication of the National Association for the Advancement of Colored People (NAACP). The latter was developed by the eminent W. E. B. Du Bois, who served as general editor; Jessie Fauset served as literary editor, a position from which she would encourage many of the younger writers. For these two publications, Black writers did not go, hat in hand, to white editors requesting publication of their work. As African Americans, both Charles S. Johnson and Du Bois were acutely aware of the need for as much African American control of publishing outlets as possible. This position, combined with their general notions of mission and service, led both editors to sponsor contests to encourage Black writing even as they regularly published what came to them voluntarily. By establishing the outlets for publication, determining the criteria, and passing judgment on the works, these editors and their staffs moved dramatically away from the censorship that had defined cross-racial publication by writers such as Paul Laurence Dunbar and Charles W. Chesnutt prior to this period. Again, an assessment of the Harlem Renaissance in this area is not to suggest that all was sweetness and light, for both Johnson and Du Bois had rather specific notions of what they believed should be published. The point is that African Americans, whatever their criteria, were making the decisions that they had not previously made except for newspapers, white-owned/Black-edited small magazines (*Voice of the Negro*), and denominational outlets (the *Christian Recorder,* the *A.M.E. Church Review*).

The claiming of creativity was even history-making in the anthologies that appeared during this period. Two of the most important were *The Book of American Negro Poetry,* edited and published by James Weldon Johnson in 1922, and *The New Negro,* edited and published by Alain Locke in 1925 (expanded from a special issue of *Survey Graphic*). Black writers had appeared in yearbooks such as William Stanley Braithwaite's *Anthology of Magazine Verse* (beginning in 1913), but Johnson's and Locke's were volumes devoted almost exclusively to African American writers. Johnson was careful to include as many up-and-coming poets as he could locate, and he expanded his original inclusions when the volume was revised and republished in 1931. Locke's volume, of course, served as the defining statement for the Renaissance, just as Hughes's "The Negro Artist and the Racial Mountain" (1926) served as the defining manifesto for younger Black writers. Locke wanted to assure his readers that the Old Negro was dead, that this was an age of unparalleled creativity by African American writers. While it has become clear that Locke, even in his seeming expansiveness, gave preferential treatment to certain kinds of writers and subjects, it is nonetheless more significant that he was doing the choosing, that an African American scholar, researcher, and writer was in charge of shaping a volume that showcased the richness of African American cultural creativity. The bountifulness of that creativity could not be constrained by the mind that offered it for public consumption. Thus the legacy of the Renaissance was measurable from even that single volume of claimed creativity.

An even more proper appreciation of the claiming of African American creativity during the Harlem Renaissance might begin in the middle of the 1920s, with the publication of the little magazine called *Fire!!* (1926). The work of Hughes, Hurston, Thurman, Richard Bruce Nugent, Gwendolyn Bennett, and a few others, it represented the efforts of younger African American writers to claim their creativity from their elders, all members of Du Bois's "talented tenth" of well-educated Blacks with leadership potential (and often "high yaller"), as well as from potential white exploiters. *Fire!!* was in bas relief against the backdrop of prevailing elder wisdom represented by the likes of Du Bois, James Weldon Johnson, and Braithwaite, all of whom espoused best-foot-forward, universalized portrayals of Black experience that could serve to bridge the gaps between Blacks and whites. *Fire!!* represented the first time a group of young African American writers consciously sought to define themselves against a larger tradition, which means that it was the first time that there were measurable *layerings* of African American literary creativity. When Nugent and Thurman flipped a coin to see who would write a story on prostitution and who on drugs, they were claiming their creativity as young writers breaking away from their elders: "If black people are pleased, it doesn't matter."

The fact that *Fire!!* exists would be reason enough to label the 1920s a noteworthy period of African American creativity. Here were several young Black writers bent upon cultural production at a time when it was not yet historically established that they indeed had a culture. That independence of spirit is no less remarkable than that exhibited by Frederick Douglass and others who escaped from slavery in the South and went on to produce narratives about their experiences. The difference is one of orchestration, not one of kind. Whereas Douglass was manipulated—though his genius nonetheless showed through that manipulation—these young writers made their own decisions about who and what to publish. They may have failed to sustain the magazine, but what they sought to accomplish is the guiding motivation for scholarly focus on the Harlem Renaissance: the documentation of African American creative genius as widespread, diverse, and ever evolving.

A careful look at Johnson's *Book of Negro Poetry* will reveal that several of the figures Johnson singled out for greatness did not make it. Of those who did, Countee Cullen, Langston Hughes, and Claude McKay have garnered critical attention worthy of their talent, and that attention continues. In 2002, when the Academy of American Poets conducted a survey to determine who was the most well-known American poet, Langston Hughes won by a landslide. It would have been difficult in the 1920s, however, for literary observers to conclude that Hughes's reputation would exceed Cullen's, for Cullen was the darling of critics and critical readers. His imitation of Keatsian poetic forms undoubtedly informed those judgments, whereas Hughes's focus on the Black masses was a bit more to the left than some elitists in the "talented tenth" tradition might have wished. Ensuing decades, especially the Black-centered 1960s, coupled with Hughes's own longevity and interaction with later writers, probably influenced ultimate scholarly and popular preference for Hughes.

Hughes and McKay, whose strong emotional sentiments overshadowed his Shakespearean sonnets, make clear the importance of audience as an ongoing, shaping force in Harlem Renaissance successes. The increase in Black audiences during the 1920s, which found their parallels in the 1960s, spurred acceptance by some of sentiments that were slightly more militant than many of Cullen's sugar-coated creations. Publication in outlets aimed primarily at Black people during the 1920s was a marked contrast to the outlets in which Dunbar and Chesnutt had published their early works, such as the *Atlantic Monthly*. Talented poets such as Hughes and McKay, along with a host of other writers during the 1920s, thus facilitated the institutionalization of African American literary arts within Black communities.

The anthologies, volumes of poetry, novels, dramas, and newspaper columns that the Harlem Renaissance has yielded make the claim more than anything else for the period having been substantive and of greater import than Locke allowed. We can certainly measure individual accomplishment, as with Hughes's focus on the blues as a source for literary creativity in *The Weary Blues,* or Jean Toomer's experimentation in *Cane* (1923), or Hurston's concern with colorphobia in *Color Struck* (1926). Of greater import is the stage-setting or path-breaking that these accomplishments pointed toward. *Fire!!* easily leads to *Black World/Negro Digest* and on to *Callaloo. Cane* anticipates works such as Ntozake Shange's *Sassafras, Cypress and Indigo* (1982), Alice Walker's *The Color Purple* (1982), and practically all of Toni Morrison's novels. Hurston is godmother to a host of African American women writers, including Walker, Tina McElroy Ansa, and Gloria Naylor. Thus institution-building and midwifing a literary tradition were functions Harlem Renaissance writers served for ensuing generations as assuredly as Alain Locke and Jessie Fauset midwifed them.

Godmothering, however, is not always altruistic, as was the case with Mrs. Mason's impact on Hurston as well as on Hughes. The issue of patronage for African American writers remains a central concern in the twenty-first century. What does a writer owe to the providers of fellowships and leisure time to write? At what point does a writer who receives such aid give up his or her autonomy to his or her work? The issue is relevant not only to isolated writers trying to find the funds for a semester's leave from teaching, but also to the choreographer or the dramatist or the musician whose creative space can be provided by funders who may or may not be sympathetic to the total direction of the project. The Harlem Renaissance gave us models for thinking through these crucial issues and for weighing the shackles as well as the opportunities of patronage across racial lines. That continues to be a source of exploration in contemporary scholars' understanding of the factors that influenced how successful some of the most important writers of the Harlem Renaissance were —or were not—in claiming their creativity.

In the early years of the twenty-first century, the Harlem Renaissance is a scholarly industry. It became institutionalized with the advent of Black studies courses and programs in American academies in the 1960s and 1970s. No scholar of African American literary studies could be taken seriously without in-depth knowledge of the Harlem Renaissance. No doctoral candidate studying for written and oral examinations could expect to be taken seriously without detailed knowledge of the Harlem Renaissance. In contrast to the 1960s, when a single survey course might have sufficed to introduce students to African American literature, today there are two and three courses designed to provide that coverage. Specialized courses focusing exclusively on the Harlem Renaissance are offered routinely. Equally as significant, graduate students in African American literary studies remain engrossed enough by the Renaissance to select writers and topics relevant to it for the subjects of their masters theses and doctoral dissertations. Their interest, in turn, has been guided in large part by the numerous scholarly studies of the Harlem Renaissance that have been published in the past thirty years. In striking contrast to Alain Locke's assessment, the Harlem Renaissance is alive and well in every college and university in the United States where students explore the multi-faceted meanings and ramifications of the literature, its producers, and its production. These three volumes are welcome additions to those ongoing dialogues and will undoubtedly provide invaluable insights that will continue to illustrate the undying significance of the Harlem Renaissance.

—Trudier Harris-Lopez, Ph.D.
J. Carlyle Sitterson Professor of English
University of North Carolina at Chapel Hill

The Gale Critical Companion Collection

In response to a growing demand for relevant criticism and interpretation of perennial topics and important literary movements throughout history, the Gale Critical Companion Collection (GCCC) was designed to meet the research needs of upper high school and undergraduate students. Each edition of GCCC focuses on a different literary movement or topic of broad interest to students of literature, history, multicultural studies, humanities, foreign language studies, and other subject areas. Topics covered are based on feedback from a standing advisory board consisting of reference librarians and subject specialists from public, academic, and school library systems.

The GCCC is designed to complement Gale's existing Literary Criticism Series (LCS) , which includes such award-winning and distinguished titles as *Nineteenth-Century Literature Criticism* (NCLC), *Twentieth-Century Literary Criticism* (TCLC), and *Contemporary Literary Criticism* (CLC). Like the LCS titles, the GCCC editions provide selected reprinted essays that offer an inclusive range of critical and scholarly response to authors and topics widely studied in high school and undergraduate classes; however, the GCCC also includes primary source documents, chronologies, sidebars, supplemental photographs, and other material not included in the LCS products. The graphic and supplemental material is designed to extend the usefulness of the critical essays and provide students with historical and cultural context on a topic or author's work. GCCC titles will benefit larger institutions with ongoing subscriptions to Gale's LCS products as well as smaller libraries and school systems with less extensive reference collections. Each edition of the GCCC is created as a stand- alone set providing a wealth of information on the topic or movement. Importantly, the overlap between the GCCC and LCS titles is 15% or less, ensuring that LCS subscribers will not duplicate resources in their collection.

Editions within the GCCC are either single-volume or multi-volume sets, depending on the nature and scope of the topic being covered. Topic entries and author entries are treated separately, with entries on related topics appearing first, followed by author entries in an A-Z arrangement. Each volume is approximately 500 pages in length and includes approximately 50 images and sidebar graphics. These sidebars include summaries of important historical events, newspaper clippings, brief biographies of important non-literary figures, complete poems or passages of fiction written by the author, descriptions of events in the related arts (music, visual arts, and dance), and so on.

The reprinted essays in each GCCC edition explicate the major themes and literary techniques of the authors and literary works. It is important to note that approximately 85% of the essays reprinted in GCCC editions are full-text, meaning that they are reprinted in their entirety, including footnotes and lists of abbreviations. Essays are selected based on their coverage of the seminal works and themes of an author, and based on the importance of those essays to an appreciation of the author's contribution to the movement and to literature in general. Gale's editors select those essays of most value to upper high school and undergraduate students, avoiding narrow and highly pedantic interpretations of individual works or of an author's canon.

Scope of Harlem Renaissance

Harlem Renaissance, the inaugural set in the Gale Critical Companion Collection, consists of three volumes. Each volume includes a detailed table of contents, a foreword on the Harlem Renaissance written by noted scholar Trudier Harris-Lopez, and a descriptive chronology of key events of the movement. The main body of volume 1 consists of entries on five topics relevant to the Harlem Renaissance, including 1) Overviews and General Studies; 2) Social, Economic, and Political Factors that Influenced the Harlem Renaissance; 3) Publishing and Periodicals during the Harlem Renaissance; 4) Performing Arts during the Harlem Renaissance; and 5) Visual Arts during the Harlem Renaissance. Volumes 2 and 3 include entries on thirty-three authors and literary figures associated with the movement, including such notables as Countee Cullen, W. E. B. Du Bois, Jessie Redmon Fauset, Langston Hughes, Zora Neale Hurston, Claude McKay, and Jean Toomer, as well as entries on individuals who have garnered less attention, but whose contributions to the Harlem Renaissance are noteworthy, such as Alice Dunbar-Nelson, Angelina Weld Grimké, Georgia Douglas Johnson, Richard Bruce Nugent, and Willis Richardson.

Organization of the Harlem Renaissance

A *Harlem Renaissance* topic entry consists of the following elements:

- The **Introduction** defines the subject of the entry and provides social and historical information important to understanding the criticism.
- The list of **Representative Works** identifies writings and works by authors and figures associated with the subject. The list is divided into alphabetical sections by name; works listed under each name appear in chronological order. The genre and publication date of each work is given. Unless otherwise indicated, dramas are dated by first performance, not first publication.
- Entries generally begin with a section of **Primary Sources,** which includes essays, speeches, social history, newspaper accounts and other materials that were produced during the time of the Harlem Renaissance.
- Reprinted **Criticism** in topic entries is arranged thematically. Topic entries commonly begin with general surveys of the subject or essays providing historical or background information, followed by essays that develop particular aspects of the topic. For example, the Publishing and Periodicals topic entry in volume 1 of *Harlem Renaissance* begins with a section providing an overview of the topic. This is followed by three other sections: African American Writers and Mainstream Publishers; Anthologies: *The New Negro* and Others; and African American Periodicals and the Harlem Renaissance. Each section has a separate title heading and is identified with a page number in the table of contents. The critic's name and the date of composition or publication of the critical work are given at the beginning of each piece of criticism. Unsigned criticism is preceded by the title of the source in which it appeared. Footnotes are reprinted at the end of each essay or excerpt. In the case of excerpted criticism, only those footnotes that pertain to the excerpted texts are included.
- A complete **Bibliographical Citation** of the original essay or book precedes each piece of criticism.
- Critical essays are prefaced by brief **Annotations** explicating each piece. Unless the descriptor "excerpt" is used in the annotation, the essay is being reprinted in its entirety.
- An annotated bibliography of **Further Reading** appears at the end of each entry and suggests resources for additional study. In some cases, significant essays for which the editors could not obtain reprint rights are included here.

A *Harlem Renaissance* author entry consists of the following elements:

- The **Author Heading** cites the name under which the author most commonly wrote, followed by birth and death dates. Also located here are any name variations under which an author wrote. If the author wrote consistently under a pseudonym, the pseudonym will be listed in the author heading and the author's actual name given in parentheses on the first line of the biographical and critical information. Uncertain birth or death dates are indicated by question marks.

- A **Portrait of the Author** is included when available.
- The **Introduction** contains background information that introduces the reader to the author that is the subject of the entry.
- The list of **Principal Works** is ordered chronologically by date of first publication and lists the most important works by the author. The genre and publication date of each work is given. Unless otherwise indicated, dramas are dated by first performance, not first publication.
- Author entries are arranged into three sections: **Primary Sources, General Commentary**, and **Title Commentary.** The Primary Sources section includes letters, poems, short stories, journal entries, and essays written by the featured author. General Commentary includes overviews of the author's career and general studies; Title Commentary includes in-depth analyses of seminal works by the author. Within the Title Commentary section, the reprinted criticism is further organized by title, then by date of publication. The critic's name and the date of composition or publication of the critical work are given at the beginning of each piece of criticism. Unsigned criticism is preceded by the title of the source in which it appeared. All titles by the author featured in the text are printed in boldface type. However, not all boldfaced titles are included in the author and subject indexes; only substantial discussions of works are indexed. Footnotes are reprinted at the end of each essay or excerpt. In the case of excerpted criticism, only those footnotes that pertain to the excerpted texts are included.
- A complete **Bibliographical Citation** of the original essay or book precedes each piece of criticism.
- Critical essays are prefaced by brief **Annotations** explicating each piece. Unless the descriptor "excerpt" is used in the annotation, the essay is being reprinted in its entirety.
- An annotated bibliography of **Further Reading** appears at the end of each entry and suggests resources for additional study. In some cases, significant essays for which the editors could not obtain reprint rights are included here. A list of **Other Sources from Gale** follows the further reading section and provides references to other biographical and critical sources on the author in series published by Gale.

Indexes

The **Author Index** lists all of the authors featured in the *Harlem Renaissance* set, with references to the main author entries in volumes 2 and 3 as well as commentary on the featured author in other author entries and in the topic volume. Page references to substantial discussions of the authors appear in boldface. The Author Index also includes birth and death dates and cross references between pseudonyms and actual names, and cross references to other Gale series in which the authors have appeared. A complete list of these sources is found facing the first page of the Author Index.

The **Title Index** alphabetically lists the titles of works written by the authors featured in volumes 2 and 3 and provides page numbers or page ranges where commentary on these titles can be found. Page references to substantial discussions of the titles appear in boldface. English translations of foreign titles and variations of titles are cross-referenced to the title under which a work was originally published. Titles of novels, dramas, nonfiction books, and poetry, short story, or essay collections are printed in italics, while individual poems, short stories, and essays are printed in body type within quotation marks.

The **Subject Index** includes the authors and titles that appear in the Author Index and the Title Index as well as the names of other authors and figures that are discussed in the set. The Subject Index also lists hundreds of literary terms and topics covered in the criticism. The index provides page numbers or page ranges where subjects are discussed and is fully cross referenced.

Citing Harlem Renaissance

When writing papers, students who quote directly from the *Harlem Renaissance* set may use the following general format to footnote reprinted criticism. The first example pertains to material drawn from periodicals, the second to material reprinted from books.

> Alvarez, Joseph A., "The Lonesome Boy Theme as Emblem for Arna Bontemps's Children's Literature," *African American Review* 32, no. 1 (spring 1998): 23-31; reprinted in *Harlem Renaissance: A Gale Critical Companion,* vol. 2, ed. Janet Witalec (Farmington Hills, Mich: The Gale Group, 2003), 72-8.

> Helbling, Mark, introduction to *The Harlem Renaissance: The One and the Many* (Westport, Conn.: Greenwood Press, 1999), 1-18; reprinted in *Harlem Renaissance: A Gale Critical Companion,* vol. 1, ed. Janet Witalec (Farmington Hills, Mich: The Gale Group, 2003), 27-38.

Harlem Renaissance *Advisory Board*

The members of the *Harlem Renaissance* Advisory Board—reference librarians and subject specialists from public, academic, and school library systems—offered a variety of informed perspectives on both the presentation and content of the *Harlem Renaissance* set. Advisory board members assessed and defined such quality issues as the relevance, currency, and usefulness of the author coverage, critical content, and topics included in our product; evaluated the layout, presentation, and general quality of our product; provided feedback on the criteria used for selecting authors and topics covered in our product; identified any gaps in our coverage of authors or topics, recommending authors or topics for inclusion; and analyzed the appropriateness of our content and presentation for various user audiences, such as high school students, undergraduates, graduate students, librarians, and educators. We wish to thank the advisors for their advice during the development of *Harlem Renaissance.*

Suggestions are Welcome

Readers who wish to suggest new features, topics, or authors to appear in future volumes of the Gale Critical Companion Collection, or who have other suggestions or comments are cordially invited to call, write, or fax the Project Editor:

Project Editor, Gale Critical Companion Collection
The Gale Group
27500 Drake Road
Farmington Hills, MI 48331-3535
1-800-347-4253 (GALE)
Fax: 248-699-8054

ACKNOWLEDGMENTS

The editors wish to thank the copyright holders of the criticism included in this volume and the permissions managers of many book and magazine publishing companies for assisting us in securing reproduction rights. We are also grateful to the staffs of the Detroit Public Library, the Library of Congress, the University of Detroit Mercy Library, Wayne State University Purdy/Kresge Library Complex, and the University of Michigan Libraries for making their resources available to us. Following is a list of the copyright holders who have granted us permission to reproduce material in this edition of *Harlem Renaissance.* Every effort has been made to trace copyright, but if omissions have been made, please let us know.

Copyrighted material in Harlem Renaissance *was reproduced from the following periodicals:*

African American Review, v. 26, Fall, 1992; v. 27, Fall, 1993; v. 31, Autumn, 1997. All reproduced by permission of the *African American Review,* formerly the *Black American Literature Forum.*/v. 32, Spring, 1998 for "The Lonesome Boy Theme as Emblem for Arna Bontemps' Children's Literature," by Joseph A. Alvarez. Copyright © 1998 by the author. Reproduced by permission of the publisher and the author./v. 32, Winter, 1998 for "Countee Cullen's *Medea,*" by Lillian Corti. Reproduced by permission of the author./v. 32, Winter, 1998 for "The World Would Do Better to Ask Why Is Frimbo Sherlock Holmes?: Investigating Liminality in Rudolph Fisher's *The Conjure-Man Dies,*" by Adrienne Johnson Gosselin. Reproduced by permission of the author./v. 33, Fall, 1999 for "And Yet They Paused and A Bill to be Passed: Newly Recovered Lynching Dramas by Georgia Douglas Johnson," by Judith Stephens. Reproduced by permission of the author.—***Afro-Americans in New York Life and History,*** v. 10, 1986. Reproduced by permission.—***American Drama,*** v. 5, 1996. Reproduced by permission.—***American Literary History,*** v. 3, 1991 for "Community and Cultural Crisis: The 'Transfiguring Imagination' of Alain Locke," by Everett Akam. Reproduced by permission of Oxford University Press and the author.—***American Literature,*** v. 43, March, 1971; v. 44, 1972; v. 47, 1975; v. 51, March, 1979. Copyright © 1971, 1972, 1975, 1979 by Duke University Press, Durham, NC. All reproduced by permission.—***American Quarterly,*** v. 17, Summer, 1965; v. 32, Winter, 1980; v. 48, March, 1996; v. 50, September, 1998; v. 51, 1999. © The Johns Hopkins University Press. All reproduced by permission.—***American Studies,*** v. 18, Spring, 1977 for "Combatting Racism with Art: Charles S. Johnson and the Harlem Renaissance," by Ralph L. Pearson. Copyright Mid-America American Studies Association Reproduced by permission.—***ANQ: A Quarterly Journal of Short Ar-***

ticles, Notes, and Reviews, v. 8, Summer, 1995. Copyright © 1985 Helen Dwight Reid Educational Foundation. Reproduced with permission of the Helen Dwight Reid Educational Foundation, published by Heldref Publications, 1319 18th Street, NW, Washington, DC 20036-1802.—***Arizona Quarterly,*** v. 39, Fall, 1983 for "Jean Toomer's *Cane*: The Search for Identity through Form," by Alan Golding. Copyright © 1983 by the Regents of the University of Arizona. Reproduced by permission of the publisher and the author.—***Black American Literature Forum,*** v. 12, Autumn, 1978; v. 14, 1980; v. 19, 1985; v. 21, Fall, 1987; v. 21, Spring-Summer, 1987. All reproduced by permission of the *Black American Literature Forum,* currently the *African American Review.*—***Black World,*** v. 20, November, 1970 for "Alain Locke," by Richard A. Long. Reproduced by permission of the author./v. 20, November, 1970 for "Voice for the Jazz Age, Great Migration, or Black Bourgeoisie," by Faith Berry. Reproduced by permission of the Gail Berry for the author./v. 21, April, 1972 for "Alain Locke & Black Drama," by Samuel A. Hay. Reproduced by permission of the author./v. 25, February, 1976 for "Renaissance 'Renegade'? Wallace Thurman," by Huel D. Perkins. Reproduced by permission of the author./v. 25, February, 1976 for "The Genesis of Locke's *The New Negro,*" by Richard A. Long. Reproduced by permission of the author./v. 25, February, 1976 for "Toward a Sociological Analysis of the Renaissance: Why Harlem?" by Jabulani Kamau Makalani. Reproduced by permission of the author.—***Callaloo,*** v. 9, 1986; v. 21, Fall, 1998. Both reproduced by permission.—***CLA Journal,*** v. 15, March, 1972; v. 16, March, 1973; v. 16, June, 1973; v. 17, September, 1973; v. 18, 1974; v. 19, 1976; v. 26, December, 1982; v. 29, September, 1985; v. 32, December, 1988; v. 32, March, 1989; v. 32, June, 1989; v. 34, March, 1991; v. 35, June, 1992; v. 37, March, 1994; v. 38, September, 1994; v. 39, December, 1995; v. 41, June, 1998; v. 42 September 1998; 42, June 1999. Copyright, 1972, 1973, 1974, 1976, 1982, 1985, 1988, 1989, 1991, 1992, 1994, 1995, 1998, 1999 by The College Language Association. All reproduced by permission.—***The Crisis,*** v. 76, March, 1969; v. 78, July, 1971; v. 90, June/July, 1983. All reproduced by permission.—***Federal Writers' Project,*** August 23, 1938; December 1, 1938; January 17, 1939; January 19, 1939; April 19, 1939. All courtesy of The Library of Congress. All reproduced by permission.—***Georgia Historical Quarterly,*** v. 80, Winter, 1996. Courtesy of the Georgia Historical Society. Reproduced by permission.—***Georgia Review,*** v. 5, Fall, 1951, renewed 1979 by the *Georgia Review.* Reproduced by permission.—***International Review of African American Art,*** v. 4, 1995. Reproduced by permission.—***Journal of Black Studies,*** v. 12, September, 1981. Copyright © 1981 by Sage Publications, Inc. Reproduced by permissions of Sage Publications, Inc.—***Journal of Negro History,*** v. 52, 1967; v. 57, 1972. Both reproduced by permission.—***Langston Hughes Review,*** v. 1, Fall, 1982. Reproduced by permission.—***Legacy: A Journal of American Women Writers,*** v. 18, 2001. Reproduced by permission.—***Markham Review,*** v. 5, Summer, 1976. Reproduced by permission.—***The Massachusetts Review,*** v. 24, Autumn, 1983; v. 28, Winter, 1987. © 1983, 1987. Both reproduced from The Massachusetts Review, Inc. by permission.—***The Modern Schoolmen,*** v. 74, May, 1997. Reproduced by permission.—***MELUS,*** v. 23, 1998. Copyright, MELUS: The Society for the Study of Multi-Ethnic Literature of the United States, 1998. Reproduced by permission.—***The Midwest Quarterly,*** v. 24, Winter, 1983. Reproduced by permission.—***Narrative,*** v. 7, May, 1999. Reproduced by permission.—***Negro American Literature Forum,*** v. 14, January, 1965; v. 6, Summer, 1972. Both reproduced by permission of the *African American Review.*/v. 5, Spring, 1971 for "The Vagabond Motif in the Writings of Claude McKay," by Mary Conroy. Copyright © 1971 by the author. Reproduced by permission of the publisher and the author./v. 10, 1976 for "Carl Van Vechten and the Harlem Renaissance" by Mark Helbling. Reproduced by permission of the author.—***New England Quarterly,*** v. 74, March, 2001 for "Encouraging Verse: William S. Braithwaite and the Poetics of Race," by Lisa Szefel. Copyright held by *The New England Quarterly.* Reproduced by permission of the publisher and the author.—***New Orleans Review,*** v. 15, 1989. Copyright © 1989 by Loyola University. Reproduced by permission.—***New York Herald Tribune Books,*** January 10, 1926. Reproduced by permission.—***The New York Times,*** February 29, 1932. Copyright 1932 by The New York Times Company. Reproduced by permission.—***The New York Times Book Review,*** August 21, 1927; March 4, 1945; Copyright © 1945, renewed 1972 by The New York Times Company; September 20, 1992 Copyright © 1992 by The New York Times Company; January 3, 1999. Copyright © 1999 by The New York Times Company. All reproduced by permission.—***The New Yorker,*** v. 74, September 27, 1998 for "Beyond the Color Line," by Henry Louis Gates, Jr. © 1998 by the author. All rights reserved. Reproduced by permission of the author.—*Novel,* v. 30, Winter, 1997. Copyright NOVEL Corp. © 1997 Reproduced with permission.—*Pacific Coast Philology,* v. 15, December, 1980. Reproduced by permission.—*Phylon: The Atlanta University of Race and Culture,* v.6, 1945; v. 9, 1948; v. 11, 1950; v. 17, 1956; v. 18, 1957; v. 21, 1960;v. 25, 1964; v. 32, 1971; v. 39, 1978; v. 40, 1979; v. 57, 1996. Copyright 1945, 1948, 1950, 1956, 1957, 1960, 1964, 1971, 1978, 1979, 1996 by Atlanta University. All reproduced by permission.—*PMLA,* v. 105, January, 1990. Copyright © 1990 by the Modern Language Association of America. Reproduced by permission of the Modern Language Association of America.—*Poetry,* v. 24, February, 1930. Reproduced by permission.—*South Carolina Review,* v. 2, May, 1970. Reproduced by permission.—*Studies in American Fiction,* v. 19, Spring, 1991. Copyright © 1991 Northeastern University. Reproduced by permission.—*Studies in Black Literature,* v. 3, Summer, 1972; v. 5, Winter, 1974. Copyright 1972, 1974 by the editor. Both reproduced by permission.—*Studies in Short Fiction,* v. 2, 1965. Reproduced by permission.—*Studies in the Literary Imagination,* v. 7, Fall, 1974. Reproduced by permission.—*Susquehanna University Studies,* v. 7, June, 1963. Reproduced by permission.—*Theatre Annual,* 1985. Reproduced by permission.—*Virginia Cavalcade,* v. 27, 1978. Reproduced by permission.—*Western American Literature,* v. 6, Spring, 1971. Copyright 1971, by the Western American Literature Association. Reproduced by permission.—*Western Journal of Black Studies,* v. 22, 1998. Reproduced by permission.

Copyrighted material in Harlem Renaissance *was reproduced from the following books:*

Anderson, Paul A. From "'My Lord, What a Morning': The 'Sorrow Songs' in Harlem Renaissance Thought," in *Symbolic Loss: The Ambiguity of Mourning and Memory at Century's End.* Edited by Peter Homans. University Press of Virginia, 2000. Copyright © 2000 by University Press of Virginia. All rights reserved. Reproduced by permission.—Baker, Houston A., Jr. From *Modernism and the Harlem Renaissance.* University of Chicago Press, 1987. Copyright © 1987 by University of Chicago Press. All rights reserved. Reproduced by permission.—Balshaw, Maria. From *Looking for Harlem: Urban Aesthetics in African American Literature.* Pluto Press, 2000. Copyright © 2000 by Pluto Press. All rights reserved. Reproduced by permission.—Barfoot, C. C., et al. From "The New Negro in Context," in *Wallace Thurman's Harlem Renaissance.* Editions Rodopi B.V., 1994. Copyright © 1994 by Editions Rodopi B.V. All rights reserved. Reproduced by permission.—Barksdale, Richard K. From "Langston Hughes and the Blues He Couldn't Lose," in *The Harlem Renaissance: Revaluations.* Edited by Amritjit Singh, William S. Shiver, and Stanley Brodwin. Garland Publishing, Inc., 1989. © 1989 Amritjit Singh, William S. Shiver, and Stanley Brodwin. All rights reserved. Reproduced by permission of the editors.—Bearden, Romare and Harry Henderson. From *A History of African-American Artists From 1792 to the Present.* Pantheon Books, 1993. Copyright © 1993 by Pantheon Books. All rights reserved. Reproduced by permission.—Bone, Robert. From *The Negro Novel in America.* Yale University Press, 1958. Copyright © 1958 by Yale University Press. Revised edition © 1965 by Yale University. Copyright © renewed 1985 by Robert Bone. Reproduced by permission of the author.—Bontemps, Arna. From *Personals.* P. Breman, 1973. Reproduced by permission of Harold Ober Associates, Inc. for the Literary Estate of Arna Bontemps.—Booker, Peter. From "Modernism Deferred: Langston Hughes, Harlem and Jazz Montage," in *Locations of Liberty Modernism: Region and Nation in British and American Modernist Poetry.* Edited by Alex Davis and Lee M. Jenkins. Cambridge University Press, 2000. Copyright © 2000 by Cambridge University Press. All rights reserved. Reprinted with permission of Cambridge University Press and the author.—Brown-Guillory, Elizabeth. From "Disrupted Motherlines: Mothers and Daughters in a Genderized, Sexualized, and Racialized World," in *Women of Color: Mother-Daughter Relationships in 20th-Century Literature.* Edited by Elizabeth Brown-Guillory. University of Texas Press, 1996. Copyright © 1996 by University of Texas Press. All rights reserved. Reproduced by permission.—Byrd, Rudolph P. From "Jean Toomer and the Writers of the Harlem Renaissance: Was He There with Them?" in *The Harlem Renaissance: Revaluations.* Edited by Amritjit Singh, William S. Shiver, and Stanley Brodwin. Garland Publishing, Inc., 1989. © 1989 Amritjit Singh, William S. Shiver, and Stanley Brodwin. All rights reserved. Reproduced by permission of the editors.—Champion, Laurie. From "Dorothy West (1907-1998)," in *American Women Writers, 1900-1945: A Bio- Bibliographical Critical Sourcebook.* Edited by Laurie Champion. Greenwood Press, 2000. Copyright © 2000 by Greenwood Press, Greenwood Publishing Group, Inc., Westport, CT. All rights reserved. Reproduced by permission of Greenwood Publishing Group, Inc., Westport, CT.—Clum, John M. From ***Ridgely Torrence.*** Twayne Publishers, 1972. Copyright © 1972 by Twayne Publishers. All rights reserved. The Gale Group.—Coleman, Leon. From ***Carl Van Vechten and the Harlem Renaissance: A Critical Assessment.*** Garland Publishing, Inc., 1989. Copyright © 1989 by Garland Publishing, Inc. All rights reserved. Reproduced by permission.—Collier, Eugenia. From "Message to the Generations: The Mythic Hero in Sterling Brown's Poetry," in ***The Furious Flowering of African American Poetry.*** Edited by Joanne V. Gabbin. University of Virginia, 1999. Copyright © 1999 by University of Virginia. All rights reserved. Reproduced by permission.—Cripps, Thomas. From "Introduction: A Monument to Lost Innocence," in ***The Green Pastures.*** Edited by Thomas Cripps. University of Wisconsin Press, 1979. Copyright © 1979 The Board of Regents of the University of Wisconsin System. All rights reserved. Reproduced by permission.—Cullen, Countee. From ***Caroling Dusk: An Anthology of Verse by Negro Poets.*** Edited by Countee Cullen. Harper & Row, 1974. Copyright © 1974 by Harper & Row. All rights reserved. Reproduced by permission of Thompson and Thompson for the Estate of Countee Cullen.—Cullen, Countee. From ***Copper Sun.*** Harper, 1927. Copyright 1927 by Harper. Renewed 1954 by Ida M. Cullen. All rights reserved. Reproduced by permission of Thompson and Thompson for the Estate of Countee Cullen.—Davis, Thadious M. From "Nella Larsen's Harlem Aesthetic," in ***The Harlem Renaissance: Revaluations.*** Edited by Amritjit Singh, William S. Shiver, and Stanley Brodwin. Garland Publishing, Inc., 1989. © 1989 Amritjit Singh, William S. Shiver, and Stanley Brodwin. All rights reserved. Reproduced by permission of the editors.—Douglas, Aaron with L. M. Collins. From "Aaron Douglas Chats about the Harlem Renaissance," in ***The Portable Harlem Renaissance Reader.*** Edited by David Levering Lewis. Viking, 1994. Copyright © 1994 by Viking. All rights reserved. Reproduced by permission.—Doyle, Don H. From the introduction to ***Mamba's Daughters: A Novel of Charleston,*** by DuBose Heyward. University of South Carolina Press, 1995. Copyright © 1995 by University of South Carolina Press. All rights reserved. Reproduced by permission.—Driskell, David. ***From Harlem Renaissance: Art of Black America.*** Harry N. Abrams, Inc., 1987. Copyright © 1987 by Harry N. Abrams, Inc. All rights reserved. Reproduced by permission.—Du Bois, W. E. B. "Editing The Crisis," in ***Black Titan: W. E. B. Du Bois: An Anthology by the Editors of "Freedomways."*** Edited by John Henrik Clarke, et al. Beacon Press, 1970. Copyright © 1970 by Beacon Press. All rights reserved. Reproduced by permission.—Durham, Frank. From ***DuBose Heyward: The Man Who Wrote Porgy.*** University of South Carolina Press, 1954. Copyright © 1954 by University of South Carolina Press. Renewed 1982 by Kathleen C. Durham. All rights reserved. Reproduced by permission.—Early, Gerald. From ***My Soul's High Song.*** Doubleday, 1991. Copyright © 1991 by Doubleday. All rights reserved. Reproduced by permission.—Ellington, Duke. From ***Music is My Mistress.*** Doubleday, 1973. Copyright © 1973 by Doubleday. All rights reserved. Reproduced by permission.—Fabre, Michel. From ***From Harlem to Paris: Black American Writers in France, 1840-1980.*** University of Illinois Press, 1991. Copyright 1991 by Board of Trustees. Used with permission of the University of Illinois Press.—Flamming, Douglas. From "A Westerner in Search of 'Negro-ness': Region and Race in the Writing of Arna Bontemps," in ***Over the Edge: Remapping the American West.*** Edited by Valerie J. Matsumoto and Blake Allmendinger. University of California Press, 1999. Copyright © 1999 by University of California Press. All rights reserved. Reproduced by permission.—Flynn, Joyce. From the introduction to ***Frye Street & Environs: The Collected Works of Marita Bonner.*** Edited by Joyce Flynn and Joyce Occomy Stricklin. Beacon Press, 1987. Copyright © 1987 by Beacon Press. All rights reserved. Reproduced by permission.—Garber, Eric. From "Richard Bruce Nugent," in ***Dictionary of Literary Biography, Volume 51: Afro-American Writers from the Harlem Renaissance to 1940.*** Edited by Trudier Harris and Thadious M. Davis. Gale Research, Inc., 1987. Copyright © 1987 by Gale Research, Inc. All rights reserved.—Govan, Sandra Y. From "A Blend of Voices: Composite Narrative Strategies in Biographical Reconstruction," in ***Recovered Writers/Recovered Texts: Race, Class, and Gender in Black Women's Literature.*** Edited by Dolan Hubbard. University of Tennessee Press, 1997. Copyright © 1997 by University of Tennessee Press. All rights reserved. Reproduced by permission.—Gray, Christine Rauchfuss. From ***Willis Richardson: Forgotten Pioneer of African-American Drama.*** Greenwood Press, 1999. Copyright © 1999 by Greenwood Press. All rights reserved. Reproduced by permission of Greenwood Publishing Group, Inc., Westport, CT.—Greene, J. Lee. From "Anne Spencer," in ***Dictionary of Literary Biography, Volume 51: Afro-American Writers from the Harlem Renaissance to 1940.*** Edited by Trudier Harris and Thadious M. Davis. Gale Research, Inc., 1987. Copyright © 1987 by Gale Research, Inc. All rights reserved.—Greene, J. Lee. From ***Time's Unfading Garden: Anne Spencer's Life and Poetry.*** Louisiana State University, 1977. Copyright © 1977 by Louisiana State University. All rights reserved. Reproduced by permission of the author.—Hayden, Robert. From the preface to ***The New Negro.*** Edited by Alain Locke. Atheneum, 1968. Copyright © 1968 by Atheneum. All rights reserved. Reproduced by permission.—Helbling, Mark. From the introduction to ***The Harlem Renaissance: The One and the Many.*** Greenwood Press, 1999. Copyright © 1999 by Greenwood Press, Inc., Westport, CT. All rights reserved. Reproduced by permission of Greenwood Publishing Group, Inc., Westport, CT.—Hemenway, Robert E. From "Zora Neale Hurston and the Eatonville Anthropology," in ***Harlem Renaissance Remembered.*** Edited by Arna Bontemps. Dodd, Mead, 1972. Copyright © 1972 by Dodd, Mead. All rights reserved. Reproduced by permission.—Henderson, Mae Gwendolyn. From "Portrait of Wallace Thurman," in ***The Harlem Renaissance Remembered.*** Edited by Arna Bontemps. Dodd, Mead & Company, 1972. Copyright © 1972 by Dodd, Mead & Company. All rights reserved. Reproduced by permission.—Herron, Carolivia. From the introduction to ***Selected Works of Angelina Weld Grimké.*** Edited by Carolivia Herron. Oxford University Press, 1991. Copyright © 1991 by Oxford University Press. All rights reserved. Reproduced by permission.—Hill, Robert A. From the introduction to ***Marcus Garvey: Life and Lessons.*** University of California Press, 1987. Copyright © 1987 by University of California Press. All rights reserved. Reproduced by permission.—Howard, Elizabeth F. From "Arna Bontemps," in ***The Scribner Writers Series.*** Gale Group, 2002. Copyright © 2002 by Gale Group. All rights reserved.—Huggins, Nathan Irvin. From "Alain Locke: Aesthetic Value-System and Afro-American Art," in ***Revelation: American History, American Myths.*** Edited by Brenda Smith Huggins. Oxford University Press, 1995. Copyright © 1995 by Oxford University Press. All rights reserved. Reproduced by permission.—Hughes, Langston. From "The Negro and the Racial Mountain," in ***African American Literary Criticism.*** Edited by Hazel Arnett Ervin. Twayne Publishers, 1999. Copyright © 1999 by Twayne Publishers. All rights reserved. Reproduced by permission of Harold Ober Associates for the Estate of Langston Hughes.—Hull, Gloria T. From "Black Women Poets from Wheatley to Walker," in ***Sturdy Black Bridges: Visions of Black Women in Literature.*** Edited by Roseann P. Bell, Bettye J. Parker, and Beverly Guy-Sheftall. Anchor Books, 1979. Copyright © 1979 by Anchor Books. All rights reserved. Reproduced by permission of the author.—Hull, Gloria T. From the introduction to ***Give Us Each Day: The Diary of Alice Dunbar-Nelson.*** W.W. Norton, 1984. Copyright © 1984 by W.W. Norton. All rights reserved. Reproduced by permission of the author.—Hurston, Zora Neale. From "What White Publishers Won't Print," in ***I Love Myself When I Am Laughing ... And Then again When I Am Looking Mean and Impressive: A Zora Neale Hurston Reader.*** Edited by Alice Walker. The Feminist Press, 1979. Copyright © 1979 by The Feminist Press. All rights reserved. Reproduced by permission of the Victoria Sanders Literary Agency for the Estate of Zora Neale Hurston.—Hutchinson, George. ***The Harlem Renaissance in Black and White.*** The Belknap Press of Harvard University Press, 1995. Copyright © 1995 by The Belknap Press of Harvard University Press. Reprinted by permission of the publisher.—Hutson, Jean Blackwell. From ***Black Bibliophiles and Collectors: Preservers of Black History.*** Howard University Press, 1990. Copyright © 1990 by Howard University Press. All rights reserved. Reproduced by permission.—Ikonne, Chidi. From ***From Du Bois to Van Vechten: The Early New Negro Literature, 1903-1926.*** Greenwood Press, 1981. Copyright © 1981 by Greenwood Press. All rights reserved. Reproduced by permission of Greenwood Publishing Group, Inc., Westport, CT.—Jimoh, A. Yemisi. From "Dorothy West (1907-1998)," in ***Contemporary African American Novelists: A Bio-Bibliographical Critical Sourcebook.*** Edited by Emmanuel S. Nelson. Greenwood Press, 1999. Copyright © 1999 by Greenwood Press. All rights reserved. Reproduced by permission of Greenwood Publishing Group, Inc., Westport, CT.—Johnson, Abby Arthur and Ronald Maberry Johnson. From ***Propaganda and Aesthetics: The Literary Politics of Afro-American Magazines in the Twentieth Century.*** University of Massachusetts Press, 1979. Copyright © 1979 by University of Massachusetts Press. All rights reserved. Reproduced by permission.—Johnson, Charles S. From "The Negro Renaissance and Its Significance," in ***The Portable Harlem Renaissance Reader.*** Edited by David Levering Lewis. Viking, 1994. Copyright © 1994 by Viking. All rights reserved. Reproduced by permission.—Johnson, Eloise. From ***Rediscovering the Harlem Renaissance: The Politics of Exclusion.*** Garland Publishing, Inc., 1997. Copyright © 1997 by Garland Publishing, Inc. All rights reserved. Reproduced by permission.—Kellner, Bruce. From "Carl Van Vechten's Black Renaissance," in ***The Harlem Renaissance: Revalua-***

tions. Edited by Amritjit Singh, William S. Shiver, and Stanley Brodwin. Garland Publishing, Inc., 1989. © 1989 Amritjit Singh, William S. Shiver, and Stanley Brodwin. All rights reserved. Reproduced by permission of the editors.—Kostelanetz, Richard. From ***Politics in the African American Novel: James Weldon Johnson, W. E. B. Du Bois, Richard Wright, and Ralph Ellison.*** Greenwood Press, 1991. Copyright © 1991 by Greenwood Press. All rights reserved. Reproduced by permission of Greenwood Publishing Group, Inc., Westport, CT.—Lang, Robert. From "'The Birth of a Nation': History, Ideology, Narrative Form" in ***The Birth of a Nation: D.W. Griffith, Director.*** Edited by Robert Lang. Rutgers University Press, 1994. Copyright © 1994 by Rutgers University Press. All rights reserved. Reproduced by permission.—LeSeur, Geta. From "Claude McKay's Marxism," in ***The Harlem Renaissance: Revaluations.*** Edited by Amritjit Singh, William S. Shiver, and Stanley Brodwin. Garland Publishing, Inc., 1989. © 1989 Amritjit Singh, William S. Shiver, and Stanley Brodwin. All rights reserved. Reproduced by permission of the editors.—Lewis, David Levering. From the introduction to ***The Portable Harlem Renaissance Reader.*** Edited by David Levering Lewis. Viking, 1994. Copyright © 1994 by Viking. All rights reserved. Reproduced by permission of Brandt & Hochman for the editor.—Locke, Alain. From "Art or Propaganda," in ***The Critical Temper of Alain Locke: A Selection of His Essays on Art and Culture.*** Edited by Jeffrey C. Stewart. Garland Publishing, Inc., 1983. Copyright © 1983 by Garland Publishing, Inc. All rights reserved. Reproduced by permission.—Locke, Alain. From "The Negro Takes His Place in American Art," in ***The Portable Harlem Renaissance Reader.*** Edited by David Levering Lewis. Viking, 1994. Copyright © 1994 by Viking. All rights reserved. Publisher, 1994. © info from verso. Reproduced by permission of the author.—Lutz, Tom. From "Claude McKay: Music, Sexuality, and Literary Cosmopolitanism," in ***Black Orpheus: Music in African American Fiction from the Harlem Renaissance to Toni Morrison.*** Edited by Saadi A. Simawe. Garland Publishing, Inc., 2000. Copyright © 2000 by Garland Publishing, Inc. All rights reserved. Reproduced by permission.—Martin, Tony. From ***Literary Garveyism: Garvey, Black Arts, and the Harlem Renaissance.*** Majority Press, 1983. Copyright © 1983 by Majority Press. All rights reserved. Reproduced by permission.—McDonald, C. Ann. From "James Weldon Johnson," in ***American Women Writers, 1900-1945: A Bio-Bibliographical Critical Sourcebook.*** Edited by Laurie Champion. Greenwood Press, 2000. Copyright © 2000. Reproduced by permission of Greenwood Publishing Group, Inc., Westport, CT.—McKay, Nellie. From "Jean Toomer in his Time: An Introduction," in ***Jean Toomer: A Critical Evaluation.*** Edited by Therman B. O'Daniel. Howard University Press, 1988. Copyright © 1988 by Howard University Press. All rights reserved. Reproduced by permission.—McLaren, Joseph M. From "Early Recognitions: Duke Ellington and Langston Hughes in New York, 1920-1930," in ***The Harlem Renaissance: Revaluations.*** Edited by Amritjit Singh, William S. Shiver, and Stanley Brodwin. Garland Publishing, Inc., 1989. © 1989 Amritjit Singh, William S. Shiver, and Stanley Brodwin. All rights reserved. Reproduced by permission of the editors.—Meche, Jude R. From "Marita Bonner," in ***Dictionary of Literary Biography, Volume 228: Twentieth-Century American Dramatists.*** Edited by Christopher J. Wheatley. The Gale Group, 2000. Copyright © 2000 by The Gale Group. Reproduced by permission.—Miller, Nina. From "'Our Younger Negro (Women) Artists': Gwendolyn Bennett and Helene Johnson," in ***Making Love Modern: The Intimate Public Worlds of New York's Literary Women.*** Oxford University Press, 1998. Copyright © 1998 by Oxford University Press. All rights reserved. Reproduced by permission.—Miller, R. Baxter. From "'Some Mark to Make': the Lyrical Imagination of Langston Hughes," in ***Critical Essays on Langston Hughes.*** G.K. Hall, 1986. Copyright © 1986 by G.K. Hall. All rights reserved. The Gale Group.—Mitchell, Verner D. From the introduction to ***This Waiting for Love: Helene Johnson, Poet of the Harlem Renaissance.*** University of Massachusetts Press, 2000. Copyright © 2000 by University of Massachusetts Press. All rights reserved. Reproduced by permission.—Parascandola, Louis J. From ***An Eric Walrond Reader.*** Wayne State University Press, 1998. Copyright © 1998 by Wayne State University Press. All rights reserved. Reproduced by permission.—Peplow, Michael W. From ***George S. Schuyler.*** Twayne Publishers, 1980. Copyright © 1980 by Twayne Publishers. The Gale Group.—Perry, Patsy B. From "Willis Richardson," in ***Dictionary of Literary Biography, Volume 51: Afro-Ameican Writers from the Harlem Renaissance to 1940.*** Edited by Trudier Harris and Thadious M. Davis. The Gale Group, 1987. Copyright © 1987 Gale Research Company.—Rampersad, Arnold. From "Langston Hughes and Approaches to Modernism in the Harlem Renaissance," in ***The Harlem Renaissance: Revaluations.*** Edited by Amritjit Singh, William S. Shiver, and Stanley Brodwin. Garland Publishing, Inc., 1989. © 1989 Amritjit Singh, William S. Shiver, and Stanley

Brodwin. All rights reserved. Reproduced by permission of the editors.—Robinson, William H. From ***Black New England Letters: The Uses of Writings in Black New England.*** Trustees of the Public Library of the City of Boston, 1977. Copyright © 1977 by Trustees of the Public Library of the City of Boston. All rights reserved. Reproduced by permission.—Sanders, Mark A. From "The Ballad, the Hero, and the Ride: A Reading of Sterling Brown's 'The Last Ride of Wild Bill,'" in ***The Furious Flowering of African American Poetry.*** Edited by Joanne V. Gabbin. University of Virginia, 1999. Copyright © 1999 by University of Virginia. All rights reserved. Reproduced by permission.—Sinnette, Elinor Des Verney. From ***Arthur Alfonso Schomburg: Black Bibliophile & Collector.*** The New York Public Library & Wayne State University Press, 1989. Copyright © 1989 by The New York Public Library & Wayne State University Press. All rights reserved. Reproduced by permission of the author.—Slavick, William H. From "Going to School to DuBose Heyward," in ***The Harlem Renaissance Re-Examined.*** Edited by Victor A. Kramer. AMS, 1987. Copyright © 1987 by AMS. All rights reserved. Reproduced by permission.—Slavick, William H. From ***DuBose Heyward.*** Twayne Publishers, 1981. Copyright © 1981 by Twayne Publishers. The Gale Group.—Stewart, Jeffrey C. From ***Rhapsodies in Black: Art of the Harlem Renaissance.*** University of California Press, 1997. Copyright © 1997 by University of California Press. All rights reserved. Reproduced by permission.—Stoff, Michael B. From "Claude McKay and the Cult of Primitivism," in ***The Harlem Renaissance Remembered.*** Edited by Arna Bontemps. Dodd, Mead & Company, 1972. Copyright © 1972 by Dodd, Mead & Company. All rights reserved. Reproduced by permission.—Sundquist, Eric J. From the introduction to ***The Oxford W. E. B. Du Bois Reader.*** Oxford University Press, 1996. Copyright © 1996 by Oxford University Press. All rights reserved. Reproduced by permission.—Tate, Claudia. From ***The Selected Works of Georgia Douglas Johnson.*** G.K. Hall & Co., 1997. Copyright © 1997 by G.K. Hall & Co. All rights reserved. The Gale Group.—Tracy, Steven C. From "To the Tune of Those Weary Blues," in ***Langston Hughes: Critical Perspectives Past and Present.*** Edited by Henry Louis Gates, Jr., and K.A. Appiah. Amistad Press, 1993. Copyright © 1993 by Amistad Press. Reproduced by permission of Henry Louis Gates, Jr.—Turner, Deborah. From ***Gay and Lesbian Literature,*** Volume 2. St. James Press, 1998. Copyright © 1998 by St. James Press. All rights reserved. The Gale Group.—Tuttleton, James W. From "Countee Cullen at 'The Heights,'" in ***The Harlem Renaissance: Revaluations.*** Edited by Amritjit Singh, William S. Shiver, and Stanley Brodwin. Garland Publishing, Inc., 1989. © 1989 Amritjit Singh, William S. Shiver, and Stanley Brodwin. All rights reserved. Reproduced by permission of the editors.—Tyler, Bruce M. From ***From Harlem to Hollywood: The Struggle for Racial and Cultural Democracy, 1920-1943.*** Garland Publishing, Inc., 1992. Copyright © 1992 by Garland Publishing, Inc. All rights reserved. Reproduced by permission.—van Notten, Eleonor. From ***Wallace Thurman's Harlem Renaissance.*** Rodopi, 1994. Copyright © 1994 by Rodopi. All rights reserved. Reproduced by permission.—Walden, Daniel. From "'The Canker Galls ... ,' or, the Short Promising Life of Wallace Thurman," in ***The Harlem Renaissance Re-Examined.*** Edited by Victor A. Kramer. AMS Press, 1987. Copyright © 1987 by AMS Press. All rights reserved. Reproduced by permission.—Walker, Alice. From "Dedication," in ***I Love Myself When I am Laughing ... And Then again When I am Looking Mean and Impressive: A Zora Neale Hurston Reader.*** Edited by Alice Walker. The Feminist Press, 1979. Copyright © 1979 by The Feminist Press. All rights reserved. Reproduced by permission.—Wall, Cheryl A. From "Zora Neal Hurston: Changing Her Own Words," in ***American Novelists Revisited: Essays in Feminist Criticism.*** Edited by Friz Fleischmann. G.K. Hall, 1982. Copyright © 1982 by G.K. Hall. All rights reserved. Reproduced by permission.—Wall, Cheryl A. From "Whose Sweet Angel Child? Blues Women, Langston Hughes, and Writing during the Harlem Renaissance," in ***Langston Hughes: The Man, His Art, and His Continuing Influence.*** Edited by C. James Trotman. Garland Publishing, Inc., 1995. Copyright © 1995 by Garland Publishing, Inc. All rights reserved. Reproduced by permission.—Wall, Cheryl A. From the foreword to ***This Waiting for Love: Helene Johnson, Poet of the Harlem Renaissance.*** Edited by Verner D. Mitchell. University of Massachusetts Press, 2000. Copyright © 2000 by University of Massachusetts Press. All rights reserved. Reproduced by permission.—Wall, Cheryl A. From ***Women of the Harlem Renaissance.*** Indiana University Press, 1995. Copyright © 1995 by Indiana University Press. All rights reserved. Reproduced by permission.—Washington, Mary Helen. From "'I Love the Way Janie Crawford Left Her Husbands': Hurston's Emergent Female Hero," in ***Zora Neale Hurston: Critical Perspectives Past and Present.*** Edited by Henry Louis Gates, Jr. and K.A. Appiah. Amistad Press, 1993. Copyright © 1993 by Amistad Press. Reproduced by permission of Henry Louis Gates, Jr.—

Washington, Sarah M. From "Frank S. Horne," in ***Dictionary of Literary Biography, Volume 51: Afro- American Writers from the Harlem Renaissance to 1940.*** Edited by Trudier Harris. Gale Research, Inc., 1987. Copyright © 1987 by Gale Research, Inc. All rights reserved. Reproduced by permission.—Willis-Braithwaite, Deborah. From ***James Van DerZee: Photographer 1886-1983.*** Harry N. Abrams, Inc., 1987. Copyright © 1987 by Harry N. Abrams, Inc. All rights reserved. Reproduced by permission.—Wintz, Cary D. From "Booker T. Washington, W. E. B. Du Bois, and the 'New Negro' in Black America," in ***Black Culture and the Harlem Renaissance.*** Rice University Press, 1988. Copyright © 1996 by Texas A&M University Press. Reproduced by permission.—Wolseley, Roland E. From ***The Black Press, U.S.A.*** Iowa State University Press, 1990. Copyright © 1990 by Iowa State University Press. All rights reserved. Reproduced by permission. Copyright to all editions of the Black Press, U.S.A. is owned by Alice A. Tait.—Woodson, Jon. From ***To Make a New Race: Gurdjieff, Toomer, and the Harlem Renaissance.*** University of Mississippi Press, 1999. Copyright © 1998 by University of Mississippi Press. All rights reserved. Reproduced by permission.—Zamir, Shamoon. From ***Dark Voices: W. E. B. Du Bois and American Thought, 1888-1903.*** University of Chicago Press, 1995. Copyright © 1995 by University of Chicago Press. All rights reserved. Reproduced by permission.

Photographs and illustrations in **Harlem Renaissance** *were received from the following sources:*

African American soldiers of the 368 Infantry, photograph. Corbis. Reproduced by permission.—Apollo Theater marquee, "See You Soon," photograph. AP/Wide World Photos. Reproduced by permission.—"Aspects of Negro Life: The Negro in an African Setting," painting by Aaron Douglas, photograph by Manu Sassoonian. Schomburg Center for Research in Black Culture, The New York Public Library, Art Resource, NY. Reproduced by permission.—"Ethiopia Awakening," sculpture by Meta Warrick Fuller, photograph. Schomburg Center for Research in Black Culture, The New York Public Library/Art Resource, NY. Reproduced by permission. Bailey, Pearl, photograph by Carl Van Vechten. Reproduced by permission of the Estate of Carl Van Vechten.—Baker, Josephine, in a scene from the 1934 film Zou Zou, directed by Marc Allegret, photograph. The Kobal Collection. Reproduced by permission.—Bennett, Gwendolyn, photograph. Reproduced by permission of Helaine Victoria Press and the Moorland-Spingarn Research Center, Howard University.—Black Cross nurses, parading down a street in Harlem during the opening of the Universal Negro Improvement Association convention, photograph. © Underwood & Underwood/Corbis. Reproduced by permission.—Bonner, Marita, sitting with her husband, William Occomy, photograph. Radcliffe Archives, Radcliffe Institute, Harvard University. Reproduced by permission.—Bontemps, Arna, photograph. Fisk University Library. Reproduced by permission.—Braithwaite, William Stanley, photograph. Fisk University Library. Reproduced by permission.—Brown, Sterling, photograph. Fisk University Library. Reproduced by permission.—Calloway, Cab, photograph by Carl Van Vechten. The Estate of Carl Van Vechten. Reproduced by permission.—Circular diagram showing difference between speech and silence (Figure A), compared with circular diagram showing the linearity of silence and speech by marking the trajectory as a circuit (Figure B). The Gale Group.—Cotton Club, Harlem, New York City, ca. 1920-1940, photograph. Corbis Corporation. Reproduced by permission.—Cover from *Black Thunder,* by Arna Bontemps. Beacon Press, 1992. Copyright 1936 by The Macmillan Company, renewed 1963 by Arna Bontemps. Reproduced by permission.—Cover from *The Crisis: A Record of the Darker Races,* edited by W. E. B. Du Bois, 1910, print.—Cover of the program for DuBose Heyward and Ira Gershwin's libretto *Porgy and Bess,* photograph. Hulton/Archive. Reproduced by permission.—Cullen, Countee, photograph. The Bettmann Archive/Corbis-Bettmann. Reproduced by permission.—Diagram showing the word fixed in the middle of a diagrammatically circumscribed cross becoming a vehicle for the attempted transcendence of silent difference and the aspiration to silent non-difference. The Gale Group.—Douglas, Aaron (oil on canvas painting), photograph. Gibbs Museum of Art/CAA. Reproduced by permission.—Du Bois, W. E. B., photograph. Fisk University Library. Reproduced by permission.—Du Bois, W. E. B. (top right), and others working in the offices of the NAACP's *Crisis* magazine, photograph. © Underwood & Underwood/Corbis. Reproduced by permission.—Ellington, Duke, and Louis Armstrong (performing), 1946, photograph. AP/Wide World Photos Inc. Reproduced by permission.—Exterior view of Abyssinian Baptist Church, New York City, c. 1923, photograph. Corbis Corporation. Reproduced by permission.—Exterior view of Lafayette Theatre in Harlem, 7th Avenue between 131st and 132nd Streets, photograph. Corbis. Reproduced by permission.—"Ezekiel Saw the

Wheels," painting by William H. Johnson. The Library of Congress.—Fauset, Jesse Redmon, photograph. The Library of Congress.—Fauset, Jessie, Langston Hughes and Zora Neale Hurston, photograph. Schomburg Center for Research in Black Culture, The New York Public Library/Art Resource, NY. Reproduced by permission.—Fisher, Rudolph, photograph. The Beinecke Rare Book and Manuscript Library. Reproduced by permission.—Frontispiece, caricature drawing by Miguel Covarrubias, from "Keep A-Inchin' along," written by Carl Van Vechten, (left to right), Carl Van Vechten, Fania Marinoff, and Taylor Gordon. Special Collections Library, University of Michigan. Reproduced by permission.—Garvey, Marcus (center), handcuffed to a deputy after he is escorted from a courtroom after being sentenced to five years in Atlanta Penitentiary for mail fraud, photograph. © Bettmann/Corbis. Reproduced by permission.—Garvey, Marcus, photograph. Consulate General of Jamaica. Reproduced by permission.—Garvey, Marcus, standing in front of a UNIA club in New York, photograph. Hulton/Archive. Reproduced by permission.—Grimké, Angelina Weld, photograph. Reproduced by permission of Helaine Victoria Press and the Moorland-Spingarn Research Center, Howard University.—Harlem bookstore known as the "House of Common Sense and the Home of Proper Propaganda" hosting the registration for the Back-to-Africa movement, photograph. © Bettmann/Corbis. Reproduced by permission.—Heyward, DuBose, photograph. The Library of Congress.—Horne, Frank, photograph. AP/Wide World Photos. Reproduced by permission.—Hughes, Langston, photograph. The Bettmann Archive/Newsphotos, Inc./Corbis- Bettmann. Reproduced by permission.—Hurston, Zora Neale, photograph. Yale Collection of American Literature, Beinecke Rare Book and Manuscript Library. Reproduced by permission of Carl Van Vechten Papers.—Jacket of *The Souls of Black Folk,* by W. E. B. Du Bois. Random House, 1996. Jacket portrait courtesy of the Bettman Archive.—The January, 1991 PLAYBILL for Langston Hughes and Zora Neale Hurston's *Mule Bone,* directed by Michael Schultz by the Ethel Barrymore Theatre, at Lincoln Center Theater, some men and one woman are sitting on a porch listening to a man playing a guitar, photograph. PLAYBILL ® is a registered trademark of Playbill Incorperated, N.Y.C. All rights reserved. Reproduced by permission.—Johnson, Charles S., photograph. Fisk University Library. Reproduced by permission.—Johnson, William H., self portrait painting. The Library of Congress.—Johnson, James Weldon, photograph. The Library of Congress.—Larsen, Nella (1891-1964), photograph. The Beinecke Rare Book and Manuscript Library. Reproduced by permission.—Larsen, Nella (shaking hands, four men to her left), photograph. UPI/Corbis-Bettmann. Reproduced by permission.—Leibowitz, Sam, Patterson, Heywood (Scottsboro boys), phototgraph. UPI/Corbis-Bettmann. Reproduced by permission.—Locke, Dr. Alain, photograph. The Library of Congress.—McKay, Claude, photograph. The Granger Collection, New York. Reproduced by permission.—Members of the NAACP New York City Youth Council holding signs and picketing for anti-lynching legislation in front of the Strand Theatre in Times Square, photograph. Courtesy of The Library of Congress. Reproduced by permission.—NAACP anti-lynching poster, photograph. Archive Photos. Reproduced by permission.—Nelson, Alice Ruth Moore Dunbar, photograph. Reproduced by permission of Helaine Victoria Press and the Ohio Historical Society.—Original typewritten manuscript from *Harlem/Good Morning, Daddy,* written by Langston Hughes. Reproduced by permission of Harold Ober Associates Incorporated for the Estate of Langston Hughes.—Parade of men, opening of the annual convention of the Provisional Republic of Africa in Harlem, carrying banners and a paintng of the "Ethiopian Christ," banner above street: "Summer Chatauqua of the Abyssinian Baptist Church," New York, photograph by George Rinhart. Corbis Corporation. Reproduced by permission.—Pedestrians walking on East 112th Street in Harlem, New York, photograph. © Bettmann/Corbis. Reproduced by permission.—Rex, Ingram, photograph. The Kobal Collection. Reproduced by permission.—Robeson, Paul, as Brutus Jones, throwing his hands up, surrounded by ghosts, scene from the 1933 film *The Emperor Jones,* photograph. ©Underwood & Underwood/Corbis. Reproduced by permission.—Robinson, Bill (with Shirley Temple), photograph. AP/Wide World Photos. Reproduced by permission.—Scene from the movie *Birth of A Nation,* 1915, photograph. The Kobal Collection. Reproduced by permission.—Schuyler, George S., photograph by Carl Van Vechten. Reproduced by permission of the Estate of Carl Van Vechten.—Smith, Bessie, photograph. New York Public Library.—Spencer, Anne, photograph. Reproduced by permission of Helaine Victoria Press and the Literary Estate of Anne Spencer.—Thurman, Wallace, photograph. Reproduced by permission of the Beinecke Rare Book and Manuscript Library.—Title page from *Anthology of Magazine Verse for 1920,* edited by William Stanley Braithwaite, all text. Courtesy of the Graduate Library, University of Michigan. Reproduced by permission.—Title page from *The Book of American Negro Poetry,* written by James Weldon Johnson, all text. Courtesy of the Graduate Library, University of Michigan. Reproduced by permission.—Title page from *Caroling Dusk,* edited by Countee Cullen, all text. Special Collections Library, University of Michigan. Reproduced by permission.—Title page from *Frye Street & Environs: The Collected Works of Marita Bonner,* by Joyce Flynn and Joyce Occomy Stricklin. Copyright © 1987 by Joyce Flynn and Joyce Occomy Stricklin. Reproduced by permission of Beacon Press, Boston.—Title page from *The Weary Blues,* written by Langston Hughes. Special Collections Library, University of Michigan. Reproduced by permission.—Toomer, Jean (foreground), sitting in front of typewriter while his wife, Marjory Latimer, stands next to him looking over his shoulder, photograph. © Bettmann/Corbis. Reproduced by permission.—Toomer, Jean, photograph. Beinecke Library, Yale University. Reproduced by permission.—Two women walking with two girls, photograph. Corbis. Reproduced by permission.—Unemployed black men talking together, 1935, Lennox Avenue, Harlem, photograph. Corbis-Bettmann. Reproduced by permission.—VanDerZee, James, photograph. AP/Wide World Photos. Reproduced by permission.—Van Vechten, Carl, photograph. AP/Wide World Photos. Reproduced by permission.—View of Lenox Avenue in Harlem, photograph. Corbis. Reproduced by permission.—Walrond, Eric, a drawing. Winold Reiss Collecection/Fisk University Library. Reproduced by permission.—West, Dorothy, Martha's Vineyard, Massachusetts, 1995, photograph. AP/Wide World Photos. Reproduced by permission.—White, Walter, photograph. Library of Congress.

● = historical event

■ = literary event

1890

● Between 1890 and 1920, about two million African Americans migrate from the rural southern states to the northern cities, where they hope to find better opportunities and less discrimination.

1908

● The Frogs, a group of African American theatrical professionals including George Walker, James Reese Europe, and Bert Williams, is founded.

● Reverend Adam Clayton Powell is named pastor of Harlem's Abyssinian Baptist Church.

1909

● The National Negro Committee holds its first meeting. The organization will evolve into the National Association for the Advancement of Colored People (NAACP) the next year.

1910

● The NAACP is founded, and prominent Black leader W. E. B. Du Bois becomes editor of the group's monthly magazine, *Crisis,* which publishes its first issue.

● The National Urban League, a merger of the Committee for Improving the Industrial Conditions of Negroes in New York, the Committee on Urban Conditions, and the National League for the Protection of Colored Women is founded under the direction of Dr. George E. Haynes.

1912

■ James Weldon Johnson's influential novel *The Autobiography of an Ex-Colored Man* is published.

1914

● Madame C. J. Walker, the first African American woman to become a self-made millionaire, moves to New York City with her daughter L'Alelia. The family moves to Harlem in 1916. The founder of a line of hair and cosmetic products for Black women, Madame Walker's fortune will finance her daughter's foray into the nightclub and literary salon business.

1917

● Jamaican-born Marcus Garvey arrives in Harlem and founds the Universal Negro Improvement Association (UNIA), an organization that urges Blacks to unite and form their own nation.

- Between 10,000 and 15,000 African Americans join the Silent Protest Parade, marching down Fifth Avenue in complete silence to protest violence against Blacks.
- The politically radical Black publication *The Messenger* is founded.
- Two of Claude McKay's poems, "Invocation" and "The Harlem Dancer," are published in the white literary journal *Seven Arts.*

1918

- Garvey's UNIA begins publishing *Negro World,* the organization's weekly newspaper.

1919

- The 369th Infantry Regiment, a highly decorated unit made up entirely of African American soldiers, returns from World War I to a heroes' welcome in Harlem.
- During the "Red Summer of Hate," African Americans react angrily to widespread lynchings and other violence directed against them, with race riots occurring in Chicago, Washington, D.C., and two dozen other American cities. The NAACP holds a conference on lynching and publishes *Thirty Years of Lynching in the United States 1889-1918.*
- Jessie Redmon Fauset becomes literary editor of *Crisis.*
- McKay publishes "If We Must Die" in the *Liberator.*

1920

- James Weldon Johnson becomes the first African American executive secretary of the NAACP.
- Garvey's UNIA holds the First International Convention of the Negro Peoples of the World in New York
- The NAACP awards the Springarn Medal to W. E. B. Du Bois for "the founding and the calling of the Pan African Congress."
- Acclaimed American playwright Eugene O'Neil's drama *The Emperor Jones* opens at the Provincetown Playhouse with Black actor Charles Gilpin in the lead role.

1921

- Harry Pace founds the Black Swan Phonograph Corporation and begins production of the "race records" that will help to bring jazz and blues music to a wider audience.
- The musical revue *Shuffle Along* opens on Broadway, delighting audiences with its high-energy singing and dancing and, many believe, providing the spark that ignites the Harlem Renaissance.
- An exhibition of works by such African American artists as Henry Tanner and Meta Vaux Warrick Fuller is held at Harlem's 135th Street branch of the New York Public Library.
- Langston Hughes's great poem "The Negro Speaks of Rivers" is published in *Crisis.*

1922

- Marian Anderson performs at New York's Town Hall, launching her career as a classical singer.
- Warrick Fuller's sculpture *Ethiopia Awakening* is shown at the "Making of America" exhibition in New York.
- The first major book of the Harlem Renaissance appears when Claude McKay's novel *Harlem Shadows* is published by Harcourt, Brace.
- James Weldon Johnson's *The Book of American Negro Poetry* is published by Harcourt, Brace.

1923

- Bessie Smith records "Downhearted Blues" and "Gulf Coast Blues," soon becoming the most famous blues singer in both the northern and southern states.
- Roland Hayes makes his New York debut, singing a program of classical music as well as African American spirituals.
- Marcus Garvey is arrested for mail fraud and imprisoned for three months.
- Joe "King" Oliver's Creole Jazz Band makes a series of thirty- seven recordings with trumpet player Louis Armstrong.
- Pianist, composer, and band leader Duke Ellington arrives in New York with his band, the Washingtonians.
- Louis Armstrong joins Fletcher Henderson's orchestra, which— performing at the famed Roseland Ballroom— becomes the most popular dance band in New York.
- Kansas City-born artist Aaron Douglas arrives in New York and begins developing a new style that will make him the official artist of the Harlem Renaissance.

- Harlem's largest and most famous cabaret, the Cotton Club, opens.
- Josephine Baker appears in *Chocolate Dandies* on Broadway.
- Roland Hayes performs at Carnegie Hall.
- The Harlem Renaissance Basketball Club is formed to provide Black athletes who have been unable to play on white teams with a league of their own.
- The National Urban League establishes *Opportunity* magazine, which will not only publish the work of Harlem Renaissance writers and artists but will help to support them through an annual contest.
- The National Ethiopian Art Players produce Willis Richardson's *The Chip Woman's Fortune,* the first drama by a Black playwright to appear on the Broadway stage.
- Jean Toomer's innovative novel *Cane* is published and Toomer is hailed as one of the most promising young authors of the Harlem Renaissance.
- The Ethiopian Art Players perform Eugene O'Neill's play *All God's Chillun Got Wings* in Washington, D.C., while in Cleveland the Gilpin Players at Karamu Theatre present *In Abraham's Bosom* by Paul Green.
- Poems by Harlem Renaissance star Countee Cullen appear in four major white publications.

1924

- James VanDerZee begins a series of photographs chronicling Marcus Garvey and the activities of UNIA.
- Filmmaker Oscar Micheaux completes *Birthright* and *Body and Soul,* the latter starring Paul Robeson.
- At the Civic Club dinner hosted by *Opportunity*'s Charles S. Johnson, promising young writers meet the influential editors and publishers who can boost their careers.
- *The Fire in the Flint,* a novel by NAACP leader Walter White, is published.
- The publication of Jessie Redmon Fauset's *There Is Confusion* marks the first Harlem Renaissance book by a woman writer.

1925

- The exciting new musical form known as jazz is showcased in the "First American Jazz Concert" at Aeolian Hall in New York.
- Small's Paradise nightclub opens in Harlem; the club will prove to be a one of the city's most popular jazz destinations.
- Marcus Garvey is convicted of mail fraud and imprisoned in the Atlanta Penitentiary.
- Marian Anderson wins a singing competition sponsored by the New York Philharmonic Orchestra.
- Artist Sargent Johnson exhibits his paintings at the San Francisco Art Association, and Archibald Motley wins a medal from the Art Institute of Chicago for his painting "A Mulatress."
- James Weldon Johnson is awarded the NAACP's Springarn Medal for his work as an author, diplomat, and leader.
- *Survey Graphic* magazine publishes *Harlem: The Mecca of the New Negro,* an issue devoted entirely to the work of Harlem Renaissance writers and artists.
- Zora Neale Hurston publishes her short story "Spunk" in *Opportunity.*
- Countee Cullen's first volume of poetry, *Color,* is published.
- Wallace Thurman moves from Los Angeles to New York and soon becomes a leader of the younger generation of Harlem Renaissance writers and artists.
- Zora Neale Hurston enters Barnard College on a scholarship, studying anthropology.
- Well-known white poet Vachel Lindsay reads the poems of the Langston Hughes, then working as a restaurant busboy, to the audience at his own poetry reading, announcing that he has discovered a bright new talent.
- The *New Negro* anthology, edited by Alain Locke, introduces the work and ideas of the Harlem Renaissance.

1926

- W.C. Handy's *Blues: An Anthology* is published, bringing wider attention to this unique African American musical form.
- Another jazz hotspot, the Savoy Ballroom, opens in Harlem with Fletcher Henderson and his orchestra established as the house band.
- The Harmon Foundation holds its first annual art exhibition of works by African American artists, and Palmer Hayden and Hale Woodruff win top awards.

- The Carnegie Corporation buys Arthur Schomburg's African American collection and donates it to the newly established Negro Reference Library at the Harlem branch of the New York Public Library.
- The NAACP-sponsored theatrical group the Krigwa Players stages three plays.
- White author Carl Van Vechten's controversial novel *Nigger Heaven* is published.
- Langston Hughes's first volume of poetry, *The Weary Blues,* is published.
- *Crisis* awards its first prizes in literature and art. Winners include Arna Bontemps, Countee Cullen, Aaron Douglas, and Hale Woodruff.
- A daring new (but short-lived) literary journal called *Fire!!* is launched by Langston Hughes, Wallace Thurman, Zora Neale Hurston, Aaron Douglas, and Richard Bruce Nugent, with artwork by Douglas and Nugent.

1927

- Duke Ellington begins a three-year stint at the Cotton Club, gaining fame and praise for his innovative style and compositions.
- Ordered to leave the United States, Marcus Garvey returns to Jamaica.
- Wealthy African American L'Alelia Walker, whose mother founded a successful Black hair and skin care business, opens a nightclub and literary salon called the Dark Tower.
- *Caroling Dusk: An Anthology of Verse by Negro Poets,* edited by Countee Cullen, is published by Harper.
- Charles S. Johnson publishes *Ebony and Topaz: A Collectanea,* an anthology of writings that originally appeared in *Opportunity.*
- Dorothy and DuBose Heyward's *Porgy,* a musical play with Black characters and themes, opens on Broadway; the work is adapted from DuBose's novel of the same name.
- James Weldon Johnson's *God's Trombones,* a book of poems modeled after sermons by Black preachers and illustrated by Aaron Douglas, is published.
- Several young Harlem Renaissance writers and artists—notably Zora Neale Hurston and Langston Hughes— accept money and other help from wealthy patron Charlotte Osgood Mason, who insists that those under her patronage call her "Godmother."
- Langston Hughes's second poetry collection, *Fine Clothes to the Jew,* features blues rhythms and Harlem-inspired imagery.

1928

- Palmer Hayden's work is featured in a one-man exhibition at a Paris art gallery, and Archibald Motley exhibits his paintings at the New Galleries in New York
- Aaron Douglas is awarded a fellowship to study at the Barnes Foundation in Pennsylvania.
- A number of important Harlem Renaissance works are published, including Rudolph Fisher's *Walls of Jericho,* Nella Larsen's *Quicksand,* Jessie Redmon Fauset's *Plum Bun,* W. E. B. Du Bois's *Dark Princess,* and Claude McKay's *Home to Harlem* (which becomes the first bestseller by a Black author).
- Poet Countee Cullen marries Yolande Du Bois, daughter of the great Black leader, in an extravagant wedding that is one of the most memorable social events of the Harlem Renaissance.
- Wallace Thurman edits another literary journal, *Harlem,* that is—like its predecessor, *Fire!!*— destined to appear only once.

1929

- The Harmon Foundation sponsors the exhibition *Paintings and Sculptures by American Negro Artists* at the National Gallery in Washington, D.C.
- The Negro Experimental Theater is founded.
- Films showcasing African American musicians debut, including *Black and Tan,* featuring Duke Ellington and his orchestra, and *St. Louis Blues,* which features Bessie Smith.
- The Broadway show *Ain't Misbehavin'* features music by piano player Fats Waller.
- The stock market crashes, ending the Jazz Age and ushering in the Great Depression.
- Wallace Thurman's play *Harlem,* written with William Jourdan Rapp, opens on Broadway, becoming the most successful such production by a Black author.
- Novels by Wallace Thurman (*The Blacker the Berry*) and Claude McKay (*Banjo*) are published, as is Countee Cullen's *The Black Christ and Other Poems.*

1930

- Aaron Douglas is commissioned to create a series of murals for the campus library at Fisk University in Nashville.
- James V. Herring creates the Howard University Gallery of Art. It is the first gallery in the United States to be autonomously curated and directed by African Americans.
- Marc Connelly's play *The Green Pastures,* notable for its African American characters and content, opens to great acclaim on Broadway.
- Langston Hughes's novel *Not without Laughter* is published.
- James Weldon Johnson's historical account of Harlem, *Black Manhattan,* is published by Knopf.
- Willis Richardson's *Plays and Pageants from the Life of the Negro* is published by Associated Publishers.

1931

- Artist August Savage opens the Savage School of Arts and Crafts in Harlem. It is the first of several art schools she will open in Harlem.

1932

- Louis Armstrong stars in the musical film short *A Rhapsody in Black and Blue.*

1933

- A number of Harlem Renaissance writers and artists find employment with the Works Project Administration (WPA), a government-sponsored program designed to put Americans back to work.
- Aaron Douglas paints murals for the YMCA in Harlem.
- The film adaptation of Eugene O'Neill's *The Emperor Jones,* starring Paul Robeson, is released. The screenplay is written by DuBose Heyward.

1934

- Aaron Douglas is commissioned to create a series of murals, which will be entitled *Aspects of Negro Life,* for the 135th Street (Harlem) branch of the New York Public Library.
- The NAACP and the American Fund for Public Service plan a coordinated legal campaign, directed by Howard University Law School vice-dean Charles H. Houston, against segregation and discrimination.
- Oscar Michaux releases his film *Harlem After Midnight.*
- Wallace Thurman's death in the charity ward of a New York hospital stuns and sobers his Harlem Renaissance friends.
- Zora Neale Hurston's first novel, *Jonah's Gourd Wine,* is published by Lippincott.
- Nancy Cunard, a British socialite, assembles and edits the *Negro Anthology,* a sprawling 855 page work that features photographs and scores for African music as well as articles on ethnography, linguistics, poetry, and political commentary. Contributors include Sterling Brown, Langston Hughes, and Zora Neale Hurston.

1935

- Harlem is the scene of a major riot sparked by anger over discrimination by white-owned businesses.
- The exhibition *African Negro Art* opens at the Museum of Modern Art in New York City.
- Carl Van Vechten debuts his first collection of photographs in *The Leica Exhibition* at the Bergdorf Goodman in New York City.
- Lippincott publishes Hurston's ethnographic study *Mules and Men,* with illustrations by Miguel Covarrubias.

1936

- African American actors Paul Robeson and Hattie McDaniel appear in director James Whales's film adaptation of Kern and Hammerstein's musical *Show Boat.*

1937

- *Their Eyes Were Watching God* by Zora Neale Hurston is published by Lippincott.

CHARLES SPURGEON JOHNSON

(1893 - 1956)

American nonfiction writer, editor, researcher, and educator.

As founder and editor of the journal *Opportunity,* Johnson offered recognition and support to many African American writers of the Harlem Renaissance by giving them the chance to publish their works, holding literary contests with prize money, and hosting honorary annual banquets. For these and other efforts, Langston Hughes credited Johnson with having "single-handedly propelled" the Harlem Renaissance into being. His books of sociological studies on race relations, including *The Negro in Chicago: A Study of Race Relations and a Race Riot* (1922), provided scientific data on the Black community that was useful for policy makers in their attempts to alleviate racial tensions. As president of Fisk University at Nashville from 1947 until his death, Johnson hired remarkable talent and was a noted educational spokesman, tirelessly advocating the need for quality teaching.

BIOGRAPHICAL INFORMATION

Johnson was born in Bristol, Virginia, in 1893, the son of the Reverend Charles Henry Johnson and Winifred Branch. Reverend Johnson, a former slave, was tutored by his master, along with the master's white son, in Latin, Greek, Hebrew, and English and American literature. The Reverend's library was avidly used by his own son later. Johnson took an interest in sociological field work at an early age, observing race relations and behavior in the barbershop which he cleaned for pay. From 1909 to 1913 he attended Wayland Academy in Richmond in lieu of high school, followed by Virginia Union University, also in Richmond, completing the four-year B.A. program a year early. For graduate studies he chose the University of Chicago, where he came under the influence of the famous sociologist Robert E. Park and his ideas of race assimilation. Johnson quickly set up research for the Urban League and began studying African American migration in the United States. In 1918 Johnson enlisted to fight in the first World War, and in the course of one year engaged in battle in France and became a noncommissioned officer. In 1919 he returned home only to find more fighting: race riots were breaking out in numerous cities around the country, notably in Chicago. Johnson immediately set to work writing a report that explained some of the factors leading to the violence and outlined recommendations for further study. The Governor's Commission on Race Relations was so impressed by Johnson's work that Johnson was made aide to the secretary; from the study emerged *The Negro in Chicago.* Johnson married Marie Antoinette Burgette, and together they moved to New York City in 1921, where they would eventually have three sons and a daughter. Johnson became director of research for the National Urban League, and founded *Opportunity,* serving as its editor from 1923 to 1928. In 1928 he moved to Nashville and became Chair of the Social Sciences Department at Fisk University, a position he held until 1947, when he assumed the presidency of the entire university. Johnson died in Louisville in 1956 after suffering a heart attack.

MAJOR WORKS

Johnson's 600-page report, *The Negro in Chicago,* was heralded for its clarity and established him as one of the country's leading sociologists. In 1927 he edited *Ebony and Topaz, A Collectanea,* which culled the best of the writing that appeared in the pages of *Opportunity*. The 1930s was Johnson's most productive decade. *The Negro in American Civilization* (1930) is a 500-page report put together for the National Interracial Conference. *Shadow of the Plantation* (1934) studies the demise of the plantation system and its effect on the workers engaged in it; further analysis of this issue is found in *The Collapse of Cotton Tenancy* (1935), which Johnson wrote with Edwin R. Embree and W. W. Alexander. *A Preface to Racial Understanding* (1936) is a text for college students. Numerous studies followed, their titles descriptive of their subject matter: *The Negro College Graduate* (1938); *Growing up in the Black Belt: Negro Youth in the Rural South* (1941); *Statistical Atlas of Southern Counties* (1941); and *To Stem This Tide: A Survey of Racial Tension Areas in the United States,* a collaborative study published in 1943.

CRITICAL RECEPTION

Johnson's studies were widely acclaimed by social scientists and noticed by Presidents Herbert Hoover, Franklin Delano Roosevelt, Harry Truman, and Dwight Eisenhower, all of whom enlisted Johnson to serve on commissions. He received countless awards and honors, chief among them honorary doctorates from Virginia Union University in 1928 and Howard University in 1941, a Doctor of Laws from the University of Glasgow, Scotland, in 1951, and a Doctor of Letters from Columbia University in 1951. Johnson was not without detractors, however: Edwin R. Embree writes, "Radicals say he is too conservative, too willing to compromise, and he admits that he believes in step by step rather than in sweeping revolution. Some people think he is too calm in the face of the evils he is studying, though his record in bringing about lasting reforms gives pause to those critics." Elmer A. Carter explains the significance of the studies made by Johnson: "At a time when the intelligence test was rapidly becoming accepted as proof of the Negro's innate inferiority, his relentless demand for the facts, for the application of scientific methods was the greatest single influence in stirring the academicians to a reexamination of test techniques and content and, finally, to the abandonment of the sweeping generalizations in the measurement of racial difference." Ralph L. Pearson quotes Johnson explaining his hopes that *Opportunity* will encourage Blacks "to effect an emancipation from their sensitiveness about meaningless symbols, and . . . [to] inculcate a disposition to see enough of interest and beauty in their own lives to rid themselves of the inferior feeling of being a Negro." Pearson explains Johnson's belief that the European model of literature must yield to the personal experience of the African American, and that Johnson felt the "emancipation of black artists was the means for a 'new freedom' for the entire race." Kathleen A. Hauke writes that Johnson's "literary voice stood for excellence, thoroughness, clarity, and nurturance. Without his quietly aggressive assistance, many of the voices who shaped the Afro-American literary canon beyond the renaissance would not have come into prominence."

PRINCIPAL WORKS

The Negro in Chicago: A Study of Race Relations and a Race Riot (nonfiction) 1922

Ebony and Topaz, A Collectanea [editor] (fiction) 1927

The Negro in American Civilization (nonfiction) 1930

Negro Housing: Report, President's Conference on Home Building and Home Ownership, Washington, D.C., 1931 (nonfiction) 1932

The Negro in Baltimore Industries: A Study of the Industrial Situation in Baltimore (nonfiction) 1932

The Economic Status of Negroes (nonfiction) 1933

Race Relations: Adjustment of Whites and Negroes in the United States [with Willis D. Weatherford] (nonfiction) 1934

Shadow of the Plantation (nonfiction) 1934

The Collapse of Cotton Tenancy [with Edwin R. Embree and W. W. Alexander] (nonfiction) 1935

Negro White Collar Projects (nonfiction) 1935

A Preface to Racial Understanding (nonfiction) 1936

The Negro College Graduate (nonfiction) 1938

Growing up in the Black Belt: Negro Youth in the Rural South (nonfiction) 1941

Statistical Atlas of Southern Counties (nonfiction) 1941

Education and the Cultural Process: Papers Presented at Symposium Commemorating the Seventy-Fifth Anniversary of the Founding of Fisk University, April 29-May 4, 1941 [editor] (essays) 1943

Patterns of Negro Segregation (nonfiction) 1943

To Stem This Tide: A Survey of Racial Tension Areas in the United States [with others] (nonfiction) 1943

Into the Main Stream: A Survey of Best Practices in Race Relations in the South [with others] (nonfiction) 1947

People vs. Property: Race Restrictive Covenants in Housing [with Herman Hodge Long] (nonfiction) 1947

Education and the Cultural Crisis (nonfiction) 1951

Bitter Canaan: The Story of the Negro Republic (nonfiction) 1987

PRIMARY SOURCES

CHARLES S. JOHNSON (ESSAY DATE 1954)

SOURCE: Johnson, Charles S. "The Negro Renaissance and Its Significance." In *The Portable Harlem Renaissance Reader,* edited by David Levering Lewis, pp. 206-18. New York: Penguin Books, 1994.

Considered a founding father of the Harlem Renaissance, Johnson was a participant in the very first gathering sponsored by Opportunity *in 1924. This essay, a contribution to a 1954 symposium at Howard University, assesses that historic meeting and how it influenced one of the most vibrant periods of African American history.*

There is a double presumptuousness about this presentation: It is not only a sort of history, constructed in large part from memory; but it is presented as history in the presence of rigid and exacting historians who regard the proper and unchallengeable enlightenment of future generations as their sacred trust.

There are, however, some compensating factors for this boldness: We are, in a sense, memorializing Alain Locke, an important maker of history who is himself inadequately recorded. And while some of the fragments of memory and experience may be compounded with a prejudiced aura of friendship, this fact itself from a collateral contemporary may have some value.

As a sociologist rather than an historian, it is expected that particular events would be viewed in the light of broader social processes, thus offering greater illumination to what has come to be recognized as a dramatic period in our national history.

American Negroes in the 1920's were just a little more than a half century on their rugged course to citizenship. This period was the comet's tail of a great cultural ferment in the nation, the "melting pot" era, a period of the ascendancy of unbridled free enterprise, of the open beginnings of class struggle and new and feeble mutterings of self-conscious labor; of muckrakers and social settlements, of the open and unabashed acceptance of "inferior and superior races and civilizations." Likewise, the era just preceding the 1920's was a period of the sullen and frustrated gropings of the agrarian and culturally sterile South, in its "colonial" dependence upon the industrial North. It had been left in indifference to settle its problem of democracy in its own way.

In the wake of Reconstruction in the South there had been for the Negro, almost total political disfranchisement, economic disinheritance, denial of, or rigid limitation of, educational opportunity, complete racial segregation, with a gaudy racial philosophy to defend it, cultural isolation with its bitter fruit of inner personal poison, followed by mass migrations and revolt, and the tortuous struggle to slough off the heavy handicaps in order to achieve more completely a new freedom.

These were a part of the backdrop of what we have called the "Negro Renaissance," that sudden and altogether phenomenal outburst of emotional expression, unmatched by any comparable period in American or Negro American history.

It is well to point out that this was not a crisis and trauma affecting only the Negroes. It was fundamentally and initially a national problem.

James Weldon Johnson, who, with W. E. B. Du Bois emerged in the period just preceding the epochal 1920's, recognized this relationship and said this:

> A good part of white America frequently asks the question, "What shall we do with the Negro?" In asking the question it completely ignores the fact that the Negro is doing something with himself, and also the equally important fact that the Negro all the while is doing something with America.

Before Johnson there had been only a few Negroes capable of articulating the inner emotional turmoil of the race in full consciousness of its role in a nation that was itself in great stress.

Frederick Douglass had been a powerful oratorical force for the abolition of slavery, convincing to a sector of the nation in his own superiority as a person. Booker T. Washington had been a social strategist, speaking to the nation from the heavy racial miasma of the deep South, with wise words of economic counsel and even wiser words of tactical racial strategy. He parried the blows of the skeptical ones and the demagogues, who spoke hopelessly and menacingly of the destiny of the millions of ex-slaves in the South, still very largely unlettered and sought the armistice of tolerance during a vital period of regional gestation, as he negotiated with the industrial strength and benevolence of the North that was in being and the industrial dreams of the South, as yet unrealized.

W. E. B. Du Bois, brilliant, highly cultured, and racially sensitive, wrote with such bitter contempt for the American racial system that his flaming truths were invariably regarded as incendiary. He got attention but scant acceptance. And there was the poet Paul Laurence Dunbar who, like Booker T. Washington, came at a dark period, when with the release of the white working classes the independent struggle of Negroes for existence had become almost overwhelming in its severity. Dunbar caught the picture of the Negro in his pathetic and contagiously humorous moods and invested him with a new humanity. He embellished a stereotype and made likeable, in a homely way, the simple, joyous creature that was the mass Southern Negro, with the soft musical dialect and infectious rhythm. William Dean Howells, in an article in *Harper's Magazine,* hailed Dunbar as the first Negro to feel Negro life esthetically and express it lyrically. But in his candid moments, Dunbar confessed to Johnson that he resorted to dialect verse to gain a hearing and then nothing but his dialect verse would be accepted. He never got to the things he really wanted to do.

The acceptability of Dunbar's verse inspired many followers, including, for a brief spell, Johnson himself. The period of Johnson, however, was one that permitted bolder exploration and he turned forthrightly to poetry of race-consciousness. They were poems both of revelation and of protest. William Stanley Braithwaite was able to say of him that he brought the first intellectual substance to the context of poetry by Negroes, and a craftsmanship more precise and balanced than that of Dunbar. His Negro sermons symbolized the transition from the folk idiom to conscious artistic expression. In naive, non-dialect speech, they blend the rich imagery of the uneducated Negro minister with the finished skill of a cultured Negro poet. In a curiously fascinating way both style and content bespoke the meeting and parting of the old and new in Negro life in America.

The commentators even farther removed from today will be able to define more clearly the influence of these social and economic forces shortly after World War I, moving beneath the new mind of Negroes, which burst forth with freshness and vigor in an artistic "awakening." The first startlingly authentic note was sounded by Claude McKay, a Jamaican Negro living in America. If his was a note of protest it came clear and unquivering. But it was more than a protest note; it was one of stoical defiance which held behind it a spirit magnificent and glowing. One poem, "If We Must Die," written at the most acute point of the industrialization of Negroes when sudden mass contact in the Northern states was flaming into riots, voiced for Negroes, where it did not itself create, a mood of stubborn defiance. It was reprinted in practically every Negro newspaper, and quoted wherever its audacious lines could be remembered. But McKay could also write lyrics utterly divorced from these singing daggers. "Spring in New Hampshire" is one of them. He discovered Harlem and found a language of beauty for his own world of color.

> Her voice was like the sound of blended flutes
> Blown by black players on a picnic day.

Jean Toomer flashed like a meteor across the sky, then sank from view. But in the brilliant moment of his flight he illuminated the forefield of this new Negro literature. *Cane,* a collection of verse and stories, appeared about two years ahead of its sustaining public mood. It was significantly a return of the son to the Southland, to the stark, natural beauties of its life and soil, a life deep and strong, and a virgin soil.

More than artist, he was an experimentalist, and this last quality carried him away from what was, perhaps, the most astonishingly brilliant beginning of any Negro writer of his generation.

With Countee Cullen came a new generation of Negro singers. Claude McKay had brought a strange geographical background to the American scene which enabled him to escape a measure of the peculiar social heritage of the American Negro which similarly lacked the impedimenta of an inhibiting tradition. He relied upon nothing but his own sure competence and art; one month found three literary magazines carrying his verse simultaneously, a distinction not to be spurned by any young poet. Then came his first volume, *Color.* He brought an uncannily sudden maturity and classic sweep, a swift grace and an inescapable beauty of style and meaning. The spirit of the transplanted African moved through his music to a new definition—relating itself boldly to its past and present.

> Lord, not for what I saw in flesh or bone
> Of fairer men; not raised on faith alone;
> Lord, I will live persuaded by mine own.
> I cannot play the recreant to these;
> My spirit has come home, that sailed the doubtful seas.

He spoke, not for himself alone, but for the confident generation out of which he came. White gods were put aside and in their place arose the graces of a race he knew.

> Her walk is like the replica
> Of some barbaric dance
> Wherein the soul of Africa
> Is winged with arrogance.

and again:

> That brown girl's swagger gives a twitch
> To beauty like a queen.

No brief quotations can describe this power, this questioning of life and even God; the swift arrow thrusts of irony curiously mingled with admiration; the self-reliance and bold pride of race; the thorough repudiation of the double standard of literary judgment. He may have marvelled "at this curious thing to make a poet black and bid him sing," but in his *Heritage* he voiced the half-religious, half-challenging spirit of an awakened generation. "He will be remembered," said the *Manchester Guardian,* "as one who contributed to his age some of its loveliest lyric poetry."

Langston Hughes, at twenty-four, had published two volumes of verse. No Negro writer so completely symbolizes the new emancipation of the Negro mind. His was a poetry of gorgeous colors, of restless brooding, of melancholy, of disillusionment:

> We should have a land of sun
> Of gorgeous sun,
> And a land of fragrant water
> Where the twilight
> Is a soft bandana handkerchief
> And not this land where life is cold.

Always there is, in his writing, a wistful undertone, a quiet sadness. That is why, perhaps, he could speak so tenderly of the broken lives of prostitutes, the inner weariness of painted "jazz-hounds" and the tragic emptiness beneath the glamour and noise of Harlem cabarets. His first volume, *The Weary Blues,* contained many moods; the second, *Fine Clothes to the Jew,* marked a final frank turning to the folk life of the Negro, a striving to catch and give back to the world the strange music of the unlettered Negro—his "Blues." If Cullen gave a classic beauty to the emotions of the race, Hughes gave a warm glow of meaning to their lives.

I return again more comfortably to my role as a sociologist in recording this period following the deep and disrupting crisis of a world war, with its uprooting of customs and people in which there developed two movements with clashing ideologies. There was reassertion with vigor of the old and shaken racial theories, with "racial purity clubs," intelligence tests "proving" the unchangeable inferiority of the Negro and other darker peoples, Congressional restrictions of immigration according to rigid racial formulas, race riots, dark foreboding prophecies of the over-running of the white race by the dark and unenlightened hordes from Asia and Africa, in Lothrop Stoddard's *Rising Tide of Color.*

These were only reflections of the new forces set loose in the world and finding expression in such mutterings as "India for the Indians," "A Free Ireland," self-determination for the smaller countries of the world.

For the just-emerging Negro who had freed himself geographically at least, there was much frustration. Perhaps the most dramatic phase of this was the Garvey movement. Here were hundreds of thousands of Negroes who had reached the promised land of the North and found it a bitter Canaan. Having nowhere else to seek haven in America their dreams turned to Africa under the powerful stimulation of the master dream-maker from the West Indies, Marcus Garvey. They would find haven in their ancestral homeland, and be free from the insults and restrictions of this nation and England, on their chance for greatness. Provisionally there were created Dukes of the Nile, Princesses of Ethiopia, Lords of the Sudan, for the weary and frustrated people whose phantom freedom in the North was as empty as their explicit subordination in the South.

Of this desperate and pathetic mass fantasy I find an editorial note in *Opportunity Magazine* in 1923 in a mood of brooding concern for the present and apprehension for the future:

> It is a symbol, a symptom, and another name for the new psychology of the American Negro peasantry—for the surge of race consciousness felt by Negroes throughout the world, the intelligent as well as the ignorant.
>
> It is a black version of that same one hundred per cent mania that now afflicts white America, that emboldens the prophets of a Nordic blood renaissance, that picked up and carried the cry of self-determination for all people, India for the Indians, A Free Ireland.
>
> The sources of this discontent must be remedied effectively and now, or the accumulating energy and unrest, blocked off from its dreams, will take another direction. Perhaps this also will be harmless, but who knows.

To this note of 1923 might be added the observation of what is happening in the Asian-African Conference in Bandung in 1955; what happened in this long interval to make it possible for twenty-nine nations that in 1923 were only muttering against colonial imperialism and now are speaking as free and independent nations collectively to preserve the peace and security of the world.

It was out of forces of such magnitude that the voices of the Negro Renaissance made themselves heard and felt. It was a period, not only of the quivering search for freedom but of a cultural, if not a social and racial emancipation. It was unabashedly self-conscious and race-conscious. But it was race-consciousness with an extraordinary facet in that it had virtues that could be incorporated into the cultural bloodstream of the nation.

This was the period of the discovery by these culturally emancipated Negroes of the unique esthetic values of African art, of beauty in things dark, a period of harkening for the whispers of greatness from a remote African past. This was the period of Kelly Miller's Sanhedrin to reassess the lost values and build upon newly-found strengths. It was the period of the reaching out of arms for other dark arms of the same ancestry from other parts of the world in a Pan-African Conference.

Significantly, Dr. W. E. B. Du Bois made his first talk after returning from the Pan-African Conference of 1923 at the first *Opportunity Magazine* dinner, sponsoring the fledgling writers of the new and lively generation of the 1920's.

The person recognized as the Dean of this youthful group was Alain Locke. A brilliant analyst trained in philosophy, and an esthete with a flair for art as well as letters, he gave encouragement and guidance to these young writers as an older practitioner too sure of his craft to be discouraged by failure of full acceptance in the publishing media of the period.

Perhaps this is the point at which to add a previously unwritten note to the history of the period. The importance of the *Crisis Magazine* and *Opportunity Magazine* was that of providing an outlet for young Negro writers and scholars whose work was not acceptable to other established media because it could not be believed to be of standard quality despite the superior quality of much of it. What was necessary was a revolution and a revelation sufficient in intensity to disturb the age-old customary cynicisms. This function became associated with *Opportunity Magazine.*

Alain Locke recognized the role and possibility of this organ for creating such a revolution and associated himself with it, first as a reviewer and appraiser of various literary and sociological efforts and later as a contributor of major articles. As a by-product of his acquaintance with France, England and Germany through frequent visits, he wrote articles on current issues affecting Negroes from the perspective of Europe: "The Black Watch on the Rhine" (1921), "Apropos of Africa" (1924) and "Back Stage on European Imperialism" (1925). These articles were of such mature sophistication and insight that *Opportunity* offered to share their publication with the *Survey Magazine* to get a larger reading public. This magazine not only published the articles jointly with *Opportunity* but requested special ones for the *Survey* readers. Thus began an important relationship with the editor of the *Survey* and *Survey Graphic.*

The first *Opportunity* contest had Alain Locke's enthusiastic support and assistance. It was a dual venture in faith: faith in the creative potential of this generation in its new cultural freedom; and faith in the confidence of the nation's superior mentalities and literary creators. Both were justified. Locke's mellow maturity and esthetic sophistication were the warrant of confidence in the possibilities of these youth as well as the concrete evidence of accomplishment. The American scholars and writers who stretched out their arms to welcome these youthful aspirants to cultural equality were, without exception, the intellectual and spiritual leaders of the nation's cultural life and aspirations. They served as judges in these contests and in this role gave priceless assistance to this first and vital step in cultural integration. They were such great figures of American literary history as Van Wyck Brooks, Carl Van Doren, Eugene O'Neill, James Weldon Johnson, Paul Kellogg, Fannie Hurst, Robert Benchley, Zona

Gale, Dorothy Canfield Fisher, Witter Bynner, W. E. B. Du Bois, Alexander Woollcott, John Macy, John Dewey, Carl Van Vechten, John Farrar and others.

They not only judged the poetry, essays, short stories and plays, but lent a supporting hand to their development in the best literary traditions.

At the first *Opportunity* dinner at the Civic Club in New York, Alain Locke was as a matter of course and appropriateness, moderator. It happens that this was one of the most significant and dramatic of the announcements of the renaissance. It marked the first public appearance of young creative writers in the company of the greatest of the nation's creative writers and philosophers. Out of this meeting came some of the first publications in the best publication tradition.

I cannot refrain from quoting briefly a poem read at this dinner by Gwendolyn Bennett:

TO USWARD
And some of us have songs to sing
Of purple heat and fires
And some of us are solemn grown
With pitiful desires;
And there are those who feel the pull
Of seas beneath the skies;
And some there be who want to croon
Of Negro lullabies.
We claim no part with racial dearth
We want to sing the songs of birth.
And so we stand like ginger jars,
Like ginger jars bound round
With dust and age;
Like jars of ginger we are sealed
By nature's heritage.
But let us break the seal of years
With pungent thrusts of song
For there is joy in long dried tears
For whetted passions of a throng.

For specific identification, it should be noted that Frederick Allen of *Harper's Magazine* made a bid for Countee Cullen's poems for publication as soon as he had finished reading them at this *Opportunity* dinner; and Paul Kellogg of the *Survey* sought to carry the entire evening's readings in an issue of the magazine. This fumbling idea lead to the standard volume of the period, *The New Negro.*

Winold Reiss, a German artist of extraordinary skill in pictorial interpretation had just completed some drawings for the *Survey* of Sea Island Negroes. The publishers Boni and Boni who were interested in a book of Winold Reiss' drawings decided to carry the literary content along with the pictures. This literary content had been carried first in the *Survey Graphic* in a special issue under the editorship of Alain Locke. As a book it became *The New Negro,* also edited by Locke, and expanded from the special issue of the *Survey Graphic* to the proportions that now make brilliant history.

The impetus to publication backed by the first recognition of creative work in the best literary tradition, swept in many if not most of the budding writers of this period, in a fever of history-making expression.

Removed by two generations from slavery and in a new cultural environment, these Negro writers were less self-conscious and less interested in proving that they were just like white people; in their excursions into the fields of letters and art, they seemed to care less about what white people thought, or were likely to think, than about themselves and what they had to say. Relief from the stifling consciousness of being a problem had brought a certain superiority to it. There was more candor, even in discussions of themselves about weaknesses, and on the very sound reasoning that unless you are truthful about your faults, you will not be believed when you speak about your virtues. The emancipation of these writers gave them freedom to return to the dynamic folk motives.

Carl Van Doren, in commenting upon this material said:

> If the reality of Negro life is itself dramatic there are, of course, still other elements, particularly the emotional power, with which Negroes live—or at least to me they seem to live. What American literature needs at this moment is color, music, gusto, the free expression of gay, or desperate moods. If the Negroes are not in a position to contribute these items, I do not know which Americans are.

As a rough cultural yardstick of the continuing repercussions of the period called the Renaissance, I have looked up the record of the youthful writers and commentators of this period for evidences of their effect upon the present state of the American culture.

An anthology called *Ebony and Topaz* carried about twenty young Negro writers, previously unknown to the great and critical public. Of those still living Langston Hughes and Sterling Brown are established poets, Arna Bontemps is a major novelist, having left his poetry with his youth; Aaron Douglas is one of the country's best-known artists; Zora Neale Hurston is a writer-anthropologist; Allison Davis is a distinguished psychologist and Abram Harris an equally distinguished economist, and both are on the faculty of the University of Chicago. Ira Reid heads the Department of Sociology at Haverford; Frank Horne is a national housing official. E. Franklin Frazier is one of the nation's most notable sociologists and a former president of the American Sociological Society, George Schuyler is a well-known columnist and John P. Davis is publisher of *Our World Magazine.*

There are others, of course, but the important thing is to show some end result of the striving.

As master of ceremonies for the first *Opportunity* dinner Alain Locke had this to say about these young spirits being launched on their careers: "They sense within their group—a spiritual wealth which if they can properly expound, will be ample for a new judgment and re-appraisal of the race."

Whether or not there has been a reappraisal of the race over these past thirty years rests with our estimates of the contributions of those who began their careers in the 1920's. It is my opinion that the great fire and enthusiasm of the earlier period, and the creative dynamism of self-conscious racial expression are no longer present. They have faded with the changed status of Negroes in American life.

With the disappearance of many of the barriers to participation in the general culture the intense race-consciousness has been translated into contributions within the accepted national standards of the special professional fields.

One of Goethe's commentators referred to his literary art as the practice of living and pointed out that his life was as much worth studying as his work. Goethe in one of his diaries said:

> People who are always harping on the value of experience tend to forget that experience is only the one-half of experience. The secret of creative living consists in relating the rough and tumble of our contact with the world outside ourselves to the work which our minds put in on this stuff of experience. The full value of experience is in seeing the significance of what has happened. Without this awareness we do not really live. Life lives us.

This, it seems to me, is the essence of the shift in Negro life and Negro appraisals of life.

The infectious race-conscious movement of the period of the "Renaissance" has been transmitted into less race-conscious scholarship. The historical research of John Hope Franklin, Benjamin Quarles and Rayford Logan appears as aspects of American history even though the subject matter may be Negroes. Similarly the sociological writing of E. Franklin Frazier, Ira de A. Reid, and Oliver Cox is in the broader context of the American society. Frank Yerby's romantic novels are best sellers and deal only incidentally with Negroes, if at all.

The most recent books by Negro authors, interestingly enough, are travel studies of other lands and people. Saunders Redding and Carl Rowan have written about India, Richard Wright and Era Belle Thompson about Africa. Meanwhile the kind of writing done by American Negroes in the 1920's is reflected in the books today by Peter Abrahams of South Africa and George Lamming of Trinidad, in the British West Indies.

In 1923 Franklin Frazier who was one of the first *Opportunity* prize winners with a bold essay on "Social Equality and the Negro" had this to say:

> The accomplishment of a consciously built-up culture will depend upon leaders with a vision and understanding of cultural processes. Nevertheless, spiritual and intellectual emancipation of the Negro awaits the building of a Negro university, supported by Negro educators, who have imbibed the best that civilization can offer, where its savants can add to human knowledge and promulgate those values which are to inspire and motivate Negroes as a cultural group.

We have in this present period, and out of the matrix of the Renaissance period, scholars who know the cultural process, and savants who have imbibed the best that civilization can offer and can and are aiding human knowledge, within the context, not of a special culture group, but of the national society and world civilization.

GENERAL COMMENTARY

ERNEST W. BURGESS (ESSAY DATE 1956)

SOURCE: Burgess, Ernest W. "Charles S. Johnson: Social Scientist and Race Relations." *Phylon: The Atlanta University Review* XVII, no. 4 (fourth quarter 1956): 317-21.

In the following essay, Burgess discusses Johnson's early years at the University of Chicago and provides capsule descriptions of his most significant books.

Charles S. Johnson spent four years in Chicago from 1917-21 in study at the University of Chicago and in research on problems of the Negro. He entered the University just as I was beginning my second year as the junior member of the department of sociology. Its staff was then the most distinguished in the country including Albion W. Small, head of the department, Robert E.

Park, and William I. Thomas, who was succeeded by Ellsworth Faris. The social philosopher Herbert G. Mead might well be added to this group since his courses in social psychology were taken by students in sociology.

Charles Johnson impressed me at once, as he did all his instructors, as a young man of unusual ability, energy, and originality. Loraine Green, also a brilliant student, and Johnson both held their own so ably in class discussions that they were living refutations of any belief other students might have in racial differences in mentality.

Robert E. Park, W. I. Thomas, and Ellsworth Faris were all intensely interested in the phenomena of race. Their studies in this country and in Africa had convinced them that observable differences between the races in mental ability and in behavior were the result of cultural and social rather than biological factors. They all held that the sociological study of racial contacts, competition, conflict, accommodation, and assimilation would yield valuable returns in contributions both to social theory and to the understanding and ultimate solution of one of humanity's most pressing problems.

Charles Johnson as a student developed an association with Park which was to continue and grow until the death of the latter in 1944 while visiting professor at Fisk University. Park had entered academic life as a member of the department of sociology of the University of Chicago at a late age—that of fifty—to begin a meteoric career. But he had an exceptional background of preparation as newspaper man, as a student of William James, George Santayana, and Josiah Royce at Harvard, of Georg Simmel and Wilhelm Windelband in Germany and later as an intimate associate of Booker T. Washington in his work at Tuskegee.

Johnson gained from Park a broad background of sociological theory which encompassed both the development of the person under cultural and other social influences and also the principles of social interaction and collective behavior so essential for the analysis and understanding of interracial relations and behavior. He also obtained from him a mastery of the use of the personal document which he was to use with effectiveness in his research. Under Park's guidance he developed an objective scientific attitude toward the highly emotional problem of race relations and a belief that an understanding of the attitudes underlying opinions and prejudices was essential for research in human behavior.

While carrying on his studies at the University Johnson began his brilliant research career. He was director of research and records (1917-19) of the Chicago Urban League of which Park was then president. He was associate executive director of the Chicago Commission on Race Relations and participated with Graham Romeyn Taylor in the study of the Chicago race riot of 1919 which led to the publication of the outstanding report ***The Negro in Chicago: A Study of Race Relations and a Race Riot.*** This volume contained an exhaustive factual and objective description of the race riot and of the events leading up to it. But it also assembled a wealth of information on the conditions of living of Negroes in Chicago and of the misconceptions, misinformations, and prejudices which constituted the hard core of the problem of race relations in the city.

This volume was, of course, a joint effort of the Commission, the executive director, the associate executive director, and of an able staff. But it bears the stamp of the characteristics which distinguish the work of Charles S. Johnson as a social scientist. It has scientific objectivity, it relies on both personal documents and statistical data, its findings are marshalled for practical application in the solution of a problem, its main objective is to obtain understanding of the factors and processes in human behavior.

The next large-scale study in which Johnson participated was begun in 1926 under the auspices of the National Interracial Conference organized by sixteen national organizations interested in improving relations between the white and the colored in this country. His services were contributed by the National Urban League where he was director of research. He was chosen as research secretary to assist the Conference in constructing a reasonably faithful contemporary picture of Negro life and the existing status of race relations. After the Conference, held in Washington, D. C. on December 16-19, 1928, Johnson was charged with the task of organizing into a book the material already gathered. The result was ***The Negro in American Civilization*** published in 1930 which brought together for the first time in challenging form the findings of social research on the Negro in this country in the perspective of race relations and attitudes.

In 1928 Johnson was appointed chairman of the department of social science at Fisk University. Under his leadership the department developed into the leading research center in race relations in the world. A series of studies was undertaken, only a few of which can be reported on here.

One group of published studies dealt with the occupational aspects of Negro living in the South. ***The Shadow of the Plantation,*** appearing in 1934, revealed the attitudes of Negroes in this type of economic organization and the personality changes taking place with the breakup of the system. ***The Collapse of Cotton Tenancy,*** written with Edwin R. Embree and W. W. Alexander, presents their findings and conclusions on tenancy in the Southern cotton belt. Johnson's book on ***The Negro College Graduate*** published in 1938 is concerned with the opposite end of the educational and occupational level from that of the cotton picker of the plantation. Some data are reported upon a grand total of 43,821 Negro college graduates from 1826-1936 and a mass of information on 5,512 living graduates who were interviewed or reached by questionnaires. The attempt in the final chapter to synthesize the social and educational philosophy of the Negro college graduate still remains the basic principle of education. "Only in terms of one's own experience can one comprehend fully and usefully the experience of others. With a deeper and sounder understanding of his own life and traditions, knowledge could then be extended to the world outside."

A basic study undertaken by Johnson for the Council on Rural Education, founded in 1934 and supported by the Julius Rosenwald Foundation, was published in 1941 under the title ***Statistical Atlas of Southern Counties.*** The Council was convinced that education must seriously take into account the social environment of Negro children. This volume consisted of a listing and detailed analysis of social economic data and indices for 1104 southern counties. The counties were classified in three ways: by major crop types, by complexity of crop operations and by urbanization and industrialization. The fact that the rural educational status of the county was associated with its classification by these indices was of significance in educational planning for rural areas.

The volume ***Growing Up in the Black Belt*** prepared for the American Youth Commission and published in 1941 represents perhaps the fullest utilization of the talents of the staff of his department. Statistical and case-study methods were carefully planned in advance. The findings provide invaluable knowledge on the personality development of southern rural Negro youth in a social environment with racial implications. Significant for sociological theory is Johnson's conclusion that the theory of southern racial relations as a caste system is only superficially true. It lacks the mutual acceptance and adjustment to a fixed status, religious sanctions for it, and the absolute impossibility of altering caste status. Instead "the southern race system is highly unstable. There is not only tension between the races but actual uncertainty in the minds of both groups as to the significance of race lines. . . . If one cannot safely predict progress in race relations, he can at least predict change."

When Gunnar Myrdal was collecting material for his study of the Negro problem, later published as *The American Dilemma,* he asked Johnson to prepare the memorandum on segregation. The data gathered were reworked by Johnson and published in 1943 in the book entitled ***Patterns of Segregation,*** a most exhaustive analysis of the subject. This volume not only describes the many different types of segregation but establishes that the color line is defined more certainly by ideology than by customs and laws. He concludes: "The effects of the unrestrained operation of the principles of racialism are conceivably as dangerous to American society as the unrestricted play of free competition in the economic sphere. Logically, it would be appropriate for government to impose controls and regulations as mandatory as those imposed on its economic life to ensure all its racial minorities not only free but equal participation in the economic and political life of the country." This statement may be taken as forecasting the historic decision of the Supreme Court in decreeing the invalidity of residential restrictive convenants and in abolishing racial segregation in schools.

Two other studies by Johnson merit brief mention. ***To Stem the Tide*** was the title of the report of a survey of racial tension areas in the United States under war conditions. Published in 1943 in the middle of World War II it highlighted the fact that Negro manpower was not being either adequately or efficiently used for national defense, either by industry or by the military services. ***Into the Main Stream*** issued in 1947 might be considered as a follow-up volume concerned with post-war circumstances. It consisted of a telling survey of the best practices in race relations in the South.

In 1946 Johnson became president of Fisk University. In his book ***Education and the Cul-***

tural Crisis appearing in 1951 he outlined his educational philosophy which had been developing during his lifetime of social research on race relations. Earlier in 1943 in his introduction to a symposium on Education and the Cultural Process he had seen education in the broader context of acculturation, one aspect of which "appears in the constant struggle to get a new society and a new solidarity." Now, raising his perspective from race relations to the larger framework of international relations he called for "a mass education which is democratic in inspiration and faithful to the idea of minority rights and which seeks to develop the best within a culture and includes all cultures." "In this way there can be a blending of East and West and the discovery of common ground in those values which are a responsibility of the higher civilizations."

On April 2, 1955, President Charles S. Johnson proudly presided at the dedication of the Social Science Building at Fisk University. For him it was a dream come true. It was named for Robert E. Park in recognition of his outstanding contributions to sociology and to the field of race relations, and as a tribute of regard and esteem from a former student and colleague. The assemblage of eminent social scientists and leaders in research in race relations at the symposium before the dedication on "Progress in Race Relations" made the occasion one of reviewing the function of research in the moving current of social action.

In the process of change in race relations in the United States, from the race riot of Chicago to the Supreme Court's decision outlawing segregation in schools and requiring integration, no one has made a greater contribution than Charles S. Johnson. The accumulated impact of his research has been tremendous because of his scientific objectivity, his caution in interpreting data, his understanding of the human element in social situations, and his discernment in coming to sound and practical application of his findings. He achieved first rank as a social scientist. He also developed as a great educator and as a social statesman to whom our government, our welfare, educational, and religious organizations and UNESCO frequently turned for counsel and guidance.

ELMER A. CARTER (ESSAY DATE 1956)

SOURCE: Carter, Elmer A. "Charles S. Johnson: Editor and 'The New Negro'." *Phylon: The Atlanta University Review* XVII, no. 4 (fourth quarter 1956): 321-24.

In the following essay, Carter discusses the cultural and historic importance of Opportunity, *the journal founded by Johnson.*

In the second issue of *Opportunity—Journal of Negro Life* (February 1923), Charles S. Johnson set forth the aims and purposes of the new magazine in a modest but challenging editorial captioned, "Why We Are." It would be difficult to find in the history of American journalism a more succinct and vivid justification for the launching of a new publication. In this forceful prose he announced the editorial policy:

> The policy of *Opportunity* will be definitely constructive. It will aim to present, objectively, facts of Negro life. It hopes, thru an analysis of these social questions, to provide a basis of understanding; encourage interracial cooperation in the working out of these problems, especially those surrounding the emergence of the Negro into a new industrial field and the consequent reorganization of habit and skill. The alarming tho' preventable death rate; the miseducation and uneducation of a million colored children with their consequent registration in defective manhood, delinquency and crime need attention.
>
> There are aspects of the cultural side of Negro life that have been long neglected. There are facts of Negro progress as well as handicaps that should be known not only for the stimulation which comes from recognition but as an antidote to a disposition not infrequently encountered to disparage unjustly the capacities and aspirations of this group.

I venture to say that no projected policy in the field of journalism has ever been carried out with more fidelity, none with more brilliance than this one. Not even the Directors of the National Urban League and the Associates of Charles Johnson in the movement at that time appreciated the conception of this venture as it existed in his mind, nor were they fully cognizant of the range of his knowledge, the variety of his intellectual interests, which successive issues of *Opportunity* were to demonstrate. A natural diffidence served to obscure these qualities. His placid countenance belied the restlessness of his mind. Beneath the apparent austerity of the pure scholar was surging curiosity, the capacity for great but controlled indignation. He was a logician who brought at once exultation and dismay to social scientists of this era.

At a time when the intelligence test was rapidly becoming accepted as proof of the Negro's innate inferiority, his relentless demand for the facts, for the application of scientific methods was the greatest single influence in stirring the academicians to a reexamination of test techniques and content and, finally, to the abandonment of the sweeping generalizations in the measurement of racial difference. In the February 1928 issue Charles Johnson was to say:

ABOUT THE AUTHOR

A FORUM FOR BLACK LITERATURE

Johnson's launching of *Opportunity,* which included the alerting of white editors and publishers to black artists and the funding of prizes for the best poetry, fiction, and visual art submitted annually, was one of the primary contributing catalysts in the creation of the Harlem Renaissance. Johnson asked his secretary, Ethel Nance, to make dossiers on black creative folk, to identify the people of promise and then entice them to come to Harlem where they could spur one another on. Sensitive to the artistic temperament and the importance of editorial reassurance, Johnson responded to submissions to *Opportunity* with utmost tact, so that even rejections encouraged. He turned down an overly long story from Angelina Grimké, after he had become "unwrapt from its fascination," telling her, "You have achieved a rare thing: that tragedy of life which escapes the melodramatic; characters which are real, unpretentious and lovable; [and] . . . good sound humor, no special pleading—all these with a delightfully competent touch."

SOURCE: Kathleen A. Hauke, "Charles Spurgeon Johnson," in *Dictionary of Literary Biography* 51: *Afro-American Writers from the Harlem Renaissance to 1940,* Gale, 1987, p. 148.

> There is a notion among certain social research students, that the mere documentation of a popular assumption gives it all that it needs of authority and finality. This is especially true of the studies which involve racial comparisons invidiously and convincingly, and so easy it is to establish these comparisons that they are growing increasingly popular as laboratory material. The wide and frequently empty gestures of fairness in comparison are meaningless so long as the zeal for truth does not penetrate the first questionable assumptions about race. The studies thus evolved become merely a laborious accumulation of figures, valuable only to those whose science is considerate enough to restrain them from inquiry into the situations behind the theories.

It was his extraordinary ability to create intellectual ferment in widely separate fields that first attracted the attention and later compelled the respect of those who had been called to plan and to fashion and to direct advanced learning in America. Honors that came to him—from Harvard, from the University of Glasgow, from our government which selected him for important educational missions—were the recognition of his contribution, not primarily to the Negro, but to learning.

Opportunity has long since ceased publication and a later generation may be totally oblivious, if not scornful, of the part this journal played in stimulating the creative urge among Negroes. In those days literary contests assumed some added fillip in the pages of *Opportunity*—essays, short stories, poetry ranging from the commonplace to the distinctive, poured from the throbbing pens of those who hurled their hearts against the color line. Inevitably, as Charles Johnson foresaw, were added other voices which could not be identified by race or color. Gradually, he lifted the young Negro's yearning to express his hopes, his dreams, his frustrations in moving prose or measured verse or in marble or stone or on canvas from contemplation of that which was sordid and mean to contemplation of that beauty which is always truth.

Most of Charles Johnson's interests and much of his work had more than parochial or racial significance. The series of articles on African art did much to acquaint not only the Negro but America with the artistic heritage of the Negro race. It was these articles which revealed to many for the first time the debt which modern painting and sculpture owe to the creations in wood and stone of the primitive African. Freely acknowledged in artistic circles in Europe, recognition of the enormous influence which these nameless artists had on the development of the masters of the age—Picasso, Soutine, Matisse, Modigliani—came tardily in America. Just now the full import of this phase of African life is being understood.

Perhaps this article should have been confined to a reprint of his last editorial published in the September 1928 issue of *Opportunity.* It was captioned, "To Negro Youth." If I had my way, I would make this statement prescribed reading for every Negro on his admission to college. I can quote the first two paragraphs:

> Negro youth facing the world today are bound by the historic implications of Negro status. These implications, both direct and insidious, have tended to warp perspective, to consume energies futilely in conflict, in disconsolate brooding, bitterness and sensitiveness; they have imposed dangerous dual standards, constricted life aims and

expectations, and contributed mightily to a defeat of the very spirit of youth. It is not too much to say that, granting all the obvious differences of race, these implications are escapable. The differences are susceptible of re-interpretation, and through this re-interpretation can come a new and vitalizing spiritual release, a freedom from within.

Human nature is plastic. It is constantly being shaped to new social attitudes. Things that appear to be a part of the order of the very universe may be altered by a sufficiently serious crisis in the life of a group. Negro youth have a right to feel that their self-expression can be more than a mere adjustment to racial policy; that it is possible to separate Negro life from the implications of Negro status; that Negro life in itself offers possibilities of the highest spiritual expression; that, in a very practical sense, it is possible to develop conscious compensations for the social disabilities of the moment; that we have in Negro life a virgin world of beauty which can yield rich satisfaction and command a new order of respect, and finally, that the freedom which these bring is a first condition of participation in the world culture.

CLARENCE H. FAUST (ESSAY DATE 1956)

SOURCE: Faust, Clarence H. "Charles S. Johnson: Educational Statesman, and Philanthropic Enterprises." *Phylon: The Atlanta University Review* XVII, no. 4 (fourth quarter 1956): 324-25.

In the following essay, Faust describes Johnson's generosity in providing his services to numerous foundations and philanthropic organizations.

Those of us who learned to know Charles Johnson well as a consequence of working with him in one of the many areas of his interest, philanthropic and foundation activities, came increasingly to depend upon his far-seeing vision, his imagination, his practical wisdom, his devotion to good causes, and his courage.

Time and again, when an important enterprise required the guidance of a wise, experienced, respected board or committee, his name would be among the first to be suggested. We had learned that where a combination of philosophic insights, practical prudence, and willingness to sacrifice time and energy were required, Charles Johnson was the man to enlist, and we had found that despite the heavy load of responsibility he already carried, he was amazingly generous in taking on yet another burden.

The range of the tasks he successfully assumed was astonishing. He was a valued participant in the efforts of the Conference on Science, Philosophy, and Religion to uncover and clarify the basic philosophical and religious problems of our time. He gave freely of his wisdom and experience to the national fellowship program for college teachers, established by the Fund for the Advancement of Education. He was a member of the national committee sponsoring the Fund's program of college self-studies. When the prospect of a tidal wave of students into our colleges and universities began to present a very serious problem of maintaining quality in education at a time of severe and hopeless shortage of college teachers, the Fund for the Advancement of Education formed a national committee on the Better Utilization of College Teaching Resources and turned once again to Charles Johnson, who generously agreed to serve on it. His counsel on matters of policy and practical procedure as a member of the Board of the Southern Education Reporting Service set up to provide full and objective information on the developments with respect to the integration of the public schools following the action of the Supreme Court in 1954 proved invaluable. In ways too numerous to mention, Charles Johnson's advice on formal boards and committees and informally on many important problems of foundation planning and procedure was sought and always generously and wisely given.

I am sure that the experience of other foundations and philanthropic organizations was like ours in the Fund for the Advancement of Education and that he was ready and useful in the service of many foundations and philanthropic enterprises.

What all of us who worked with him came to respect and admire was the sweep of his imagination and the depth of his insight into long-range problems, his clarity about the fundamental purposes and ends of education, and his great practical wisdom with respect to means for accomplishing these ends. He was imaginative without being impractical. He was deeply devoted to and confident of progress without losing sight of practical difficulties. He saw practical difficulties without being discouraged or despairing, and he was never unduly bound by the traditional or conventional ways of procedure.

His fine balance was reflected in his superb sense of humor, so that even in the most difficult and tense situations he was able to rise above the oppressive concerns of the moment in flashes of humorous insight. Time and again, after prolonged discussion of a complicated and difficult problem, he would go to the heart of it with an apt and brilliant summary observation.

Charles S. Johnson was truly an educational statesman whose breadth and depth and range of view, together with his practical prudence, have affected the work of philanthropic organizations and foundations, and through them American education, in a wide range of ways that have and will long continue to enrich American higher education. We in foundations will greatly miss his counsel, his warm-heartedness, his steady friendship.

RALPH L. PEARSON (ESSAY DATE 1977)

SOURCE: Pearson, Ralph L. "Combatting Racism with Art: Charles S. Johnson and the Harlem Renaissance." *American Studies* 18, no. 1 (spring 1977): 123-34.

In the following essay, Pearson discusses Johnson's belief that quality African American art, when recognized as such by whites, would help lead to racial equality.

Until the appearance of Patrick Gilpin's essay, "Charles S. Johnson: Entrepreneur of the Harlem Renaissance,"[1] the important role of Johnson as a cultivator of the Harlem Renaissance was described in a paragraph or two by historians and literary critics. In his recent analysis of the Renaissance as a cultural movement encompassing all the arts, Nathan Irvin Huggins merely cites Johnson as editor of *Opportunity* and then comments on the role of *Opportunity* in the Renaissance, ". . . even more than the others [*Crisis; The Messenger*], *Opportunity* believed its motto—'Not Alms but Opportunity'—to apply to the arts. It sponsored a literary contest in the 1920s that became a major generating force in the renaissance."[2]

Describing Johnson's entrepreneurial activities such as the Civic Club dinner of May 21, 1924, which brought "together the black literati and the white publishers,' and the *Opportunity* contests, Professor Gilpin argues persuasively that it was "in reporting and promoting black culture in the United States and the world at large that Johnson and *Opportunity* found their forte."[3] He reveals also Johnson's concern with "placing the New Movement into historical and sociological perspective." This observation leads to provocative suggestions of the importance Johnson ascribed to "the serious development of a body of literature about Negroes" for blacks as an "ethnic group"; and to literature as "a great liaison between races."[4] But Gilpin never develops the sociological and historical implications of these observations for Johnson's role as entrepreneur of the Renaissance. This essay proposes to fill the gap by analyzing how Johnson expected the revelation of black artistic talent to be a liaison between the races, as well as to affect the self-image of blacks as an ethnic group.

A major source of racial antagonism in America, Johnson believed, was the misunderstanding and ignorance of the two races about one another.[5] Johnson's opinion was shared by Alain Locke, who wrote in 1925,

> It does not follow that if the Negro were better known, he would be better liked or better treated. But mutual understanding is basic for any subsequent cooperation and adjustment. The effort toward this will at least have the effect of remedying in large part what has been the most unstatisfactory feature of our present stage of race relationships in America, namely the fact that the more intelligent and representative elements of the two race groups have at so many points got quite out of touch with one another.[6]

Johnson spent much of his life as a sociologist, first with the National Urban League and later at Fisk University, engaging in sociological studies that exposed the conditions of black life in America. As his friend Edwin Embree wrote, his role was one of interpreting "colored people to whites and white people to Negroes, Southerners to Northerners, rustics to city dweller, analyzing people's problems so that they can understand themselves."[7]

But interpreting the races to one another meant more than exposing the inferior social and economic conditions to which blacks were condemned by white discrimination and prejudice. As important for altering race relations was emphasis upon black achievements. "There are facts of Negro progress as well as handicaps that should be known not only for the stimulation which comes from recognition," Johnson wrote, "but as an antidote to a disposition not infrequently encountered to disparage unjustly the capacities and aspirations of this group."[8]

The Harlem Renaissance provided just the opportunity for blacks to reveal their capacities as artists. Gilpin suggested, but never developed, Johnson's conception of the Renaissance as a tool for altering racial patterns when he wrote, "Johnson's motivation in beginning the *Opportunity* contests appears to be that of a skilled, shrewd and pragmatic entrepreneur who saw a flourishing of black culture as but another road for combatting white racism while aiding black people."[9]

In September, 1927, Johnson himself described the *Opportunity* contests as a way to stimulate "not merely an interest in Negro life and in the work of the artists of the race, but work of a character which stands firmly and without apology along with that of any other race."[10] Artistic work that equalled the quality of any other race would surely undermine white arguments of innate black inferiority. Johnson assumed, of course, that whites would react to evidence of black artistic talent as an argument for racial equality. This assumption, Huggins notes, was widespread among black intellectuals in the 1920's: "Inequities due to race might best be removed when reasonable men saw that black men were thinkers, strivers, doers, and were cultured, like themselves. Harlem intellectuals, with their progressive assumptions, saw themselves as the ones most likely to make this demonstration."[11]

Johnson feared, of course, that the use of art to combat racism would fail because whites were predisposed to ignore black achievements. Occasionally this frustration turned to cynicism. Referring to ***Ebony and Topaz,*** a collection of black art, fiction, poetry and essays he edited, Johnson chided, "It is not improbable that some of our white readers will arch their brows or perhaps knit them soberly at some point before the end. But this is a response not infrequently met with outside the pages of books. There is always an escape of a sort, however, in ignoring that which contradicts one's sense, even though it were the better wisdom to give heed."[12] In a less cryptic moment Johnson told a friend what he hoped white reaction would be to evidence of black talent: "The best use of the volume is in its presentation to some white person who needs a succinct, face value presentation of Negro competence. . . ."[13]

Equally in need of "a succinct, face value presentation of Negro competence" were blacks themselves. Johnson was among the earliest sociologists to emphasize the psychological toll discrimination and segregation had taken on blacks and to combat the behavioral adjustments the race made to survive and function in American society.[14] He fought the resulting sense of inferiority so many of his race had lived with because he knew that until blacks conceived of themselves as equals with other races they could not begin to relate, and so be treated, as equals. Charles V. Hamilton, in his 1968 essay analyzing the meaning of Black Power, described well the change Johnson sought in the self-conception of many blacks: "The black man must change his demeaning conception of himself, he must develop a sense of pride and self-respect. Then, if integration comes, it will deal with people who are psychologically and mentally healthy, with people who have a sense of their history and of themselves as whole human beings."[15]

Johnson sought to alter the self-image of many blacks not with demands or accusations that would further alienate the races, but with ideas and programs that were achievable within the racial atmosphere of the 1920's. He remained constantly aware of the social milieu in which he was seeking to reorient race relations. Publishing *Opportunity* magazine, he wrote in 1928, was one way to encourage Negroes to think more objectively about their role in the race problem, as well as "to effect an emancipation from their sensitiveness about meaningless symbols, and . . . [to] inculcate a disposition to see enough of interest and beauty in their own lives to rid themselves of the inferior feeling of being a Negro."[16]

Who better than black artists themselves could capture the "interest and beauty" of black lives that could emancipate much of the race from feelings of inferiority. Here, then, is the framework for understanding how the Harlem Renaissance became for Johnson a means to change the self-image of many blacks and, in the end, to alter race relations. Evidence of black talent equal to that of other races could be an important step in the direction of race pride. Nathan Huggins describes the effect of black literary publications in *The Messenger, Liberator, Crisis* and *Opportunity* in just this way: "The tone and the self-assurance of these magazines were the important thing. They gave a sense of importance to blacks who read them. They gave answers that always had failed the porter, the barber, the maid, the teacher, the handyman. They were the Negro's voice against the insult that America gave him."[17]

But to succeed as artists and, consequently, as uplifters of the race's image, Johnson argued, blacks must use their own experiences as the basis for their creativity. They had to free themselves from the hold white cultural values exercised upon their art, just as white artists had found it imperative to reject European standards as the arbiter of their work:

> It was the dull lack of some idealism . . . that held America in a suspended cultural animation until it sought freedom thru self-criticism and its own native sources of beauty. In the same manner, American Negroes, born into a culture which they did not wholly share, have responded falsely to the dominant patterns. Their expression has been, to borrow a term which Lewis Mumford employs in referring to Americans in relation to Europe, 'sickly and derivative, a mere echo of old notes.'

> There has been the same self-deception of 'boasting and vain imagination[,]' the same indifference to the spiritual refinement of the beautiful, the same dull seeking of an average level, and the same mystifying sense of an imponderable shortcoming which led inevitably to inferior feeling and apology. The form of expression merely has been different.[18]

The lives of black men and women were replete with deeds and words worthy of being captured in poetry and story, in music and portrait. Survival itself, while trapped in the snares of slavery and Jim Crow, could provide inspiration for creativity. "There is a thrilling magnificence and grandeur," Johnson wrote, ". . . in the thread of unconquerable life thru two centuries of pain."[19] The folk life of the race included untapped sources for creative inspiration. "The vast sources of this field for American literature," Johnson reminded aspiring black artists, "cannot be escaped. . . . There is here a life full of strong colors, of passions, deep and fierce, of struggle, disillusion—the whole gamut of life free from the wrapping of intricate sophistication."[20]

So important was the black artists' use of black experiences to Johnson that he described their utilization of folk material as "a new emancipation." Gone was the "sensitiveness" that only a decade before denied the existence "of any but educated Negroes" and opposed Negro dialect, folk songs or anything that "revived the memory of slavery." Black artists were now sensitive "to the hidden beauties" of the black experience and expressed "a frank joy and pride in it."[21]

The emancipation of black artists was the means for a "new freedom" for the entire race. Addressing a graduating class of black students in 1928, Johnson argued, ". . . that the *road to a new freedom for us* lies in the discovery of the surrounding beauties of our lives and environment, and in the recognition that beauty itself is a mark of the highest expression of the human spirit."[22] Black artists of the Renaissance were capturing the beauty of black lives. In their work blacks could discover countless reasons for pride in their race. Simultaneously white men and women could experience the revelation of a long suppressed race with artistic talent, a history and culture equal to that of other races.

Johnson's race relations philosophy dictated, however, that racial pride be not a tool for further racial separation or for a Garveyite dream of African glory, but a lever for achieving equality in American society. His sense of realism convinced him that there was no value in pursuing a separatist course. Blacks were a distinct minority segment of American life and institutions. Those institutions were givens in their environment. The racial injustices of American society would not be eliminated by seeking to create another society, but by altering the racial habits of functioning institutions through such tools as research and education, negotiation and persuasion, confidence and achievement within the race itself.[23]

Equality within American society did not mean the loss of racial identification or "becoming a black Anglo Saxon," as Gilpin phrased it. Indeed, a careful reading of Johnson's published and unpublished writings conveys his conception of black Americans as a separate ethnic group within American society—an ethnic group that could contribute to, as well as draw upon, the society's cultural mainstream.[24]

The poems, essays and art that Johnson published as editor of *Opportunity,* as well as of *Ebony and Topaz,* reflected clearly this "conception of black Americans as a separate ethnic group within American society" that could both contribute to and draw upon that society's cultural mainstream. The poem of Waring Cuney spoke of the beauty of the brown body:

> She does not know
> Her beauty
> She thinks her brown body
> Has no glory.
>
> If she could dance
> Naked,
> Under palm trees
> And see her image in the river
> She would know.
>
> But there are no palm trees
> On the street
> And dish water gives back no images.[25]

While Helene Johnson's *Sonnet To A Negro in Harlem* expressed disdain for the white man's values:

> You are disdainful and magnificent—
> Your perfect body and your pompous gait,
> Your dark eyes flashing sullenly with hate,
> Small wonder that you are incompetent
> To imitate those whom you so despise—
> Your shoulders towering high above the throne,
> Your head thrown back in rich, barbaric song,
> Palm trees and mangoes stretched before your
> eyes.
> Let others toil and sweat for labor's sake
> And wring from grasping hands their need of
> gold.
> Why urge ahead your supercilious feet?
> Scorn will efface each footprint that you make.
> I love your laughter arrogant and bold
> You are too splendid for this city street.[26]

A similar theme was struck at the conclusion of Edna Worthley Underwood's marvelous short story, "La Perla Negra":

> She [La Perla Negra] had gone back to the wild undisciplined life of her race. She must have different things. She must have the healed dance under the stars—at night—and the fight that followed. She must feel hunger, discomfort and weariness. She must feel upon her faultless, grey-marble shoulders, the overseer's lash. She must burn up her youth, her beauty in a frenzy of feverish life; in toil, in the brittle dawn, by the edge of the cane field. She must have the fierce things of her blood.
>
> Not yet was the white man's life, with its weakening trivialities, for her.
>
> She had escaped from that consuming disease we call civilization.[27]

Frank Horne's poem in the December, 1925, issue of *Opportunity,* "On Seeing Two Brown Boys in a Catholic Church," compares vividly the fate that awaits these boys with that of Christ—a fate decreed by the white man's civilization in which they live:

> And Gethsemane
> You shall know full well
> Gethsemane . . .
>
> . . . . .
>
> And in this you will exceed God
> For on this earth
> You shall know Hell—

Readers of *Ebony and Topaz* were exposed to the achievements of "Juan Latino, Magister Latinus,"[28] as well as to "Four drawings for Mulattoes" by Richard Bruce and the paintings of Sebastian Gomez, known as "Mulatto de Murillo."[29] Johnson published in *Ebony and Topaz* a short piece on "Gullah" by Julia Peterkin in which she underscored the unique contributions blacks who spoke this language were making to American culture: "And this language which is not easily understood except by a trained ear, is not only beautiful, but its whimsical words and phrases, its quaint similes and shrewd sayings are undoubtedly a permanent enrichment of American language and literature."[30]

The conception of the Renaissance as a tool for fostering black cultural autonomy, which could then contribute to the nation's cultural life, has been seriously questioned by Huggins. Rather than contributing to the national culture as a distinct ethnic group, he argues, "black men and American culture have been one—such a seamless web that it is impossible to calibrate the Negro within it or to ravel him from it."[31] These divergent views underscore differing conceptions of the relationship between blacks and the remainder of American society, not the benefit of historical perspective allowed by the passage of decades. Johnson himself reflected on the meaning of the Renaissance in the mid-1950's and spoke again in terms of a distinct "self conscious and race conscious" movement that "could be incorporated into the cultural bloodstream of the nation."[32]

If black artists were to contribute to the nation's "cultural bloodstream" and simultaneously make art a liaison between the races, they would have to produce works equal in quality to those produced by artists of other races. Being the best Negro author in a particular genre benefited neither the artist nor the race. "As Negro writers come into their estate it is expected that what they produce shall approach the standards set by the accepted writers of the country."[33] Not only would failure to meet accepted standards of quality perpetuate the widely held opinion that blacks were innately inferior, but it would also threaten interest in what black authors wrote. Furthermore, the possibility existed that authors with a polished style but little information might usurp the audience interested in literature about the black experience. Therefore, Johnson told *Opportunity* contest entrants, ". . . the cult of competence must be courted assiduously. We must write to be known; we must write well to be heard at all."[34]

And when black men wrote so well that their excellence achieved recognition in literary anthologies, Johnson applauded the achievement as more than an individual accomplishment: ". . . to the glory of their skill, it speaks for Negroes."[35] This articulation of the significance of individual success for an entire race underscores the importance of the Harlem Renaissance for Johnson's race relations philosophy—for surely this display of artistic skill called into question traditional white attitudes about blacks, as well as the image blacks had of their own race.

During the past decade several scholars have questioned the meaning of the Harlem Renaissance for black independence and/or equality. As noted, Nathan Huggins rejects the Renaissance as an expression of black cultural autonomy. The autonomous ethnic culture Johnson and others saw expressed in the Renaissance had little independent ballast to support it. Huggins concedes that blacks did achieve a maturity of racial conceptualization and an appreciation of folk roots and culture which permitted partial emancipation from the "embarrassment of past conditions" as a result of the Renaissance. But these achievements led to a "naive faith in the possibility of creating an ethnic culture." When, in fact, black artists were unable to free themselves from emulation of white values.[36]

In his study of *Harlem: The Making of a Ghetto* Gilbert Osofsky questioned the sincerity of whites who seemed genuinely attracted to black art—individuals to whom the meaning of black creativity for race relations should have been most obvious. The attraction of the New Negro and the Renaissance, Osofsky contends, was the challenge they represented to traditional American values. That generation of Americans who discovered "newness" all around it—New Humanism, New Criticism, New Masses, New Poetry and so on—"also found a 'New Negro'; and the concept became a cultural weapon: 'Another Bombshell Fired into the Heart of Bourgeois Culture.'"[37]

The traditional view of the Negro as Sambo did not change, Osofsky argued. Instead new characteristics were attributed to him that made him exciting. He was "expressive," "primitive," "exotic," possessing an "innate gayety of soul." Such characteristics were captivating when compared with the puritanical and repressed culture of white America. Still, the black man remained a toy with which the players would tire. What remained with a degraded, suppressed race.[38]

Charles Johnson was not unaware of the artificiality which attached itself to what he considered to be a genuine cultural expression of black life and experiences. He was sensitive to the shallowness which could overtake an artistic movement such as the Renaissance once it appeared to have captivated public attention. Concerned that the Renaissance was moving in that direction he wrote in 1927,

> The public has recently given a sudden ear to the submerged voices of dark Americans; hearing has brought a measure of interest and this interest, in characteristic American fashion has catapulted itself into something very much like a fad.[39]

In a March, 1926, *Opportunity* editorial he had enumerated the dangers to the legitimacy of the Renaissance: the "shortsighted exploiters of sentiment"; the "immediate and prematurely triumphant ones who think that Negro writers have fully arrived"; and the "superficial ones, inebriated with praise and admission to the company of writers, who are establishing by acceptance, a double standard of competence as a substitute for the normal rewards of study and practice, and in many instances, lack talent." Unless the exploiters of public interest were curbed, Johnson feared the Renaissance would indeed be a fad "to be discarded in a few seasons" instead of a "sound wholesome expression of [artistic] growth."[40]

The Renaissance was shattered by the Depression, Huggins believes, "because of naive assumptions about the centrality of culture, unrelated to economic and social realities." Black intellectuals "were comrades in this innocence with many white intellectuals of the time."[41] By the time the Depression ended the Renaissance, Charles Johnson had joined the faculty of Fisk University. One must conclude, however, that his role as one of the "entrepreneurs" of the Renaissance was not grounded upon "naive assumptions about the centrality of culture, unrelated to economic and social realities." His encouragement of black cultural achievements through art assumed only that blacks were a distinct ethnic group which had a unique contribution to make to the nation's cultural mainstream.

Even if the assumption of ethnic distinctiveness is questionable, there is no doubt of his awareness of the economic and social realities of the society in which black artists labored. Johnson's entrepreneurial activities reveal a clear understanding of which groups and individuals controlled opportunities in the arts and of their past attitudes about black artists.

And if blacks were unable to emancipate themselves from the values of white society, as Johnson occasionally felt they had or were doing, he was realistic enough to see in the Renaissance a tool for altering the black self-image. His most unrealistic social goal for the movement was that it might affect white attitudes toward the black race. It was an unrealistic goal not because only a relatively few whites knew of black art, but because whites were not prepared to grant blacks the same distribution of talent and mediocrity that characterizes other races. No rational proof would convince whites that the black race included individuals with abilities and capabilities equal to those of individuals from other races.

Charles Johnson did not stand alone in his interpretation of the meaning of the Renaissance for his race, as well as for interracial relations. His contemporary, and another significant entrepreneur of the movement, Alain Locke wrote, too, of "emancipation" from "a warped social perspective" and of the emergence of "a new group psychology." That "new group psychology" was characterized by a "more positive self-respect and self-reliance," "a repudiation of the double standard of judgment with its special philanthropic allowances" and a "desire for objective and scientific appraisal; and finally the rise from social disillusionment to race pride. . . ."[42]

The social element, so dominant in the art of the Renaissance, was an expression of that emancipation, "an idiom of experience, a sort of added enriching adventure and discipline, airing subtler overtones to life, making it more beautiful and interesting, even if more poignantly so."[43] Just as did Johnson, Locke interpreted the use of the social element as artistically significant for its contribution to the cultural mainstream: "The new motive, then, in being racial is to be so purely for the sake of art. Nowhere is this more apparent, or more justified than in the increasing tendency to evolve from the racial substance something technically distinctive, something that as an idiom of style may become a contribution to the general resources of Art."[44]

By the mid-1920's, W. E. B. DuBois was challenging Locke's assertion that black art and literature drew upon social experience "purely for the sake of art." Reviewing *The New Negro* in the *Crisis* DuBois wrote,

> Mr. Locke has newly been seized with the idea that Beauty rather than Propaganda should be the object of Negro art and literature. His book proves the falseness of this thesis. This is a book filled and bursting with propaganda but it is propaganda for the most part beautifully and painstakingly done.
>
> . . . if Mr. Locke's thesis is insisted on too much it is going to turn the Negro renaissance into decadence. It is the fight for Life and Liberty that is giving birth to Negro literature and art today and when, turning from this fight or ignoring it, the young Negro tries to do pretty things or things that catch the passing fancy of the really unimportant critics and publishers about him, he will find that he has killed the soul of Beauty in his Art.[45]

While Johnson shared DuBois' view that black art and literature should be used in the fight for life and liberty, "used" in the sense of "proving" to both races that blacks could create works of art qualitatively as significant as those of other races, he agreed with Locke that beauty must be one of the objectives, even of art with social themes. In fact, only a few months prior to his review of Locke's book, DuBois committed the support of the *Crisis* to the cause of Black writers in the following terms: "We shall stress Beauty—all Beauty, but especially the beauty of Negro life and character; its music, its dancing, its drawing and painting and the new birth of its literature."[46]

Art became propaganda for DuBois because he judged the creations of both black and white authors inaccurate portrayals of black life. Whites wanted to hear only about the "dregs" of black life, and black authors responded because only that way could they get manuscripts accepted by white publishers. Art as propaganda would be committed to beauty, but beauty defined *only* by standards of Truth ("the highest handmaiden of imagination, . . . the one great vehicle of universal understanding") and Goodness ("the goodness in all its aspects of justice, honor and right"). Thus an artist searching for beauty must use criteria of truth and justice, which in DuBois' terms make art a form of propaganda.[47]

Using such criteria, DuBois found little to praise in the works of either black or white authors. He condemned Van Vechten's *Nigger Heaven* as "an insult to the hospitality of black folk"; McKay's *Home to Harlem* as an effort "to paint drunkenness, fighting, lascivious sexual promiscuity and other absence of restraint" without a "well-conceived plot"; and Arno Bontemps' *God Sends Sunday* as the tandem volume to *Home to Harlem.* Praise was reserved for works such as Langston Hughes' "Sorry for a Banjo" and Countee Cullen's "Ballad of the Brown Girl."[48]

By the late 1920's DuBois did not share the concern of Johnson and Locke that black artists, while drawing upon themes from the life of the race, become part of, and contribute to, the nation's cultural mainstream. In fact, Francis Broderick argued, DuBois was seeking to direct the efforts of black artists toward only one end:

> . . . and all DuBois's platitudes about truth, beauty, and right could not conceal his insistence that Negro artists refuse to submit to the 'passing fancy of the really unimportant critics and publishers' and that they use their talent in the direct service of the race. Down that road lay cultural separation.[49]

Charles Johnson was aware of the irrationality of white racism that led men like DuBois to advocate separatism. As a teacher and scholar he spent much of his life combatting racism through sociological studies and education, but he avoided disillusion with this approach to race relations by resisting the temptation to expect racism to evaporate in the face of persuasive arguments. For example, his hope that white racial attitudes might be affected by evidence of black talent was tempered by his awareness that, as he wrote in *Ebony and Topaz,* "There is always an escape of a sort . . . in ignoring that which contradicts one's sense, even though it were the better wisdom to give heed."[50] Johnson's perceptions of the races reflected the insights of the sociologist and the humanist. The failure of the Renaissance to affect white racism, as he hoped, is not a blot upon his understanding of American race relations but upon white America's self-perception and understanding of other men and races.

Notes

1. Patrick Gilpin, "Charles S. Johnson: Entrepreneur of the Harlem Renaissance," in Arna Bontemps, ed., *The Harlem Renaissance Remembered* (New York, 1972), 215-246.
2. Nathan I. Huggins, *Harlem Renaissance* (New York, 1971), 29.
3. Gilpin, 223.
4. *Ibid.,* 238.
5. See, for example, "Public Opinion and the Negro," *Opportunity,* 1 (October, 1923), 201-206.
6. Alain Locke, "The New Negro," in Alain Locke, ed., *The New Negro* (New York, 1968 edition), 8, 9.
7. Edwin Embree, *Thirteen against the Odds* (Port Washington, New York, 1968), 55.
8. "Why We Are," *Opportunity,* 5 (September, 1927), 254.
9. Gilpin, 226.
10. "The Opportunity Contest," *Opportunity,* 5 (September, 1927), 254.
11. Huggins, 5.
12. "Introduction," Charles S. Johnson, ed., *Ebony and Topaz: A Collectanea* (New York, 1927), 11.
13. Letter, Charles S. Johnson to Jesse O. Thomas, December 10, 1927, National Urban League papers, Manuscripts Division, Library of Congress.
14. See "Public Opinion and the Negro," 204-206; and S. P. Fullinwider, *The Mind and Mood of Black America* (Homewood, 1969), 107-115.
15. Charles V. Hamilton, "An Advocate of Black Power Defines It," *New York Times Magazine* (April 14, 1968), 79.
16. "The Rise of the Negro Magazine," *Journal of Negro History,* 13 (1928), 19.
17. Huggins, 30.
18. "An Address to the Graduating Classes of Virginia Union University and Hartshorn College" (June 6, 1928), Fisk University Library, Johnson papers, 9-10.
19. *Ibid.,* 11.
20. "Introduction," 12-13.
21. *Ibid.,* 12.
22. "An Address . . ." My underlining. See also "Out of the Shadow," *Opportunity,* 3 (May, 1925), 131; "On Writing about Negroes," *Opportunity,* 3 (August, 1925), 227-228.
23. See, for example, "The Social Philosophy of Booker T. Washington," *Opportunity,* 6 (April, 1928), 102-105.
24. Gilpin, 237-238.
25. Waring Cuney, "No Images," *Opportunity,* 4 (June, 1926), 180.
26. Helene Johnson, "Sonnet to a Negro in Harlem," *Ebony and Topaz* (New York, 1927), 148.
27. Edna Worthley Underwood, "La Perla Negra," *Ibid.,* 62.
28. Arthur Schomburg, "Juan Latino, Magister Latinus," *Ibid.,* 69.
29. *Ibid.,* 73-75.
30. Julia Peterkin, "Gullah," *Ibid.,* 35.
31. Huggins, 309.
32. "The Negro Renaissance and Its Significance," Johnson papers, 8.
33. "To the Contestants," *Opportunity,* 4 (January, 1926), 6.
34. *Ibid.*
35. "Stories and Poetry of 1926," *Opportunity,* 5 (January, 1927), 5.
36. Huggins, 304, 307.
37. Gilbert Osofsky, *Harlem: The Making of a Ghetto* (New York, 1968 edition), 183-184.
38. *Ibid.,* 184.
39. "Some Perils of the Renaissance," *Opportunity,* 5 (March, 1927), 68.
40. "A Note on the New Literary Movement," *Opportunity,* 4 (March, 1926), 80.
41. Huggins, 303.
42. *The New Negro,* 10-11.
43. *Ibid.,* 48.
44. *Ibid.,* 51.
45. W. E. B. DuBois, "Our Book Shelf," *Crisis,* 31 (January, 1926), 141.
46. DuBois, "Art," *Ibid.,* 30 (May, 1925), 8.
47. DuBois, "Criteria of Negro Art," *Ibid.,* 32 (October, 1926), 296.
48. Francis L. Broderick, *W. E. B. DuBois: Negro Leader in a Time of Crisis* (Stanford, 1959), 158-159.
49. *Ibid.,* 160.
50. *Ebony and Topaz,* 11.

FURTHER READING

Bibliography

Bibliography of Charles S. Johnson's Published Writings. Nashville: Fisk University Library, 1947, 16 p.

Compiled by the staff of the library in honor of Johnson's inauguration as president.

Biographies

Gilpin, Patrick. "Charles S. Johnson: Entrepreneur of the Harlem Renaissance." In *The Harlem Renaissance Remembered,* edited by Anna Bontemps, pp. 214-46. New York: Dodd, Mead and Company, 1972.

Focuses on Johnson's life in New York and his fostering of the Harlem Renaissance.

Robbins, Richard. *Sidelines Activist: Charles S. Johnson and the Struggle for Civil Rights.* Jackson: University Press of Mississippi, 1996, 223 p.

Examines Johnson's efforts to make the arts a viable means of expression for African Americans.

Criticism

Embree, Edwin R. "Charles S. Johnson—A Scholar and a Gentleman." In *Thirteen against the Odds.* 1944. Reprint, pp. 47-70. Port Washington, N.Y.: Kennikat Press, Inc., 1968.

Provides a biographical sketch and discusses the criticism that Johnson was too careful to avoid controversy in his writing.

Build the Future: Addresses Marking the Inauguration of Charles Spurgeon Johnson. Nashville: Fisk University Press, 1949, 100 p.

Collection of speeches honoring Johnson.

Huggins, Nathan Irvin. "Harlem: Capital of the Black World." In *Harlem Renaissance,* pp. 13-51. New York: Oxford University Press, 1971.

Compares and contrasts three Harlem magazines: Crisis, The Messenger, *and* Opportunity, *noting Johnson's role as editor.*

OTHER SOURCES FROM GALE:

Additional coverage of Johnson's life and career is contained in the following sources published by the Gale Group: *Black Writers,* Eds. 1, 3; *Contemporary Authors,* Vol. 125; *Contemporary Authors New Revision Series,* Vol. 82; and *Dictionary of Literary Biography,* Vols. 51, 91.

GEORGIA DOUGLAS JOHNSON

(1877 - 1966)

(Full name Georgia Blanche Douglas Camp Johnson) American poet, playwright, short story writer, and composer.

As the author of four volumes of verse, numerous plays, short stories, essays, and songs, Johnson was one of the most productive artists of the Harlem Renaissance and one of the first African American female poets to achieve a national reputation. Beginning in the style of the genteel school, Johnson wrote romantic, personal poetry centered on the experiences of a woman, with no explicit mention of race. In the mid-1920s, after she began associating with other authors in weekly salons that she hosted at her home in Washington, D.C., Johnson's writing changed to protest racism and injustice, with her thoughts expressed in numerous plays illustrating the horrors of lynching. These Saturday night salons altered the focus of Johnson's writing and gave other emerging Black writers encouragement and inspiration from already established authors. Johnson's own work was not always appreciated in her lifetime, sometimes being judged as unfashionable or criticized for what it lacked. In recent years, however, critics have reevaluated her work, recognizing that it provides scholars with an opportunity to assess the development of female African American authors across several different literary movements due to Johnson's lengthy writing career.

BIOGRAPHICAL INFORMATION

Johnson was born Georgia Blanche Douglas Camp in Atlanta, Georgia, probably in 1877, to Laura Douglas, who was half Black and half Native American, and George Camp, who was half Black and half white. Johnson's earliest schooling took place in Rome, Georgia, then continued in Atlanta. She graduated from Atlanta University's Normal School in 1893 and started teaching in Marietta, Georgia. In 1902 she quit her job and attended the Oberlin Conservatory of Music and the Cleveland College of Music, where she studied composition, piano, and violin. In 1903 she left Ohio and returned to Atlanta, taking the post of assistant principal at a local school. She resigned later in the same year and married Henry Lincoln Johnson. Although he actively discouraged his wife's writing activities, Johnson published "Omnipresence" in the June 1905 issue of *Voice of the Negro.* Johnson, her husband, and their two sons moved to Washington, D.C., in 1910 where Henry became involved in government and politics. In 1916 *Crisis* published three of Johnson's poems—"Gossamer," "Fame," and "My Little One"—in three separate issues. Her first book, *The Heart of a Woman and Other Poems* (1918), was soon followed by *Bronze: A Book of Verse* (1922). When Johnson's husband died in 1925, however, she found little time for writing. Paying for college expenses for her two sons, Johnson worked assorted jobs as a substitute teacher, a file clerk, and eventually Commissioner of Conciliation in the Labor Department from 1925 to 1934. During this time she hosted some of the greatest of emerging Black writers, including Jean Toomer, W. E. B. Du Bois, Alice Dunbar-Nelson, and Langston Hughes. Her literary salon is credited with nurturing their talent and providing them and dozens of others with a sense of community. Beginning in the 1930s and continuing throughout the rest of her life, Johnson sought fellowships in order to continue with her writing projects, but she was mostly unsuccessful. In 1965 Atlanta University awarded her an honorary doctor of letters degree. Johnson died of a stroke in 1966 in Washington, D.C. Many of her manuscripts and letters, stored in her basement, were discarded on the day of her funeral, indicative of her relative obscurity as a writer in the latter portion of her life.

MAJOR WORKS

Johnson's reputation is based primarily on her first three collections of verse. *The Heart of a Woman and Other Poems* is comprised of sixty-two short lyrical poems, mostly written in quatrains. The poems deal with specific feelings, such as sympathy or despair, in fairly conventional terms, or sometimes abstractly, with no mention of race. *Bronze: A Book of Verse* contains fifty-six poems in a wide range of forms, including sonnets and free verse, in addition to quatrains. The poems reflect the changes occurring in Johnson's life as she moved from the genteel school to become an active participant in the New Negro Movement, which would eventually be termed the Harlem Renaissance. In this book Johnson attests to her interest in Black history and the struggles of her race through slavery. *An Autumn Love Cycle* (1928), consisting of fifty-eight poems of varying lengths, explores the development of a love affair from a promising beginning to the desperate, bitter end; there is no mention of race. Johnson's last book of verse, *Share My World,* was published in 1962; it collects poetry written over a period of many years, including poems that were sent annually as gifts to friends. Johnson wrote dozens of one-act plays, but only four were published in her lifetime, and most of the others are now lost. Johnson's first play, *Blue Blood,* was performed in New York in 1926 and was published in 1927. Its subject matter is the rape of Black women by white men in the South following the Civil War. The one-act *Plumes* (1927) won *Opportunity* magazine's first prize in its drama competition. Its story concerns a poverty-stricken Black mother agonizing over whether to pay a doctor to operate on her ailing daughter and perhaps save her life, or to spend the money on a respectable funeral for her; the child dies before her mother decides. The other two produced plays concern runaway slaves: *Frederick Douglass* (1935) depicts Douglass's visit with a woman whom he would later marry, immediately before his escape to Massachusetts, and *William and Ellen Craft* (1935) shows the couple's love for each other. *Safe* (1929), although it was not produced, is one of Johnson's most famous lynching plays. In it, a woman in labor hears a lynch mob and the cries of their captive outside her home. She gives birth, but upon realizing it is a boy, she strangles the baby, saying that "Now he's safe—safe from the lynchers." Some of Johnson's previously unpublished short stories appeared in print for the first time in 1997 in *The Selected Works of Georgia Douglas Johnson.*

CRITICAL RECEPTION

Although Johnson received a certain amount of critical acclaim in her lifetime and had national exposure, her career suffered somewhat by being caught between the genteel age and the age of the New Negro. Generally holding the belief that the best way to achieve acceptance and popularity in society was through the merits of the art itself, Johnson began her career with the raceless poetry found in *The Heart of a Woman and Other Poems.* While this collection is dismissed by some as too conventional, Gloria T. Hull finds the apparent sentimentality undercut by irony and quiet sedition. Although *Bronze* was possibly Johnson's most widely read and critically acclaimed work immediately after publication, Hull considers it her weakest, reading like "obligatory race poetry." Du Bois concludes in the book's introduction, however, that "as a revelation of the soul struggle of the women of a race it is invaluable." *An Autumn Love Cycle* is generally considered Johnson's finest achievement. Claudia Tate extols its power, poignancy, and focus. Some critics reacted negatively to it, deeming the return to raceless poetry accommodationist. Judith L. Stephens, who found some lost plays of Johnson, concentrates on her lynching plays, finding them rich in material for "studying relations among race, gender politics, and aesthetics; they permit us to see more clearly the impact of racism and to understand art as a force of resistance as well as a force of renewal." Much of Johnson's work is no longer extant, and some that may have survived is not readily identifiable as her own because she used numerous pseudonyms: two that are known are Paul Tremaine and John Temple. Tate lists many unpublished plays, collections of verse, short stories, and songs. Some of these were probably not finalized for publication, and some failed to materialize for lack of funds, as all of Johnson's works were published at her own expense. Recently four boxes of Johnson's papers were found undamaged in her attic and now reside at Howard University. Previously unknown works, letters, and documents have allowed scholars to gain new insight into Johnson's life and work.

PRINCIPAL WORKS

The Heart of a Woman and Other Poems (poetry) 1918

Bronze: A Book of Verse (poetry) 1922

Blue Blood (play) 1926

A Sunday Morning in the South (play) 1926

Plumes (play) 1927

An Autumn Love Cycle (poetry) 1928

Safe (play) 1929

Blue-Eyed Black Boy (play) 1930

Frederick Douglass (play) 1935

William and Ellen Craft (play) 1935

Share My World (poetry) 1962

The Selected Works of Georgia Douglas Johnson (poetry, plays, short stories) 1997

GENERAL COMMENTARY

WINONA L. FLETCHER (ESSAY DATE 1985)

SOURCE: Fletcher, Winona L. "From Genteel Poet to Revolutionary Playwright: Georgia Douglas Johnson." *Theatre Annual* (1985): 41-64.

In the following essay, Fletcher examines Johnson's plays and contemporary critical and public reaction to them, noting that her confrontational works of social protest were not well received.

Most Literary artists have only their own personal choices and limitations to confront in the creation of a new work. Black writers seldom are granted this freedom. They share with other artists concerns for finding the most appropriate words, techniques, styles, and forms; then, they must deal with barriers forced upon them as blacks in America. Among their added concerns are (1) how to escape such labels as "raceless writers," or "writers with inferiority complexes;" (2) avoid the stronghold of stereotypical images; (3) overcome the dilemma of the "dual audience" (black and white); and (4) mollify internal disagreements within the race. Faced with all these barriers, black writers have usually chosen one of four avenues:

> First: Transcend the bonds of race; escape into romanticism, idealism, "art for art's sake," pretend "we are all alike" or, when differences must be acknowledged, appeal for sympathy and understanding. Write "raceless literature."
>
> Second: March up to the barriers fully clad in protective armor; recognize and call the barriers by their proper name, "Racism," and attack them with all the rage and fortitude they can muster. Write literature of confrontation, agit-prop, social protest.
>
> Third: Write folk literature.
>
> Fourth: Baptize themselves totally in the race; raise the level of consciousness and black integrity through understanding and appreciation of their worth; rise so high above the boundaries that they seem not to exist as barriers. Write consciousness-raising literature.

Particularly for those who choose the second route, social protest, a perplexing question arises. Can they find success in America?

To experience the poignant lyrics of Georgia Douglas Johnson is to sense black success, failure, and fortitude firsthand. The text and sub-text of her soulful words reveal the entire inheritance of choices bequeathed black writers. For example: "I believe in the ultimate justice of fate . . . / That the heart of humanity strikes the same chord." (**"Credo"**); "Oh, let's build bridges everywhere . . ." (**"Interracial"**); "Bid you storm the sullen fortress built by prejudice and wrong." (**"To My Son"**); "The strong demand, contend, prevail; the beggar is a fool!" (**"The Suppliant"**); "Life charges through my veins— / Mixed forces guide the reins / And I must on." (**"The Man To Be"**).[1]

When Mrs. Johnson turned from "art for art's sake" to "art with a purpose" or social protest, she also transformed from a poet to a poet-dramatist, thus enabling us to address the specific question of this essay: Did social protest from a black perspective successfully find a place in American drama of the thirties?

For the purpose of this essay, the following definitions are assumed:

> Success: To be widely read and produced and judiciously evaluated.
>
> Failure: To be denied exposure.
>
> Fortitude: Endurance of mental and physical anguish; guts to keep going in spite of it all.

Georgia Douglas Johnson, like her better-known contemporary, Langston Hughes, was granted a rich professional life that spanned several generations of writers. Born in Atlanta, Georgia in 1886, she authored her first volume of poetry in 1918 and published poems and dramas in anthologies and journals for every subsequent decade until her death at the age of eighty in 1966. As an active pioneer in women's and civic movements and a woman who wrote because "she loved to write," she became the first "woman of color" to gain general recognition as a poet after Francis Harper (1825-1911).[2] Mrs. Johnson received a good education in the public schools of Atlanta, at Atlanta University and at Oberlin College in Ohio. For a brief time, she taught in the South, married Henry Lincoln Johnson, a lawyer, and moved to Washington, D.C. when he was appointed Recorder of Deeds under President Taft. Their Washington home soon became the center for literary gatherings of black intellectuals in the area. When her play, ***Plumes,*** was awarded the first prize in the *Opportunity Magazine* Annual Drama Contest (1927), Mrs. Johnson revealed her artistic aspirations to the general public:

> Long years ago when the world was new for me, I dreamed of being a composer—wrote songs, many of them. The words took fire and the music smouldered and so, following the lead of friends and critics, I turned my face toward poetry and put my songs away for a while. . . . Then came drama. . . .[3]

Mrs. Johnson's words suggest the breadth of her talent. As a symbol of success she can be encapsulated best by the words which poured from her own heart and pen and by the voices of those who shared her creative world at the beginning of her long career.

Georgia Douglas Johnson was formally introduced to the reading public as the first black feminist poet in 1918 with the publication of her anthology of poetry, ***The Heart of a Woman and Other Poems.*** William Stanley Braithwaite, prominent black poet, publisher, and college professor, took the responsibility for this act:

> The poems in this book are intensely feminine and for me this means more than anything else that they are deeply human. We are yet scarcely aware, in spite of our boasted twentieth-century progress, of what lies deeply hidden . . . in the heart of a woman.
>
> To look upon what is revealed (in this book) is to give one a sense of infinite sympathy; to make one kneel in spirit to the marvelous patience, the wonderful endurance, the persistent faith, which are hidden in this nature. . . .
>
> It is a kind of privilege to know so much about the secrets of woman's nature, a privilege all the more cherished when given, as in these poems, with such exquisite utterance, with such a lyric sensibility.[4]

By 1922, Mrs. Johnson had been admitted to the circle of men and women whose names fill the books of famous black Americans—W. E. B. Du Bois, Countee Cullen, William S. Braithwaite, Sterling Brown, Benjamin Brawley, Jessie Fauset, Angelina Grimke, Langston Hughes, Zora Neale Hurston, James Weldon Johnson, Claude McKay, Willis Richardson and others. While she remained intensely concerned with the thoughts and feelings of women, and specifically with black women—"Don't knock on my door, little child,. . . . / I must not give you birth!"[5], she also reached out to the men who blazed the trail from slavery through Reconstruction and were then knocking on closed doors of segregation and racism. "Grandly isolate as the god of day—" she wrote in tribute to W. E. B. Du Bois.[6] Du Bois honored her second anthology of poetry with a forthright foreword:

> Those who know what it means to be a colored woman in 1922—and know it not so much in fact as in feeling, apprehension, unrest and delicate yet stern thought—must read Georgia Douglas Johnson's ***Bronze***. . . . none can fail to be caught here and there by a word—a phrase—a period that *tells a life history or even paints the history of a generation*. . . .
>
> I hope Mrs. Johnson will have a wide reading. Her word is simple, sometimes trite, but it is singularly sincere and true, and *as a revelation of the soul struggle of the women of a race it is invaluable* (emphasis added).[7]

Apparently ***Bronze*** was widely read, for there followed numerous reviews and critiques of it by readers "touched—even captured—by the strange force of its burning enthusiasm." Zona Gale, commenting on Mrs. Johnson's verse in *Literary Digest* International Book Review, expressed regret that the American Indians never had one of their number to speak out for them, but was joyous over the presence of black voices now being heard:

> But the colored peoples have voices, crying with power over the barriers, and among such utterances the lyric voice of Georgia Douglas Johnson, but passionate and plaintive . . . She speaks for the colored people of America, 'the mantled millions,' 'children of sorrow, dethroned by a hue,' those, in fine, 'who walk unfree, though cradled in the hold of liberty.' . . . Never have they who are 'the fretted fabric of a dual dynasty,' made by the mingling of dark and light, found a voice at once more delicate and clear.[8]

Then followed an outburst of sensibility rarely felt for a black writer in 1923—and even more rarely expressed:

> We who are as strangely insensible to this tragedy among us as were the Romans to the crucifixion of lions and of Christians, must *keep this little book for those who will be better able to appraise its place.* We must keep it, a varied and piercing record, *to 'gem the archives of a better day.'*
>
> (emphasis added)[9]

A sense of the intense conviction, the fortitude that sustained this early black writer through the decades of development and change, is captured by Effie Lee Newsome of Birmingham, Alabama, who reviewed ***Bronze*** for *Opportunity Magazine*:

> It has been stated that authors can convince only to the extent of their persuasion: Georgia Douglas Johnson has molded with the very pulsations of her heart.
>
> Her heart—for this is the potent factor in her creative force—has molded a ***Bronze*** *that challenges not altogether with the sharp angles of accusation, but as well with the graceliness of heart's call to heart for sympathy in the problems of a race; . . .*
>
> This book [is] burnished, in spite of all, now here, now there, with a brave 'Optimism' that can glow thus:
>
> 'We man our parts within life's tragic play.'
>
> (emphasis added)[10]

Despite the reviewer's reference to Mrs. Johnson's race, Mrs. Johnson's reputation at the beginning of her career was clearly based on her choice to write "raceless" poetry and to associate with "The Genteel School" of writers. "Much of her work transcends the bounds of race," wrote one contemporary authority, Benjamin Brawley; he continues, "in earlier work Mrs. Johnson cultivated especially the poignant, sharply chiselled lyric that became so popular with Sara Teasdale and some other writers a decade or two ago."[11]

Black writers of The Genteel School were integrationists, comparable to those of the 1950's and 1960's in their beliefs that the best hope for acceptance into American society was by being "like everybody else" and by proving that "we're as good" as the rest. Writers such as Arna Bontemps, Du Bois, Jean Toomer, Sterling Brown, and Georgia Douglas Johnson were primarily concerned with writing that could be "judged on its artistic merit and fidelity to truth;" their search was for universal themes and literature that did not call attention to Negro authorship. Their aim was to show how courageous, dignified, and capable the Negro was in spite of all he had to endure.[12] "The New Negro," as envisioned by Alain Locke, had not yet emerged as a literary force. The Genteel School, because of its affinity to the traditional modes, was perceived by its followers as a wiser, safer, and sometimes *only* choice for a black writer who wanted to be read widely and who sought success in a society molded by white standards—literary and otherwise.

By the mid-twenties, surrounded by writers of The New Poetry Movement which repudiated sentimentality, optimism, didacticism, romantic escape, and 'poetic' diction, and by black artists who were to shape "The Harlem Renaissance" (the black artistic explosion of the era), Mrs. Johnson began to move toward more race-conscious writing.[13] "There came into her verse a deeper, more mellow note."[14] In 1924, as a guest at a dinner to pay tribute to "the younger school of Negro writers," Mrs. Johnson must have been visibly moved by Alain Locke's eloquent speech. As "Dean of the New Negro Movement," he spoke of the new currents manifest in the writing of the new school: "They sense within their group . . . a spiritual wealth which if they can possibly expound will be ample for a new judgement and reappraisal of the race." Undoubtedly, she bristled at a white publisher's admonition to black writers "to avoid reflecting in their writings the 'inferiority complex' so frequently apparent in much of the writing published." With affinity and affirmation, she heard Miss Jessie Fauset, whose novel, *There is Confusion,* motivated the dinner tribute, call Dr. Du Bois her "best friend and severest critic." With compassion and understanding, she sat as Du Bois was introduced from "the older school" and as he felt compelled to explain "that the Negro writers of a few years back were of necessity pioneers, and much of their style was forced upon them by barriers against publication of literature about Negroes of any sort."[15]

The years of the New Negro Renaissance were, undoubtedly, years of deep reflection for Georgia Douglas Johnson. Cedric Dover, writing of her importance twenty-five years later, proclaimed her "definitely of it; but equally definitely not in it."[16] As Du Bois had explained at the tribute dinner, Johnson, like other early writers, had pursued the course encouraged by circumstances of the time and had gained success. Now she was faced with the "consciousness-raising" of the New Negro Writers. These artists ranged from the so-called "Nigger Heaven" devotees to the "Locke School" who wanted to proclaim the beauty of being a Negro and to "scrap the fictions, garret the bogeys and settle down to a realistic facing of facts."[17]

Having been called the creator of raceless lyrics, "a feminist without color" and even "hedonistic;" having unknowingly fallen prey to the persuasive myth that Negro folk material actually stood in the way of assimilation and integration by continuing to present the Negro as "an inferior being;" having tried at any cost to avoid the derogatory images of the black man that minstrels had implanted in the minds of white America, Mrs. Johnson felt a strong need to re-evaluate the means of expression that led to her success and to try new themes and forms. ***Bronze*** had shown a move in this direction when she ceased to be "just a woman" and became a "colored woman" expressing specific emotions and feelings growing out of her experience of blackness. Carl Van Doren, recognizing perhaps that the leap to racial consciousness was a precarious one for black writers, had cautioned the new Negro writers in their enthusiasm to retain that quality of the "race not given to self-destroying bitterness . . . [and to] strike a happy balance between rage and complacency—that balance in which passion and humor are somehow united in the best of all possible amalgams for the creative artist."[18] He might also have sensed that without this "balance" black writers could negate their chances for success in the larger society.[19]

Mrs. Johnson came at this moment in her life to the inevitable dilemma faced by all black writers—how to write the truth from a black point of view and yet find acceptance in a predominantly white society; how to continue to achieve by standards that threatened or denied black essence, or risk failure by defying them in order to preserve one's racial integrity. Caught on the horns of this dilemma, she wrote:

> Long have I beat with timid hands upon life's
> leaden door,
> Praying the patient, futile prayer my fathers
> prayed before,
> Yet I remain without the close, unheeded and
> unheard,
> And never to my listening ear is borne the
> waited-word.
> Soft o'er the threshold of the years there comes
> that counsel cool:
> The Strong demand, contend, prevail; the beggar
> is a fool!
>
> —**"The Suppliant"**[20]

The poem clearly announces the decision which Mrs. Johnson reached at this stage in her writing; the decisions quite obviously affected the writing which followed. She turned to prose in the form of dramatic literature and began to focus on themes of intense social protest. The decisions also contributed to a period of failure—at least to get published and produced.[21] Nevertheless, the new direction afforded her personal rewards and the adulation of contemporaries who fearlessly took up the banner of agit-prop writing in the late twenties and thirties.[22] Mrs. Johnson's entrance into the arena of social criticism coincided with the end of the "effulgence of the 'twenties," as Dover calls it, with the shocking after-effects of the 1929 stock market crash, and with the start of the Great Depression. Undoubtedly, these abrupt changes in society contributed to the changes that occurred in her writing and provoked the transition to a social critic whose "end product is not to rework his vision to produce a finished and complete poem, but to re-work society or to create a new society."[23] The soul of the black American dictates the inevitability of this transformation inasmuch as "the social critic sees himself as a materialist or realist," not as an idealist.[24] Idealism becomes the only logical explanation for the early black writers who retained their optimism and proclaimed themselves "integrationists" in a land where integration in practice did not exist. The Negro artist, as exemplified by Mrs. Johnson's long and ardent struggle, continued to believe that full integration could be attained, however. These artists also exhibited the fortitude to hang on to the dream articulated so memorably by Martin Luther King again thirty years later.

By the fall of 1935 when the United States government made its first effort to inaugurate a nationwide, federally sponsored theatre as a part of President Roosevelt's New Deal and Works Progress Administration, Mrs. Johnson was well on her way to becoming a dramatist of social protest. Hallie Flanagan, Federal Theatre Project National Director, in a much publicized address to launch the project, had declared that "the theatre must grow up (and) become conscious of the implications of the changing social order, or the changing social order (would) ignore, and rightly so, the implications of the theatre."[25] Encouraged by conspiring events in society and persuaded by friends and critics to try drama, she had found it a living avenue.[26]

During the "full lean years" of the thirties, as George Mason Brown described the period, Mrs. Johnson shared the creative world with several well-known playwrights—Eugene O'Neill, Paul Green, Elmer Rice, Maxwell Anderson and others. She was joined by other newcomers who later became the major dramatists of the twentieth century American stage—Lillian Helman, Arthur Miller, and Tennessee Williams.

> The theatre of the thirties was often referred to as a 'left theatre,' a 'Roosevelt theatre,' a 'theatre of creeping socialism' or worse. The record shows that this was mostly hogwash. The theatre then *reflected what was going on in the world around it.*
>
> (emphasis added)[27]

Obviously some playwrights were freer than others to write about what "was going on in the world" and to gain success in so doing. What was going on in the world of the black American and what s/he was driven by a moral, social, and artistic conscience to write was seldom welcomed by the general public. Only a few black literary creations slipped past the censors if the themes, forms and styles did not continue to perpetuate the old myths and stereotypes "acceptable" to the American theatre-going public. Langston Hughes' drama *Mulatto* and the story of its Broadway run is one of the few success stories to which blacks can relate with pride from this decade. Its theme of miscegenation and angry lynch mobs terminates with the mulatto son's death by his own hands—and some scholars believe accounts for its toleration in the thirties. On the other hand, Abram Hill's realistic three act drama, *Hell's Half Acre,* which opens on an aftermath of a lynching in Georgia and erupts with social problems that were going on around the United States—lynch mobs, disenfranchisement, segregated facilities, miseducated blacks, and numerous other results of racism, never got further than the readers of The Federal Theatre Project and is unknown as a drama today. Two stirring moments from the drama illustrate untouchable subjects and illuminate the failure of Hill and Mrs. Johnson, as well as that of other black writers of social protest. The moments occur in the play when the so-called educated blacks and "the less fortunate, average men" cannot agree on how to solve a problem:

> DR. SMALLS: We are more militant than you . . . though it may not appear that way. . . . We fight and discuss things at a round table. . . . We fight verbally with the powers that be.
>
> WILL: (Thin, yellow Negro, about 30) Then all we got to do is sit down with a bunch of ignorant crackers . . . and say you all got to stop lynching me and they'll say all right. . . .[28]

Later when the educated Negroes see the light, Dr. Smalls admits that "I thought it would be evolutionary rather than revolutionary. . . . I was wrong."

The lynching which takes place in Hill's drama is based on the perennial argument that "a black man will rape the first white woman he sees and, thus, must be stopped at all costs." A mandatory character in both the real life and stage versions of this "drama" is the indignant white "victim" whose primary testimony is based on a remark similar to Daisy's in Hill's drama: "You dare question the integrity of a white woman!" (II,2,1)

The use of the "black male-white female rape argument" is the basis for most of the dramas on the lynching theme written in the thirties—and also continued to be the argument most frequently heard in society. The real facts from the period do not support this argument, but that made little difference to anybody. Willie Snow Etheridge, writing in 1930, stated that "during the first nine months of this year, there were twenty-one lynchings. . . . Twenty of the twenty-one victims were Negroes. And though the familiar chorus of rape which follows each lynching stanza swelled as loudly these nine months as ever before, *only seven of the twenty-one were even accused of rape.* This proportion is in accord with the records for the past forty-four years. . . . of the 4,287 persons lynched from 1885 through 1929, only 884 were charged with rape or attempted rape. This is one-fifth or 20.6 per cent of the total."[29]

Encouraged by expectations that the Federal Theatre would be a haven for fledgling playwrights, that experimental productions not likely to get produced elsewhere would be mounted, that plays of social protest were welcomed, and that playwrights' serious dramatic efforts would be judged on their merits, Georgia Douglas Johnson submitted at least five plays to the Federal Theatre Project between 1935 and 1939, the year the project closed. *None* were accepted for production in any of the producing units of FTP. Three of the plays submitted are specifically on the theme of lynching and rape; two are historical sketches based on the desperation of slaves to escape from servitude to freedom. The lynch mob lurks ubiquitously in the minds of the author and the characters of both of these dramas. A brief analysis of the dramas and of the FTP playreaders' evaluations of them can lead to an understanding of why Mrs. Johnson, and black playwrights in general, failed in the American theatre of the thirties—and any time when their serious dramas expose the evils of a racist society.

In the one-act drama, ***Blue-eyed Black Boy,*** Jack Walter, a 21 year-old black man on his way home from work, innocently brushes against a white woman, is charged with attempted attack, arrested and jailed. He becomes the intended victim of a lynch mob. Jack's mother, hearing the lynch mob moving toward the jail to get her son, in desperation, retrieves a small ring from a secret hiding place. She then sends the black doctor, who is soon to marry her daughter, in haste to the governor with a message from "Pauline who gave birth to a son 21 years ago." She adds with emphasis:

> PAULINE: Just give him the ring and say, Pauline sent this, she says they goin' to lynch her son born 21 years ago, mind you say twenty one years ago—then say—listen close—look in his eyes and you'll save him.[30]

The ring and the message are delivered, the governor remembers, the militia is called out, the lynching is stopped, and Jack is sent home safely to his mother.

Like many of the revolutionary dramas of the sixties that are reminiscent of the social protest plays of the thirties, ***Blue-eyed Black Boy*** is a tightly structured drama with compressed action. The entire playing time of the script is less than twenty minutes. Johnson, having already exhibited technical aptitude of high quality in her writing, handles exposition with inference and understatement, plants a note of suspense, and concentrates on protesting the social realism of black women and their mulatto sons. The dialogue distinguishes between the simple dialect of the uneducated, older characters and the more polished speech of the young, educated characters. The audience never sees the blue-eyed boy and, while this contributes to the suspense, the omission might have contributed to the play being attacked as an "incomplete drama."

One FTP reader dismissed the "playlet" as a pointless bit of melodrama without significance, and rejected it as "too amateurish to consider." Another felt that "it (was) fine as a little theatre piece although it does not reach crucendos (sic) or does not solve the problem" and rejected it as "too amateurish" also. A third reader complimented it as a "very well constructed playlet (that) develops some suspense (sic)," adding that "it is obviously designed to discourage lynchers and to show that proud governors have slack moments." But his judgment of it as a play was "merely so-an-so."

The note which this reader added under "Audience Appeal" is of particular significance in this discussion:

> It would appeal to many audiences composed of men and women who have feverish ideas about the lynching 'Down South.' Its rather unhealthful matter would interest and delight many loose-thinking, race-baiting persons both black and white.[31]

The three readers did not agree on the merits of the play; however, they all agreed to reject it. Their comments leave much to speculation. To see the intention of the play as "designed to discourage lynchers and exhibit governors' slack moments" is to fail to acknowledge the real problem in society which the playwright is protesting—the victimization of black women and their sons. Referring to "accused rape and lynching" as "a rather unhealthful matter" should qualify for the Guiness Book of Records as the "understatement of the century." To perceive of this unhealthful material being a delight to blacks under *any* condition is to acknowledge the chasm between black and white thinking at its widest. One is forced to wonder how much racial fear and bias, deliberate or subconscious, entered into the rejection of the drama.

Safe, a play which Mrs. Johnson apparently submitted along with ***Blue-eyed Black Boy,*** is set in a three-room cottage of a simple black family in a southern town in 1893. A young wife awaits the imminent birth of a child as a crazed lynch mob passes by dragging their sobbing black victim. The young boy's agonizing pleas for his mother shatter the expectant mother's composure. Almost before the laughter of the crowd and the cries of the victim die down, she goes into labor and delivers her child. The healthy cry of the newborn babe is heard from the adjoining room and shortly thereafter the doctor emerges to announce the birth of a fine son—BUT:

> DR. JENKINS: She asked me right away, 'Is it a girl?' . . . And I said, 'no child, it's a fine boy,' and then I turned my back a minute to wash my hands in the basin. When I looked around again she had her hands about the baby's throat choking it. I tried to stop her, but its little tongue was already hanging from its mouth—it was dead! Then she began, she kept muttering over and over again 'Now he's safe—safe from the lynchers! Safe!'[32]

The three readers who evaluated ***Safe*** were more impressed by it than the readers who responded to ***Blue-eyed Black Boy***; only one of the three readers read both plays. However, they were all aghast at the notion that a lynching could take place for no obvious "good reason" and impugned the playwright for suggesting this in her drama:

> An extremely dramatic, tragic piece. But the glaring weakness of utter exaggeration is too bright—and it fails not because the idea is not dramatic,

> but because it follows from an absurdity—that they lynch Negro boys 'Down South' for defending themselves from thieves. In fact, the crime that produces lynching is vastly fouler.[33]

Clearly this reader has fallen victim to the myth that "only rape produced lynching down South" and expects the playwright to protect this myth by ignoring the truth. Another reader responded

> Laying aside such questions as the authress' (sic) negative, timid and even false philosophy, this play lacks conviction and feeling. The story is told so casually and factually that it becomes little more than an amplified but unconvincing statement that the sight of a lynching drove a Negro mother crazy.[34]

In some other plays, as for instance in dramas of Henrik Ibsen, factual treatment of social evils, dramatization of psychological conflict, reversal of action, etc. are viewed as evidence of "dramatic genius." When employed by Ms. Johnson, they motivate reactions of: "utter exaggeration," "an absurdity," "negative and false philosophy," "lacks conviction and feeling." The playwright, instead of society, becomes the accused and must, therefore, be indicted. The black-white chasm deepens, making black playwrights' chances of acceptance and success more dubious.

One reader was less offended by the theme of lynching and wrote honestly:

> In this play about lynching, Miss Johnson just begins to show the horror of this national shame. I wonder why she is not brave enough to show the whole truth. . . . She reaches a great dramatic climax, but still, I believe she could show the suffering and anxiety of these poor people in a much greater way, but her efforts are to be commented (sic) because it is truly a nice piece of work for a little theatre.[35]

One is instantly struck by the criticism "not brave enough to show the whole truth." Is the reader objecting to being denied the opportunity to *see* enacted on stage the birth and subsequent murder of the baby? Mrs. Johnson's choice of "offstage" violence is certainly not her invention and probably reflects her earlier inclination toward gentility. The decision does not weaken the structure of the drama; even this reader acknowledges that "it reaches a great dramatic climax." Perhaps the reader intended the emphasis in his phrase to be on "the whole truth." If so, what truth, or rather *whose* truth, does he have in mind? The protagonist's truth is undeniably and emphatically expressed by her decision to kill her newborn babe rather than to hear his death cries at the hands of a raving lynch mob eighteen years later.

Finally, Mrs. Johnson's use of the "law of economy" in the writing of ***Safe*** in no way diminishes the degree of "suffering and anxiety" of her characters. The explosive conclusion is as powerful as the eruption of a volcano. No one could possibly look only at the first trickle of hot lava without sensing what boils deep inside.

One of the reviewers admonished the playwright to "REWRITE IT!" and recommended it "with reservations," but apparently the drama never went any further than in the rejected file at the FTP Playreaders Service. Until ***Safe*** was recovered and placed in the George Mason University Special Collections and Archives, it was lost to the theatrical world.

Three copies of ***A Sunday Morning in the South*** are also preserved in the Archives at George Mason; one copy includes the music of the drama. Two versions of the script provide an opportunity to see Mrs. Johnson, the playwright, at work trying to follow the suggestion of the reader who told her to re-write her other play. In the second version, the play has been compressed from a "one-act play in two scenes" to "a one-act play in one scene." A new character is added to facilitate the action of going after "the good white man"—in this instance a woman, who will save the innocent victim, thus opening the way for the protagonist to remain on stage throughout the entire action. Also, in this version, the dialogue is truer to the dialect and rhythm pattern of the black speech of the characters portrayed; the exposition and the didacticism of the author are less intrusive. The second version is overall a more tightly written play, but it loses some dramatic impact by having the news of the lynching reported by a third party rather than having the protagonist receive the information firsthand.[36]

The action of ***A Sunday Morning in the South*** takes place in 1924 in a humble cottage occupied by a grandmother, Sue Jones, and her two young grandsons, Tom (19) and Bossie (7). Church music is heard from nearby as a neighbor, on her way to morning services, reports that a white woman has claimed "rape by a young black man." They all suspect that the rape charge is untrue but know it will fan more racial hatred and shudder at the thought of what will happen if the young man is found. Almost immediately, two white officers come with the girl who vaguely identifies Tom as the man who raped her. Despite the grandmother's pleas and assurance that Tom was at home asleep all night, the 19 year old boy is arrested and supposedly taken to jail. Sue (in the second version) sends for help from "Miss Vilet, the good white woman," but learns that Tom is lynched before anybody can save him. The shock of the news kills Sue as the curtain falls.

Of the three plays specifically on lynching, this was the only one that met with the approval of all the FTP readers. Their acceptance and recommendations did not lead to a production of the script, however. The reports read from the terse to the enthusiastic:

> Very simple and inexpensive. The second set (this reader read version one) may be only a back drop for smaller groups. No difficulties (of production) and (of audience) Labor, Negro, liberal, Radical (sic)[37]
>
> Here is the first Piece I have read about lynching that truthfully shows the futility of resisting the insane minds of a lynching mob *with gentility*. All sence (sic) of reasoning is lost, justice is forgotten and an innocent youth is sacraficed (sic) on the altar of race hatred and gigotry (bigotry).
>
> Miss Johnson handles the theme, one of the many causes of mob maddness (sic) and with deftness gives dramatic emphasis to this evil.
>
> her (sic) characters appear as if from life. It has Tenseness (sic) and reality. *It is not offensive to either group.* It is a great sermon agins't (sic) this national shame. I recommend for Little Theatre. (emphasis added)[38]

The clue to approval of ***Sunday Morning*** may be found in the reader's phrase "it is not offensive to either group." The persistent dilemma of which audience to address rears its head again, but sympathy for the characters seems to overcome the need to take sides and makes the play more acceptable. Subtextual statements on the hypocrisy of the Christian religion may also have touched sensitive chords in the readers' consciences. Nevertheless, the play was *not* given a production by The Federal Theatre Project.[39]

Although Mrs. Johnson's other two scripts submitted to FTP are not social protest dramas of the thirties, they deserve a brief discussion here. Both ***Frederick Douglass*** and ***Ellen and William Craft*** are set in the days of slavery and concern the efforts of slaves to escape to the North and freedom.[40] In the first play, Frederick tells Anne, his "sweetheart freewoman," "I'm a-workin' for freedom an' you," and saves every penny he can to get to "that great big free country up North." His plans change, however, when he learns that his old master has arrived in town with intentions to send him back to the plantation where he cannot buy his freedom. He must escape immediately. In ***Ellen and William Craft,*** a beautiful octaroom slave, whose "pretty white face is (her) curse," is trying to avoid exploitation by her master by escaping with her "brown slave fiance" via the Underground Railroad. When news comes that "De white folks done found all about de underground," Ellen agrees to cut off her long hair and don Marse Charles' suit which Aunt Mandy is mending; she becomes the "spittin image of her daddy, ole Marse Charles," and boards the *real* train to Philadelphia, accompanied by her "slave William."

It is difficult to determine just when ***Frederick Douglass*** was submitted to the Federal Theatre National Service Bureau since the readers' reports are dated from June 29, 1936 to September, 1938. One report for ***Ellen and William Craft,*** dated June 29, 1936, has been found. Mrs. Johnson may have submitted all five of her plays at the same time in 1936 or she may have turned from the lynching theme after failure to have her plays accepted and couched her protest in themes and forms that came closer to "the happy balance between rage and complacency" that Van Doren had noted as a necessity for success. In any event, one reader saw ***Craft*** as a "competent romantic script, not of an experimental type, suitable for showboat production," and all recommended it. ***Frederick Douglass*** was viewed as "excellent material for a play, which is not yet written," and "not a finished play but merely the statement of a potentially dramatic incident which the author has apparently been artistically unable to develop." There is cause for speculation about how much Mrs. Johnson's decision to let the "smart Negro slaves" (as one reader calls them) outsmart the white masters contributed to this feeling of incompleteness on the part of the readers. Two of the three readers rejected the script and complained that "the authoress writes in so factual and casual manner" and that "interesting facts are set forth but with scarcely more artistry than say in a newspaper item." It is ironical that the FTP Living Newspaper productions, one of the project's most innovative and publicized creations, were at this very time breaking attendance records dramatizing "factual news items." Even this choice, however, seemed closed to black playwrights. The one known Living Newspaper script written exclusively from a black perspective and one that dramatizes nearly all the racial injustices in the entire history of black life in America was rejected by the FTP National Service Bureau.[41] The script, *Liberty Deferred* by Abram Hill and Frank Silvera, remains in the "unproduced files" at George Mason University Special Collections and Archives.

What then can be concluded from this examination? If the answer to the question posed—did social protest from a black perspective successfully find a place in the American drama of the thirties—is based on the experiences of Georgia Douglas Johnson, it must be an unqualified No. Mrs. Johnson, as a poet of "raceless writing" and even as a race-conscious poet and as a playwright of Negro folk life, gained recognition and critical acclaim. In other words, when she pursued avenues one, three, and four of the choices given earlier in this essay, society welcomed, or at least acknowledged, her artistry. When she turned to avenue two—social protest—she failed, not because she exhibited less ability as a writer, but because society was not ready for her writing. Apparently Mrs. Johnson forsook the writing of drama and concentrated again on writing poetry where social protest was more "acceptable" by society. She continued to write and to publish poetry until her death in 1965.

When Mrs. Johnson's experiences are projected beyond the decade of the thirties in order to generalize about black dramatists' probable success as writers of social protest, the response is still problematic. Even fifty years later—even after the revolutionary sixties—perplexing questions remain unresolved. Why do black dramatists who know best the grim realities of racism fail as social protesters in the American theatre? Why, on the other hand, do white writers receive critical acclaim for plays of social protest, for instance, *Stevedore,* a play on race and union conflicts, by George Sklar and Paul Peters? Or is the secret to success found in black-white collaboration as *Turpentine,* labeled a "folk drama" but primarily concerned with an uprising and racial problems in a turpentine camp? The play is credited to J. Augustus Smith, black dramatist, and his white collaborator, Peter Morell. Like a refrain from an old song of the past, Van Doren's words come back to haunt the black dramatist: "strike a happy balance between rage and complacency." But on a theme such as rape and lynching can rage be tempered? Should it be? How can black anger, bitterness and frustration be expressed in a manner that a white audience can tolerate, endure, support—even pay to see it? Yet protest is surely wasted if only the victims are "enlightened."[42]

Assuming an occasional black protest drama slips past the censors and draws a black and white audience, how much can white "liberals" take of the sins and evils of society before their sensitivity is strained beyond endurance? Those who are already convinced of racial superiority are not likely to feel guilty and can hardly be expected to patronize efforts to produce such feelings. On the other hand, most blacks can tolerate "ugliness" only in small doses and agit-prop dramas run the risk of fanning smouldering rage. Compromise, concessions, conciliatory writing, detachment and retreat from social protest are well-known, but unacceptable, routes for the black playwright who wants to employ "sharp angles of accusation," as has been said of Mrs. Johnson's writing in the thirties. Despite the inestimable accomplishments of black theatre made by the Federal Theatre Project, it did not solve the problem of social protest from a black perspective.

We can now only hope to settle down—again—to a realistic facing of the facts and pray for sustained determination, resilience, and fortitude, as black dramatists, and others, continue to search for answers to these perplexing concerns. Perhaps the efforts of Georgia Douglas Johnson will not only "gem the archives of a better day," but inspire those of us living in "this better day"—fifty years later, to force change and bring an end to racism in our society.

Notes

1. The poems cited here can be found in: "Credo," *Phylon,* XVII, No. 4 (1956), p. 316; "Interracial," *Phylon,* V, No. 2 (1944), p. 188; "The Man To Be," *Phylon,* XVII, No. 2 (1956), p. 1972. "The Suppliant" is documented in note 20. "To My Son" appears on p. 380 in *The New Negro Renaissance,* see note 12 following. *Black American Writers Past and Present: A Biographical and Bibliographical Dictionary* by Theresa G. Rush, Carol F. Myers, and Esther Spring Arata is a good reference for the sources of many of the poems, but there is a great need for a comprehensive collection of Johnson's writing. See Fletcher's biographical essay on Georgia Douglas Johnson in the volume on Afro-American writers before 1955, *Dictionary of Literary Biography,* for more information.
2. Francis Harper was a popular black poet and lecturer; she was involved in the abolitionist movement, Women's Christian Temperance Union, and the underground railroad.
3. Mrs. Johnson wrote a brief statement to accompany a photograph which was published on p. 204 of *Opportunity,* July, 1927.
4. Georgia Douglas Johnson, *The Heart of a Woman and Other Poems,* Boston, Cornhill, 1918. Braithwaite, who wrote the introduction, was a black poet/critic, essayist and professor of creative literature at Atlanta University (1878-1962).
5. Georgia Douglas Johnson, "Black Woman," in *Bronze,* Boston, B. J. Brimmer Co., 1922, p. 43.

6. Line from "To W. E. B. Du Bois—Scholar," in *Bronze,* p. 92.
7. Foreword to *Bronze.*
8. As reported in *Opportunity,* December, 1923, p. 355.
9. "Bronze," *Opportunity,* July, 1923, p. 218.
10. Effie Lee Newsome, review of *Bronze, Opportunity,* December, 1923, p. 377.
11. Benjamin Brawley, *The Negro Genius,* New York, Dodd and McClelland, 1937, p. 219. Sara Teasdale (1884-1933), American poet, won the Pulitzer Prize for *Love Songs* in 1917. Known for the evocative intensity of her lyrics.
12. Michael W. Peplow and Arthur P. Davis, *The New Negro Renaissance: An Anthology,* New York, Holt, Rinehart and Winston, 1975, p. 70.
13. See statement on The New Poetry Movement in Sterling A. Brown, Arthur P. Davis and Ulysses Lee, *The Negro Caravan,* New York, Dryden Press, 1941, p. 280.
14. Brawley, p. 219.
15. As reported in "The Debut of the Younger School of Negro Writers," *Opportunity,* May, 1924, p. 143.
16. Cedric Dover, "The Importance of Georgia Douglas Johnson," *Crisis,* December, 1952, pp. 633-636.
17. For information on the artists of these schools of writing see *The New Negro Renaissance,* p. 142 and p. 389.
18. Carl Van Doren, "The Younger Generation of Negro Writers," *Opportunity,* May, 1924, p. 144.
19. See Fanin S. Belcher's monumental study, "The Place of the Negro in the Evolution of the American Theatre, 1767-1940," diss. Yale University, 1945, p. 399, for an interesting black perspective. Belcher's complaint concerns too little color and too much violence and he cites Mrs. Johnson's *Plumes* as "the usual example" of a desirable blend of "craftsmanship and imagination." Belcher's dissertation is infinitely more useful to scholars now that Neil Conboy and James V. Hatch have prepared an index of proper nouns for it. Published in *Black American Literature Forum,* 17, No. 1, Spring, 1983.
20. *The Negro Caravan,* p. 340.
21. Johnson's third volume of poetry, *An Autumn Love Cycle,* was published in 1928; her fourth volume, *Share My World: A Book of Poems,* did not appear until 1962.
22. For a concise yet comprehensive statement on the social forces that altered Negro life in America after WWI, see *The Negro Caravan,* p. 279.
23. Chester J. Fontenot, Jr., "Angelic Dance or Tug of War?" in *Black American Literature and Humanism,* R. Baxter Miller (ed.), Lexington, Kentucky, University of Kentucky Press, 1981, p. 41.
24. Fontenot, p. 41.
25. FTP papers give the date of Flanagan's speech as October 8, 1935. The Federal Theatre is well documented in Hallie Flanagan's *Arena: The History of Federal Theatre.* For specifics on black participation, see Ronald Ross, "The Role of Blacks in the Federal Theatre, 1935-1939," in *The Theatre of Black Americans,* II, Errol Hill (ed.), Englewood Cliffs, Prentice-Hall, 1980, p. 33; E. Quita Craig, *Black Drama of the Federal Theatre Era,* Amherst, University of Massachusetts Press, 1980; and *Free, Adult, Uncensored, The Living History of the Federal Theatre Project,* John O'Connor and Lorraine Brown (eds.), Washington, New Republic Books, 1978.
26. *Opportunity,* July, 1927, p. 204.
27. Harold Clurman, "Groups, Projects, Collectives," *Theatre Arts,* September, 1960, p. 18.
28. All excerpts from Abram Hill's drama, *Hell's Half Acre,* are from the typescript preserved in the Special Collections and Archives at George Mason University, Fairfax, VA.
29. Willie Snow Etheridge, "Southern Women Attack Lynching," *The Nation,* December 10, 1930, p. 647. Readers willing to risk painful revulsion, fear and anxiety may gain a new perspective on lynching and rape from this and similar articles in the journals of the era, e.g., Paul Blanshard, "They Are Not Always Lynched," *The Nation,* January 13, 1932, p. 42; "The States Right to Condone Lynching," *Opportunity,* February, 1923, p. 4; "I Am Opposed to Lynching, But—," *The Crisis,* December, 1922, p. 70; and from W. E. B. Du Bois' satirical opinion column, "A University Course in Lynching," *The Crisis,* June, 1923, p. 55. See also Bettina Aptheker, *Woman's Legacy, Essays on Race, Sex, and Class in American History,* Amherst, University of Massachusetts Press, 1982.
30. This and all subsequent excerpts from and references to the dramas discussed are taken from typescripts preserved in the Special Collections and Archives at George Mason University.
31. These comments and all subsequent quotations from and references to FTP Readers' reports are taken from the Playreading Department files, Bureau of Research and Publication, Federal Theatre Project, preserved at George Mason University.
32. Quotation from typescript of *Safe,* FTP Archives at GMU.
33. Charles Gaskill, FTP reader.
34. John Birassa, FTP reader.
35. C. C. Lawrence, FTP reader.
36. FTP readers liked both versions of the script, but tended to prefer the two-scene script.
37. Reader not identified.
38. C. C. Lawrence, FTP reader.
39. *Sunday Morning in the South* is, perhaps, the best known of Mrs. Johnson's plays. Its publication in James Hatch and Ted Shine, *Black Theatre U.S.A.: Forty-five Plays by Black Americans 1847-1974,* made it available to the public for the first time. Hatch's and Shine's introduction to the play is one of the best sources on Mrs. Johnson's personal life after the thirties.
40. Belcher, p. 407, lists the play as *Frederick Douglass Leaves for Freedom,* when it was presented by The New Negro Theatre in Los Angeles in 1940.
41. See E. Quita Craig's *Black Drama of the Federal Theatre Era,* pp. 63-65, for a fascinating account of the pros and cons of *Liberty Deferred*'s rejection.

42. I am forced to disagree with Quita Craig's conclusion, p. 54, that Georgia Douglas Johnson's plays "are written directly and unequivocably for a black audience." See her well documented, but controversial study.

CLAUDIA TATE (ESSAY DATE 1997)

SOURCE: Tate, Claudia. Introduction to *The Selected Works of Georgia Douglas Johnson,* pp. xvii-lxxx. New York: G. K. Hall & Co., 1997.

In the following excerpt, Tate traces Johnson's writing career, describes her approach to female desire and eroticism, and analyzes her disagreements with some younger male artists of the Harlem Renaissance.

Greater sophistication would spoil the message. Fortunately, to the gift of a lyric style, delicate in touch, rhapsodic in tone, authentic in timbre, there has been added a temperamental endowment of ardent sincerity of emotion, ingenuous candor of expression, and happiest of all for the particular task, a naive and unsophisticated spirit.

—Alain Locke, Foreward to ***An Autumn Love Cycle*** by Georgia Douglas Johnson (1928)[1]

The erotic is the nurturer or nursemaid of all our deepest knowledge. . . . Our erotic knowledge empowers us, becomes a lens through which we scrutinize all aspects of our existence, forcing us to evaluate those aspects honestly in terms of their relative meaning within our lives. . . . [W]hen released from its intense and constrained pellet, [the erotic] flows through and colors my life with a kind of energy that heightens and sensitizes and strengthens all my experiences.

—Audre Lorde, "The Uses of the Erotic" (1984)[2]

[R]emember that others judge us by past performances . . . but we judge ourselves by that which we dream and hope to do—our possibilities.

—Georgia Douglas Johnson[3]

Rereading a (Woman) Poet of the New Negro Renaissance

Georgia Douglas Johnson was the most anthologized woman poet of the New Negro Renaissance. While she also wrote one-act plays, short stories, and songs, her reputation rests on three collections of lyrical verse—***The Heart of a Woman*** (1918), ***Bronze: A Book of Verse*** (1922), and ***An Autumn Love Cycle*** (1928).[4] Primarily written in the ballad stanza, the poems in these collections focus on recalled love, lost youth, and inevitable death. Although she racialized ***Bronze,*** a work that anticipated Gwendolyn Brooks's *A Street in Bronzeville* (1945), Johnson has generally been understood by her critics as a traditionalist and an advocate of genteel culture, who adhered to the Romantic[5] conventions of the nineteenth-century Anglo-literary establishment.

Johnson's somewhat anachronistic verse did not constitute a retreat from the harsh social reality of African Americans during the first decades of the twentieth century. Rather, Johnson's poetic style was part of her strategy of "compensatory conservatism,"[6] which veiled her criticism of racial and gender oppressions behind the demeanor of "the lady poet." This perspective offered her the means to describe freedom, beauty, and especially her renegade sensuality without the censure of her peers. One persistent element of this veiled strategy is irony. What she praised, she also undercut with interrogating whimsy and thereby inscribed a furtive critique of the gender conventions of her day. Thus, beneath the veneer of Johnson's traditionalist verse and genteel public persona, labored a "bold modernist imagination"[7] that used erotic desire to idealize disappointment and irony to cushion the pain.

By recovering Johnson's erotic imagination from clichés about Victorian femininity, I want to suggest that we late-twentieth-century readers can appreciate Johnson's recurring depictions of sensual and often highly sexual perceptions, feelings, actions, and longings in especially her verse but also in her short stories and plays as the calculated attempts of a middle-aged black woman to define and preserve her subjectivity. Johnson used writing to define her life, shape her ambitions, determine her relationships, and accept her disappointments. Her love lyrics in particular are not sentimental abstractions but complex instruments for her intense self-reflection and retrospection. As letters from Johnson's admirers and her unpublished works suggest, writing love poetry was also the means by which she celebrated *and* camouflaged actual romantic conquests and idealized emotional injury.[8]

Johnson was a fascinating woman, who for various reasons—some obvious, others not—failed to fulfill her ambition to be a major poet. Because Johnson's formative years coincided with the period of U.S. modernization, when literature became one staple of a highly politicized mass culture, her life and work form a provocative perspective from which to reread the intersections of race, gender, class, and sexuality. Her career as a woman poet during the New Negro Renaissance also provides an excellent context for reviewing the literary fates of her black female contemporaries such as Zora Neale Hurston, Nella Larsen, Jessie Fauset, Angelina Grimké, and Alice Dunbar-Nelson. Thus Johnson's importance as a literary figure is a product of the volume of her writings and her transitional position in two cultural maps of U.S. literary history.

Neither a subscriber to Victorian ideology nor a fully modern woman, Johnson stood between

FROM THE AUTHOR

INSPIRATION

Many years ago a little yellow girl in Atlanta, Georgia, came across a poem in a current paper that told of a rose struggling to bloom in a window in New York City. A child tended this flower and her whole life was wrapt [sic] up in its fate. This poem was written by William Stanley Braithwaite, years before the world knew how marvelous was his mind. Some one told the reader of these lines that the writer was colored and straightway [sic] she began to walk upward toward him.

SOURCE: Georgia Douglas Johnson, from the introduction to a collection of her poems in *Caroling Dusk: An Anthology of Verse by Negro Poets,* edited by Countee Cullen, Harper, 1927.

those of the generation who understood sex as the husband's conjugal right, race as fixed, and poetry as sedate, speculative wonder on the one extreme, and those of the next generation who assumed sexual liberty, fluid racial identities, and a poetic sensibility of social activism on the other. Her contemporaries describe her verse as possessing "exquisite artistry," "poignant pathos," "ardent sincerity," and "ingenuous candor of expression."[9] Despite the fact that Johnson is everywhere concerned with eroticism, this term is effaced in commentaries about her work—probably because her contemporaries feared that any mention of sexuality would invite the racist stereotype of the essential licentiousness of black people. Alain Locke, the veritable dean of the New Negro Renaissance, comes the closest to recognizing Johnson's persistent lyrical ardor in his foreword to ***An Autumn Love Cycle,*** her third collection of verse, and therefore provides an incisive illustration of how Johnson's black contemporaries read female sexuality.

In the foreword to Johnson's ***An Autumn Love Cycle*** (hereafter referred to as ***Autumn***) Locke promises a gender-sensitive reading of this work by addressing Johnson's somewhat unreserved display of emotions, indeed, her intense sensuality. By commenting on how "the emotions of woman . . . have yet to be carried beyond the platitudes and sentimentalizations of man made tradition" (xv), Locke intimates that Johnson explores what is fundamentally a woman-centered tradition of eroticism—"the Sapphic cult of love"—to describe "the ecstasy of life" (xviii). Adding that Johnson "probes under the experiences of love to the underlying forces of natural instinct which so fatalistically control our lives," Locke implicitly draws on Freudian psychology to explain as instinctive the curious yoking of passion and melancholy in Johnson's poetry.

Locke seems to have detected a libidinal impulse in her verse beyond maternal devotion, indeed, one of transgressive ardor. However, the conventions of his age and race evidently prevented him from publicly addressing his discovery. As a result, Locke retreats from examining the censored content and substitutes an analysis of "the tragic poignancy of Motherhood" (xviii). However, no sooner has he has placed Johnson's transgressive passion in the context of maternal virtue than he concedes that motherhood cannot subsume womanhood. The "real dilemma of womanhood," he explains, encompasses "the antagonisms of the dual role of Mother and Lover" (xviii-xix). But rather than examine this conflict, Locke abandons the project by allowing the powerful cultural valence of motherhood to bind female desire.

For Locke and his contemporaries, female desire was to be bound to motherhood, and motherhood was understood, accordingly, as "the consummation of love" and "the expiation of [female] passion" (***Autumn,*** xviii). Although Locke was well aware that Johnson did not address motherhood in this rather candid collection of love poetry, I suspect that he mentions the maternal institution, which is a prominent theme in ***Bronze,*** published six years earlier, to harness Johnson's renegade passion to respectability. By binding Johnson's depictions of female desire to motherhood, Locke subjugates the power of female sexuality to maternity by insisting that she "has gone straight to the mine of the heart" to explore "her own subjective experience" undoubtedly as a widowed mother (xix), for he believed her work to be "abstractly confessional of a woman's way and view of love."[10] By framing ***Autumn*** in this way, Locke forecloses the possibility of a "philosophical yield" in her work (xix). For despite his comment on the novelty, indeed, the power of Johnson's eroticism, Locke ultimately follows the gender prescriptions of his age and circumscribes her poetry within a patriarchal economy in which the feminine signifies the body and feelings of the mother and not the mind and ardor of the poet.

Locke not only fashions Johnson to fit early twentieth-century cultural prescriptions of woman as mother, he also portrays her as fitting the description of "the average Negro writer," despite his implicit use of this category to designate male writers. According to Locke the "average" black writer of the early twentieth century was "characteristically conservative and conformist on general social, political and economic issues, [and] something of a traditionalist with regard to art, style and philosophy, with a little salient of racial radicalism jutting out in front—the spear-point of his position."[11] Although these characteristics ostensibly fit Johnson, the label—"average Negro writer"—obscures the fact that she was an ambitious, mature woman, writing when female desire was closely regulated by, to invoke Locke, the "man made tradition," and when the old and new generations were competing to define the aesthetic of New Negro literature.

From the perspective of present-day readers, Johnson is not usually regarded as a "New Negro" but rather as a member of what Robert Bone has labeled "the rear guard."[12] For Bone and us as well, the New Negro or Harlem Renaissance is generally characterized by the works of the younger generation of black writers, "the young Turks," who were mostly male—principally Langston Hughes, Claude McKay, and Wallace Thurman. This is not surprising inasmuch as they were the most productive members of this younger generation who would overshadow the writers of Johnson's generation. The young Turks were also destined to become the dominant canonical figures, because their black nationalistic values were resurgent during the 1960s and early 1970s, when scholars of African-American culture rewrote the literary history of the New Negro Renaissance. These two periods are analogues. As literary historian Nathan Huggins has perceptively observed, the militant self-assertion of those who saw themselves as New Negroes determined "their search for ethnic identity and heritage in folk and African culture, and their promotion of the arts as the agent which was to define and to fuse racial integrity resonate [in] what we hear about us now, fifty years later."[13] As a result, the black aesthetic of the late 1960s and 1970s redefined the New Negro Renaissance as a prototype of the Black Arts Movement. This redefinition distinguished the young Turks as innovative and progressive, as Huggins, Bone, and Darwin Turner (and others) have argued, while classifying the writers of Johnson's generation—W. E. B. Du Bois, Jessie Fauset, William Stanley Braithwaite, for example—as reactionary integrationists, indeed, as "old" Negroes. This viewpoint has helped to obscure Johnson's prominence as the lady poet of the Renaissance.

Recent interpretative strategies of feminism, deconstruction, and cultural studies, however, suggest that we should question such literary topographies at the same time that we begin to reassess the significance of Johnson's work. For we now know that powerful racialist and gendered assumptions (as illustrated) predetermined the literary representations of eros. Because Johnson was a woman, indeed, a lady, her constituency automatically relegated her to the status of a very minor poet and a muse for masculine ambition during a period when African-American art became intensely politicized. I contend that Johnson's feminized voice was not a retreat from but a radical engagement with the politicized aesthetic of the Renaissance. She used that voice to create a space to enact her own literary ambitions and to formalize an erotic agency that on the one hand, white culture had denied to women and black people in general and on the other hand, black culture had denied to women of the race. Because the Renaissance (and modernism as well) called into question prior social and literary meanings, it offered Johnson an opportunity to mask her appropriation of the masculine prerogative to critique her culture and express sexual agency.

The Renaissance also provided the occasion for a contest between elite and folk culture among black artists. In the words of Locke, the former held that "assimilation was the prevailing idea in Negro endeavor," and the latter "pointed in the direction of distinctive achievement[,] a capitalization of the race's endowments and particular inheritances of temperament and experience."[14] However, as Locke further insisted, the movement from the assimilationist position "was not separatist" in motivation, but "a minority promotion move—an attempt to capitalize" on one's own culture, to move "from propaganda to art, from cultural parade to self-expression" ("A Decade of Negro Expression," 7). As a result, the writers of the younger generation defined themselves in opposition to the then reigning standards of assimilationist literature. To accomplish this task they fastened the "older" generation of writers, which would include Johnson, to a rigidly defined bourgeois conservatism so as to highlight their own originality, liberalism, and self-assertiveness. Even though the older writers—Locke, Du Bois, Fauset, Braithwaite (Johnson's mentor), and Johnson herself—held more varied artistic and social attitudes than the young Turks would ascribe to them, the elders still tended to regard art as a vehicle for racial uplift, as evidence of social advancement.

The elders did not agree that art must address racial topics to accomplish this task. Du Bois's writings are always tinged with racial propaganda, while Braithwaite's poetry suggests no aura of race. Nevertheless, Du Bois and Braithwaite, like their black contemporaries, were conditioned by a post-Reconstruction ethos that made social equality within an integrated political context the goal. They still believed that African Americans could use their "production of literature and art" to demonstrate their "intellectual parity" with white Americans.[15] But unlike Braithwaite, Du Bois was prepared to move beyond demonstration and deploy black literature as a weapon for social justice. Johnson held both positions. She wrote love poems about erotic self-awareness that endorsed Anglo-literary conventions and thereby earned the approval of Braithwaite. But she also wrote racial protest verse and plays with a passionate indignation that pleased Du Bois. Hence Johnson evidently did not strive to make her writings reflect a consistent position but allowed them to delineate an ideological dissidence that embraced the objectives of *both* bourgeois assimilation and folk nationalism.

By contrast, the younger generation of artists, Hughes in particular, attempted to unify their positions under the mantle of political manifestos. Not interested in proving themselves worthy to a white audience, these writers repudiated the "uplift" mission for art. They used art to define black cultural identity. To illustrate the bifurcation of the generational positions, I refer to their 1926 launching of the ill-fated *Fire!!* Principally established by Hughes, Thurman, Hurston, and Gwendolyn Bennett, the quarterly was "Devoted to the Younger Negro Artists." According to Hughes, *Fire!!* "would burn up a lot of old, dead, conventional Negro-white ideas of the past, *épater le bourgeoise* into a realization of the existence of the younger Negro writers and artists."[16] In *Fire!!* they defined their collective artistic agenda by shocking some of the black bourgeois intelligentsia, according to Locke, with their "strong sex radicalism" and, hence, their outspoken repudiation of "any special moral burden of proof."[17] Although Du Bois was among those who disapproved of the young Turks' radical sexuality, he nevertheless celebrated the flowering of Negro literature in the decade of the twenties. For Du Bois that development was fostered by propaganda. In "Criteria of Negro Art," for example, published in the Du Bois edited *Crisis,* he encouraged young black artists "to fight their way to freedom" of expression by refusing to cater to either the white public's demand for black primitivism or the black middle-class's demand for bourgeois propriety.[18] And still, as Du Bois's 1926 *Crisis* survey on black representation reveals, he felt that writers and publishers who overemphasized "the sordid, foolish and criminal among Negroes" would "convinc[e] the world that this and this alone is really and essentially Negroid." Such representation would prevent "white artists from knowing any other types and black artists from daring to paint them."[19]

Georgia Douglas Johnson shared Du Bois's position. In response to the *Crisis* survey questions, she appealed to black artists to let "the world see those who have proven stronger than the iron grip of [racial] circumstance. Let the artist cease to capitalize on the frailties of the struggling or apathetic mass. . . . Depict the best, with or without approbation, and renown."[20] What Johnson meant here by "the best" had little to do with technique and everything to do with class. Like many of her black contemporaries, she felt that black writers had concentrated on portraying "the Negro farthest down" and that "the time is about ripe" for stories that tell "the history of our great middle class"—its "hopes, dreams, yearnings, heartbreaks and yes, even the joys and fulfillments of today."[21]

Nevertheless, Johnson's emphatic endorsement of middle-class values and her very close friendships with Thurman and Hughes in particular undoubtedly complicated her response to *Fire!!*. Johnson's reaction can be deduced from Thurman's undated letters to her. In the fragment of one letter, presumably written before *Fire!!*'s appearance, he requests her assistance in finding subscribers. In another, on *Fire!!* letterhead, addressed to Johnson as "Dear God-mother," he seeks her sympathy and possibly her aid by describing his poor health and financial woes, while accepting her apparent chastisement by mentioning without complaint his receipt of the copy of *Fire!!* that she returned.[22] In this way she expressed her disapproval of *Fire!!*.

The debate over aesthetic values was more than a dispute over black representation. It was a controversy among factions of black writers who disagreed on whether art could or should define a unique black identity. One faction held that the New Negro Renaissance was "unmitigated bunk,"[23] and the other used a racialized aesthetic to mount a heroic effort to assault the racist American landscape. For example, in "Negro-Art Hokum," published in *The Nation* in 1926, black journalist George S. Schuyler attacked the New Negro Renaissance by insisting that Negro art in America was "non-existent": "Negro art there has been, is, and will be among the numerous black nations of Africa; but to suggest the possibility of any such development among the ten million colored people in this republic is self-evident foolishness" (662). Schuyler went on to exclaim that "it is sheer nonsense to talk about 'racial differences' as between the American black man and the American white man" (663). The "Aframerican," Schuyler insisted, "is merely a lampblack Anglo-Saxon" (662).

In response to Schuyler, Hughes published his most famous essay—"The Negro Artist and the Racial Mountain"—in the next issue of *The Nation.* Here Hughes emphatically affirms "the duty of the younger Negro artist . . . to change through the force of his art that old whispering, 'I want to be white,' hidden in the aspirations of his people, to 'Why should I want to be white? I am a Negro—and beautiful!'"[24] This essay became a veritable manifesto for black writers of the new generation:

> We younger Negro artists who create now intend to express our individual dark-skinned selves without fear of shame. If white people are pleased we are glad. If they are not, it doesn't matter. We know we are beautiful. And ugly too. The tom-tom cries and the tom-tom laughs. If colored people are pleased we are glad. If they are not, their displeasure doesn't matter either.
>
> (694)

The New Negro writer then is not one who simply demands the opportunity to address topics beyond Victorian respectability. According to Locke, a sympathetic elder, who looked back at the Renaissance from the vantage point of the mid-thirties, the New Negro writer was one who gradually converted "race consciousness from a negative sense of social wrong and injustice to a positive note of race loyalty and pride in racial tradition" ("Propaganda or Poetry," 70). Hence, art became the mode of redress during the decade of the twenties, as in the black literature of the post-Reconstruction era, because African Americans of both periods had no hope of ameliorating the vicious social oppression with civil appeals to due process of the law. As we shall see, for Johnson art was also a means to recuperate shattered hopes. Johnson's volume of poetry ***Bronze*** and her folk plays were her defenses against the reentrenchment of institutionalized racism whereby black Americans alone would define the terms of their emotional interdependencies.

The interracial hostility of post-World War I matched that of the post-Reconstruction. Segregation, discrimination, and disenfranchisement, mob violence, lynching, and full-scale race riots were the rule rather than the exception. However, the war had conditioned black people to respond aggressively to social injustice. Black soldiers had fought to make the world safe for democracy. They abandoned the accommodationist position of Booker T. Washington and declared their readiness, in the words of Du Bois, "to fight a sterner, longer, more unbending battle against the forces of hell in our own land."[25] The swelling ranks of the National Association for the Advancement of Colored People (NAACP), which was founded in 1910, reflected black America's growing discontent and its willingness to use militant agitation to demand racial justice. *The Crisis* magazine, the official publication of the NAACP, proclaimed the battle cry. In its pages black Americans not only declared war on racism but on white cultural dependency as well. The New Negro literature was a part of their declaration of independence.

The decided emphasis on the black cultural aesthetics of the Renaissance supported a different objective than that defined by the artistic formulas of the post-Reconstruction period. During that era African-American writers sought to demonstrate their intellectual parity by appropriating Western, genteel, artistic models as the means for promoting social assimilation. Black poets, for example, published works that either avoided or idealized black identity. Black poets like Paul Laurence Dunbar (best known for nostalgic dialect verse) and Braithwaite, as well as such lesser-known poets as Mary Weston Fordham, Priscilla Jane Thompson, Josephine D. Heard, and H. Cordelia Ray, as scholar Joan R. Sherman explains, "emulate[d] the white literary establishment's inspirational, romantic, and sentimental poetry on orthodox subjects."[26] This poetic model shaped Johnson's formative experience as a poet. Such a model, as Sterling Brown would later explain, required the repression of a historicized black identity:

> References to race were avoided or else couched in abstract, idealistic diction. Valuably insisting that Negro poets should not be confined to problems of race or pictures of Negro life, these poets too often committed a costlier error out of timidity at being Negroes: they refused to look into their own hearts and write.
>
> (45)

These poets seem not to have questioned their use of Western literary forms or expectations and their subsequent artistic colonization. Their poetry was a passive political strategy for cultural if not social assimilation.

During the New Negro Renaissance, though, race was the quintessential topic of the new aesthetic. The historical fact of segregation was recast from the black rather than the white perspective as separatism for enhancing race pride. "To be black," in the words of literary scholar Benjamin Brawley, "ceased to be matter for explanation or apology; instead it became something to be advertised and exploited: thus the changed point of view made for increased racial self-respect."[27] Assimilation was no longer the prevailing ideal in the distinctive achievements of black artists; rather they now capitalized, as Locke argued, on "the race's endowments and particular inheritances of temperament and experience."[28] Despite their nationalistic redefinition of the politics of racial separation, black people still held the desire to participate in United States polity as full citizens. Into the culturally complex, turbulent, and paradoxical domain of the New Negro ventured Georgia Douglas Johnson with a life-long determination to be recognized as a serious poet.

An Ambitious, Dynamic, and Spirited Woman

Georgia Blanche Douglas Camp was born on September 10, 1877, in Atlanta, Georgia, to Laura (neé Douglas) and George Camp, who were respectively half black and Native American, and half black and white.[29] In an autobiographical sketch Johnson recalls that her first school days were in Rome, Georgia, and while still a young child, she moved to Atlanta with her mother (Davis and Freeman, 2). Johnson seems to have been somewhat estranged from her mother, for she mentions in the sketch that her mother was "rather resentful of her daughters" (Johnson and her half sisters) and that her childhood was very lonely. Johnson does not refer to her father beyond mentioning his racial background. Presumably her parents separated sometime around the move to Atlanta. At this time her mother resumed her maiden name, Douglas, an action suggesting that her union with George Camp might have been a common-law marriage. Within a year or two she remarried and became Laura Spaulding.[30] Despite Johnson's apparent ambivalence toward the mother, Johnson displaced her patrimonial name at the time of her marriage and unconventionally proclaimed herself to be Georgia *Douglas* Johnson and not Georgia Camp Johnson. This act of self-naming transformed the daughter's conflicted devotion into fidelity to her mother.

In 1893 she finished Atlanta University's Normal School and began teaching in Marietta, Georgia. In 1902, after working as a schoolteacher for nearly a decade, she resigned to attend the Oberlin Conservatory of Music. A year later she returned to Atlanta where she worked as an assistant principal in the local school system. Shortly after assuming this position she resigned to marry Henry Lincoln Johnson, an Atlanta attorney, on September 28, 1903.[31] In 1910 she and Henry Sr. relocated in Washington, DC, with their two young sons, Henry Lincoln Jr. (1906-c. 1990[32]) and Peter Douglas (1907-1957). In Washington Henry Sr. ("Link") established a law firm. In 1912 President Taft appointed him to a four-year term as the Recorder of Deeds, a position traditionally held by a black man since Frederick Douglass. This appointment securely placed the Johnsons into elite black society.

Although Johnson was circumscribed by middle-class matrimony and maternity, she was not "a conventional housewife" (Shockley, 348). She gave expression to her creative impulses by writing stories, poems, and songs, teaching music, and performing as a church organist. The dining room table, according to her good friend writer Alice Dunbar-Nelson, was routinely cluttered with papers, a typewriter, and literary journals, much to her husband's disapproval.[33] According to Johnson herself, "He thought a woman should take care of her home and her children and be content with that" (quoted in Hull, 167). Even though her husband "tried to discourage" her ambition to write, he seems not to have been a major obstacle. She wrote volumes of poetry. In fact she ironically dedicated her first two collections of verse, ***The Heart of a Woman*** (1918) and ***Bronze*** (1922), to her somewhat critical spouse.

Sometime around 1920 Johnson began arranging informal gatherings for writers at her home at 1461 "S" Street, Northwest, in Washington. Johnson's home (which she would later call the "Half Way House") offered a convenient place for comfortable rest and relaxation for her black friends and associates who traveled between the North and the South when segregated public accommodations were the rule. Johnson ritualized these meetings as her literary salon. Publicly documented in Gwendolyn Bennett's "Ebony Flute" columns in *Opportunity*[34] and privately recalled in Dunbar-Nelson's diary entries as well as in the correspondence of Renaissance notables, Johnson's "Saturday Nighters Club" offered the most celebrated black writers of the period a place to share their work and discuss literature. Writers of the young generation—for example, Jean Toomer, Countee Cullen, Anne Spencer, Jessie Fauset, Marita Bonner, Willis Richardson, Montgomery Gregory, and Bruce Nugent as well as Hughes, Thurman, Hurston, and Bennett of *Fire!!*—met in various combinations at Johnson's home with those of the old generation—Du Bois, Dunbar-Nelson, Locke, James Weldon Johnson, Angelina Grimké, and Braithwaite, among others.

Johnson's affectionate rapport with these literary personalities is recorded in their letters to her. For example, Toomer mentions their mutual affinity for music. His appreciation for rhapsody made him an exceptionally sensitive reader of Johnson's love lyrics. In his letter of March 4, 1920, he remarks, "I read your lines and I swear that as love lyrics[,] aiming not at the rhythmic subtleties and virtuosities of the genius but at the true expression of emotion and feeling filtered thru the imagination[,] they come nearer [to] my heart than anything I've read. Send me some more."[35] The exchange of manuscripts, musings, aspirations, ideas, and advice between Johnson and Toomer was typical of the rapport that she developed with many of the writers of the Renaissance. Unfortunately, Toomer's response to Johnson's poetry was less than sincere; unbeknownst to Johnson, he was a patronizing reader of her work. In Toomer's letter to John McClure, editor of the *Double Dealer,* he describes Johnson's verse as having "Too much poetic jargon, too many inhibitions check the flow of what I think to be real (if slender) lyric gift."[36] While there may be other reasons for Toomer's callous disapproval of Johnson's poetry, his criticism calls attention to Johnson's anxiety of authorship engendered by the social constraints that regulated the erotic expression of black bourgeois women.

On September 10, 1925, Henry Sr. died of a stroke. His death ended Johnson's career as the "housewife-writer" and began her life as a wage earner (Hull, 184). As a widow, she had the personal and emotional space to write but little time. From 1925 to around 1934 she had to work outside the home in a series of nine-to-five public service jobs to pay her sons' tuitions and to support herself. Her income enabled Henry Jr. to complete Bowdoin College and Howard University Law School and Peter to finish Dartmouth College and Howard University Medical School.

Despite the demands on her time, Johnson continued to write. In 1926 her one-act play ***Blue Blood*** won honorable mention in the *Opportunity* contest. The following year ***Plumes,*** another one-act play, won first prize in the 1927 competition. The *Opportunity* prize marked the peak of Johnson's career. From the perspective of 1927, Johnson undoubtedly believed that her career was in its ascendancy. By 1928, though, the tide was changing. She was unable to secure a commercial publisher for ***An Autumn Love Cycle*** and as a result published it (just as she had earlier published ***The Heart of a Woman*** and ***Bronze***) at her own expense in 1928. In a 1928 feature article in the Pittsburgh *Courier,* Johnson revealed her rising anxiety about the difficulty of publishing additional works. The article referred to five books that "could, on short notice, be prepared for the publishers if she had the time to do it."[37] I suspect that Johnson used this announcement to invite queries about her work in the hope of attracting a publisher. Most of these works were finished, as she would recall in her "Catalogue of Writings," but they were never published.

Undoubtedly, the stock market crash of 1929 and the ensuing Great Depression further diminished opportunities for Johnson to find publishers for her work. The crash dismantled the patronage that supported the Renaissance and left the New Negro writers struggling to survive. Black artists could no longer afford to visit Washington, DC, with regularity, and their absence caused Johnson's Saturday Nighters Club to disband in the thirties. Without the intense stimulation of first-rate artists, Johnson's writing suffered. She settled into the pattern of recycling old poems in small local magazines and became a closeted fiction writer.

In 1941 Johnson was invited to join The Writers' Club, Inc. of Washington, DC, a group of local black writers, most of whom had connections with Howard University. The club was incorporated on April 16, 1941, and lasted until 1960. According to the club's constitution "this organization exists for the purpose of stimulating more creative writing among those who have had their writings accepted by periodicals or publishers of note."[38] In addition to Johnson, the better-known members were dramatist Owen Dodson, poet and playwright May Miller Sullivan, archivist Dorothy Porter and her artist husband, James, dramatist Willis Richardson, historian-diplomat Merze Tate, and poet-scholar Sterling Brown. Although Johnson's attendance was spotty during the first years of the group, after 1948 she seldom missed a meeting. Dorothy Porter Wesley recalled that Johnson was always "very stiff, still, and quiet" as she sat wrapped in a big fur coat. Not gregarious like her good friend May Miller Sullivan, Johnson read her poetry in a very evenly measured voice that invited listeners but no commentary.[39] Johnson probably knew that her time to mature into a first-rate poet had passed. Therefore, she settled into the role of an antiquated, minor sage.

The minutes of nearly two decades of the triannual meetings of the D.C. Writers' Club preserve a record of Johnson's literary activities and reveal that she remained an enormously energetic woman during the last years of her life. For example, the minutes of the May 19, 1951, meeting report the publication of her serial story in *True Confessions.* This work corroborates Gloria Hull's speculation that Johnson, like Wallace Thurman, supplemented her meager income by writing for "pulp" serials under pseudonyms (203). The minutes also report that Decker Press (Prairie City, IL) published her poetry collection *Friendship Fires* and that her poems appeared in anthologies published in the Netherlands, Czechoslovakia, Sweden, China, Israel, and South America.[40]

Despite her prominence during the Renaissance and her tremendous productivity, Johnson was to witness the publication of a only few short stories and several poems after the twenties. The Boston-based *Challenge* magazine published two stories—**"Gesture"** and **"Tramp Love"** in 1936 and 1937 respectively—under the name of Paul Tremaine (a male-narrative appropriation whose significance I shall discuss below). Johnson's serial story in *True Confessions,* noted in the minutes of the Writers' Club, was probably also published under a pen name. These acts of pseudonymous authorship are reminiscent of her submission of ***Plumes*** to the 1927 *Opportunity* contest under the name of John Temple. The circumstances of publication for these works and probably others during the decade of the 1920s prompted Dunbar-Nelson to write in her "As in a Looking Glass" column of May 13, 1927, that "Georgia Douglas Johnson has as many aliases as Lon Chaney had faces. One is always stumbling upon another nom de plume of hers" (quoted in Hull, 202). Scholars will probably never recover all of her published works because they appear under signatures not associated with Johnson on pages of no longer extant publications.[41] This practice was symptomatic of her intense anxiety of authorship, for she was fully convinced, and rightly so, that her readers would be more likely to treat her works seriously if she disassociated her black and female self from them.

Johnson also wrote a weekly column, "Homely Philosophy," from 1926 to 1932, syndicated to Negro newspapers, including the Pittsburgh *Courier,* Boston *Guardian,* New York *News,* Chicago *Defender,* New York *Amsterdam News,* Philadelphia *Tribune,* and New York *Age* (Hull, 185). As the titles of representative columns—"Starting All Over Again," "Look Up at the Sky," "The Winner," "Visions," "A Smile on the Lips," and "Find Pleasure in Common Things"—suggest, these somewhat clichéd bits of wisdom were Johnson's attempt "to bring cheer into the homes of Americans during the Great Depression" (Donlon, 641).[42] When juxtaposed to Johnson's M. V. Strong columns on social commentary on such topics as integration, the 1964 Civil Rights Bill, the 1964 presidential campaign, and building character, we can begin to reconstruct Johnson's active public life. Moreover, when Johnson's activism is placed alongside her syndicated "Beauty Hints by Nina Temple" (also published in *The Negro Woman's World*), we can appreciate how Johnson found very pragmatic ways to express all sides of her personality. For example, "Nina Temple" is not concerned with promoting cosmetics for artificial beautification, but rather she advises her readers to "Powder your face with sunshine." In another column she advises her readers to associate the ardor of love with the fullness of life: "Verily this is true. He who loves not, lives not and he who loves most, lives most."[43] Taken together, these columns help us to understand Johnson's appreciation of love, beauty, and hopefulness as the bases for an existential strategy. She used her delight in sensuality and her selective memory to define the life she endorsed in all of her writings. Furthermore, when we understand that she wrote to sustain her subjectivity and optimistic outlook, it becomes clear how she could be so productive without prospects for publication. Believing that "the greatest mistake is in giving up,"[44] Johnson used writing to define an independent identity for herself and to add purpose and cohesion to her life.

Johnson thrived on talk about all forms of art. She recognized the significance of her salon to literary history. In the early 1940s she shared her plans to publish a book about her literary salon with the members of the Writers' Club. She planned not only to recall dozens of anecdotes but to include letters and original poems of famous Renaissance writers. In a book manuscript Johnson assembled her account of the complex interplay of literary influence that materialized in her living room on Saturday nights. Although the manuscript is no longer extant, a list of the participants, some letters from them, and fragments of their original verse have survived. Almost as tragic as the loss of this manuscript has been the persistence of scholars in fashioning Johnson as a literary hostess rather than as a serious writer in her own right. The role of muse for male ambition diminished the critical appreciation of her talent and fated this enormously energetic and ambitious woman to literary marginality. And yet Johnson is also responsible for her fate. She seems to have deliberately elected the role of muse as a means of maintaining her contact with the most talented artists of the twenties in the hope of expanding the limited alternatives for developing her writing.

Throughout Johnson's declining years she was remarkably vigilant but unfortunately unsuccessful in securing publishers for her post-Renaissance works. Occasionally, she published a poem or a story in black periodicals like *Phylon, Journal of Negro History, Challenge, Negro Digest, Negro Voices, The Observer,* the Baltimore *Afro-American,* and the Washington-based *The Negro Woman's World.* No doubt, remembering her good fortune as the Renaissance's premiere lady poet during the decade of the twenties fortified her resolve not to abandon her ambition. Even after she was forgotten Johnson continued to write lyrical poetry throughout her long life, now and then slipping a poem into correspondence to friends. She also remained active in many political, racial, and cultural organizations, regularly went to the movies, and during the 1940s ran a correspondence club for "[l]onely people all over the world."[45]

Johnson's correspondence club suggests her ingenuity and persistence, as well as her ability to stretch the truth in her claim that "This club has been running successfully for 30 years."[46] Johnson named the club "One World: Washington Social Letter Club, Inc.," and ran it under the name M. Strong primarily during the Second World War. Wartime provided Johnson with an abundance of lonely people as potential members. However, the commanders of DC-area military bases wanted to restrict her epistolary activities. On at least two occasions the commanders asked her not to promote her club among the enlisted men in the interest of national security. No doubt Johnson's venture had two purposes: recreational and financial. Like the people whom she targeted, Johnson longed for a fuller life and the excitement of meeting new people. Moreover, the application fee of two dollars supplemented her dwindling income.

Johnson frequently itemized her writings as a part of her persistent but unsuccessful application to funding agencies. For example, she applied to the Harmon Foundation[47] from 1927 to 1930, to the Guggenheim Foundation in 1929, the Rosenwald Fund in 1942 and 1944, and the John Hay Whitney and the Guggenheim Foundations in 1950. Her age was always a problem. In the 1928 Harmon Foundation application, as Gloria Hull notes, Johnson falsified her birthday. Here she states that she was born in 1888 and therefore was forty-two. As it turns out, she was not forty-seven, as Hull suspected, but actually fifty-one. In the 1950 Whitney application, she attempted to make her maturity work to her benefit by explaining to one respondent that "one would need age in order to qualify for the thing I would do" and by requesting that he refer to her as "the mother of the Negro Poets."[48]

If the letters of recommendation written in her behalf to the Harmon Foundation and the Rosenwald Fund are typical, it is no wonder that Johnson's applications were unsuccessful. For during the cycles of Harmon applications, Braithwaite, Du Bois, Carter G. Woodson, and James Weldon Johnson repeatedly "damned her with faint praise." Johnson's application to the Rosenwald Fund generates the same kind of response from A. Philip Randolph. Although these avid "race men" wrote supportive letters, they could not conceal their belief that writing love poetry was a superfluous endeavor when compared to social activism.[49] Moreover, because all of her advocates with the exception of James Weldon Johnson were generally unfamiliar with or unsympathetic to the aesthetic and critical language of the white literary establishment, they could not describe Johnson's work in terms that the establishment would appreciate. In addition, the more extreme segregation of Washington and Atlanta versus New York City probably conditioned her not to seek the assistance of white mentors. She may also have been afraid of success, like many talented women who accepted their lack of opportunity rather than risk responsibility for their own failure. As a result of all or some of these reasons, Johnson's frequent applications for funding were doomed to failure.

And yet, despite rejection after rejection, somehow Johnson remained hopeful. In a March 2, 1950, letter to Harold Jackman, whom she addresses as "My Dear son," Johnson characterized her perseverance in pursuing funding: "You would be surprised to know how many foundations I have tried, and more surprised to learn that each one, said, 'no,' but *most* surprised, to learn that I have still high hopes—am looking with my heart's bright eyes to the bright tomorrow."[50] This was one of many letters to Jackman in which Johnson preserved her literary ambitions by sharing her ideas, mentioning self-promotional undertakings, and asking for his advice and assistance. Although she was greatly disappointed with each rejection, she continued to apply for funding until the last years of her life. In 1963, three years before her death, as her correspondence reveals, Johnson inquired about Ford Foundation grants.[51]

The letters between Johnson and Jackman, cast with the mutual affection of surrogate mother and son, suggest that she and Jackman were kindred spirits.[52] Although Johnson maintained a similar history of correspondence with Langston Hughes, the relationship with Jackman was more intense. They seem to have written to each other more frequently and over a longer period of time than the other correspondents. With tender affection, he helped Johnson to preserve her literary ambitions and to maintain her ego as a poet. Although she insisted in her letters to Jackman that she was "utterly refusing to grow old" (March 2, 1950), that she was "not dimming out but carrying on with more intensity as the days march!" (March 27, 1951), and that she was still "Hoping with my heart's bright eyes" (December 2, 1952), Johnson knew that her time was running out.[53]

Always anticipating that "bright tomorrow," Johnson prepared her "Catalogue of Writings" in the last years of her life and deposited it in the archive at Atlanta University either in 1963 when she attended the Baccalaureate Services[54] or in 1965 when she returned to her alma mater to receive the honorary degree Doctor of Letters. Her care in safeguarding the survival of the catalogue suggests that she intended for it to serve as a research guide for future literary scholars, as by the 1960s most of her works remained unpublished. Moreover, it was also clear to Johnson that her early success in the New Negro Renaissance was long forgotten. As her letter written to Jackman two decades before would suggest, these circumstances did not seem to burden her unduly. In that letter of August 8, 1944, she writes of her works that it "seems I must go to that last peaceful abode without getting them printed . . . but why should I be worrying, Balzac left forty unpublished books."[55] According to her catalogue, Johnson left behind seventeen books.

This well-organized directory seems to be Johnson's effort to convince her posterity of her former literary prominence and continued productivity despite the neglect she suffered. She concludes the catalogue by summarizing statements in recognition of her early renown. In this last section, entitled "Reviews and Tributes," Johnson cites references to herself as "the modern Sappho" (John White of the *Washington Times-Herald*), "the foremost woman poet of her race" (Braithwaite), and "one of the finest and most distinctive voices in the renaissance of American Poetry" (Clement Wood[56]). But more important than these accolades, the catalogue lists her unpublished books:

1. "Little Eagles," a book of inspirational thought for "aspiring youth"
2. "Bridge to Brotherhood," a collection of seventy-seven poems
3. "Little Philosophies," several booklets for inspiring human progress
4. "My Bible," a collection of "heartwarming, heartlifting thoughts"
5. "Homely Philosophies," a collection of vignettes on commonplace wisdom
6. "One and One Makes Three," a novel about the life of a child born to parents much like Johnson and her husband
7. "The Black Cabinet," a biography of her husband, Henry Lincoln Johnson, cast against the history of the Republican politics[57]
8. a book of seventeen short stories, related to her by a real or fictitious person named Gypsy Drago
9. "Literary Salon," the story of the literary meetings at her home on "S" Street
10. a collection of twenty-one short stories
11. a collection of ten short-short stories
12. three one-act black historical plays
13. four primitive life plays ("Plumes," "Blue Blood," "Red Shoes," and "Well-Diggers")

14. three stories of "average Negro life"

15. six plays of "average Negro life"

16. eleven lynching plays

17. twenty-four copyrighted songs

Despite Johnson's inability to find publishers for these works, she made plans for new books, which she lists in her private papers as "Glittering Fire," "Ride Atilt," "Sundry," "Destiny's Darling," "Psychological," "My Anthology," "Prefaces," and "Lovelight."[58]

Johnson wrote in numerous genres and formats; nevertheless, it was undoubtedly poetry that sustained her artistic life and vigor. For Johnson, writing poetry was a way of intensely experiencing life. For this reason it is not surprising that she was still publishing poetry up until her death and entering literary contests during her last decade. Sometimes her efforts met with success. She won a prize for poetry awarded by *Flame Magazine* (Avalon, TX) in 1959.[59] Her poems appeared in poetry journals like *Poetry Digest* (Milldale, CT) and *New Athenaeum* (Crescent City, FL). In 1962, four years before her death, Johnson published her last poetry collection, ***Share My World.***

Johnson's literary ambition and her identity as a writer were very important to her. As she lay dying at Howard University's Freedman's Hospital on May 14, 1966, her close friend May Miller Sullivan comforted her by sitting "by her bedside stroking her hand and repeating quietly over and over 'Poet Georgia Douglas Johnson.'"[60] Remembering that she had been a poet seems to have greatly consoled her in her final hours. After Johnson's death Miller Sullivan, probably responding to Johnson's deathbed request, beseeched Henry Jr. "to preserve the barrels of papers that his mother kept at home," but to no avail (Fletcher, 163).

Johnson correctly anticipated her own literary recovery. Not only did she deposit her "Catalogue" at Atlanta University, she also labeled her letters and annotated the carbon copies of individual poems with publication information. Sadly, she overestimated her family's appreciation for the mildewed manuscripts, rotting in the basement of her home. Henry Jr. undoubtedly did not realize their value, for immediately after the funeral, according to Owen Dodson, her manuscripts were treated as so much rubbish:

> I do know that she had a great deal of unpublished material—novels, poems, essays, memoirs, remembrances, all kinds of things. But as the car stopped in front of her house, the men were cleaning out the cellar, and I clearly saw manuscripts thrown into the garbage. I said, "A lifetime to the sanitation department!"[61]

Perhaps Dodson was too overcome with grief to offer the sanitation workers a few dollars in order to salvage Johnson's papers for posterity. An opportunity forever lost.

Like the other scholars of Johnson's life and works, I too believed that all of her manuscripts and personal papers were forever lost, until I learned that on January 6, 1992, the Manuscript Division of Howard University retrieved enough documents from the attic of Johnson's "S" Street House to fill four large boxes. Among an assortment of miscellaneous items are included fragments of many of the unpublished works, unpublished poetry, old photographs, correspondence, newspaper clippings, issues of old journals, typescripts of her syndicated columns, and information about her correspondence club. Fortunately, all was not lost.

The Lyrical Lady

A member of the old guard of Negro writers by birth, Georgia Douglas Johnson was a woman and a poet who understood feminine gender conventions. They stipulated that women could be muses for male ambition, but they were not to harbor similar ambitions for themselves. As Johnson's poem "Woman" (which she published rather late in her career in *Opportunity* in 1947[62]) indicates, she was well aware of the protocol that prescribed woman's sanctioned relation to man:

> UNSELFISH, silent potently
> Behind each man of history
> A woman stands, upon whose strength
> He leans to cast his shadow's length.
>
> She is his stairway to the sky,
> His bow of hope, his inward eye,
> His rhythm, yea his very breath
> That plays betwixt his lips and death.
>
> Aye, some brave woman without crown
> Behind each male-throne huddles down,
> A sentinel to guard his sleep,
> A bosom where he kneels to weep.
>
> To woman then! whose urge to live
> Is summed within the right to give,
> To merge her own identity
> Into another's entity!

While this poem commemorates the conventional wisdom that behind every successful man there is a woman, it harbors a feminist reproach inscribed in her critique of masculine dependency on feminine strength and talent. The tension signaled by the punctuation of the final line insinuates a cynicism that interrogates the conventional wisdom of the very virtues that the poem purportedly salutes. Had Johnson written more poems like this one and published them in small women's journals like *The Negro Woman's World,* there would have been a significant feminist record in which to place her writings. Instead of persistently pursuing this course, Johnson seems to have tried to fit her poetic sensibility to the vicissitudes of a conservative marketplace. She maintained her posture as "the lady poet," recycled old poems, and wrote what she thought would see print, rather than develop her work by exploring the complex critical sensibility that shaped her own life and vision. Even when her writing ventured beyond the routine she masked her efforts behind pseudonymous names. Without a circle of supportive and yet critical colleagues, Johnson was not able to focus her writing on the complicated social and sexual life she lived, except in a few furtive works.

Johnson's public persona would only allow the feminist in her to peek out from behind the veil of the lady. She seems only to have nurtured her feminist critique in her unpublished works and in her pseudonymously and posthumously published stories. What becomes immediately apparent on examining Johnson's life is that she did not make her complicated social and sexual attitudes the explicit focus of her writing. Neither did she allow her extensive circle of gay, lesbian, and bisexual black artists to inform her writing.[63] She seems to have possessed what late-twentieth-century scholarship defines as a feminist sensibility and sensuality. She refused to subscribe to a patriarchal sexuality that designated women as male property and that condemned homoeroticism as immoral, although she reined in these transgressive attitudes in her writing within a Victorian ethos.

Johnson undoubtedly understood the consequences of abandoning the posture of the lady for she knew that black women writers who dared to follow their literary aspirations were hampered by the double burden of bourgeois respectability in a black patriarchal order. Not only were black writers of Johnson's epoch expected to observe the anachronistic artistic customs of the post-Reconstruction period (1885-1915) that defined art as the measure of civilization, black women writers were also expected to prove to both white and black America, by self-consciously endorsing chaste literary conventions, that they did not remotely resemble the Jezebel stereotype. Hence early twentieth-century black women's writing was generally refined with a vengeance. Johnson knew she faced a different battle than that commonly associated with the Harlem Renaissance. While Hughes and Schuyler debated over whether poets who happened to be black were poets or black poets, Johnson understood the gendered politics of art. Much to the detriment of her writing, Johnson also seems also to have sought flattery rather than candid constructive criticism of her work. She might have swayed from convention, but she didn't visibly rock the boat.

For Johnson the contest was not whether she was a poet or a black poet but whether she could secure recognition as a poet during an age that inherently understood poetry as a masculine art form. Despite this obstacle, Johnson did have one advantage; poetry was the dominant genre of the New Negro Renaissance, and it was anthologized in a plethora of poetry collections. The most prominent of these include *The Book of American Negro Poetry* (1922), edited by James Weldon Johnson; *Negro Poets and Their Poems* (1923), edited by Robert T. Kerlin; *An Anthology of Verse by American Negroes* (1924), edited by Newman I. White and Walter C. Jackson; *Caroling Dusk* (1927), edited by Countee Cullen; and *Ebony and Topaz* (1927), edited by Charles S. Johnson. Each of these works accorded Johnson a prominent place in the Renaissance.

I suspect, though, she guaranteed her place by electing the feminine role of the lady poet and muse and by appealing to friends rather than daring the originality she was capable of voicing. Had she dared to fulfill her potential, the literary politics of the Renaissance might have regarded her as an aberration and accorded her little or no recognition. No doubt Johnson calculated her odds and placed her bet where she had the greatest chance for winning recognition. The results of such conservative politicking were short-lived at best. By the 1960s and 1970s anthologies of African-American literature either mention Johnson as a "minor" writer or omit her altogether.[64] During the 1980s, the second decade of the resurgence of the women's movement, Johnson's identity as a literary *woman* activates her partial recovery. And now in the 1990s the scholarly focus on understanding how race, gender, class, and sexuality mediate artistic subjectivity, production, and reception has enhanced her presence in an increasingly more complex rendering of the United States literary landscape.[65]

However, the changing scholarly ethos does not fully explain how Johnson managed to secure recognition during the New Negro Renaissance only to be "lost" and recovered during successive literary ages. Did she achieve her reputation as "the lady poet" of the Renaissance by writing volumes of poetry alone? Or did she assure her recognition by fashioning herself for this role? I offer the following analogy as an answer to these questions.

During a visit with Johnson and her husband, Alice Dunbar-Nelson recalls (on October 1, 1921) in her diary that Henry Sr. was more impressed with her teaching Johnson "how to put on hats" than with their discussion of the "manuscript of her new book."[66] If knowing "how to put on hats" was publicly sanctioned feminine knowledge, the mature Johnson learned her lesson well. She was seldom seen in public without a hat, as her numerous photographs reveal. I suspect that like the properly dressed lady wearing a stylish hat, Johnson's feminine comportment in both appearance and writing was the basis of her construction of self-confidence and insured as well her acceptance as a (woman) poet of the Renaissance.

While her contemporary Zora Neale Hurston also wrote about subjects that addressed the female domain, Hurston's now legendary manner and immodest commentary emphatically challenged masculine authority. Georgia Douglas Johnson did not ostensibly challenge the gender conventions of her age. In fact, critics frequently remark on how ladylike she was. For example, the Pittsburgh *Courtier* columnist Geraldyn Dismond provides the following impression of Johnson: "From the place [Johnson] occupies in the Negro renaissance, I had expected to see a brusque, cold-blooded individual whose efficiency and belief in sex equality would be fairly jumping at one. I imagined she was engrossed in herself and work, sophisticated and self-sufficient."[67] Contrary to her expectation, Dismond explains that Johnson "is very sensitive, retiring and absolutely feminine." Johnson's work is a synecdoche of this feminine persona. For as Dismond remarks, Johnson's writing reflects "the charm of her quiet dignity and tender sympathy" (8).

During the early stages of her career Johnson had looked to William Stanley Braithwaite to provide her with a poetic model. In an autobiographical sketch that she wrote for Countee Cullen's *Caroling Dusk,* Johnson recalls Braithwaite's influence by describing herself as "a little yellow girl in Atlanta, Georgia, [who, many years ago] came across a poem in a current paper that told of a rose struggling to bloom in a window in New York City. A child tended this flower and her whole life was wrapt [*sic*] up in its fate. This poem was written by William Stanley Braithwaite."[68] This critic and editor of the *Anthology of Magazine Verse* from 1913 to 1929, and himself author of several volumes of verse, objected to having his poems "classified indiscriminately as 'Negro' poetry," as Sterling Brown has recalled, for "he is concerned nowhere in his poems with race but wishes them to be 'art for art's sake.'" According to Brown, Braithwaite's "lines are graceful; at their best, exquisite," though "the substance is thin."[69] This description of Braithwaite's verse ostensibly fits Johnson's poetry. However, when Locke wrote about Johnson, he did not compare her to Braithwaite but to another American minor woman poet—Sara Teasdale (1884-1933)—who also wrote compact, conventional romantic lyrics about melancholic introspection and intuition and published several of them in Braithwaite's editions of *Anthology of Magazine Verse.*

From a late-twentieth-century perspective, Locke's invocation of Teasdale's poetry to characterize Johnson's verse might seem a ready comparison, governed by gender conventions that aligned women writers only with other women. Nevertheless, there are many important similarities between the two women. Teasdale was the first woman poet to achieve a national reputation for voicing a woman's point of view and emotions as well as the first to compile an anthology, *Love Songs* (1917), organized around a coherent view of women's attitudes on love.[70] This was Teasdale's most popular work, and it probably influenced Johnson's ***The Heart of a Woman*** (1918). In addition, Teasdale's favorite poem, "Arcturus in Autumn" (1922), lyricizes a midlife, eroticized melancholy that would also dominate Johnson's ***An Autumn Love Cycle*** (Drake, 213). Whereas Teasdale was divided between self-fulfillment and Victorian moral imperatives, Johnson seems to have been a freer spirit, who eroticized despair but not self-destruction.

Johnson and Teasdale were popular among their respective constituencies. However, unlike Johnson, Teasdale's large readership translated into tangible rewards of cash prizes and royalties. Most important, for the upper, white middle class, love poetry was not an extraneous concern; it reinforced the gender roles to which this class subscribed. But for the black population, mired in racism, bigotry, and poverty, lyrical expressions of genteel love must have seemed superfluous when compared to art with an explicit political agenda. Though they shared the erotic milieu, both women suffered from their failure to attend to the changing expectations for poetry. Rather than consistently focus their verse on the complexity of the self and the world, they relied on genteel formulas of sedate feminine reflection. As a result, they were not entirely innocent victims of a modern(ist) influence. Johnson slipped into obscurity when the Renaissance was inscribed into literary history as an inherently masculine aesthetic movement,[71] and Teasdale became marginalized when the new critics canonized modernist poetry.

In the mid-twenties, though, Johnson was a mature woman, who undoubtedly saw that her effort to bloom as a poet had much in common with the tenement rose in Braithwaite's poem. In her autobiographical sketch in *Caroling Dusk,* Johnson revealed that his languishing rose provided her with a metaphor for her persona that enabled her to reconcile her ambition to be a prominent poet with the gender conventions of black bourgeois aesthetics. This figurative model allowed her to veil her aspirations and disguise her grievances, and, unfortunately, retarded the development of her verse.

In another autobiographical sketch, published in the *Opportunity* "Contest Spotlight" in 1927, she relied on caprice, rather than frailty, to invite assistance: "If I might ask of some fairy godmother special favors, one would sure be for a clearing space, elbow room, in which to think and write and live beyond the reach of the Wolf's fingers."[72] Rather than presume to develop her art and risk revealing her disappointment, Johnson concealed her desperate petition for assistance behind the mask of guileless, feminine whimsy. In striking contrast to Johnson's calculated caprice, in the same article Arna Bontemps assertively expressed his gratitude to the *Opportunity* judges for awarding him "the Pushkin award again" by claiming, "At least it would seem that matrimony and fatherhood do not especially shorten one's luck" ("Spotlight," 204). I have to wonder what Johnson might have thought when she read his comment, for matrimony and motherhood habitually circumscribed her possibilities, despite her effort to recast her roles as wife, widow, and mother to her advantage.

Johnson's preoccupation with the emotional tenor of the female domain suggests that she used ***The Heart of a Woman*** and her projection of feminine comportment to solicit the appellation and role of "the lady poet" for herself in the unfolding drama of the New Negro Renaissance. Because she laid claim to the feminine domain of poetic expression from the vantage point of the lyrical wife and mother, and because she wrote more poetry than her black female contemporaries—Anne Spencer, Jessie Fauset, Helene Johnson, and Alice Dunbar-Nelson—Johnson gained recognition as the premier woman poet of the New Negro Renaissance. Unfortunately, this self-selected domain offered her little opportunity to develop her verse outside its parameters. Johnson's emphatically self-determined feminine voice, subject matter, and demeanor also invited early anthologists to regard her work as feminine effusion and to segregate the work of other women writers similarly. By appropriating "the heart of a woman" as the domain of female poetic expression, Johnson handed anthologists a gendered category that reified the segregation of male and female writers in anthologies as distinctive gendered voices throughout most of the twentieth century.

While anthologists of the twenties did not regularly adhere to sex segregation in their volumes, by the thirties, when the Renaissance was beginning to be inscribed into literary history, the women writers' section was a standard feature of anthologies and critical texts. For example, the 1935 edition of Robert Kerlin's *The Negro and His Poetry,* originally published in 1923, represented the poetry of the Renaissance in two chapters. One chapter, entitled "The Present Renaissance of the Negro," was composed entirely of male poets. Its complementary chapter, entitled "The Heart of Negro Womanhood," contained the works of Miss Eva A. Jessye, Mrs. J. W. Hammond, Mrs. Alice Dunbar-Nelson, Mrs. Georgia Douglas Johnson, Miss Angelina W. Grimké, Mrs. Anne Spencer, and Miss Jessie Fauset. While a few women poets were dispersed throughout the other six chapters, the overwhelming proportion of the poets were male, and most of the women were catalogued in the women's section with their marital status marked by the polite title—Miss and Mrs. It was not long before male scholars unquestioningly leaped from the assumption that feminine emotion was the subject of women's art to simply discussing their lives and not their works, that is, if they addressed women writers at all.[73]

Before we late-twentieth-century readers censure Johnson for inviting the emotional platitudes that trivialized her works, we should be mindful that the choices for Johnson may very well have been to be a "lady poet" or to receive no recognition at all. I suspect that her self-conscious adoption of an intensely feminine authorial posture was a calculated risk. For she seems to have gone out of her way to align her small poems with the feminine poetic imagination and to please Braithwaite by entitling her first collection of poetry ***The Heart of a Woman.***[74] Before examining Johnson's major collections of poetry, I refer to their forewords to characterize their reception.

Braithwaite's foreword to ***The Heart of a Woman,*** published in 1918, sets the tone for the reception of this work and those that follow. He writes that the

> poems in this book are intensely feminine and for me this means more than anything else that they are deeply human. We are yet scarcely aware, in spite of our boasted twentieth-century progress, of what lies deeply hidden, of mystery and passion, of domestic love and joy and sorrow, of romantic visions and practical ambitions, in the heart of a woman.[75]

As Gloria T. Hull, Johnson's biographer, astutely notes, Braithwaite broaches the possibility that Johnson could speak for humankind rather than only for women before backing off with clichés "about the secrets of a woman's nature," as Locke was also to do in his foreword to ***Autumn,*** discussed above (Hull, 157; Braithwaite, ix). In 1922 James Weldon Johnson similarly acknowledges ***The Heart of a Woman*** in *The Book of American Negro Poetry.* "It may be," he writes here, "that her verse possesses effectiveness precisely because it is at the pole opposite to adroitness, sophistication, and a jejune pretension to metaphysics. Her poems are songs of the heart, written to appeal to the heart" (181). James Weldon Johnson praises her for being "neither afraid nor ashamed of her emotions" and adds that "the principal theme of Mrs. Johnson's poems is the secret dread down in every woman's heart, the dread of the passing of youth and beauty, and with them love" (xliv). Moreover, he exalts "her ingenuously wrought verses," which "through sheer simplicity and spontaneousness" exude "a note of pathos or passion that will not fail to waken a response, except in those too sophisticated or cynical to respond to natural impulses" (*The Book,* xliv). Thus, in self-consciously gendered praise he appreciates her verse by regarding it not as art but as natural, transparent, feminine self-expression, in contrast to cultivated artistic creation, which is by implication to be associated with masculine expression.

In the foreword to ***Bronze,*** published in 1922, W. E. B. Du Bois racializes James Weldon Johnson's gendered response. In this rather short introduction, Du Bois describes the volume by explaining that it reveals "what it means to be a colored woman in 1922—and to know it not so much in fact as in feeling, apprehension, unrest and delicate yet stern thought." He concludes by hoping that "Mrs. Johnson will have [a] wide reading. . . . Her word is simple, sometimes trite, but it is singularly sincere and true, and as a revelation of the soul struggle of the women of a race it is invaluable."[76]

Gloria Hull asks why Johnson would permit "such a bald, condescending statement to be printed" and concludes that she must have felt that any word from Du Bois "was a boon" (Hull, 163). I suspect that Johnson had locked herself into the consequences of a bad decision by following Braithwaite's recommendation to ask Du Bois to write this foreword.[77] Even when Du Bois uses more flattering language in the foreword, like "stern thought," his failure to elaborate on this, among other passing remarks, makes the entire foreword fade into clichés about femininity. Six years later Alain Locke's foreword to ***An Autumn Love Cycle*** seals this typecasting. Even though Locke momentarily departs from the predictable tributes, he nevertheless settles on proclaiming that Johnson "has set herself" to the task of "documenting the feminine heart" (xv). These somewhat flattering and reductive readings of feminine sensibility would restrict a broader appreciation of Johnson's poetic imagination and entice her into duplicating worn lyrical strategies.

The Heart of a Woman and Other Poems has been labeled by anthologists and scholars alike as "a book of tidy lyrics" that voices "the love-longing of a feminine sensibility" (Hull, 157). However, beneath Johnson's ostensible concern with the "intensely feminine" "secrets of a woman's nature" (Braithwaite, vii and ix) is her persistent depiction of a soaring human imagination, her own. Despite disappointment and an unrelenting awareness of mortality, despite the confinement of convention, Johnson records moments of intense introspection and sensuality in lyrics characterized by their evanescence. As Gloria Hull has also noted, the dreams, dead hopes, sympathy, and pain depicted in this and the other collections of Johnson's verse are not simply lyrical monuments dedicated to universal feelings but "masked autobiographical utterances of the author herself" about unfulfilled desire (158).

Heart begins with Johnson's most anthologized poem—**"The Heart of a Woman"**:

> The heart of a woman goes forth with dawn,
> As a lone bird, soft winging, so restlessly on,
> Afar o'er life's turrets and vales does it roam
> In the wake of those echoes the heart calls home.

The heart of a woman falls back with the night,
And enters some alien cage in its plight,
And tries to forget it has dreamed of the stars
While it breaks, breaks, breaks on the sheltering
bars.

If one fails to heed the figuration of this woman's heart, as did the male critics of the Renaissance, this heart is presumed to be defined by feminine pathos. A close reading of this poem, however, reveals that Johnson portrays this female heart not as pulsating corporeality, seeking physical love, but as the classic incarnation of the unfettered imagination—the soaring bird—found in Romantic poems like Wordsworth's "To a Skylark." Hence, by identifying this heart with a bird, "soft winging, so restlessly on," Johnson associates a woman's heart with the traditional image of the poetic imagination, probably with the hope that feminine heart and poetic imagination would appear not simply as complements but as synecdoches for one another.

By caging this bird in the last stanza, Johnson clearly invokes the caged bird of Paul Laurence Dunbar's "Sympathy." While Dunbar's birdlike poetic spirit "beats his bars and would be free," Johnson's spirit, burdened with sentiment and obligation, "tries to forget it has dreamed of the stars" and surrenders to "the sheltering bars." Dunbar's influence on her writing is evident, but no one seems to have noticed the allusion, no doubt because Dunbar was depicting the limitations of race, while Johnson addressed gender confinement. And yet both of them would agree that "the world was an affair of masks."[78]

"The Dreams of the Dreamer," the second poem in ***Heart,*** repeats the cry of despair that will reverberate throughout this collection. In this poem Johnson depicts the predicament of the imagination as inevitable disappointment; for mortality ends all dreams:

The dreams of the dreamer
Are life-drops that pass
The break in the heart
To the soul's hour-glass
The songs of the singer
Are tones that repeat
The cry of the heart
'Till it ceases to beat.

Weary despair, caused by frequent loss, is the recurring theme of the collection. Although the persona recalls in "Pendulum" that she has "swung to the uttermost reaches of pain" to "rebound to the limits of bliss, / On the rapturous swing of an infinite kiss," death is her ultimate lover: "O shadows! take me to your breast / For I am tired—I would rest" ("Tired"). In "Smothered Fires" Johnson portrays her persona as "A woman with a burning flame / Deep covered through the years / With ashes," who utters "a sigh of victory / She breathed a soft—good-night!" During the Renaissance her readers assumed that the flame referred to the ardor of physical love and the vigor of youth. This flame was never associated with burning female ambition. Moreover, her contemporaneous critics assumed that her persona voiced the plight of an overly emotional woman rather than an idealized consciousness, struggling to recover lost hope by means of passionate conviction, imagination, and fantasy. Such reductive readings would help to seal Johnson's literary marginality.

Several poems in ***Heart*** depict marriage as another event for summoning "plaintive melod[ies]" of "shattered hopes that lie / As relics of a bygone sky" (**"Dead Leaves"**). Here marriage is emblematic of other dreams unfulfilled. In these poems there is no promise of sexual embrace, companionate unity, but only the painful separation of death. Erlene Stetson has detected the subtle subversion in ***Heart*** by observing that its poems "are iconoclastic romantic deconstructions of male fantasy."[79] The recurring theme of romantic disillusionment in ***Heart*** has caused Gloria Hull to underscore Stetson's observation by adding that ***Heart*** is "quietly seditious" (157). Undoubtedly, these feminist scholars are responding to Johnson's insistence that a woman's life is not circumscribed by romantic rapture and domestic reward (contrary to traditional sexual ideology) but rather conditioned by the same blighting despair that mars all who live with unfulfilled aspirations.

Current feminist scholarship, as Hull and Stetson illustrate, has the tools to analyze what Johnson's contemporaneous critics were unable to recognize as her deconstruction of romantic love. For example in **"Foredoom,"** Johnson laments that "Her life was dwarfed, and wed to blight, / Her very days were shades of night, / Her every dream was born entombed, / Her soul, a bud,—that never bloomed." Because the critics of her day were distracted by conventional beliefs that a woman's life was circumscribed by the domestic consequences of romantic love, they buried the poetic lamentations of Johnson's first collection under platitudes about "the secret dread down in every woman's heart" of not being loved (James Weldon Johnson, *The Book,* xliv).

Bronze, Johnson's second collection of verse, seems a more hopeful work than ***Heart*** because

FROM THE AUTHOR

"THE SUPPLIANT"

Long have I beat with timid hands upon
life's leaden door,
Praying the patient, futile prayer my
fathers prayed before,
Yet I remain without the close,
unheeded and unheard,
And never to my listening ear is borne
the waited word.
Soft o'er the threshold of the years there
comes this counsel cool:
The strong demand, contend, prevail;
the beggar is a fool!

SOURCE: Georgia Douglas Johnson, "The Suppliant," from *Bronze: A Book of Verse,* Brimmer, 1922.

her persona is not engaged in tragic introspection but absorbed in social dialogue with self-affirmed racial confidence. Du Bois's foreword calls attention to this message, which gives him the occasion to celebrate the book as an "invaluable" "revelation of the soul struggle of the women of the race" (7). Alain Locke observes in his *Crisis* review that there is "a certain fresh breeze of faith and courage" in this collection.[80] According to him ***Bronze***'s "healthy, humanistic optimism" about "the saving grace of mother-heart" is "insinuated between the lines of her poems" (161). For Locke these features meant that "Mrs. Johnson has at last come to her own—if not also in a peculiar way into her own" (161). Three decades later Cedric Dover would explain that the subject of ***Bronze*** "is the heart of a colored woman aware of her social problem."[81] More recently Erlene Stetson has claimed that ***Bronze*** is "unabashedly racial and strident"; for Johnson is no longer engaged in "the task of documenting the feminine heart" (29). Despite all of these emphatic proclamations of the racial significance of ***Bronze,*** the work continues to mourn a woman's languishing ambition. However, these themes are now masked behind the mantle of racial restrictions.

In ***Bronze,*** Johnson turned to the trope of race rather than love to commemorate her self-awareness. ***Bronze*** was not the first occasion for Johnson to address race in her poetry. As early as 1917 she was writing racial verse, as her correspondence to Arthur Schomburg indicates.[82] However, ***Bronze*** was to be her only collection of racial poetry. In the author's note to this work, Johnson explains that "This book is the child of a bitter earth-wound. I sit on the earth and sing—sing out, and of, my sorrow." Johnson goes on to racialize and aggregate her sorrow by exhorting that "God's sun shall one day shine upon a perfected and unhampered people" (3). In this way Johnson conceals her own personal despair behind the suffering of her race. Just as the commentators on ***Heart*** were distracted by the title of the collection, its title poem, and excessive effusion of female commiseration, ***Bronze*** distracts its readers with the standard racial fare. For the opening section of ***Bronze,*** entitled **"Exhortation,"** persuaded her critics, anthologists, and readers to see that "[p]ractically all the poems are racial in theme."[83] However, a close reading of the collection reveals that a third of the poems are not expressly racial but rather the traditional romantic lyrics on love, lost dreams, and sorrow. Another third repeats these themes, but Johnson marks them slightly with racial signifiers like "veil," "sable strain," and "dusky child." And the final third of the collection either depicts typical situations of racial oppression or celebrates advocates of the race in commemorative verse.

Bronze was probably Johnson's most commercially successful book because it was packaged as a work of strong racial awareness. It is not my intention to question in any way Johnson's feelings of racial solidarity. It *is* my intention, however, to suggest that the success of this work is directly related to her readers' enthusiastic recognition that she was depicting the racial oppression and optimism that they shared. Nevertheless, personal cries of impending despair (**"Let Me Not Lose My Dream," "Calling Dreams,"** and **"Sorrow Singers,"** for example) are prominent features of ***Bronze,*** which make the collection reminiscent of ***Heart.***

These cries of desperation dominate Johnson's third collection, ***An Autumn Love Cycle*** (1928). This collection of love poems is divided into five sections with titles that allude to a musical arrangement: The Cycle, Contemplation, Intermezzi, Penseroso, Cadence. In the already mentioned foreword, Alain Locke writes that with "maturing power and courage of expression," Johnson returns to "the task which she has set [for] herself—documenting the feminine heart." Locke attempts to open space for

Johnson's topic beyond the "time-old" and "hackneyed" sentiments of male privilege (xv), but then retreats to the safety of maternal banality. Although respectful of Johnson and her subject, Locke, like the reviewers of ***Heart,*** still regards the female heart alien to poetic imagination in ***Autumn.*** He finds that Johnson expresses the "yearning of woman for candid self-expression" presumably about love in "a simple, declarative style"; the collection's ingenuity lies in its candor, naivety, and unsophistication (xvii-xviii).

Although ***Autumn*** received favorable reviews, gender conventions sharply polarized what is presumed to define the feminine and masculine sensibility. Each reviewer still regarded the collection as a document of a woman's heart rather than of her imagination. What made this book more gratifying for readers than ***Heart*** is Johnson's poetic treatment of poignant narrative events that focus the emotional response. Nevertheless, insofar as Cedric Dover was concerned, Johnson's return "to the personal notes of her first poems," diminished rather than enlarged her vision. According to him, "The poet is again overwhelmed by herself" (634). And yet, this collection reflects Johnson's profound self-reflection and subtle poetic expression. Perhaps Dover was disheartened by what he saw in ***Autumn*** as Johnson's "politics of wait and accommodation" (Stetson, 33). Johnson's female contemporary Anne Spencer made a similar comment about its accommodationist tenor. She observed that in ***Autumn*** "the author has come to terms with life, signed the valiant compromise, the Medean alternative, delivering her awareness over to pain."[84] Blanche Watson's review of ***Autumn*** in the *Chicago Defender* repeated similar observations but concluded by claiming that "altogether it is a soul-satisfying book."[85]

In contrast to these general accolades, Alice Dunbar-Nelson speculates that the power of ***Autumn*** is more directly tied to remembered pleasure than accommodation and pain. Writing in her journal, Dunbar-Nelson concedes that "You might call it poetic inspiration, if you will, but it looks suspiciously to me as if Georgia had an affair, and it had been a source of inspiration to her" (quoted in Hull, 175). One of Johnson's last published poems, **"Magdalen,"** in ***Share My World,*** as well as an unpublished poem entitled **"You,"** raises this question again. In **"You"** the speaker proclaims, "I'd mount the cross of thorns for you / And hold the feat sublime / If, as I go you whisper love / 'I loved you all the time.'" And in **"Magdalen"** the speaker "stand[s] at the judgment bar" imploring God's grace: "I have kept the commandments with never a pause / Save the one You see written there, / But You are my Judge and I hope You can find / Some grace for a flaw so grim / For I loved a mortal far more than my life / And forfeited heaven for him."

When Dunbar-Nelson's speculation and these two poems are juxtaposed to two love letters written to Johnson, I am led to suspect that Johnson had several affairs. One such letter is probably the only extant erotic letter (written in Moscow on ** 17, 1926) authored by Du Bois. Here he writes, "I'm thinking of you. I'd like to have you here." He closes the letter by imploring her to "Please come down [to * * *] half-dressed with pretty stockings. I shall kiss you." In the fragment of another letter addressed to "My darling, sweet Georgia," Maxwell Hayson chides his "literary pet" on her unreadable penmanship.[86] These letters in concert with **"Magdalen"** and **"You"** as well as other poems suggest that Johnson's eroticism was not confined to the intensity of poetic expression in ***Autumn.***

The confidence that Anne Spencer associates with Johnson's Medean self-awareness greets us in the opening poem of ***Autumn*—"I Closed My Shutters Fast Last Night."** Here the persona brings her ". . . heart forlorn, / Restoring it with calm caress / Unto its sheltered bower, / While whispering: 'Await, await / Your golden, perfect hour.'" Unlike in **"The Heart of a Woman,"** the persona's forlorn heart need not break on the "sheltering bars" of "some alien cage" but can rest comfortably with the expectation of fulfillment. Even though this collection embraces rather than yearns for love's satisfaction, the moment of satiation is fleeting: "Oh night of love, your groves of strange content / project a thralldom over coming days" (**"Oh Night of Love"**). Rather than mourn the impossibility of satisfaction as in ***Heart,*** in ***Autumn*** Johnson uses memory to mystify gratification by returning once again to love as the trope for envisioning delight and time as the promise of its fruition:

> How my heart sinks when I beheld the sad reflection of my face,
> A wan and wistful wound, with oh, such meager grace;
> How can you hold me dear withal and conjure charms withdrawn.
> Or does Autumn twilight hold a charm unknown to dawn?
>
> (**"How My Heart Sinks"**)

Johnson was a modern romantic,[87] who believed that her imagination held the power to perceive the hidden knowledge of daily experience, and this knowledge had the power to transform her sensibility. Because she followed her own inspiration, which did not entirely adhere to the New Negro aesthetic, critics defined her verse as excessively personal. However, when her verse is associated with the carpe diem tradition of seventeenth-century love poetry, it achieves fresh insight and humanistic appeal. This tradition casts desire in a cautionary tale, according to Andrew Marvell, to

> . . . roll all our strength and all
> Our sweetness up into one ball,
> And tear our pleasures with rough strife
> Through the iron gates of life:
> Thus, though we cannot make our sun
> Stand still, yet we will make him run.
> (from "To His Coy Mistress")

But from Johnson's point of view, her persona is no longer like Marvell's young, innocent mistress, implicated by the word "we," but an experienced and mature woman, longing once again to savor past delight. This is the recurring theme of ***Autumn.*** For example, the persona of "Le Soir" speculates that age holds a residual of the bounty of youth: ". . . Hope's blossoms spray / In lush profusion / P'er the edge of Day." In "Welt" the persona imagines meeting her young self as one would meet a lover:

> Would I might mend the fabric of my youth
> Which daily flaunts its tatters to my eyes,
> Would I might compromise awhile with truth
> Until love's moon, now waxing, wanes and dies.
>
> For I would go a further while with you
> And drain this Cup of Joy so passing fair,
> Which meets my parching lips like cooling dew
> 'Ere time has brushed cold fingers through my hair.

Indeed, throughout this third collection, the beloved self is figured as the youthful gleam in the Other's aged eye.

Poetry that idealized nature, the individual, and romantic love liberated Johnson by offering her an opportunity to represent her humanity without accentuating her double, indeed triple consciousness as a black American woman. These traditional themes provided her with the means to construct an identity that countered the familiar stereotypes about black women. For Johnson, a broad conceptualization of love not as maternal or connubial devotion nor finite sexual ardor but rather as a metaphysical eroticism was the means for transcending one's human limitations and experiencing the sublime. However, Johnson's modernist impulses made the sublime not a state realized but one sustained by desire. Also typical of the modernist poet, religious faith is tinged in her verse with skepticism, and death is depicted as the ultimate reality that "the timeless and transcendental space" of the lyric cannot alter.[88] Johnson then seems poised at the crossroads of two traditions. She was a modernist in her close attention to metaphoric detail of the fleeting moment of sublime awareness, and she was a Victorian in her refusal to abandon poetic conventions of form and beauty as the last vestiges of permanence.

Johnson's Plays

Johnson captured the arrested moment of personal awareness not only in her verse but in her plays as well. During the twenties, while Johnson was writing poetry and hosting her salon on "S" Street, she turned to playwriting with her unique version of Negro folk drama. Although she wrote dozens of one-act plays, only four were published during her lifetime: ***Blue Blood*** and ***Plumes*** in 1927 and ***Ellen and William Craft*** and ***Frederick Douglass*** in 1935. ***Blue Blood*** and ***Plumes*** were reprinted in Locke's *Plays of Negro Life* (1927). ***A Sunday Morning in the South, Safe,*** and ***Blue-Eyed Black Boy*** (written circa 1926, 1929, and 1930, respectively) were published posthumously.[89] Two of Johnson's unpublished plays are included here—***Starting Point*** (circa 1931), which is a part of the Langston Hughes file in the Beinecke Rare Book and Manuscript Library at Yale University, and ***Paupaulekejo*** (circa 1926), which surfaced in Johnson's papers at Howard University.

The folk Negro as dramatic subject was a spinoff of the American folk drama movement, influenced by the plays of John Millington Synge and the tour of the Abbey Players in 1911.[90] In 1917 Ridgely Torrence's New York production of *Three Plays for Negro Theatre* stimulated the interest of white artists in black subject matter. In rapid succession the productions of Eugene O'Neill's *The Dreamy Kid* in 1919, *The Emperor Jones* in 1920, and *All God's Chillum Got Wings* in 1924, Paul Green's *In Abraham's Bosom* in 1926, for which he won a 1927 Pulitzer Prize, and Marc Connelly's *The Green Pastures* in 1930 defined the Negro as prime dramatic material. However, white playwrights (even those who were sympathetic) focused on the primitivism and exoticism of black culture and thereby shaped Negro characters to fit familiar stereotypes.

In response to these stilted roles, black playwrights assumed authority for the authentic presentation of black culture. Dramatist Montgomery Gregory, who was a frequent patron of Johnson's salon, probably best expressed this endeavor when he claimed in Locke's *The New Negro* that the Negro "alone can truly express the soul of his people."[91] Gregory organized and directed the Howard Players of Howard University between 1919 and 1924. He also issued the call for "a national Negro Theater where the Negro playwright, musician, actor, dancer, and artist in concert shall fashion a drama that will merit the respect and admiration of America" (Locke, 159). Gregory insisted that "the only avenue of genuine achievement in American drama for the Negro lies in the development of the rich veins of folk-tradition of the past and in the portrayal of the authentic life of the Negro masses of to-day" (Locke, 159). When Du Bois established the Krigwa Little Theatre Movement in 1926 in the basement of the 135th Street Library in Harlem, he repeated the call for self-defined Negro drama. Insofar as Du Bois was concerned, authentic Negro theatre was by, about, for, and near black people.[92]

Several black women responded to these calls for artistic action. In addition to Johnson, Dunbar-Nelson, May Miller Sullivan, Marita Bonner, Mary Burrill, and Eulalie Spence provided dozens of mostly one-act plays about the experiences of black people, particularly those of black women. Almost all of these women were connected with the N.A.A.C.P. Drama Committee, and following Du Bois's manifesto they wrote for church congregations, students, and lodges rather than Broadway. Their plays synthesize social protest (especially protest against lynching), genteel propriety, black history, religion, fantasy, and feminism in various combinations.[93] Unfortunately, until the advent of feminist scholarship, they were routinely erased from literary history.[94]

Like Johnson's racial verse, writing plays about Negro life allowed her to abandon the lyrical monologue of the forlorn self and to engage the polyvocality of social discourse. She took to playwriting just as she had to poetry and wrote about twenty plays, making her one of the most prolific black women playwrights of the Renaissance. Two were powerful antilynching plays. ***Safe*** (reminiscent of Angelina Grimké's 1919 short story "The Closing Door") dramatizes the utter desperation of a black mother who strangles her newborn son to free him from the future threat of lynchers. And ***A Sunday Morning in the South,*** which foreshadows Gwendolyn Brooks's 1960 epic poem lamenting the lynching of Emmett Till—"A Bronzeville Mother Loiters in Mississippi. Meanwhile, a Mississippi Mother Burns Bacon"—in the *Bean Eater,* depicts the lynching of an innocent young black man.

Johnson also published two historical plays probably written for school production: ***William and Ellen Craft*** and ***Frederick Douglass.*** Interestingly, these two plays focus on intimate moments in the lives of these runaway slaves that were effaced in abolitionist documents. ***William and Ellen Craft*** recreates the Crafts' summoning their mutual conviction in love as they prepare to escape. ***Frederick Douglass*** reconstructs Douglass's last visit with his future first wife, Anne Murray, before his escape to Massachusetts. While these plays reveal Johnson's efforts to recover aspects of a black heroic past through drama, ***Blue Blood*** and ***Plumes*** earned her her reputation as a playwright.

Blue Blood and ***Blue-Eyed Black Boy*** are about miscegenation, a theme to which Johnson had a special affinity because of her own mixed-blood heritage. In these works Johnson reveals how tangled were the racial strains of citizens of a country that purportedly upheld strict separation of the races. ***Blue Blood,*** which won honorable mention in the 1926 *Opportunity* play competition, was produced that year by the Krigwa Players of New York City with May Miller Sullivan and Frank S. Horne in the principal roles (Smith, 581). The success of ***Blue Blood*** anticipates that of ***Plumes.***

Plumes is Johnson's most celebrated play. It recalls a poor black mother trying to decide whether to allow a doctor to operate on her daughter and possibly save her life or to reserve the doctor's fee for her elaborate funeral, complete with plumed horses. Before the woman can decide, the child dies. While scholars have read ***Plumes*** as an indictment on poverty and superstition, I suggest that the play, like ***Autumn,*** also represents the inevitability of death and Johnson's steadfast conviction that only love can preserve human dignity. Thus the mother's final display of love for her daughter is more important than trying to postpone the certainty of death.

Starting Point dramatizes the failure of youth to live up to its potential. Thus, like death, failure seems inevitable. By setting the play in Charleston, South Carolina, and referring to Cat Fish Row, Johnson offered her commentary on the very popular *Porgy,*[95] staged by DuBose and Dorothy Heyward in 1927. Rather than subscribe to the "happy darky" plot sanctioned by the white literati, Johnson critiqued that story with another about an old black couple, Martha and Henry Robinson, who attempt to live out their ambition through their son, Tom. They work and scrape to send Tom to a northern medical school. The opening scene foreshadows Tom's fate. Here his parents share the trouble of a friend, whose son has become involved in the numbers racket. When Tom unexpectedly visits his parents with Belle, his new, blues-singing wife, the old couple expect the worst. At this point in the plot Johnson complicates the anticipated ending. While Belle's name, manner, and singing suggest a tawdry woman whom the old couple regard as inappropriate for their ambitious son, she proves to be kind and sincere by insisting that Tom tell his parents about his involvement in the numbers racket. Moreover, she insists that he quit the hustling life and relieve his parents by assuming his father's menial job. As in Johnson's other plays, the title and ironic ending make her point with poignant economy. The Robinsons are representative of ambitious black families who in spite of their labor find themselves never getting beyond the "starting point." The play is also a poignant statement about Johnson's own failure to live up to her potential.

Johnson's ***Paupaulekejo: A Three-Act Play*** is penned under the name of John Tremaine. Like the stories **"Tramp Love"** and **"Gesture,"** discussed below, Johnson's use of this nom de plume signals sexual content she evidently thought needed to be masked with masculine authority.[96] This is a miscegenation play set in Africa. Rather than relying on the often forced sexual pairing of white men and black women, which was the staple of American miscegenation stories, Johnson reverses the racial and sexual identities of the couple and depicts a story of probable miscegenation by consent.

The principal action concerns the devout effort of Claire, a white missionary's daughter, to teach Paupaulekejo, the half-caste son of the chief, about Christian love. Depending on the reader's racial ideology, Paupaulekejo either learns the lesson too well or fails to learn it at all. He falls in love with Claire, and she evidently loves him. However, Claire's father convinces her that she's been bewitched and arranges for her to leave. At their farewell, Paupaulekejo embraces her and then "plunges [a] knife into Claire's heart and then into his own. They fall on [a] couch." Despite Paupaulekejo's belief that in death they can be together, as the curtain falls the black maid, perhaps out of jealousy, endorses the racial hegemony by separating the lovers and embracing the dead Paupaulekejo herself. Again, Johnson relies on the ironic ending to make her point: convention rivals even fateful intention.

Johnson's Short Stories

The dramatic irony that distinguished Johnson's plays can also be found in her extant stories. As in the plays, Johnson focuses on poignant moments to present the subtlety and utter paradox of complex motives and conflicted awareness. Such complexity often results in indeterminate meaning but always in the protagonist's acceptance of the finality of fate with resignation. **"Free"** was originally a part of her Harmon application and recently posthumously published.[97] **"The Smile"** surfaced in her papers at Howard University. As mentioned, **"Gesture"** and **"Tramp Love"** were originally published in *Challenge: A Literary Quarterly* in 1936 and 1937, respectively, under the name of Paul Tremaine.

"Free," recalled in third-person narrative, recounts the unconventional resolution of a love triangle after the funeral of the principal agent, elderly Dr. Paul Ryan. His wife, Martha, expects finally to be "free" of the young nurse Rose Delaney, whom the doctor invited to share their home for twenty-five years as their alleged daughter. While Martha waits to hear the reading of his will, she muses, "At last, boss in her own house, and out [Rose]'d go! Her friends had taunted her long enough[;] she'd show them how she'd handle the situation." Martha is dumbfounded when the will names both women as equal beneficiaries. However, Rose volunteers to leave, announcing that "'anything Mrs. Ryan suggests will be all right with me.'" As Rose starts to leave, Martha is suddenly aware that Rose is no longer a young woman but old like herself. She realizes that over the years in spite of her determination, she had grown attached to Rose's attending to her needs and keeping her unobtrusive company. At the threshold of their parting, the two women embrace: "Mrs. Ryan flung open her arms and cried brokenly, 'Rose!'"

The title and the early plot of the story invite us to anticipate the wife's liberation from an adulterous marriage, then complicates that possibility. However, the resulting tension turns to irony as "free" takes on another meaning—freedom from the patriarchal conventions that define women as antagonistic contestants for male affection to acknowledge their own mutual dependence and affection. Johnson complicates even this meaning in her masterful ending, for she goes yet one step farther to reveal how custom condemns women to share complicity in their own oppression. She has Martha initiate the display of the women's mutual affection at the end of the story. But Johnson leaves the story's outcome uncertain. She refuses to disclose whether Martha has the strength of her own conviction to thwart public opinion and invite Rose to live with her.

"The Smile" is a more conventional story about unrequited love, which, like all of Johnson's plots, draws on irony to reveal how the capriciousness of life defeats best intentions. The story is about Florence Rowe, a woman of thirty-five, who longs for a "smart, sophisticated, modern romance," like the ones she reads about in serials. When she inherits a small legacy from her aunt, Florence resigns from her teaching position to travel to the French Riviera. No sooner does she arrive than she is involved in an accident that disfigures her face. Facial reconstruction and a series of events transform the plain Florence into the beautiful, literary sophisticate Flordé, whose lips are forever frozen into "a faint, skeptical, cynical smile." When she meets Gene, the "most brilliant and cynical of the younger writers, they are drawn to each other. . . . The fact that she was ten years older than he ceased to matter."[98] After the death of his mother, she lovingly consoles him, and he begins to return her affection. But on gazing into her face, he becomes full of loathing and retreats in horror. Unable to understand what prompted his behavior, she catches "a glimpse of herself in a mirror—smiling, aloof, cool."

"Gesture"[99] is the first of Johnson's two "on the road" stories. Cast in third-person, presumably masculine narration, **"Gesture"** recalls the refusal of a young man, tramping across an Arizona desert, to accept a condescending offer for a ride from a rich woman. Here Johnson seems to be experimenting with a masculine perspective to project on the one hand, spontaneity, leisure, and impulsiveness routinely forbidden to women, and on the other hand, freedom constructed as mobility typically ascribed only to whites. Moreover, this masculine mask allowed Johnson to claim "an authority of experience," as scholar Thadious M. Davis explains in another context, for sexual topics "usually denied to the female, especially to one who surveyed them without moral commentary."[100] The nameless young man can "lay flat on his back gazing up into the dusty skies" and then yawn and stretch "luxuriously" without the threat of a white vigilante carting him off to jail to protect the virtue of white women. He is "free, white, and twenty-one." Johnson uses him to construct the "courtesy of the road" of the West, which is not dependent on class position, in contrast to the rigid social proprieties of the East.

Johnson is more comfortable with constructing her male persona in the second "on the road story"—**"Tramp Love."**[101] Here Johnson returns to her conventional first-person narrative position to dramatize the brief encounter between a tramp and a female hitchhiker during the Great Depression. Again, Johnson frees her story from the well-known sexual stereotypes associated with black women by implying that her narrator is a white man. Unlike **"Free,"** the plot of **"Tramp Love"** requires little delineation because the plot of the one night stand is so familiar. However, Johnson reverses the conventional sexual responses of the male and female characters to liberate the latter from sexual prescription even while she relies on stock devices to portray them. For instance, the young woman has "very blond" hair and she wears "white slacks and seem[s] quite neat and trim." Her comment on paying for a ride "the only way a poor girl could pay" concedes her rather cavalier acceptance of the sexual protocol of the road. "At first," she admits, "it was rather hard to take, but one learns it doesn't matter. A bath in the morning, and one forgets the bad taste. . . . I keep going and going. Doing the best I can. . . . hoping and dreamin' that a day will come when I can get a break, a good guy, a fairy prince." As she and the tramp talk, she realizes that he's not like the others who have tried to lay claim to her body. She likes the tramp and asserts that "We're alike." Believing that she can make him happy at least momentarily, she propositions him. The tramp refuses, realizing that a night of pleasure would make him even more unhappy after she left. Rather than spend the night with him, she hitches a ride, determined to get to another town that night, and the tramp jumps a freight car. As the girl leaves, she "turn[s] and look[s] back" and "[doesn't] wave," gestures suggesting her capturing the moment for future savoring. **"Tramp Love"** repeats another theme central to Johnson's canon: disappointment finds solace in recalling arrested desire.

Johnson's Poetic Finale

Share My World, published in 1962, is Johnson's last collection of verse. Like ***The Heart of a Woman, Bronze: A Book of Verse,*** and ***An Autumn Love Cycle,*** Johnson arranged to have ***Share*** published at her own expense. This fourth collection is the most modest in size, number of poems, and appearance. The cover sketch of ***Share*** by Effie Newsome repeats the theme of her frontispiece sketch for ***Autumn.*** Both sketches feature the same female face. However, ***Autumn***'s cover foregrounds the woman's enlarged heart, droplets (rain or tears), and falling leaves, while ***Share***'s cover replaces the heart, droplets, and leaves with the globe of the Earth, planets, and stars. In ***Autumn*** the erotic object is reflected as the Other, and the persona savors the sensual and, indeed, transformative power of love, while mourning the passage of youth. But in ***Share*** a lifetime of experiences has taught the persona life's ultimate wisdom: she learns that love's object is the desiring self. The erotic object then is not so much another person but her own subjectivity, conditioned by earthly existence: "the bubble of life's joy" caught "Within my eager fingers / A fragile, fairy meteor / That never, never lingers" (**"The Bubble"**). Thus, rather than reflected onto another, the erotic object in ***Share*** is *desire* itself. And for Johnson poetry was both a metaphor and a metonymy for desire.

Share is Johnson's last major tribute to her erotic subjectivity. In the opening poem, entitled **"Share My World,"** she proclaims the power of faith, prayer, and love, mediated by her poetic imagination, to "rebuild [her] shattered world." In **"Your World"** Johnson invokes the trope of the soaring bird of her most famous poem, **"The Heart of a Woman,"** to acknowledge that her persona "used to abide / In the narrowest nest in a corner / My wings pressing close to my side. / But I sighted the distant horizon / Where the sky-line encircled the sea / And I throbbed with a burning desire / To travel this immensity." The persona's "burning desire" to go to the horizon is reminiscent of Zora Neale Hurston's Janie in *Their Eyes Were Watching God* (1937). Like Janie, Johnson's persona commemorates her persistence in pursuing lifelong dreams, even though they are seldom realized. In **"I Gaze into the Sun"** the persona explains the preservation of desire as the blinding and exhilarating experience of daring "To look at life aflame." In **"The Gift of Years"** the lines—"The mellow years have brought to me / Many a precious thing, / The infinite peace of forgetting, / The joy of remembering"—are again reminiscent of *Their Eyes Were Watching God.* On the opening page of the novel the narrator remarks on how "women forget all those things they don't want to remember, and remember everything they don't want to forget. The dream is the truth."[102] For Johnson's persona the dream is to preserve and cultivate desire.

"The Audacious" is the final poem of ***Share My World*** and Johnson's tribute to a daring life of creative possibility. Whether she actually fulfilled this ambition is difficult to determine. By what standards do we measure her literary aspirations, assess her talent, and place her in literary history? Johnson believed that the seventeen unpublished works left in the basement of her "S" Street home would distinguish her achievement and secure her reputation, but they are no longer extant. Yet, a close examination of Johnson's extant writings (most of which are assembled here for the first time) reveals the emotional complexity, the artistic sophistication, and verbal acuity typically associated with highly respected writers. Not only do these characteristics demand that we reevaluate Johnson's writings, but when they are appreciated in the context of a problematized analysis of her life, we can also begin to understand how race, gender, and class have delimited a black woman's artistic endeavors.

Women writers of the New Negro Renaissance faced basically two choices. If they wanted an exceptional career, they had to step beyond the conventional feminine roles and risk social censure. Or if they were unwilling to challenge these conventions, they had to learn to accept the label of "minor" permanently affixed before their endeavors. The pragmatic Johnson tried to consolidate these choices with predicable results. Although her persistence in pursuing her writing career was exceptional, her dependency on the appreciation of Braithwaite, Locke, Du Bois, and others like them underdeveloped her talent. In addition, without a sustained, first-rate literary community, Johnson could not dispel her authorial anxiety and publicly risk venturing beyond the accepted lyrical mode. She needed supportive and competent criticism rather than polite flattery. And she certainly needed the time that financial assistance could provide to test her ability.

Johnson realized that she should invest her talent in more substantial literary forms than modest love lyrics if she were to garner sustained critical attention. By the time Johnson won the *Opportunity* contest for ***Plumes,*** she was a single parent, who found it necessary to work a full-time job to maintain her "S" Street home and to finance the completion of her sons' educations. Hence, during the formative period of her career, finding enough time to devote to her writing became a serious problem. Longer works demanded greater commitments of her time and concentration; nevertheless, in addition to poetry

Johnson also wrote impressive amounts of fiction, drama, and exposition. But publishers were not interested in these longer works. Consequently, she concentrated on publishing tidy lyrics in the hope of keeping her public reputation alive. Unfortunately, that reputation was confined to the minor role of the lady poet of the New Negro Renaissance. This was the only uncontested position available to her, and she chose a nonoppositional stance for herself.

The circumstances of Johnson's personal life also dictated the literary risks she was and was not willing to take. Unlike Zora Neale Hurston, who rejected the posture of the lady, renounced social acceptance, and spent her talent pursuing her own aspirations, Johnson chose modest security within social conventions. In addition, like most black literary women of her epoch (Jessie Fauset, Anne Spencer, and Helene Johnson, for example), Johnson generally acquiesced to gender conventions. She was conditioned by the social codes of her age, region, and race to assert and defend her claim to ladyhood. Furthermore, her experience as a wife for over two decades reinforced that conditioning. Thus Johnson learned to mediate female desire within the parameters of a racially contested black patriarchy in which the fair-skinned woman was the esteemed sexual object. These factors shaped her writing and necessitated the masking of her more innovative and transgressive works behind pseudonyms or burying them in the basement of her home.

By contrast, the exceptionally talented Hurston was not acquiescent to the gender conventions of female subordination, and she was neither agent nor object of a "color struck" black society. Moreover, Hurston refused to be reticent and "act like a lady." As a result, she was severely ridiculed, censured, and, in fact, ostracized for her unorthodox behavior. Furthermore, Hurston was ill suited for the role of wife, even though she married at least twice. And whether from fate or choice, she had no children. Instead of the traditional life of gendered convention, Hurston sought intellectual and sexual experience outside the borders of wife and mother.

Rather than risk venturing toward the mythic horizon, like the audacious Hurston, who for her effort left behind an extraordinary literary legacy for scholars to recover and appreciate, Johnson accepted recognition for writing traditional love lyrics and hoped that the large volume of her unpublished works would rescue her reputation. Rather than, like Hurston, hazard expeditions in unfamiliar places, Johnson clipped roses in her own backyard. Hurston's final years in obscurity, sickness, and poverty attest to the high price she paid for her absolute devotion to her career as a writer and folklorist. While Johnson tried "to snatch the stars / From out the purple blue," as the lines of **"The Audacious"** report, she stood firmly on the ground. Johnson was prudent, discreet, and dependable. By contrast, Hurston spent her life "jumping at the sun," and she paid exorbitantly for the uncommon undertaking. There is no evidence to suggest that either woman regretted her decision, and in no way do I wish to appear judgmental. My intention is to represent the severe limitations they both experienced as black women writers.

Given the publication date of **"The Audacious"** in 1962, two years after Hurston's death, we can read it as a more fitting tribute to her than to the more prudent Johnson. Johnson did manage to grasp a few "stars." Equally significant is her vigilance in keeping her literary aspirations at the center of her life for half a century. ***Share My World*** is Johnson's memorial to that life and the key to understanding her tremendous productivity. Although Johnson wrote for recognition, and during her lifetime was at best trivialized and at worst forgotten, writing allowed her to nourish her imagination, arrest the delight of desire, and endure the insults of time.

Notes

1. Alain Locke, Foreword to *An Autumn Love Cycle* by Georgia Douglas Johnson (New York: Harold Vinal, 1928), xvii-xviii.

2. Audre Lorde, "Uses of the Erotic: The Erotic as Power," in *Sister Outsider* (Trumansburg, NY: Crossing Press, 1984), 56-7.

3. Undated letter to Theresa Davis and Charles Freeman at Fisk University Special Collections. Davis and Freeman wrote "A Biographical Sketch of Georgia Douglas Johnson and Some of Her Works" (Nashville, TN: Y.M.C.A. Graduate Schools, 1931). References to this letter appear parenthetically as "Davis and Freeman" in the introduction.

4. Johnson financed the publication of these three collections as well as *Share My World.*

5. I use the uppercase "R" in "Romantic" to distinguish the conventions of nineteenth-century romanticism from the more reductive tradition of romantic love normally associated with women.

6. This is Susan Lanser's term.

7. Jeffrey C. Stewart, "Alain Locke and Georgia Douglas Johnson, Washington Patrons of Afro-American Modernism," *G. W. Washington Studies* 12 (July 1986): 37.

8. I thank Jeffrey Stewart for sharpening this observation.

9. The first two quotations are taken from Robert Kerlin's *Negro Poets and Their Poems* (Washington, DC: Associated Publishers, 1923, 1935), 148. The second two quotations are taken from Alain Locke's foreword, xvii-xviii.

10. "Georgia Douglas Johnson: An Appreciation," written July 20, 1920. This document is a part of the Locke papers at Howard University's Moorland-Spingarn Research Center.

11. Alain Locke, "Propaganda or Poetry?" *Race* 1 (Summer 1936): 70.

12. See Robert Bone, *The Negro Novel in America* (New Haven: Yale University Press, 1964).

13. Nathan I. Huggins, *Harlem Renaissance* (New York: Oxford University Press, 1971), 7.

14. Alain Locke, "A Decade of Negro Self Expression," An Occasional Paper (Chapel Hill, NC: Trustees of the John F. Slater Fund, 1928), 7.

15. James Weldon Johnson, *The Book of Negro Poetry,* vii. *An Anthology of Verse by American Negroes,* ed. Newman I. White and Walter C. Jackson (Durham, NC: Trinity College Press, 1924), also shares this perspective: "It is therefore no longer to be doubted that the Negro will make his contribution to American poetry, if there is any poetry in him to contribute. And whether there is any poetry in him may be partly judged from the quality of what has hitherto been produced" (1-2). This viewpoint is essentially an enlightenment tenet, held over from the post-Reconstruction period. For the formulation of the relationship between art and activist politics, also see my *Domestic Allegories of Political Desire* (New York: Oxford University Press, 1992), 83-87.

16. Langston Hughes, "In the Twenties," *Saturday Review of Literature* 22 (June 22, 1940): 13. Other founders of *Fire!!* include John Davis, Aaron Douglas, Arthur Huff Fauset, and (Richard) Bruce Nugent.

17. Alain Locke, "Fire: A Negro Magazine," *The Survey* (August 15-September 15, 1927): 563.

18. William E. B. Du Bois, "The Criteria of Negro Art" (originally published in *The Crisis* 32 [October 1926]); reprinted in *W. E. B. Du Bois: The Crisis Writings,* ed. Daniel Walden (Greenwich, CT: Fawcett, 1972), 289.

19. "The Negro in Art, How Shall He Be Portrayed: A Symposium" ran in 1926 in the April (pp. 278-80), May (pp. 35-36), June (pp. 71-73), August (pp. 193-94), September (pp. 238-39), and November (pp. 28-29) issues of *The Crisis.* The seven questions in the survey focused on speculating about the consequences of the recurring negative portrayals of black people in art. Question 7 summarizes Du Bois's concern: "Is there not a real danger that young colored writers will be tempted to follow the popular trend in portraying Negro character[s] in the underworld rather than seeking to paint the truth about themselves and their own social class?" The quotation in the introduction is a paraphrase of question 6, which appears on the first page of the *Crisis* surveys.

20. Georgia Douglas Johnson's response to the symposium on "The Negro in Art: How Shall He Be Portrayed," *The Crisis* 34 (August 1926): 193.

21. Georgia Douglas Johnson, "Book Chat," Norfolk *Journal and Guide* (October 4, 1930): 12.

22. Both letters are a part of Johnson's file at the Moorland-Spingarn Research Center at Howard University.

23. George S. Schuyler, "The Negro-Art Hokum," *The Nation* 122 (June 16, 1926): 662.

24. Langston Hughes, "The Negro and the Racial Mountain," *The Nation* 122 (June 23, 1926): 694.

25. W. E. B. Du Bois, "Returning Soldiers," *The Crisis* 18 (May 1919): 14.

26. Joan R. Sherman, "Introduction," *Collected Black Women's Poetry,* vol. 2 (New York: Oxford University Press, 1987), xxix. In addition to volume 2, see volumes 3 and 4 for selections of these poets' verse.

27. Benjamin Brawley, "The Negro Literary Renaissance," *Southern Workman* 56 (1927): 177.

28. Locke, "A Decade of Negro Self Expression," 7.

29. The biographical information on Johnson's life is derived from Gloria T. Hull, *Color, Sex and Poetry: Three Women Writers from the Harlem Renaissance* (Bloomington: University of Indiana Press, 1987), 115-211; Winona Fletcher, "Georgia Douglas Johnson" in *Afro-American Writers from the Harlem Renaissance to 1940,* vol. 51; *The Dictionary of Literary Biography,* ed. Trudier Harris (Detroit: Gale, 1987), 153-64; Anne Allen Shockley's *Afro-American Women Writers, 1746-1933: An Anthology and Critical Guide* (Boston: G. K. Hall, 1988), 346-53; Jessie Carney Smith, "Georgia Douglas Johnson," in *Notable Black American Women* (Detroit: Gale, 1992), 578-84; and Jocelyn Hazelwood Donlon, "Georgia Douglas Johnson," in *Black Women in America: An Historical Encyclopedia,* ed. Darlene Clark Hine (Brooklyn, NY: Carlson, 1993), 640-42. Hull and Smith list the repositories of Johnson's papers. References to these works appear parenthetically in the introduction under the author's name. In addition, I gleaned information from Johnson's papers at the Moorland-Spingarn Research Center at Howard University.

30. It seems that Laura Douglas had a daughter, Elizabeth Douglas, between marriages. After her marriage to Spaulding, she had at least three more children: Henry, Willie (a daughter), and Roy Spaulding. See Johnson's letter of January 5, 1962, to Rev. William Holmes Borders and Roy Spaulding's letter of September 22, 1959, to Johnson. Both letters are in Johnson's file at Howard University.

31. Henry Sr. received the A.B. degree from Atlanta University (ca. 1888) and the LL.B. from the University of Michigan (ca. 1892).

32. The code of the District of Columbia restricts access to information concerning the death of its residents not in the public domain; thus 1990 is an approximate date of the death of Henry Lincoln Johnson Jr.

33. *Give Us Each Day: The Diary of Alice Dunbar-Nelson,* ed. Gloria T. Hull (New York: Norton, 1984), 87.

34. See, for example, "The Ebony Flute" (July 1927): 212; (October 1926): 322; and (November 1926): 356-58.

35. Toomer's letter is a part of Johnson's file at Howard University. Gloria T. Hull claims that the literary salon was Toomer's idea. See Hull, *Color, Sex and Poetry,* 165.

36. See Toomer's letter of October 6, 1922, to John McClure, the editor of *Double Dealer* (a journal published

in New Orleans). Toomer's remark is quoted in George B. Hutchinson, "Jean Toomer and the 'New Negroes' of Washington," *American Literature* 63, no. 4 (December 1991): 683. The McClure letter is a part of the Jean Toomer papers in the Beinecke Rare Book and Manuscript Library at Yale University.

37. Floyd Calvin, "Georgia Douglas Johnson Fears She Won't Have Time to Complete All of the Work She Has Planned," Pittsburgh *Courier,* 7 July 1928, 6. Quoted in Hull, *Color, Sex and Poetry,* 165.

38. The records of the Writers' Club, Inc. of Washington, DC, are preserved at the Moorland-Spingarn Research Center at Howard University.

39. Interview with Dorothy Porter Wesley at her home in Washington, DC, on December 22, 1993.

40. See the minutes of May 14, 1949, and May 2, 1959, of the Writers' Club at the Moorland-Spingarn Research Center. In Johnson's "Catalogue of Writings" in the Cullen-Jackman Collection at Atlanta University Library, she lists some of these anthologies. They include *Half-Caste,* edited by Cedric Dover in London; *American Authors,* edited by Anna Lenah Elgstrom in 1927 in Sweden; *Black and White Ladyship,* edited by Nancy Cunard in 1931 in London; and *Russian Anthology,* edited by R. Magidoff in 1934 in Russia.

41. Gloria Hull notes, for example, that in a letter to Harold Jackman, Johnson refers to a magazine (in Fort Worth, TX) publishing her serial story "Double Exile" (203). This story may or may not have been published under her name. In addition, Johnson's papers at Howard University reveal a wealth of information about her likely publishers, which in addition to those listed in the text of the introduction include the Christopher Publishing Company in Boston; Different Press in Corpus Christi, Texas; and *Brief Stories* magazine in Philadelphia. Also, the editor of *Guinea Times* (Accra, Ghana) thanks Johnson for sending her articles. In the absence of the full body of her manuscripts, locating these works is very difficult if not impossible. However, there are fragments of Johnson's manuscripts and published writings in her file at Howard University that suggest that in addition to M. Strong, Mary V. Strong, John Tremaine, Paul Tremaine, and John Temple, Johnson used the names Nina Temple, Ninevah Gladstone, Miriam Nosra, Lorraine Lillith, and Bessie Brent Winston to cloak her authorship. Although Johnson identifies Thomas H. Malone as a poetry-writing friend of her deceased husband, and the mysterious Gypsy Drago as a black man who believed he was white, these probably are additional names appropriated by Johnson.

42. The first four columns are a part of Johnson's file at Howard University.

43. The fragments of her manuscripts and newspaper clippings at the Moorland-Spingarn Research Center document that she wrote syndicated columns under the name Mary V. Strong during the 1940s and 1950s. These fragments also suggest that she may have used the names Tom Malone and John Sutton. I suggest that her acquisition of a post office box—P.O. Box 6345, Washington 9, DC—was to facilitate her correspondence in a variety of names and the management of her correspondence club under the name M. Strong.

44. This is one of Johnson's "Wise Sayings" that completed each manuscript page of "M. V. Strong Talks" and "Beauty Hints by Nina Temple." See Johnson's file at Howard University.

45. Jessie Carney Smith lists Johnson as a member of the following organizations: the American Society of African Culture, the (New York City) Civic Club, the District of Columbia Women's Party, the League for Abolition of Capital Punishment, the (District of Columbia) Matrons, the National Women's Party, the Poet Laureate League, the Poets League of Washington, the Republican Club of Washington, the Virginia White Speel Republican Club, and the Writers League Against Lynching. In addition, Johnson was in charge of publicity for the Eastern Area Conference of Negro Republican Women and a member of the First Congregational Church. See Smith, *Notable Black American Women,* p. 582, and her undated letter to James Weldon Johnson in her archive at Fisk University. In her autobiographical sketch, Johnson also identifies her habit of regularly attending the movies.

46. An application form for the club is a part of Johnson's file at the Moorland-Spingarn Research Center.

47. Information regarding Johnson's application to the Harmon Foundation was secured from the Harmon Foundation Records in the manuscripts division of the Library of Congress (folder #53).

48. Correspondence to Robert Weaver (March 14, 1950) in Johnson's papers at Howard University.

49. Braithwaite writes (June 18, 1927) in response to the question about the quality of her achievement that she has "deep feeling, imaginative substance, to which she has given poignant lyric expression." Woodson writes (September 17, 1928), "She has a bait of poetic genius." Du Bois writes (September 17, 1928, and April 16, 1929, respectively) in response to the same question, "I know that many competent people regard her work very highly," and "Her work has received high praise." In 1928 Du Bois additionally writes, "I think Mrs. Johnson has a real poetic gift and succeeds after work in giving it adequate expression." In 1929 he adds, "Mrs Johnson has an unusually sincere, interesting literary message." James Weldon Johnson's praise was fainter still. In an April 16, 1929, recommendation, he responds to the question about his estimation of the public opinion about her achievement with the single word "Yes." Later he adds that "[s]he has done some very beautiful lyric poetry." See the Harmon Foundation Records in the manuscript division of the Library of Congress. A. Philip Randolph sent a copy of his letter to Johnson, which is among her private papers at Howard University.

50. Letter to Harold Jackman from Georgia Douglas Johnson (March 2, 1950) in the Countee Cullen-Harold Jackman Collection of the Woodruff Library, Special Collections, of Atlanta University.

    Harold Jackman (1901-1961) established the Countee Cullen Collection of Negro Cultural Memorabilia, also known as the Countee Cullen-Harold Jackman Collection of Atlanta University. Described as a Renaissance man by his contemporaries, Jackman was born in London and lived in Harlem for thirty-seven years. He was the associate editor of *Challenge: A Literary Magazine,* contributing editor of *Phylon: Atlanta University Quarterly,* and a member of the executive board of the Negro Actors Guild of America, Inc. For additional biographical information see *Harold Jackman,* compiled by the Harold Jackman Memorial Committee, 1973, at the Moorland-Spingarn Research Center at Howard University, and *Who's Who in Harlem: The 1949-1950 Biographical Register* (New York: Magazine and Periodical Printing and Publishing, 1950).

51. In response to Johnson's query, Chester Kerr of Yale University Press provides Johnson with the address of the Ford Foundation in his letter dated July 2, 1963.

52. David Levering Lewis mentions that Johnson "mothered [Bruce Nugent's] neuroses when he returned to Washington in 1924." See Lewis's *When Harlem Was in Vogue,* 196. Gloria Hull also mentions that Johnson had an affinity for mothering a group of homosexual young black men (which in addition to Jackman and Nugent included Glenn Carrington and Wallace Thurman) whom she called her sons. She was also very close to Angela Grimké, Mary Burrill, and Alice Dunbar-Nelson. See *Color, Sex and Poetry,* 187-88. In a letter of May 26, 1958, to Langston Hughes, Johnson mentions that she wants Grimké to recuperate at her home in Washington. Moreover, she informs him that Grimké has written two novels and a book of verse "that should be printed. . . . It would be a great loss if it were not." This letter is a part of Hughes's papers in the Beinecke Library.

53. These letters are a part of the Cullen-Jackman file in the Woodruff Library at Atlanta University.

54. A copy of the program is in her papers at the Moorland-Spingarn Research Center at Howard University.

55. This letter is a part of the Cullen-Jackman file in the Woodruff Library at Atlanta University.

56. Born in 1888, Clement Wood was a white man from Alabama, who studied at Yale Law School but became a poet. According to *The University of Alabama Alumni News* (May-June 1921), his poem "De Glory Road" possesses "all the musical swing and rhythm" of black America (112). His sociological novel *Nigger,* published in 1922, sympathetically portrayed a poor black family from slavery in the South to exploitative wage-labor force in the urban North.

57. A fragment, including the "Author's Word," "Contents," and "Chapter I: A Statesman Is Born," is extant in Johnson's papers at the Moorland-Spingarn Research Center.

58. Several copies of Johnson's "Catalogue" as well as the table of contents for "Lovelight" appear in Johnson's file at the Moorland-Spingarn Research Center at Howard University.

59. See Johnson's "Catalogue of Writings" at the Woodruff Library at Atlanta University. Several copies of this document are held by the manuscript division of the Moorland-Spingarn Research Center. Johnson also states that she won first prize for the story "The Skeleton" in a contest sponsored by the *Washington Tribune.*

60. Quoted in Winona Fletcher, *Georgia Douglas Johnson,* 163. Also see Johnson's obituary in *The Baltimore Afro-American Way* (May 28, 1966): 18.

61. Gloria T. Hull, *Color, Sex and Poetry,* 210. In the August 1944 letter to Jackman, Johnson mentions that she has "quite a lot of unpublished material from Jean Toomer, Bruce Nugent, etc." The "etc." referred to the young writers who regularly attended her "S" Street salon.

62. Georgia Douglas Johnson, "Woman," *Opportunity* 25 (January-March 1947): 16.

63. While Johnson maintained close friendships with many homosexuals, no clear evidence has surfaced to suggest that she was herself homosexual or bisexual. Yet, Johnson did pen three sonnets, signed "G. D. J.," that may suggest a lesbian relationship with Grimké. The sonnets are included in Grimke's papers at Howard University. I thank Barbara Foley for calling my attention to this material. Also see note 52.

64. During the late 1930s and 1940s Johnson was anthologized in poetry collections and discussed in studies on black literature. For example, Sterling Brown's *Negro Poetry and Drama* (1937; reprint, New York: Atheneum, 1968) includes Johnson in a discussion of women poets from 1914 to 1936. *The Negro Caravan* (1941; reprint, New York: Arno, 1970), ed. Sterling Brown, Arthur Davis, and Ulysses Lee, contains four of Johnson's poems. *The Poetry of the Negro, 1746-1949,* ed. Langston Hughes and Arna Bontemps (New York: Doubleday, 1949), contains eight of her poems.

    By the 1960s Johnson's poetic presence begins to fade away in anthologies and literary scholarship. For example, only one poem, "I Want to Die While You Love Me," appears in *Kaleidoscope, Poems by American Negro Poets,* ed. Robert Hayden (New York: Harcourt, Brace, 1967). *Dark Sympathy: Negro Literature in America,* ed. James Emanual and Theodore Gross, (New York: Free Press, 1968), includes one poem each written by two Harlem Renaissance writers, Rudolph Fisher and Eric Walrond and no works of women writers of the Renaissance. Dudley Randall's *The Black Poets* (New York: Bantam, 1971) contains selections from McKay, Toomer, and Tolson but none of Johnson's poems, indeed, no work of women poets of the Renaissance. Randall's *Black Poetry* (Chicago: Broadside, 1969) similarly anthologizes Frank Horne, Hughes, Bontemps, and Cullen. *Cavalcade: Negro American Writings from 1760 to the Present,* ed. Arthur Davis and Saunders Redding, (Boston: Houghton Mifflin, 1971), does not mention Johnson at all. Houston Baker's *Black Literature in America* (New York: McGraw-Hill, 1971) discusses Cullen, Toomer, McKay, Fisher, and Hughes but no woman writer of the Renaissance period. Davis's *From the Dark Tower* (Washington, DC: Howard University Press, 1974) only mentions Johnson in the claim that she was not less talented than Anne Spencer. This scholarship sets the pattern of Johnson's exclusion until the second wave of the women's movement slowly reverses it by focusing on the recovery of women's writings.

65. For example, see *Shadowed Dreams: Women's Poetry of the Harlem Renaissance,* ed. Maureen Honey (New Brunswick, NJ: Rutgers University Press, 1989).

66. Gloria T. Hull, ed., *Give Us Each Day: The Diary of Alice Dunbar-Nelson* (New York: Norton, 1984), 87-88.

67. Geraldyn Dismond, "Through the Lorgnette," Pittsburgh *Courier,* 29 October 1927, 8,

68. Countee Cullen, ed. *Caroling Dusk: An Anthology of Verse by Negro Poets* (New York: Harper, 1927), 74.

69. Sterling Brown, *Negro Poetry and the Drama* (1937; reprint, New York: Atheneum, 1968), 50.

70. William Drake, *Sara Teasdale: Woman and Poet* (New York: Harper & Row, 1979).

71. Thadious Davis explains that the sexual chauvinism of the New Negro Renaissance took a decided turn for the worse after the 1926 *Opportunity* Civil Club dinner. Masked as an occasion to honor Jessie Fauset, who had been touted as the "midwife" of the Renaissance, the dinner was actually a promotional ploy for the magazine. From this moment on, Davis explains, the leadership of the New Negro Renaissance became misogynistic. According to Davis, *Opportunity*'s editor, Charles S. Johnson, used the magazine to counter if not block Fauset's further development as a literary leader by elevating Locke to that position. When Locke became the dean of the New Negro Renaissance, Davis writes, "the unspoken antagonism toward women and the latent sexual rivalry triumphed. Women were largely excluded from decision-making circles, particularly after 1926 when Fauset, seemingly disillusioned both with the turn of events and with her mentor Du Bois, resigned from her position on *Crisis*" to begin "a year of study in France." See Thadious M. Davis, *Nella Larsen: Novelist of the Harlem Renaissance* (Baton Rouge: Louisiana State University Press, 1994), 159-60.

72. "The Contest Spotlight," *Opportunity* (July 1927): 204. References to this work appear parenthetically in the introduction as "Spotlight."

73. See, for example, Hughes's "In the Twenties," mentioned above, in which he refers to Hurston's personality rather than her work, and Darwin Turner's *In Minor Chord: Three Afro-American Writers and Their Search for Identity* (Carbondale: Southern Illinois University Press, 1971), in which he discusses Hurston's life rather than her work.

74. A September 2, 1917, letter to Arthur Schomburg in which Johnson questions the title suggests that it may have been Braithwaite's choice. This letter is a part of the Schomburg file at the Schomburg Center for Research in Black Culture.

75. William Stanley Braithwaite, introduction to *The Heart of a Woman and Other Poems* by Georgia Douglas Johnson (1918); reprint (Freeport, NY: Books for Libraries Press, 1971), vii.

76. See the foreword to *Bronze* (Boston: Brimmer, 1922), 7.

77. See Braithwaite's letter, dated December 12, 1921, in which he writes, "About the introduction: that is really a thing you would have to decide, but if Mr. Du Bois wrote an introduction there is no doubt it would add to the distinction and appeal of the book." This letter is a part of the William Stanley Braithwaite file in the James Weldon Johnson Collections at the Beinecke Library at Yale.

78. *The Paul Laurence Dunbar Reader,* ed. Jay Martin and Gossie H. Hudson (New York: Dodd, Mead, 1975), 266.

79. Erlene Stetson, "Rediscovering the Harlem Renaissance: Georgia Douglas Johnson, 'The New Negro Poet,'" *Obsidian* (Spring/Summer 1979): 28.

80. Review of *Bronze* by Alain Locke in "Notes on the New Books," *The Crisis* (February 1923): 161.

81. Cedric Dover, "The Importance of Georgia Douglas Johnson," *The Crisis* 59 (December 1952): 634.

82. See note 75.

83. Newman I. White and Walter C. Jackson, eds. *Anthology of Verse by American Negroes* (Durham, NC: Trinity College Press, 1924), 225.

84. Anne Spencer, "The Browsing Reader," review of *An Autumn Love Cycle, The Crisis* 20 (March 1929): 87.

85. Blanche Watson, "The Bookshelf," review of *An Autumn Love Cycle,* entitled "A Document of a Woman's Heart," *Chicago Defender,* Part 2, 16 March 1929, 1.

86. Maxwell Hayson is described as a "colored" poet on the card catalogue entry at Howard University's Moorland-Spingarn Research Center. One work of his is on file there, a five-page "An Ode of Welcome to Samuel Coleridge-Taylor," published in 1906. Both letters are in Johnson's file at Howard University. In addition to Hayson, Toomer and Fauset also comment on Johnson's illegible handwriting.

87. "Modern romantic" is the label that Ronald Primeau ascribes to Johnson in "Frank Horne and the Second Echelon Poets of the Harlem Renaissance" in *Harlem Renaissance Remembered,* ed. Arna Bontemps (New York: Dodd, Mead, 1972), 265.

88. Chavina Hosek and Patricia Parker, eds., *Lyric Poetry Beyond New Criticism* (Ithaca, NY: Cornell University Press, 1985), 199. References to this work appear parenthetically in the introduction as *Lyric Poetry.*

89. Johnson submitted at least five plays of social protest (*Blue-Eyed Black Boy, Safe, A Sunday Morning in the South, Frederick Douglass,* and *William and Ellen Craft*) to the Federal Theatre Project between 1935 and 1939, the project's final year. None were accepted for publication. After reviewing the readers' commentary at the Federal Theatre Project archives at George Mason University, Winona L. Fletcher speculates that Johnson "forsook the writing of drama and concentrated again on writing poetry, which evidently was more acceptable to white publishers." See Winona L. Fletcher, "From Genteel Poet to Revolutionary Playwright: Georgia Douglas Johnson," *The Theatre Annual* 40 (1985): 41-64.

    Plumes was originally published by Samuel French (New York, 1927). It was reprinted that year in *Plays of Negro Life: A Source Book of Native American Drama,* ed. Alain Locke and Montgomery Gregory (New York: Harper, 1927). *Blue Blood* was originally published by Appleton-Century (New York, 1927). It was reprinted in *Fifty More Contemporary One-Act Plays,* ed. Frank Shay (New York: Appleton-Century, 1938). *Frederick Douglass* and *William and Ellen Craft* were originally published in *Negro History in Thirteen Plays,* ed. Willis Richardson and May Miller (Washington, DC: Associated Publishers, 1935). *A Sunday Morning in the South* was originally published in *Black Theatre, U.S.A.: Forty-Five Plays by Black American Playwrights, 1847-1974,* ed. James V. Hatch and Ted Shine (New York: Free Press, 1974). *Safe* and *Blue-Eyed Black Boy* were recovered from the Federal Theatre Project research division, Fenwick Library, George Mason University, and published in *Wines in the Wilderness: Plays by African Americans,* ed. Elizabeth Brown-Guillory (New York: Greenwood, 1990).

    Johnson's unpublished plays, which apparently are no longer extant, included the following in categories of her designation. Her primitive life plays were *Red Shoes* and *Well-Diggers.* Her plays of average Negro life were *Jungle Love, Little Blue Pigeon, Scapegoat, The New Day: A Brotherhood Play, One Cross Enough, Holiday,* and *Sue Baily.* Her lynching plays were *Safe, A Bill to be Passed, And Still They Paused, Camel-Legs, Miss Bliss, Heritage,* and *Midnight and Dawn.* These works are listed in Johnson's "Catalogue of Writings." For a partial listing see also Perkins, 243-48.

For additional discussions on black theatre during the twenties and women's participation in black drama, see Nellie McKay, "Black Theater and Drama in the 1920s: Years of Growing Pains," *Massachusetts Review* 28 (Winter 1987): 615-26; Nellie McKay, "'What Were They Saying?' Black Women Playwrights of the Harlem Renaissance," in *The Harlem Renaissance Re-Examined,* ed. Victor Kramer (New York: AMS, 1987), 129-47; Doris E. Abramson, "Angela Weld Grimké, Mary T. Burrill, Georgia Douglas Johnson, and Marita O. Bonner: An Analysis of Their Plays," *Sage* 22 (Spring 1985): 9-12; and Jeanne-Marie A. Miller, "Georgia Douglas Johnson and May Miller: Forgotten Playwrights of the New Negro Renaissance," *C.L.A. [College Language Association] Journal* 33 (June 1990): 349-86.

90. See Leslie Catherine Sanders, *The Development of Black Drama: From the Shadows to Selves* (Baton Rouge: Louisiana State University Press, 1988), 8-10, 13-23 for a summary of the relationship of American folk drama and Negro folk drama.

91. Alain Locke, ed., *The New Negro* (1925; reprint, New York: Atheneum, 1969), 159.

92. See W. E. B. Du Bois, "Krigwa Little Theatre Movement," *The Crisis* 32 (July 1926): 134. Krigwa was the acronym for the Crisis Guild of Writers and Artists; however, Du Bois changed the "C" to "K." See *Black Female Playwrights,* ed. with an introduction by Kathy A. Perkins (Bloomington: University of Indiana Press, 1989), 5.

93. Elizabeth Brown-Guillory, *Their Place on the Stage: Black Women Playwrights in America* (Westport, CT: Greenwood, 1988), 5.

94. For example, Doris Abramson's study *Negro Playwrights in the American Theatre, 1925-1959* (New York: Columbia University Press, 1959) outlines the development of Negro theatre without mentioning any black women playwrights of the New Renaissance era.

95. The play was based on the 1925 novel *Porgy* by DuBose Heyward.

96. Under the name Paul Tremaine, Johnson also published a review of Boston mayor James Michael Curley's *I'd Do It Again: A Record of All My Uproarious Years, New Republic* 137 (September 9, 1957): 17-19. Here Johnson clearly appropriates the unquestioned authority of white masculinity to critique not only Curley's book and his political character but to participate in one of the principal organs of hegemonic discourse.

97. I could not find the manuscript of "Free" in the Harmon file at the manuscript division of the Library of Congress. The story is published in *The Sleeper Wakes: Harlem Renaissance Stories by Women,* ed. Marcy Knopf (New Brunswick, NJ: Rutgers University Press, 1993), 55-59. Johnson's "Catalogue" refers to one apparently nonextant story, "Holiday."

98. This character seems based on Jean Toomer.

99. "Gesture" was originally published in *Challenge: A Literary Quarterly* 1, no. 1 (June 1936): 13-17. The quarterly was edited and copyrighted by Dorothy West.

100. Davis's observation concerns Nella Larsen's adoption of the name Allen Semi for the publication of two stories in *Young's Realistic Stories* magazine. However, Davis's observation fits Johnson and other women writers hampered by Victorian notions about the appropriate topics for women writers. See Davis's *Nella Larsen: Poet of the Harlem Renaissance,* 173.

101. "Tramp Love" was originally published in *Challenge: A Literary Quarterly* 2, no. 1 (Spring 1937): 3-11.

102. Zora Neale Hurston, *Their Eyes Were Watching God* (1937; reprint, New York: Harper Perennial, 1990, 1.

JUDITH STEPHENS (ESSAY DATE 1999)

SOURCE: Stephens, Judith. "'And Yet They Paused' and 'A Bill to Be Passed': Newly Recovered Lynching Dramas by Georgia Douglas Johnson." *African American Review* 33, no. 3 (fall 1999): 519-22.

In the following essay, Stephens describes the circumstances surrounding the creation of two recently discovered lynching plays by Johnson.

My recent discovery of Georgia Douglas Johnson's "lost" lynching plays ends a scholarly quest of many years and confirms Johnson's status as the leading playwright of the genre. The typescripts, dating from the 1930s and found among the NAACP papers at the Library of Congress on June 11, 1999, make possible a more thorough study of the six one-acts comprising the body of work Johnson specifically referred to as her "lynching plays" or "plays on lynching."[1] Since Johnson was the most prolific playwright of lynching drama, such a study can provide a clearer understanding of her contributions to this uniquely American dramatic genre, as well as the conditions of its production and reception.

Plays representing the history of lynching in the United States are only beginning to be understood as a distinctly American dramatic genre, a type of theatre that began to appear at least as early as 1905 and continues to evolve on the contemporary stage.[2] As the first anthology to address how the horrors of lynching have been represented in American theatre, *Strange Fruit: Plays on Lynching by American Women,* edited by Kathy A. Perkins and Judith L. Stephens (Indiana UP, 1998), reveals the historical continuity of the genre and speaks to its prior neglect in theatre history and dramatic criticism.

The fact that Johnson is known primarily as one of the leading poets of the Harlem Renaissance but has, until recently, remained invisible as the leading playwright of an unrecognized dramatic genre speaks loudly to the genre's status and critical reception, as well as to the precarious position Johnson occupied as a black woman writer in the 1920s and '30s. In her recent review of *Strange Fruit,* Eileen Cherry's comment that lynching dramas "may not present the picture that America wants to see of itself" provides insight into why the genre has been neglected in the recorded history of American theatre (224-25).

This note describes the conditions surrounding the production of ***And Yet They Paused*** and ***A Bill to be Passed,*** provides brief synopses of the plays, and locates the texts in relation to Johnson's more familiar and accessible lynching dramas: ***Sunday Morning in the South, Safe,*** and ***Blue-Eyed Black Boy.*** I am indebted to the work of scholars such as James V. Hatch, Ted Shine, Winona L. Fletcher, Margaret Wilkerson, Sandra Richards, Kathy Perkins, Bernard L. Peterson, Nellie McKay, Gloria T. Hall, Cheryl Wall, Elizabeth Brown-Guillory, and Claudia Tate, whose writing on Johnson brought the importance of her work to my attention.

According to correspondence in the NAACP files, in June of 1936 Johnson sent Walter White, Executive Secretary of the NAACP, several of her plays on the subject of lynching, but White returned the plays in January of 1937 on the grounds that they "all ended in defeat and gave one the feeling that the situation was hopeless despite all the courage which was used by the Negro characters."[3] Johnson graciously replied that she understood the point that White was making but added, "Yet, it is true that[,] in life, things do not end usually ideally[;] however, it is a point that I shall keep in mind if I write others or perhaps rewrite these."[4] Today Johnson's words are prophetic, since we know that, despite the NAACP's considerable and sustained efforts, the United States Congress never enacted any federal anti-lynching legislation. In her letter to White, Johnson mentioned that her lynching plays were under consideration for publication by Samuel French, but since her more recent "Catalogue of Writings" does not list these dramas among her published plays, it seems clear that French rejected them. Winona Fletcher's valuable 1985 article in *Theatre Annual* documents Johnson's submission of her lynching dramas to the Federal Theatre Project between 1935 and 1939, as well as the result that none were accepted for production in any of the producing units of the FTP. These historical records provide a glimpse into the struggle Johnson faced in seeing her lynching dramas published or produced in her lifetime, especially in the 1920s and 1930s when the brutality of lynching was not an uncommon occurrence in society.

In January of 1938 the NAACP called upon Johnson to write a short play to be used in the then-current "fight against lynching," but a request for last-minute revisions in the script prevented its inclusion in a mass anti-lynching demonstration, as originally planned. Correspondence shows that Johnson was asked to draw on the Congressional Record in dramatizing the specifics of the struggle to pass a federal anti-lynching bill. The NAACP assured Johnson that her scripts would be kept by the organization and made available to "the numerous white and colored groups throughout the country who constantly write us for anti-lynching plays."[5]

The NAACP file of 1937-38, titled "Anti-Lynching Bill Play," contains three typed scripts by Georgia Douglas Johnson, and correspondence concerning the writing of the plays. Two scripts, each fourteen pages long (with one script including three additional pages of songs) are slightly different versions of ***And Yet They Paused,*** which depicts the struggle to pass a federal anti-lynching bill through the U.S. House of Representatives. The third script, ***A Bill to be Passed*** (sixteen pages, plus three pages of songs), portrays the successful passage of the bill in the House and ends with a call to continue the struggle for passage in the Senate. A brief (four-and-one-half-page) additional ending scene by Robert E. Williams (currently unknown, but possibly an NAACP staff member) is attached to Johnson's third script and represents the historic filibuster carried out by Southern Senators to defeat the Wagner-Van Nuys Anti-Lynching Bill. Williams's scene ends with a commentator as well as the character of Walter White, then Executive Secretary of the NAACP, urging audience members to fight on.

All three of Johnson's scripts call for the onstage action to occur in two different locations: a black church in Mississippi and a hallway outside the doors of the House Chamber. All three include a scene in which a young boy enters the church and painfully describes, to the congregation, an extremely brutal lynching occurring outside. Joe Daniels, the victim of the lynching, is accused by the white mob of bootlegging and murder. The three episodes consisting of the black church service, the arguing over the anti-lynching bill in the halls of Congress, and the brutal lynching of Joe Daniels form a central triad that simultaneously binds the incidents together and allows them to illuminate, challenge, and contradict one another.

Each script includes the black congregation singing "Walls of Jericho," "Go Down, Moses," and "Sisters Don't Get Weary." The technique of using spirituals to accompany the action of a lynching drama was used before by Johnson in what is probably her best known work in the genre, ***Sunday Morning in the South.*** In an artistic gesture that points to the pervasiveness of racial separation in the United States, Johnson wrote one version of ***Sunday Morning in the South*** with music coming from a black church, and another from a white church. Her technique of employing sound effects and vivid verbal description to convey the events of an off-stage lynching to on-stage listeners is also seen in ***Safe*** and ***Blue-Eyed Black Boy,*** Johnson's other two contributions to the genre.

Finally, all of Johnson's lynching dramas include the medium of prayer, which reveals the constant presence of a spiritual dimension embedded in these stark dramas of social realism. To borrow a phrase from dramaturg Sydné Mahone, Johnson's plays effect a "spiritual realism" which "uses theatre to reveal the unseen through that which is seen" (xxxi-xxxii). The unique convergence of a political and spiritual voice found in Johnson's lynching dramas affirm her status as an important pioneer in the tradition of African American women playwrights.

An examination of the artistic techniques Johnson used to set forth the brutality and injustice of lynching attests to her skill as an innovative playwright and suggests the unique vision Johnson possessed as an African American artist/activist. Her position as the most prolific playwright of lynching drama testifies to her vision of theatre as "art for life's sake" and her struggle to bring such a theatre into being.[6]

Lynching dramas, written in the anti-lynching tradition by both black and white playwrights, are perhaps the only collection of performance texts providing a sustained portrayal of white Americans as terrorists. According to bell hooks,

> To name that whiteness in the black imagination is often a representation of terror: one must face a palimpsest of written histories that erase or deny, that reinvent the past to make the present vision of racial harmony and pluralism more plausible. To bear the burden of memory one must willingly journey to places long uninhabited, searching the debris of history for traces of the unforgettable, all knowledge of which has been suppressed.
>
> (342)

The recovery of the lost lynching plays of Georgia Douglas Johnson brings to light a vital part of African American culture that is continually under the threat of erasure. These plays also provide scholars with a newly complete unit of Johnson's work that commands a central position in a distinctly American theatrical genre, a type of drama that is only now beginning to gain recognition. In addition to their value as a unique contribution to American dramatic literature and theatre history, the dramas provide a new site for studying relations among race, gender politics, and aesthetics; they permit us to see more clearly the impact of racism and to understand art as a force of resistance as well as a force of renewal.

Notes

1. See Georgia Douglas Johnson's "Catalogue of Writings" in the Georgia Douglas Johnson Papers, Moorland-Spingarn Research Center, Howard U, Washington, DC. A typescript of these papers indicates that Johnson wrote six one-act lynching dramas, not eleven, as previously reported.
2. See my numerous articles on the genre.
3. "Anti-Lynching Bill Play, 1936-1938," NAACP Papers, Box C-299, Manuscript Reading Room, Library of Congress. All correspondence concerning Johnson's typescripts is in this file.
4. Letter from Johnson to Walter White, 19 Jan. 1938.
5. Letter from Miss Jackson, Special Assistant to the Secretary, NAACP, to Johnson, 7 Feb. 1938.
6. dele jegede's essay on Yoruban arts contrasts an African view of "art for life's sake" with the Western concept of "art for art's sake."

Works Cited

"Anti-Lynching Bill Play, 1936-1938." NAACP Papers, Box C-299. Manuscript Reading Room, Library of Congress.

Brown-Guillory, Elizabeth, ed. *Wines in the Wilderness: Plays by African American Women from the Harlem Renaissance to the Present.* New York: Praeger, 1990.

Cherry, Eileen. Rev. of *Strange Fruit: Plays on Lynching by American Women,* ed. Kathy Perkins and Judith L. Stephens. *Theatre Journal* 51.2 (1999): 224-25.

Fletcher, Winona. "From Genteel Poet to Revolutionary Playwright: Georgia Douglas Johnson." *Theatre Annual* 30 (1985): 41-64.

———. "Georgia Douglas Johnson." *Afro-American Writers from the Harlem Renaissance to 1940.* Dictionary of Literary Biography 51. Ed. Trudier Harris and Thadious M. Davis. Detroit: Gale, 1987. 153-64.

———. "Georgia Douglas Johnson." *Notable Women in the American Theatre.* Ed. Alice Robinson, Vera M. Roberts, and Millie Barranger. New York: Greenwood, 1989. 473-77.

Hatch, James V., and Ted Shine, eds. *Black Theatre U.S.A: Plays by African Americans.* 2nd ed. New York: Free P, 1996.

hooks, bell. "Representing Whiteness in the Black Imagination." *Cultural Studies.* Ed. Lawrence Grossberg, Cary Nelson, and Paula Treichler. New York: Routledge, 1992. 338-47.

Hull, Gloria T. *Color, Sex and Poetry: Three Women Writers of the Harlem Renaissance.* Bloomington: Indiana UP, 1987.

jegede, dele. "Art for Life's Sake: African Art as a Reflection of an Afrocentric Cosmology." *The African Aesthetic: Keeper of the Traditions.* Ed. Kariamu Welsh-Asante. Westport: Greenwood, 1993. 237-47.

Johnson, Georgia Douglas. "Catalogue of Writings." Georgia Douglas Johnson Papers. Moorland-Spingarn Research Center, Howard U, Washington, DC.

Mahone, Sydné, ed. *Moon Marked and Touched By Sun: Plays By African-American Women.* New York: Theatre Communications Group, 1994.

McKay, Nellie. "What Were They Saying?: Black Women Playwrights of the Harlem Renaissance." *The Harlem Renaissance Re-examined.* Ed. Victor A. Kramer. New York: AMS P, 1987. 129-47.

Perkins, Kathy A., ed. *Black Female Playwrights: An Anthology of Plays before 1950.* Bloomington: Indiana UP, 1989.

Perkins, Kathy A., and Judith L. Stephens, eds. *Strange Fruit: Plays on Lynching by American Women.* Bloomington: Indiana UP, 1998.

Peterson, Bernard L., Jr. *Early Black American Playwrights and Dramatic Writers: A Biographical Directory and Catalogue of Plays, Films, and Broadcasting Scripts.* New York: Greenwood, 1990.

Richards, Sandra L. "African American Women Playwrights and Shifting Canons." Unpublished essay. 1992.

Stephens, Judith L. "The Anti-Lynch Play: Toward an Interracial Feminist Dialogue in Theatre." *Journal of American Drama and Theatre* 2.3 (1990): 59-69.

———. "Anti-Lynch Plays by African American Women: Race, Gender, and Social Protest in American Drama." *African American Review* 26 (1992): 329-39.

———. "The Harlem Renaissance and the New Negro Movement." *The Cambridge Companion to American Woman Playwrights.* Ed. Brenda Murphy. Cambridge: Cambridge UP, 1999. 98-117.

———. "Lynching, American Theatre and the Preservation of a Tradition." *Journal of American Drama and Theatre* 9.1 (1997): 54-65.

———. "Racial Violence and Representation: Performative Strategies in Lynching Dramas of the 1920s." Forthcoming in *African American Review* 33.4 (1999).

———. "Revisiting Representations of an American Race Ritual: Early Lynching Dramas, 1905-1920." Forthcoming in *The Imagined Self: Re-visioning the African American Text.* Ed. Wilfred D. Samuels. University: U of Alabama P, 2000.

Tate, Claudia. "Introduction." *The Selected Works of Georgia Douglas Johnson.* New York: Hall, 1997. xvii-lxxx.

Wall, Cheryl A. *Women of the Harlem Renaissance.* Bloomington: Indiana UP, 1995.

Wilkerson, Margaret B. *9 Plays By Black Women.* New York: Mentor, 1986.

FURTHER READING

Biography

Fletcher, Winona L. "Johnson, Georgia Douglas." In *Notable Women in the American Theatre: A Biographical Dictionary,* edited by Alice M. Robinson, Vera Mowry Roberts, and Milly S. Barranger, pp. 473-77. Westport, Conn.: Greenwood Press, 1989.

Overview of Johnson's life and career.

Criticism

Dover, Cedric. "The Importance of Georgia Douglas Johnson." *Crisis* 59 (December 1952): 633-36, 674.

Discusses Johnson's contributions to literature and the Harlem Renaissance.

Hull, Gloria T. *Color, Sex, & Poetry: Three Women Writers of the Harlem Renaissance.* Bloomington: Indiana University Press, 1987, 256 p.

Provides feminist perspective criticism of Johnson and other women of the Harlem Renaissance.

McKay, Nellie. "'What Were They Saying?': Black Women Playwrights of the Harlem Renaissance." In *The Harlem Renaissance Re-Examined,* edited by Victor A. Kramer, pp. 129-47. New York: AMS Press, 1987.

Examines Johnson's plays in relation to those written by some of her female peers, including Alice Dunbar-Nelson, Angelina Weld Grimké, and Myrtle Livingston.

Perkins, Kathy A. and Judith L. Stephens. Introduction to *Strange Fruit: Plays on Lynching by American Women,* edited by Kathy A. Perkins and Judith L. Stephens, pp. i-x. Bloomington: Indiana University Press, 1998.

Provides historical background and critical contexts for lynching plays by Johnson and others.

Stephens, Judith L. "The Anti-Lynch Play: Toward an Interracial Feminist Dialogue in Theatre." *Journal of American Drama and Theatre* 2, no. 3 (fall 1990): 59-69.

Discusses the manner in which Johnson appeals to the collective conscience of white women by demonstrating that they are part of the system of exploitation and violence that leads to lynch mobs.

———. "Lynching, American Theatre, and the Preservation of a Tradition." *Journal of American Drama and Theatre* 9, no. 1 (winter 1997): 54-65.

Examines the social conditions that led to the creation of lynching dramas and discusses the relative neglect of these plays by modern scholars.

OTHER SOURCES FROM GALE:

Additional coverage of Johnson's life and career is contained in the following sources published by the Gale Group: *Black Writers,* Ed. 1; *Contemporary Authors,* Vol. 125; *Dictionary of Literary Biography,* Vols. 51, 249; and *World Poets.*

HELENE JOHNSON

(1907 - 1995)

American poet.

Johnson distinguished herself as one of the youngest poets of the Harlem Renaissance and as one of the first to address the issue of race directly in her work. Along with her cousin, the short story writer and novelist Dorothy West, Johnson moved in the highest circles of the Harlem literary elite, which included Countee Cullen and Zora Neale Hurston. Between 1925 and 1935 Johnson was accounted one of the most promising young poets of the literary movement, though she published only about twenty-four poems in that decade.

BIOGRAPHICAL INFORMATION

Little is known about Johnson's life. She was born July 7, 1907, in Boston, the only child of Ella Benson Johnson and George William Johnson. She never knew her father, as her parents separated soon after her birth, but she grew up with her mother's family—the minister Benjamin Benson, his daughters (Johnson's aunts), and their children, including Johnson's first cousin Dorothy West. They lived in Brookline, a suburban section of Boston, and spent summers in the town of Oak Bluffs, on Martha's Vineyard, where Benson worked as a carpenter. Johnson and West were well educated as girls, attending the prestigious Boston Girls' Latin School and taking writing courses at Boston University. They were members of The Saturday Evening Quill Club, a group of aspiring African American writers. In 1925 Johnson published her first poem in the African American journal *Opportunity*. That poem, "Trees at Night," won an honorable mention in the journal's literary contest. In 1926 she published a poem in Wallace Thurman's journal *Fire!!*, her work appearing alongside poems by Langston Hughes. In 1927 the two cousins moved to New York to study writing through the Columbia University Extension Division, thus landing in Harlem. When Johnson sold a poem to *Vanity Fair*, she became a Harlem celebrity. The market crash of 1929 eventually took its toll on the Harlem Renaissance, and its writers dispersed. Johnson returned to Boston and published very little. Her cousin West edited *Challenge: A Literary Quarterly*, to which Johnson contributed poems in 1934 and 1935. Johnson married William Hubble in 1933, which both Johnson and later historians point to as the end of her poetry career. They had one child, Abigail, and Johnson worked as a civil service employee. She soon returned to New York City and lived in Manhattan for the rest of her life. She died on July 6, 1995.

MAJOR WORKS

As one of the minor poets of the Harlem Renaissance, Johnson has fewer than ten poems accounted as her major works. Many of them were published in Countee Cullen's anthology, *Caroling Dusk: An Anthology of Verse by Negro Poets* (1927). From her first poem, "Trees at Night," Johnson turned to nature for her images as well as her themes. In addition to nature, the intersection of race and gender, and the many forms of love, were the most frequent motifs of her poetry. Though she used a more colloquial, free-form style, she was influenced by the lyrics of older poets she admired, especially Walt Whitman, Alfred Lord Tennyson, Percy Bysshe Shelley, and Carl Sandburg. Many of her poems call for African Americans to reject wholesale assimilation. In "Magula" (1926) Johnson tells the hero of her poem to beware of selling "the passionate wonder of your forest / For a creed that will not let you dance." Though her work preceded the heyday of the civil rights movement, she urged Black Americans to continue their struggle for equality. In "The Road" (1926) she invited African Americans to "Rise to one brimming golden, spilling cry." Other important titles include "My Race" (1925), "Metamorphism" (1926), "Bottled" (1927), "Summer Matures" (1928), "Sonnet to a Negro in Harlem" (1928), and "Let Me Sing My Song" (1935).

CRITICAL RECEPTION

Johnson's poems were received with enthusiasm, particularly by Zora Neale Hurston. She won several honorable mentions through the National Urban League's journal, *Opportunity*, in contests judged by James Weldon Johnson, Robert Frost, Carl Sandburg, Countee Cullen, and other contemporary poets. Since 1935 several authors have lamented Johnson's abrupt disappearance from the literary scene, suggesting that the promise of her early works, written mainly while she was barely twenty years old, would likely have borne greater fruit had she continued practicing her art. Gloria T. Hull, echoing the sentiments of other critics, has suggested that being a woman was particularly disadvantageous for poets of the Harlem Renaissance, which she called "a predominantly masculine affair." Not until 2000 were Johnson's poems collected, and so this has limited the amount of scholarship on her poetry. Johnson is remembered as one of the leading minor poets of the Harlem Renaissance, her poems reflecting some of its major concerns as well as capturing its atmosphere and energy.

PRINCIPAL WORKS

"Trees at Night" (poem) 1925; published in the journal *Opportunity*

"Magula" (poem) 1926; published in the journal *Palms*

"The Road" (poem) 1926; published in the journal *Opportunity*

"Let Me Sing My Song" (poem) 1935; published in the journal *Challenge*

This Waiting for Love: Helene Johnson, Poet of the Harlem Renaissance (poetry) 2000

GENERAL COMMENTARY

GLORIA T. HULL (ESSAY DATE 1979)

SOURCE: Hull, Gloria T. "Black Women Poets from Wheatley to Walker." In *Sturdy Black Bridges: Visions of Black Women in Literature,* edited by Roseann P. Bell, Bettye J. Parker, and Beverly Guy-Sheftall, pp. 69-86. Garden City, N.Y.: Anchor Books, 1979.

In this essay, Hull surveys the development of Black women's poetry in America, placing Johnson among the major women poets of the Harlem Renaissance, and suggesting that her poems strongly reflect the dominant themes of Harlem Renaissance literature.

In certain ways, the often garish spotlight which has been focused on contemporary Black women poets such as Nikki Giovanni, June Jordan, and others has, ironically, tended to obscure the already shadowy literary past by suggesting that Black female poets are something new. Granted that they are among the strongest voices in this current explosion of Black poetry, and that it is normal for contemporary readers (and sometimes even scholars) to be more familiar with modern writers. Yet, despite the implications of this present emphasis, the tradition of Black women poets goes back much further than the 1960s. In fact, Black American literature begins with a female poet, and an imposing line of her successors stretches from that time forward.

These women who wrote before the modern period have received neither the popular nor the critical attention which they deserve—even though growing interest in the field makes knowing what has gone before that much more imperative. Studying them teaches us that significant numbers of Black women have always written poetry and accords this earlier work its rightful esteem. It also gives a necessary perspective on the present poets by placing them in their appropriate, rich tradition. In this way, a body of literature, which is too often perceived as isolated and fragmented, assumes a coherent shape; and this, in turn, works to correct the myopic view taken toward Black women writers and Black poetry in general.

Even before a formal literary history began, slave women were, no doubt, helping to produce the earliest Black poetry—the spirituals and secular songs. One of the curious and distinguishing characteristics of this folk poetry is its lack of an identifying sexual framework—that is, a reader cannot tell if the consciousness or voice behind the song is male or female. Yet, surely, women are to be counted among the "Black and unknown bards."

This beginning period, rich in oral literature, is correspondingly sparse in formal, written poetry. However, the eighteenth century brought the first poem by a Black American and the emergence of the first widely known Black American poet. Both of these writers were women. Lucy Terry, a sixteen-year-old slave girl, witnessed an Indian raid on her village of Deerfield, Massachusetts, and left behind the best account of the massacre in fourteen naïve tetrameter couplets called "Bars Fight, August 28, 1746." The work was not published until 1893 and survives today because of its historical importance.

Phillis Wheatley, on the other hand, is the major Black writer of the period. Quite a bit has already been written about her. Students of literature are familiar, if only in outline, with her genius and remarkable history: how she was kidnaped from the African coast of Senegal when she was five or six years old and brought to America, where, in the nurturing atmosphere of the Wheatley household, she learned to speak and read English in sixteen months and to write creditable poems in six years. And they also know of her abstract elegies and occasional poems modeled after the English neoclassic poets. The table of contents of her 1773 *Poems on Various Subjects, Religious and Moral* is illustrative of this preoccupation and influence:[1] "Thoughts on the Works of Providence," "An Hymn to the Morning," "On Recollection," "On Imagination," and then in a particularly calamitous time, these four poems: "To a Lady on her coming to North America with her Son, for the Recovery of her Health"; "To a Lady on her remarkable Preservation in a Hurricane in North Carolina"; "To a Lady and her Children on the Death of her Son, and their Brother"; and, finally, "To a Gentleman and Lady on the Death of the Lady's Brother and Sister, and a Child of the Name of Avis, aged one year"—very complete and descriptive titles, typical of their day.

Almost equally well known is the common criticism of Wheatley for her lack of race consciousness—at least of a kind which would have led her to personally empathize with the average slave or protest against the institution of slavery in her writings. All of these bits and pieces form a prevailing idea of her which one critic has summed up in this way: "Phillis Wheatley was a pathetic little Negro girl who had so completely identified herself with her eighteenth century Boston background that all she could write was coldly correct neo-classical verse on dead ministers and even deader abstractions."[2] There is truth in this common view, but there are also corrective observations which need to be made.

The first is that her poetry is not as imitative and moribund as most commentators make it sound. Some of her images and conceits display an originality which shows that many of her thoughts are fresh ideas of her own even if her rhythm is almost always Pope's—for example, these lines from the hurricane poem just mentioned:

> Aeolus in his rapid chariot drove
> In gloomy grandeur from the vault above:
> Furious he comes. His winged sons obey
> Their frantic sire, and madden all the sea.

Secondly, Phillis Wheatley was conscious of herself as a poet, a Black poet, a Black female poet, as the numerous references to herself in her poems attest—their stylization notwithstanding. One should also remember that she was a thorough New England Puritan, and it is partly her Christianity which compels her to look upon deliverance from her native land as the blessing which she describes it to be in one of her best-known poems, "On Being Brought from Africa to America." Furthermore, her personality was naturally delicate and reticent. After being feted on both sides of the Atlantic, she and an infant child died in the squalor of a cheap Boston boardinghouse—a circumstance which is of course another tragic writer's tale, but also a chilling commentary on the precariousness of Wheatley's status as a Black female poet.

The period from 1800 to 1865 was a time of antislavery agitation and utilitarian literature. All resources, including the pens of writers, were marshaled for the abolitionist cause. Understandably, the slave narrative, the speech, and the essay flourished to the relative neglect of more belletristic literary genres. However, the poetry which was written shows its political involvement. George Moses Horton, who earned from twenty-five to fifty cents each for the eighteenth-century-style love lyrics which he wrote for University of North Carolina students, also complained against his slavery and entitled the 1829 volume of his poems

Hope of Liberty. A second major poet, James M. Whitfield, added Byronic misanthropy to his forceful denunciation of America.

The key female poet of this period (there is only one other), Frances Harper, is a better technician than Horton and ranks well with Whitfield. In addition to her abolitionist themes, she has subjects and moods which give her greater variety and also reveal her special qualities as a woman writer. The editors of *The Negro Caravan* call her "easily the most popular American Negro poet of her time."[3] This popularity stemmed from the fact that she took her poetry to the people—just as did the young Black poets of the 1960s and '70s. As a widely traveling lecturer of the Anti-Slavery Society, she spoke to packed churches and meeting halls, giving dramatic readings of her abolitionist poems which were so effective that she sold over fifty thousand copies—an unheard-of figure—of her first two books, mostly to people who had, in the words of her fellow abolitionist William Still, "listened to her eloquent lectures."[4]

Essentially this poetry is message verse, dependent on an oratorical and histrionic platform delivery for its effect. Harper leans heavily on the poetic and emotional appeal of sensory imagery, as can be seen in these characteristic lines from "Bury Me in a Free Land":

> I could not rest if I heard
> the tread
> Of a coffle gang to the
> shambles led,
> And the mother's shriek of
> wild despair
> Rise like a curse on the
> trembling air.

Harper's speaking and writing did not end with 1865, for the fight against slavery was only one of the many battles which engaged her during her lifetime. She was also deeply involved in religious, feminist, and temperance movements—with no apparent conflict or lack of energy—which is comparable today to being in the Black Liberation, the Women's Liberation, the Jesus, and the ecology/health-food movements. She combined these interests in her writing as well as in her life to produce a fairly extensive body of quite readable poetry.

From her feminism comes "A Double Standard," a poem spoken by a seduced and abandoned young woman who addresses the reader or listener in these terms:

> Crime has no sex and yet today
> I wear the brand of shame;
> Whilst he amid the gay and proud
> Still bears an honored name.

The social double standard is directly condemned in the final lines:

> And what is wrong in woman's
> life
> In man's cannot be right.

She also wrote about Vashti, the Persian Queen in the Bible who gave up her throne rather than shame her womanhood. And included in her corpus are temperance poems like "Nothing and Something"; a mother, confident that her son would not ". . . tread / In the downward path of sin and shame," was not alarmed about alcohol, but she became quite concerned when that only son ". . . madly cast in the flowing bowl / A ruined body and sin-wrecked soul." In her forms (as is obvious), Harper relies mainly on the ballad stanza and rhymed tetrameters.

Her last volume of poems, *Sketches of Southern Life,* 1872, presents a Black heroine, Aunt Chloe, who is very well drawn and is firmly set in the folk-life milieu which would furnish the dialect poets with their materials. Its "Learn-to-Read" epitomizes Harper's manner and catches up most of her themes. Although the "Rebs" hated the schools established for ex-slaves—education of Blacks ". . . was agin' their rule"—Aunt Chloe is determined to learn to read:

> So I got a pair of glasses,
> And straight to work I went
> And never stopped till I could read
> The hymns and Testament.

She also moves into her own "little cabin," where she feels ". . . as independent / As the queen upon her Throne."

After Mrs. Harper herself, there were no more queens on her poetry throne for a long while—nor kings either, for that matter. A. A. Whitman wrote extremely long versified romantic tales à la Scott and Byron which were very popular with both Black and white readers near the end of the nineteenth century (William Cullen Bryant, for instance, liked him). And, during the same period, Henrietta Ray published her mannered, bookish poetry. On the whole, the Reconstruction-backlash period from 1865 to 1915 was not congenial to Black literary activity. But near the end of the century, a crop of writers auguring the Renaissance began to spring up—chief among which were Dunbar and the whole slough of dialect poets.

When Gwendolyn Brooks was a little girl writing verses, her mother encouraged her by predicting that she would be "the lady Paul Laurence Dunbar."[5] In his own time, however, Dunbar had no such female counterpart. But even before that, not one of the dialect poets who are usually encountered is a woman. This is a significant—and in certain ways, a gratifying—fact, but one is not altogether sure of what it means. There does not seem to be anything inherently masculine in either the content or the manner of this largely plantation-and-minstrel-tradition-based dialect verse. Conceivably, women could just as easily have imagined or reminisced about cooking, kissing, and raising children in the ante bellum South as the men did about eating, courting, and coonhunting. Or a woman poet could have followed the lead of Harper in her Aunt Chloe poems and given realistic and human depictions of folk life as Dunbar does in the best of his dialect work. But none of them did.

At any rate, there is no major female poet in this period—although Dunbar's wife, Alice Dunbar-Nelson, produced some poems, one of which, "Sonnet," is almost always anthologized. But the most arresting poem which she wrote is a three-stanza lyric called "I Sit and Sew," in which she protests against her apparently petty occupation when real work is needed for the war. The poem could read as a rebellion against the chafing confinement of a "woman's place." She writes:

> But—I must sit and sew.
> The little useless seams,
> the idle patch;
>
> . . . . .
>
> It is no
> roseate dream
> That beckons me—this pretty
> futile seam,
> It stifles me—God,
> must I sit and sew?[6]

The picture presented by the Harlem Renaissance years—roughly from 1915 to 1930—is, of course, very different from that of the preceding period. Black literature flourished. The major writers were poets—Johnson, McKay, Cullen, Hughes. And there were women poets, too, seven of whom are worthy of note—Angelina Grimke, Anne Spencer, Georgia Douglas Johnson, Jessie Fauset, Effie Lee Newsome, Gwendolyn Bennett, and Helene Johnson. But none of them is considered "major." A serious investigator naturally wonders why and tries to determine if this is a valid judgment. The answer which emerges after a closer study of their poetry and their lives is a mixed one. First the poetry.

The most prolific writer was Georgia Douglas Johnson. Between 1918 and 1938, she published three volumes of poems. (Four years before her death in 1966, she brought out a final book.) This was enough to make her the first Black woman after Harper "to gain general recognition as a poet."[7] However, a modern reader does not usually find her efforts very impressive—mainly because of the sameness of her themes and manner, and her conventional style. She writes either melancholy love lyrics or muted, attenuated poems of racial protest. Illustrative of the first type is this stanza from her poem "Welt":

> Would I might mend the
> fabric of my youth
> That daily flaunts its
> tatters to my eyes,
> Would I might compromise
> awhile with truth
> Until our moon now waxing,
> wanes and dies.

This lyric gathers up the themes of youth, aging, time, love, and death, which recur in these poems.

The personae and characters are usually women (such as the suffering outcast in "Octoroon"), and her poetry almost always has a definite feminine voice. For example, in her first book, *The Heart of a Woman* (1918), she talks about a "woman with a burning flame" which was kept covered and hushed until death, and in the title poem, she likens the heart of a woman to a bird which "goes forth with the dawn" but

> falls back with the night,
> And enters some alien cage
> in its plight,
> And tries to forget it has
> dreamed of the stars,
> While it breaks, breaks,
> breaks on the sheltering bars.

Representative of her handling of the race theme is ["The Suppliant"]:

> Long have I beat with timid hands
> upon life's leaden door,
> Praying the patient, futile prayers
> my fathers prayed before,
> Yet I remain without the close,
> unheeded and unheard,
> And never to my listening ear
> is borne the waited word.
>
> Soft o'er the threshold of the years
> there comes this counsel cool:
> The strong demand, contend, prevail;
> the beggar is a fool!

Almost all of her poems are in the ballad stanza, which she sometimes stretches out into heptameter couplets. The diction is predictably poetic with, every now and then, a fresh word or image. She uses parallel and balanced phrases for rhythm and development of thought (especially in her heptameter racial poems), and resorts to inversion for the sake of meter and rhyme.

A better and more interesting poet is Anne Spencer. When asked by Cullen to write her biographical notice for his 1927 anthology, *Caroling Dusk,* she responded with the following paragraph:

> Mother Nature, February, forty-five years ago forced me on the stage that I, in turn, might assume the role of lonely child, happy wife, perplexed mother—and, so far, a twice resentful grandmother. I have no academic honors, nor lodge regalia. I am a Christian by intention, a Methodist by inheritance, and a Baptist by marriage. I write about some of the things I love. But have no civilized articulation for the things I hate. I proudly love being a Negro woman—it's so involved and interesting. We are the PROBLEM—the great national game of TABOO.[8]

Her civilized articulation about things that she loves includes poems as varied as their titles: "Before the Feast of Shushan," "At the Carnival," "The Wife-Woman," "Dunbar," "Letter to My Sister," "Lines to a Nasturtium," "Neighbors," "Questing," and "Creed." Her forms are an eccentric mixture of free verse and rhymed, iambic-based lines. The result works, but it defies precise categorization. She also exhibits something of a predilection for casting herself into roles. For instance, "Shushan" is a dramatic monologue spoken by a King (the material is the same biblical story treated by Harper in "Vashti"). In trying to make love to Vashti, he calls her Sharon's Rose and then says:

> And I am hard to force
> the petals wide;
> And you are fast to suffer
> and be sad.
> Is my prophet come to teach
> a new thing
> Now in a more apt time?[9]

Not surprisingly, Spencer liked Browning. She even wrote a light poem about him, bemoaning the fact that "Life-long, poor Browning never knew Virginia"—which is her native state. It is full of biographical references and allusions to his work ("Pippa Passes," for example) which show her familiarity with him. This kind of dramatic distancing is surprising, appearing as it does during a time of intensely self-centered lyric poetry.

Spencer also has a sense of woman-self and a female identity which comes through in her poems, notably in her "Letter to My Sister," in which she gives advice about how a woman must live; although

> It is dangerous for a woman
> to defy the gods;
> To taunt them with the
> tongue's thin tip,
> Or strut in the weakness
> of mere humanity,
> it is even worse if you
> Dodge this way or that,
> or kneel or pray,
> Be kind, or swear agony drops
> Or lay your quick body over
> your feeble young.

Even though Spencer's poetic instincts are not unerring (she can be obvious and predictable), her work is attractive because of the originality of her material and approach, and because of her terse—almost elliptical—style, apt or unusual diction, vivid images and metaphors, and the occasionally modern lines, which stop the reader with their precise wording and subtly pleasing sounds and rhythms. It is difficult to choose one poem which adequately conveys Spencer's essence. "At the Carnival" might, or "The Wife-Woman," but both of them need to be quoted entirely, yet are too long. "For Jim, Easter Eve," then, best serves the purpose. The persona, after comparing her garden "with old tombs set high against / The crumbled olive tree—and lichen" to Gethsemane, continues:

> what is pain but happiness here
> amid these green and wordless
> patterns,—
> indefinite texture of blade and
> leaf:
> Beauty of an old, old tree,
> last comfort in Gethsemane.

Spencer wrote before the Harlem Renaissance (note that she was forty-five years old in 1927), but was first published during that era. Her uniqueness was apparent even then. Editors who printed her work used phrases like "independent, unconventional style"[10] and "first Aframerican woman poet to show so high a degree of maturity,"[11] and Sterling Brown called her "the most original of all Negro women poets."[12] Not enough is known about her, and the biographical basis of her poems remains a tantalizing question. She is still alive, over ninety years old, in Lynchburg, Virginia, where she has spent almost all of her life.

Anne Spencer did not write racial protest poems. However, the same statement cannot be made about the last Renaissance poet who will be looked at in detail, Helene Johnson. The youngest of the Harlem group, she took "the 'racial' bull by the horns,"[13] and she also wrote poems in the new colloquial-folk-slang style popular during that time. Of all the women poets, her work most reflects the themes which are commonly designated as the characteristic ones of the Renaissance. Her

"Sonnet to a Negro in Harlem" is pro-Black and militant and calls to mind the work of Claude McKay. In **"Poem,"** she gushes over the "Little brown boy / Slim, dark, big-eyed" who croons love songs to his banjo down at the Lafayette:

Gee, brown boy.
I loves you all over.
I'm glad I'm a jig.
I'm glad I can
Understand your dancin'
and your
Singin', and feel all the
happiness
And joy and don't care in you.[14]

"Bottled" presents her notion that a Black man dancing on Seventh Avenue in Harlem has been bottled just as has some sand from the African Sahara sitting on the shelf of the 135th Street public library. Finally, she has a poem which expresses a pro-African primitivism which should be better known than it is, since it is superior to some of the more frequently encountered works on this theme. It is entitled **"Magalu"** [**"Magula"**] and seems to be a fantasy about meeting Magalu, "dark as a tree at night, / Eager-lipped, listening to a man with a white collar / And a small black book with a cross on it." She enters the scene and ends the poem like this:

Oh Magalu, come!
Take my hand and I
will read you poetry
Chromatic words,
Seraphic symphonies,
Filled up your throat with laughter
and your heart with song.
Do not let him lure you
from your laughing waters,
Lulling lakes, lissome winds.

The bulk of Helene Johnson's poems are more conventional lyrics. In them, she uses much descriptive imagery and frequently treats young love and youthful sensuality.

Now, briefly, a word about each of the four remaining poets. Angelina Grimke wrote commonplace lyric poetry before the Renaissance, but first saw it published then. Her strength lies in her notable use of color imagery. The poem of hers most often reprinted, "Tenebris," envisions a huge black shadow hand plucking at the blood-red bricks of the white man's house. Jessie Fauset, though primarily a novelist of four published books, is usually represented in poetry anthologies by her love poems. Some of these are distinguished by the French titles which she gave them and her sometimes humorous and ironic cast of mind. Effie Newsome wrote primarily children's verse based on nature lore. And, finally, there is Gwendolyn Bennett, whose poetry is rather good. She was, by occupation, an artist, and consequently in her work she envisions scenes, paints still lifes, and expresses herself especially well in color.

Looking back over this group of seven female poets of the Harlem Renaissance and assessing their impact and collective worth, we can begin to see why they are not better known or more highly rated. In the first place, they did not produce and publish enough: Grimke no book, Spencer no book, Fauset no book, Newsome no adult book, Bennett no book, Helene Johnson no book—which means that six of the seven did not collect a single volume of their work. And the one who did, Georgia Johnson, is not the best poet—though she was the most popular. And even here, her popularity is uncharacteristic of the new themes and forms of the Renaissance. Except for Helene Johnson perhaps, this same factor was operative in the cases of the other six writers.

Furthermore, since the Renaissance was a predominantly masculine affair, these poets did not benefit from being insiders. Though Fauset held her quiet literary gatherings, these women—as women—did not fraternize with the male writers and artists. Nor did they have much opportunity to do so. Fauset lived in New York, and Bennett and Helene Johnson were there for a while—but, on the whole, they were not based in the city which was the cultural center of the Renaissance. In fact, most of them were at one time or another a part of the Washington, D.C., social and literary circle which revolved around Georgia Johnson, whose husband had a government appointment in the Capitol. Thus, they were out of the mainstream in more ways than one.

For these reasons, then, these poets represent a group of talented individuals who did not produce enough, or, in a worldly-wise fashion, parlay their talent into "fame." So, lamentably, they end up being "interesting," "minor"—a kind of secondary wave which helped to make up the Renaissance tide.

After this glorious and busy period, the country and Black literary activity went into a slump. What poetry there is, is tinged with depression, socialism, and sometimes protest. Between 1930 and 1945, the major poet was Margaret Walker and the most important poetic event the appearance of her 1942 volume *For My People,* brought out as No. 41 of the Yale Series of Younger Poets, making her the first Black poet to appear in that prestigious group. At the time of its publication,

Walker was a twenty-seven-year-old professor of English at Livingston College in Salisbury, North Carolina, her first teaching position after she had received a master of arts degree from the University of Iowa's School of Letters two years earlier.

For My People is divided into three sections. The first seeks to define the poet's relationship to "her people" and her native Southland, and it begins with the well-known title poem, a work which anticipates the material and the manner of the rest of the section:

For my people everywhere
singing their slave songs repeatedly:
their dirges and their ditties
and their blues and jubilees,
praying their prayers nightly
to an unknown god, bending their
knees humbly to an unseen power.[15]

The form of "For My People" is the most immediately striking thing about it. Drawing on free-verse techniques, on the Bible, on the Black sermon (her father was a preacher), Walker fairly overwhelms the reader with her rhetorical brilliance. She continues this same method and approach in the poems in the collection—reciting her heritage of "Dark Blood," tracing Black people's blind belief in gods from Africa to America, singing of her "roots deep in southern life," and decrying the fact that she is not as strong as her grandmothers were in "Lineage," one of the simplest and nicest poems in this group:

My grandmothers are full of
memories
Smelling of soap and onions
and wet clay
With veins rolling roughly
over quick hands
They have many clean words to say.

Part II of *For My People* is made up of ballads about Black folk heroes known and unknown, famous and infamous. Traditional subjects are "Bad-Man Stagolee" and "Big John Henry." But no less worthy are "Poppa Chicken," the "sugah daddy / pimping in his prime"; the "Teacher," who was a "sap" about women; and "Gus, the Lineman," who "had nine lives / And lived them all." Two of the best of these ballads have heroines as their central figures—Molly Means, "a hag and a witch: / Chile of the devil, the dark, and sitch," and Kissie Lee, a tough, bad gal, whose account ends like this:

She could shoot glass doors
offa the hinges,
She could take herself
on the wildest binges.
And she died with her boots on
switching blades
On Talladega Mountain
in the likker raids.

In these tall tale and ballad narratives, Walker adheres pretty closely to the traditional ballad stanza, varying it with four-beat couplets and spicing it up with dialect speech which she is successful at orthographically representing.

The final section, composed of only six poems, is much shorter than the first two. These are sonnets (with the form freely handled) in which Walker gazes back on her childhood, writes about experiences she has had since leaving the South (such as talking to an Iowa farmer), and expresses needs and struggles common to all human beings. Her craftsmanship is not always smooth in this section, but some of her best lines conclude the poem entitled "Whores":

Perhaps one day they'll all
die on the streets
or be surprised by bombs
in each wide bed;
learning too late in
unaccustomed dread
that easy ways, like whores
on special beats,
No longer have the gift
to harbor pride
or bring men peace,
or leave them satisfied.

On the whole, *For My People* is a good book. Unlike many volumes of poetry, one can read it from cover to cover without getting bored or inattentive—probably because of the narrative interest of Part II. Walker is best with these poems and with her unique "for my people" style, but not as sure or deft in her handling of the sonnets.

The volume was (and is) significant for many reasons. First, its mood coincided with the Depression and hard times of the 1930s, and also with the social consciousness and militant integrationism of that and the following decade. In style, it was different in a worthwhile way from what had been written during the Renaissance. Her attention to Black heroes and heroines was also timely and helped to communicate the *négritude* of the volume and the delving for roots which is one of its major themes.

After Margaret Walker's *For My People,* Gwendolyn Brooks published *A Street in Bronzeville* in 1945 and went on to win the Pulitzer Prize (the first Black to do so) in 1950 for her 1949 volume *Annie Allen.* From this point on, Black women are well represented in poetry. In the 1950s and early '60s, Margaret Danner, Naomi Madgett, and Gloria Oden are significant. In the 1960s, poetry exploded (as did Black America) and in this second Renaissance, women were not left out. Walker, after a twenty-eight-year poetic silence, published two more books of poems. Brooks, also of an earlier period, has gone through changes and remained current, productive, and good. And important new names have appeared, including Audre Lorde, Sonia Sanchez, Lucille Clifton, Nikki Giovanni, Mari Evans, June Jordan, and Alice Walker. These writers show all of the characteristics of the poetry of the Black sixties while revealing, at the same time, their wonderful woman/ human selves. They are a large and exciting group and, as a group, are of a higher order or quality and achievement than the comparable group of Black male poets.

Whereas, in the thirty years from 1915 to 1945, one could name only about fourteen female poets, the number swells to near fifty for the almost thirty years following—and it is constantly growing. When proportionate figures are compared, more of the Black women who are writers are primarily poets as compared to the men, showing that more women than men have turned to this form of creative and literary expression. In it, they have wrought well.

Notes

1. Phillis Wheatley, *Poems on Various Subjects, Religious and Moral* (London: Bell, 1773). Quotations from her poems are from this first edition.
2. Arthur P. Davis, "Personal Elements in the Poetry of Phillis Wheatley," *Phylon,* 14 (1963), 192.
3. Sterling A. Brown, Arthur P. Davis, and Ulysses Lee, eds., *The Negro Caravan* (New York: Arno Press and the New York *Times,* 1969), p. 293.
4. Quoted from William H. Robinson, Jr., ed., *Early Black American Poets* (Dubuque, Iowa: Wm. C. Brown, 1971), p. 27. Quotations from Harper's poetry are also taken from this collection.
5. Gwendolyn Brooks, *Report from Part One* (Detroit: Broadside Press, 1972), p. 56.
6. Robert T. Kerlin, ed., *Negro Poets and Their Poems,* 2nd ed. (Washington, D.C.: Associated Pubs., 1938), p. 146.
7. James Weldon Johnson, ed., *The Book of American Negro Poetry,* rev. ed. (New York: Harcourt, Brace & World, 1931), p. 181. All quotations of her poems are from this work except "The Supplicant," which is taken from Langston Hughes and Arna Bontemps, eds., *The Poetry of the Negro, 1746-1970* (Garden City, N.Y.: Doubleday & Company, 1970), p. 76.
8. Countee Cullen, ed., *Caroling Dusk: An Anthology of Verse by Negro Poets* (New York: Harper & Brothers, 1927), p. 47.
9. Johnson, p. 214. All other quotations of her work come from Hughes and Bontemps.
10. Kerlin, p. 158.
11. Johnson, p. 213.
12. Sterling Brown, *Negro Poetry and Drama* (1937) (New York: Atheneum Publishers, 1969), p. 65.
13. Johnson, p. 279.
14. Ibid., p. 280. "Magalu" is quoted from Hughes and Bontemps, p. 263.
15. Margaret Walker, *For My People* (New Haven: Yale University Press, 1942), p. 13. This is the source for all citations of her poetry.

CHERYL A. WALL (ESSAY DATE 2000)

SOURCE: Wall, Cheryl A. Foreword. In *This Waiting for Love: Helene Johnson, Poet of the Harlem Renaissance,* edited by Verner D. Mitchell, pp. ix-xiii. Amherst: University of Massachusetts Press, 2000.

In this essay, Wall discusses the long-felt need for a collection of Johnson's poetry. She briefly mentions Johnson's place among the larger lights of the Harlem Renaissance and expores the forward-looking nature of her writings.

In many years of teaching courses on the Harlem Renaissance, I have learned to look forward to the days I introduce Helene Johnson's poems to my students. Few have heard of her, and almost none have encountered her work. But their delight in her poems almost never fails to equal my own. Two of Johnson's lyrics are among my favorites: **"Sonnet to a Negro in Harlem"** and **"Poem."**

Addressing the young migrant, newly arrived in Harlem, the sonneteer proclaims:

> You are disdainful and magnificent—
> Your perfect body and your pompous gait,
> Your dark eyes flashing solemnly with hate;
> Small wonder that you are incompetent
> To imitate those whom you so despise—

The qualities of contempt and resplendence reinforce each other, even as they repel and attract those passersby who hold the Negro in their gaze. If the poem's subject is destined never to adapt to urban life, he finds solace in the fierceness of his pride. My students applaud the swagger and recognize the rage. So does the speaker who concludes, "You are too splendid for this city street!" Despite its dated references to palm trees and "barbaric" song, the sonnet's representation of alienation in the inner city seems as current as hip-hop.

My other favorite is tied more tightly to its time. **"Poem"** celebrates the African American popular culture that so defined the zeitgeist of the 1920s that the decade was dubbed the Jazz Age. Written in free verse black vernacular, the poem

FROM THE AUTHOR

"LITTLE BROWN BOY"

Gee, boy, when you sing, I can close my
 ears
And hear tom-toms just as plain.
Listen to me, will you, what do I know
About tom-toms? But I like the word,
 sort of,
Don't you? It belongs to us.

SOURCE: Helene Johnson, from "Little Brown Boy," in *American Negro Poetry,* edited by Arna Bontemps, revised edition, Hill and Wang, 1974.

addresses the crooning, tap-dancing, process-wearing, banjo-playing "jazz prince," who inspires it. But the poem's language collapses the distance between audience and performer. The terms of address are deeply personal: "Gee, boy, I love the way you hold your head / and the way you sing, and dance, / And everything." **"Poem"** is a performance piece, one in which Helene Johnson responds to the call of the musicians she has admired on the stage of Harlem's Lafayette Theater. As my students perform it in class, I think they begin to understand better the pride and exhilaration that defined the moment "when Harlem was in vogue."[1]

The ease with which Johnson moves from the rigor of the sonnet to the free idiom of "your shoulders jerking the jig-wa" is impressive. So too is the grace with which she slips the yoke of racial politics. Johnson offers no apologies for her love of laughter, dance, music, and color. While she seems always aware of a larger clash of cultures, she is impatient with constraints imposed on the behavior of ordinary people ostensibly for reasons of progress or propriety. She seems to recognize that these constraints in fact reflect racist and sexist thinking. Yet Johnson never seems to take herself or her "situation" too seriously. The leavening of humor is ever at hand. Consequently, it is always a disappointment to have to tell my students that Helene Johnson was a poet of great promise, who wrote only a handful of poems and who, like several other mysterious women, disappeared from the Harlem Renaissance leaving barely a trace.

This Waiting For Love comes then as an unexpected and most welcome gift. Here Verner Mitchell has collected all thirty-four of Helene Johnson's published poems, many of which have not been reprinted since they first appeared in various small magazines of the 1920s and 1930s: *The Saturday Evening Quill, Palms, Opportunity, Harlem,* and *Challenge.* Even many of us who are Johnson admirers do not know poems like **"Night," "Cui Bono?," "Regalia,"** and **"Futility,"** the poem that gives this volume its title. Moreover, those poems we recognize including **"Bottled," "Fulfillment," "A Missionary Brings a Young Native to America,"** and **"A Southern Road"** seem new in the context of this volume. Not only does the imagery of **"A Southern Road"** anticipate the imagery of Billie Holiday's famous song "Strange Fruit," but its use of religious metaphors to protest lynching also looks back to poems by Claude McKay and forward to those by Gwendolyn Brooks. Johnson's statement is distinctive nonetheless. **"Invocation"** and **"Summer Matures"** explore the erotic, but from a safe distance. In the former, distance derives from the poem's many classical allusions; in the latter, the speaker invokes flora and fauna "riotous, rampant, wild and free," but only to cover her grave. As I reread **"Magula,"** one of Johnson's most richly textured poems, the phrase "chromatic words" struck me as a perfect gloss for my two favorite poems. Color and music are what they evoke for me.

In addition to the poems and an excellent introduction that locates Helene Johnson's work in the context of the Harlem Renaissance, Verner Mitchell has compiled a chronology of her life that begins to lift the veil that she placed over it. She guarded her privacy so jealously that it was only in the 1970s that scholars discovered her married name, though she had wed William Warner Hubbell in 1933. I well remember my excitement in February 1987, when I read a brief notice in the *New York Times* that announced a reading of the works by "one of the last surviving Harlem Renaissance poets." It had taken place the night before. At the time I was doing research for my book, *Women of the Harlem Renaissance.* Every reference I consulted gave only the same few facts about Johnson's girlhood, just as every anthology reprinted the same few poems. I had often wondered whether Johnson was still alive. Reading that notice I could scarcely believe that she had given a poetry reading—*or*—that I had missed it.[2] Immediately, I called the theater where the reading had taken place. The manager gave me the name and number of Johnson's daughter, Abigail McGrath, who told me that her eighty-year-old mother declined to be interviewed but suggested that I send any questions that I had in writing. Many months later, Johnson returned my questionnaire. The handwritten answers were too brief not to seem grudging. Everything about the exchange made me feel that my inquiries were invasive. Despite my disappointment, I could not help but admire Johnson's finely honed sense of irony. In response to my final question that asked if she were surprised by the continuing interest in the Harlem Renaissance, Johnson answered sharply: "never surprised by repetition."

I have good reason, therefore, to be impressed by the amount of new information that Verner Mitchell has uncovered about Johnson's life. Here are fresh facts concerning her childhood, one that she shared with her cousin, who grew up to be the novelist Dorothy West. These discoveries complicate the conventional wisdom about their privileged background. Here too is correspondence between Johnson, West, and Zora Neale Hurston, who sublet her New York apartment to the cousins while she collected folklore in the South. Hurston had met Johnson and West when all were feted at *Opportunity* magazine's Second Annual Literary Awards Dinner in May 1926. As Mitchell documents, their friendship outlasted the Harlem Renaissance. In addition to her links to Hurston and West, Mitchell uncovers important connections between Johnson and other literary and visual artists, including Gwendolyn Bennett, Lois Mailou Jones, and Wallace Thurman.

Johnson's last published poem, **"Let Me Sing My Song,"** appeared in 1935 in *Challenge,* the journal Dorothy West founded in an attempt to revive the spirit of the Harlem Renaissance. The journal was short-lived, despite a subsequent attempt by associate editor Richard Wright to ally it with radical politics. But Helen Johnson did not stop "singing." She ceased to publish but she continued to write. ***This Waiting for Love*** includes thirteen previously unpublished pieces. **"He's About 22. I'm 63"** (written circa 1970) offers irrefutable proof that Johnson's sense of humor remained intact.

After Helene Johnson died on 6 July 1995, the *New York Times* published an obituary that was accompanied by a selection of poems, under the heading "A Voice of Youth From a Renaissance." It was wonderful to see her legacy honored, even for one day. ***This Waiting for Love*** is an enduring tribute, one that provides the opportunity for a new generation of readers to discover the vibrant poetry of Helene Johnson. Answer the invitation that is extended to Magula:

> Oh Magula, come! Take my hand and I will read
> you
> poetry,
> Chromatic words,
> Seraphic symphonies, . . .

Notes

1. Langston Hughes, *The Big Sea* (1940; reprint, New York: Hill and Wang, 1993), 227.
2. I have since learned that Johnson did not appear in person; instead, she recorded her poems on a tape, which she sent to the reading.

VERNER D. MITCHELL (ESSAY DATE 2000)

SOURCE: Mitchell, Verner D. Introduction. In *This Waiting for Love: Helene Johnson, Poet of the Harlem Renaissance,* pp. 3-20. Amherst: University of Massachusetts Press, 2000.

In this essay, Mitchell provides an overview of Johnson's life and career, including her relationship with her cousin, the fiction writer Dorothy West. Mitchell concludes with a study of Johnson's poem "Magula."

Students of the Harlem Renaissance have long appreciated Helene Johnson's talent. But because so many of her poems are located in older, often inaccessible journals (*Challenge, Fire!!, Harlem, The Messenger, Palms,* and so on) teaching and even reading her work has been difficult. Eugene B. Redmond accordingly captures a long-standing sentiment in his 1976 study, *Drumvoices: The Mission of Afro-American Poetry.* He dubs Johnson an important minor poet whose entire "output should be collected and published in book form."[1] The following volume, ***This Waiting for Love,*** is the first book ever published on Johnson and an answer to Redmond's call. The volume makes Johnson's poetry from the twenties and thirties, as well as previously unpublished poems from the sixties, seventies, and eighties, available to her many enthusiasts. More important, it brings Johnson's art to new generations of readers.

As the title ***This Waiting for Love*** suggests, Johnson's poems defy the genteel conventions that governed many early twentieth-century female writers. Her verse also offers a penetrating insight into 1920s America, particularly into the artistic community. Several of her poems respond to aesthetic and political conflicts during the Harlem Renaissance. They counter, for example (as does Langston Hughes's celebrated 1926 essay "The Negro Artist and the Racial Mountain"), the aesthetics of older writers such as Alain Locke and W. E. B. Du Bois. Recall Locke's comments about jazz: "Unfortunately, but temporarily, what is best known are the vulgarizations; and of these 'Jazz' and by-products are in the ascendancy."[2] Recall, too, Du Bois's caustic reaction to Claude McKay's 1928 novel *Home to Harlem:* "for the most part [it] nauseates me, and after the dirtier parts of its filth I feel distinctly like taking a bath."[3] Johnson's dialogue and dispute with members of the literary establishment make her, at a minimum, an important and powerful foremother. Her role can perhaps be best illustrated through a sustained reading of her 1926 poem **"Magula."** But first, some background information on the poet and on what some term the "radical" nature of her verse.

Johnson was born 7 July 1906, in Boston, Massachusetts, to Ella Benson Johnson, of Camden, South Carolina, and George William Johnson, of Nashville, Tennessee. She was an only child.[4] Shortly after her birth her parents separated, and thus she never knew her father or her father's parents. Her mother's parents, Benjamin Benson and Helen Pease Benson—after whom Johnson was named—had been born into slavery in South Carolina.[5]

> Mama [Johnson's grandmother] was born a slave, bound to obedience. . . . All too soon she was bound again. For at fifteen she was bound in marriage to my nineteen-year-old grandfather. . . . Then Mama was bound forever by her batches of babies, her girlhood over before it was ever experienced.[6]

After his wife's death, Benjamin Benson, a minister, followed three of his daughters—Ella, Minnie, and Rachel—north to Massachusetts. There he summered in the town of Oak Bluffs on Martha's Vineyard Island, and earned his living as a carpenter. Rachel's daughter and Johnson's first cousin, the novelist and short story writer Dorothy West, would later live in Oak Bluffs (on property bought by her grandfather Benjamin Benson)[7] until her death in August 1998, at age ninety-one.

Johnson and West grew up together at 478 Brookline Avenue, in the Brookline section of Boston. They spent most of their summers at Oak Bluffs. As West explains, "The house that I grew up in was four-storied, but we were an extended family."[8]

> My mother's mother had eighteen children, and, later on—because my father [a greengrocer in downtown Boston] was doing quite well—many of my mother's sisters and nephews and nieces came to live with us. All of us had different complexions—at one end there was a blond kid and at the other end there was me. . . . My mother was a light woman, and my Aunt Minnie looked white. Those were the two people who brought me up. There were four of us children. They were my first cousins. A blond kid, an olive-skinned kid, a golden-skin kid, and me.[9]

Johnson, the eldest of the cousins, was the golden-skin kid. She was also the prototype for the character Vicky, in West's novel *The Living Is Easy.* Chapter 19 of the novel captures the excited little cousins on a Christmas morning: "Victoria was the first to scamper out of bed, where she lay beside Lily, her mother. Vicky was seven, a tall, butter-colored, red-cheeked child, whose seniority of six months over Penny [Aunt Minnie's daughter, Jean] and ten months over Judy [Dorothy West] made her the unquestioned leader of the little girls."[10] Chapter 29 presents the cousins, now fifth-graders, as avid readers and aspiring writers: "Restless, fun loving Vicky could be sobered and inspired by the simple act of opening a book. She turned pages tenderly, not wanting to break the ebony thread that wove itself into a wonderful pattern of words. And the words were the explanation of life, the key to understanding. She, the child of Cleo's [Aunt Rachel's] heart, was the child whose intelligence equaled Cleo's hope."[11]

According to T. J. Bryan, Johnson "credited her early interest in writing to her mother, who provided her with new experiences; to the supplemental education she received at home; and to her exploration of library books."[12] Johnson and West attended Boston's Lafayette School, the Martin School, and the prestigious Boston Girls' Latin School. After Girls' Latin, they took writing courses at Boston University and joined The Saturday Evening Quill Club, an organization of aspiring black Boston writers. The 1929 number of the club's annual, *The Saturday Evening Quill,* features West's story "Prologue to a Life" as well as seven of Johnson's poems.

In April of 1926, the cousins, now ages nineteen and eighteen, traveled from Boston to New York City for a brief visit. The following year, still full of zest and awe, they returned to the city. This time the cousins came to stay and to continue their education, enrolling in Columbia University's Extension Division, where they studied with the novelist John Erskine.[13] Soon after their move, they were ushered gently into the heart of Harlem's literary renaissance by the able and witty raconteur Zora Neale Hurston. Wallace Thurman's satirical roman à clef, *Infants of the Spring* (1932), presents Hurston as Sweetie May Carr and famously details the cousins' entrance:

> Sweetie May was accompanied by two young girls, recently emigrated from Boston. They were the latest to be hailed incipient immortals. Their names were Doris Westmore [West] and Hazel Jamison [Johnson]. Doris wrote short stories. Hazel wrote poetry. . . . Raymond [Thurman] liked them more than he did most of the younger recruits to the movement. For one thing, they were characterized by a freshness and naïveté which he and his cronies had lost. And, surprisingly enough for Negro prodigies, they actually gave promise of possessing literary talent.[14]

The events that led them to move, in West's words, to "the magical city of New York" had been set in motion three years earlier.[15] Toward the end of 1924 Johnson submitted a poem, **"Trees at Night,"** to the Urban League's official magazine, *Opportunity*. Her poem was accepted for publication and eventually appeared in the journal. Then, when the Urban League held its first annual literary awards ceremony in May 1925, **"Trees at Night"** won an honorable mention. Encouraged by her success, Johnson decided to enter three poems in the 1926 contest, and West, at Johnson's urging, penned and submitted a short story. West reports that in due time they received invitations to the awards ceremony, and they were "overwhelmed with joy."[16]

They persuaded their parents—Rachel and Isaac West and Ella Johnson—to let them go to New York City to attend the awards dinner on May 1. Neither was disappointed. Johnson's **"Fulfillment," "Magula,"** and **"The Road,"** won first, fourth, and seventh honorable mentions, and West's "The Typewriter" shared the second-place prize for fiction along with Hurston's short story "Muttsy." For West, sharing the prize with the older writer was unsettling, but, as she explains, that initial, somewhat awkward meeting resulted in a lifelong friendship:

> God, with whom I had lengthy conversations in my childhood and presumed had got to know me and my aspirations, allowed me to share a second prize with the now legendary Zora Neale Hurston. At first she had mixed feelings about sharing a prize with an unknown teenager. But in time I became her little sister, and my affection for her has never diminished. In time I was to play my part in the Harlem Renaissance. I was nineteen and its youngest member.[17]

Thus at the 1926 *Opportunity* awards dinner, cousins West and Johnson began their long friendship with Zora Neale Hurston. And in so doing, they received their first taste of Harlem's magic.[18]

West has been best known for her 1948 novel *The Living Is Easy,* although she is currently in the midst of a literary rebirth, owing to her well-received memoir *The Richer, The Poorer: Stories, Sketches, and Reminiscences* (1995), and her best-selling 1995 novel *The Wedding.* She finished the latter work with the help of her Martha's Vineyard neighbor Jacqueline Onassis. "To the memory of my editor, Jacqueline Kennedy Onassis," reads the book's gracious dedication. "Though there was never such a mismatched pair in appearance, we were perfect partners." "It's interesting that so much is happening and so many people have called," West beamed in a 1995 interview. "At my age it didn't have to happen."[19]

Johnson, by contrast, is still relatively unknown. Surely much of her popular and critical neglect can be explained by the fact that heretofore there has been no available volume of her writings. Also, unlike West, who continued to write (and never married), Johnson took a lengthy hiatus from her writing when she married William Hubbell and had to help support her family. The couple's only child, Abigail McGrath, recalls her father working for the Brooklyn shipyard and her mother working both inside the home and outside, as a civil service employee. Years later, speaking of the writer's need for "a certain laxity," Johnson explained: "It's very difficult for a poor person to be that unfastened. They have to eat. In order to eat, you have to be fastened and tightly. . . . [Y]ou don't have too much time to go in another direction. And to write anything (it can be poetry or anything at all), you have to have time. You have to sit and rock like a fool or look out the window, and something will come by."[20] Johnson last published a poem in May 1935, two years after her marriage.

Over the years, Johnson generally remained out of the public eye. Always painfully shy, she declined an invitation to give a public poetry reading (at New York City's Off Center Theater) as recently as February 1987, at age eighty.[21] The following year, West's wide-ranging interview with Katrine Dalsg rd shed light on the cousins' early days in Manhattan. We learned, for example, that after arriving in the city, they shared a room at the Harlem YWCA. Later, when "Zora got a grant [and] went South," recalls West, "Helene and I took over her apartment."[22] West also discussed their friendships with such luminaries as Claude McKay, A'Lelia Walker, Wallace Thurman, Carl Van Vechten, Countee Cullen, and Langston Hughes.

From the early 1960s to the early 1980s, Johnson lived at 210 Thompson Street, her "dream" apartment in Greenwich Village. She always loved Greenwich Village, and she particularly enjoyed the young people she came to know from her outings to Judson Poet's Theater and Washington Square Park (both two blocks from her apartment).[23] With the exception of a few years on Cape Cod in the 1980s, Johnson lived her entire adult life (over half a century) in New York City. She died in Manhattan on July 6, 1995, the day before her eighty-ninth birthday.[24]

Four years younger than poets Gwendolyn Bennett and Langston Hughes, Johnson is described in the July 1926 edition of *Opportunity* as "perhaps the youngest of the new group of Negro poets" (232). Miss Johnson "possesses true lyric talent," observed James Weldon Johnson in 1931. "She is one of the younger group who has taken . . . the 'racial' bull by the horns. She has taken the very qualities and circumstances that have long called for apology or defense and extolled them in an unaffected manner."[25] Over a half century later, Patricia Liggins Hill notes that "Johnson's racial poems established her during the 1920s as one of the brightest lights shining among the up-and-coming young poets. One has to wonder," she adds, "what the literary fate of this talented poet would have been if she had received the patronage and critical attention enjoyed by several of the male poets of the time."[26] Similarly, in a 1998 interview, the Pulitzer Prize-winning poet Yusef Komunyakaa observes that Johnson was the youngest and most talented of the Harlem Renaissance poets. "It's a shame," he continues, "that she was unable to reconcile the demands of working nine to five and writing."[27]

Another who sang Johnson's praise was a judge for the 1926 *Opportunity* contest, Robert Frost. Frost called Johnson's **"The Road"** the "finest" poem submitted.[28] Perhaps he thought that Johnson's "nature" poems, set in her beloved New England, echoed his! **"The Road,"** also reminiscent of Whitman's "Song of the Open Road," uses nature as a controlling metaphor in a captivating expression of racial pride. Most of Johnson's early poems (published between May 1925 and June 1926) focus on nature. Trees become "Slim Sentinels / Stretching lacy arms / About a slumbrous moon" in **"Trees at Night"**; the sea in **"Metamorphism"** is "This sudden birth of unrestrained splendor." And in **"Fulfillment,"** a poet longs

To climb a hill that hungers for the sky,
To dig my hands wrist deep in pregnant earth,
To watch a young bird, veering, learn to fly,
To give a still, stark poem shining birth.

After Johnson moved to New York City, she saw poverty up close—witnessing, in particular, the hard time African Americans had, and personally experiencing the glass ceiling. In time, she drifted away from the lighthearted nature verse, and, notes her daughter, "her personality became more radical, politically, socially, and economically."

When contemplating how to organize the poems in this collection, I considered arranging them chronologically within three thematic categories: Nature, Race and Gender, and Love. The difficulty, of course, is that thematic groupings always overlap. In which group, for instance, would one place **"A Southern Road,"** a poem that protests a lynching, but a poem whose controlling metaphor is a beautiful southern road? Because so many of Johnson's poems resist thematic categories, I eventually decided simply to present them according to their original publication dates. An advantage to this chronological arrangement is that the reader will be able to study the progression and evolution of Johnson's poetics.

I take the book's title from the brief 1926 poem **"Futility."**

It is silly—
This waiting for love
In a parlor.
When love is singing up and down the alley
Without a collar.

Like Andrew Marvell's "To His Coy Mistress" and Gwendolyn Brooks's "a song in the front yard," **"Futility"** renders a ringing endorsement of love without coyness or shame. And in rejecting bourgeois rituals of courtship, it exemplifies the air of defiant sensuality present in so much of Johnson's verse.

Although her love poetry usually focuses on erotic themes, Johnson also deals with less controversial images of love. Her octave **"Mother,"** to cite one example, meditates on a mother's love of Christ and the intense love shared by mother and daughter. At the opposite end of the spectrum, and thematically more representative of Johnson's verse, are **"The Little Love,"** ***"Cui Bono?,"*** **"Foraging," "He's about 22. I'm 63,"** and the long dramatic monologue **"Widow with a Moral Obligation."** In the latter work, the widow, having sensed the presence of her long dead husband, runs away from her new "friend." I quote the opening lines:

Won't you come again, my friend?
I'll not be so shy.
I shall have a candle lit
To light you by.
I shall have my hair unbound,

My gown undone,
And we shall have a night of love
And death in one.
I was very foolish
To have run away before,
But you see I thought I heard
Him knocking at the door . . .

As the above poems partially illustrate, Johnson's preferred form was the free verse of Whitman or Hughes, rather than the more formal structures of the nineteenth-century British Romantics, preferred by Cullen and to a lesser extent by McKay. Nonetheless, on occasion, she did write sonnets. Her favorite subjects were love, protest, female sexual awakenings, the importance of the African past, the sensuousness of nature, and black cultural pride—matters considered inappropriate by the genteel readers of the early twentieth century. Indeed, Johnson's willingness to challenge accepted boundaries—both aesthetic and political—is likely the most prominent feature of her poetry.

I conclude my introduction with a reading of one of Johnson's more overtly political poems, **"Magula."** This poem succinctly illustrates the "radical" nature of Johnson's verse. As critic Maureen Honey notes, "The radical nature of [Johnson's] poetry lies not only in its employ of what was considered non-poetic language, but also in Johnson's praise of those aspects of Black culture most despised by whites. She loved insouciance, sensuality, vivacity, and celebrated them."[29]

"Magula" was first published in the October 1926 number of *Palms.* The list of contributors to this special issue, guest edited by Countee Cullen, reads like a Harlem Renaissance "Who's Who." Established writers Jessie Fauset, Du Bois, Locke, William Stanley Braithwaite, Georgia Douglas Johnson, and Anne Spencer contributed pieces, as did several of the younger ones: Gwendolyn Bennett, Walter White, Arna Bontemps, Bruce Nugent, Clarissa Scott Delaney, Langston Hughes, and, of course, Helene Johnson.

Subsequent collections in which **"Magula"** appeared, from *Caroling Dusk: An Anthology of Verse by Negro Poets* in 1927, to *Shadowed Dreams: Women's Poetry of the Harlem Renaissance* in 1989, incorrectly identify the poem as "Magalu." I have retained Johnson's original spelling. The poem is a free-verse dramatization of the inner mythic "good person / bad person" struggle for the titular character's heart and soul. To that end, it dramatizes a metaphoric tug-of-love for an African woman's affections. Johnson adeptly delays the moment of confrontation, creating first an expectation of pleasure with the two-word sentence, "Summer comes." Against this background, the poem sprinkles animated images of the natural world. At this level it caters to shallow consumers of Renaissance literary production, giving them exactly what they look for and want—a flashy, exotic vision of Africa. By poem's end, however, Johnson has deftly destabilized those expectations.

Summer comes.
The ziczac hovers
'Round the greedy-mouthed crocodile.
A vulture bears away a foolish jackal.
The flamingo is a dash of pink
Against dark green mangroves,
Her slender legs rivalling her slim neck.

The rich word play on "bears" invites interpretation. First, "bears" meshes harmoniously with the other animal appellations (ziczac, crocodile, vulture, jackal, flamingo); second, it shows the vulture "bearing" away the foolish jackal; and, third, it hints that the vulture and jackal are entwined in an intimate and fatal embrace ("bear" hug). Is the ziczac moments away from a similar fate? In drawing our attention to the flamingo's fragility and vulnerability—her slender legs and slim neck—the poem seems to support this reading. Such a reading suggests an extended analogy between the devoured or soon-to-be devoured animals and vulnerable Magula.

Critic Erlene Stetson posits a more upbeat reading. According to her, the ziczac is "an Egyptian species of plover who warns the crocodile of approaching danger by its cry."[30] Thus, the ziczac and crocodile are symbolic soul mates, and the ziczac's warning both foreshadows and parallels the speaker's plea to Magula. An added benefit of Stetson's reading is that it locates the poem in Africa. Consequently, the pretty flamingo, "a dash of pink / Against dark green mangroves," becomes a rich foil against the dark Magula:

The laughing lake gurgles delicious music in its throat
And lulls to sleep the lazy lizard,
A nebulous being on a sun-scorched rock.
In such a place,
In this pulsing, riotous gasp of color,
I met Magula, dark as a tree at night,
Eager lipped, listening to a man with a white collar
And a small black book with a cross on it.

In this world view, "dark" retains its pre-Western meaning; not a vehicle of fear and the demonic, darkness is a coequal member of the rainbow's "pulsing, riotous gasp of color." Danger then comes not from the darkness, but from the glaring absence of camouflage between pink/dark green, and dark/white. Threatening dark Magula is the "man with a white collar." His "small black book" is an enticing trap to dark Magula, but it is also an extension of the constraining collar which seeks to stifle Magula's dance.

The opening lines, then, are action-packed portraits of the African wild. There is an aura of danger, but this danger contributes a sense of excitement which is preferable to a staid and colorless (black book and white collar) world without dance. Having established a static frame with the end-stopped "Summer comes," the poem rushes forward—hovering, bearing, rivalling, laughing, pulsing—toward the central meeting, when it again stops. All eyes, accordingly, converge on unprotected Magula.

Suggestive of 1920s Harlem, the laughing lake's soothing syncopation vibrates with "delicious music," lulling the lazy lizard to sleep. Magula, too, is susceptible to hypnosis. But unlike the laughing lake's emancipating rhythms, the music produced by the man is foreign, unnatural, and confining. Therefore the poem forcefully rejects the constraining, universalizing polemic of the white collar and the black book. Notice that the "nebulous being on a sun-scorched rock," the chameleon-like lizard, unites with the speaker's chromatic words to embody the rainbow's "pulsing, riotous gasp of color." In contrast, the man with the white collar spurns diversity, seeing only in black and white, and offering a creed that will not let Magula dance. Given the centrality of dance to African culture, any creed which rejects dance would be psychically and physically harmful for Magula. Critic Beverley Bryan, writing in *The Heart of the Race* (1986), correctly discerns the importance of dance in African culture: "Alongside music, dance has been our most important form of cultural expression. . . . Historically dance has always been integral to Black culture. There is literally a dance for everything, back in the land of our ancestors—a dance for death, for birth, for weddings, for social occasions, for everything you can imagine."[31]

Next, the poem's "I" enters, offering—with Whitman-esque affection—poetry that can rescue Magula from the alien tempter with the white collar:

Oh Magula, come! Take my hand and I will read
  you
  poetry,
Chromatic words,
Seraphic symphonies,
Fill your throat with laughter and your heart
  with song.
Do not let him lure you from your laughing
  waters,
Lulling lakes, lissome winds.
Would you sell the colors of your sunset and
  fragrance
Of your flowers, and the passionate wonder of
  your forest
For a creed that will not let you dance?

Clearly the speaker is a poetic guide who can lead Magula away from that which threatens her. But precisely where will the speaker steer Magula? Exploring possible answers to this question will show the boldness and beauty of Johnson's artistic vision.

During the antebellum era, black women were stereotyped as loyal mammies who were innately equipped only for nursing white children, scrubbing floors, and an array of other domestic chores that their "delicate" mistresses would not perform. In point of fact, from John Wheatley's Massachusetts to Thomas Jefferson's Monticello, "faithful" black females were forced to tend other people's households. By the time of Johnson's writings, however, the stereotype had curiously become inverted. No longer dependable mammies, black women were now seen as lascivious and sexually insatiable, unsafe near any household.[32] Thus, when the poetic guide implores Magula to realize the beauty of her flowers and the passionate wonder of her forest, the guide is rejecting societally imposed definitions and constraints for black female sexuality and personhood. Defiantly shunning the man's creed, the wise guide seeks to focus Magula's attention to the wonder of her laughing waters, lulling lakes, lissome winds: natural bridges leading to the deepest sites of passion and wholeness. Once secure in the loving embrace of her own forest, Magula's heart will blossom with song and her feet with dance.

Some, no doubt fearful that artistic explorations of passion would fuel negative stereotypes, strove to mute the black music and dance. The distinguished Harlem Renaissance philosopher and Rhodes Scholar Alain Locke, for example, described jazz as "a submerged and half-inarticulate motive in Negro doggerel," a "mere trickery of syncopation." Similarly, he called the "Jazz school" of Negro poetry a "vulgarization."[33] Writing in his "New Negro" essay of 1925, Locke insists that socially conscious artists should eschew vulgar forms so they can then function as "the advance-guard of the African peoples" to rehabilitate "the race in world esteem. . . . The especially cultural recognition they win should in turn prove the key to that revaluation of the Negro which must precede or accompany any considerable further betterment of race relationships."[34] **"Magula's"** appearance in October of 1926 clearly indicates that Johnson was unwilling to suppress the colors of her sunset or to adhere to any creed that would not let her dance.

Later that same year (1926) Johnson and Hurston helped organize the avant-garde journal *Fire!!*, subtitled *A Quarterly Devoted to the Younger Negro Artists.* Its inaugural issue featured a number of erotic drawings, Wallace Thurman's vignette of a sixteen-year-old prostitute "Cordelia the Crude," Gwendolyn Bennett's "Wedding Day," the story of a former boxer and jazz musician left at the altar by a white prostitute, and Richard Bruce Nugent's "Smoke, Lilies, and Jade," the first African American work to openly explore homosexuality.[35] By challenging forthrightly the Victorian sensibilities of Locke and others in the black literary establishment, the publication of *Fire!!* was the culminating act of a movement that Arnold Rampersad describes (in something of an overstatement) as the students, the younger writers, dispensing with their dean, Alain Locke.[36]

In noting that Helene Johnson's "imagination was clearly activated by the sights and sounds of jazz age Harlem," Maureen Honey endorses my interpretation of a Magula at home, both in the vibrant and exciting world of Harlem's Jazz Age, and beside the "laughing waters, / Lulling lakes, lissome winds" of dark Africa. Concerning **"Magula,"** she writes that "the speaker warns a young African woman not to be seduced by a missionary to whom she is eagerly listening."[37] Although Honey's reading is convincing, Johnson's rich art resists restrictive interpretations, demanding that it be viewed from several different angles, open to many perspectives. How, for example, do we know that Magula is a woman? The flamingo is female, and the man is definitely male, but the poem provides no other references to gender. The poem goes to considerable lengths to sidestep gender; in fact, the "I" narrator is arguably both and neither male/female, much like the narrator of Toni Morrison's *Jazz.* Furthermore, the name Magula is indeterminate, one which resists gender constructions. From this perspective, Magula becomes a composite of dark youth—both male and female. And poet Johnson is seeking to save not just one child, but an entire race, an entire people. It is here in Johnson's goal that I find the compelling vitality of her art.

This Waiting for Love recognizes Helene Johnson as an important literary foremother. It celebrates the import of her life and art. Now her laughing lake can gurgle its delicious music to all Magulas present and future.

Notes

1. Eugene B. Redmond, *Drumvoices: The Mission of Afro-American Poetry, A Critical History* (Garden City, N.Y.: Anchor, 1976), 207.
2. Alain Locke, "The Negro in American Culture" (1929), in *Black Voices,* ed. Abraham Chapman (New York: Mentor, 1968), 524.
3. W. E. B. Du Bois, "Two Novels," *The Crisis* 35 (June 1928): 202.
4. Cheryl A. Wall, unpublished mail interview with Helene Johnson, June 1987.
5. T. J. Bryan, "Helene Johnson," in *Notable Black American Women,* ed. Jessie Carney Smith (Detroit: Gale, 1992), 587.
6. Dorothy West, *The Richer, the Poorer: Stories, Sketches, and Reminiscences* (New York: Anchor, 1995), 186.
7. Bryan, "Helene Johnson," 587.
8. West, *The Richer, The Poorer,* 167.
9. Rachel West lists her mother's and stepmother's nineteen children, some of whom died in infancy, from oldest to youngest: Robert, Wilkie, David, Ella, Carrie (also known as Dolly), Rachel, Mattie, Isabella, Minnie, Bennie, Jessie, Scotter, Eugene, Scipio, Emma, Belton, Sarah, Malcom, and Ruth (Dorothy West Papers, Schlesinger Library, Harvard University). Quoted in Katrine Dalsg rd, "Alive and Well and Living on the Island of Martha's Vineyard: An Interview with Dorothy West, October 29, 1988," *The Langston Hughes Review* 12.2 (Fall 1993): 29, 32.
10. West, *The Living Is Easy* (1948; reprint, New York: The Feminist Press, 1982), 198.
11. Ibid., 299-300.
12. Bryan, "Helene Johnson," 589.
13. Gwendolyn Bennett, "The Ebony Flute," *Opportunity* (December 1926): 391; (January 1927); 28-29.
14. Thurman, *Infants of the Spring* (1932; reprint, Boston: Northeastern University Press, 1992), 230-31.
15. West, *The Richer, the Poorer,* 2.
16. Ibid., 2.
17. Ibid., 2-3.
18. On May 7, 1927, during *Opportunity's* third and final literary contest, West received a Buckner Award for her story "An Unimportant Man." Johnson's "Summer Matures" and "Sonnet to a Negro in Harlem" won the second and fourth prizes for poetry, respectively. For a list of award winners for all three years, see *Opportunity* (May 1925): 142-43; (May 1926): 156-57; (June 1927): 179.
19. Quoted in V. R. Peterson, "Talking with . . . Dorothy West," *People* 43 (March 6, 1995): 36-37. In August 1997, another first lady, Mrs. Hillary Clinton, traveled to Oak Bluffs and helped West celebrate her ninetieth birthday. The event was televised internationally on Cable News Network.

20. Quoted in Bryan, "Helene Johnson," 590. Abigail McGrath discussed her mother's life and art with me during telephone interviews conducted in January 2000.

21. "Poetry," *New York Times* (February 8, 1987): C13. The event was scheduled to help launch the City's Black History Month festivities. Abigail McGrath founded the Off Center Theater with her husband, Tony McGrath.

22. Dalsg rd, *Alive and Well,* 30.

23. Abigail McGrath, during a telephone interview with author, January 2000. In the 1960s, Judson Poet's Theater (now Judson Memorial Church) was a hub of experimental theater, music, and dance.

24. Abigail McGrath and "Obituary," *New York Times* (11 July 1995).

25. J. W. Johnson, *The Book of American Negro Poetry* (1931; reprint, New York: Harcourt, 1983), 279.

26. Patricia Liggins Hill, ed., *Call & Response: The Riverside Anthology of the African American Literary Tradition* (New York: Houghton Mifflin, 1998), 918.

27. In February 1998, Komunyakaa and I discussed Johnson at length.

28. Quoted in Gwendolyn Bennett, "The Ebony Flute," *Opportunity* (September 1926): 292.

29. Honey, "Introduction," *Shadowed Dreams: Women's Poetry of the Harlem Renaissance* (New Brunswick: Rutgers University Press, 1989), 28.

30. Erlene Stetson, *Black Sister: Poetry by Black American Women,* 1746-1980 (Bloomington: Indiana University Press, 1985), 79.

31. Beverley Bryan, Stella Dadzie, and Suzanne Scafe, eds. *The Heart of the Race: Black Women's Lives in Britain* (London: Virago Press, 1985), 202-3.

32. A more sustained examination of these two binary images, such as the one Patricia Hill Collins provides in *Black Feminist Thought: Knowledge, Consciousness, and the Politics of Empowerment* (New York: Routledge, 1991), shows that both stereotypes were actually produced and engendered, quite paradoxically, during American slavery.

33. Locke, "The Negro in American Culture," 524, 532.

34. Locke, "The New Negro," in *The New Negro: Voices of the Harlem Renaissance* (1925; reprint, New York: Macmillan, 1992), 5, 14-15.

35. This first and only issue of *Fire!!* also contains Hurston's play "Color Struck" and short story "Sweat" and Johnson's poem "A Southern Road."

36. Arnold Rampersad, *The Life of Langston Hughes* (New York: Oxford University Press, 1986), 135. For more on Locke and the Harlem Renaissance, see my essay "Alain Locke: Philosophical 'Mid-Wife' of the Harlem Renaissance," in *The Critical Pragmatism of Alain Locke,* ed. Leonard Harris (New York: Rowman & Littlefield, 1999), 191-98.

37. Honey, "Introduction," 28.

FURTHER READING

Bibliography

Griffin, Barbara L. J. "Helene Johnson." In *African American Authors, 1745-1945: A Bio-Bibliographical Critical Sourcebook,* edited by Emmanuel S. Nelson, pp. 290-96. Westport, Conn.: Greenwood Press, 2000.

Cites reviews, scholarship, and other documents relating to Johnson's life and works.

Biography

Pace, Eric. "Helene Johnson, Poet of Harlem, 89, Dies." *New York Times* (11 July 1995): D19.

Reviews the life and works of Johnson as part of her obituary.

Criticism

Ferguson, Sally Ann H. "Dorothy West and Helene Johnson in *Infants in the Spring.*" *Langston Hughes Review* 2, no. 2 (1983): 22-24.

Discusses Wallace Thurman's depiction of Johnson and her cousin in his satirical novel of the Harlem Renaissance.

Redmond, Eugene B. "A Long Ways from Home: Minor, or Second-Echalon Poets of the Renaissance." In *Drum Voices: The Mission of Afro-American Poetry,* pp. 139–203. New York: Anchor Books., 1976.

Dicusses the major themes of Johnson's poetry and presents her as one of several African American poets whose writing had an impact on the larger culture.

OTHER SOURCES FROM GALE:

Additional coverage of Johnson's life and career is contained in the following sources published by the Gale Group: *Contemporary Authors,* Vol. 181; *Dictionary of Literary Biography,* Vol. 51; and *World Poets.*

JAMES WELDON JOHNSON

(1871 - 1938)

(Born James William Johnson) American poet, novelist, editor, critic, and publisher.

Having established himself as a songwriter, poet, editor, and activist, Johnson took on the role of promoting the work of young poets during the Harlem Renaissance. He edited *The Book of American Negro Poetry* (1922), which showcased the talent of new writers, and encouraged others to have their work published. Johnson's novel, *The Autobiography of an Ex-Coloured Man,* written in 1912 and re-released in 1927, also inspired Renaissance authors with its theme of racial conflict and racial pride, and his poetry called for a spiritual reconnection with African American heritage. As an academic, leader of the NAACP, diplomat, and one of the most distinguished Black men of letters in the early twentieth century, Johnson worked to promote Black culture, fight for African American rights, and bridge the gap between Blacks and whites.

BIOGRAPHICAL INFORMATION

Johnson was born on June 17, 1871, in Jacksonville, Florida, to a middle-class, church-going family. Johnson was encouraged by his parents, who home-schooled him for a time, to study English literature and music in the European tradition. After graduating from Stanton School in Florida, he attended Atlanta University where he began writing poetry. After graduation in 1894, he took a job as the principal of Stanton. He continued to write poetry and published a newspaper, *The Daily American,* which focused on African American issues. The paper was in circulation less than one year. Johnson then studied law, became the first African American to be admitted to the bar in Florida, and began his own law practice. When his brother, John Rosamond, completed his studies in music at the New England Conservatory, Johnson collaborated with him on musical compositions, providing the poems which served as lyrics. The brothers' most famous song was "Lift Every Voice and Sing" (1900), written on the occasion of Lincoln's birthday; it became very popular in the Black community and became known as the "Negro National Anthem." Johnson and his brother also attained some success writing songs for Broadway with Bob Cole. Johnson left New York in 1906 to work with the diplomatic corps, first as U.S. Consul to Venezuela and then as Consul to Nicaragua. In 1910, Johnson took a brief leave to marry Grace Nail of New York. While employed by the diplomatic corps, Johnson had poems published in *Century Magazine* and *The Independent* and published *The Autobiography of an Ex-Coloured Man* (1912) anonymously. In 1913 Johnson changed careers again, working for *New York Age* as an editorial writer. In 1916 he was appointed field secretary for the National Association for the Advancement of Colored People

(NAACP), and from 1920 to 1930 he served as the organization's executive secretary, fighting in particular for anti-lynching legislation. During this time Johnson continued to write poetry and nonfiction, compiled anthologies of Black writing, and became a leader of the younger generation of poets of the Harlem Renaissance. In 1929 he took a position as a professor of creative writing at Fisk University and in 1934 accepted a concurrent position at New York University, the same year he published *Negro Americans, What Now?* Johnson was killed in a car accident in Great Barrington, Massachusetts, in June 1938.

MAJOR WORKS

Johnson wrote important works in a number of genres. His 1900 lyric "Lift Every Voice and Sing," first performed by the Stanton chorus for the ninety-first anniversary of Lincoln's birth, gained in popularity over the years to become the NAACP's official anthem. Johnson's only novel, *The Autobiography of an Ex-Coloured Man,* is now his best-known work. It tells the story of a light-skinned African American musician who rejects his Black roots for a life of material comfort in the white world. It explores the theme of "passing," which was a common subject among Harlem Renaissance writers. Johnson was the first to explore this subject and to write about white society from a Black perspective.

Although Johnson's novel is his most famous work, most critics consider his greatest achievement to be his poetry. His 1917 volume *Fifty Years and Other Poems* includes poems written in dialect as well as free verse, covering such subjects as racial pride, love, brotherhood, and self-sufficiency. Thereafter Johnson abandoned dialect verse, as seen in his most critically acclaimed work, *God's Trombones* (1927). Johnson declared that he reached back to the sermons of his childhood to create these "Seven Negro Songs of Free Verse," which capture the creativity of the oral tradition of the Black preacher.

Johnson also made important contributions as an editor and a mentor to other Black writers. Because of his work on Broadway and with the NAACP, he knew many of New York's influential publishers, producers, and patrons. He used his connections to help young artists get their work into print and in 1922 published *The Book of American Negro Poetry,* an anthology of poetry by Black Americans beginning with Paul Laurence Dunbar. In 1931 he published a revised edition to include works by Harlem Renaissance writers, including Langston Hughes and Sterling Brown, whose work came to prominence after 1922. Johnson also wrote a nonfiction work chronicling the achievements of Black artists in New York in *Black Manhattan* (1930). His 1933 autobiography, *Along This Way* provides details not only of his own life but of African American customs and manners, and his extended essay, *Negro Americans, What Now?* urges Blacks to take pride in their culture and to fight for racial justice through peaceful means and integration.

CRITICAL RECEPTION

During his lifetime Johnson achieved success in a great variety of endeavors, and he enjoyed distinguished careers as an educator, songwriter, poet, journalist, and activist. The anonymously published work *The Autobiography of an Ex-Coloured Man* was widely praised when it appeared in 1912, but Johnson did not immediately acknowledge its authorship because he did not want to associate himself with a story that might be rejected as dishonest. He eventually claimed it as his work in 1927, and the novel's theme of racial pride made it an important work for other writers of the Harlem Renaissance. Johnson was a respected leader of the movement because of his efforts in promoting other writers as well as advancing his own work, such as *God's Trombones,* which sought to acknowledge the power of the African American spirit. Modern critics also see Johnson's work as central to the Renaissance and view his mature poetry as groundbreaking, with its use of a new "folk idiom" rooted in African American traditions. Johnson's *The Autobiography of an Ex-Coloured Man,* was the first novel to subordinate racial protest to artistic considerations and thus was a prototype for other Renaissance artists. Scholars have examined the autobiographical elements of the novel, its use of irony and psychological elements, and its theme of "passing." The work has also enjoyed a wide readership outside of academia and has been praised for its universal appeal despite its racial theme.

PRINCIPAL WORKS

The Autobiography of an Ex-Colored Man (novel) 1912; re-released as *The Autobiography of an Ex-Coloured Man* in 1927

Fifty Years and Other Poems (poetry) 1917

The Book of American Negro Poetry [editor] (poetry) 1922; revised 1931

The Book of American Negro Spirituals [editor] (song lyrics) 1925

The Second Book of American Negro Spirituals [editor] (song lyrics) 1926

God's Trombones: Seven Negro Sermons in Verse (poetry) 1927

Black Manhattan (nonfiction) 1930

Saint Peter Relates an Incident of the Resurrection Day (poetry) 1930

Along This Way: The Autobiography of James Weldon Johnson (memoir) 1933

Negro Americans, What Now? (nonfiction) 1934

PRIMARY SOURCES

JAMES WELDON JOHNSON (SONG DATE 1900)

SOURCE: Johnson, James Weldon. "Lift Every Voice and Sing." 1900.

Johnson wrote this song (with his brother J. Rosamond Johnson composing the music) in celebration of the birthday of Abraham Lincoln. The song was originally performed in Jacksonville, Florida, by a choir of children. The work became so popular over time that it has come to be known as "The Negro National Anthem."

"LIFT EVERY VOICE AND SING"

Lift every voice and sing
Till earth and heaven ring,
Ring with the harmonies of Liberty;
Let our rejoicing rise
High as the listening skies,
Let it resound loud as the rolling sea.
Sing a song full of the faith that the dark past has
taught us,
Sing a song full of the hope that the present has
brought us.
Facing the rising sun of our new day begun,
Let us march on till victory is won.

Stony the road we trod,
Bitter the chastening rod,
Felt in the days when hope unborn had died;
Yet with a steady beat
Have not our weary feet
Come to a place for which our fathers sighed?
We have come over a way that with tears has
been watered,
We have come, treading our path through the
blood of the slaughtered,
Out from the gloomy past,
Till now we stand at last
Where the white gleam of our bright star is cast.

God of our weary years,
God of our silent tears,
Thou who hast brought us thus far on the way;
Thou who hast by Thy might
Led us into light,
Keep us forever in the path, we pray.
Lest our feet stray from the places, our God,
where we met Thee,
Lest, our hearts drunk with the wine of the
world, we forget Thee,
Shadowed beneath Thy hand,
May we forever stand.
True to our God,
True to our native land.

JAMES WELDON JOHNSON (NOVEL DATE 1912)

SOURCE: Johnson, James Weldon. "Chapter 1." In *Autobiography of an Ex-Colored Man.* Sherman, French, 1912.

Originally published anonymously in 1912, this novel did not garner much attention until it was republished under Johnson's name. Many suggest that it is more a chronicle of the author's life than a work of fiction, as he contended. Johnson later wrote his actual autobiography, Along This Way, *to eliminate the confusion.*

I know that in writing the following pages I am divulging the great secret of my life, the secret which for some years I have guarded far more carefully than any of my earthly possessions; and it is a curious study to me to analyze the motives which prompt me to do it. I feel that I am led by the same impulse which forces the un-found-out criminal to take somebody into his confidence, although he knows that the act is likely, even almost certain, to lead to his undoing. I know that I am playing with fire, and I feel the thrill which accompanies that most fascinating pastime; and, back of it all, I think I find a sort of savage and diabolical desire to gather up all the little tragedies of my life, and turn them into a practical joke on society.

And, too, I suffer a vague feeling of unsatisfaction, of regret, of almost remorse, from which I am seeking relief, and of which I shall speak in the last paragraph of this account.

I was born in a little town of Georgia a few years after the close of the Civil War. I shall not mention the name of the town, because there are people still living there who could be connected with this narrative. I have only a faint recollection of the place of my birth. At times I can close my eyes and call up in a dreamlike way things that seem to have happened ages ago in some other world. I can see in this half vision a little house—I am quite sure it was not a large one—I can remember that flowers grew in the front yard, and that around each bed of flowers was a hedge of varicolored glass bottles stuck in the ground neck down. I remember that once, while playing around in the sand, I became curious to know whether or not the bottles grew as the flowers did, and I proceeded to dig them up to find out; the investigation brought me a terrific spanking, which indelibly fixed the incident in my mind. I can remember, too, that behind the house was a shed under which stood two or three wooden wash-tubs. These tubs were the earliest aversion of my life, for regularly on certain evenings I was plunged into one of them and scrubbed until my skin ached. I can remember to this day the pain caused by the strong, rank soap's getting into my eyes.

Back from the house a vegetable garden ran, perhaps seventy-five or one hundred feet; but to my childish fancy it was an endless territory. I can still recall the thrill of joy, excitement, and wonder it gave me to go on an exploring expedition through it, to find the blackberries, both ripe and green, that grew along the edge of the fence.

I remember with what pleasure I used to arrive at, and stand before, a little enclosure in which stood a patient cow chewing her cud, how I would occasionally offer her through the bars a piece of my bread and molasses, and how I would jerk back my hand in half fright if she made any motion to accept my offer.

I have a dim recollection of several people who moved in and about this little house, but I have a distinct mental image of only two: one, my mother; and the other, a tall man with a small, dark mustache. I remember that his shoes or boots were always shiny, and that he wore a gold chain and a great gold watch with which he was always willing to let me play. My admiration was almost equally divided between the watch and chain and the shoes. He used to come to the house evenings, perhaps two or three times a week; and it became my appointed duty whenever he came to bring him a pair of slippers and to put the shiny shoes in a particular corner; he often gave me in return for this service a bright coin, which my mother taught me to promptly drop in a little tin bank. I remember distinctly the last time this tall man came to the little house in Georgia; that evening before I went to bed he took me up in his arms and squeezed me very tightly; my mother stood behind his chair wiping tears from her eyes. I remember how I sat upon his knee and watched him laboriously drill a hole through a ten-dollar gold piece, and then tie the coin around my neck with a string. I have worn that gold piece around my neck the greater part of my life, and still possess it, but more than once I have wished that some other way had been found of attaching it to me besides putting a hole through it.

On the day after the coin was put around my neck my mother and I started on what seemed to me an endless journey. I knelt on the seat and watched through the train window the corn and cotton fields pass swiftly by until I fell asleep. When I fully awoke, we were being driven through the streets of a large city—Savannah. I sat up and blinked at the bright lights. At Savannah we boarded a steamer which finally landed us in New York. From New York we went to a town in Connecticut, which became the home of my boyhood.

My mother and I lived together in a little cottage which seemed to me to be fitted up almost luxuriously; there were horse hair covered chairs in the parlor, and a little square piano; there was a stairway with red carpet on it leading to a half second story; there were pictures on the walls, and a few books in a glass-doored case. My mother dressed me very neatly, and I developed that pride which well-dressed boys generally have. She was careful about my associates, and I myself was quite particular. As I look back now I can see that I was a perfect little aristocrat. My mother rarely went to anyone's house, but she did sewing, and there were a great many ladies coming to our cottage. If I was around they would generally call me, and ask me my name and age and tell my mother what a pretty boy I was. Some of them would pat me on the head and kiss me.

My mother was kept very busy with her sewing; sometimes she would have another woman helping her. I think she must have derived a fair income from her work. I know, too, that at least once each month she received a letter; I used to watch for the postman, get the letter, and run to her with it; whether she was busy or not, she would take it and instantly thrust it into her bosom. I never saw her read one of these letters. I knew later that they contained money and what was to her more than money. As busy as she generally was, she found time, however, to teach me my letters and figures and how to spell a number of easy words. Always on Sunday evenings she opened the little square piano and picked out hymns. I can recall now that whenever she played hymns from the book her tempo was always decidedly largo. Sometimes on other evenings, when she was not sewing, she would play simple accompaniments to some old Southern songs which she sang. In these songs she was freer, because she played them by ear. Those evenings on which she opened the little piano were the happiest hours of my childhood. Whenever she started toward the instrument, I used to follow her with all the interest and irrepressible joy that a pampered pet dog shows when a package is opened in which he knows there is a sweet bit for him. I used to stand by her side and often interrupt and annoy her by chiming in with strange harmonics which I found on either the high keys of the tremble or the low keys of the bass. I remember that I had a particular fondness for the black keys. Always on such evenings, when the music was over, my mother would sit with me in her arms, often for a very long time. She would hold me close, softly crooning some old melody without words, all the while gently stroking her face against my head; many and many a night I thus fell asleep. I can see her now, her great dark eyes looking into the fire, to where? No one knew but her. The memory of that picture has more than once kept me from straying too far from the place of purity and safety in which her arms held me.

At a very early age I began to thump on the piano alone, and it was not long before I was able to pick out a few tunes. When I was seven years old, I could play by ear all of the hymns and songs that my mother knew. I had also learned the names of the notes in both clefs, but I preferred not to be hampered by notes. About this time several ladies for whom my mother sewed heard me play and they persuaded her that I should at once be put under a teacher; so arrangements were made for me to study the piano with a lady who was a fairly good musician; at the same time arrangements were made for me to study my books with this lady's daughter. My music teacher had no small difficulty at first in pinning me down to the notes. If she played my lesson over for me, I invariably attempted to reproduce the required sounds without the slightest recourse to the written characters. Her daughter, my other teacher, also had her worries. She found that, in reading, whenever I came to words that were difficult or unfamiliar, I was prone to bring my imagination to the rescue and read from the picture. She has laughingly told me, since then, that I would sometimes substitute whole sentences and even paragraphs from what meaning I thought the illustrations conveyed. She said she not only was sometimes amused at the fresh treatment I would give an author's subject, but, when I gave some new and sudden turn to the plot of the story, often grew interested and even excited in listening to hear what kind of a denouement I would bring about. But I am sure this was not due to dullness, for I made rapid progress in both my music and my books.

And so for a couple of years my life was divided between my music and my school books. Music took up the greater part of my time. I had no playmates, but amused myself with games—some of them my own invention—which could be played alone. I knew a few boys whom I had met at the church which I attended with my mother, but I had formed no close friendships with any of them. Then, when I was nine years old, my mother decided to enter me in the public school, so all at once I found myself thrown among a crowd of boys of all sizes and kinds; some of them seemed to me like savages. I shall never forget the bewilderment, the pain, the heart-sickness, of that first day at school. I seemed to be the only stranger in the place; every other boy seemed to know every other boy. I was fortunate enough, however, to be assigned to a teacher who knew me; my mother made her dresses. She was one of the ladies who used to pat me on the head and kiss me. She had the tact to address a few words directly to me; this gave me a certain sort of standing in the class and put me somewhat at ease.

Within a few days I had made one staunch friend and was on fairly good terms with most of the boys. I was shy of the girls, and remained so; even now a word or look from a pretty woman sets me all a tremble. This friend I bound to me with hooks of steel in a very simple way. He was a big awkward boy with a face full of freckles and a head full of very red hair. He was perhaps fourteen years of age; that is, four or five years older than any other boy in the class. This seniority was due to the fact that he had spent twice the required amount of time in several of the preceding classes. I had not been at school many hours before I felt that "Red Head"—as I involuntarily called him—and I were to be friends. I do not doubt that this feeling was strengthened by the fact that I had been quick enough to see that a big, strong boy was a friend to be desired at a public school; and, perhaps, in spite of his dullness, "Red Head" had been able to discern that I could be of service to him. At any rate there was a simultaneous mutual attraction.

The teacher had strung the class promiscuously around the walls of the room for a sort of trial heat for places of rank; when the line was straightened out, I found that by skillful maneuvering I had placed myself third and had piloted "Red Head" to the place next to me. The teacher began by giving us to spell the words corresponding to our order in the line. "Spell first." "Spell second." "Spell third." I rattled off: "T-h-i-r-d, third," in a way which said: "Why don't you give us something hard?" As the words went down the line, I could see how lucky I had been to get a good place together with an easy word. As young as I was, I felt impressed with the unfairness of the whole proceeding when I saw the tailenders going down before twelfth and twentieth, and I felt sorry for those who had to spell such words in order to hold a low position. "Spell fourth." "Red Head," with his hands clutched tightly behind his back, began bravely: "F-o-r-t-h." Like a flash a score of hands went up, and the teacher began saying: "No snapping of fingers, no snapping of fingers." This was the first word missed, and it seemed to me that some of the scholars were about to lose their senses; some were dancing up and down on one foot with a hand above their heads, the fingers working furiously, and joy beaming all over their faces; others stood still, their hands raised not so high, their fingers working less rapidly, and their faces expressing not quite so much happiness; there were still others who did not move or raise their hands, but stood with great wrinkles on their foreheads, looking very thoughtful.

The whole thing was new to me, and I did not raise my hand, but slyly whispered the letter "u" to "Red Head" several times. "Second chance," said the teacher. The hands went down and the class became quiet. "Red Head," his face now red, after looking beseechingly at the ceiling, then pitiably at the floor, began very haltingly: "F-u—". Immediately an impulse to raise hands went through the class, but the teacher checked it, and poor "Red Head," though he knew that each letter he added only took him farther out of the way, went doggedly on and finished: "—r-t-h." The handraising was now repeated with more hubbub and excitement than at first. Those who before had not moved a finger were now waving their hands above their heads. "Red Head" felt that he was lost. He looked very big and foolish, and some of the scholars began to snicker. His helpless condition went straight to my heart, and gripped my sympathies. I felt that if he failed, it would in some way be my failure. I raised my hand, and, under cover of the excitement and the teacher's attempts to regain order, I hurriedly shot up into his ear twice, quite distinctly: "F-o-u-r-t-h, f-o-u-r-t-h." The teacher tapped on her desk and said: "Third and last chance." The hands came down, the silence became oppressive. "Red Head" Began "F—" Since that day I have waited anxiously for many a turn of the wheel of fortune, but never under greater tension than when I watched for the order in which those letters would fall from "Red's" lips—"o-u-r-t-h." A sigh of relief and disappointment went up from the class. Afterwards, through all our school days, "Red Head" shared my wit and quickness and I benefited by his strength and dogged faithfulness.

There were some black and brown boys and girls in the school, and several of them were in my class. One of the boys strongly attracted my attention from the first day I saw him. His face was as black as night, but shone as though it were polished; he had sparkling eyes, and when he opened his mouth, he displayed glistening white teeth. It struck me at once as appropriate to call him "Shiny Face," or "Shiny Eyes," or "Shiny Teeth," and I spoke of him often by one of these names to the other boys. These terms were finally merged into "Shiny," and to that name he answered good-naturedly during the balance of his public school days.

"Shiny" was considered without question to be the best speller, the best reader, the best penman—in a word, the best scholar, in the class. He was very quick to catch anything, but, nevertheless, studied hard; thus he possessed two powers very rarely combined in one boy. I saw him year after year, on up into the high school, win the majority of the prizes for punctuality, deportment, essay writing, and declamation. Yet it did not take me long to discover that, in spite of his standing as a scholar, he was in some way looked down upon. The other black boys and girls were still more looked down upon. Some of the boys often spoke of them as "niggers." Sometimes on the way home from school a crowd would walk behind them repeating:

> Nigger, nigger, never die,
> Black face and shiny eye.

On one such afternoon one of the black boys turned suddenly on his tormentors and hurled a slate; it struck one of the white boys in the mouth, cutting a slight gash in his lip. At sight of the blood the boy who had thrown the slate ran, and his companions quickly followed. We ran after them pelting them with stones until they separated in several directions. I was very much wrought up over the affair, and went home and told my mother how one of the "niggers" had struck a boy with a slate. I shall never forget how she turned on me. "Don't you ever use that word again," she said, "and don't you ever bother the colored children at school. You ought to be ashamed of yourself." I did hang my head in shame, not because she had convinced me that I had done wrong, but because I was hurt by the first sharp word she had ever given me.

My school days ran along very pleasantly. I stood well in my studies, not always so well with regard to my behavior. I was never guilty of any serious misconduct, but my love of fun sometimes got me into trouble. I remember, however, that my sense of humor was so sly that most of the trouble usually fell on the head of the other fellow. My ability to play on the piano at school exercises was looked upon as little short of marvelous in a boy of my age. I was not chummy with many of my mates, but, on the whole, was about as popular as it is good for a boy to be.

One day near the end of my second term at school the principal came into our room and, after talking to the teacher, for some reason said: "I wish all of the white scholars to stand for a moment." I rose with the others. The teacher looked at me and, calling my name, said: "You sit down for the present, and rise with the others." I did not quite understand her, and questioned: "Ma'm?" She repeated, with a softer tone in her voice: "You sit down now, and rise with the others." I sat down dazed. I saw and heard nothing. When the others were asked to rise, I did not know it. When school was dismissed, I went out in a kind of stupor. A few of the white boys jeered me, saying: "Oh, you're a nigger too." I heard some black children say: "We knew he was colored." "Shiny" said to them: "Come along, don't tease him," and thereby won my undying gratitude.

I hurried on as fast as I could, and had gone some distance before I perceived that "Red Head" was walking by my side. After a while he said to me: "Le' me carry your books," I gave him my strap without being able to answer. When we got to my gate, he said as he handed me my books: "Say, you know my big red agate? I can't shoot with it any more. I'm going to bring it to school for you tomorrow." I took my books and ran into the house. As I passed through the hallway, I saw that my mother was busy with one of her customers; I rushed up into my own little room, shut the door, and went quickly to where my looking-glass hung on the wall. For an instant I was afraid to look, but when I did, I looked long and earnestly. I had often heard people say to my mother: "What a pretty boy you have!" I was accustomed to hear remarks about my beauty; but now, for the first time, I became conscious of it and recognized it. I noticed the ivory whiteness of my skin, the beauty of my mouth, the size and liquid darkness of my eyes, and how the long, black lashes that fringed and shaded them produced an effect that was strangely fascinating even to me. I noticed the softness and glossiness of my dark hair that fell in waves over my temples, making my forehead appear whiter than it really was. How long I stood there gazing at my image I do not know. When I came out and reached the head of the stairs, I heard the lady who had been with my mother going out. I ran downstairs and rushed to where my mother was sitting, with a piece of work in her hands. I buried my head in her lap and blurted out "Mother, mother, tell me, am I a nigger?" I could not see her face, but I knew the piece of work dropped to the floor and I felt her hands on my head. I looked up into her face and repeated: "Tell me, mother, am I a nigger?" There were tears in her eyes and I could see that she was suffering for me. And then it was that I looked at her critically for the first time. I had thought of her in a childish way only as the most beautiful woman in the world; now I looked at her searching for defects. I could see that her skin was almost brown, that her hair was not so soft as mine, and that she did differ in some way from the other ladies who came to the house; yet, even so, I could see that she was very beautiful, more beautiful than any of them. She must have felt that I was examining her, for she hid her face in my hair and said with difficulty: "No, my darling, you are not a nigger." She went on: "You are as good as anybody, if anyone calls you a nigger, don't notice them." But the more she talked, the less was I reassured, and I stopped her by asking: "Well, mother, am I white? Are you white?" She answered tremblingly: "No, I am not white, but you—your father is one of the greatest men in the country—the best blood of the South is in you—" This suddenly opened up in my heart a fresh chasm of misgiving and fear, and I almost fiercely demanded: "Who is my father? Where is he?" She stroked my hair and said; "I'll tell you about him some day." I sobbed: "I want to know now." She answered, "No, not now." Perhaps it had to be done, but I have never forgiven the woman who did it so cruelly. It may be that she never knew that she gave me a sword thrust that day in school which was years in healing.

JAMES WELDON JOHNSON (ESSAY DATE 1914)

SOURCE: Johnson, James Weldon. "What Is Your Brain Power?" *New York Age* XXVIII, no. 9 (November 26, 1914): 4.

In this essay, Johnson assesses intellect, the human power to reason and analyze.

The essential differences among engines are differences in horse power. The essential differences among men are differences of brain-power.

A 10 horse-power engine cannot accomplish the work of a 60 horse-power engine; nor can a 10 brain-power man accomplish the work of a 60 brain-power man.

Then why are you content to run around as a 10 brain-power man when it is possible for you to be a man of 20, of 30, of 40, of 50, of 60 brain-power?

There is no mystery about developing and increasing brain-power; it is as simple as developing and increasing muscular strength. We develop muscular strength by physical exercise. We develop brain-power by mental exercise [which] consists in thinking.

Do not confuse the development of brain-power with the securing of an education. Securing an education may result in increased brain-power, and it may not. There is many an educated fool, and there are not a few unlettered wise men. A man with an education is one who has learned something. A man with developed brain-power is one who has thought out something.

In the vaudeville theatres there are often given exhibitions of educated horses and dogs and monkeys, etc., but these are in no degree exhibitions of brain-power.

Reading does not necessarily produce increased brain-power. A man may read one thousand books and never have an original thought about what he reads, such a man is not developing brain-power, he is merely educating himself, storing his mind with information, useful or otherwise. On the other hand, to read one great thought and then to think it through, to unravel it, to get at the inside of its meaning, to chew, swallow and digest it mentally, will produce increased brain-power. Thinking the thought through gives the brain the proper exercise; making the thought your own gives the brain the proper food, and it gains strength and power.

In truth, without reading any book at all, a man may observe life about him, and, by thinking over his observations, increase his brain-power. Indeed, this has been the method followed by those men who are the world's mental giants.

Do you wish to make a simple experiment in measuring brain-power? Well, you can do it at any place where you catch people at leisure, with nothing to do; just watch and see how they do it. The best place, perhaps, is in a subway or elevated train or in any street car. You get into the car and you have a twenty minute ride before you; use your eyes on the people around.

Notice that fellow doubled up in the corner seat and fast asleep with his mouth open; you will be liberal if you give him credit for more than 10 brain-power. See that young girl gazing vainly around or listlessly out the window; do not give her more than 20 brain-power. There are some people who are reading; according to what and how they are reading, you may mark them 30 or 40 or 50 brain-power. There is a man sitting there, oblivious to everything around him; you can see by the expression of his eyes and his face that he is thinking, thinking out some important question, weighing it up and down and deciding how he shall act; promptly mark him down 60 brain-power.

Accomplishment in life depends upon brain-power, and the magic of securing increased brain-power consists in thinking. Not in memorizing, but in thinking.

Brain-power is the power to take hold of the problems of life and reduce them to the best solutions possible. It is, in a word, the power to decide. It is the power to decide questions ranging all the way from the small affairs of everyday life to the problems of metaphysical philosophy.

Brain-power is employed not alone in building a great bridge or in arguing a great law case or in writing a great book; it may be employed in running a farm or in digging post-holes.

Men who possess developed brain-power become the directors of men who are lacking in it, and thereby their superiors. If it is necessary for one man to decide for another where and how the post-holes should be dug he becomes that man's superior.

As it is with individuals so it is with races. Those races which are to-day the backward races are those running on a low mental speed. They are those races that are not thinking and, so, are not developing increased brain-power. Perhaps at one time they were running at higher speed, but they have allowed their mental engines to slow down, and, as a result, they have fallen behind.

How shall we increase our brain power? By thinking. And how shall we do that? Why, simply by doing it. In most people the mind is lazier than the muscles. It is difficult to keep it on the job. It likes to loaf. It shirks and runs away. When you begin to think you will probably find that after a few moments concentration the mind is wandering far off in other fields. You must take hold of it bodily and put it back to work. The oftener you do this the less you will find you need to do it; the mind will begin to stick to its work and enjoy it. The time will come when you will find yourself able to tackle a thought, to think it through logically and clearly to the end, and to decide what action to take.

Don't be a 10 or 20 brain-power man. Make yourself a man of 30, 40, 50 or 60 brain-power.

GENERAL COMMENTARY

EUGENIA W. COLLIER (ESSAY DATE 1960)

SOURCE: Collier, Eugenia W. "James Weldon Johnson: Mirror of Change." *Phylon* 21, no. 4 (winter 1960): 351-59.

In the following essay, Collier contends that Johnson's poetry reflects the changes that took place between the turn of the century and the 1920s in the way African American folk elements and dialect were handled by Black writers.

At the turn of the twentieth century the American reading and listening public was amusing itself with a fascinating literary toy. The toy was Negro dialect poetry, popularized by white local colorists after the Civil War, and perpetuated by a young Negro poet, Paul Laurence Dunbar, and his imitators. Poetry in Negro dialect consisted mainly of rhymed and metrical misspelling; its subject matter seldom rose above the stereotype of the black-faced buffoon. It was tremendously popular, and anyone with a knack for elocution could make his audience laugh or cry with readings from Dunbar's poems or perhaps something from Daniel Webster Davis' *Weh Down Souf.*

Later a subtle change began to occur in America's literary taste. The confusion of the '20's, the despair of the Depression, the disillusionment and the fear began to yield a new kind of poet and a different kind of poetry. A small part of the change was a tendency by certain Negro poets to a more penetrating depiction of folk life as artistic material. In this change, dialect became more flexible in rhythmic pattern and rhyme scheme; folk experience as expressed in spirituals, jazz, and the blues was basic to the new dialect; folk idioms and speech patterns rather than mere misspellings were fundamental. At its best the new dialect, in subject matter and in form, reached a level of artistry never attained by the best of the Dunbar school.

The change in the handling of folk material in poetry by Negro writers, from traditional dialect to an imitation of the idiom, is most apparent in the work of James Weldon Johnson, a Floridian born in 1871, one year before the birth of Dunbar. In addition to his careers as professor of creative literature, author, and critic, Johnson had been public school teacher and principal, lawyer, writer of musical comedy, diplomat, and official in the newly organized National Association for the Advancement of Colored People. In his dialect poetry Johnson never had Dunbar's facility for sophisticated rhythm and rhyme; he did, however, have an artistic integrity, a more faithful rendition of social truth as he saw it, which is seldom evident in Dunbar's plantation tradition poems. Two threads ran continuously throughout Johnson's varied careers: a concern for basic human rights, especially that of social equality for the Negro, and an interest in creative expression. These two threads were constantly becoming interwoven. In his work as Field Secretary for the NAACP, a position he held for fourteen years, he had many experiences which he expressed in his literary works.

In 1917, some eleven years after Dunbar's death, Johnson published his first book of poetry, ***Fifty Years and Other Poems,*** containing works previously published in various periodicals. Most of the book consists of adequate (but for the most part, unremarkable) standard English poems; one section, **"Jingles and Croons,"** contains Johnson's dialect poetry. The dialect is written in the Dunbar tradition in form and in subject matter. It is not nearly so polished as Dunbar's; rather, it is quite artificial and occasionally almost clumsy. The attempt at imagery is not nearly so successful as Dunbar's, and the rhythm is often faulty.

Compare, for example, the two poets' handling of the same idea. Dunbar's superior flexibility, ease of handling, mastery over imagery are apparent. Both poems are titled **"A Banjo Song."** Johnson writes:

W'en de banjoes wuz a-ringin',
An' de darkies wuz a-singin',
Oh, wuzen dem de good times sho!
All de ole folks would be chattin',

An' de pickaninnies pattin',
As dey heah'd de feet a-shufflin' 'cross de flo'.

An' how we'd dance, an' how we'd sing!
Dance tel de day done break.
An' how dem banjoes dey would ring,
An' de cabin flo' would shake!

Come along, come along,
Come along, come along,
Don't you heah dem banjoes a-ringin'?
Gib a song, gib a song,
Gib a song, gib a song,
Git yo' feet mixed up fu' a-wingin'.

W'ile de banjoes dey go plunka, plunka plunk,
We'll dance tel de ole flo' shake;
W'ile de feet keep a-goin' chooka, chooka,
chook,
We'll dance tel de day done break.[1]

Dunbar, on the other hand, writes in part:

'Bout de time da night is fallin'
An' my daily wu'k is done,
An' above de shady hilltops
I kin see de settin' sun;
When de quiet, restful shadders
Is beginnin' jes' to fall,—
Den I take de little banjo
F'om its place upon de wall.

Den my fam'ly gadders roun' me
In de fadin' o' de light,
Ez I strike de strings to try 'em
Ef dey all is tuned er-right.
An' it seems we're so nigh heaben
We kin hyeah de angels sing
When de music o' dat banjo
Sets my cabin all er-ring.[2]

The subject matter of **"Jingles and Croons,"** then, follows the Dunbar school: lovers, lullabies, simple pleasures, sentiment, faith—a faith in which one prays for a Christmas turkey rather than for the more basic needs of life. This was the sort of treatment which the "eye dialect" of the Dunbarists seemed best able to portray. Yet there is even in these poems a subtle difference from Dunbar, the beginnings of the use of dialect to express something more than the surface pleasures and pains of a simple people. For Johnson tells of a bacchanal which is held not for the purpose of a little innocent fun, but for the purpose of forgetting very real troubles. Another unmistakable bit of truth is observed in **"Tunk,"** a poem based upon a real child whom Johnson taught during a summer in a backwoods Georgia schoolroom. The poem tells of the folk Negro's eagerness for education for his children.

At about this time, the early 1920's, America was again experiencing an upheaval of basic values. The World War brought with it profound social changes and an examination of what these changes meant. Expansions in industry had caused swift and constant migration to the cities, and this migration in turn brought about serious social problems, problems which could not be ignored. The war which had professed to make the world safe for democracy did not bring about the opportunities which Negroes had expected, and several influential groups began to demand that something be done to make America safe for democracy. These were the days of the Red Scare, the reawakened Ku Klux Klan, labor strikes, and brutal race riots. The plight of labor and the plight of the Negro were demanding national attention.

An interest in the common man had become more and more important in American poetry in general. The influence of Whitman had shown itself in the works of Moody and Markham; the Imagists were experimenting with form and subject matter; young poets like Pound, Lindsay, Frost, Masters, and Sandburg were writing of the commonplace with a strength and power new to American *belles lettres.*

Negro poets were beginning to join the concern with social awareness and the seeking for a linguistic medium in which to express it. To James Weldon Johnson two things became evident: that folk experience was a rich source of poetic material, a source virtually untouched by colored writers; and that traditional dialect with its emphasis on mispronunciation and its adherence to strict metre and rhyme had not been used as a successful means of interpreting the folk. The experiences of a lifetime contributed to Johnson's realization. Unlike Dunbar, Johnson had had direct and meaningful contact with the Southern folk in their native background. Born and reared in the deep South, Johnson was profoundly moved by his experiences with the folk during a summer of teaching in rural Georgia when he was not yet out of his teens; here he lived and worked with farm Negroes and gained an insight into their lives. Later his work as public school principal, lawyer, and newspaperman brought him in further contact with the people. The experiences and the feelings expressed by the folk in spirituals, work songs, and blues were more real to him than the unnumbered Christmas parties celebrated by the dark folk in the works of the Southern white local colorists.

In 1900 when he was still writing poems in Dunbar dialect, Johnson read Whitman's *Leaves of Grass.* Recalling this incident in his autobiography, ***Along This Way,*** he stated, "I got a sudden realization of the artificiality of conventionalized

Negro dialect poetry; of its exaggerated geniality, childish optimism, forced comicality, and mawkish sentiment; of its limitation as an instrument of expression to but two emotions, pathos and humor, thereby making every poem only sad or funny."[3] During a visit to Johnson's home (at which time Dunbar wrote a dozen poems in the course of a few days), Dunbar himself agreed that traditional dialect, although demanded by the public, was indeed "narrow and limited" as a medium of expression.

These personal experiences, together with the social and cultural climate of America during the early 1920's, were influential in Johnson's shift to the use of folk idiom in Negro poetry. For several years Johnson had recognized the poetic possibilities of the "old-time Negro sermon" and had planned to use this subject matter in a way similar to a composer's use of folk music as a theme for serious musical expression. He recognized the sermon's "characteristic qualities: imagery, color, abandon, sonorous diction, syncopated rhythms, and native idioms"[4] well before he began to write poetry exploiting these characteristics. One Sunday while participating in a program for the NAACP at a small Western church, he heard the sermon of a visiting minister who preached the old-fashioned fiery type of sermon Johnson had heard in his childhood. Immediately Johnson jotted down on his program the nucleus of a poem, **"Creation,"** which became the first in the series he published seventeen years later as ***God's Trombones: Seven Negro Sermons in Verse.***

In ***God's Trombones*** Johnson discarded conventional dialect. Many years after the poems were written he stated:

> It was not my intention to paint the picturesque or comic aspect of the old time Negro preacher. . . . My aim was to interpret what was in his mind, to express if possible, the dream to which, despite limitations, he strove to give utterance. I chose a loose rhythmic instead of a strict metric form, because it was the first only that could accommodate itself to the movement, the abandon, the changes of tempo, the characteristic syncopations of the primitive material.[5]

Compare Johnson's treatment of death in his earlier traditional dialect with his treatment of the same theme in an old-time sermon from ***God's Trombones.*** **"De Little Pickaninny's Gone to Sleep"** resembles Dunbar's "Two Little Boots" in its saccharine sentiment as well as in its inaccurate rendering of pronunciation; Dunbar's poem, however, is more skillfully done. Johnson's **"Go Down Death"** has much more dignity than **"De Little Pickaninny"** and is much more effective in its rendition of actual speech.

In **"De Little Pickaninny"** Johnson wrote:

> Cuddle down, ma honey, in yo' bed,
> Go to sleep an' res' yo' little head,
> Been a-kind o' ailin' all de day?
> Didn't have no sperit fu' to play?
> Never min'; to-morrer, w'en you wek,
> Daddy's gwine to ride you on his bek,
> 'Roun' an' roun' de cabin flo' so fas'—
> Der! He's closed his little eyes at las'.
>
> Mandy, w'at's de matter wid dat chile?
> Keeps a-sighin' ev'y little w'ile;
> Seems to me I heayhd him sorta groan,
> W'at's dat far-off light dat's in his eyes?
> Dat's a light dey's borrow'd f'om de skies;
> Fol' his little han's across his breas'.
> Let de little pickaninny res'.[6]

Later in **"Go Down Death,"** included in ***God's Trombones,*** he wrote:

> While we were watching round her bed,
> She turned her eyes and looked away,
> She saw what we couldn't see;
> She saw Old Death. She saw Old Death
> Coming like a falling star.
> But Death didn't frighten Sister Caroline;
> He looked to her like a welcome friend.
> And she whispered to us: I'm going home,
> And she smiled and closed her eyes.
>
> And Death took her up like a baby,
> And she lay in his icy arms,
> But she didn't feel no chill.
> And Death began to ride again—
> Up beyond the evening star,
> Out beyond the morning star,
> Into the glittering light of glory,
> On to the Great White Throne.[7]

The effectiveness of Johnson's use of the idiom as expression can be seen again in comparing the interpretation of the Biblical story of Moses as treated in the Negro spiritual, in Dunbar's traditional dialect, and in Johnson's idiomatic usage. The Moses story was popular among the slaves, who saw in the plight of the Hebrew children something of their own situation, and who hoped for deliverance from slavery as God had delivered the Hebrews from slavery in Egypt. The spiritual "Go Down Moses" was so strong in its protest that on many plantations slaves were forbidden to sing it. Johnson maintains this note of protest in his adaptation of the theme to the words of the fire-and-brimstone colored preacher, in his **"Let My People Go."** The note of protest in Dunbar's "An Antebellum Sermon" is quite ineffectual, weakened further by its expression in traditional dialect; Dunbar's preacher has none of the verve of Johnson's, has none of the dignity of Johnson's, seems rather to be cute and clownish, rendering the poem shallow and ineffective.

Sang the folk in "Go Down Moses":

When Israel was in Egyptland
Let my people go
Oppressed so hard they could not stand
Let my people go.

Go down, Moses,
Way down in Egyptland
Tell old Pharaoh
"Let my people go."

"Thus saith the Lord," bold Moses said,
"Let my people go;
If not I'll smite your first-born dead
Let my people go."

Go down, Moses,
Way down in Egyptland
Tell old Pharaoh
"Let my people go!"

Said Dunbar's preacher in "An Antebellum Sermon":

We is gathered hyeah, my brothahs,
In dis howlin' wildaness,
Fu' to speak some words of comfo't
To each othah in distress.
An' we chooses fu' ouah subjic'
Dis—we'll 'splain it by an' by;
An' de Lawd said, 'Moses, Moses,'
An' de man said, 'Hyeah am I.'

Now ole Pher'oh down in Egypt,
Was de wuss man evah bo'n
An' he had de Hebrew chillun
Down dah wukin' in his co'n;
'Twell de Lawd got tihed o' his foolin',
An' sez he: "I'll let him know—
Look hyeah, Moses, go tell Pher'oh
Fu' to let dem chillun go."

"An' ef he refuse to do it,
I will make him rue de houah,
Fu' I'll empty down on Egypt
All de vials of my powah."
Yes, he did—an' Pher'oh's ahmy
Wasn't wuth a ha'f a dime;
Fu' de Lawd will he'p his chillun,
You kin trust him evah time.

Seven stanzas later the Dunbar preacher concluded:

But when Moses wif his powah
Comes an' sets us chillun free,
We will praise de gracious Mastah
Dat has gin us liberty;
An' we'll shout ouah halleluyahs,
On dat mighty reck'nin' day,
When we'se reco'nised ez citiz'—
Huh uh! Chillun, let us pray![8]

Johnson's preacher began:

And God called Moses from the burning bush,
He called in a still, small voice,
And he said: Moses—Moses—
And Moses listened,
And he answered, and said:
Lord, here am I.

And the voice in the bush said: Moses,
Draw not nigh, take off your shoes,
For you're standing on holy ground.
And Moses took off his shoes,
And Moses looked at the burning bush,
But he saw no man.

. . . . .

And God said to Moses:
I've seen the awful suffering
Of my people down in Egypt,
I've watched their hard oppressors,
Their overseers and drivers;
The groans of my people have filled my ears
And I can't stand it no longer;
So I'm come down to deliver them
Out of the land of Egypt,
And I will bring them out of that land
Into the land of Canaan;
Therefore, Moses, go down,
Down into Egypt,
And tell Old Pharaoh
To let my people go.[9]

In the language of ***God's Trombones*** Johnson found a much more flexible medium than Dunbar dialect for the interpretation of folk material. Traditional dialect attempts (sometimes unsuccessfully) a strict fidelity in metre and in rhyme scheme; Johnson adapted to an artistic form the rhythms of an actual sermon, the accents of actual speech and intonation. He freed himself from the necessity to rhyme, thus subordinating strict poetic form to the artistic interpretation of his subject matter. In ***God's Trombones*** Johnson approximated the vivid imagery of the folk, an imagery far superior to any he attained in the ***Fifty Years*** dialect poems and certainly an imagery which rivaled the best of Dunbar's. Johnson used all the tricks of the folk preacher's trade—hyperbole, repetition, juxtaposition, personal appeal to his listeners, the knack of making Biblical happenings have an intense meaning to current life. Johnson even used punctuation and capitalization to achieve his effect—dashes to indicate the frequent and dramatic pauses, capitalization to emphasize important words, such as "Old Earth" and "Great White Throne." The sensitive reader cannot fail to hear the rantings of the fire-and-brimstone preacher; the extremely sensitive reader may even hear the unwritten "Amens" of the congregation. Johnson does this without misspellings. He uses folk idioms such as "I'll make me a world," the description of God making man "like a mammy bending over her baby," frequent use of the dialectic prefix "a," as in "a-shuddering" and "a-bursting."

James Weldon Johnson reflected the change from stilted poetics to the more natural poetry of living, a change which was taking place in Negro poetry as well as in American poetry in general. The 1920's and early 1930's witnessed the emergence of the New Negro poets, who used their talents in various ways to express truth as they perceived it, with a vigor and a beauty largely lacking in previous poetry by Negroes. Some of these poets, notably Langston Hughes and later Sterling Brown, utilized the idiomatic folk patterns as an effective artistic instrument. The Rastus and Lishy Davis of the old Dunbar tradition were fortunately fading. James Weldon Johnson played a significant part in their demise.

FROM THE AUTHOR

A MEASURE OF GREATNESS

The final measure of the greatness of all peoples is the amount and standard of the literature and all they have produced. The world does not know that a people is great until that people produces great literature and art.

SOURCE: James Weldon Johnson, excerpt from the preface to *The Book of American Negro Poetry*, edited by Johnson, Harcourt, Brace, 1922.

Notes

1. James Weldon Johnson, *Fifty Years and Other Poems* (Boston, 1917), p. 17.
2. Paul Laurence Dunbar, *Complete Poems* (New York, 1925), p. 267.
3. Johnson, *Along This Way* (New York, 1931), pp. 158-59.
4. *Ibid.*, p. 335.
5. *Ibid.*, p. 336.
6. Johnson, *Fifty Years*, p. 21.
7. Johnson, *God's Trombones: Seven Sermons in Verse* (New York, 1927), p. 29.
8. Dunbar, *op. cit.*, p. 305.
9. Johnson, *God's Trombones*, pp. 45-46.

LYNN ADELMAN (ESSAY DATE 1967)

SOURCE: Adelman, Lynn. "A Study of James Weldon Johnson." *Journal of Negro History* 52, no. 2 (April 1967): 128-45.

In the following essay, Adelman presents a biographical study of Johnson, demonstrating how the poet responded to both personal and social/political problems.

The period running roughly from the 1890's to the 1930's was a particularly harsh one for the American Negro. It was characterized in many ways by a deterioration in the Negro's status both in the South and the North. And although the Negro made some important gains, especially in the latter part of this period, the South's capitulation to racism and to the Jim Crow code of discrimination, which began in the 1890's, ran unabated until well into the depression years.[1] These conditions placed heavy demands on Negro leadership, which was itself torn, at least until 1915, by the bitter split between Booker T. Washington and W. E. Du Bois and their followers.

The adult life of James Weldon Johnson spanned approximately these years. Johnson lived from 1871 until 1938. Study of his career yields substantial insight into the period and into the way in which it affected an individual Negro. Johnson's problems and responses were, to be sure, not altogether typical, for he was an unusually gifted and versatile person. But in some ways both his personal career and the nature of the leadership which he provided demonstrate the difficulties the Negro faced and the harsh limitations on the possible approaches to those difficulties.

I.

Johnson had the benefit of an unusual childhood.[2] He was born in Jacksonville, Florida, where his family provided a comfortable and culturally stimulating home. His father was a native of New York and held the position of headwaiter at the St. James Hotel. The St. James was a haven for wealthy tourists[3] and the Johnson family became familiar, at least as spectators, with an aristocratic way of life. Johnson's mother was the daughter of Stephen Dillet, who was the Postmaster of the city of Nassau and one of the best known Negroes in the Bahamas. She was proud, sensitive, and musically talented; her unique background of Nassau and New York had given her no conception of her "station." From this proud and cosmopolitan home, Johnson gained a deep sense of dignity.

Other factors worked to his advantage. His childhood years were spend in that hazy period in the history of Southern race relations before the violent settlement of the Negro's position had been reached. Systematized discrimination and segregation did not come until later. And in this period—when attitudes had not yet hardened into laws—Jacksonville was considered a particularly good town for Negroes. Thus, Johnson was able to grow up free of the effects of the ghetto or the slum. He never learned to view his Negritude as a burden. When he finally did encounter the problem of race he was able to meet it on a more or less rational level and with an already keen intelligence.

At the age of sixteen Johnson entered Atlanta University. Because of the lack of a Negro high school in Jacksonville, his parents sent him to Atlanta for both his high school and college educations. Thus, he was at Atlanta for practically all of his early manhood and the impact of the school upon him was profound. Atlanta was Johnson's introduction to the problem of race. Awareness of race was pervasive and the subject was constantly discussed. The school sought to foster a sense of mission in its students. It had been founded twenty years before by a white philanthropist whose hope was to develop individual Negro talent, provide inspiration and leadership for Negro communities, and train teachers.[4] Johnson began to write poetry with racial themes and he began to think of his purpose in life as one peculiar to a Negro.

So, too, did the school's philosophy of education influence him. Atlanta stressed the classical liberal education. This became central in Johnson's thinking. He would consistently argue that education was the most potent weapon in the Negro's struggle;[5] that the liberal education, in particular, could improve and uplift the Negro. Concerning Booker Washington's emphasis on vocational training, Johnson once pointed out that Washington himself had been liberally educated.[6] In stressing academic education, Johnson—who was proud of his own intellectual accomplishments—generalized, in part, from his own experience. This experience may, in some ways, have limited his perspective on the race problem. He seemed sometimes to underestimate the many barriers impeding Negroes from gaining an education. His exhortations, while certainly sensible, occasionally seemed naive as, for example, when he urged Harlem Negroes to spend more time in the library.[7]

II.

Johnson graduated from Atlanta in 1894. Having by this time become well thought of by the Negroes in Jacksonville, he was offered and accepted the job as principal of Stanton School, which was the elementary school that he had attended and the largest Negro school in Florida. At Stanton he was both a teacher and an administrator and he made a distinguished record. By adding one grade each year, he made Stanton a high school as well as a grade school. His ability was widely recognized, leading, in 1900, to his election as President of the Negro State Teachers Association.

Teaching and school administration, however, were not entirely fulfilling either his ambition or the sense of responsibility to his race which had been developed at Atlanta. These feelings were strong ones and in 1895 they impelled him to start a newspaper. *The Daily American,* as the paper was called, was aimed primarily at the Negro and was to provide an instrument for the expression of the Negro's feelings. According to one of Johnson's first editorials, the *American* would champion the rights of the Negro but would criticize him when he deserved it. It would be Republican in politics, objective in its news coverage, and adamant in its fight against wrongdoing, both in personal conduct and in government.[8]

With the *American,* for the first time Johnson assumed the role of spokesman for his people and exhorter to them. Alternately he urged the Negro to demonstrate his proven ability[9] and to strive to improve himself. Present but less conspicuous in his editorials was the bitter indictment of discrimination and prejudice which would characterize his work for the *New York Age* twenty years later. The difference in tone was part of the difference in the situations. At the time of the *American* he was a young man trying to gain support for a new paper, in a time and place where there was virtually no tradition of strong Negro protest.

Johnson was seeking most to increase respect for the Negro in the eyes of both Negroes and whites. The *American* itself was a symbol of this purpose. Its prosaic style, its puritanical emphasis on clean living and clean government, its explicit attempts at objectivity all were part of his attempt to improve the image of the Negro. Each copy was to be proof that Negroes were not illiterate and irresponsible.

The paper made a good start, but failed after eight months of publication because of insufficient financial support. Johnson himself was not sure whether the failure was because the Negroes of Jacksonville were not yet ready for such a paper, or because of his own failings.[10] It was clear that in seeking to provide a voice for the Southern Negro and to encourage pride and self respect Johnson was waging a lonely and uphill struggle. Virtually everything in the Southern system tended to beat against the black man's pride. As Paul Buck has written: "Early in life the Negro child learned the hazards of the color line. It was the lot of every Negro to accept, as most of his race did, the badge of inferiority or to carry within his inner soul an important yet agonizing spark of rebellion against the fateful injustice of his position."[11]

With the failure of the *American,* another side of Johnson came to the fore. He decided to take up the study of law and arranged to "read law" in the office of Thomas Ledwith, a young white lawyer whose father had been a prominent Republican. Here was the more conventional aspect of his ambition asserting itself. While he wanted to serve his race, he also wanted to succeed in a way more or less unrelated to race. The tension between these two sides of him would be a consistent theme for many years of his life.

He studied law for eighteen months and then, at the urging of Ledwith, decided to take the Florida bar examination. At that time there were several Negro lawyers in Jacksonville but none had been admitted through open examination in a state court. Johnson's examination was an ordeal, with one of the examiners calling him a "nigger" and walking out, but his answers were right and he managed to pass.

Law, however, was not the career for him. He opened an office, but practiced only for a short time. Although he was not unsuccessful in getting business, he may have seen that opportunities for Negro lawyers in the South were limited. Few were able to devote themselves to practice and fewer appeared in court. For a Negro client, white counsel often was more helpful than the best Negro representation.[12]

Besides this, he had found a new interest. His brother Rosamond, who was a musician, wanted him to help compose a comic opera. Rosamond was to write the lyrics and James, the words, the ultimate plan being to sell it in New York. Johnson was receptive to the idea. He had been writing verse since college and he was fascinated by the world of theatre and music, which his brother, who had spent seven years studying and working in the North, inhabited.

Together they produced **"Toloso,"** a comic opera satirizing United States imperialism, and in the summer of 1899, set out for New York. Although the opera itself was never produced, the trip was an important one in their lives. **"Toloso"** served as a passport to the inner circles of the Negro show business world. Johnson was exposed to Negro artists and he saw for the first time the great potentialities of Negro art. His love of New York, which he had visited as a child, was revived. Although he returned to Jacksonville in the fall, it was only a few years later that Johnson left Jacksonville for good. Between 1899 and 1902, he spent his winters at the Stanton School and his summers in New York, writing songs and musical comedies. In the summer of 1900, he and Rosamond formed a combination songwriting-vaudeville team with Bob Cole. And in the summer of 1902, as they became increasingly successful, Johnson resigned from Stanton.

Show business was his fourth new venture in the five years since Atlanta. This darting from one project to another was a commentary on the conditions in which he found himself. A particular kind of identity crisis was involved. There were no clear paths for Johnson to follow. He was a talented and ambitious Negro living in a society which had little place for such types. As the plight of the Negro laborer at this time was poor, so too was that of the Negro aristocrat. As John Hope Franklin has put it: ". . . the American melting pot, so far as Negroes were concerned, was not boiling; it was hardly simmering."[13] Johnson's desire to be a racial spokesman had been dampened by the failure of the *American.* Being a lawyer in Florida offered an uncertain future and a high school principalship was not enough for a life's work. One of the few areas of opportunity was the world of show business. It lacked the dignity and the seriousness which were so much a part of him, but it offered glamor and excitement.

III.

In the years between 1900-1906, the team of Cole and the Johnson Brothers flourished. They were among the top composers of American popular music and were signed to a lucrative contract by Klaw and Erlanger, a major theatrical firm. Johnson lived at the Marshall Hotel and was a leading figure in New York's Black Bohemia. He and his partners toured the United States and played the Palace Theater in London. They lived the gay life—in a three-month stay in Europe they spent some ten thousand dollars and had to borrow money to tip the ship's steward on the return trip.[14]

Artistically, Johnson's work was less successful. Before becoming a professional songwriter, he had written essentially two kinds of poetry: more or less conventional verse, sometimes with racial themes, and dialect poems. The dialect, at that time, posed a particular problem for an aspiring Negro poet. Dialect, which had first been popularized by white local colorists after the Civil War, consisted mainly of rhymed and metrical misspellings. It was widely accepted as the verse best fitted to describe Negro life, and Negro poets generally wrote in dialect. The subject matter of dialect, however, rarely rose above the stereotype of the harmless plantation Negro.[15] It rendered an inaccurate and often insulting picture of the Negro.

Johnson had mixed feelings about the dialect. He liked it because of its particularly Negro quality but he saw its limitations, or as he later wrote, its "artificiality . . . exaggerated geniality, childish optimism, forced comicality, and mawkish sentiment . . ."[16] Further, he had had some success with conventional form in expressing racial themes. In 1900 he wrote **"Lift Every Voice and Sing,"**[17] a powerful poem which, when set to music, later came to be adopted by Negroes as a Negro National Anthem.

During his tenure in show business, however, he was unable to break away from the dialect. Such a course was made more difficult by the demands of his new profession. As show business represented something of a compromise for him, so his writing saw the same compromise. Negro entertainers were bound largely by the white man's stereotypes and prejudices; the time had not yet come for the Negro rebel, in politics or in art. Johnson, as yet, was no exception.

Even while he continued to write dialect, however, Johnson was able to express more than surface emotions. In **"A Banjo Song,"**[18] for example, he wrote of a plantation bacchanal held not for innocent fun but to forget very real troubles.[19] And he strove consciously to avoid portraying the stereotype of the happy, gluttonous Negro.[20]

Johnson was never entirely satisfied by show business and these feelings persisted. In 1903 he wrote to the Atlanta University newspaper, reassuring it that he had not given up life's serious pursuits. He also found time to study literature at Columbia, and to head a Colored Republican Club in New York. When he returned from Europe the sense that show business was neither dignified enough nor important enough continued to weigh heavily upon him. He began to consider the suggestion of Charles Anderson, a politician, that he try for a position in the United States Consular Service. Two of his qualifications were fluent Spanish and past service for the Republican Party. He passed the examination, and in 1906 he took the next step in his already staccato career when he received the appointment as United States Consul in Puerto Caballo, Venezuela at a starting salary of $2,000.

IV.

Johnson was, of course, not the first Negro in government service. McKinley alone appointed twice as many Negroes to federal positions as had any previous President.[21] As a consul his primary duties were to overlook international commercial affairs and to assist American citizens. He found the work enjoyable and sometimes exciting—as when he became at least peripherally involved in the turbulence of Latin American politics—and after a time he began to consider making it his life's work. In 1909 he received a promotion to consul at Corinto, Nicaragua, with a thousand dollar increase in pay. His years in Latin America were productive in other ways. In February of 1910, on one of his trips to New York, he married Grace Nail, who came from a wealthy long-established Negro family in Brooklyn.

Residence in Latin America also had a good effect on his development as an artist. Musical comedy had been a hindrance in many ways. He had been hemmed in by the demands of his audience, and the gay life which he led was not conducive to the expression of deep feeling. In Latin America there was no immediate audience and few distractions. Removed from the American racial scene, he could observe with greater clarity.

Nearly all his poems now were racial in theme. He was able to discard completely the dialect, and the feelings which he expressed were no longer the dialect's "pathos and humor." Particularly noteworthy were such poems as **"O Black and Unknown Bards"** and **"Mother Night."** Some of his poems were protests, a note not often heard in Negro poetry since before the Civil War. An example is **"O Southland"**[22] which begins,

O Southland, fair Southland
Then why do you still cling
To an idle page
To a dead and useles thing?

He also found time to write a novel, ***The Autobiography of an Ex-Coloured Man,***[23] the story of a Negro who is able to "pass." The hero of the story wanders through the American South, to New York, and to Europe, having adventures and making various observations on the race question. He ultimately marries a white girl and decides to pass permanently. The book was revolutionary in several respects. Its treatment of the miscegenation theme was new in that both parties were aristocrats.[24] Further, Johnson portrayed a dimension of Negro life rarely present in stories about Negroes. Consider this description of his hero's life in Black Bohemia:

> . . . my regular time for going to bed was somewhere between four and six o'clock in the morning. I got up late in the afternoon, walked about a little, then went to the gambling house or the club.[25]

The novel was, in its own way, a statement of racial pride. Johnson's hero leads a life that would make anyone envious and, in the end, he has the last laugh on the white man by intermarrying. The novel was, in fact, frightening to its author. Johnson was worried about its potential shock effect and had no desire, with a possible government career ahead of him, to become controversial. Also, he had hopes that the story would be taken as true. He, thus, chose to publish it anonymously. The book, published in 1912, turned out to be a financial success and received no particular denunciation;[26] in 1927 it was republished by Knopf above its author's name.

Johnson's hopes of a career in the foreign service were not to be fulfilled. In 1913, when Woodrow Wilson took office, he was expecting his second promotion and, in fact, had been nominated by President Taft to be Consul to the Azores. When no action was taken on the matter Johnson went to Washington to talk to Secretary of State Bryan. The Wilson Administration's attitude toward the Negro was equivocal, if not hostile; its policy regarding the foreign service was generally to substitute neophyte Democrats for experienced men.[27] Bryan was not encouraging and Johnson left feeling victimized by race and politics. Shortly afterward he resigned from the Consulate.[28]

His frustration was, of course, nothing new. Now forty-two, he had come some way since Atlanta University—publisher, educator, lawyer, composer, artist, and diplomat—yet in a way he was back where he began. In none of his pursuits—except the *American*—had he failed, but each had brought frustration. He had started as a Negro in the South, trying to make his own way and to improve the lot of his race, but his efforts had been blocked by Negro indifference and white prejudice. He had gone North and found that there, too, opportunities were limited. He was a successful songwriter but had to write juvenile and sometimes demeaning verse. The latest roadblock had come in government service. In some ways, he had been a Negro doing white men's work. Not since his short-lived publishing attempt was his work directly related to the Negro struggle. His poems indicated his feelings, but his time had been spent living the good life in Negro Bohemia or being a functionary in Latin America, far away from the turbulence of racial conflict.

After 1913, Johnson turned back to the central issues and identified himself totally with the cause of the Negro. While this course was, in part, forced upon him by the circumstances in which he found himself, he did not choose it reluctantly. His ambition to be a leader and a spokesman had only been in abeyance. None of this was clear to him in 1913. First he went to Jacksonville to gather his thoughts. But Jim Crow signs were more common and Grace Nail Johnson was unhappy. In 1914 they headed for New York and when, several weeks later, he was offered the job as head of the editorial staff of the *New York Age,* New York's oldest Negro newspaper, Johnson quickly accepted.

V.

Johnson's editorship of the *Age* thrust him to the forefront of American Negro spokesmen. For the first time he had to face squarely and state his position on the many issues of the day. The outlines of his thought had already been made clear in ***The Autobiography of an Ex-Coloured Man.*** Underlying all his ideas was the belief that the race problem was, at root, a question of attitude. The Negro, through years of subjugation, had become apathetic and resigned.[29] The problem of white attitudes lay mainly in their misconceptions about the Negro. Johnson realized that the myth of inferiority was often a cover-up for complex emotional forces, but he believed that the first step towards equality was to prove that inferiority was nonsense. Thus, he advocated a two-pronged approach of seeking to awaken the Negro and to enlighten the white.[30]

Johnson turned with alacrity to his new role as agitator. He wrote a daily column called **"Views and Reviews,"** which contained the strongest race protests he had yet uttered. No longer was he inhibited by worries about a career as a diplomat; his only responsibility now was to the Negro. Johnson passionately defended the Negro and the Negro's ability. No important Negro activity missed his attention. He praised Negro artists and performers and defended the Negro soldier.[31] He also berated the Negro for not helping himself in such columns as **"Cut Out the Comedy."**[32]

Nor did he hesitate to attack prejudice. Particularly biting were such pieces as **"Tom Watson, Apostle of Prejudice"**[33] and **"Staying in the Ditch"**[34] which opened as follows:

> We doubt that Mississippi has ever produced a man who has contributed to the progress of the world.

He could see the debilitating effect of racism on both its protagonists—"The solving of the race problem," he said, "involves in large measure the salvation of the black man's body and the white man's soul."[35]

The freedom and power evident in his editorials could also be seen in the poetry he was now writing. Besides his own maturity, the spirit of the times was more conducive to militance. People were using the term "New Negro," whose spirit was, perhaps, best represented by Du Bois. This new feeling had not yet reached Negro art but Johnson was to lead the way. The Harlem Renaissance was imminent.

The best example of this spirit in Johnson's work is his poem **"Brothers—American Drama,"**[36] written in 1916, about the burning of a Negro by a white mob. It was a thoroughly realistic social justice poem[37] and the most vigorous poem yet heard from any Negro poet.[38] The horror of the burning is vividly described:

> Now let it blaze again. See there!
> He squirms! He groans!
> His eyes bulge wildly out.

But Johnson's calm wisdom is also present. The act is

> The bitter fruit . . . of planted seed;
> The resultant, the inevitable end
> Of evil forces and the powers of wrong.

Thus, after 1913, Johnson seemed to find himself as a spokesman and a poet. In both media he spoke with increasing strength. His efforts did not go unnoticed. In 1916 Joel Spingarn, president of the recently formed NAACP, invited him to attend a conference on questions relating to the Negro at Amenia, New York. The Amenia Conference was an important event both for the Negro and for Johnson. It marked the first time that Negro leadership was more or less united, a unity caused partly by the death of Washington and partly, said Du Bois, "by the concentration of effort . . . which rising race segregation, discrimination, and mob murder were compelling us to follow."[39]

Johnson, according to Arthur Spingarn, "hit it off perfectly with everybody."[40] After the Conference the NAACP's Board of Directors, headed by the Spingarns and Du Bois, decided they wanted Johnson in the Association. The only problem, both for the Association and for Johnson, involved Johnson's ideological position.[41] During the long conflict between Washington and Du Bois, Johnson had never really taken sides. His thinking was much closer to that of Du Bois, which his editorials, emphasizing full equality and denouncing race prejudice, clearly showed. But Johnson had long been close to Washington and owed him a debt of gratitude; for it was only through Washington's efforts that Johnson had received his appointment in the Consulate.[42] And even had he wanted to criticize Washington he would have been prevented by the policy of the *Age,* which at one time had been partially owned by Washington, of never criticizing Washington in print.[43] The Association, not sure of his position but hoping to bring him into their camp, offered him a position. Johnson accepted and, in 1916, assumed the newly created position of Field Secretary, beginning what was to be his major work for the next fifteen years.

VI.

Johnson's principal duties as Field Secretary were organization and expansion. His first major contribution was to convince the Board of the importance of organizing a Southern section. In January 1917, he began an organizing tour of the South addressing conferences in every major city. Johnson was encouraged by the response of Negroes at the mass meetings. Walter White, then in his early twenties, described the meeting in Atlanta and Johnson's approach as follows:

> The . . . meeting . . . was so packed with eager faced Negroes and even a few whites that we had difficulty wedging the platform party through the crowd to enter the auditorium. Mr. Johnson, calm, slender, and immaculate, stood hazardously between the footlights and a painted backdrop . . . There was none of the sonorous flamboyant oratory of that era in the meeting . . . only the quiet irrefutable presentation of the facts and the need to wipe out race prejudice before the hate . . . destroyed both the victims and the perpetrators.[44]

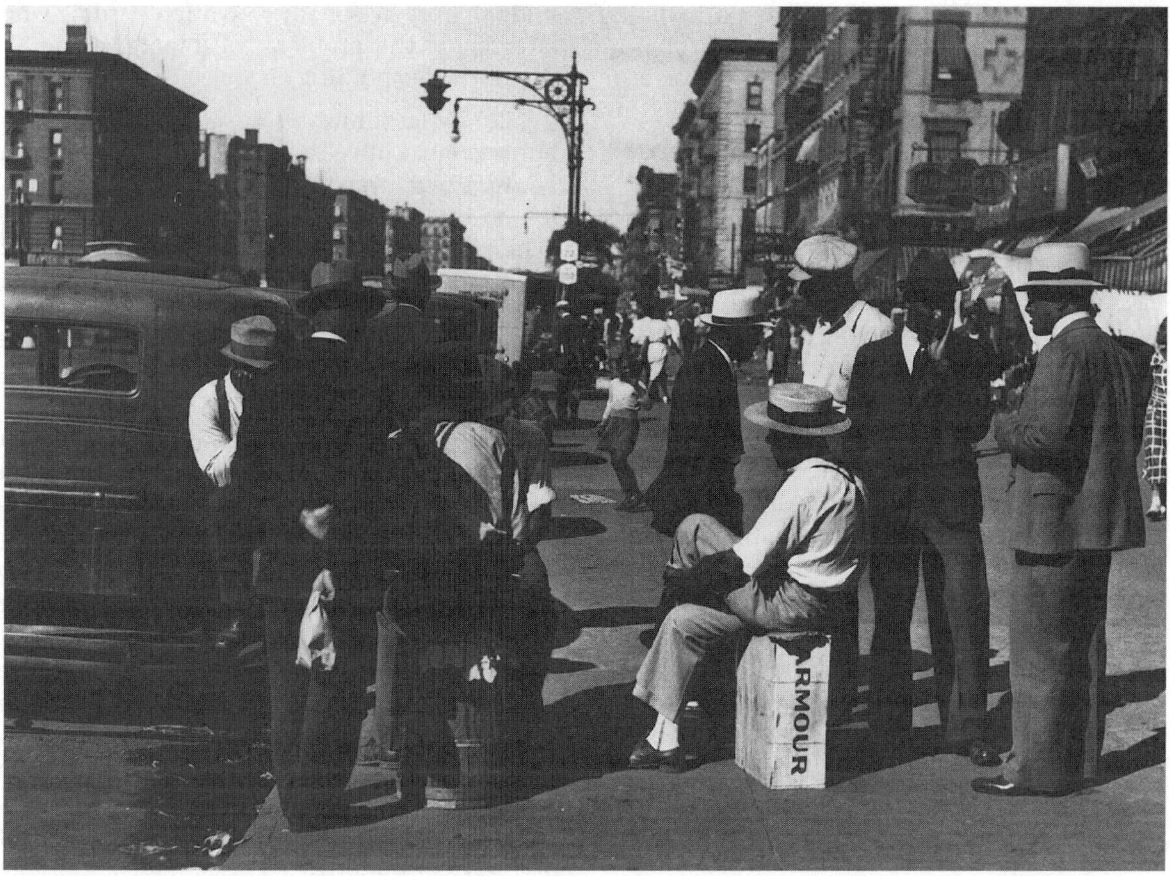

Unemployed Black men on Lennox Avenue in Harlem in 1935. Johnson wrote about the status of educated men of color in the United States.

The sum of Johnson's efforts was an organizational success for the Association. By 1919, there were 155 Southern branches, over half of its total number.[45]

The general outlook for the Negro at this time, however, was bleak. The War and the migration of Negroes from South to North and from country to city were bringing new racial tensions, tensions which erupted in Coatesville, in East St. Louis, and elsewhere. The Association was also having its problems. It was threatened by the black nationalism of Marcus Garvey, and it was divided internally, mainly by Du Bois, who insisted on running the *Crisis* independently of the Association and who had already caused the resignation of Oswald Garrison Villard. Its leadership was faltering as Executive Secretary, John Shillady, had been frightened since being beaten by a mob in Austin, Texas. Besides this, it had already been branded by many as radical and irresponsible.[46]

In 1920, these problems were thrown squarely into Johnson's lap. The Board of Directors appointed him to succeed Shillady as Executive Secretary. He was to be the first Negro to hold this position. His first act was characteristic. He accepted; but only on the condition that his salary at least equal Shillady's.[47]

Johnson was not as sure of himself as his demand to the Board might have indicated. The problems he faced were grave and often he had no answers to them. One of these problems was the Negro laborer, who was just beginning to be heard from. Jobs for unskilled laborers were rare and the Negro was, as the saying went, "the last to be hired, the first to be fired." High wartime wages had only whetted his appetite.

Johnson recognized the problem and was deeply concerned. He saw the grim struggle for existence that was the real, behind-the-scenes story of Harlem.[48] He could make, however, no effective response. He advocated a pragmatic, more or less opportunistic policy, stressing organization, if possible, in white unions, otherwise in Negro associations. He also suggested boycotts and an effort to convince whites of the abilities of Negro laborers.

Johnson rarely took any action particularly aimed at helping the Negro laborer. Probably there was little he could have done; but it was also true that he was hard pressed to personally involve himself in the laborers' struggle. He had little in common with the laborer. Du Bois pointed out that Johnson, except for isolated incidents, never had any personal contact with the urban laborer.[49] Johnson abhorred a working class philosophy. So middle class was his orientation that in a later book on the alternatives facing the Negro, he had to be urged even to mention Communism.[50] As an artist and an intellectual, a psychological approach to prejudice appealed to him more than did an economic one.

Another evidence of the difficulties of Johnson's and the NAACP's pragmatic and necessarily long-range approach was the rise of Garveyism in the 1920's. Garvey's effect on the unlettered and inexperienced Negro urban element was magnetic; by 1923 Garvey could legitimately claim at least a half million supporters.[51] Johnson could not help but admire Garvey, who had awakened Negroes in a way that he himself could never do. But he had no sympathy for "Back to Africa." Garveyism was to him the "Apotheosis of the Ridiculous."[52] He felt no great bond with Africa. Although he felt some cultural unity with the African people,[53] he took little interest in plans that included Negroes of the world, such as Du Bois's Pan-African Congress.

More than that, he loved America. He felt little of the despair or the bitterness of a Du Bois. He tended to generalize from his own life. Wasn't he himself an example of the distance a Negro could go? Whatever his frustrations had been, he was very much at home in a white culture. Du Bois even criticized him for too often asking advice from whites.[54] He was not only an American Negro, who, as C. Vann Woodward has pointed out, is possessed of a realism bred into his bones and marrow,[55] but he was an American Negro for whom that realism was not an unpleasant one.

Johnson was somewhat more successful in other areas. One of the Association's major efforts in the years 1921-24 was to pass the Dyer Anti-Lynching Bill. Johnson spent much of those years lobbying in the halls of Congress. The bill passed the House in 1922, but succumbed to the Senate in 1924. Although an anti-lynching bill was not passed until 1937, the effort had aroused substantial enthusiasm among American Negroes. Johnson also made an investigation of the brutality of the U. S. Marines and of U. S. imperialism on the island of Haiti. He wrote an expose[56] and told the story personally to Warren Harding who later made the problem a campaign issue although he did nothing once elected.

But by far Johnson's most important contribution as Executive Secretary was in building the NAACP. Here, the qualities which left him helpless in the face of Garveyism served him well. When he began, in 1920, the organization had few funds, faltering leadership, and an insecure reputation. Under his leadership all this changed. He was a masterful fund raiser. From a state of near bankruptcy in 1920 the NAACP was by 1930 a financially stable organization. Johnson's distinguished style and personality were, according to Arthur Spingarn, the Association's greatest selling point.[57]

Johnson also brought to the NAACP courageous leadership; during his tenure the leadership moved from the Board of Directors to the Executive Secretary.[58] The ideology of the Association did not change under him. The objectives remained full political, economic, and social equality. The methods remained lobbying, propaganda, and legal reform. Johnson's contribution was to maintain and implement these principles in a period when the Association could have been destroyed by timidity.

Furthermore, Johnson was the crucial force in maintaining the harmony and integrity of the Association. His mere presence was a cohesive force. Mary White Ovington ascribed to Johnson the quality of "sweet reasonableness." "Given authority," she said, "he knew when and when not to use it."[59] Johnson and Du Bois, for example, worked well together. "They got along," said Carl Van Vechten, "because Johnson got along with Du Bois."[60] No other act demonstrated his "sweet reasonableness" more than did his resignation. In 1930 he took a year's leave of absence because of ill health. During his absence he delegated most of his responsibility to Walter White. When Johnson returned he found that White had become accustomed to the job and would be unhappy to give it up. The job was still Johnson's, but he had no desire for a power struggle within the Association.[61] Johnson, the reasonable man, stepped down.

VII.

Johnson lived seven more years in which he taught and continued to write. The poetry he had written during his years with the NAACP was the finest he had ever done and among the best Negro poetry that had been written. He had found a new form, the idiom, which could express themes and emotions peculiar to the Negro but which, unlike the dialect, was pure and truthful and did not smack of the minstrel stage.[62] He had arrived at this form by studying the traditional Negro folk sermons, and in it he wrote such poems as **"The Creation," "Go Down Death"** and **"Let My People Go."**[63] There were also several books including an autobiography. In 1938 he was killed in an automobile accident in Great Barrington, Massachusetts.

Johnson had started out to build a life of his own and be an asset to his race. Circumstances limited the life of his own; all had to go to the race. As a race leader there were also limitations. Du Bois called Negro leadership in the 1920's both a great success and a colossal failure. But whatever ideological or tactical criticisms one might make of Johnson and others, the most imposing fact about the period is that a foundation was created for the road ahead.

Notes

1. C. Vann Woodward, *The Strange Career of Jim Crow* (New York, 1955), p. 102.
2. For some of the biographical information about Johnson's early years this paper relies on his autobiography, *Along This Way* (New York, 1933).
3. Thomas Davis, *History of Jacksonville, Florida and Vicinity* (Jacksonville, 1925), p. 488.
4. Willard Range, *The Rise and Progress of Negro Colleges in Georgia, 1865-1949* (Athens, Ga., 1951), p. 21. 90% of Atlanta graduates became teachers. See *Atlanta University Catalogue,* 1877-78 (Atlanta), p. 7.
5. See, e.g., Johnson's class oration at Atlanta in 1892 (James Weldon Johnson Collection, Yale University, New Haven, Conn.).
6. Johnson to Florida *Times Union,* December 21, 1897 (James Weldon Johnson Collection).
7. See Johnson's editorial, "The Harlem Public Library," *New York Age,* Nov. 5, 1914 (James Weldon Johnson Collection).
8. *Daily American,* probably May, 1895 (James Weldon Johnson Collection). There are no known extant copies of the *American* and all references are to clippings in the Johnson Collection.
9. Johnson tried, for example, to persuade the Negroes of Jacksonville to enter a display in the Jacksonville Exposition of 1895. *Daily American,* probably June, 1895 (James Weldon Johnson Collection).
10. Johnson, *Along This Way,* pp. 139-40.
11. Paul Buck, *The Road to Reunion 1865-1900* (New York, 1959), pp. 300-01.
12. See Gunnar Mydal, *An American Dilemma* (New York, 1944), p. 326.
13. John Hope Franklin, *From Slavery to Freedom* (New York, 1947), p. 405.
14. Oswald G. Villard, "Issues and Men," *The Nation,* CXLVII (July, 9, 1938), p. 44.
15. Eugenia Collier, "James Weldon Johnson: Mirror of Change," *Phylon,* XXI (Winter, 1960), 351.
16. Johnson, *Along This Way,* pp. 158-59.
17. In Robert Eleazer, *Singers in the Dawn* (Atlanta, 1934), p. 22.
18. In James Weldon Johnson, *Saint Peter Relates an Incident: Selected Poems* (New York, 1935), p. 73.
19. Collier, "James Weldon Johnson: Mirror of Change," *loc. cit.,* pp. 352-53.
20. Sterling Brown, *Negro Poetry and Drama* (Washington, D. C., 1937). Johnson's pop music is also of relatively high quality; see, e.g., "Mandy," "The Maiden with the Dreamy Eyes," "The Congo Love Song" (James Weldon Johnson Collection).
21. Franklin, *From Slavery to Freedom,* p. 427.
22. The poems mentioned in this paragraph and others are collected in James Weldon Johnson, *Fifty Years and Other Poems* (Boston, 1917).
23. New York, 1912.
24. Sterling Brown, *The Negro in American Fiction* (Washington, D. C., 1937), p. 105.
25. Johnson, *The Autobiography of an Ex-Coloured Man,* p. 113.
26. Interview with Carl Van Vechten, Feb. 11, 1960.
27. Paul Haworth, *The United States in Our Own Times 1865-1920* (New York, 1920), p. 23.
28. Johnson, *Along This Way,* pp. 291-93.
29. Of the lower class Negroes, he wrote, in *The Autobiography of an Ex-Coloured Man,* of their "unkempt appearance, the shambling, slouching gait and loud talk and laughter," p. 56.
30. The fullest exposition of Johnson's views on Negro strategy is his *Negro Americans, What Now?* (New York, 1934).
31. See Bolton Smith, "The Negro in Wartime," with a rejoinder by James Weldon Johnson, 1918 (James Weldon Johnson Collection).
32. *New York Age,* March 3, 1917 (James Weldon Johnson Collection).
33. *Ibid.,* Sept. 2, 1915 (James Weldon Johnson Collection).
34. *Ibid.,* Feb. 6, 1918 (James Weldon Johnson Collection).
35. Johnson quoted by Walter White, *A Man Called White* (New York, 1948), p. 34.
36. In Johnson, *Saint Peter Relates An Incident: Selected Poems,* p. 27.
37. Margaret Just Butcher, *The Negro in American Culture* (New York, 1956), p. 122.
38. Brown, *Negro Poetry and Drama,* p. 51.
39. W. E. B. Du Bois, *Dusk of Dawn* (New York, 1940), p. 243.

40. Interview with Arthur Spingarn, March 4, 1961.
41. *Ibid.*
42. *Ibid.*
43. See Emma Thornbrough, "More Light on Booker T. Washington and the *New York Age*," *Journal of Negro History,* XLIII (Jan., 1958), p. 34-49.
44. White, *A Man Called White,* p. 34.
45. NAACP, *Annual Report,* 1919, p. 9.
46. Franklin, *From Slavery to Freedom,* p. 439.
47. Interview with Arthur Spingarn.
48. James Weldon Johnson, *Black Manhattan* (New York, 1930), p. 161.
49. Interview with W. E. B. Du Bois, March 1, 1961.
50. Interview with Arthur Spingarn.
51. Franklin, *From Slavery to Freedom,* p. 482.
52. *New York Age,* Aug. 19, 1922 (James Weldon Johnson Collection).
53. See James Weldon Johnson, *Native African Races and Cultures* (Charlottesville, 1927).
54. Interview with W. E. B. Du Bois.
55. C. Vann Woodward, "Comment," *Studies on the Left,* VI (Nov.-Dec., 1966), 42.
56. James Weldon Johnson, "Self Determining Haiti," *The Nation,* CXI (Sept. 4-Sept. 25, 1920), 2878.
57. Interview with Arthur Spingarn.
58. *Ibid.*
59. Mary White Ovington, *The Walls Came Tumbling Down* (New York, 1947), p. 177.
60. Interview with Carl Van Vechten.
61. Interview with W.E.B. Du Bois.
62. Brown, *Negro Poetry and Drama,* p. 68.
63. These poems and others are collected in James Weldon Johnson, *Gods Trombones* (New York, 1927).

RICHARD A. LONG (ESSAY DATE 1971)

SOURCE: Long, Richard A. "A Weapon of My Song: The Poetry of James Weldon Johnson." *Phylon* 32 (winter 1971): 374-52.

In the following essay, Long discusses the development of both the form and the content of Johnson's verse.

The verse output of James Weldon Johnson falls into four groups: lyrics in standard English, poems in the dialect tradition, folk-inspired free verse, and a long satirical poem. The first two groups are contemporary and were published in the volume ***Fifty Years and Other Poems*** (Boston, 1917). The prayer and seven Negro sermons of the third group constitute ***God's Trombones*** (New York, 1927). The last group is represented by the poem **"Saint Peter Relates an Incident of the Resurrection Day,"** privately printed in 1930, and republished with a selection of earlier poems in 1935.

The early poetry of Johnson belongs to the late nineteenth century tradition of sentimental poetry in so far as its techniques and verse forms are concerned, seldom rising above the mediocrity characteristic of American poetry in the period 1890-1910, during which it was written for the most part. In purpose, however, Johnson's early verse was a species of propaganda, designed sometimes overtly, sometimes obliquely, to advance to a reading public the merits and the grievances of blacks. In this sense the poetry of Johnson is an integral part of a coherent strain in the poetry of Afro-Americans beginning with Phillis Wheatley:

> Remember, Christians, Negroes, black as Cain,
> May be refined, and join th' angelic train.
> (Phillis Wheatley, "On Being Brought from Africa to America")

More particularly, we may note the relationship of Johnson's early poetry to that of Paul Lawrence Dunbar, his much admired friend and contemporary. Though they were about the same age, Dunbar was by far the more precocious, and his virtuosity had an obvious impact on Johnson, though little of Dunbar's verse bears any obvious burden of racial protest, in spite of the real personal suffering Dunbar underwent because of misunderstanding and neglect that he ascribed to his color.

Another factor of importance in the early verse of Johnson is his composition of verses to be set to music by his brother J. Rosamond Johnson; the search for euphony and piquancy and the use of devices such as internal rhyme betrays the hand of the librettist.

The division of Johnson's poetry into standard lyrics and dialect verse, as in the case of Dunbar's poetry, reflects a self-conscious distinction made by the author himself. Johnson's first collection of his poetry, which appeared eleven years after Dunbar's death, presents forty-eight standard poems, followed by a segregated group of sixteen **"Jingles and Croons."** The dialect poems reflect of course a literary tradition of their own since in point of fact the themes and forms of such dialect poetry as was written by Dunbar and Johnson and many others reflect no tradition of the folk who used "dialect." In point of fact, it is useful to remember that the dialect poets learned mainly from their predecessors and employ for the most part uniform grammatical and orthographic conventions which suggest that they did not consciously seek to represent any individual or regional dialect. Johnson himself gives a brief account of the dialect literary tradition in his introductions to Dunbar and other dialect poets in ***The Book of American Negro Poetry*** (New York, 1931).

One of Johnson's dialect poems, because of its popular musical setting, is widely known and thought by many to be a genuine folk-product. The low-key sentimentality of **"Sence You Went Away"** is nevertheless that of the stage and not of real life. The last stanza will illustrate the point:

Seems lak to me I jes can't he'p but sigh,
Seems lak to me ma th'oat keeps gittin' dry,
Seems lak to me a tear stays in ma eye,
Sence you went away.

The other dialect poems in Johnson's first collection which should be classified among the "croons" are **"My Lady's Lips Are Like De Honey," "Nobody's Lookin' But de Owl and de Moon," "You's Sweet to Yo' Mammy Jes de Same," "A Banjo Song."** The titles are sufficiently indicative of their range and content. The "jingles" are frequently in the form of dramatic monologue, and while they (partly because of their later publication), have never become platform rivals to Dunbar's monologues, **"Tunk (A Lecture on Modern Education)"** and **"The Rivals"** can challenge comparison. The first is an exhortation to a truant schoolboy in which the light duties of white folks in offices are contrasted with the labors of black folks in the fields. The second is an old man's reminiscences of a crucial episode in the courtship of his wife. Both poems are written in long line rhyming couplets, Johnson's preferred verse form for his dialect verse, though a variety of stanza forms and rhyme schemes is employed, some with great versatility as the refrain from **"Brer Rabbit, You's de Cutes' of 'Em All"** illustrates:

"Brer Wolf am mighty cunnin',
Brer Fox am mighty sly,
Brer Terrapin an' 'Possum—kinder small;
Brer Lion's mighty vicious,
Brer B'ar he's sorter 'spi'cious,
Brer Rabbit, you's de cutes' of 'em all."

Of the standard poems of Johnson collected in ***Fifty Years,*** at least ten are more and less overtly on the race problem and among these are several of Johnson's most important poems. In contrast, the more generalized poems have hardly more than a passing interest except for a group of six poems **"Down by the Carib Sea"** in which Johnson treats images from his Latin-American experience as a U.S. consul in Venezuela and Nicaragua. Unfortunately, even here, conventionality of diction vitiates what might have been a poetic expression of enduring interest and value.

The group of ten race poems includes three of the "appeal" genre in which the black poet addresses his white compatriots and invites an improvement in their attitudes toward the blacks. This genre of Afro-American poetry runs from Phillis Wheatley to Gwendolyn Brooks, and may be said to have been already conventional when Johnson essayed it, though the sincerity with which he takes up the form cannot be doubted. In the short poem **"To America"** he asks:

How would you have us, as we are?
Or sinking 'neath the load we bear?

. . . . .

Strong willing sinews in your wings?
Or tightening chains about your feet?

"O Southland" makes the poet implore

O Southland, fair Southland!
Then why do you cling
To an idle age and a musty page,
To a dead and useless thing.

And in **"Fragment"** he declares

See! In your very midst there dwell
Ten thousand blacks, a wedge
Forged in the furnaces of hell. . . .

The somewhat stern Calvinistic fervor of this poem suggests that the system is foredoomed to divine malediction.

Another genre in the race poems is that of pointing out the virtuous black and inviting sympathy and understanding. **"The Black Mammy"** and **"The Color Sergeant"** illustrate this genre. The theme of the Black Mammy who has nursed with tenderness the white child who may some day strike down her own black child has its own kind of immortality, combining as it does the mawkishness of mother love with America's quaint racial customs. **"The Color Sergeant"** is based on a real incident in the Spanish-American War and may be said to prefigure the Dorie Miller and similar poems of succeeding wars.

A lynching poem is called **"Brothers"** and is a stilted dramatic exchange between a lynch victim and the mob who burn him alive. The division of objects from the ashes is intended perhaps to recall the casting of lots for Christ's clothes:

"You take that bone, and you this tooth, the
chain—

Let us divide its links; this skull, of course
In fair division, to the leader comes."

Still another poem which I classify as a race poem because of its obvious symbolism and because Johnson places it at the end of that group in the arrangement of the poems in ***Fifty Years*** could be read simply as a poem of ghostly circumstance. **"The White Witch"** describes a beauteous apparition who lures young men to their death. The poem's progenitors are the Romantic literary ballads. It is possible that Johnson had heard of the Jamaican ghost legend of the White Witch of Rose Hall, but there is no obvious patterning of his scenario on the legend.

In two of the race poems Johnson addresses black people specifically. One of these is the famous ode to the dead creators of the spirituals, **"O Black and Unknown Bards."** The harmony and dignity of the poem are fully deserving of the praise it has received. The poet marvels continually:

There is a wide, wide wonder in it all,
That from degraded rest and service toil
The fiery spirit of the seer should call
These simple children of the sun and soil.

But his conclusion seems timid and apologetic,

You sang far better than you knew; the songs
That for your listeners' hungry hearts sufficed
Still live,—but more than this to you belongs:
You sang a race from wood and stone to Christ.

The bulk of the poems written by Johnson which fall into the two categories just discussed were written before 1910. The poem which serves as the title poem to his first collection is itself a commemorative poem written in 1912 to mark the fiftieth anniversary of the Emancipation Proclamation. The poem begins with an apostrophe to his fellow blacks:

O brothers mine, today we stand
Where half a century sweeps our ken. . . .

He then invokes the scene of the first blacks arriving in Jamestown in 1619. And from these few (aided, as the poet does not note, by the energetic exploitation of the slave trade) have come a race "ten million strong / An upward, onward marching host."

He goes on to declare

This land is ours by right of birth,
This land is ours by right of toil;
We helped to turn its virgin earth,
Our sweat is in its fruitful soil.

He cites the labors of blacks and their frequent defense of the flag. He observes that despite these things blacks are maltreated and persecuted, but he urges

Courage! Look out, beyond, and see
The far horizon's beckoning span!
Faith in your God-known destiny!
We are a part of some great plan.

And the poem closes with expression of faith in God's intentions for the best. The poem is in twenty-six octosyllabic quatrains, rhyming a b a b, in ***Fifty Years and Other Poems.*** Johnson abridged it to twenty stanzas for its appearance in ***The Book of American Negro Poetry.*** In the 1935 collection it appears as a poem of twenty-four stanzas, with a prefatory note.

One poem, related in tone and character to **"Fifty Years,"** written in 1900, was not included in ***Fifty Years and Other Poems,*** but was included in the 1935 collection. This is the famous song lyric **"Lift Every Voice and Sing,"** known far and wide as the "Negro National Anthem." Its heroic language, fully sustained by the harmonies of J. Rosamond Johnson, have played a role in the life of black America that no patriotic song could have fulfilled.

We have come over a way that with tears has
been watered,
We have come, treading our path through the
blood of
the slaughtered,
Out from the gloomy past,
Till now we stand at last
Where the white gleam of our bright star is cast.

The second decade of the twentieth century was a period of innovation and change in American poetry. The establishment of *Poetry Magazine,* the Imagist manifesto, the appearance of Frost, Masters, Sandburg, Lindsay and Pound all bespeak the new spirit. The annual anthologies of Magazine verse edited by William Stanley Braithwaite beginning in 1913 which were one of the chief forums of the new spirit despite Braithwaite's own conservatism were surely well-perused by his friend James Weldon Johnson. Accordingly, it is not surprising to find a sudden modification in Johnson's poetic practice develop during this decade, for his poem **"The Creation"** precedes by almost a decade its publication with companion pieces in ***God's Trombones*** in 1927. He recounts his immediate inspiration for **"The Creation"** in the Preface to ***God's Trombones***:

. . . He [a rural black preacher] strode the pulpit up and down in what was actually a very rhythmic dance, and he brought into play the full gamut of his wonderful voice. . . . He intoned, he moaned,

> he pleaded—he blared, he crashed, he thundered. I sat fascinated; and more, I was, perhaps against my will, deeply moved; the emotional effect upon me was irresistible. Before he had finished I took a slip of paper and somewhat surreptitiously jotted down some ideas for the first poem, **"The Creation."**

"The Creation" was conceived, as it were, in the heat of the moment. Only gradually did Johnson develop the series of poems which constitute the seven sermons and the opening prayer of ***God's Trombones.*** The principles he employed in writing these poems, based closely on the practice of the folk preacher, are explained in the Preface. He explains why he did not write them in dialect (in the sense of an attempted indication of folk speech):

> First, although the dialect is the exact instrument for voicing certain traditional phases of Negro life, it is, and perhaps by that very exactness, a quite limited instrument. Indeed, it is an instrument with but two complete stops, pathos and humor. This limitation is not due to any defect of the dialect as dialect, but to the mould of convention in which Negro dialect in the United States has been set, to the fixing effects of its long association with the Negro only as a happy-go-lucky or a forlorn figure. . . .
>
> The second part of my reason for not writing these poems in dialect is the weightier. The old-time Negro preachers, though they actually used dialect in their ordinary intercourse, stepped out from its narrow confines when they preached. They were all saturated with the sublime phraseology of the Hebrew prophets and steeped in the idioms of King James English, so when they preached and warmed to their work they spoke another language, a language far removed from traditional Negro dialect. It was really a fusion of Negro idioms with Bible English; and in this there may have been, after all, some kinship with the innate grandiloquence of their old African tongues. To place in the mouths of the talented old-time Negro preachers a language that is a literary imitation of Mississippi cotton-field dialect is sheer burlesque.

Johnson says in the Preface that "the old-time Negro preacher is rapidly passing." Nothing could have been further from the truth. "Oldtime" Negro preaching is not only fully present in 1971 in large churches as well as in store-front meeting rooms, but its eloquence has dominated political forums and civil rights meetings, sometimes to the exclusion of action. This eloquence underlies much of the prose of Ellison and Baldwin as well as that of many writers of the sixties.

The medium Johnson chose for the sermon poems is a cadenced free verse which very effectively reflects the rhythmical speech of the folk preacher. Johnson uses the dash to indicate "a certain sort of pause that is marked by a quick intaking and an audible expulsion of the breath. . . ." The arrangement of prayer and sermons in ***God's Trombones*** is

> Listen, Lord—A Prayer
> The Creation
> The Prodigal Son
> Go Down Death—A Funeral Sermon
> Noah Built the Ark
> The Crucifixion
> Let My People Go
> The Judgment Day.

"Listen, Lord," "The Creation," "Go Down Death," and **"The Crucifixion"** are generally of a more exalted interest than the other pieces, but all of them capture effectively the imagery, the intensity, the sly humor, and the hypnotic grandeur of the black sermon tradition. In **"Listen, Lord"** the blessing of God is invoked on the preacher in these terms

> Put his eye to the telescope of eternity,
> And let him look upon the paper walls of time.
> Lord, turpentine his imagination,
> Put perpetual motion in his arms,
> Fill him full of the dynamite of thy power,
> Anoint him all over with the oil of thy salvation,
> And set his tongue on fire.

The actual events of awful moments are iterated in **"The Crucifixion"**:

> Jesus, my lamb-like Jesus,
> Shivering as the nails go through his feet.
> Jesus, my darling Jesus,
> Groaning as the Roman spear plunged in his
> side;
> Jesus, my darling Jesus,
> Groaning as the blood came spurting from his
> wound.
> Oh, look how they done my Jesus.

In **"Noah Built the Ark"** Satan is depicted with familiarity:

> Then pretty soon along came Satan.
> Old Satan came like a snake in the grass
> To try out his tricks on the woman.
> I imagine I can see Old Satan now
> A-sidling up to the woman.
> I imagine the first word Satan said was:
> Eve, you're surely good looking.

After the story of the exodus is told in **"Let My People Go"** the preacher concludes with a magnificent coda:

> Listen!—Listen!
> All you sons of Pharaoh.
> Who do you think can hold God's people
> When the Lord God himself has said,
> Let my people go?

The general technique developed by Johnson for ***God's Trombones*** constitutes a giant leap from his archaizing early poetry. Unfortunately the many pressures of his life as a public man and as a cultural mentor prevented him from utilizing his new freedom in a substantial body of work, though the continuing popularity of ***God's Trombones*** since its initial publication and its appeal to a broad stratum of readers have given this slim volume an importance in American poetry enjoyed by few other works of comparable scope.

A special irony of Johnson's creations is that they have often themselves reentered the folk stream they were intended to fix and commemorate, and have in turn sustained through countless recitations the continuation of a living tradition.

While Johnson expressed no overt ideological objectives concerning his verse sermons, it is significant that they were not offered either in the spirit of his early standard verse or of his "jingles and croons." The sermons are an assertion of black pride and black dignity with no reference to perspectives and standards of others.

A further direction in his poetic practice was revealed by Johnson in the long satirical poem **"Saint Peter Relates an Incident of the Resurrection Day."** Johnson describes the genesis of the poem in the third person in his 1935 foreword:

> . . . The title poem of this volume was originally printed in 1930, in an edition of 200 copies for private distribution. In the summer of that year the author was busy on the manuscript of a book. He read one morning in the newspaper that the United States government was sending a contingent of gold-star mothers to France to visit the graves of their soldier sons buried there; and that the Negro gold-star mothers would not be allowed to sail on the same ship with the white gold-star mothers, but would be sent over on a second and second-class vessel. He threw aside the manuscript on which he was working and did not take it up again until he had finished the poem, **"Saint Peter Relates an Incident of the Resurrection Day."**

The poem, arranged in six sections of varying length, presents St. Peter, long after Resurrection Day, recounting to some of the heavenly host the unburying of the Unknown Soldier. The discovery that the man who had been honored by generations of Americans in his magnificent tomb was black is the O'Henryesque reversal in the poem. The limpidity of Johnson's handling of the theme in quatrains of rhyming couplets, a favorite meter for narration and monologue with him in his earlier verse, is illustrated by his description of the reaction to the Klan's suggestion that the soldier be reburied:

> The scheme involved within the Klan's suggestion
> Gave rise to a rather nice metaphysical question:
> Could he be forced again through death's dark portal,
> Since now his body and soul were both immortal?

The publication of **"Saint Peter Relates an Incident of the Resurrection Day"** in 1935 provided the occasion for Johnson to issue a new selection of his poems. Thirty-seven poems, including eight in dialect, from ***Fifty Years and Other Poems*** were reprinted, as well as **"Lift Every Voice and Sing."** Four additional poems were a sonnet **"My City,"** a celebration of Manhattan, and **"If I Were Paris,"** a lyric of twelve lines, both in his earlier manner; a free-verse poem **"A Poet to His Baby Son"** written in a later colloquial manner; and a translation from the Cuban poet Placido, **"Mother, Farewell!"** a sonnet which Johnson had published in the 1922 edition of ***The Book of American Negro Poetry*** and again in the 1931 revised edition. ***Fifty Years and Other Poems*** had included the translation of another poem of Placido.

An untitled envoy, the last poem in ***Fifty Years and Other Poems,*** contains the following lines, central to its thought:

> . . . if injustice, brutishness and wrong
> Should make a blasting trumpet of my song;
> O God, give beauty and strength—truth to my words. . . .

Eighteen years later a revised and now titled **"Envoy"** closes the second and final selection of Johnson poems:

> . . . if injustice, brutishness, and wrong
> Stir me to make a weapon of my song;
> O God, give beauty, truth, strength to my words.

In this revision two important points are presented in capsule. Johnson continued to revise and modify his poems, a fact which should be taken account of in any future study devoted primarily to the texts. The second point is that Johnson's conception of the function of the poet, the black poet particularly, had evolved from the apologetic tradition, in which racial justice is implored and in which an attempt to show the worthiness of blacks is made by showing their conformism, to a militant posture, in which the poet uses his talent as a weapon with concern only for beauty, truth and strength. In both phases, Johnson was a poet who recognized the propriety of propaganda. His earlier concern was with influencing opinion ("a blasting trumpet"); his later concern was asserting the verities, with a willingness "to make a weapon of my song."

TITLE COMMENTARY

The Autobiography of an Ex-Coloured Man

ROBERT E. FLEMING (ESSAY DATE 1971)

SOURCE: Fleming, Robert E. "Irony as a Key to Johnson's *The Autobiography of an Ex-Coloured Man.*" *American Literature* 43, no. 1 (March 1971): 83-96.

In the following essay, Fleming contends that Autobiography of an Ex-Coloured Man *is not only about American race relations but is a deeply ironic character study of a marginal man who is not completely aware of the significance of his story.*

James Weldon Johnson's only novel, ***The Autobiography of an Ex-Coloured Man*** (1912), has frequently been lauded for its objective presentation of Negro manners in various parts of the country, from rural Georgia to New York City. While this recognition of the novel's sociological importance is merited, it has tended to draw attention from the artistic elements of the work; those critics who admire the novel often do so for the wrong reasons. For example, the highly respected black critic Sterling A. Brown states that the novel is important because it is "the first to deal with Negro life on several levels, from the folk to the sophisticated," but goes on to say that it is "rather more a chart of Negro life than a novel."[1] While Hugh M. Gloster praises Johnson's restrained handling of racial questions, he treats the novel as if it were little more than a frank commentary on racial relations offered by a Negro who has dropped the mask usually worn before whites.[2] Only Robert A. Bone has pointed out one of the most notable features of the work, its ironic tone.[3] ***The Autobiography*** is not so much a panoramic novel presenting race relations throughout America as it is a deeply ironic character study of a marginal man who narrates the story of his own life without fully realizing the significance of what he tells his readers.

It is the irony of ***The Autobiography*** which sets it apart from a number of novels which deal with a similar theme, for it belongs to a class of novels which was by no means new in 1912. The general theme of the tragic mulatto who fits into neither culture had been employed by such authors as Harriet Beecher Stowe in *Uncle Tom's Cabin* (1852), William Wells Brown in *Clotel; or, the President's Daughter* (1853), and Charles W. Chesnutt in *The House behind the Cedars* (1900) and *The Marrow of Tradition* (1901). However, none of these books, whether by white or black authors, goes beyond the stereotyped view of the tragic mulatto, whose appeal to the reader is made on the basis of a high percentage of white blood, and whose difficulties are external and primarily physical.[4] George and Eliza Harris from *Uncle Tom's Cabin* illustrate the stereotype admirably: George is so light-complexioned that at one point he passes for a Spaniard simply by donning the right clothes; his difficulties and those of his wife are physical dangers connected with the evils of slavery. The white reader is evidently expected to feel a different kind of sympathy for the mulatto than for stoical, coal-black Uncle Tom; in addition, the reader's sympathy is intended to bring about the abolition of slavery—the external evil which gives rise to the conflicts of the novel. ***The Autobiography,*** on the other hand, features a protagonist-narrator born after the emancipation of slaves and so light that he may choose the race to which he will belong. External difficulties such as the fear of discovery are almost nonexistent; rather, emotional conflicts become the major concern of the novelist. Johnson's ironic technique is well-suited to such material.

Johnson's ironic handling of his material also separates his novel from a number of works published in the twenties. In spite of the fact that they follow Johnson's lead in using the "passing" theme, novelists like Walter White (*Flight,* 1926), Jessie Fauset (*Plum Bun,* 1928), and Nella Larsen (*Passing,* 1929) are relatively straightforward in their treatment of their characters. None of these three novels makes its point by the sustained and many-faceted irony which is the chief artistic merit of ***The Autobiography of an Ex-Coloured Man.***

On the first page of ***The Autobiography,*** Johnson establishes the tone of the novel and suggests the complexity of the narrator. The ex-colored man begins by analyzing his motives for revealing "the great secret of [his] life"; while he feels a perverse sort of pride in his accomplishment, he also has a "savage and diabolical desire to gather up all the little tragedies of [his] life, and turn them into a practical joke on society."[5] However, the second paragraph suggests that the account is to be read not only as a boast but also as a confession; the narrator admits, "And, too, I suffer a vague feeling of unsatisfaction, of regret, of almost remorse, from which I am seeking relief, and of which I shall speak in the last paragraph of this account" (p. 3). The reader who turns to the end of the book at this point finds the key to one of the central ironies of the novel: the practical joke may, after all, be on the narrator, who laments "a vanished dream, a dead ambition, a sacrificed talent" and struggles to free himself of the fear that he has "chosen the lesser part" or sold his "birthright for a mess of pottage" (p. 211). The narrator's first paragraph gives the reader the impression of a self-assured man with a rather objective, analytical approach to what promises to be a searching and honest account of his life. However, the second and last paragraphs alert the reader to the fact that the narrator-protagonist is in reality disturbed, torn by doubt; therefore, his statements should be examined carefully to determine the psychological facts concealed by superficial meanings. The unreliable nature of the narrator is thus suggested, and the reader who keeps this in mind will appreciate ***The Autobiography*** as a novel rather than as a guidebook to Negro life, as an account of emotional and psychological responses rather than as a mere history of the protagonist's social and financial rise in the world.

The main character's relationship with his father and mother, treated mainly in chapters 1 through 3, illustrates Johnson's ironic use of the unreliable narrator. An examination of what the narrator tells us suggests that he harbors an unrealized resentment toward each of his parents. The father, in particular, is treated harshly, although he is not overtly criticized for his treatment of the narrator and his mother. The narrator's earliest memories of his father center not on traits of character or physique but on the material objects associated with him: shiny boots or shoes, a gold watch and chain, the slippers his small son must bring him, and the coins doled out as presents. When the father is about to send his mistress and son north so that his white fiancée will not learn about them, he drills a hole in a gold piece and ties it around his son's neck. The narrator wryly comments, "More than once I have wished that some other way had been found of attaching it to me besides putting a hole through it" (p. 6). This flawed gold piece serves as a fitting symbol for most gifts the white man has given the black as well as for the white man's materialistic values, values which the protagonist later adopts as his own. The father's action evokes suggestions of slavery, and his choice of a going-away present is another example of his substitution of material gifts for overt recognition. Another suggestion of a master-slave relationship occurs later when the father comes to visit: he addresses his son as "boy" and the son responds, "yes, sir" (p. 34). Thus the reader is prepared to recognize the irony in the mother's statement to her son that his father is "a great man, a fine gentleman" who loves them both very much (p. 38); moreover, there is a sort of double-edged irony in her assertion that "the best blood of the South" is in her son (p. 18). The relationship between father and son is epitomized in one incident: the father sends his son a new upright piano; however, the boy wonders why the gift was not a grand piano. Clearly, although the narrator tells of his father's kindness and his own emotional indifference in purely objective terms, the suggestiveness of the illustrative details and the psychologically revealing nature of apparently casual remarks make the reader aware of the protagonist's true feelings—resentment toward the father and his strictly materialistic expressions of affection.

While the narrator states that he loves his mother very much, there is evidence that Johnson attempted to convey more ambivalent feelings, the negative aspects of which are primarily subconscious. The mother's closeness to her son, her loving embraces, her desire to see him well educated—these are balanced by less admirable characteristics. She does not tell her son that he is partly black until he has been ridiculed as a "nigger" by schoolmates, and she hides the reality of his illegitimacy from him as long as possible. Even such minor details as the mother's practice of scrubbing him "until [his] skin ached" (p. 4), as if to make him even more white than he is, suggest that she accepts the white world's value system, and thus helps to create the confused marginal being that her son becomes. The incident which is most indicative of the son's subconscious feelings about his mother occurs when, after several years, the father first visits them in the North. The mother is obviously delighted, but the son, awkward and embarrassed, soon rushes off to a musical rehearsal where he is to accompany a white violinist, a girl with whom he is infatuated. Although he is under no great pressure to invent an alibi for being late, he tells his teacher that his mother is seriously ill, near death. Subconsciously then, the narrator reveals his feelings: jealousy of the love his mother has for his father, and, possibly, resentment of her black race, which has so lowered his position in the eyes of his classmates and of himself. The wish-fulfillment element in the lie is not admitted by the narrator even when his mother really does die shortly thereafter; he attributes his pang of guilt to having prophesied her death. The protagonist's great love for his mother is an important factor in his attempt to accept his black identity, just as his hidden resentment of her "tainted blood" is one of the underlying factors in his ultimate rejection of the black race.

Johnson's most notable irony is reserved for the narrator's comments about himself. It is significant that passages which deal with his reactions and feelings are characterized by a neoromantic style, by sentimental and rather inflated diction. The narrator views himself in romantic terms, as a tragic hero whose flaw is the black blood he has inherited from his beloved mother. Yet the reader, responding to the irony which undercuts the romantic pose, is more likely to view him as an antiheroic or pathetic character, frequently indulging in self-pity and unable to accept his total identity and assume his position in a race for which he feels little sympathy or admiration. Indeed, at times the reader suspects that the main character may have the makings of a first-class bigot in his own personality. Because the narrator's view of himself is distorted and because his narrative is, in a sense, an attempt to justify his decisions, the reader must question everything the main character says about himself.

The narrator strikes many ironic notes in telling about his boyhood. One of his small but meaningful memories is his preference for the black keys on the piano. This choice would seem to suggest that the protagonist feels that "black is beautiful," that he is subconsciously drawn to his mother's race even before he is aware of his mixed parentage. However, closely juxtaposed to this memory is an account of how some black classmates were mistreated:

> Sometimes on the way home from school a crowd would walk behind them repeating:
>
> "Nigger, nigger, never die,
> Black face and shiny eye."
>
> On one such afternoon one of the black boys turned suddenly on his tormentors and hurled a slate; it struck one of the white boys in the mouth, cutting a slight gash in his lip. At sight of the blood the boy who had thrown the slate ran, and his companions quickly followed. We ran after them pelting them with stones until they separated in several directions. I was very much wrought up over the affair, and went home and told my mother how one of the "niggers" had struck a boy with a slate. I shall never forget how she turned on me. "Don't you ever use that word again," she said, "and don't you ever bother the coloured children at school. You ought to be ashamed of yourself."
>
> (pp. 14-15)

It is, ironically, only a short time after his participation in this attack that the main character is shocked to find himself classified with these pariahs when the principal of his school divides the class into white and colored. The protagonist is surprised by the reactions of the two races: the black children in the class, some of whom he has persecuted, say that they have known his secret all along but would not unmask him; however, his former friends jeer, "You're a nigger too" (p. 16). This experience and the realization that his mother belongs to the black race make the narrator determined to consider himself black and to live his life accordingly. This is the first of several courses chosen by the protagonist, who vacillates between opposing bigotry in society and learning to live within the system, until his final capitulation.

Even before his humiliating discovery, the main character has admired a black boy, the leading scholar of their class. Without meaning harm, he has tagged the black classmate with the nickname "Shiny," an obvious pun on the racial slur, "shine." After he realizes that he is identified with the black children, the main character feels an even closer tie with Shiny. At their graduation ceremony, Shiny's well-delivered oration profoundly moves the protagonist:

> . . . the effect upon me of "Shiny's" speech was double; I not only shared the enthusiasm of his audience, but he imparted to me some of his own enthusiasm. I felt leap within me pride that I was coloured; and I began to form wild dreams of bringing glory and honour to the Negro race. For days I could talk of nothing else with my mother except my ambitions to be a great man, a great coloured man, to reflect credit on the race and gain fame for myself.
>
> (pp. 45-46)

However, the same incident illuminates the other side of the protagonist, for he also speculates on the enthusiastic reaction of the largely white audience. Instead of accepting this response as a matter of course, the narrator admires the whites' willingness to overlook race when a performance is sufficiently superior. He believes that "the explanation . . . lies in what is a basic, though often dormant, principle of the Anglo-Saxon heart, love of fair play" (p. 45). It is ironic that elsewhere the narrator holds these same white parents accountable for the cruel bigotry their children exhibit toward the black students.

From time to time throughout the novel, the narrator interrupts the movement of the story to generalize about Negro life and experience, and the reader can hardly help being struck by the objective tone of his observations. After he knows he is a Negro, he comments:

> And this is the dwarfing, warping, distorting influence which operates upon each and every coloured man in the United States. He is forced to take his outlook on all things, not from the view-point of a citizen, or a man, or even a human being, but from the view-point of a *coloured* man. It is wonderful to me that the race has progressed so broadly as it has, since most of its thought and all of its activity must run through the narrow neck of this one funnel.
>
> (p. 21)

Although the protagonist has apparently accepted his membership in the race he is describing, his attitude toward black people is curiously aloof. In the next section of the novel, chapters 4 through 10, the main character's experiences provide him with opportunities to observe many facets of Negro life, but he consistently views that life as an outsider might and constantly reverts to white values, attitudes, and responses. The fact that the narrator's observations of black life in America have been so highly praised by readers and critics adds an element of irony that Johnson may not have foreseen.

After his mother's death, the main character decides to attend Atlanta University, for the South holds a "peculiar fascination" for him; it is there, he feels, that he must work out his destiny and start toward his goal of becoming "a great coloured man." However, there is an ironic gap between his expectations and the reality he finds in Atlanta. The Pullman porter whom he asks for directions takes him to an unsavory boarding house in a run-down section of the city. The protagonist's first response to the race which he has decided to join is less than hearty:

> Here I caught my first sight of coloured people in large numbers. I had seen little squads around the railroad stations on my way south, but here I saw a street crowded with them. They filled the shops and thronged the sidewalks and lined the curb. I asked my companion if all the coloured people in Atlanta lived in this street. He said they did not and assured me that the ones I saw were of the lower class. I felt relieved, in spite of the size of the lower class. The unkempt appearance, the shambling, slouching gait and loud talk and laughter of these people aroused in me a feeling of almost repulsion.
>
> (pp. 55-56)

His stomach turns when he is taken to a greasy basement restaurant, "the best place in town where a coloured man could get a meal" (p. 57). The culmination of his disillusionment occurs when all his plans are thwarted because his money is stolen, ironically by the very porter who has served as his guide.

Unable to enter the university or to find work in Atlanta, the narrator travels to Jacksonville, Florida, a city Johnson knew well. Perhaps because Jacksonville is smaller than Atlanta and presented a less harsh aspect in the late nineteenth century, the main character is not so confused or appalled and is able to think about what he sees there. Once again adopting that clinical tone so characteristic of his comments on the black race, he analyzes the socioeconomic classes of black people in the South and points out the curious relationships between the three classes and the white Southerner. The servants, directly dependent on their white masters, are generally liked and frequently treated with real kindness; the desperate criminal class is easily controlled by the law and by extralegal terrorism; but the bourgeois class presents a social and economic threat to the whites, who systematically ridicule and ostracize the independent workmen and tradesmen. Objective analyses like this one, which occupies eight pages in the 1927 edition of the novel, have encouraged readers and critics to consider ***The Autobiography*** a sociological guidebook with only a suggestion of plot; but such disgressions tell us something about the narrator as well. He is able to view "his" race in detached sociological terms because he never feels a part of it. He never succeeds in his attempts to find his identity within the race to which the country's laws and customs consign him, the race which he embraced because it was his mother's. This ability to step outside the race is a reminder of the ironic gap between his true character and the flattering self-portrait the narrator draws of a man earnestly attempting to do what he knows is right. However, beneath his air of detachment, the reader is allowed to glimpse an individual whose racial identity changes because he bases his life on unstable principles. The protagonist's vacillating principles as well as his changing "color" were emphasized by Johnson's alternate title for the novel, *The Chameleon.*[6]

The protagonist experiences a different black culture in New York, where he is introduced to the black gambling houses and the "sporting life." Still the sociological analyst, he notes a curious attitude among white New Yorkers. Rather than isolate the Negro as do the Southerners, the New York upper classes enjoy slumming trips into black places of amusement. Ironically, the fact that the narrator is himself an observer of black life enables him to recognize and classify the motives of the slummers:

> There was at the place almost every night one or two parties of white people, men and women, who were out sight-seeing, or slumming. They generally came in cabs; some of them would stay only for a few minutes, while others sometimes stayed until morning. There was also another set of white people who came frequently; it was made up of variety performers and others who delineated "darky characters"; they came to get their imitations first-hand from the Negro entertainers they saw there.
>
> There was still another set of white patrons, composed of women; these were not occasional visitors, but five or six of them were regular habituées. . . . I always saw these women in company with coloured men. They were all good-looking and well dressed, and seemed to be women of some education.
>
> (pp. 107-108)

Because of the prudish literary conventions of 1912, Johnson's narrator is not very explicit about black-white sexual relationships, but his reaction to the sight of one white woman with her black gigolo is revealing: "I shall never forget how hard it was for me to get over my feelings of surprise, perhaps more than surprise, at seeing her with her black companion; somehow I never exactly enjoyed the sight" (p. 109). Not even the constrained understatement can conceal the fact that his reaction is that of a white man.

The narrator's ability as a rag-time pianist attracts the attention of a New York millionaire, who becomes his friend and patron and offers to take him to Europe. The narrator seems oblivious to the unintentional irony in the millionaire's invitation: "'I think I'll take you along instead of Walter.' Walter was his valet" (p. 124). In a way, the millionaire replaces the father in the master-servant relationship which seems to characterize the protagonist's experiences with white men. While the narrator states with pride that his patron treats him "as an equal, not as a servant" (p. 130), we also learn that the millionaire "fell into a habit which caused me no little annoyance; sometimes he would come in during the early hours of the morning and, finding me in bed asleep, would wake me up and ask me to play something" (p. 131). Johnson uses the European trip to throw certain characteristics of American racial attitudes into relief, but the trip also takes the protagonist away from the difficulties of the life he has tried to lead. Accepted as a white man in Europe, he again dreams of becoming "a great coloured man" and plans to do so by using his musical talent: "I made up my mind to go back into the very heart of the South, to live among the people, and drink in my inspiration firsthand. I gloated over the immense amount of material I had to work with, not only modern rag-time, but also the old slave songs—material which no one had yet touched" (pp. 142-143). The irony of his exploiting the music of the Negro escapes him.

On his way to the South, he encounters two men whose racial attitudes impress him. The first of these is a black doctor whom he meets on the ship. A member of what Du Bois called the "talented tenth," the doctor is described by the narrator as "the broadest-minded coloured man I have ever talked with on the Negro question" (p. 151). The narrator seems unaware that his high opinion of the doctor is determined by the many similarities between the man and himself. Like the protagonist, the doctor can discuss the "Negro question" in objective, detached terms. Only when his personal freedom is threatened does the doctor become emotionally involved enough to resent racial prejudice; on being informed that a man has attempted to have him evicted from the dining room, the doctor responds:

> I don't object to anyone's having prejudices so long as those prejudices don't interfere with my personal liberty. Now, the man you are speaking of had a perfect right to change his seat if I in any way interfered with his appetite or his digestion. . . . but when his prejudice attempts to move *me* one foot, one inch, out of the place where I am comfortably located, then I object.
>
> (p. 150)

Also like the protagonist, the doctor deplores the fact that some classes of black people are not so cultivated as he, and in some ways he can sympathize with Southern attitudes. When the two men visit some of the doctor's friends in Boston, the narrator's comments are significant:

> I could not help being struck by the great difference between them and the same class of coloured people in the South. In speech and thought they were genuine Yankees. The difference was especially noticeable in their speech. There was none of that heavy-tongued enunciation which characterizes even the best-educated coloured people of the South. It is remarkable, after all, what an adaptable creature the Negro is.
>
> (pp. 152-153)

Thus, even in the midst of his resolve to become a great black man, the narrator feels shame for all but the most acculturated of his race; his standards are white standards, and may cause the reader to recall the millionaire's observation, "My boy, you are by blood, by appearance, by education, and by tastes a white man" (p. 144).

The second important encounter occurs in a smoking car in the South. Accepted as white, the narrator listens as a Texan defends an extreme anti-Negro position against three Northerners: an apologetically liberal professor, a cautious Jewish businessman, and a Civil War veteran who appears to be a sympathetic spokesman for the liberal cause until he reveals his own prejudice. Ironically, the narrator feels most sympathetic toward the racist Texan: "I must confess that underneath it all I felt a certain sort of admiration for the man who could not be swayed from what he held as his principles" (p. 165). The total absence of any emotional response to the Texan's slurs is another indication of the fact that the main character does not feel like a member of the insulted race. In spite of all his experiences, his psychological orientation has not changed since he was a boy, joining the whites who chased the "niggers" home from school.

The incident to which the main character attributes his decision to pass for white is indeed traumatic. After a successful trip through the rural South, during which he collects lyrics and music and observes the spontaneous reactions of Negroes at camp meetings, the narrator witnesses a burning. Unable to help or to leave the scene, he watches as the whites chain their victim to a stake, pile wood around him, and ignite the fuel with coal oil. The narrator's reaction is notable for two reasons: he seems to feel no pity for the victim, yet for himself he feels humiliation and shame. Just as in previous comments on Negroes, the narrator is distant and unsympathetic in describing the man being burned: "There he stood, a man only in form and stature, every sign of degeneracy stamped upon his countenance. His eyes were dull and vacant, indicating not a single ray of thought" (pp. 186-187). However, the effect the scene has on him is intensely emotional:

> I walked a short distance away and sat down in order to clear my dazed mind. A great wave of humiliation and shame swept over me. Shame that I belonged to a race that could be so dealt with; and shame for my country, that it, the great example of democracy to the world, should be the only civilized, if not the only state on earth, where a human being would be burned alive.
>
> (pp. 187-188)

While the reader probably sympathizes with the shame the character feels for his country, he undoubtedly wonders at the man's lack of hostility toward the white Americans who are burning the Negro. The narrator goes on to justify to himself the decision he has made:

> I argued that to forsake one's race to better one's condition was no less worthy an action than to forsake one's country for the same purpose. I finally made up my mind that I would neither disclaim the black race nor claim the white race; but that I would change my name, raise a moustache, and let the world take me for what it would; that it was not necessary for me to go about with a label of inferiority pasted across my forehead. All the while I understood that it was not discouragement or fear or search for a larger field of action and opportunity that was driving me out of the Negro race. I knew that it was shame, unbearable shame. Shame at being identified with a people that could with impunity be treated worse than animals.
>
> (pp. 190-191)

Thus he decides to take the step toward which he has unconsciously been moving from the beginning, but there is bitter irony in the fact that the narrator chooses to ally himself with the persecutors rather than the persecuted, to be one of those who can, without shame or remorse, treat other human beings as animals.

As he has certainly foreseen, everyone who meets him assumes that he is white, and he rises quickly, both socially and financially. For a time he enjoys the sensation of playing a practical joke on white society and thinks how surprised his new acquaintances would be if he revealed his true identity. However, the joke recoils on him when he falls in love and wonders whether to reveal his secret to the girl. While he is agonizing over the decision, he and the girl encounter Shiny, who, in contrast with the main character, has made a distinct effort to help black people by teaching in a black Southern college. Emboldened by his loved one's friendly response to Shiny, the main character tells her the truth about himself, only to feel himself "growing black and thick-featured and crimphaired" (p. 204). She bursts into tears, and the narrator sums up his own feelings by confessing, "This was the only time in my life that I ever felt absolute regret at being coloured, that I cursed the drops of African blood in my veins and wished that I were really white" (p. 205). This statement, as the reader has had ample opportunity to see, is false. From the time he was first called "nigger" by his schoolmates, the main character has fought against being classified as a Negro. It is only at this point, however, that he permits himself to recognize the revulsion against his black blood, his inheritance from his beloved mother.

Eventually the girl accepts the protagonist as he is (something he has never been able to do himself) and marries him. They live happily until she dies after bearing him two children. Near the end of the novel the narrator at last faces his life honestly: "Sometimes it seems to me that I have never really been a Negro, that I have been only a privileged spectator of their inner life; at other times I feel that I have been a coward, a deserter, and I am possessed by a strange longing for my mother's people" (p. 210). An address by Booker T. Washington causes the ex-colored man to reflect again and to feel "small and selfish" compared to those who "are publicly fighting the cause of their race" (p. 211). Ironically, in spite of his efforts to ignore the advice of his millionaire friend, he has followed it—"make yourself as happy as possible" (p. 146). However, the happiness of being a successful white man now seems insufficient recompense for his unfulfilled dreams of contributing to Negro musical achievement. Self-realization has come at last, if only reluctantly and tentatively, and the ex-colored man fears that he has been the real victim of the practical joke he has played on society. The low keyed ending of the novel is much more effective and realistic than the melodramatic conclusions so typical of earlier black novels on the "tragic mulatto" theme.

Although Johnson wrote no other novels, his achievement in ***The Autobiography of an Ex-Coloured Man*** deserves recognition. The book has a significant place in black literature because it overthrows the stereotyped black character, employed even by early black writers, in favor of one that is complex and many-sided. Johnson gains depth and subtlety by using the first-person point of view rather than the third-person favored by his contemporaries. Moreover, his skill in using an unreliable narrator who reveals more than he intends—indeed, more than he knows—adds important psychological dimensions to the main character and his story. Finally, Johnson's skill in conveying his vision of black life in America through irony rather than by means of the heavy-handed propagandistic techniques of his predecessors marks a new, more artistic direction for the black novelist.

Notes

1. "A Century of Negro Portraiture in American Literature," *Massachusetts Review,* VII (Winter, 1966), 73-96.
2. *Negro Voices in American Fiction,* rev. ed. (New York, 1965), pp. 78-83.
3. *The Negro Novel in America,* rev. ed. (New Haven, 1965), pp. 46-49.
4. Before Johnson's publication of *The Autobiography,* the only authors to explore possibilities beyond the tragic mulatto stereotype were William Dean Howells (*An Imperative Duty,* 1892) and Mark Twain (*Pudd'nhead Wilson,* 1894).
5. New York, 1927, p. [3]. Page references to the novel, hereafter cited parenthetically in the text, are to this edition. The Hill and Wang American Century Edition of *The Autobiography* (1960) is identical in text and pagination.
6. In *Along This Way: The Autobiography of James Weldon Johnson* (New York, 1933), p. 238, Johnson tells how his brother J. Rosamond Johnson suggested *The Chameleon* as a title: "I also debated with myself the aptness of *The Autobiography of an Ex-Colored Man* as a title. Brander Matthews had expressed a liking for the title, but my brother had thought it was clumsy and too long; he had suggested *The Chameleon.* In the end, I stuck to the original idea of issuing the book without the author's name, and kept the title that had appealed to me first. But I have never been able to settle definitely for myself whether I was sagacious or not in these two decisions. When I chose the title, it was without the slightest doubt that its meaning would be perfectly clear to anyone; there were people, however, to whom it proved confusing."

JOSEPH T. SKERRETT, JR. (ESSAY DATE 1980)

SOURCE: Skerrett, Joseph T., Jr. "Irony and Symbolic Action in James Weldon Johnson's *The Autobiography of an Ex-Colored Man.*" *American Quarterly* 32 (winter 1980): 540-58.

In the following essay, Skerrett explores the problem of irony in Autobiography of an Ex-Colored Man *in relation to Johnson's own autobiography.*

James Weldon Johnson's only novel, ***The Autobiography of an Ex-Coloured Man,*** has divided its readers over the years into two distinct camps. One group, which includes Sterling Brown, Hugh Gloster, David Littlejohn, Stephen Bronz, and Nathan Huggins, feels that Johnson's narrator and his opinions are more or less direct reflections of their author.[1] The other group, whose membership includes Robert Bone, Edward Margolies, Eugenia Collier, Robert Fleming, and Marvin Garrett, argue that Johnson's treatment of his narrator is essentially ironic.[2]

Such disagreement over a fiction so brief and seemingly simple is remarkable, but not at all unintelligible. As Wayne Booth has pointed out in his *Rhetoric of Fiction,* the trouble with irony in narrative is that the signposts which indicate its presence are often lost to the reader's sight. Booth delineates these "troubles" into three broad areas, any one of which is sufficient to make the proper reading of a work problematic. In some cases, he says, "there is no warning, either explicitly or in the form of gross disparity of word and deed," that irony is the mode; in other cases "the relationship of the ironic narrator to the author's norms is an extremely complex one, and the norms are themselves subtle and private"; and in still other cases "the narrator's own mental vitality dominates the scene and wins our sympathy."[3]

In ***The Autobiography of an Ex-Coloured Man*** all three of these obstacles are present. Most of the critical readers who see little or no irony in the narrative, I would argue, have been taken in by the narrator's tone—they have been won over by what Booth would call Johnson's "mental vitality." The style of the narration is forceful and effective, and the opinions and attitudes are those of a plausible, eminently respectable gentleman of a post-Victorian cast. The racial situation of the narrator is, of course, also instrumental in eliciting sympathetic responses from the reader. There is undeniably a tragic aspect to the effect racial prejudice has on this talented musician's life, much as there is, say, in the purely social aspect of the hero's situation in Thomas Hardy's *Jude the Obscure.* But Jude does not tell his own story and thus cannot, as this nameless narrator can, obscure by sincerity of tone those personal failings which play so large a role in the working out of his fate.

At the same time, Johnson gives little explicit warning that his narrator is not to be taken at face value. The framing of the "history" of his life by two opening and two closing paragraphs on his present attitude toward that history, does, I think, warn the reader that another construction can be put on the "practical joke on society" that the narrator thinks he has played. Bone, Garrett, Margolies, Collier and Fleming—as well as all other readers who insist that the book is ironic in nature—have built their arguments on these passages, proceeding thence to demonstrate real disparities between word and word or word and deed in the narrator's life-story. The opposition, however—Brown, Bronz, Littlejohn, Gloster, Huggins—will not allow that this frame points to any larger realizations than the narrator's feelings of remorse, longing, and waste as he looks back across his life. Thus the debate is perpetuated.

The one "trouble" area that has not been ravaged in this battle over irony in Johnson's novel is the question of the author's norms. The assumption that this sensitive, talented young musician is only a front for the sensitive, talented young writer and poet who created him has dominated criticism of the book, even the criticism of some in the *pro*-irony camp. They have accepted the narrator's digressions on race and culture, on travel and sexuality, on music and religion as thinly fictionalized versions of Johnson's opinions, and seen in them no dramatic or characterizing function. Undeniably some of the narrator's views were shared by his creator; anyone who has read Johnson's preface to ***The Book of American Negro Spirituals*** will recognize there material used earlier in the novel.[4] By the same token, however, anyone who has read Johnson's autobiography, ***Along This Way*** (published in 1933), will realize that while some of the events related there were used in the novel, the personality and much of the life experience of the young James Weldon Johnson have little or no resemblance to the narrator's. The odd fact that both these major prose works are "autobiographies" (one in name, one in fact), presents itself as another knot in the tangle of this question. But if we are to extricate an accurate image of the author's norms from the morass of assumption, myth, error, and plain old confusion, we must begin with ***Along This Way.*** In the absence of other routes to a solution, the problem of irony in ***The Autobiography of an Ex-Coloured Man*** must be approached from a side which can reveal something of the author's relationship with his creation.

* * *

Along This Way is not one of those autobiographies in which the author "tells all" in a rush of breathless confessional prose. Johnson was too reticent, too Victorian for that sort of thing. His is a public story of a public life; the private life—love, sex, marriage—and most of the stronger emotions are only glimpsed if seen at all, and they are subordinated to the revelation of Johnson's personal reactions to his public achievements.

Thus Johnson records the circumstances in which his only novel came to be written. The facts are these: in 1906 James Weldon Johnson gave up a career as a successful writer of material for Broadway entertainments and accepted an appointment as United States Consul to Puerto Caballo, Venezuela. On this diplomatic assignment he completed the manuscript of a novel which he had begun shortly before his departure from New York. Not long before he left for Venezuela, Johnson met Grace Nail, who was to become his wife a few years later; he was also introduced to the white Jewish fiancée of his black Jacksonville childhood friend, D. After a visit home, Johnson returned to Venezuela and completed ***The Autobiography of an Ex-Coloured Man*** in late October or early November of 1908. It was published anonymously, by a small Boston firm, in 1912. Not until its republication in 1927 did Johnson publicly acknowledge his authorship.[5]

The situation of the narrator in the novel in no way resembles these facts. Johnson was certainly not fictionalizing his immediate experiences (not that there weren't the makings of fiction in them; his commentary on his role in the various Nicaraguan and Venezuelan political upheavals in ***Along This Way*** are dramatic and exciting). Yet there are in the novel both events and personalities drawn from experience and related again, as such, later, in ***Along This Way.*** For example, the millionaire who in the novel takes the narrator to Europe surely resembles the white physician who befriended Johnson in Jacksonville during his college years and took him on a trip to New York. Similarly, a number of experiences of the narrator resemble events from the life of Johnson's lifelong friend, D. Given the pattern of reticence that has been noted in Johnson's personality, it is the more remarkable that these two relationships are so thoroughly explored in ***Along This Way.***

Indeed, the depth and complexity of Johnson's relationship with D. and the physician, when viewed in light of the use he makes of them in writing his novel, bolster the suggestion that Johnson's involvement with the narrator is personally charged, despite the surface disparity between their conditions. If Johnson in his role as creator either consciously or unconsciously distanced himself from his personal experiences and innermost feelings, then we may be right in searching "between the lines" for the real revelations of the work.

Kenneth Burke's theory of "symbolic action" provides a framework upon which this problem may be stretched, the better to read between the lines of it. In proposing a fully articulated theory of the creative act, Burke insists on using "everything that is available" by way of material, including, of course, biographical data.

> The main ideal of criticism, as I conceive it, is to use all that is there to use. And merely because some ancient author has left us scant biographical material, I do not see why we should confine our study of a modern author, who has left us rich biographical material, to the same coordinates as should apply in studying the work of the ancient author. If there is any slogan that should reign among critical precepts, it is that "circumstances alter cases."[6]

Burke's position is that authors, at least in some works of literature, may be attempting to deal with difficult personal "situations" by unconsciously objectifying them into "strategies"—that is, fictions. He defines the act of writing, therefore, as "the adopting of various strategies for the encompassing of situations." These strategies "size up the situation," name its parts anew (and symbolically transform them) and in thus renaming and restructuring the complex of painful circumstances enable the writer to take a new attitude toward his "situation." The relabelling of the burden enables the sufferer to escape from its limitations. By unconsciously objectifying the elements of his "situation," the author is able to transform it into a "benefit."

FROM THE AUTHOR

THINKING THE THOUGHT THROUGH

Reading does not necessarily produce increased brain-power. A man may read one thousand books and never have an original thought about what he reads, such a man is not developing brain-power, he is merely educating himself, storing his mind with information, useful or otherwise. On the other hand, to read one great thought and then to think it through, to unravel it, to get at the inside of its meaning, to chew, swallow and digest it mentally, will produce increased brain-power. Thinking the thought through gives the brain the proper exercise; making the thought your own gives the brain the proper food, and it gains strength and power.

SOURCE: James Weldon Johnson, excerpt from his editorial "What Is Your Brain-Power?" in *New York Age*, November 26, 1914.

The "situation" Johnson is attempting to encompass in his novel is a complex of relationships between himself and his old friend, D. Since D. had been a friend from childhood, this "situation" includes most aspects of Johnson's life—professional, social, sexual, racial. From the distance of Puerto Cabello, Johnson symbolically objectified problems he could not confront directly back in New York—where he had written a draft of two chapters of his novel.

The relationship with D., as Johnson records it in ***Along This Way,*** is the relationship of an individual to an alter ego.

> But it was at school, when I was about eight years old that I formed my closest boyhood friendship. D. and I were unlike each other in more ways than

> one, yet we instantly became chums and mutual confidants—a relationship that was to run through boyhood, youth, and early manhood, and strangely to influence, cross and interact upon both our lives.
>
> (33)

Later, while recounting their days together at Atlanta University, Johnson remarks that although D. was only three months his senior, he was "more mature and far more sophisticated." In contrasting himself with D., Johnson's attitude is a mixture of jealousy and mild disapproval: "He had an unlimited self-assurance, while I was almost diffident; and he had inherited or acquired a good share of his father's roughness and coarseness. He had a racy style of speech, which I envied; but many of his choicest expressions I was unable to form in my mouth" (76). Yet even in the relatively puritanical atmosphere of Atlanta University in the 1890s, D. was popular with students and faculty alike. There was, Johnson notes, a "definite charm" about his very rakishness, and he was, "underneath his somewhat ribald manner, tender-hearted and generous."

D. was also physically prepossessing:

> Moreover, he was extremely good-looking, having, in fact, a sort of Byronic beauty. He was short. . . . His head, large out of proportion to his height, was covered with thick, dark brown hair that set off his pale face and fine hazel eyes. The only thing that marred his looks was the frequent raising of the drooping corners of his mouth in a cynical curl. But speaking of his face as pale does not convey the whole truth; for neither in color, features, nor hair could one detect that he had a single drop of Negro blood.
>
> (76)

If I am right, this particular physiognomical anonymity of D. is a cornerstone in the structuring of the novel. But that is only a minor aspect of Johnson's overall use of biographical material. Time and again in ***Along This Way*** he stresses D.'s self-confidence in contrast to his own struggles against reserve and timidity. Speaking of childhood kissing games, Johnson records his paralysis in the face of "fly to the east / fly to the west / fly to the very one that / you love the best": "I stood shamefaced . . . I simply could not expose my delicate desires to the crowd" (34). This shyness was with him still at Atlanta University, where he conquered it to become a prize-winning public speaker. This protective attitude toward the ego, so lightly touched upon here, is one of the elements of the narrator's character which has foundations in aspects of both Johnson's and D.'s characters, and which Johnson is, I believe, attempting to exorcise in himself by the writing of ***The Autobiography of an Ex-Coloured Man.***

Johnson's career in Jacksonville after his graduation from Atlanta University, first as teacher and then as principal at the colored high school, and later as an attorney, no less than his childhood and education, were closely tied to the progress of D.'s life. Finding his friend again, after his [Johnson's] first year of teaching, Johnson heard out D.'s adventures "in Negro sporting circles" which make their way into the novel in the form of the narrator's first experiences in similar circles in New York. Johnson's personal link to D.'s more colorful personality and audaciousness were strengthened:

> I sat late into the night listening to his adventures. He related incident after incident in his racy, half-cynical manner, giving a punch to the whole recital by his not meager command of profanity. He caused me to laugh heartily over some of his most dire situations. I knew that he had acted recklessly, but I admired, perhaps envied, the way in which he could challenge life.
>
> (138)

This envy did not surface as the two reestablished their alter ego relationship. Joint activities abounded: D. became Johnson's associate on the staff of the Jacksonville *Daily American,* a short-lived Negro daily newspaper; when the paper failed, Johnson prepared D. for the Florida bar exam. Their subsequent joint practice lasted until broken up by Johnson's decision to go to New York and work in the theatre with his brother Rosamond. ***Along This Way*** and other material tell us that the relationship remained unclouded throughout this period of close contact between 1895 and 1902. Yet dissonance must also have played a part in this harmony. Johnson had a definite if mild contempt for portions of his friend's personal behavior:

> Throughout our lives, D. in all his love affairs had sooner or later made me a sort of confessor. He frequently did something that I should rather have lost a finger than do, he would read me most ardent letters from his lady loves; I recall, in particular, letters he received for several years from a girl he met at the University of Michigan, letters too tender, too sincere, yes, too sacred to be seen by a third pair of eyes; yet he read them to me. It may have been an injustice to him, but I always suspected that the act was not purely confidential in its nature, but was more or less mixed with vainglory.
>
> (241)

Johnson's envy of "the way in which he could challenge life" was a jealousy of D.'s easygoing relationship with the world, a kind of freedom

Johnson did not himself feel. He was, as we have previously noted, reserved in general, and cautious in his explorations of persons and possibilities. Moreover, there was a sort of psychological insecurity with which he was saddled. Somewhat later, in the midst of his Broadway successes, he was filled with doubt. "I was not able," he said, "to feel completely that our success was real. This trait has persisted in me through all the years of my manhood. When successes with me seemed brightest, there has never failed to lurk somewhere the shadow of doubt" (194).

This anxiety and doubt could not be shaken off. Even in 1933, when he was writing ***Along This Way,*** he was plagued by anxiety dreams that must have played a role in the development of his career generally:

> For many years now I have been disturbed by a frequently recurring dream, the pattern of which is: I am taking a terribly difficult examination, on the passing of which my future and my means of existence depend; I awake before I know the result of the test, and sometimes seconds pass in the effort to shake off the dream and seize the reality.
>
> (194)

In his conscious mind, Johnson felt free of the debilitating feelings of inferiority and fear of failure that plagued so many blacks in his generation. He had been raised in a physically healthy family environment, in relatively comfortable middle-class circumstances, had attended college, and was otherwise also on the track of achievement and success. Yet in coming to terms with the "planned wrong, concerted injustice, and applied prejudice" that was the lot of the black American, he was also aware of a conscious effort of resistance: "Here was a deepening but narrowing experience; an experience so narrowing that the inner problem of a Negro in America becomes that of not allowing it to choke and suffocate him" (78). Johnson considered his background a great benefit in this resistance. The fact that he had been raised "free from undue fear or esteem for white people as a race" he considered "the most fortunate thing" in his whole life, for otherwise "the deeper implications of American race prejudice might have become a part of [his] subconscious" as well as of his conscious self (78). But the subconscious did absorb the natural anxiety that Johnson felt in his daily existence. This anxiety was suppressed there and emerged only in dreams—and in fiction.

Johnson's psychic strategies for dealing with this general challenge of maintaining his identity in the face of constant race-based attacks are basically of two types. One is role-playing. Situations of stress are often accompanied by his acting out of possible roles within them. Thus when he becomes principal of the Stanton School in Jacksonville, he acts out various of his predecessors' behavior patterns (128). On several occasions, recorded in ***Along This Way,*** his ability in idiomatic Spanish allowed him to "pass" for some other kind of brown-skinned man than an American Negro. In these situations his goal was to avoid the potential unpleasantness inherent in "a suddenly presented situation that involved 'race'" (88). Johnson was personally familiar, then, both with the concept of impersonation and the experience of "passing"—if not for white, then at least for some other kind of non-Negro.

His other characteristic pattern of crisis behavior is one of withdrawal. He notes early in ***Along This Way*** his thankfulness for a well-developed ability to focus his attention on what had to be done and to wipe out intruding and potentially enervating perceptions by an act of will (75). It is decidedly not a pattern of fear and flight. Johnson's withdrawals are strategic: they are undertaken as much to strengthen and refresh his sense of purpose as to escape the difficulty at hand. He was quite explicitly conscious of the psychic power this technique gave him: "the ability to withdraw from the crowd while within its midst never failed to yield me the subtlest and serenest of pleasures" (75). And there was a release of pressure involved in withdrawing from one situation in order to explore another. In ***Along This Way,*** he records his response to finally mailing in his resignation from the Stanton School, which he did in order to take up full-time theatre work in New York:

> As the letter dropped into the box, a load dropped from my shoulders. I at once became aware of an expanse of freedom I had not felt before. Immediately it seemed that the goal of my efforts was no longer marked by a limit just a little way in front of my eyes but reached out somewhere toward infinity.
>
> (189)

The sense of adventure is mixed with a rejection of limitation. The fear of stagnation, of impotence, of entrapment, begins to surround the idea of continuing in the principalship, and therein, curiously, lies the insecurity, in the feeling that his work there will have no lasting and satisfying meaning. Johnson's examination results are not reported in his dream precisely because he feared a negation of all his efforts by the hostile forces which surrounded him. "Always," for him, "the sense of security is greater in the struggle to succeed" (194). Thus he exhibits a long pattern of restlessness and constant shifting of careers (teacher, lawyer, lyricist, writer, diplomat, politician, professor, to name the major ones).

D.'s arrival in New York in the spring of 1905 found Johnson ready for, and, I believe, precipitated, an imminent withdrawal on his part from the New York theatrical scene. Johnson was already "making a mental shift and adjustment" regarding his work with his brother Rosamond and singer Bob Cole (222). He had for several semesters been studying drama at Columbia, under Brander Matthews' appreciative and friendly direction, and he revived in himself the desire to do literary work more serious than his theatre pieces. Furthermore, he had recently returned from strongly contrasting tours with his partners: one altogether pleasant and triumphant trip to Paris, Brussels, and London, and one extended tour of the western United States where they met, head-on, the kinds of prejudicial treatment and gross affrontery that revolted Johnson most deeply. The question of what he, James Weldon Johnson, could do with his talents in "the constant struggle to renerve their [black people's] hearts and wills against the unremitting pressure of unfairness, injustice, wrong, cruelty, contempt, and hate" had thus been forcibly restored to the forefront of his attention (205-06). At the back there burned the general question of race identity, which incidents such as those encountered on his western trip were likely to fuel. Johnson had once been asked point-black by a white man in a Jacksonville bicycle shop, "What wouldn't you give to be a white man?" As he tells it in ***Along This Way,*** he was, even after countering the insolence, deeply disturbed by the question:

> I thought: I must go over this question frankly with myself; I must go down to its roots; drag it up out of my subconsciousness, if possible, and give myself the absolutely true answer. I made a sincere effort to do this. I watched myself closely and tried to analyze words, actions, and reactions.
>
> (136)

In 1895, Johnson was convinced that the answer he gave in the bicycle shop that day was the true one: he wouldn't give anything to be just *any* white man, certainly not such a one as had asked the question. By 1933 he did not wish to be anyone but himself, though, like "every intelligent Negro in the United States" he had "toyed with the Arabian Nights-like thought of the magical change of race" (136). This secure adherence to his racial and personal identity had been achieved in the interim, partly through the symbolic "outering" of the inner conflict in the form of the novel. But in any case, the period of Johnson's theatrical work was fraught with race-based anxieties and discontent.

D.'s arrival in New York brought this simmering discontent to a boil, and elicited from Johnson a characteristically ambiguous response: on the one hand, he was glad to have his old friend so close by; on the other, he thought the shift from Jacksonville to New York a mistake on D.'s part:

> As D. had disapproved of my moving to New York, so I had disapproved of his. And I felt that my advice was more disinterested than was his. The personal element could hardly be absent from the advice he had given me: unwillingness to have our companionship and partnership broken, and dislike of my living in the great metropolis and his remaining in the small city. I was glad enough to have D. in New York, but I felt that, in leaving Jacksonville, he was doing a foolish thing to himself.
>
> (222)

Johnson's decision, soon thereafter, to drop his work in the musical theatre was a withdrawal, a choice of freedom from "the disagreeable business of traveling around the country under the conditions that a Negro theatrical company had to endure" (223). But he was also, I think, choosing freedom from the special pressures that D.'s renewed presence must have brought—suppressed resentment of the benefits D.'s racial anonymity brought him, pressure to achieve status and distinctions they had hoped for in a shared past. The alter ego relationship now imposd a special burden: "The feeling came over me that, in leaving New York, I was not making a sacrifice, but an escape; that I was getting away, if only for a while, from the feverish flutter of life, to seek a little stillness of the spirit" (223). "A little stillness of the spirit" was needed, most of all to provide time for the writing he wanted to do. D.'s opposition to his taking up the diplomatic post was strong; the irony of it was not lost on Johnson:

> And so, while D. was setting himself up in New York, I was pulling up my stakes. Once again our seesaw of advice and counter-advice got into action. His expression of opinion, this time, was sharper than it was on my leaving my school position and law practice to move to New York.
>
> (223)

Despite his old friend's objections, Johnson sailed for Venezuela in early summer, 1906, taking with him a draft of two chapters of ***The Autobiography of an Ex-Coloured Man,*** written that spring. If Kenneth Burke is correct in saying that writing a novel is, sometimes, a way of "settling a score with the world . . . symbolically, on paper," then I think it reasonable to suggest that the score Johnson was settling had a great deal to do with his suppressed attitudes toward D. and the aspects of D.'s personality that he saw in himself.

* * *

The novel Johnson wrote during the next two years contains nothing of this complex "situation" that is not greatly displaced or distorted, as the situations of everyday conscious existence are displaced and distorted in dreams. The narrative does not, however, have a dreamlike or surreal quality. On the contrary, it is convincing as a "personal history" precisely because of its concreteness. Johnson achieves a satisfying realism of character, setting, and incident, while avoiding the deterministic naturalism of so many of his contemporaries. The studies with Brander Matthews are put to good use: the book is structured around a series of "dramatic" scenes whose power allows Johnson liberally to intersperse digressions, in the voice of the narrator, on music, race relations, Europe, history, and other subjects.

This form had been a long time in coming together. In an early notebook—dating from at least his college days—Johnson had recorded random notes and possible titles for essays. "Reasons why I am glad I'm Afro-American," "How it feels to be colored," "How to escape the———of caste," "Opportunity of being in at the making of a race," all reflect the concern he was, of course, feeling about the meaning of his racial identity in relation to the kind of creative and satisfying life he hoped to lead. There are also notes here on projected fictional works. **"The Man Without a Race: Story of Two Brothers"** invites speculation as to content, but nothing more concerning it follows. However, other notes for stories and plays cast light in its direction. In "The Sins of the Fathers" Johnson proposed a melodrama involving unknowing incest between the white daughter and bastard Negro son of a Southern planter, culminating in the accidental death of the son and the suicide of the guilty father; another note suggests only a broad plot line—"Blind man, great poet, young amanuensis who steals his name and glory." A plot for a "romantic operetta" has a young mulatto slave lose his "quadroon" bride-to-be to the master's son, just home from college for the Christmas holiday. In "The Man and the Maid" a fortune hunter really falls in love with a young girl he believes to be a maid, but who, of course, turns out to be a mining heiress posing as a maid "to gather material for a society novel she hopes to write." Ostensibly these ideas have little in common beyond their nineteenth-century conventionality; nor do they outwardly anticipate the achievement of Johnson's one completed work of fiction. But on closer scrutiny, similarities can be discerned. First, there is the "tragic" element, the race-founded sufferings of the mulatto slave and the bastard son of the planter. Second, there is the posed possibility of writing race-free works such as "The Man and the Maid." Third, there is the theme of displacement shared by works in both categories. The great poet whose "name and glory" are stolen by his secretary provides a prime example of the displaced, but almost all these plots turn on some such displacement of identity. Furthermore, a slightly later note reinforces the pervasive nature of this theme: "Trace the growth of the sacrificing love of a man for a woman who sees only the tinsel of life"; when the woman awakes to the great love he bears her, it has, alas died. Johnson never devised a title for this notion, but he wanted to use the name of "some animal that gives its life substance to support another body."[7]

These adolescent fantasies are characterized by images of identity displacement through tandemness, symbiosis, and parasitism, as well as disguise. Duality is a prime concern in Johnson's imagination—would that we knew the projected fate of those two brothers in "The Man Without a Race" that was never written! In any case, ***The Autobiography of an Ex-Coloured Man*** is a summation of all the themes Johnson wanted to deal with in his youthful fantasizing: music, miscegenation, high society, the race question, and displacement of identity—all play major roles in the novel. Moreover, Johnson's interest in duality, I would venture, had matured to the point where he could take a double view of his narrator, at once "tragic" and "ironic." This new double attitude is an expression of Johnson's ambiguous feelings toward D. and toward those aspects of his own consciousness that most resembled D.'s. In the novel, Johnson symbolically works out his quarrel with the part of himself that D. as alter ego most clearly represented and, as it were, replicated, undercutting his narrator's "tragic" complaint by juxtaposing to it blindly unheroic behavior on the narrator's part.

The "tragic" element lies in the narrator's situation. He is, like Johnson—and also, of course, like D.—a talented and intelligent black American. Like D., but unlike Johnson, he is in skin color, hair texture, and facial features indistinguishable from a white man. Indeed, his father is a wealthy Southern white who sends the narrator and his mother north to Connecticut when he marries, and the narrator does not know he is a Negro until he is ten years old and is told so by a teacher in the Connecticut schools. Thence his problem lies in coming to terms with this fact. The narrator is a fine natural musician, but he discovers that he cannot make the most of this talent because of the prejudicial society in which he lives. During his tour of Europe, late in the novel, he asks himself the very question that so worried Johnson back in New York—in his [Johnson's] case with regard to literature: "What am I doing but wasting my time and abusing my talent? What use am I making of my gifts? What future have I before me following my present course?"[8]

It is more than circumstantial that a trip to Europe leads to soulsearching in both Johnson and his character. Eugenia Collier has suggested that the journey metaphor is the structural key to the novel. In such a reading, the trip to Europe would represent the farthest outreach of the narrator's psychic swing from imagined whiteness in childhood, through exploratory blackness, and finally, into permanent pretended whiteness. The European tour is the apogee of both his physical travels and his psychic flight from identity; as such, it is only fitting that he here gains a companion, a guide who voices for him the indirect and unutterable desires of his inner self.

On his own trip to London and the Continent, a few years earlier, Johnson had travelled with his brother Rosamond and his partner, Bob Cole. The narrator's companion, however, is a rich, young white bachelor. In his notes for the novel, Johnson sketched the idea:

> Met rich bachelor who wanted me to travel in Europe—went as his valet—this bachelor one of many whites who have [——————— dagia (?) neuralgia (?) nostalgia (?)] Al John's millionaire friend.[9]

Despite the rather dim reflection of author-experience in narrator-experience that this note proffers, I think a more certain source for the character is the Dr. Summers for whom Johnson worked during one of his college summers, and who took him on a trip to New York and Washington, D. C.—as his valet.

This Dr. Summers had been an inspiration to Johnson's interest in literature; Johnson had shown him his poems and received from him "the first worthwhile literary criticism and encouragement" he had ever gotten. His exposure to the cosmopolitan, ether-sniffing physician had left its mark: he made the doctor his "model of all that a man and a gentleman should be." Like a surrogate father, Dr. Summers "clarified, strengthened, and brought into some shape the ambition to write" that had been mostly latent in Johnson for years. Johnson's admiration for him, for treating him during that summer as an equal in all areas and for encouraging his literary efforts, survived the shock of the discovery, some years later, that the physician had taken his own life.

Suicide is one of many similarities between the narrator's rich white millionaire and his creator's white physician. The millionaire is not an experimenter with drugs, but the narrator's evaluation of his behavior places him at least potentially in the line of it:

> As I remember him now, I can see that time was what he was always endeavoring to escape, to bridge over, to blot out; and it is not strange that some years later he did escape it forever, by leaping into eternity.
>
> (143)

The egalitarian relationship that existed between Johnson and Dr. Summers is mirrored in the relationship between the narrator and his millionaire bachelor—but the image is not without distortion. The millionaire's democratic attitude toward the narrator is tinged with evil. Playing the piano for the bachelor late at night, the narrator muses on the essentially closed nature of his companion's personality:

> During such moments, this man sitting there so mysteriously silent, almost hid in a cloud of heavy-scented smoke, filled me with a sort of unearthly terror. He seemed to be some grim, mute, but relentless tyrant, possessing over me a super-natural power which he used to drive me on mercilessly to exhaustion.
>
> (121)

The bachelor comes to represent, then, a demonic force in the narrator's life, a powerful impetus which urges him to abandon his black identity and escape into whiteness. The trip to Europe with this millionaire is the most extreme of a series of psychic escapes and avoidances which comprise the narrator's "strategies" for dealing with his own "tragic" problem—being black. A wolf in sheep's clothing, the bachelor functions as a classical tempter, voicing for the narrator "the ultimate solution" which his subconscious self cannot "outer"—and which, for the moment, the conscious self decidedly rejects.

The bachelor argues speciously and misleadingly, at first in terms of flattery which distorts objective fact: he tells the narrator, "My boy, you are by blood, by appearance, by education, and by tastes a white man." The narrator takes in this opener without objection, though he knows that his mother was a Negro and that he is a Negro, precisely because he has all along desired to be white. The bachelor moves to an argument based on a cynicism that distorts values: he asks the narrator, "Now why do you want to throw your life away amidst the poverty and ignorance, the hopeless struggle, of the black people of the United States?" The narrator voices no objection to this questionable bit of prophecy and pride. And so the bachelor continues, now advising the narrator to reject his black heritage entirely and to give up "this idea you have of making a Negro out of yourself." The support he offers for this position is a pseudo-scientific rationalist view of the world: "Perhaps some day, through study and observation, you will come to see that evil is a force, and like the physical and chemical forces, we cannot annihilate it; we may only change its form" (145-46). This is, of course, the reasoning of the damned. The bachelor is a Mephistophelean figure, satanically suggesting to the narrator an attitude that would as well ease his conscience as it would enable him to avoid the pain and suffering of a commitment to his black identity. The image of the gentlemanly Dr. Summers has thus been radically transformed in Johnson's subconscious mind, and his effete ether-sniffing alienation has been rejected as a temptation which, in spite of its democratic aura, could only lead to real or symbolic self-annihilation.

The narrator rejects the bachelor's temptations, but he cannot save himself from the hellish torments caused by the awareness of previously suppressed desires. The bachelor's alienation is his own writ large; the bachelor's arguments are his own subconscious feelings "outered" for him by another. Consciously he recognizes the selfishness and egotistical cowardice in his mentor's position, but he finds, he says, "reason and common sense" there, too. Along similarly mixed principles, "in accordance with [his] millionaire's philosophy," he decides to return to the United States, to "voice all the joys and sorrows, the hopes and ambitions of the American Negro, in classical music form" (147-48). The real tragedy of the narrator, then, is that he cannot see far enough into himself; he does not realize that once he begins to act "in accordance with [his] millionaire's principles" he has, in effect, yielded his black identity totally, for this black identity is structured about antithetical premises to those of the bachelor. The narrator's most important identity characteristic is his artistic nature, his musical creativity. It is this ability at music that sustains him in the New York gambling houses, where he gained the title of "professor" for his clever ragtime improvisations. Through music he met the bachelor and escaped the "lower world" of the gambling clubs (115). The music of blackness and the "principles" of millionaires will not mix. As Fleming quite correctly points out, money and whiteness are associated in the novel; the narrator's white father gives him the pierced gold piece, the millionaire gives him the experience of Europe—and his poisoned advice—and the narrator ends as a "white" real estate speculator. The cynical principles of both his father and the millionaire lead him away from his blackness and the arts of expression with which it is associated.[11]

The characteristic blindness of the narrator to his own real emotions and desires is the foundation of the ironic structure which counterweighs his pathetic telling of his own story. The individual ironies are small but many. At one point the narrator compares Anglo-Saxon covertness to Gallic openness in discussing the difference between London and Paris. The attitude cannot with evidence be imputed to Johnson, for there is no such disparagement of London or of the British in his comments on his own travels there and in France in 1905. The praise for the frankness of the Parisians and for "the peculiar cleanliness of thought belonging to things not hidden" serves far more certainly as ironic counterpoint to the bachelor's proposals and the narrator's subsequent choice of "passing" as a way of life (138). Similarly, the narrator's lack of sympathy for the professor on the train in Chapter 10 is an ironic comment on his own lack of commitment to his identity. He has almost unreserved praise for the vulgarly racist Texan, but only contempt for the cautious, timid but liberal teacher:

> Yet I must confess that underneath it all I felt a certain sort of admiration for the man who could not be swayed from what he held as his principles. Contrasted with him, the young Ohio professor was indeed a pitiable character.
>
> (165)

Both here and later, the narrator exhibits behavior typical of the psychological sellout; he expresses admiration for traits of the oppressor which are directly related to their mastery and his subjugation—"their notions of chivalry and bravery and justice" (189). By pretending to be a white man on the train trip from Nashville to Atlanta, the narrator renders himself impotent in the conversation on the race question. He has numbed himself to the pain of such discussions, and now does not participate in them at all.

Numbness and alienation of course carry over into his excursion to the Georgia backwoods, which Eugenia Collier calls "the zenith of the narrator's trip into blackness, the point where physical and psychological journeys merge into one vital totality." Yet though the narrator enters these dark woods with no companion at his side, his false-Virgil has already planted, and the narrator's soul nurtured, the seeds of his destruction. His subconscious conceives itself as *white,* not *black,* and so he remains, in the face of folk preaching and communal singing, the alienated outsider:

> I was a more or less sophisticated and non-religious man of the world, but the torrent of the preacher's words, moving with the rhythm and glowing with the eloquence of primitive poetry, swept me along, and I, too, felt like joining in the shouts of "Amen! Hallelujah!"
>
> (177)

But he does not join with the black community in the shout: "Arrived at last at the point where he must come to grips with his real self—or rather with his two warring selves," the narrator discovers the irrevocable whiteness of his soul.[12] Thus, when shortly after this he witnesses a lynching, his reaction is, ironically, not a reinforcement of his identity as a threatened and oppressed black man, but rather a reinforcement of his fear of pain and his mechanisms of escape and avoidance:

> I finally made up my mind that I would neither disclaim the black race nor claim the white race; but that I would change my name, raise a moustache, and let the world take me for what it would; that it was not necessary for me to go about with a label of inferiority pasted across my forehead. All the while I understood that it was not discouragement or fear or search for a larger field of action and opportunity that was driving me out of the Negro race. I knew that it was shame, unbearable shame. Shame at being identified with a people that could with impunity be treated worse than animals.
>
> (190-91)

This self-made "man without a race" loses the name of hero in thus finally accepting the bachelor's advice to pass for white, to abandon the racial struggle. When he returns to New York, he follows not the black path of art and creation, but the white path of commerce and accumulation: "I had made up my mind that since I was not going to be a Negro, I would avail myself of every possible opportunity to make a white man's success; and that, if it can be summed up in any one word, means 'money'" (193). And it is only when he has later lost a large part of what mattered in what he had gained by "passing" that he realizes the final truth: that his action has annihilated both his cultural identity and his artistic creativity:

> When I sometimes open a little box in which I still keep my fast yellowing manuscripts, the only tangible remnants of a vanished dream, a dead ambition, a sacrificed talent, I can not repress the thought that, after all, I have sold my birthright for a mess of pottage.
>
> (211)

This realization that his most meaningful self, the black and creative self to which he had never given expression, lies withered and impotent in that little box of manuscripts, casts a final, reductive, and ironic light back along the course of the narrator's "tragic" life. The potential black leader and hero is reduced to a white petty bourgeois; the potential composer is reduced to a minor capitalist, a dabbler in real estate. He has really made no progress at all, for his real estate dealing is in fact only a glorified form of the gambling which had so often reduced him to ignominious nakedness during his early days in New York. As Garrett usefully suggests, the narrator's intention in telling his story—to "play a practical joke on society"—has been, in fact, the ironic instrument of his undoing.[13] He has revealed himself in his pathetic and pitiable nakedness and weakness without knowing that he did so.

* * *

Johnson's relationship with his creature, the narrator, is expressed through an almost hermetically sealed structural irony. The clues are few, tangential, and undramatic. The narrator is allowed to maintain his posture as "tragic" victim though the air grows thick with images of duplicity, compromise, covertness, hypocrisy, and cowardice the closer the narrator approaches the abandonment of his black identity. In his epiloguelike closing paragraphs, the narrator defends his course of action, troubled with small remorse for his "vanished dream, dead ambition," and "sacrificed talent"—the victim to the end. But in an earlier draft of this ending, Johnson brought him closer to a full realization of what he has done:

> I feel that I have been a deserter, a coward. I have an unrealizable longing for the people of my youth. I know a score of colored men who were my peers at schools who are today engaged in the making of a race, to whom thousands and even millions look with respect, devotion, veneration and love, and I feel that I, the selfish, the self-seeking, have buried my talents in a napkin, have

> sold my heritage for a mess of pottage. I know now that the very soul-trying ordeals that I have avoided would have brought out of me all the best that was in me.[14]

In the published text, this paragraph is expanded to three; the score of colored men admired by millions is reduced to one, Booker T. Washington (though a black youth from the narrator's school days is dramatically introduced into the episode of the narrator's courtship, with fine effect); the box of yellowing manuscripts is introduced as a more concrete image of the narrator's wasted talents. The changes are all effective in dramatizing the scene and maintaining the integrity of the narrator's tone. But the clear self-indictment of the last sentence in the early draft is softened to the perhaps and after all more characteristic uncertainty of "sometimes it seems to me that I have never really been a Negro" (211).

Even so, it seems that the confusion of some readers stems from their failure to grasp that James Weldon Johnson is intimately involved with both sides of this structure, with both the "tragic" and the "ironic." He is sympathetic with the narrator's "situation"—it is, after all, a version of his own—but he rejects the "strategy" the narrator chooses to solve his problem. "True irony," Kenneth Burke insists, "is based upon a sense of fundamental kinship with the enemy, as one *needs* him, is indebted to him, is not merely outside him as an observer but contains him *within,* being consubstantial with him."[15] The narrator of ***The Autobiography of an Ex-Coloured Man*** is a projection of Johnson and of his alter ego, D.; through the duality of the tragic/ironic narrative, Johnson "outers" and then exorcises the weakness he saw so clearly in (and shared with) D.—the temptation to desire and to seek a less heroic, less painful identity than their blackness imposed on them. The novel is Johnson's most adequate, most final answer, to the insolent question he was asked that day in the bicycle shop in 1895.

In the spring of 1909—if not earlier—D. chose to sell his heritage; he married his Jewish fiancée and began to "pass." Whether he received in return a mess of pottage we do not know. But he did commit suicide in 1930, financially ruined by the collapse of Florida real estate values, in which he had invested heavily.[16]

Johnson returned to New York that same spring and revived his courtship of Grace Nail. He returned to Latin America, taking up a new post as American consul in Corinto, Nicaragua. Within the year, he was back in New York to marry Grace and take her to Corinto. At the election of Woodrow Wilson in 1912 Johnson left the diplomatic service with the feeling that he had "found himself" there. "I feel my power to do better than before but I also feel the lack of incentive," he wrote to Matthews after completing the novel.[17] The pressure had been relieved in the process of symbolically restructuring his psychic "situation" into a novel. The creation of ***The Autobiography of an Ex-Coloured Man*** had thus served as a therapeutic—or symbolic—slaying of a hesitant and reluctant old self, and a fortification of Johnson's personal confidence for the years of leadership work that lay ahead.

Notes

1. Steven Bronz, *Roots of Negro Social Consciousness: The 1920's: Three Harlem Renaissance Writers* (New York: Libra Books, 1964); Sterling Brown, *The Negro in American Fiction* (Washington, D. C.: Associates in Negro Folk Education, 1937); Hugh Gloster, *Negro Voices in American Fiction* (Chapel Hill: Univ. of North Carolina Press, 1948); Nathan Huggins, *Harlem Renaissance* (New York: Oxford Univ. Press, 1971); David Littlejohn, *Black on White: A Critical Survey of Writing by American Negroes* (New York: Viking, 1969).
2. Robert Bone, *Negro Novel in America* (New Haven: Yale Univ. Press, 1965); Eugenia Collier, "The Endless Journey of an Ex-Coloured Man," *Phylon,* 32 (1971), 365-73; Robert E. Fleming, "Irony as a Key to Johnson's *The Autobiography of an Ex-Coloured Man,*" *American Literature,* 43 (Mar. 1971), 83-96; Marvin P. Garrett, "Early Recollections and Structural Irony in *The Autobiography of an Ex-Coloured Man,*" *Critique,* 13 (Summer 1971), 5-14; Edward Margolies, *Native Sons: A Critical Study of Twentieth Century Negro American Authors* (Philadelphia: J. B. Lippincott, 1968).
3. Wayne C. Booth, *The Rhetoric of Fiction* (Chicago, Univ. of Chicago Press, 1961), 324.
4. James Weldon Johnson, *The Book of American Negro Spirituals* (New York: Viking, 1925), 22-23.
5. Johnson, *Along This Way* (New York: Viking, 1943), 201-39 *passim;* Johnson refers to his friend as D. throughout *Along This Way.* Benjamin Brawley's identification of him, in a letter to Johnson dated Oct. 17, 1933, goes unchallenged by the author. There are also a few corroborating but unilluminating letters from the man named by Brawley. The James Weldon Johnson Correspondence is housed along with the James Weldon Johnson Papers in the James Weldon Johnson Memorial Collection of Negro Arts and Letters in the Yale University Library.
6. Kenneth Burke, *The Philosophy of Literary Form: Studies in Symbolic Action* (New York: Random, 1957), 21.
7. James Weldon Johnson Papers (hereafter JWJ Papers), MS, vol. 3, n.p.
8. Johnson, *The Autobiography of an Ex-Coloured Man* (New York: Knopf, 1927), 142.
9. JWJ Papers, MS, vol. 2, n.p.
10. Johnson, *Along This Way,* 97-99.
11. Fleming, "Irony as a Key," 86.

12. Collier, "Endless Journey," 371.
13. Garrett, "Structural Irony," 12-13.
14. JWJ Papers, MS, vol. 2, n.p.
15. Burke, *A Grammar of Motives* and *A Rhetoric of Motives* (New York: World Publishing, 1962), 514.
16. Johnson, *Along This Way,* 391.
17. JWJ Papers, MS, vol. 2. A rough draft of the letter is scrawled on the back of a manuscript sheet. Another draft, with the same wording, is in the Brander Matthews letter file in JWJ Correspondence.

RICHARD KOSTELANETZ (ESSAY DATE 1991)

SOURCE: Kostelanetz, Richard. "James Weldon Johnson." In *Politics in the African American Novel: James Weldon Johnson, W. E. B. Du Bois, Richard Wright, and Ralph Ellison,* pp. 19-25. New York: Greenwood Press, 1991.

In the following essay, Kostelanetz discusses the political, moral, and emotional ambiguities of "passing" in The Autobiography of an Ex-Coloured Man.

> James Weldon Johnson was an avant-gardist, who fathered modern Afro-American fiction. Within ***The Autobiography of an Ex-Colored Man,*** Johnson established the concept of the invisible man. It was on that rock that Wright and Ellison built their church.
>
> —Joe Johnson, in a personal letter to Richard Kostelanetz (1990)

James Weldon Johnson's sole novel, ***The Autobiography of an Ex-Colored Man*** (1912), treats a subject recurrent in early African-American writing, the experience of a very fair-skinned African-American who passes into white society. Indeed, the theme appeared in what was long regarded as the first novel attributed to a black American author, *Clotel, or the President's Daughter* (1853), by William Wells Brown, an expatriate abolitionist. In the original edition, his mulatto protagonist Clotel is traced to Thomas Jefferson's lecherous adventures; however, in the later American edition, as Robert A. Bone observed, "An anonymous senator is substituted for Jefferson, and the plot is altered accordingly."[1] The point of Wells Brown's novel is that once Clotel's part-black origins are disclosed, she is still considered a slave and, thus, subject to recapture. Charles Chesnutt, perhaps the first major Afro-American fiction writer, portrayed in *The House Behind the Cedars* (1900) a young woman, Rena, the master's daughter by a colored mistress, who decides to pass into white society. Upon the eve of her wedding to a white man, her racial background is revealed, and as a result the marriage is cancelled. Heartbroken, she lets her life disintegrate. The moral of Chesnutt's story holds that the major risk of passing is that discovery can ruin one's life. Given this background, it is scarcely surprising that a spate of novels about passing appeared in the 1920s: Jessie Fauset's *There Is Confusion* (1924) and *Plum Bun* (1928), Nella Larsen's *Quicksand* (1928), and Walter White's *Flight* (1926).[2]

James Weldon Johnson's novel is an unsentimental and more complex exploration of the subject and a superior work of art, although esthetically marred by numerous polemical digressions, sometimes of considerable perception, on "the Negro problem." Originally published anonymously by Sherman, French and Company in 1912, ***The Autobiography of an Ex-Colored Man*** was restored to its author when it was republished fifteen years later, at the height of the negro renaissance, with Carl Van Vechten's introduction. The book is a fictional memoir whose first-person narrator is so intimate and honest with his readers that they would, unless warned otherwise, accept his words as authentic autobiography; a later, equally successful model of autobiographical artifice is Ralph Ellison's *Invisible Man.* In fact, ***The Autobiography,*** like Ellison's novel, is not in the least autobiographical, except in the sense that certain events have their symbolic equivalents in Johnson's own life.[3] The effectiveness of the artifice is, of course, a basic measure of Johnson's fictional artistry.

The novel's theme is the many ambiguities of passing—moral, political, emotional; and its predominant action is the nameless narrator's shifting sympathies for white or black identity. Born in Georgia, the son of a white man by his family's favorite black servant, the narrator grows up with his mother in Connecticut, attending a racially mixed elementary school. He unwittingly identifies with white peers in the squabbles with "the niggers" until a white teacher says to his class, "I wish all of the white scholars to stand for a moment":

> I rose with the others. The teacher looked at me and, calling my name, said: "You sit down for the present, and rise with the others." I did not quite understand her, and questioned "Ma'm?" She repeated, with a softer tone in her voice: "You sit down now, and rise with the others."
>
> (16)

However, as his community is not aggressively racist, the narrator remains only dimly aware of his racial origins until high school. There, a dark-skinned friend nicknamed "Shiny" instills in the narrator some awareness of his heritage:

> I read with studious interest everything I could find relating to coloured men who had gained prominence. My heroes had been King David, then Robert the Bruce; now Frederick Douglass was enshrined in the place of honor.
>
> (46)

Thus, when forced to select a college from the two possible alternatives presented to him—his father's recommendation, Harvard; or his mother's, Atlanta—he decides on the latter. Once there, however, he finds himself unable to register because his "inheritance" (money from his father) is stolen. He thinks of explaining his predicament to the school's authorities; but as he approaches their offices, "I paused, undecided for a moment; then turned and slowly retraced my steps, and so changed the whole course of my life." (63) In traveling to Florida, he undergoes a symbolic dark night of suffering in a womblike setting. "Twelve hours doubled up in a porter's basket for soiled linen, not being able to straighten up. The air was hot and suffocating and the smell of damp towels and used linen was sickening." (65) He emerges reborn to a new existence in the African-American community of Jacksonville.

As a cigar-maker, he learns of both the impregnable structure of Southern discrimination and the exclusive habits of the black middle class. Finding himself doomed to remain an outsider in the South, unfulfilled in his ambitions, this narrator, like so many analogous characters in later African-American fiction, heads north to New York City. Once there, he gravitates to the major black bohemia of the early twentieth century, in the West Twenties between Sixth and Seventh Avenues, first making his way as a successful gambler and then as a pianist of ragtime music. In this milieu he discovers freedom of movement but little discernible stability—opportunistic drifters, white widows on the make, sporting men capable of sudden violence. A disagreeable experience with the last element drives the narrator to befriend a millionaire white man who, out of admiration for his piano playing, offers to become his patron. At the novel's turning point, the narrator and his benefactor go off to Europe; and the narrator, now posing as a white man, enters high-class international society.

Still, he does not claim his white identity at once. At a Paris theater, he recognizes the man two seats away as his father, but he refuses the temptation to announce his presence. Later becoming disillusioned with his patron's way of life—a constant quest for novelty to assuage the boredom of purposelessness—the narrator remembers his childhood ambition to become an Afro-American composer and collector of African-American folk materials. Despite the millionaire's not-unperceptive warning that "the idea you have of making a Negro out of yourself is nothing more than a sentiment," the narrator returns to America to pursue his self-determined task. In each Southern town he visits he is faced with the possibility of passing for white, but each time he reaffirms blackness:

> In thus traveling about through the country I was sometimes amused on arriving at some little railroad station town to be taken for and treated as a white man, and six hours later, when it was learned that I was stopping at the house of the colored preacher or school-teacher, to note the attitude of the whole town change.
>
> (172)

Just as an earlier incident of violence propelled him out of black bohemia into his white patron's beneficence, so his witnessing of a Southern lynching initiates another collapse of personal purpose and integrity. The narrator experiences a second rebirth with a new vow: "I would neither disclaim the black race nor claim the white race; but . . . I would change my name, raise a mustache, and let the world take me for what it would." (190) Behind this decision is a patent rationalization for cowardice and pure self-interest: "Shame at being identified with a people that would with impunity be treated worse than animals." (191) However, it is still a credible outcome of his experience.

He returns to New York, takes a well-paying job, invests his money in real estate, and strikes up a relationship with a Caucasian woman. The specter of his past identity confronts him when he and his fiancee accidentally meet his childhood friend Shiny in a museum; but in cutting short Shiny's approach, the narrator rejects a last tie to the past.[4] He marries the white woman, who bears him a boy and a girl, only to die suddenly; and he assumes responsibility for his children. The book's final passage conveys his continued ambivalence over passing:

> My love for children makes me glad that I am what I am and keeps me from desiring to be otherwise; and yet, when I sometimes open a little box in which I still keep my fast yellowing [music] manuscripts, the only tangible remnants of a vanished dream, a dead ambition, a sacrificed talent, I cannot repress the thought that, after all, I have chosen the lesser part, that I have sold my birthright for a mess of pottage.
>
> (211)

The price of passing is not only a loss of heritage and the sacrifice of one's self-chosen mission but guilt over an opportunistic materialism equal to that of Esau in Genesis (25:29-34). So famished from toiling in the fields, we remember, Esau frivolously exchanged "his birthright" with his brother Jacob for "bread and pottage of lentils."

Some of the book's meaning stems from its relationship to Afro-American folk blues, that tightly organized lyric form in which the singer narrates the reason for his sadness, usually attributed to his failure to attain the ideal role he conceives for himself. In a successful blues song, the singer makes his personal predicament a realized metaphor for the human condition.[5] Here the subject of the blues is selling out one's dreams for material rewards. Johnson was, of course, aware of the folk blues tradition, not only from his experience writing show tunes with his brother Rosamund but also from a desire to appropriate the heritage for literature. In his actual autobiography, ***Along the Way*** (1933), Johnson wrote of his early days:

> I now began to grope toward a realization of the importance of the American Negro's cultural background and his creative folk-art, and to speculate on the superstructure of conscious art that might be reared upon this.[6]

This statement echoes what Johnson wrote in the introduction to ***The Book of American Negro Poetry*** (1922):

> What the colored poet in the United States needs to do is something like Synge did for the Irish; he needs to find a form that will express the racial spirit by symbols from within rather than by symbols from without, such as the mere mutilation of English spelling and punctuation.[7]

In the novel, then, Johnson's narrator expresses a disenchantment of a special kind—a blues about being white, but black. Passing produces not only the individual's alienation from his natural milieu but feelings of the blues, expressed particularly as a guilty self-identification with Abraham's least-favored grandson, Esau. In the political sense then, the novel suggests that passing—an African-American's total assimilation into white culture—signifies opportunistic rejection of one's heritage for the meagre "mess of pottage" of material comfort.

Notes

1. Robert A. Bone, *The Negro Novel in America* (New Haven, Conn., 1958), 30. Regarding William Wells Brown, see Richard Bardolph, *The Negro Vanguard* (New York, 1961), 66-70.
2. See Hugh M. Gloster, *Negro Voices in American Fiction* (Chapel Hill, N.C., 1948).
3. Though quite dark in complexion, Johnson could pass for a Latin American by speaking Spanish; he once accompanied a Spanish-speaking white friend in the first-class coach on a Southern train. John Hope Franklin, "Introduction," *Three Negro Classics* (New York, 1965), xv; James Weldon Johnson, *Along the Way* (New York, 1933), 65.
4. According to folklorist Roger D. Abrahams, the name "Shiny" is "generic for any male Negro." *Deep Down in the Jungle* . . . (Hatboro, Pa., 1964), 116.
5. For insights into the esthetic character and purpose of the blues, this writer is indebted to an unpublished paper by Stanley Edgar Hyman that subsequently appeared in his posthumous book, *The Critic's Credentials* (New York, 1978). For an abridged version of Hyman's ideas, see "Those Trans-Atlantic Blues," *The New Leader, 44,* 35 (October 16, 1961), 24-25. See also Harold Courlander, *Negro Folk Music, U.S.A.* (New York, 1963), 128-45; Ralph Ellison, *Shadow and Act* (New York, 1964), 78-79.
6. Johnson, *Along the Way,* 133.
7. Johnson, ed., *The Book of American Negro Poetry* (New York, 1922), 41.

God's Trombones

COUNTEE CULLEN (ESSAY DATE 1927)

SOURCE: Cullen, Countee. "And the Walls Came Tumblin' Down." *The Bookman* 66, no. 2 (October 1927): 221-22.

In the following essay, Cullen favorably reviews the poems of God's Trombones, *crediting Johnson for replacing dialect with a new medium of expressing the Black idiom in poetry.*

> And seven priests shall bear before the ark seven trumpets of rams' horns; and the seventh day ye shall compass the city seven times, and the priests shall blow with the trumpets.
>
> And it shall come to pass, that when they make a long blast with the ram's horn, and when ye hear the sound of the trumpet, all the people shall shout with a great shout; and the wall of the city shall fall down flat. . . .

James Weldon Johnson has blown the true spirit and the pentecostal trumpeting of the dark Joshuas of the race in ***God's Trombones,*** composed of seven sermon-poems and a prayer. The seven sermons are like the seven blasts blown by Joshua at Jericho. **"The Creation," "The Prodigal Son," "Go Down Death—A Funeral Sermon," "Noah Built the Ark," "The Crucifixion," "Let My People Go,"** and **"The Judgment Day,"** they are all great evangelical texts. And the magnificent manner in which they are done increases our regret that Mr. Johnson was not intrigued into preaching "The Dry Bones In the Valley," the *pièce de résistance* in the repertoire of every revivalist to whom a good shout is a recommendation of salvation well received.

An experiment and an intention lie behind these poems. It will be remembered that in ***The Book of American Negro Poetry*** Mr. Johnson spoke of the limitations of dialect, which he compared to an organ having but two stops, one of humor and one of pathos. He felt that the Negro poet needed to discover some medium of expression with a latitude capable of embracing the Negro experience. These poems were written with that purpose in view, as well as to guarantee a measure of permanence in man's most forgetful mind to that highly romantic and fast disappearing character, the old time Negro preacher.

The poet here has admirably risen to his intentions and his needs; entombed in this bright mausoleum the Negro preacher of an older day can never pass entirely deathward. Dialect could never have been synthesized into the rich mortar necessary for these sturdy unrhymed exhortations. Mr. Johnson has captured that peculiar flavor of speech by which the black sons of Zebedee, lacking academic education, but grounded through their religious intensity in the purest marshalling of the English language (the King James' version of the Bible) must have astounded men more obviously letter-trained. This verse is simple and awful at once, the grand diapason of a musician playing on an organ with far more than two keys.

There is a universality of appeal and appreciation in these poems that raises them, despite the fact that they are labeled "Seven Negro Sermons in Verse", and despite the persistent racial emphasis of Mr. Douglas' beautiful illustrations, far above a relegation to any particular group or people. Long ago the recital of the agonies and persecution of the Hebrew children under Pharaoh ceased to chronicle the tribulations of one people alone. So in **"Let My People Go"** there is a world-wide cry from the oppressed against the oppressor, from the frail and puny against the arrogant in strength who hold them against their will. From Beersheba to Dan the trusting wretch rich in nothing but his hope and faith, holds this an axiomatic solace:

> Listen!—Listen!
> All you sons of Pharaoh,
> Who do you think can hold God's people
> When the Lord himself has said,
> Let my people go?

In considering these poems one must pay unlimited respect to the voice Mr. Johnson has recorded, and to the pliable and agony-racked audience to whom those great black trombones blared their apocalyptic revelations, and their terrible condemnation of the world, the flesh, and the devil. Theirs was a poetic idiom saved, by sincerity and the heritage of a colorful imagination, from triteness. If in "Listen, Lord", they addressed the Alpha and Omega of things in a manner less reverent than the frigidity of the Christian's universal prayer, it is not to be doubted that their familiarity was bred not of contempt, but of the heartfelt liberty of servitors on easy speaking terms with their Master. What people not so privileged could apostrophize Christ so simply and so humanly as merely "Mary's Baby"?

In like manner certain technical crudities and dissonances can be explained away. The interpolation here and there of a definitely rhymed couplet among the lines of this vigorous free and easy poetry will not jar, when one reflects that if poetry is the language of inspiration, then these black trumpeters, manna-fed and thirst-assuaged by living water from the ever flowing rock, could well be expected to fly now and then beyond their own language barriers into the realms of poetic refinements of which they knew nothing, save by intuitive inspiration. And if on occasion the preacher ascended from *you* and *your* to *thee* and *thou,* this too is in keeping with his character.

To me **"The Creation"** and **"Go Down Death"** are unqualifiedly great poems. The latter is a magnificent expatiation and interpretation of the beatitudes; it justifies Job's "I know in Whom I have believed" to all the weary, sorrow-broken vessels of earth. It is a revelation of to what extent just men shall be made perfect. The repetitions in **"The Crucifixion"** are like hammer-strokes of agony.

It is a tribute to Mr. Johnson's genius that when a friend of mine recently read **"Go Down Death"** to an audience in Mr. Johnson's own natal town, an old wizened black woman, the relic of a day of simpler faith and more unashamed emotions than ours, wept and shouted. Perhaps many a modern pastor, logically trained and multi-degreed might retrieve a scattering flock, hungry for the bread of the soul, by reading one of these poems as a Sunday service.

SUSAN J. KOPRINCE (ESSAY DATE 1985)

SOURCE: Koprince, Susan J. "Femininity and the Harlem Experience: A Note on James Weldon Johnson." *College Language Association Journal* 29, no. 1 (September 1985): 52-6.

In the following essay, Koprince claims that a study of the women in God's Trombones *helps to explain Johnson's enchantment with 1920s Harlem.*

God's Trombones (1927), James Weldon Johnson's collection of folk sermons in verse, has long been celebrated for its innovative language[1]—in particular, for its rhythmic, free-verse lines, which recreate the art of the "old-time Negro preacher."[2] But these poetic sermons can also be examined profitably in terms of the literary characters which occur in them. A study of the women in Johnson's sermons, for example, not only reveals the poet's attitude toward the female sex, but, in a broader sense, helps to explain his enchantment with Harlem during the 1920s—the same Harlem which Johnson evokes so vividly in his cultural treatise ***Black Manhattan*** (1930).

Several poetic sermons in ***God's Trombones*** make clear Johnson's view of women as powerful temptresses. The poem **"Noah Built the Ark"** introduces the figure of Eve, the archetypal temptress "With nothing to do the whole day long / But play all around in the garden" (p. 32) with her consort, Adam. Although Eve disobeys God out of vanity ("You're surely goodlooking," Satan tells her, offering her a mirror), Adam does so out of uxoriousness and a fatal desire for this beautiful, sensuous woman. "Back there, six thousand years ago," says Johnson, "Man first fell by woman— / Lord, and he's doing the same today" (p. 33).

Johnson describes the temptress even more explicitly in his sermon **"The Prodigal Son."** Here the prodigal son journeys to the great city of Babylon, where he associates with "hot-mouthed" and "sweet-sinning" women (pp. 24-25). Dressed colorfully in yellow, purple, and scarlet, and adorned with bright jewelry, the women are "Perfumed and sweet-smelling like a jasmine flower," and their lips are "like a honey-comb dripping with honey" (p. 24). Much in the manner of Eve, these temptresses usher a man into a world of sin and profligate living, confounding his powers of reason with their sexual allure and bending him completely to their will.

But Johnson also presents a different image of women in ***God's Trombones***: that of the saintly mother, the sympathetic and loving comforter. In his sermon **"The Crucifixion,"** for instance, Johnson pictures the Virgin Mary at the scene of her son's death, weeping as she watches "her sweet, baby Jesus on the cruel cross" (p. 42). In **"Go Down Death,"** the poet celebrates the simple human dignity of Sister Caroline, a wife and mother who has "borne the burden and heat of the day" and "labored long in [God's] vineyard" (p. 28). When at last it is Sister Caroline's turn to be comforted, Death takes her in his arms like a baby and then places her "On the loving breast of Jesus" (p. 30). This last image, it should be noted, transfers the maternal role from Sister Caroline to Christ; and the Savior Himself becomes her eternal comforter:

> And Jesus took his own hand and wiped away
>   her tears,
> And he smoothed the furrows from her face,
> And the angels sang a little song,
> And Jesus rocked her in his arms,
> And kept a-saying: Take your rest,
> Take your rest, take your rest.
>
> (p. 30)

The deification of maternal love is likewise evident in Johnson's well-known poem **"The Creation,"** where the act of divine creation is compared to a scene of maternal devotion, and where God Himself is portrayed as the tender-hearted mother of mankind:

> This Great God,
> Like a mammy bending over her baby,
> Kneeled down in the dust
> Toiling over a lump of clay
> Till he shaped it in his own image;
>
> Then into it he blew the breath of life,
> And man became a living soul.
>
> (p. 20)

In the poet's view, motherhood is sacred, partly because the earthly mother shelters and nurtures her offspring, but also because, like the Divine Maker Himself, she has the power to create new life.

So important for Johnson is this dichotomy between the sensual and the spiritual, between the whorish and the maternal, that he employs it not only to describe the women of ***God's Trombones,*** but to depict Harlem of the twenties in his cultural study ***Black Manhattan.*** Just as Johnson tends to divide women into two extreme types—the sexual temptress and the saintly mother—so does he picture Harlem as a city containing the extremes of sensuality and spirituality. For Johnson, Harlem is at once a voluptuous temptress and a spiritual mother—a force which inspires both amorous passion and creative genius—a city which is seductive and vibrant.

Thus, like the "sweet-sinning" women of Johnson's poems, Harlem is "farthest known as being exotic, colorful, and sensuous."[3] The city is noted not only for its flashy night life, with music, dancing, and laughter, but for its underworld "of pimps and prostitutes, of gamblers and thieves, of illicit love and illicit liquor, of red sins and dark crimes" (p. 169). Just as the prodigal son in

Johnson's poem is tempted to "[waste] his substance in riotous living" (p. 24), so may the visitor to Harlem "nose down into lower strata of life" (p. 160). He may become initiated, explains the author, "in all the wisdom of worldliness" (p. 169). This black metropolis entices "the pleasure-seeker, the curious, the adventurous, the enterprising, the ambitious, and the talented of the entire Negro world"; indeed, *"the lure of it,"* says Johnson, "has reached down to every island of the Carib Sea and penetrated even into Africa" (p. 3; italics added).

Yet Harlem of the twenties is also a life-giving force, a kind of spiritual and artistic mother. The city can boast, for example, of an abundance of churches, which serve as a crucial stabilizing force in the community. Like mothers, these churches provide their members with a sense of identity and belonging, offering not only spiritual inspiration, but the feeling of being part of an extended family.[4] Harlem's ability to bring about the *"birth* of new ideas" (p. 231) and "opportunities for the *nurture and development* of talent" (p. 226; italics added) is also a maternal characteristic. As the center of the Negro Renaissance and the repository of a new black culture, Harlem possesses a truly regenerative force. The spiritual (or maternal) side of Harlem comprises more, in other words, than mere religiosity. According to Johnson, Harlem encourages black people to believe in their own potential and to discover for themselves their unique powers and abilities. Like a mother, this black city ultimately builds self-confidence; it gives a new hope and vitality to the individual creative artist.[5]

Although Johnson's image of women in ***God's Trombones*** can indeed be compared with his image of Harlem in ***Black Manhattan,*** one distinction should be kept in mind; whereas Johnson divides women into two different roles—temptress and mother—he unites these two roles in the city of Harlem itself. Harlem thus resembles not an individual woman, but womankind, for it expresses all aspects of femininity, from gaiety and sensuous charm to spiritual emotion and creative vigor. Like a temptress, Harlem lures the black man, exhilarates him, and overwhelms him; but like a mother, it also shelters him, inspires him, and gives him his identity. For James Weldon Johnson, Harlem of the twenties was much more, therefore, than a place to which to "jazz through existence" (p. 161); it was the scene of the black people's cultural rebirth—the home of their racial awakening.

Notes

1. See, for example, Jean Wagner, *Black Poets of the United States,* trans. Kenneth Douglas (Urbana: Univ. of Illinois Press, 1973), pp. 377-84; and Richard A. Long, "A Weapon of My Song: The Poetry of James Weldon Johnson," *Phylon,* 32 (Winter 1971), 374-82.
2. James Weldon Johnson, Pref., *God's Trombones: Seven Negro Sermons in Verse* (New York: Viking, 1927), p. 2. Future references are to this edition.
3. James Weldon Johnson, *Black Manhattan* (1930; rpt. New York: Atheneum, 1968), p. 160. Future references are to this edition.
4. According to Johnson, a Harlem church is really much more than a place of worship: "It is a social centre, it is a club, it is an arena for the exercise of one's capabilities and powers, a world in which one may achieve self-realization and preferment" (p. 165).
5. In his preface to *Black Manhattan* (New York: Atheneum, 1968), Allan H. Spear emphasizes that "Johnson's vision of Harlem was more a dream than a reality." By 1930 the city was already largely transformed from a "community of great promise" to a saddened ghetto.

Along This Way

WILLIAM STANLEY BRAITHWAITE (ESSAY DATE 1933)

SOURCE: Braithwaite, William Stanley. "*Along This Way*: A Review of the Autobiography of James Weldon Johnson." *Opportunity* 11, no. 12 (December 1933): 376-78.

In the following review, Braithwaite notes Johnson's depiction of the duality facing African Americans and praises his brilliant description of Black life, ethics, and manners.

For many of us contemplating the perusal of this ***Autobiography*** of "Jim" Johnson, there was a kind of eagerness which set up a rare and peculiar scale of anticipations. Of all the works produced by Negro authorship since the so-called literary renaissance in the early nineteen-twenties, no single work intrigued the curiosity concerning the intimacies and relationships of a conspicuously successful figure in the aesthetic and controversial life of the race and the nation, as the record of this man who has been educator, lawyer, popular song-writer, librettist, translator, poet, novelist, editor, journalist, orator, diplomatist, and as a publicist the spear-head of a militant organization, shot in all directions over the country in a crusade to pierce the armor of American race-prejudice, oppression, and injustice.

Since the "Up From Slavery" of Booker T. Washington a generation ago, there have been, in this era of bumper-crops in autobiographies, but two stories of self-recorded Negro lives, that I recall, presented to the general public: Dr. Moton's "What the Negro Thinks" and Taylor Gordon's "Born To Be," antiphonal as they are in environment and purpose; with such fleeting glimpses, in supplement, as Dr. Du Bois, Benjamin Brawley and Claude McKay, have given us of fragments of their lives in periodical contributions. In a sense this ***Autobiography of James Weldon Johnson*** is unique, quite apart from the many-gifted character of its subject, for it takes shape and expression out of the qualities which make that character to become both a challenge to, and a triumph over, the critical authorities of American life.

There is a dual emphasis that should be laid upon any consideration of this pulsing human story, a duality that will be secretly recognized by every intelligent reviewer of the book in the literary press, but seldom, I fear, to be recorded by them in print. To date I have failed to notice, in any of the reviews of the book, this distinction made, or commented upon. This duality of which I speak is the duality of every gifted Negro whose physical life, by chance or circumstance of his public activities, is forced into the pattern of the eternal *problem,* but whose spiritual life transcends that pattern and adds to the radiance of the universal vision of mankind. Therefore, we are confronted with columns, in the white press, summarizing the many episodes related in the ***Autobiography,*** of the author's personal experiences with prejudice and attempted discriminations, which inevitably precipitate a tragic, humiliating, or humorous climax. These experiences have been common to countless numbers of humble Negroes, with little variations from the attitudes and reactions taken by the more gifted and famous; but these experiences will not be corrected nor eliminated from the social and civic consciousness of American life until that consciousness has become saturated with a recognition of the verities which this thrilling, and often, fascinating, story of James Weldon Johnson's life teaches on its spiritual and cultural side.

In the familiar shaping of an epigrammatic idea, God makes James Weldon Johnson a creative artist, but he made himself a race-agitator. He had an intellectual motivation for the cause into which he threw the energies and devotions of his manhood's prime; and while the heat of debate, the tactics and strategies were pursued with ardour and often with consummate skill, there was none of the passion nor exalted moods of rationalization, which forged the spirit of Douglass or Washington or Du Bois on the anvil of a diabolical oppression. If these race champions, Douglass, Washington, and Du Bois, flame across the pages of race and American history with a greater glory for stirring the hearts of their people with higher hopes and clearer visions, and a more determined effort to realize them, than James Johnson, that same history will record in its footnotes and appendices, that with Booker T. Washington he stands forth as one of the two best organizers of a racial program.

The fourteen years that James Johnson gave to his labors with the N. A. A. C. P. were years for which the race should be immensely grateful. They left him weary, and I believe, somewhat disillusioned. Not the Negro, I hasten to explain, was disillusioned, but the man, the artist. And one cannot fully understand this mood without reading with particular attention the last ten or fifteen pages of this ***Autobiography.***

That all through these fourteen years of organization and agitation, James Johnson was disturbingly aware of the creative impulses which haunted his more prosaic duties, he gives testimony near the end of his ***Autobiography,*** in the statement: "I got immense satisfaction out of the work which was the main purpose of the National Association for the Advancement of Colored People; at the same time, I struggled constantly not to permit that part of me which was artist to become entirely submerged. I had little time and less energy for creative writing."

There is a bit of wistful pleading in the statement; to me like the mystic echo of the Voice that spoke gently but radiantly in the Galilean hills, "I am the true vine. . . . Now ye are clean through the word which I have spoken unto you." And the implication interposes like a thin veil through which one peers along the vista of this ***Autobiography*** to behold a dim pageantry of ideals and realities, half fantasy, half tragical, of a human soul. One hears echoing out of this dim recess of a spirit, sensitive to the harsh and intimidating taboos of American life, the symphonic movements of experience which carried that spirit in triumph upon the crest of the environment that would quell and silence it. This is the other aspect of that dual character of this ***Autobiography*** of which I spoke, the spiritual element which lifts the individual out of the prescribed pattern into which an hypocritical concept has woven him, and gives him a symbolic balance in the ultimate scheme of social unity in a free democracy.

There are four sections of Mr. Johnson's ***Autobiography*** which fascinated me. The first two are of great significance to the race as ideals of attainment to be emulated. First is the story of the author's parentage, childhood and youth, up to and through those years which carried him to the threshold of his college life; they are chronicled with a fullness and charm which make these pages a lone and singular contribution of Negro authorship to American literature. Next is Mr. Johnson's invasion, with his brother Rosamond and Bob Cole, of the musical and theatrical world and the brilliant success they achieved in contributing songs and librettos to many of the best-known light operas of the opening years of the century. I only regret that Mr. Johnson did not write with the same anecdotal detail about the personalities and associations, which he knew in the later years of his literary successes. Perhaps he thought the associates and the famous figures of the musical portion of his career, when he was still a young man, had receded sufficiently into the past to give him the freedom to sketch them and the affairs of their world more copiously and intimately, while his friendships and associations in the more recent world of American letters, as well as that other world of the more sombre hue, wherein notable and self-sacrificing men and women of both races were pledged together in a warfare of service against injustice, were too well-known and in the public view, for him to write about them with the same detachment and freedom. Rich as the ***Autobiography*** is with the crowded figures of notable men and women in the aesthetic world of yesterday and today, it would have been made richer by the intimate portraitures of the author's immediate contemporaries.

The third section of the ***Autobiography*** which stirred and entranced me was the leading part Mr. Johnson took in the fight for the Dyer Anti-Lynching Bill. His account of this fight to enact into Federal legislation a remedy for the most shameful deeds of violence and lawlessness of which America was guilty above all other nations making up the civilized society of today, is, though compressed into a comparatively few pages, an epic of fortitude, tact, patience and perseverance. And the fourth recital of Mr. Johnson's colorful career, is the description of his visit to Japan as a member of the Institute of Pacific Relations, to attend the Conference at Kyoto.

Why this latter episode of his career should so impress me I cannot explain to my satisfaction. It covers scarcely more than twelve or fifteen pages. It had been nothing unusual for American Negroes, from Frederick Douglass, Mary Church Terrell, Dr. Robert R. Moton, Dr. Du Bois, John Hope to young Richard Hill, through the struggling years when the race was winning the intellectual right to a representation in world movements for the betterment of human society, to attend foreign conferences as accredited delegates. These, however, met in Europe. Could it be that there was something racially significant that the Institute of Pacific Relations Conference which took Mr. Johnson to Japan, and to that Garden Party given for its members by the Emperor of Japan, was more than an intellectual and social gesture? Did one, as one read Mr. Johnson's simple, but impressive, description of the affair and the picture of the arrival of the Imperial family and court upon the scene, feel some magic by which the spectacle was transformed into an allegory of the Past and Future, of Time and Race? If an allegory is evoked did it fuse the spirit of the dark people who had mastered with the dark people who were rising to a mastery of their own? And the framework to hold the allegory, the fact that both dark peoples had been freed of a bondage but a few years apart!

James Weldon Johnson has lived a crowded life and he has recorded it minutely in this ***Autobiography,*** which is incontestably the first work of its kind in American literature. Unlike any other autobiography, that of Frederick Douglass, Booker T. Washington, or even Dr. Moton, it escapes from that category of racial recitals in the narrower sense, and remains the narrative of a man who for sixty years of his life has passed through an amazing series of social and intellectual adventures and events which lifted him steadily to a foremost place as an American citizen. And yet I think, the word brilliant must be used to describe the picture which Mr. Johnson has composed of the *social life, the domestic manners and habits, loyalties, and ethical foundations,* which pertain to the lives of Negroes. As Colonel Higginson told a skeptical and indifferent nation a generation or two ago, that the Negro like all other peoples was "intensely human," in his ideals and aspirations, in his habits and conduct, and nowhere in a literal record of his experiences have we had so brilliant a presentation of this truth as in this ***Autobiography.*** Except for that menacing shadow which eternally hovers along the boundary line of the Negro's contact with the objective mood and sentiment of a self-deluded Nordic superiority, page after page of this ***Autobi-***

ography might well be the chronicle of an upper middle-class American gentleman, his family and friends. But like all individuals of exceptional spiritual gifts, there are moments when the spirit of the author is hard pressed with problems and decisions which to solve and make, affect him purely as an individual; beyond their consequences he had to make note, because of that Man-Negro dualism upon which fate and circumstance placed its accent at critical stages of his career. How hampered his career might have been otherwise if Mr. Johnson had lacked that sense of humor and philosophic detachment which so plentifully sprinkles the pages of his ***Autobiography,*** it is not difficult to see.

On arriving in France with his brother and Bob Cole, preparatory to the theatrical engagement for which the latter two were booked in London, Mr. Johnson writes: "From the day I set foot in France, I became aware of the working of a miracle within me. I became aware of a quick readjustment to life and to environment. I recaptured for the first time since childhood the sense of being just a human being. I need not try to analyze this change for my colored readers; they will understand in a flash what took place. For my white readers . . . I am afraid that any analysis will be inadequate, perhaps futile. . . . I was suddenly free; free from a sense of impending discomfort, insecurity, danger; free from the conflict within the Man-Negro dualism and the innumerable maneuvers in thought and behavior that it compels; free from the problem of the many obvious or subtle adjustments to a multitude of bans and taboos; free from special scorn, special tolerance, special condescension; special commiseration; free to be merely a man."

I could wax either sentimental or philosophic over that paragraph. Any estimate of the confession Mr. Johnson makes, of the emotions that moved him on arriving in France, is certain to be colored by both moods. But I venture to predict that an America acquainted with this ***Autobiography*** as it should be—and as I think it will be—will be cleansed of much in its heart that is contemptible and unjust, and will make it unnecessary in the future for one of her citizens to express such a mood. A life such as Mr. Johnson has lived, a career such as he has achieved and a record such as he has made of both in the pages of this ***Autobiography,*** is one of the surest guarantees of that fulfillment in the future.

FURTHER READING

Bibliography

Fleming, Robert E. *James Weldon Johnson and Arna Bontemps: A Reference Guide.* Boston: G. K. Hall, 1978, 149 p.

Annotated bibliography of criticism about Johnson's work published between 1905 and 1976.

Biography

Jackson, Miles, Jr. "James Weldon Johnson." *Black World* 19, no. 8 (1970): 32-4.

Provides a brief portrait of Johnson through excerpts from his letters.

Criticism

Brawley, Benjamin. Review of *Fifty Years and Other Poems. The Journal of Negro History* 3, no 2 (April 1918): 202-03.

Lauds the simple, direct, and sensuous expression of Johnson's poems.

Bone, Robert. "James Weldon Johnson." In *The Negro Novel in America,* revised edition, pp. 45-9. New Haven: Yale University Press, 1965.

Considers Johnson to be the only true artist among early African American novelists, but finds occasional lapses in his work despite its overall merits.

Brooks, Neil. "On Becoming an Ex-Man: Postmodern Irony and the Extinguishing of Certainties in *The Autobiography of an Ex-Colored Man." College Literature* 22, no. 3 (1995): 17-29.

Suggests that a postmodern approach can help readers to understand Johnson's narrative position and the arguments concerning race.

Carroll, Richard A. "Black Racial Spirit: James Weldon Johnson's Critical Perspective." *Phylon* 32 (1971): 344-64.

Asserts that the essential feature of Johnson's literary criticism is "blackness."

Cataliotti, Robert H. "The Most Treasured Heritage of the American Negro: James Weldon Johnson." In *The Music in African American Fiction,* pp. 58-73. New York: Garland Publishing, Inc., 1996.

Discusses the tension between individual and communal expression in The Autobiography of an Ex-Colored Man, *which Cataliotti says is a pivotal work in the representation of music in the African American literary tradition.*

Faulkner, Howard. "James Weldon Johnson's Portrait of the Artist as Invisible Man." *Black American Literature Forum* 19, no. 4 (1985): 147-51.

Considers The Autobiography of an Ex-Colored Man *to be a masterpiece of control.*

Favor, J. Martin. "For a Mess of Pottage: James Weldon Johnson's Ex-Colored Man as (In)authentic man." In *Authentic Blackness: The Folk in the New Negro Renaissance,* pp. 25-52. Durham, NC: Duke University Press, 1999.

Considers the critical discourse of Johnson's novel.

Fleming, Robert E. "The Composition of James Weldon Johnson's 'Fifty Years.'" *American Poetry* 4, no. 2 (1985): 147-51.

Examines the lost stanzas of the poem "Fifty Years," which reveal far more bitterness than the final version.

Franklin, Vincent P. "James Weldon Johnson: The Creative Genius of the Negro." In *Living Out Stories, Telling Our Truths: Autobiography and the Making of the African-American Intellectual Tradition,* pp. 95-138. New York: Scribner, 1995.

Detailed study tracing Johnson's life and career and discussing his major works.

Goellnicht, Donald C. "Passing as Autobiography: James Weldon Johnson's *The Autobiography of an Ex-Coloured Man.*" *African American Review* 30, no. 1 (1996): 17-33.

Discusses the preface of the novel and the problematic stance of the narrator to questions of race.

Hawkins, Alphonso. "Redefining the Text: The Spiritual in James Weldon Johnson's *Along This Way.*" *The Western Journal of Black Studies* 20, no. 1 (1996): 48-56.

Shows how Johnson's autobiography reconstructs a persona that has characteristics of the African American spiritual.

Kostelanetz, Richard. "The Politics of Passing: The Fiction of James Weldon Johnson." *Negro American Literature Forum* 3 (1969): 22-4, 29.

Discusses Johnson's sophisticated, complex exploration of the ambiguities of "passing."

Levy, Eugene. "Ragtime and Race Pride: The Career of James Weldon Johnson." *Journal of Popular Culture* 1 (1968): 357-70.

Examines Johnson's career as a songwriter, from his composition of "coon songs" to his recognition of the artistic and racial importance of Black folk music and ragtime.

Mason, Julian. "James Weldon Johnson: A Southern Writer Resists the South." *College Language Association Journal* 31, no. 2 (1987): 154-69.

Claims that Johnson resisted being Southern, and that this is evident in The Autobiography of an Ex-Colored Man.

Mencken, H. L. "Is Mutare Potest Aethiops Pellum Suam. . . ." *The Smart Set* LIII, no. 1 (September 1917): 138-44.

Reviews The Autobiography of an Ex-Colored Man, *focusing on the treatment of North and South.*

Monroe, Harriet. Review of *God's Trombones. Poetry* 30, no. 5 (August 1927): 291-93.

Praises God's Trombones *as Johnson's highest achievement.*

O'Sullivan, Maurice J., Jr. "Of Souls and Pottage: James Weldon Johnson's *The Autobiography of an Ex-Coloured Man.*" *College Language Association Journal* 23 (1979): 60-70.

Discusses the ambivalence and lack of reconciliation in Johnson's novel.

Payne, Ladell. "Themes and Cadences: James Weldon Johnson's Novel." *Southern Literary Journal* 11, no. 2 (1979): 43-55.

Maintains that the themes and cadences of Johnson's The Autobiography of an Ex-Colored Man *are Black and Southern.*

Pisiak, Roxanna. "Irony and Subversion in James Weldon Johnson's *The Autobiography of an Ex-Coloured Man.*" *Studies in American Fiction* 21, no. 1 (1993): 83-96.

Claims that the ambiguity of color lines and the manner in which race is developed through the use of language are the major themes of The Autobiography of an Ex-Colored Man.

Ruotolo, Cristina L. "James Weldon Johnson and the Autobiography of an Ex-Colored Musician." *American Literature* 72, no. 2 (2000): 249-74.

Examines the role of music in the narrator's experience and identity in The Autobiography of an Ex-Colored Man.

Saunders, James Robert. "The Dilemma of Double Identity: James Weldon Johnson's Artistic Acknowledgment." *Langston Hughes Review* 8, no. 1-2 (spring-fall 1989): 68-75.

Discusses the dilemma Johnson faced about whether to accept mainstream values or to hold on to Black ways that were deemed inferior.

Sheehy, John. "The Mirror and the Veil: The Passing Novel and the Quest for American Racial Identity." *African American Review* 30, no. 3 (1999): 401-15.

Examines novels by W. E. B. Du Bois, Johnson, and others to reveal what they say about African American identity.

Smith, Valerie. "Privilege and Evasion in *The Autobiography of an Ex-Colored Man.*" In *Self-Discovery and Authority in Afro-American Narrative,* pp. 44-64. Cambridge: Harvard University Press, 1987.

Discusses the use of autobiography in Johnson's work of fiction.

Stepto, Robert B. "Lost in Quest: James Weldon Johnson's *The Autobiography of an Ex-Colored Man.*" In *From Behind the Veil: Study of Afro-American Narrative,* pp. 95-127. Urbana: University of Illinois Press, 1991.

Explores the manner in which Johnson's novel fuses aspects of authenticating rhetoric with aspects of generic narrative form and examines the Ex-Colored Man's Club as a fresh expression of an African American ritual ground.

White, Walter. "Negro Poets." *The Nation* CXIV, no. 2970 (June 7, 1922): 694-95.

Presents a favorable review of The Book of American Negro Poetry.

Wilson, Sondra Kathryn. Introduction to *James Weldon Johnson: Complete Poems,* pp. xv-xxi. New York: Penguin Books, 2000.

Discusses Johnson's life and works, suggesting that his writing is especially distinctive for its universality.

OTHER SOURCES FROM GALE:

Additional coverage of Johnson's life and career is contained in the following sources published by the Gale Group: *African American Writers,* Eds. 1, 2; *Black Literature Criticism,* Vol. 2; *Black Writers,* Eds. 1, 3; *Children's Literature Review,* Vol. 32; *Concise Dictionary of American Literary Biography, 1917-1929; Contemporary Authors,* Vols. 104, 125; *Contemporary Authors New Revision Series,* Vol. 82; *Dictionary of Literary Biography,* Vol. 51; *DISCovering Authors Modules: Multicultural Authors* and *Poets; DISCovering Authors 3.0; Exploring Poetry; Major 20th-Century Writers,* Eds. 1, 2; *Poetry Criticism,* Vol. 24; *Poetry for Students,* Vol. 1; *Reference Guide to American Literature,* Ed. 4; *Something about the Author,* Vol. 31; and *Twentieth-Century Literary Criticism,* Vols. 3, 19.

NELLA LARSEN

(1891 - 1964)

American novelist and short story writer.

Although her career was cut short by scandal, Larsen is considered an important African American novelist, and her two novels, *Quicksand* (1928) and *Passing* (1929), are ranked among the best fiction of the Harlem Renaissance. Both novels portray the lives of middle-class African Americans of mixed ancestry with skillful use of narrative and symbolism. Larsen's novels dispelled the myth of the "tragic mulatto" that had been depicted in earlier fiction, and treated the complex subject of "passing" and African American "double consciousness" in a convincing, lucid, and dignified manner. Her works are absent of rhetoric, and she avoided promoting causes—of African Americans, women, or other groups—in her writing. Rather, her works present intricate psychological, modernist studies of the interconnections between race, gender, sexuality, and class.

BIOGRAPHICAL INFORMATION

Larsen was born in Chicago on April 13, 1891, to a Danish mother, Mary Hanson Walker, and an African American father, Peter Walker. Her parents separated shortly after her birth, and her mother married a white man, Peter Larsen. Larsen grew up in Chicago, attended Fisk University and the University of Copenhagen, and in 1912 moved to New York to train as a nurse. In 1915 she moved to Alabama, where she took a job as head nurse at John Andrew Memorial Hospital and Nurse Training School, but in 1916 she returned to New York and took a nursing post there. In New York she met Elmer Imes, a physicist, whom she married in 1919. During this time she also began her acquaintance with Black artists of the burgeoning movement that would later be known as the Harlem Renaissance. Her interest in literature began to grow, and she started writing. She published two articles about Danish games in the *Brownies' Book,* a children's magazine edited by Jessie Redmon Fauset. In 1921 she took a job at the New York Public Library and attended library school at Columbia University. She continued writing, publishing several stories under the pseudonym of Allen Semi. In 1928 she published her first novel, *Quicksand,* which received widespread critical acclaim. Her second novel, *Passing,* followed in 1929. In 1930 Larsen won a Guggenheim Foundation Fellowship—the first African American woman to do so—but the same year, she was accused of plagiarism. Her short story "Sanctuary," published in *Forum* magazine, apparently bore a close resemblance to a story published in 1922. Larsen eventually proved her innocence, but the incident destroyed her writing career; her next novel was rejected by her publisher. In 1933 Larsen was engaged in a crudely sensationalized divorce from Imes, and after that she retreated from public view. She worked as a nurse in Brooklyn and withdrew from her Harlem friends. Though there is evidence that she worked on up to two other novels, she never published her writing again. She was found dead in her apartment at age 72 in March 1964.

MAJOR WORKS

Both Larsen's novels have elements of autobiography, portraying women whose racial and sexual confusion contribute to their unfulfilled quest for an identity. *Quicksand* is the story of Helga Crane, a woman of mixed race who struggles with her racial identity. Her family rejects her because of her dark skin, and she goes South to teach at a Black school, where she once again feels out of place. In *Passing*, the protagonist Clare "passes" in white society, but reunites with her acquaintance, Irene, who knows of Clare's heritage but is also afraid that her light-skinned friend is a threat to her marriage. Although the work deals with the subject of "passing," it also explores deeper questions of identity, sexuality, economics, racism, and self-doubt.

CRITICAL RECEPTION

When Larsen's novels first appeared she was hailed by many as a visionary novelist who convincingly depicted the psyche of middle-class bicultural women. The works were praised in particular for their insights into their characters' psychology. Larsen received the Harmon Award for Distinguished Achievement among Negroes in 1928 and a Guggenheim Foundation Fellowship on the strength of her novels. However, she never regained her literary stature after the accusations of plagiarism in 1930. By the mid-1930s her work was all but forgotten, and it remained largely ignored until the 1970s. Critics since then have admired Larsen's work, although some have faulted the weak endings of her novels. Still others see the endings as fitting in with the themes of the novels, as they eschew easy answers, reject polemics, and explore the complexity and contradictions inherent in issues of gender, race, sexuality, and identity.

PRINCIPAL WORKS

Quicksand (novel) 1928

Passing (novel) 1929

An Intimation of Things Distant: The Collected Fiction of Nella Larsen [edited by Charles R. Larson] (fiction) 1992

PRIMARY SOURCES

NELLA LARSEN (SHORT STORY DATE 1930)

SOURCE: Larsen, Nella. "Sanctuary." *Forum* 83 (January 1930): 15-18.

The following short story is significant to Larsen's career in that she was accused of plagiarizing another work to create it. Though she was later cleared of the charge, the allegation had a tragic effect on her career, as she was unable to find publication again in her lifetime.

I

On the Southern coast, between Merton and Shawboro, there is a strip of desolation some half a mile wide and nearly ten miles long between the sea and old fields of ruined plantations. Skirting the edge of this narrow jungle is a partly grown-over road which still shows traces of furrows made by the wheels of wagons that have long since rotted away or been cut into firewood. This road is little used, now that the state has built its new highway a bit to the west and wagons are less numerous than automobiles.

In the forsaken road a man was walking swiftly. But in spite of his hurry, at every step he set down his feet with infinite care, for the night was windless and the heavy silence intensified each sound; even the breaking of a twig could be plainly heard and the man had need of caution as well as haste.

Before a lonely cottage that shrank timidly back from the road the man hesitated a moment, then struck out across the patch of green in front of it. Stepping behind a clump of bushes close to the house, he looked in through the lighted window at Annie Poole, standing at her kitchen table mixing the supper biscuits.

He was a big, black man with pale brown eyes in which there was an odd mixture of fear and amazement. The light showed streaks of gray soil on his heavy, sweating face and great hands, and on his torn clothes. In his woolly hair clung bits of dried leaves and dead grass.

He made a gesture as if to tap on the window, but turned away to the door instead. Without knocking he opened it and went in.

II

The woman's brown gaze was immediately on him, though she did not move. She said, "You ain't in no hurry, is you, Jim Hammer?" It wasn't, however, entirely a question.

"Ah's in trubble, Mis' Poole," the man explained, his voice shaking, his fingers twitching.

"W'at you done now?"

"Shot a man, Mis' Poole."

"Trufe?" The woman seemed calm. But the word was spat out.

"Yas'm. Shot 'im." In the man's tone was something of wonder, as if he himself could not quite believe that he had really done this thing which he affirmed.

"Daid?"

"Dunno, Mis' Poole. Dunno."

"White man o' niggah?"

"Cain't say, Mis' Poole. White man, Ah reckons."

Annie Poole looked at him with cold contempt. She was a tiny, withered woman—fifty perhaps—with a wrinkled face the color of old copper, framed by a crinkly mass of white hair. But about her small figure was some quality of hardness that belied her appearance of frailty. At last she spoke, boring her sharp little eyes into those of the anxious creature before her.

"An' w'at am you lookin' foh me to do 'bout et?"

"Jes' lemme stop till dey's gone by. Hide me till dey passes. Reckon dey ain't fur off now." His begging voice changed to a frightened whimper. "Foh de Lawd's sake, Mis' Poole, lemme stop."

And why, the woman inquired caustically, should she run the dangerous risk of hiding him?

"Obadiah, he'd lemme stop ef he was to home," the man whined.

Annie Poole sighed. "Yas," she admitted slowly, reluctantly, "Ah spec' he would. Obadiah, he's too good to you all no 'count trash." Her slight shoulders lifted in a hopeless shrug. "Yas, Ah reckon he'd do et. Emspecial' seein' how he allus set such a heap o' store by you. Cain't see w'at foh, mahse'f. Ah shuah don' see nuffin' in you but a heap o' dirt."

But a look of irony, of cunning, of complicity passed over her face. She went on, "Still, 'siderin' all an' all, how Obadiah's right fon' o'you, an' how white folks is white folks, Ah'm a-gwine hide you dis one time."

Crossing the kitchen, she opened a door leading into a small bedroom, saying, "Git yo'se'f in dat dere feather bald an'Ah'm a-gwine put de clo's on de top. Don' reckon dey'll fin' you ef dey does look foh you in mah house. An Ah don' spec' dey'll go foh to do cat. Not lessen you been keerless an' let 'em smell you out gittin' hyah." She turned on him a withering look. "But you allus been triflin'. Cain't do nuffin' propah. An' Ah'm a-tellin' you ef dey warn's white folks an'you a po'niggah, Ah shuah wouldn't be lettin' you mess up mah feather bald dis ebenin', 'cose Ah jes' plain con' went you hyah. Ah done kep'mahse'f outen bubble all mah life. So's Obadiah."

"Ah's powahful 'bliged to you, Mis' Poole. You shuah am one good 'omen. De Lawd'll mos' suttinly—"

Annie Poole cut him off. "Dis ain't no time foh all dat kin' o' fiddle-de-roll. Ah does mah duty as Ah sees et 'shout no thanks from you. Ef de Lawd had gib you a white face 'stead o' dat dere black one, Ah shuah would turn you out. Now hush yo' mouf an' git yo'se'f in. An' don' git movin' and scrunchin' undah dose covahs and git yo'se'f kotched in mah house."

Without further comment the man did as he was told. After he had laid his soiled body and grimy garments between her snowy sheets, Annie Poole carefully rearranged the covering and placed piles of freshly laundered linen on top. Then she gave a pat here and there, eyed the result, and, finding it satisfactory, went back to her cooking.

III

Jim Hammer settled down to the racking business of waiting until the approaching danger should have passed him by. Soon savory odors seeped in to him and he realized that he was hungry. He wished that Annie Poole would bring him something to eat. Just one biscuit. But she wouldn't, he knew. Not she. She was a hard one, Obadiah's mother.

By and by he fell into a sleep from which he was dragged back by the rumbling sounds of wheels in the road outside. For a second fear clutched so tightly at him that he almost leaped from the suffocating shelter of the bed in order to make some active attempt to escape the horror that his capture meant. There was a spasm at his heart, a pain so sharp, so slashing, that he had to suppress an impulse to cry out. He felt himself falling. Down, down, down . . . Everything grew dim and very distant in his memory . . . Vanished . . . Came rushing back.

Outside there was silence. He strained his ears. Nothing. No footsteps. No voices. They had gone on then. Gone without even stopping to ask Annie Poole if she had seen him pass that way. A sigh of relief slipped from him. His thick lips curled in an ugly, cunning smile. It had been smart of him to think of coming to Obadiah's mother's to hide. She was an old demon, but he was safe in her house.

He lay a short while longer, listening intently, and, hearing nothing, started to get up. But immediately he stopped, his yellow eyes glowing like pale flames. He had heard the unmistakable sound of men coming toward the house. Swiftly he slid back into the heavy, hot stuffiness of the bed and lay listening fearfully.

The terrifying sounds drew nearer. Slowly. Heavily. Just for a moment he thought they were not coming in—they took so long. But there was a light knock and the noise of a door being opened. His whole body went taut. His feet felt frozen, his hands clammy, his tongue like a weighted, dying thing. His pounding heart made it hard for his straining ears to hear what they were saying out there.

"Evenin', Mistah Lowndes." Annie Poole's voice sounded as it always did, sharp and dry.

There was no answer. Or had he missed it? With slow care he shifted his position, bringing his head nearer the edge of the bed. Still he heard nothing. What were they waiting for? Why didn't they ask about him?

Annie Poole, it seemed, was of the same mind. "Ah don' reckon youall done traipsed way out hyah jes' foh yo' healf," she hinted.

"There's bad news for you, Annie, I'm 'fraid." The sheriff's voice was low and queer.

Jim Hammer visualized him standing out there—a tall, stooped man, his white tobacco-stained mustache drooping limply at the ends, his nose hooked and sharp, his eyes blue and cold. Bill Lowndes was a hard one too. And white.

"W'atall bad news, Mistah Lowndes?" The woman put the question quietly, directly.

"Obadiah—" the sheriff began—hesitated—began again. "Obadiah—ah—er—he's outside, Annie. I'm 'fraid—"

"Shucks! You done missed. Obadiah, he ain't done nuffin', Mistah Lowndes. Obadiah!" she called stridently, "Obadiah! git hyah an' splain yo'se'f."

But Obadiah didn't answer, didn't come in. Other men came in. Came in with steps that dragged and halted. No one spoke. Not even Annie Poole. Something was laid carefully upon the floor.

"Obadiah, chile," his mother said softly, "Obadiah, chile." Then, with sudden alarm, "He ain't daid, is he? Mistah Lowndes! Obadiah, he ain't daid?"

Jim Hammer didn't catch the answer to that pleading question. A new fear was stealing over him.

"There was a to-do, Annie," Bill Lowndes explained gently, "at the garage back o' the factory. Fellow tryin' to steal tires. Obadiah heerd a noise an' run out with two or three others. Scared the rascal all right. Fired off his gun an' run. We allow et to be Jim Hammer. Picked up his cap back there. Never was no 'count. Thievin' an' sly. But we'll git 'im, Annie. We'll git 'im."

The man huddled in the feather bed prayed silently. "Oh, Lawd! Ah didn't go to do et. Not Obadiah, Lawd. You knows dat. You knows et." And into his frenzied brain came the thought that it would be better for him to get up and go out to them before Annie Poole gave him away. For he was lost now. With all his great strength he tried to get himself out of the bed. But he couldn't.

"Oh, Lawd!" he moaned. "Oh, Lawd!" His thoughts were bitter and they ran through his mind like panic. He knew that it had come to pass as it said somewhere in the Bible about the wicked. The Lord had stretched out his hand and smitten him. He was paralyzed. He couldn't move hand or foot. He moaned again. It was all there was left for him to do. For in the terror of this new calamity that had come upon him he had forgotten the waiting danger which was so near out there in the kitchen.

His hunters, however, didn't hear him. Bill Lowndes was saying, "We been a- lookin' for Jim out along the old road. Figured he'd make tracks for Shawboro. You ain't noticed anybody pass this evenin', Annie?"

The reply came promptly, unwaveringly. "No, Ah ain't sees nobody pass. Not yet."

IV

Jim Hammer caught his breath.

"Well," the sheriff concluded, "we'll be gittin' along. Obadiah was a mighty fine boy. Ef they was all like him—I'm sorry, Annie. Anything I c'n do, let me know."

"Thank you, Mistah Lowndes."

With the sound of the door closing on the departing men, power to move came back to the man in the bedroom. He pushed his dirt-caked feet out from the covers and rose up, but crouched down again. He wasn't cold now, but hot all over and burning. Almost he wished that Bill Lowndes and his men had taken him with them.

Annie Poole had come into the room.

It seemed a long time before Obadiah's mother spoke. When she did there were no tears, no reproaches; but there was a raging fury in her voice as she lashed out, "Git outer mah feather baid, Jim Hammer, an' outen mah house, an' don' nevah stop thankin' yo' Jesus he done gib you dat black face."

GENERAL COMMENTARY

THADIOUS M. DAVIS (ESSAY DATE 1989)

SOURCE: Davis, Thadious M. "Nella Larsen's Harlem Aesthetic." In *The Harlem Renaissance: Revaluations*, edited by Amritjit Singh, William S. Shiver, and Stanley Brodwin, pp. 245-56. New York: Garland, 1989.

In the following essay, Davis claims that Larsen was driven to writing fiction by her intense desire for prestige and recognition.

"I do so want to be famous," Nella Larsen wrote to Henry Allen Moe of the Guggenheim Foundation. She was in Spain for the completion of her year as the foundation's first black woman to receive a fellowship in creative writing: "The work goes fairly well. But I like it. Of course, that means nothing because I really can't tell if it's good or not. But the way I hope and pray that it is [is] like a physical pain. I do . . . want to be famous."[1] The statement in context is innocent enough, but it is an indication of the attitudes and values Larsen held throughout the 1920s and early 1930s when she was writing fiction.

At thirty-seven, Larsen had published her first novel, ***Quicksand,*** brought out by Knopf, but which she had considered submitting to Albert and Charles Boni, for as she said: "It would be nice to get a thousand dollars . . . and publicity."[2] ***Quicksand***'s reception in 1928 fueled her determination to be a famous novelist. She promptly decided that she "was asking for the Harmon Award," because as she assessed her chances, "Looking back on the year's output of Negro literature I don't see why I shouldn't have a book in. There's only Claude McKay besides.—Rudolph [Fisher] is just too late—. . . .[3] She immediately sought out recommendations from James Weldon Johnson, W. E. B. Du Bois, and Lillian Alexander when she discovered that one had to be *nominated* for the Harmon Award.

Larsen had already shaved two years off her age in order to comply with the image of youth promoted during the Renaissance. The daughter of an interracial union, Larsen had come a long way by the end of the 1920s when she no longer admitted to being from a working-class background on Chicago's South Side. However, it was not simply upward mobility that she sought during the Renaissance; by then, she had already been married to a physicist since May 1919. She was seeking instead to become someone important in her own right.

Nella Larsen, novelist, emerged from a particular cultural configuration—Harlem of the New Negro Renaissance; perhaps no other could have produced her. While her art was dependent upon a number of factors, it was obviously linked to her historical situation. With an influx of 87,417 blacks during the 1920s, the 25-block area above 125th Street was, as James Weldon Johnson declared, "the greatest Negro city in the world."[4] Harlem provided a place for black life, in Alain Locke's view, to seize "its first chances for group expression and self-determination. . . . There is a fresh spiritual and cultural focusing. We have, as the heralding sign, an unusual outburst of creative expression."[5] This "unusual outburst of creative expression" was possible in a particular environment not only conducive to black creativity, but also to inspire participation in that creativity.

In April 1927, when Nella Larsen and her husband Elmer Imes moved from Jersey City to an apartment in Harlem's 135th Street, they arrived seeking proximity to the "cultural Capital." Larsen especially welcomed the move as the convergence of her social and literary interests. Her initial aim was imitative; she wanted to join herself through writing to a particular phenomenon. The creative activity, whether a Zora Neale Hurston telling stories, an Aaron Douglas drawing illustrations, a Countee Cullen or Langston Hughes writing poetry, inspired confidence in artistic potential and promised rewards for involvement.

For Larsen, the activity was like a whirlwind. As she stated: "It has seemed always to be tea time, as the immortal Alice remarked, with never time to wash the dishes between while."[6] Her actions were controlled by her conscious desire to achieve recognition and were perhaps controlled too by her unconscious hope to belong. While for some the stirrings in Harlem may have been racial and aesthetic, for Larsen they were primarily practical. Her objective was to use art to protract her identity onto a larger social landscape as emphatically as possible.

Larsen had made her decision to become part of the growing number of "New Negro" writers in 1925 when, as Arna Bontemps recalled, "It did not take long to discover . . . the sighs of wonder, amazement and sometimes admiration . . . that here was one of the 'New Negroes.'"[7] The reception accorded young artists motivated Larsen to turn to writing, at first stories, which early in 1926 she sold to a ladies magazine. These stories, and especially her first novel, ***Quicksand*** (1928), were part of her attempt to "cash in" on the cultural awakening, to stake her own claim for the recognition and development of identity that other authors were accorded. Basically, it was not enough to write; it was *essential* to publish.

The writer during the Renaissance was just as often *made* as born. Walter White had written *The Fire in the Flint* (1924) in response to a wave of white interest in race material. And others had answered the call by publishers for "Negro" works by producing poetry, fiction, and drama. In that milieu it was possible to become a writer with an announcement to "friends" that a project was under way or through a notice that a publisher was searching for "Negro" materials. In 1927, for example, Larsen wrote to her friend Dorothy Peterson, "You'd better write some poetry, or something. I've met a man from Macmillan's who's asked me to look out for any Negro stuff and send them to him."[8] She would and did believe that any and all of her intelligent, lively friends could and would want to produce "poetry, or something" in order to take advantage of the opportunities for recognition and prestige that publishing, particularly with a white firm, would bring. Talent or inclination or aptitude or inspiration had little to do with it.

Larsen herself had become known as a budding writer even before an audience had seen her fiction; rumor had it as early as the start of 1926 that she was writing a novel. "How do these things get about?" she asked Van Vechten, and added, "It is the awful Truth. But, who knows if I'll get through with the damned thing. Certainly not I."[9]

The two prongs of inspiration for Larsen were public acclaim and social activity, both intricately tied to the climate for publishing things "Negro." In this she may have been similar to others; there were, however, writers who wrote out of a different set of aesthetic values, such as Georgia Douglas Johnson, who revealed in 1927:

> I wrote because I love to write. . . . If I might ask of some fairy godmother special favors, one would sure to be for a clearing space, elbow room in which to think and write and live beyond the reach of the wolf's fingers.[10]

Nella Larsen, however, functioned in what Gilbert Osofsky called the "myth world of the twenties."[11] Described in 1929 as having a "satin surface,"[12] she revealed her ritual for reading a good book: "a Houbigant scented bath, the donning of my best green crepe de chine pyjamas, fresh flowers on the bedside table, piles of freshly covered pillows and my nicest bed covers."[13] Her pretentious description portrays not merely a sense of aesthetic pleasure, but also the degree to which she was removed from ordinary black life.

Drawn to the class of blacks and of whites who could ignore the poverty that Harlem bred along with the possibilities for its residents, Larsen responded to a world of glitter and potential that distanced itself from the teeming masses. In the process, she created precarious boundaries for her work and life: "I'm still looking for a place to move. . . . Right now when I look out into the Harlem streets I feel just like Helga Crane in my novel. Furious at being connected with all these niggers."[14] Being ensconced in a five-room apartment was not enough to make her forget that she was trapped among lower-class blacks whom she once described as "mostly black . . . quite shiftless, frightfully clean and decked out in appalling colours."[15] When she found a better apartment on Seventh Avenue, which she called "Uncle Tom's Cabin,"[16] she would more readily admit "that she would never pass" because, as she told a reporter, "with my economic status it's better to be a Negro [sic]."[17] She might have added—especially if she could be labeled one of the "talented tenth" of the race and associate with people accustomed to prestige, position, and comfort.

But, as Langston Hughes pointed out in *The Big Sea* (1940): "All of us knew that the gay sparkling life of the so-called Renaissance . . . was not so gay and sparkling beneath the surface. . . . I thought it wouldn't last long. . . . for how could a large and enthusiastic number of people be crazy about Negroes forever?"[18] Whereas Hughes's assessment is familiar, Alain Locke's is not. In 1936, eleven years after his confident pronouncements in *The New Negro,* and after the Harlem riots of March 1935, Locke wrote another Harlem essay for *Survey Graphic,* "Harlem: Dark Weather Vane," in which he broke what he called a "placid silence and Pollyanna complacency" about "the actual predicament of the mass of life in Harlem": "For no cultural advance is safe without some sound economic underpinning . . . and no emerging elite—artistic, professional or mercantile—can suspend itself in thin air over the abyss of a mass of unemployed [people] stranded in an over-expensive, disease-and crime-ridden slum . . . for there is no cure or saving magic in poetry and art, an emerging generation of talent, or international prestige and interracial recognition, for unemployment, . . . for high rents, high mortality rates, civic neglect, capitalistic exploitation."[19] Locke includes the two elements that were key components of Nella Larsen's Harlem aesthetic; the two are "international prestige" and "interracial recognition."

Partly because she was a black person in a predominantly white world in Chicago and a nobody in the primarily bourgeois world of elite blacks in New York, Larsen sought a career in writing as a way to become somebody. The single claim that she could and did make about being special was that she was a mulatto, daughter of "a Danish lady and a Negro from the Virgin Islands," as she wrote in her 1927 author's publicity sketch for Knopf; later, once ***Quicksand*** had been published, she could point out that she had not worked outside her home for three years, inflate her educational background and previous employment, and emphasize that her husband had a Ph.D. in physics and worked *downtown* for an engineering firm.

Larsen had married well, but the marriage did not guarantee her acceptance or prominence or make her comfortable within the black elite. She had neither college credentials to call upon, nor a prominent family to smooth her way. What she had was ambition and drive and intelligence. The ambivalences in her fiction and ultimately in her life result perhaps more from her attempts to enter into a class that never knew her for the person she had been in her early life—the child of a working-class immigrant family; it is the background that Larsen could never reveal once she had transformed herself from Nell*ie* to Nell*a*, member of a black society that was not only race conscious, but class conscious as well.

Larsen wanted her own life to become a kind of fairy tale, "like a princess out of a modern fairy tale," as she observed of Fania Marinoff, Van Vechten's wife.[20] But discontented with life in the limelight of her prince, she desired her *own* spotlight, as is indicated by her transition from calling herself Nella *Imes* to Nella Larsen, or Nella Larsen Imes when necessary, after she had finished her first novel. She confessed in 1929 that she "would like to be twenty-five years younger [and that] she want[ed] things—beautiful and rich things."[21]

Nella Larsen as a novelist was driven not by an inner need to write, but by a craving for what she called "fame" and what Locke described as prestige or recognition. Larsen, however, was not the only one whose values emphasized prestige and recognition: others such as Richard Bruce Nugent, Wallace Thurman, Albert Rice, Walter White, or Gwendolyn Bennett also wanted the fame that was almost assured by being part of the New Negro movement. I would not criticize the effort that such individuals put into their writing or dismiss the fact that the writing itself functioned as a means of insight.

I do not question Nella Larsen's effort or seriousness of purpose. Her hard work is a persistent refrain in her letters: "I have been working like a coloured person," she stressed repeatedly, and she would also, as she said, "sweat blood over her work, and console herself with Van Vechten's maxim: 'Easy writing makes bad reading.'"[22] Moreover, she saw herself as a serious novelist, despite being one who would underline the appositive "novelist" after her name in news items noting her attendance at social functions before sending the clippings to her friends. She never gave her occupation as anything other than "writer," and never referred to herself except as "novelist." My doubts about her work lie, therefore, in the somewhat inexplicable area of motivation and intention. I believe that Larsen's commitment to writing may have been inextricably linked to tangible social rewards. She seems to have valued social popularity on the same level as her writing, and it may well be that the publicity she received as one of the two black women *novelists* in the 1920s forced her to take the production of work seriously so that she could sustain her new identity.

Larsen "worked" privately on her writing and publicly on her social standing. She promoted herself on the stage that encouraged her transformation. Because she was bound by the larger expectations of the Renaissance and her own internal pressure to achieve, the measure she set for herself was public acknowledgment of her work and productivity. One result was the intensification of a split between her work as a creative process and her work as a source of public recognition—the standard by which she, like Locke and others, measured achievement. Because one of her objectives remained constant—reaping the benefits of social prominence—she was forced to set unreasonably short deadlines for her finished work and that self-imposed restriction ultimately frustrated her.

The tension between individual work and social interaction was exacerbated by her own underlying conception of writing, her Harlem aesthetic: writing was a "product," which could, upon reception, confirm self-identity as well as very self-worth. Larsen had in the Renaissance a formidable model for understanding writing in the contexts of upward mobility, status, and achievement, not in the private creative process but in the public end result. The result validates the power of the black writer to define the self in the larger world, yet validates as well the power of the larger world to determine and arbitrate the conditions of that validation.

Though Hughes had warned in 1926 that the "present vogue in things Negro . . . may do as much harm as good for the budding colored artist," and that the "Negro artist works against an undertow of sharp criticism and misunderstanding from his own group and unintentional bribes from the whites,"[23] his message was not heard distinctly. Tangible production was the most viable means of asserting the existence of the "New Negro" and measuring achievement. Locke's 1925 announcement of "outbursts of creative expression"—that is to say, published works—as a "heralding sign" established the stage in a way that he may not have fully intended. Achievement for Larsen and other racially defined writers was thus seemingly construed as public acknowledgment without which the creative act was incomplete. Achievement consisted of both publication and reception by an audience, preferably a white one.

Considered in this context, Walter White's letter to Claude McKay on 20 May 1925 is revealing:

> Things are certainly moving with rapidity . . . so far as the Negro artist is concerned. Countee Cullen has had a book of verse accepted by Harper . . . and . . . Knopf accepted a volume by Langston Hughes. Rudolph Fisher . . . has had two excellent short stories in *The Atlantic Monthly*. . . . James Weldon Johnson is at work on a book of Negro spirituals. . . .
>
> The Negro artist is really in the ascendancy. . . . There is unlimited opportunity . . . you will be amazed at the eagerness of magazine editors and book publishers to get hold of promising writers.
>
> Let me as a friend urge you to get your novel ready for publication as soon as possible.[24]

The trap here is evident. The black individual generally has an internal barometer that measures, accurately or not, his or her own selfhood in a society whose locus of meaning has little to do with the meaning of blackness. However, the black individual, who for whatever reasons wants and needs a validation of the self in the external world, may well resort to what that world has accepted as worthy of measurement.

This awareness is one that McKay had formulated when he responded to White's letter: "I am so happy about the increased interest in the creative life of the Negro. It is for Negro aspirants to the creative life themselves to make the best of it—to discipline themselves and do work that will hold ground firmly [to] the very highest white standards. Nothing less will help Negro art forward; a boom is a splendid thing but if the masses are not up to standard people turn aside from them after the novelty has worn off."[25] McKay shifts his focus away from White's emphasis on quantity and publication to "the creative life" and quality; albeit he too leaves "white standards" as the aesthetic measure.

For Larsen, too, in the sparkling social world of the Renaissance with its interracial conclaves and its hope for uplift, the printed product evidenced the New Negro's reality. Each group of published works was carefully added to the list of verifiable products, of achievement of oneself and the race; each writer's productivity was dutifully proclaimed in the records for the year. It is not surprising, then, that this tallysheet approach could not last, that most writers did not endure, so that in a retrospective view of the Renaissance, one can marvel not at the lists of works produced during a relatively brief period, but instead take note of the casualties—those black writers who, for whatever conjunction of personal factors and external causes, simply did not make it into the next decade, or if into it, then not out of it. By 1936 Locke himself was to observe, "indeed, [we] find it hard to believe that the rosy enthusiasms and hope of 1925 were more than bright illusions or a cruelly deceptive mirage. Yet after all there was a renaissance, with its poetic spurt of cultural and spiritual advance, vital and significant but uneven accomplishments. . . ."[26]

Few would quarrel with Locke here, and few would challenge his interpretation of the accomplishments as being "vital and significant but uneven." Too few have, however, asked why the accomplishments were so uneven. One answer to that question might pose as well an answer to the questions of why the Renaissance ended so abruptly—a question that is more frequently answered, but in such a way as to link not aesthetics but economics to the decline of the movement.

Perhaps another answer to the question may lie in the particular and personal motivations of individual writers, in the impetus for their will to create. Their aesthetics thus emphasized both the product and the status that came with it, these two being more important to them than either artistic creativity or economic gain.

For a brief time, one of these authors, Nella Larsen, captured the spirit of a unique time for modern black writers. She praised the activity as "writing as if [one] didn't absolutely despise the age in which [one] lives. . . . Surely it is more interesting to belong to one's own time, to share its peculiar vision, catch that flying glimpse of the panorama which no subsequent generation can ever recover."[27] In her own words, in her own "flying glimpse of the panorama," Larsen saw a world of middle-class blacks that became the basis for her fictional vision, but she saw, too, the complexities of personal identification with that world. While it cannot be claimed that she saw either steadily or whole, it is evident that the angle and the scope of her vision resulted from her particular involvement with her time. Perhaps then, like others such as Thurman, Larsen was more acutely a victim of the New Negro Renaissance than has been assumed. Had she completed her three novels in progress, she might have emerged from her age with a more substantial canon, and with more of the fame that she so wanted. Yet that canon, in all probability, would not have altered the estimation of her relationship to her age, even though she had the individual talent to transcend "hack work," as she herself once labeled her early stories.[28] Larsen was a writer inspired to write by the confluence of activities in the Harlem of the Renaissance, and limited as well by that very inspiration.

Notes

1. Letter to Henry Allen Moe, 11 January 1931, in the John Simon Guggenheim Foundation Files. Hereafter referred to as GFF.
2. Letter to Carl Van Vechten, 1 July 1926, in the James Weldon Johnson Collection, Beinecke Rare Book and Manuscript Library, Yale University, New Haven, Connecticut. Hereafter referred to as JWJC.
3. Letter to Carl Van Vechten, n.d., circa 3 September 1928, JWJC.
4. James Weldon Johnson, "The Making of Harlem," in *Survey Graphic,* 6 (March 1925), 635.
5. Alain Locke, "Foreword," in *The New Negro* (New York: Albert & Charles Boni, 1925), p. xvii.
6. Letter to Carl Van Vechten, Monday [1925], Carl Van Vechten Collection, New York Public Library, New York. Hereafter, CVVC.
7. Arna Bontemps, *Personals* (London: Paul Bremen, 1963), p. 4.
8. Letter to Dorothy Peterson, Thursday 21st [1927], JWJC.
9. Letter to Carl Van Vechten, 1 July 1926, JWJC.
10. Georgia Douglas Johnson, "The Contest Spotlight," *Opportunity* (July 1927), p. 204.
11. Gilbert Osofsky, *Harlem: The Making of a Ghetto, Negro New York, 1890-1930* (1965; rpt. New York: Harper & Row, 1968).
12. Mary Rennels, *The New York Telegram,* 13 April 1929.
13. Letter to Carl Van Vechten, Friday sixth. [1926], JWJC.
14. Letter to Dorothy Peterson, Tuesday 19th [1927], JWJC.
15. Letter to Fania Marinoff and Carl Van Vechten, 22 May 1930, JWJC.
16. Letter to Carl Van Vechten, 1 May 1928, JWJC.
17. Mary Rennels, *New York Telegram,* 13 April 1929.
18. Langston Hughes, *The Big Sea: An Autobiography* (New York: Knopf, 1940), pp. 227-228.
19. Alain Locke, "Harlem: Dark Weather-Vane," *Survey Graphic,* 25 (August 1936), 457-462, 493-495.
20. Letter to Carl Van Vechten, Wednesday [1926], CVVC.
21. Rennels, *New York Telegram,* 13 April 1929.
22. Letter to Carl Van Vechten, 7 April 1931, JWJC.
23. Langston Hughes, "The Negro Artist and the Racial Mountain," *The Nation,* 23 June 1926, pp. 692-694; reprinted in *Voices from the Harlem Renaissance,* ed. Nathan Irvin Huggins (New York: Oxford University Press, 1976), p. 307.
24. In NAACP Papers, Library of Congress, Washington, D.C.
25. Letter to Walter White, 25 June 1925, NAACP Papers, Library of Congress, Washington, D.C.
26. Locke, "Harlem: Dark Weather-Vane," *Survey Graphic,* 25 (August 1936), 457.
27. Letter to Carl Van Vechten, Monday [1925], CVVC.
28. Guggenheim Application, 14 November 1929, GFF.

BETTYE J. WILLIAMS (ESSAY DATE 1995)

SOURCE: Williams, Bettye J. "Nella Larsen: Early Twentieth-Century Novelist of Afrocentric Feminist Thought." *College Language Association Journal* 39, no. 2 (December 1995): 165-78.

In the following essay, Williams maintains that Larsen's novels show her to be an early twentieth-century "Afrocentric feminist"—a highly visible woman who recognized and critiqued existing social structures, and who challenged systems of race, class, and gender oppression that affect African American women.

African-American slave women were among the first feminists in the United States. Through subversive tactics and resistance, they challenged

FROM THE AUTHOR

PASSING

She wished to find out about this hazardous business of "passing," this breaking away from all that was familiar and friendly to take one's chances in another environment, not entirely strange, perhaps, but certainly not entirely friendly.

SOURCE: Nella Larsen, excerpt from *Passing*, Knopf, 1929.

their subordination and denigration.[1] Often ignored by African-American men and American feminists, African-American women struggled, by way of the lecture platform and the written word, for both political and sexual equality. Their legacy is evident in paradigms established by courageous and outspoken African-American forebears like Sojourner Truth, Anna J. Cooper, and Frances Ellen Watkins Harper. One can uncover in the speeches and texts of these women writers an inclusive view of how systems of race, gender, and class oppression constrain self-actualization.[2] Centering feminist concerns in her novels of elite African-Americans, Nella Larsen treats as complex and significant the struggle of her protagonists to form positive self-definitions in the face of multiple systems of oppression.

Larsen was outraged by prevailing concepts and stereotypic images of African Americans during the Harlem Renaissance. No social class was exempt from disparagement. For instance, striving to live an image of refinement, the African-American burgeoisie were viewed as materialistic and passionless, and working-class women were presented as primitive, exotic, and/or wanton. Clearly these stereotypes were dehumanizing and unfair. By examining ***Quicksand*** (1928) and ***Passing*** (1929), I will attempt in this discourse to project Larsen as an early twentieth-century Afrocentric feminist.[3]

Broadly directed, Afrocentric feminist thought includes disparate meanings.[4] First, it declares the visibility of African-American women. Second, because it empowers African-American women to interpret and define their reality, it asserts self-definition. Third, it offers another concept of the social relations of domination and resistance. Fourth, it challenges the three systems of control/oppression (race, class, and gender) that heavily affect African-American women. Patricia Hill Collins points out, "Systems create new possibilities for an empowering Afrocentric feminist knowledge. They [address] and [debate] in the sociology of knowledge concerning the truth."[5] Last, Afrocentric feminist ideology presumes an image of African-American women as powerful, independent subjects. In ***Quicksand*** and ***Passing,*** Larsen posits the foregoing in her narrative design and paints her protagonists as resisting subjects rather than objects of oppression.

During the 1920s the eclipse of Victorian standards encouraged African-American men to appreciate and respect a wider spectrum of African-American women. Feminism and femininity dominated the conversation of the era. Sexual freedom and sexual liberation were other subjects of great concern. Evident in Harlem and the major cities in the United States, African-American women embraced the beauty ethos of the time. Paula Giddings notes that African-American women of the 1920s were "breaking out of the hard-edged chrysalis of a stereotyped past."[6] In 1925, Elise McDougald wrote about the "colorful pageant of individuals . . . each differently endowed . . . with traces of the race's history left in physical and mental outline on each."[7] African-American novelists—especially Larsen and W. E. B. Du Bois—were demanding absolute social equality, which included dispelling denigrating images of African-American womanhood.

Larsen made bold strides toward self-definition in her public stance. Even though tragedy and disappointments were a part of her personal and professional life, she worked out a pattern of survival that permitted her to transcend the marginality that circumscribed her. Being separated from Elmer Imes (her husband) for some time when she commenced writing *Quicksand,* Larsen centered the book on her own preoccupations—sex and the dissolution of nuptials. During the Harlem Renaissance, the refined intelligentsia were held to codes of conduct steeped in Victorianism. Being a modern woman, Larsen rebelled against the rigid code of behavior demanded of this class. Even though her stance was considered radical by the standards of that time, her candor on the subject made her a pioneer in the crusade against sexual repression. My own view is that Larsen's repressed sexuality is the subplot of ***Quicksand.***[8] Thus, attempting such a private, race-dividing issue and bursting barriers to emancipate women from systems of bondage and unhappiness, Larsen ranked with and transcended previous African-American feminists.

In the light of the latter assertion, Larsen's feminist stance requires a backward glance, a glimpse into an era of staunch nineteenth-century Afrocentric feminists who refused to be thwarted by petty restrictions. Pointing out in 1831 that racial and sexual oppression were the fundamental causes of African-American women's poverty, Maria W. Stewart (1803-1879) challenged African-American women to reject false claims of their womanhood. Stewart's is the earliest recorded call of social and political disparagement:

> O, ye daughters if Africa, awake! Awake? Arise! No longer sleep nor slumber, but distinguish yourselves. Show forth to the world that you are endowed with noble and exalted faculties. . . . Shall it any longer be said of the daughters of Africa, that they have not ambition, they have no force? By no means. . . . Possess the spirit of independence. . . . Possess the spirit of men, bold and enterprising, fearless and undaunted. Sue for your rights and privileges. . . . We need never think that anybody is going to feel interested in us, if we do not feel interested for ourselves.
>
> (30, 37-38)

Making herself a "warrior" and "potential martyr" for the "cause of oppressed Africa" and urging African-American women to forge self-definitions of self-reliance and independence, Stewart crusaded boldly and militantly for change. Richardson summarizes Stewart's appeal to the "daughters of Africa":

> [To] develop their highest intellectual capacities, to enter into all spheres of the life of the mind, and to participate in all activities within their community from religion and education to politics and business, without apoligy to notions of female subservience.
>
> (xiv)

Being aware of the conservative traditional sphere of influence allotted to women, Stewart made an effort to redefine African-American women's domestic situation. While she was mute (or suggested very little) about sexual abuse in her speeches, Stewart suggested activism as a tactic of empowerment (21-22). In both the formulation and the articulation of ideas central to the struggle for African-American freedom and human rights, Stewart was a predecessor to influential champions of African-American female activism.

Using their voices and pens during a period called the "club women's era," post-Reconstruction African-American activists organized themselves into a powerful political force by raising issues that affected African-American womanhood. Besides Cooper and Harper, Pauline E. Hopkins, Ida B. Wells Barnett, Fannie Barrier Williams, and Mary Church Terrell were the giants during this period of African-American women's political activism.[9] The preceding feminists galvanized the African-American populace with activist concerns. Their speeches and texts are significant, for they illustrate a tradition of joining scholarship with activism. For example, Harper wrote *Iola Leroy, or Shadows Uplifted* (1892) to intervene in and influence political, social, and cultural debate "concerning the status of 'the Negro' as 'Jim Crow' practices threatened to extinguish the last hopes for a black political presence in the South."[10] Besides nationalist concerns, what shaped *Iola Leroy* was an assertion of female values and actions upon the political life of the culture and the nation. In corroboration with Harper but written from a Northern conviction, Hopkins' *Contending Forces: A Romance Illustrative of Negro Life North and South* (1901) was the most detailed exploration of the parameters of African-American womanhood and the limitations of African-American manhood at the turn of the century.[11] By 1916, the menbers of the National Association of Colored Woman (NACW) could point to a long list of achievements. Being both an intellectual and activist group, NACW wanted to be accountable to and engage themselves against "the achievements of their forebears who had not been free."[12] Preceding the National Association for the Advancement of Colored People (NAACP) and the Urban League, NACW articulated Afrocentric feminist thought and sustained itself, without white-American largesse, as the first national African-American organization to deal with the needs of the race.

With an assertiveness like that of her NACW predecessors, Larsen articulated Afrocentric feminist thought in her fiction. First, she situated race, gender, and class as interlocking systems of oppression. Second, by placing African-American women as subjects, she offered transformed images of African-American womanhood, especially with regard to one class—the intelligentsia.[13] Unlike Jessie Redmon Fauset, who explored feminist concerns[14] but bowed to social pressures and manners, Larsen exercised artistic integrity.[15] Last, Larsen fostered a sensitivity to sexual politics.

By 1920s standards, Larsen was an unconventional African-American woman. She resisted in her personal life and in the lives of her fictive characters "the expected, the traditional, 'the correct.'"[16] Responding to "a world of glitter and potential that distances itself from the teeming masses," Larsen sought to become important in her own right:

> She had married well, but the marriage did not guarantee her acceptance or prominence or make her comfortable within the black elite. . . . She desired her own spotlight, as is indicated by her transition from calling herself Nella Imes to Nella Larsen or Nella Larsen Imes when necessary, after she had finished her first novel.[17]

Besides taking an active part in Harlem's refined social circles, Larsen wore her dresses short, bobbed her hair, smoked cigarettes, rejected religion, and lived in defiance of the rules that most African-American women of her education and means were bound by.[18] Moreover, her unorthodoxy led to open resentment from many African-American males who were loyal to the Garvey Movement and the NAACP. On one occasion, Walter White (active in the NAACP) chastised her for insensitivity and "fondness for burlesque."[19]

Afrocentric feminist thought posits authentic experience as a guage for credibility. Based on many of her real-life experiences, Larsen dramatizes that lived events/situations deconstruct myth, fiction, and fantasy. Joining biography with art and reacting against the inaccurate portrayal of mulatto protagonists described in T. S. Stribling's *The Birthright* (1992), Larsen used her fiction to affirm self.[20] In African-American circles, *Birthright* was recognized as being filled with racist assertions, stereotypical thinking, and disparaging images of African-American womanhood. Larsen's resistance to the novel is evident in the themes and narrative strategy of her texts. Perhaps most significantly, Larsen moves in ***Quicksand*** beyond stereotype in providing nonbiological motivations for her protagonist's sense of alienation and powerlessness.

Placing self as subject and center in ***Quicksand,*** Larsen offers an exploration of how one's personal life is shaped by interlocking systems of race, gender, and class oppression.[21] Using Helga as her voice, Larsen challenges, resists, undermines, and assaults ideologies of African-American female victimization. As a subject, Helga is not a long-suffering victim but a diverse and intense protagonist who asserts her independence and self-will in the midst of struggle. Larsen projects Helga's experiences as a series of movements from a woman totally victimized by society and by men to a growing, developing woman whose consciousness allows her to have some control over her own life. As Audre Lorde maintains in "The Master's Tools Will Never Dismantle the Master's House," Helga struggles for self-defined consciousness which rejects the "master's images."[22] After Naxos, Chicago, Harlem, and Copenhagen, Helga takes charge of her life. Through the varied experiences that encompassed race, class, and sex, Helga's multiple strategies of resistance represent physical actions to bring about change. Nikki Giovanni's assertion best describes Helga's transformation:

> People are rarely powerless, no matter how stringent the restrictions. We've got to live in the real world. If we don't like the real world . . . change it. And if we can't change it, we change ourselves. We can do something. . . . Effective change occurs through action.[23]

Afrocentric feminist thought encourages empowerment through resistance and activism. Helga's movements take psychic and physical forms. Psychically, she moves from stereotype to self-actualization. In Harlem, after seeing Robert Anderson with Audrey Denny in a nightclub, she flees into the "psychic depths of self."[24] Two years later, upon being rebuffed by Anderson, she flees to religion. Physically aware of her political impotence at Naxos (which generated the initial flight), she moves full circle—from South to North, with time out in Copenhagen, and back to the South. In the removals, she eagerly greets each event/situation, becomes restive and pessimistic, then retreats from the experience in disgust and anger. My point here is that with Larsen's narrative manipulation, Helga resists the thickets of racial and sexual oppression by taking flight.

Afrocentric feminist thought suggests that there is always choice and power to act, no matter how desperate the situation appears to be. Larsen did not project her protagonists as passive, unfortunate recipients of multiple systems of abuse. For example, wearing a mask of stoic indifference for survival in order to prevent others from hurting her, Helga frantically moves from one place to another in pursuit of an environment which would allow her some individuation and self-expression.[25] Even though her quest ends in a quagmire, the final experience offers her contemplation, hope and a new sense of self.

Sisterhood is a recognizable source of connectedness, although it is not new to African-American women. With centrality in the family and the church, which are both women-centered Afrocentric institutions, African-American women share concrete knowledge of what it takes to be well-defined women. In Afrocentric feminist thought, dialogue validates and empowers because it provides women with deeper, more meaningful self-definitions. New knowledge claims are worked out in dialogue—rarely in isolation.[26] As Bell Hooks asserts, "Dialogue implies talk between two subjects, not the speech of subject and object."[27] After Anderson spurns Helga's suggestion of an affair, her subsequent turmoil is marked by a number of asphyxiation metaphors. Disoriented by his rebuff, Helga receives solace among sisters in the Harlem church, which becomes "a kind of transcendent women's room."[28] The church women attend her until she achieves a temporary catharsis. About two years later, female parishioners in the Alabama church attempt the same role played by the women in the Harlem mission.

Afrocentric feminist thought challenges systems (race, gender, class) of oppression. Consumerism, capitalism, and sexuality are thoroughly intertwined in ***Quicksand.*** Hazel V. Carby says, "Helga was brought to a recognition of her exchange value which denied her humanity while cementing her fragile dependence on money."[29] Using her uncle's conscience money to escape to Copenhagen, Helga is packaged in order to advance the social fortunes of her well-to-do relatives and the artistic future of Axel Olsen, a fashionable portrait painter. Unlike Naxos, where she is required to be a lady, Helga is made, in Copenhagaen, into an exotic female "other." Cheryl A. Wall reminds, "Helga is a symbol of the unconscious, the unknowable, the exotic, and the passive."[30] It is Olsen's portrayal which demonstrates most sharply the confluence of racism and sexism. Desiring to recreate her, Katrina Dahl and Olsen urge Helga to capitalize on her "difference." However, resenting being a "decorative sexual object," Helga recognizes their selfish motives and uses innumerable tactics that include reticence, cold formality, denial, reserve, aloofness, and stoic politeness to undermine their subjugation of her. Decentering Olsen, Helga evokes a declaration of independence; "I'm not for sale. Not to you. Not to any white man. I don't care at all to be owned."[31] Through self-assertion, Helga subverts subjugation and victimization.

Motherhood is a basic tenet in Afrocentric feminist thought. It serves as a site where women express and learn the power of self-definition and value, respect each other, inspire and support self-reliance, and encourage female empowerment. Sharing only a few weeks with Helga, Hayes-Rore (who is a race advocate) is an indispensable "presence" as a mother figure to Helga. It is her advice, recommendations, and sense of well-being that shapes Helga's life. Further, the extended family and the powerful community "othermothers" offer a range of models of African-American motherhood. Besides emphasizing protection by shielding daughters from the penalties attached to their race, class, and gender status by teaching them how to protect themselves, "othermothers" share mothering tasks, provide emotional support, and foster a sense of empowerment in young girls. Creating "othermothers" in ***Quicksand,*** Larsen suggests that "shapers of lives" need not be biological mothers. In the Alabama episode, Larsen posits nurse Hartley as Helga's confidante and an "othermother" to Helga's children.

During the 1920s, African-American female sexuality was acknowledged and commercialized. The Freudian themes of "sexual abandon" and "free love" invaded both the popular and artistic cultures. For instance, Van Vechten's *Nigger Heaven* (1926) and Claude McKay's *Home to Harlem* (1928) set the pattern that would dominate the literary treatment of African-American sexuality in the decade. Risking the exotic, primitive designation in Helga's portrayal, Larsen confronted the restraint of passion and the repression of female sexuality and desire. Yet Larsen created Helga as a sexual being as well. Carby reminds, "[Larsen's] sexual politics tore apart the very fabric of the romance form."[32] In corroboration with Carby's reflections, Deborah E. McDowell asserts that Larsen's treatment of African-American female sexuality can be regarded as something pioneering, something of a trailblazer in the African-American female literary tradition.[33]

That African-American women love African-American men is a major Afrocentric feminist theme that Larsen centers in ***Quicksand.*** It is after Anderson's wedding that Helga acknowledges a long-repressed sexual attraction for him. Through the narration, Helga greets him with eagerness, then retreats in disgust and anger. The foregoing is an embodiment of sexual conflict and repression. Hortense E. Thornton says, "Helga's inability to allow herself authentic sexual expression assumes a significant role in her dilemma."[34] Like Helga, Anderson is frustrated by sexual passivity. As members of the intelligentsia, both live the self-conscious existence of their class. For both, class rigidity forces emotional fragmentation and unhappiness.

Besides repressed sexuality, Larsen could write firsthand of blighted hopes and broken relationships. In almost every instance, Helga is treated like a dependent. For one, her relation with James Vayle is made difficult because she lacks "sufficient" background. Second, with Anderson and the Harlemites, she is unable to accept the reality of natural sexual responses. Third, as the wife of a Southern minister, she is sketched not as a "helpmate" but from a biological-regenerative standpoint. However, the Helga of the final scene is a woman who makes decisions based on feelings. Larsen explains:

> She wanted not to leave them if that were possible. The recollection of her own childhood, lonely, unloved, rose too poignantly before her for her to consider calmly such a solution. . . . But to leave them would be a tearing agony, a rending of deepest fibers. . . . No. She couldn't desert them.[35]

Despite being chained to her children and buried among the common folk in Albama, Helga empowers herself through self-knowledge. At last, she recognizes her inability to alter her marital state and the dilemma of her children.

Finally, women who seek self-definitions run the risk of being ostracized. Because they resist or challenge dominant ideologies, Afrocentric feminists generally face rejection, expulsion, or a devaluation of their knowledge claims. Larsen and her fiction were a part of the "paring process." Her texts threatened conventional 1920s ideologies and opened up, first, new paradigms for arriving at the truth and, second, fresh insights about African-American women. Although the claims of the novelist were ignored, discredited, or absorbed and marginalized into existing paradigms, Larsen called into question the legitimacy of knowledge depicting African-American women. Before the 1950s, only a few African-American women writers embraced Afrocentric feminist thought and defied dominant ideologies. Larsen made a courageous attempt.

Notes

1. For example, born a slave (1803) in Hartford, Connecticut, Maria W. Stewart was the first African-American woman to lecture in defense of women's rights and leave extant copies of her texts. From 1832 to 1834 she constructed a series of arguments citing feminists precedents drawn from biblical, classical, and historical sources. See Marilyn Richardson, ed., *Maria W. Stewart: America's First Black Woman Political Writer* (Bloomington: Indiana UP, 1987) xiv-xx; further references are included in the text. See, also, Sharon Harley and Rosalyn Terborg-Penn, eds., *The Afro-American Woman: Struggles and Images* (Port Washington, NY: Kennikat, 1978) 28-30.

2. Unlike African-American male writers who involve confrontation with individuals outside the family and community in their work and American feminists who focus generally on economic and gender/sex issues rather than race, African-American women writers treat, as significant, relationships within the family and community, between women and men, and among women.

3. For both *Quicksand* and *Passing,* I am using the editions published by Rutgers UP, 1986.

4. As Patricia Hill Collins and other African-American feminists assert, Afrocentric feminist thought is a term that is "widely used yet rarely defined" because it "encompasses diverse and contradictory meanings" (see Patricia Hill Collins, *Black Feminist Thought: Knowledge, Consciousness, and the Politics of Empowerment* [New York: Rouledge, 1992] 19). This text is particularly instructive to my formulation of Larsen as an early twentieth-century Afrocentric feminist. Also see Barbara Christian, *Black Feminist Criticism: Perspectives on Black Women Writers* (New York: Pergamon, 1986) and Deborah King, "Multiple Jeopardy, Multiple Consciousness: The Context of Black Feminist Ideology," *Signs* 14 (1988): 47-72.

5. Collins 202, 22.

6. Paula Giddings, *When and Where I Enter: The Impact of Black Women on Race and Sex in America* (New York: Doubleday, 1984) 185.

7. Elise McDougald, "The Double Task: The Struggle of Negro Women for Race and Sex Emancipation," *Survey Graphics* March 1925: 691, as reported in Amritjit Singh, William S. Shriver, and Stanley Brodwin, eds., *The Harlem Renaissance: Revaluations* (New York: Garland, 1989) 7.

8. Larsen's personal distress (her marital status and its consequences) is evident in Helga's agony.

9. Stewart is the foremother to the preceding group of 1890s feminists and novelists. It is in their writings that Stewart's radical crusade for women's rights realized fruition. Cooper was an activist educator during the 1890s. See Mary Helen Washington's introduction, *A Voice from the South* (New York: Oxford UP, 1988) xxvii-liv and Louise Daniel Hutchinson, *Anna J. Cooper: A Voice from the South* (Washington, D.C.: Smithsonian Institution Press, 1981).

10. Hazel V. Carby, *Reconstructing Womanhood: The Emergence of the Afro-American Woman Novelist* (New York: Oxford UP, 1977) 64.

11. Pauline E. Hopkins, *Contending Forces: A Romance Illustrative of Negro Life North and South* (1901; New York: Oxford UP, 1988).

12. *Giddings,* 138.

13. Philip Randolph and Chandler Owen, who were political radicals, published *The Messenger.* Like the other news organs of the day (*Crisis* and *Opportunity*), *The Messenger* extolled a new image of the African-American woman. See the anonymous article, "Negro Womanhood's Greatest Needs," *Messenger* 5 July 1923: 757.

14. See *There Is Confusion* (1924), *Plum Bun* (1929), *The Chinaberry Tree* (1931), and *Comedy, American Style* (1933), in addition to her essays in *Crisis,* appearing from 1919 through 1926.

15. Deborah E. McDowell, "The Neglected Dimensions of Jessie Redmon Fauset," in Marjorie Pryse and Hortense J. Spillers, eds., *Conjuring: Black Women, Fiction, and Literary Tradition* (Bloomington: Indiana UP, 1985) 86-104.

16. The quote comes from Marita Golden, foreword, *An Intimation of Things Distant,* ed. Charges R. Larson (New York: Doubleday, 1992) viii.

17. Thadious Davis, "Nella Larsen's Harlem Aesthetic," *The Harlem Renaissance: Revaluations,* ed. Singh, Shriver, and Browdin, 250.

18. Mary Helen Washington, "Nella Larsen: Mystery Woman of the Harlem Renaissance," *Ms Magazine* 9.6 (December 1980): 50.

19. William Bedford Clark, "The Letters of Nella Larsen to Carl Van Vechten: A Survey," *Resources for American Literary Sources for American Literary Study* 8 (1978): 197.

20. Heralded by white American critics as revolutionary in its treatment of African Americans, Stribling's *Birthright* employed the concept of primitivism in describing certain behavior traits of its mulatto characters. Of Cissie Dildine, the mulatto heroine, Stribling says, "She is flexuous and passionate, kindly and loving, childish and naively wise. . . . For all her precise English, she is untamed, perhaps untamable" (264).

21. According to Paule Marshall, the self is "the ability to recognize one's continuity with the larger community" (see Mary Helen Washington, "I Sign My Name," *Mothering the Mind: Twelve Studies of Writers and Their Silent Partners,* ed. Ruth Perry and Martine Watson Broronley [New York: Holmes and Meier, 1984] 159). Sońia Sanchez points to the preceding version of self by stating, "We must move past always focusing on the 'personal self' because there's a larger 'self.' There's a 'self' of Black people" (see Claudia Tate, ed., *Black Women at Work* [New York: Holmes and Meier, 1984] 134).

22. Cherrie Moraga and Gloria Anzaldúa, eds., *This Bridge Called My Back: Writings by Radical Women of Color* (New York: Kitchen Table, Women of Color Press, 1981) 112. The "master's images" intimated in Lorde's article are concerns of the oppressor, such as domination, subjugation, denigration, victimization, objectification, as well as discourse/language.

23. Claudia Tate, ed., *Black Women at Work* (New York: Continuum, 1983) 68.

24. *Quicksand* 61-62.

25. Hortense E. Thorton, "Sexism as Quagmire: Nella Larsen's *Quicksand,*" *CLA Journal* 16.3 (1973): 288.

26. These claims are reinforced by Mary Field Belenky, Blythe McVicker Clinchy, Nancy Rule Goldberger, and Jill Mattuck Tarule, *Women's Ways of Knowing* (New York: Basic Books, 1986); see, also, Carol Gilligan, *In a Different Voice* (Cambridge: Harvard UP, 1982).

27. Bell Hooks, *Talking Back: Thinking Feminist, Thinking Black* (Boston: South End Press, 1989) 131.

28. Cheryl Wall, "Passing for What? Aspects of Identity in Nella Larsen's Novels," *Black American Literature Forum* 20 (1986): 107.

29. Hazel V. Canby, "The Quicksands of Representation: Rethinking Black Cultural Politics," *Reconstructing Womanhood: The Emergence of the Afro-American Woman Novelist* (New York: UP, 1987) 172-73.

30. Wall 102.

31. *Quicksand* 87.

32. Canby, *Reconstructing Womanhood* 18.

33. Deborah E. McDowell, introduction, *Quicksand* and *Passing* xxxi.

34. Thornton 290.

35. *Quicksand* 135.

C. ANN MCDONALD (ESSAY DATE 2000)

SOURCE: McDonald, C. Ann. "Nella Larsen (1891-1964)." In *American Women Writers, 1900-1945: A Bio-Bibliographical Critical Sourcebook,* edited by Laurie Champion, pp. 182-91. Westport: Greenwood Press, 2000.

In the following essay, McDonald presents a biography of Larsen, discusses her major writings (including her posthumously published short fiction), and surveys the reception of her work.

Biography

An important clue to understanding Nella Larsen's early life came with the discovery by Thadious M. Davis of Larsen's birth certificate and consequently her name at birth. Born Nellie Walker on April 13, 1891, Larsen was, according to that certificate, the "colored" daughter of Mary Hanson Walker, a twenty-two-year-old Danish woman, and Peter Walker, a "colored" cook. Little else about her father's identity can be gleaned from the birth certificate, since his nationality, age, and birthplace are not recorded. One possible clue to his identity is found in the given names of Larsen's father and stepfather. What at first seems like coincidence—both men were named Peter—gives way to a more calculated possibility on further inspection: The two names may have belonged to the same man. Compounding the seeming coincidence is the fact that Peter Walker faded out of existence, with no evidence of his death beyond hearsay, around the same time that Peter Larson entered the scene. No official document records Walker's death, nor does his name appear in any public record or directory after 1891. In addition to the problems concerning Larsen's father, her relationship to her mother and sister is problematic as well; at times, both women denied knowledge of Larsen's existence. Apparently, the family found it necessary both to create a new identity for the father and to erase any evidence of the daughter. The reasons for this cover-up can be found in the issues of race and class that eventually became the thematic cornerstone of Larsen's fiction.

Mary, Anna, and Peter Larson were officially documented "white"; only Nellie Walker Larson and Peter Walker received the designation "colored." In her later years, Larsen described her father as "West Indian, but light-skinned" (qtd. in Davis 45). If Peter Walker was indeed Peter Larson, then one can assume that he was light-skinned enough to pass for white. The birth of obviously "colored" Nellie Walker, however, would have revealed his African heritage, thus warranting the designation "colored" for not only the child but also the father on Nellie Walker's birth certificate. The establishment of "white" Peter Larson in place of "colored" Peter Walker as head of the household allowed the family to adopt the racial designation of white—excepting, of course, Nellie Walker Larson, who stood on the outside as the black stepchild. The racial designation of white was a stepping-stone in Peter Larson's upward social mobility. Being white meant that Larson could work as a railroad conductor, a position that offered prestige and financial security. Eventually, the Larsons moved from a middle-class interracial neighborhood—one where Nellie fit in—to an all-white neighborhood that represented an upward move in class position that could not include the darker child. Whether Peter Larson was Larsen's white stepfather, or whether he was "colored" Peter Walker now passing as white, the Larson's upward mobility necessitated the removal of Nella Larsen from that family. Through firsthand experience, Larsen learned both the connections between race and class and the requirements for passing into the middle class that she later explored in her novels.

Larsen enrolled in Fisk University's Normal School in 1907, at which time she became permanently estranged from her family. She studied to be a nurse from 1912 until 1915, and after her graduation she worked in the Tuskegee Institute as the head nurse of the John Andrew Memorial Hospital and Nurse Training School. Finding the Institute as stifling as Helga Crane finds Naxos in ***Quicksand,*** Larsen went to New York and took a nursing job there. Shortly thereafter, she met Elmer Imes, a scientist, and in 1919, they were married. Growing tired of nursing, Larsen went to work as a librarian at the Harlem branch of the New York Public Library (NYPL). During this time, Larsen became involved with the literary artists of the Harlem Renaissance. Eventually, she left the position at the NYPL and concentrated on writing fiction. In 1926, *Young's Realistic Stories Magazine* published two of her short stories under the pseudonym Allen Semi, which was her married name spelled backwards. In 1928, ***Quicksand,*** for which she won the Harmon Award, was published, followed by the publication of ***Passing*** in 1929. Her success as a writer appeared to continue with *Forum*'s publication in 1930 of her short story **"Sanctuary."**

Shortly after *Forum* published **"Sanctuary,"** a scandal occurred concerning the possibility that Larsen had plagiarized a story by Sheila Kaye-Smith entitled "Mrs. Adis." Eventually, Larsen convinced the editors of *Forum* that the story was her own by producing several rough drafts, but the scandal damaged her reputation and perhaps, as some scholars speculate, her confidence in herself as a writer, since it was her last piece of published fiction. That same year, Larsen received the Guggenheim Fellowship (she was the first African American woman to do so), and she used the money to travel to Europe, where she worked on a novel, *Mirage,* which was subsequently rejected by Knopf. Though she most likely worked on at least one more novel, Larsen failed either to finish or to publish it. Other events—the failing U.S. economy and the waning interest by the public at large in African American writers—most likely contributed to the end of Larsen's literary career. Certainly the possibility exists that her later novels were not of publishable quality, though the lack of extant manuscripts prohibits scholars from making such a judgment. Whatever the cause or causes—economic depression, lack of public interest, a talent run dry, or a ruined literary reputation—the publication of **"Sanctuary"** effectively marks the end of Larsen's literary career.

In 1933, Larsen divorced Imes as a result of his affair with a white woman. After her marriage ended, Larsen eventually drifted out of the public eye, and she spent the last thirty years of her life as Mrs. Imes, a nurse who lived and worked in Brooklyn. On March 30, 1964, the body of Mrs. Nella Imes was discovered in her apartment. Most likely, she had been dead about a week, a testament to the solitary life she had exchanged for the hustle and bustle of literary Harlem. Larsen's literary career, however, comprised only a small portion of her life—from the publication of two articles in *Brownies' Book* in 1920 to 1930 and the publication of **"Sanctuary"**—and that career produced two significant novels. Furthermore, during the last thirty years of her life she conducted a successful nursing career. Though the temptation exists to see Larsen's life as a tragedy, one in which a talented woman was swallowed up by the nothingness of literary obscurity, in fact hers was a life well-lived, and the novels and short stories she produced in the late 1920s have left a legacy to the times in which she lived as well as a wealth of wisdom for generations to come.

Major Works and Themes

Larsen's identity as an African American woman certainly influences her work. Both ***Quicksand*** and ***Passing*** examine what it meant to be a black woman in early twentieth-century America. However, in a time when black writers were urged to promote the political causes of the black race in their work, Larsen avoided writing purely polemical novels about race. As Cheryl A. Wall points out in *Women of the Harlem Renaissance,* "Larsen's novel [***Quicksand***] is not a polemic for any cause. She scorned purpose novels and mocked the sometimes sententious rhetoric of racial uplift" (117). Likewise, Larsen's work avoids uplifting visions of emancipated Woman and therefore does not fit a certain feminist agenda of nearly propagandistic feminine success. Her novels and short stories are a complex presentation of the crossroads between race, gender, and class that do not offer inspirational messages about these categories of identity. In fact, ***Quicksand*** and ***Passing*** each reveal the failure of both race unity and feminist sisterhood and present instead characters divided by the demands of upward class mobility. Furthermore, Larsen's writing offers a glimpse into the futility of seeking affirmation in categories of identity since, as Helga Crane finds out, identity itself is ultimately unstable. In both her short stories and novels, Larsen embarks on the modernist's examination of constructed identities and reveals in her work an early twentieth-century understanding of the subject's desire for transcendence and the ultimate frustration of that desire, using as her rubric for examination the cross sections between gender, race, and class.

Passing and the controversial **"Sanctuary"** both examine the complexities of race and class in relation to race loyalty. In **"Sanctuary,"** Annie Poole must choose between familial loyalty and loyalty to the black race. Jim Hammer is a black man who inadvertently murders Annie's son, Obadiah. Clearly, Annie has a lack of respect for Jim that is based on class difference: To her, Jim is "no 'count trash" and "nuffin' . . . but a heap o' dirt" (***Intimation*** [***An Intimation of Things Distant***] 23). Nevertheless, when he comes to her for protection from the white law officers who pursue him, Annie's loyalty to her race demands that she harbor Jim, "siderin' all an' all, how Obadiah's right fon' o' you, an' how white folks is white folks" (***Intimation*** 23). Both her son's apparent loyalty to the race despite class difference—for Annie, Obadiah is "too good" to his lower-class acquaintances (***Intimation*** 23)—and her understanding of the nature of white people compel Annie Poole to "hide [Jim] dis one time" (***Intimation*** 23). Furthermore, Annie tells Jim, "Ef de Lawd had gib you a white face 'stead o' dat dere black one, Ah shuah would turn you out" (***Intimation*** 24). The race loyalty Annie expresses is relatively unproblematic, since at the time both she and Jim believe that he has killed a white man. Eventually, however, the identity of the murdered man is revealed, and at this point, the race loyalty she feels for Jim overrides her feelings of loyalty to her son. After telling the white sheriff that "Ah ain't sees nobody pass" (***Intimation*** 26), Annie Poole returns to the room where Jim is hiding and tells him, "Git outer mah feather baid, Jim Hammer, an' outen mah house, an' don' nevah stop thankin' yo' Jesus he done gib you dat black face" (***Intimation*** 27). Due to a sense of race loyalty, Annie *has* enabled Jim to "pass"—that is, to remain safely undetected by "white folks." This loyalty, however, comes with a price: Annie Poole must surrender her chance to avenge her son's death. Nonetheless, the short story illustrates a clear race unity that overcomes class distinction.

In ***Passing,*** the metaphor of "passing" again represents the idea of protecting a member of the black race from the dangers posed by "white folks," though Irene Redfield does not conquer the constraints of class that Annie Poole overcomes. In fact, Irene not only fails to place race above class but also sacrifices gender ties to the comforts of a middle-class lifestyle. This sacrifice becomes evident when Irene suspects that her husband, Brian, is having an affair with Clare Kendry, who is passing for white. Irene tries to think of a plan to end the affair between her friend and her husband, and she considers revealing Clare's secret to John Bellew, Clare's white, bigoted husband. As she contemplates betraying her friend, Irene finds herself torn between what she sees as her own self-preservation and her loyalty to the black race:

> She was caught between two allegiances, different, yet the same. Herself. Her race. Race! The thing that bound and suffocated her. Whatever steps she took, or if she took none at all, something would be crushed. A person or the race. Clare, herself, or the race. It was, she cried silently, enough to suffer as a woman, an individual, on one's own account, without having to suffer for the race as well. It was a brutality, and undeserved. Surely, no other people as cursed as Ham's dark children.
>
> (***Quicksand*** 225)

In this passage, Irene describes what she sees as the burden of race loyalty, a sense of obligation that is for her the curse of black people. She is unwilling to betray Clare, however, and well aware of the danger Clare would face if her husband—a white threat similar to the sheriff in **"Sanctuary"**—should discover Clare's secret. Nevertheless, Irene's desire for middle-class comfort is threatened by Clare's possible connection to Brian, which eventually overrides Irene's sense of loyalty to Clare's blackness.

In the novel's resolution, John Bellew discovers Clare's secret, leaving her, as Irene surmises, free to take Irene's husband. Irene's tie to Brian is not based on love or even sexual desire but on the lifestyle he can provide for her and their sons. Brian's own desire to leave the medical profession has remained a constant threat to Irene, since without the doctor husband she has acquired she would not be able to live the middle-class life to which she is accustomed. Seeing Clare, who has always wanted the life Irene leads, as a threat to her bourgeois security and comfort, Irene pushes Clare from an open window to her death. Clearly, Irene has chosen self-preservation over race loyalty; her motivation is a desire for class comforts that rely on the presence of a male figure. Earlier in their lives, Clare, the daughter of a violent alcoholic, envied the fact that Irene had a stable, caring father. Knowing that to have Irene's life means to have the man in that life, Clare apparently attempts to take that man—at least in Irene's mind. Just as Clare's ability to pass for white and therefore escape the oppressive class position of her past depended upon her husband, her entrance into the black bourgeoisie would depend on her attachment to a man. In a world where men define women's social status, Clare and Irene can afford neither gender nor race loyalty but instead become combatants in a class-based battle.

"The Wrong Man" is a "passing" story that focuses on class rather than race, yet it also touches upon the idea of unstable identities in such a way that it ties together the main concerns of Larsen's work. Julia Romley, the story's protagonist, has, through marriage, obtained an upper-class position that hides her early, lower-class position. The attendance at a party of Ralph Tyler's, a man who knows the details of her sordid past, threatens to expose her and cause her to "lose everything—love, wealth, and position" (***Intimation*** 5). Clearly, this story addresses the same gender and class issues that Larsen examines more fully in ***Passing:*** Without a man, a woman cannot make the social climb necessary to happiness and contentment. Likewise, the story underscores the idea of the unstable, constructed identity, an idea that is obviously at the heart of the concept of passing, where one deliberately creates a public identity that is in contrast to the private self. Unstable identity becomes the ironic punchline of this story, as Julia, while pleading with a man who stands in darkness, asks that he not expose her true identity—then realizes that she has "told the wrong man" (9).

"Freedom" offers a glimpse into Larsen's modern obsession with the instability of identity and a frustrated desire for transcendence. In **"Freedom,"** the unnamed focal character attempts to gain freedom by leaving his girlfriend. Once he does, he creates an image of her in his mind, envisioning her life without him. Eventually, he finds that she is not at all as he "visualized" (***Intimation*** 15). Instead, she died in childbirth without knowing that her lover was gone. This contrast between his image of his lover and the actuality of her existence is a realization that "spoiled his life," since it reveals the instability of the identity he created for her (***Intimation*** 16). Ultimately, he comes to realize that his freedom is also an illusion: "He had reached out toward freedom—to find only a mirage; for he saw quite plainly that now he would never be free. It was she who had escaped him" (***Intimation*** 16). In other words, the man realizes that freedom from the constraints of the physical world comes only with death. In the end, he, like his lover, finds freedom in death, stepping through an open window in a moment that foreshadows both Clare Kendry's death and Helga Crane's descent into the quicksand of her own physical life.

Quicksand is a novel that fully explores both the search for an identity that is characterized by race, class, and gender and the inevitable failure to find that identity. Throughout the novel, Helga Crane fashions herself according to other people's ideas about race, class, and gender, only to find that none of the identities she adopts satisfy her longing to belong. In what seems to be an uncharacteristic moment for Helga, she wanders into a church ceremony where black men and especially women experience a religious frenzy and ecstasy that eventually envelops Helga. As she has done before, Helga adopts this new identity with apparent abandon, believing that the wild, spiritual elation she experiences will provide her with the sense of belonging and transcendence for which

Nella Larsen receiving the Harmon Award for Distinguished Achievement among Negroes in 1928.

she has been searching. In the end, however, she is smothered by her life as preacher's wife, and she realizes that her sense of suffocation is not unlike the feeling of oppression that has haunted her throughout the novel:

> [I]n some way she was determined to get herself out of this bog into which she had strayed. Or—she would have to die. She couldn't endure it. Her suffocation and shrinking loathing were too great. Not to be born. Again. For she had to admit that it wasn't new, this feeling of dissatisfaction, of asphyxiation. Something like it she had experienced before. In Naxos. In New York. In Copenhagen. This differed only in degree. And it was of the present and therefore seemingly more reasonable. The other revulsions were of the past, and now less explainable.
>
> (***Quicksand*** 134)

Clearly, Helga's attempts to find belonging and identity have resulted in feelings of "dissatisfaction, of asphyxiation" (***Quicksand*** 134). The freedom she longs for can be found—as it is found in **"Freedom"**—through death, an escape from the body that represents a rather morbid, hopeless transcendence. However, Helga "wanted not to leave" her children, remembering "her own childhood, lonely, unloved" (***Quicksand*** 135). She tells herself that leaving her children would be different from her own abandonment as a child, since "[t]here was not an element of race, of black and white. They were all black together" (***Quicksand*** 135). Clearly, Helga sees her children as having racial unity and therefore a sense of belonging that Helga (and perhaps Larsen) did not experience as a child. In the end, Helga is unable to escape from the life of the body, and she sinks into the oppression of birthing her fifth child. Rather than promoting racial prosperity or gender triumph, the novel—like Larsen's work in general—uses race, gender, and class as the lenses through which we view the unstable, trapped self in search of an ever-elusive transcendence.

Critical Reception

Like many writers of the Harlem Renaissance—women especially—Larsen's work was largely ignored until the early 1970s when feminist critics resurrected numerous literary careers, Larsen's included. Her novels, however, met with critical praise at the time of publication. A contemporary review of ***Quicksand*** called the book "an articulate and sympathetic first novel"; in the *World Telegram,* a reviewer claimed, "The book makes you want to read everything that Nella Larsen will ever write" (qtd. in Wall 116). W. E. B. Du Bois wrote a favorable review of ***Quicksand,*** stating that Larsen "has done a fine, thoughtful and courageous piece of fiction" that revealed a "subtle comprehension of the curious cross currents that swirl about the black American" (qtd. in Wall 117). ***Passing*** likewise garnered favorable reviews, and in general, Larsen was seen as a talented writer and literary artist. Furthermore, she received in 1928 the Harmon Award for Distinguished Achievement among Negroes (the Bronze Medal for literature) for ***Quicksand*** and a Guggenheim Fellowship, based on the positive reception of her first novels, to write a third. That she never lived up to the promise of the Guggenheim remains a source of wonder to critics. Indeed, the charges of plagiarism that were labeled against **"Sanctuary"** harmed her sterling literary reputation and cooled what had been a warm critical reception.

From the outset, however, critics have been puzzled and displeased by the endings of Larsen's novels. According to Deborah E. McDowell in the introduction to ***Quicksand** and **Passing,*** reviewers "consistently criticized the endings of her novels *Quicksand* (1928) and *Passing* (1929), which reveal her difficulty with rounding off stories convincingly" (xi). In general, such criticism has arisen from scholars who want Larsen's works to present a more uplifting, politically inspiring outcome for her African American heroines. Helga's descent, for example, into the quagmire of motherhood and wifedom provides a shocking end to a novel in which the heroine searches so convincingly for a strong identity, rejecting for the most part overtly sexist and racist offerings before she sinks into the quicksand of an oppressive married life. Likewise, Irene's murdering of her childhood friend does not provide a positive model for solidarity among either women or black people.

Contemporary critics, however, are choosing to take the novels on their own terms, recognizing in them richly woven tales that resist polemical conclusions. For example, McDowell argues that the controversial endings "if examined through the prism of black female sexuality . . . make more sense" (xii). McDowell suggests that rather than prescribing how things should be for women, Larsen's work provides a compelling critique of how things are:

> [The endings of Larsen's stories] show her grappling with the conflicting demands of her racial and sexual identities and the contradictions of a black and feminine aesthetic. Moreover, while these endings appear to be concessions to the dominant ideology of romance—marriage and motherhood—viewed from a feminist perspective, they become much more radical and original efforts to acknowledge a female sexual experience, most often repressed in both literary and social realms.
>
> (xii)

From this perspective, the endings do make sense. Whereas Larsen's contemporaries argued that the endings marred her work, McDowell suggests that happier endings, though they might satisfy a political agenda, would simply provide pat answers for complicated questions. Clearly, Larsen's work goes beyond solving the political and social problems of any particular era. Instead, her stories offer an investigation into categories of identity. Finally, Larsen remains true to her modern perspective by rejecting any possibility for transcendence—political or personal—and her work ultimately rejects polemics in favor of complexity.

Bibliography

Works by Nella Larsen

"Playtime: Danish Fun." *Brownies' Book* 1 (1920): 219.

"Playtime: Three Scandinavian Games." *Brownies' Book* 1 (1920): 191-92.

Rev. of *Certain People of Importance,* by Kathleen Norris. *Messenger* 5 (1923): 713.

[Pseud. Allen Semi]. "Freedom." *Young's Realistic Stories Magazine* 51 (1926): 241-43.

[Pseud. Allen Semi]. "The Wrong Man." *Young's Realistic Stories Magazine* 50 (1926): 243-46.

Quicksand. New York: Knopf, 1928.

"Moving Mosaic or N.A.A.C.P. Dance, 1929" (excerpt from *Quicksand*). All-Star Benefit Concert for the National Association of Colored People Forrest Theater, New York, program booklet, 8 Dec. 1929.

Passing. New York: Knopf, 1929.

Rev. of *Black Sadie,* by T. Bowyer Campbell. *Opportunity* 7 (1929): 24.

"The Author's Explanation." *Forum* 83 (1930): xli-xlii.

"Sanctuary." *Forum* 83 (1930): 15-18.

An Intimation of Things Distant: The Collected Fiction of Nella Larsen. Ed. Charles R. Larson. New York: Anchor, 1992.

Studies of Nella Larsen

Beemyn, Brett. "A Bibliography of Works by and about Nella Larsen." *African American Review* 26 (1992): 183-88.

Blackmore, David L. "'That Unreasonable Restless Feeling': The Homosexual Subtexts of Nella Larsen's *Passing.*" *African American Review* 26 (1992): 475-84.

Chandler, Karen M. "Nella Larsen's Fatal Polarities: Melodrama and Its Limits in *Quicksand.*" *CLA Journal* 42 (1998): 24-47.

Christian, Barbara. *Black Women Novelists: The Development of a Tradition, 1892-1976.* Westport, CT: Greenwood, 1980.

Clemmen, Yves W. A. "Nella Larsen's *Quicksand:* A Narrative of Difference." *CLA Journal* 40 (1997): 458-66.

Conde, Mary. "Passing in the Fiction of Jessie Redmond Fauset and Nella Larsen." *Yearbook of English Studies* 24 (1994): 94-104.

Davis, Thadious M. *Nella Larsen, Novelist of the Harlem Renaissance: A Woman's Life Unveiled.* Baton Rouge: Louisiana State University Press, 1994.

duCille, Ann. "Blues Notes on Black Sexuality: Sex and the Texts of Jessie Fauset and Nella Larsen." *Journal of the History of Sexuality* 3 (1993): 418-44.

Esteve, Mary. "Nella Larsen's 'Moving Mosaic': Harlem, Crowds, and Anonymity." *American Literary History* 9 (1997): 268-86.

Haviland, Beverly. "Passing from Paranoia to Plagiarism: The Abject Authorship of Nella Larsen." *Modern Fiction Studies* 43 (1997): 295-319.

Hostetler, Ann E. "The Aesthetics of Race and Gender in Nella Larsen's *Quicksand.*" *PMLA* 105 (1990): 35-46.

Huggins, Nathan. *Harlem Renaissance.* New York: Oxford University Press, 1971.

Hutchinson, George. "Nella Larsen and the Veil of Race." *American Literary History* 9 (1997): 329-50.

Larsen, Charles R. *Invisible Darkness: Jean Toomer and Nella Larsen.* Iowa City: University of Iowa Press, 1993.

Little, Jonathan. "Nella Larsen's *Passing:* Irony and the Critics." *African American Review* 26 (1992): 173-82.

Madigan, Mark J. "Miscegenation and 'The Dicta of Race and Class': The Rhinelander Case and Nella Larsen's *Passing.*" *Modern Fiction Studies* 36 (1990): 523-29.

McDowell, Deborah E. Introduction. *Quicksand and Passing.* By Nella Larsen. Ed. Deborah McDowell. New Brunswick: Rutgers University Press, 1986. ix-xxxv.

McLendon, Jacquelyn Y. *The Politics of Color in the Fiction of Jessie Fauset and Nella Larsen.* Charlottesville: University Press of Virginia, 1995.

Monda, Kimberly. "Self Delusion and Self Sacrifice in Nella Larsen's *Quicksand.*" *African American Review* 31 (1997): 23-41.

Ramsey, Priscilla. "Freeze the Day: A Feminist Reading of Nella Larsen's *Quicksand* and *Passing.*" *Afro-Americans in New York Life and History* 9 (1985): 27-41.

———. "A Study of Black Identity in 'Passing' Novels of the 19th and Early 20th Century." *Studies in Black Literature* 7 (1976): 1-7.

Sato, Hiroko. "Under the Harlem Shadow: A Study of Jessie Fauset and Nella Larsen." *The Renaissance Remembered.* Ed. Arna Bontemps. New York: Dodd, 1972. 63-89.

Silverman, Debra B. "Nella Larsen's *Quicksand:* Untangling the Webs of Exoticism." *African American Review* 27 (1993): 599-614.

Sullivan, Nell. "Nella Larsen's Passing and the Fading Subject." *African American Review* 32 (1998): 373-86.

Tate, Claudia. "Nella Larsen's *Passing:* A Problem of Interpretation." *Black American Literature Forum* 14 (1980): 142-46.

Thornton, Hortense. "Sexism as Quagmire: Nella Larsen's *Quicksand.*" *CLA Journal* 16 (1973): 285-91.

Wall, Cheryl A. *Women of the Harlem Renaissance.* Bloomington: Indiana University Press, 1995.

Washington, Mary Helen. "Nella Larsen: Mystery Woman of the Harlem Renaissance." *Ms.* Dec. 1980: 44-50.

Williams, Bettye J. "Nella Larsen: Early Twentieth-Century Novelist of Afrocentric Feminist Thought." *CLA Journal* 39 (1995): 165-78.

Youman, Mary. "Nella Larsen's *Passing:* A Study in Irony." *CLA Journal* 18 (1974): 235-41.

TITLE COMMENTARY

Quicksand

HORTENSE E. THORNTON (ESSAY DATE 1973)

SOURCE: Thornton, Hortense E. "Sexism as Quagmire: Nella Larsen's *Quicksand.*" *CLA Journal* 16, no. 3 (March 1973): 285-301.

In the following essay, Thornton contends that the protagonist of Quicksand *should not be seen as fitting the "tragic mulatto" formula, since the novel is more properly seen as an exploration of sexual desire and discrimination against women.*

Nella Larsen represents one of several unlaureled Black women who contributed greatly to the development of the Afro-American novel. Writing during the Harlem Renaissance, Miss Larsen distinguished herself as the author of two novels, ***Quicksand*** (1928) and ***Passing,*** (1929),[1] both of which treat the experiences of cultured, middle class mulatto heroines. On the merits of ***Quicksand,*** she received the Harmon Foundation bronze medal, and in 1930 she earned a Guggenheim Fellowship to travel to Europe in search of material for a third novel which she never completed.[2] That Miss Larsen's novels are partly autobiographical can be gleaned from certain facts about her life. Born in Chicago in 1893 to a Danish mother and West Indian father, Nella Larsen experienced a difficult childhood when her father died and her mother remarried a white man with whom she had other children. Miss Larsen's educational experiences were varied: she audited classes at the University of Copenhagen, and in New York she earned a certificate in library science and a nursing degree. She was married to Elmer S. Imes, a physicist; their marriage ended in divorce. She died in Brooklyn in 1963.

In ***Quicksand*** Miss Larsen relates the experiences of her heroine Helga Crane, mulatto offspring of a Danish mother and West Indian father. Upon her father's desertion of her mother, Helga has an unhappy childhood with the white man her mother marries and the children of that union. After her mother dies, Helga's education at Devon, an all Black college, is financed by her maternal uncle, Peter Nilsson. When the novel opens, Helga has decided to terminate her employment as an English teacher at Naxos, a southern Black institution whose educational system she can no longer stomach because of its policy of "uplift," of dulling the minds of its students so that they would fit securely into the pattern set for them by the white man. Helga leaves Naxos for Chicago in the middle of the spring term. When her efforts to obtain a loan from her Uncle Peter are thwarted by her confrontation with his new wife, Helga searches constantly for jobs. With luck, she obtains a speech-editing position with Mrs. Hayes-Rore, a prominent Black uplift spokeswoman, with whom she travels to New York. Securely employed by a Black insurance company, with the assistance of Mrs. Hayes-Rore, Helga remains in New York, living with Mrs. Hayes-Rore's niece, Anne Grey. She essentially enjoys an exciting life, has lots of friends, attends dinner parties, plays, cabarets. After a year and a half Helga becomes restless. With an unexpected $5,000 check from her Uncle Peter, Helga decides to go to Denmark in search of a happy future. She is well received by her aunt and uncle, the Dahls, who generously embellish her with clothes and friends. Eventually Helga resents being displayed in Copenhagen where she is flaunted, observed, and painted. Disgustingly she refuses the marriage proposal of Axel Olsen, an eccentric portrait artist, upon confirming that he had, in fact, intended a concubinage before being forced into his proposal. After two years, Helga leaves Copenhagen for New York with the intent of attending Anne Grey's marriage to Dr. Anderson, formerly principal of Naxos (the man whose memory she has been unable to shake since her departure from Naxos). While in New York, Helga becomes cognizant of the awakening of new feelings within her. For the first time, she is sexually attracted to someone. Anderson kisses her at a party, an incident upon which she places great significance. She is dumbfounded when he apologizes for his misdirected kiss. Angered, embarrassed, hurt, Helga weakens mentally and physically. One evening upon searching for shelter from a rainstorm, she despondently strays into religious services being held in a storefront church where she is "saved." Dissolving into emotion and clasping the crutch of religion, Helga marries a visiting minister, the Reverend Mr. Pleasant Green, a colorless, paunchy man who breaks one of the Lord's commandments with her after church services. He takes her to live with him at his parsonage in a rural Alabama town. The novel ends with Helga pregnant with her fifth child.

In her "Ebony Flute" column of May 1928, a column written monthly for *Opportunity,* Gwendolyn Bennett announced the publication of ***Quicksand.***

> Nella Larsen's ***Quicksand*** has just arrived. And let me say that many folks will be interested to hear that this book does not set as its tempo that of the Harlem cabaret—This is the story of the struggle of an interesting cultured Negro woman against her environment. Negroes who are squeamish about writers exposing our worst side will be relieved that Harlem night-life is more or less submerged by the psychological struggle of the heroine . . . .
>
> (p. 153)

Miss Bennett's announcement hints at an issue of the Harlem Renaissance which was of concern to certain older-generation intellectuals, especially W. E. B. Du Bois and Benjamin Brawley: the "negative" representation of Black life in some of the works being published. Cases in point were Carl Van Vechten's *Nigger Heaven* (1926), Claude McKay's *Home to Harlem* (1928), both best-selling novels, and Langston Hughes' *Fine Clothes to the Jew* (1927).[3]

The subject matter of ***Quicksand*** is varied, but the novel reveals that the issues of racism and sexism are no doubt concerns of Miss Larsen in that she exposes the racial and sexual prejudice which Helga, a perceptive, responsible woman, confronts in her cross-cultural quest for a sense of her place in life, her identity. When one considers the complex events of the novel, it becomes possible to argue that Helga's tragedy was perhaps more a result of sexism than of racism. The novel assumes picaresque proportions as Helga frantically moves from one place to another in pursuit of an environment which will allow her free expression. Despite what some may label as snobbishness in her character, or cowardice, one must admire this young woman, who because of the hardships of her youth, wears a stoic mask of indifference for survival, a mask worn solely to prevent others from hurting her. Understandably, Helga's childhood taught her to be suspicious of the affections of others, thus crippling her adaptability to the events experienced in her adult life. Helga optimistically pursues a variety of experiences with hopes of realizing a sense of self being and retreats from each experience with feelings of disillusionment, indifference, and restiveness. What is significant about her fortunes, or misfortunes, is that she assumes the responsibility for every failure she undergoes. She is not the type of person to shift the blame for her decisions on others.

Miss Larsen chose as the epigraph for ***Quicksand*** the final stanza of Langston Hughes' poem "Cross."

> My old man died in a fine big house.
> My ma died in a shack.
> I wonder where I'm gonna die,
> Being neither white nor black?

In this poem, the persona retracts the curses which he placed upon both his white father and Black mother for the responsibility of his birth. He is obviously a "cross" between them, a mulatto. The poem reveals his resignation to live with the "cross" he must bear as a person caught between two cultures. As I reflect upon the critics' appraisals of ***Quicksand,*** it seems to me that Nella Larsen's decision to use the Hughes poem as epigraph was not in the best interest of her novel. As I shall argue in this paper, Helga's plight is not to be explained solely in terms of her racial heritage, and possibly can be best understood through considering her sex. She was a woman, just as her creator, living in a male-dominated society, a woman who repressed her sexuality and thus placed herself in a most vulnerable situation leading to her tragic degeneration. Unfortunately, few of Larsen's critics have been able to see beyond Helga's race. To label Helga's plight as typical of the tragic mulatto motif, as many critics have, is to reduce Miss Larsen's novel to a melodramatic fantasy intended to titillate readers still hanging on to certain myths about the myriad advantages of the Caucasian blood strain.

Sterling Brown's "A Century of Negro Portraiture in American Literature" records the origin and use of the tragic mulatto stereotype by both white and Black authors.

> The tragic mulatto stereotype stemmed from the antislavery crusade, whose authors used it, partly to show miscegenation as an evil of slavery, partly as an attempt to win readers' sympathies by presenting central characters who were physically very like the readers. Antislavery authors, Harriet Beecher Stowe included, held to a crude kind of racism. Their near-white characters are the intransigent, the resentful, the mentally alert—for biological, not social reasons. In the pro-slavery argument, the mixed blood characters are victims of a divided inheritance and proof of the disastrous results of amalgamation. Most of the villains in reconstruction fiction are mixed bloods, 'inheriting the vices of both races and virtues of neither.' The mulatto, or quadroon, or octoroon heroine has been a favorite for a long time; in books by white authors the whole desire of her life is to find a white lover; then balked by the dictates of her society, she sinks to a tragic end. In our century, Negro authors have turned the story around; now after restless searching, she finds peace only after returning to her own people. In both cases, however, the mulatto man or woman is presented as a lost, unhappy, woebegone abstraction.[4]

A cursory examination of ***Quicksand*** may well lead a reader to the conclusion that Nella Larsen is an example of an author who "turned the story around," for on one level Helga searches restlessly as evidenced by her odyssey from Naxos to Chicago to New York to Copenhagen to New York and finally to rural Alabama. But Helga is not a "lost, unhappy, woebegone abstraction." Instead, she is a sensitive woman, an individual, who throughout her life because of society's taboos has repressed a significant part of her being. Helga's inability to allow herself authentic sexual expression assumes a significant role in her tragic dilemma at the novel's end.

In his recent book, *Harlem Renaissance,* Nathan Huggins contends that "None of the novels that came out of Harlem in the renaissance took its audience for granted" (exceptions being Toomer's *Cane* and Thurman's *Infants of the Spring*).[5] Huggins argues that within the novels, context and circumstance assume importance over the characters peopling them. Of Nella Larsen he states:

> Nella Larsen came as close as any to treating human motivation with complexity and sophistication. But she could not wrestle free of the mulatto condition that the main characters in her two novels had been given. Once she made them mulatto and female the conventions of American thought—conditioned by the tragic mulatto and the light-dark heroine formulas—seemed to take the matter out of the author's hands.[6]

Whereas Mr. Huggins is to be commended for his opinion that Miss Larsen "came as close as any to treating human motivation with complexity and sophistication," his implication that Miss Larsen's control of subject matter was lost once she chose light-skinned women as her heroines is open to question. Nevertheless, his argument that Larsen's audience, pre-conditioned by the tragic mulatto formula, would undoubtedly fail to see deeply in her heroines' motivation, is quite useful in explaining the critics' failure to perceptively understand Helga's motivation.[7]

A brief examination of some of the critical assessments of ***Quicksand*** reveals the extent to which Miss Larsen's critics were influenced by the tragic-mulatto motif, thus limiting their analyses. Robert Bone in *The Negro Novel in America,* sees Helga Crane as "a neurotic young woman of mixed parentage, who is unable to make a satisfactory adjustment in either race."[8] Though he recognizes Helga's sexuality as having thematic significance, he labels her attitude toward sex as prudish, and argues that she "allows herself to be declassed by her own sexuality" (p. 105) without explaining the male's role in this situation. Saunders Redding in *To Make a Poet Black* contends: "The chief personages of ***Quicksand*** and ***Passing,*** white to all superficial appearances, attempt to find life across the line. Helga Crane of ***Quicksand,*** she of the Swedish mother [*sic.* Helga's mother is Danish] and the Negro father, is driven back by hereditary primitivism. . . ."[9] Hugh Gloster in *Negro Voices in American Fiction* states ". . . it is hardly deniable that Helga Crane is a convincing portrait of the tragic mulatto. Sensitive because of her questionable background, Helga cannot integrate herself into either race."[10]

The above observations were all written by men who gave very little consideration to the fact that Helga Crane of ***Quicksand*** was a woman living in a male chauvinistic society wherein social roles, including sexual behavior, were, and still are to a great extent, defined by men and by women who accept male dominance.[11] Miss Larsen's female critics read ***Quicksand*** more perceptively and sympathetically as evidenced by the following statement of Adelaide Cromwell Hill.

> ***Quicksand*** helps us to see how one Black woman viewed the problem of the Black community, its relation to White society, the survival of the individual Black person in a totally White society abroad, and *the basic problem of sex as it expresses itself for Black women and for those males, Black or White, available or attractive to them* [italics mine].[12]

Another perceptive analysis of Helga's dilemma is that found in a review of the book written for *Opportunity,* July 1928, by Eda Lou Walton.

> To tell the story of a cultivated and sensitive woman's defeat through her own sex-desire is a difficult task. When the woman is a mulatto and beset by hereditary, social and racial forces over which she has little control and into which she cannot fit, her character is so complex that any analysis of it takes a mature imagination. This, I believe, Miss Larsen is too young to have the [sic] book, ***Quicksand,*** is a first novel. The attempt is to present Helga Crane not as a young colored woman, but as a young woman with problems unique to her temperament, and her background one largely of her own choice.
>
> (p. 212)

Whereas Miss Walton is conscious of Nella Larsen's intention, she argues that Larsen's purpose was not fulfilled because she lacked the necessary maturity to develop a complex character. Miss Walton sees no continuity in the development of Helga's character and argues that Helga's characterization is incomplete, lacks wholeness and consistency.

> As portrayed, the character is not quite of one pattern. Now it is Helga the aesthete, the impulsively intelligent girl whom we feel; now it is Helga, the mulatto, suffering from an inferiority complex about her mixed ancestry, her lack of social status. Since she is supposedly complex, her character should be turned to us as a jewel of many facets. Instead we get it as a piece of bright red glass or as smoke colored.
>
> (p. 212)

Sterling Brown also questions the continuity of Helga's character.

> Helga Crane is buffeted around, but does not attain tragic stature. The attempt to reveal a self-centred, harrassed personality is commendable, but is not helped by scenes like the one in which the sophisticated heroine attends a church meeting, and there, overwhelmed by the frenzy, begins to yell like one insane, and to weep torrents of tears.[13]

I take issue with the above reading of Helga's dilemma by first of all disagreeing with Brown's statement that Helga does not attain tragic stature. His statement indicating that Helga "attends a church meeting" is distortive for it suggests that she went purposely to the church services when, in fact, she accidentally stumbled into the meeting in search of shelter from a rain storm.

That Helga's character is consistently developed can be shown best through an examination of Larsen's narrative structure. She chose the third person omniscient point of view to delineate Helga's tragedy, a point of view which is both objective and interpretive and which effectively zooms the reader very close to Helga's character. Dialogue is minimized, which undoubtedly dissatisfies those readers who object to too much telling and not enough dramatic presentation. In presenting Helga's motivations and conflicts, Miss Larsen chose a structure resembling a downward spiral. As Helga optimistically, enthusiastically enters a new experience (e.g., Naxos, Harlem, Copenhagen), a new curve is formed, but each curve extends a bit lower than the preceding one, thus suggesting the successive stages of Helga's degradation. Miss Larsen cohesively connects these curves through careful selection, arrangement, and repetition of details which serve well in illuminating Helga's tragedy so that a recognizable pattern is evident: Helga eagerly greets each experience; she becomes restive, discontented with the experience; and she pessimistically retreats from the experience in disgust and anger. When we meet the Helga of the final episodes in the novel, after Anderson's rejection of her sexual overtures, she is at a very depressed ebb. And from this point on in the novel, through frequent references to asphyxiation, Miss Larsen projects the vise of the social and mental quicksand in which her heroine is sinking. In fact, we learn that Helga's self-knowledge of her tragic situation was quite instrumental in increasing her anguish. "I can't stay in this room any longer. I must get out or I'll choke" (p. 183).

Complementing her tightly controlled plot, Miss Larsen skillfully coheres atmospheric setting and time. In the opening chapter of the novel we find Helga alone in her room in the shadowy soft gloom of the evening. As chapter two opens, Helga awakens as the sun streams in a "golden flow" through her window. Larsen traces the movement of the sun as Helga converses with her co-worker Margaret Creighton. "She [Helga] was watching the sunlight dissolve from thick orange into pale yellow. Slowly it crept across the room, wiping out in its path the morning shadows" (p. 41). With the opening of chapter three, Larsen continues to trace the sun's path as Helga scurries in the early heat of the morning to confer with Dr. Anderson, the college principal. "On one side of the long, white, hot sand road that split the flat green, there was a little shade, for it was bordered with trees. Helga Crane walked there so that the sun could not so easily get at her" (p. 44).

With excellent dexterity, Miss Larsen describes the seasons accompanying Helga's discontent. Helga leaves Naxos for Chicago in the early spring and arrives in New York several weeks later. The flashback in chapter eight recounts Helga's years of experiences in New York. "A year thick with various adventures had sped by since that spring day on which Helga Crane had set out away from Chicago's indifferent unkindness for New York . . ." (p. 84). Spring feeds into late summer (one and one-half years in New York) when Helga receives the letter from her uncle which makes possible her trip to Copenhagen. She crosses the sea when ". . . the weather was lovely with the

FROM THE AUTHOR

A PROTECTIVE IMMUNITY

Lies, injustice, and hypocrisy are a part of every ordinary community. Most people achieve a sort of protective immunity, a kind of callousness, toward them. If they didn't, they couldn't endure.

SOURCE: Nella Larsen, excerpt from *Quicksand*, Knopf, 1928.

serene calm of the lingering September summer . . ." (p. 114). Helga says goodbye to Denmark after two years, and when she returns to New York, "A summer had ripened and fall begun" (p. 160). In addition to associating the seasons with Helga's plight, Miss Larsen associates Helga's love of bright colors with her waning condition. At the novel's beginning, she introduces us to Helga's colorful surroundings which she enjoys tremendously; these colors fade, however, as Helga's life in Alabama dissipates her. Here she is surrounded in browns and very dull lifeless objects.

Larsen skillfully displays the extent to which Helga's sex and her attitudes toward it serve as a handicap in her full realization of self. In her relationship with the various male characters in the novel, Helga is shown as an object to be pursued, courted, and adored. In each case she is dependent upon these men for some aspect of her existence, and she is rarely accepted as a sensitive human being.

When she goes to her Uncle Peter for a loan, she is met by his new wife who rejects Helga. Later he guiltily pays her off as he impresses upon her why he must terminate his relationship with her. He freely gives her "an old man's advice" to visit her Aunt Katrina in Denmark and not to do as her mother had done—marry a Black man. Helga has to depend on him for money, which she resents, because she, in her helplessness, feeds his "oft-repeated conviction that because of her Negro blood she would never amount to anything . . ." (p. 32). So when we meet Helga at Naxos, the only real family ties she has are those loose links to Uncle Peter.

Helga's lack of family ties is responsible for her having sought solace in the clutches of Jim Vayle who is from a most respectable "first family" in Black society. He could provide her with the prerequisite social background, elevating her from being a "nobody" to the privileged stature of a "somebody." The social environment of Naxos requires "ladyness." Vayle is well shaped in the Naxos mold and is pleased with his contours. Therefore, in Naxos, we see Helga very much conscious of her role as Vayle's fiancee, a role which requires that she deny her sexuality so as not to disturb Vayle's ideas of her "ladyness." She realizes that relinquishing her relationship with him would amount to social suicide, so she chooses to sacrifice her sexuality.

> She was, she knew, in a queer indefinite way, a disturbing factor. She knew too that something held him, something against which he was powerless. The idea that she was in but one nameless way necessary to him filled her with a sensation amounting almost to shame. And yet his mute helplessness against that ancient appeal by which she held him pleased her and fed her vanity—gave her a feeling of power. At the same time she shrank away from it, subtly aware of possibilities she herself couldn't predict.
>
> (p. 34)

Once her illusion of Naxos's greatness is shattered and she sees the institution for what it is, "a showplace in the Black Belt, exemplification of the white man's magnanimity, refutation of the black man's inefficiency" (p. 28), she rejects both Naxos and Jim Vayle.

When Helga sees Jim Vayle again at a party in Harlem she notices that he has not changed. She entreats him to relax, assuring him "This isn't Naxos, you know. Nobody's watching us, or if they are, they don't care a bit what we do" (pp. 169-170). But Vayle, very secure in his new position as assistant principal of Naxos, is as pompous as ever in his limited world view. He cannot see life as extending beyond Naxos, is disgustingly intolerant of the racial mixing at the party, and advances the Du Boisian "talented tenth" philosophy in his proclamation "We're the ones who must have the children if the race is to get anywhere" (p. 174). Throughout their conversation Helga mocks him and listens to him proclaim what she knew all along, the fact that he never understood her or accepted her right to be what she was: "Well, Helga, you were always a little different, a little dissatisfied, though I don't pretend to understand you at all. I never did . . ." (p. 171).

Dr. Anderson is perhaps the only male character who accepts Helga's individuality. When she goes to him to discuss her resignation from Naxos, we are informed that "For some reason she had liked him . . ." (p. 45). In this meeting and other meetings with him later in the novel, much emphasis is placed on the gaze of his gray eyes, which makes Helga very uncomfortable.

> His gaze was on her now, searching.
>
> (p. 50)
>
> Just what had happened to her there in that cool dim room under the quizzical gaze of those piercing gray eyes?
>
> (pp. 53-54)
>
> . . . Helga was conscious of the man's steady gaze. The prominent gray eyes were fixed upon her, studying her, appraising her.
>
> (p. 95)
>
> And another vision, too, came haunting Helga Crane; level gray eyes set down in a brown face which stared out at her, coolly, quizzically, disturbingly. And she was not happy.
>
> (p. 97)

It seems apparent that Larsen's emphasis on Anderson's eyes foreshadows the appearance of Axel Olsen's portrait of Helga. Dr. Anderson's eyes are a mirror from which is reflected the sexually appealing woman that Helga is. He respects her professional capabilities and almost succeeds in influencing her to remain at Naxos. At the same time, he sees the sensual side of Helga. That he perceives her dilemma is seen in a statement he makes when they are together at a party in Harlem: "You haven't changed. You're still seeking for something, I think" (p. 95).

In Chicago Helga has no real contact with men, except that Nella Larsen shows how a woman cannot safely walk on the public streets without being accosted by men who assume that she is willing to prostitute her body. During weeks of job searching, we are told that no one wanted Helga's services. "At least not the kind that she offered. A few men, both white and black, offered her money, but the price of the money was too dear. Helga Crane did not feel inclined to pay it" (p. 70).

The young Black men whom Helga dates in New York offer her an exciting social life. They take her to elaborate parties, theaters, cabarets, but she soon tires of this round of activity. "The tea to which she had so suddenly made up her mind to go she found boring beyond endurance, insipid drinks, dull conversation, stupid men" (p. 97). Helga becomes unwilling to hear the race problem rehashed by Anne and her New York friends: "Why, Helga wondered, with unreasoning exasperation, didn't they find something else to talk of? Why must the race problem always creep in? She refused to go on to another gathering. It would, she thought, be simply the same old thing" (p. 97). Helga is as contemptuous of the "uplift" as was Nella Larsen.[14] "'Uplift,' sniffed Helga contemptuously, and fled before the onslaught of Anne's harangue on the needs and ills of the race" (p. 98).

In Copenhagen Helga is paraded through Danish high society by her aunt and uncle, the Dahls, who are intent on advancing their social fortunes at her expense. She meets a variety of young Danes who eagerly wine and dine her for various superficial reasons such as her exotic racial difference or her healthy vivacity. At first Helga is very content with the spotlight she occupies, even though she feels "like nothing so much as some new and strange species of pet dog being proudly exhibited" (p. 123). She revels in the attentions and flattery of the men. "She liked the compliments in the men's eyes as they bent over her hand. She liked the subtle half-understood flattery of her dinner partners" (p. 124). In her role as narrator-observer, Nella Larsen relates the scornful attitude of the Danish women toward Helga. "The women too were kind, feeling no need for jealousy. To them this girl, this Helga Crane, this mysterious niece of the Dahls, was not to be reckoned seriously in their scheme of things. True, she was attractive, unusual, in an exotic, almost savage way, but she wasn't one of them. She didn't at all count" (p. 124).

Helga as object is projected poignantly in the scene when she and Axel Olsen meet for the first time.

> With Fru Dahl he came forward and was presented. "Herr Olsen, Herr Axel Olsen." To Helga Crane that meant nothing. The man, however, interested her. For an imperceptible second he bent over her hand. After that he looked intently at her for what seemed to her an incredibly rude length of time from under his heavy drooping lids. At last, removing his stare of startled satisfaction, he wagged his leonine head approvingly.
>
> (p. 125)

The arrogant Axel, we learn later, is intent upon a concubinage. He offers marriage to Helga only after she ignores his first overture for the informal arrangement. In his theatrical proposal, he commends Helga for her previous sexual restraint. Marriage to her would be a unique, rewarding experience for Axel, as suggested in his statement "It may be that with you, Helga for wife, I will become great. Immortal" (p. 149). Helga rejects Olsen's sexist offer firmly and refuses to soothe his wounded ego. She will not be owned. "But you see, Herr Olsen, I'm not for sale. Not to you. Not to any white man. I don't at all care to be owned. Even by you" (p. 150). Importantly, in this episode we get a glimpse of Axel's portrait of Helga. Ironically, he accentuates her sensuality, an aspect of her personality that she represses. In rejecting the picture Helga thinks "It wasn't, she contended, herself at all, but some disgusting sensual creature with her features" (p. 152).

The unveiling of Helga's portrait takes on great symbolic significance in relation to the remainder of the novel. Olsen insists that this picture of Helga represents "the true Helga Crane. Therefore—a tragedy" (p. 152). As Helga views the picture, she thinks about Olsen's statement, but refuses to accept its truth. Nathan Huggins aptly describes Helga's reaction: "She is disturbed, however, not merely because Axel Olsen exposes, through his portrait of her, Helga's sensual and primitive nature, but because she sees by this sudden insight the key to her acceptance by the painter as well as her Danish relatives. He senses a tiger, an animal within her which he wants to possess—to ravish and to be ravished—through marriage if necessary" (*Harlem Renaissance,* p. 158).

The picture forces the reader to reflect upon Helga's attitude toward the men in her life up to her present involvement with Olsen. At Naxos, her physical relationship with Jim Vayle did not surpass a few kisses. As she questions Olsen's vague proposal of a liaison, she thinks, "Had he insinuated marriage, or something less—and easier?" (p. 145). To Helga, Olsen is seeking sex with no marriage obligations, and when she discovers that he had in fact meant sex with "no strings," she exclaims coldly ". . . in my country the men, of my race at least, don't make such suggestions to decent girls" (p. 148). It is significant that in her rejection of Olsen she stresses their racial differences, causing one to question the extent to which her acknowledgement of race is used as a mask for her sexual repression.

After the incident involving the portrait, the novel takes a turn in its presentation of Helga's attitude toward her sexuality. Previously her various friends, suitors, and acquaintances had manipulated her to advance their own selfish ends. Helga assumes a new role of aggressor, or manipulator of events. Upon returning to Harlem, her sexual overture to Dr. Anderson is rebuffed. Rebounding from this crushing blow to her ego, she wanders into revival services being held in a storefront church, is swept into the frenzy of the worshippers, and is "saved."

Miss Larsen's treatment of Helga's conversion is a tour de force in the sense that she brings to a meaningful focus all of what Helga's life has meant to her. As Helga accidentally enters the church meeting, she hears "a song which she was conscious of having heard years ago—hundreds of years it seemed" (pp. 184-185). With this is established Helga's strong sense of identity with her Black slave heritage. Helga is conscious of how very inappropriate or ridiculous it is that she should be in such holy surroundings, which is certainly consistent with the Helga of whom we are told earlier in the novel ". . . was not religious. She took nothing on trust" (p. 71). She carefully observes what is happening around her and to her. "Helga Crane was amused, angry, disdainful as she sat there, listening to the preacher praying for her soul. But though she was contemptuous, she was too well entertained to leave" (p. 187). The meeting later takes on "an almost Bacchic vehemence" (p. 188). Helga becomes enchanted, and through her vision the church meeting is transformed into an orgy, a "horror" in which she uncontrollably participates. Her conversion is highly reminiscent of John Grimes' conversion in Baldwin's *Go Tell It on the Mountain.*[15]

Walking home with the Reverend Mr. Pleasant Green, Helga considers her new freedom and a possible sexual union with him. "No. She couldn't. It would be too awful. Just the same, what or who was there to hold her back? Nothing. Simply nothing. Nobody. Nobody at all" (p. 192). Helga decides that she will no longer acquiesce to society's taboos and consciously uses her sexuality to maneuver Green into marriage. With her marriage to the good Reverend, Helga's tragic life reaches its summit. Clearly her sex becomes her undoing, for despite her disgust for her husband she struggles through the days and anticipates the nights. "And night came at the end of every day. Emotional, palpitating, amorous, all that was living in her sprang like rank weeds at the tingling thought of night, with a vitality so strong that it devoured all shoots of reason" (p. 202).

As with her previous experiences, Helga convinces herself that her new experience as the wife of Reverend Green will have a positive effect on her life. But with this experience, the downward spiral is completely spun. There is no other direction in which Helga can go. With the vanishing of the luster of religion, Helga recognizes that she hates her husband; she becomes fully cognizant of "the quagmire in which she had engulfed herself" (p. 218). So at the book's end, the tough Helga of Naxos, Chicago, Harlem, Copenhagen, who has survived heartbreak, scorn, and prejudice is no longer capable of fighting. Helga's struggle ends as she finds herself pregnant with her fifth child. Her womb entraps her so much that through childbearing she is left a tragic lifeless shell.

Whereas some readers may have difficulty in accepting Helga Crane in the Reverend Mr. Pleasant Green environment, this does not suggest any failure on Miss Larsen's part, for she has created in Helga a tragedy of a person oppressed by a system that discriminates unmercifully against Blacks as well as against women. Helga's struggle for self identity, for a way of shaking the smallness and enclosure of her life, takes her through an expansive gamut of experiences encompassing race, class, and sex. After Naxos, Chicago, New York, and Copenhagen, Alabama follows logically. When the reader carefully weighs the excruciating circumstances of Helga's life, the irony of her undoing through her sex, not her race, achieves prominence.

Notes

1. Both novels were reprinted in paperback editions in 1971 as a part of the Macmillan Company's African / American Library series. In this paper, all quotations from *Quicksand* are from the African / American Library edition.
2. Miss Larsen was the first Black woman to be awarded a Guggenheim Fellowship. Other Black recipients preceding her were Walter White (1927), Countee Cullen and Eric Walrond (1928).
3. For several months in 1926, *The Crisis* invited Black and White writers to participate in a controversial forum, "The Negro in Art: How Shall He Be Portrayed." Included among the participants were Hughes, Cullen, Jessie Fauset, Georgia D. Johnson and Carl Van Vechten.
4. Originally published in *The Massachusetts Review* (Winter 1966). Quoted from Abraham Chapman, *Black Voices* (New York: The New American Library, 1968), p. 570.
5. *Harlem Renaissance* (New York: Oxford University Press, 1971), p. 236.
6. *Ibid.*
7. In my Winter Quarter 1972 Harlem Renaissance course at Ohio State University, very few of my students felt that Helga Crane's dilemma was solely that of the tragic mulatto archetype.
8. *The Negro Novel in America,* Rev. ed (New Haven: Yale University Press, 1965), p. 102.
9. *To Make a Poet Black* (Chapel Hill, N. C.: University of North Carolina Press, 1945), p. 117.
10. *Negro Voices in American Fiction* (Chapel Hill, N. C.: University of North Carolina Press, 1948), p. 143.
11. W. E. B. Du Bois is an exception. That he feels Helga's race is subordinate in her dilemma is reflected in his review written for *The Crisis,* 35 (1928), p. 202: "Nella

Larsen . . . has seized an interesting character and fitted her into a close yet delicately woven plot . . . Helga is typical of the new, honest, young fighting Negro woman—the one on whom 'race' sits negligibly and Life is always first and its wandering path is but darkened, not obliterated by the shadow of the Veil."

12. "Introduction" to *Quicksand* (New York: The Macmillan Company, 1971), p. 12. Unfortunately the publishers are guilty of advancing the tragic mulatto motif as seen in their sensational blurb on the back cover of the book.

13. *The Negro in American Fiction* (New York: Atheneum, 1969), p. 142.

14. In various samples of her correspondence to Carl Van Vechten and others in the James Weldon Johnson Collection at Yale University, Nella Larsen expresses her reservations about the "uplift."

15. One questions the extent to which Miss Larsen's novel may have directly or indirectly influenced James Baldwin's *Go Tell It on the Mountain* and Ralph Ellison's *Invisible* Man. As mentioned, the description of Helga's conversion is not unlike John Grimes' conversion in the storefront church designated by Baldwin as The Temple of the Fire Baptised. Larsen states of Helga "Her religion was to her a kind of protective coloring, shielding her from the cruel light of an unbearable reality" (p. 208). The sounds from outside Harlem can be heard within Baldwin's temple, suggesting the sordid reality of Harlem which the saints must face at the end of the service despite the temporary shield provided by the temple. On the other hand, the global scope of Helga's experiences is not unlike the sojourn of Ellison's narrator. Even closer resemblances are found in the descriptions of the southern Black colleges. The students at Naxos must listen to the pronouncements of the white southern preacher just as Ellison's narrator and his classmates must assemble on Founder's Day to be brainwashed by Homer A. Barbee, Norton, and other trustees of their institution.

Passing

CLAUDIA TATE (ESSAY DATE 1980)

SOURCE: Tate, Claudia. "Nella Larsen's *Passing*: A Problem of Interpretation." *Black American Literature Forum* 14, no. 4 (1980): 142-46.

In the following essay, Tate praises Passing *as a work of subtlety and psychological ambiguity, claiming that the novel's artificiality was intentional rather than an indication of Larsen's limitations as a writer, as some critics have suggested.*

Nella Larsen's ***Passing*** (1929) has been frequently described as a novel depicting the tragic plight of the mulatto.[1] In fact, the passage on the cover of the 1971 Collier edition refers to the work as "the tragic story of a beautiful light-skinned mulatto passing for white in high society."[2] It further states that ***Passing*** is a "searing novel of racial conflict. . . ."[3] Though ***Passing*** does indeed relate the tragic fate of a mulatto who passes for white, it also centers on jealousy, psychological ambiguity and intrigue. By focusing on the latter elements, ***Passing*** is transformed from an anachronistic, melodramatic novel into a skillfully executed and enduring work of art.

Set in a romanticized region of Harlem's Sugar Hill in 1927, where beautiful Black socialities swirl about in designer gowns, sip tea from antique china cups and jaunt between home and resort, the world of ***Passing*** is, as Hoyt Fuller says in the Introduction to the 1971 edition, as unreal, "artificial and ultimately as lifeless as a glamorous stage set" (p. 19). Fuller's assessment is certainly accurate enough. We must assume, however, that Larsen was equally aware of the novel's obvious artificiality, and therefore could not have intended to pass off this fantasy land as a fictive replica of external reality. I suggest that ***Passing***'s social pretentiousness is not, as critics have frequently said,[4] a deficiency of Larsen's artistic vision but an intentional stylistic device.

The story is told from the point of view of the principal character, Irene Redfield, whose observations and interpretations account for every detail of the unfolding narrative. The story begins with Irene recalling the events surrounding her renewed friendship with a childhood acquaintance, Clare Kendry. During their chance meeting, Irene recalls the events of the past twelve years in flashbacks. The recollection of past events presents a rather comprehensive picture of the two women, both of whom are light-skinned enough to be mistaken for white. Irene is a socialite, married to a successful Black physician, Brian Redfield, and they live in a fashionable section of Harlem. Clare is married to a wealthy white man, John Bellew, who is unaware of her racial identity. Although Clare's domestic life is comfortable, she grows increasingly weary of its monotony, and as a result she seeks excitement by socializing with Irene and her Harlem friends without Bellew's knowledge. Clare's frequent association with Irene makes Irene envious of Clare's extraordinary beauty. In fact, she becomes obsessed with envy once she suspects that Brian and Clare are romantically involved. The climax occurs when Bellew follows Clare to a social gathering at the residence of a Black couple, where he surmises that she too is Black. During his angry outburst and the resulting confusion, Clare mysteriously falls to her death through an open window, bringing the story to its tragic conclusion.

Ostensibly, ***Passing*** conforms to the stereotype of the tragic mulatto. However, many factors make such an interpretation inadequate. The conventional tragic mulatto is a character who "passes" and reveals pangs of anguish resulting from forsaking his or her Black identity. Clare reveals no such feelings; in fact, her psychology is inscrutable. Moreover, Clare does not seem to be seeking out Blacks in order to regain a sense of racial pride and solidarity. She is merely looking for excitement, and Irene's active social life provides her with precisely that. An equally important reason for expanding the racial interpretation is that alone it tends to inhibit the appreciation of Larsen's craft. Larsen gave great care to portraying the characters; therefore, the manner of their portrayal must be important and ultimately indispensable to interpreting ***Passing***'s meaning. Thus, the "tragic mulatto" interpretation not only is unsuited to the book's factual content, but also disregards the intricately woven narrative.

An understanding of ***Passing*** must be deduced not merely from its surface content but also from its vivid imagery, subtle metaphors, and carefully balanced psychological ambiguity. For example, although the story has a realistic setting, it is not concerned with the ordinary course of human experience. The story develops from a highly artificial imitation of social relationships which reflect Irene's spiritual adventures. These characteristics are more compatible with the romance than with the tragedy. But for the purposes of this study ***Passing*** is treated as a romance of psychological intrigue in which race is more a device to sustain suspense than merely a compelling social issue.

The work's central conflict develops from Irene's jealousy of Clare and not from racial issues which are at best peripheral to the story. The only time Irene is aware that race even remotely impinges on her world occurs when the impending exposure of Clare's racial identity threatens to hasten the disruption of Irene's domestic security. Race, therefore, is not the novel's foremost concern, but is merely a mechanism for setting the story in motion, sustaining the suspense, and bringing about the external circumstances for the story's conclusion. The real impetus for the story is Irene's emotional turbulence, which is entirely responsible for the course that the story takes and ultimately accountable for the narrative ambiguity. The problem of interpreting ***Passing*** can, therefore, be simplified by defining Irene's role in the story and determining the extent to which she is reliable as the sole reporter and interpreter of events. We must determine whether she accurately portrays Clare, or whether her portrait is subject to, and in fact affected by, her own growing jealousy and insecurity. In this regard, it is essential to ascertain precisely who is the tragic heroine—Irene who is on the verge of total mental disintegration or Clare whose desire for excitement brings about her sudden death.

Initially, ***Passing*** seems to be about Clare Kendry, inasmuch as most of the incidents plot out Clare's encounters with Irene and Black society. Furthermore, Irene sketches in detail Clare's physical appearance down to "[her] slim golden feet" (p. 127). Yet, she is unable to perceive the intangible aspects of Clare's character, and Larsen uses Irene's failure as a means of revealing disturbing aspects of her own psychological character.

Irene tells us that Clare is a "lovely creature" (p. 42); in fact she is "just a shade too good-looking" (p. 120). Irene is fascinated by Clare's eyes, which she says are "strange[ly] languorous" (p. 120), provocative and magnificent. Her frequent references to Clare's eyes do not refer merely to a physical feature, but become a symbolic statement of Clare's total mystery. More important to the story, though, than Clare's beauty (which we must remember is related entirely through Irene's sensibilities) is its emotional effect on Irene. Clare makes Irene "[feel] dowdy and commonplace" (p. 128), thus making her constantly aware that she is comparatively mediocre in the light of Clare's sheer loveliness, which is "absolute and beyond challenge" (p. 60). As a result, Irene becomes more insecure, and she tries to mitigate her growing discontent with suspicions about Clare's fidelity.

Long before we encounter Clare Kendry, Larsen creates a dense psychological atmosphere for her eventual appearance. In the very first paragraph of the narrative, Larsen describes Clare's letter from Irene's point of view:

> It was the last letter in Irene Redfield's little pile of morning mail. After her other ordinary and clearly directed letters the long envelope of thin Italian paper with its almost illegible scrawl seemed out of place and alien. And there was, too, something mysterious and slightly furtive about it. A thin sly thing which bore no return address to betray the sender. Not that she hadn't immediately known who its sender was. Some two years ago she had one very like it in outward appearance. Furtive, but yet in some peculiar, determined way a little flaunting. Purple ink. Foreign paper of extraordinary size.
>
> (p. 29)

Larsen uses ambiguous and emotional terminology to refer to Clare's letter: "alien," "mysterious," "slightly furtive," "sly," "furtive," "peculiar," "extraordinary." Repeated references to the letter's beguiling unobtrusiveness and its enthralling evasiveness heighten the mystery which enshrouds both the almost illegible handwriting and its author. The letter itself is animated with feline cunning—"a thin sly thing." From one perspective the letter is insubstantial; from another, it possesses "extraordinary size." The letter rejects every effort of precise description. Provocative, bewitching, vividly conspicuous and yet elusive, the letter resembles the extraordinary physical appearance of Clare Kendry as she is later described, sitting in Irene's parlor:

> Clare, exquisite, golden, fragrant, flaunting, in a stately gown of shining black taffeta, whose long full skirt lay in graceful folds . . . her glistening hair drawn back . . . her eyes sparking like dark jewels. . . . Irene regretted that she hadn't counselled Clare to wear something ordinary and inconspicuous.
>
> (pp. 127-28)

In the next paragraph of the introductory section there are numerous references made to danger which incite a sense of impending disaster. The suspense is associated first with the letter and then with Clare. The letter is, to use T. S. Eliot's term, "an objective correlative," in that it objectifies abstract aspects of Clare's character, and its very presence reflects her daring defiance of unwritten codes of social propriety. Like Clare herself, the letter excites "a little feeling of apprehension" (p. 32), which grows in intensity to "a dim premonition of impending disaster" (p. 115), and foreshadows the story's tragic ending.

The letter, therefore, is a vivid though subtle narrative device. It foreshadows Clare's actual arrival and characterizes her extraordinary beauty. It also suggests abstract elements of Clare's enigmatic character which evolve into a comprehensive, though ambiguous portrait. Furthermore, it generates the psychological atmosphere which cloaks Clare's character, rendering her indiscernible and mysterious.

Irene is literally obsessed with Clare's beauty, a beauty of such magnitude that she seems alien, impervious, indeed inscrutable. Upon meeting Clare in Chicago, "Irene [felt that] . . . about the woman was some quality, an intangible something, too vague to define, too remote to seize" (p. 43). On one occasion we are told that "Irene turned an oblique look on Clare and encountered her peculiar eyes fixed on her with an expression so dark and deep and unfathomable that she had for a short moment the sensation of gazing into the eyes of some creature utterly strange and apart" (p. 77). On another occasion, Irene puzzles "over that look on Clare's incredibly beautiful face. . . . It was unfathomable, utterly beyond any experience or comprehension of hers" (pp. 84-85). Irene repeatedly describes Clare in hyperbole—"too vague," "too remote," "so dark and deep and unfathomable," "utterly strange," "incredibly beautiful," "utterly beyond any experience. . . ." These hyperbolic expressions are ambiguous. They create the impression that Clare is definitely, though indescribably, different from and superior to Irene and other ordinary people.

Irene's physical appearance, on the other hand, is drawn sketchily. We know that she has "warm olive skin" (p. 95) and curly black hair (p. 40). Though Irene is not referred to as a beauty, given her confidence and social grace, we are inclined to believe that she is attractive. Despite the fact that little attention is given to Irene's physical portrayal, her encounter with Clare provides the occasion for the subtle revelation of her psychological character. Hence, the two portraits are polarized and mutually complementary—one is purely external, while the other is intensely internal.

Irene is characterized as keenly intelligent, articulate and clever. In this regard, the social gatherings seem to be more occasions for her to display a gift for witty conversation than actual events. Whether in the midst of a social gathering or alone, Irene often falls prey to self-dramatization, which is half egoism and half ironic undercutting for the evolving story. She also never cares to know emotional rapture, but prefers instead "only to be tranquil . . . [and] unmolested . . ." (p. 178). Hence, her personal feelings are confined to an outer shell of superficial awareness. Although she is further portrayed as possessing an acute awareness of discernment, she tends to direct this ability entirely toward others and employ hyperbole rather than exact language for its expression. Her perceptions, therefore, initially seem generally accurate enough, until she becomes obsessed with jealousy.

As the story unfolds, Irene becomes more and more impulsive, nervous and insecure, indeed irrational. She tends to jump to conclusions which discredit her credibility as a reliable source of information. For example, on several occasions Irene assumes that Clare questions her racial loyalty (pp. 63, 93 and 108). On another occasion, she assumes that Clare is involved with the man who escorted her to the Drayton Hotel dining room (p. 74). And eventually, she concludes that Clare and Brian are having an affair (pp. 149 and 173). Each of her assumptions may indeed be correct, but we observe no tangible evidence of their support; consequently, we cannot know with any certainty whether or not Irene's suspicions are true.

Although we only know the external details of Clare's life, we observe the total essence of Irene's psychology. We have also noted that thematic information is seldom communicated directly, but implied through dramatic scenes. Hence, Irene's character, like Clare's, achieves cohesion from the suggestive language Irene employs (especially when describing Clare), the psychological atmosphere permeating her encounters with Clare, and the subtle nuances in characterization. The realistic impact of incidents in and of themselves neither fully characterizes Irene nor conveys the novel's meaning. Meaning in ***Passing,*** therefore, must be pieced together like a complicated puzzle from allusion and suggestions. Irene gives form to Clare, but we are left with the task of fashioning Irene from her reflections of Clare's extraordinary beauty.

The ambiguous ending of ***Passing*** is another piece of the puzzle. The circumstances surrounding Clare's death support several interpretations. The most obvious interpretation is that Irene in a moment of temporary insanity pushed Clare out of the window. This interpretation has received widest acceptance, although the manner in which Larsen dramatizes Irene's alleged complicity receives no serious attention at all. Critics take her involvement in Clare's death for granted as merely a detail of the plot.[5] A close examination of the events surrounding Clare's death, however, reveals that the evidence against her, no matter how convincing, is purely circumstantial. No one actually observes Irene push Clare, and Irene never admits whether she is guilty, not even to herself. We are told only that

> [Irene] ran across the room, her terror tinged with ferocity, and laid a hand on Clare's bare arm. One thought possessed her. She couldn't have Clare Kendry cast aside by Bellew. She couldn't have her free.
>
> Before them stood John Bellew, speechless now in his hurt and anger. Beyond them the little huddle of other people, and Brian stepping out from among them.
>
> What happened next, Irene Redfield never afterwards allowed herself to remember. Never clearly.
>
> (p. 184)

At this moment Clare falls through the open window, and Irene responds by saying that "she wasn't sorry. [That she] was amazed, incredulous almost" (p. 185). Larsen provides no clarification for Irene's remark or its emotional underpinning. We do not know whether she is simply glad that Clare is permanently out of her life by means of a quirk of fate, whether she does not regret killing her, or whether she has suffered momentary amnesia and therefore does not know her role in Clare's death. In fact, Larsen seems to have deliberately avoided narrative clarity by weaving ambiguity into Irene's every thought and expression. For example, shortly after Clare's fall, Irene wonders what the other people at the party may be thinking about the circumstances surrounding Clare's death. Her speculations further cloud the narrative with other possible explanations for Clare's death. Irene wonders, "What would the others think? That Clare had fallen? That she had deliberately leaned backward? Certainly one or the other. Not . . ." (p. 185). A literal interpretation of this passage suggests that Clare may have accidentally fallen through the open window, or that she may have committed suicide. The passage can also be interpreted to mean that Irene hopes that the guests will mistakenly assume her innocence in their effort to arrive at a more agreeable explanation than murder. Of course, the passage may merely reflect Irene's genuine attempt to deduce what the others would necessarily conclude in light of her innocence. A few moments later, Irene fiercely mutters to herself that "it was an accident, a terrible accident" (p. 186). This expression may be merely her futile effort at denying involvement in murder. Or, it may be her insistence that she is indeed innocent, though she suspects that no one will believe her. Or, she could be uncertain of her involvement and struggling to convince herself that she is innocent. In all cases we must be mindful that there is still no tangible proof to support one interpretation over another. Although we may be inclined to accept the conventional interpretation, we must remember that all evidence is circumstantial, and we cannot determine Irene's guilt beyond a reasonable doubt.

In reference to other explanations for Clare's death mentioned above, we note that the possibility of accidental death is the least satisfying interpretation. Consequently, we disregard it, despite its being a plausible assumption as well as the conclusion which the authorities reach.

The last alternative—suicide—tends to be inadvertently neglected altogether, inasmuch as Clare's motives are not discernible. Nothing is left behind, neither note nor explaining discourse, to reveal her motives. However, this interpretation does deserve consideration, since it enhances the ambiguous conclusion and draws heavily on Larsen's narrative techniques of allusion and suggestion.

Early in the text we are given the circumstances surrounding the death of Clare's father. When his body was brought before her, she stood and stared silently for some time. Then after a brief emotional outburst, "[s]he glanced quickly about the bare room, taking everyone in, even the two policemen, in a sharp look of flashing scorn. And, in the next instance, she . . . turned and vanished through the door [never to return]" (p. 31). The last scene in the story bears a striking resemblance to this, and the motives for Clare's behavior in the early scene suggest a possible motive for her suicide. "Clare stood at the window, as composed as if everyone were not staring at her in curiosity and wonder. . . . One moment Clare had been there . . . the next she was gone" (pp. 184-85). In both instances Clare surveys the fragments of her life, and in both she vanishes, leaving behind a painful situation which she cannot alter. In the latter, she is utterly alone, and suicide is the ultimate escape from the humiliation that awaits her.

Passing's conclusion defies simple solution. I cannot resolve this problem by accepting a single explanation, since Larsen, on one hand, deliberately withheld crucial information that would enable me to arrive at a definite conclusion, and on the other, she counter-balanced each possible interpretation with another of equal credibility. Although I am unable to determine Irene's complicity in Clare's death, this dilemma is neither a deterrent to appreciating Larsen's meticulous narrative control nor an evasion of my critical responsibility. To the contrary, my admission of uncertainty is my honest response to the work, given only after serious consideration of my position as a literary critic. In fact, my inability to arrive at a conclusion in and of itself attests to Larsen's consummate skill in dramatizing psychological ambiguity. I realize that this critical posture is not a popular one. Of course, I could insist, as many critics have done, that Irene pushed Clare out of that window.[6] To build a case for this interpretation would not be difficult. But to do so would be forcing the work to fit the demands of critical expectations rather than allowing the work to engender meaningful critical response. This approach would be of no service to the work and ultimately discredit the criticism itself. What I am certain of, though, is that ***Passing*** is not the conventional tragic mulatto story at all. It is an intriguing romance in which Irene Redfield is the unreliable center of consciousness, and she and not Clare Kendry is the heroine.

Larsen's focus on a mulatto character, the plagiarism scandal surrounding her short story, **"Sanctuary,"** published in 1939,[7] and aspects of her personal life probably account for the sparsity of serious, critical attention given to her work. Critics, of course, hastily comment on Larsen's skill as they either celebrate other Harlem Renaissance writers or look ahead to the socially conscious writers of the '30s. Few address the psychological dimension of Larsen's work.[8] They see instead a writer who chose to escape the American racial climate in order to depict trite melodramas about egocentric black women passing for white. This critical viewpoint has obscured Larsen's talent and relegated ***Passing*** to the status of a minor novel of the Harlem Renaissance. But Larsen's craft deserves more attention than this position attracts. ***Passing*** demands that we recognize its rightful place among important works of literary subtlety and psychological ambiguity.

Notes

1. Robert A. Bone, *The Negro Novel in America,* rev. ed. (New Haven: Yale University Press, 1966), p. 102; Sterling Brown, *The Negro in American Fiction,* rev. ed. (New York: Atheneum, 1969), p. 143; Nick A. Ford, *The Contemporary Negro Novel: A Study in Race Relations* (Boston: Meador, 1936), pp. 50-51; Hugh M. Gloster, *Negro Voices in American Fiction* (Chapel Hill: The University of North Carolina Press, 1948), pp. 146-47; Saunders Redding, *To Make a Poet Black* (Chapel Hill: The University of North Carolina Press, 1939), pp. 117-18; Amritjit Singh, *The Novels of the Harlem Renaissance* (University Park: The Pennsylvania State University Press, 1976), pp. 98-100; Mary Mabel Youman, "Nella Larsen's *Passing:* A Study in Irony," *C.L.A. Journal,* XVIII, No. 2 (1974), 235-41.

2. Hoyt Fuller, cover remarks, *Passing* by Nella Larsen (New York: Collier, 1971). Future references to the text of *Passing* will appear parenthetically in the text.

3. Fuller, cover remarks.

4. Bone et al.

5. Bone et al.

6. Bone et al.

7. See: Adelaide Cromwell Hill, Introduction to Nella Larsen's *Quicksand* (New York: Collier, 1971), p. 16.

8. Amritjit Singh in *The Novels of the Harlem Renaissance* discusses the manic-depressive behavior of Helga Crane, the heroine of Larsen's *Quicksand,* (pp. 102-103) but psychological analysis is not employed in his discussion of *Passing* (pp. 99-100).

MERRILL HORTON (ESSAY DATE 1994)

SOURCE: Horton, Merrill. "Blackness, Betrayal, and Childhood: Race and Identity in Nella Larsen's *Passing.*" *CLA Journal* 28, no. 1 (September 1994): 31-45.

In the following essay, Horton claims that the themes stressed by previous critics of Passing, *such as marital stability, the protagonist's emotional turbulence, and social class, actually have their genesis in the main issue taken up by the novel, that is, the problem of racial identity.*

Charles R. Larson has written that "the primary theme" of Nella Larsen's ***Passing*** (1929) "is not race . . . but marital stability."[1] For Claudia Tate, "racial issues . . . are at best peripheral to the story"; for Tate, "the real impetus" of ***Passing*** is the protagonist's "emotional turbulence" (143). As we shall see, critics dealing with ***Passing*** often subsume the issue of race under issues such as the ones above, or "social class." It has also been suggested that the title of the novel refers to "sexual orientation" as well as race: that the characters who pass for white are also passing for heterosexual. What I want to do is to suggest that the other themes and issues in ***Passing*** have their genesis in the childhood of the author and the childhood games of her characters, and are reducible to the issue of racial identity, a fact that the novel's protagonist realizes when she ponders what action to take in order to save her marriage from her childhood friend:

> She was caught between two allegiances, different, yet the same. Herself. Her race. Race! The thing that bound and suffocated her. Whatever steps she took, or if she took none at all, something would be crushed. A person or the race.[2]

Passing is the story of two women, Irene Redfield and Clare Bellew, who are black by birth and by culture, but whose light skin allows them to "pass for white." A chance meeting between the two women renews an old friendship, and Clare, who has completely passed into the white world, is increasingly attracted to Irene's Harlem milieu. Clare's husband, a wealthy white racist, is unaware of her origin; he discovers it, however, and Clare either throws herself from a window, falls, or is pushed.

In "Nella Larsen's Harlem Aesthetic," Thadious M. Davis says that Larsen's work resulted from a complicated blend of racial and socioeconomic motivation. Davis cites several sources, including the following part of a letter from Larsen to Carl Van Vechten in which Larsen describes "her ritual for reading a good book: "a Houbigant scented bath, the donning of my best green crepe de chine pyjamas, fresh flowers on the bed side table, piles of freshly covered pillows and my nicest bedcovers."[3] Larsen's association of literature with upper-class accoutrements is interesting because Davis says Larsen "wanted her own life to become a kind of fairy tale, like a princess out of a modern fairy tale, as she observed of Fania Marinoff, [Carl] Van Vechten's wife" (Davis 250). And Larsen justified her search for a new apartment by writing Dorothy Peterson: "I'm still looking for a place to move. . . . Right now when I look into the Harlem streets I feel just like Helga Crane in my novel [***Quicksand***]. Furious at being connected with all these niggers"; she referred to the new apartment as "Uncle Tom's Cabin" (Davis 248).

Davis notes that Larsen's one claim to "specialness" was that "she was a mulatto, daughter of a Danish lady and a Negro from the Virgin Islands" (Davis 249-50). Indeed, "two key components of Nella Larsen's Harlem aesthetic" were "international prestige" and "interracial recognition"—both of which were dependent on her race—and Larsen's "aesthetic" led to, first, a "split between her work as a creative process and her work as a source of public recognition," and then to an intensification of this split (Davis 249, 251). What we get here is the sense of an artist who is involved in a symbiotic, not-altogether-desired relationship: she does not particularly care for lower- or middle-class black culture and is ambivalent about her own racial heritage, but she believes that only by being measured against other blacks can she attain the public and financial recognition that she requires. Here we recall Larsen's statement to an interviewer from the New York World: "[W]ith my economic status it's better to be a Negro" (Quoted in Davis 249). For Larsen, the Harlem Renaissance was both an opportunity and a restriction: a crucible of sorts. The tension between the object of Larsen's art, the world of Harlem, and "the complexities of personal identification with that world," is embodied in the two main characters of ***Passing,*** her second and final published novel.[4]

Mary Mabel Youman sees in ***Passing*** the thematic duality of race vs. class, and she comes down on the side of class. Youman believes that Irene "has sold her birthright for a mess of pottage," like the biblical Esau, and writes that this "selling-out" is demonstrated by Irene's emphasis on economic and social standing, security, her aloofness toward her black servants, and the antiseptic raising of her children.[5]

Certainly, class is an extremely important factor in Irene's life; Larsen seems to say that it plays a crucial motivational role in the life of the passer and that it also shapes, restricts, and ultimately controls certain behavior. The scene in which Irene and Clare have tea with their childhood friend Gertrude demonstrates that these three women form a socio-economic spectrum, so to speak. Gertrude, also capable of passing, is married to a white butcher and represents the lower end of the spectrum; Clare is also married to a white man, "some sort of international banking agent" who, when younger, "turned up from South America with untold gold"; Clare represents the upper-end of the spectrum (Larsen 56, 42). Irene's husband Brian is a black medical doctor, incapable of passing, who has never been to South America but wants to emigrate in order to escape racist American society (217). Irene represents the center.

Irene is annoyed with Gertrude's middle-class gaucheness and with both Clare and Gertrude for being married to white men (54-55). Later, Irene admits to herself that her "annoyance"

> arose from a feeling of being outnumbered, a sense of aloneness, in her adherence to her own class and kind; not merely in the great thing of marriage, but in the whole pattern of her life as well.
>
> (56)

We know little about "the whole pattern" of Irene's life, but we do know that her father is a college graduate, and therefore that Irene probably grew up in a middle-class environment; certainly, Clare seems to have envied Irene's economic status (28, 41). Irene's own "class and kind" would seem to be middle-class blacks, whose rarity is implicit in Irene's sense of aloneness. Irene would have less reason, relatively speaking, to be dissatisfied with her childhood than Clare to be with hers; Irene's relative satisfaction with her status would have created in her the strong race and class identity which the above quote reveals.

Irene's position *between* the middle-class Gertrude and the upper-class Clare is suggestive of her desire to "have it both ways," "to have her cake and eat it, too": to live in an upper-class world that is black. The Redfield's economic and social position allows Irene to participate in all the activities of a comparably situated white woman, activities such as charity work and bridge games. Irene wants "black" emotional security and familiarity, and "white" financial security: she wants to play it safe, a symbolic example of which is that even though Clare's husband has returned from South America with "untold gold," Irene refuses to let Brian seek riches there (99-101). The maintenance of this safety, this tightrope act, depends on husband Brian and is the center of Irene's world—and she fears Clare might disrupt it.

Youman's focus on class leads to the cultural and spiritual price of passing. Only passers are invited to Clare's tea, and the only mutual childhood friend that Clare, Gertrude, and Irene discuss is a man who is also capable of passing and has passed over into a Jewish milieu—"no longer a Negro or a Christian" (62). Clare seems aware of an overall cost of passing when she tells Irene, "[M]oney's awfully nice to have. In fact, all things considered, I think, 'Rene, that it's even worth the price" (44). And Irene does not want husband Brian to talk to their oldest son about sex, a fact which leads Youman to argue that Irene's attitude toward sex is a function of a class-induced spiritual crisis (238). The implication is that social class, sexuality, and spirituality combine in the passer to create a worldview that both physically and mentally isolates passers from both their native and adopted cultures.

One exorbitant price paid by all the women of ***Passing*** is celibacy, which helps lead Deborah E. McDowell to contend that "[h]aving established the absence of sex from the marriage of [Irene and Clare], Larsen can flirt, if only obliquely, with the idea of a lesbian relationship."[6] The novel unquestionably contains sensuous actions: Clare kisses Irene's head and bare shoulder, and Irene strokes Clare's bare arm; moreover, Irene is almost constantly fascinated by Clare's spectacular good looks and enchanting laughter. McDowell explains Larsen's sexual subtext thusly:

> [T]he novel's clever strategy derives from its surface theme and central metaphor—passing. It takes the form of the activity it describes. Implying false, forged, and mistaken identities, that it functions on multiple levels: thematically, in terms of the racial and sexual plots, and, strategically, in terms of the narrative's disguise.
>
> (160)

In *Sororophobia,* Helena Michie argues that McDowell is wrong to imply that the subject of race is merely a "cover" for lesbian sexuality; for Michie a "hierarchicization of the two plots" is "unnecessary and untrue" to the novel's complexity because "racial passing and sexuality are inextricable," a fact which Michie says creates an "erotics of passing."[7] I accept and adopt Michie's phrase "erotics of passing," but reject "a lesbian reading" of the relationship between Irene and Clare.[8] I argue that Larsen artistically combines the two types of passing not to provide a surreptitious "tale within a tale," but to express the powerful emotional and psychological underpinnings of "passing" which, like the roots of culture, class-consciousness, and sexuality, are established in childhood.

Sigmund Freud concludes his "Creative Writers and Day-Dreaming" with the argument that a writer's "[p]hantasies, when we learn them, repel us or at least leave us cold. But when a creative writer presents his plays . . . or tells us what we are inclined to take to be his personal day-dreams"—i.e., books, plays, poems, etc.—we accept them because the writer thus "softens the character of his egoistic day-dreams by altering and disguising it."[9] Such egoism, says Freud, has its origins in childhood, during which the child at play "creates a world of phantasy which he takes very seriously—that is, which he invests with large amounts of emotion" (Freud 443).

We have reason to believe that race and childhood emotions were more than usually intertwined in the case of Nella Larsen. Charles R. Larson tells us that on the 1910 census form for Nella's family, Larsen's white mother claimed to have had only one child, Nella's younger, white half sister, Anna, and to have only one child, again Anna, living at home (Larson xix). Larson further notes: "[N]ot only was Nella no longer living with [her family] (she would have been nineteen) but she had also been written out of their lives" (Larson xix). According to Larson, "[s]omething traumatic happened to Nella between the years 1894 (when her mother married [a white man]) and the time of the 1910 census," and he believes that the novel ***Quicksand*** contains clues: "When Helga [Crane] declines her Danish suitor's proposal, she informs him, 'If we were married, you might come to be ashamed of me, to hate all dark people. My mother did that'" (Larson xix). When Nella died, her half sister Anna inherited the estate and said to a family friend, "Why, I didn't know that I had a sister" (Larson xx). Whatever this "something traumatic" was, then, it seems likely that Nella attributed it to her race; whatever "it" was, it certainly happened either in Nella's childhood or early youth—Larson speculates that Nella "was removed from the Larsen household sometimes around the age of nine or ten. . . . It had to have been early enough for her sister, Anna, to have forgotten about her" (Larson xx).

We know little about Nella Larsen's childhood, but we do know that Larsen's mother, Mary Hanson, was white, and therefore that Nella's Oedipal phase intimately involved a white woman. We cannot psychoanalyze Larsen's fictional characters, but scholars such as Thadious Davis and Charles R. Larson have provided us with enough biographical information about Larsen to suggest that ***Passing*** is indeed a therapeutic exploration of issues in the black race that Nella Larsen found difficult to reconcile.

Freud says that the child's play is determined solely "by the wish to be big and grown," and that when the child becomes adult, he or she cannot give up his or her pleasurable child's play:

> [H]e knows he is expected not to go on playing or phantasying any longer, but to act in the real world; on the other hand, some of the wishes which give rise to his phantasies are of a kind which it is essential to conceal. Thus he is ashamed of his phantasies as being unpermissable.
>
> (Freud 438)

Artistic adults formalize their childhood play via art. This art, says Freud, either corrects or attempts to correct "unsatisfying reality." Among other things, art is aesthetic; significantly, Freud's word for aesthetic pleasure is the German equivalent for "fore-pleasure," which, as Peter Gay notes, "links aesthetics to sexual pleasure" (Freud 436). Here, we begin to see how racial passing in fictional characters might appear sensuous without necessarily suggesting the sexual orientation of those characters or of their creator.

By filling in the spaces of this "erotics of passing," we can see that black children who "pass"—regardless of whether they grow up to be authors—probably learn to do so *as a game* and become progressively more alert to the advantages of *simply being able to play the game.* As with any childhood game, passing exacts an emotional investment from its players, and if the child continues to play as he or she ages, then the initial cost of passing expands to fit the child's changing emotional state. Adult passing allows the fulfillment of childhood fantasies, is the maturation of those fantasies; Clare is in the World Series of passing.

Clare is celibate because she is afraid to reveal her race to her husband. But when Gertrude, who has no such fear, confides that she, too, is celibate, and says, "Nobody wants a dark child," Irene counters "in a voice of whose even tones she was proud": 'One of my boys is dark'" (61). Irene's pride in her "even tones," rather than in her son, suggests that the issue of "dark children" is a highly emotional one for her, and we cannot be certain that her "even tones" do not mask shame.

Given Irene's "even-toned" protest and her failure to echo her friends' assertions of celibacy, readers may logically infer that at this point Irene is *not* celibate and is therefore morally superior to her friends because she is not afraid to produce another "dark" child. But in ***Passing***'s Part 2, which occurs two years after Part 1, we learn that Irene's husband, Brian, considers sex "a joke," "a grand joke, the greatest in the world" (105). The probable source of Brian's cynicism is not revealed until Part 3, where we learn that Irene—despite considering her husband "extremely good-looking"—and Brian have separate bedrooms (93, 187). While it is impossible to determine when separate sleeping arrangements began—before or after the Chicago trip—it seems that Irene, despite her protestation to Gertrude, was then, or shortly afterward became, celibate. I contend that if Irene became celibate after the Chicago trip, she did so under the influence of her friends: her fellow passers brought Irene up-to-date on the rules of the game. On the other hand, if Irene's celibacy predates the Chicago trip, then her prim class-consciousness prevents her from acknowledging emotional solidarity with her friends.

Unlike Clare's husband, both Gertrude's and Irene's are aware of their wives' race, so their wives are not celibate due to the conventionally romantic fear of discovery found in passing novels, i.e., unless all three women are lesbians, Gertrude's and Irene's overt motivation logically cannot be the same as Clare's.[10] Indeed, both Gertrude's husband and mother-in-law tell her that her fear of having a "dark" child is "silly" (60). That the women, however, feel a covert emotional constraint against producing "dark" children reveals in them the depths of the emotional and psychological effects of passing. Irrationally, Gertrude tolerates her white family's gentle ridicule, and Irene even risks her husband's departure for Brazil, simply in order to avoid having another child. And Clare is willing to humiliate Gertrude and Irene by forcing them to "pass" in front of her husband, who proceeds to describe blacks in repulsive terms, just to impress them with her accomplishment of "passing over completely" (66-70). Psychologically, Clare, Gertrude, and Irene are still so profoundly attached to their childhood game of passing that they view even their sexual, mature lives as part of the game.

Larsen's emphasis on social class implies that what we might call "upward mobility" is perhaps the primary impetus for playing the game beyond childhood. However, economic considerations also must have been involved in the initial phases of passing. The novel is bracketed, so to speak, by window scenes: the Drayton Hotel window overlooking Lake Michigan, and Felise Freeland's apartment window, through which Clare falls. Picture three little girls—Gertrude, Irene, and Clare—standing on a Chicago sidewalk and peering through the exotic and attractive window of some commercial establishment that they are legally and, to varying degrees, economically prohibited from entering. Picture the girls daring one another to enter the store; surely, something of this sort was the genesis of Clare's transformation and of what we will see is Irene's secret desire to pass into the white world.

Irene and Clare reunite atop an upper-class, whites-only Chicago hotel, the Drayton, where both happen to be visiting: both women are passing, playing the game. Overlooking the exclusive lakefront, the roof of the Drayton represents the social and economic pinnacle whose heights both women, against all odds, have achieved. The women do not immediately recognize each other, but Irene notes that Clare's manner with the waiter, "coming from another woman, would have been classed as just a shade too provocative" (16). But "there was something that made [Irene] hesitate to name it that. A certain impression of assurance, perhaps" (16). Irene looks away from the woman, as a polite middle-class woman should—only to suddenly realize that she, Irene, is now in turn being scrutinized by the woman: "Did that woman, could that woman, somehow know that here before her very eyes on the roof of the Drayton sat a Negro?" (18).

As Irene later tells her white friend Hugh Wentworth, "[t]here are ways [of detecting passing]. But they're not definite or tangible" (141). Moreover, we know that Irene has little respect for whites' ability to perceive these intangibles—"white people were so stupid about such things"; thus, her confusion over the beautiful and strange white woman's stare (18-19). Because Clare exhibits the intangible racial signs only vaguely—they are masked by their whiteness and confidence—Irene senses them only vaguely and does not associate them with blackness. Clare's self-confidence, which Irene consistently labels as "brazen," hides her even from other passing blacks. But Clare senses these intangibles in Irene and does *not* politely turn away, as did Irene, thus allowing herself time to recall her childhood friend (17).

Therefore, the reunion between the two women takes place because of Clare's lower-class brazenness, precisely the quality of Clare's that the straight-laced Irene consistently finds most objectionable and yet most fascinating: "Stepping always on the edge of danger. Always aware, but not drawing back or turning aside. Certainly not because of any alarms or feeling of outrage on the part of others" (4). To Irene, Clare's blond beauty is remarkable because it is an unusually "white" beauty even for a passer. Irene's attraction to Clare is the attraction of the starlet to the star, of the meek child to the brave, of the amateur passer to the professional. For Clare, passing is an adventure to be experienced to the fullest; Irene secretly envies her friend's attitude, and Clare, a more experienced participant in the game, knows this and uses it to insinuate herself into Irene's Harlem life.

Clare's involvement in Irene's life takes a metaphorically sexual form of seduction, but this is a two-way seduction, because while Clare wants the exposure to black life which Harlem affords, Irene wants to know what it would be like to achieve complete whiteness, as we see in a good example of the speakerly text:

> The truth was, [Irene] was curious. There were things that she wanted to ask Clare Kendry. She wished to find out about this hazardous business of "passing," this breaking away from all that was familiar and friendly to take one's chances in another environment, not entirely strange, perhaps, but certainly not entirely friendly. What, for example, one did about background, how one accounted for oneself. And how one felt when one came into contact with other Negroes. But she couldn't.
>
> (35-37)

Irene initially spurns the seduction, which has the predictable effect of increasing the ardor of the lover, and soon Clare becomes almost a fixture in Redfield's social life.

One of the conventions of "passing fiction" is the return, or attempted return, of passers to black culture. Robert E. Fleming divides the conventional "difficulties experienced by characters in the passing novel" into two categories; "the practical"—essentially, the various ways in which a "passer" may be "found out"; and "the psychological"—essentially, guilt, loneliness, and loss of self-esteem."[11] And Robert Bone observes that "the invariable outcome [of passing] . . . is disillusionment with life on the other side . . . a new appreciation of racial values, and an irresistible longing to return to the Negro community."[12] In the passer, appreciation of one's racial values is made possible by comparing those native values to one's adopted, white values; and, of course, one cannot return to a place one has never been. My point is that *passers seek to return to a culture which they knew in childhood.*

Irene allows Clare to take part in her life partly because of self-titillation—Clare's blond good looks and wealth make her a celebrity—and partly, as she says, due to Clare's stated psychological and emotional need for blacks, a need which Irene understands and has managed to balance (129). Moreover, it satisfies Irene's ego to pity Clare and to know that the ultra-successful Clare prefers Irene's game to her own. We can see Clare's tacit recognition of this altered state of affairs when she writes Irene: "It may be, 'Rene dear, it may just be, that after all, your way may be the wiser and infinitely happier one. I'm not sure just now. At least not so sure as I have been" (82).

Soon Irene comes to believe that Clare is having an affair with her husband, it is this belief which highlights the potential for unreliability inherent in the central consciousness-style narrator: Are Brian and Irene really having an affair? It is impossible to arrive at an objective answer, but Charles R. Larson writes that Nella's husband, Elmer Imes, was a "notorious womanizer" and that "[b]y the time ***Passing*** was published, the fault lines in Nella Larsen's . . . marriage were so unstable that it was only a matter of time before the relationship would end" (xv). Near the time of the divorce, Elmer had a white mistress, "and Nella herself was said to have jumped out of a window and broken her leg" (xvii). The parallels between Larsen's life and art, then, are inconclusive but obviously suggestive.

Since Irene is ***Passing***'s central consciousness, events in the novel are necessarily filtered through her perception; if the reader questions the probability of an affair between Brian and Clare, the reader must also question Irene's subjective perceptions about other events, including Irene's fateful meeting with Mr. Bellew on the streets of New York. Irene believes that the affair is real, and I note the shrewdness and tenacity with which she has maintained her "life in the middle," to which, as we have seen, even Clare pays tribute: Irene never makes a judgment which is not borne out by the narrative's action. At the Drayton Hotel, Irene senses something vaguely amiss about Clare—and Clare turns out to be passing. Irene knows of Brian's dislike of medicine and of his desire to emigrate to Brazil, and she is always so ready to tenaciously combat both that Brian simply prefers to avoid the subjects (99-101). Irene is even cynically aware of the ulterior motives that prominent whites—such as Hugh Wentworth—have to frequent Harlem society (125). And Irene's one, prophetic objection to Clare's visits to Harlem is that Mr. Bellew might discover his wife's race (122, 147). Finally, convinced of Brian's infidelity, Irene skillfully initiates the events that lead to Mr. Bellew's discovery that Clare is black, and to her death.

One day while shopping with her obviously black friend, Felise, Irene accidentally encounters Clare's husband, John Bellew.

> His hat came off. He held out his hand, smiling genially. But the smile faded at once. Surprise, incredulity, and—was it understanding?—passed over his features. He had, Irene knew, become conscious of Felise, golden, with curly black Negro hair, whose arm was still linked in her own. She was sure, now, of the understanding in his face, as he looked at her again and then back at Felise. And displeasure.
>
> (183)

Rather than provide an explanation which will preserve her passing status and protect Clare, Irene gives Bellew "the cool appraising stare which she reserved for mashers," and walks on (183). We know that Irene was forced by Clare into passing in front of Mr. Bellew in Chicago, so Irene's "cutting" of him might simply be revenge. But we also know that on the previous day Irene contemplated betraying Clare:

> Strange, she had not before realized how easily she could put Clare out of her life! She had only to tell John Bellew that his wife—No. Not that! But if he should somehow learn of these Harlem visits—Why should she hesitate? Why spare Clare?
>
> (180)

Clare's initial cost of passing is high: betrayal; she deserts her culture to pass into the white world. But the cost of rejoining black culture, Larsen seems to say, is also betrayal—and death. Prior to the party at which Clare dies, Clare meets Irene at the latter's home and kisses her friend's "bare shoulder" (195). If Irene is correct about Clare and Brian's relationship, then Clare's kiss must be seen as a Judas-like kiss of betrayal, and here again we see the confluence of the spiritual and sexual prices that the women of ***Passing*** pay. But just as Clare and Irene "seduced" one another, so they almost simultaneously betray one another, for after Clare's kiss, Irene is described as wondering: "[W]hy didn't she go on and tell Clare about meeting Bellew? Why couldn't she" (195-96).

Clare's attempt to rejoin black culture is made possible by Irene. However, Irene realizes that she will be the one who is "crushed" by her friend's reversal of course, so to speak: Clare will get Brian, and Irene will lose the economic foundation of her upper-middle-class life and a part of her identity (180). This observation leads us to a third sense of the term "passing." Clare wants to return to black culture, while Irene, as we have seen, has a conflicted, secret childhood ambition to "pass" into the white world. In a sense, then, Clare's death is the result of the two women colliding while "passing" one another. The collision kills Clare and leaves Irene stunned and just as racially ambivalent as ever, for while Irene is glad that Clare is dead, she nonetheless mourns her friend's whiteness: Clare's "glorious body mutilated" (213).

Soon after Clare's death, "a strange man, official and authoritative," shows up and, like a referee, pronounces what is apparently the official bureaucratic verdict regarding Clare's fall: "Death by misadventure" (215-16). With Irene's intervention, Clare's adventure has taken a wrong turn and the game is over. The "game" was motivated by economic desire and certainly yielded financial rewards, but it also yielded spiritual and sexual bankruptcy and, for Irene, a continuing ambivalence regarding her identity.

Notes

1. Charles R. Larson, introd., *An Intimation of Things Distant: The Collected Fiction of Nella Larsen,* Larson ed. (New York: Doubleday, 1992) xv. Hereafter cited parenthetically in the text.
2. Nella Larsen, *Passing* (New York: Knopf, 1929) 180. Hereafter cited parenthetically in the text.
3. Thadious M. Davis, "Nella Larsen's Harlem Aesthetic," *The Harlem Renaissance: Revaluations,* ed. Amritjit Singh (New York: Garland, 1989) 248. Hereafter cited parenthetically in the text.
4. According to Charles R. Larson, after *Passing* Nella wrote three novels, all of which were rejected by publishers (xviii). I do not know whether the unpublished manuscripts are extant.
5. Mary Mabel Youman, "Nella Larsen's *Passing:* A Study in Irony," *CLA Journal* 18 (Dec. 1974): 237-38.
6. Deborah E. McDowell, introd., *Quicksand and Passing,* by Nella Larsen (Brunswick: Rutgers UP, 1986) 153. Hereafter cited parenthetically in the text.
7. Helena Michie, *Sororophobia: Differences among Women in Literature and Culture* (New York: Oxford UP, 1992) 152.
8. Michie's acceptance of McDowell's "lesbian reading" of Clare and Irene's relationship is based on an interpretation of the gazes between the two women in the Drayton Hotel scene; Michie's interpretation seems to be a version of the psychological idea of "the looking-glass self," the idea that we construct our individual psychologies and worldviews through a complex visual process of identifying with, and differentiating ourselves from, others. However, what are we to make of the "gaze," or stare, which Gertrude gives Irene: "[Irene] discovered . . . a woman staring up at her with such intense concentration that her eyelids were drawn as though the strain of that upward glance had paralyzed them" (Larsen 194)? In a lesbian reading of *Passing,* where does Gertrude fit in?

9. Sigmund Freud, "Creative Writers and Day-Dreaming," *The Freud Reader,* ed. Peter Gay (New York: Norton, 1989) 443. Hereafter cited parenthetically in the text.

10. Robert W. Fleming, "*Kingswood Royal* and the Black 'Passing' Novel," *Critical Essays on Sinclair Lewis,* ed. Martin Bucco (Boston: G. K. Hall, 1986) 214.

11. Fleming 214.

12. Quoted in Fleming 215.

FURTHER READING

Biography

Davis, Thadious. *Nella Larsen, Novelist of the Harlem Renaissance: A Woman's Life Unveiled.* Baton Rouge: Louisiana State University Press, 1994, 496 p.

Biography and study of Larsen's works that attempts to remove the aura of mystery and misconceptions surrounding her life and discover how the author transcended barriers of race, class, and gender to pursue her dream of becoming a writer.

Criticism

Barnett, Pamela E. "'My Picture of You Is, after All, the True Helga Crane': Portraiture and Identity in Nella Larsen's *Quicksand.*" *Signs* 20, no. 3 (1995): 575-600.

Examines the representation of Larsen's protagonist in Quicksand *and the author's own quest for self-identity.*

Blackmer, Corinne E. "The Veils of the Law: Race and Sexuality in Nella Larsen's *Passing.*" *College Literature* 22, no. 3 (1995): 50-67.

Takes up the issue of "passing" through the interface of literature, politics, and law as they relate to race and sex, using Larsen's novel as a point of discussion.

Blackmore, David L. "'That Unreasonable Restless Feeling': The Homosexual Subtexts of Nella Larsen's *Passing.*" *African American Review* 26, no. 3 (1992): 475-84.

Claims that Larsen hints at same-sex desire between the characters of Irene and Clare and also in the case of Brian.

Brody, Jennifer DeVere. "Clare Kennedy's 'True' Colors: Race and Class Conflict in Nella Larsen's *Passing.*" *Callaloo* 15, no. 4 (1992): 1053-65.

Reexamines Passing *as a work concerned with the simultaneous representation and construction of race and class within a circumscribed community.*

Butler, Judith. "Passing, Queering: Nella Larsen's Psychoanalytic Challenge." In *Female Subjects in Black and White: Race, Psychoanalysis, Feminism,* edited by Elizabeth Abel, Barbara Christian, and Helene Moglen, pp. 266-84. Berkeley: University of California Press, 1997.

Psychoanalytic reading of Larsen's Passing *that considers the importance of sexual difference.*

Chandler, Karen M. "Nella Larsen's Fatal Polarities: Melodrama and Its Limits in *Quicksand.*" *College Language Association Journal* 42, no. 1 (1998): 24-47.

Explores Larsen's use of melodrama to illuminate her vision of the moral and cultural uncertainty of the modern Black woman.

Clark, William Bedford. "The Heroine of Mixed Blood in Nella Larsen's *Quicksand.*" In *Identity and Awareness in the Minority Experience: Past and Present,* edited by George E. Carter and Bruce L. Mouser, pp. 225-38. La Crosse: Institute for Minority Studies, University of Wisconsin-La Crosse, 1975.

Examines the notion of identity in Larsen's work.

———. "The Letters of Nella Larsen to Carl Van Vechten: A Survey." *Resources for American Literary Study* 8 (1978): 193-99.

Shows how Larsen's letters to Carl Van Vechten offer insights into her personality.

Clemmen, Yves W. A. "Nella Larsen's *Quicksand*: A Narrative of Difference." *College Language Association Journal* 40, no. 4 (1997): 458-66.

Discusses the narratalogical motivations of the multidirectional plot of Quicksand, *which ultimately defies easy categorization or explanation.*

Conde, Mary. "Europe in the Novels of Jessie Redmon Fauset and Nella Larsen." In *Difference in View: Women and Modernism,* edited by Gabriele Griffin, pp. 15-26. London: Taylor and Francis, 1994.

Claims that Fauset and Larsen had pessimistic views about Europe as a solution for the characters in their novels.

———. "Passing in the Fiction of Jessie Redmon Fauset and Nella Larsen." *Yearbook of English Studies* 24 (1994): 94-104.

Examines the works of Fauset and Larsen and how they show that "passing" does not change any reality but only exploits the fiction that Black people are necessarily black.

Cutter, Martha J. "Sliding Significations: Passing as a Narrative and Textual Strategy in Nella Larsen's Fiction." *"Passing" and the Fictions of Identity,* edited by Elaine K. Ginsberg, pp. 75-100. Durham: Duke University Press, 1996.

Discusses the literary implications of passing in Larsen's fiction.

Davis, Thadious M. "Introduction." In *Passing,* by Nella Larsen, pp. vii-xxiii. New York: Penguin Books, 1997.

Study of the novel that discusses the phenomenon of "passing," provides background for the work, and discusses the racial issues raised.

Debo, Annette. "Changing Cultural Scripts: Nella Larsen's *Passing* and the Reconstruction of Modernism." *In Process* 1 (1996): 36-52.

Discusses Larsen's work in the context of Modernism.

DuCille, Ann. "Blues Notes on Black Sexuality: Sex and the Texts of Jessie Fauset and Nella Larsen." *Journal of the History of Sexuality* 3, no. 3 (1993): 418-44.

Identifies "blues inscriptions," or concerns with black female desire and erotic relationships, in the works of Fauset and Larsen.

———. "The Bourgeois, Wedding Bell Blues of Jessie Fauset and Nella Larsen." In *The Coupling Convention: Sex, Text, and Tradition in Black Women's Fiction,* pp. 86-109. New York: Oxford University Press, 1993.

Explores the way Fauset and Larsen use the metaphor of coupling to critique the social practices and gender choices that limit women's choices and narrowly define their roles.

Esteve, Mary. "Nella Larsen's 'Moving Mosaic': Harlem, Crowds, and Anonymity." *American Literary History* 9, no. 2 (1997): 268-86.

Discusses Larsen's depiction of crowd behavior in Quicksand.

Favor, J. Martin. "A Clash of Birthrights: Nella Larsen, the Feminine, and African American Identity." In *Authentic Blackness: The Folk in the New Negro Renaissance,* pp. 81-110. Durham, NC: Duke University Press, 1999.

Considers the critical discourse of Larsen's texts.

Gray, Jeffrey. "Essence and the Mulatto Traveler: Europe as Embodiment in Nella Larsen's *Quicksand.*" *Novel* 27, no. 3 (1994): 257-70.

Discusses the novel's protagonist's move to Europe in the hopes of escaping racism.

Grayson, Deborah R. "Fooling White Folks: Or, How I Stole the Show: The Body Politics of Nella Larsen's *Passing.*" *Bucknell Review* 39, no. 1 (1995): 27-37.

Examines some political implications of the motif of passing in Larsen's work.

Hardwig, Bill. "'A Lack Somewhere': Lacan, Psychoanalysis, and *Quicksand.*" *Soundings* 80, no. 4 (1997): 573-89.

Discusses Larsen's work in the context of Lacan's psychological ideas.

Haviland, Beverly. "Passing from Paranoia to Plagiarism: The Abject Authorship of Nella Larsen." *Modern Fiction Studies* 43, no, 2 (1997): 295-318.

Discusses Larsen' paranoia and that of her fictional characters, and claims that the author assumed the position of plagiarist that insured the end of her career as a writer.

Hering, Frank. "Sneaking Around: Idealized Domesticity, Identity Politics, and Games of Friendship in Nella Larsen's *Passing.*" *Arizona Quarterly* 57, no. 1 (2001): 35-60.

Argues that Passing shows idealized domesticity and identity politics to be dangerous responses to segregation.

Hostetler, Ann E. "The Aesthetics of Race and Gender in Nella Larsen's *Quicksand.*" *PMLA* 105, no. 1 (1990): 35-46.

Claims that the emphasis on color in Quicksand *advances a thematics of race and gender.*

Howard, Lillie P. "'A Lack Somewhere': Nella Larsen's *Quicksand* and the Harlem Renaissance." *The Harlem Renaissance Re-Examined,* edited by Victor A. Kramer, pp. 223-33. New York: AMS, 1987.

Sees the novel as depicting the search for identity that was common among African Americans during the period of the Harlem Renaissance.

Hutchinson, George. "Nella Larsen and the Veil of Race." *American Literary History* 9, no. 2 (1997): 329-49.

Reviews two works about Larsen: Thadious Davis's Nella Larsen, Novelist of the Harlem Renaissance: A Woman's Live Unveiled *and* Invisible Darkness, *by Charles R. Larson.*

———. "*Quicksand* and the Racial Labyrinth." *Soundings* 80, no. 4 (1997): 543-71.

Explores notions about race in Larsen's work.

Johnson, Barbara. "The *Quicksands* of the Self: Nella Larsen and Heinz Kohut." In *Female Subjects in Black and White: Race, Psychoanalysis, Feminism,* edited by Elizabeth Abel, Barbara Christian, and Helene Moglen, pp. 252-65. Berkeley: University of California Press, 1997.

Applies Heinz Kohut's psychological theory of "Self Psychology" to the protagonist of Quicksand.

Lackey, Michael. "Larsen's *Quicksand..*" *Explicator* 59, no. 2 (winter 2001): 103-106.

Discusses the jazz scene in the novel.

Larson, Charles R. *Invisible Darkness: Jean Toomer and Nella Larsen.* University of Iowa Press, 1993, 241 p.

Presents biographies, compares their lives and work, and considers why Larsen and Toomer "failed" as writers according to conventional standards.

Lay, Mary M. "Parallels: Henry James's The Portrait of a Lady and Nella Larsen's *Quicksand.*" *CLA Journal* 20 (June 1977): 475-86.

Compares the two novels to and tries to account for their heroines' very different endings despite their similarities.

Lewis, Vashti Crutcher. "Nella Larsen's Use of the Near-White Female in *Quicksand* and *Passing.*" In *Perspectives of Black Popular Culture,* edited by Harry B. Shaw, pp. 36-45. Bowling Green: Popular, 1990.

Discusses the stylistic and social implications of passing in Larsen's work.

Madigan, Mark J. "Miscegenation and 'the Dicta of Race and Class': The Rhinelander Case and Nella Larsen's *Passing.*" *Modern Fiction Studies* 36, no. 4 (1990): 523-29.

Shows how the details of a controversial divorce case of the time provide a historical subtext for Larsen's novel.

McDowell, Deborah E. "'That nameless . . . shameful impulse': Sexuality in Nella Larsen's *Quicksand* and *Passing.*" In *Black Feminist Criticism and Critical Theory,* edited by Joe Weixlmann and Houston A. Baker, Jr., pp. 139-67. Greenwood: Penkevill, 1988.

Examines the dialectic between pleasure and danger in Larsen's novels and discusses their treatment of Black female sexuality.

McLendon, Jacquelyn Y. "Self-Representation as Art in the Novels of Nella Larsen." In *Redefining Autobiography in Twentieth-Century Women's Fiction: An Essay Collection,* edited by Janice Morgan and Colette T. Hall, pp. 149–68. New York: Garland, 1991.

Argues that Larsen's works are not merely autobiographical but are critiques of conventional narrative forms and subjects, whereby the author creates a distinctive art out of personal experience.

———. "Nella Larsen: Overview." *Feminist Writers,* edited by Pamela Kester-Shelton, pp. XXX-XXX. Detroit: St. James Press, 1996.

Overview of Larsen's novels and their main themes of middle-class values, appearance vs. reality, entrapment, and the psychological effects of racial dualism and marginality on a Black bourgeois women.

McMillan, T. S. "Passing Beyond: The Novels of Nella Larsen." *West Virginia University Philological Papers* 38 (1992): 134-46.

Examines the motif of passing in Laresen's works.

Monda, Kimberly. "Self-Delusion and Self-Sacrifice in Nella Larsen's *Quicksand.*" *African American Review* 31, no. 1 (1997): 23-39.

Treats Larsen's criticism of the emotional and sexual self-sacrifice of repression.

Nelson, Emmanuel S. "Nella Larsen (1891-1964)." In *African American Authors, 1745-1945: A Bio-Bibliographical Critical Sourcebook,* edited by Emmanuel S. Nelson, pp. 316-23. Westport: Greenwood, 2000.

Provides a biography, discusses Larsen's major works, and assesses her reputation.

Rhodes, Chip. "Writing Up the New Negro: The Construction of Consumer Desire in the Twenties." *Journal of American Studies* 28, no. 2 (1994): 191-207.

Discusses Heyward's Porgy *as an example of a "Negrotarian" novel and compares Heyward's attitudes toward capitalism to those of Nella Larsen in her novel* Quicksand.

———. "Primitive Desires and the Desire for the Primitive: DuBose Heyward and Nella Larsen." In *Structures of the Jazz Age: Mass Culture, Progressive Education, and Racial Discourse in American Modernism,* pp. 170-96. London: Verso, 1998.

Compares how the "new Negro" was written up in Heyward's Porgy *and Larsen's* Quicksand.

Sato, Hiroko. "Under the Harlem Shadow: A Study of Jessie Fauset and Nella Larsen." In *Harlem Renaissance Remembered,* edited by Arna Bontemps, pp. 83-89. New York: Dodd, Mead, 1972.

Overview of Larsen's work that considers her one of the best Black writers of her day and an artist who uses a wide perspective in her novels.

Silverman, Debra B. "Nella Larsen's *Quicksand*: Untangling the Webs of Exoticism." *African American Review* 27, no. 4 (1993): 599-614.

Discusses the representation of the exotic Black female body in Larsen's novel.

Sullivan, Nell. "Nella Larsen's *Passing* and the Fading Subject." *African American Review* 32, no. 3 (1998): 373-86.

Discusses Larsen's search for recognition and racial identity that are mirrored in her novel's characters.

Tate, Claudia. "Desire and Death in *Quicksand,* by Nella Larsen." *American Literary History* 7, no. 2 (1995): 234-60.

Offers a psychological reading of Quicksand *to address the novel's complex textual subjectivity, which previous analyses have overlooked.*

Wall, Cheryl A. "Nella Larsen: Passing for What?" In *Women of the Harlem Renaissance,* pp. 85-138. Bloomington: Indiana University Press, 1995.

Claims that Larsen's most effective act of passing was masking her subversive themes in her fiction.

Youman, Mary Mabel. "Nella Larsen's *Passing*: A Study in Irony." *College Language Association Journal* 18 (1974): 235-41.

Claims that the title of Passing *is ironic, and that the protagonist of the novel is really the character Irene, and that she is the one who "passes."*

OTHER SOURCES FROM GALE:

Additional coverage of Larsen's life and career is contained in the following sources published by the Gale Group: *African American Writers,* Eds. 1, 2; *Black Literature Criticism,* Vol. 2; *Black Writers,* Ed. 1; *Contemporary Authors,* Vol. 125; *Contemporary Authors New Revision Series,* Vol. 83; *Contemporary Literary Criticism,* Vol. 37; *Dictionary of Literary Biography,* Vol. 51; *DISCovering Authors Modules: Multicultural Authors*; and *Feminist Writers.*

ALAIN LOCKE

(1885 - 1954)

(Born Arthur LeRoy Locke) American philosopher, social and political theorist, critic, and essayist.

For his active promotion of African and African American culture, Locke is considered one of the central figures of the Harlem Renaissance. As editor of the literary anthology *The New Negro: An Interpretation* (1925), which contained work by the best Black writers of the day—Langston Hughes, Countee Cullen, Zora Neale Hurston, James Weldon Johnson, Claude McKay, and Jean Toomer—Locke brought serious critical attention to African American writers for the first time. His aesthetic, political, and cultural writings urged African Americans to look to their African roots and aspire to the highest level of artistic excellence.

BIOGRAPHICAL INFORMATION

Born in Philadelphia to parents who were both teachers, Locke grew up in a middle-class household. He was a talented student, and after high school he entered Harvard University, graduating magna cum laude in 1907 with a degree in philosophy. He received a Rhodes scholarship to Oxford University, where he earned a B.Litt. in 1910. He also studied philosophy at universities in Paris and Berlin. After he returned to the United States in 1911, Locke toured the South, witnessing first-hand the environment of racial prejudice and poverty in which Black Americans lived and conceiving an urgent need to promote the cultural achievement of African Americans. In 1913, Locke joined the faculty of Howard University as a professor of English, philosophy, and pedagogy. When he proposed teaching a course on race relations at the university in 1915, he was denied permission to do so. In 1916, Locke began his doctoral studies at Harvard and graduated with a Ph.D. in philosophy in 1918. Soon thereafter, he was made chair of the philosophy department at Howard, where he actively promoted African art exhibits and Black culture. He traveled to Africa in 1924, and the following year he and several other African American professors were fired from Howard for seeking parity in the wages earned by Black workers and their white counterparts. For the next three years, Locke wrote prolifically and established relationships with numerous artists, writers, and philanthropists. In 1925, he compiled *The New Negro,* which would become, according to many critics, the standard-bearer for the Harlem Renaissance. After he was rehired by Howard in 1928, Locke continued to promote Black literature and art. Around 1935, when the Harlem Renaissance movement began to lose its initial force and focus, Locke became more active in the fields of philosophy and adult education, helping to form the Associates in Negro Folk Education in 1936. Locke continued to teach, write articles and books, edit periodicals, travel, and lecture until his death in New York in 1954.

MAJOR WORKS

Beginning in 1904, Locke wrote articles about race, culture, literature, and education for a number of publications, establishing a name for himself as a leading Black intellectual. With the publication of *The New Negro,* an anthology of literature containing work by some of the best Black artists of the early twentieth century, he made his mark as a American cultural figure. The work began as a special Harlem issue for the periodical *Survey Graphic,* which Locke later expanded into an anthology of fiction, poetry, drama, and essays. The quality and variety of work collected in *The New Negro* challenged the perception of African Americans among Black and white readers alike. This volume also brought attention to the African roots of Black America. According to many critics, *The New Negro* signaled the beginning of the movement that came to be known as the Harlem Renaissance. The collection included Locke's essays "The New Negro," in which he discusses the distinct identity of African Americans; "Negro Youth Speaks," an analysis of the "voice" of the new generation of Black Americans; and "The Negro Spirituals," which emphasizes specifically African American forms of artistic expression. Other volumes in which Locke promoted writings by Black writers included *Four Negro Poets* (1927), *Plays of Negro Life: A Source-Book of Native American Drama* (1927), *A Decade of Negro Self-Expression* (1928), and *The Negro in America* (1933). He also reviewed literature by and about African Americans in *Opportunity* and *Phylon,* two of the most important periodicals about Black literature, culture, and art. Locke actively promoted the idea that Black writers should look not to white culture but to their African roots for aesthetic inspiration. In *The Negro and His Music* (1936) and *The Negro in Art* (1940), he traces the history of Black aesthetic practices to African folk traditions. In addition to writing and editing twelve book-length volumes, Locke published hundreds of articles and essays and lectured widely. The motivating ideas behind much of Locke's work were the uniqueness of Black culture and racial relations in the United States. His essays on these subjects were compiled in *Race Contacts and Interracial Relations: Lectures on the Theory and Practice of Race* (1992).

CRITICAL RECEPTION

While Locke was an important figure in initiating and guiding the Harlem Renaissance, he was not universally admired even during the heyday of the movement. His detractors, including W. E. B. Du Bois, found that his ideas about what should and should not constitute "Negro" literature and aesthetics were too rigid. There is also some indication that there were power struggles within the movement between Locke and Walter White for ideological control. However, even those who disagreed with Locke in terms of his philosophy and cultural theories held him in high esteem for his tireless energy in promoting African American art and literature. He was viewed by many Black writers as a figure who united the movement, and he himself declared that he was a "philosophical mid-wife to a generation of younger Negro poets, writers, and artists." Today, his work is still valued for the insight it provides into the Harlem Renaissance period as well as the evolving awareness of the Black experience in America.

PRINCIPAL WORKS

The New Negro: An Interpretation [editor] (poetry, fiction, drama, and essays) 1925

Four Negro Poets [editor] (poetry) 1927

Plays of Negro Life: A Source-Book of Native American Drama [with Montgomery Gregory; editor] (dramas and essays) 1927

A Decade of Negro Self-Expression (bibliography) 1928

The Negro in America (bibliography) 1933

The Negro and His Music (nonfiction) 1936

Negro Art: Past and Present (nonfiction) 1936

Americans All: Immigrants All [editor] (essays) 1939

The Negro in Art: A Pictorial Record of the Negro Artist and of the Negro Theme in Art (nonfiction) 1940

When Peoples Meet: A Study in Race and Culture Contacts [with Bernhard J. Stern; editor] (nonfiction) 1942

Le Role du Negre dans la Culture des Ameriques (nonfiction) 1943

The Negro Artist Comes of Age: A National Anthology of Contemporary American Artists [editor] (poetry, essays, and drama) 1945

Race Contacts and Interracial Relations: Lectures on the Theory and Practice of Race (lectures) 1992

PRIMARY SOURCES

ALAIN LOCKE (ESSAY DATE 1928)

SOURCE: Locke, Alain. "Art or Propaganda?" *The Critical Temper of Alain Locke: A Selection of His Essays on Art and Culture,* edited by Jeffrey C. Stewart, pp. 27-28. New York: Garland Publishing, Inc., 1983.

In the following essay, which originally appeared in 1928, Locke employs biblical and literary allusions to elucidate the artistic freedom required of African American artists.

Artistically it is the one fundamental question for us today.—Art or Propaganda. Which? Is this more the generation of the prophet or that of the poet; shall our intellectual and cultural leadership preach and exhort or sing? I believe we are at that interesting moment when the prophet becomes the poet and when prophecy becomes the expressive song, the chant of fulfillment. We have had too many Jeremiahs, major and minor;—and too much of the drab wilderness. My chief objection to propaganda, apart from its besetting sin of monotony and disproportion, is that it perpetuates the position of group inferiority even in crying out against it. For it lives and speaks under the shadow of a dominant majority whom it harangues, cajoles, threatens or supplicates. It is too extroverted for balance or poise or inner dignity and self-respect. Art in the best sense is rooted in self-expression and whether naive or sophisticated is self-contained. In our spiritual growth genius and talent must more and more choose the role of group expression, or even at times the role of free individualistic expression,—in a word must choose art and put aside propaganda.

The literature and art of the younger generation already reflects this shift of psychology, this regeneration of spirit. David should be its patron saint: it should confront the Philistines with its five smooth pebbles fearlessly. There is more strength in a confident camp than in a threatened enemy. The sense of inferiority must be innerly compensated, self-conviction must supplant self-justification, and in the dignity of this attitude a convinced minority must conform a condescending majority. Art cannot completely accomplish this, but I believe it can lead the way.

Our espousal of art thus becomes no mere idle acceptance of "art for art's sake," or cultivation of the last decadences of the over-civilized, but rather a deep realization of the fundamental purpose of art and of its function as a tap root of vigorous, flourishing living. Not all of our younger writers are deep enough in the sub-soil of their native materials—too many are pot-plants seeking a forced growth according to the exotic tastes of a pampered and decadent public. It is the art of the people that needs to be cultivated, not the art of the coteries. Propaganda itself is preferable to shallow, truckling imitation. Negro things may reasonably be a fad for others; for us they must be a religion. Beauty, however, is its best priest and psalms will be more effective than sermons.

To date we have had little sustained art unsubsidized by propaganda; we must admit this debt to these foster agencies. The three journals which have been vehicles of most of our artistic expressions have been the avowed organs of social movements and organized social programs. All our purely artistic publications have been sporadic. There is all the greater need then for a sustained vehicle of free and purely artistic expression. If Harlem should happily fill this need, it will perform an honorable, and constructive service. I hope it may, but should it not, the need remains and the path toward it will at least be advanced a little.

We need, I suppose in addition to art some substitute for propaganda. What shall that be? Surely we must take some cognizance of the fact that we live at the centre of a social problem. Propaganda at least nurtured some form of serious social discussion, and social discussion was necessary, is still necessary. On this side: the difficulty and shortcoming of propaganda is its partisanship. It is one-sided and often prejudging. Should we not then have a journal of free discussion, open to all sides of the problem and to all camps of belief? Difficult, that,—but intriguing. Even if it has to begin on the note of dissent and criticism and assume Menckenian scepticism to escape the commonplaces of conformity. Yet, I hope we shall not remain at this negative pole. Can we not cultivate truly free and tolerant discussion, almost Socratically minded for the sake of truth? After Beauty, let Truth come into the Renaissance picture,—a later cue, but a welcome one. This may be premature, but one hopes not,—for eventually it must come and if we can accomplish that, instead of having to hang our prophets, we can silence them or change their lamentations to song with a Great Fulfillment.

GENERAL COMMENTARY

EUGENE C. HOLMES (LECTURE DATE 1955)

SOURCE: Holmes, Eugene C. "Alain Locke—Philosopher, Critic, Spokesman." *The Journal of Philosophy* LIV, no. 5 (28 February 1957): 113-18.

In the following lecture, originally delivered at a memorial meeting for Alain Locke at New York University in 1955, Holmes sketches Locke's philosophical views.

Alain Leroy Locke was a teacher of philosophy for over forty years. His philosophical contributions were not numerous, but he did produce essays which were both seminal and germinal in content and in influence. These philosophical ideas were the seasoned results of his life-long interests in art, literature, the theatre, value theory, and philosophical pacifism. Perhaps his greatest contributions lay in a transcending and pervasive influence upon a generation of artists, students, colleagues, and followers. For this reason alone, there are needed many-faceted reassessments of the man's career as a teacher, scholar, critic, and spokesman—the latter in the quite special sense that Locke was a Negro who knew that the scientific facts concerning the Negro heritage had to be known.

His training for the philosophical enterprise was exceptionally rigorous, in the Philadelphia public and normal schools, at Harvard where he won Phi Beta Kappa, at Oxford where he was a Rhodes scholar and where he won a B.Litt., at Berlin where he studied under Brentano, Meinong, and Natorp, and in Paris where he studied under Bergson and others. At Harvard he sat under James, Sheffer, Münsterberg, Palmer, Adams, Royce, and Santayana. His work in value theory was with Perry and Royce. Much of his tutelage at Harvard was under the sympathetic guidance of Horace Meyer Kallen, a life-long friend who was at Oxford at the same time as Locke.

When Locke came to Howard University in 1912 as an instructor in education and philosophy, he was forced to undergo quite an orientation in an institution just out of its swaddling clothes as an academy for the newly manumitted freedmen and just emerging as a coëducational college. Locke wished to put something of his training into practice in this almost alien academic environment. His efforts were met with success because he was able to introduce philosophy, esthetics, and anthropological thinking into this young institution. He was successful in developing the first Negro college theatre and the first art gallery, and he saw to it that library facilities were widened. He knew that there had to be a real community of scholars at Howard, Negro and white. Academic freedom and freedom to express had to be encouraged, and he succeeded in making philosophical analysis of all educational problems the fulcrum around which the new education at Howard centered. In many ways, this was a one-man revolution undertaken by a courageous, physically small scholar, who knew that for years this would be the only reward for putting philosophy to work and the only way to practice educational philosophy and the classical philosophy of his teachers. This meant also new developments in general education, antipodal to the philanthropy-geared industrial and agricultural practices of the Hamptons and Tuskegees. It meant that orientation courses for freshmen and general logic for all students could be organized and developed in an atmosphere where scholarship and culture could become the goal for the new type of students.

As for himself, he was a true peripatetic, an ambassador, going over much of the western world, telling Europe of Negro art, going to Africa and collecting African art and connecting this with the Negro heritage. He lectured for a year in Latin America and in Haiti. His lecture tours over all America, guest and visiting professorships, all served to make the Locke message about Negro art and ***The New Negro*** known to the academic and art world. Being invited to the Harvard Academic Festival in Salzburg in 1950 as a guest professor was a crowning point and culmination in Locke's career.

Alain Locke possessed and professed as a philosophical credo the view of humanity that there is a uniqueness of the personality, an individuation of the psyche and the soma which are essentially communicable. This indefeasibility of the individual's experiences is physical and ethical, allowing for the development of man's own inner personality and freedom. As a sensitive member of a minority group he saw in retrospect that the Negro scholar's ability to withstand the infirmities of the American scene is a dialectic phase of the democratic process which must necessarily aid in bringing to fruition the dream of a community of Negro scholars. This was his sensitivity about American history, and it led him to an identity with the great leader, the self-taught Frederick Douglass, and to mutual understanding, if sometimes mild controversy, with W. E. B. DuBois.

Locke's philosophic productions, though not numerous, were best represented by three essays:

"The Problem of Classification in Theory of Value," his doctoral dissertation at Harvard (1918); an essay contributed to *American Philosophy, Today and Tomorrow* (1935), entitled **"Values and Imperatives"**; and another in *Freedom and Experience,* a Festschrift presented to Horace Kallen, entitled **"Pluralism and Ideological Peace"** (1947). He was primarily the philosopher's philosopher, who, because of his extensive training, scintillated in the *conversazioni* in New York, Cambridge, Oxford, Paris, Rome, and Salzburg.

At a Memorial for Locke, I noted certain resemblances between Locke and the late Santayana:

> There was to friends who knew both men rather well, a certain resemblance between Alain Locke and George Santayana. Each professed a philosophic faith which, however diverse from the other's, was at one with it in the spirit of friendly hospitality to all sorts and conditions of men and ideas. Each had multitudes of acquaintances, yet hardly any intimates. Each was a man alone, personally uncommitted and essentially lonely. Santayana was a Spaniard who grew up in America but could identify himself neither with the land of his birth nor the land of his growth. Locke was a Negro who was born in America, and grew up in America, but was denied, because of the color of his skin, complete identification with the land of his birth and growth.
>
> Both were men of discriminating sensibility and disciplined intellect, by education and preference free and at home in the world of letters and the arts. Santayana, having entered that world, never went outside it to the day he died. Locke, on the contrary, did not feel at liberty to retain his refuge in it, much as he might have wished to. He came to see in his own personal situation an exemplar of the situation and problems of every human being, wherever in the world people are penalized for some difference entirely unrelated to their qualities as persons or their competence as thinkers or craftsmen or artists.

Locke's esthetic, literary, and anthropological contributions to what he termed value relativism and cultural pluralism, and his identification with international movements, also made him, for a time at least, more sympathetic to Bahaism than to the more familiar creeds. His co-editorship with Bernhard Stern of the volume, ***When Peoples Meet*** (1947), was an earnest of his well-considered belief in the values of cultural anthropology, and the expert critical analyses accompanying the selections showed his scholarship and deep insight into a science he helped to foster and nurture. This was closely allied to his understanding of the biological theory and the genetics propounded by his close friend, the late Ernest E. Just. The fusion of the meritorious aspects of the biological sciences bolstered his own theory and practice of value theory and led him to a life-long conviction that philosophy belongs more properly to social philosophy than to metaphysics.

He used philosophical ideas to illuminate his experiences as a critic and as an expert in the arts, producing such works as ***The New Negro*** (1925), ***The Negro in Art*** (1940), ***The Negro and His Music*** (1941), ***Negro Art, Past and Present,*** and ***Race Contacts and Interracial Relations.***

In all of this critical expertise, Locke employed no ultimates or absolutes. There was, rather, the furbishing of the new—the New Negro and the burgeoning artist—subjected to criticism and analysis and subject only to the inviolate ethos which Locke thought of as democratically based. His friendship with young, struggling artists, his sponsorship of the growing youth movements, and his vision of the new youth taking a rightful place in the democratic milieu were reflections of the philosophical liberalism he professed. Professional philosophizing was turned into the kind of critical analysis which Locke equated with progress in the growth of the personality.

The development of Locke's axiological views supplied him with a *Weltanschauung* as a philosophy of life in the here and the now, the projection of value judgments into the milieu of contemporary problems. This was not a vague and actionless *modus vivendi,* but rather a system of perspectives with respect to the individual as an active participant. The belief in a value relativism was of course a rejection of all absolutes, theological as well as metaphysical. He once wrote, "We must realize more fully that values create imperatives as well as the more formally super-imposed absolutes, and that norms control our behavior as well as guide our reasoning."

This affirmation meant that a world without values would be meaningless, colorless positivism, and behavioristic pragmatism. The values of the Whitmanesque, democratic common man were to be carried on in individual and group behavior in only the most practical way. "Whether then on the plane of reason or that of action, whether 'above the battle' in the conflict of 'isms' and the 'bloodless battle of ideas' or in the battle of partisans with their conflicting and irreconcilable ways of life, the same essential strife goes on, and goes on in the name of eternal ends and defined ultimates. Our quest for certainty, motivated from the same urge, leads to similar dilemmas. The blind practicality of the common man and the disinterested practicality of the philosopher yield similar results and rationalizations."[1]

Value anarchy was rejected also, as well as any descriptive analysis of personal or class interests. The major problem for American philosophy, Locke thought, is the resolution of those conflicts so inherent in the American philosophical tradition—truth and error, means and ends, goodness and evil. And, he thought, a resurgence of some normative principles of objective validity for values is the answer—a functional version of value norms and a search for normative principles within the immediate context of valuation. The plea that Locke made in 1935 bore fruit. He asked that there be a more direct approach to the problem of value ultimates residing in their functional roles as stereotypes of feeling-attitudes and dispositional imperatives of action choices. This meant a more scientific understanding of the operative mechanisms of valuation. In this clarion call he proved himself a trailblazer, and twenty years ago he predicted that "once contemporary American thought turned systematically to the analysis of values, its empirical and functionalist approach would be considerably in its favor."

His own analytic work in value theory was abstract and schematic, and it was designed to rework the scientific value-judgments of the Austrian School and Brentano. But he was never "above the battle" even in this abstruse field, for he applied valuational judgment to American social action, free enterprise, colonialism, imperialism, war, discrimination, and the deprivation of human rights, which he associated with value anarchy. Always interested in peace, he could write, "Repose and action, integration and conflict, acceptance and projection as attitudes, create natural antinomies, irresolvable orders of values; and the only peace a scientific view of value can sanction between them is one based not upon priority and precedence but upon parity and reciprocity."[2]

Locke always returned to what he called the common denominator order of factual reality and objectivity, but he added that values are not to be reduced to this denominator. Since our imperatives are likely to be with us, we must establish some principle for regulating them—practical humane imperatives and constants of social science.

> In such a perspective, Nordicism and other rampant racialisms might achieve historical sanity or at least prudential common-sense to halt at the natural frontiers of genuinely shared loyalties and not sow their own eventual downfall through forced loyalties and the counteractions which they inevitably breed. Social reciprocity for value loyalties is but a new name for the old virtue of tolerance, yet it does bring the question of tolerance down from the lofty thin air of idealism and chivalry to the plane of enlightened self-interest and the practical possibilities of value-sharing. As a working principle it divorces proper value loyalty from unjustifiable value bigotry, releases a cult from blind identification with creed and dogma, and invests no value interest with monopoly or permanent priority.[3]

Since there was no immediate expectation of any transvaluation of values, Locke's belief in relativism led him to foresee the end of absolutism and totalitarianism in every form. "Cultural relativism . . . is the culminating phase of relativistic philosophy, and it is bound to have a greater influence than any other phase of relativism upon our conception and practise of values."[4]

Locke thought that the reciprocity and tolerance which might emerge once there was a genuine sense of value-sharing would lead to integration in a real direction. These views were the natural outgrowth of his perspective as to brotherhood values and the other-regarding outlook of scientifically-minded persons who had no regard for bigotry, "race," or inferiority-value anarchy. His prescience was more Cassandra-like than he himself admitted in 1935.

> But if reciprocity and tolerance on the large scale are to await the incorporation of the greater community the day of our truce of values is far off. Before any such integrations can take place, the narrowness of our provincialisms must be broken down and our sectarian fanaticisms lose some of their force and glamour. A philosophy aiding this is an ally of the larger integration of life . . . such reconstruction will never bring us to a basis of complete cultural uniformity or commonmindedness about values. Whatever integrations occur . . . whether of thought and social system . . . cultural and value pluralism of some sort will still prevail. Indeed in the atmosphere induced by relativism and tolerance such differentiation is likely to increase rather than just continue. . . . But a theoretical break has come, and seems to have set in simultaneously from several quarters . . . the convergence of these trends indicates a new center for the thought and insight of our present generation, and that would seem to be a philosophy and a psychology, and perhaps too, a sociology, pivoted around functional relativism.[5]

As a critic, Alain Locke may not take his place with the immortals and perhaps not with the New Criticism, for his vision was more stereoscopic. His critical acumen opened new paths for others to follow and this broad view made him a spokesman in the best sense. His humility never allowed for bombast or pompousness. He was too conscious of his limitations and too aware of the circumstances which circumscribed his own career. It is fitting to recall Locke's own self-estimate when he was asked, in 1934, for a self-analysis. He replied that he would like to claim as his life motto the Greek principle, "Nothing in excess," but that he had to wear another badge, "All things with a reservation," his badge of circumstances.

Notes

1. "Values and Imperatives," *American Philosophy, Today and Tomorrow,* ed. by Horace M. Kallen and Sidney Hook (New York, 1935), p. 315.
2. *Ibid.,* p. 326.
3. *Ibid.,* p. 327.
4. *Ibid.,* p. 327.
5. *Ibid.,* p. 328.

WILLIAM STANLEY BRAITHWAITE (LECTURE DATE 1955)

SOURCE: Braithwaite, William Stanley. "Alain Locke's Relationship to the Negro in American Literature." *Phylon* 18, no. 2 (1957): 166-73.

In the following lecture, first delivered before the Alain Locke Memorial Committee Workshop in 1955, Braithwaite claims that Locke's purpose in his writing was to liberate and gain recognition for the African American "soul."

You will note that in the title selected for this address there is an emphasis on Negro authorship rather than on Negro literature. There is intended a subtlety of implication which reflects, and I hope convincingly to the discerning mind, the spirit of Alain Locke. He was a scholar in philosophy in which he took for his chief concept the theory of values. The doctrine of values, which Thoreau pursued with such dismay to the Puritan skeptics, has always seemed to me the keystone of philosophic thinking, for if the function of philosophy is to estimate and appraise the worth and inevitability of human thought and action, then it is only by determining values can standards be established for the guidance and operation of human conduct and relationships. These standards serve the interests of society, interchangeable as they are with heritage and tradition which are the props of conformity; but it is the individual that counts in the maintenance of standards, for out of reason and emotion, the imagination and intuition, with their interactions of reality and illusion, is compounded the kind of society that prevails in one era or another. I never have been able, though I confess that better Hegelian minds than mine can, to separate aesthetics from philosophy—philosophy to my belief being the science of Truth, if I may use the term science as connoting method rather than formula or finality, and aesthetics being the science of Beauty. Thus we have the two motivating energies, as Henry Adams would say, sustaining the spirit of man.

How, one may ask, do these observations concern Alain Locke's relationship to Negro authorship? Very decidedly, and effectively, I would reply. And to confirm the reply, we will have to glance cursorially, as the limitation of time and occasion imposes, at the history of Negro authorship.

From the beginnings in the 1760's to the antebellum period there was produced some verse, verse of moral reflections and indignant protest against the conditions of slavery, in techniques wholly imitative of English models; there were slavery-songs which we call "spirituals," and work-songs which gave vocal expression to the unremitting and exploited labor on the plantations of the South. These spirituals and worksongs are the first genuine folk-expression in America. From Eighteen Hundred to the close of the Civil War, there was a continuous stream of prose writings, crowned with the unique production of slave-narratives, autobiographical records of fugitive bondsmen, out of which materials of harrowing and dramatic escapes were fashioned the first attempts at creative expression, the novels of Martin R. Delany, Frank J. Webb, and William Wells Brown. One cannot read the narratives of Gustavus Vassa, Frederick Douglass, and William Wells Brown, the most impressive among the large body of these writings, without deep respect and admiration for the character and spirit of a handicapped people who for two centuries and a half had been assimilating slowly and agonizingly the mores of Western civilization. It was more truly during this period than at any later period that the Negro passed *per aspera ad astra,* and reached that glory through the sheer and indomitable exercise of his will.

As a contemporary historian, Richard Bardolph, of the University of North Carolina, says of this period, from 1831 to 1865:

> [It was] in the nation's social history preeminently the time of the rise of the common man, effectuated by wide-ranging reform efforts increasingly channeled into the anti-slavery movement. The Negro leadership adjusted itself easily to this formula and, convinced of the futility of slave-revolts on the Turner model, worked now in close association with a growing army of northern folk who espoused positive programs.

Through this period, not in single and isolated instances, but in a group consciousness the Negro expressed and gave clearance to the articulated impulse of his nature as a human being. That consciousness was wholly dominated and tempered by the institution of slavery and its far-reaching influence upon the civil, political, and social character of American life both in the North and the South. The spirit of the Negro was fueled but from one source, Christianity, in whose hope lay the single promise of his escape from the suppressions and discriminations hedging in his participation as a member of a democratic society. In his effort to escape he wrote furiously and voluminously, and created a body of discoursive and subjective literature out of a natural aptitude for self-expression. Indeed, the period historically may be compared to the Saxon period in Britain, when the conversion to Christianity was the all-absorbing inspiration for literary expression. It is true there were no alliterative verse Beowulfs or Cademons, but the prose writers to whom I have just referred were inspired by the hope of freedom as the Saxon writers were inspired by the exalted visions of Christianity. Those Saxon writers were the fertile soil in which Chaucer flowered, just as surely as the slave narratives were the fertile soil in which flowered the talents of Dunbar.

The name of Dunbar brings us to the third period of Negro authorship—the period from 1896 to the death of Dunbar in 1906—with a scattering of minor and ineffectual rhymsters revolving satellites in orbits of the major figures, Dunbar and Chesnutt. In Dunbar and Chesnutt were first expressed the sensibility of an aesthetic form in Negro authorship that found evocation in the adequate techniques of specific artistic mediums. It was this matter of form that up to the second decade of the Twentieth Century was the undiscovered continent for Negro authorship. The Negro, however, has not been alone in regarding form as the structure of language in all its variations of prose and verse; or in the plastic arts, modelling of clay as it is cast into bronze or polished in marble, as exemplified by a Phidias or a Rodin, or in the pictorial arts as exemplified by a Raphael or a Rubens, by a Picasso or a Matisse. Form is a compound of abstract elements that make up the thoughts and feelings of mankind—his desires and dreams, his joys and sorrows, his hopes and despairs, and which imbue the materials of his experiences, as the spirit imbues the flesh and makes of those experiences a manifest in the materials and techniques serving as a witness to man's troubled or serene consciousness.

The literature of the Negro that I have alluded to in the foregoing was a legacy handed down to serve as a springboard for re-conversion for some perceptive Twentieth Century mind. Please be reassured that what I am about to say is wholly in the aesthetic sense. There was, indeed, this flood of literature, a body of splendid content; but it lacked a soul, and again, I remind you that I am speaking in the aesthetic sense. The mind that gave it a soul was Alain Locke's. At first it was a timid soul, either unaware of, or a bit mistrustful of, its sanctions. But it developed with confidence and conviction under his gentle and encouraging urgency. And suddenly, at the end of the first quarter of this Century it blossomed in ***The New Negro*** that he fathered. Negro authorship had come of age and received the inheritance his wise mind and transcendent idealism had prophesied.

That evolutionary work—and mind you, I do not call it revolutionary—was the expression of a mind and spirit that had been tutored in the universal law of humanity—that law of "unity in diversity," as Locke called it. A law whose highest doctrine, he adds, may be, to quote him, "carried out to a practical degree of reciprocity." This was the demand that Locke made of Negro authorship, and along with it, the concomitant demand for its recongition by the white world. We can interpret the writings as contained in ***The New Negro*** as specifically of literary interest, and, perhaps, its greatest importance lies not always directly on the surface, but indirectly in the potentiality of a new literary concept in the intellectual and imaginative development of the Negro in authorship. For Locke's discerning spirit elevated the worth and significance of Negro life, and he included in the work essays dealing with the subjects of social, economic, artistic and civil importance woven into the fabric of human relations which give design to the patterns of American democracy.

One of the essential requisites for an emancipated Negro authorship, was, as I have hinted, the possession of a soul. Locke did not demand, nor would he have had any sympathy with, the divorce of Negro authorship from the interest of Negro life. He repeatedly extolled the richness and variety of Negro life and character, but his passionate concern was that the Negro as an artist should treat them on the same high level of interpretation and execution as the best artists of other races. One of Locke's great masters was G. Lowes Dickinson, the English Platonist, who had declared in his Ingersol Lecture at Harvard that there was no difference between the races of man, except in the growth of the soul. And that affirmation was echoed by Locke, particularly in its application to Negro life when he stated in his Foreward to ***The New Negro,*** that "Negro life is not only establishing new contacts and founding new centers, it is finding a new soul."

With this acquisition of a new and developing soul, there is another observation which Locke made, of tremendous importance to Negro authorship. His leadership in cultural aspiration, in the breaching of barriers that obstructed the paths to a full participation in the aesthetic expression of Negro authorship was established inevitably with this assertion:

> It was rather the necessity for fuller, truer self-expression, the realization of the unwisdom of allowing social discrimination to segregate him mentally, and a counter-attitude to cramp and fetter his own living—and so the 'spite-wall' that intellectuals built over the 'color-line' has happily been taken down.

In this, the refusal to be segregated mentally, and in a counter-attitude, to be cramped and fettered, he previsioned a result that was the main responsibility of Negro authorship. It laid a difficult, but not impossible, burden upon that authorship.

That Locke was confident Negro authorship was capable of bearing the burden is attested to time and again in his writings. Unlike any of his contemporaries, he knew that the roots of the American Negro's imagination were fertilized in the primitive arts of Africa. All the Negro intellectuals were stirred only by the political and economic significance of Africa and deplored often in undisciplined invectives her exploitation by the European overlords. But Locke discovered a cultural heritage that may have given the American Negro his basic attributes for artistic expression. The heritage as a factual record of continuity was severed by slavery. Wrote Locke:

> We will never know and cannot estimate how much technical African skill was blotted out in America. The hardships of cotton and rice-field labor, the crudities of the hoe, the axe and the plow reduced the typical Negro hand to a gnarled stump, incapable of fine craftsmanship even if the materials, patterns, and artistic incentives had been available. But we may believe there was memory of beauty; since by way of compensation, some obviously artistic urges flowed even with the peasant Negro toward the only channels of expression left open—those of song, graceful movement and poetic speech.

The memory of beauty! What an exalted declaration of a heritage that was to sprout impoverished as a plant for nigh three centuries, until under some miraculous bestowal of fertilization it was to blossom and flower—and that flowering due largely to the beneficial spirit of Alain Locke.

That is too much to claim for this man, you will think, whose memory we are this day honoring. But show me another who had the intensified and cultural dedication to exercise the shaping influence that was his. In saying this, I do not intend to minimize the knowledge and the desire of many who sought to encourage and inspire their compatriots, but their efforts ran in less exalted channels, channels that ran through the temporary realities of material things and affairs. Locke's was that enduring field of the imaginative representation of human emotions and actions, symbolized and pictured in narrative and rhythm, which constitute a flowering of the human soul that approaches nearest to the divine. Behind all this was the shadowy tapestry of a race whose most assertive identities were tangled in a wave of civilization that would distort and devalue its most precious self-expansion of physical growth and an imposed delusion of spiritual serenity. The transient and confused conditions of human life make it imperative that some transcendent quality of faith be found, above the routine practice of prayer and sacrament, to assure man of his spiritual integrity, of his collaborative sense as a child of nature. Beyond his physical observation and relationship exist a realm of immeasurable, abstract, and everlasting Reality. It has been the unceasing aspiration of man, both in the mood of reverence and defiance, in all ages, and by all peoples, however divergent in racial origins, to penetrate that realm by some measurement of his consciousness. The most effective effort has been made through man's imagination. The borderline of that penetration exists in Sir Arthur Eddington's dictum that the greatest thing in the physical universe is the brain of man. But this is only an arrival at the bourne. To cross it we must accept the concept of that rebellious Puritan, and great American novelist, Nathaniel Hawthorne, in all of whose romances was pursued one imaginative doctrine, the throwing of man's soul against Eternity. Here was a measurement, however infinitesimal, of man's worth and destiny, adumbrating his inheritance both as a child of God and of nature.

What a circuitous way, may well be your charge, that I have taken to declare that this was Alain Locke's profound purpose in his philosophic-aesthetic writings and promptings on Negro authorship: that the soul of the Negro be thrown against Eternity!

FROM THE AUTHOR

THE VOICE OF THE NEW NEGRO

The Younger Generation comes, bringing its gifts. They are the first fruits of the Negro Renaissance. Youth speaks, and the voice of the New Negro is heard.

SOURCE: Alain Locke, excerpt from *The New Negro,* A. and C. Boni, 1925.

In an essay Locke wrote on the **"Orientation of Hope"** for the *Baha'i World,* he set down this pregnant phrase: "For those of us who are truly dawn-minded." In its context it has an application to his attitude towards Negro authorship. Further, in the same essay he wrote this: "It is the occasion and opportunity of convincing many who were skeptical because they could not see the impending failure of the old order." Here in a differing concern was Locke's re-affirmation of his insight into the literary progress that was to function freely without psychological restrictions, when the 'spite-walls' were demolished, and the mentality of the Negro artist was uncramped and unfettered by the wasteful intensity of a counter-attitude.

This dawn-mindedness of Locke's broke the new day of Negro authorship. It was he who introduced the phrase that described the first group-flowerings of writings by Negro authors. It was the "heralding sign," an "unusual outburst of creative expression," which enabled him to say in the final sentence of his Foreword to ***The New Negro*** that, "Justifiably, then, we speak of the offerings of this book embodying these ripening forces as culled from the first fruits of the Negro Renaissance."

It was a period of enlightenment, too, this proclaimed Renaissance of creative expression, of which Locke was the propelling spirit as surely as was Erasmus the propelling spirit of the Northern Renaissance in the early Sixteenth Century. Locke glowed with the same humanism which made Erasmus quicken the thirst of optimism and faith among the multitude. As with Erasmus humanism ceased to be the exclusive privilege of the few, so with Locke his humanistic philosophy was based on the common acquaintance and appreciation of the Negro's creative works by his own as well as by the peoples of other races.

There is one more principle in the hierarchy of Locke's program for the liberation and recognition of the Negro author, which he insisted upon as essential, and to which I shall refer briefly. In a sense it was the most important, for it was the keystone of the aesthetic edifice he built in all his writings and teachings. This was the doctrine of objectivity. He was aware, and painfully so, as many of us have been, of the physical proscriptions of Negro life—he had himself tasted them in spite of his intellectual triumphs—and it was his passionate devotion to the effort that the Negro artist should not be depressed and hindered by mental and emotional proscriptions. How many times in the old days of our association and discussions when he visited me at Arlington did he with that delicate but penetrating dialectic and logic of which he was a master insist that the Negro author, if he was to become fully emancipated, must of necessity work in a mood of objectivity. And what, pray, did he mean by being objective? Simply, the release from self-pity, from the illogical conviction that the Negro was the only people to suffer indignities, that the need for sympathy should be made imperative by the exposure of sore wounds, rather then by the therapeutic healing by the inner spirit, and that the imagination alone, however encased in the shell of ethnic varieties of human flesh, was subject to the same determinations. This objectivity of Locke's demand for the Negro author reminds me of the quintessential summation made by dear old Colonel Thomas Wentworth Higginson, when he solved the whole racial problem, and especially for the enlightenment of the American nation, by declaring that like all other people "the Negro was intensely human." This was what Locke meant by the objective mood, and through its exercise and manifestation by the Negro author the latter could destroy the stereotypes and produce instead of lifeless automatons and clichéd experiences a vitality of characterization and the mutations of human experience.

In this way would the Negro author, especially in his fiction, achieve a comedy of manners. The models were a Jane Austen, a William Dean Howells, an Edith Wharton, or an E. M. Delafield. Jessie Fauset in four novels, published a quarter of a century ago, was an example of the unity in diversity which was Locke's artistic credo for the new era. In Miss Fauset's *There Is Confusion, Blum Bun, The Chinaberry Tree,* and especially in the devastatingly ironic *Comedy: American Style,* was

Locke's credo practiced with distinction. I mention this author and these novels because they fulfill the aesthetic theories Locke preached for the spiritual marriage of race and art. And I shadow the mention with the regretful knowledge that they stand alone in this particular genre of the Negro's literary activity.

I want to close by bringing to your attention an episode in a novel by Wallace Thurman, entitled *Infants of the Spring,* because it shows how directly Locke announced, in one instance, and to those most concerned, his gospel of aesthetic liberation. In brief outline, the story is this: A Negro lady of intelligence and means, without gifts of artistic expression herself, but devoted to the cause of Negro culture, gave her somewhat pretentious home to a group of poets, musicians and composers, painters and novelists, where they could live and work in freedom from economic pressures. The group was inter-racial, lived a free Bohemian life, and in all things of cultural intent regarded themselves as intellectual reformers. The dwelling was called Niggeratti Manor. They were drifting aimlessly upon a springtide of emotion, each with his or her individual idiosyncrasy of dream and idealism, without as a community being grounded in the virtuous fundamentals of life and art. One of the members heard of a man whom he thought could bring them a message of enlightenment and confidence, and they invited him to come to New York and address them. This man was a Dr. Parkes, who had achieved a notable reputation in the inner circles of both white and Negro intellectualism, and also in the academic world of both races. Dr. Parkes was a thin, but palpable disguise of Alain Locke. Of this there is no doubt when you read the novelist's description of Dr. Parkes' personality:

> He was a mother hen clucking at her chicks. Small, dapper, with sensitive features, graying hair, a dominating head, and restless hands and feet, he smiled benevolently at his brood. Then in his best continental manner, which he had acquired during four years at European universities, he began to speak.

And what, this commentator asks, did he say? There were some things that his audience of Negro artists did not like, and particularly about their psychological roots in Africa by virtue of a remembered beauty. Here is what Dr. Parkes said:

> 'You are the outstanding personalities of a new generation. On you depends the future of your race. You are not, as were your predecessors, concerned with donning armor, and clashing swords with the enemy in the public square. You are finding both an escape and a weapon in beauty, which beauty when created by you will cause the American white man to reestimate the Negro's value to his civilization, cause him to realize that the American black man is too valuable, too potential of utilitarian accomplishment, to be kept downtrodden and segregated.
>
> 'Because of your concerted storming up Parnassus, new vistas will be spread open to the entire race. The Negro in the South will no more know peonage, Jim Crowism or loss of ballot, and the Negro everywhere in America will know complete freedom and equality.
>
> 'But,' and here his voice took on a more serious tone, 'to accomplish this, your pursuit of beauty must be vital and lasting. I am somewhat fearful of the decadent strain which seems to have filtered into most of your work. Oh, yes, I know you are children of the age and all that, but you must not, like your paleface contemporaries, wallow in the mire of post-Victorian license. You have too much at stake. You must have ideals. You should become . . . well, let me suggest your going back to your racial roots, cultivating a healthy paganism based on African traditions.'
>
> The reference to the African traditions brought forth a volley of protest and rejection from the assembled artists. 'What old black pagan heritage?' asked one. 'How can I go back to African ancestors when their blood is so diluted and their country and times so far away?' another questioned. And this sentiment was unequivocally affirmed by one who said flatly, 'I ain't got no African spirit!'
>
> 'I think you have missed the point,' responded Dr. Parkes. 'I mean you should develop your inherited spirit.'

What Alain Locke in the guise of Dr. Parkes was trying to tell this group of young hopefuls was that Western civilization and culture were the fruits of the remembered beauty of the Greeks—a people who had also known slavery—and that similarly, the literature produced by the Negro in modern America should be leavened by the remembered beauty bequeathed by primitive Africa. He did not demand, or even remotely suggest, that the mores, nor the landscape, of primitive Africa be used as materials for the body or framework of literature by Negro authors; but that modern life, all its tragedies and comedies, all its romances and social complexities, and racial dramas, was at hand to be informed and made lustrous by the spirit of a remembered beauty.

And that spirit of beauty which was Alain Locke is before us today leading, as a ball of fire by night and a pillar of cloud by day, to the promised land of literary fulfillment, that we may add a new glory to American culture!

DOUGLAS K. STAFFORD (ESSAY DATE 1961)

SOURCE: Stafford, Douglas K. "Alain Locke; The Child, the Man, the People." *The Journal of Negro Education* 30, no. 1 (winter 1961): 25-34.

In the following essay, Stafford claims that Locke's childhood years did more to shape his work than has been acknowledged.

A discussion of Alain Locke's thought would ordinarily go back to his years with James, Santayana, Royce, and von Muensterburg, a sound enough beginning and one on which almost any interested student might base a revealing and stimulating study. This ought to be done some day. But there is another, less well known side to his intellectual genesis, the story of a precocious only child. No one need say that without those great teachers in later life his work would most likely have been of a different caliber, being less ably undertaken. What I want to say is that the earlier years did far more to shape the vein and tenor of his work than is usually guessed. To probe cautiously into the influences surrounding his childhood may unfold naturally the growth of his thought and teaching. There being no biography, only those who knew him well or listened to him carefully may see how this is so. This memoir is only one testimony, and many more are needed to round out the story of this man and his outlook.

With most of us purest epistemic accident dictates that no two people should know us in quite the same way. With reassurance as frequently as with regret, one reflects how this is but the nature of things, being severely valid in that thing we call knowing people. With Locke this kaleidoscopic effect is calculated with both cleverness and good faith. It arises with the simple wish both to be whatever a friend needed most and to bless that friend by letting him give whatever happened to be his most cherished gift. He did not bring his friends together. They will recall, I believe, how seldom anyone else was encountered at Grove Street in the Village or at that marvellously cluttered set of rooms in Washington down R Street from the Charles Hotel. He set almost as great a store upon the individuality of those he knew as upon his own privacy. These ways made of him a riddle which, sensible as it may have been in his lifetime, may be ready now for an illumination intended to help understanding rather than to pry.

He liked it quiet. His annoyance went unconcealed, a thing rare in this most urbane of men, when a doorbell, the telephone, or a backfiring automobile interrupted the delicate spell of two thinking people alone together. It was there, not at the New School, Howard University, The American Seminar in Austria, or at the University of Wisconsin, that he did his finest teaching. He did his best when he was thinking aloud. Uttered reflection, even from the lips of a master, is gravid with tension when heard in the classroom. Too many different people are there, and Alain Locke seemed always aware of what was fitting. His standards were high, but they tempted him neither to strain the intellectual range of his students unduly nor to relinquish his touching respect for those hypersensitivities bequeathed them by culture. The teacher who deals with the individual in surroundings precisely as he would have them can liberate his pupil's mind with deft shocks and sudden starts. As the group grows and the situation is less of the master's own making, the mind must be more gently separated from its prejudices and led less precipitously from the limits of its own provinciality. Locke knew this, and, beloved as it may have made him, it possibly robbed his classroom of his most vital presence. He had no such problem in the dimly lit chamber where, behind a massive black piano, the ashes of his mother reposed in a finely embellished casket. Schonberg's *Verklærte nacht* bewitched the air. His hand would find a shoulder, only to rest there in a contentment too eloquent and rare for its proper name in the Western World unless somehow known as the moment of the "I and Thou." For these reasons he kept his friends apart. In this way an inescapable condition of human existence became in his knowing hands the poetry of shared private experience, the paradox which gives to the varied texture of beauty its unifying thread.

He was a Negro child of Northern Reconstruction, a fertile seedbed for ambiguous experience. This will be hard for some to understand, regarding as they do that post-bellum bitterness as an exclusively Southern phenomenon. A closer look, however, reveals that critical ebb in Northern morale of which Dorothy Canfield Fisher has so candidly written. Those who had marched, sometimes under sordid duress, sometimes like crusaders, and given so much did not witness what they had hoped for. They experienced a stage of painful embarrassment and restless disillusionment when the new colored citizens did not at once seem fit to carry the responsibilities of full-grown men. There were some unpleasant second thoughts about things now found readily understandable. The irresponsible output of Southern apologists for a lost cause did nothing to bring clarity to a scene of uncertain transition. The

North itself, in its more thickly populated areas, had found a new use—or abuse—for the Negro: he could be used to account for the economic frustrations of the working white man. Alain Locke grew up in Philadelphia, but he was not untouched by the tragic era. The late eighteen hundreds brought chafing marginality into his life early enough to spare him its more damning impact in adulthood. He was just far enough removed from Jim Crow at its most brutal to let him know quite soon the subtler meanings of racial dynamics.

His mother was happily a woman who knew to articulate the ostensibly obvious until she could divine the place of her family in a society more clearly and far sooner than society had made up its own mind. She knew and taught her son that authors of social tone did not necessarily understand what gave them their power any more than they saw what took it away. She was convinced that the ultimate shibboleth was social intelligence. One ceased to be the passive clay of communal momentum insofar as he knew where the forces gathered and how they were spent.

She was one of the earliest followers of Felix Adler, that honest young Rabbi who in 1876 founded the Ethical Culture Society. The movement attracted her not at all for its tenet of sex purity, considerably more for its concern with the working classes, and won her over for its stress upon continued intellectual development. Aside from the Society of Friends it was in many ways the most liberal of respectable organizations open to the Negro, explicitly providing for his participation in all its projects. Its programs were usually educational and extended from the Kindergarten to the university in scope. Many wisely question its equation of religion and morality but the mother of Alain Locke saw in this a pathway to both desirable character formation and spiritual development untrammeled by sectarian bias and superstition. There was too much of terror and hysteria in Negro Protestantism, and the more restrained bodies of worship seemed sterile if not merely indifferent where the need for social change was concerned. She had not borne a son to preserve a dogma that offered no more than emotional escape or empty respectability. Her acute aesthetic sense allowed her to save for him the poetry, music, and truth of Negro Protestantism while sparing him its brutal frenzy and then pitiful temporal helplessness.

Those two talked about everything. Nothing was taken for granted. Nothing was spared their scrutiny. They tried to pinpoint the moral quality in every relationship. All their conversations displayed the same disdain for taboo and thirst after rationality, and then they put their thoughts away, knowing they would spend their lives talking about them over and over again in the same and different ways. This explicit approach to growing up once prompted him to make the remark least worthy of him and his subject I ever heard. "Sterling Brown," he once muttered," is a highly talented man, but he would have been a great genius if his father had not been a Baptist minister." What he really meant was that he, Alain Locke, could not have looked upon American civilization with his peculiarly creative perspective had *his* father been that Baptist minister.

It is really very hard to say just what his father was to him. Alain found it hard to remember anything more than a vague series of quite probably unfair impressions. The blurred paternal image lends itself to more understanding if we look at what loomed dismally above it. Even today it is difficult for the colored father to fill his role in a manner convincing and other than disquieting to his young. They learn early and know well (especially boys) the limits beyond which his authority can not extend. Save under the most fortunate circumstances, his position is ambiguous: asserted master at home; hemmed in by social usage, conciliatory if not servile elsewhere—a complex posture, one frighteningly suited to leave unsated childhood's hunger after security. Folk wisdom has telescoped the matter, and E. Franklin Frazier has documented it in his studies of the Negro family. "Ain't nobody free in this country," the saying goes, "but white men and colored women." Rub out the more salient flaws in this gem and see what you have. The situation was worse and more puzzsling then. The Negro was expected to stay in his place, but nobody, North or South, had told either himself or the Negro what place had been set aside. The courts had not heard Plessy and Ferguson, and the ruling had yet even to be barbarized.

This much he recalled to me about his father, who died when his son was quite young. The man had, he said, a great mustache and sometimes tried to give paternal kisses. The son found the hirsute mass unpleasant, like a wiry mesh, coarse, insensate, and meaninglessly interposed between faces that should have met.

Alain remembered that he had once been struck, the only time, he said. His father intended to punish him for some wrong, an offense long forgotten by the time he told the story—an interesting lapse in one whose right hand monitored his left in a fashion so scrupulous as to delight one eminent analyst, his good friend Benjamin Karpman. His mother was more forceful than he could recall at any other time. She drew her son close, shielding his body as if anticipating a thorough thrashing, and vowed to leave her husband if he ever struck the child again. That denouement pleased and comforted him all his life, and he seemed to think it a critical moment in his education.

But there was much more to it than this. He was frail from infancy, and it early became apparent that he was afflicted with a rheumatic heart. He remembered the bicycle schedule gratefully as the most helpful medical advice. He was to ride one block and walk two until he reached stages when different combinations were prescribed. He followed these instructions religiously. He was intelligent about his heart as he was about everything else, and it did not utterly fail him until after retirement.

How did so frail a boy fare away from home? "I never had a fight," he said, smiling with poorly disguised pride but weeks before his final illness. "I was always too polite to invite one. No empty, senseless pride, you see. Now and then some boy was determined, but there were ways out. I walked backward, never taking my eyes from him. Soon a bigger boy would come to my rescue, warning my enemy, 'you leave Roy Locke alone; he's a good boy.'"

But his upbringing was not entirely of the tough-minded variety. He was profoundly though gently influenced by Froebelian pedagogy. Everyone knows that Mrs. Carl Schurz set up the first American Kindergarten in 1855, and Miss Elizabeth Peabody's little school in Boston is almost equally well known. But this innovation, while not to be confused with countless vestiges of the dame school, was somewhat more widely spread than is generally supposed. Some philanthropic body, quite possibly the Ethical Culture Society, had imported a Froebelian teacher to Philadelphia. Alain regretted that the years had left her in apparent anonymity and spoke lovingly in his old age of the days he had spent in her care.

She faced him with Froebel's toy-symbols, forms which, their designer had intended, neither conveyed a denotation nor played with some set of mind. If the master of Keilhau was correct, his tools for children were sufficiently indeterminate to throw the child back onto pre-lingually developed resources. The hope is that the child may enjoy some awareness of what he is like and wants before we undertake explicitly to tell him what answers are best. Fulfilling an idealist blueprint of mind and knowledge, the child arranges his own world, one genuinely pervaded by unity, since here the very first articulate ideas are of the child's own making. The self is not an alloy of inner and outer forms. Unity is said further to be nurtured in this system because the mind is left free from external pressure to discover in itself the bond of oneness belonging to all creatures.

Alain credited these experiences with what was his most striking personal trait, an unusual freedom from inner conflict. He was able, he felt, to distinguish between those things belonging to his temperament and earliest sub-conscious learning on the one hand, and on the other those objective necessities in society demanding respect. The two may exist in harmonious union, but they are obviously not the same. The difference between the two (a difference which Froebel seems obscurely to deny, but one with which Ethical Culture must sooner or later concern itself) must not be a point of wasteful friction. It must be refined by intelligent examination and behavior; hence, his charming dictum, "all things with qualifications." He could envision no spontaneous individuality inherently unable to enjoy a productive existence in any environment—provided, of course, that both were clearly conceived. Clarity here depends as much upon being honest as upon being keen regarding what really belongs to oneself, for individuality is corrupted when we mistake what looks good in another and seems to pay off, for our very own. Such clarity does not preclude forthright borrowing, adoption, exchange, or even the hybrid development. It does, however, bar denying parts of oneself and blindly taking on alien superficialities to which one can not offer the harmony which relies upon fertile fields and understanding care. Alain Locke made a career of expounding the niceties of this argument in terms of diverse peoples and cultures, but the outlook itself stems from his childhood. He found out then that one must first recognize the genuineness of whatever marks him off from others before he can take a fruitful moral stance before his environment.

His first explicitly sexual experience took place in a neighboring cellar where a darkroom had been set up. He could revisit the interlude more than half a century later, as throughout his life, without shame, embarrassment, or apology. There was, at least on his part, no clumsy adolescent fumbling of the kind that can distort later erotic attitudes. It was, he said, just as he had expected and wanted it to be. This discovery of his most secret self came when he awakened with another in an unlighted room to some part of the universe that he could sense and know in no other way. He had sinned against no one. Consenting equally, they had joined in a new way the total rhythm, however varied or enriched with seeming dissonance its cadence. There was no need for slyly written notes or the awful waste of childlishly concealed passion. He went straight home and told his mother. They talked sensibly about the event and what it could mean.

The only surprise to him later in this was the naturalness with which he found himself this close to another besides his mother. His only pets were fish and birds, and, as he once laughingly remarked, "You can't get much interaction there." He went about on boyish jaunts, peer, but of a different species. "I think," he mused, "those white boys must have looked upon me in much the same way as ducks upon a chicken." Race was not the only thing. How could they figure out a fellow forbidden by health from doing those things they took for granted as the only possible meaningful stuff of which to make a boy's life? The puzzle was not at all unscrambled by his intelligent and ungrudging acceptance of his condition. He did not even call them limitations, bridles upon a Penrod or Tom Sawyer will, simply because he had no such will. His enlightened upbringing, the security he drew from a deeply felt kinship with things he was not and could never be, made his strongest wish to be what and how he Alain Locke could be without unrealistically denying his ties to the world around him.

An anecdote may show his feelings and behavior better. He shared this story with me in April of 1954, during that weekend on which I last saw his living face. He had always told me stories, recollections of Claude McKay's unpublished notes on Russia, Countee Cullen's Easter Sunday visits as a young man, how he and Fen had called on John Dewey to offer Cordon Bleu and birthday greetings—always interesting, often beautiful. Many times the humor was more than a trifle too sophisticated for his listener, but he never, I believe, told the same story twice to anyone. But this time he told me tale after tale of his childhood, and I truly shuddered, thinking back to that superstition that we see and speak of our earliest years more frequently and vividly as death draws nearer. (Minutes later, I asked if he would do some certain thing "if he got well." His response was sharp. "You mean *when* I get well". He apologized in a moment, explaining that death, as Wittgenstein has remarked, is not an experience since we do not survive it. To this he added that it is not to be feared, but we need not take it into account.) This week-end, but weeks before Arthur Fawcett sent me the news and Professor Ulich reminded me that "he would not want us to grieve," he told me the very simple but important story of the swimming hole.

We were walking about in Washington Square, and he was speaking of Rimbaud in a very special tone and Bodenheim when his verse still showed promise. He reminded me, as he need not have, that he had introduced me to that courtly derelict on just such a stroll as this years before. He raised his furled umbrella, that object so much a part of him that his students and friends knew so well as his cane, and pointed out Mrs. Roosevelt's rooms in a nearby hotel. (He knew if one were a frightened, uninformed person in New York, but he played the host without making him feel the country cousin.)

It was then.

"I have waded from time to time at resorts, but I never swam and never wished to. I understand temptation but I never wished to do things that would harm me if I understood how they would. No horses or fast cars. I tried once with my mother to drive, and we decided that it was not for us. Too late, you see? No skill. But I used to go swimming with those boys. I might dangle a foot, but the most important thing was watching the clothes. A prankster, you see, could tie them into knots or make off with them. The joke was not yet threadbare. It was a filthy hole, but I sat on the bank. Besides, they had to provide for me, make me necessary. They couldn't understand me, but they liked me and had to have me involved. Don't forget now, that I saw them as the chicken sees the ducks—where the chicken is brighter, of course." He laughed, not at them, but with the delicious flavor of the memory.

The surface of the bank was slick with mud. He was squatted upon its crest, discovering the changing curves and shapes of moving bodies. The appearing and disappearing flesh robbed him of control. Pink, tan, and youthfully fuzzed sinews sped into and out of the murky mess. He was fairly hypnotized. His staunchest and most admired defender stood poised to dive from a coarse old plank, his dripping body gleaming in the sunlight. Alain gasped and fell in. The diver never plunged. The whole naked troop came to his rescue, begging, even before they could be sure he was alive, that he say nothing to his mother of the accident, lest he not be allowed to come with them again. "I'm sorry," he gasped, "but I'll have to tell my mother. She'll let me come back." They wrung out his clothes, dried him with theirs, and watched him head homeward for a long talk with his mother, they fearful all the while that "the chicken" would come no more.

> "Failure to face facts has made America and made it sick. Men crossing the continent with near primitive tools. The Founding Fathers ignored the absence of concrete precedents for their dreams until those hopes became phrases which no one could discount. Before the country knew it they were hallowed traditions and institutions. Over all the years when Negroes were being funneled into this country no one took a really clear-eyed look at the frightful size of the colored population that was building up. Even today the figure is more than most minds can handle. We scoffed at the technical obstacles to nuclear fission. And so we have that, but we shelter ourselves in just the same way from other things like facts about race, sex and economics. We read, we talk, we sometimes listen, but we are too seldom cerebral enough. When it is done, we say "nevertheless" or "still" and go on to state in less clear terms our favorite superstitions.
>
> "Face the facts, child, face the facts and then be intelligent about them. That is what induction means when it's most valuable—except that today we must escape the statistical illusion. And something else, you see, to learn just how the brain can take shortcuts when a significant variable has been subconsciously selected—perhaps the only one worth the time it takes to observe it—in a particular case, that is.
>
> "Everything, everything, you see, child, everything with qualifications.
>
> "Oh, you know what will happen to Negroes. These new opportunities will get them into a great deal of nonsense. Middle class American nonsense, of course, but we can't afford it. That won't keep us out of it, though. And then we will flow into certain—say teaching, civil rights, religion—jobs, you know, where whitefolk have long pictured us, whether with hope, resentment, or ridicule. Oh, they will complain, as about Jews in science and finance, for the number will seem much larger no matter how one is arguing."

This is the way in which he chatted, now gravely, now with ironic levity, but always scintillating. His gifts were numerous, but his instinct for the cultural interplay of aesthetic developments was without equal. Here his mind was daringly seminal. He set out to tell the Negro his fortune with this gift, pointing out the future, how he could and would grow in the arts. His erudition, a store of learning used almost carelessly here and there, could conjure up the past, holding up the mirror of gifted tribes and races held captive. It cleared away the film that obscured the long gone Jew in Egypt and the learned Greek in Rome to reflect the future of a thinking and creating Negro in the United States. His essays in ***The New Negro*** are more than dimly reminiscent of those pronouncements in the *Autobiographies* of William Butler Yeats on the shape of Irish letters to come. "As with the Jew," he wrote, "persecution is making the Negro international." These words did not refer to the colored expatriate artist who remains in some cases so long abroad that he risks losing the very roots from which his work sprang. He was drawing once more upon that childhood insight into the discovery of oneself when confronted with the indeterminate symbol; the toy-gift of Froebel is now the universal issue of human existence as coarsely marred by a majority culture, but the effect is much the same. The learner is thrown back onto his inner resources, those things which are truly his. The pupil is the Negro artist and thinker who has first to discover nature in himself before delineating his true kinship with the external. Private experience was not to be censored with reference to the social values of some group that seemed to be better off and probably was. Only when sufficiently grounded in the natural self is one ready to fill in the hiatus with an intelligence that qualifies. More than anything else, the Negro had to be taught to be himself.

"Be yourself." The byword on first hearing belongs in the aura of the cracker-barrel, and one thinks of David Harum. But this is not a mere folksly admonition against putting on airs. Alain Locke began nearly half a century ago saying this to a race whose environment has conspired over long generations to conceal from it its true selves through stereotype and related misrepresentation. The teacher knew how hard his advice was to follow, mainly because one technique of dominance had long been to tell the Negro and everybody else what he was like, basing portrayal of his character solely on the parts the white man had found it convenient to have him play. Having in mind the work of Sterling Brown, Harold E. Adams, and Guy P. Johnson, Professor Locke wrote in ***When Peoples Meet,*** "Once the majority has acquired its status through power, the problem of its maintenance arises. Auxiliary weapons are more useful for that . . . Prestige has already been shown to be one of the main devices of power, but behind that, even, there is need of tradition and rationalizations. These are the cultural and ideological weapons . . . Since majority group interests and policy are basically so similar, it is not surprising to discover that majority rationalizations have so much in common. Back of them all is the prevalent tendency to personify social groups and dramatize ideologically social issues and conflicts . . . these polarize, in sharpened contrasts, favorable and unfavorable characterizations. Around these stereotypes of rivalry and conflict, elaborate historical rationalizations are built, the most elaborate of which are racial myths."

Not only had the Negro, in order to be himself, to resist "elaborate historical rationalizations," but he had to look with dignity and assurance upon the truth of the matter. Majority value taught that no beauty could be found in his face. Nothing in his habits of linguistic expression was worth preserving save for laughable quaintness. Where white superstition is often mystic, religious, or mythological, that of the Negro was pure, simple ignorance. The deepest and most intimate parts of his being, imperfectly noted, superficially sensed, were the gimmicks for lowest comedy on another's stage.

It was then and still is, to a lesser degree, hard for a Negro to be himself. It took courage and prophetic authority to tell him to try it. But Alain Locke could say this for many reasons. No one could say of a man so well educated that he did not know what things were done and valued in white society. His years at Harvard, Oxford, and Heidelberg had given him, along with the manifold other contacts he enjoyed, ample opportunity to examine the values of the West. These things he had learned well, and he knew them to be important even when ludicrous, but he was never overawed. They were not for slavish aping, but for intelligent, modifying interaction, where the Negro has so studied himself that he can teach as much as he can learn. Froebel's child acts in time as strongly upon nature and society as they later come to work upon him. Professor Locke wrote: "Civilization is largely the product and residue of this ever-widening process of culture, contact, interchange, and fusion . . . cultural exchange passes in reciprocal streams from the conqueror to the conquered and from the conquered to the dominant groups. It is not always the dominant stock or the upper classes who are carriers or importers of culture. Societies have just as frequently received infiltrations of alien culture from the bottom through the absorption of conquered and subject groups."

Alain Locke could teach the Negro to be himself, this simple but awfully difficult thing, because he himself had learned it so well. He had accepted the lifetime of the near invalid, the high feminine component in his nature, and whatever else distinguished his mind and personality from that of others. In many instances he shrewdly turned his seeming liabilities into enviable assets. I think no one ever heard him speak with bitterness about any of his traits or the way in which they were looked on by others.

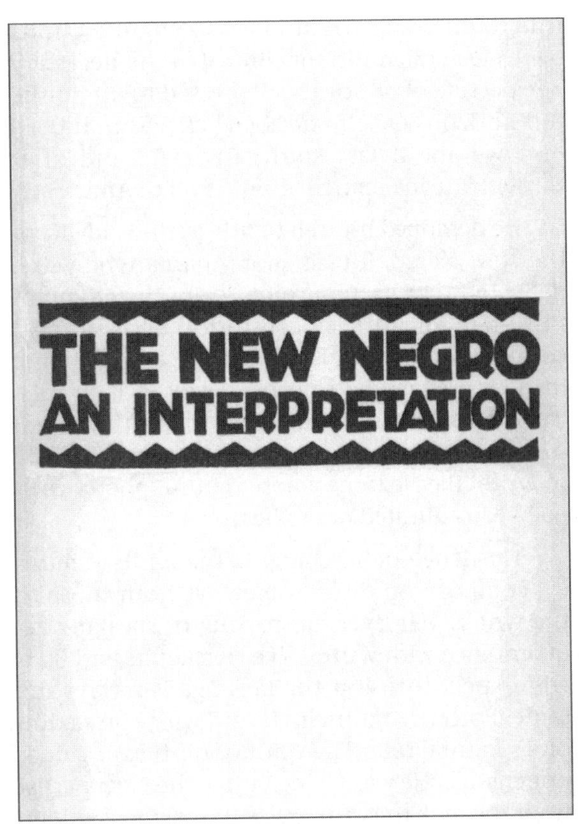

The New Negro: An Interpretation, edited by Alain Locke, with book decorations and portraits by Winold Reiss.

If anything is more difficult than being oneself, it is probably relating one's identity with good sense to others. This second step is essential to the productive life. The first alone is perilous. We are sometimes so stunned and even horrified by the ostensible distance between ourselves and the rest of the world that we retreat and lapse into spiritual coma from which the only exit is through a hatred that gnaws no less viciously at our own vitals than at those of others. So grim is this second step that the mere prospect of it is often enough to drive one back from the first.

Alain Locke directed his most detailed teachings at the Negro artist. He told the writer for instance, that the ethnic flavor could be preserved without abortive dialect, reminding him of his good fortune in having "never broken kinship with nature." He congratulated him on his efforts in the late Twenties at abandoning the wail and the sentimentality of decadent romanticism, suggesting that the aesthetic value of his craft would win more souls through subtle satire and honest taste than through crass protest. "It is no longer true that the Negro mind is too engulfed in its own social dilemnas for control of the necessary perspective of art; or too depressed to attain the full horizons of self and social criticism. Indeed . . . we are at last spiritually free, and offer through art an emancipating vision to America."

He described himself rightly as the midwife of the New Negro, for he, more than anyone else, delivered that peculiar mind from the womb of third-rate romanticism. Historical necessity had conceived it there, and the want of self-respecting imagination might well have caused it to miscarry. The earliest Negro writers tried either clumsily to write like genteel white men or ridiculously to write like Negroes whose natural poetry they had been educated not to hear.

The details of his charge to the spirits of musical composition differ somewhat from those to the writer. Whoever has passing or speaking acquaintance with writers like Herskovits and Boas will expect this. But the message is always the same: Portray convincingly and with conviction one's natural role. The spirit of his blessing does not change. He was trying to free the Negro artist from the embarrassing waste of seeking a golden fleece that he would not find, purely because it had never had a place in his mythos. To create was to take from the guarded branch a lambskin colored like a metal not yet found and still to be named.

But Alain Locke was not a Negro philosopher addressing himself exclusively to a Negro audience. To read his dissertation, ***The Problem of Classification in a Theory of Value*** or his essay in the Kallen *Festschrift* is, I think to see that he might well have said the same kind of thing to any people. In his own subtle way he intended it, indeed, at least for all the United States. I have in mind first such traditional bits of utter nonsense as the Colonial Complex which for so long dominated American thought and art and which among the masses has yet to be totally exorcised. And then there is the reverse side of the coin impressed with the necessity of forgetting the language and ways of one's immigrant parents and the fallacious belief that the melting pot does its work on the first day of public school. Much more widely spread is the readiness to overlook the fact that what is called the white man in America is after all but an agglutination of minorities having little more than approximate pigmentation in common. There is no telling how much we have lost and are still losing in the way of creativity because no one has yet said effectively to more of us that we must be ourselves.

This pressing need reminds me of Professor Locke's contribution, **"The Need for a New Organon in Education,"** to the Ninth Symposium on Science, Philosophy, and Religion. "This generally conceded goal of an 'integrated' education is, of course, the old humanist ideal and objective of the best possible human and self-understanding. But it recurs in our age in a radically new context, and as something only realizable in an essentially scientific way. Instead of being based as before on the Universal, common character of man, abstractly and rationally conceived, it rests on the concrete study of man in all his infinite variety. If it is to yield any effective integration, that must be clearly derived from an objective appraisal and understanding of the particularities of difference, both cultural and ideological. These it must trace to the differentiating factors of time, place, and circumstance, largely on the framework laid down by recent cultural anthropology. The modern version of the "proper study of mankind is man" is, therefore a comprehensive, comparative study of mankind with realistic regard for difference, instead of a rationalistic study with a zeal for commonalities and conformities."

RICHARD A. LONG (ESSAY DATE 1970)

SOURCE: Long, Richard A. "Alain Locke." *Black World* 20, no. 1 (November 1970): 87-90.

In the following essay, Long focuses on Alain Locke's contributions to the development of the Harlem Renaissance.

In a sense the Harlem Renaissance became fully conscious of itself at the same time that the world became conscious of it. The agency of this dual consciousness was one and the same—Alain Locke's, ***The New Negro.*** The anthology grew out of the special Harlem number of Survey Graphic which Alain Locke had carefully prepared and which was published in March 1925. ***The New Negro,*** appearing at the end of the year, confirmed the expectations which had been raised. Behind Alain Locke's editorial achievement lay the literary and artistic activity of the Crisis, edited by W. E. B. Du Bois, and of Opportunity, edited by Charles S. Johnson. Jessie Fauset was Du Bois' assistant at the Crisis for literature, while Alain Locke himself, from the founding of Opportunity by the Urban League in 1923, had contributed largely to its development both directly and indirectly.

In the "Foreword" to ***The New Negro*** Locke announced as its aim the cultural and social documentation of the new Negro. Who was the new Negro who in fact needed such documentation? Out of the fulcrum of World War I, the attendant cityward migration of the Black masses, the wave of race riots (real ones), had emerged a spirit of protest and defiance quite at variance with that traditionally ascribed to the American Black, and it was the full documentation of this spirit as reflected in the writings, both imaginative and analytical, of a large number of spokesman to which Locke wished to give wide currency. Locke asserted: "There is a fresh spiritual and cultural focusing . . . There is a renewed race-spirit that consciously and proudly sets itself apart."

Race-spirit is a concept that recurs frequently in Alain Locke's own contributions to ***The New Negro.*** I have proposed the term *ancestralism* to describe the totality of this concept in Locke's thinking, for it had several aspects. In his essay, "The Legacy of the Ancestral Arts," he stated, "We ought and must have a school of Negro art, a local and a racially representative tradition." The ancestralism of Alain Locke was grounded in a profound respect for the African past and for the folk spirit developed in the American South. This orientation unites him with two of his most eminent contemporaries, Du Bois and Carter G. Woodson; but, whereas they were essentially time-minded as historians, Locke—from the vantage point of philosophy and esthetics—had a more subtle and elusive perception of the meaning of the past.

Bringing the names Du Bois, Woodson, and Locke into conjunction dramatizes certain parallels among them which should not be lost. All were Harvard Ph.D.'s. All had studied in Europe: Du Bois in Berlin, Woodson in Paris, Locke at Oxford (England). Each could be extremely outspoken, but observed in his general manner a standard of decorum which can best be described as "old world," and that decorum was itself a rejection of the essential crudity of the American environment and an affirmation of *Black* dignity.

The special significance and inspiration which underlay Locke's perception of race as embodied in ancestralism was fully realized and expressed by only one of the figures of the Harlem Renaissance, Langston Hughes. Only he manifested that sense of an independent and valid culture which could and must be reflected in the world of art. Sterling Brown, too, gives expression to this, but his work is grounded rather exclusively in the folk tradition without that larger world reference which Alain Locke wished to see expressed. Jean Toomer had, of course, anticipated this concern in *Cane,* but his voice was scarcely heard after ***The New Negro*** consecrated his position.

There is, then, a very special relationship between Locke's theories and Hughes' work in the Twenties. Happily, Hughes has documented some of this in *The Big Sea.* But Alain Locke's awareness and concern went far beyond literary expression. The appearance of decorative designs by the young Aaron Douglas in ***The New Negro*** was a token of his devotion to the plastic arts and a complement to his essay on the art of Africa, a tradition he was among the first to treat. His association with Edith Isaacs of Theatre Arts Monthly in the presentation of the Blondiau Collection of Congo art in 1927 was of great significance.

The concern of Locke with the drama was given positive expression in the anthology of plays of Negro life which he edited with Matthew Gregory. His involvement with the drama was no casual thing. Together with Gregory and Ernest Just he had been active with the players at Howard University as early as 1912. His conception of the role of drama for the Negro artist as expressed in the 1927 article, "The Negro and the American Stage," is still unrealized in the consistent practice of any dramatist.

In his essay, "The Negro Spirituals," in ***The New Negro*** Alain Locke gives evidence of his great sensitivity for and knowledge of music. His analytical observations on the spirituals were two generations ahead of any thinking on the subject and are still the most sensible things said in print that can be understood by a layman. Alain Locke was especially devoted to the singer Roland Hayes, perceiving in him a man of deeply-felt folk origin who attained through his wholesome sense of his own tradition mastery of others, treating them all with artistic priority. Locke was, of course, fully acquainted with Harry T. Burleigh, Edward H. Boatner, Hall Johnson, John Wesley Work and many other arrangers of Negro spirituals.

* * *

Throughout the Twenties, particularly through the pages of Opportunity, the attention of Alain Locke ranged widely over the areas of literature, art, music, and world affairs. This activity accompanied his teaching at Howard University, his yearly voyages for travel and study in Europe, and his active encouragement of young Black writers, artists and scholars wherever he found them. He also entered into contact with such Afro-French intellectuals as René Maron, Paulette Nardal, and Jean Price-Mars, and later contributed to *Le Monde Noir.*

It is no exaggeration to say that the Harlem Renaissance as we know it is marked strongly by the presence of Alain Locke, and would have been something rather different without him and the role of mentor which he filled with modesty and elegence.

SAMUEL A. HAY (ESSAY DATE 1972)

SOURCE: Hay, Samuel A. "Alain Locke and Black Drama." *Black World* 21 (April 1972): 8-14.

In the following essay, Hay examines Locke's ideas about drama as a means for expressing the African American experience.

Movements in Western drama abound. From classicism to the *avant-garde,* automatism to *agit-prop,* they, like cells undergoing mitosis, keep coming, *ad taedium.* Black drama, too, shows signs of developing this splinter-group syndrome. I was struck recently by a query posed to a fledging Black dramatist, "Are you a Black experience or a revolutionary type?" The question was probably informed by the Black drama issue of *The Drama Review,* whose contents are listed under the titles "Black Revolutionary Theater" and "Theater of Black Experience." The origin and intellectual fountainhead of this division (or typing) can be traced to a 1927 essay, **"The Negro and the Theater,"**[1] by the then Dean of Black letters, Professor Alain Locke.

An eminent scholar and aesthetician, Locke theorized that modern American drama, "for all its frantic experimentation, is an essentially anemic drama, a something of gestures and symbols and ideas and not overflowing with the vital stuff of which drama was originally made. . . ." He felt that the Black dramatic art should "have the courage to develop its own idiom, to pour itself into new moulds." It should be noted that these remarks precede by nearly a half century Amiri Baraka's recent call for new Black dramatic forms.[2] And Larry Neal's contention that Black Art must "speak to the spirital and cultural needs of Black people"[3] parallels Locke's position that "Art must serve Negro life . . . [and] should stimulate the group life culturally and give it the spiritual quickening of a native art." (Race-spirit is a frequently recurring concept in Locke's literature, notes Richard A. Long, who proposes the term *ancestralism* "to describe the totality of this concept in Locke's thinking.")[4] Furthermore, as indicated by Locke's dictum that "Negro drama must grow in its own soil and cultivate its own intrinsic elements [because] only in this way can it become truly organic, and cease being a rootless derivative," he had a sound notion of what the constituents of Black drama should be. He states: "One can scarcely think of the complete development of Negro dramatic art without some significant artistic reexpression of African life, and the tradition associated with it."

But Locke felt that the development of an authentic Black drama was being hampered by historical controversy and social issues, which "clouded out the dramatic colors of Negro life into the dull mass contrasts of the Negro problem." Black drama's focusing on Black problems "was too partisan for fair dramatic balancing forces and too serious for either aesthetic interest or *artistic detachment.*" (Emphasis added.) Detachment, he felt, was a prerequisite for "great art." And because Black dramatists were incapable of such detachment, he advises them to refrain from addressing social issues:

> Race drama has appeared to them [Black dramatists] a matter of race vindication, and pathetically they have pushed forward their moralistic allegories or melodramatic protests as dramatic correctives and antidotes for race prejudice.

Black problem drama, in other words, was but propaganda, "which—pro-Negro as well as anti-Negro—scotched the dramatic potentialities of the subject." Realizing that these remarks are extracted from the social and artistic contexts that prompted them, I nevertheless wish to focus on Locke's concepts (1) of reality in drama, (2) of the need for artistic detachment, and (3) of propaganda and art. This examination, hopefully, will not only eradicate the apparent dichotomy between the two types of Black drama, but, by advancing some principles of Black drama, will limit the potential of further divisions.

Locke's definition of the types is quite applicable today:

> Two quite contrary directions compete for the artist's choice. On the one hand is the more obvious drama of social situation, focusing on the clash of the race life with its opposing background; on the other, the apparently less dramatic material of the folk life and behind it the faint panorama of an alluring race history and tradition. The creative impulse is for the moment caught in this dilemma of choice between the drama of discussion and social analysis and the drama of expression and artistic interpretation.

Reality, Locke asserts, should be the source of Black drama. But his concept of depicting reality in drama is somewhat fatuous. "Folk drama," he writes, "has no objective but to express beautifully and colorfully the folk life of the race." But the very nature of playwriting dictates against this notion. Even the naturalist, whose tendency it is to picture things as they are without assigning a hierarchy of significance, chooses situations from life, modifies them, interprets them, and perfects them in terms of specific dramatic purpose. And that purpose, more often than not, is to comment on some aspect of his existence. Although the comment may be so subtle that it gives the impression that the drama is but "beautiful and colorful" entertainment, it, nevertheless, is a comment. We should not be duped into thinking that any form of drama is but a passive portrayal of the surface characteristics of "what is." Drama is an historically concrete representation of the inner processes, the contradictions, and the ceaseless development of reality. The dramatist, therefore, must capture and transmit through his drama the latent potentialities of reality, so that the viewer can see a process of change, of development, and of evolution in the organization of the artistic representation. In other words, Black drama should not only reflect reality, but should create it. Hence, one of the primary requirements of *all* Black drama is that it be teleological.

Locke's designation of "detachment" as the prerequisite of "great art" does not acknowledge the fact that drama, like all art, is an inseparable part of life and history. The dramatist and his environment are an indissoluble entity. Locke intimates this point by indicating that, "Negro drama must grow in its own soil and cultivate its own intrinsic elements." His call for Black dramatists to detach themselves from their "intrinsic elements" negates his own dictum. As Emmanuel Kant's *Critique of Pure Reason* suggests, the dramatist is a synthesis of external things and internal causes. And we must admit that the external and internal natures of both the dramatist and his society are so intense, so influential, and so intertwined that the creative process demands a perfectly functioning consciousness of both. Although man has a psychic and a physical nature, and his society is a compendium of structures (oftentimes based upon superstitutions, lies, and desires for political and cultural hegemony), neither the man nor his society can be separated, explored, and represented at will. Attempts to do so result in a distortion of reality or, in Locke's own words, "the covering of life with the illusion of happiness and spiritual freedom." As indicated by his enthusiasm for Eugene O'Neill's *The Emperor Jones,* Locke apparently is willing to grant the dramatist such license. Of course, this is consonant with his notion that folk drama "has no objective but to express beautifully and colorfully the folk life of the race." But *The Emperor Jones,* with all of its Collective Unconscious suggestions, and all other illusion-lending dramatic forms, has no place in Black drama because these elements sublimate the Black man into purely mental processes. Black people do not generally relate to such illusionistic forms. Quite interesting is Langston Hughes's report of the Black reaction to a production of *Jones* at the old Lincoln Theatre in Harlem:

> The audience didn't know what to make of *The Emperor Jones* on a stage where "Shake That Thing" was formerly the rage. And when the Emperor started running naked through the forest, hearing the Little Frightened Fears, naturally they howled with laughter.
>
> "Them ain't no ghosts, fool!" the spectators cried from the orchestra. "Why don't you come on out o' that jungle back to Harlem where you belong?"
>
> In the manner of Stokowski hearing a cough at the Academy of Music, Jules Bledsoe stopped dead in his tracks, advanced to the footlights, and proceeded to lecture his audience on manners in the theater. But the audience wanted none of *The Emperor Jones*. And their manners had been all right at all the other shows. . . . So when Brutus continued his flight, the audience again howled with laughter. And that was the end of *The Emperor Jones* on 135th Street.[5]

Although entertaining, the expressionistic form (as well as its derivates) does not connect the inner life of the Black man, its essential traits, and essential conflicts with the social and historical factors that have shaped that inner life. By reducing man to a sequence of unrelated experiential fragments, the dramatist perpetuates the notion that man's acts can be separated from his motives or thoughts. Hence, such portrayals show not only a splintered man alienated from his society, but a man who is incapable of relating meaningfully to that society. The Black man becomes, in a sense, a solitary agent riveted to a meaningless existence. Additionally, he is portrayed as an impotent, static character incapable of structuring his existence, or even influencing the components of that existence.

Nobel Prize-winner Samuel Beckett is presently the *ne plus ultra* of this development in Western drama. And although John O'Neal, co-author of *The Free Southern Theatre,* reports some favorable Black reactions to FST's production of Beckett's *Waiting for Godot,* one wonders to what extent does the viewing of two despairing, vegetating clowns, engaged in the activity of waiting, contribute to the activation of Blacks to seek change. I suppose that it was hoped that after viewing the play and discussing its content with the actors, Blacks, by a process of induction, would more clearly see their situation and the need for change. Such knowledge, however, is only the desired end and, because of the reliance on revelation, could just as easily be missed—or worse—ignored. This leads us to another principle of Black drama, the use of revelation.

Western drama thrives on revelation, which is the gradual dispensing of information about the characters and the theme. The rationale is that a performance, being a creation in time, can at the outset show only a little of each character as it appears and must of necessity make up the sum of what is known of each, bit by bit, as the play progresses. Each speech and each action adds to the audience's knowledge of the character and of the play's theme, so that when the play ends, the knowledge is as complete as the whole play requires, or as the dramatist wishes. I hold no brief against revelation *per se.* In fact, if the dramatist wishes to create other than static and stock characters, predictable situations, and ideas that are obvious after the first two minutes, revelation should be utilized. Unfortunately, too many Black dramatists use so little revelation that their works are unmoving, unentertaining, and uniformative.

But modern Western dramatists tend to occupy the opposite end of the spectrum. They hold that the more subtle and "sophisticated" (read *obscure*) the revelation, the more engaging and meaningful the play. Edward Albee's *Tiny Alice* serves as an illustrative example. I remember well the baffled expressions on the viewers' faces as they left the theater. I recall also my fellow students' comments made about the meaning of the play in a writing seminar. Another more recent example—although not totally for the same reason—is *We Righteous Bombers,* supposedly by Kingsley B. Bass, Jr. Again, people (this time Black) left the theater puzzled, which can possibly be attributed to the dramatist's use of a borrowed form. "The whole play," writes Larry Neal (and I agree), "is abstracted (or stolen) from Albert Camus' *Les Justes.*"[6] With qualifications, I concur with Karenga's assertion that borrowing itself is not necessarily damaging to an art form. But "what is important," he writes, "is the choice of what one borrows and how he shapes it in his own images."[7] . . . *Bombers* is not so reshaped. Black dramatists should eschew borrowing not only Western structural elements, forms, characterizations, and language styles, but the attitudes about revelation. Black drama should entertain and inform Black people, not send them home to put together the pieces of a puzzle.

But the Black dramatist should avoid the other extreme of "sophisticated" revelation, didacticism. The reason Locke advised Black dramatists that "the future of Negro drama lies with the development of the folk play" as opposed to the "Negro problem play" is that "the Negro dramatist's advantage of psychological intimacy [needed for the writing of the problem play] is for the present more than offset by the disadvantage of the temptation to counter partisan and propagandist attitudes." The art-propaganda issue has long troubled aestheticians, and Locke's sensitivity is prompted by his somewhat inconsistently applied theory that drama should be written from "purely aesthetic attitudes." Yet he states that "one of the main reactions of Negro drama must and will be the breaking down of those false stereotypes in terms of which the world still sees us." I find it difficult to believe that Locke did not see the incompatibility of the two concepts. Any review of the historical relationship between society and the theater reveals that the theater is only an effective weapon for changing attitudes, beliefs, and conditions when it vociferously addresses specific problems. I direct your attention to 1776, when John Leacock's *Fall of the British Tyranny* was produced. Washington had ordered that all slaves be discharged from the Army because of uncertainty about their loyalty. Immediately following the production of Leacock's play, which advanced the proposition that all slaves who killed their masters be freed, the British made the theme national policy. Washington countered by rescinding the order and welcoming the Blacks into battle. Such examples are plentiful in theater history. No play informed by "purely aesthetic attitudes" is capable of "breaking down false stereotypes," or anything else, save a viewer's endurance.

Black dramatists need not concern themselves with the art-propaganda controversy, even if critics (including some Blacks) do disseminate the idea that most "Black Revolutionary" dramas are but propaganda tracts. I tend to agree with Mordecai Gorelik's suggestion that "propaganda ceases to be propaganda . . . as soon as it becomes art. Perhaps it also ceases to be propaganda when it coincides with our beliefs."[8] Eric Bentley agrees: "People who profess themselves to be opposed to propaganda in art nearly always turn out to be opposed only to the propaganda of 'the other side,' propaganda on 'our side' not being propaganda at all, but Truth. . . ."[9] My concern is not that Black drama might be propagandistic, but that it might be didactic and boring. Obviously some of the pieces being cranked out and labeled "Black drama" are but dramatized essays, about as theatrical as some of Plato's dialogues. The serious Black dramatist must study his craft. He should study world drama, paying attention to the Irish and to the socialist realists (specifically, Alexei Abruzov's *It Happened in Irkutsk* and Vladimir Mayakovsky's *The Bedbug,* a good example of how comedy can be used to inform). And, of course, special attention should be given to successful Black drama prototypes, some of which are: Baraka's *Black Mass* and *Slave Ship,* Ed Bullins' *Goin' a Buffalo* and *In New England Winter,* Jimmy Garrett's *And We Own the Night,* N. R. Davidson's *El Hajj Malik,* and many, many others.

Of course these comments are not meant to be *formulae* for Black drama. (The creative process should be spared such.) Neither do I contend that all Black dramatists are obligated to write "revolutionary" drama. But I do contend that when a drama is labeled "Black," it should adhere to some specific principles, other than "by, for, and about Black people." The case for the need of all Black drama to be revolutionary rests upon history, which shows that drama can be an effective weapon for change when the drama itself is revolutionary. A dramatist's portraying illusions, or detaching himself from his elements, or staging puzzles, or cudgeling viewers with dramatized discourses is hardly a means of effecting change. In a sense, Revolutionary Black Drama *is* folk drama—fully developed. Professor Locke seems to be predicting such a development: "With life becoming less a problem and more a vital process for the younger Negro, we shall leave to the dramatist not born to it the dramatization of the race problem. . . ."

Notes

1. First appeared in *Theatre,* Edith J. R. Isaacs, ed. (Boston, 1927), pp. 290-303. An edited version entitled "The Negro and the American Stage" is in Lindsay Patterson's *Anthology of the American Negro in the Theatre* (N. Y., 1967), pp. 21-24.
2. "A Symposium on *We Righteous Bombers,*" *Black Theatre Magazine* (April, 1970), 16-25.
3. "The Black Arts Movement," TDR XII (Summer, 1969), 15-25.
4. "Alain Locke: Cultural and Social Mentor," *Black World* XX (Nov., 1970), 88.
5. *The Big Sea* (N. Y., 1940), pp. 258-259.
6. "Symposium."
7. "On Black Art," *Black Theatre Magazine,* 9.
8. *New Theatres for Old* (N. Y., 1961), p. 363.
9. *The Life of the Drama* (N. Y., 1964), p. 136.

NATHAN IRVIN HUGGINS (LECTURE DATE 1973)

SOURCE: Huggins, Nathan Irvin. "Alain Locke: Aesthetic Value-System and Afro-American Art." *Revelation: American History, American Myths,* edited by Brenda Smith Huggins, pp. 111-14. New York: Oxford University Press, 1995.

In the following lecture, which was originally delivered in 1973, Huggins contends that Locke wanted African American art to display similar concerns with technique, discipline, and authenticity, qualities that he found to be intrinsic to African art.

Alain Locke would be especially gratified that a symposium of this character, sponsored by the *Harvard Advocate,* is given in his honor. His gratitude would go beyond his pleasure in being honored at Harvard, the University of his graduate training. It would stem, rather, from the fact that the *Harvard Advocate,* long an organ generating Euro-American letters, has at last made itself instrumental in celebrating Afro-American writers. From Locke's point of view, this symposium would mark a coming of age for both the *Advocate* and black American literature.

For almost half a century, Alain Locke has been respected for his role as interpreter of the Harlem Renaissance, for his identifying and support of young black artists, for his unfailing enthusiasm about the high cultural calling of black men and women of talent. But we have tended to use Locke as a lens through which to see writers like Langston Hughes, Countee Cullen, and Sterling Brown, and artists like Aaron Douglas; and we have tended to ignore the philosophical and theoretical grounds on which all of his efforts rested. This is especially ironic since his academic training was in philosophy, and since it has often been noted that his special interest was aesthetics. We should have wanted to look deeper, to understand the source of Locke's thought. It was not until I read his dissertation that I realized how much of a single piece was his scholarly work and his criticism.

Locke's dissertation, entitled **"The Problem of Classification in Theory of Value,"** which was done here at Harvard in 1917, is a quite technical work which proposes, for all fields of value, a classification system suitable for comparison and analysis across the various fields.

Locke had no intention of attacking traditional views of aesthetic values, which held aesthetics to be strictly contemplative and sui generis. Rather, he wanted to find, in the roots of human experience, the genetic source—the blueprint—from which ultimate aesthetic value could be derived.

Traditional thinking did not allow for the possibility that human experience directed toward other values—economic, hedonistic, moral, or ethical—could produce the psychological circumstances in which aesthetic values could be realized. If you found pleasure eating, you could not derive from that experience any aesthetic value.

Locke denied this. He claimed that through the experience, one could discover "enjoyment beyond mere satisfaction in eating." Likewise, one could discover in the religious experience, or the jazz performance, those qualities which stood on their own grounds as values in themselves.

To use his words, "psychologically" such aesthetic value "consists of such relationships that the presentation as a whole or the activity as a process induces a form-quality in feeling, which as long as it lasts or holds is felt to be the intrinsic ground of its own valuation and [the intrinsic ground] of wishing to persist . . . for the sake of maintaining the attitude and its component feeling qualities."

These qualities, growing out of generalized experience, Locke called pre-aesthetic values. But he found in them those genetic patterns of the form-feeling which would be manifest, in its purest state, in the fully developed and abstract aesthetic values. In other words, one could find inherent in the most ordinary and generalized experience a sense of contrast, a sense of rhythm, a sense of climatic order, a sense of summating. However primitive these senses might be in any given experience, they may evoke, according to Locke, rudimentary aesthetic values which are suggestions of themselves in a purer, abstract state.

Alain Locke's role in the 1920s and 1930s can be understood in terms of these ideas. They formed the basis for the cultural pluralism that characterized his work; they explain his persistent demand that Afro-American art achieve universalizing forms; they explain his belief in a process by which art-forms (such as jazz and dance), emerging out of generalized human experience, could ultimately be developed and abstracted into the quintessential purity of form to be found in fully developed aesthetic values. One can see here a debt to two of his teachers at Harvard: it is a fusing of the philosophical idealism of Josiah Royce with the psychology of William James. But Locke's thinking had a special charge: to serve the refinement of Afro-American culture.

We can now understand why African art had such a special meaning for Locke. Here was an art, created out of the religious and community experiences of a non-white people, that exhibited the discipline and purity of form that could be called *classic.* In every sense, African art demonstrated intrinsic aesthetic value.

This not only supported his theory but also represented the promise of Afro-American art. He did not expect Afro-American art to imitate African forms, but he hoped that the existence of African art would suggest to black Americans the possibilities of their own expression.

Locke acted as agent for the realization of sophisticated Afro-American art. There was, in his mind, a need for an authoritative voice to assert the validity of the Afro-American art enterprise. There was a need for someone to mediate between the folk art and the goals of classical expression, to articulate and define possibilities, to point the way. There was a need for someone to identify those values and techniques, derived from Afro-American sources, which had found their way into universal currency. Alain Locke wanted to fulfill all those needs.

To Locke, the Afro-American had to be held to his true experience. The temptation to imitate, to merely please and entertain, was the greatest danger, especially since black Americans had been persuaded that such was their role. Black artists could learn from Africa. But even there they had to be careful. The Afro-American, according to Locke, was actually the African "turned inside out." Whereas the African's dominant arts were decorative and craft arts—sculpture, metal working, weaving—the Afro-American's had been literature, song, dance, music, and later, poetry. The African was technical, rigid, controlled, disciplined, "thus, characteristic African art expression is sober, heavily conventionalized, restrained." On the other hand, black Americans were "freely emotional, sentimental and exuberant, so that even the emotional temper of the American Negro represents a reversal of his African temperament." Locke did not intend that the Afro-American give up his character, but he did hope that he could learn from the African to have a respect for technique and craft, a respect for discipline and form, and, through the agency of African art, an appreciation of forms of beauty that would better fit his own reality than those imposed by European sources.

Interestingly enough, Locke's notion of the African's character stood at odds with the characterizations of naïve exuberance, spontaneity, and sentimentality which were being imagined by Claude McKay and Countee Cullen, and which were, in time, to define negritude.

Doubtless the best example of Locke's theory at work is his discussion of jazz. For him, there were two types of worthwhile jazz: first, "that which, rising from the level of ordinary popular music, usually in the limited dance and song-ballad forms, achieves creative musical excellence." This we may call the "jazz classic." The other is that type of music which successfully transposes the elements of folk music, in this case jazz idioms, to the more sophisticated and traditional music forms. This latter type has become known as "classical jazz."

While he was appreciative of both the "jazz classic" and "classical jazz," it is clearly the latter he valued most, since only it could realize what he called universal and sophisticated values. He found in some Afro-Cuban music the development of formal ballet and chamber music, which were to him suggestive of the future of jazz.

In 1936, when he wrote ***The Negro and His Music,*** Locke found the influence of jazz already widespread. "It has educated the general musical ear to subtler rhythms, unfinished and closer harmonies, and unusual cadences and tone qualities. It has also introduced new systems of harmony, new instrumental techniques, and novel instrumental combinations."

And as if to demonstrate the validity of his theory of progress of preaesthetic values, he asserted, "The greatest accomplishment to date excepting the joy of the music itself, lies in the fact that there is now no deep divide between our folk music and the main stream of world music. That critical transition between being a half-understood musical dialect and a compelling variety of world speech has been successfully made."

For Locke, it was all progressive: stages leading to higher stages until it was all capped by universal values and forms. As he put it, "Every successive step in the general popularity of the Negro theme brings the Negro and the white American artist closer together, in this common interest of the promotion of Negro art over the common denominatory of the development of native American art." The ultimate end was an American art, in part defined by Afro-American forms, participating in universal aesthetic value.

It is hard to know how Locke would view it all now. But if music, dance, and theater are any measure, the vital force of Afro-American expression has so perfused American culture that it is sometimes impossible to recognize it for what it is. That might please him, but he would still want to search for his universal forms.

EVERETT AKAM (ESSAY DATE 1991)

SOURCE: Akam, Everett. "Community and Cultural Crisis: The 'Tranfiguring Imagination' of Alain Locke." *American Literary History* 3, no. 2 (1991): 255-76.

In the following essay, Akam attempts to rescue Locke's reputation from charges that he was an apolitical, naïve utopian and an integrationist who rejected revolutionary cultural ideas.

Black studies labors under the burden of a heavy irony. The Harlem Renaissance, that period of African-American cultural flowering from the mid-1920s to the mid-30s, has too often been an object of dismissal by influential scholars. Guided by Alain Locke, America's first black Rhodes scholar and life-long advocate of racial democracy, the renaissance, also known as the New Negro movement, nurtured such well-known figures as Zora Neale Hurston, Langston Hughes, Claude McKay, Jean Toomer, Bessie Smith, Duke Ellington, Louis Armstrong, and many others. Yet the movement that provided the foundation for modern black cultural expression falls far short of the high standards held by such scholars as Harold Cruse, Henry Louis Gates, Jr., Nathan Huggins, and Sterling Stuckey.[1]

The explanation for this irony lies in yet another. Searching for a theoretical synthesis of neo-Marxism and cultural nationalism, attempting to establish a conception of black identity not shackled to Eurocentric standards, these scholars have promoted autonomous cultural nationalism and militant socialism as the necessary foundation for black identity and communal life. Thus, while conceding that African-Americans possess a dual consciousness, or an identity composed of elements from a unique black cultural heritage as well as American traditions, these intellectuals pit the claims of autonomy or particularism against those associated with the communal ground of a shared culture. Cruse and his intellectual progeny have therefore admitted the dialectical nature of African-American identity, a dialectic suggested by the hyphen itself, even as they pursue the nationalist element exclusively in what amounts to a reductionist, dichotomous schema. In their view, real (nationalist) consciousness opposes false (integrationist) consciousness, and the choice facing black Americans is stark: either develop autonomous forms or face being "integrated out of existence" (Cruse 437).

The exclusion of the third alternative implicit in the idea of dual consciousness, combined with the Marxist assumptions that continue to inform this kind of thinking, explains why these scholars dismiss the renaissance, often with much contempt. For them, the New Negro movement represents an integrationist ploy by bourgeois "black yea-sayers" anachronistically struggling "to uphold the American virtues of progressivism, individualism, and self-reliance" (Huggins 141).

Alain Locke, the guiding spirit of the renaissance, shrank from the revolutionary implications of cultural and political autonomy, so the charge goes. Only a "militant, card-carrying, gun-toting socialist who refused to turn the cheek," according to Gates, was truly worthy of the title of New Negro. Locke's aesthetic efforts, aimed at transforming racial attitudes through the medium of art and formal culture, instead "transformed the militancy associated with this trope and translated this into an apolitical movement of the arts" (Gates 147). Such naive utopianism, wrongly attributing power to art and language, constituted no more than a "fantasy of indirect liberation" conducted in the "non-place of language" (Gates 132). By attempting to construct an identity for black Americans from biblical and pre-Marxist traditions, Locke indulged in a misguided effort "to recreate a race by renaming it." Unenlightened by postmodern thought, he could not realize that "this black and racial self," the New Negro, "does not exist as an entity or group of entities but 'only' as a coded system of signs, complete with masks and mythology" (Gates 132).

Yet the very lives of the ideal theorists of culture championed by Stuckey, for example, testify to the bankruptcy of neo-Marxist nationalism as a source for the creation of identity. The life of W. E. B. Du Bois, who rightfully commands respect, nevertheless resembled more the unfinished arc of a pendulum swinging out of time than the steady and fulfilling course suggestive of a successful synthesis. Moreover, Stuckey's claim that Paul Robeson reconciled his roots with socialism also appears dubious. After all, Robeson's ideal theorist of culture was Josef Stalin, and Robeson's celebration of a life spent as a "'Negro wandering through the world'" (Stuckey 344) conveys more the pain of an open wound and spiritual homelessness than the healing effect of self-knowledge and rootedness. Without an adequate understanding of dual consciousness, therefore, we only perpetuate the lonely sense of being an "orphan in history" (Cowan). A reappraisal of the renaissance and Locke's transfiguring imagination has been long overdue.

1. Culture and Democracy

As a student at Yale from 1904 to 1907 and again in 1916-17, Locke absorbed the intellectual contradictions embodied in such diverse figures as William James, Ralph Barton Perry, Josiah Royce, George Santayana, and Barrett Wendell. As late as 1923, while teaching philosophy at Howard University, where he would stay for most of his career, Locke, like Wendell, held a conception of culture indebted to Matthew Arnold. Against a philistine cult of utility, Locke opposed its mirror image. Sweetness and light, provided by the canon of the Western tradition, could serve as a common ground capable of uniting black and white on the lofty plane of high culture (**"Ethics"** [**"Ethics of Culture"**]).

Only two years later, however, Locke rejected the Arnoldian concept. The influences of James, Santayana, Randolph Bourne, and Van Wyck Brooks, Locke's classmate, loosened the hold of the genteel tradition on Locke's thought and life. By the time he served as editor for the special issue of the *Survey Graphic* that launched the Harlem Renaissance in March 1925, Locke had repudiated that tradition, regarding it as a cul-de-sac for black Americans. Self-cultivation demanded self-denial as the price of admission to the Anglo-Saxon world.

The evidence for this had accumulated steadily in Locke's life. At Oxford in 1907, his presence at a Thanksgiving dinner held by the American Club was opposed by white Southerners. When Horace Kallen, another Rhodes scholar and Locke's friend, wrote Wendell on Locke's behalf, Wendell replied in the racist terms that permeated the genteel tradition and refused to involve himself in Locke's predicament. "Professionally I do my best to treat negroes with absolute courtesy. It would be disastrous to them," however, he continued, "if they be gentlemen at heart, to expose them in private life, to such sentiments of repugnance as mine, if we were brought into anything resembling formal relations." Wendell's racism was typical, as he himself made clear to Kallen. Anything other than formal courtesy, he said, Locke had "no right to expect from men of my race and time."

Locke found his alternative in Bourne's cosmopolitanism. Bourne's vision of a "trans-national America" called for a reconstruction of American life, not mindless conformity to the standards of Anglo-Saxon governing classes. The failure of assimilation reflected a failure by Anglo-Saxons to transform the "colony into a real nation, with a tenacious, richly woven fabric of native cultures." Without such a cultural center, freedom at best meant no more than the "right to do pretty much as one pleases, so long as one does not interfere with others" ("Trans-National" 111). Rather than the impoverished negative freedom of classical liberalism, American life offered the materials for a positive freedom based on a vibrant cosmopolitanism. And this realm of positive freedom Bourne had discovered in culture itself, in culture understood as "democratic cooperation in determining the ideas and purposes and industrial and social constitutions of a country" (111). In all its forms, the demand for cultural democracy was inseparable from a radical call for participatory democracy in all spheres of life. Not reducible to a question of efficiency and technical expertise, Bourne's cosmopolitanism expressed the "poetic vision" necessary to a truly democratic "beloved community" (112).

The Harlem Renaissance promised to give life to that poetic vision. This New Negro movement represented the cultural revolt of the romantic tradition against the growing cultural authority of the liberal Enlightenment in American life. Cosmopolitan culture as a public discourse, Locke recognized, opposed both the concept of culture as a conflict-free war against nature conducted under the generalship of a new class and the neo-Kantian, Arnoldian understanding of culture as a noetic realm untainted by use. Both were underpinned by a separation of facts from values, technical from moral reason. Locke therefore advanced a critical theory of society rooted in aesthetic vision.

In his assault on the racial and class power that undergirded the genteel tradition, Locke wielded the "philosophical sword" of pragmatism (**"Pluralism"** [**"Pluralism and Intellectual Democracy"**] 53). Following James's rejection of foundationalism, Locke regarded the renaissance as the fulfillment of the pragmatist demand that philosophy meet the "pressing practical demand for a revaluation of social values" (**"Cultural"** [**"Cultural Relativism"**] 1). Such a reconstructed "philosophy of culture" confronted the pretensions of Western cultural absolutism with the "intensive particularism" of an anthropology that unmasked "most of our scales of social value" as constituting "social rationalizations suiting our particular pet purposes" (1).

Accordingly, all philosophies of culture, Locke suggested in **"Cultural Relativism,"** a revealing talk given at Harvard in 1930, contained a tendency toward chauvinism. An acknowledgment of cultural relativism would serve as a corrective to hubris, "would reveal," that is, "the limitations and unfinalities of our prime social values independently of historical perspective, or cultural breakdown or defeat" (2). A sense of limits, made possible by the acceptance of cultural pluralism, suggested that cultural values, like history itself, could not legitimately be justified by reasons of power. Indeed, Locke's relativist perspective could "even cut under the irrationalisms that support our naive partisanships and our cultural apologetics" (2).

Not content with unmasking alone, Locke offered the concept of cultural relativism as an alternative to cultural absolutism and radical subjectivism, the "two planes of our social thought" (2). By regarding social cultures as "functional differentiations" possessing "environmental adequacy" as the criterion of their "practicability, efficiency," and "endurance," a rational observer could recognize that every type possesses "inevitable shortcomings" (5). Demands for cultural conformity to Anglo-Saxon values, which were presented as representing the highest stage of the "ladder concept of social evolution" (6), were themselves irrational, a true irony for a culture that regarded itself (and still does, of course) as the very epitome of reason and progress. At the same time, the recognition that cultural values are "relative both in time and space," and that no particular type of culture "could legitimately lay claim to be universal if it could be" (6), encouraged an authentically rational loyalty on the part of its citizens. An acceptance of tragedy opened the way to a view of values as provisional truths subject to modification through experience and public conversation with others. Locke therefore found in cosmopolitan culture the democratic community championed by Royce, James, Brooks, and Bourne.

Locke's deconstruction formed the necessary prelude to the reconstruction of a communal world premised on the possibility of intersubjective understanding, itself a mode of reason distinct from both foundationalist objectivity and the radical subjectivism of the will typical of some forms of the romantic tradition. Philosophy and culture needed some means capable of nurturing allegiance to particular values, traditions, and institutions without promoting a "corresponding distortion of view in our evaluation of divergent cultures" (9). Loyalty to particular values, when viewed from the Lockean perspective of "functional equivalence," served to "unify and focus our group life" (8). Dethroning absolutes therefore amounted to an acknowledgment of hubris, of humankind's propensity to regard the self and its desires as the measure of the good. Such an acknowledgment led, in turn, to the "more objective view that my patriotism and your patriotism, my sectarianisms and yours, though differing and often opposing one another, are functionally equivalent—and objectively identical." The attitude of "cold relativism" would reveal "many or most of our over-values as useful fictions, historically necessary and pardonable, but variable in time and tenable only within functionally determined limits" (10).

Values, rightly regarded as provisional truths subject to revision as a result of experience and discourse with others, could foster a political community premised on democracy and the cultivation of difference within the context of a shared culture created by all. With the realization of the cosmopolitan ideal, which owed much to the classical vision of the polis, as well as to the Puritan acknowledgment of sin, the "tradition of ethnic unity, of a race or nation, or of the finality and universality of a particular religion" could finally be left behind (10). Contrary to the view of the liberal Enlightenment, however, and unlike John Locke, Alain Locke clearly hoped to avoid a political community that avoided coerced conformity only at the expense of public values. "We will suspect this relativism if we feel that it will develop indifferent neutrality," he warned; rather, the "consciousness of the meaning of difference should beget a loyalty the price of which is not intolerance—and a fundamental unity in difference which does not require uniformity" (14).

To use the language of Western philosophy, Locke pursued a conception of practical reason that accepted Hegel's critique of Kant, while retaining the latter's insight concerning the necessity for values that possess an *ought* character as a precondition for the existence of the moral community. Values and moral reason, Locke realized, did not occupy a noumenal realm that required the transcendence of the heteronomous natural world of cause and effect; such Kantian moral reason could never guide action in the empirical world by virtue of its radically transcendental quality. At the same time, however, neither was moral or practical reason constituted solely by the expedient reactions of an agent to the dictates of an ever-shifting and contingent necessity; the mere selection of efficient means chosen to secure desired ends begged the question of which ends should be chosen. As such, the latter case pertained to efficiency, or technical reason. The exercise of practical reason, in truth, joined considerations of value with consequences and means, a fruitful marriage disallowed by the Kantian insistence that the realm of moral freedom could be realized only through transcendence of the realm of necessity, the heteronomous natural world of particularism and empirical phenomena.[2]

Locke's synthesis therefore rejected the established antithesis of universalism versus historicism and an ethics of principle versus the exercise of moral judgment in the context of history and culture, which Hegel termed *Sittlichkeit.* Moreover, these values thus recast possessed both a "private" and a "public" character. Whereas the former expressed the legitimate demands associated with the particularisms of being-in-the-world, the latter derived authority through the process of a democratic discourse that both encouraged plurality and subjected its claims to the light of justification within the public sphere. Consequently, self- and group-realization, associated in the liberal tradition with John Stuart Mill, was inseparably intertwined with democratic participation in public life. This nexus, then, formed the heart of Locke's cosmopolitan ideal, an ideal that regarded language and art as the mode of practical reason.

2. Values and Identity

With this in mind, we may see just how inadequate and misleading recent interpretations of Locke and the renaissance have been. Far from being a naive utopian, Locke integrated the inclusionary demands for racial, economic, and political democracy with his concept of cosmopolitanism as moral discourse in such a way as to challenge, rather than affirm, the tradition of liberalism. His essays on the New Negro, for example, linked the emergence of a distinctive African-American identity to a national spiritual awakening and coming of age. The conventional view of cultural values had fostered a model of race relations that opposed two different but related extremes which, when taken as a whole, presented black Americans with an oppressive and unnecessary choice between assimilation and nationalism.

The consequence of this restrictive model, Locke brilliantly recognized, required black Americans to choose between being black or being American. In other words, the opponents of assimilation accepted the assimilationist premise that Anglo-Saxon cultural values were not subject to democratic discourse and debate by a plurality of culturally different subjects. If assimilationists demanded the renunciation of black identity as the price of acceptance into the dominant culture, cultural nationalists such as Marcus Garvey also expected that blackness could only be achieved as a consequence of withdrawal. In the face of the power exerted by this unnecessary choice, the third possibility—namely that these demands for inclusion as well as identity were crucially connected—was never envisioned, as Locke realized. The irony of this choice lay in the subsequent expectation that the price of identity entailed either a psychic or physical departure from the very country and culture that black Americans helped to build. Ultimately, in both cases, self-renunciation for an abstract ideal paradoxically formed the undesirable and unnecessary outcome.

The dehumanizing effect of this confusion about values tainted all aspects of racial relations and revealed itself in the white attitude toward the black American, who was regarded as "more of a formula than a human being—a something to be argued about, condemned or defended," to be "kept down," or "in his place," or "helped up," to be "worried with or worried over, harassed or patronized, a social bogey or a social burden" (**"New"** [**"The New Negro"**] 3). The New Negro, however, aided by the forces of industrialization and black migration, expressed the "transformed and transforming psychology" that "permeates the masses" (7). This psychology of self-esteem and the recognition of black beauty in the face of white denial constituted nothing less than the capacity for self-definition premised on the values of black traditions. The black construction and expression of identity premised on African-American cultural traditions gave birth to a spiritual emancipation that made philanthropy and the sociological treatment of the Negro as a "problem" obsolete. "It is a social disservice to blunt the fact that the Negro of the Northern centers has reached a stage where tutelage, even of the most interested and well-intentioned sort," Locke wrote in **"The New Negro,"** "must give place to new relationships, where positive self-direction must be reckoned with in ever increasing measure. The American mind," he warned, "must reckon with a fundamentally changed Negro" (8).

Even an older generation of black intellectuals had "idols of the tribe to smash." White paternalism and black defensiveness shared a common and debilitating assumption. "If on the one hand the white man has erred in making the Negro appear to be that which would excuse or extenuate his treatment of him," Locke pointed out, "the Negro, in turn, has too often unnecessarily excused himself because of the way he has been treated" (**"New"** 10). Contrarily, however, the liberating effect of self-identity lay in the refusal of the black American to regard himself simply as a victim who, through no fault of his own, had failed to attain the white cultural standard. The acceptance of a special status premised on victimization as an "extenuation for his shortcomings" ceded the capacity for definition to a culturally dominant majority (10-11). After all, the essence of victimization lies precisely in the incapacity to influence or control the alien forces and values that direct destiny and form identity.

Relatedly, Locke also criticized those black intellectuals who, like Du Bois, sought to employ artistic expression as a deliberate means of racial advancement. Art as race propaganda also paradoxically surrendered the capacity for self-definition because the self-conscious wish to disprove the Sambo stereotype inadvertently undermined authentic self-expression. In other words, white standards retained their power by defining the very terms of racial expression. Consequently, such "cautious moralism and guarded idealizations" represented further manifestations of "all those pathetic over-compensations of a group inferiority complex which our social dilemmas inflicted upon several unhappy generations" (**"Negro Youth"** [**"Negro Youth Speaks"**] 48). Released from the constraints imposed by putting the best racial foot forward, black artists of the renaissance were freed from the "hard choice between an over-assertive and an appealing attitude" (48). Stilted self-consciousness and racial rhetoric could at last be laid aside. "Our poets have now stopped speaking for the Negro—they speak as Negroes," Locke wrote in **"Negro Youth Speaks."** "Where formerly they spoke to others and tried to interpret, they now speak to their own and try to express. They have stopped posing, being nearer the attainment of poise" (48).

A self-consciously moralistic art, which critics have wrongly accused Locke of advancing, actually reproduced in the realm of formal culture the Anglo-Saxon cult of technical reason. "Race leaders" articulated unrepresentative values and reduced aesthetic consciousness to a merely instrumental role, transforming the art object into a kind of battering ram used to "fight social battles and compensate social wrongs" (**"Negro Youth"** 50). Aesthetic consciousness, properly understood, however, offered a "transfiguring imagination," a capacity to see the world not only as it was, but also as it could be. Such a consciousness, long identified by the romantic tradition with what William Blake termed poetic vision, combined "pure art values" with the "poetry of sturdy social protest" (52). Unlike the confinement of art to "classes, cliques, and coteries" typical of industrial society, Locke's modernism sought to infuse social and political life with the liberated spirit of art and beauty more typical of premodern culture (52). Consequently, out of the "ashes of materialism," the New Negro, expressing the twofold vision of romanticism and the primitive, found beauty within the self and, in turn, offered "through art an emancipating vision to America" (53).

3. Aesthetic Vision and Cultural Transformation

The New Negro movement challenged the notion of values as opaque and given, and it identified the capacity for the construction of a new democratic culture informed by humane values as the very essence of a fulfilled selfhood. Thus it reconciled the expression of a black identity rooted in Africa with the role of the black masses as conscious collaborators in the creation of a postgenteel American culture. Through the recovery of nativity and a realization of the crucial importance of premodern group traditions, the New Negro would serve as a rich alternative to a desiccated individualism premised on abstract rights and the accumulation of property. American culture, premised on the subjugation of nature, elevated technical mastery of the natural world by an abstract individual free of all modes of authority to the realm of the moral itself. "Nordicism" or "Puritanism" had its origins in a regressive desire for absolute control and the denial of death on the part of culturally and historically disembodied individuals. Although Locke never fully elaborated his charge, he often suggested that the Western project of technical mastery was premised on such a futile rebellion of human pride against the limitations imposed by the human condition, a condition marked by finitude and death. Rather than fostering an acknowledgment of human dependency and the existence of powers as well as ends higher than our own, liberal individualism rooted the very capacity for moral agency itself in an antagonistic relationship to the natural world and its creatures. The human world, according to the liberal Enlightenment, constituted a moral world free from natural causal determination only to the extent that man as a producer subdued and transformed a seemingly limitless nature regarded as essentially indifferent to human needs. By these lights, human freedom and self-fulfillment were synonymous with the colonization of the world in conformity to the demands of the human will, with its ubiquitous desire for comfort, security, and the avoidance of death.

The power of Locke's critique of the Anglo-Saxon worldview originated not in its condemnation of mastery as a form of selfish fulfillment, but rather in the insight that mastery ultimately proved to be self-defeating. A culture that equated self-fulfillment and moral agency with conquest and private rights lost all sense of connection with those human capacities that made identity and selfhood possible. The denial of mortality and limitation in truth formed a lonely prison in which the deepest needs for connection and community with the world and others are repressed for the sake of control and invulnerability. The appropriation of the earth and the domination of so-called primitive people by Westerners armed with an imposing technology therefore represented a needless and dehumanizing psychopathology that defeated its own purpose and oppressed those who knew another, more satisfying way of life.[3]

Although both Huggins and Cruse fault Locke for neglecting black nativity, Locke's vision found its inspiration in "ardent respect and love for Africa, the motherland" (**"Negro Youth"** 52-53). Aesthetically rich African culture offered an antidote to America's "social poison" (52) precisely because its peoples had never lost their sense of connection to and dependence upon the natural world. Indeed, an embrace of human vulnerability and dependence formed the very heart of African cultural wisdom. The consciousness denigrated by the West as "primitive" and "underdeveloped" offered a "return to nature, not by way of the forced and worn formula of romanticism, but through the closeness of an imagination that has never broken kinship with nature" (52).

In his writings on African sculpture, for example, Locke, like John Dewey and Lewis Mumford, revealed the consequences of the separation of beauty from utility, a separation that informed the very foundation of industrial society and the cult of progress. A culture that regarded art as "artificial, borrowed, non-utilitarian, and the exclusive product and possession of cliques and coteries" (**"Art Lessons"** [**"Art Lessons from the Congo"**]) expressed the liberal Enlightenment's project of mastery and psychopathology of disconnection. African art therefore confronted industrial society, with its separation of creative planning and execution, as a subversive presence, a form suffused with a consciousness that refused to accept the distinction between fine and decorative art, beauty and use. In regarding African art as applied, a pejorative term in the West, "we fail to see," Locke wrote, "how irrelevant such a distinction is for a culture where fine and decorative art have never been separated out, and where things can be superlatively beautiful and objects of utility at the same time" (**"Art Lessons"**). Locke therefore rejected the Arnoldian aesthetic rival to the cult of instrumental reason because it too sundered a unitary concept of reason as at once moral, aesthetic, and instrumental. The Arnoldian wing of romanticism, furthermore, restricted creativity to an aesthetic elite just as philistinism fostered the growth of a managerial class premised on the separation of conceptual thought from execution in the industrial sphere. In both cases, personal fulfillment through the exercise of judgment and the creation of durable objects of beauty was restricted to the few, to "classes, cliques, and coteries" (**"Collection"** [**"A Collection of Congo Art"**]).

In contrast, Locke praised the African artist, who approached the vocation with a humility that placed the art object above the self in importance. Unlike the European modernist, who was "always working with the idea of authorship and a technically formal idea of expressing an aesthetic," the "native African sculptor, forgetful of self and fully projected into the idea, was always working in a complete fusion with the art object" (**"African"** [**"African Art: Classic Style"**]). By foregoing a self-conscious authorship and by reverentially creating a useful object of beauty, the sculptor, paradoxically, was at the same time "naive and masterful, primitive and mature." European modernism, although properly cherishing the timeless quality and powerful simplification of form in African sculpture, never grasped its true essence of reverence and connection, a spirit born of an acceptance of human limitation and dependence. Like much of European culture, European modernism was also trapped in the worship of technique, which alone could never yield the emancipating vision required by the spiritual crisis of the West.

The point of Locke's contrast lay in the paradox that self-forgetfulness, rather than attempts at mastery, offered the way to authentic self-fulfillment. The European modernist, who represented the epitome of the unmediated urge to dominate, self-consciously imposed on the art object the desire for recognition, power, and a form of immortality. The unmediated extension of the self's desire for boundlessness deprived the art object of any measure of autonomy, however. In other words, the self-conscious authorship of the modernist reflected the Enlightenment's confused identification of human freedom and moral reason with the subjugation of nature and the elimination of all constraints on the human will.

The African art object, in contrast, reflected the capacity of premodern consciousness to sublimate the hope for transcendence of the human condition into the creation of durable objects possessing beauty, utility, and permanence. By thus contributing to the creation of a stable and aesthetically rich human world that acknowledged its dependence on nature, the African artist secured a sense of selfhood through the exercise of creative judgment, as well as a kind of immortality based on remembrance. Forsaking mastery of the world, the sculptor mixed the totality of his or her personality with the natural material, thereby creating a union in which the autonomy and bounds of each were at once respected and simultaneously unified in a new creation, the art object conceived both as self-expression made possible by devotion to a vital tradition and as a loving contribution to an enduring life-world that outlasts its dying inhabitants.

Locke's cosmopolitanism therefore reflected the moral vision captured by the primitive art form's fusion of beauty and use, practical and technical reason. As the bearer of a premodern moral consciousness worthy of revitalization in the search for democratic community and authentic self-fulfillment, the art object uttered a truth recognizable by all who would listen. The "cosmic emotion" of "gifted pagans" and African-American artists promised to add the "motives of self-expression and spiritual development to the old and still unfinished task of making material headway and progress" (**"New"** 15-16).

4. A Community of Understanding

The most directly political consequence of this aesthetic theory was its critique of a politics of pure power and foundationalist cultural values. Racial relations were, in an important sense, a continuation of aggression that made power the paramount attribute. For if moral agency and civilization itself were synchronous with the development of technical mastery and subjugation, then preindustrial traditions and values were by definition inferior and even irrational. The bearers of such traditions were simultaneously subjected to demands for conformity, to genocide, and to exploitation as well. The mentality that refused to acknowledge the boundary between self and other, as recent studies of narcissism suggest, tended to obliterate that which it could not shape in its own image.

Contrarily, a cosmopolitan coalition of oppressed hyphens could offer a counterexample of a communitarian "gentleness of spirit," which could prevent the "rapid rise of a definite cynicism and the counter-hate and a defiant superiority feeling" (**"New"** 13). While black counterhatred was understandable, it served only to perpetuate the very values that the oppressed hoped to overthrow. A defiant cultivation of blackness as a new form of privileged consciousness, in other words, would only mirror the worst features of the Western political-cultural tradition—the exertion of power without the need for a common ground of authority or the moral legitimation that public justification brings.

Consequently, Locke denounced the particularisms that would undermine the common cause of social justice and perpetuate the fragmentation of the public world. He rejected racial divisiveness for a solidarity of the oppressed and grounded his political ethics in a "mental passive resistance" that stressed the "oneness of humanity" as well as love of the other (**"New"** 13; **"Unity"** [**"Unity through Diversity"**]). Locke's ideal therefore rejected the interconnected extremes of subjectivist self-assertion and its opposite of self-denial for the public good, for he had seen that the former invited the latter. Locke's alternative, intersubjectivity grounded in a public discourse, offered a communal world of shared meaning, not a one-sided pursuit of power in a war of each against all. At the same time, the common ground of culture, understood in Bourne's terms, also provided an alternative to the identification of particularism with some hypothesized universal. Locke confronted racism and class exploitation through an appeal to the American moral conscience and the "country's professed ideals" of the democratic community premised on an equality of power, property, and dignity, all of which aimed at authentic fulfillment through participation in a public sphere (**"New"** 13, 12).

5. Play as Alternative to Reason as Domination

Locke's modernist "recoil from the machine age," his indictment of a joyless industrial capitalism that separated planning from execution, and his praise of the "half-submerged paganism of the Negro" gathered his concerns into a far-ranging and penetrating reappraisal of American life (**"Beauty"** [**"Beauty Instead of Ashes"**] 24). Art and cultural concerns were permeated with a political dimension of the widest possible scope. Art, based upon a fusion of beauty with use and rooted in the vital context of culture, gave expression to the dialectical relationship between the particular and the communal. Kallen's musical metaphor of a transnational, self-directing orchestra playing a distinctively American music was taken up by Locke and developed as an example of the possibilities suggested by cosmopolitanism. Traditional black gospel, for example, reflected the creative merger of African and American influences by African-Americans, who infused white culture with black spiritual values, resisting domination by whites. Gospel therefore formed the direct expression of the black group spirit with its heroic resistance to domination and materialism. That musical tradition nurtured black life and, in turn, offered the material for a national music that would both retain and transcend the roots of its origin. Rejecting the commercialized jazz of Tin Pan Alley and the cloistered classics secluded behind the walls of the "conservatory and the taboos of musical respectability," Locke looked instead to "art-music" or classical jazz (**"Toward a Critique"** [**"Toward a Critique of Negro Music"**] 110). Art-music retained its connection to the various folk traditions but also broadened their appeal to a cosmopolitan audience. No single tradition would dominate, and all groups could recognize their particular contributions in the new form. In any case the former was never intended to supplant folk music, which represented the roots to richly nurturant ethnic traditions.

As in Locke's political theory, a cosmopolitan music reconciled creative individuality with a communal setting devoted to difference and harmony. Locke therefore praised the spiritual as authentically African and American, while calling at the same time for the creation of a "super-jazz" being explored by Duke Ellington and Louis Armstrong. Contrary to the charges of his critics,

Locke took a very close look at jazz and condemned, not its creative potential or its joy, but its exploitation by an industry premised on the degradation of culture into a commodity. By the same token, no mere grafting of native material to classical form would do, and Locke heavily criticized the "artificial hybrids" of Aaron Copland, George Gershwin, and Paul Whiteman, while praising the efforts of Ellington, Edmund Jenkins, William Grant Still, and William Dawson (**"Toward a Critique"** 110).

Locke's contempt for Tin Pan Alley, a contempt forcefully expressed in his 1936 work, ***The Negro and His Music,*** was seconded at the time by Armstrong, who also lamented that the commercialized jazz pumped out by a culture machine "makes a good musician tired, for they are the very ones who are doing most to break up these worn-out patterns" (***Negro and His Music*** 94). The culture industry represented another form of the Western penchant for subordinating a sharply contracted world of art to profit, creativity to debased utility, spirit to accumulation, and the sacred to the profane. Authentic jazz, that "spirit-child" of black musicians, as Locke called it (110), healed the fragmentation of modern life. Rejecting a mechanical organization that isolated judgment in the hands of the composer, the jazz group unified conception and execution, judgment and technical virtuosity. "Much of the musical superiority and force of jazz," Locke wrote, "comes from the fact that the men who play it create it" (97). Creativity and judgment flourished among all members of the group as improvisation balanced the power of the composer and conductor. The result formed a music that "comes alive from the activity of the group, like folk-music originally does, instead of being a mere piece of musical execution" (97). Within the communal group that liberated selfhood, the mastery of cultural material more closely resembled play than the sterility of technical mastery. And this insight—that specific practices rooted in play reconciled the individual and communal modes of existence within a loving reverence for self and other—constituted the black gift of beauty to a new America (**"Beauty"**).

6. Locke and the Struggle for the Jamesian Legacy

The Harlem Renaissance ultimately failed to yield a sustained cosmopolitanism based on an "art vitally rooted in the crafts, uncontaminated by the blight of the machine, and soundly integrated with life" (**"American Negro" ["The American Negro as Artist"]** 179). Locke's conception of a self-fulfilling paganism and creative playful spontaneity was corrupted by an emerging culture of consumption and fun morality. "Faddist negrophiles" (**"Spiritual" ["Spiritual Truancy"]** 66) and the culture industry converted Harlem, the black Mecca, into an exotic entertainment colony of the erotic, epitomized by the Cotton Club. Harlem as a spiritual center for cultural renewal was in this way corrupted into a kind of forerunner of Club Med, the self-styled "antidote for civilization." Even many black artists and writers had misunderstood the modernist impulse or allowed themselves to be co-opted by the fashionable cult of the Negro. Indeed, these "spiritual truants" had betrayed the black masses by creating a new stereotype rather than a new Negro, a stereotype of black instinctual spontaneity that complemented, rather than challenged, a civilization based on degrading work and dehumanizing leisure (**"Spiritual"** 63).

The transfiguring imagination was also beset by a new demand for the subordination of art to technical reason. Marxism redirected the quest for a native radicalism into the demand that art carry out the revolutionary role assigned by historical necessity. In response, Locke attacked the subordination of art to the demands of a political theory heavily influenced by positivism and the Enlightenment's penchant for the domination of nature. Proletarian culture substituted the "clank and clatter of propaganda" for a "quieter, more indigenous radicalism" that combined a leftist turn of thought with a "real enlargement of native social consciousness and a more authentic folk spokesmanship," Locke argued in 1936 (**"Propaganda" ["Propaganda—Or Poetry?]** 55). Marxism ultimately failed to recognize that the "color line and its plight are definitely linked up with the class issue" (55). This ideology without roots in American life therefore forced an overly neat distinction between class and race, and promoted the "class angle" over race, which it deemed misleading. In truth, Locke believed, these issues were intertwined, and there existed a "high compatibility between race-conscious and class-conscious thought" (55). The task confronting the younger generation of intellectuals was "not to ignore or eliminate the race problem, but to broaden its social dimensions and deepen its universal human implications" (55).

During the 1930s and beyond, Locke resisted pseudoradicalism with the same determination that he had displayed against corporate capitalism. His commitment to a populist position saved him from the epiphanic journey of those who, like Kallen, had embraced fascism and communism only to be disillusioned by the Soviet "betrayal of socialism." During the postwar period, Kallen exalted the moral superiority of corporate capitalism and "pluralism" over "totalitarianism," whereas Locke attacked the radical empiricists who sought to identify democracy with a cult of facts and a normatively neutral pragmatism.

Locke therefore engaged Cold War liberals in a struggle over the legacy of William James. In **"Pluralism and Intellectual Democracy,"** written in 1942, Locke argued against the likes of Sidney Hook that a "pluralistically tempered" James had never advocated the "banishment of values from public life" (54). Although James had proposed "giving up for good and all the 'game of metaphysics' and the 'false' and categorical rationalizing of values," Locke pointed out that James had never advocated "sterilizing the 'will to believe' or abandoning the search for pragmatic sanctions for our values" (54). The pragmatist's philosophical "sword of pluralism," having slain foundationalist monism, was meant as a preparation for moral discourse concerning values (53). Radical empiricism, however, had abolished intellectual absolutism only to replace it with a stultifying worship of existing relations of power and inequality. Ironically, pluralists like Kallen, who had once condemned the Anglo-Saxon melting pot, were now transformed by their values into proponents of a new version of 100% Americanism.

Again Locke identified the common confusion concerning values that united Marxism and Cold War liberalism. The idea that the world could be neatly divided into facts and values was no more than a chimera of the liberal Enlightenment and its foundation of Baconian science. The world of morally neutral facts and method constituted an illusion precisely because values profoundly influenced the process of cognition, penetrating the very process of "recognizing reality" (**"Values"** 118). But just as there were no facts without values, so too were there no values without facts. As values oriented the subject in his or her construction of reality, the empirical world simultaneously exerted a profound influence on the attitude of the subject toward the object. Indeed, this complex interplay formed the very nature of values. Neither inhering solely in the object, nor determined by transcendental reason, nor yet by a transhistorical subject, values represented "personal attitudes toward an object of interest," attitudes that were intended to guide action in the world (126).

Consequently, values were not gratuitous additions to reality, nor did they embody what Sheldon Wolin has insightfully called the undebatable perceptions of a "selfless instrument of divine truth" (51). Rather, values formed the essential foundation for the public world of a shared culture. As such, they constituted morally cogent claims capable of generating both debate and agreement by virtue of their public character. In that sense, values, as James and Dewey had argued, resembled scientific hypotheses that were subject to experimentation and verification or rejection by a community of inquirers. Unlike the hypotheses found within the esoteric community of positivist science, however, values were properly the domain of all citizens by virtue of their exoteric moral education and shared moral languages. A conversation about the how and the ought of public life substituted reasons for Reason, and the formation and transformation of values in the interpretive light of tradition and experience formed the highest expression of democracy.

Shortly before his death in 1954, Locke finally found the political movement that embodied the cosmopolitan ideal. The emerging civil rights movement combined opposition to class and racial oppression with a commitment to the spiritual values of equality and dignity in a "third stage" of social protest (**"Stretching"** [**"Stretching Our Social Mind"**] 3). In the "'common cause' type of movement," each group simultaneously pursued its own goals and interests while finding unity with other oppressed groups on the common ground of shared subjugation and commitment to the democratic ideal (3). Such a movement, appropriating the "share-cropper lesson" (**"Negro Group"** 46) of populism, united people of various cultural and racial groups, "not as representatives of particular groups but as co-workers and collaborators in a common cause in which, however, their special group interests are soundly and usefully incorporated" (**"Stretching"** 4).

As equal collaborators in the movement, black Americans rejected the special status of victim, a status that threatened to perpetuate paternalism and powerlessness while dividing the forces of radical opposition. Rather, the third stage expressed a "rational fraternity" premised on a "commonality of interests" that Locke had believed to be at the heart of the great community for almost thirty years (**"Frontiers"** [**"Frontiers of Culture"**] 6). Drawing from the republican tradition the notion of politics as a practice devoted to selfhood and the public good, the movement embraced the values of nonviolent opposition as Locke's sought-for alternative to a politics premised on power, domination, and racialism. A nonviolent moral agency recognized the dignity of the other and also bridged class and racial differences by appealing to a common humanity and shared traditions.

The third-stage movement at the same time broke down the narrow notions of citizenship associated with the republican tradition by welcoming the dispossessed, the culturally different, and the powerless. The values of democracy and community were therefore broadened to include the objective of Locke's modernism—namely, the exercise of moral reason through an ongoing and inclusive dialogue concerning the meaning of the democratic tradition and the good under constantly changing historical conditions.

Although Locke did not live to see the full potential of the civil rights movement, he recognized, as few other cultural critics have, that racism is one manifestation of a fundamental crisis of values. A culture premised on the subjugation of nature and the sanctity of private rights destroys the very ethnic traditions that, along with fulfilling work and democratic participation, make personal identity possible. "Nothing is more galvanizing than the sense of a cultural past," Locke once wrote (**"Note"** [**"A Note on African Art"**]). And nothing is more conducive to mass amnesia, he might well have continued, than the inadequately public philosophy of the liberal Enlightenment.[4]

Rather than assigning values to an impoverished private sphere, on the one hand, or presenting values as unalterable Truth in a public sphere characterized by domination, on the other, we might revitalize Locke's cosmopolitan ideal. By foregoing the quest for certainty and by calling a truce in the war against nature, we may finally begin to build a truly democratic community. If we cherish the moral ideals of Kant and John Locke, but recognize that the transfiguring imagination of Alain Locke more adequately shows us the way toward realizing those ideals, then we will have more to look forward to than the extremes of disconnection on the one hand or the explosions of Howard Beach, Bensonhurst, and Central Park on the other.

Notes

Material from the Alain Locke Papers is quoted with the permission of the Moorland-Spingarn Research Center at Howard University, Washington, DC.

1. While a number of works on the Harlem Renaissance are available, see Cruse; Gates; Huggins; Lewis; and Stuckey for the dominant interpretation. Unfortunately, we still lack a biography of Locke.
2. For a useful treatment of these issues, see Benhabib; Rorty; and Smith.
3. In this sense, Bourne and Locke anticipated the more recent studies of narcissism by Lasch and Chasseguet-Smirgel. See also McWilliams. For more on this theme in Bourne's thought, see works by Blake.
4. For a discussion of this theme and its importance in the premodern world, see Arendt, who, according to Washington, influenced Locke.

Works Cited

Arendt, Hannah. *The Human Condition.* Chicago: U of Chicago P, 1958.

Benhabib, Selya. "In the Shadow of Aristotle and Hegel: Communicative Ethics and Current Controversies in Practical Philosophy." *Philosophical Forum* 21 (1989-90): 1-31.

Blake, Casey. *Beloved Community: The Cultural Criticism of Randolph Bourne, Van Wyck Brooks, Waldo Frank, and Lewis Mumford.* Chapel Hill: U of North Carolina P, forthcoming.

———. "The Young Intellectuals and the Culture of Personality." *American Literary History* 1 (1989): 510-34.

Bourne, Randolph. "Trans-National America." Resek 107-23.

Chasseguet-Smirgel, Janine. *The Ego Ideal: A Psychoanalytic Essay on the Malady of the Ideal.* Trans. Paul Barrows. New York: Norton, 1985.

Cowan, Paul. *An Orphan in History: Retrieving a Jewish Legacy.* Garden City: Doubleday, 1982.

Cruse, Harold. *The Crisis of the Negro Intellectual: A Historical Analysis of the Failure of Black Leadership.* New York: William Morrow, 1967.

Gates, Henry Louis, Jr. "The Trope of a New Negro and the Reconstruction of the Image of the Black." *Representations* 24 (1988): 129-55.

Harris, Leonard, ed. *The Philosophy of Alain Locke: Harlem Renaissance and Beyond.* Philadelphia: Temple UP, 1989.

Huggins, Nathan Irvin. *Harlem Renaissance.* New York: Oxford UP, 1971.

Lasch, Christopher. *The Culture of Narcissism: American Life in an Age of Diminishing Expectations.* New York: Norton, 1978.

Lewis, David Levering. *When Harlem Was in Vogue.* New York: Vintage, 1982.

Locke, Alain. "African Art: Classic Style." Stewart 151.

———. "The American Negro as Artist." Stewart 176-79.

———. "Art Lessons from the Congo." Stewart 137.

———. "Beauty Instead of Ashes." Stewart 24-25.

———. "A Collection of Congo Art." Stewart 148.

———. "Cultural Relativism." Harvard Philosophy Club. Cambridge, 7 Feb. 1930. Alain Locke Papers.

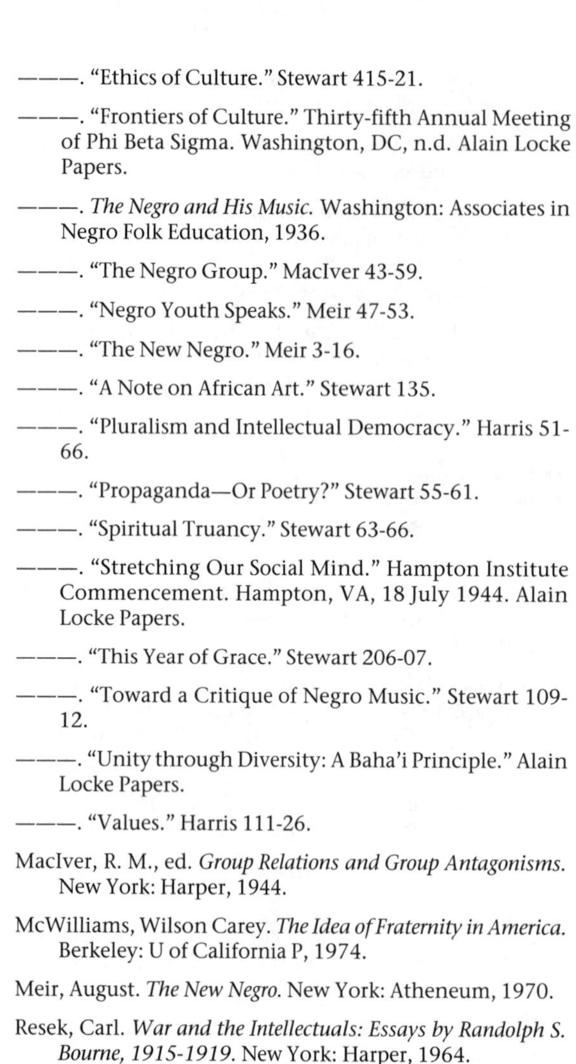

———. "Ethics of Culture." Stewart 415-21.

———. "Frontiers of Culture." Thirty-fifth Annual Meeting of Phi Beta Sigma. Washington, DC, n.d. Alain Locke Papers.

———. *The Negro and His Music.* Washington: Associates in Negro Folk Education, 1936.

———. "The Negro Group." MacIver 43-59.

———. "Negro Youth Speaks." Meir 47-53.

———. "The New Negro." Meir 3-16.

———. "A Note on African Art." Stewart 135.

———. "Pluralism and Intellectual Democracy." Harris 51-66.

———. "Propaganda—Or Poetry?" Stewart 55-61.

———. "Spiritual Truancy." Stewart 63-66.

———. "Stretching Our Social Mind." Hampton Institute Commencement. Hampton, VA, 18 July 1944. Alain Locke Papers.

———. "This Year of Grace." Stewart 206-07.

———. "Toward a Critique of Negro Music." Stewart 109-12.

———. "Unity through Diversity: A Baha'i Principle." Alain Locke Papers.

———. "Values." Harris 111-26.

MacIver, R. M., ed. *Group Relations and Group Antagonisms.* New York: Harper, 1944.

McWilliams, Wilson Carey. *The Idea of Fraternity in America.* Berkeley: U of California P, 1974.

Meir, August. *The New Negro.* New York: Atheneum, 1970.

Resek, Carl. *War and the Intellectuals: Essays by Randolph S. Bourne, 1915-1919.* New York: Harper, 1964.

Rorty, Richard. *The Consequences of Pragmatism: Essays 1972-1980.* Minneapolis: U of Minnesota P, 1982.

Smith, Steven B. "Hegel's Critique of Liberalism." *American Political Science Review* 80 (1986): 121-39.

Stewart, Jeffrey C. *The Critical Temper of Alain Locke: A Selection of His Essays on Art and Culture.* New York: Garland, 1983.

Stuckey, Sterling. *Slave Culture: Nationalist Theory and the Foundations of Black America.* New York: Oxford UP, 1987.

Washington, Johnny. *Alain Locke and Philosophy: A Quest for Cultural Pluralism.* New York: Greenwood P, 1986.

Wendell, Barrett. Letter to Horace Kallen. 3 Nov. 1907. Horace Kallen Papers. American Jewish Archives, Cincinnati, Ohio.

Wolin, Sheldon. *Politics and Vision: Continuity and Innovation in Western Political Thought.* Boston: Little, 1960.

LEONARD HARRIS (ESSAY DATE 1997)

SOURCE: Harris, Leonard. "Alain Locke: Community and Citizenship." *The Modern Schoolmen* 74, no. 4 (May 1997): 337-46.

In the following essay, Harris considers Locke's understanding of the concepts of race and community.

Alain L. Locke believed that persons should be cosmopolitan rather than partisan; "culture-citizenship" rather than parochial-citizenship.[1] Locke argued that persons should aspire to be citizens of the world and cosmopolitan in the sense of appreciating the complexity and similarities of the human community. Culture-citizenship for Locke requires that persons appreciate cultural goods across lines of parochial or partisan identity. Consequently, all forms of nationalism, ethnic loyalty, racial preference and tribal allegiances held less merit than commitment to culture-citizenship. One might thus understand Locke to favor group transcendence norms over norms associated with partisan causes. I argue that Locke has an interesting way of uniting the group transcendence norms of culture-citizenship or cosmopolitanism with a concept of "community" as an inherently socially constructed entity. This argument provides insight into an apparent paradox in Locke's works: Locke argues for reasoned commitment to partisan causes and yet ardently promotes cosmopolitanism.

Locke argued for partisanships, particularities, differentiations, specificities, cultural uniquenesses, and the justification of commitment to relatively closed parochial communities, as *Gesellschaft* and *Gemeinschaft.* Locke advocated cultural pluralism. *Gesellschaft* is defined as an association where members freely join to pursue a limited set of interests; *Gemeinschaft* is defined as an association where members are born into the group. A joined community, i.e., *Gesellschaft,* involves persons living as if each is the embodiment of the other. *Gemeinschaft,* communities formed through unchosen obligations such as communion in families, neighborhoods, or language groups, also requires that individuals live vicariously through the other, albeit, with little to no historical choice. In both cases, members hold their community associations in high regard and live vicariously through its definitions. Communities are thus enlivened by vicarious identities continually molded through experiences.[2] The interaction between individuals and groups, especially for pragmatists, creates value exchanges, transitions, transactions and integrations.

African American cultural identity, in particular, was defended by Locke. Locke defends the entitlement of African Americans to their culture, inclusive of the "racial element" in African American life because of its value as a source of advocacy against oppression and its value as a font of universalizable cultural goods.[3] In effect, group transcendent norms are not automatically favored nor presented by Locke as abstract or general norms substantively divorced from particularities.

The conflict between cosmopolitan identity and partisan identity is resolved by Locke in the following way: All persons have a consciousness of kind (how the kind is defined is socially and historically determined); consciousness of kind is asymmetrically associated with a particularity because consciousness of kind does not cause any particular identity, however all particular identities are parasitic on the existence of human inclinations to have a consciousness of kind; particularities, as social entities or groups are social constructions and subject to change ("anabsolute").[4] I consider these various ideas in Locke's works as a way of understanding how he views communities as socially constructed while allowing for reasoned partisan commitments.

FROM THE AUTHOR

A RACE CAPITAL

Here in Manhattan is not merely the largest Negro community in the world, but the first concentration in history of so many diverse elements of Negro life. . . . In Harlem, Negro life is seizing upon its first chances for group expression and self-determination. It is—or promises at least to be—a race capital.

SOURCE: Alain Locke, excerpt from his foreword to *The New Negro*, A. and C. Boni, 1925.

Communities, in my interpretation of Locke, are characteristically social constructions.[5] That is, they do not exist because of biological natures that require we bind with certain types; rather, they exist because of historical experiences, situations, popular conceptions, material interests, and conflicting values. Common values and experiences provide a sense of familiarity, warranted or imagined, and constitute individuals and communities.

There is an interaction, for Locke, between the individual and the community. The interaction helps create and shape the common character of individuals and communities. Locke did not believe, however, that communities have ontological standing. That is, communities were not objective social entities distinct from, and irreducible, to its members. In a Weberian sense, social entities, inclusive of communities, should not be reified.[6] The existence of a group is not to be treated as a phenomenon imposed upon consciousness or having agency independent of the vagaries of value shifts. Rather, groups function in terms of how persons interpret and define themselves as members. It is in the context of socially constructed communities that, for Locke, it makes sense to discuss culture and citizenship.

Citizens are persons with both legal and social standing, i.e., they hold requisite rights, privileges, and responsibilities even if they are not member's of one's community as *Gemeinschaft.* Citizens, to the extent that they are identified with a community, are also frequently raciated, i.e., seen as members of a common race or group of races. Paradigmatic citizens, from the standpoint of racist Americans, for example, are white heterosexual families. Rejecting race, *mutatis mutandis,* meant for Locke rejecting ideals of community and citizenship as raciated ideal types.

In a 1935 article, **"Values and Imperatives,"** Locke provides a broad view of community.[7] Writes Locke, "All philosophies, it seems to me, are in ultimate derivation philosophies of life and not of obstruct, disembodied 'objective' reality; products of time, place and situation, and thus systems of timed history rather than timeless eternity."[8] In a similar vain, group identities are derivative.

A group that is "anabsolute" is a group that functions as if it were an absolute feature of objective reality, but is in fact "ana"; as if. Such groups are variously stable, rigid, or well formed. They are, in effect, ontologically ambiguous. Ambiguous, in part, because they appear to be caused to exist because of some feature of human nature. Heterosexual nuclear families, for example, are not simply caused to exist by some feature of universal human nature, such as love for one's affiliates; it falsely appears as if human nature is the sole cause of some particular social characteristic. Analogously, any given ethnic group or racial group exists for numerous reasons, one of which is not that caring for affiliates causes a particular group to exist. Groups appear as if they are stable or natural. However, anabsolutes are not absolute, composite, stable, or independent of our values.[9] Nor is it the case that anabsolutes are the inalterable consequence of universal human nature.

Features of social entities are for Locke always subject to change. The geographical boundaries of nations, as well as religions or languages understood as paradigmatic of cultural groups, are subject of change. Moreover, the meaning of a given group to its members, for example, what traits are understood as honorable, is subject to change. Nations, races, or classes are always subject to intrinsic revaluation. If nations, races, or classes are understood as ontologically real, it is still the case that the features of such entities are anabsolute.

At least two ideas of Locke's value theory suggest that social groups are inherently ambiguous, and thereby anabsolute. The first is Locke's view that social constructions are forms of categorization that reflect our valuations in an effort to make sense out of our world.[10] Value judgments on Locke's account make sense of initial value experiences. Value judgments form categories, such as race, culture, nation, or class, as well as, value fields, such as agitation or repose. These categories or entities may be useful and they may have fairly well grounded referents.

Similar to Dewey and other pragmatists, Locke was staunchly against using provisionally useful abstractions and distinctions as if they were real entities. He was also against distinctions such as subject and object, stimulus and response, means and ends, individuals and society, culture and nature, mind and reality, or truth and falsity as though they were words picking out things with independent natures or distinct phenomenon and thereby forming binary opposition. There are for classical pragmatists no absolute certainties external to experience. James' famous dictum is instructive: "All 'homes' are in finite experience, finite experience as such is homeless. Nothing outside the flux secures the issue of it."[11]

Social entities are not pure, stable, static, finite, and essential phenomenon. The desire for a thoroughly efficient and effective criteria of reference, one that picks out things with finite individual natures, bespeaks an important modernist desire: the desire for certainty about the entities through which we invest or commit our individual identities and cultural values.

Locke held that "values are rooted in attitudes, not in reality, and pertain to ourselves, not to the world." However, "value pluralism does not invite value anarchy" if we accept some norms as "functional and native to the process of experience."[12] Reciprocity and tolerance were, for Locke, normative goods that could be useful in defeating loyalty to value tribes. Jorge Garcia in "African-American Perspectives, Cultural Relativism, and Normative Issues: Some Conceptual Questions" is right in noting that Locke does not develop a worked out moral argument for reciprocity and tolerance to be followed by persons with conflicting value loyalties.[13] If, however, one set of values native to experience involves imaginary bonding, stressed values, and a forever broadening sense of interchangability with kinds of persons, then it may make sense to treat social entities as functioning in various ways without a codified moral system.

Various "value tribes" or social entities may be identical in the sense that valuation is always involved, but they are certainly not "on par" or of equal worth for Locke. Garcia contends that ". . . any strong nonrankability thesis [i.e., that values between groups are on par] is implausible in functionalist forms of relativism, since such forms have built into whatever function they take as definitive of moral codes, a nonrelativized standard for evaluation of such codes."[14] Garcia is concerned here with moral foundations. However, if I consider his concern as the kind of concern the methodological individualist has for insisting on criteria of reference, then Locke's approach defeats the criticism—the methodological individualist criticism that entities should not be admitted into our ontology unless they have an identity as established by a criteria of reference. The reason this is so is because race, for Locke, does not refer to a living reality. The concept of race was also condemned for failing to satisfy reasonable criteria of reference and condemned as a social entity without reference because of its pernicious meanings and functions. Similar reasoning methods are available to defeat paganist proliferation of entities. However, whether a group exists as a social construction, anabsolute, depends on values defining group conceptions and behavior.

Social entities are, in concert with other pragmatists, provisionally useful concepts for Locke. That is, persons are subjects; and social entities at best function as if they were substances, but always fail tests of identity. We can use fairly stringent criteria for the one, but not for the other because social entities are inherently ambiguous. Treating the two as "either" one "or" the other (as satisfying or failing to satisfy stringent criteria of reference) is misguided. Entities, such as consumers, corporations, women, men, the working class, elites, professionals or parents are categories which entail the way persons almost invariably function when they hold the requisite social characteristics.

It is useful to think that consumers, corporations, the working class, elites, professionals, and parents are entities for purposes of categorizing, describing, predicting, logic, computing, and analyzing collective behavior. The nature of such entities, however, is not necessarily coterminous with individual persons as agents. It is mistaken on this account to believe that groups match unambiguous social entities, i.e., that the ontology of entities is instantiated by an ability to define, count, and predicate in ways that give us excellent descriptive and often predictive power. Social entities are ontologically and inherently ambiguous—not because we lack the knowledge to define the boundaries but (or possibly also) because the boundaries do not exist as rigid externalities. If, for example, sexuality, mothering, reproduction, and sex-affective production are individually not the causes of, nor strictly symmetrical to, "women," it does not follow on this interpretation that the social entity of "woman" is simply a mythology, an egregious reification, lacking any agency. It follows that to the extent that a group is a nonnatural social entity, it is variously ambiguous, anabsolute.

Africans, Europeans, Asians, consumers, corporations, working class, elite, professional, parents, and disabled children may be understood as social entities, albeit, of different sorts, because they tend to function more or less like substances. Their function may or may not go out of existence, but whether or not we proceed as if they are substances should not be contingent on a realist ontology but on a radical, if not revolutionary, pragmatist argument concerning their pernicious or liberating constitution.

Possibly, one problem with this approach is that we expect, or hold a background assumption, that entities in general are not ambiguous and that social entities should be as congruent as natural entities; possibly we want to confer existence on phenomenon only if they exist as undifferentiated social kinds or neatly definable social entities. The way Locke treats the value categorization of social entities, as phenomenon which are not necessarily symmetrical or coterminous with the subject, allows a broader range of considerations for addressing what entities should fit into our ontology.[15]

The following discussion of the importance of instincts and the disjunction between instincts and any particular, always transient, identity, will be used to help clarify the character of Locke's commitment to particularities. Analogous to the transient character of groups, individuals are always engaged, on Locke's account, in transvaluations, revaluations, transactions, and transfigurations, and value transfers from one field to another. Social constructions or categories such as race, nation, and class are lived experiences through the vagaries of our instincts. On Locke's account, "human society must [have] a [certain homogeneity based upon] consciousness of kind."[16] "Kinds" are contingent social entities.

One feature of what Locke means by consciousness of kind is that it is an instinct as a sort of inclination or latent potential. This is a motivation that is invested in each person and manifest in every social grouping. In addition, what counts as a kind is contingent on social and historical circumstances in conjunction with physical limitations. Kind consciousness is analogous to a free variable because it is never a cause but always a potential source of sustenance. The relationship between a social group and a kind consciousness is thus asymmetrical.

The asymmetry between universality and particularity, and the inherent ambiguity of social entities, is one that allows Locke to deny the existence of natural races and maintain support for the raciated community of African Americans.[17] The cultural specificity of African Americans, which includes the reality of racialism, is not seen by Locke as a biologically based group, but a social-historical group with cultural goods that can contribute to a broader community.

Race as a biological category does not exist for Locke, yet, race is considered a category with contributions to make to culture and not antithetical to universal civilization. I want to sketch one way this view might be refigured: When it references that feature of a culture that has, as one feature it must navigate, erroneous identification as a race.

In **"Race Contacts and Inter-racial Relations: A Study of the Theory and Practice of Race,"** a series of lectures given in 1915-1916 with the aid of the Howard University chapter of the National Association for the Advancement of Colored People (NAACP), Locke argued against the idea that races exist and were biologically caused to express cultural traits.[18] Locke held that races were socially constructed, i.e., social races, and that cultures were the manifestation of stressed values, always subject to transvaluation and revaluation. Social races are groups falsely identified as a biological kind coterminous with a social or cultural kind, e.g., white, black, Negro, Caucasian, Mongolian do not exist in nature but in how we self define and are defined by others in various cultures.[19] There is no unfettered, unmediated, uninterpreted access to racial qualia. There is nothing natural about racial entities. Even if there is a biological entity, for example, "Negro," there is no social entity that matches this group, especially given the myriad of interracial and cross-racial unions over the centuries.

Locke's rejection of the idea that biological races exist and necessarily express cultural traits went beyond early twentieth century ways of understanding communities, and thereby, citizenship. Communities were often understood as racial or ethnic kinds, thereby representing ontological entities. It is arguable, for example, that the working class is an ontological entity, i.e., an embodied collective group with agency. Workers are citizens of various countries, but as members of the class of workers with ontological status, they arguably have agency *qua* workers. Locke rejected the idea that races are ontological entities cutting across communities. There is nothing biologically natural or socially codified about racial categories that render them definable as ontological entities; social race identity cuts across citizenship status but does not form an ontological entity.

There are several meanings of "race" in Locke's works which were not always neatly distinguished. One meaning is a biological sense grounded on notions of physical racial types. Locke criticized racial classification theories that equated racial types with "definite cultural traits and heredity."[20] Categories determined by strict averages of physical characteristics do not fit all the possibilities of racial cross mixing and intermixtures arising from very mobile persons. Moreover, "[t]his tendency toward identifying cultural aptitudes with ability to survive has constantly to be discounted and combatted."[21] The erroneous link of racial types with culture, aptitude, and survivability renders the use of biological concepts of race, especially to imply social significance, fundamentally problematic.

Another sense of "race" is what Locke terms "culture-type or social race." This is the concept at the basis of Wagley's "On the Concept of Social Race in the Americas": "A 'social race' is the perception by others and self perceptions of group identity understood as a kind of person [*sic. race*] coterminous with a social or cultural kind."[22] A "social race" is a "social entity" in the sense that it is a conceptual phenomenon that references to definable individual members. On Locke's account, "[i]nstead therefore of regarding culture as expressive of race, race by this interpretation is regarded as itself a culture product."[23] "Race" here consists of the "stable and stock character" of ethnic traits, social heredity, relatively stable reactions, rates of assimilation and affection. Group bonding traits are not rooted in any inherent biologically inherited traits, psychological natures, or constant unchanging forms of valuation. Rather, ". . . race may itself be regarded as one of the operative factors in culture since it determines the stressed values which become the conscious symbols and tradition of the culture."[24] Stressed values help account for cultural continuity and persistence. "Race operates as tradition, preferred traits and values."[25]

It is important to note that race as biology, in relation to the meaning of race as a social entity, is irrelevant. As Wagley and more recently St. Clair Drake's two volume *Black Folks* note, biological significance for a social race plays a strictly social role.[26] In America, for example, the "one drop" rule applies, i.e., one drop of Black blood makes a person Black.[27] The quintessential "Black" person is of dark African heritage. The identity of Black is thus always degenerative. Only white people can bear white children; but any partner that includes someone with any heritage of Black identity makes the offspring Black. The biological import, for example, what diseases a person is susceptible to by virtue of an overwhelming Jewish or Anglo-Saxon heritage; whether a person's heart rate, hair type, blood characteristics, skin features or body size is all congruent with being Japanese is irrelevant if it turns out that there is one sub-saharan African anywhere in their background. Moreover, actual color is irrelevant. A person that appears white, but is known to have anywhere in one's background 'one-drop' of Black blood is, on the one-drop rule American account, Black. Actual biology is irrelevant to the designation. Social heredity matters in social race, not biological heredity. As Locke contends in "Who and What is Negro,' 1942, in response to the question of what counts as distinctively or uniquely "Negro": "[t]here is, in brief, no *'The Negro'*."[28] There are only cultural styles, themes, or idioms that make a work of literature more or less common to Afro-American culture, i.e., stressed values.

These distinctions between the senses of "race" are not intended to suggest that Locke never believed in the existence of biological race in a weak sense, i.e., in the sense that some physical features such as heart rates or hereditary diseases can be limitedly categorized as types. The distinctions are intended to provide a closer interpret of Locke, to clarify how race, as a designation is most often used, and to provide a conceivably defensible refigured conception of social race as a community construction.

Race unity, as a form of bonding, was especially pernicious for Locke. The social and cultural groups formed in part because of the pernicious existence of racialism were at best provisionally defensible forms of association if they were associations open to internal and external revaluations. Thus, "The Negro" does not exist for Locke not only because the concept of race as a biological type is itself erroneous and because race as a biological type coterminous with a culture is indefensible, but also because "The Negro" is not *sui generis* or a static social construction. Moreover, there is no reason why the racialism endemic to America or African American culture should be permanent as a cultural dynamic.[29]

Philosophers have often relied on ontological stringency, i.e., that some array of features can sufficiently define the boundaries and members of a social entity. We expect, or hold a background assumption, that entities in general are not ambiguous and that social entities should be as congruent as natural entities to be treated like nature, i.e., we want to confer existence on phenomena in a *sui generis* fashion. However, if social entities are inherently ambiguous, arguments for the entitlement of, or commitment to, a social entity are arguments that reference an enigmatic phenomena. The way Locke treats the value categorization of social entities, as phenomena which are not necessarily symmetrical or coterminous with the subject, allows a broader array for addressing what entities should fit into our ontology.

Locke, I believe, accepts that feature of experience which involves imaginary bonding, stressed values, and transvaluations as a basis of all social connectedness. Yet, entities are inherently ambiguous; they are not fixed absolutes or substances but socially constructed phenomena which function like common sense notions of substance—subject to critique, not subject to criteria of reference that compel us to match the subject with the social. The subject and the social object are not pure identities or pure opposites.

Avoiding reification of particularities is crucial, for Locke, as well as seeing that universalities or group transcendent norms arise from particular value loyalties. Cosmopolitanism can only arise from a refiguration of particularities. Effective moral agency occurs through relationships formed in community.[30] A reasoned commitment to a particularity should include consideration of a particularity's actual and potential capacity as a conduit to a broader, provisionally transcendent, culture and community. Culture-citizenship, is consequently, a form of cosmopolitan pluralism.[31]

Notes

I am indebted to comments on an earlier version to participants of the Second Henle Conference, Nature vs. Nurture, Saint Louis University, April 1996.

1. See for an argument against the idea that Locke was an atavist, Leonard Harris, "Identity: Alain Locke's Atavism," *Transactions of the Charles S. Peirce Society,* XXVI:1 (Winter 1988):65-84. Also see Leonard Harris, *The Philosophy of Alain Locke* (Philadelphia: Temple University Press, 1989).

2. See for Locke's voluminous works on universal aesthetic values in literature, African American literature in particular, and advocacy, Jeffrey C. Stewart, *The Critical Temper of Alain Locke: A Selection of His Essays on Art and Culture* (New York: Garland Publishing, 1983).

3. See for a discussion of various approaches to Locke on community Archie Epps, Nathan I. Huggins, Harold Cruse, Albert Murray, Ralph Ellison, "The Alain L. Locke Symposium," *Harvard Advocate* (December 1, 1973):9-29.

   See for an exploration of Locke's ontological relativism and his similarity to Derrida, Ernest D. Mason, "Deconstruction in the Philosophy of Alain Locke," *Transactions of the Charles S. Peirce Society* XXIV:1 (Winter, 1988):85-106.

4. I argue for this interpretation of Locke in "Alain Locke and Community," *Journal of Ethics,* forthcoming, and "Rendering the Subtext: Subterranean Deconstruction Project," ed., Leonard Harris, *The Philosophy of Alain Locke: Harlem Renaissance and Beyond,* pp. 279-289.

5. See also "Identity: Alain Locke's Atavism," *Transactions of the Charles S. Peirce Society,* XXVI:1 (Winter 1988):65-84, and "The Characterization of American Philosophy: The African World as a Reality in American Philosophy," *Quest: Philosophical Discussions,* 11:1 (June 1988):25-36.

6. See Max Weber's "Objectivity in Social Science," in *Max Weber: Sociological Writings,* ed., Wolf Heydebrand, (New York: Continuum, 1994), pp. 248-258.

7. Locke, Alain, "Values and Imperatives," in Leonard Harris, *The Philosophy of Alain Locke,* pp. 31-50.

8. Alain Locke "Values and Imperatives," in Leonard Harris, editor, *The Philosophy of Alain Locke, Harlem Renaissance and Beyond* (Philadelphia: Temple University Press, 1989), p. 34.

9. See for example, Ernest D. Mason, "Deconstruction in the Philosophy of Alain Locke," pp. 85-106.

10. George Mason, "Alain Locke's Philosophy of Value," in Russell J. Linneman, ed., *Alain Locke: Reflections on a Modern Renaissance Man, a Modern Renaissance Man* (Baton Rouge: Louisiana State University Press, 1982), pp. 34-50.

11. James, William, *Pragmatism: A New Name for Some Old Ways of Thinking, The Works of William James* (Cambridge: Harvard University Press, 1975), p. 125.

12. "Values and Imperatives," in *The Philosophy of Alain Locke,* pp. 31-32.

13. Garcia Jorge, "African-American Perspectives, Cultural Relativism, and Normative Issues: Some Conceptual Questions," *African-American Perspectives on Biomedical Ethics* (Washington D.C.: Georgetown University Press, 1992), pp. 11-18.

14. Ibid., 16-17.

15. Further consideration of conditions that should define a phenomenon's existence is not a topic I will discuss here except to note that theories of explanation that rely on stable entities may fail either to explain or predict well because entities are treated as inalterable essential substances. Conversely, theories that consider social entities abstractions without substance and thereby reject explanations in favor of descriptions or depictions may not be informative because they fail to consider entities as functioning like substances. Social entities, considered as either stable substances or vacuous associations, aggregates, groups, or serials fail to accept "ambiguity" as a real condition of possibility.

16. Alain Locke, *Race Contacts and Interracial Relations,* ed., Jeffrey C. Stewart, (Washington D.C.: Howard University Press, 1992), p. 79. Also see p. 66.

17. See Leonard Harris, "Identity: Alain Locke's Atavism," pp. 65-84.

18. See Alain Locke, *Race Contacts and Interracial Relations.*

    Also see for Locke's ideas on race relations Ernest Mason, "Locke on Race and Race Relations," *Phylon,* 4:4 (1979):342-350 and Ernest D. Mason, "Alain Locke's Philosophy of Value," Russell J. Linnemann, ed., *Alain Locke* (Baton Rouge: Louisiana State University) pp. 1-16.

19. See for the concept of social race, Alain Locke, "Theoretical Conceptions of Race," in *Race Contacts and Interracial Relations,* pp. 1-19.

    Also see Charles Wagley, "On the Concept of Social Race in the Americas," *Contemporary Cultures and Societies of Latin America* (New York: Random House, 1965) 531-532. Also see David-Hillel Ruben, "The Existence of Social Entities," *Philosophical Quarterly,* 34:129 (October 1982):295-310.

20. *Race Contacts,* "The Problem of Race Classification," p. 166.

21. *Race Contacts,* "The Problem of Race Classification," p. 172.

22. See Charles Wagley, "On the Concept of Social Race in the Americas," *Contemporary Cultures and Societies of Latin America,* pp. 531-532. Also see David-Hillel Ruben, "The Existence of Social Entities," *Philosophical Quarterly,* 34:129 (October 1982):295-310.

23. "The Concept of Race as Applied to Social Culture," *The Philosophy of Alain Locke,* p. 193.

24. Ibid., p. 194.

25. Ibid., p. 195.

26. See Max Weber, "Objectivity' in Social Science," in *Max Weber: Sociological Writings,* ed., Wold Heydebrand, (New York: Continuum, 1994), pp. 248-258.

27. See St. Clair Drake, *Black Folks Here and There* (Los Angeles: Center for Afro-American Studies, 1987).

28. See James F. Davis, *Who is Black* (Pennsylvania: Pennsylvania State University Press, 1991).

29. Locke, Alain. "Who and What is 'Negro,'" *The Philosophy of Alain Locke,* 1942, p. 210.

30. See for an excellent argument of this sort, David B. Wong, "On Flourishing and Finding One's Identity in Community," *Midwest Studies in Philosophy* XIII (1988):324-341.

31. See Leonard Harris, "Identity: Alain Locke's Atavism," *Transactions of the Charles S. Peirce Society,* XXVI:1 (Winter, 1988):65-84.

FURTHER READING

Bibliography

Tidwell, John Edgar, and John Wright. "Alain Locke: A Comprehensive Bibliography of His Published Writings." *Callaloo* 3, (1981): 175-92.

Most thorough primary bibliography to date.

Criticism

Burgett, Paul Joseph. "Vindication as a Thematic Principle in Alain Locke's Writings on the Music of Black Americans." In *The Harlem Renaissance: Revaluations,* edited by Amritjit Singh, William S. Shiver, and Stanley Brodwin, pp. 139-57. New York: Garland Publishing, 1989.

Discusses Locke's writings on jazz, particularly in The Negro and His Music.

Harris, Leonard. "Rendering the Text." In *The Philosophy of Alain Locke: Harlem Renaissance and Beyond,* edited by Leonard Harris, pp. 10-21. Philadelphia: Temple University Press, 1989.

Overview of Locke's life and his philosophy of radical pragmatism.

Helbling, Mark. "Alain Locke: Ambivalence and Hope." In *Analysis and Assessment,* edited by Gary D. Wintz, pp. 393-402. New York: Garland Publishing, 2000.

Emphasizes that Locke's background as a philosopher informs his intellectual, artistic, and social commentary.

Hutchinson, George B. "The Whitman Legacy and the Harlem Renaissance." *Walt Whitman: The Centennial Essays,* edited by Ed Folsom, pp. 201-16. Iowa City: University of Iowa Press, 1994.

Discusses the influence of Walt Whitman on Locke, James Weldon Johnson, Jean Toomer, and others.

Kallen, H. M. "Alain Locke and Cultural Pluralism." *The Journal of Philosophy* 54, no. 5 (February 1957): 119-27.

Examines Locke's pluralism as discussed in his essays "Value and Imperatives" and "Pluralism and Ideological Peace."

Long, Richard A. Review of *Race Contacts and Interracial Relations,* edited by Jeffrey C. Stewart. *African American Review* 29, no. 1 (spring 1995): 152-53.

Review of Locke's lectures on race that sees the author's views as foundational to the Harlem Renaissance.

Lott, Tommy. "DuBois and Locke on the Scientific Study of the Negro." *Boundary 2* 27, no. 3 (fall 2000): 135-52.

Compares W. E. B. Du Bois's and Locke's views on the scientific study of race, noting a fundamental difference in their attitudes to anthropology but showing that both men viewed the only criteria for race as cultural.

McLeod, A. L. "Claude McKay, Alain Locke, and the Harlem Renaissance." *Literary Half-Yearly* 27, no. 2 (July 1986): 65-75.

Claims that Locke did not fully appreciate Claude McKay's artistic talent and describes the antipathy between the two men.

Napier, Winston. "Affirming Critical Conceptualism: Harlem Renaissance Aesthetics and the Formation of Alain Locke's Social Philosophy." *Massachusetts Review* 39, no. 1 (spring 1998): 93-112.

Discusses Locke's method of cultural empowerment for Blacks using art as a means of achieving material and political goals.

Scruggs, Charles W. "Alain Locke and Walter White: Their Struggle for Control of the Harlem Renaissance." *Black American Literature Forum* 14 (1980): 91-9.

Argues that White and Locke challenged one another for the leadership of the Harlem Renaissance and shows that the system of patronage and the publishing situation for Black writers were more complicated than had been previously thought.

Washington, Johnny, *Alain Locke and Philosophy: A Quest for Cultural Pluralism.* Westport, Conn.: Greenwood Press, 1986.

Comprehensive formulation and evaluation of Locke's philosophy.

———. *A Journey into the Philosophy of Alain Locke.* Westport, Conn.: Greenwood Press, 1986.

Study of the political, cultural, and economic ideas of Locke.

OTHER SOURCES FROM GALE:

Additional coverage of Locke's life and career is contained in the following sources published by the Gale Group: *Black Literature Criticism Supplement; Black Writers,* Eds. 1, 3; *Contemporary Authors,* Vols. 106, 124; *Contemporary Authors New Revision Series,* Vol. 79; *Reference Guide to American Literature,* Ed. 4; and *Twentieth-Century Literary Criticism,* Vol. 43.

CLAUDE MCKAY

(1889? - 1948)

(Born Festus Claudius McKay; also wrote under the pseudonym Eli Edwards) Jamaican-born American poet, novelist, essayist, and journalist.

Although he was not a native of the United States and spent little time there during the 1920s and 1930s, Jamaican-born McKay is considered, with Langston Hughes and Jean Toomer, to be one of the three central figures of the Harlem Renaissance. Because of his radical politics, bohemian lifestyle, identification with the Black masses, and contempt of bourgeois values, McKay was a controversial figure in his day. But his poetry of resistance, particularly his famous sonnet "If We Must Die," struck a chord with Blacks all over the world, initiating the tone of the Harlem Renaissance movement, and inspiring later generations of Black poets. McKay's writing was rooted in English Romantic poetry, but he used traditional forms to give new voice to the social and political concerns of peoples of African descent as well as to write about his Jamaican homeland and romantic love. His writings reflect too his beliefs in the power of traditional African folk cultures and the need for Blacks to return to their African roots and their relationship with the natural world. His volume of poetry *Harlem Shadows* (1922) and his novel *Home to Harlem* (1928) were defining works of the Harlem Renaissance, and his later novels inspired the founders of the Négritude movement—another literary movement whose proponents tried to classify a Black-based, African-based aesthetic based on the ideas of the Harlem Renaissance. McKay was criticized by some prominent Black intellectuals during his own day because of his lifestyle, his political beliefs, and his shifting loyalties, but others, including Langston Hughes, acknowledged their literary debt to him. Modern scholars are divided as to the literary merits of McKay's poetry and fiction, but he is generally considered to have had a profound impact on the development of an authentic African American literature rooted in the dignity and pride of its racial heritage.

BIOGRAPHICAL INFORMATION

McKay was born Festus Claudius McKay in Sunny Ville, Jamaica, in 1889 or 1890, the youngest of eleven children. At an early age McKay was sent by his parents, who were farmers, to live with his oldest brother, a schoolteacher, so he might receive the best education possible. McKay was an avid reader and began to write poetry at the age of ten. In 1907 he met Walter Jekyll, an Englishman living in Jamaica who became his mentor and encouraged him to write dialect verse. In 1912 McKay published *Songs of Jamaica* and *Constab Ballads,* both written in dialect and recording his impressions of Black life in his native land. Also in 1912, McKay traveled to the United States to attend Tuskegee Institute in Alabama. It was in Alabama that he first encountered the harsh realities of American racism that would form the basis for much of his subsequent writing. He remained in the American South only a few months, leaving to study agriculture at Kansas State University and then moving in 1914 to New York, where he opened a restaurant and married his childhood sweetheart, Eulalie Imelda Lewars. His wife returned to Jamaica within a year to give birth to their daughter. The restaurant failed, and McKay took a series of menial jobs. In 1917 he published two poems, "Invocation" and "The Harlem Dancer," under the pseudonym Eli Edwards. More poetry followed, and in 1919 he published in the socialist magazine the *Liberator* the sonnet "If We Must Die," a call to Blacks to resist the white mobs that were attacking them during the period of racial violence known as the Red Summer of 1919. Thereafter McKay became a regular contributor to the *Liberator* and other left-wing publications.

From 1919 to 1921 McKay lived in England, where he worked for the British socialist journal *Workers' Dreadnought.* He continued to write in England, when he returned briefly to the United States, and then during his twelve-year travels through Europe, the Soviet Union, and Africa. His first published novel, *Home to Harlem,* was critically acclaimed but sparked controversy because of its realistic portrayal of Harlem life. In 1930 McKay moved to Morocco, but returned to the United States in 1934 because of financial difficulties. He was accepted into the Federal Writers Project in 1936 and finished his autobiography, *A Long Way from Home,* in 1937. He also published essays and articles in left-leaning journals such as the *Nation,* the *New Leader,* and the *New York Amsterdam News* and produced a nonfiction work, *Harlem: Negro Metropolis* (1940). McKay became a U.S. citizen in 1940 and several years later converted to Catholicism, a move that surprised his audience and friends. In 1944 McKay moved to Chicago and worked for the Catholic Youth Organization. He suffered congestive heart failure and died in 1948.

MAJOR WORKS

By the time he immigrated to the United States in 1912, McKay was an established poet in Jamaica. His early volumes of dialect verse, *Songs of Jamaica* and *Constab Ballads,* describe the beauty, strength, and self-sufficiency of rural and city folk in his native Jamaica and decry their poverty and the racist treatment they suffered at the hands of the British. In his American poems McKay continued to write about racial issues, describing the injustices of Black life in the United States and the racism he encountered as a Black immigrant. His 1919 sonnet "If We Must Die" was revolutionary in its content and tone, as it urged Blacks in no uncertain terms to actively resist white oppression. If Blacks must die at the hands of racists, the poet urges, they must not go lying down, likes hogs about to be slaughtered; they should go down fighting. McKay uses the traditional sonnet form to offer a powerful new message of resistance and pride to the Black masses.

McKay also wrote nonpolitical poems, many of which he published in a volume of pastoral lyrics, *Spring in New Hampshire* (1920). However, McKay was ashamed that the collection omitted his protest verse, and two years later he published *Harlem Shadows,* which included "If We Must Die" and other militant poems. During this time McKay also wrote articles on political issues for the *Liberator* and other magazines. When he moved to the Soviet Union in 1923, he continued to work as a journalist and published his articles analyzing American racism in *Negry v Amerike* (1923; *The Negroes in America*). He also published a volume of short stories, *Sudom lincha* (1925; *Trial by Lynching*). While in Europe, McKay wrote *Home to Harlem,* which he had published in the United States. The novel tells the story of poor, working-class Black immigrants in Harlem. The novel's characters, including the protagonist, Jake, are mostly poor, ignorant, and dispossessed but McKay presents them with sympathy and shows their rough, hard-drinking ways. They are depicted also as happier and more courageous than educated, middle-class people. This theme is continued in McKay's second novel, *Banjo* (1929), which describes the exploits of an expatriate African American musician in Marseilles. The stories in McKay's collection *Gingertown* (1932) are different in style and tone from his first two novels, with their Jamaican setting and pastoral mood. This mood is reflected too in his final novel, *Banana Bottom* (1933), which tells the story of Bita Plant, who returns to Jamaica after being educated in England and struggles to form an identity that reconciles her new aesthetic values with her native roots.

In the final years of his life McKay published two works of nonfiction: an autobiography, *A Long Way from Home,* and *Harlem: Negro Metropolis,* a work that earned him little recognition at the time but remains an important historical source. His second autobiography, *My Green Hills of Jamaica,* was published posthumously in 1979.

CRITICAL RECEPTION

McKay's two volumes of verse published in Jamaica earned him a medal from the Jamaican Institute of Arts and Science, making him the first Black writer to be so honored. In the United States his work was less warmly received, although he did soon find a home in radical literary circles. The liberal publisher Max Eastman, for example, published his poetry and took him on the editorial staff of the *Liberator.* When McKay's poem "If We Must Die" was published in the *Liberator* in 1919, it brought him instant fame among Blacks and was the rallying cry for the Harlem Renaissance. The poem became so well known that Winston Churchill used it in a speech against the Nazis during World War II, and many Black civil rights groups in the United States invoked it during the 1960s. McKay's other works received mixed reviews both during and after his life. *Harlem Shadows* was praised by many Black intellectuals as the first collection of poetry that truly dealt with racial issues. The volume was a landmark publication for the Harlem Renaissance because it showed other Black writers that questions of race could be dealt with in thought-provoking, serious literature. McKay's first novel, *Home to Harlem,* had minor commercial success and was widely praised for its realistic depiction of Black life, but some critics, including W. E. B. Du Bois, lambasted it. It was seen by some as portraying negative elements of Black society and of pandering to white tastes and stereotypes of African Americans. *Banjo* and *Gingertown* garnered little notice during his life, but McKay's final novel, *Banana Bottom,* appealed to readers because of its realistic depictions of the Jamaican landscape. Today it is considered McKay's finest novel and is admired for its affirmation of Black culture.

During his life McKay was regarded as the *enfant terrible* of the Harlem Renaissance because of his unconventional sexual preferences (he was bisexual) and unabashed championing of the Black masses. Some important intellectuals, including Alain Locke, criticized him because of his shifting political allegiances and rejection of communism (although McKay remained a committed socialist). Critics today view McKay as an important figure in the Harlem Renaissance, although some regard his work as being uneven and stylistically immature. Critics generally do not rank McKay's works with those of Hughes or Toomer, but many credit McKay with ushering in a new chapter for Black writing in the United States and beyond. He was the first writer to focus on issues of racism and equality and inspired the best writers of his own and subsequent generations to do the same.

PRINCIPAL WORKS

Constab Ballads (poetry) 1912

Songs of Jamaica (poetry) 1912

Spring in New Hampshire and Other Poems (poems) 1920

Harlem Shadows (poetry) 1922

Negry v Amerike [*The Negroes in America*] (essays) 1923

Sudom lincha [*Trial by Lynching: Stories about Negro Life in North America*] (short stories) 1925

Home to Harlem (novel) 1928

Banjo: A Story without a Plot (novel) 1929

Gingertown (short stories) 1932

Banana Bottom (novel) 1933

A Long Way from Home (memoir) 1937

Harlem: Negro Metropolis (nonfiction) 1940

My Green Hills of Jamaica and Five Jamaican Short Stories (memoir) 1979

PRIMARY SOURCES

CLAUDE MCKAY (POEMS DATE 1922)

SOURCE: McKay, Claude. "America." "If We Must Die," and "Spanish Needle." In *Harlem Shadows: The Poems of Claude McKay,* pp. 6, 24, 53. New York: Harcourt Brace and Company, 1922.

The following three poems, including McKay's best-known verse piece, "If We Must Die," originally published in The Liberator *in 1919, were compiled from his 1922 collection.*

"AMERICA"

Although she feeds me bread of bitterness,
And sinks into my throat her tiger's tooth,
Stealing my breath of life, I will confess
I love this cultured hell that tests my youth!
Her vigor flows like tides into my blood,
Giving me strength erect against her hate.
Her bigness sweeps my being like a flood.
Yet as a rebel fronts a king in state,
I stand within her walls with not a shred
Of terror, malice, not a word of jeer.
Darkly I gaze into the days ahead,
And see her might and granite wonders there,

Beneath the touch of Time's unerring hand,
Like priceless treasures sinking in the sand.

"IF WE MUST DIE"

If we must die, let it not be like hogs
Hunted and penned in an inglorious spot,
While round us bark the mad and hungry dogs,
Making their mock at our accursed lot.
If we must die, O let us nobly die,
So that our precious blood may not be shed
In vain; then even the monsters we defy
Shall be constrained to honor us though dead!
O kinsmen! we must meet the common foe!
Though far outnumbered let us show us brave,
And for their thousand blows deal one death-
blow!
What though before us lies the open grave?
Like men we'll face the murderous, cowardly
pack,
Pressed to the wall, dying, but fighting back!

"THE SPANISH NEEDLE"

Lovely dainty Spanish needle
With your yellow flower and white,
Dew bedecked and softly sleeping,
Do you think of me to-night?

Shadowed by the spreading mango,
Nodding o'er the rippling stream,
Tell me, dear plant of my childhood,
Do you of the exile dream?

Do you see me by the brook's side
Catching crayfish 'neath the stone,
As you did the day you whispered:
Leave the harmless dears alone?

Do you see me in the meadow
Coming from the woodland spring
With a bamboo on my shoulder
And a pail slung from a string?

Do you see me all expectant
Lying in an orange grove,
While the swee-swees sing above me,
Waiting for my elf-eyed love?

Lovely dainty Spanish needle,
Source to me of sweet delight,
In your far-off sunny southland
Do you dream of me to-night?

GENERAL COMMENTARY

ROBERT A. SMITH (ESSAY DATE 1948)

SOURCE: Smith, Robert A. "Claude McKay: An Essay in Criticism." *Phylon* 9, no. 3 (third quarter 1948): 270-73.

In the following essay, Smith discusses McKay's poetry and considers whether his protest affected the quality of his poetry.

Claude McKay fits into a pattern of thought which had its genesis directly after World War I. He did not agree with the theory of passive resistance, or of complacent nonchalance, as did some Negro writers. His strongest attribute was the extreme dislike for prevailing standards of racial discrimination; hence he lost no opportunity, when writing, to attack the *status quo.*

The period into which he found himself thrust was a virtual whirligig. During it, Negroes in great numbers shifted from an agrarian to an urban habitat. When they reached the North, for this is where the majority went, they found some avenues of employment hitherto closed to them, now opened wide. Politics, social rights, government positions, and better jobs generally, converged on the race, and the recipients began to strike out in some of these areas. Negroes were used as strike breakers in the steel mills of Pittsburgh; they were used as cheap labor in many other industries, and they also entered in great numbers the various professional fields.

This wholesale exodus was not, however, without certain repercussions. Whites found themselves having to work beside Negroes. Negroes showed up beside whites in the theatres and at the beaches. All of this the whites resented and they did not fail to make it known. The result was a series of race riots in many of those areas, during the year of 1919.

Along with this change in conditions and philosophy, there was a marked evolution on the part of Negro poets and their work. The change is obvious when the poetry of this period is compared with that of the writers of other times. Phillis Wheatley was not concerned with social protest. Paul Laurence Dunbar was satisfied to write of the lowly Negro in most of his poems. Even a poet as late as William Stanley Braithwaite wrote objectively, and advised Claude McKay to do the same.[1] Previously, most poets had written for the love of the art; now they decided, for the most part, to use their poetry as *media* for attacking race prejudice in all of its ramifications. Negroes had no swords, so the poets took up pens for them. Foremost in this movement was Claude McKay, whose vituperation was the extreme.

In 1911, through the aid of a friend, McKay published a group of poems entitled ***Songs of Jamaica.*** This book brought him recognition from The Institution of Arts and Sciences. The poems in the collection are, for the most part, written in

West Indian dialect, and they delve deeply into the souls of the natives. All are simple, but represent lowly subjects interestingly treated.

During his tenure as a constable McKay wrote many poems, all of which were collected and published in 1912 as ***Constab Ballads.*** Most of these poems are also written in the native dialect, and are excellent interpretations of West Indian life and folk-lore. One of the funniest in this group is the naive song of the jackass driver on the road.

This dialect of the British West Indian corresponds to that of the Negroes in Charleston, South Carolina, and the neighboring islands. As for the other poems in the group, some are excellent; others are inconsequential. However, folklore usually involves simple subjects, true to life. Occasionally, the author makes a mistake in dialect, but none is tremendously important. Here or there he misplaces a word, or is inconsistent in his rime. These errors are the sort one would expect to find in the work of a beginner, or in that of an immature writer.

Shortly after this book was published, McKay came to the United States. With the intention of completing his education, he entered a Negro college in the South. Not satisfied with the institution chosen, Tuskegee Institute, he stayed only three months before leaving for Kansas State College. Here he studied for two years.

New York now beckoned to him, and he heeded its call, partly because he wanted to try his fortune there, and partly because he had received a legacy which he wished to enjoy. The legacy was soon spent, and McKay found himself completely broke. He was then forced to obtain various types of employment such as waiting table, dishwashing, cleaning houses and hotels, serving as a janitor, and working as a longshoreman. During the years of 1917, 1918, 1919, he managed to get material published in *The Seven Arts, The New Masses, The Liberator,* and *Pearson's Magazine.*

In 1919 McKay went abroad, visiting several European countries, including England, Belgium, and Holland. He lived in London for a year and while there published another group of poems, ***Spring in New Hampshire.*** The title poem is representative, and can be read with some appreciation. All of these poems were later reprinted in ***Harlem Shadows.***

Two years later found the author back in the United States, but he remained only for a short period. After accepting a position as associate editor of the *Liberator,* he again went abroad, this time to Russia and to Berlin. Later, in 1921, he had published ***Harlem Shadows,*** his best known collection of poems. This book spoke the passionate language of a persecuted race, and its author did not make the least attempt to disguise his feelings. He did not attempt to please his white readers; his voice is a direct blast at them for their policy of discrimination. Many of the poems are saturated with protest. For example, in the octet of **"Enslaved,"** McKay traces the ills and suffering of the race during its sojourn in various lands; then in the sestet he calls for the complete destruction of "the white man's world." One can easily find here the philosophy of a race expressed in the few lines of a poem. This is not the poetry of submission or acquiescence; this is not the voice of a gradualist; or is this the naive dialect of the jackass driver. It is one of scorching flame, a voice conscious of persecution, that dares to strike back with vehemence.

McKay's brother, his tutor, was an independent thinker, inculcating the idea of freedom of thought into the mind of young Claude. As a result of his ideas the latter found himself in difficulty as a constable. Later, in the South, he was faced with the problem of discrimination. His attempts at independent thought never ceased, however, and he drifted toward the Left, identifying himself with radical artists of various types. He joined them in their attacks on discrimination. Through all of this storm and stress, however, he constantly denied being a Communist. Other writers, as well as he, used the arts in fighting the racial problem. They decried injustice by the use of caustic diatribes. McKay was simply defiant in his protest poetry. So much so was he, that in many instances this characteristic completely obscures his lyricism.

In the title poem, **"Harlem Shadows,"** one finds various shades of this protest, yet there is also some semblance of beautiful lyricism. There are some good interpretations of life in Harlem, Negro section in upper Manhattan. The poem is mediocre, but reveals the author's bitterness toward the conditions which produce the Negro prostitutes of Harlem. I question the poet's choice of such as a title poem for his book. Certainly this is a sordid aspect of the race to thrust forward. In addition, it is not the best poem in the collection. The greatest justification that can be found for it is that it is realistic, and accurately describes a phase of existing life.

One must admit that the author's most powerful dudgeon lay in this protest poetry. Whether he wrote an epigram, a sonnet, or a longer poem, his thought is sustained. He expressed the deepest resentment, but even when doing so his feelings were lucid. He did not stumble as he attempted to express himself. This dynamic force within his poetry caused him to be constantly read and re-read by his admirers and critics. They realized that here was a man of deepest emotions, as well as one who was a skilled craftsman.

In the sonnet, McKay had found a verse form peculiarly adaptable to his taste and ability. His talent was diversified, but this form with its rise and fall seemed quite the thing for the thought which he wished to convey to his readers. Sonnets that bear out this idea are **"America," "If We Must Die,"** and **"The Lynching." "America"** does not show McKay's bitterness. It gives advice to Negro Americans to face squarely the tests and the challenges that come to them as a persecuted minority. **"If We Must Die"** reflects the author's acrimony toward the lynchers of Negroes. Written during the epidemic of race riots which swept the country in 1919, its theme is: "fight back; do not take a beating lying down".

Other poems which in content are racial protest are: **"In Bondage," "Outcast," "The White City,"** and the **"Barrier."** The rebellious philosophy in McKay may be traced back through his turbulent youth, and his affiliation with radical organizations and people.

Occasionally, however, one sees another side of McKay. When he puts down his rancor, his lyricism is entirely clear. He paints pictures that are beautiful; especially is this true when he describes scenes of his native islands. One sees in the poet a sort of nostalgia for home, for relatives, and for the scenes of childhood days, long past. It is in this idyllic mood that McKay appears in an entirely different light. Possibly one of the best poems of this sort is **"Flame-Heart."** It contains beautiful lines of description such as "The poinsettia's red, blood red in warm December," and "Sweet with the golden threads of the rose apple." **"To One Coming North"** and **"The Tropics in New York"** are in the same vein. Although not concerned with the West Indies, they do picture scenes of nature and peacefulness. Their mood is one of quietness also. Others in this group show McKay's range and facility. There is sheer delight in reading them, and the collection would be richer with more of the same tone. For further reading I recommend: **"To O. E. A.," "Romance," "Summer Morn in New Hampshire,"** and **"Spring in New Hampshire."**

McKay took upon himself a tremendous task when he chose to be the leading spokesman of an oppressed race. The question always arises as to whether a poet loses any or all of his effectiveness when he takes upon his shoulders the problem of fighting. Does one's lyrical ability become clouded by his propaganda or bombast? is another question. This, it seems, may or may not be true. In the case of McKay, what he has had to say, for the most part has been important. Literary history is full of humanitarians who attacked conditions that were unsavory. Some were successful in their attacks; others were not. Although he was frequently concerned with the race problem, his style is basically lucid. One feels disinclined to believe that the medium which he chose was too small, or too large for his message. He has been heard.

Notes

1. Claude McKay, *A Long Way From Home* (New York, 1937), p. 27.

WAYNE COOPER (ESSAY DATE 1964)

SOURCE: Cooper, Wayne. "Claude McKay and the New Negro of the 1920's." In *Analysis and Assessment, 1940-1979,* edited by Cary D. Wintz, pp. 485-94. New York: Garland Publishing, Inc., 1996.

In the following essay, originally published in Phylon *in 1964, Cooper discusses McKay's life and major works and assesses his place in the New Negro movement, which was the broader Black cultural, social, and political movement of which the Harlem Renaissance was a part.*

As used in the 1920's, the term "New Negro" referred to more than the writers then active in the Negro Renaissance. The New Negro also included the Negro masses and especially the young. "For the younger generation," Alain Locke wrote in 1925, "is vibrant with a new psychology."[1] This new spirit he described as basically a renewal of "self-respect and self-dependence."[2]

The new confidence which characterized Negroes in the twenties resulted from many forces. Prior to World War I, militant new leaders had arisen. By demanding immediately full civil liberties and an end to segregation, men such as W. E. B. DuBois had inspired a greater self-assertiveness in their people. World War I and the resulting mass migration of Negroes to the urban North further disrupted old patterns of life and created new hopes, as well as new problems. The fight for democracy abroad led to greater expectations at home. The bloody race riots of 1919 did not kill these hopes, although the remarkable popularity of Marcus Garvey and his black nationalism indicated the Negro masses could not forever contain their frustrated aspirations.[3] As the Negro people entered the twenties, the "promised land" of the old spirituals still seemed far away. But their new militancy demonstrated that the long journey down the bitter desert years of history had strengthened, not weakened, their determination to reach the good life ahead.

That sudden flowering in literature called the Negro Renaissance gave voice to the new spirit awakening in Negroes in the twenties.[4] In addition, the Negro Renaissance became a part of the general revolt by the writers of the decade against the gross materialism and outmoded moral values of America's new industrial society. Negro writers found new strength in their own folk culture. As Robert Bone has written, "The Negro Renaissance was essentially a period of self-discovery, marked by a sudden growth of interest in things Negro."[5]

Of all the Renaissance writers, Claude McKay was one of the first to express the spirit of the New Negro.[6] His first American poems appeared in 1917. Before the decade of the Negro Renaissance had begun, he was already winning recognition as an exciting new voice in Negro literature.[7] A brief examination of his early career will perhaps reveal more clearly some of the important characteristics of the New Negro of the 1920's.

Claude McKay was born September 15, 1889, on the British West Indian island of Jamaica. There he grew to manhood. In 1912, at the age of twenty-three, he came to the United States to study agriculture at Tuskegee Institute. In Jamaica, McKay had already established a local reputation as a poet, having produced before he left two volumes of dialect poetry, ***Song of Jamaica*** and ***Constab Ballads.***[8]

These volumes revealed McKay to be a sensitive, intelligent observer of Jamaican life. Of black peasant origin himself, he used the English dialect of rural Jamaica to record lyrically the life of his people. In evaluating McKay's Jamaican verse, Jean Wagner has recently written:

> Here, we are far from the dialect of the Dunbar school, inherited from the whites, who had forged it in order to perpetuate the stereotype of Negro inferiority, and at best fix them in their role of buffoons charged with diverting the white race. . . .[9] All things being equal, McKay's portrait of the Jamaican peasant is in substance that of the peasant the world over. Profoundly attached to the earth, he works the soil with a knowledge gained from age long habit; although a hard worker, the Jamaican, like his counterpart the world over, is condemned to exploitation.[10]

On the eve of his departure to the United States, McKay appeared to be an ambitious, talented young man with a fine future in Jamaica. In his poetry he had closely identified himself with its people. He had also revealed a deeply sensitive, independent spirit, keenly responsive to the good and evil in both man and nature.

Like many before him, however, he was strongly attracted to the United States. Years later, he wrote that America then seemed to him, "a new land to which all people who had youth and a youthful mind turned. Surely there would be opportunity in this land, even for a Negro."[11] Although far from naïve, McKay had never experienced firsthand American racial prejudice, and he seemed to have been totally unprepared for its vicious effects.

His initiation into the realities of Negro American life must certainly have been a swift one. Landing in Charleston, South Carolina, in the summer of 1912, he proceeded to Alabama's Tuskegee Institute. In 1918, McKay recorded in *Pearson's Magazine* his first reaction to Southern racial prejudice.

> It was the first time I had ever come face to face with such manifest, implacable hate of my race, and my feelings were indescribable. At first I was horrified; my spirit revolted against the ignoble cruelty and blindness of it all. . . . Then I found myself hating in return, but this feeling could not last long for to hate is to be miserable.[12]

Accompanying this statement were several poems, which, McKay said, had been written during his first year in America. "I sent them so that you may see what my state of mind was at the time."[13] Among them was one of his most eloquent polemics—**"To the White Fiends."** This poem shows a personality unaccustomed to servility and murderously aroused against the brutish debasement of Southern prejudice. If the poet could not physically defeat it, he, nevertheless, could throw a revealing light on its moral inferiority.

> Think you I am not fiend and savage too?
> Think you I could not arm me with a gun
> And shoot down ten of you for every one of my
> black brothers murdered, burnt by you?
> Be not deceived, for every deed you do
> I could match—out-match: Am I not Afric's son,
> Black of that black land where black deeds are
> done?
> But the Almighty from the darkness drew
> My soul and said: Even thou shalt be a light
> Awhile to burn on the benighted earth,
> Thy dusky face I set among the white
> For thee to prove thyself of higher worth;
> Before the world is swallowed up in night,
> To show thy little lamp: go forth, go forth![14]

Soon tiring of what he described as "the semi-military, machine-like existence"[15] at Tuskegee, McKay transferred to Kansas State College, where he remained until 1914. In that year he was given several thousand dollars by an English friend.[16] Having decided his future lay in writing, not agricultural science, he took the money and went to New York City.

Once there, literary success did not come quickly. In fact, during his first year in New York, little time seems to have been devoted to writing. As he described it, through "high-living" and "bad investments" he soon managed to lose all his money.[17] His marriage to a Jamaican girl shortly after his arrival in New York lasted almost as briefly as his money.[18] "My wife," McKay wrote in 1918, "wearied of the life [in New York] in six months and went back to Jamaica."[19] McKay himself made a different decision. "I hated to go back after having failed at nearly everything so I just stayed here and worked—porter . . . janitor . . . waiter—anything that came handy."[20]

He also wrote, "If I would not," he said, "graduate as a bachelor of arts, I would graduate as a poet."[21] Within two years, Waldo Frank and James Oppenheim accepted for *Seven Arts Magazine* two of his sonnets, **"The Harlem Dancer"** and **"Invocation."**[22] A year later he was discovered by Frank Harris, who brought him to public notice again in *Pearson's Magazine.* Shortly afterwards, McKay met Max Eastman and his sister, Crystal. A lifelong friendship resulted.

At the time, Max Eastman was editor of *The Liberator,* then America's most openly Marxist literary magazine.[23] Through the *Liberator,* McKay quickly became identified with the radical-bohemian set in Greenwich Village. In 1919, Eastman and his staff were eagerly praising the young communist government of Russia, violently denouncing the repressive post-war hysteria at home, and writing stories and poems that ranged from fighting proletariat propaganda to tender pieces of home and mother. Few magazines, then or now, could match the *Liberator* in enthusiasm. Despite its flamboyancy, however, it was rich in talents. "On the surface," Robert Aaron has written, "*The Liberator* reflected the aimless, pointless life of the village." Yet, as Aaron pointed out, after World War I, it displayed a "toughness and militancy in its social attitudes,"[24] which belied its bohemian character.

Into such an atmosphere McKay fitted well. Eastman has described him then as a very black, handsome, high-spirited young man, with peculiar, arched eyebrows which gave him a perpetually quizzical expression.[25] Another old radical, Joseph Freeman, remembered also in his autobiography McKay's charm and wit.[26]

If McKay was sometimes given to abandoned gaiety, in the summer of 1919 he had good reason to exhibit a greater seriousness, as well as toughness. 1919 was the year of the Great Red Scare, one desperate phase of the effort to return to pre-war "normalcy." For Negroes, the year turned into a nightmare of bloody riots and violent death.[27] From June until January there occurred no less than twenty-five riots in major urban centers throughout the country.[28] The Chicago riot of July was the worst. When it was over, authorities counted 38 Negroes and whites dead, over 520 injured, and 1,000 families homeless.[29] Like all Negroes, McKay felt the emotional effects of such battles.

In the July issue of the *Liberator*[30] there appeared, along with six other poems, his now famous **"If We Must Die."** Today, it is the one poem by which McKay is most widely known. **"If We Must Die"** was a desperate shout of defiance; almost, it seemed a statement of tragic hopelessness. At the same time, it loudly proclaimed that in Negroes the spirit of human courage remained fully alive. Here is the poem which brought McKay to the alert attention of the Negro world. If not a great poem it, nevertheless, must certainly have expressed the attitude of many Negroes in 1919.

> If we must die, let it not be like hogs
> Hunted and penned in an inglorious spot,
> While round us bark the mad and hungry dogs,
> Making their mock at our accursed lot.
> If we must die, O let us nobly die,
> So that our precious blood may not be shed in
> vain; then even the monsters we defy
> Shall be constrained to honor us though dead!
>
> . . . . .
>
> What though before us lies the open grave?
> Like men we'll face the murderous, cowardly
> pack,
> Pressed to the wall, dying, but fighting back!

After his appearance in *The Liberator,* McKay entered more fully into the literary world. His career through the twenties reads, in fact, like a romance of the decade itself. Through the generosity of friends, he went to England in late 1919 and stayed for more than a year, working part of the time for Sylvia Pankhurst's socialist paper, *The Workers' Dreadnought.* While there his third book of poems, ***Spring in New Hampshire,*** appeared.[31]

Upon his return to the United States in 1921, he became for a brief time co-editor of *The Liberator* with Michael Gold. Before leaving that job because of policy differences with Gold,[32] McKay's first American book of poems, ***Harlem Shadows,***[33] appeared. During this period, he also made a brief first acquaintance with many leading Negro intellectuals, among them James W. Johnson and W. E. B. DuBois.[34] But before the end of 1922, he was off again, this time to Russia.

McKay was among the first Negroes to go to Russia after the Civil War which had brought the Communists into undisputed power. He arrived during Lenin's period of ideological retrenchment, when the New Economic Policy allowed a limited amount of free enterprise and personal freedom. Because of his black complexion, McKay immediately attracted the attention of people in the street. Although not a party member, or even definitely committed to Marxist principles, McKay's popularity with the crowds in Moscow and Leningrad helped win him favor among higher party circles. Sen Katayama, then Japan's leading Communist, got McKay admitted to the Fourth Congress of the Communist International.[35] But above all, as McKay wrote James Weldon Johnson in 1935, "It was the popular interest that irresistibly pushed me forward."[36] His trip soon turned into one long triumph of personal popularity.

After meeting Trotsky in Moscow, he was sent on a long and elaborate tour of Soviet army and naval bases. Besides Trotsky, he met Zinoviev and other top Communists, as well as many leading Russian literary figures.

Despite McKay's sincere attraction to the Communist Revolution, he never fully committed himself to its ideology. In the 1930's, he was viciously attacked by American Communists for going back on his principles; but, as he wrote James Weldon Johnson in 1935, he went to Russia as "a writer and free spirit"[37] and left the same. He wrote Johnson then and later repeated in his autobiography that he had desired in 1922 the title, "creative writer," and had felt it would mean more to Negroes in the long run.[38]

Throughout the twenties, and to a large extent throughout his life, McKay remained what Frederick Hoffman called the "aesthetic radical."[39] This was the artist who, typical of the twenties, stoutly affirmed the value of his non-social personality. He considered himself "the natural man," willing in an age of conformity to be only himself. That McKay shared this attitude is evident in all his writings.

Like other Negro writers of the twenties (most notably, Langston Hughes), he shared, to some degree, the same feeling of alienation that characterized Gertrude Stein's "lost generation." Thus, in 1918, McKay could write: "And now this great catastrophe [World War I] has come upon the world, proving the real hollowness of nationhood, patriotism, racial pride, and most of the things one was taught to respect and reverence."[40] His affiliation with *The Liberator* and his trip to Russia were part of a personal search for new moral and social standards.

McKay's trip to Russia marked the beginning of his long twelve-year exile in Europe. From Russia, he went briefly to Germany, then to France, where he lived for a number of years. In the late twenties, he journeyed to Spain and then to Morocco in North Africa where he remained until his return to the United States in 1934.[41]

Why did McKay spend twelve years wandering through Europe and North Africa? He never felt himself to be a typical expatriate. In his autobiography, he gave perhaps the main reason for his long expatriation.

> Color consciousness was the fundamental of my restlessness . . . my white fellow-expatriates could sympathize but . . . they could not altogether understand . . . unable to see deep into the profundity of blackness, some even thought . . . I might have preferred to be white like them . . . they couldn't understand the instinctive . . . pride of a black person resolute in being himself and yet living a simple civilized life like themselves.[42]

The place of Negroes in the modern world was the one great problem that obsessed McKay from his arrival in the United States until his death in 1948.[43] For a while after World War I, he undoubtedly thought that in Communism Negroes might find a great world brotherhood.

In the twenties, he turned from international communism but not from the common Negro, with whom he had always closely identified. He came to the conclusion that in Negro working people there existed an uninhibited creativity and joy in life which Europeans, including Americans, had lost. In their folk culture lay strength enough for their salvation. McKay felt Negroes should not lose sight of their own uniqueness and the value of their own creations while taking what was valuable from the larger European civilization. He laid much emphasis on the need of Negroes to develop a group spirit.[44]

Among Negro writers of the twenties, McKay was not alone in his discovery of the folk. In fact,

FROM THE AUTHOR

ON THE IMPORTANCE OF GROWTH AND DEVELOPMENT

Nations, like plants and human beings, grow. And if the development is thwarted they are dwarfed and overshadowed.

SOURCE: Claude McKay, excerpt from "Out of the War Years: Lincoln, Apostle of a New America," in *New Leader* 13, February 1943.

of central importance to the Negro Renaissance was its emphasis on Negro folk culture. Jean Toomer, for example, celebrated the black peasants of Georgia, and in the following verses, associated himself with their slave past:

O Negro slaves, dark purple ripened plums
Squeezed, and bursting in the pine-wood air,
Passing, before they stripped the old tree bare
One plum was saved for me, one seed becomes

An everlasting song, a singing tree,
Caroling softly souls of slavery,
What they were, and what they are to me,
Caroling softly souls of slavery.[45]

In enthusiastic outbursts, youthful Langston Hughes was also loudly proclaiming the worth of the common folk.[46]

To a certain extent, the New Negro's emphasis on the folk was heightened by the new attitude toward Negroes exhibited by many white writers of the twenties. After World War I certain white writers such as Gertrude Stein and Waldo Frank thought they saw in Negroes beings whose naturally creative expressiveness had not been completely inhibited by the evil forces of modern civilization.[47] As the twenties progressed, Negroes and their arts enjoyed a considerable vogue. Primitive African art became popular among many intellectuals. Jazz, of course, became popular in the twenties. Negro singers found a greater public receptivity, and the blues entered American music. In many respects, American Negroes had in the twenties a favorable opportunity for a reassessment of their past accomplishments and future potentials.

The great emphasis on the primitive and the folk led however to some naïve delusions. Just as whites had previously built a stereotype of the happy, simpleminded plantation Negro, many people in the twenties stereotyped Negroes as unfettered children of nature, bubbling over with uninhibited sexual joy and child-like originality. To the extent that Negro writers accepted such an image, they limited the depth and richness of their own evaluations of American Negro life.[48]

While he was in Europe, McKay produced three novels which reflected his own interest in the Negro folk. They were ***Home to Harlem*** (1928),[49] ***Banjo*** (1929), and ***Banana Bottom*** (1933). He also produced a volume of short stories entitled ***Gingertown*** in 1932.[50] To a considerable extent, McKay's view of the Negro common folk was influenced by the newer stereotype of Negroes. ***Home to Harlem,*** his first novel, is the story of Jake, a Negro doughboy, and his joyful return to Harlem after World War I. Jake seems to have been McKay's ideal type—an honest, carefree worker whose existence, if a rather aimless one, is not complicated by pettiness or unnecessary worry over things that do not immediately concern him. Contrasted to Jake is Ray (McKay himself), an educated Negro, who is torn between two ways of life—Jake's and the more serious though conventional one imposed upon him by education. While the virtues of the common folk are contrasted to the doubts and confusion of the educated, McKay takes the reader on a tour of Harlem cabarets and rent parties.

His unvarnished view of Harlem night life delighted many white readers of the twenties and dismayed not a few middle-class Negroes.[51] The latter felt that an undue emphasis on the Negro lower class would damage their fight for civil rights and further delay their just battle for liberty. McKay was not the only writer of the Negro Renaissance to upset respectable Negro society.[52] One of the chief results of the Negro Renaissance was to force the Negro middle class to reevaluate their relationship to the Negro masses.

McKay's second novel, ***Banjo,*** told the story of the Negro beachboys of Marseilles, and further contrasted the free life of common Negroes with the frustrations of those caught in the more sophisticated web of modern civilization. In his third novel, ***Banana Bottom,*** he idealized the folk culture of Jamaica.

In some ways, Claude McKay differed radically from the typical New Negro writer of the twenties. For one thing, he was a Jamaican and did not become an American citizen until 1940. For another, he was older by some ten years than most writers of the Negro Renaissance; and except for a brief period, he did not live in the United States at all in the twenties.

He was also unique in the extent to which he associated with the larger literary world. Most Negro writers of the twenties had depended on Negro publications for a start. McKay's first successes were in white magazines—*Seven Arts, Pearson's,* and *The Liberator.* As an editor of *The Liberator* for a brief while, he was probably the only Negro writer of the time to hold such a position on an important American publication. McKay was at least partly responsible for the greater degree of communication that existed between Negro and white writers in the twenties. On the eve of his departure for Russia in 1922, James Weldon Johnson gave him a farewell party, and invited prominent writers of both races. Years later Johnson wrote to McKay concerning that event:

> We often speak of that party back in '22. . . . Do you know that was the first getting together of the black and white literati on a purely social plane. Such parties are now common in New York, but I doubt if any has been more representative. You will remember there were present Heywood Broun, Ruth Hale, F. P. Adams, John Farrar, Carl Van Doren, Freda Kirchway, Peggy Tucker, Roy Nash—on our side you, DuBois, Walter White, Jessie Fauset, [Arthur] Schomburg, J. Rosamond Johnson—I think that party started something.[53]

Although McKay's career differed somewhat from that of the typical Negro writer of the twenties, he represented much that was characteristic of the New Negro. His movement from rural Jamaica to the big city and the literary world of the twenties is itself symbolic of the larger movement by Negro people from the rural South to the broader horizons of the urban North. His early interest in Communism was only one indication that the New Negro would no longer be unaffected by world events. World War I had ended American isolation for both Negroes and whites.

In his prose, McKay stressed the value of the common Negro and joined other Negro Renaissance writers in a rediscovery of Negro folk culture. But it is for his poetry that McKay will be longest remembered. For in his poetry, he best expressed the New Negro's determination to protect his human dignity, his cultural worth, and his right to a decent life.

Notes

1. Alain Locke (ed.), *The New Negro* (New York, 1925), p. 3.
2. *Ibid.*, p. 4.
3. Two recent general discussions of the New Negro of the twenties are found in Robert A. Bone. *The Negro Novel in America* (New Haven, 1958), pp. 51-107; and Jean Wagner, *Les Poetes Negres des États-Unis* (Paris: Librairie Istra, 1963), pp. 161-207.
4. Wagner, *op. cit.*, p. 161.
5. Bone, *op. cit.*, p. 62.
6. Wagner, *op. cit.*, p. 211.
7. McKay first became widely known after the appearance of his poem, "If We Must Die," in *The Liberator* (July, 1919), 20-21.
8. Claude McKay, *Songs of Jamaica* (Kingston: Aston W. Gardner and Co., 1912); *Constab Ballads* (London, 1912).
9. Wagner, *op. cit.*, p. 219.
10. *Ibid.*, p. 220.
11. McKay, *My Green Hills of Jamaica* (Unpublished mss. in the Schomburg Collection, New York Public Library), p. 80, written in the mid-1940's.
12. *Pearson's Magazine* (September, 1918), 275.
13. *Ibid.*
14. *Ibid.*, p. 276.
15. *Ibid.*
16. Letter from McKay to James Weldon Johnson, March 10, 1928, in the McKay folder of Johnson Correspondence (James Weldon Johnson Collection, Yale University Library).
17. Countee Cullen (ed.), *Caroling Dusk, An Anthology of Verse by Negro Poets* (New York, 1927), p. 82.
18. Marriage certificate in the McKay Papers (Yale University Library).
19. *Pearson's Magazine* (September, 1918), 276.
20. *Ibid.*
21. McKay, *A Long Way From Home* (New York, 1937), p. 4.
22. Wagner, *op. cit.*, p. 215.
23. For a good discussion of *The Liberator* and its origins see, Daniel Aaron, *Writers on the Left, Episodes in American Literary Communism* (New York, 1961), pp. 5-108.
24. *Ibid.*, p. 92.
25. In McKay, *The Selected Poems of Claude McKay* (New York, 1953), p. 110.
26. Joseph Freeman, *An American Testament, A Narrative of Rebels and Romantics* (New York, 1936), pp. 243, 245-46, 254.
27. John Hope Franklin, *From Slavery to Freedom, A History of American Negroes* (New York, 1947), pp. 471-73.
28. *Ibid.*
29. *Ibid.*, pp. 473-74.
30. *The Liberator* (July, 1919), 20-21.
31. McKay, *A Long Way From Home*, pp. 59-91.
32. *Ibid.*, pp. 138-41. See also, Aaron, *op. cit.*, p. 93.

33. McKay, *Harlem Shadows* (New York, 1922).

34. McKay, *A Long Way From Home,* pp. 108-15.

35. *Ibid.,* pp. 165-66.

36. Letters from McKay to James Weldon Johnson, May 8, 1935, in the McKay folder of the Johnson Correspondence (James Weldon Johnson Collection, Yale University Library).

37. *Ibid.*

38. *Ibid.*

39. Frederick J. Hoffman, *The Twenties, American Writings in the Postwar Decade* (New York, 1955), pp. 382-84.

40. *Pearson's Magazine* (September, 1918), 276.

41. McKay, *A Long Way From Home,* pp. 153-341, contains an account of his travels through Europe and North Africa. A briefer account is in Wagner, *op. cit.,* pp. 215-17.

42. McKay, *A Long Way From Home,* p. 245.

43. For McKay's views on race toward the end of his life, his "Right Turn to Catholicism" (typewritten ms. in the Schomburg Collection, New York Public Library) is especially important.

44. These ideas were presented by McKay in two novels, *Banjo* (New York, 1929), and *Banana Bottom* (New York, 1933). He discussed the idea of a "group soul" in *A Long Way From Home,* pp. 349-54.

45. In Wagner, *op. cit.,* p. 292.

46. Langston Hughes, "The Negro Artist and the Racial Mountain," *The Nation* (June 23, 1926), 694.

47. For a general discussion of this topic, see Wagner, *op. cit.,* pp. 174-77. Also, see Hoffman, *op. cit.,* pp. 269-71.

48. Bone, *op. cit.,* pp. 58-61.

49. *Home to Harlem* (New York, 1928).

50. *Gingertown* (New York, 1932).

51. Here are two extreme views of McKay's *Home to Harlem.* The first reflects Negro middle-class opinion.

> Again, white people think we are buffoons, thugs and rotters anyway. Why should we waste so much energy to prove it? That's what Claude McKay has done.
> (Clipping from the *Chicago Defender,* March 17, 1928, in McKay Folder, Schomburg Collection, New York Public Library.)

Now, another view:

> [*Home to Harlem* is] . . . beaten through with the rhythm of life that is the jazz rhythm . . . the real thing in rightness. . . . It is the real stuff, the low-down on Harlem, the dope from the inside.
> (John R. Chamberlain, Review of *Home to Harlem, New York Times,* March 11, 1928, p. 5.)

52. Langston Hughes, *The Big Sea, An Autobiography* (New York, 1945), pp. 265-66.

53. Letter from Johnson to McKay, August 21, 1930, in the McKay Correspondence (Yale University Library).

MARY CONROY (ESSAY DATE 1971)

SOURCE: Conroy, Mary. "The Vagabond Motif in the Writings of Claude McKay." *Negro American Literature Forum* 5 (spring 1971): 15-23.

In the following essay, Conroy discusses the elements of vagabondage in McKay's personal life and his writing, which she says are gestures to escape the harshness of life.

That ***A Long Way from Home***[1] should be the first reprint of Claude McKay's writing is indeed appropriate, since this autobiography captures the vagabondage of McKay's life from which he distilled a central motif in his fiction and poetry. This motif of vagabondage, as evident in McKay's picaresque novels, in his conception and definition of sexual vagabondage, in his dramatization of psychological vagabondage, and in his own religious vagabondage, offers poignant insights into both the creative and biographical aspects of McKay's life and thought.

The Negro primitive of McKay's second novel, ***Banjo,***[2] is a man on the move, much like his creator, whose worldly and worldwide experiences convince him, as they had convinced McKay before him, that the black man can depend only upon his own ingenuity to cope with life. This on-the-road quality and the necessity to live by wit naturally suggest certain picaresque qualities which the novel further demonstrates.

The three-fold division of the episodic adventures in ***Banjo*** indicates an obvious relationship to the picaresque. Part I centers on Banjo himself, that "great vagabond of lowly life" (**Bj** [***Banjo***] 11), who has come to Marseilles from the heart of Dixie, via a stretch in the Canadian army during World War I. More to celebrate his own instinctive joy than to earn money—for which he has absolutely no regard—Banjo forms an orchestra whose music expresses his own life; that is, the "rough rhythm of darkly carnal life" (**Bj** 57). Part II concerns the meeting of Banjo and Ray, the educated middle-class American Negro, who discovers "the veritable romance of Europe" (**Bj** 68) in the Marseilles waterfront where he sees the primitive purity of the black man's instinctive life. The Negroes in the Ditch, as the area is nicknamed, in their carefree living have somehow resisted the dehumanization that accompanies the progress of Western civilization. In the Ditch Ray comes to understand that civilization threatens "to rob him of his warm human instincts" (**Bj** 163); therefore, he resolves not to let "civilization . . . take the love of color, joy, beauty, vitality, and nobility out of *his* life and make him like the poor mass of its pale creatures" (**Bj** 164). Although Ray's formal education unites him to those "pale creatures," he decides that rather than "lose his soul," those warm human facets of life, he will "let intellect go to hell and live on instinct!" (**Bj** 165).

Part III of ***Banjo*** dramatizes Ray's eventual realization that "close association with the Jakes and Banjoes had been like participating in a common birthright" (**Bj** 321). So that he may enjoy that birthright, Ray decides to join Banjo in perpetual vagabondage. As is consistent with the picaresque tradition, there is no formal ending to Banjo, but rather a tapering-off; for the novel, as it concludes, suggests a sequel which would celebrate Banjo's and Ray's continued adventures on the road. Despite this three-fold structure, the novel gives the poetic impression of a formless form which accurately reflects the endless and constantly changing chaos of vagabond life.

Robert Alter in *Rogue's Progress,* a study of picaresque novels, notes:

> The picaroon, before all else, is an outsider. Granted, he is an outsider who can make and keep friends, and in this respect he remains distinct from the tortured and isolated outsiders of twentieth-century fiction, but the way he chooses is nevertheless a devious and personal way, not the straight, clearly-marked, foot-worn path of society at large.[3]

As a black man, Banjo, despite his beachboy friends, is automatically an outsider in the picaroon sense described by Alter. Banjo's steps, like the traditional picaroon's, tread away from the broad highway to the "twisting, garbage strewn by-ways," which, as Alter further observes, "have in general been considered off-limits for the more respectable heroes of traditional narratives."[4] Indeed, McKay's realistic description of one of Banjo's pathways, Boody Lane (actually Rue de la Bouterie near the Marseilles waterfront), conforms to Alter's observation:

> It was a few yards of alleyway with a couple of drinking-dens, a butcher shop, and hole-in-the-wall rooms where the used-up carnivora of the city find their final shelter. A slimy garbage-strewn little space of hopeless hags, hussies, touts, and cats and dogs forever chasing one another about in nasty imitation of the residents. The hub of low-down proletarian love, stinking, hard, cruel. A ditch abandoned by the city to pernicious manure, harmless-appearing on the surface. Yet ignorant seamen tumbling into it had been relieved of hundreds and thousands of francs, and many of the stupid, cold-blooded murders of the quarter might be traced there.
>
> (**Bj** 87)

Banjo exists ambivalently in the typical picaroon position, in the undefined twilight zone between the respectable world and the violence of the Ditch's underworld. He will not ingratiate himself to the white tourists of the port nor will he lower himself to pimp for the Ditch's prostitutes. Rather, in picaroon fashion, Banjo scuttles for a day-to-day existence, relying upon luck and good-natured rascality as his means of survival. Because Banjo's rascality often borders on actual crime, his sense of morality is questioned by those who weigh morality on a conventional scale. In reality, Banjo is eminently moral. Like Huck Finn, that picaroon of nineteenth-century American fiction, Banjo discards the trappings of orthodox morality to espouse a truer morality of humanity's inner spirit.

The novel's episodic structure, the delineation of Banjo's social role as an outsider, his awareness of both the hypocrisy of the socially acceptable life and the potential violence of the underworld, as well as Banjo's unorthodox morality, are the obvious features of the novel's picaresque underpinnings.

Without question, these same vagabond elements in McKay's personal life were frequently extreme psychological gestures to escape the harshness of life, having thus only a tangential relationship to the picaresque tradition. Such an escape gesture is highlighted in McKay's short story **"Truant,"**[5] in which Barclay Oram, disgusted in his role as a "dutiful black boy among proud and sure white men" (**Gt [*Gingertown*]** 143) abandons his wife and child and flees from "the huge granite gray walls of New York" (**Gt** 152). The fiction of Barclay is the fact of McKay. In partially explaining his own decision to go to Russia in 1921, McKay confessed that he had wishes to "escape from the pit of sex and poverty, from domestic death, from the *cul-de-sac* of self-pity, from the hot-syncopated fascination of Harlem, from the suffocating ghetto of color-consciousness" (**ALW [*A Long Way from Home*]** 150).

Very much as Ralph Ellison's *Invisible Man* is shuttled from place to place in the North because Bledsoe's letters instruct white folk, in effect, to "Keep This Nigger-Boy Running,"[6] McKay wrote his own letter—and to himself—and the message was identical. McKay rationalized that the black man should "go, better than stand still, keep going" (**ALW** 150). Ironically, McKay had wanted his autobiography to be entitled *Keep Going* rather than ***A Long Way from Home.***[7] McKay's preferred title suggests that for him there was no home, but only the endless pursuit of an elusive home of momentary happiness. Like the hero of his second novel, ***Banjo,*** McKay held before himself "a dream of vagabondage that he was perpetually pursuing" (**Bj** 11).

Throughout his writing McKay employs a sexual metaphor to capture this notion of never-ending vagabondage with its escape from the confining and oppressing and its pursuit of a home of happiness and peace. An examination of the facets of sexual vagabondage in McKay's writings will clarify this.

The precarious nature of the sexual relationship in McKay's writing is a reflection of the vagabond's constant mobility. Very early in ***Banjo,*** the title character's attitude toward Latnah, the Arab-black girl who invites him to live with her in the Ditch, embodies the ongoing aspect of sexual vagabondage.

> Banjo had taken Latnah as she came, easily. It seemed the natural thing to him to fall on his feet, that Latnah should take the place of the other girl to help him now that he needed the help. Whatever happened, happened. Life for him was just one different thing of a sort following the other.
>
> (**Bj** 27)

The phrase, "to fall on his feet," is, in a sense, the literal expression of this sexual vagabondage; that is, to Banjo, who "took all women as one" (**Bj** 170), it seems perfectly reasonable that he should move on, away from one particular woman (in this case, "the other girl") and toward another woman (Latnah) who will respond sexually. The woman as a person is not important; she can be Latnah or Chere Blanche or any hussy of the Ditch. What is important is that she sexually respond totally and completely to the man who has need of her. In that response, it is the intensity, not the duration, that matters.

Later in the novel when Banjo explains why he has returned to live with Chere Blanche, who had previously jilted him for a wealthy white man, he says: "I was fed up with everything and just had to have some human pusson close to me . . . I just had to take what was ready and willing" (**Bj** 234). Sex, then, operates here as an escape from reality since it is used to block out the "everything" with which Banjo is "fed up."

In somewhat the same manner the vagabond's mobility is captured in McKay's love poems in which love is most frequently reduced to the orgastic moment. The poems celebrate loves that exist only "for one perfect hour!" and lovers who are lovers "for one night only."[8] There is the beloved who "went with the Dawn" (**SP** [***Selected Poems***] 98) and the lover who confesses

> My wounded heart sinks heavier
> than stone,
> Because I loved you longer than
> a day!
>
> (**SP** 107)

Again, as in ***Banjo,*** the momentary nature of the sexual relationships stresses the intensity rather than the duration of the emotion.

In one love poem, a lyric is the metaphor for the physical act of love. McKay structures the poem on the fact that the lyric is in itself sufficient as an artistic creation; but as the addition of appropriate music to a lyric perfects that artifact, so too, the physical act of love accompanied by words of love—even if the words be untrue—perfects the sexual act. For McKay the following is **"Romance"**:

> To clasp you now and feel your
> head close-pressed,
> scented and warm against my
> beating breast;
>
> To whisper soft and quivering
> your name,
> And drink the passion burning
> in your frame;
>
> To lie at full length, taut,
> with cheek to cheek,
> And tease your mouth with kisses
> till you speak
>
> Love words, and words, dream words,
> sweet senseless words,
> Melodious like notes of mating
> birds;
>
> To hear you ask if I shall love
> you always,
> And myself answer: Till the
> end of days;
>
> To feel your easeful sigh of
> happiness
> When on your trembling lips I
> murmur: Yes;
>
> It is so sweet. We know it is
> not true.
> What matters it? The night must
> shed her dew.
>
> We know it is not true, but it
> is sweet—
> The poem with the music is
> complete.
>
> (**SP** 96)

The sexual act in the previous poem intimates a flight from reality, an escape, since it attempts to block out the truth of the situation between the lovers which is revealed at least negatively in the accompanying words.

In both fiction and poetry, then, as the previous illustrations exemplify, McKay uses the sexual metaphor to capture the never-ending, on-going nature of the vagabond and to embody the escape aspect of vagabondage. But, there is a further dimension to this. Sometimes McKay suggests that the black man separated from the happiness of his racial homeland hopes to come closer spiritually to that home by means of the sexual act. This is evident in Part III of ***Banjo,*** when Ray, the intellectual-gone-vagabond, spends the night with a black woman. In describing that night, McKay compares the woman's body to the soft brown earth, and the man is a tree nourished in that earth: "Warm brown body and restless dark body like a black root growing down in the soft brown earth" (**Bj** 283). Since in McKay's fiction and poetry, the soil is equated to a place of peace and joy for the black man, a homeland, one can here infer that McKay is expanding the soil-home equation: the woman is the soil which is the homeland. It follows, then, that in intimacy with the woman, the black man is united to his homeland.

A poem can illustrate this expanded equation. In **"Flower of Love"** (**SP** 97) McKay envisions the body of the loved one as the flower reminiscent of the tropical home where he experienced happiness and peace. McKay says in part:

> In this moment rare and tense
> I worship at your breast.
> The flower is blown,
> The saffron petals tempt my amorous mouth,
> The yellow heart is radiant now with dew
> Soft-scented, redolent of my loved South;
> O flower of love!
> I give myself to you.

The woman-soil-home equation is further substantiated in a passage from ***Banjo,*** as McKay indicates that Ray was actually seeking his homeland by means of the sexual act:

> Ray's hankering was for scenes of tropical shores sifted through hectic years. Salty-warm blue bays where black boys dive down deep into the deep waters, where the ships shear in on foamy waves and black youths row out to them in canoes and black pilots bring them in to anchor.
>
> (**Bj** 284)

Since, however, the sexual act is a surrogate in this instance, it cannot result in authenticity. McKay points out that after the act Ray "dreamed instead of Harlem," the illusory homeland of the black man. The Negro in McKay's writing, in spite of his attempt to reach a racial homeland by means of sexual intimacy, remains, like the author himself, not only "a long way from home," but in endless pursuit. He is on the road indefinitely.

A thematic variation of sexual vagabondage, psychological vagabondage, is dramatized in five Harlem-set short stories in ***Gingertown.*** Each of these stories is fashioned out of the psychological torture of its main black character who fails to identify totally with his race and thus tries to deny the existence of the tragic barrier that has been erected between the races. The usual McKay metaphor for this racial barrier is the separation of lovers:

> I must not see upon your face
> Love's softly glowing spark;
> For there's the barrier of race,
> You're fair and I am dark.
>
> (**SP** 80)

In each of these stories the main character attempts to psychologically bypass that racial barrier by means of a devious love exploit which moves the character some distance away from the race with which he has temporarily refused to identify. For a limited time the character in this psychological vagabondage experiences an idyllic happiness reminiscent of that experienced in a racial homeland; ultimately, however, this sinuous psychological vagabondage boomerangs, leaving the character ashamed of his attempts to escape his race and renewing and sharpening his racial frustrations.

McKay dramatizes Angie Dove of **"Near-White"** (**Gt** 72-104) attempting the racial metamorphosis symbolized in a hit song of the 20's. McKay writes that the "butterfly craze had hit the belt hard. . . . New York had chosen to make it the song and dance of the season, all America had followed suit, and Harlem had gone quite crazy." Thus the reader is forewarned that Angie's flight from blackness will be characterized by the seasonal brevity of the butterfly. Light enough to "pass" as white, Angie Dove has fallen in love with John, a white man who does not know that she is Negro. Because she is confident that John's love for her is stronger than any racial barrier, Angie decides to tell him of her race. She poses a hypothetical question to John, asking him if he would continue to love a woman were he to learn that she was black. His blunt answer—"I'd sooner love a toad!" ends Angie's enchanted flight.

> She dropped the broken stick of herself in the easy chair. She thought of that delicious night, they two [Angie and John] together, how his eyes had glowed over her flesh and his lips had praised, and she shuddered, remembering the sweet caress of his hand . . . their bodies warm together . . .
>
> A toad! A toad! O god! a toad!
>
> (**Gt** 104)

Quite accurately the vet from the Golden Day rationalizes in the *Invisible Man* that the white woman is "the most easily accessible symbol of freedom"[9] for the black man in American society which has driven him to seek symbolic freedom. As LeRoi Jones points out:

> For the black man, acquisition of a white woman always signified some special power the black man had managed to obtain (illicitly, therefore, with a sweeter satisfaction) within white society. It was also a way of participating more directly in white society.[10]

Miscegenation, the concern of **"Highball"** (**Gt** 105-138), is another mode of skirting the racial barrier; but it, like the "passing" in **"Near-White,"** is in McKay's presentation a temporary escape, leading the black man to a renewed awareness of his alienation.

Although a successful blues singer, the Negro Nation Roe is never quite sure of himself among his newly-acquired white artist friends. When Myra, a disreputable and near-alcoholic white woman, is attentive to him, Nation is flattered and believes that she brings "the alien white world close to him." After he divorces his black wife and marries Myra, Nation is convinced that his white friends who exclude Myra from their parties are discriminating against her because she had married a Negro. Unaware that Myra's previous reputation and her present boorishness really account for his friends' actions, Nation angrily leaves a gathering to which Myra has not been invited and decides to return to his Harlem apartment to be with her, to comfort her. As Nation opens the apartment door, he realizes that Myra is not alone; he hears Myra and her own white friends toasting him: "There was a general clinking of glasses and a tipsy young male voice cried: 'Here's to prune, prune, our nation . . . al prune'" (**Gt** 136). When Nation storms into the room, Myra and her guests flee. Standing alone in the room, Nation realizes that his white marital vagabondage has ended ingloriously, reinforcing the reality and the impenetrability of the racial barrier. "He quivered. His heavy frame shook. He knelt down against the liquor stained piano and bellowed like a wounded bull" (**Gt** 138). This happens as Nation acknowledges to himself that his black wife would never have hurt him so.

A curious similarity exists between Angie's discovery that she is a toad and Nation's realization that he is just another prune. By having Angie's and Nation's vagabondage boomerang with the flinging of verbal insults, McKay emphasizes the precarious nature of the bridge of affection between the races, since a single word charged with racial emotionalism can destroy the bridge with unmitigating finality. McKay makes it clear that Angie will never try to meet a John again, and Nation is finished with all the Myras.

Two other Harlem stories deal with "yellow fever," or the desire for a mate who has light skin and white features (the psychological implication being: if you can't marry a white person, marry someone who looks white). In the first, **"Mattie and Her Sweetman"** (**Gt** 55-71), McKay somewhat humorously tells of a homely spade-black woman in her fifties who pays one of the yellow boys of the Black Belt to live with her. When Jay, her codfish-complexioned strutter, openly insults her about her blackness at a social gathering, Mattie comes to accept the fact that she cannot escape her blackness in loving a yellow boy. Alone, she returns to her flat. Later when Jay impatiently pounds on the door, Mattie opens the window and throws the bundle of his belongings at him on the sidewalk, saying, "Theah's you' stuff. Take a walk." Mattie's "yellow fever" has been cured by a verbal insult!

The second "yellow fever" story tells of a black woman's attempt to sidestep the racial barrier in a romance with a light-complexioned Latin, but in contrast to the rather humorous development in the previous story this vagabondage is aborted by violent murder. Tillie, the wife of a Negro hotel worker, Uriah Worms, meets Manuel, the Cuban barber the Black Belt has nicknamed "The Prince of Porto Rico" (**Gt** 32-54). Tillie's infatuation grows until she arranges a romantic tryst with the Prince in her apartment. Anonymously informed of the affair, Uriah returns to the apartment, finding Manuel with Tillie. After chasing the barefooted and a pajama-clad Prince down the fire escape, Uriah follows him into a deserted alley where he shoots and kills him.

In the final story of psychological vagabondage, McKay reveals the attempt of a black woman to "bleach-out" the racial barrier. Since his hair, color, and features differ from the Anglo-Saxon norm of beauty whose importance American culture has exaggerated, the Negro begins to be ashamed of his racial features, which he assumes are the barrier to his "belonging." For the Black wanting to be assimilated into the mainstream, the next logical assumption is to believe that if he can alter his racial features, he will "belong." Thus, investing in "kink-no-more" hair processes, bleaching creams, antiseptic soaps, copious deodorants and perfumes, the Negro feels he is purchasing an entrance into American society and therefore destroying the racial barrier.

With Bess, the cabaret entertainer in **"Brownskin Blues"** (**Gt** 1-31), McKay dramatizes the futility of this maneuver. Because her boyfriend has left her for a high-yellow girl, Bess feels that she must win Rascoe back by bleaching her coffee-colored skin. In a desperate attempt to become "high-yellow," she mixes numerous lotions and salves and applies the steaming mixture to her face. To deaden the pain the mixture causes, she sniffs a bit of cocaine but falls asleep while the horrid mixture burns and disfigures her face. This disfigurement, which emphasizes Bess's separateness from the admired "high yallers," does not alienate her from the authentic members of the race but rather brings her closer. To conclude the story McKay has Jack Newell, whose complexion is "the color and coarseness of brown wrapping paper" (**Gt** 2) propose marriage. After Jack's proposal, Bess admits the futility of bleaching-out the racial barrier; moreover, she realizes that happiness is found in accepting her own race.

The five stories of psychological vagabondage as a unit argue that the racial barrier does indeed exist and that it cannot be removed or even skirted through experiments in passing, miscegenation, or "bleaching-out." The stories, then, reaffirm McKay's belief that not even the surging passion of lovers can overcome the racial barrier. By dramatizing so forcefully that sexual relationships are powerless to scale the barrier, McKay suggests, most especially in **"Brownskin Blues,"** that happiness—although certainly not idyllic happiness—is found only in an unforced, ungrudging acceptance of the heritage of one's race.

The acceptance of this racial heritage has demanded (and still demands) that the black man possess exceptional human courage. The maintaining and reinforcing of such courage has been traditionally linked to the black church. The Swedish social scientist Gunnar Myrdal goes so far as to claim that "the chief 'function' of the Negro church has been to buoy up the hopes of its members."[11] With perhaps more personal authority, Richard Wright admits that black churches "are where we dip our tired bodies in cool springs of hope, where we retain our wholeness and humanity despite the blows of death from the Bosses."[12] McKay's personal search for the "cool springs of hope" inspired in him a religious vagabondage which separated him from the institutional church of his youth, led him to agnosticism as well as to Communism (which were spiritual forces in his life), and culminated in his conversion to Catholicism in 1944.

At that time McKay admitted that he previously "never had any faith in revealed religion."[13] Such a stance no doubt stemmed from his unhappy acquaintance with institutional religion. At the turn of the century in Jamaica, the missionaries were oriented toward an essentially Fundamentalist interpretation of the Bible. Knowing the Jamaican Negro's slave origin and affronted by his seeming lack of sexual restraint, the missionaries regarded the black man as the descendant of Noah's son Ham, father of Canaan, who in Genesis (9:23-27) is cursed into slavery because of his sexual perversion. Moreover, since the Negro in his blackness and particular features is distinctive, and, in addition, had been forced into exile almost everywhere in the world, the missionaries associated the Negro with Cain's God-given mark and his condemnation to unending exile (Genesis 4:10-16). References and allusions in McKay's dialect poems make it clear that these mythical condemnations were widely believed by the Jamaican Negro.[14]

It was therefore difficult for McKay, an intelligent and racially proud Negro, to accept Christianity. McKay reveals this in a dialect poem in which a peasant rationalizes:

> . . . lookin' close at t'ings
> [Christian teachings] we hab to
> pray quite hard
> Fe swaller wha' him [the Christian
> preacher] say an' don't think bad
> o' Gahd.
>
> (**SJ** [***Songs of Jamaica***] 56)

Since Christianity as McKay knew it in Jamaica viewed the black man so negatively, it is not surprising that as a very young man he abandoned the institutional Church.

Espousing agnosticism under his brother's tutelage, McKay furthered his estrangement from institutional religion by his interest in evolution. Evolution was particularly attractive to McKay because as he explains in **"Cudjoe Fresh from**

De Lecture" (**SJ** 55-58), evolution erases the scriptural condemnations of the Negro and stresses the equality of all races. McKay describes Cudjoe (Cousin Joe) coming from an evolutionary lecture and meeting his cousin George. Cudjoe speaks:

> . . . dis man tell us 'traight 'bout how de whole t'ing [creation] come, an' show us widout doubt how Gahd was not fe blame; How change cause eberyt'ing fe mix up 'pon de eart', An' dat most hardship come t'rough accident o' birt'.

It was indeed more reasonable for McKay to view race as an "accident o' birt'" rather than the personification of Biblical curses.

In a later verse of the same poem, Cudjoe explains that the black race was actually a natural development to ensure a balance in all things:

> No cos say we get cuss mek fe we
> 'kin come so,
> But fe all t'ings come 'quare,
> same so it was to go.

McKay's own explanatory note to these lines of dialect is: "It is not because we were cursed (Gen. IX, 25) that our skin is dark; but so that things might come square, there had to be black and white." (**SJ** 56) In addition to removing the Biblical curses and providing a balance in nature, evolution offers the remote possibility that this "accident o' birt'" may be reversed. As Cudjoe expresses it:

> But suppose eberyt'ing could tu'n
> upside down,
> Den p'raps we'd be on top. . . .
>
> (**SJ** 57)

This remote possibility is more favorable than the unalterable word of scripture which irrevocably seemed to condemn the black man.

Moreover, evolution, even as the illiterate Cudjoe can reason, provides the further possibility that in time the black man's status will be improved. History supports this possibility, since, as Cudjoe admits, the Negro race progressed since it left Africa for temporary slavery in Jamaica. After the Jamaican emancipation, the Negro, according to Cudjoe, is better off than he would have been, had he remained in Africa:

> Yes, Cous' Jarge, slabery hot fe
> dem dat gone befor';
> We gettin' better times, for those
> we no know;
> But I t'ink it do good, tek we
> from Africa
> An' lan' us in a blessed place as
> dis a ya.
> Talk 'bouten Africa, we would be
> deh till now,
> Maybe some half-naked—all day
> dribe buccra cow,
> An' tearin' t'rough de bush wid
> all de monkey dem,
> Wile an' uncibilize', an' neber
> comin' tame.

McKay's dissociation from the institutional church of his youth and his affection for the rather simplistic scientific inquiry he aligned with agnosticism are, by testimony of his dialect poems, mutually rooted in his concern for racial equality. It was this same concern for racial equality which moved McKay to adopt Communism as a spiritual force in his life. Whereas other American writers felt, as Arthur Koestler analyzes, that Communism was "the logical extension of the progressive humanistic trend . . . the continuation and fulfillment of the great Judeo-Christian tradition,"[15] McKay thought that Communism was the human and spiritual force that would improve the black man's status throughout the world. As Stephen Bronz correctly perceives in *Roots of Racial Consciousness,* McKay's idealistic appraisal of Communism appears in an article written in 1921, in which McKay ways, "I love to think of Communism liberating millions of city folk to go back to the land."[16] The metaphorical extension of this idealism seems to be the hope that Communism would enable the harassed black man of the urban ghettoes to return to the idyllic happiness of the peasantry.

When McKay later came to believe that Communism's concern for the black man served only the Party's purposes, his hope in Communism was destroyed. Since "the edifying flight of the guardian angel of Communism, toting . . . a black baby in his bosom to the realms of democracy, [had] ended with broken wings and the black baby [was] dumped down . . . in its ugly old cradle,"[17] McKay abandoned Communism.

Toward the end of his life McKay felt that the Catholic Church was lifting the black baby that Communism had failed. His final conversion to Catholicism in 1944 is best explained—on the rational level, at least—by the Church's opposition to Communism and the racial equality that the Church seemed to offer. After McKay was hired by Bishop Bernard J. Sheil to teach and research at the Sheil School of Social Studies in Chicago, he became increasingly more aware of the first real effort being made by the Catholic Church to correct the interracial conflicts which had developed within it and to help the black man it had previously failed to recognize. Although the effort was feeble, and even at times totally ineffective, it did offer hope to McKay.

The thirteen sonnets published after his conversion show that McKay had faith in the Church's effort to ensure harmonious racial relations. The glory of the Middle Ages for McKay is that then the Church gave birth to racial equality and protected *all*. In the sonnet entitled **"The Middle Ages"** McKay describes the Church as

> . . . brooding over all points
> of view
> Like a grand tree, rooted in faith
> supreme,
> Its glory and its strength pro-
> tecting all.[18]

McKay's view of the Middle Ages did not blind him to the reality of the 20th Century. In another poem he admits that fifteen million American Negroes must go to their knees praying that racial discrimination will end (**SP** 44). Yet McKay is confident that within the Church **"The New Day,"**[19] the promised time when "all black and brown and white, / Together work and play in harmony," will dawn. In addition to this hope for racial harmony, McKay looked to the Church for ultimate solace. In several sonnets, the black man becomes the Christ-figure, wounded and thorn-crowned (**SP** 50), who like Joe Christmas in Faulkner's *Light in August,* treads the "classic road" of lonely suffering (**SP** 51). But these sonnets of lonely suffering always voice as well McKay's conviction that because the black man has suffered on earth, he will be more highly rewarded in heaven.

The "eternal quest" of the black man, which McKay in a 1920 love poem (**SP** 107) defines as the search for sexual love, he seems to redefine in religious terms at the end of his life. Very much like the literary vagabonds he had created, then, McKay, the religious vagabond, had simultaneously attempted to escape the unpleasant racial realities of life and to pursue the happiness inherent in racial harmony. In the solace afforded by the Church, McKay had hoped to destroy—at least within his mind—that racial barrier that had only further frustrated his literary characters. That he actually did destroy that racial barrier is questionable; but his literary vagabondage around that barrier and his own religious vagabondage provide, hopefully, various insights into his life and his thought.

Notes

1. Claude McKay, *A Long Way from Home* (New York: Harcourt, Brace and World, Inc., 1970). Hereafter cited in text, abbreviated ALW, and followed by page reference.
2. *Banjo* (New York: Harper and Bros., 1929). Hereafter cited in text, abbreviated Bj, and followed by page reference.
3. *Rogue's Progress* (Cambridge, Massachusetts: Harvard University Press, 1964), p. 71.
4. *Rogue's Progress,* p. 62.
5. *Gingertown* (New York: Harper and Bros., 1932), pp. 139-162. Hereafter cited in text, abbreviated Gt, and followed by page reference.
6. *Invisible Man* (New York: New American Library, 1953), p. 35.
7. See: McKay Correspondence in James Weldon Johnson Collection, Beinecke Rare Book and Manuscript Library, Yale University. Letter of Laurence Roberts to McKay, June 15, 1936.
8. *Selected Poems* (New York: Bookman, 1953), p. 94; p. 99. Hereafter cited in text, abbreviated SP, and followed by page reference.
9. *Invisible Man,* p. 139.
10. LeRoi Jones, *Home* (New York: Morrow and Company, 1966), p. 23.
11. *An American Dilemma* (New York: Harper and Row, 1962), p. 936.
12. *12 Million Black Voices* (New York: Viking Press, 1941), p. 131.
13. "On Becoming a Roman Catholic," *Epistle,* II (Spring, 1945), p. 43.
14. *Songs of Jamaica* (Kingston, Jamaica: Gardner and Co., 1912). In particular, see "Cudjoe Fresh from de Lecture," pp. 55-58; "Killin' Nanny," p. 83; "My Native Land," pp. 84-85. Hereafter cited in text, abbreviated SJ, and followed by page reference.
15. Quoted in Daniel Aaron, *Writers on the Left* (New York: Harcourt, Brace and World, 1961), p. 157.
16. "How Black Sees Green and Red," *Liberator,* IV (June, 1921), p. 20.
17. "Lest We Forget," *Jewish Frontier,* VII (January 1940), p. 10.
18. "The Middle Ages," *Catholic Worker,* XIII (May 1946), p. 5.
19. "The New Day," *Interracial Review,* XIX (March, 1946), p. 37.

RICHARD PRIEBE (ESSAY DATE 1972)

SOURCE: Priebe, Richard. "The Search for Community in the Novels of Claude McKay." *Studies in Black Literature* 3 (summer 1972): 22-30.

In the following essay, Priebe claims that a dominant theme in McKay's novels is the search for community, and that this search is defined by economic and cultural oppression.

> Whence all this passion toward conformity anyway?—diversity is the word. Let man keep his many parts and you'll have no tyrant states. Why, if they follow this conformity business they'll end up by forcing me, an invisible man, to become white . . .
>
> (Ralph Ellison, *Invisible Man*)

Though Claude McKay's first novel ***Home to Harlem,*** made the *New York Herald Tribune's* best seller list when the book first appeared, his writing was generally ignored for almost forty years. Now virtually every anthology of Afro-American literature includes selections of his poetry, and his work is beginning to appear in anthologies of West Indian literature. Generally rejected by black intellectuals during his lifetime, the Jamaican-born writer is being posthumously claimed by those in his native land as well as the United States. The question of whether he is an American or Caribbean writer is a moot one, though it does point to some interesting aspects of his work, aspects which we will be examining in the course of this paper. We will, at any rate, sidestep the question by referring to him as Afro-American, employing the term in its widest sense to include all black writers of North and South America, as well as the Caribbean.[1]

If we look at the ideas presented in McKay's three novels, ***Home to Harlem, Banjo,*** and ***Banana Bottom,*** an intriguing, though complex and often confusing pattern emerges. But controlling this pattern we perceive the dominant theme of a search for community. Jake tries to find a place for himself in the United States, and fails; Banjo tries to establish a sense of stability in his life as a vagabond in Europe, but he too fails. Finally, Bita finds a place among the peasants of Jamaica. As Kenneth Ramchand has noted, "Art reveals possibilities. Mr. Naipaul's observed Tulsi world is a copy of a society from which it is necessary to escape. In ***Banana Bottom,*** Claude McKay imagined a community to which it is possible to belong."[2] Seen as the key element in the matrix within which these novels develop as related units, this theme will aid us in understanding many of the apparently contradictory elements, as well as the relationships between the various characters within each separate work. While Ramchand has done quite an interesting job in discussing the theme of community in ***Banana Bottom,*** he has built his analysis on what he sees to be weaknesses in the other novels. Moreover, he fails to come to terms with rather similar "weaknesses" in ***Banana Bottom.*** We are told that in the earlier novels "there is a self-conscious straining for a polemic effect,"[3] and "blatant manipulating of character and event . . ."[4] These statements can just as easily be applied to ***Banana Bottom,*** but more importantly we might accept them without accepting any concomitant negative value which they are intended to convey.

If we try to evaluate McKay's novels in terms of the conventions established by other British and American novelists, we will indeed find them rather weak. As Don L. Lee, Imamu Baraka, Addison Gayle and other writers and critics have effectively argued, the world (i.e., the western world), has all too long evaluated the art of Third World peoples in terms of a narrowly defined aesthetic. In literary criticism this has come to be realized in the so-called "new criticism" which excludes consideration of purpose and external matters in the process of evaluation.[5] Though critics such as Gayle do not seem to exclude the possibility of using new critical methods as tools, however limited, for aiding one in coming to grips with the perceptions a given work offers, they are just as bent as the new critics on exploring literature along racial lines.

We seem to be moving away from the subject at hand, though only to define a worthwhile approach. All literature deals with perceptions—perceptions not merely about what is, but also about what is possible. In this, of course, there should be an important process of selection. Ralph Ellison has written, "The function, the psychology, of artistic selectivity is to eliminate from art form all those elements of experience which contain no compelling significance."[6] Unfortunately he also makes a rather specious argument about the distinction between art and sociology. With any oppressed people their "elements of experience" which will be of the most "compelling significance" will not be the same as those of a more comfortable group of people. To reduce this to the simplest of terms, they will be those elements which are concerned with surviving and escaping the oppressed situation. At this point we can establish our frame of reference with the words of Frantz Fanon: "Every colonized people—in other words, every people in whose soul an inferiority complex has been created by the death and burial of its local cultural originality—finds itself face to face with the language of the civilizing nation; that is, with the culture of the mother country. The colonized is elevated above his jungle status in proportion to his adoption of the mother country's cultural standards . . ."[7] To the extent, then, that a people are economically oppressed, so will they be culturally oppressed. This of course, is not the same thing as being "culturally deprived,"[8] but rather a result of being made to think that that is the case.

What we have here are a series of frames, each one leading to finer perceptions about McKay's novels. We are at first working backwards to get at the largest frame since each perception is contingent upon a larger one. Thus, the economic and cultural oppression defines the search for community which in turn defines the nature of the perceptions with which the novels deal. To the critic who wishes to intrude with that much abused term "universal values" we are ready with a reply. A person who fails to recognize that Freud's theories of psychoanalysis are based on the culture specific problems of bourgeois Europeans will get nothing universal out of those theories. Nor will one who is unwilling or unable to see that Shakespeare's "Hamlet" reflects the problems of a specific bourgeois European, be able to see beyond these problems into anything universal. Likewise, the person who wishes to stalk universals in Claude McKay's work, must first understand the series of frames within which the work is created. We could approach the novels as we would "Hamlet" and perhaps we could partially respond to Ray, a young man from the West Indies who has assimilated a lot of Western values. But we would only come to terms with part of him, and almost nothing of Jake, Banjo, or Bita, all of whom are in tune with a different rhythm of life.

The following is one of the most interesting, however debatable statements in Ramchand's essay on McKay's novels: "The Cultural dualism towards which McKay developed raises problems of three kinds for the artist. Characterization of the primitive Negro would run close to the White man's stereotype; the polemic novelist might be tempted into passionate statement at the expense of imaginative rendering; and the celebration of one race in exclusive terms could harden into a denial of the possibilities of life and our common humanity.

Home to Harlem and ***Banjo*** are not exempt from weaknesses along these lines . . ."[9] First we might assert that cultural dualism per se is precisely what McKay was struggling against, and that his novels represent a progressive movement away from that conflict in which, as Fanon has asserted, "white and black represent the two poles of the world . . ."[10] Then we must look closely at exactly what McKay's "primitive Negro" is like, explore the aesthetic value of "passionate statement," namely nondramatic versus dramatic rendering, and finally examine the question of celebrating one's race.

As Ramchand and other critics have pointed out, the reaction by black intellectuals to ***Home to Harlem*** was bad, and the reaction to ***Banjo*** even worse.[11] The reason is rather obvious. To the degree that McKay's novels rejected bourgeois values, to that extent were they rejected by those people who were striving to be recognized as a part of that class which the novels were rejecting. True, both books could be read with the selective sensibility of a bigoted white looking for confirmation of certain racial prejudice, and we might reasonably conjecture that for this reason ***Home to Harlem*** enjoyed a success similar to Carl Van Vechten's *Nigger Heaven.* But all this tells us more about the people who read it than it does about the novel itself.

If anything, we should reverse the value judgements afforded by the black critics who reviewed McKay's novels and assert that in so far as McKay is uncertain about bourgeois values, as long as cultural dualism is the most pervasive element in the novels, the novels are flawed with an inconclusiveness which interferes with our perception of any well wrought or effective gestalt. In ***Home to Harlem*** the frenetic quality of the implied author's voice counterpoints the illusion of Jake's being reconciled to a stable ethical world which he has defined within the imposed limitations of "a white folk's war," the "white folks' business," "the white man's chu-chu," and the "white man's city."[12] The technique is an effective one, but McKay tends to overdo it. In fact it is this very deluge of exclamation marks and hyphenated words, this sense of imbalance which leaves the reader with a feeling of dissatisfaction with the structure of the novel.

It is significant that the novel begins at sea. One vision having failed him, Jake is in the process of moving towards another. We are informed that: "In the winter he sailed for Brest with a happy chocolate company. Jake had his own daydreams of going over the top. But his company was held at Brest. Jake toted lumber—boards, planking, posts, rafters—for the hundreds of huts that were built around the walls of Brest and along the coast—to house the United States soldiers.

Jake was disappointed . . . Toting planks and getting into rows with his white comrades at Bal Musette were not adventure" (p. 3). Of course, it was not an adventure. It was simply a repetition of the rather oppressive circumstances he had experienced all his life. He had tried to fit into "white folks' business" at home; he had tried to do it abroad: he had tried to even do it through that most obvious means, sex. But in all cases he found there was a barrier he was not allowed to cross, the vision was shattered and the girl seen to be "a creature of another race—of another world" (p. 5).

Hence we have his frenetic ruminations over his return to Harlem, musings which we have said will set the tone of the novel:

> "Oh, them legs!" Jake thought. "Them tantalizing brown legs . . . Barron's Cabaret! . . . Leroy's Cabaret! . . ."
>
> "Harlem for mine!" cried Jake. "I was crazy thinkin' I was happy over heah. I wasn't mahself. I was like a man charged up with dope every day. That's what it was . . ."
>
> (p. 5)

But this again is more of an assertion of what Jake wants than a vision of what he will find. For the present he is tied down to the harsh reality of the ship, a microcosm of the only world he has truly known. He works hard, gets little pay and eats rotten food, in return for which he is able to have his vision of a promised land to which the ship is taking him. There is no doubt about what Jake thinks of the ship for we are told in the opening line of the novel that "All that Jake knew about the freighter on which he stoked was that it stank between sea and sky" (p. 1).

Within the mode of realism that McKay employs we are carefully led to see the ethical construct of Jake's existence. Jake loves Harlem, the night-life as well as the daily rhythmic patterns of those who live there, but he also feels he must work in order to justify his existence. He refuses to have a girl take care of him, or be anyone's "sweetman". Moreover, he has strong feelings about what his relationship to his work must be. At one point he gets a job working with Teddy as a stevedore only to find that he has been hired as a scab laborer. He is unwilling to continue with his job, but at the same time he does not wish to get involved with labor unions as he is suspicious of any organization where whites are in the position of absolute control: "Nope, I won't scab, but I ain't a joiner kind of fellah," said Jake. "I ain't no white folks' nigger and I ain't no poah white's fool. When I longshored in Philly I was a good union man. But when I made New York I done finds out that they gived the colored mens the worser piers and holds the bes'n a' them foh the Irishmen. No, Pardner, keep you' card. I take the best I k'n get as I goes mah way . . ." (p. 25).

If we merely take Jake's words at their face value, we will simply see Jake as a free-wheeling, happy-go-lucky guy who has made a decision to define his existence in relation to wine, women, and song plus a certain amount of necessary work. But in doing this we will misread the novel and be blind to the rather perceptive relationships that McKay has presented. Though he presents a convincing facade, Jake is an alienated individual. How else can we explain the fact that in the middle of the novel he leaves the Harlem he loves in order to work on a train? No matter what he emotionally feels for the community he is unable to find the work which is necessary to sustain his personal dignity.[13] How else can we explain the fact that he is a man unable to find any sense of meaningful permanence in his relationships with women? In the end, despite the fact that he has found Felice, the girl he has been looking for through most of the novel, he is disgusted with himself for getting involved in a fight with Teddy. Jake thinks about returning once again to sea to escape the "stinking mess" (p. 175) he has found at home. But he knows the ship is no different so he is easily won over by Felice's idea of going to Chicago, "Le's go to Chicago . . . I hear it's a mahvelous place foh niggers." (p. 176) Visions of a promised land again are fixed in Jake's mind, and nothing will be allowed to stand in the way of that vision. He loves Felice, but he needs his dignity more. When she goes to get her good luck charm and fails to promptly return, he makes up his mind to go to Chicago without her: "I kain't believe she'd ditch me like that at the last moment . . . Anyhow, I'm bound foh Chicago. I done made up mah mind to go all becausing a her, and I ain'ta gwinta change it whether she throws me down or not . . ." (p. 179). Even though Felice does come back we know that Jake will find neither the relationship to work that he needs nor the relationship with Felice that he wants. Prophecy is fulfilled when we again meet him in ***Banjo,*** but we need not step out of the structure of ***Home to Harlem*** to see it.

The novel, then, is rather effectively framed between arriving and departing, for these actions, despite Jake's optimism, significantly reflect the recurring patterns of expectation and frustration which are the parameters that define his life. Yet even more significant is the rather dynamic action which goes on within that framework. In exploring the relationships between Jake and his work and Jake and his women, McKay has lifted the veil and shown that beneath the stereotyped smile are the vital life forces which are continually forcing the expansion of the constricting parameters: "Haunting rhythm, mingling of naive wishfulness and charming gaiety, now sheering over into mad riotous joy, now, like a jungle mask, strange, unfamiliar, disturbing, now plunging headlong into the far dim depths of profundity and rising out as suddenly with a simple, childish grin. And the white visitors laugh. They see the grin only. Here are none of the well-patterned, well made emotions of the respectable world. A laugh may finish in a sob. A moan end in hilarity. That gorilla type wriggling there with his hands so strangely hugging his mate, may strangle her tonight. But he has no thought of that now. He loves the warm wiggle and is lost in it . . ." (p. 178). None of the devastating harshness of Richard Wright is conveyed here, yet we are still given a glimpse at a potential Bigger Thomas.

Where ***Home to Harlem*** is a hot pulsating exploration of realities and potentials, fraught with movement and dramatic action, ***Banjo*** is more a calmly meditative exploration of those realities and potentials, presented discursively with little action. For Ramchand to criticize the characterization of Ray in ***Banjo,*** asserting that the ideas he discusses "do not strictly arise out of the presented life of the novel," is like faulting Shakespeare for not writing his later plays in the same style in which he wrote his earlier ones, or more precisely, faulting Kafka or Camus for not having enough dramatic action in their novels. Though ***Banjo*** has nothing of the relatively tight organization that McKay's realism brings into ***Home to Harlem,*** neither has it so many of the excessively jazz-like apostrophes which threaten to collapse that structure. Thus, where Ray's intellectualism seems something of an incongruous element in ***Home to Harlem,*** it fits into the looser, more episodic, but reflective structure of ***Banjo*** as a foil to Banjo's intuitive response to life.

As Ramchand has pointed out, we do not see Ray as an aggrieved individual debating with himself, but that is not the type of person which the structure demands. Bugsy, Goosey, and Banjo are men who have much to be aggrieved about, and it is only at the end of the novel that Ray comes to fully realize the injustice he has done in using his intellect to cut himself off from the masses of his black brothers who are like them. Yet even when we first meet him we learn that "In America he had lived like a vagabond poet, erect in the racket and rush and terror of that young creation . . ." but that "Now he was always beholden . . ." (p. 65). In Europe he comes to experience and finally understand what the oppressed already know. Unfortunately, towards the end his presence is far too intrusive as he functions well in the novel only so long as he is merely a backdrop like the European setting, for Banjo and the other beach boys.

A central conflict in ***Banjo*** that each of the main characters tries to come to terms with is the question of their presence on soil which is essentially foreign to all of them. In being foreign territory, Europe is seen by each of them, at one time or another, as neutral territory where they might eventually find what they have been denied elsewhere, namely a sense of belonging to a community. Yet each one of them is denied any really free movement outside the boundaries of the Marseilles ghetto (the Ditch) and each is fronted with the same alienation we found in Jake. Thus, the seemingly static structure of ***Banjo*** is actually quite dynamic. Ray, the objective observer, is forced to become an involved participant due to his interaction with the beach boys; Europe, a seemingly neutral area, is revealed as an essentially hostile place in interaction with Benjo and his friends.

Without Banjo the novel would simply be a rather perceptive study of alienated blacks in an exile situation, but his presence is a force which pulls disparate people and elements together. The story is not really allegorical, but McKay is dealing with types who loosely represent various forces among blacks; and Banjo has a symbolic function in that he is the only one capable of holding them all altogether. The problem is that there is no place he can lead his people and hence the novel ends as inconclusively as ***Home to Harlem.***

We still need to look at these men and their relationships much more closely. Banjo's life is spent in pursuit of the ephemeral. "His life was a dream of vagabondage that he was perpetually pursuing and realizing in odd ways, always incomplete but never unsatisfactory" (p. 11). It would seem that he really doesn't want anything stable in his life, but Banjo is too realistic to pursue that which he cannot get. When he says that "the banjo is preeminently the musical instrument of the American Negro" (p. 49) he is asserting more of a metaphysical truth than anything physically real. "The sharp noisy notes belong to the American Negro's loud music of life—an affirmation of his hardy existence in the . . . tumultuous civilization . . ." (p. 49). The dichotomy is rather simple. It is a choice between death and life, and Banjo opts for life. This is made quite clear when he is playing his instrument: "Shake to the loud music of life playing to the primeval round of life . . . Death over there! Life over here! Shake down Death and forget his commerce . . ." (p. 57).

While Banjo is a man without a place, he is quite aware of his past and realizes that to disassociate himself from it would most certainly be the same as death. Goosey, for example, is always talking about racial progress which he defines in terms of assimilating white culture. Because of this he is continually down on Banjo and his instrument: "Banjo is bondage. It's the instrument of slavery. Banjo is Dixie. The Dixie of the land of cotton and massa and missus and black mammy. We colored folks have got to get away from all that in these enlightened and progressive days. Let us play the piano and violin, harp and flute. Let the white folks play the banjo if they want to keep on remembering all the Black Joes singing and the hell they made them live in" (p. 90). But obviously Goosey has missed the point. Banjo replies, "All that you talking about slavery and bondage ain't got nothing to do with our starting up a li'l' orchestry . . ." (p. 90). Despite Goosey he does eventually succeed in getting a band together and though it has but a momentary existence, the point is made. A group of individuals wishing to form a community must first define their values. If they share a common fund of experience in their heritage, then that is where they should look first. The music that they play, the expressive harmony of their group, will be in direct proportion to their familiarity with the instruments they choose.

Goosey would more than willingly crawl out of his skin if he could. "In speaking of Negro people Goosey always avoided the word 'Negro' and 'black' and used instead 'race men,' 'race women,' or 'race'" (p. 115). In Goosey's argument with Ray concerning Ray's writing about the blacks in the Ditch, McKay effectively anticipates those who were to later criticize him for writing ***Banjo.*** When Goosey exclaims, "But the crackers will use what you write against the race!" (p. 115). and goes on to inquire about what Ray could possibly find "to make a practical thing of the white proverb, 'Let down your bucket where you are.'" The reply is a two-edged sword and the irony as well as the literal assertion are worth exploring.

"The white proverb" is the same one Booker T. Washington used in his famous Atlanta address of 1885. He too saw it as a practical assertion but unwittingly fell into the hands of those who were all too willing to use the idea as an aid to continued oppression. Men such as Booker T. Washington will "advance" the race about as far as Goosey would, and McKay is cutting back at them with the same irony Ellison later employs in the *Invisible man* when he makes use of the same proverb.[14] Yet he is also using it to cut forward, though with a different sense of understanding about the proverb. There is no need to emulate another culture, for as Ray points out, there is always sufficient gold in one's own culture however much another would have you believe it is dirt. The results of servile emulation are always grotesque, but more importantly they are contingent on a large base of people who are further exploited in the process. Ray remembers what it was like in college when his fellow students kept talking about getting into upper-class society: "It was funny and it was sad. There was hardly one of them with the upper class bug on the brain who didn't have a near relative—a brother or sister who was an ignorant chauffeur, butler, or maid, or a mother paying their way through college with her washtub" (p. 116).

None of this is merely idle dialogue tangential to the aesthetic construct of the novel. We have an organic interrelatedness of structures in which the discursive element is but a part. The aesthetics, that is the perceptions, are all tied to social concerns, but that makes them no less artistically wrought. Ray's argument about the need for one to avoid cutting himself off from his roots is corroborated by McKay's use of dialect, a counterpointed jazz rhythm (though not as obtrusively as in ***Home to Harlem,*** and folklore. The use of dialect is rather obvious, the counterpointed rhythm we can see in the music which pulls the beach boys together while other forces are at work pulling them apart, scattering them, and even killing some. A study of the three folktales which are narrated near the middle of the book, would be rewarding, but a few comments shall suffice for now.

All three tales are directly concerned with specious appearances and thus echo the major thematic elements of the book, namely the relationships between the black man and the white man, and between the black man and his black brother. Ray tells a tale of an old lady who tried to steal a charm from her young niece who she was supposed to be bringing up. In the end we have justice with forgiveness rather than punishment, much in the same way that Banjo forgives Bugsy's dissembling. The "bad relative" is forgiven as "flesh and blood of the same family" (p. 121). The Senegalese tells a story of a leopard who tries to catch and kill all the other animals by sweet talking them into a trap. A monkey outwits him and shares all the leopard had hoarded with the remaining animals. So too the men of the Ditch have been cajoled by the merchants into wasting their money, often getting nothing in return. But opposed to the law of the jungle that these merchants operate under is the communal law of sharing as practiced by Banjo and his friends. Finally, in Bugsy's tale we learn about Sam, a man who "wasn't nonetall satisfied to be the bestest darky foh the boss folks. He aimed to be the biggest darky ovah all the rest a darkies" (p. 124). He learns, in short, that one of the easiest ways for a black to get ahead is through accommodating the white man's image of the black man. Sam learned his stereotype, "And from that time the American darky started playing coon and the white man is paying him for it" (p. 125).

The third tale deviates from the first two in a significant manner. The concern with survival through accommodation is in sharp contrast with the implied strategies for overt self-assertion. Both extremes of covert manipulation and overt assertion are shown to be cul-de-sacs when taken separately. Goosey, as we have seen, exists in a state of living death as he bends too much. Bugsy, an individual happiest "when he was breathing some militant resentment" (p. 167), literally dies because he would not bend enough. The point is made quite clear in one of the most powerfully descriptive passes in the book. Banjo comes into the room where Bugsy has just died and sees him lying there "like a macabre etched by the diabolic hand of Goya. With clenched fists and eyes wide open, as if he were going to spring at an antagonist, even if he were God himself . . ." (p. 259). Shortly before this Ray had spoken to a third type, Lonesome Blue, whose inaction represents an equally self-defeating approach to life. Ray's remarks refer to the type of flexibility which is needed. "The two go-getting things in this white man's civilization are force and cunning. When you have force or power you make people do things. When you haven't you are cunning." (p. 241).

Here we have the realities and possibilities. The realities all relate to surviving in the corrupt wasteland of "this white man's civilization," while the possibilities relate to meaningful group solidarity which will be expressive of the type of creative harmony that Banjo's group of friends together represent. Despite the similarity of the ending with that of ***Home to Harlem,*** the net result is a much more stable structure. The tentative conclusion has been supported by the tentative synthesis of the above power-cunning dialectic. Banjo and Ray cannot go to the West Indies with their friends as the two have found only a moral framework without a clear course of action. They will not like Goosey, uncertain of what is to come, stoop to carrying their own piece of soil around in a glass jar. Nor like Jake can they assert a blind optimism of the next place being better than the last. Rather they opt for the carpe diem life of vagabondage.

In ***Banana Bottom*** the physical journey has ceased. The aborted return to the West Indies in Banjo has now taken place, and the community so frenetically sought for in ***Home to Harlem*** will be found. The conditions for this community have already been sketched in ***Banjo.*** There will be no economic oppression by companies like the Dollar Line, no emotional repression as capitalized on by the films of the Blue Cinema, and there will be no pressure toward any cultural uniformity. The pluralistic ideal stated by Ray is the same one asserted by Ellison's *Invisible Man*[15] and must be the sine qua non of the community: "To me the most precious thing about human life is difference. Like flowers in a garden, different kinds for different people to love. I am not against miscegenation. It produces splendid and interesting types. But I should not crusade for it because I should hate to think of a future in which the identity of the black race in the Western World should be lost in miscegenation" (p. 208).

Perhaps with the intent of gaining more aesthetic distance between himself and his material McKay has gone back into his past for the setting, Jamaica, and switched to a female protagonist, Bita Plant. The result, at any rate, is the most controlled and carefully executed of McKay's novels. Moreover, the volume, pitch, and timbre of the narrator's voice are all modulated to the dramatic structure. This is not to say that the counterpointed rhythm in ***Home To Harlem*** and ***Banjo*** are not effective, for the resultant jarring dissonance corroborates the ideational structure in which the dialectic of dualism is taking place. Rather, in ***Banana Bottom*** a synthesis is occurring and the narrator's voice is in harmony with that synthesis.

The plot is simple, but it would be a mistake to also conclude that the entire construct is facile. Bita is presented from the beginning as an archetypal earth-mother figure whose soul is rooted deeply in the soil and the communal spirit of those who make their living from it. Others who are shrouded in their ethnocentric vision of the world, view her "rape" by Crazy Bow as an unfortunate event to be washed away by seven years of education in England. But she herself was an active participant in the sensual communion. When Bita subsequently returns she searches for her place in the world of Banana Bottom, a process more like an emergence from a cocoon than a rediscovery of something which was lost, eventually culminating in a tragi-comic ending of death and marriage.

Ramchand's analysis of Bita's progressive involvement with the community is generally a good one. What we need to look at is the symbolic structure of that progression in order to comprehend it as a well-wrought logical conclusion to the conflicts presented in the other two novels. Bita's education is continually referred to by the Craigs as an experiment, and we are able to enjoy a certain amount of dramatic irony as we perceive that she is much too strong a person to be manipulated as an object in an experiment. Yet in a much broader, naturalistic sense, she is a character involved in an experiment to see whether a community is possible posited on the assumptions we discussed above.

Though Priscilla Craig is portrayed as one who hypocritically hides her own selfish interests under the guise of Christian concern, her husband, Malcolm truly does have an unselfish desire to help others. But where they both go wrong with Bita is in seeing her as a plastic soul to be molded into the fixed form of a "Christian" being. At the other extreme are Busha Glengley and his son, Arthur, who are both "so absorbed in the bodies of Negroes" that they never have "any time to find out anything about their souls" (p. 130). Between these two extremes we have Squire Gensir who is concerned neither with exploiting their souls nor their bodies, but learning from the simple, yet complex totality of their being. The paradox has fascinated the old man so much that he has devoted his life to studying it and incorporating essential elements of the natives' mode of existence into his own life style. The result is a Thoreau-like transcendentalism in which the artificial elements in life are abandoned in order to get in tune with a natural harmony:

> "Once a visitor remarking how simple was his way of living, the squire replied that it had been difficult to achieve.
>
> "Difficult? Why there's no difficulty in living like this. You have nothing to worry about. It's so primitive."
>
> The squire replied that primitive living was more complex than his visitor imagined . . . It was easy for hampering things to heap up in the homes of all classes of people, because it is traditional in human nature to cling tenaciously to things that have no more place in material or spiritual living than manure, and as the home is cluttered up so is the mind."
>
> (p. 120)

Against this background an intricate pattern of ironic developments emerges. The Craigs hope to "save" Bita, yet all they can produce themselves is an idiot child, the owl-like Patou. They look down on the "insanity" of Crazy Bow, yet his withdrawal from reality, and eventually his death, is the result of their culture and its emphasis on a conforming material and spiritual achievement as opposed to the self-expressive, however eccentric, achievement of genius. They want to lift Bita out of her blackness through marriage with a "cultured" young man, who turns out to be a minister who makes love with animals. Finally, though it begins to dawn on Malcolm Craig that "many of those natives whom they were seeking to advise as mentors and ministers might prefer their own particular pattern of life," (p. 226). Priscilla remains adamant in her convictions. In fact, thinking back over her experiences in a sewing circle she conducted, she concludes there is no hope for the blacks. Their dishonesty in stealing her knitting needles is seen as symptomatic of their innate moral weakness:

> "But perhaps it might have been only one person responsible," said Mr. Craig. "A case of kleptomania."
>
> Mrs. Craig was amazed at her husband: "Kleptomania, Mr. Craig! How could such a crime of high society exist among such backward people? It was just plain downright stealing."
>
> (p. 228)

It is between the antinomies of spirit and flesh that Bita is able to move more freely than Squire Gensir who is limited by his intellectual distance from total involvement in the community of Banana Bottom. Despite her intellectual development during her years in England, Bita, on returning home, immediately responds to the sights, sounds, smells, and feeling of the community in a manner that comes easily to her sensual nature. It is, after all, here and not England where she grew up, yet the expatriate experience gave her the distance she needed to understand as well as feel this: "Bita mingled in the crowd, responsive to the feelings, the color, the smell, the swell and press of it. It gave her the sensation of a reservoir of familiar kindred humanity into which she had descended for baptism. She had never had that big moving feeling as a girl . . ." (p. 40). But this is only the beginning of the baptismal experience which is to further include the joy and excitement of eating "pure native cooking," (p. 53) of surreptitiously getting away from the Craigs and attending a tea meeting, of swimming in the nude in her favorite childhood swimming hole, and finally of allowing herself to be drawn into the communal spirit of an atavistic dance:

> "The scene was terrible but attracting and moving like a realistic creation of some of the most wonderful of the Annancy tales with which her father delighted and frightened her when she was a child. Magnetized by the spell of it Bita was drawn nearer and nearer into the inner circle until with a shriek she fell down. . . ."
>
> (p. 250)

This dance comes at the end of a long drought which is a symbolic manifestation of the "Thoughts of a dry brain" we have seen Mrs. Craig attempt to foist off on Bita. Then, during the drought another tenant of that house, Evan Vaughan, tries in a much grosser manner to do to the entire town what Mrs. Craig had attempted with Bita, but "The common fetish spirit" was a much "Stranger, stronger thing than that of the Great Revival" (p. 250). And we might add, it was a much more real experience to Bita than anything the artificial environment of Priscilla Craig could offer. Nevertheless we see that "The Revival had upset the common ways of life among the rural folk" (p. 255). A return to normal activity would not be a smooth one. Crazy Bow is put in a straight jacket for attacking Patou, and Arthur Glengley attempts to assault Bita sexually. The rain finally comes, but it comes in such a severe storm that it threatens to destroy the village. Bita's father, Jordan Plant, and Malcolm Craig are drowned while attempting to ford a flooded stream, and Priscilla, having lost all purpose in her life, also dies.

The destruction by the storm is as much a necessary prelude to the marriage of Bita to Jubban, as is her baptism into the life of the village. The debris of the old colonial order needed to be swept away in order for Bita and Jubban to realize the society in which they wish to raise their children, a society where one finds "The same age-old soil nourishing a variety of plants—the great common instructor imparting general knowledge to all alike—the scientific investigator as well as the ignorant self-taught cultivator." (p. 275)

Robert Bone could not have been further from the point when, referring to ***Banana Bottom*** he stated that "McKay uses sex as the chief means of dramatizing his theme. He understands that the major conflicts in a woman's life will be sexual . . .[16] Bone's own male chauvinism aside, we see that the sexual conflict in Bita is only a part of the larger cultural conflict which she resolves in the course of the novel. The sexual rebellion against the sterile life the Craigs wish to impose on her is no greater than her intellectual rebellion. She, like Squire Gensir, consciously opts for a life of simple rural felicity. Moreover, the conflict is essentially no different than the one experienced by Jake, Ray and Banjo. In none of the novels does McKay "use" sex as his major approach to dramatizing his theme. To read them in this manner is to repeat the mistakes of his early critics.

Yet the point remains that the same conflict is dramatized in three different ways. The differences, however, are more related to the form than the characters themselves. ***Home to Harlem*** is structured as slice of life realism revealing Jake as an individual struggling to assert his ethical sensibility within the dualistic world in which he must live. ***Banjo*** is more a collection of impressionistic vignettes further exploring the possibilities open to those who must live with that dualism. ***Banana Bottom*** is a naturalistic novel in the sense of Zola's ideal of le roman experimental. Bita reacts instinctively to forces that are beyond the understanding of people like the Craigs, but more importantly she serves as an experiment by McKay to see whether or not the hypotheses he developed in his other novels can really be carried out. Though all three novels were published separately, and must be seen as representing three different forms, we should probably look at the novels as one single work for there is a strong sense of thematic unity in the prevailing conflict between two cultures and the progressive resolution of that conflict leading to the sense of community found in the village of Banana Bottom. For McKay the idea of dualism changes from a pernicious state tearing the black man apart to a liberating state which allows for many disparate views. To the extent that it disappears as an antagonizing force with which the protagonists must contend, we might say that it is replaced with a higher sense of unity. After all, there is room for many different plants in McKay's garden.

The result of this analysis is that we may see more clearly McKay's genius and his faults. In so far as there is a rather intricate relationship between the formal and thematic structures, and a germane relationship between those structures and elements of "compelling significance" to Afro-Americans, his work is extremely successful. Nor, however, is it any less successful for whites who are finally being forced to face the realities of a pluralistic world. Unfortunately, McKay's rather rough style is a divisive factor which militates against our unqualified participation in his search for a community in that world.

Notes

1. Perhaps a more accurate term would be "Neo-African". While avoiding the strictly racial bias of the other terms it covers the aesthetic approach of a much wider range of peoples than does the term "Afro-American". But again such polemics are not essential to this paper. See Janheinz Jahn, *Neo-African Literature* (New York, 1969).
2. *The West Indian Novel and its Background* (London, 1970), p. 273.
3. Ibid., p. 249.
4. Ibid, pp. 256-257.
5. See Addison Gayle, "Cultural Hegemony: The Southern White Writer and American Letters," *Amistad I* (New York, 1970), pp. 1-24.
6. Ralph Ellison, *Shadow and Act* (New York, 1964), p. 94.
7. Frantz Fanon, *Black Skin, White Masks* (New York, 1967), p. 18.
8. See Roger Abrahams, *Positively Black* (Englewood Cliffs, New Jersey, 1970).
9. Ramchand, p. 245.
10. Fanon, pp. 44-45.
11. See Ramchand, p. 250.
12. *Home to Harlem* (New York, 1965), pp. 5, 26, and 145. All parenthetical page references are to this edition and the following: *Banjo* (New York, 1957); *Banana Bottom* (New York, 1970).
13. The narrator tells us, "Jake had taken the job on the railroad just to break the hold that Harlem had upon him" (p. 66). But this affords no answer to why he cannot relate to places or women in any permanent way.
14. See *Invisible Man* (New York, 1952), p. 31.
15. Ibid., p. 499. (See quote at beginning.)
16. *The Negro Novel in America* (New Haven, 1970), p. 73.

EUGENIA COLLIER (ESSAY DATE 1972)

SOURCE: Collier, Eugenia. "The Four-Way Dilemma of Claude McKay." *CLA Journal* 15 (March 1972): 345-53.

In the following essay, Collier examines McKay's poetry and discusses a series of dilemmas in which McKay was caught.

In the heart of black Chicago is a pair of crumbling old buildings on whose walls Black people, in a time of trouble, painted pictures that portray the important aspects of their lives. One wall is the Wall of Respect. Black heroes are painted there—Martin Luther King, Marcus Garvey, Muhammad Ali, Malcolm of course. The other wall is the Wall of Truth, on which are painted scenes of Black America's tragedy and triumph. One picture is particularly impressive. It shows a black man, cut down and dying in front of a wall. The body is beautiful and powerful, the face stern and unyielding even in death, the splash of blood, red and shocking. Clutched in the hand is a paper on which is scribbled a poem. If one stands close enough to the painting, one can read these words:

If we must die, let it not be like hogs
Hunted and penned in an inglorious spot,
While round us bark the mad and hungry dogs,
Making their mock at our accursed lot.
If we must die, O let us nobly die,
So that our precious blood may not be shed
In vain; then even the monsters we defy
Shall be constrained to honor us though dead!
O kinsmen! We must meet the common foe!
Though far outnumbered let us show us brave,
And for their thousand blows deal one
deathblow!
What though before us lies the open grave?
Like men we'll face the murderous, cowardly
pack,
Pressed to the wall, dying, but fighting back![1]

This poem, written over fifty years ago, is the best-known work of Claude McKay, the fiery Jamaican who was so vital a part of the Harlem Renaissance. **"If We Must Die"** has given courage to many who faced overwhelming odds: Winston Churchill read it to his people during the dark days when German bombers nightly rained destruction on Britain. Jews in concentration camps knew this poem. And Black people in America today recognize its meaning in their life-and-death struggle with destructive forces in their own native land. Critics have sometimes pointed out flaws in this poem, in terms of Western poetic principles. But the fact remains that the poem's expression of unflinching courage and defiance has gripped generations of oppressed people.

"If We Must Die" was one of the first published poems of the Harlem Renaissance. Claude McKay was one of the first of the Harlem Renaissance writers, and one of the most significant. He was different from the other poets in several ways: He was not a native American; he was already a poet of some note before the Twenties; his first three volumes of poems were published outside the United States; moreover, he spent most of the decade of the Twenties abroad. Yet his poetry is so representative of the Harlem Renaissance, his spirit so strong and driving that his influence on this important literary movement is incalculable.

McKay wrote other things besides poetry. As editor of the *Liberator* he wrote essays and editorials. Later he wrote several novels and an autobiography. Yet it is as a poet that McKay achieves his greatest stature. And this is good, since of all forms of writing, it is poetry that best expresses the innermost truth of man.

In poetic style McKay is primarily a lyricist, virtually confining himself to the lyric forms of the English romantics. He especially favors the sonnet. In diction, too, and in tone McKay resembles the romantics. But superimposed upon the Western forms is the unmistakable stamp of blackness. McKay's sonnets fairly burst with passion: his images are bold and brilliantly executed; his themes are rooted in the dark reality of black experience. Even his tender love lyrics are tinged with tragedy.

I am particularly intrigued by McKay's themes. I have never been able *to buy* the critical theory that content is subordinate to form. *What* a poem says is vitally important; otherwise the poet has created a pretty but useless thing, a mere bauble, like a woman who is beautiful and well-designed but, unfortunately, frigid. Theme is the core of a poem, around which all other poetic dimensions revolve.

An examination of the themes of McKay's poetry reveals an interesting thread which runs through most of his works: that McKay, like other Black men in white America, is caught in a series of dilemmas. He is removed geographically and culturally from his native soil; he is a living paradox; he must struggle constantly to maintain his Black identity among forces which would bleach it white and thus destroy it. For this presentation I decided to examine these themes and to explore what I call the four-way dilemma of Claude McKay.

The first and most obvious dilemma is one of geography. Like many blacks, McKay was far from home. A great many Black individuals find it necessary to leave home to seek opportunity elsewhere, or perhaps to escape the intolerable conditions of rural locales. Though life leads one into many different paths so that it is often impossible and even undesirable for one to return, still the longing for home lurks just behind consciousness and often reveals itself in unexpected ways. Though McKay left Jamaica for a different reason (to attend an American agricultural college), and though he came to love America, still he expresses in many tender poems a nostalgia for his native land. For example, in **"Flame Heart"** McKay examines his memories of Jamaica through a series of brilliant sense images. In **"Home Thought"** he insists with a kind of ESP, "Oh, something just now must be happening there! / That suddenly and quiveringly here / Amid the city's noises, I must think / Of mangoes leaning to the river's brink." Among the best of the poems of Jamaica is **"The Tropics in New York"**:

Bananas ripe and green, and ginger-root,
   Cocoa in pods and alligator pears,
And tangerines and mangoes and grape fruit,
   Fit for the highest prize at parish fairs,

Set in the window, bringing memories
   Of fruit-laden trees laden by low-singing rills,
And dewy dawns, and mystical blue skies
   In benediction over nun-like hills.

My eyes grew dim, and I could no more gaze;
   A wave of longing through my body swept,
And, hungry for the old, familiar ways,
   I turned aside and bowed my head and wept.

The geographical dilemma is merely symbolic of the second dilemma—this, too, is meaningful to many Blacks. That is a kind of racial homesickness for Africa. Perhaps it is true that we share a racial unconscious, that deep within us beat the jungle drums of our ancestors. Writers in the past have recognized this; the concept of *Négritude* defines it; youngsters today, with their Afros and dashikis, live it. Yet there *is* a dilemma. The very term "Afro-American" expresses the twoness of the person who reflects the dual and often conflicting heritage of Africa and America, the person who is neither wholly African nor wholly American, and yet somehow is both.

In several poems McKay expresses this recognition of his origin, the influence of Africa upon his psyche, his longing for a homeland which he has never seen. In **"To the White Fiends"** he admonishes, "Be not deceived; for every deed you do / I could match—out-match: Am I not Afric's son, / Black of that black land where black deeds are done?" Another poem, **"In Bondage,"** begins, "I would be wandering in distant fields / Where man, and bird, and beast, live leisurely . . ." For eight lines the poem describes the idyllic life of peace and happiness in a primitive society—probably the Africa of his ancestry; "For," as he continues, "Life is greater than the thousand wars / Men wage for it in their insatiate lust." The dilemma emerges in the couplet which ends the poem: "But I am bound with you in your mean graves, / O black men, simple slaves of ruthless slaves."

One can be "bound" by bonds other than ropes that tie the hands. **"Outcast"** expresses the dilemma of the Western Black man, tormented by a longing for an Africa never seen, alienated in the land of his birth.

Words felt, but never heard, my lips would
frame;
For the dim regions whence my fathers came
My spirit, bondaged by the body, longs.
Words felt, but never heard, my lips would
frame;
My soul would sing forgotten jungle songs.

I would go back to darkness and to peace,
But the great western world holds me in fee,
And I may never hope for full release
While to its alien gods I bend my knee.
Something in me is lost, forever lost,
Some vital thing has gone out of my heart,
And I must walk the way of life a ghost
Among the sons of earth, a thing apart.

For I was born, far from my native clime,
Under the white man's menace, out of time.

The third dilemma is closely akin to W. E. B. Du Bois' concept of double-consciousness. Du Bois describes this dilemma thus: "It is a peculiar sensation, this double-consciousness, this sense of always looking at one's self through the eyes of others, of measuring one's soul by the tape of a world that looks on in amused contempt and pity. One ever feels his two-ness—an American, a Negro; two souls, two thoughts, two unreconciled strivings, two warring ideals in one dark body, whose dogged strength alone keeps it from being torn asunder."[2] Double-consciousness involves seeing a double image of oneself: that is, seeing oneself through the eyes of the white man and at the same time maintaining (if possible) a self-image which is very different and much more humane. Double-consciousness means playing the white man's game while retaining, at the same time, a firm conviction of what is real and what is sham. Black children learn the rules of double-consciousness before they learn the rules of Hide and Go Seek.

McKay himself was adept at the game. A celebrated Black poet functioning in the world of white intelligentsia, he often collided with the white man's image of him. Several of McKay's poems reflect the workings of double-consciousness. **"The Harlem Dancer,"** for example, plays the part that poverty and prejudice have assigned her. But the poet recognizes that "her self is not in that strange place."

Perhaps the clearest picture of double-consciousness is seen in **"White Houses."** In this poem one sees the ironic view of the Black man as "A chafing savage down the decent street." Let a Black man stroll through an exclusively white neighborhood. To the residents, and especially to the policeman on the beat, he will indeed appear to be savage, sinister, out of place among decent people. But the poem reveals that the savagery resides in the racism of white America. The Black man maintains a higher degree of "civilization." He must struggle every second to contain the honest passion which threatens to explode. The poem is tense. The images are replete with violence carefully controlled.

Your door is shut against my tightened face,
And I am sharp as steel with discontent;
But I possess the courage and the grace
To bear my anger proudly and unbent.
The pavement slabs burn loose beneath my feet,
A chafing savage, down the decent street;
And passion rends my vitals as I pass,
Where boldly shines your shuttered door of
glass.
Oh, I must search for wisdom every hour,
Deep in my wrathful bosom sore and raw,
And find in it the superhuman power
To hold me to the letter of your law!
Oh, I must keep my heart inviolate
Against the potent poison of your hate.

The fourth dilemma involves the paradox of the Black man, poor and hated, in an America that is affluent and idealistic. The very presence of the Black man is a denial of American ideals. This is *not* the land of the free. We do not *all* have the rights of liberty and the pursuit of happiness. Being upright and hard-working does not assure *all* of freedom from want. And so the Black man is a living paradox. The fourth dilemma, then, is the conflict between the American dream and the American reality. The Black man lives this conflict daily.

McKay's poems demonstrate this dilemma mainly in their sympathetic portrayal of Black people imprisoned in economic deprivation in the midst of American affluence. In **"The Tired Worker,"** for eight lines the worker anticipates the coming of night, of rest for the weary body, the tired hands, the aching feet. Night comes. For two lines the worker begins to relax. But immediately "dreaded dawn" arrives again, and the worker cries out in futile rebellion, "O let me rest! / Weary my veins, my brain, my life! Have pity! / No! Once again the harsh, the ugly city."

One of McKay's most famous poems, **"Harlem Shadows,"** shows the paradox of the Black man's lot in America. The poem is a sad, tender, loving, compassionate view of Harlem prostitutes, whom the poet sees as symbolic of the destruction which racism has wreaked upon Blacks. The sounds of the poem are soft; the poet uses soft consonants and avoids loud and exciting high vowels. The rhythm is the slow, contemplative iambic pentameter. The poem itself is a paradox—a gentle whisper and at the same time a bitter indictment.

I hear the halting footsteps of a lass
  In Negro Harlem when the night lets fall
Its veil. I see the shapes of girls who pass
  To bend and barter at desire's call.
Ah, little dark girls, who in slippered feet
  Go prowling through the night from street to
    street!

Through the long night until the silver break
  Of day the little gray feet know no rest;
Through the lone night until the last snow-flake
  Has dropped from heaven upon the earth's
    white breast,
The dusky, half-clad girls of tired feet
  Are trudging, thinly shod, from street to
    street.

Ah, stern harsh world, that in the wretched way
  Of poverty, dishonor and disgrace,
Has pushed the timid little feet of clay,
  The sacred brown feet of my fallen race!
Ah, heart of me, the weary, weary feet
  In Harlem wandering from street to street.

If McKay is an honest poet (and the profound emotion of his work leads us to believe that he is), then we must conclude that he is torn by these four dilemmas: (1) longing for sunny Jamaica and simultaneously a devotion to the sidewalks of Harlem; (2) the opposing and equally compelling styles of Africa and the West; (3) double-consciousness; (4) his paradoxical role as a living denial of America's expressed ideals and demonstrated affluence. These dilemmas are the bitter fruit of the racism which tore Black people from Africa to begin with and has kept them enslaved ever since. The result is the serious identity problem which is a recurring theme in Black literature.

This identity problem is evident in McKay's life and works. For example, when he went abroad, he went not to Africa but to Europe. Eventually he did travel to Morocco, but there he felt keenly his difference from Moroccans. He was more at home in Russia than in Africa.

Perhaps the most significant manifestation of his identity problem, the result of all the various dilemmas, is his choice of Western forms for his poetry. It is true that one can find imperfections in McKay's works. Sometimes the emotion seems too big for the work, seems to overflow the tidy meters and carefully prescribed rhymes. Sometimes the images seem too bold for the poem to contain. Sometimes the diction seems too inhibited to express the fire of the message. Sometimes McKay seems to strive for a kind of poetic polish—as if the polish were the poem!

I wonder what kind of works McKay would have produced had he used for his models not the Western romantics but the poet-musicians of Africa. Suppose that instead of the highly "artistic" forms of Western lyrics, McKay had employed the surging rhythms of African music—music not "written" for "scholars" but growing out of the experiences of *people* to accompany them as they are born and married, as they worship their gods and work their fields and bury their dead. But the Western world "held him in fee" and any question of what he might have done is merely academic.

In closing, I think the poet himself should have the last word. In **"Baptism"** we see the poet enduring and transcending the dilemmas which racism has inflicted upon him. He wrote the poem following an incident in which he went, accompanied by a white friend, to review a play for his newspaper. Upon arriving at the theater, McKay was unceremoniously jim-crowed into the Negro section of the theater. He sat through the performance enraged. Later he expressed his burning rage in this poem:

Into the furnace let me go alone;
Stay you without in terror of the heat.
I will go naked in—for thus 'tis sweet—
Into the weird depths of the hottest zone.
I will not quiver in the frailest bone,
You will not note a flicker of defeat;
My heart shall tremble not its fate to meet,
Nor mouth give utterance to any moan.
The yawning oven spits forth fiery spears;
Red aspish tongues shout wordlessly my name.
Desire destroys, consumes my mortal fears,
Transforming me into a shape of flame.
I will come out, back to your world of tears,
A stronger soul within a finer frame.

Notes

1. All McKay poems are taken from *The Selected Poems of Claude McKay* (New York: Harcourt, Brace and World, Inc., 1953).
2. W. E. B. Du Bois, "Of Our Spiritual Strivings," *The Souls of Black Folk.*

MICHAEL B. STOFF (ESSAY DATE 1972)

SOURCE: Stoff, Michael B. "Claude McKay and the Cult of Primitivism." In *The Harlem Renaissance Remembered,* edited by Arna Bontemps, pp. 126-46. New York: Dodd, Mead, 1972.

In the following essay, Stoff discusses the notion of "primitivism" that was reflected in McKay's art but not in the author's own life.

When asked why he had never visited Gertrude Stein while they were both in Paris, Claude McKay replied, "I never went because of my aversion to cults and disciples."[1] McKay, a major poet and novelist of the Harlem Renaissance, was less than accurate in expressing a distaste for cults. In his art, he employed the images of the cult of primitivism in vogue among white contemporaries. Similarly, he pursued a primitive life-style as he struggled with the special problems of the black intellectual. McKay's success on the aesthetic level would not be matched in life.

"'The most moving and pathetic fact in the social life of America today,'" wrote Malcolm Cowley about the 1920s, "'is emotional and aesthetic starvation.' And what is the remedy?"[2] The search for that remedy elicited a multitude of responses, all of which seemed motivated by a frantic desire to escape. The physical act of expatriation and the spiritual immersion of the self in art were two mechanisms employed by young intellectuals to flee the materialism and artistic stagnation of modern America. The fear and repugnance engendered by the Machine Age also evoked a third response—the intellectual retreat into the primitive.

The cult of primitivism which gripped many American intellectuals during the 1920s manifested itself in a number of ways. The rising interest in jazz, the study of African art forms, and the examination of tribal cultures were all variations on the theme of the primitive. The Negro as the uncorrupted remnant of preindustrial man became the central metaphor in this cult.[3] Against the background of a tawdry culture stood the instinctive, sensual black man whose "dark laughter" represented a fundamental challenge to the effete civilization of white America. The Negro was transformed into a cultural hero serving as the protagonist in a series of white literary efforts. Eugene O'Neill's *The Emperor Jones* (1920) and *All God's Chillun Got Wings* (1924), Waldo Frank's *Holiday* (1923), Ronald Firbank's *Prancing Nigger* (1924), Sherwood Anderson's *Dark Laughter* (1925), and Carl Van Vechten's *Nigger Heaven* (1926) are merely a sampling of that new genre.

The primitivism in Claude McKay's art manifests itself even in his earliest efforts. As a Jamaican youth, McKay composed a series of dialect poems later published in two volumes: ***Songs of Jamaica*** (1912) and ***Constab Ballads*** (1912). Both thematically, through their emphasis on everyday peasant life, and stylistically, through their use of native dialect, these poems reveal McKay's fascination with Jamaican folk culture. They capture the exotic and earthy qualities of the black peasantry with a lyrical sensitivity reminiscent of Robert Burns. McKay might have been exposed to Burns through his acquaintance with Edward Jekyll, an English recluse living in Jamaica. Years later, McKay recalled the seminal role the Englishman played in awakening the young poet to the beauty of the Jamaican folk-art tradition:

> And when I sent them [his poems] on to Mr. Jekyll, he wrote back to say that each one was more beautiful than the last. Beauty! A short while before I never thought that any beauty could be found in the Jamaican dialect. Now this Englishman has discovered beauty and I too could see where my poems were beautiful. Also, my comrades and sometimes the peasants going to the market to whom I would read some of them. They used to exclaim, "Why they're just like that, they're so natural." And then I felt fully rewarded for my efforts.[4]

McKay derived a special satisfaction from the approval of his peers. That formative recognition reinforced his affection for the cultural roots of Jamaica and provided a base for a widening perception of other folk heritages.

McKay's depiction of the Jamaican peasant is integrally related to a stereotyped image of the world's peasantry. His peasants have a universality of condition and reaction which allows them to be exchanged with peasants of any nationality. This conception is consistent with McKay's later claim: "As a child, I was never interested in different kinds of races or tribes. People were just people to me."[5] In describing McKay's image of the Jamaican peasant, the French literary critic Jean Wagner has written:

> All things being equal, McKay's portrait of the Jamaican peasant is in substance that of the peasant the world over. Profoundly attached to the earth, he works the soil with a knowledge gained from age long habit; although a hard worker, the Jamaican, like his counterpart the world over, is condemned to exploitation.[6]

This perception of common qualities among the world's masses later furnished McKay with a theoretical basis for his own peculiar vision of the ideal political state. At this early point in his life, the concept of a "universal peasantry" heightened his sensitivity to folk-art traditions of other cultures. That interest supplied him with a foundation for much of his work.

McKay emigrated from Jamaica in 1912 at the age of twenty-two. He carried with him not only a deep regard for the Jamaican peasantry but also a special vision of the island itself. He retained that vision until his death in 1948. The image of Jamaica as paradise permeates all his recollections of the island. In McKay's first American poems and in his later autobiographical material, Jamaica becomes the metaphorical equivalent of Eden. Its simplicity and freshness offered refuge from the complexities of a modern, industrialized world.[7] Two stanzas from the poem **"North and South"** are typical of the nostalgic, pastoral strains found in McKay's early work:

> O sweet are the tropic lands for waking dreams!
> There time and life move lazily along,
> There by the banks of blue and silver streams
> Grass-sheltered crickets chirp incessant song;
> Gay-colored lizards loll all through the day,
> Their tongues outstretched for careless little flies.
>
> And swarthy children in the fields at play,
> Look upward, laughing at smiling skies.
> A breath of idleness is in the air
> That casts a subtle spell upon all things,
> And love and mating time are everywhere,
> And wonder to life's commonplaces clings.[8]

The exotic setting and sensory images give a sensual flavor to the poem. These device are reemployed in conjunction with themes of innocence and uncorruptibility in other Jamaican poems:

> What days our wine thrilled bodies pulsed with joy
> Feasting upon blackberries in the copse?
> Oh some I know! I have embalmed the days,
> Even the sacred moments when we played,
> All innocent of passion, uncorrupt,
> At noon and evening in the flame-heart's shade.
> We were so happy, happy I remember,
> Beneath the poinsettia's red in warm December.[9]

McKay did not lose the vision of Jamaica as an undefiled Eden where instinct and sensation reigned supreme. Although he never returned to his island home, he was forever swept back thematically to his preindustrial, peasant origins.[10] In 1947, a year before his death, McKay wrote, "I think of a paradise as something of a primitive kind of place where there are plenty of nuts and fruits and flowers and milk and wild honey. Jamaica has all of this."[11] Recapturing the lost innocence of that Eden provided one of the major themes in McKay's life.

McKay was also obsessed with describing the social role to be played by the intellectual. His membership in a visible and oppressed minority further complicated matters. In essence, the entire body of his art can be seen as a mechanism through which he sought to transform these personal problems into public issues.[12] Such a transformation entailed an insistent reference to a recurring pattern of images. That pattern was the juxtapositioning of the instinctive black man and the educated Negro. These images defined, with increasing precision, McKay's own concepts and made them salient within a broader cultural context.

McKay's earliest use of this construction came in the first of his three novels, ***Home to Harlem.*** The book was published in 1928, the sixth year of McKay's expatriation from America. Its appearance initiated a violent debate among the black literati over the propriety of its theme and subject matter. Many of McKay's peers agreed with Langston Hughes's evaluation. Hughes argued that because it was so "vividly alive," ***Home to Harlem*** could legitimately be labeled, as "the first real flower of the Harlem Renaissance."[13]

The elder black literary figures and much of the established Negro press were revolted by what they believed to be overtly crude allusions in McKay's book. Claiming the book was not representative of Negro life, this Old Guard expressed its shock and indignation at the lasciviousness of the novel. Its very existence, they suggested, was a calculated affront to the black community. W. E. B. Du Bois's reaction was typical of the initial reviews:

> ***Home to Harlem*** for the most part nauseates me, and after the dirtier parts of its filth I feel distinctly like taking a bath. . . . It looks as though McKay has set out to cater to that prurient demand on the part of white folk for a portrayal in Negroes of that utter licentiousness which convention holds white folk back from enjoying—if enjoyment it can be labeled.[14]

The controversy enveloping ***Home to Harlem*** was merely the surfacing of an underlying tension engendered by conflicting visions of the Harlem Renaissance. The Old Guard saw the Renaissance as a vehicle for social amelioration. The Renaissance would not only demonstrate the intellectual achievements of the black man, but would also uplift the masses to some arbitrary level of social acceptability.[15]

It was precisely this view of the Harlem Renaissance, this venture in cultural pretension, that McKay's work fundamentally challenged. His notion of a renaissance was an aggregation of ". . . talented persons of an ethnic or national group working individually or collectively in a common purpose and creating things that would be typical of their group."[16] In 1929, McKay defined the problems one faced when speaking of a "racial renaissance." He delineated the tactics and sources to be employed in creating such a movement:

> We educated Negroes are talking a lot about a racial renaissance. And I wonder how we're going to get it. On one side we're up against the world's arrogance—a mighty cold hard white stone thing. On the other the great sweating army—our race. It's the common people, you know, who furnish the bone and sinew and salt of any race or nation. In the modern race of life we're merely beginners. If this renaissance is going to be more than a sporadic scabby thing, we'll have to get down to our racial roots to create it. . . . Getting down to our native roots and building up from our people is . . . culture.[17]

For McKay, this meant the conscious and studied illumination of a black folk-art tradition whose central themes would be the indestructible vitality of the primitive black man and the inextricable dilemma of the educated Negro.

Home to Harlem is a vivid glimpse of the lower depths of black life in urban America. Its peripatetic plot and dialect-oriented style are consistent with its thematic emphasis on the black man as the unrestrained child of civilization. Set in New York's black ghetto, the novel establishes Harlem as a carnal jungle. Our senses are subjected to a barrage of erotic images: "Brown girls rouged and painted like dark pansies. Brown flesh draped in colorful clothes. Brown lips full and pouted for sweet kissing. Brown breasts throbbing with love."[18] At the core of this physical world lies the cabaret Congo, "a real little Africa in New York." Forbidden to whites, the Congo is a distillation of Harlem life. Its atmosphere is filled with the "tenacious odors of service and the warm indigenous smells of Harlem." Its allusions to the unrepressed African culture provide an apt setting for the return of the novel's hero, Jake Brown.

Jake, an Army deserter, is introduced as the natural man whose actions are guided by intuition. He is the instinctive primitive, deeply rooted in the exotic mystique of Africa. As he walks down Lenox Avenue, he is overcome by the pulsations of Harlem life. "His flesh tingled," the narrator tells us, and "he felt as if his whole body was a flaming wave." Jake and Harlem are inexorably bound by a "contagious fever . . . burning everywhere," but burning most fervently in "Jake's sweet blood." That primitive passion sustains Jake and represents a profound threat to the cultural rigidity of modern society.

In contrast to Jake, McKay inserts himself as the Haitian immigrant Ray. Ray represents the cultivated intellect, the civilized black whose education has sensitized his mind but paralyzed his body. Intellectually, Ray can comprehend the cluster of sensations and emotions about him, yet he lacks the naturalness of action and spontaneity of response that are the hallmarks of a Jake Brown. Although envious of Jake, Ray harbors the obsessive fear that "someday the urge of the flesh . . . might chase his high dreams out of him and deflate him to the contented animal that was the Harlem nigger strutting his stuff."[19]

The result is a vision of the intellectual, and especially the black intellectual, as social misfit. Ray is capable of sensing and recording life, but he is unable to live it. "He drank in more of life," writes McKay, "than he could distill into active animal living." There is no outlet for his immense store of emotional energy. Robbed by his "white" education of the ability to act freely and impulsively, Ray remains little more than a "slave of the civilized tradition." Caught between two cultures, he is immobilized. "The fact is," he tells Jake as he flees to Europe,

> . . . I don't know what I'll do with my little education. I wonder sometimes if I could get rid of it and lose myself in some savage culture in the jungles of Africa. I am a misfit—as the doctors who dole out newspaper advice to the well-fit might say—a misfit with my little education and constant dreaming, when I should be getting the nightmare habit to hog in a lot of dough like everybody else in this country. . . . The more I learn the less I understand and love life.[20]

The implications of Ray's final statement are not only applicable to McKay's personal problems but related to a broader cultural phenomenon. Notions of escape, alienation, and crude commercialism were by no means uniquely black images. They were embraced by intellectuals of varying hues in the twenties.[21] McKay's use of these themes places the black experience into a larger cultural context. Blackness only added a further convolution to the already complex problem of the intellectual's social adaptability.

Ray's expatriation leaves the fundamental questions raised by the novel unresolved. The continuing focus on Jake, and his reunion with the "tantalizing brown" girl Felice,[22] imply that only the instinctive primitive can survive happily in white civilization, its dehumanizing tendencies are irrelevant to his innately free existence. The intellectual, defiled by the process of civilization, is doomed to wander in search of that potency of action he has irrevocably lost.

McKay's second novel, ***Banjo,*** published in 1929, pursues the issues raised in ***Home to Harlem.*** Although the scene has shifted to Marseille's harbor district, the structural dualism characterizing ***Home to Harlem*** is present once more.

Lincoln Agrippa Daily, familiarly known as Banjo, replaces Jake Brown while McKay again enters as Ray. The dichotomy is now expanded and more lucidly articulated.

In ***Banjo*** there is a sharpening of figurative focus and a widening of thematic scope. With the character Banjo, McKay adds a new dimension to the earthy black and provides a more concise definition of his own racial conceptions. At the same time, Ray's disposition has progressed from a confused uneasiness with American life to a coherent denunciation of western civilization. This increased clarity of imagery allows McKay to move toward a resolution to the quandary of the black intellectual.

The primitive black is given additional depth in ***Banjo.*** The loose plot, an account of the lives of a group of beach boys in the port city of Marseille, provides a background for the development of the protagonist, Banjo. He is the same intuitive vagabond originally described in ***Home to Harlem***—with one significant difference. While Jake is nebulously characterized as a laborer, Banjo is depicted as an artist. He is a jazzman whose life is the embodiment of his art. Like the songs he plays, Banjo is unrestrained, free-spirited, and vibrantly alive. McKay immediately establishes the intimate relationships between Banjo and his music: "I never part with this instrument," Banjo says in the opening pages of the novel. "It is moh than a gal, moh than a pal; it's mahself."[23]

After equating the protagonist with his instrument, McKay explains the aesthetic function of the banjo:

> The banjo dominates the other instruments; the charming, pretty sound of the ukelele, the filigree notes of the mandolin, the sensuous color of the guitar. And Banjo's face shows that he feels that his instrument is first. . . . The banjo is preeminently the musical instrument of the American Negro. The sharp, noisy notes of the banjo belong to the American Negro's loud music of life—an affirmation of his hardy existence in the midst of the biggest, the most tumultuous civilization of modern life.[24]

The instrument is the cultural expression of American Negro folk-art, and Banjo represents the prototype black folk-artist lustily proclaiming the vitality of his race. His music, "the sharp, noisy notes of the banjo," is not derived from a pretentious adaptation of European culture. Drawing inspiration from the "common people," Banjo's art represents the truest expression of black culture.

FROM THE AUTHOR

A LONG WAY FROM HOME

I have nothing to give but my singing. All my life I have been a troubadour wanderer, nourishing myself mainly on the poetry of existence. And all I offer here is the distilled poetry of my experience.

SOURCE: Claude McKay, the concluding lines to his autobiography *A Long Way from Home,* Furman, 1937.

Again juxtaposed to this earthy, intuitive black man is the intellectual Ray. Recently expatriated from America, Ray comes to Marseille in search of an artistic haven where he could "exist *en pension* proletarian of a sort and try to create around him the necessary solitude to work with pencil and scraps of paper."[25] Ray has not given up his earlier passion for writing, and although he is occasionally forced to work as a laborer, he never renounces his "dream of self-expression." Once in the Vieux Port, he finds, instead of solitude, a band of beach boys whose free and undisciplined lifestyle is particularly appealing to Ray's vagabond sensibilities. As a result, he immediately establishes an intimate relationship with the members of the group and especially with their leader, Banjo. At this point, the linear progression of the plot becomes of secondary importance, and the novel is reduced to a vehicle for the delineation of Ray's (*i.e.,* McKay's) brief against civilization and the formulation of a solution to his intellectual quandary.

McKay's condemnation of Western civilization in ***Banjo*** is inexorably tied to the psychological problems arising from his blackness. In 1937 he wrote, "What, then, was my main psychological problem? It was the problem of color. Color-consciousness was the fundamental of my restlessness."[26] And it is color-consciousness which is the fundamental of Ray's hatred for civilization. "Civilization is rotten,"[27] Ray proclaims, and in the following passage, McKay defines the sociological basis of Ray's sentiments:

> He hated civilization because its general attitude toward the colored man was such as to rob him of his warm human instincts and make him inhu-

> man. Under it the thinking colored man could not function normally like his white brother, responsive and reacting spontaneously to the emotions of pleasure or pain, joy or sorrow, kindness or hardness, charity, anger, and forgiveness. . . . So soon as he entered the great white world, where of necessity he must work and roam and breathe the larger air to live, that entire world, high, low, middle, unclassed, all conspired to make him painfully conscious of color and race. . . . It was not easy for a Negro with an intellect standing watch over his native instincts to take his own way in this white man's civilization. But of one thing he was resolved: civilization would not take the love of color, joy, beauty, vitality and nobility out of *his* life and make him like one of the poor masses of its pale creatures.[28]

Although the imagery utilized in the preceding passage is applied to the peculiar condition of the black man, this vision of a devitalizing, dehumanizing civilization is part of the larger, biracial indictment of American culture. While McKay's attack is rooted in color-consciousness, its targets remain remarkably similar to those of the general assault. McKay finds the fraudulence and duplicity of Western civilization in a multitude of situations beyond its psychological effect on individual black men. The arduous but profitable exercise of lifting the "white man's burden" was, for McKay, a particularly noxious undertaking of the civilized world. Under the guise of Judeo-Christian morality, Western civilization succeeded in its drive to commercialize and exploit the "uncivilized" masses of the earth. Furthermore, McKay saw the trend toward cultural standardization as effectively robbing the world of its "greatest charm"—ethnic diversity. The result was the creation of a sterile, monolithic culture in which "the grand mechanical march of civilization had leveled the world down to the point where it seemed treasonable for an advanced thinker to doubt that what was good for one nation or people was also good for another."[29] Yet Ray does commit the "treasonous" act of disputing this conceptualization. And it is in his dissent that he arrives at an uneasy resolution of the problem which has plagued him through two novels.

In the closing pages of the novel, Ray explains that he has always wanted "to hold on to his intellectual acquirements without losing his instincts. The black gifts of laughter and melody and simple sensuous feelings and responses."[30] It is in this rather untenable position that his problem lies. Given a world in which the terms intellect and instinct have been assigned opposing definitions, it seems improbable that one figure can plausibly synthesize both qualities. Ray's attempt at such a synthesis is achieved through his decision to join Banjo in the vagabond life. Thematically, this decision represents a rejection of the standardized white civilization and an affirmation of the cultural diversity of the beach boys' existence.

Nevertheless, we are uneasy with the solution Ray has developed, and in his closing monologue, he unwittingly defines the source of our dissatisfaction. Although he hopes to learn from Banjo how to "exist as a black boy in a white world and rid his conscience of the used-up hussy of white morality,"[31] Ray realizes that "whether the educated man be white or brown or black, he cannot, if he has more than animal desires, be irresponsibly happy like the ignorant man who lives simply by his instincts and appetites."[32] However, "irresponsible happiness" is the essence of a Jake or a Banjo. Ray's inability to adopt this posture precludes the possibility of his successfully embracing their lifestyle or their method of survival in the white world. Despite his delusions, Ray remains the same "misfit" at the conclusion of ***Banjo*** that he was when he expatriated from America in ***Home to Harlem.***

In ***Banana Bottom,*** the third and last of his novels, McKay achieves an aesthetic structure which permits the formulation of a viable resolution to the predicament of the educated black man. This resolution is viable in that it does not contradict any of the definitions set worth in the novel, and it is consistent with McKay's affirmation of the primitive elements of black life. This new form is attained by abandoning the structural dualism of his earlier works in favor of a single protagonist. In this way, McKay frees himself from the limitations imposed by the rigid polarizations of instinct and intellect in separate characters. No longer constricted by Ray's inability to reject even a part of his cerebral existence, or Jake's (and by extension, Banjo's) static, unattainable sensuality, McKay now produces a novel in which the main character can credibly embody both instinct and intellect.

The plot of ***Banana Bottom*** is relatively simple. Set in the West Indies, the story commences with the rape of a young Jamaican peasant girl, Bita Plant. Following the incident, Bita becomes the ward of the Craigs, a white missionary couple who, with an air of condescension, take pity on the girl. In the best Anglo-Saxon missionary tradition, they see in her the golden opportunity for demonstrating to their peasant flock "what one such girl might become by careful training [and] . . . by God's help."[33] As a result, they send her to a finishing school in England with the hope of "redeeming her from her past by a long period of education."[34] After a six-year absence, Bita returns to Jamaica only to find that, for all her education, she is irrepressibly attracted to the island's peasant life. Despite the Craigs' insistence on her marriage to a black divinity student and on the devotion of her life to missionary work, Bita rejects their civilized world in favor of the simplicity of peasant life.

The novel derives its power from the dynamic tension established between the conflicting value systems of Anglo-Saxon civilization and the Jamaican folk culture. This thematic dichotomy first manifests itself in the contrasting reactions to Bita's rape. Priscilla Craig expresses her shock and indignation with an unveiled sanctimony. The "over-sexed" natives, she comments, are "apparently incapable of comprehending the opprobrium of breeding bastards in a Christian community."[35] On the other hand, the village gossip, a peasant woman named Sister Phibby, reacts with a knowing smile indicating her "primitive satisfaction as in a good thing done early."[36]

McKay expands and sustains the tension of contrary value systems through the ever-present antagonism between the civilized Christ-God of retribution and puritanical repression, and the African Obeah-God of freedom and primeval sensuality. Throughout the novel, the white missionaries and native ministers are constantly troubled with the problem of wandering flocks which "worship the Christian God-of-Good-and-Evil on Sunday and in the shadow of the night . . . invoke the power of the African God of Evil by the magic of the sorcerer. Obi [is] resorted to in sickness and feuds, love and elemental disasters."[37] And although the missionaries struggle desperately to win the native populace, it is the Obeah-God who rules Jamaica, and it is the primitive African value system which is at the core of the peasant culture.

Of peasant origin and possessing a cultivated intellect, Bita Plant represents McKay's first successful synthesis of two cultures. When she finds it necessary to choose a lifestyle, it is a relatively easy decision. As opposed to Ray, she is not fraught with the vague uncertainties and questioning doubts over her ability to survive in either culture. Bita has readily internalized the concept of her blackness and willingly accepted her racial origins. Bearing no warping hatred for white civilization, she is characterized by an assertive self-confidence derived from a sense of her own innate worth:

> . . . a white person is just like another human being to me. I thank God that although I was brought up and educated among white people, I have never wanted to be anything but myself. I take pride in being colored and different, just as any intelligent white person does in being white. I can't imagine anything more tragic than people torturing themselves to be different from their natural, unchangeable selves.[38]

For Bita, intellect and education are the handmaidens of instinct. Her return to peasant life provides a source of sustenance and vitality for her total existence: "Her music, her reading, her thinking were the flowers of her intelligence, and he [Bita's peasant husband] the root upon which she was grafted, both nourishing in the same soil."[39]

In Bita Plant, McKay at last succeeds in framing an aesthetic solution to the black intellectual's problem of social incongruence. By rejecting not intellect nor education but rather the "civilized" value system in favor of the primitive values of a black folk culture, the intellectual can ultimately escape the stigma of "misfit." On the surface, this solution does not seem to differ from the one developed in ***Banjo.*** Yet in ***Banana Bottom,*** McKay makes an important distinction not present in his earlier work. For the first time, McKay distinguishes between education, or the cultivation of the intellect, and the necessary acceptance of the value system implied by that education. Ray's failure to make this distinction is the source of his problem. Believing, on the one hand, that a rejection of civilization implies a rejection of intellect, and at the same time, desiring desperately to hold his intellectual acquirements, Ray is immobilized. He can neither remain in a white world which denies his humanity, nor move into a black world which denies his intellect. However, once the distinction is made, the element of conflict between instinct and intellect is removed. Bita, who rejects the civilized value system but not her intellect, can move easily from one world to another without impairing either instinct or intellect. Unfortunately, it is one of McKay's personal tragedies that although he is capable of making this distinction in his art, he is unable to make it in his life. "My damned white education," he wrote in his autobiography, "has robbed me of much of the primitive vitality, the pure stamina, the simple unswaggering strength of the Jakes of the Negro race."[40]

McKay's *art* can be seen as a coherent attempt to articulate and resolve the personal problems of the black intellectual through an aesthetic retreat into primitivism. His *life,* like the lives of most men, presents a less consistent pattern. If there is any overriding theme, it is found in the vision

McKay holds of himself. "All my life," he wrote in 1937, "I have been a troubadour wanderer."[41] The role of artistic nomad is the thread connecting McKay's diverse preoccupations. By choosing this image, he transforms metaphor into reality and captures the elusive elements of instinct and intellect. The primitive, liberated black man, and the sensitive, eloquent artist merge in the vagabond poet who, like Bita Plant, is capable of sensually experiencing and rationally expressing life. However, the image is not the man. It is, rather, a convenient but unsuccessful vehicle through which McKay attempts to realize in life the primitive vision he sought so desperately in art.

In describing his Jamaican boyhood, McKay unwittingly identifies the two themes from which the image of the vagabond poet springs. These themes underlie McKay's life and ultimately destroy the efficacy of the role he adopts. The first of these is revealed in the following description of the changes which accrued as a result of McKay's early recognition as a poet: "People knew that I was a poet, and that made me different, although I wanted so much to be like them. . . . I tried to be as simple as simple, but they would never accept me with the old simplicity."[42] McKay sensed that becoming a poet made him different, and he associated that difference with a loss of the innate simplicity characteristic of his peasant culture. At the same time, McKay possessed a "romantic feeling about different races and nations of people until [he] came to America and saw race hatred at work in its most virulent form."[43] The second theme is the painful color-consciousness instilled by this virulent race hatred in a young, romantic Claude McKay. The vagabond poet was a mechanism designed to escape the denigrating effects of color-consciousness and to regain the lost simplicity and vitality of a primitive past.

McKay first struck the pose of the vagabond poet on his trip to Russia in 1922, the first year of his twelve-year expatriation from America. Describing himself as an "undomesticated truant,"[44] McKay explained, "I went to Russia as a writer and a free-spirit and left the same."[45] In reality, the "spiritual freedom" of McKay's truant pose is rigidly conditioned by the predispositions previously discussed. As in his Jamaican boyhood, two motivational streams are discernible. One is the overwhelming desire to "Escape from the pit of sex and poverty, from domestic death, from the cul-de-sac of self-pity, from the hot syncopated fascination of Harlem, from the suffocating ghetto of color-consciousness."[46] The other is the quest for lost simplicity and vitality. Both these needs would seek satisfaction in McKay's special vision of the Russian Revolution.

In March 1922, mere months before he left for Russia, McKay attended a performance of the Moscow Ballet in New York City and wrote a review comparing it to the American theater. His reaction was predictable but revealing: "A very vital thing is lacking [in the American theater], and one realizes what it is only after seeing naturally simple people like the Russians and Negroes on the stage."[47] Given his image of a universal peasantry, it is understandable that he would envision the hardy Russian stereotype as being derived from the same earthy stock as the Jamaican peasant. From here it is a relatively small step to the vision of the Communist revolution as a biracial, international movement of such kindred spirits as the Negro and the Russian. McKay wholeheartedly affirmed that vision[48] as it spoke directly to his desire for an escape from color-consciousness.

Concomitantly, the power of the Russian Revolution was particularly appealing to McKay, especially in the light of the unique goal he assigned to the movement. "For my part," he wrote in a *Liberator* article, "I love to think of communism as liberating millions of city folk to go back to the land."[49] Far from the destination Lenin, Trotsky, or Marx had in mind after the removal of the chains, this idyllic return to the simple life and values of the soil is typically McKay's. It fulfills the second of his driving motivations—the quest for lost simplicity. The Russian pilgrimage thereby becomes a desperate effort both to lose color-consciousness and to recapture a primitive, pastoral life-style. Truancy has been transformed into frantic flight and pursuit, and freedom, rigidly controlled by these dual obsessions, into bondage. In the end, the vagabond poet becomes an untenable characterization because the metaphor of McKay's thought does not correspond to the reality of his actions.

The Russian experience was typical. The pattern of escape and quest under the guise of the vagabond poet was repeated; only the location differed. Interestingly enough, McKay's devotion to this image quite often caused sharp discrepancies between the recollection and the reality of a given event. In his autobiography, McKay described his stay in Marseille in terms conjuring up the image of the "troubador wanderer" who can immerse himself in the "great gang of black and brown humanity."[50] In a telling letter written during his stay, he related the following impressions of the city:

> And here I am . . . existing, trying to write, in swarms of flies and bugs and filth, when, maybe, my stories converted and sent to America might change my wretched situation a little. . . . Now I am terribly disappointed, utterly desperate, absolutely fed up. . . . Marseille is my last and cheapest stand. I don't want to be driven out of here by hunger and want. . . . After all, the few things I manage to turn out are the only joy I have.[51]

The self-portrait painted in this letter is quite different from the figure created in the memoirs. Instead of the vibrantly alive, vagabond poet, we now have the struggling artist "existing" amid filth and squalor. He derives joy not from the sensuous experience of life, as the autobiographical passage suggests, but rather from the "few things" he is able to write. Unable to adopt fully the primitive life-style he pursues, McKay is destined forever to live, in his own words, "on the edge of native life,"[52] always observing but never fully participating.

Claude McKay was an integral part of the American literary movement of the 1920s. Responsive to metaphors embodied in the cult of the primitive, McKay's art served to reinforce the image of the Negro as the simple, liberated, uncorrupt man. At the same time, his work provided the means by which McKay made his personal problem of social incongruence part of the larger cultural phenomenon expressing itself in the white expatriate movement. His life represented a less successful effort. Forever seeking fulfillment of his desires to escape color-consciousness and recapture lost innocence, McKay was doomed to an existence directly opposed to the life he apotheosized in his art. It is McKay's special and tragic irony that although he clung tenaciously to the conception of himself as a "free spirit," his obsessions condemned him to a life of slavery.

Notes

1. Claude McKay, *A Long Way from Home,* Arno Press, 1969, p. 248.
2. Malcolm Cowley, *Exiles Return* (New York, 1951), p. 77.
3. *Ibid.* See also Frederick J. Hoffman's discussion of the image of the black man in the cult of primitivism in his *The Twenties* (New York, 1949), pp. 306-08.
4. Claude McKay, "My Green Hills of Jamaica" (1947), unpublished manuscript in Claude McKay Folder, James Weldon Johnson Collection, Yale University Library, hereafter referred to as McKay Folder. By kind permission of Hope McKay Virtue, p. 62.
5. *Ibid.,* p. 51.
6. Jean Wagner, *Les Poètes Nègres des Étas-Unis* (Paris, 1963), p. 220, quoted in Wayne Cooper, "Claude McKay and the Negro of the 1920's," *Phylon* (Fall, 1964), pp. 297-306.
7. Claude McKay's *Harlem Shadows* (New York, 1922) contains many of the Jamaican poems alluded to in this paragraph (*e.g.,* "Flame-Heart," "North and South," "Home Thoughts," "The Tropics in New York"). The poems cited here have been more recently reprinted in Claude McKay, *The Selected Poems of Claude McKay* (New York, 1953). The biographical material can be found in McKay's "My Green Hills" and "My Boyhood in Jamaica," *Phylon* (June 1953), pp. 134-45.
8. McKay, *Harlem Shadows,* p. 17.
9. *Ibid.,* "Flame-Heart," p. 9.
10. It is unclear from either McKay's autobiography (*A Long Way*) or his personal letters (McKay Folder), why he never returned to Jamaica. His later emphasis on the degenerating effects of civilization and Anglo-Saxon education suggest that the answer might lie in the admonishment of his favorite author, D. H. Lawrence. "Man," wrote Lawrence, ". . . can't successfully go back to Paradise—There is a gulf in time and being. I could not go back so far. Back to their uncreat condition."
11. McKay, "My Green Hills" (Fragmentary MS), p. 8.
12. This vision of the intellectual as one who seeks to make public issues of personal problems was first introduced to me in a series of lectures given by Warren I. Sussman at Rutgers University. For a more concise definition of the concept, see Warren I. Sussman's "The Expatriate Image" in *Intellectual History in America, Vol. II,* pp. 145-57.
13. Letter from Langston Hughes to Claude McKay, 5 March 1928 (McKay Folder).
14. W. E. B. Du Bois, "The Browsing Reader," *The Crisis* (June 1928), p. 202. For additional examples of similar responses see Aubrey Bower, *Amsterdam News,* 21 March 1928; "Ferris Scores Obscenity," *Pittsburgh Courier,* 31 March 1928; Burton Roscoe, "The Seamy Side," *The Bookman* (April 1928), p. 183.
15. See McKay's *A Long Way* (pp. 306-23) for a more detailed account of this conflict as well as his description of the New Negro movement and the Harlem Renaissance.
16. *Ibid.,* p. 321.
17. Claude McKay, *Banjo* (New York, 1929), p. 200.
18. Claude McKay, *Home to Harlem* (New York, 1928), p. 8.
19. *Ibid.,* p. 264.
20. *Ibid.,* p. 274.
21. For a discussion of these themes among white expatriates see Malcolm Cowley's *Exiles Return.*
22. Felice is a black girl Jakes meets in the opening chapters of the novel. He subsequently loses her. Translated from the Spanish, her name signifies joy or happiness.

23. McKay, *Banjo*, p. 6.
24. *Ibid.*, p. 49.
25. *Ibid.*, p. 66.
26. McKay, *A Long Way*, p. 245.
27. McKay, *Banjo*, p. 163.
28. *Ibid.*, pp. 163-64.
29. *Ibid.*, pp. 324-25.
30. *Ibid.*, pp. 322-23.
31. *Ibid.*, p. 322.
32. *Ibid.*, p. 323.
33. Claude McKay, *Banana Bottom* (New York, 1933), p. 17.
34. *Ibid.*, p. 31.
35. *Ibid.*, p. 16.
36. *Ibid.*, p. 15.
37. *Ibid.*, p. 135.
38. *Ibid.*, p. 169.
39. *Ibid.*, p. 313.
40. McKay, *A Long Way*, p. 229.
41. *Ibid.*, p. 354.
42. McKay, "My Green Hills," p. 69.
43. *Ibid.*, p. 51.
44. McKay, *A Long Way*, p. 150. McKay often used truant to express the same primitive energy, simplicity, and innate freedom implied in his use of the term vagabond. For a more complete discussion of McKay's concept of the black man as truant, see his short story "Truant" in his *Gingertown* (New York 1932), pp. 143-62.
45. Letter from Claude McKay to James Weldon Johnson, 8 May 1935 (McKay Folder). By kind permission of Hope McKay Virtue.
46. McKay, *A Long Way*, p. 153.
47. Claude McKay, "What Is Lacking in the Theater," *The Liberator* (March 1922), pp. 20-21.
48. Claude McKay, "How Black Sees Green and Red," *The Liberator* (June 1921), pp. 17-20.
49. *Ibid.*
50. McKay, *A Long Way*, p. 277.
51. Letter from Claude McKay to Louise Bryant Bullitt, 24 June 1926 (McKay Folder). By kind permission of Hope McKay Virtue.
52. McKay, *A Long Way*, p. 332.

GETA LESEUR (ESSAY DATE 1989)

SOURCE: LeSeur, Geta. "Claude McKay's Marxism." In *The Harlem Renaissance: Revaluations*, edited by Amritjit Singh, William S. Shiver, and Stanley Brodwin, pp. 219-31. New York: Garland Publishing, Inc., 1989.

In the following essay, LeSeur discusses McKay's sympathies and disappointments with Communism in the 1920s and 1930s.

Claude McKay remains today part of the acknowledged literary triumvirate of the Harlem Renaissance. He shares this prestigious position with Langston Hughes and Jean Toomer. Each in his own way made a lasting contribution to Afro-American literature and politics because of the uniqueness each possessed. McKay, however, was perhaps the most controversial of the three, because of his involvement with Marxism early in his career. The two primary dilemmas of McKay's life were as follows: the first was to resolve for himself whether socialism indeed was the answer to the "Negro question"; the second, the role of the black artist in a society that gives judgmental statements on both. The years 1922-1923, when he visited Russia to assess the workings and values of Marxism, were crucial for McKay. It took a lifetime to resolve these dilemmas and yet they were never satisfactorily resolved for him or his public. It was only during his final years that he found peace in the spiritual world of Catholicism.

In his study *Roots of Negro Racial Consciousness*, Stephen H. Bronz regards McKay's early understanding of socialism as having been "rooted in . . . racial equality and a return to the soil."[1] Bronz claims that McKay had not really seen Marxist doctrine in relation to the reform of industrialism. This view is difficult to comprehend since McKay's knowledge and early experience of Jamaican communal life is evident in such works as ***Banana Bottom*** (1933) and **"Boyhood in Jamaica."** The emphasis on beauty and peace in an agrarian setting should explain his initial view of Marxism as applicable to racial prejudice and agrarianism, but it does not. McKay's 1921 description of himself as a "peasant" by birth and upbringing, i.e., one possessed by "the peasant's passion for the soil," is highly reminiscent of the mood and language of his autobiography. It is also peculiar, but true, that his peasant identity explains both McKay's appreciation of English Romantic poetry and his initial devotion to Marxism. Such a limited vision of a highly complex social and economic theory was "romantic," and foreshadowed an inevitable disillusionment.

McKay was strongly committed to international socialism, which in itself is far-reaching and utopian. His poetic outlook precluded objectivity, which most persons with political aspirations for uniting mankind should have. Men like McKay often fail because their romantic vision clouds the logical procedural tactics necessary to socialist goals. Even though McKay considered himself a poet first, the roles he had envisioned for himself posed a conflict in his soul or "rebel heart." The idea of being international, like most of McKay's other traits, was carried over into almost everything he did, including his letters to Max Eastman.[2] He mentions to Eastman that he would like to write a study about Russia, but adds, "I am paying for the penalty of being too naively internationally-minded . . . all that, in a subtle way, works against . . . me."[3]

In 1922 McKay left for Russia after having had a disagreement with his friend and editor, Max Eastman, over an edition of *The Liberator,* a socialist magazine devoted to art and literature. As an editor on the magazine and the only black there, McKay saw the feasibility of writing a chapter about the race question in America. Eastman and another editor, Mike Gold, thought the objective of the magazine would be lost if McKay emphasized this kind of issue; consequently, no gains would be made for the blacks. McKay obviously disagreed, and in extended correspondence between him and Eastman, there were charges and countercharges about where each specifically stood on the race question. Eastman wrote to McKay that

> . . . there was never any disagreement between you and the editors of the Liberator, so as far as I am aware, about the proper Communist policy toward the race question in the United States. . . . The disagreement which arose after I left was a disagreement about how to further those policies, along with the others for which the Liberator stood, in that particular magazine.[4]

Eastman insists that the effect of publishing McKay's article on the race question in *The Liberator* would be the "opposite" of the one desired. He goes on in this very lengthy letter to dissect McKay's capability as a writer of such a chapter. He continues,

> You cannot take two opposite positions with the same lofty and condescending tone of voice in the same chapter. . . . [It] will irritate and tend to alienate from you every one of them, and if they have, as you say they have, the "broadcast sympathetic social and artistic understanding of the Negro" of any white group in America, your chapter is a poor beginning of an effort to extend that understanding.[5]

The reader of this lengthy cryptic letter can assume that Eastman was not only angry but was indicating to McKay that there was also something wrong with his journalistic sense. Interestingly, a few years later while writing pieces for *Pravda* and *Izvestia,* McKay admitted that he had not quite mastered the knack of "journalese." His closeness to the subject matter in these cases resulted in the natural poetizing that got in the way of the objective perspective needed. To feel strongly about a subject is one thing, but to present it effectively is another. Paradoxically, however, one observes an acute sense of audience awareness throughout McKay's writing, even more so in the pieces he wrote during his Russian visit.

McKay's response to Eastman's attack was no less harsh and analytical. Max Eastman has a memo in the manuscripts that reads, "Claude's Brain Storm in Moscow." It is not clear why he calls it that, but McKay goes through the origin of the argument or disagreement with Eastman and *The Liberator* staff, and writes, ". . . The Liberator group, revealed to me that [it] did not have a class-conscious attitude on the problem of the American Negro." McKay appears to contradict himself because, in fact, he had not discussed the labor movement seriously with *The Liberator* staff; rather, he tells us that "I discussed [it] seriously only with the radical Negro group in New York."[6] This last comment by McKay to Eastman could have been one of the sensitive points that made Eastman not wish to print the chapter. Perhaps he sensed that groups sympathetic to McKay's view would reflect an ideological perspective contrary to the socialist position already established by *The Liberator.* It is obvious, too, that McKay and Eastman were at odds regarding their views on the right of a free press. McKay goes further to say that Eastman did not even want to discuss Irish and Indian questions, because they were "national issues." McKay felt, however, that Eastman had said nothing at all on any pertinent racial issues, including the Negro in the Revolution. This is hardly a credit to a magazine's chief editor. By way of supporting his argument for the publication of the chapter in *The Liberator* on his experience, McKay said that the article **"He Who Gets Slapped,"** which appeared in the May 1922 issue, got practical results. The most personal attack on Eastman, though, is a response to the Tom Paine/Lenin analogy in an earlier Eastman letter. He says:

> . . . Tom Paine was of his time and so is Lenin. To me there is no comparison. During the age of the French Revolution, Paine performed herculean tasks in England, France and America, and if you had in your whole body an ounce of the vitality that Paine had in his little finger, you, with your wonderful opportunities, would not have missed the chances for great leadership in the class struggle that were yours in America.[7]

Despite such "brainstorms," the two men remained lifelong friends, and their correspondence regarding all kinds of problems, literary, political, and personal, continued.

There had been many rumors and assumptions regarding Claude McKay's trip to Russia and they persisted for a long time. McKay had to live with not only rumors about how and why he went, but also whether he was Communist, Socialist, Marxist, or his own brand of any of these. It is no wonder, then, that critics have called his autobiography, ***A Long Way from Home*** (1937), unbalanced.[8]

Like Hurston's *Dust Tracks on a Road,* McKay's ***Long Way*** is a peculiar autobiography. The reader discovers very little about the innermost depths of McKay, the essential human being. The book is aimed mostly at clearing the air and setting the record straight about the annoying things in his life, from his first arrival in Harlem to his journeys to Europe and Africa. Three segments are devoted to his experiences, good and bad. Perhaps one of the most interesting is the section, "The Magic Pilgrimage," which consists of seven chapters dealing with the Russian Revolution, "Blackness" as an asset, the hostility of American Communists toward McKay, and the gossip that had been written about him.

Certain aspects of Communism excited McKay, and others repelled him. He had always felt the importance of belonging to a group because the group afforded strength, distinction, and assurance. Yet, one's individual identity can be lost in the group, and this was a dilemma he never quite resolved. The forsaking of Communism on these same grounds came about with time and experience in Russia. He had been to England in 1920-1921, had worked with the Pankhurst group there, and thought at that time that Marxism indeed was the answer to the race issue. It is interesting that McKay thought of England as the place of his first real active indoctrination. As a child of colonialism, with its class distinctions, McKay returned to the Mother Land to find that Englishmen were as much into socialism as colonialism. Perhaps that was a reinforcement for his subsequent leanings and European initiation. What was to haunt McKay and make him think of Communism as "dry rot" was that it, like the white patrons and the black bourgeoisie, attempted to exercise control over black writers and artists.

The Communist "killing off" of creativity was one of the experiences in Russia that he abhorred, and he saw it happening as he milled around with the "intelligentsia" transformed into "comrade workers." So, to set the record straight, McKay recorded in detail his entire Russian sojourn in "The Magic Pilgrimage." He became the darling of Russia, the first black to receive that honor even though he was not in 1923 an official candidate to the Fourth Congress of the Third Internationale. The mulatto officially appointed as a delegate to the Congress faded into the background as the dark McKay became the symbol of the Communist cause, an American prize who appeared like a miracle to the Russians. The timing for both him and the Russians was right.

In ***A Long Way from Home,*** he cites the fact that a cartoon had appeared in the American papers depicting him on a magic carpet sailing over the clouds from Africa (not the U.S.) into Moscow, and that his visit was much like that. In that "Moscow Brain Storm" letter can be found the clearest parallel to what McKay's real presence indicated for the Russians. He relates an earlier experience in New Hampshire about a black man in a white environment who is "down" on life, but eager to know the identity of both himself and his oppressor. He says:

> . . . I went into that hotel with the full knowledge that I was not merely an ordinary worker, but that I was also a Negro, that I would not be judged on my merits as a worker alone, but on my behavior as a Negro. Up there . . . the Negro (as in thousands of other places in America) was on trial not as a worker but as a strange species. And I went into that hotel to work for my bread and bed, and also for my race. This situation is forced upon every intelligent Negro in America. . . .[9]

The letter is important because it shows that despite the excitement, exposure and speeches, McKay didn't lose sight of who and what he represented. That portion of the letter to Max Eastman illustrated that he was clearly knowledgeable of his position. If the letters or words were transported from New Hampshire to Moscow, they would become equally meaningful in his understanding of his Russian experience and his role there. While enjoying the luxury of a "roaring good time," McKay was not naive, but took in all he saw, listened eagerly, and observed all facets of Russian life. To him, the Russian people and their politics were one. While McKay found many discrepancies in the socialism of Max Eastman, his co-workers at *The Liberator,* the black radicals, and American Communists in general, he admitted readily that his "senses were stormed by Moscow before the intellect was touched by the forces of Revolution."[10]

He had already observed that many Russians were "raggedy" and lived in poor housing, and in mingling with them he found that the majority did not understand the true nature of Communism. Some knew only that Lenin had replaced the Czar and that he was a "greater little father." Then, at the Fourth Congress McKay noticed that the American Communists were split on the direction the party should take. The more McKay became aware of what was going on with the American Communist delegation, the more he perceived their actions as affecting party unity negatively. The tension there was so great that they contemplated moving the party headquarters to another country. For the Russian Communists, however, McKay was an omen of good luck and while he was in Russia, only the actions and behavior of the American Communists who lied about the progress of the party takeover in America disturbed him.

There were obvious differences between the Russian and American labor organizations also. McKay admired the organization and platform of the Finnish delegation and saw a possible application of their tactics as a redemption for blacks. The Finns voted as a bloc, were never unprepared, and controlled their delegation because they had proper organization and money. As McKay says in ***A Long Way from Home,*** "every other racial group in America is organized except Negroes. What Negroes need is political union for strength like the Finns."[11] He also concluded that the only place where illegal and secret radical propaganda was necessary was among the Negroes of the South.[12] These thoughts and ideas were to find their way into some short stories he wrote in Russia for *Izvestia.* In Russia, Eastman, the pure American Marxist, was "shrugged off" at the Congress while McKay was asked to address the group, a fact McKay does not reveal in his autobiography although it is recorded elsewhere. The omission seems to be a deliberate one on McKay's part, in order to highlight the honors and attention accorded him in Russia.

McKay had many other concerns regarding the radical left, one of which was the explosive issue of the so-called "Jewish question." From his days on *The Liberator,* he had become aware of it much as he recognized the problems of the Irish, the blacks, and the American Indians. Jews, like Negroes, posed a problem for society, and he saw them as an oppressed, "lynched" people, among the masses of classless men. In a letter to Max Eastman, he asks:

> . . . Do you think the Communist leaders and the rank and file could by a single stroke change the minds of humanity that have been warped by hundreds of years of bourgeois traditions and education?[13]

He realized that the Communist regime had not swept away the deep-rooted prejudice against Russian Jewry. Max Eastman was also aware of similar problems in the U.S. and prior to McKay's observation had written:

> . . . The situation of the Jew in Russia before the revolution is the one thing in the world comparable to the situation of the Negro in the United States. A proletarian Revolution has occurred, or is occurring here. The persecution of Jews had ceased. The two most powerful men in the government at this moment are Jews. The race problem in its basic outlines has disappeared. For you, *the leading revolutionary figure in the Negro world* . . . to imagine that the race problem will be solved by the proletarian revolution (the triumph of labor) is really a tragedy.[14]
>
> [emphasis added]

Eastman calls McKay "the leading revolutionary figure in the Negro World," an honor and recognition that McKay did not assume for himself. McKay, however, responded to Eastman's description in giving more serious thought to his subsequent statements on race and revolution.

McKay goes on to tell Eastman that his revolutionary acts started back in 1920 in London when he sold "Red" literature on the street corners of London and also when he did propaganda work among the colonial soldiers. When he discussed political and race problems with fellow workers on *The Liberator* in 1921, McKay was not play-acting, but was very seriously committed despite the Justice Department's persecution. Eastman, like most people, had been deceived by him due to his "everlastingly infectious smile." This guise of a relaxed attitude might have endeared McKay to the Russian people, too. He did not have the intensity and brooding attitude of a typical dedicated Communist. His was the image they expected and wanted, naive and primitive, and they used his "innocence" to further their aims. It is no wonder, then, that they found his early poetry, that with which they were familiar, proletarian—although his fascination was with the past, not the future, and his point of view romantic.

When McKay finally left Russia in 1923 after seeing much of the country and its political and social workings, he was leaving at the height of his popularity. He had read his poem, **"If We Must Die,"** in the spirit in which he wrote it. The poem evokes the ethos of radicalism and comradeship the Russians admired:

> If we must die, let it not be like hogs
> Hunted and penned in an inglorious spot,
> While round us bark the mad and hungry dogs,
> Making their mock at our accursed lot.
> If we must die, O let us nobly die,

> So that our precious blood may not be shed
> In vain; then even the monsters we defy
> Shall be constrained to honor us though
> Oh kinsmen! we must meet the common foe!
> Though far outnumbered let us show us brave,
> And for their thousand blows deal one
> deathblow!
> What though before us lies the open grave?
> Like men we'll face the murderous, cowardly
> pack,
> Pressed to the wall, dying, but fighting back![15]

He had written a summary of these ideas for Trotsky, whom he had met there, and published them in *Pravda.* Russia had gotten a few poems out of him and some short stories. Though still puzzled by Trotsky's famous phrase, "Permanent Revolution," he moved on to view his Russian experience in retrospect. Although Russia had already "had her revolution," he found that Trotsky's statement, "one must be *Right* against the Party," contained practical wisdom of the highest order.

McKay did not meet Lenin or Stalin, but found Trotsky to be a magnetic personality. "Trotsky," he said, "wanted to know about Negroes, organization, political position, schooling, religion, grievances, and social aspirations." Trotsky told him that Negroes needed to be "lifted up" equal to whites and they must have education through all phases of their life. When Eastman wrote the book *When Lenin Died,* McKay thought highly of it and praised Eastman by saying that he [Eastman] was:

> . . . mountain high above any American leader. You occupy on your own ground as sure and important a place as did Lenin & Trotsky themselves. . . . It seems to me that you've given us one of the finest and most balanced political treatises of these times, a crystal-clear analytic study of the cooperative work of Lenin & Trotsky—their faults—their weakness—their greatness. And whatever happens to Trotsky this little book of yours will live and interest the world so long as it remembers Lenin & Trotsky. . . .[16]

While in Russia, McKay was supposed to write a book on the Russian Revolution for Negroes, but this never materialized. He had managed to write several articles, not all of which were "adulatory." The book commissioned to be written was ***Negry v Amerike*** (***The Negroes in America***) (1923) and had as its epigraph Walt Whitman's straightforward lines:

> My call is the call of Battle
> I nourish active Rebellion.[17]

The Russian experience stayed with McKay all his life. It left its great imprint on him. It is apparent not only from the content of the autobiography, but also from the letters written after 1930 upon returning to New York. In New York, he wrote to Max Eastman that he had eaten with a group of colored Communists whom he couldn't convince that he was not a Trotskyite, so, "some of them were sorry they had eaten with me. . . ." Also,

> . . . The Third Communist Internationale seems to me by far a greater tragedy than Trotsky. . . . [It] looks like a stuffed carcass and it seems to me it will be so as long as its siege remains in Russia. . . .[18]

From 1939 to 1944, when McKay joined the Catholic Church, his reflections became more somber and philosophical. He was asked to work with the CYO (Catholic Youth Organization) and advise them on the development of Communism, but he admitted that he had not followed the party's development or Russia "since Lenin died." Upon his conversion to Catholicism, he states that the Communists had no need to "gloat" over his conversion:

> Although I was once sympathetic to their cause I was never a Communist. I had a romantic hope that Communism would usher in a classless society and make human beings happier. All I saw in Russia was that Communism was using one class to destroy the other. . . . Besides, communism is quite a primitive ideal and I don't see how modern society could go back to it.[19]

McKay went to Russia to view a great social experiment which, in reality, was not an answer to his own problems. He had argued with his friend, editor, and former boss Max Eastman about the positive effect of writing a chapter in *The Liberator* about the Negro question. Eastman saw it as negative and destructive to the magazine and the black masses. McKay, on the other hand, bound by duty, felt that this was positive and constructive. He felt that blacks needed to organize themselves into a power group and the closest thing he saw as a model was an international Communism separate from whites.

The real source of McKay's discontent was the beginning of his realization that the concept of a universal proletariat was not the solution to the black man's struggle. The Russian experience was enriching and confusing, as he did not see there the utopian solidarity he had envisioned. However, he used the experience, enjoyed the lionizing, managed to further a writing career (in prose), and came out of it still a "poet," not a politician.

For a few years McKay clung to the illusion that Marxism was the answer for the black man, and even when that illusion was shattered, he still wrote about the trip to Russia with a degree of nostalgia. The fact that he spent a large portion of his autobiography, ***A Long Way from Home,*** on this two-year phase of his life is evidence enough that Russia had made a lasting impact on him. Until his conversion to Catholicism, in the last few years of his life, the concept of a proletarian revolution was the strongest of all his temptations to desert his belief in a pure black identity.

Notes

1. Stephen H. Bronz, *Roots of Negro Racial Consciousness* (New York: Libra Publishers, 1964), pp. 76-77.
2. McKay's unpublished letters are in the Lily Library, Indiana University, Bloomington. The references and excerpts are from the McKay Mss. there.
3. McKay letter to Eastman, 25 November 1934.
4. Eastman letter to McKay, March 1923.
5. Ibid., pp. 3-5.
6. McKay letter from Moscow, 3 April 1923.
7. Ibid.
8. Claude McKay, *A Long Way from Home* (New York: Harcourt, Brace and World, 1937).
9. McKay letter from Moscow, 3 April 1923.
10. McKay, *A Long Way from Home,* p. 138.
11. Ibid., p. 174.
12. Ibid., pp. 177-178.
13. McKay letter to Eastman, 18 May 1923.
14. Eastman letter to McKay, 12 April 1923.
15. Claude McKay, *Selected Poems* (New York: Bookman, 1953), p. 36.
16. McKay letter to Eastman, Avignon, May 1925.
17. Claude McKay, *The Negroes in America,* trans. from the Russian by Robert J. Winter (New York: Kennikat Press, 1979).
18. McKay letter to Eastman, 9 May 1934.
19. McKay letter to Eastman, 30 June 1944.

CHARLES J. HEGLAR (ESSAY DATE 1995)

SOURCE: Heglar, Charles J. "Claude McKay's 'If We Must Die,' *Home to Harlem,* and the Hog Trope." *ANQ: A Quarterly Journal of Short Articles, Notes, and Reviews* 8, no. 3 (summer 1995): 22-26.

In the following essay, Heglar discusses the use of "hog" as a trope for unreflecting complacency in "If We Must Die" and Home to Harlem.

In the sixty-five years since the publication of ***Home to Harlem,*** readers have missed Claude McKay's skillful use of irony in the novel's conclusion. Critics—among them Robert Bone (68), Arthur Davis (40), Nathan Huggins (122), Wayne Cooper (242-43) and Tyrone Tillery (85-86)—have noted the episodic, almost picaresque plot, in which Jacob Brown searches for his happiness in the person of Felice, the woman he meets when he returns to Harlem after deserting the A. E. F. in France. But they do not consider the ironic significance of the reunion of Jake and Felice in Part III of the novel and her suggestion that they move to Chicago.[1] I believe that McKay's choice of Chicago as the city of refuge and the spring of 1919 as the season of departure emphasizes the restrictions of both black and middle-class life. Further, McKay reenforces his ironic commentary by skillfully developing the trope of blacks as "hogs" trapped in the city. Indeed, those familiar with McKay's poem **"If We Must Die"** should have noticed the deployment of the trope in ***Home to Harlem*** and its effect on the novel's conclusion.

According to Arthur P. Davis, "**'If We Must Die'** is the best known of McKay's poems. During the [Harlem] Renaissance it became a kind of rallying cry for young Negro writers, who felt it expressed their own spirit of defiance" (38). Although McKay later claimed that the sonnet was a universal statement, when it was initially published in July 1919, in *Liberator* magazine, James Weldon Johnson, an active participant in both the NAACP and the Harlem Renaissance, had no doubt that it was inspired by the summer of race riots—especially the riot in Chicago—that came to be called "The Red Summer of 1919" (341). The first four lines of the poem establish McKay's disdain for passivity in the face of degradation and violence; in addition, these lines present the "hog" as a trope for unreflecting acceptance of the status quo:

> If we must die, let it not be like hogs
> Hunted and penned in an inglorious spot,
> While round us bark the mad and hungry dogs,
> Making their mock at our accursed lot.

The great popularity of the poem maintained McKay's reputation as an artist for the next nine years while he struggled as an expatriate fiction writer. It is within the context of the poem's "hog" trope and the author's attitude toward Chicago as a riot site in the summer of 1919 that Felice's suggestion in Part III to move there should be read. Moreover, McKay's foreshadowing throughout the three-part novel and his use of details in Part III reenforce such a reading.

Throughout the novel, Jacob Brown searches for Felice after his one-night affair with her on his first day back in Harlem; he hopes for a lasting relationship within Harlem, although by the end of the novel he must move once again. In Part II,

McKay contrasts Jake's aspirations with those of his intellectual friend, Ray, who rejects a relationship with Agatha because he sees marriage in terms of complacency and atrophy. He believes that were he to marry her, he would become "one of the contented hogs in the pigpen of Harlem, getting ready to litter little black piggies" (263). Ray also rejects institutional education, which Jake respects and admires, because Ray feels that "modern education is planned to make you a sharp, snouty, rooting hog" (243). In both instances, Ray uses "hog" in the same sense that McKay used the term in **"If We Must Die"**: as a trope for unreflecting complacency.

While Ray's thoughts on marriage and education expand the trope to include a blind drive for middle-class conformity, he also uses the figure in contemplating racial injustice. Even as he considers escape from Harlem and America, he wonders "what would become of that great mass of black swine, hunted and cornered by slavering white canaille" (155)! In fact, the novel refers several times to the restrictions that would lead to the racial violence of the "Red Summer." For example, in Part I, Jake is involved in a violent confrontation between black scabs and white union workers on the docks of New York, which directs attention to the economic competition that frequently erupted in racial violence during the post-war period. Jake refuses to scab, but because he is aware of union discrimination against blacks, he also refuses to join the union (44–46). In Part III, Jake notes the residential segregation that causes the overcrowding of blacks (285, 287) and the struggle of whites in "Block Beautiful" to prevent blacks from moving into a white neighborhood bordering Harlem (300–01). In Part II, Ray, whom McKay describes as a "touchstone of the general emotions of his race," reacts to the harsh attitudes toward and actions against blacks that would deteriorate into wide-ranging violence in the summer of 1919: "Any upset—a terror-breathing Negro-baiting headline in a metropolitan newspaper or the news of a human bonfire in Dixie—could make him miserable" (266).

After Ray escapes Harlem and the United States as a waiter on a steamer bound for Europe, McKay focuses Part III on the reunion of Jake and Felice, who initially had planned to spend their lives in Harlem. Their fear that someone has overheard Zeddy's threat to expose Jake as an Army deserter leads Felice to suggest that they move to Chicago—she has heard "it's a mahvelous place foh niggers" (333). McKay foreshadows the irony of their flight to a city about to be torn by a race riot in several places in Part III of the novel. The section begins with a chapter, "Spring in Harlem," which establishes that the time of their departure is prior to the summer. McKay also reminds the reader that the year is 1919, especially in the final chapter.[2] At one point McKay notes, in reference to World War I, that "the war was just ended" (317). Elsewhere, he refers to the imminent murder of the musician James Reese Europe during 1919 and to Prohibition (1920–1933), which "was on the threshold of the country and drinking was becoming a luxury" (319).

Thus, when Felice mentions Chicago as a good place for black people in the spring before "The Red Summer of 1919," it is obvious that McKay is dooming, through irony, Jake and Felice's move away from Harlem. Moreover, he seems to foretell that Jake will become one of the "hogs / Hunted and penned in an inglorious spot" if he settles into a conventional marriage in Harlem or Chicago. This point is confirmed in McKay's next novel, ***Banjo: A Story Without a Plot*** (1929), when Jake reappears in Marseilles as a seaman who could not stand being pent up in either Chacago or—after he, Felice, and his son return—Harlem.

As Richard Priebe points out, "Jake is an alienated individual," who is unable to find a community in the United States due to racial and bourgeois restraints (24). Thus it is erroneous to see McKay's Harlem as A. Robert Lee does: "an irresistible black 'city' of the senses" (71). Especially in terms of the "hog" trope, ***Home to Harlem*** is better read as a modernist novel in which the alienated individuals Jake and Ray search for a home or community but are unable to find one. In the end, both characters find more of a home in their quest for values and in other individuals with a similar outlook than they do in Harlem. Perhaps where one is "penned" is less important than that one is "penned."

Notes

1. Prior to the 1980s, most critics, such as Bone, Davis, and Huggins, attempted to place McKay within both the Harlem Renaissance and the primitivism movement. Since 1980, critical attention has shifted to a biographical or historical reading of McKay, such as those of Cooper and Tillery; Tillery serves as the clearest example in structuring his reading of *Home to Harlem* around the idea that "McKay had lived both a Jake-like and a Ray-like life" (85). From a broader historical perspective, both A. L. McLeod and P. S. Chauhan read McKay, a native of Jamaica, as a colonial writer. Finally, there is the trend represented by A. Robert Lee that focuses on the literary presentation of Harlem as an idea and a metaphor.

2. No critic has noticed that the novel actually begins and ends in 1919. In the first chapter, "Going Back Home," McKay has Jake celebrating New Year's Day, 1919, in London. Significantly in terms of McKay's interest in the race riots in the United States of the same summer, "that summer Jake saw a big battle staged between colored and white men of London's East End" (7). Apparently, McKay was so intent on making the racial violence of the summer of 1919 a part of his novel that he skewed the chronology of the plot. The events of Part III should take place a year later, in 1920, but the novel begins and ends in 1919 without an internal explanation for McKay's very clear dating of events in both sections.

There are several possible explanations for the lack of critical attention to this detail. Most obviously, it is not the kind of repetition that one would be alert for in reading the novel, and most critics have read the novel with emphasis on other elements (see note 1). Second, critical attention to the "episodic," "picaresque," and "primitive" qualities of the novel may have diverted attention from the repetition of dates and the importance of the time frame in terms of the "Red Summer." Finally, in combination with the prior possibilities, readers may have missed the date because McKay used calendar dates in Part I, but in Part II he used references to contemporary events for which the reader must supply the calendar date.

Works Cited

Bone, Robert. *The Negro Novel in America.* Rev. ed. New Haven: Yale UP, 1965.

Chauhan, P. S. "Rereading Claude McKay." *College Language Association Journal* 34 (1990): 68–80.

Cooper, Wayne C. *Claude McKay: Rebel Sojourner in the Harlem Renaissance, A Biography.* Baton Rouge: Louisiana State UP, 1987.

Davis, Arthur P. *From the Dark Tower: Afro-American Writers 1900 to 1965.* Washington: Howard UP, 1974.

Huggins, Nathan Irvin. *Harlem Renaissance.* New York: Oxford UP, 1971.

Johnson, James Weldon. *Along This Way: The Autobiography of James Weldon Johnson.* 1933. New York: Viking, 1990.

Lee, A. Robert. "Harlem on My Mind: Fictions of a Black Metropolis." *The American City: Literary and Cultural Perspectives.* Ed. Graham Clarke. New York: St. Martin's Press, 1988. 62–85.

McKay, Claude. *Banjo: A Story without a Plot.* New York: Harcourt, 1929.

———. *Home to Harlem.* New York: Harper & Brothers, 1928.

McLeod, A. L. "Claude McKay as Historical Witness." *Subjects Worthy of Fame: Essays on Commonwealth Literature in Honour of H. H. Anniah Gowda.* Ed. A. L. McLeod. New Delhi: Sterling, 1989. 62–71.

Preibe, Richard. "The Search for Community in the Novels of Claude McKay." *Studies in Black Literature* 3 (1972): 22–30.

Tillery, Tyrone. *Claude McKay: A Black Poet's Struggle for Identity.* Amherst: U of Massachusetts P, 1992.

TITLE COMMENTARY

"If We Must Die"

ROBERT A. LEE (ESSAY DATE 1974)

SOURCE: Lee, Robert A. "On Claude McKay's 'If We Must Die'." *CLA Journal* 18, no. 2 (1974): 216-21.

In the following essay, Lee offers a close reading of McKay's most famous poem, "If We Must Die," and says that from a sociological as well as a literary perspective it should be read as a racial poem.

Through a reading of Claude McKay's **"If We Must Die,"** I want to consider certain matters of literary theory. Should a poem be read as specifically (narrowly) as possible? Or should we read generally, finding a universal truth from the specific illustration? Secondly, *must* a poem by a member of a racial minority be read as a racial poem?

If we must die, let it not be like hogs
Hunted and penned in an inglorious spot,
While round us bark the mad and hungry dogs,
Making their mock at our accursed lot.
If we must die, O let us nobly die,
So that our precious blood may not be shed
In vain; then even the monsters we defy
Shall be constrained to honor us though dead!
O kinsmen! we must meet the common foe!
Though far outnumbered let us show us brave,
And for their thousand blows deal one deathblow!
What though before us lies the open grave?
Like men we'll face the murderous, cowardly pack,
Pressed to the wall, dying, but fighting back!

McKay makes use of the elements of prosody to construct a finely wrought sonnet. The sonnet's overt form is English, with the structure of three quatrains and a final couplet giving the conventional effect of sequential argument and concluding moral apothegm. Yet the theme is simultaneously expressed by the Italian sonnet form's division into sections of eight and six lines, situation and resolution. The end-stop/run-on pattern of the lines of **"If We Must Die"** reinforces this tension in the poem: three lines in the octave are run-on lines: numbers one, six, and seven; and the resulting effect is one of immediacy, urgency. But in the sestet, as the counterargument becomes persuasive, controlled, and dominant, all lines are end-stopped. The calm force of the speaker's tone in the latter part of the poem is further suggested by the two caesuras in line fourteen (the only instance of two caesuras in one line in the poem), and by the caesura in line thirteen, between "murderous" and "cowardly."

There is also, I think, a heard but unwritten pause between "cowardly" and "pack," as the adjectives condemning the "they" of the poem are stressed.

Another fact in the development of the poem is the progression of the images created by the pronouns and epithets. The condemned "we" of the poem (primarily, but, according to McKay, not exclusively black people) begin as "hogs." Moreover, the imagery is that of chase ("hunted") and certain entrapment ("penned"); but worst of all, the hogs can achieve no vestige of self-respect by their actions; they will die in an "inglorious spot." Conversely, the "they" (whites, generally, all oppressors) are initially dogs, animals which probably have more agreeable connotations than hogs. In the second quatrain, the dogs evolve to "monsters," becoming more terrifying and awesome in the suggestion of non-humanness. At the same time, the hogs gain a measure of humanization: their blood is now "precious"; they can "defy" the monsters, an act which suggests an attained dignity. The dogs now suffer their first setback, as they will be "constrained" (reversing the entrapment image earlier connected with the hogs) to "honor us." The "we" of the poem have acquired self-respect and even the respect of their antagonists. In the third quatrain, also the beginning of the sestet, the hogs progress further, from the acquisition of human but individual honor to the attainment of brotherhood and solidarity: they become "kinsmen." This solidarity is also implied throughout the poem by the repetition of pronouns: six occurrences of "us," five of "we," two of "our." But the dogs remain "common." McKay is deliberately ambiguous here; common means both mean and low and also allied. They are denigrated in their meanness. Though "they" may ultimately win the battle, metaphorically "they" have lost it.

The loss is specified in the final couplet. "We" are now "men"; "they" have devolved from superiority to parity to a "pack," one which is both "murderous"—if criminal at least possessing some suggestion of redeeming action—but also "cowardly"—thus undercutting even such negative attainment. The positions of the opening of the sonnet are effectively reversed. "They," the oppressors, have not moved from their animal-like nature. But though "pressed," though "dying," the oppressed "we" are fighting—and the participles suggest continuing action, survival, and escape from the parallel "if we must die" clauses which begin the first and second quatrains, and which dominate the octave. This newly attained stature is also suggested by the movement into the future tense of "we'll face the murderous, cowardly pack." The former inevitability of "if we must die" is undercut by the sense of futurity now present. The combination of the future tense and the participles denotes duration and ultimate triumph.

Tonal discrimination between "they" and "we/us" is emphasized in other ways. The "mad" and "hungry" adjectives first attached to the dogs suggest a failure of reason, a lack of valid motivation. The hunted flee with cause; the hunters have none. Oppression has a life of its own, but not a rationale. The "k" consonance of the dog's bark is heard again in the fourth line, as the dogs are "making their mock" at the "accursed" lot of the hogs. Such consonance is urgent and harsh, and further suggests the dogs' irrationality. This sound pattern contrasts with the formal, almost stately effect of line five, where the "o" assonance of "O let us nobly die" suggests a calm and inevitable dignity. This "o" assonance is repeated in line nine, where it is joined by a mellow "m" consonance: "O kinsmen! we must meet the common foe!" And the formal praise for "we" is made certain by the "b"-"d" chiasmus in line eleven, where the "o" assonance is also reheard: "And for their thousand blows deal one death blow." This line is extraordinarily well made. The slight sibilance of the repeated "th" sound, the "o" assonance of the "for," which leads to the heavily accentuated vowels of "one" and "blow(s)," finally, the climactic "b"-"d" chiasmus, all work to suggest an attitude of solemnity and control. The sounds in this line have a totally different purpose and effect than those lines about the mad, hungry, barking dogs, in which the consonance is clipped and stammering.

Throughout the poem, McKay uses different rhythms and sound patterns to describe the contending sides. Generally, the "we" of the poem are alluded to or specified in lines which are formal, balanced, and whose musical qualities suggest order and strength. Conversely, "they" are described in a hard, sharp language, with suggestions of disorder. The fifth line, "If we must die, O let us nobly die," and the eleventh, "and for their thousand blows deal one deathblow," are the clearest examples of the parallel verbal structure and the use of sound devices in an harmonic, balanced way. Other lines reveal this effect as well. Line nine, for example ("O kinsmen! we must meet the common foe") is nearly perfectly balanced, with the lone "e" assonance of "we" and "meet," the "m" alliteration and "t" consonance of "must meet" and the "k" alliteration of "kinsmen" and "common" being surrounded by the formal, apostrophic "o" and "foe." Similarly, in line seven the pattern of "n" assonance (". . . In vain; then even the monsters we defy") moves into the similar "m" sound of "monsters," which word signals a sound change to the hard "d" of "defy." The "d" sound, harsh and dissimilar to the "n" and "m" sounds, is associated with the "they," and is repeated in "constrained" and "dead." Nearly every line reveals this dominant technique of McKay. For the "us" of line twelve ("What though before us lies the open grave"), the dominant sound is the three-times repeated "o" assonance, a sound consistently associated with "us" throughout the poem. For the "they" of line thirteen (". . . the murderous, cowardly pack") the harsh "d" and "k" sounds predominate—and these sounds have been associated with "they" from the outset of the poem, beginning in lines three and four.

It is likely that there is no inherent meaning in sounds. But the assignment of particular sounds to particular verbal structures is a common technique in poetry, and the result of such verbal felicity is that meaning *does* begin to inhere in the respective structures and their sounds. Tone, and hence value, is communicated not only by the denotative and connotative *facts* of the poem, but the prosodic *facts* of rhythm, meter, sound. Though the language specifies inferiority, pain, and probably death for "us" from the beginning of this poem, McKay's subtle use of his poetic material makes quite clear that the foredoomed "we" of the poem are its secure and inevitable victors.

McKay's use of the material of his trade makes a first-rate verbal structure; *in itself* **"If We Must Die"** is a fully realized work of art. However, art is not self-contained, and its implications and inferences, both purposeful and accidental, cannot be ignored. Our initial questions dealt with the specific dramatic context and with the issue of whether or not the poem *must* be read racially. Knowledge of McKay's race invites such a reading; ignorance of it would, I think, lead to a more generalized theme—the conflict between any oppressor and any group of oppressed people. McKay himself argued forcefully that the poem is universal in scope when he stated the poem is for all men, the "abused, outraged and murdered, whether they are minorities or nations, black or brown or yellow or white, Catholic or Protestant or Pagan. . . ." But limited and general readings are seldom exclusive, and with this poem, as with others, it is reasonable and fair to allow that such a general theme will be inevitably suggested by the poem's specifics. Yet, such rationale may ultimately denude literature. To read insistently toward the universal is ultimately to reduce literature to a convenient list of a few rubrics (myth is the fashionable term) on the order of conflict, reconciliation, and the like. Surely, all literature does not move toward the widest universality; criticism should accept the virtues of limitations. We have known at least since Aristotle that it is the individual and unique that is the essence of literature. The acceptance of the particular, therefore, seems an act of critical fealty to the understanding of art.

Still, several phrases in the poem have echoes of literary allusions and other, apparently fortuitous, but wide-ranging references that are difficult to account for unless the poem is read in a larger framework than only that of racial conflict. The grammatically awkward "let us show us brave" is reminiscent of Marvell's "Now let us sport us while we may." Yet, any connection between Marvell's speaker (no matter how one reads his tone) and McKay's seems strained. As well, the speaker's wish that his blood "may not be shed / In vain" has strangely Lincolnesque overtones. A connection between Lincoln and the subject matter of this poem, *via* race, can easily be made; but such a case seems to merge unwillingly the specifically historical and the generally human. Finally, the hortatory cries of the speaker, no matter the depth of emotion, verge on the banal. The cry, "we must meet the common foe!", rings of the locker room almost as much as it does of the far more serious field of racial strife. But, to therefore read the poem as a generalized statement of human conflict, applicable to any similar context, is to allow sports contests to be a legitimate subject matter of this poem, or, somewhat more seriously, is to say the poem is about the conflict between generations. Such readings are not universal; they are reductive. They deny the urgency of the racial situation with which the poem is directly concerned; they presuppose slackness in the language of this poem.

Therefore, I suggest severe limits on the reading of a poem; above all, its context must be understood as specifically as possible. One *must* read **"If We Must Die"** as a racial poem—or allow the poem to be interpreted, because of these various allusions and suggestions, as a poem about *any* conflict. The conflict between the white man and the black becomes no—or little—different from the conflict between lover and coy mistress; the conflict becomes resolvable through the agency of a nineteenth century president, whose deeds may have been instrumental in ending slavery, but whose actions did not end human bigotry, prejudice, and oppression. The specific may well lead to the general. But this poem, and black people throughout the country, point to the uniqueness of their situations. From both a sociological and a literary point of view, it is crucial to see what is solely, uniquely, and fundamentally racial in **"If We Must Die."**

Home to Harlem

W. E. B. DU BOIS (REVIEW DATE 1928)

SOURCE: Du Bois, W. E. B. "Two Novels." *Crisis* 35, no. 6 (1928): 202, 211.

In the following excerpt, Du Bois offers an appraisal of McKay's Home to Harlem.

I have just read the last two novels of Negro America. The one I liked; the other I distinctly did not. I think that Mrs. Imes, writing under the pen name of Nella Larsen, has done a title, thoughtful and courageous piece of work in her novel [*Quicksand*]. It is, on the whole the best piece of fiction that Negro America has produced since the heyday of Chesnutt and stands easily with Jessie Fauset's *There is Confusion,* in its subtle comprehension of the curious cross currents that swirl about the black American.

Claude McKay's ***Home to Harlem,*** on the other hand, for the most part nauseates me, and after the dirtier parts of its filth I feel distinctly like taking a bath. This does not mean that the book is wholly bad. McKay is too great a poet to make any complete failure in writing. There are bits of ***Home to Harlem,*** beautiful and fascinating: the continued changes upon the theme of the beauty of colored skins; the portrayal of the fascination of their new yearnings for each other which Negroes are developing. The Chief character, Jake, has something appealing, and the glimpses of the Haitian, Ray, have all the materials of a great piece of fiction.

But it looks as though, despite this, McKay has set out to cater for that prurient demand on the part of white folk for a portrayal in Negroes of that utter licentiousness which conventional civilization holds white folk back from enjoying—if enjoyment it can be called. That which a certain decadent section of the white American world, centered particularly in New York, longs for with fierce and unrestrained passions, it wants to see written out in black and white, and saddled on black Harlem. This demand, as voiced by a number of New York publishers, McKay has certainly satisfied, and added much for good measure. He has used every art and emphasis to paint drunkenness, fighting, lascivious sexual promiscuity and utter absence of restraint in as bold and as bright colors as lie can.

If this had been done in the course of a well-conceived plot or with any artistic unity, it might leave been understood if not excused. But ***Home to Harlem*** is padded. Whole chapters here and there are inserted with no connection to the main plot, except that they are on the same dirty subject. As a picture of Harlem life or of Negro life anywhere, it is, of course, nonsense. Untrue, not so much as on account of its facts, but on account of its emphasis and glaring colors. I am sorry that the author of *"Harlem Shadow's"* stooped to this. I sincerely hope that he will some day rise above it and give us in fiction the strong, well-knit as well as beautiful theme, that it seems to me he might do.

RICHARD K. BARKSDALE (ESSAY DATE 1972)

SOURCE: Barksdale, Richard K. "Symbolism and Irony in McKay's *Home to Harlem.*" *CLA Journal* 15, no. 3 (March 1972): 338-44.

In the following essay, Barksdale argues that Home to Harlem *is a study in symbolic conflict between disorder and order and between the rational and the animalistic.*

Traditionally, there have been two rather disparaging views of Claude McKay's ***Home to Harlem***—a novel, incidentally, not written in Harlem but in France while McKay was on an extended twelve-year sojourn in Europe and North Africa. The first point of view is that it is not a well-made novel; proponents of this view charge that its plot lacks unity and is pock-marked by episodicity; there is no character development and far too much "atmosphere"—too many lyrical arpeggios to the intoxicating, soul-swaying beauty of the Black Experience. These critics usually conclude that a good poet like McKay would inevitably produce a poorly made work of fiction, for it is written that good poets do not good novelists make. A second disparaging point of view is that ***Home to Harlem*** is full of a repugnant realism. It exposes the seamy underside of Black community life where pimps, whores, gamblers, and slicksters congregate and where real, true-to-life bedbugs bite. Critics representing this group share the reaction of W. E. B. Du Bois who, after reading ***Home to Harlem,*** felt unclean and in need of a bath. Certainly, there is much in the novel which would have given offense to the sensitivities of a Black bourgeoisie which in the Harlem of the late 1920's was interested in leading the Black community to the best kind of accommodation to, and respect from, a racist America. To these leaders ***Home to Harlem***'s Black settings reeked of a racial hedonism and exoticism scarcely compatible with accepted notions of racial progress.[1] In their view a carefree hedonist like Jake, with his boundless and roaming sexual appetite, fitted the white man's racial and social stereotyped view of the Black male and could do little to enhance the Black man's image within the large community. To many of these critics it seemed as though McKay, after the manner of Van Vechten in his *Nigger Heaven,* had written ***Home to Harlem*** in order to give white America a guided tour through the "joy belt" of lower class Black life, to display in lurid colors its gay savagery, panting animalism, and emotional exuberance.[2] By so doing, they charged, the novelist merely confirmed the white American's highly prejudiced notion that the Black man was the kind of slothful, sexual animal who could not be easily assimilated into the fabric of American society.

Fortunately, the passage of time has helped to erode or modify these hostile critical judgments of McKay's first novel. Now, as George Kent implies in his essay on "The Soulful Way of Claude McKay,"[3] critics have come to believe that the racial settings of ***Home to Harlem*** are positive and racially affirming rather than negative and racially demeaning; these settings, they believe, recapture the *elan* of the Black Experience in all of its color and rich emotional variety. The novel's episodicity of plot, it is also argued, is the common mark of a picaresque novel like ***Home to Harlem.*** Indeed, in this interpretation Jake becomes a flawed hero but a very likeable one—a sort of Black Tom Jones, good-hearted and virile and ensnared only by an occasionally unhappy sexual liaison. Like his white English counterpart of two centuries past, his motives are always good and unsullied. He does not customarily strike or beat women; he carefully avoids physical confrontations with his quarrelsome friends; in many instances, he is a peacemaker with an instinct for rational withdrawal from overly complex situations. Above all, he has a sexual magnetism that attracts women of all ages and kinds—even old, toothless Aunt Hattie in whose "aged smoke-red eyes" there appears a sensual gleam when she rubs "her breast against Jake's shoulder." So Jake may be a carefree hedonist, but he is also something of a paragon among men—a man of proper instincts moving in a society in which so many men are governed by improper instincts.

The fact that Jake is so sharply differentiated from his associates in moral outlook and in his almost completely self-sufficient individualism suggests another interpretation of ***Home to Harlem*** that goes far beyond the conclusion that the novel is no more than a naturalistic *exposé* of Black urban ghetto life of the late 1920's. Such an interpretation posits that the novel is actually a study in symbolic conflict—a symbolic conflict that occurs on two levels. On the first level the conflict is between order and disorder, order being symbolized by Jake and disorder by the characters and settings which furnish the background for the action in the novel. In such an interpretation, Jake becomes a wise primitive who has been blessed with an intuitive sense of order. Whether working on the boat, whether working as longshoreman or as a pullman car cook, he has it "together." Apparently, he is rarely, if ever, troubled or insecure or overwhelmed or incapacitated by doubt, fear, or uncertainty. In this sense he is different from Zeddy, Congo Rose, Billy Biasse, and Ray who either become disconcerted by the disorder surrounding them or deeply involved in that disorder. This is not to say that Jake is an outsider or a neutralist or an observer who stands apart. Like Ellison's much more intellectualized hero of a later date, Jake participates in the seething disorders that swirl around him, but unlike Ellison's hero he always carefully extricates himself in time to remain his own man. He does not have to suffer the happy accident of falling out of the world of time and space into a hole of self-discovery.

There are at least four situations of maximum disorder in which Jake emerges as a symbol of order. One is the party at Susy's apartment in Brooklyn which the author invests with a disorderliness that is almost *surréal,* largely because of the bizarre and distorted appearance and behavior of Susy, Miss Curdy, and Strawberry Lips. According to McKay's description, "Gin-head Susy" is "wonderfully created." Not only is she "chocolate-to-the-bone," but she has a "majestic chest" and, on her high heels, she towers "like a mountain."[4] Her friend, Miss Curdy, is even more grotesque and *surréal* in appearance. She is a

> putty-skinned mulatress with purple streaks on her face. Two of her upper front teeth had been

> knocked out and her lower lip slanted pathetically leftward. She was skinny and when she laughed she resembled an old braying jenny.
>
> (p. 33)

Strawberry Lips completes the trio; he is so called because he is a "burnt-cork black" with "stage-red" lips. McKay describes them as "Marvellous lips. Salmon-pink and planky." (p. 38) It would seem that by their very appearance the author has programmed this trio for some kind of disorder. Inevitably, a fight breaks out at the party and in the ensuing confusion Jake leaves, condemning the general area of Myrtle Street in Brooklyn as a sort of "sewer" of human experience. Throughout the entire Brooklyn incident, he stands out as a symbol of order in conflict with an enveloping pattern of disorder.

Such is also true of the role Jake plays as a cook on the Pullman diner. During the bitter fight between the pantryman and the chef, Jake is an interested but relatively uninvolved observer. As the disorder in the dining car mounts, leading to the egg-stealing climax, not even Ray, the widely read and informed intellectual, can remain detached from the swirling controversy. McKay observes at this point: "Only Jake was keeping his head in the kitchen." (p. 97) And, after the incident is over and the chef has been transferred and demoted to second cook on another run, Jake tells the gleeful and victorious pantryman:

> Ise with yu buddy . . . and now that wese good and rid of him, I hope that all we niggers will pull together like civilization folks.
>
> (p. 99)

Here Jake is obviously a spokesman for social cohesion and racial solidarity and the order that he thinks is implicit in the word "civilization."

There are two other incidents in the novel in which Jake as the symbol for order is in conflict with persons symbolic of disorder.[5] These two incidents differ from the two described above, however, for in neither of the two to be described is Jake merely an interested observer or friendly non-participant. In both of these incidents he is provoked to violent reaction and becomes momentarily involved in the disorder. The first incident occurs when Congo Rose rakes her nails across his face in order to provoke him into some form of physically violent reaction. Almost involuntarily, Jake "slaps her down," but immediately thereafter, as a non-violent man of order, he is smitten with remorse:

> Walking down the street, he looked at his palms "Ahm shame o' you, hands," he murmured. "Mah mother uester tell me, 'Nevah hit no woman,' but that hussy jest made me do it . . . jest *made* me. . . . Well, I'd better pull outa that there mud-hole. . . . It wasn't what I come back to Gawd's own country foh. No, siree!"
>
> (p. 62)

The last sentence in Jake's comment has significant ironic implications, as will be demonstrated below; but the major thrust of his self-recriminating statement is that he has violated his own code of orderly conduct.

His reaction to his quarrel with Zeddy over Felice is similarly self-recriminating, but in this instance McKay goes to some lengths to explain how a man of order like Jake feels after he has pulled a gun and threatened to shoot his best friend:

> The miserable cock-fights, beastly, tigerish bloody. They had always sickened, saddened, unmanned him. . . . Why should love create terror? Love should be joy lifting man out of the humdrum ways of life. He had always managed to delight in love and yet steer clear of the hate and violence that govern it in this world. . . . Yet here he was caught in the thing that he despised so thoroughly. . . . Oh, he was infinitely disgusted with himself to think that he had just been moved by the same savage emotions as those vile, vicious, villainous white men who, like hyenas and rattlers, had fought, murdered, and clawed the entrails out of black men over the common, commercial flesh of women. . . .
>
> (p. 173)

This explication reveals the racial nature of Jake's code of order. It is evidently rooted in a deep desire for alienation from the disorders he has beheld in the white world—in Brest, France and on London's East Side. And, of course, one can assume that here Jake is the spokesman for the world-travelling expatriate Claude McKay.

The symbolic conflict between disorder and order in ***Home to Harlem*** is reinforced by another level of symbolic conflict—a conflict between the rational and the animalistic. The novel is filled with animal imagery to describe disorderly and violent situations or people. In Jake's view love somehow provokes men into "cock-fights" that are "beastly, tigerish, bloody." The white men in London who fought over women were "hyenas and rattlers." When Zeddy advances on Jake with an open razor (p. 172), he is like "a terrible bear." In the fight that breaks out in Susy's apartment in Brooklyn, one combatant leaps at his enemy of the moment "like a tiger-cat" and the other responds like "an enraged ramgoat" (p. 39). Billy Biasse is named "The Wolf" because of his avid rapacity as a pimp and gambler, and the chef on the railroad diner is a "dirty rhinoceros," the ugliest animal in all of Africa (p. 89). And at the end of the episode about Rosalind and Jerco, Jerco is described in his death by suicide as "a great black boar in a mess of blood." (p. 139)

Inevitably, an interpretation of ***Home to Harlem*** stressing symbolic conflict between order and disorder, reinforced by a conflict between the rational and the animalistic, implies that the novel is more than just an *exposé* of the "joy belt" of Harlem. McKay meant to provide more than a guided tour through the bars, buffet flats, speakeasies, gambling joints, and whorehouses of the sprawling Black city. The implication is that Harlem represents disorder as much as Brest or London and that Jake, the wise primitive and man of order, finds the place to which he has returned not "Gawd's own country," but a snare and a delusion. So one may justifiably hypothecate that the title of the novel is ironic, for in a world in which men are everywhere disorderly and animalistic, a man like Jake can never truly find a "home." Certainly, Jake's creator, Claude McKay, found no home in Harlem, for he was absent from the Black man's mecca and metropolis for a twelve-year span which covered some of the most exciting and creative years of the Harlem Renaissance. As the novel ends, Jake is on his way to Chicago to find another "home" with Felice, whose name means "happiness." One may assume that there he finds the ordered kind of pleasure he is seeking, but in ***Banjo,*** McKay's second novel, Jake explains to Ray that he has been happy but he is ready to move on to some other city. So it is and will be for all men who, like Jake, want to escape the "mud-hole" of human disorder. They will keep moving on in a fruitless quest and never truly find a "home"—not even in Harlem.

Notes

1. In his *A Long Way from Home* (New York: Lee Furman, 1937), McKay wrote that he refused James Weldon Johnson's invitation to return to Harlem because "the resentment of the Negro intelligentsia against *Home to Harlem* was so general, bitter, and violent. . . ." See p. 306.
2. According to Sterling Brown, McKay denied that *Home to Harlem* was influenced by Van Vechten's book. See Brown, *The Negro in Am. Fiction* (New York: Atheneum, 1969), p. 134.
3. *Black World,* XX (November 1970), 37-51.
4. Claude McKay, *Home to Harlem* (New York: Pocket Books, Inc., 1965), p. 31. All subsequent references in this paper are taken from this edition of the novel.
5. It should be stated in this context that Robert Bone, although viewing Jake as an unfettered primitive, sees some symbolic conflict in *Home to Harlem.* In his view the conflict is not between order and disorder but between instinct and reason, Jake symbolizing instinct and Ray symbolizing reason. Bone concludes that because McKay never brings these two characters to a point of conflict, the novel is an artistic failure. See Bone. *The Negro Novel in America* (New Haven: The Yale Press, rev. ed., 1965), p. 69.

FURTHER READING

Biographies

Giles, James R. *Claude McKay.* Boston: Twayne Publishers, 1976, 170 p.

Study of McKay's life and works, with separate chapters on the major poems, novels, short stories, and nonfiction.

Goldweber, David. "Home at Last: The Pilgrimage of Claude McKay." *Commonweal* (10 September 1999): 11-13.

Discusses McKay's conversion to Catholicism.

Ojo-Ade, Femi. "Claude McKay: The Tragic Solitude of an Exiled Son of Africa." In *Of Dreams Deferred, Dead or Alive: African Perspectives on African-American Writers,* edited by Femi Ojo-Ade, pp. 65-81. Westport, Conn.: Greenwood Press, 1996.

Examines McKay's cultural alienation and his search for identity.

Criticism

Breitinger, Eckhard. "In Search of an Audience: In Search of the Self: Exile as a Condition for the Works of Claude McKay." In *The Commonwealth Writer Overseas: Themes of Exile and Expatriation,* edited by Alastair Niven, pp. 175-84. Brussels: Didier, 1976.

Discusses McKay's alienation and exile as a Black Jamaican writing for a primarily white audience.

Chauhan, P. S. "Rereading Claude McKay." *CLA Journal* 34, no. 1 (1990): 68-80.

Disagrees with those who think McKay's works reflect the consciousness of the Harlem Renaissance, pointing instead to a colonial sensibility that stems from McKay's Jamaican heritage.

Condit, John Hillyer. "An Urge toward Wholeness: Claude McKay and His Sonnets." *CLA Journal* 22, no. 4 (1979): 350-64.

Contends that McKay sought as a man and a poet to resolve his universality and individuality on as transcendent a plane as possible.

De Barros, Paul. "The Loud Music of Life: Representations of Jazz in the Novels of Claude McKay." *Antioch Review* 57, no. 3 (summer 1999): 306-17.

Claims that jazz music was a key element in McKay's novels.

Greenberg, Robert M. "Idealism and Realism in the Fiction of Claude McKay." *CLA Journal* 24, no. 3 (1981): 237-61.

Contends that in terms of style and attitude toward representation, McKay is a realist, but in his approach to his characters' inner lives he is a moral and philosophical idealist.

Griffin, Barbara Jackson. "The Road to Psychic Unity: The Politics of Gender in Claude McKay's *Banana Bottom.*" *Callaloo* 22, no. 2 (1999): 499-508.

Uncovers the patriarchal features of Banana Bottom.

Hansell, William H. "Jamaica in the Poems of Claude McKay." *Studies in Black Literature* 7, no. 3 (1976): 6-9.

Examines McKay's idealistic portrayal of his native land.

Hathaway, Heather. *Caribbean Waves: Relocating Claude McKay and Paule Marshall.* Bloomington: Indiana University Press, 1999, 200 p.

Cross-cultural study of McKay and Marshall, two African Caribbean writers, emphasizing their status as migrants.

Jay, Paul. "Hybridity, Identity and Cultural Commerce in Claude McKay's *Banana Bottom.*" *Callaloo* 22, no. 1 (1999): 176-94.

Shows how McKay offers a critique of absolutist discourses grounded in race, nationalism, and ethnicity but often in terms that reinforce the ideology he seeks to displace.

Jones, Bridget. "With *Banjo* by My Bed: Black French Writers Reading Claude McKay." In *Analysis and Assessment, 1980-1994,* edited by Cary D. Wintz, pp. 202-09. New York: Garland Publishing, Inc., 1996.

Study of McKay's influence on French readers and the Négritude movement.

Keller, James R. "'A Chafing Savage, Down the Decent Street': The Politics of Compromise in Claude McKay's Protest Sonnets." *African American Review* 28, no. 3 (1994): 447-56.

Contends that McKay used the sonnet, a form of the white majority, to challenge the dominant power structure.

Kent, George E. "The Soulful Way of Claude McKay." *Black World* 20, no. 1 (1970): 37-51.

Explores McKay's sensibility as a poet—his emotional, psychic, and intellectual responses to life—as well as his concept of the embattled soul that pervades his work.

Krishnamurthy, Sarala. "Claude McKay (1889-1948)." In *African American Authors, 1745-1945: A Bio-Bibliographical Critical Sourcebook,* edited by Emmanuel S. Nelson, pp. 338-48. Westport, Conn.: Greenwood Press, 2000.

Presents a biography, discussion of major works and themes, survey of critical reception, and bibliography of secondary sources.

Lowney, John. "Haiti and Black Transnationalism: Remapping the Migrant Geography of *Home to Harlem.*" *African American Review* 34, no. 3 (2000): 413-29.

Maintains that the decreased American attention to Haiti's ongoing ordeal is the unstated political subtext of Home to Harlem.

McLeod, A. L. "Claude McKay, Alain Locke, and the Harlem Renaissance." *Literary Half-Yearly* 27, no. 2 (July 1986): 65-75.

Claims that Alain Locke did not fully appreciate McKay's artistic talent and describes the antipathy between the two men.

Nicholls, David G. "The Folk as Alternative Modernity: Claude McKay's *Banana Bottom* and the Romance of Nature." *Journal of Modern Literature* 23, no. 1 (1999): 79-94.

Maintains that Banana Bottom *argues for a return to "folk" roots not for the sake of nostalgia but to offer an analysis of the modern global economy.*

North, Michael. "Quashie to Buccra: The Linguistic Expatriation of Claude McKay." In *The Dialect of Modernism: Race, Language, and Twentieth-Century Literature,* pp. 100-26. New York: Oxford University Press, 1994.

Discusses McKay's use of language as an expatriate writer.

Pyne-Timothy, Helen. "Perceptions of the Black Woman in the Work of Claude McKay." *CLA Journal* 19, no. 2 (1975): 152-64.

Analyzes McKay's sensitive discussion of the role and personality of the Black woman.

Ramchand, Kenneth. *The West Indian Novel and Its Background.* New York: Barnes and Noble, 1970, 295 p.

Sees McKay as the forerunner of West Indian fiction.

Smith, Robert P., Jr. "Rereading *Banjo*: Claude McKay and the French Connection." *CLA Journal* 30, no. 1 (1986): 46-58.

Examines Banjo *and the historical meeting of African American, African French, and Caribbean French literati in Paris in the 1920s and 1930s.*

Spencer, Suzette A. "Swerving at a Different Angle and Flying in the Face of Tradition: Excavating the Homoerotic Subtext in *Home to Harlem.*" *CLA Journal* 42, no. 2 (1998): 164-93.

Offers a homoerotic reading of Home to Harlem *and a homoerotic exegesis of three characters in the novel.*

Timothy, Helen P. "Claude McKay: Individualism and Group Consciousness." In *A Celebration of Black and African Writing,* edited by Bruce King, Kolawole Ogungbesan, and Iya Abubakar, pp. 15-29. Oxford: Oxford University Press, 1975.

Shows how McKay expresses his individual conscience and the consciousness of his race.

OTHER SOURCES FROM GALE:

Additional coverage of McKay's life and career is contained in the following sources published by the Gale Group: *African American Writers,* Eds. 1, 2; *American Writers Supplement,* Vol. 10; *Black Literature Criticism,* Vol. 3; *Dictionary of Literary Biography,* Vols. 4, 45, 51, 117; *DISCovering Authors: British Edition*; *Exploring Poetry*; *Gay & Lesbian Literature,* Vol. 2; *Literature and Its Times,* Vol. 3; *Poetry Criticism,* Vol. 2; *Poetry for Students,* Vol. 4; *Poets: American and British*; *Reference Guide to American Literature,* Ed. 4; *Twentieth-Century Literary Criticism,* Vols. 7, 41; *World Literature Criticism*; and *World Poets.*

RICHARD BRUCE NUGENT

(1906 - 1987)

(Also wrote as Richard Bruce) American short story writer, poet, and artist.

Nugent was Harlem's most prominent bohemian. As one of the board of editors for the short-lived journal *Fire!!*, Nugent worked with and befriended Langston Hughes, Zora Neale Hurston, Gwendolyn Bennett, and Wallace Thurman. In *Fire!!* he published the story that has in some ways defined his career: "Smoke, Lilies, and Jade"—the story of a gay encounter between two African American men. "Smoke, Lilies, and Jade" was the first openly homosexual piece of fiction from an African American writer. Nugent was also well known for his talent in the visual arts, with his murals and illustrations providing a backdrop for much of the social and literary activity of the Harlem Renaissance.

BIOGRAPHICAL INFORMATION

Nugent was born in Washington, D.C., on July 2, 1906. His parents, Richard Henry Nugent and Pauline Minerva Bruce, moved in the higher circles of Black society in Washington. His father was a Pullman porter, a position reserved for light-skinned Blacks well-trained in polite customs. Pauline was the mixed-race daughter of Sandy Bruce, a Black man, and a French woman; two of her brothers had "passed" as white well enough to join the Navy. His father died when Nugent was still a teenager, and Nugent moved with his mother to Manhattan. He worked at a series of menial jobs, eventually landing work at the catalog house Stone, Van Dresser, which sparked his interest in art. When, at eighteen, he informed his mother that he would no longer work at a traditional job, but would instead work on his art, she sent him back to Washington, where his grandmother still lived. There he met the influential poet Georgia Douglas Johnson, who introduced him to Langston Hughes; his grandmother had a connection to the family of Alain Locke, who published his story "Sadhji" in *The New Negro* in 1925. With these connections, Nugent found himself soon able to return to New York, where he met Wallace Thurman. Thurman and Nugent became fast friends, living together in the house in Harlem they called "Niggerati Manor," from Thurman's appellation of the Black literati of Harlem. "Niggerrati Manor" was a focal point of Harlem intellectual society, figuring largely in Thurman's satirical novel about the Renaissance, *Infants of the Spring* (1932). In that novel, Nugent appears as Paul Arabian, a bohemian artist of erotic drawings. Nugent did not work, and his literary production was small, so he continued to be poor and dependent. When in 1926 he and his friends launched the journal *Fire!!*, he contributed to its untimely demise after just one issue. The controversy aroused by the gay lovers in "Smoke,

Lilies, and Jade" offended some readers, but the more material problem for *Fire!!* was that Nugent, who distributed the journal, collected the earnings and kept them for himself. Nugent also toured with the Dubose Heyward play *Porgy* (1927) when Heyward had struggled to find a suitable cast. The *Porgy* cast also included Thurman and fiction writer Dorothy West. The play toured the East Coast and Midwest before going to Europe in 1929. After his return to New York, several of Nugent's attempts at publication were thwarted by the instability of the journals to which he contributed. The advent of the Depression, in some ways the death knell of the Harlem Renaissance, also prevented Nugent from playing the carefree bohemian. He worked with art projects sponsored by the federal government, continued to contribute an occasional piece to literary journals, and worked on a series of gay romances. In the 1960s and 1970s, he focused primarily on the visual arts, though he published a short story, "Beyond Where the Star Stood Still," in 1970. He outlived many of his Harlem compatriots, making him an invaluable source of living history in his later life. His open acknowledgement of his homosexuality made him a celebrated figure in the early Gay Rights movement as well. He continued to work on his art and speak widely about the Renaissance until his death in 1987.

MAJOR WORKS

Given the scant nature of his literary output, Nugent has few works that could legitimately be called "major." An important exception, however, is the story "Smoke, Lilies, and Jade," which made history in African American literature. The story focuses on nineteen-year-old Alex, an artist whose love of writers like Oscar Wilde and Boccaccio mirrored Nugent's own literary interests. Alex is approached by a handsome stranger, whom he instantly takes home. After a night with the man, Alex, who also has a female lover, concludes that he can be bisexual and love both a man and a woman. Nugent's short story "Sadhji," about the wife of an African chief and her bisexual love interest, Mrabo, eventually became a one-act musical drama performed at the Eastman School of Music. Nugent also worked on an unpublished memoir entitled *Gentleman Jigger* (likely around 1930), which provides a wealth of information about his life among the Harlem literati, particularly Hughes and Thurman. Nugent is also well known for his very distinctive style in the visual arts. His drawings combine erotic and art deco elements and showcase his experiments with color. Nugent contributed drawings to *Fire!!*, the anthology *Ebony and Topaz* (1927), and the journal *Opportunity*, in addition to the murals he and Aaron Douglas painted in Harlem's basement cabarets.

CRITICAL RECEPTION

Critics since the 1920s have responded as much to Nugent's unconventional lifestyle as to the quality of his work. The appearance of *Fire!!* drew barbs even from Nugent's supporters. Alain Locke gave the most balanced critique, suggesting that while the efforts of Nugent and his friends to shock and outrage were not wholly inappropriate, the "effete" influence of decadents like Oscar Wilde was, at best, regrettable. Many of Nugent's friends were important proponents of his art: Thurman thought him genuinely talented and Hughes rescued his poems from the trash. Modern critics have focused primarily on the homosexual themes of his work, or on his relationships with other, more prolific, writers of the Harlem Renaissance. The absence of a large body of collected works may also have limited scholarly response to Nugent's writings; a collected selection of his writings was not published until 2002. Moreover, many critics have suggested that Nugent's life was his work—his bohemian style, his peculiar embodiment of "the New Negro"—which has meant that later writing on Nugent is more often biographical than literary. Nugent's prominent role in the Harlem Renaissance, however, has ensured that his life, his writing, and his art will continue to attract interest.

PRINCIPAL WORKS

Sadhji, for Ballet, Chorus, and Bass Soloist (musical drama) 1961

Lighting Fire (nonfiction) 1982

Gay Rebel of the Harlem Renaissance: Selections from the Work of Richard Bruce Nugent (poetry, fiction, essays) 2002

GENERAL COMMENTARY

THOMAS H. WIRTH (ESSAY DATE 1985)

SOURCE: Wirth, Thomas H. "Richard Bruce Nugent." *Black American Literature Forum* 19, no. 1 (1985): 16-17.

In this essay, Wirth presents a brief biography of Nugent that reviews his role in the Harlem Renaissance. Wirth addresses Nugent's relationships, his artwork, and his work with Fire!!, *suggesting that Nugent's unconventional and unapologetic lifestyle was as important to the culture of the Harlem Renaissance as his artistic productions.*

Richard Bruce Nugent is a phenomenon who was not supposed to exist—an Afro-American artist influenced by Michelangelo, Beardsley, and Erte who devoured the novels of Firbank and Huysmans and wrote stream-of-consciousness prose.

Now 78, Nugent was born in Washington, D.C., to a family of impeccable position in Afro-American society, and attended Dunbar High School. After the death of his father in 1920, his mother moved to New York, where he joined her a few months later. Handsome, intelligent, charming, and young, he soon found his way from West 18th Street, where they lived, to Greenwich Village.

He held a succession of jobs, ranging from bellhop at the Martha Washington Hotel to apprentice with the catalog house of Stone, Van Dresser, where he received his first training in art. Eventually he announced to his mother that he was going to be an artist and would not take another job—whereupon she sent him back to Washington to live with his grandparents.

There he became a favorite of Georgia Douglas Johnson. At one of her famous salons, he met Langston Hughes. Alain Locke, whose mother was a good friend of Nugent's grandmother, also attended the salons frequently, and he included Nugent's story **"Sadhji"** in *The New Negro* in 1925. Hughes rescued Nugent's first poem, **"Shadow,"** from the wastebasket and sent it to *Opportunity,* where it was published in October 1925.

Nugent accompanied Hughes on a trip to New York, where Hughes introduced him to Carl Van Vechten and Wallace Thurman. Nugent decided he had had enough of Washington and stayed. Eventually, he moved with Thurman to the infamous "Niggerati Manor" on West 136th Street, the setting for Thurman's roman à clef about the Harlem Renaissance, *Infants of the Spring,* in which Nugent appears as a major character, Paul Arbian. Arbian/Nugent is an artist who "indolently" creates "voluptuous geometric designs" and "erotic drawings" which "are nothing but highly colored phalli."

"Niggerati" was the appellation Thurman invented for the group of young, adventurous, and relatively unconventional Harlem intellectuals to which he and Nugent belonged. Others in the group were Hughes, Zora Neale Hurston, Aaron Douglas, Gwendolyn Bennett, and John P. Davis. Nugent worked with Douglas, accompanying him to lessons with Winold Reiss and helping him execute murals on the walls of basement cabarets. Nugent reports that some of these were executed in two colors—red and blue. When they were viewed under blue light, the African past was visible; under red light, the scene shifted to the modern city.

In November, 1926, the Niggerati published *Fire!!*—the first Afro-American "art quarterly." Although it lasted only one issue (for financial reasons), *Fire!!* was one of the most brilliant achievements of the Renaissance. It was a cooperative venture, free from the restraints imposed by the need to please patrons and publishers (who tended to be white), and independent of sponsoring organizations with "larger" political and social objectives. Aaron Douglas did the cover, decorations, and three wonderful, whimsical line drawings which are unlike any of his other work. Nugent, writing under the name of "Richard Bruce," contributed two brush-and-ink drawings and **"Smoke, Lilies, and Jade,"** which Hughes discreetly characterized as "a green and purple story in the Oscar Wilde tradition." It was, in fact, the first literary work on an openly homosexual theme to be published by an Afro-American writer.

Silhouettes in brush and ink such as those in *Fire!!* and the illustration accompanying this article are an important segment of Nugent's oeuvre. Four such pieces on a mulatto theme appear in Charles S. Johnson's *Ebony and Topaz* (1927). Numerous others, mostly unattributed, appeared throughout the late twenties and early thirties in *Opportunity.* They are highly stylized and instantly recognizable as Nugent's work. The influence of Aaron Douglas is evident, but Douglas' comparable work is sober, often heroic in its subject matter, incorporating regular arcs and straight lines rather than Nugent's s-curves. Nugent's figures move; the dance is one of his favorite themes. He illustrated an article by Thurman on jazz dance which appeared in the May 1928 issue of *Dance* magazine.

Line drawings, executed in pen and ink or pencil, are also an important aspect of Nugent's work. He experimented extensively with color in his drawings, using Japanese dyes which were normally used to color photographs. In 1930 he executed a series on the theme of Salomé in which unexpected juxtapositions of colors, strongly idiosyncratic stylistic elements, and unconventional composition emphasizing the borders rather than the center combine to stunning effect.

Throughout his working life, Nugent has been legendary for his erotic, art-deco drawings. These show the strong influence of Beardsley and Erte, but the style is distinctly Nugent's. Eroticism is an element in nearly all of Nugent's work. But "erotic" must be sharply distinguished from "pornographic." With their elegant style and exquisite colors, even the most explicit of Nugent's drawings are simply too beautiful to arouse the viewer sexually.

Nugent also works in oil and pastel. His oils are more "serious" than his graphics, with his distinctive stylistic qualities less in evidence. Nonetheless, they are effective. *The American,* for example, is an intense, full-face portrait of an Afro-American executed in very dark tones. Equally striking is a close-up portrait of a Cuban prisoner, whose intense expression contrasts with the strong sunlight and the blue background—the color of the Caribbean sky.

Nugent has been persistently unconventional in both his life and his work. He has refused to pursue a "career." He does not permit others to impose on him their definitions of who he ought to be, either as an artist, an Afro-American, or a "man." He has insisted on freedom when freedom was not allowed. His real masterwork has been the living of his life.

ERIC GARBER (ESSAY DATE 1987)

SOURCE: Garber, Eric. "Richard Bruce Nugent." In *Dictionary of Literary Biography,* Vol. 51: *Afro-American Writers from the Harlem Renaissance to 1940,* pp. 213-21. Detroit, Mich.: Gale Research, 1987.

In this essay, Garber surveys Nugent's life and career, focusing on his connections with the elite of the Harlem Renaissance. He discusses the stories "Smoke, Lilies, and Jade" and "Sadhji" and notes Nugent's involvement with the journal Fire!!

Richard Bruce Nugent was a singular figure during the Harlem Renaissance but his importance was due as much to his unique personal style, sense of humor, and world view as to his modest literary output. He was the ultimate bohemian, thumbing his nose at social, political, and sexual conventions. He knew, and worked with, many of Harlem's artistic luminaries, and his participation in the period's arts and letters added a bold and individual voice to the era's search for Afro-American identity.

Nugent was born to a family of modest means but high social position in Washington, D.C., black society. His parents, Richard Henry Nugent and Pauline Minerva Bruce, were artistically inclined and made sure the arts figured prominently in their sons' education. Gary Lambert Nugent, Richard's younger brother, eventually developed a distinguished career as a jazz dancer. The future writer attended Dunbar High School, but when Richard was thirteen, his father died and the family moved to New York City. There the young man fell in love with the diversity and adventure of Manhattan. He roamed its streets and neighborhoods for hours, finding excitement everywhere. He worked at numerous odd jobs, from bellhop to errand boy. After several years he decided to become an artist and announced to his mother that he would no longer be seeking employment. Appalled, Mrs. Nugent promptly packed her son's bags and sent him to his grandmother's home in Washington.

Bruce Nugent, as he was by then known, did not stay long. One summer evening in 1925, at one of Georgia Douglas Johnson's famous artistic "at-homes," Nugent met Langston Hughes. Their rapport was immediate and they quickly became friends. Nugent was captivated by the rising young poet's handsome appearance, his worldly experiences, his gentle manner, and his literary success. Hughes opened his new friend's eyes to the possibilities of the emerging New Negro and gave strong support to Nugent's impulse for creative expression. When Hughes returned to New York to attend a Krigwa Theatre dinner in his honor, Nugent came with him. Nugent later remembered this as being the point at which his "period of excitement and happiness and work began."

With Hughes's assistance, Nugent rapidly immersed himself in the exciting Harlem artistic scene. His quick, sometimes cutting, sense of humor, his good looks and intelligence, and his unorthodox mode of living made him a favorite among the loose-knit group of rebellious young artists which Wallace Thurman and Zora Neale Hurston wryly called "The Niggerati." The Niggerati were on the cutting edge of the Renaissance of Afro-American culture and included such artists as Hughes, Thurman, Hurston, Countee Cullen, Harold Jackman, and Aaron Douglas. With his new Niggerati friends Nugent attended dinners sponsored by the NAACP and *Opportunity* magazine, the official monthly of the National Urban League; listened to Jean Toomer's Gurdjieff lectures; socialized at the parties of A'Lelia Walker and the Carl Van Vechtens; and frequented disreputable nightspots along 133th Street and in Greenwich Village. He was continually without money, relying on his indulgent friends for a place to stay and something to eat. His wardrobe consisted of whatever clothing was around. Many of his poems and drawings were composed on pieces of scrap paper. In his long, first-person narrative **"Smoke, Lilies, and Jade,"** Nugent depicts a young artist named Alex who bears an unmistakable resemblance to the author.

> . . . he wondered why he couldn't find work . . . a job . . . when he had first come to New York he had . . . but he had only been fourteen then was it because he was nineteen now that he felt so idle . . . and contented . . . or because he was an artist . . . he should be ashamed that he didn't work . . . but . . . Alex . . . was content to lay and smoke and meet friends at night . . . to argue and read Wilde . . . Freud . . . Boccaccio and Schnitzler. . . .

Nugent wonders why Alex feels so different from other people and imagines him as "The Tragic Genius."

Nugent enjoyed shocking the prudish with his overtly erotic drawings and poetry and his tales of amorous adventure, many of which were unabashedly homosexual. The notoriety he gathered was sufficient to prompt him to assume the pseudonym "Richard Bruce" to avoid parental disapproval, but his reputation only helped endear him to his new friends. Fellow poet Albert Rice described him as "the bizarre and eccentric young vagabond poet of High Harlem." John P. Davis later recalled that "Nugent was a true bohemian in every sense of the word. In no ways a *poseur,* he was simply and basically a nonconformist who refused to accept so-called middle class standards of any kind."

One of the most vivid pictures available of Nugent during this period can be found in Wallace Thurman's 1932 novel *Infants of the Spring.* Thurman intended his novel, a satiric roman à clef in which most of the Harlem Renaissance participants appear in thin disguises, to be a serious assessment of the New Negro movement. Nugent appears as Paul Arbian, "a Negro painter whose subjects are bizarre and erotic." Unapologetically bisexual, Arbian is a talented but indolent artist, always quick with his wit and ready to celebrate, but unwilling to work: the quintessential bohemian. "I'm an artist," proclaims Arbian; "I think Oscar Wilde is the greatest man that ever lived. Huysmans' Des Esseintes is the greatest character in literature, and Baudelaire is the greatest poet." A rebel, he refuses to follow the racial aesthetics called for by Dr. A. L. Parkes, Thurman's caricature of Alain Locke. When asked if he has any racial pride at all, Arbian replies coolly, "Fortunately, no. I don't happen to give a good goddam about any nigger except myself." Thurman's Paul Arbian, despite his flippancy and lack of discipline, possesses genuine artistic talent, a trait the author clearly felt Nugent shared.

Nugent's first published poem, **"Shadows,"** actually had to be rescued from the trash can by Langston Hughes before it could be sent to *Opportunity* and, eventually, published. In **"Shadows"** Nugent voices his feelings of alienation, a situation he finds accentuated by his race.

> A silhouette am I
> On the face of the moon
> Lacking color
> Or vivid brightness
> But defined all the clearer
> Because I am dark,
> Black on the face of the moon.

"Shadows" was reprinted in 1927 in Countee Cullen's poetry anthology *Caroling Dusk.*

Nugent was among the artists and writers asked for contributions by Alain Locke for what was to become his showcase for Afro-American culture and art, *The New Negro* (1925). Locke's anthology contained **"Sadhji,"** Nugent's first published short story. Locke and Nugent had known each other for years, their families being friends, and Locke knew the eccentric youth had talent. Nugent's submission to the project had been a striking black-and-white wash drawing of a young African woman. Locke praised the drawing highly but asked Nugent for a brief written explication to accompany it. Evidently the short, two-page narrative Nugent returned was more useful than his graphic; when *The New Negro* appeared, Nugent's tale was illustrated by Aaron Douglas.

In **"Sadhji"** Nugent introduces two themes which would recur throughout his work: his reliance on moral, often Biblical, narratives and his fascination with human sexuality, particularly homosexuality. Sadhji is the beautiful wife of an aging African chieftain named Konombjo, whom she deeply loves. She is secretly coveted by Konombjo's son, Mrabo, who patiently awaits his father's death, anticipating his subsequent betrothal to his stepmother. In turn, Mrabo is loved by Numbo, "a young buck [who] would do anything to make Mrabo happy." To help his lovestruck Mrabo, Numbo murders the elderly chieftain on a hunting expedition, but instead of bringing happiness to Mrabo, the murder brings only misery. When Sadhji learns of her husband's death she throws herself on his funeral pyre. Mrabo is left alone. This simple morality tale is

FROM THE AUTHOR

"SMOKE, LILIES, AND JADE"

. . . he wondered why he couldn't find work . . . a job . . . when he had first come to New York he had . . . but he had only been fourteen then was it because he was nineteen now that he felt so idle . . . and contented . . . or because he was an artist . . . he should be ashamed that he didn't work . . . but . . . Alex . . . was content to lay and smoke and meet friends at night . . . to argue and read Wilde . . . Freud . . . Boccaccio and Schnitzler . . .

SOURCE: Richard Bruce Nugent (writing as Richard Bruce), excerpt from "Smoke, Lilies, and Jade," in *Fire!!* 1, November 1926.

told in a terse, abbreviated fashion, brief sentence fragments punctuated entirely with ellipses. The style is self-conscious but effective.

Locke saw considerable potential in this short African melodrama and continued to encourage Nugent's work on a dramatic version. The resulting one-act play with original musical score by William Grant Sill was published in Locke's and Montgomery Gregory's *Plays of Negro Life* (1927) and was produced in 1932 at the Eastman School of Music in Rochester, New York.

In the summer of 1926 the "Niggerati" began work on a new literary periodical designed to break with the older black literary establishment and to forge a new Afro-American aesthetic. They called their fledgling quarterly *Fire!!,* after a spiritual Hughes had written with composer Hall Johnson. Thurman, Hughes, and Hurston were designated editors, John P. Davis served as business manager, and Nugent was in charge of distribution. The publication was to be financed by contributions but ultimately had to be subsidized by Thurman. Aaron Douglas designed a stunning black and red cover for the magazine's first edition. Thurman, Hurston, and Gwendolyn Bennett contributed stories. Poetry was submitted by Hughes, Cullen, and Arna Bontemps, and Arthur Huff Fauset wrote an essay condemning the hypocrisy of the intelligentsia. Nugent contributed two brush-and-ink drawings and his fictionalized self-portrait **"Smoke, Lilies, and Jade,"** which he submitted on a roll of toilet paper. His first version of the story had been accidentally thrown away; written on Nugent's customary paper scraps it had been mistaken for trash.

"Smoke, Lilies, and Jade" (1926) was the first literary work on an explicitly homosexual theme to be published by an Afro-American. The story is intentionally subjective and, like ***Sadhji,*** punctuated entirely by ellipses. It begins with its autobiographical protagonist, Alex, lost in deep Proustian reverie. He eventually clears his thoughts, rises, and takes to the streets, looking for excitement. At four o'clock one morning, while walking home from a night of merriment, Alex is approached by a sexually attractive stranger. They exchange pleasantries, then Alex invites the man home. ". . . No need for words . . . they had always known each other . . . as they undressed by the blue dawn . . . Alex knew he had never seen a more perfect being . . . his body was all symmetry and music. . . ." A night of lovemaking leaves Alex in confusion about his sexuality (he is already involved with a woman), but his doubts are quickly resolved. ". . . He loved them both . . . there . . . he had thought it . . . actually dared to think it . . . One *can* love two at the same time . . . one *can* love. . . ." Nugent's defense of homosexual love was quite remarkable in its day, and it has lost little of its immediacy through the years.

The editors of *Fire!!* had intended the journal to be controversial, and the inclusion of **"Smoke, Lilies, and Jade"** insured that. Artists such as Thurman and Nugent were rebelling against the desires of the Afro-American intelligentsia to portray only the uplifting sides of black life. They wanted the freedom to depict all aspects of their experiences as Afro-Americans, from the bourgeois to the bohemian. Thurman decided that in order for *Fire!!* to be truly daring, two particularly sensational pieces were needed: one on homosexuality, the other on prostitution. He and Nugent had flipped a coin to determine who would write what. Thurman's tawdry tale of a sixteen-year-old prostitute, "Cordelia the Crude," was a result of the toss, and it equally outraged middle-class Afro-American sensibilities. The reviewer for the *Baltimore Afro-American* wrote: "I have just tossed the first issue of *Fire!!* into the fire." Alain Locke, in his review of the journal in the *Survey,* noted, "This is left-wing literary modernism with deliberate intent." While he supported the editors' anti-Puritan efforts, he deplored the "effete echoes of contemporary decadence" he found in their pages. In apparent response to the overt homosexuality expressed, Locke counseled that "Back to Whitman would have been a better point of support than a left-wing pivoting on Wilde and Beardsley." The negative reaction was not limited to academic critics. Nugent remembers going to Gregg's Restaurant with Thurman a few days after *Fire!!* was released.

> As we passed through, conversation parted before us like before the prow of a boat and closed after us as we passed by. . . . Not a soul spoke to us. We were in trouble—very deep trouble.

The ostracism did not last long; *Fire!!*'s chief problems were financial. The issue had cost more than anticipated. The printer had never been paid. Nugent, in charge of distribution, had often literally eaten up the profits. As a result, *Fire!!* never published a second issue.

After the demise of *Fire!!,* Nugent spent several years as a cast member of Dubose Heyward's play *Porgy,* touring the United States and Europe. In 1928 he contributed an essay to Wallace Thurman's second periodical effort, *Harlem: A Forum of Negro Life.* Though the contents were solid, featuring articles by Walter White, Langston Hughes, and Theophilus Lewis, *Harlem* proved as ephemeral as *Fire!!* and survived for only one issue. *Gumby's Book Studio Quarterly,* which was to have published Nugent's **"The Tunic With a Thousand Eyes,"** a stylized version of the Biblical story of Salome, seems never to have made it past the page proof stage. Apparently production of the *Quarterly* halted when its publisher, Alexander Gumby, became gravely ill with tuberculosis in the early 1930s.

The Depression forced some changes in Nugent's life-style, but he continued to work in the creative arts. He worked with the Federal Arts Project and the Federal Theatre. He contributed to the "Negroes of New York" manuscript funded by the Federal Writers' Project. The Harmon Foundation exhibited his artwork during the early 1930s. He contributed to Dorothy West's *Challenge* and *New Challenge* and to the poetry magazine *Trend.* After World War II, Nugent's creativity was encouraged by his close friend Bernard Kay. It was during this time that Nugent began to write a series of vaguely pornographic homosexual romances. None of these novels has ever been published.

The 1960s was a period of great energy for Nugent. Along with Romare Bearden and several others, Nugent founded the Harlem Cultural Council. He was particularly enthusiastic about the *Dancemobile* and the *Jazzmobile* projects. His Christmas story **"Beyond Where the Star Stood Still"** was published in the December 1970 issue of the *Crisis.* The story concerns a special gift that Herod's painted young catamite offers to the newborn Jesus. Nugent's elliptical style is missing, but his favored themes of homosexuality and biblical mythology remain.

Recognition has come slowly to Richard Bruce Nugent. The surge of interest in Afro-American history has brought what Nugent describes as a "growing multitude of people who have taped interviews with me in a quest for first-hand impressions of the Negro Renaissance." He has been consulted for works on jazz dance and the Harlem literary scene, for biographies of Langston Hughes, Zora Neale Hurston, Paul Robeson, and A'Lelia Walker. His early defense of homosexuality has been rediscovered by the Gay Rights movement, a cause which Nugent embraces. He appears briefly in the 1984 documentary film about gay history, *Before Stonewall.* He continues to write and draw and charm his visitors in Hoboken, New Jersey.

ELEONORE VAN NOTTEN (ESSAY DATE 1994)

SOURCE: van Notten, Eleonore. "Niggeratti Manor and Beyond." In *Wallace Thurman's Harlem Renaissance,* pp. 169-211. Amsterdam: Rodopi, 1994.

In this essay, van Notten discusses Nugent as a major figure in author Wallace Thurman's life. Drawing from Nugent's unpublished memoir Gentleman Jigger *and interviews with Nugent, van Notten describes Thurman and Nugent's time together in Harlem and the so-called "Niggeratti Manor."*

Of the nine years Wallace Thurman worked as a writer in Harlem, the first four were the most successful, both professionally and socially. Between December 1925 and December 1929, Thurman published articles, book reviews, editorials, poems, short stories, and a novel. In addition, Thurman edited two little magazines, finished his collection of essays "Aunt Hagar's Children," completed most of the manuscript of a second novel, and co-authored several plays and articles.

During the following five years, from 1929 until his death in 1934, the number of Thurman's publications decreased significantly. Apart from a second novel *Infants of the Spring,* only four publications from this period can be identified: one book review (1930), one co-authored novel (1932), and two co-authored film scripts (1934). Thurman's modest literary production, particularly in relation to the almost feverish creativity of the previous four years, is a reflection of his disillusion with his own potential as a writer.

Thurman's frequent absences from New York and his growing sense of isolation during these last years of his life are also symptomatic of his growing disinterest in Harlem life and in the Harlem Renaissance as an artistic movement.

The rise and fall of Thurman's literary prominence between 1925 and 1929 was linked to the course of his career as leader of Harlem's bohemian avant-garde. As an editor at *The Messenger* and particularly as the editor-in-chief of *Fire!!* magazine, Thurman had earned himself a position of authority among Harlem's younger generation of writers and artists. Conversely, the failure of Thurman's second magazine *Harlem* (1928), and his growing inability to cope with the strains and tensions of Harlem life from May 1928 onwards, marked the beginning of his decline as a pivotal force in this group.

Other factors, involving Thurman's Harlem friends and associates, contributed to the deterioration of his position. By the end of 1927, the collective spirit of rebellion which had become the trademark of the younger generation had begun to fade, partly as a result of the prolonged absence from Harlem of some of the *Fire!!* seven, particularly Hurston, Nugent, and Hughes. Hurston, for example, left for the South in search of folklore as early as December 1927. Nugent went on tour with *Porgy* only a few months later. And Hughes spent the summers of 1928 and 1929 away from Harlem working on his first novel *Not Without Laughter* (1930).[1] In addition, the old guard, which had inspired much of the rebellion of Harlem's younger generation, no longer served as a counterforce. By the end of the decade, organizations such as the N.A.A.C.P. and the National Urban League were no longer convinced that the arts could function effectively as an instrument in the advancement of the race. After 1927, both *The Crisis* and *Opportunity* suspended their literary contests indefinitely. Jessie Fauset and Charles S. Johnson, two of the three so-called midwives of the Renaissance,[2] resigned from their respective editorial positions.

Between his arrival in Harlem in September 1925 and his move to Niggeratti Manor in November 1926, Thurman moved at least five times. Following his short stay at the Strahans and his subsequent retreat to Mount Morris Park, Thurman lived, successively, at 666 St. Nicholas Avenue, at 137th Street, and at 314 West 138th Street.[3] During his early years in Harlem, Thurman developed several close and lasting friendships, in particular with Jeanette Randolph, Georgia Washington, Helene Grant, Theophilus Lewis, Richard Bruce Nugent, William Jourdan Rapp, Langston Hughes and Harald Jan Stefansson. The various accounts of Thurman's rooms and his creative living arrangements reveal his talent for turning his quarters into a meeting place for others. Rampersad describes how Thurman's place was invariably "the center of a whirlwind of activity, of laughter and carousing but also of intense, rebellious creativity."[4] Thurman's bohemian fringe lifestyle not only fitted his outsider position but also endorsed anti-social behaviour, unorthodox sexual relationships and other attitudes consistent with a counter-culture mentality.

To a large extent, Thurman's bohemianism developed through his friendship with Richard Bruce Nugent. Just as Mencken's artist-iconoclast provided Thurman with a model to accommodate and to some degree redeem his marginalized social position, Nugent's bohemianism provided Thurman with an appropriate lifestyle.

1. Bruce Nugent

Richard Bruce Nugent was born in Washington on 2 July 1906, the son of Richard Henry Nugent (Harry) and Pauline Minerva Bruce. At the time of Bruce Nugent's birth, his father Harry was working as a Pullman porter. This position, curiously, is an indication of the family's somewhat elitist social position. Traditionally the Pullman Company recruited its black porters from the ranks of the light-coloured and well-trained former house-hold slaves.[5] The railroad company, furthermore, entrusted the recruitment and instruction of new young porters to their experienced older co-workers so that the position of Pullman porter became more or less hereditary until well into the twentieth century. The job was looked upon as one of the few options for black males to secure themselves a relatively prosperous life and to provide a college education for their children.[6] Although salaries were low and the Pullman porter had to buy his own uniforms and meals, through ingenuity and discretion weighty tips could be had. Furthermore, the Pullman porter's travels, and the continuous enforcement of the rules of etiquette customary among his clientele, generated a bearing of urbane elegance which was quite unusual for both blacks and whites at that time.[7]

Nugent's mother Pauline was the second youngest of thirteen children born to Sandy Bruce and his French wife. Twelve children were of a light complexion. Indeed two boys passed for white and joined the Navy.[8] In ***Jigger*** [***Gentleman Jigger***] Nugent describes parts of his family history:

> After a whirlwind courtship, the brown and handsome Charles Henry Brennon [Richard Henry Nugent] the second, had succeeded in marrying the pale and personable Palma Minerva Steward [Pauline Minerva Bruce]. Against all precedent, because it was the motto of the new race and social order to marry as near white as possible. Of course the brown and handsome Harry as everyone called him, had done excellently by himself. He had married into one of the oldest and most aristocratic of these new-race families, and taken to his bosom a maiden fair as fair.[9]

Pauline Bruce Nugent shared all of Washington's prejudicial attitudes with regards to the preferred skin tones of her race in that she perceived skin-tone as an indication of class and moral character. Bruce Nugent remembers that his mother made an effort not to transfer her racial biases to her sons Richard and Gary Lambert, or Pete, as he was called. She never criticized their friends on the basis of colour or religion, Nugent recalls. At other times, however, Nugent describes his mother's antagonistic reactions to his friendships with darker coloured blacks, notably Dorothy West and Wallace Thurman.[10]

In addition to Nugent's self-concept of social sophistication, his idiosyncratic lifestyle and artistic bent can also be traced to his family background. "My parents were what we would now call Bohemian," he explains, and could "afford" to be "because they had the safety of their name behind them":

> Not that they were completely hedonistic, but they did believe in living their lives and they happened to be interested in music, the theatre, arts etc. and some of those things were in bad taste in Washington. Artists were, the theatre was, in as bad taste in Washington as it was in any of the strongholds of the WASPs."[11]

After Henry Nugent's death in 1920,[12] Pauline Nugent moved the family to New York City. His formal education at an end at the age of fourteen, Bruce Nugent worked as a delivery boy, a bellhop and eventually at a catalogue house where he received some training in art. He took over his own education by reading Wilde and Huysmans and by exploring New York, particularly Greenwich Village. At the age of eighteen Nugent announced to his mother that he had decided to become an artist and would no longer work. Pauline Nugent's response was to send her son back to Washington to live with his grandmother.[13] During this "exile," as he called it, Nugent frequented Georgia Douglas Johnson's salon where he met Langston Hughes in the summer of 1925. When Hughes returned to New York to attend a Krigwa Theatre dinner, Nugent went with him and never looked back.

There are indications that Thurman first met Nugent in late December 1925 or January 1926.[14] They were introduced by Hughes at the cafeteria of the YWCA in Harlem. Nugent's recollection of the event reveals an initial ambivalence towards Thurman. His retrospective account of this first meeting is recorded on tape:

> Langston and I were going into the YWCA cafeteria which was one of the best places to eat and I, as usual, I was bewitched by the smell of food and the sight of it, and in the middle of it Langston said "Oh, there is Wally, Wally Thurman." Well, I had admired Wally Thurman. I thought he was one of the most brilliant black men I'd ever read. . . . I had some kind of hero-worship for him. I looked over to where he pointed and there was this little black boy, man. He was little enough for me to think of as a boy, with this kind of sneering black nose. . . . Well, all of my prejudices, all of my Washingtonian prejudices came out. The idea of this brilliant man being so black! Well, I couldn't forgive him that. I found some excuse to leave soon, and that was it.[15]

Nugent's tape-recorded account is strikingly similar to the description of the same event in ***Jigger***:

> It was just as Bruce was succumbing to the invitation of cafeteria cooking, that Langston pointed toward a table and said, "There's Wally." It was a distinctly unpleasant shock. So unpleasant that Bruce lost all desire for food. Silent and empty-handed he followed Langston to Wally's table. So this was the brilliant Wallace Thurman. The Negro of whom he had hoped so much. This little black boy with the charming smile and sneering nose. With shifty eyes, and a nervous, unpleasant laugh. There was no mirth in either his voice or his eyes when he laughed. Bruce decided that he wasn't to be trusted. He was too balck [sic]. His mother had always warned him not to trust black people. That they were evil. And Bruce was Pauline's child.[16]

Nugent's account of the recognition of his own colour bias at the time of his first encounter with Thurman is consistent with his recollection of the event in several of his published interviews.[17] In these interviews, Nugent also recounts the follow-up to the first meeting. He explains how he went to Thurman's office at *The Messenger* to apologize for his behaviour and how from then on a remarkable friendship began to develop.[18]

Nugent's interpretation of the event, in ***Jigger,*** provides an insight into some of the racial preconceptions within the black community itself, at least as Nugent understood them:

> His [Thurman's] instinctive distrust of light complectioned Negroes was something Pellman [Thurman] was trying to overcome. . . . Thruout Stuart's [Nugent's] stumbling apology Raymond Pellman was silent. He recognized the sincerity and was furious at the trust he saw Stuart have that his apology would of course be accepted. . . . Stuart was more naive, after the manner of those who have always held themselves aloof thru some belief in their superiority. . . . It never occurred to him that Pellman might not be able to forgive him for having even for a while, having [sic] objected to his blackness. . . . After all, Stuart had condescended to accept Pellman—oh quite equally.[19]

Nugent further suggests that Thurman was particularly sensitive to manifestations of intraracial colour prejudice. In one of his later interviews, Nugent explains: "Wally was very conscious of his being Black in a Black society that put Black down and put mulatto coloring up." This awareness, according to Nugent, "was a very important psychological fact in Wally's life."[20] Nugent's reading of Thurman's colour-consciousness parallels a similar assessment by Nathan Gray, Thurman's friend in Salt Lake City. Gray points out that Thurman suffered the effects of his dark complexion more intensely in his relationships with other blacks than in his relationships with whites.[21]

Thurman became acutely aware of the prevailing colour code within the black race during his time at the University of Southern California. Indeed, in his autobiographical novel *The Blacker the Berry,* campus life at USC is Thurman's setting for some of his protagonist's most baffling and painful encounters with the lighter members of her race. Thinly disguised as fiction, the novel reads like a cathartic psychoanalytic account of Thurman's own experiences. In "Stepchild," Thurman describes his personal approach in the effort to minimalize the harmful effects of internalized racial bigotry:

> He had consciously detached himself from any local considerations, striven artfully for a cosmopolitan perspective. He knew that there was a certain amount of discomfort, a certain amount of interference, inevitably to be expected from one's fellow men, no matter what happened to be one's color or race or environment. . . . He was not interested in races or countries or people's skin color. He was interested only in individuals, interested only in achieving his own salvation and becoming if possible a beacon light on Mount Olympus.[22]

Thurman's defense mechanism was essentially escapist. Adopting a posture of detachment and intellectual superiority, Thurman tried to immunize himself from the traumas of racism. By ridiculing the prevailing social system from the distance assumed by artist-iconoclasts, Thurman believed he had sufficiently removed himself from direct contact with an offensive and potentially harmful environment. And by trivialising the possible psychological fallout of racism on himself, he tried to nullify its more persistent destructive consequences. Thurman believed that racial transcendence was not only necessary to survive in American society but also a prerequisite for his career as a writer and critic. In a letter to Hughes, Thurman wrote that objectivity was imperative to the success of his dual career as Harlem Renaissance "literary historian" and as a black realist writer whose work, he felt, must not be tainted by propaganda.[23] Thurman maintained that "to shake off the psychological shackles" of race, was "the duty of those who have the will to power in artistic and intellectual fields."[24]

Once again, even in his choice of words, Thurman demonstrates his intellectual debt to both Nietzsche and Mencken for the origin of his ideas. Yet, as we will see, this ultra-rational approach to a very personal predicament could not completely immunize Thurman against the effects of what must have been daily encounters with racial bigotry. To a man of Thurman's complexion, race, in all its ramifications, constituted a permanent and inescapable force. And, despite his pronouncements to the contrary, racism, particularly among blacks themselves, must have dictated his personal development, his ideas, and his actions.

Time and again Thurman tries to convince others that even under trying circumstances his response is one of controlled detachment and contempt. Yet his understanding of racism as inherent to the uneducated mob, which in Thurman's perception included most of humankind with the notable exception of the artist-iconoclast elite, could not but generate an exceedingly cynical view of the world. This cynicism, which bordered on misanthropy at times, made him more and more destructive over the years, both in his relationships with others and in his attitude towards himself. At the time of his first meeting with Nugent, however, Thurman was still relatively in control and just beginning to make his mark as one of the aspiring leaders of Harlem's younger generation.

Thurman and Nugent complemented each other in a number of ways. Nugent found his friendship with Thurman both interesting and expedient. He recognized not only skin colour as one of Thurman's remarkable features but also his intelligence. Furthermore, Thurman, unlike Nugent, always managed to earn money. "Wally practically supported me," Nugent explains on tape.[25]

To Thurman, Nugent was a much needed ally and a ready follower. In ***Jigger,*** Nugent offers the following insight into the Thurman-Nugent partnership through their respective fictional counterparts Rusty Pelman and Stuart Brennan. Against the background of one of the meetings of the seven *Fire!!* editors, Nugent writes:

> They were the New Negroes. But mostly they were Rusty and Stuart. For Rusty knew he was the nucleus and Godhead inspiration of the group, and Stuart had decided it also and attached himself to Rusty. And Rusty was shrewd enough to recognize and utilize the complement of Stuart's nature. And the rest of them accepted this state.[26]

Socially, the roles of leader and follower were reversed. As Nugent repeatedly points out, his significance to Thurman was as a counterbalance to the latter's racially induced sense of insecurity.[27] Nugent was an independent spirit, and explicitly so. After one *Opportunity* dinner, for example, Carl Van Vechten recorded in a letter to Langston Hughes:

> As I went out William Pickens caught my arm to ask me who the 'young man in evening clothes' was. It was Bruce Nugent, of course, with his usual open chest and uncovered ankles. I suppose soon he will be going without trousers.[28]

In ***Jigger,*** too, Nugent's persona Stuart is depicted as a character who consciously decides to become a notorious artist "with a flair for drawing and exhibitionism . . . oddities of dress and conversation."[29] From the numerous accounts of Nugent's early years in New York, Stuart Brennan appears to be a replica image of Nugent himself.

Nugent, unlike Thurman, was entirely his own man. He did not seek the approval of others for his conduct and regarded his own judgement as sufficient in the assessment of his worth. In one of his interviews, Nugent reports why Thurman may have found him interesting. "What Wally admired in me," Nugent explains, was

> my brashness, my social background, to a certain extent my looks . . . and my ability to get along with people. I had a greater ability to get along with people than he did. So frequently if there was going to be something that he was going to attend he would take me along because I could get along with the people which meant that he got along with the people better.[30]

In Nugent's estimation this self-confidence was used by Thurman to compensate for his own social vulnerability and self-consciousness. Furthermore, Nugent's eccentricities which, as he himself indicates, were often calculated to shock, amused Thurman. They eventually found their way into Thurman's *Infants* in the character of Paul Arbian, Niggeratti Manor's consummate bohemian.

2. Black Bohemia

In November of 1926, Thurman and Nugent, who had shared lodgings virtually from the day of their first meeting, together moved into new quarters at 267 West 136th Street. The residence, nicknamed Niggeratti Manor, was owned by Iolanthe Sidney, who ran an employment agency and sponsored a variety of worthy causes. She put one of her two large houses in Harlem at the disposal of young, indigent black artists. The larger and more attractive of the two (on Lenox Avenue) was designated for the benefit of pullman porters who needed accommodation during their layovers in New York City.[31]

From 1926 to 1928 Richard Bruce Nugent and Wallace Thurman formed the core of Harlem's black bohemia centred at Niggeratti Manor. In a personal review of *Infants of the Spring,* the novel which records and analyzes life at the Manor, Thurman writes:

> Bohemianism, in the popular sense of the term, came to the present author too late to be the youthful fourteen year old adventure it should have been, and too early to be clarified by twenty five year old maturity. It came during that uncertain middle period of his life, (he was eighteen then), when it was alternately fascinating and repellant, more the former than the latter, but sufficiently both to unbalance him.[32]

The fact that Thurman links bohemianism to a specific age is telling. He intimates that while it may suit the fourteen-year-old adolescent it can unbalance those, like himself, who engage in it at eighteen. In fact, Thurman was twenty-four when he met Nugent, some ten years too old in his own estimation to adopt a bohemian lifestyle. Indeed, in the *Infants* review, Thurman deliberately makes himself six years younger by crossing out what he had originally designated as his age in the typescript and by inserting "eighteen" in his own hand.

Theophilus Lewis, in one of his accounts of Thurman's arrival in Harlem in September 1925, describes how Thurman almost immediately became the "leader of [the] shock-proof young sophisticates."[33] He quickly became "an urban animal," Lewis reports, "who loathed the ways of life and points of view of the country and small town [and who] practised the virtues of city life with an ardor that all but amounts to religious fervor."[34] Yet Thurman's ambivalence about Harlem's bohemia and his leading role in it was never quite resolved, as Hughes indicates in *The Big Sea.* Hughes describes Thurman as, "a strange kind of fellow, who liked to drink gin, but *didn't* like to drink gin . . . who adored bohemianism, but thought it wrong to be bohemian . . . [who] liked to waste a lot of time, but always felt guilty wasting time."[35] Hughes further explains that Thurman felt that the "Negro vogue . . . had flattered and spoiled" Harlem's younger generation and had mostly provided them the opportunity "to drink gin and more gin so that they were drunk most of the time instead of producing good art."[36]

In Thurman's correspondence, however, the focus is predominantly on the more amusing sides of his bohemian existence. In a letter to Fay Jackson, for example, Thurman writes: "There is a bunch of us more or less communistic in spirit. If one has, he shares. If not, we all do without. And I am sure we have more fun than perspiring mortals with both belly and pocketful."[37] It is interesting to note that Thurman's letter to Jackson, dating from May 1928, was written during one of his frequent retreats from the hectic bohemian life in Harlem, when Thurman tried to restore his physical and mental health and work without interruption. Despite Thurman's fondness for certain aspects of communal living, he clearly recognized its limitations. He quickly found that bohemianism interfered with his writing and generated prolonged periods of near starvation. In a letter to Hughes from early 1927, Thurman reports that his employers at *The World Tomorrow* had offered him money to buy a new overcoat.[38] They felt sorry for my "freezing carcass," Thurman explains.[39] Thurman also records that he was not only struggling to pay off various debts incurred from the publication of *Fire!!* but also that he had seriously fallen behind in room rent and could only eat when free meals were offered.

Thurman's studio at Niggeratti Manor attracted a host of frequent visitors with artistic aspirations. Typically, Thurman himself was sceptical about their artistic quality or potential: "There are many never-will-be-top-notch literary, artistic and intellectual strivers in Harlem as there are all over New York. Since the well advertised 'literary renaissance,' it is almost a Negro Greenwich Village in this respect," Thurman declared.

With a headstart of at least ten years, the Village as a hotbed of revolutionary change in manners and morals and as the most notable centre of the bohemian avant-garde in the United States, made a compelling role model for other artistic centres, including Harlem.[40] Greenwich Village's "first lady" Mabel Dodge pointed out in her memoirs that Harlem's black younger generation had too hastily and too uncritically accepted the Village as their beacon light. "When a man or a race has to make a new adaptation," Dodge declared, "it is sometimes unsuccessfully hurried, like an apple that is rotted before it is ripe, as are many of the Negroes in Harlem."[41]

Dodge's judgment parallels evaluations by both Locke and Thurman. Locke described the Niggeratti as "pot-plants seeking a forced growth,"[42] and Thurman selected from *Hamlet* a comparable metaphor of impaired growth for his epigraph to *Infants of the Spring,* reflecting his assessment of the Harlem Renaissance as seriously compromised from its inception.[43] Among the movement's major flaws, in Thurman's estimation, were its racial self-consciousness and the faddist forces surrounding it. He grieved over the New Negroes, including himself "as a lost generation, pandering to tourists on the safari for queer dives in Harlem."[44] Dorothy West agrees that Thurman "not only understood himself but he also understood his period. He recognized its artificiality, its high-blown divorce from reality."[45]

Thurman's comparison of Harlem with Greenwich Village as equally lacking in artistic excellence is not surprising. Of the Niggeratti only Nugent made contact with the white avant-garde downtown. Thurman, according to Nugent, hardly ever went there. He was convinced of the superiority of Europe where the arts were concerned, so much so that he virtually overlooked such literary figures as Eugene O'Neill, F. Scott Fitzgerald, Sherwood Anderson, and Sinclair Lewis, all of whom had close links with the Village. In Thurman's estimation it was the idea of a lost generation which linked Harlem to Greenwich Village; the idea of a promising younger generation which squandered its talents in bohemianism and dissipation.

Within a year of Thurman's arrival, Harlem had grown into one of New York City's major tourist attractions. The commercializing of black life affected all layers of Harlem's population. Although night life was booming, the average black Harlemite was not the beneficiary. Instead, as Hughes points out, they resented the nightly influx of white New Yorkers, trooping into Harlem after sundown, "flooding the little cabarets and bars where formerly only colored people laughed and sang, and where now the strangers were given the best ringside tables to sit and stare at the Negro customers—like amusing animals in a zoo."[46] In this development, Harlem again seems to have followed Greenwich Village which some five years earlier had turned into "a side-show for tourists, a peep-show for vulgarians," as Floyd Dell describes it.[47]

Naturally, white interest in Harlem life also affected the representation of blacks in the arts. Zora Hurston writes in a letter to Hughes: "It makes me sick to see how these cheap white folks are grabbing our stuff and ruining it."[48] "My only consolation being," Hurston continues, "that they never do it right and so there is still a chance for us."[49] Yet *Opportunity* was quick to point at the various exploitative practices by blacks themselves. A 1927 editorial refers specifically to blacks who trooped into Harlem, entering the fields of music, dance, and literature with no legitimate claim to distinction other than their complexions. There is a danger, the magazine points out, "that the alloys will accomplish more harm than the real can accomplish benefits."[50]

In a similar vein, Bruce Forsythe writes about blacks in film, for *Flash* magazine:

> I saw intelligent and cultured Negroes, men and women of charm, manner and education, deliberately concreting the old, old Nordic conception of the Race. The best entertainers are hiring themselves out in ridiculous form; fine actors are tossing their art and pride at the dollar, magazines with enormous circulations are printing things that make every self-respecting person blush with shame, writers of talent are doing nigger hack work; musicians are bastardizing their art. There is a great scratch and scramble for the few dollars the Nordic is willing to pay.[51]

Langston Hughes voiced similar complaints when he reported that, "the lindy-hoppers at the Savoy began to practice acrobatic routines, and to do absurd things for the entertainment of the whites, that probably never would have entered their heads to attempt merely for their own effortless amusement. . . . Some critics," Hughes concluded, "say that is what happened to certain Negro writers, too."[52]

One such critic was Thurman's fellow Menckenite George Schuyler who declared that this was the time in Harlem when, in his words, "some of the most ridiculous doggerel won poetry prizes."[53] Another critic, Sterling Brown, provides what is perhaps the most penetrating retrospective assessment of the period, particularly in his appraisal of Thurman's artistic milieu. Its revolt, in Brown's view, was one more of youth than of race, more similar to than different from its white counterpart:

> Gay with youth, heady from attention, caught up along with much of America in ballyhoo, flattered by influential creators, critics, and publishers who had suddenly discovered the dark world at their doorstep, many Negroes helped to make a cult of Harlem. They set up their own Bohemia, sharing in the nationwide rebellion from family, church, small town, and business civilization, but revolt from racial restrictions was sporadic. Rash in the spurt for sophistication (wisdom was too slow and did not pay off), grafting primitivism on decadence, they typified one phase of American literary life in the twenties. A few magazines such as *Fire* and *Harlem* flared like rockets; good experiments jostled against much that was falsely atavistic and wilfully shocking.[54]

Nugent's conclusion in ***Jigger*** that the Niggeratti wasted much of their time discussing rather than producing art is not unlike Brown's implicit judgment on the Renaissance' overall lack of literary output. In the final analysis, the artistic achievements of the niggeratti, Nugent suggests, were limited and disappointing:

> Wallie had written four articles that had been published and paid for. Zora had written any number of short stories, one of which had been published. She then had disappeared, had gone south to further her studies in Anthropology. Gwenny had written one story since the advent of 'The Current' [*Fire!!*], been kicked out of her position, and married. She was now somewhere in Georgia. . . . Aaron had settled down to smug married life and supported his family by drawing mediocre jackets for negro books.[55]

Most of the niggeratti's group activities, Nugent further points out, were stimulated by alcohol.

Although Nugent's evaluation may have been overly pessimistic, he correctly calls attention to one of the principal weaknesses of the Renaissance's second and final stage. When, in November 1926, Thurman and Nugent moved into the Manor, the Jazz Age was at its height. Prohibition had generated a temper of defiance to the point that the consumption of alcohol and the accompanying lifestyle became a banner of revolt for the bohemian fringe milieu. From all accounts, the residents of 267 were no different. According to Nugent, the manor was the house of parties. "Someone was always coming in with a bottle of gin," Nugent remembers. And although not drunk all the time, Nugent recounts, "we certainly were moist."[56] Hughes recalls how at Thurman's parties "you met the bohemians of both Harlem and the Village."[57] Arthur Davis remembers in some detail how as a college boy he would frequent the parties "at Thurman's house":

> Thurman was a charming host with a hearty laugh and a keen sense of the phony. His parties tended

to have a broader social mixture than those at the Tower. There one found in addition to writers and artists, truck drivers and other workers, theatrical people from downtown, and always, it seems, a disproportionate number of white girls. The sky was the limit at Thurman's parties.[58]

Thurman was at "the peak of his popularity," as his friend Theophilus Lewis points out, when Niggeratti Manor was the talk of the town. Lewis further suggests that although rumours about "wild nights" and "delirious days" may not have been entirely groundless they were perhaps exaggerated.[59]

This was also Thurman's view. In a letter to Fay Jackson, Thurman explains why outsiders might come away with a distorted image of life at the Manor:

> I expected Eddie Myers to tell some rather fantastic tales. He seemed quite bawled over by what everyone is wont to call our bohemian life. He happened to drop in, as is usually the case, just when we all felt reckless and were on a long distance drunk. You know how such things happen and you also know how outsiders ignore all but the bizarre and regale other outsiders with tales of "queerness" and licentiousness.[60]

Despite Thurman's clarifications the bohemian lifestyle was one of the defining features of life at the Manor, and Thurman was fascinated by it.

3. Niggeratti Manor: The First Year

With the beginning of 1927, Thurman and his fellow Niggeratti still found themselves the subject of some attention as a result of their *Fire!!* publication two months earlier. On the second of January, for example, they were invited to read from their little magazine at the Civic Club. Hemenway reports that four of the seven editors took part in the event: Hurston, Hughes, Bennett, and Thurman.[61] From Thurman's correspondence, however, it would appear that Hughes did not attend. "The Fire meeting was great," he writes in a letter to Hughes. "I read your poetry and made a grand hit. From now on I substitute pour vous."[62]

Thurman could be justifiably proud of his own literary production as well. Between March and December 1927 he published six articles. The magazines which took his work were mostly liberal left-wing publications, including *The Haldeman-Julius Quarterly* which identified itself as "a debunking magazine" and as "an enemy of sham and hypocrisy."[63] The subject matter of Thurman's articles of this period can be divided thematically into two fairly even groups: black literature and black life in Harlem. Thurman's third and most enduring theme, his personal struggle with a potentially destructive race-consciousness, invariably intrudes in these writings as well as in his novels *The Blacker the Berry* and *Infants of the Spring.*[64]

In many respects 1927 was one of the more successful years of Thurman's adult life, not only as a writer but also as the recognized spokesman for Harlem's younger generation. In this capacity, Thurman granted an interview to the prominent leftist writer and journalist Granville Hicks. In his subsequent article entitled "The New Negro: An Interview with Wallace Thurman," published in *The Churchman* of 30 April 1927, Hicks writes:

> Nobody can hope to understand the young negro without studying the negro achievements in art and letters. I wanted a representative of that movement, and I found him in the person of Wallace Thurman, whom I first saw seated at a desk in the new offices of *The World Tomorrow.* There he was, black and smiling, eager to tell me about himself, his friends, their hopes and their accomplishments.[65]

Through Hicks, Thurman reiterates his view that the Renaissance's artistic objectives must always take precedence over social and racial concerns: "Socially we want to win recognition for the negro at the same time that we break down the desire, which seems to be growing within the race, *not* to be a negro," Thurman declares, "but mostly we want to create good literature and good art.[66] At the time of the Hicks interview, Thurman appears to have managed to combine a promising writing career with a bohemian lifestyle. Furthermore, Thurman also experimented with two new genres, the novel and the play. The new literary forms would complement his already versatile literary opus. A discussion of his first play will follow. . . .

4. Thurman and the Theatre

In the autumn of 1927 Thurman found himself a job which would stand him in good stead as a budding playwright. Together with some of his bohemian friends, Thurman answered a call for black performers to try out for parts in the ambitious stage adaptation of Du Bose Heyward's novel *Porgy* (1925) by New York's Theatre Guild.[67] From his various references to Heyward, it is safe to assume that Thurman approved of Heyward's portrayal of black life. In September 1924, in his article "Nephews of Uncle Remus," for example, Thurman writes: "No negro has written about his own people as beautifully or as sympathetically as has Du Bose Heyward, the author of 'Porgy', purely because the negro writer, for the most part, has seen fit to view his own people as sociological problems rather than as human beings."[68]

The stage adaptation of the novel had been a joint venture between Heyward and his wife Dorothy Hartzell Kuhns.[69] It is interesting to note that Heyward was never part of New York City's interracial intellectual milieu. He always remained a white southern gentleman from Charleston, South Carolina.[70] In one of his numerous articles on the staging of *Porgy,* Heyward describes some of the early challenges in the production of the play: "Of the many unknown quantities that were encountered in the highly experimental production of 'Porgy' by the Theater Guild," he writes, "the most interesting, the most unknown, and in the final analysis the most satisfactorily solved was that presented by the cast."[71]

Both Bruce Nugent and Theophilus Lewis comment on the experimental character of *Porgy.* Nugent recalls that initially the Theatre Guild had been faced with the challenge of finding black actors for the play.[72] Despite the relative abundance of amateur theatre groups such as the Lafayette Players, the Harlem Community Players, and the Krigwa Players, in Harlem during the 1920s there was a limited interest in the portrayal of black life on the stage.[73] Anderson points out that small black amateur companies tended to produce conventional and often tame melodramas of middle-class life.[74] Theophilus Lewis, the most prominent black drama critic of the Harlem Renaissance, offers the following explanation:

> The fundamental problem with the upper-class or "higher intellect" black theater patron [i.e. Du Bois' Talented Tenth] was that he went to the theater and often ignored his own tastes as well as the desires of the lower classes in the audience and demanded instead that the performance be geared to a set of standards alien to both—to white standards. . . . What we call the Negro Theatre is an anaemic sort of thing that does not reflect Negro Life, Negro fancies or Negro ideas.[75]

Another obstacle facing Heyward's production was what Lewis calls "the absence of actors with an understanding of the dignity of their calling."[76] Whereas many of the amateur black theatre groups pandered to the white theatrical traditions, most of the professional black actors of the day, Lewis suggests, "were willing to play for low humor and obscenity."[77] In short, black theatre during the first half of the decade had not been able to generate a class of players from which Heyward could recruit black actors for his play. Ultimately, the successful approach, Heyward wrote, "was to use a drag net, and bring in every available actor of the least promise."[78] Among those caught in the net were Dorothy West, Wallace Thurman, and Richard Bruce Nugent.

According to Nugent, who gave various detailed accounts of his experiences as one of the residents of "Catfish Row," a "cattle call" had gone out in Harlem by means of local newspapers and bill boards to find black actors.[79] Although the Theatre Guild was particularly interested in blacks who could sing, dance, and whistle, Nugent recalls that some, including himself, who did not meet these criteria were hired nevertheless.[80] According to Alexander Woollcott, drama critic for the *New York World,* the play was cast with "a wild, untrained, tatterdemalion horde of players."[81]

Much of the success of *Porgy* was due to the play's director Rouben Mamoulian. Of mixed Armenian and Russian descent, Mamoulian had received his training for the theatre in Moscow. His interpretation and treatment of *Porgy* was, at

ABOUT THE AUTHOR

NUGENT'S CONTRIBUTION TO THE HARLEM RENAISSANCE

Despite the modest size of his published oeuvre, Richard Bruce Nugent is a significant figure of the Harlem Renaissance. He was a key member of the group of younger African American writers and artists who created the legendary publication *FIRE!!* in November 1926—a group that included Langston Hughes, Zora Neale Hurston, Aaron Douglas, and Wallace Thurman. Nugent was the first African American to write from a self-declared homosexual perspective; his work therefore occupies an honored place in the now-burgeoning literature of the gay black male. An openly gay black youth who moved in circles—white and black—where same-sex erotic interest was pervasive but rarely acknowledged publicly, Nugent illuminated, through his life and work, conundrums of race, sex, and class that are of considerable current interest.

SOURCE: Thomas H. Wirth, in *Gay Rebel of the Harlem Renaissance,* Duke University Press, 2002.

least in part, the result of an enlightening experience in one of Harlem's makeshift churches. Leigh Whipper, who played the dual roles of undertaker and crab man, had taken Mamoulian up to Harlem: "I had to tell him [Mamoulian] how to be colored," Whipper explained. "I carried him to one of these store front churches. And when he came out of the store front church he was sold. He had never seen anything like it in all his life and it was just what he wanted."[82]

Porgy opened 10 October 1927 at Broadway's segregated Guild Theatre where it ran for some two hundred and seventeen performances.[83] In May 1928, it moved to the Republic Theatre where it ran for another hundred and thirty-seven performances.[84] Later in the year, the play went on tour along the East Coast and throughout the Midwest.[85] In the spring of 1929, it was produced at His Majesty's Theatre in London. C. B. Cochran, the London producer, wrote that he "would rather be responsible for putting on 'Porgy' than for all the other plays and entertainments presented in London during [his] lifetime."[86]

Although only three of the Catfish Row denizens (Thurman, Nugent, and West) can be identified as Harlem literati, Nugent suggests that Harlem's bohemians were hired in droves because they were black and available. Availability may have been one of the reasons which kept others such as Hughes, Hurston, Davis, Bennett, and Douglas from joining. West suggests that there were only four, Thurman, Nugent, herself, and a man whose name she cannot remember. "We were totally obnoxious," she recalls.[87] "We were a little group of four little writers who stuck together and everybody hated us."[88]

From Thurman's participation in *Porgy,* it can be assumed that by the time rehearsals began in September 1927 he was no longer working as circulation manager at *The World Tomorrow.* Unlike Bruce Nugent, however, who went on tour with *Porgy,* including to Europe, Thurman left the cast after about six weeks. The various theatre programmes of the play do not list Thurman's name after the first week in December. The precise reason for Thurman's departure remains unclear. Dorothy West suggests that Thurman left only one week after he won a battle (including a strike) over pay. The supers, according to West, initially made only about $17.00 per week.[89] In one of her later interviews, West adds that Thurman had decided to stick his neck out for higher pay. When the salaries were finally raised Thurman was fired, West claims.[90] Bruce Nugent confirms Thurman's involvement in the strike:

> Wallie only stayed with it [*Porgy*] thru rehearsals and six weeks after the opening. That was long enough to start excitement. He incited a strike among the extras. Then when the fight was at its height, left the show.[91]

Nugent further indicates that Thurman left *Porgy* to prepare the production of his play *Harlem,* co-authored by William Jourdan Rapp.

Accounts of exactly where and when Thurman and Rapp first met vary. According to Van Vechten and Nugent, the first meeting took place at the editorial offices of *Dance Magazine* where Thurman was preparing an article. The article in question, entitled "Harlem's Place in the Sun," was published in the journal in May 1928 with illustrations by Nugent. Other sources suggest that Thurman knew Rapp before May 1927 and that their meeting probably took place at Rapp's editorial office at the *American Monthly.*[92] Thurman's May 1927 article "Harlem: A Vivid Picture of the World's Greatest Negro City," published in Rapp's *American Monthly,* seems to support this claim.[93] Rapp's own record of his first meeting with Thurman indicates that they probably met early in 1927. Rapp writes:

> About two years ago a young negro from Salt Lake City walked into the office of a young editor from the sidewalks of New York. He bore a card of introduction from a young minister . . . who had known the editor during his foreign correspondent days in the Near East. Out of this meeting came *Harlem,* the drama of New York's Black Belt which is now chilling audiences at the Apollo Theatre.[94]

Thurman and Rapp's introduction and subsequent friendship not only resulted in the production of their co-authored play *Harlem,* but also initiated their collaboration on at least two other plays and numerous newspaper articles.[95] Rapp, to whom Thurman would dedicate his unpublished collection of essays "Aunt Hagar's Children" became one of Thurman's closest and most loyal friends. Rapp frequently acted on Thurman's behalf, providing outlets for the publication of his articles and, in 1929, mediating and negotiating Thurman's separation from his wife Louise Thompson. It was with Rapp that Thurman left instructions to be carried out after his death. "He is the most energetic man I know being happiest when there is much work to do," Thurman writes of his friend and collaborator. "He is generous of his time and money and I have never known him to be bored or pessimistic. He keeps his sense of humour even when doing the hack work he must sometimes do in order to eat," Thurman concludes.[96]

William Jourdan Rapp (1895-1942) was the son of a Jewish cigar manufacturer and merchant. He was born 17 June 1895 in New York City.[97] Rapp, who graduated with a BS degree from Cornell in 1917, worked briefly as a Health Inspector in the Department of Health of New York City before enlisting as a bacteriologist in the Medical Corps of the United States Army. He served in France for two years. Six months before his discharge in August 1919, Rapp worked at the Pasteur Institute in Paris. Upon his return to the U.S., he became a Milk Inspector for New York City's Health Department but resigned in April 1920.

During the following four years, Rapp was an Overseas Secretary of the International Committee of the YMCAs of North America but was loaned to the American Red Cross and the Near East Relief on various occasions. He worked in Turkey for two years, making his headquarters at Smyrna and Constantinople. In 1922 and 1923 his headquarters were based in Athens where he directed a social survey of the city, specifically studying conditions relating to children. A synopsis of his findings was submitted to the second World Conference of YMCA Workers Among Boys in Austria in June 1923. As a member of the Athens American Relief Committee, Rapp, at the request of the U.S. State Department, travelled to remote parts of the Balkans to investigate the refugee situation.

In 1924, Rapp moved to France to study and write. His publications include articles on various aspects of the Near East and appeared in periodicals such as *Current History* and *The Nation*. That same year his book *When I Was a Boy in Turkey* was published by Lothrop in Boston. The book was published in a series which came to be known as: "The Children of Other Lands Books." Other titles included *When I Was a Boy in Greece, When I Was a Boy in Persia, When I Was a Boy in Denmark*, etc.[98] In 1926, Rapp was hired by Macfadden Publications. At *American Monthly*, he worked together with George Sylvester Viereck as a co-editor. Then, he became an editor at *True Story* magazine, a position which he held until shortly before his death in 1942. Rapp was also connected with some twenty-three radio programs as consultant, author, and producer.

Meanwhile, Rapp worked as a free-lance "feature writer" for several New York based periodicals including the *New York Times*. During the second half of the 1920s, Rapp began to gain prominence as a playwright. Although as early as 1919 a first play had been translated for productions in Greece and France respectively, it is doubtful if this ever reached the stage. After 1925, however, five of Rapp's plays were produced in New York City under the titles *Whirlpool, Hilda, Cassidy, Substitute for Murder, The Holmeses of Baker Street*, and *Harlem*, in collaboration with Wallace Thurman. *Harlem* was the first play in their co-authored dramatic trilogy *Color Parade*. The second, *Jeremiah the Magnificent*, dealt with the life and work of Marcus Garvey and his Back to Africa Movement. The third, called *Harlem Cinderella*, also referred to as *Black Cinderella*, dealt with the complexities of colour prejudice within black society, a subject close to Thurman's heart.[99]

For Rapp and Thurman, black life in Harlem provided the inspiration for various co-authored scripts and articles. Their first collaboration, after much revision and reworking, eventually resulted in the production of the play *Harlem*. Known under a variety of names including *Cordelia the Crude, City of Refuge, Black Mecca*, and *Black Belt*, the title was ultimately changed to *Harlem* only days before its week-long try out at the Boulevard Theatre in Jackson Heights, Queens, New York, beginning on 11 February 1929.[100] On 20 February, *Harlem*, now subtitled *An Episode of Life in New York's Black Belt*, opened at the Apollo Theatre on 42nd Street, West of Broadway. The play was produced by Edward A. Blatt and directed by Chester Erskin.[101]

A close examination of Thurman's co-authored work is outside the scope of this study. There is evidence, however, that Thurman supplied most of the details on black life for all three of his plays with Rapp. Richard de Rochemont claims that Rapp was "the deviser of the plot of the play" while Thurman provided "dialogue and background."[102] This division of responsibilities seems plausible since Thurman was in the best position to provide the local colour, as it were, and the realistic details of black life.

Much of the writing and rewriting of *Harlem*, which took up almost two years, was done at Rapp's house at 88 Morningside Drive in New York. "Ours has been one of those collaborations you read about . . . no quarrels over pet ideas or sulkings because of their exclusion, which is set down here more in admiration of Bill Rapp than in praise of myself," Thurman would admit retrospectively.[103] During the early months of the project, Rapp became increasingly aware of the practical consequences of an interracial friendship. Eating out in the company of Thurman allowed him to sample the workings of racism in midtown Manhattan during the 1920s. Frequently they were refused service or were served in isolated corners. At Sardi's, one of New York City's best known theatrical restaurants, Thurman and Rapp were asked to leave through the back door.[104]

It appears from Thurman's correspondence that within six months after his move to Niggeratti Manor he had begun writing his first play. The scenario for *Harlem* was loosely based on Thurman's short story "Cordelia the Crude," published in *Fire!!* in 1926. The three-act melodrama was set against the backdrop of one of Thurman's favourite night-spots, the Harlem rent-party. In what is most likely a very early draft, entitled *Cordelia the Crude,* Thurman presents a portrait of a newly arrived black southern family and their struggle to adapt to the unfamiliar urban environment of Harlem. Thurman contrasts the antics of his pragmatic heroine Cordelia with the pathetic struggles of her parents. In the synopsis of the play, Cordelia is described as "a strong willed over-sexed, prematurely mature Negro girl with sturdy limbs and form."[105] The parents are portrayed as "a hard pushed, hard working pair, bewildered by their new environment, unable to cope with conditions; they accept each new assault docilely with just a few shivers of protestation and surprise."[106]

The first manuscript of the play was offered to literary agent Frieda Fishbein in December 1927.[107] On 9 January 1928, a standard Dramatic Contract was negotiated and signed between the two playwrights Rapp and Thurman, and Crosby Gaige. Gaige, according to the contract, agreed to the production of "a certain play or dramatic composition provisionally entitled *Black Mecca* for the sum of $500." Gaige also agreed to produce the play before the first of November 1928.[108]

5. Niggeratti Manor: The Final Year

Within a month after the signing of the contract rehearsals were under way, yet it would take another year before the play eventually opened on Broadway in February 1929. By then Gaige's option had expired, and *Black Mecca,* by now renamed *Black Belt,* had passed through the hands of Horace Liveright, Lee Shubert, the Theatre Guild, and many others.

Although Thurman still found himself in poor health at the beginning of the new year (1928), his fortunes appeared to have taken a turn for the better. In a letter to Hughes he writes:

> I am up again, weak in the knees, but happy. Crosby Gaige has taken my play. I will be on Broadway soon. Rehearsals may start within ten days. Also I have a job, reader for Boni-Liveright. And I am signed up for three more plays. . . . The novel is about re-written. . . . It is a novelty to be eating regularly once more. I hope it continues. Fire debts!!!! I am still being harassed. I paid off one completely. But the Mutual Aid is still waiting and fretting. No news or scandal. I am practically in seclusion. Not a bit well. Tonsils swollen, necked puffed out like a balloon on one side. Dizzy in the head, etc. etc. Soon as inflammation goes from tonsils out they come. Bastards. . . . Send me a book of some kind as a peace offering and write me damn you, write me.[109]

The contract with Gaige for the production of Thurman's play could not have come at a more propitious time. From one of the co-authored articles by Thurman and Rapp on the production of *Harlem,* it would seem that within a month after the signing of the contract the play had been cast and rehearsals had begun. By now Thurman could barely restrain his excitement. "Play all cast," he writes to Hughes, "and what a cast!!"[110] There may have been other reasons for Thurman's sense of exhilaration at this time. In a letter to Hughes he writes: "I'm in love!" The object of his affections, however, was not revealed.[111]

Meanwhile, Crosby Gaige had joined forces with Al Lewis, another producer, who demanded significant changes, particularly in the third act of the play. Lewis, according to Thurman and Rapp, "went to see 'Porgy' and returned enthusiastic about the 'wow' funeral in that play, and suggested, [that] 'Black Belt' get its 'wow' by inserting a christening in its third act. We thought this over and rejected it."[112]

It seems that only one month after the play was cast, it was taken out of rehearsal and the cast dismissed.[113] "I hear Wallace Thurman's play 'Black Belt' is not going to try-out this spring as has been planned, but is to be staged in September," Harold Jackman writes to Claude McKay in April, noting also that Thurman was bitterly disappointed by the postponement.[114] Thurman's disappointment was acute enough to serve as a catalyst for one of his increasingly frequent escapes from Harlem. "I have disappeared!" he writes to Hughes in early May. "Harlem was too hectic for me."[115] The same information was sent to others. To Fay Jackson, for example, Thurman writes:

> I have disappeared. No one in New York or rather only about three people know where I am. One is my collaborator [William Jourdan Rapp]. The other my best friend [Harald Jan Stefansson]. The third my best pal, a girl [Jeanette Randolph]. . . . I had to do it. Harlem was too hectic. I grew weary, surfeited. I couldn't work.[116]

Twelve days later he writes to Jackman:

> This disappearing act is really a glorious gesture. I never felt so well in my life, nor was my mind ever more alert and active. Two weeks, country air, disciplined living, and regular meals have done much to counteract the effects of much more hectic living in Harlem.[117]

Although Thurman's disappointment over the suspension of his play can be easily understood, it alone can hardly account for the frustration evident in his letters. It would seem that at this point in Thurman's career there was a growing realization that he could no longer successfully combine a bohemian lifestyle with the discipline of writing. Dorothy West recalls that Thurman "had no privacy except on the infrequent occasions when he literally pushed his companions out of his quarters and wrote for a stretch of 48 hours or else escaped."[118] During Thurman's spells of isolation he would always increase dramatically the output of work. During these particular three weeks away from Harlem, Thurman, as he told Jackman, was able to do "a prodigious amount of serious reading," finish a first draft of a play, write some "15,000 words on a new novel, and two articles."[119]

In addition to Thurman's literary ventures there may also have been some activity of a more romantic nature during this period as can be inferred from Thurman's letter to Fay Jackson in Los Angeles in which he writes:

> I am not married! Where on earth did you hear that news. Not now or ever. I don't believe in it. It's too enervating and sheep like. And since I have no paternal instincts would be a dead waste of time, talent and industry. If I ever mate up it will be free love and brief.[120]

No convincing evidence can be found, however, to support the suggestion implicit in Jackson's letter that Thurman had even met his future wife Louise Thompson at this point. Rampersad suggests that Thompson only arrived in Harlem in June 1928 and then later was hired by Thurman as a typist. What should be noted, however, is that there are no indications in Thurman's letters and other writings that he considered marriage incompatible with his sexual orientation. Rather, he considered marriage incompatible with his life as an artist.

6. Louise Thompson

On 22 August 1928 Thurman married Louise Thompson.[121] Thompson was born in Chicago on 9 September 1901.[122] She took her degree in business administration from Berkeley in 1924 and worked briefly as a teacher in Pine Bluffs, Arkansas. In 1926, she began teaching at Hampton Institute, Virginia. In October 1927, she supported a student strike in protest of the school's tolerance of racism and the timidity with which it handled its white philanthropic sponsors. Thompson's anonymous account of the strike appeared in *The Crisis* of December 1927.[123] Six months later, in June 1928, she accepted a scholarship in sociology from the National Urban League and moved to New York, where, as a friend of Aaron Douglas, she was introduced to Harlem's artistic and intellectual milieu.[124] Nugent who, like Thurman, met Thompson shortly after her arrival, defines her as "a very pretty girl, very sweet-seeming . . . a sort of no-nonsense girl." Nugent further concedes that he had no liking for her and that Thompson did not like him.[125]

Although Thurman's friendship with Thompson probably began at Niggeratti Manor, Nugent's most vivid memory of them as a couple dates from the summer of 1928, after Thurman had moved to a rooming house at 128th Street between Lenox and Fifth Avenue. Nugent, also a tenant there, recalls that Thurman was not feeling well at the time and Louise Thompson looked after him while she typed his manuscripts. "I had respect for her ability to make Wallie work, and keep on working," Nugent reports. But "I had a great dislike for a jealously that she had about Wallie."[126] Nugent suggests that Thompson, who was very possessive after her marriage, had only "peripheral knowledge or acquaintance with the people surrounding Wallie," including himself. Nugent concludes that he got along with Louise Thompson only because it was important to Thurman but not on any personal basis.[127] To Nugent, Thurman's marriage to Thompson was just another example of Thurman's destructive nature:

> if it wasn't Louise it was going to be Oscar or somebody. If it wasn't either of those two he was going to drink too much. He was born to die. . . . I think I always felt . . . it is not going to last forever.[128]

Even though Nugent's retrospective position unavoidably colours his perception of Thurman, some of his comments are revealing. "It was always clear to me," Nugent asserts on tape, "that Wallie was going to mess up his life," just as he ruined Louise Thompson's (and that of some of his friends).[129]

Thurman's alleged carelessness about himself and others can be explained on a variety of levels: as a consequence of his cultivated detachment from a society that marginalized him, in the context of his search for materials for his writing, and as a result of his experimental approach to life. In "Stepchild," for example, Thurman writes:

> His future method of procedure became more outlined. It would be his religious duty to ferret deeply into himself—deeply into his race, isolating elements of universality, probing, peering, stripping all in the interest of garnering literary material to be presented truthfully, fearlessly, uncompromisingly. A new laboratory experiment had been inaugurated.[130]

Thurman's understanding of his life in terms of "a new laboratory experiment," was motivated, at least in part, by the need for authentic subject-matter for his writing. It also helps to explain the self-referential character of much of his work and his alleged insensitivity towards friends and associates. If their significance was to any extent proportional to their degree of usefulness to Thurman's writing career, it would follow that the integrity of Thurman's friendships might be called into question. He frequently flaunted his ability to collect "colorful personalities," Dorothy West remembers. He "surrounded himself with a queer assortment of the 'lost generation'. . . . He saw them clearly and could evaluate them in a half-dozen brutal words, she recalls."[131] In *Infants,* Thurman's persona Raymond Taylor is depicted, pad in hand, eagerly recording other people's experiences and life stories. "He saw himself heightening and distilling [them] . . . for his own literary use," the narrator points out.[132] And Thurman's own persona in the novel only overcomes his reluctance to visit a friend in prison because he is "bent on completing his experiment."[133] Thurman's reported ruthless manner in his dealings with others was well known to Nugent. "Wallie had a fascination for people that only the devil could have, an almost diabolical power," Nugent records in his interview with David Lewis.[134]

From Thurman's correspondence and from Nugent's statements on the matter, it would appear then that Thurman's impulsive marriage to Louise Thompson fitted his penchant for experimentation and diversity. According to West, Thurman had an "oft-repeated philosophy of doing everything once before he died."[135] Nugent believes that Thurman was interested primarily in the idea of the so-called companionate marriage which was coming into vogue.[136] The concept of this nuptial arrangement was advanced and defined during the 1920s by Judge Ben B. Lindsey who presided over the Juvenile Court of Denver at the time. Lindsey identified it as: "a legal marriage with legalized Birth Control, and with the right to divorce by mutual consent for childless couples, usually without payment of alimony."[137] Felix Adler, a scholar and contemporary of Lindsey, explains in one of his articles on marriage and divorce: "birth control had reduced the social significance of marriage and left it a private matter of concern only to those persons forming an alliance."[138] Lindsey was not in favour of the so-called trial marriage, but he wanted acknowledgment and recognition of the reality that marriage contained an element of risk. In 1927, the experimental nature of the companionate marriage caused controversy on a national scale when Mr. and Mrs. Haldeman-Julius, friends of Judge Lindsey's, permitted the companionate marriage of their foster daughter to one of her fellow students at the University of Kansas.[139]

Some six weeks after his marriage to Thompson, Thurman attempts to clarify his views on the arrangement in a letter to Claude McKay:

> Things do happen. Since I last heard from you several things have happened to me. First, I got married, which action I, who never [sic] and still do not believe in marriage for an artist of any type, will not try to explain. It's just one of those inexplainable things that happens even to the best of us. My only point of extenuation is that I happen to have married a very intelligent woman who has her own career and who also does not believe in marriage and who is as anxious as I am to avoid the conventional pitfalls into which most marriages throw one. I assure you ours is a most modern experiment, a reflection of our own rather curious personalities.[140]

Not surprisingly, Thurman identifies his bride in terms of her intelligence, professional independence, and unconventional personality, all three characteristics which he clearly admired in himself. Dorothy West, who knew both Thurman and Thompson before and after their brief period of cohabitation, reports in one of her interviews how Thompson ("a little bitty woman") arrived in New York, accompanied by a 'great big mother' who was anxious to see her daughter married to "somebody who was in the arts."[141] Like Nugent, West was not naturally drawn to Thompson. And like Nugent, she rather uncritically took Thurman's side.

> Louise married Wallie and we all went crazy, because we said, "it'll never work," and so forth and so on and so on. And I was in the middle, I don't know why, because Wallie used to come to me and tell me his story . . . [and] Louise would come on her lunch hour into my little apartment. . . . She was a chain smoker. . . . Louise liked me bet-

ter than I liked her. . . . She was totally outside the Renaissance. Well, you know what I mean, she was married to Wally, and nobody liked her.[142]

West's assertion that Louise Thompson was uniformly disliked by Thurman's friends is incorrect. West fails to mention Thompson's friendship (albeit short-lived) with Hurston and her life-long friendship with Hughes, for example. After the break-up of her marriage with Thurman, Thompson, on 2 October 1928, was hired by "godmother" Osgood Mason to work as a stenographer for Hughes at $15.00 a month. Rampersad reports: "With her mother ill, the money and the flexible hours were truly a godsend. Their large apartment at 435 Convent Avenue, near the City College of New York, Rampersad writes, became a second home for Hughes."[143]

In one of her articles on Thurman, West suggests that the marriage, at least in the beginning, was much more traditional than Thurman would have others believe.[144] West recalls how Thurman, "forsook his old haunts and attempted the transition from bachelorhood and bohemianism to the life of conventional family man by going eagerly to a new address with his wife and also his mother-in-law, for whom he had real affection."[145] However, Thurman's attempt at conventional family life, if true, was on the whole unsuccessful. The couple moved to a new apartment at 90 Edgecombe Avenue with Thompson's mother in tow. West's recollections of Thurman's attachment to his mother-in-law, furthermore, seem somewhat at odds with suggestions in a letter by Zora Hurston. "Wally should perk up," Hurston writes to West: "I know that it is annoying for his mother-in-law to keep on living and pestering him, but then there are gunmen on the East Side who hire out for as low as $25.00. He should be a very happy man by Thanksgiving."[146] By Thanksgiving, however, Thurman's marriage could not be saved. By the end of November, Thurman, true to form, fled Harlem. From his retreat once again Thurman explains his actions in a letter to Hughes:

> Can I let you in on a secret, one which you will not divulge to your new as yet unidentified inamorata? Ostensibly I am in Salt Lake because my mother is ill. I received two hectic telegrams advising me to leave at once. I dashed to my publishers. They gave me the necessary $150, and I left. Tehee. On my arriving in Salt Lake my mother of course was quite surprised to see me as was every-one else save Mignon, my first love, whom I had wired to send those telegrams. It's almost too good to keep, but I swear I'll murder you if you ever breathe it to a soul. I just had to flee. I was fed up on New York, on the magazine, and on married life (yes it's all over, but I dare you to mention that either.)[147]

Harold Jackman, knowing of Thurman's disappearance and the possibility of a ruse, writes to Countee Cullen in early December:

> Did Edward tell you that he saw Wallace in Chicago? Wallace is now in Salt Lake City. He received a telegram from home (so the story goes) saying his mother was very ill and to come right away. I think that Wallace went there so there shouldn't be any talk when he left his wife. And of course, as I predicted, *Harlem* is no more.[148]

The new year of 1929 would bring both success and failure in Thurman's career and personal life. His "nomad" play *Harlem,* as he now called it, was unexpectedly revived after it came to the notice of Chester Erskin. Rapp fills in some of the details:

> A young actor, play reader, stage manager, vaudeville sketch writer, and occasional director by the name of Chester Erskin got hold of one of the original copyrighted copies of the play. . . . Erskin liked the play and decided he wanted to do it. He interested a theatrical publicity man by the name of C. A. Leonard. Both of them interested young Edward A. Blatt, who wanted to become a producer and bought the option unseen. We settled back to await its expiration. Imagine our surprise when these three young men actually produced the play under the title *Harlem.*[149]

In January, Thurman was back with Thompson in their apartment at 90 Edgecombe ("woe is me," he writes to Hughes)[150] not only busily preparing for the upcoming opening of his play at the beginning of February but also for the publication of his first novel *The Blacker the Berry* that same month. On the 19th of January, the Thurmans had a little party at their Edgecombe address. "Yes, he is with his wife again," Jackman reports, "but for how long I don't know."[151] According to one of his letters to Rapp, Thurman stopped living at the apartment he shared with Thompson sometime in February.[152] Dorothy West claims that it was Thompson who left Thurman on the night before the opening of *Harlem* on Broadway. What Thurman failed to see, West explains, is "the fact that she could desert him at a crucial hour [made her] as much a failure as a writer's wife as he was as a conventional husband." With the deterioration of his marriage, West claims, Thurman for the first time became unsure of himself. Scandalous gossip surrounded the disunion.[153] To Thurman's close friends, however, nothing was scandalous, West recalls. Thurman's break-up only proved their opinion that "Thurman was not the marrying kind."[154]

According to Louise Thompson, who was interviewed by Rampersad on 23 May 1984, the improbable marriage had already collapsed after a few weeks, and in a welter of recrimination:

> "I *never* understood Wallace," she would later admit. "He took nothing seriously. He laughed about everything. He would often threaten to commit suicide but you knew he would never try it. And he would never admit he was a homosexual. *Never, never,* not to me at any rate."[155]

From Thurman's point of view, particularly as stated in his letter to McKay, the marriage lasted at least a little longer than Thompson attests. However, her comments on Thurman's behaviour fit descriptions by others, especially with regard to Thurman's "general disregard for established custom," as West describes it. "He laughed very hard when things hurt him most," she recalls.[156] "Everything was a joke to Wally," Aaron Douglas confirms in an interview of June 1978.[157] And Arna Bontemps in one of his retrospective articles on the Harlem Renaissance remembers Thurman's fascination with Raphael Sabatini's hero Scaramouche in the novel of the same title. Something of an anti-hero, he is predominantly identified by his "gift of laughter and [his] sense that the world was mad."[158] Thurman felt it applied to himself, Bontemps reports.[159]

Thurman emphatically rejected Thompson's charge of his homosexuality. By way of explanation to Rapp, Thurman linked Thompson's allegations to her discovery of the story of his arrest in the Harlem subway station in 1925. "By some quirk fate," Thurman writes to Rapp, the story of the incident reached Louise:

> just at the time she was fighting me for money settlement. She told Ernst. He verified the story, and they threatened to make charges that I was homosexual, and knowing this and that I was incapable of keeping up my marital relationship had no business marrying. All of which Louise knew was a lie. The incident was true, but there was no evidence therein that I was homosexual and Louise also knew that tho there had been sexual incompatibility it had been her fault, not mine. She had to have an operation while I was in Salt Lake, remember, in order to make an entry possible, and because by that time I had lost all sexual feeling for her and tho there was a consummation of the sexual act I was blackmailed thusly. The alibi being that she had been so upset by this vile disclosure that it had ruined her life.[160]

Three weeks later, in another letter to Rapp, Thurman writes:

> I will succumb to no more sentimental pleas that we discuss matters between ourselves in an adult way. . . . I have the trump cards. She can not get any judge to grant her that which I have not. We have our agreement drawn up to prove that I tried to do my share. If she brings up this homo-sexual business, she will get nowhere. She has already admitted to Swerling that after her operation all was well sexually between us and neither can she bring up that knowledge of that one incident in my life disgusted her so that she was unable to have further intercourse with me, for she did, on the very day I left New York, April the sixth.[161]

Thurman's activities on the sixth of April seem to contradict his earlier assertion about his lack of sexual interest in Thompson. Nugent's judgment that Thurman was bisexual seems closer to the mark, as we will see later. There is no evidence that Louise Thompson knew of Thurman's relationships with men, other than the subway incident. Indeed, it was Thurman's friendship with Jeanette Randolph, one of Thurman's life-long female friends, which seems to have incensed Louise Thompson. In a letter to Rapp Thurman writes:

> I would like to have a nice poke at the honorable Louise's jaw. She seems intent on making me as miserable as possible, writing ridiculous letters to my folks and doing all she can to alienate friends of mine from me. She flatters me. I could never be the villain she has tried to make some people believe existed. Her latest is to write to Miss Randolph (whom you will remember) who had asked her in all friendliness to lunch. Louise responded in a hysterical letter, alleging that I had flaunted my friendship with Jeannette to her during our married life, and striven hard to make her (Louise) believe that Miss Randolph and I were committing adultery.[162]

Wallace Thurman never divorced Louise Thompson. Although the financial aftermath of the separation would cause considerable irritation on both sides, evidence suggests that they remained in touch until Thurman's death in 1934. Rampersad writes that Thurman, three years after the separation, "still claimed to love his wife."[163] And Thompson suggests that she visited Thurman during the terminal phase of his illness.[164] Six years after Thurman's death, Louise Thompson married the black communist leader and civil rights lawyer William L. Patterson in 1940. Thompson now lives in Oakland and is in the process of writing her autobiography.

Thurman's frequent absences from Harlem from 1928 onwards reflect his growing disillusion with the artistic potential of the Harlem Renaissance and with his own role in it. Some two months after the publication of his first novel *The Blacker the Berry* and the opening of his play *Harlem,* both in February 1929, Thurman left Harlem for Salt Lake City and the West Coast. After his return in September, he would concentrate his professional activities almost exclusively outside the black artistic milieu.

Notes

1. Rampersad I 163, 172-73.
2. The third was Alain Locke.
3. JWJ/WTP.
4. Rampersad I 132.
5. Terry Pindell, *Making Tracks: An American Rail Odyssey* (New York: Holt, 1990) 159.
6. Pindell 159.
7. Pindell 162.
8. RNP/Tapes.
9. Nugent, *Jigger.* This story is repeated in RNP/Tapes.
10. RNP/Tapes.
11. RNP/Tapes.
12. Nugent's stream-of-consciousness account of his father's death is part of "Smoke, Lilies and Jade," published in *Fire!!* in 1926.
13. RNP/Tapes.
14. Both in *Jigger* and on tape, Nugent reports that at the time of their first meeting he lived with his mother at 660 St. Nicholas Avenue, only a few doors away from Thurman who lived at number 666.
15. RNP/Tapes.
16. Nugent, *Jigger.* See illustration 1.
17. LC/Oral/Nugent. Kisseloff, *You Must Remember This.* Richard Bruce Nugent, interview trans., Hatch-Billops Collection, New York, 4 Apr. 1982. Hereafter HB/ Oral/Nugent.
18. Nugent's mother Pauline, who had explicitly warned her son against Thurman because of his dark complexion, was appalled to learn of her son's apologies. RNP/ Notes.
19. Nugent, *Jigger.*
20. HB/Oral/Nugent.
21. EVN/Oral/Gray.
22. Thurman, "Stepchild."
23. Wallace Thurman, letter to Langston Hughes, n.d., Los Angeles/FJP.
24. Thurman, "Stepchild."
25. LC/Oral/Nugent, RNP/Tapes.
26. Nugent, *Jigger.*
27. RNP/Tapes.
28. Carl Van Vechten to Langston Hughes, n.d.; librarian's notation 1927, JWJ.
29. Van Vechten to Hughes.
30. RNP/Tapes.
31. Sidney's interest in the plight of Pullman porters had been stirred by her friendship with the labour leader A. Philip Randolph, one of the founding editors of *The Messenger* in 1917 and founder of the Brotherhood of Sleeping Car Porters in 1925. RNP/Tapes.
32. Wallace Thurman, rev. *Infants of the Spring,* by Wallace Thurman, unpub. ts., 2 pp., n.d., *Contempo* Papers, U of Texas at Austin.
33. Theophilus Lewis, "Wallace Thurman is Model Harlemite."
34. Theophilus Lewis, "Wallace Thurman is Model Harlemite."
35. Hughes, *The Big Sea* 238.
36. Hughes, *The Big Sea* 238.
37. Wallace Thurman, letter to Fay Jackson, n.d.; internal evidence suggests May 1928, Los Angeles/FJP.
38. Wallace Thurman, letter to Langston Hughes, n.d.; internal evidence suggests early 1927, JWJ/WTP.
39. Thurman to Hughes.
40. Munson 73.
41. Mabel Dodge Luhan, *Movers and Shakers* (New York: Harcourt, 1936) 363.
42. Locke, "Art or Propaganda."
43. Thurman, *Infants.* See also Chapter 7 [of *Wallace Thurman's Harlem Renaissance*].
44. Sterling A. Brown, "The New Negro in Literature (1925-1955)," *The New Negro Thirty Years Afterward.*
45. West, "Elephant's Dance" 83.
46. Hughes, *The Big Sea* 225.
47. Munson 79.
48. Zora Neale Hurston, letter to Langston Hughes, 20 Sept. 1928, JWJ.
49. Hurston to Hughes.
50. "Some Perils of the Renaissance," Editorial, *Opportunity* March 1927: 68.
51. Bruce Forsythe, "Movies and Pride," *Flash* 29 June 1929, Los Angeles/FJP.
52. Hughes, *The Big Sea* 226.
53. CU/Oral/Schuyler 106.
54. Sterling A. Brown, "The New Negro in Literature," *The New Negro Thirty Years Afterward* 59.
55. Nugent, *Jigger.* See bibliography for the correct number of Thurman's magazine publications.
56. RNP/Tapes.
57. Hughes, *The Big Sea* 249.
58. Arthur P. Davis, "Growing Up in the New Negro Renaissance," *Negro American Literature Forum* Fall 1986: 55.

59. Theophilus Lewis, "Harlem Sketchbook."

60. Wallace Thurman, letter to Fay Jackson, n.d.; internal evidence suggests May 1928, Los Angeles/FJP.

61. Hemenway 50.

62. Wallace Thurman, letter to Langston Hughes, n.d., JWJ/WTP. In the letter, the word "I" is underlined three times.

63. "The Truth about America: The *Haldeman-Julius Monthly* exposes Bunk and Hypocracy." Editorial. *Haldeman-Julius Quarterly* Oct. 1926: 251.

64. On 22 Apr. 1927 Jackman wrote in a letter to Cullen that Thurman had just completed his first novel *The Blacker the Berry,* JWJ/WTP. About one month later Thurman informed Hughes that he had submitted his novel to Doubleday, JWJ/WTP.

65. Hicks, "An Interview with Wallace Thurman" 10.

66. Hicks, "An Interview with Wallace Thurman," 11.

67. "'Porgy:' The Play That Set a Pattern," *Theatre Arts,* Oct. 1955: 33. In 1935 the Theatre Guild would produce the musical version of the play (score by George Gershwin) under the title *Porgy and Bess.*

68. Thurman, "Nephews."

69. Anderson 275.

70. William H. Slavick, "Going to School to DuBose Heyward," *The Harlem Renaissance Re-examined,* ed. Victor Kramer (N.Y.: AMS P, 1987) 67.

71. Du Bose Heyward, "The Casting and Rehearsing of 'Porgy'," *The New York Sun* 22 Oct. 1927.

72. RNP/Tapes.

73. Freda L. Scott, "Black Drama and the Harlem Renaissance," *Theatre Journal* Dec. 1985: 426-39; and James V. Hatch and Ted Shine, eds., *Black Theatre U.S.A.: Forty-five Plays by Black Americans, 1847-1974* (N.Y.: Macmillan, 1974).

74. Anderson 275. Du Bose Heyward, "Author of 'Porgy' Reveals Sources of Melodrama," *New York American* 27 Nov. 1927. J. Mercer Burrell records that the first black actor engaged in serious drama (as opposed to vaudeville) was Ira Aldridge from Baltimore. Aldridge left for England in the 1850s where he played Shakespeare, particularly Othello. NY/Gumby.

75. Theodore Kornweibel, "Theophilus Lewis and the Theatre of the Harlem Renaissance," *The Harlem Renaissance Remembered,* ed. Arna Bontemps (N.Y.: Dodd, 1972) 182.

76. Kornweibel, "Theophilus Lewis."

77. Kornweibel, "Theophilus Lewis."

78. RNP/Tapes.

79. RNP/Tapes. The play was set in Catfish Row, a small seaside community in South Carolina.

80. RNP/Tapes.

81. Alexander Woollcott, rev. *Porgy,* by Du Bose Heyward, *New York World* 11 Oct. 1927: 13.

82. Leigh Whipper, interview trans., Hatch-Billops Oral History Collection, New York, Jan. 1972.

83. "Porgy: The Play that set a Pattern," NY/Gumby.

84. "Porgy," NY/Gumby.

85. RNP/Tapes.

86. C. B. Cochran, "Why I Produced 'Porgy,' as told by the English Producer for the London 'Bystander,'" *New York Amsterdam News* 5 June 1929.

87. Dorothy West, interview trans. Black Women Oral History Project, Schlesinger Library, Radcliffe College, 6 May 1978. Hereafter Radcliffe/Oral/DWP.

88. Radcliffe/Oral/DWP.

89. West, "Elephant's Dance" 82.

90. Radcliffe/Oral/DWP.

91. RNP/Tapes.

92. NYPL/CVVP. In Apr. 1927, *American Monthly* published an article by Frederick Millar entitled, "Jazz—A Stepping Stone," illustrated by Richard Bruce (Nugent).

93. Countee Cullen describes Thurman's article as "riotous with that sharp staccato writing affected by so many modern young writers." Cullen further points out that Thurman presented an unrecognizable portrait of Harlem as a habitat of "human checkers automatically moving on a huge crazy-quilt and getting nowhere at all." Countee Cullen, "The Dark Tower," *Opportunity* June 1927: 180.

94. William Jourdan Rapp, "The Making of Harlem: The Story of a Strange Collaboration," n.d; internal evidence suggests Feb. or March 1929, JWJ/WTP.

95. Thurman and Rapp's co-authored articles mostly deal with the production of the play *Harlem.* They include titles such as: "The Negro Made Human," "How Harlem Got to Broadway," "Casting and Directing Harlem." See Bibliography for a more comprehensive list.

96. Wallace Thurman, "My Collaborator," unpub. ms., 2 pp., n.d., JWJ/WTP.

97. For the biographical section on William Jourdan Rapp I have made extensive use of the introduction to the William Jourdan Rapp Papers, U of Oregon Library, Eugene, Oregon and Rapp's personal papers and correspondence in this collection. The William Jourdan Rapp Papers will be referred to hereafter Oregon/WRP.

98. W. F. Gregory, letter to William Jourdan Rapp, 19 March 1923, Oregon/WRP.

99. On 31 Oct. 1929 the *Philadelphia Tribune* reported that C. A. Leonard, formerly associated with Edward A. Blatt productions, was planning the imminent production of a play about Marcus Garvey and the U.N.I.A entitled *Jeremiah the Magnificent* with the opening date set for February 1930. Leonard further announced that Paul Robeson was being considered for the leading role. Klotman suggests that the failure of another play about Garvey entitled *Sweet Chariot* may have caused potential producers to shy away from the production of *Jeremiah* which appears to have been performed only once, after Thurman's death. Klotman, *DLB,* vol 51: 268.

100. Oregon/WRP.

101. Oregon/WRP.

102. De Rochemont.

103. Thurman, "My Collaborator."

104. "Obstacles in Way of Playwright," *Amsterdam News* 3 Apr. 1929: 13.

105. Wallace Thurman, "Synopsis of *Cordelia the Crude,* A Melodrama in Three Acts," unpub. ts., 3 pp., n.d., JWJ/WTP.

106. Thurman, "Synopsis."

107. JWJ/WTP.

108. JWJ/WTP.

109. Wallace Thurman, letter to Langston Hughes, n.d., JWJ/WTP. There is no extant information about Thurman's position at Boni-Liveright. On 21 May 1928 the League for Mutual Aid reported to William Jourdan Rapp the payment of $100 covering Thurman's debt. JWJ/WTP.

110. William Jourdan Rapp and Wallace Thurman, "Detouring 'Harlem' to Times Square," *The New York Times* 7 Apr. 1929.

111. Wallace Thurman, letter to Langston Hughes, n.d.; internal evidence suggests March 1928, JWJ/WTP.

112. Rapp and Thurman, "Detouring 'Harlem'."

113. Rapp and Thurman, "Detouring 'Harlem'."

114. Harold Jackman, letter to Claude McKay, 22 Apr. 1928, Atlanta/CJMC. Jackman further informed McKay that he had read the manuscript copy of *The Blacker the Berry* which Thurman had just completed and which he felt was "very good."

115. Wallace Thurman, letter to Langston Hughes, n.d.; internal evidence suggests early May 1928, JWJ/WTP.

116. Wallace Thurman, letter to Fay Jackson, 5 May 1928, Los Angeles/FJP.

117. Wallace Thurman, letter to Harold Jackman, postmarked 17 May 1928, JWJ/WTP.

118. West, "Elephant's Dance" 80.

119. Wallace Thurman, letter to Harold Jackman, postmarked 17 May 1928, JWJ/WTP.

120. Wallace Thurman, letter to Fay Jackson, n.d.; internal evidence suggests May 1928, Los Angeles/FJP.

121. Klotman, *DLB,* vol. 51: 260.

122. The principal sources used in the biographical section on Louise Thompson are: Kellner, *Dictionary;* Rampersad I; Lewis, *When Harlem Was in Vogue;* Phyllis Klotman's entry on Thurman in *DLB,* vol. 51; Dorothy West's article "Elephant's Dance."

123. Louise Thompson, "The Hampton Strike," *The Crisis* Dec. 1927: 345-47.

124. Kellner, *Dictionary* 354.

125. RNP/Tapes.

126. RNP/Tapes.

127. RNP/Tapes.

128. RNP/Tapes.

129. RNP/Tapes.

130. Thurman, "Stepchild."

131. West, "Elephant's Dance" 80.

132. Thurman, *Infants* 82-83.

133. Thurman, *Infants* 203.

134. LC/Oral/Nugent.

135. West, "Elephant's Dance" 81.

136. LC/Oral/Nugent.

137. Quoted in: Robert H. Elias, *"Entangling Alliances with None"* (New York: Norton, 1973) 15.

138. Elias 15.

139. As noted before Thurman's monograph "Negro Life in New York's Harlem" was published in the Oct., Nov., Dec. 1927 issue of the *Haldeman-Julius Quarterly.* In 1928 the article was reissued in the Haldeman-Julius Little Blue Book Series.

140. Wallace Thurman, letter to Claude McKay, 4 Oct. 1928, JWJ.

141. Radcliffe/Oral/DWP.

142. Radcliffe/Oral/DWP.

143. Rampersad I 174. For a discussion of Thompson's relationships with Locke, Hurston, and Hughes see Rampersad I and II. The Alain Locke Papers at Howard U. contain an undated letter to Charlotte Osgood Mason with a "Memorandum re Louise Thompson," Howard/ALP.

144. West, "Elephant's Dance" 80.

145. West, "Elephant's Dance" 80.

146. Zora Neale Hurston, letter to Dorothy West, n.d., Radcliffe/DWP.

147. Wallace Thurman, letter to Langston Hughes, n.d.; internal evidence suggests the end of Nov. 1928, JWJ/WTP.

148. Harold Jackman, letter to Countee Cullen, 6 Dec. 1928, Tulane/CCP.

149. Rapp and Thurman, "Detouring 'Harlem' to Times Square."

150. Wallace Thurman, letter to Langston Hughes, n.d., JWJ/WTP.

151. Harold Jackman, letter to Countee Cullen, 25 Jan. 1929, Tulane/CCP.

152. Wallace Thurman, letter to William Jourdan Rapp, n.d.; internal evidence suggest July 1929, JWJ/WTP.

153. West, "Elephant's Dance" 81.

154. West, "Elephant's Dance" 81.

155. Rampersad I 172.

156. West, "Elephant's Dance" 79.

157. Charles L. James, "On the Legacy of the Harlem Renaissance: A Conversation with Arna Bontemps and Aaron Douglas," *Obsidian* June 1978: 51.

158. Bontemps, "The New Black Renaissance." Bontemps refers to Rafael Sabatini, *Scaramouche the Kingmaker* (1921).

159. Bontemps, "The New Black Renaissance."

160. Wallace Thurman, letter to William Jourdan Rapp, 7 May 1929, JWJ/WTP. Ernst Swerling was Thurman's lawyer.

161. Wallace Thurman, letter to William Jourdan Rapp, 1 June 1929, JWJ/WTP.

162. Wallace Thurman, letter to William Jourdan Rapp, n.d., JWJ/WTP. According to Nugent, Thurman had an affair with Jeanette Randolph. RNP/Notes.

163. Rampersad I 213.

164. Kellner, *Dictionary* 354.

Abbreviations

Amherst/DBP: W. E. B. Du Bois Papers. University of Massachusetts at Amherst.

Atlanta/CJMC: Cullen-Jackman Memorial Collection. Robert W. Woodruff Library, Atlanta University, Atlanta.

"Aunt Hagar": Wallace Thurman, unpub. collection of essays completed in 1929.

Berry: Wallace Thurman, *The Blacker the Berry* (1929; New York: Arno, 1969).

CU/Oral: Columbia University, Oral History Collection, New York.

CU/Oral/CVV: Carl Van Vechten, interview trans., CU/Oral, New York, 1960.

CU/Oral/Schuyler: George Schuyler, interview trans., CU/Oral, New York, 1960.

CU/Gumby: L. S. Alexander Gumby Collection of Negroiana. Columbia University, New York.

DLB: Dictionary of Literary Biography (Detroit: Bruccoli/Gale Research Co.).

EVN/Oral/Dawson: Fairrie L. Dawson, personal interview, Salt Lake City, 20 Dec. 1991.

EVN/Oral/Gray: Nathan Gray, personal interview, Salt Lake City, 20, 22 Dec. 1991.

EVN/Oral/Kelly: Marcella Kelly, personal interview, Salt Lake City, 18 Dec. 1991.

EVN/Oral/C.Thornton: Clarence Thornton, personal interview, Salt Lake City, 21 Dec. 1991.

EVN/Oral/G. Thornton: Gladys Thornton, personal interview, Salt Lake City, 23 Dec. 1991.

HB/Oral/Nugent: Richard Bruce Nugent, interview trans., Hatch-Billops Collection, New York, 4 Apr. 1982.

Howard/ALP: Alain Locke Papers. Moorland-Spingarn Research Center, Howard University, Washington, D.C.

Infants: Wallace Thurman, *Infants of the Spring* (1932; Boston: Northeastern UP, 1992).

Jigger: Richard Bruce Nugent, *Gentleman Jigger,* unpub. ms. 122 pp./ unpub. ts. 84 pp., n.d.; external evidence suggests 1930. RNP.

Jigger/Sect.1: Richard Bruce Nugent, fictional rendering of Wallace Thurman's family history, unpub. ts. 6 pp. n.d.; external evidence suggests 1930. RNP.

JWJ: James Weldon Johnson Memorial Collection. Beinecke Rare Book and Manuscript Library Collection, Yale University.

JWJ/CVVP: Carl Van Vechten Papers. James Weldon Johnson Memorial Collection. Beinecke Rare Book and Manuscript Library, Yale University.

JWJ/DPP: Dorothy Peterson Papers. James Weldon Johnson Memorial Collection. Beinecke Rare Book and Manuscript Library, Yale University.

JWJ/HJP: Harold Jackman Papers. James Weldon Johnson Memorial Collection. Beinecke Rare Book and Manuscript Library, Yale University.

JWJ/LHP: Langston Hughes Papers. James Weldon Johnson Memorial Collection. Beinecke Rare Book and Manuscript Library, Yale University.

JWJ/WTP: Wallace Thurman Papers. James Weldon Johnson Memorial Collection. Beinecke Rare Book and Manuscript Library, Yale University.

JWJ/WTP/Ms.1: Wallace Thurman, one of two autobiographical sketches, untitled, unpub. ms. 2 pp., n.d.; internal evidence suggests 1929. JWJ/WTP.

LC/Oral/Nugent: Richard Bruce Nugent, interview, David Levering Lewis, Sept. 1974, May 1977, Library of Congress, Washington D.C.

Los Angeles/FJP: Fay M. Jackson Memorial Collection. Los Angeles.

Negro Life: Wallace Thurman, *Negro Life in New York's Harlem: A Lively Picture of a Popular and Interesting Section* (Girard: Haldeman-Julius, Little Blue Book 494, 1928). Previously published under the same title in the *Haldeman-Julius Quarterly,* Oct., Nov., Dec., 1927.

NYPL/CVVP: Carl Van Vechten Papers. New York Public Library, New York.

Oregon/WRP: William Jourdan Rapp Papers. University of Oregon, Eugene.

Radcliffe/DWP: Dorothy West Papers. Radcliffe College, Cambridge, MA.

Radcliffe/Oral/West: Dorothy West, interview trans., Radcliffe College, 6 May 1978.

RNP: Richard Bruce Nugent Papers. Private Collection of Dr. Thomas Wirth, Elizabeth N.J.

RNP/Bio: Richard Bruce Nugent, *Wallace Thurman Ex-editor: A Biography,* unpub. ms. 1 p., n.d. RNP.

RNP/Notes: Notes by Dr. Thomas Wirth summarizing meetings and telephone conversations with Richard Bruce Nugent, dating from 1981 and 1983. RNP.

RNP/Tapes: 15 audio-taped, 90 minute interviews with Richard Bruce Nugent dating from 1983. RNP.

SLC Directory: Salt Lake City Directory.

"Stepchild": Wallace Thurman, "Notes on a Stepchild," one of two autobiographical sketches, unpub. ts. 10 pp., n.d.; external evidence suggests 1929, included in "Aunt Hagar's Children." JWJ/WTP.

Tulane/CCP: Countee Cullen Papers. Amistad Research Center, Tulane University, New Orleans.

FURTHER READING

Bibliography

Sample, Maxine J. "Richard Bruce Nugent." In *African American Authors, 1745-1945: A Bio-Bibliographical Critical Sourcebook,* edited by Emmanuel S. Nelson, pp. 349-52. Westport, Conn.: Greenwood Press, 2000.

Provides a brief biography in addition to a bibliography of sources on Nugent.

Criticism

Balashaw, Maria. "'Black Was White': Urbanity, Passing, and the Spectacle of Harlem." *Journal of American Studies* 33, no. 2 (1999): 307-22.

Analyzes Nugent's writing along with that of Rudolph Fisher and Nella Larsen to illuminate the issues of modernity and subjectivity in Harlem Renaissance literature.

Cobb, Michael L. "Insolent Racing, Rough Narrative: The Harlem Renaissance's Impolite Queers." *Callaloo* 23, no. 1 (2000): 328-51.

Focuses on Nugent's treatment of beauty and Black male homosexuality in "Smoke, Lilies, and Jade."

McBreen, Ellen. "Biblical Gender Bending in Harlem: The Queer Performance of Nugent's *Salome.*" *Art Journal* 57, no. 3 (1998): 22-28.

Addresses Nugent's artistic depictions of Salome and the influence of Oscar Wilde on his work, emphasizing the themes of gender and identity.

Silberman, Seth Clark. "Looking for Richard Bruce Nugent and Wallace Henry Thurman: Reclaiming Black Male Same-Sexualities in the New Negro Movement." *In Process: A Graduate Student Journal of African-American and African Diasporan Literature and Culture* 1 (1996): 53-73.

Compares Nugent's treatment of homosexuality in the short story "Smoke, Lilies, and Jade" to that of Thurman in Infants of the Spring and The Blacker the Berry.

OTHER SOURCES FROM GALE:

Additional coverage of Nugent's life and career is contained in the following sources published by the Gale Group: *Black Writers,* Ed. 1; *Contemporary Authors,* Vol. 125; *Dictionary of Literary Biography,* Vol. 51; *Gay & Lesbian Literature,* Vol. 2.

WILLIS RICHARDSON

(1889 - 1977)

American playwright, essayist, and editor.

Richardson was a pioneer of Black theater in America. He was driven by a desire to create a theater that would offer an authentic representation of African American experience and social conditions, and that would supplant the images of Blacks created by minstrel shows and other stereotypical characterizations. He was the first Black writer to have a Broadway production of a non-musical play mounted—his one-act play, *The Chip Woman's Fortune* (produced in 1923)—and the first to compile, edit, and write collections of plays for children. Along with W. E. B. Du Bois, Richardson believed that theater should be educational, even propagandistic for a righteous cause, and he was influential in encouraging African American drama through the essays he published on Black theater and through his many plays, which were available for performance in theaters, schools, and by civic and church groups.

BIOGRAPHICAL INFORMATION

Richardson was born in Wilmington, North Carolina, but his parents moved to Washington, D.C., after the 1898 riots in Wilmington. In Washington, Richardson attended the first African American public high school in the United States, the M Street School (later called Dunbar High School). There his English teacher, Mary Burrill, a playwright herself, encouraged him to write and showed his work to Howard University professor Alain Locke, a primary figure in the Harlem Renaissance movement. Angelina Grimké also taught English at the school and took an interest in Richardson's writing. Seeing a performance of her play *Rachel* (1916) encouraged Richardson's ambition to become a playwright. He did not, however, depend solely on playwrighting for his livelihood. In 1911 Richardson began working in the U.S. Bureau of Engraving and Printing in Washington, D.C., remaining there until his retirement in 1954. He married Mary Ellen Jones in 1914, and they had three children. Richardson died in 1977.

MAJOR WORKS

Richardson's first plays were four one-act children's works—*The Children's Teasure* (1921), *The Dragon's Tooth* (1921), *The Gypsy's Finger Ring* (1921), and *The King's Dilemma* (1921)—published in *Brownie's Book,* a magazine founded by W. E. B. Du Bois. Incorporating realistic detail and techniques borrowed from the fairy-tale genre, these works were mostly didactic, intended to teach universal brotherhood. *The Deacon's Awakening* (1920), the first play Richardson wrote for adults, deals with the theme of women's right to vote. Richardson's most famous play, *The Chip*

Woman's Fortune, which had a pioneering run on Broadway in 1923, is a domestic folk drama which highlights an unjust jail sentence and an unfair job furlough. Richardson also developed and elucidated his ideas for an African American theater in a series of four articles written for *Opportunity* magazine in 1924 and 1925. He put these ideas into practice as a playwright, as director of the Little Theater group in Washington, D.C., and through his personal contact with African American drama professors, notably Locke. Richardson's other plays—*Mortgaged* (1924), *The Broken Banjo* (1925), *Compromise* (1925), and *The Flight of the Natives* (1927) among them—are likewise one-act domestic dramas that derive from African American folk tradition, stress a sense of community, and teach positive values. In addition, Richardson edited three anthologies of drama—two of which were of his own works, and one that included the plays of other Black dramatists.

CRITICAL RECEPTION

Despite the fact that his work of the 1920s and beyond had an important influence on the development of Black theater, and that *The Chip Woman's Fortune* was praised in a 1923 review in the *New York Times* as "a wholly convincing transcript of everyday character," Richardson rather quickly fell into obscurity. Christine Gray Rauchfuss has written, "[t]he man who was at one time considered the hope and promise of black drama, whose work had been in great demand by little-theater groups and drama clubs . . . died remembered by few others than his family and African American theater historians." Yet Richardson's plays enjoyed a revival in the late 1960s and the 1970s, with several of his works republished and performed by African American theater groups. By the turn of the present century scholars were beginning to recognize Richardson's importance, but less often for his individual dramatic accomplishments than because, in Helene Keysser-Frank's words, he was "the first black writer to make a serious commitment to drama for and about black life."

PRINCIPAL WORKS

"The Hope of a Negro Drama" (essay) 1919

The Deacon's Awakening (play) 1920

The Children's Treasure (juvenilia) 1921

The Dragon's Tooth (juvenilia) 1921

The Gypsy's Finger Ring (juvenilia) 1921

The King's Dilemma (juvenilia) 1921

The Chip Woman's Fortune (play) 1923

Mortgaged (play) 1924

"The Negro and the Stage" (essay) 1924

The Broken Banjo (play) 1925

Compromise (play) 1925

The Fall of the Conjurer (play) 1925

"The Negro Audience" (essay) 1925

The Bootblack Lover (play) 1926

Rooms for Rent (play) 1926

The Flight of the Natives (play) 1927

The House of Sham (play) 1929

The Idle Head (play) 1929

Plays and Pageants from the Life of the Negro [editor] (plays) 1930

Sacrifice Travels, Myths, and Legends in the New World (play) 1930

The Black Horseman (play) 1931

Negro History in Thirteen Plays [editor, with May Miller] (plays) 1935

Miss or Mrs. (play) 1941

The King's Dilemma and Other Plays for Children (juvenilia) 1956

GENERAL COMMENTARY

PATSY B. PERRY (ESSAY DATE 1987)

SOURCE: Perry, Patsy B. "Willis Richardson." *Dictionary of Literary Biography,* Vol. 51: *Afro-American Writers of the Harlem Renaissance to 1940,* edited by Trudier Harris, pp. 236–44. Detroit, MI: Gale Research Company, 1987.

In the following essay, Perry traces Richardson's life and career, emphasizing his role as a pioneer in Black theater in America.

Emerging at the beginning of the New Negro Renaissance, Willis Richardson wrote serious drama portraying the lives of black people. Truly a pioneer, he was the first black to have a Broadway production of a nonmusical, one-act play—***The Chip Woman's Fortune*** (produced in 1923)—and the first to compile, edit, and write collections of black plays for young people: ***Plays and Pageants from the Life of the Negro*** (1930) and, with May Miller, ***Negro History in Thirteen Plays*** (1935). Richardson wrote three of the twelve dramas in ***Plays and Pageants*** and five of those in ***Negro History in Thirteen Plays.*** In addition he encouraged others to write and to produce "Negro plays," and in all of his work, including children's plays and critical essays on contemporary theater, he attempted to interest his readers in high Negro drama which he described as "a mine of pure gold."

Convinced that neither the stereotypical "darkies" of white dramatists nor sterile Negro characters like those of Angelina Grimké's *Rachel* (1920) came close to capturing the richness, diversity, and beauty of his race, Richardson wrote forty-two individual plays that ranged from fairy tales of the future and romanticized actions of famous black leaders to realistic representations of ordinary blacks who suffer from their own weaknesses or society's shortcomings. Richardson acted to prevent the consequences of a challenge posed in 1926 by W. E. B. DuBois: "Suppose the only Negro who survived some centuries hence was the Negro painted by white Americans in the novels and essays they have written. What would people in a hundred years say of black Americans?" To Richardson's credit, after only fifty years, more or less, his pioneer efforts have resulted in dramatizations of the soul of black people, a soul "truly worth showing."

Willis Richardson was born on 5 November 1889, in Wilmington, North Carolina, the son of Willis Wilder and Agnes Ann Harper Richardson. Summarizing his early years for *Crisis* magazine, Richardson said his family moved to Washington, D.C., following the Wilmington riots of 1898 and that he was "Graduated from the M St. [later Dunbar] High School in 1910." While still in high school, he became interested in drama and was encouraged by his English teacher, Mary Burrill, who was writing and staging her own plays. His serious study of the drama was delayed, however, while he established himself as a government employee and began a family.

In 1911 he became a clerk in the U.S. Bureau of Engraving and Printing in Washington, D.C., and on 1 September 1914, he married Mary Ellen Jones. The couple had three children: Jean Paula in 1916; Shirley Antonella in 1918; and Noel Justine in 1920.

According to Richarson, in about 1916 he "saw a performance of Angelina Grimké's 'Rachel' and by that was influenced to study the technique of the Drama." Subsequently from 1916 to 1918 he was enrolled in a correspondence course in poetry, drama, and the novel, after which he "began to write plays." Among the first of these were four one-act children's dramas published in the *Brownies' Book,* a monthly magazine founded by DuBois and designed especially for "Children of the Sun": ***The King's Dilemma*** (December 1920), ***The Gypsy's Finger Ring*** (March 1921), ***The Children's Treasure*** (June 1921), and ***The Dragon's Tooth*** (October 1921). In ***The Children's Treasure,*** Richardson employs realistic details to teach a lesson in charity as five children, including the most selfish one among them, contribute their savings toward the rent of a poor neighbor facing eviction. In the other three plays he focuses on the future and employs the techniques of the fairy tale. In ***The King's Dilemma,*** Richardson dramatizes the beginning of democracy succeeding rule by kings. ***The Gypsy's Finger Ring*** is about the age of freedom following the periods of chattel slavery and peonage; ***The Dragon's Tooth*** projects a future time of love and brotherhood to be realized through children. The plays were in keeping with the major purpose of the *Brownies' Book,* which was to "teach Universal Love and Brotherhood for all little folk—black and brown and yellow and white."

In sharp contrast to the ideal subjects of his children's plays, Richardson's first one-act play for adults, ***The Deacon's Awakening,*** deals with an immediate sociopolitical concern, women's efforts to engage in their newly won right to vote. The protagonist, David Jones, a church deacon, abandons his crusade to identify for disciplinary action all aspiring women voters when he discovers that his wife and daughter are organizers and active members of the Voting Society. Although ***The Deacon's Awakening*** was published in *Crisis* in November 1920 and performed in 1921 by the St. Paul Players of Minnesota, it brought little recognition to its author. Richardson described the stage production as "not much of a success" and himself as still "unheard of" in 1921. In retrospect, however, he should be credited with exploring what was, in 1921, a highly volatile subject in words which are familiar even today. Readers can clearly understand Mrs. Jones's position when she outlines the unfair treatment of girls from birth onward and protests further denial of their opportunities. Classified as a domestic protest drama, ***The Deacon's Awakening*** is one of a group of plays through which Richardson expresses concern about enfranchisement, equal access to education, and employment opportunities. He skillfully blends these subjects in a scene during which Deacon Jones and Sol threaten to remove their daughters from Howard University as their punishment for having joined the Voting

Society. Mrs. Jones intervenes with a convincing argument in favor of women's rights of citizenship, education, and economic independence.

In 1923 Richardson gained recognition with the production of ***The Chip Woman's Fortune*** in Chicago, Washington, and New York. In New York it opened at Harlem's Lafayette Theatre on 7 May 1923 and, after eight performances, moved to Broadway, where it premiered at the Frazee Theatre on 15 May 1923. Director Raymond O'Neil's Ethiopian Art Players presented it with Oscar Wilde's *Salome* and a jazz rendition of Shakespeare's *Comedy of Errors.* Recalling the steps which led to Broadway, Richardson stated in a March 1972 interview that: the Ethiopian Art Players originally were organized in Chicago "and they put on Negro plays, but they didn't know any Negro playwrights, or black playwrights, or whatever you want to call them, so they wrote to *Crisis* and Dr. DuBois put me in touch. They put on Oscar Wilde's *Salome* and my play ***The Chip Woman's Fortune.*** They went to New York and played at the Frazier [*sic*] Theater and the reviews were so good that they sold lots of tickets. . . ."

Perhaps it is more accurate to say, however, that the reviews were mixed. On 8 May 1923, *New York Times* drama critic John Corbin wrote: "As a curtain raiser to *Salome,* . . . ***The Chip Woman's Fortune,*** a one-acter by Willis Richardson, was offered. The piece is trifling and at times amusing." On 20 May 1923, Corbin had only praise for Richardson's play, especially for its development of characters: "***The Chip Woman's Fortune*** . . . is an unaffected and wholly convincing transcript of everyday character. No one is glorified or otherwise tricked out to please; no one is blackened to serve as a 'dramatic' contrast. I am referring, of course, to points of essential character, not to that matter of walnut stain. . . . Willis Richardson has limned half a dozen characters candidly, sympathetically, truly." It is futile to make conjectures about the reasons for Corbin's reevaluation of ***The Chip Woman's Fortune.*** The facts that the play is still anthologized and that it can be read seriously support his second, more detailed assessment of it as a "convincing transcript." Briefly it is the story of Aunt Nancy, who has maintained herself as a member of Silas's household by collecting bits of wood and coal for fuel and by nursing Silas's invalid wife. Faced with the loss of both his job and the prized Victrola for which he has failed to make payments, Silas asks Aunt Nancy's help. She explains, however, that the money which she has saved is for her son, Jim, who is soon to be released from prison. While they are engaged in this discussion, Jim arrives and generously divides Aunt Nancy's fortune with Silas and his family who had taken care of her during his absence. While the play ends on a relatively happy note, there is mild protest in the suggestions that both Jim's imprisonment and Silas's furlough from his job may have been unjust. Describing it as a "miniature folk drama," editor Burns Mantle included ***The Chip Woman's Fortune*** in *The Best Plays of 1922-23* and *The Year Book of the Drama in America.*

Though Richardson was never again to see one of his works on Broadway, he became an influential playwright among theater groups in black high schools, colleges, churches, and communities. As early as 1919 Richardson issued the call for a national Negro theater "able to send a company of Negro Players with Negro Plays across our own continent [and] . . . to the artistic peoples of Europe." While citing the Irish National Theater as an excellent model, he reminded his readers that the Irish possessed no richer resources than did black Americans. He himself used black folk materials and urged the development of a sophisticated theater audience that would respect and sustain the national theater he envisioned. In four essays written for *Opportunity* magazine, he defined and developed his criteria for serious drama. In **"The Negro and the Stage"** (October 1924), he held that "the theater should always, and seriously, be considered as an educational institution side by side with the school." In **"The Negro Audience"** (April 1925), he outlined the following points as "things which should matter . . . if the Negro drama is to prosper and become 'a thing of beauty and a joy forever': whether the characters are well drawn, whether the dialogue is natural, whether the ending is consistent and whether the whole thing is interesting and logical." Focusing on "the peasant class of the Negro group" in **"Characters"** (June 1925), Richardson described that class as being "different and interesting," important qualities for theater. Finally, in **"The Unpleasant Play"** (September 1925), he challenged the Negro writer to "make his audience hear the truth, or nothing." Recognized as "the great spirit encouraging the creation of a Negro Theater movement," Richardson supplied original plays for black producers; directed the Little Theater group in Washington, D.C.; and established contacts with professors of drama, chiefly Alain Locke and Montgomery Gregory of Howard University.

On 29 March, 1924, the Howard Players produced ***Mortgaged,*** Richardson's one-act domestic drama exploring the friction between the two Fields brothers. John, a struggling research scientist, is made to feel great indebtedness to Tom, an unscrupulous businessman, who has financed several of John's research projects. When John learns that his chemical formula has been purchased, he offers to underwrite Harvard University expenses for Tom's two children, a somewhat embarrassing offer since Tom had earlier agreed to send John's son to Harvard only if John left his research laboratory for another job. In their anthology *The New Negro Renaissance* (1975) Arthur P. Davis and Michael Peplow included ***Mortgaged*** under the heading "Best-Foot-Forward Literature," a school of writing which emphasized progressive ideas. Stressing the value of scientific contributions over materialistic interests, ***Mortgaged*** is a prime example of this tradition based on the talented-tenth philosophy of DuBois. In May 1925 ***Mortgaged*** was again performed in a drama tournament by the Dunbar Dramatic Club of Plainfield, N.J. Recalling the event, Richardson made the following evaluation: "The rare thing about this occasion was that out of the eight or ten clubs producing plays, one Negro club produced a Negro play by a Negro author. The play, which I consider one of my poorest, gained fourth place among some of the best American one-acters."

The Broken Banjo, produced by the Krigwa players in New York City on 1 August 1925, is another of Richardson's one-act domestic dramas. The main character, Matt Turner, is obsessed with his banjo to the point of neglecting his wife, Emma. His meager existence—having been forced to live for a time on Emma's wages and currently reduced to purchasing secondhand shoes for her—affords him little comfort. His only joy is the banjo, which he plays at every opportunity. He is equally zealous in his attempts to rid his household of Sam, his wife's parasitic brother, and Adam, her cousin. During one of their dreaded visits, Sam accidentally breaks Matt's banjo as he tries to take it away from Adam. Sam narrowly escapes Matt's angry assault with the startling announcement that he had witnessed the murder of "old man Shelton." Until this time, Matt had thought that his unintentional but lethal blow to Shelton had gone unobserved. Matt struck out in anger when, in parrying blows, Shelton had shattered his banjo. Now a second time, Matt's beloved banjo is broken. Bereft of music, both literally and figuratively, Matt leaves with a police officer to whom Sam has revealed details of the Shelton murder. In its 30 October 1925 issue, *Crisis* announced that ***The Broken Banjo*** had won the seventy-five-dollar first prize in the Amy Spingarn Contest in Literature and Art. Eugene O'Neill, who served as one of the contest evaluators, commented: "I am glad to hear that the judges all agreed on ***The Broken Banjo*** and that the play was so successfully staged. Willis Richardson should certainly continue working in this field." *Crisis* published this play in its issues for February and March 1926. Following its production in 1934 by the Atlanta University Summer Theatre, the play earned the following comment from Sterling Brown: "the acting of the entire cast had a zest to it that gave dramatic body to a play that in the reading had seemed somewhat thin. There was no question of the play's taking."

In 1925 Richardson finished ***Compromise,*** another one-act domestic drama. It is the story of two families—the black Lees and the white Carters—and the tragic events which the Lees suffer at the hands of the Carters. Having "accidentally" killed Joe Lee, Ben Carter compromised with Joe's father, Jim Lee, by paying him $100, money with which Jim buys entough strong drink to kill himself. Seven years later, when Alec Lee discovers that Jack Carter has impregnated his sister, he breaks Jack's arm. In this situation, however, no compromise is possible; Ben Carter is "goin' to put the sheriff on" Alec. Though the curtain falls with Alec's mother vowing to save him, ***Compromise*** makes the point that for southern blacks in the 1920s there was no justice; their very lives were "compromised." ***Compromise*** was included in Alain Locke's *The New Negro* (1925), and Richardson described the drama as one in which he had "some confidence." It was the first produced by the Gilpin Players at Karamu House, Cleveland, Ohio, on 26 February 1925. Subsequently it was staged by the Krigwa Players in New York, on 3 May 1926, and by the Howard Players, on 8 April 1936.

Richardson's ***The Flight of the Natives*** and ***The Idle Head*** are two additional one-act dramas of the 1920s which explore racial dilemmas of past and present times. Produced by the Krigwa Players in Washington, D.C., on 7 May 1927, ***The Flight of the Natives*** describes the daring escape of six slaves from a South Carolina plantation in 1860. Having suffered lashings, the treachery of slave informers, and threats of being sold down the river, these slaves effect their escape by using their combined strengths. In a concise analysis of this drama, James Hatch cites two important features: Richardson's rejection of the "contented slave" image and his use of the "group protagonist" rather than a central hero whose chances of escape, under the watchful eyes of slavery, would have been slight. Indeed heroes or rebellious slaves paid for their status by being made "examples of" to frighten other slaves into submission. In ***The Idle Head*** (1929), Richardson continues his exploration of southern peonage. Through the time of this drama is some sixty years following the end of chattel slavery and the setting is the Broadus home rather than a slave cabin, George Broadus is far from being a free man. Admired by his mother for his natural independence, George is denied any demonstration of this manly trait; he is, in fact, blacklisted because he will not grin, bow, or answer to "Sambo." Unable to secure a job and feeling guilty about his inability to aid his mother, George pawns a valuable pin which a white woman had forgotten to remove from a garment sent to be laundered. As the curtain falls, he is carried off to jail—without regard to circumstances—in much the same way that an intractable slave was sold down the river for any similar infraction of his master's law. Whether or not Richardson consciously drew parallels, it is clear that these two dramas make a poignant statement that conditions for southern blacks had not improved much since slavery time. ***The Idle Head*** was published in April 1929, in the *Carolina* magazine, a literary publication of the University of North Carolina at Chapel Hill.

In 1930, at the request of Carter G. Woodson, founder of the Association for the Study of Negro Life and History, Richardson compiled his first anthology ***Plays and Pageants from the Life of the Negro.*** In the introduction he cites Woodson as "the real editor of the pageants" and provides evaluative comments on the contributors, including Thelma Duncan, Maud Cuney-Hare, John Matheus, May Miller, Edward J. McCoo, Inez M. Burke, Dorothy C. Gwinn, and Frances Gunner. Richardson also classifies the works according to theme, temper, and level of difficulty, assuring his audience of having collected "the best material of its kind, . . . plays and pageants suitable for every reasonable need of School, Church, or Little Theater Group." Among the plays Richardson included three of his own that represented his wide range: the children's fairy tale ***The King's Dilemma***; ***The House of Sham,*** a domestic satire; and ***The Black Horseman,*** a historical drama. In ***The King's Dilemma,*** a white prince, having discovered equality in love and friendship, refuses the king's command to give up his black friend; he is happy when the kingdom is dissolved and the people are given power to govern themselves. First produced in the Washington, D.C., public schools, ***The King's Dilemma*** won the Public School Prize on 21 May 1926. ***The House of Sham,*** neatly summarized in its title, satirizes the exploitative practices and shallow strivings of a middle-class black family headed by John Cooper, who admits to having stolen and done "everything else crooked" in his efforts to appear wealthy. In short he is proven to be bankrupt both materially and morally. John Cooper's opposite can be found in ***The Black Horseman,*** a one-act drama picturing King Massinissa as the embodiment of nobility, bravery, and steadfastness. Ruler of Numidia, Africa, in 204 B.C., King Massinissa resists the treacherous bribes of a Carthaginian prince and saves his nation. This drama was first produced on 12 October 1931 by the Playground Athletic League of Baltimore, Maryland.

In 1935 Richardson published five additional one-act historical dramas in his second anthology, ***Negro History in Thirteen Plays,*** which he edited with May Miller. In the preface Richardson and Miller state that they "have not attempted to reproduce definitive history, but have sought to create the atmosphere of a time past or the portrait of a memorable figure." Richardson's plays, ***Antonio Maceo, Attucks, the Martyr, In Menelik's Court,*** and ***Near Calvary,*** do indeed provide memorable portraits, but, perhaps more important, they epitomize the sterling qualities which Richardson saw as intrinsic in black people. Only in ***The Elder Dumas,*** Richardson's fifth drama in this collection, does he present a prominent black figure in unflattering terms.

In both ***Antonio Maceo*** and ***Attucks, the Martyr*** brave warriors die in the service of their countries. General Maceo, a Cuban freedom fighter, leads a successful rebellion against Spain but is assassinated when his unscrupulous physician betrays him. Crispus Attucks, a fugitive from slavery, leads an attack against British soldiers and is the first to be killed in America's fight for independence from England. Though ***In Menelik's Court*** and ***Near Calvary*** do not have clearly focused battlegrounds, they both support Richardson's insistence upon the bravery of black men through explicit comments or through specific actions. For example, in characterizing his people, Menelik II, Emperor of Abyssinia, says, "We do not betray our enemies when they trust us. Our hands are brown and we play a fair game—always above the table." Later, when it is revealed that one of the servants has turned traitor, Menelik contrasts him with the Italian spies and reminds him that nothing was expected from the Italians "but everything was expected of [him], an Abyssinian." In ***Near Calvary*** Simon bravely carries Jesus' cross, and Laban, when questioned by Caesar's soldiers, admits his belief in Jesus despite the fact that his confession could result in his death. In sum it is Richardson's point that "When men are black and brave they are never traitors."

In ***The Elder Dumas,*** however, Richardson reveals the unseemly practices of a writer grown careless but, at the same time, overly sensitive to criticism. Alexandre Dumas pére, the French mulatto playwright and novelist, is charged with writing hurriedly, representing as his own the ideas of other writers, and sacrificing sound creative achievements for quick financial profits. Perhaps Richardson implies an even greater charge against the elder Dumas, for he presents his character as being more interested in physical retaliation against the critic than in an honest assessment of his criticism.

In 1956, after more than two decades without a major drama publication or production, Richardson issued his third and final collection, ***The King's Dilemma and Other Plays for Children.*** In this collection he included ***The Dragon's Tooth, The Gypsy's Finger Ring, The King's Dilemma,*** and the Easter play ***Near Calvary.*** Emphasizing the importance of love, racial harmony, justice, and equality, these children's dramas bring Richardson back to his original purpose and audience. Perhaps weary of trying to influence mature readers and disappointed that black professional actors and producers had ignored his works, Richardson came to believe that children would be the hope for a world in which a national black drama might flourish.

During the last decade of his life, however, Richardson witnessed a general revival in black drama and a specific interest in his contributions. Between 1969 and 1975, for instance, several of his most popular dramas were republished, including ***The Chip Woman's Fortune*** in Lindsay Patterson's *Anthology of the American Negro* (1967) and in Darwin Turner's *Black Drama in America* (1971). ***The Broken Banjo*** was collected in Richard Barksdale and Kenneth Kinnamon's *Black Writers of America* (1972); ***The Idle Head*** and ***The Flight of the Natives*** appeared in Hatch and Ted Shine's *Black Theater, U.S.A.* (1974); and ***Mortgaged*** was included in Davis and Peplow's *New Negro Renaissance* (1975). Moreover, as a part of the Oral Black Theatre History Collection of City College, New York, Richardson was interviewed in March 1972 by Hatch and his assistants. And in Wilmington, North Carolina, Richardson's birthplace, a community theater group was established in 1974 as the Willis Richardson Players. Just a few days after Richardson's death, his achievements were cited at AUDELCO's Fifth Annual Theatre Awards program on 21 November 1977 in Harlem, New York. Efforts to reintroduce and recognize more fully Richardson's pioneering contributions signaled the arrival of that sophisticated theater audience which he had envisioned at the start of his career.

FREDA SCOTT GILES (ESSAY DATE 1996)

SOURCE: Giles, Freda Scott. "Willis Richardson and Eulalie Spence: Dramatic Voices of the Harlem Renaissance." *American Drama* 5, no. 2 (1996): 1-22.

In the following essay, Giles examines the dramatic techniques used by Richardson and Eulalie Spence to achieve a realistic depiction of African Americans' experience on the stage.

Though the Harlem Renaissance, a seminal period in African American arts and letters which reached its zenith between the end of World War I and the advent of the Great Depression, has left a lasting literary legacy, relatively little is written, outside of scholarly circles, of the drama which that era produced. For example, a recently published study intended for a general audience, *The Harlem Renaissance; Hub of African-American Culture, 1920-1930* by Steven Watson (New York: Pantheon, 1995), devoted less than two of its 180 pages of text to non-musical drama. There are a number of possible reasons for this neglect. Perhaps most significantly the fact that while the necessary infrastructure for the production of serious drama, in the form of African American professional and little theatres, was in the process of nearly exponential growth, production opportunities remained too limited to allow much opportunity for developing African-American playwrights. Very few African-American playwrights were given widespread attention nor were their works printed for general distribution in other than African-American journals. The mainstream professional theatre had made some accomodation to the African-American performer, because the Euro-American playwrights of this time were exploring what they felt to be the African-American experience in their quest for a new American drama. Producers looked to Euro-American playwrights like Paul Green (*In Abra-*

ham's Bosom) and Eugene O'Neill (*The Emperor Jones, All God's Chillun Got Wings*) for serious drama on the "authentic" black experience in the United States.

The first non-musical play of African-American authorship to reach Broadway was Willis Richardson's ***The Chip Woman's Fortune*** in 1923. Though there were literally hundreds of non-musical Broadway productions during the decade of the 1920's, only three other non-musical plays of African-American authorship were produced there: *Appearances* by Garland Anderson (1925); *Meek Mose* by Frank Wilson (1928); and *Harlem* by Wallace Thurman in collaboration with a Euro-American playwright, William Jourdan Rapp (1929). In 1927, Eulalie Spence's *Fool's Errand* was presented on Broadway in a Little Theatre competition and won publication by Samuel French; this and ***The Chip Woman's Fortune,*** which was published in a collection of one-act plays by Appleton (*Fifty More One-Act Plays,* edited by Frank Shay) in 1928, were the only plays of African-American authorship exposed to Broadway which were printed by mainstream presses in their own time. Not that Broadway production or mainstream publication validate the merits of these playwrights' works, but pointedly, until recent years, the exclusion of these works left behind by the playwrights of the Harlem Renaissance has made them less readily accessible to the public than those of poets, novelists, and essayists of the same era. Additionally, the fact that African-American theatre critics of the time, such as Theophilus Lewis and Romeo Daugherty, have been largely ignored by most theatre historians adds to the relative obscurity of the drama they critiqued.

Another possible reason why Harlem Renaissance drama is less talked about is that the dramatists, catering mainly to the needs of little theatres and African-American journals, wrote primarily in the one-act form; one-acts were popular at the time and believed to be more suitable for the amateur companies, black and white, which were springing up all over the country. Though a good one-act play is as difficult to write as any other dramatic form, it seems to carry less critical weight in the present day.

Most important among the reasons for the underrepresentation of the drama in the literary canon of the Harlem Renaissance is the possibility that in the eyes of history, Harlem Renaissance drama has been found wanting primarily for its perceived lack of political commitment. During the Black Arts Movement of the 1960's, when overt nationalism was stressed as an essential value in all forms of cultural expression, Larry Neal, one of the most highly regarded African-American theatre critics of the time, surmised that the Harlem Renaissance was "essentially a failure" because "it did not address itself to the mythology and the life styles of the Black community" and did not "link itself concretely to the struggles of the community" (Neal 39). This evaluation reflects the ongoing, long standing debate over the nature and definition of an African-American aesthetic and the drama which should be created from it. It might be fair at this time to take another look at Harlem Renaissance drama to see if this judgement against it is overly harsh. One way of doing so would be to examine the aesthetic choices in representative works by two of the dramatists most produced by African-American little theatre companies during the 1920's, Willis Richardson and Eulalie Spence. These two playwrights made major contributions to the development of an African-American drama within the context of intense debate and aesthetic confusion—the necessary chaos which precedes the concretization of a movement.

During the period in which it was produced, Harlem Renaissance drama was viewed as an essential cultural element by the movement's intellectual leadership, not only because an effective counterattack against the overwhelmingly powerful minstrel stereotypes imbedded in the American consciousness was needed, but also because it seemed that a window of opportunity had finally opened which would enable African-Americans to internally and externally value the culture they had created as African people immersed in European cultures in the New World. Theatre, in the Euro-American sense of the word, was not directly connected to this culture.[1] In the mainstream commercial theatre, which catered to the prejudices and predispositions of white audiences, the African-American had not only been marginalized as character to a subordinate stereotype on the stage but also relegated as audience to a seat in the balcony of the theatre itself to insure nearly total invisibility. Black stock companies, which operated in theatres in black communities such as those at the Pekin Theatre in Chicago or the Lafayette Theatre in New York, primarily reproduced for black patrons the offerings of the commercial white theatre. Little had been done to build an inherently African-American theatre. The Harlem Renaissance signalled those interested in building such a theatre that the time was now right.

The intellectual leadership of the Harlem Renaissance thought that drama could serve an important purpose as cultural ambassador to white America and also act as a conduit for indigenous African-American culture in a tradition similar to the emergence of folk culture in Ireland's Abbey Theatre or the Moscow Art Theatre. However, those who were attempting to frame this new Negro theatre became deeply divided over the mixture of aesthetic and ideological elements involved. W. E. B. DuBois and Alain Locke, two of black drama's godfathers at this time, embodied the debate, and represented divisions which have persisted to the present day. In DuBois' view, "All art is propaganda," and drama should present social issues for open debate. DuBois, a great admirer of the "problem plays" of George Bernard Shaw, saw black drama as a weapon to be wielded against oppression. In pursuit of this goal, DuBois instituted a literary contest in *The Crisis,* the journal he edited for the NAACP; he tried to start a pageant association, having written and produced a black history pageant, "The Star of Ethiopia," which had been viewed by thousands in New York, Philadelphia, Washington, and Los Angeles; he founded a little Negro theatre in Harlem, the Krigwa Players; and finally, he published a manifesto declaring that there must be a national Negro theatre, and it must be "by us . . . for us . . . about us . . . and near us" (DuBois 134).

Locke agreed on the need for a national theatre which expressed authentic African-American culture, but he thought that African-American drama should avoid political issues and instead exhibit unique aspects of its culture within themes thought to be "universal." Locke favored folk plays which did not foreground racial issues.

Though both thought the African-American playwright could tell the story better, neither DuBois nor Locke felt that white playwrights should avoid the African-American as a dramatic subject. DuBois corresponded with Eugene O'Neill and included him among *The Crisis* contest judges; contest rules, however, stipulated that all entrants be African-American. When Locke published the first anthology devoted to the African-American as a dramatic subject, *Plays of Negro Life,* he included plays by five African-American and five Euro-American playwrights. Neither Locke nor DuBois looked further than the European traditional and experimental forms which had already been created for the structure of the drama of African-American life; perhaps this Euro-centrism contributed to the confusion over what African-American drama should be.

In addition to the heated arguments over the nature, purpose, and audience for African-American drama, cultural leaders debated whether there were enough unique features in African-American culture to engender a distinctly African-American art form. In *The Nation,* conservative African-American critic George Schuyler declared that the black American was nothing more than a "lamp-blacked Anglo-Saxon," so thoroughly assimilated into Euro-American culture, particularly the further he/she climbed the economic ladder to the middle class, as to be indistinguishable from the Euro-American except by physical features (Schuyler 662). He was answered in the same magazine by Langston Hughes, an African-American poet who would later become a significant figure in black theatre, that the perceived idiomatic idiosyncracies of Black culture, such as the blues, jazz, spirituals, and modes of vocal expression were in reality the retentions of African culture upon which a drama of African-American experience could be built. He added that the Black artist should not be burdened in his/her pursuit of the truths of Black life by restrictions based on the fears and prejudices of audiences and critics, no matter what their color (Hughes 693-694).

According to James Weldon Johnson, who had written for the Broadway musical theatre with his brother, John Rosamond, the audience was another problem. In his essay "The Dilemma of the Double Audience," he describes the perceptions of the white audience and the black audience of what black life and black people were like as so different that plays had to be written with only one or the other audience in mind. Catering to a white audience might bring financial rewards, but would most likely offend the black audience. Writing for the black audience, so sensitized to stereotyping that it was extremely self-conscious about images and issues projected on the stage, carried its own set of difficulties (Johnson 477). It was amid this maelstrom of issues that Willis Richardson and Eulalie Spence sought out an authentic voice for the African-American character in drama. They managed to please not only DuBois and Locke, but black and white audiences as well.

Prior to the publication of *Plays of Negro Life,* Locke had edited another seminal anthology, *The New Negro.* Among this collection of essays on all aspects of arts and letters, Locke included only one drama, ***Compromise,*** by Willis Richardson. ***Compromise*** illustrates the dilemma black play-

FROM THE AUTHOR

LETTER TO ALAIN LOCKE

. . . my family moved to Washington in August 1899 after the awful riot of the previous November. So I obtained the basis of my education in the high and secondary schools of this city. Whatever literary education I have (and I consider that more important than the other) I gained by years of reading and hard study of . . . Poetry, Drama, and the Novel. . . .

SOURCE: Willis Richardson, to Alain Locke, in a letter dated August 9, 1925, regarding the inclusion of Richardson's play *Compromise* in *The New Negro* anthology, August 9, 1925, Alain Locke Papers, Moorland-Springarn, Research Center, Howard University.

wrights faced when trying to write about African-American life: there was practically no way to separate political and social issues.

Compromise is a folk drama set in rural Maryland, in the kitchen of the Lee family. The main characters are Jane Lee, a widowed mother of three struggling to keep the family's farm afloat, and her white neighbor, Ben Carter. The lives of the Lees and the Carters had been entangled for over a generation. Some years prior to the action of the play, the well-to-do Ben accidently shot and killed Jane's eldest son. He had "compromised" with Jane's husband, Jim, and compensated the family with a hundred dollars for their loss. Jim drank himself to death with the money. Ben has now come to Jane to speak with her about her other son, Alec, who has grown to manhood and refuses to forget the killing. Jane shares her son's unrequited anger ("If ma old man had 'a' shot your boy Jack down out a tree like you done Joe, would you be so friendly? Would you be laughin' and grinnin' at us on the road?"), but she makes another compromise with Ben, that he will pay for the education of the remaining children. After Ben reluctantly agrees, it is revealed that his son has impregnated Jane's eldest daughter. Alec finds Ben's son and beats him in a fight, breaking his arm. Ben angrily calls off the deal and vows to send Alec to prison. The play closes with the family helping Alec to escape, as Jane laments, "I oughtn't 'a' compromised" (Locke, *New Negro* 168-195).

Without overt mention of race or racism, Richardson has revealed the effects of living in a social system in which the powerful act without fear of legal retribution and bend the system to crush the least act of protest by the powerless. The irony behind Ben's need to be smiled at by Alec is made perfectly clear. The victims recognize their position and have learned that compromise cannot buy safety. Yet Richardson was viewed as a non-political playwright.

Though Richardson (1889-1977) was born in Wilmington, North Carolina, most of his youth and adult life were spent in Washington, D.C., where he eventually found a career in the U.S. Bureau of Printing and Engraving. Richardson had been an avid theatre-goer from an early age, but when he saw the production of *Rachel,* a powerful anti-lynching drama by Angelina Grimke presented by the Drama Committee of the Washington branch of the NAACP in 1916, he was inspired to try his hand as a playwright. After study of his craft through a correspondence school (no other formalized study was available to him), he began submitting his work to W. E. B. DuBois at *The Crisis.* DuBois published a Richardson essay, **"The Hope of a Negro Drama,"** in the November 1919 issue, in which Richardson defined black drama as "the play that shows the soul of a people." Though he admired *Rachel,* he believed that its propagandistic themes and stilted, melodramatic structure were not the ideal. It is revealing that he selected *Three Plays for a Negro Theatre* by white playwright Ridgely Torrence, as closer to what black drama should be:

> When I say Negro plays, I do not mean merely plays with Negro characters. . . . Miss Grimke's *Rachel* is nearer the idea . . . it is called a propaganda play and a great portion of it shows the manner in which Negroes are treated by white people in the United States. That such a work is of service will be acknowledged by anyone who will examine any of the plays by Shaw, Galsworthy and Brieux. Still there is another kind of play; the play that shows the soul of a people . . . Mr. Ridgely Torrence has accomplished it. "Granny Maumee," "The Rider of Dreams," and "Simon the Cyrenian" are Negro plays; and we can never thank Mr. Torrence enough for the beginning of a movement we hope to continue
>
> (Richardson, **"Hope"** 339)

Torrence's all black cast plays had been produced on Broadway in 1917. They were critically, though not commercially, successful, and were generally viewed as a major step forward in the presentation of the African-American character onstage. Actually, Torrence wrote two versions, one for a black cast and one for a white cast, of one of the plays, *The Rider of Dreams*; the white cast version was published.

Richardson's first produced play was ***The Deacon's Awakening,*** (presented by The Players, a St. Paul, Minnesota, little theatre group, in 1921); the play had been published in *The Crisis* in 1920. Although the play avoided any references to racial issues and could be presented by a white cast, its focus is still political, as the central conflict concerns a deacon who vehemently opposes a women's suffrage group which has formed in his church, only to discover that his own wife and daughter are the group's leaders. Richardson, in fact, included some form of politically charged material in nearly all of his works, even the "neutral" folk dramas and children's plays.

In 1922, a white producer, Raymond O'Neil, organized a company of African-American actors which would eventually become known as the Ethiopian Art Players, and set out on a commercial tour. The bulk of the company's repertory consisted of plays by European playwrights, including Oscar Wilde, Moliere, George Buchner, and Shakespeare.

Richardson had sent two one-act plays to O'Neil, ***The Chip Woman's Fortune*** and ***The Broken Banjo*** (a somber folk drama in which a black man who has killed a white man in a fight is betrayed to the authorities by his brother-in-law), which O'Neil accepted for use as curtain raisers for the other plays. When the company played a short Broadway run in 1923, opening with an evening composed of ***The Chip Woman's Fortune*** and Wilde's *Salome,* Richardson became the first African-American author of a non-musical work to be seen in the leading venue for the commercial theatre in the United States. ***The Chip Woman's Fortune*** is notable for a number of other reasons.

First of all, it was a comedy, a genre often avoided by African-American playwrights of the era due to the fear that ethnic characters and humor would be misinterpreted as minstrel stereotypes. Although his play was misunderstood by some of the mainstream critics, Richardson proved that African-American characters could be placed in humorous situations without deprecation. He dramatized a black family which endured a domestic crisis and concomitant misunderstandings resolved through mutual cooperation and affection.

Silas, a porter, is the husband of Liza and father of eighteen-year-old Emma. The family has taken in a boarder, Aunt Nancy, who ekes out a living following coal wagons, collecting the coal chips which fall off and selling them. Aunt Nancy has recently nursed Liza through "a spell of sickness" through her knowledge of roots and herbs. She has also become a surrogate grandmother and confidante to Emma. The action of the play begins when Aunt Nancy returns from her work glowing with a secret. When Silas enters, he glumly informs the family that he has been temporarily laid off from his job. Though he is not indebted to the white storeowner who employs him, Silas is being punished for being in debt to another white storeowner: he's been unable to meet the payments on the family's one luxury, the victrola. Not only has he been laid off, but men are coming to repossess the victrola. Silas fears he may lose his job completely. Silas believes that Aunt Nancy has buried her savings in their back yard, and tries to persuade her to hand the money over. Aunt Nancy wants to help, but has been saving money to give to her son, who is due to be released from prison that very day. Silas questions her decision to sacrifice so greatly for a "jail bird," but Aunt Nancy cautions against sitting in judgement:

> Goin' to the pen ain't nothin.' Some o' the best men in the world's been to the pen. It ain't the goin' to the pen that counts, it's what you go there for. . . . If the Lord had a got locked up for stealin' somethin' or killin' somebody do you think people would be praisin' him like they do?
>
> (Hamalian 178)

Aunt Nancy does not fully excuse her son for responding violently when he found his girlfriend two-timing him with another man (he beat them both), but she believes that her son Jim has learned a great lesson and deserves another chance. Jim enters the scene in time to stop the repossession of the victrola and shows his gratitude for the family's treatment of Aunt Nancy by handing over enough money to pay for it. As Jim and Aunt Nancy leave to find an apartment, Silas prepares to return to work, and the lights fade on Emma dancing the shimmy to the music from the victrola.

Richardson created a human comedy based on a realistic situation. In the lives of his characters, what should have been a problem develops into a crisis; though it is not directly stated, much of the blame can be placed on racism. The unseen bosses and the legal system showed a pronounced lack of compassion. However, Richardson kept his focus on the family's relationships and the loyalty and friendship that saved the day.

Richardson used dialect, thought to be an essential stylistic element by black and white playwrights of the era, but did not exaggerate it. He was making a conscious effort to lend his characters dignity and counter the prevailing images of African-Americans on the stage: "Most of the [black] plays and players seemed to be put on the stage just to be laughed at. My play was about ordinary black people" (Richardson 1974). Drawn from observation and memory, his early writing style was primarily naturalistic/realistic. Concerned that the slices of life he created be served up with minimal distortion, he firmly believed that the option to write in dialect should not be denied the African-American playwright. Sometimes criticized in the African-American community because of the brutal misconception of African-American speech, this practice translated into a stage dialect which had become a staple of commercial theatre and film. He wrote that the peasant class was less likely to lose sight of its own culture in order to more closely imitate the dominant culture. They provided the best true reflection of African-American culture, and he sought to capture the speech patterns of this class: "[Plays built around black bourgeois characters] will not have the strength of those written around the peasant class of the Negro group." (Richardson **"Characters"** 183) Rather than being ashamed of dialect, the African-American performer should appreciate it: "Not only is the Negro's dialect more sweet-toned, but his use of the perfect English is warmer and more soothing than the Caucasian's." (Richardson, **"Negro"** 310)

The Chip Woman's Fortune garnered praise from Burns Mantle, Heywood Broun, and most of the other reviewers who attended opening night on Broadway at the Frazee Theatre on May 7, 1923. Alexander Wollcott of the New York Herald illustrates the condescension which tempered the praise:

> Delightful . . . a sketchy morsel of darky life which the company was able to present most engagingly. If all the rejoicing must be confined to this curtain raiser it is because it is the stuff of which a true negro [sic] theater will one day take form to the permanent enrichment of the American stage. Those who groan at the mulatto "Salome" do so because there are so many players who can play "Salome" and so few who can give such plays as ***The Chip Woman's Fortune.***
>
> (Woollcott 12)

Broadway dismissed Richardson with a pat on the head. The Ethiopian Art Players retained ***The Chip Woman's Fortune*** when it changed its main production to a jazz version of *The Comedy of Errors* during the second week of its repertory run, but could not generate enough interest to extend the run past May 20. The African-American press had supported the efforts of the company, especially during a pre-Broadway engagement at the Lafayette Theatre in Harlem: "Many expected that this would be just an insignificant little something to kill the time before . . . 'Salome,' but the merit of this little piece and the acting proved a distinct shock of satisfaction" ("Wonderful" 5). Some black audience members did try to support the Ethiopian Art Players on Broadway, but black audiences were not entirely welcome. Though segregated seating was not legal in New York, black audience members, even those from the press, were barred from the orchestra, for fear that white patrons would not tolerate integrated seating ("Colored Factor" 23). Richardson could not interest any of the commercial theatre's literary agents in his work (Richardson interview 1974), and returned to the Little Negro Theatre.

The Broadway exposure did gain Richardson a long sought after opportunity to see some of his works produced by the Howard Players, the little theatre founded by Alain Locke and Montgomery Gregory, and Richardson garnered more awards through *The Crisis* and *Opportunity* (the journal of the Urban League) literary contests. In April 1928 *Carolina Magazine* printed two of Richardson plays, ***The Idle Head*** and ***Flight of the Natives,*** in a special number on black drama.

Richardson edited his first anthology, ***Plays and Pageants from the Life of the Negro*** (Washington, D.C.: Associated Publishers), in 1930. Three of his own works, ***The King's Dilemma, The House of Sham,*** and ***The Black Horseman*** are included in this volume of eight plays and four pageants. Richardson branched out into a broad range of styles; in addition to folk plays of the black underclass and middle class, he created kings and queens and recreated historical figures:

> Although some of Richardson's plays were influenced by the folk tradition of Ridgely Torrence and Paul Green, many of the others were unique in their glorification of the Black hero long before the world was to affirm that "Black is Beautiful" . . . Richardson was one of the first Black playwrights to write romantic plays of Black history.
>
> (Peterson 114)

By projecting black characters as heroes, Richardson offered white audiences unaccustomed images and situations, for, as James Weldon Johnson remarks, "American Negroes as heroes form no part of white America's concept of the race" (Johnson 479). The projection of such a hero, no matter how mild the context, made the work political and controversial, at least in terms of the mainstream white audience, which could not accept the "universality" of such a hero, even though that hero had been drawn according to the European dramatic and theatrical conventions upon which American theatre modeled itself.

Historian Carter G. Woodson, who had played a major role in the preparation and editing of ***Plays and Pageants from the Life of the Negro,*** requested that Richardson compile a second anthology, this time of plays with black historical themes. ***Negro History in Thirteen Plays,*** coedited by May Miller, was published in 1935. Richardson contributed five plays to this anthology: ***Antoneo Maceo,*** about the betrayal of the Cuban patriot; [Crispus] ***Attucks the Martyr***; ***The Elder Dumas,*** a rather unflattering portrait of Alexandre Dumas pere; ***Near Calvary,*** a treatment of the story of Simon the Cyrenian which was broadcast on the radio program *Voice of America* on July 7, 1936 (Peterson 123); and ***In Menelik's Court,*** a love story set amid the intrigue of a 1898 Italian plot against the Ethiopian throne.

After the publication of ***Negro History in Thirteen Plays,*** Richardson's output of new plays dropped sharply. In 1941, ***Miss or Mrs.*** was produced by the Bureau of Engraving Dramatic Club in Washington, and then little was heard from Richardson until the publication of his third and final anthology, ***The King's Dilemma and Other Plays for Children,*** in 1956. Some of Richardson's earliest writing efforts, included in this compilation, had been plays for children, commissioned for a short-lived youth journal edited by DuBois, *The Brownies' Book.*

Richardson's body of dramatic work, most of which was produced during the 1920's and 1930's, includes ten full-length plays which were never produced or published. One of these is a full-length version of ***The Chip Woman's Fortune.*** His forty one-act plays proved extremely popular with black little theatre companies, stock companies, colleges and amateur groups. Nineteen of his one-act plays were published.

No black playwright during the Harlem Renaissance period was as prolific as Richardson, but perhaps the most popular among black theatre groups after Richardson was Eulalie Spence (1894-1981). Spence's family emigrated from Nevis, British West Indies; most of Spence's youth and all of her adult life were spent in New York. Spence graduated from the New York Training School for Teachers, and did additional coursework at City College and Columbia University, where she took a course in playwriting taught by Hatcher Hughes, who would eventually win the 1928 Pulitzer Prize for his melodrama *Hell-Bent for Heaven.* Spence gained playwriting and acting experience with Columbia's Laboratory Players and the National Ethiopian Art Theatre, a group based in Harlem but affiliated with the American Academy of Dramatic Art. Spence and two of her sisters joined DuBois' newly formed Krigwa Players in 1925.

Despite her exposure to DuBois and his ideas, Spence fell firmly in line with the opinions of Alain Locke. In an essay she wrote for *Opportunity,* "A Criticism of the Negro Drama," Spence outlined a very pragmatic vision for African-American drama, based on her observation that drama in the United States was twenty to thirty years behind the novel and short story in freedom of selection of subject matter. Neither black nor white audiences were prepared to support a black Shaw or Galsworthy:

> Many a serious aspirant for dramatic honors has fallen by the wayside because he would insist on his lynching or his rape. The white man is cold and unresponsive to this subject and the Negro, himself, is hurt and humiliated by it. We go to the theatre for entertainment, not to have old fires and hates rekindled.
>
> (Spence 180)

Spence made comedy her specialty and was especially adept at exploring the urban landscape, particularly in Harlem. Her first produced play was probably *Foreign Mail,* a light comedy which took second place in the 1926 *Crisis* competition and was staged by the Krigwa Players in 1927 on the same bill as one of Spence's serious dramas, *Her.*

The title character of *Her* is a ghost which haunts the top floor flat in a Harlem apartment house. However, in her telling of the ghost's story, Spence builds a reasonable amount of suspense and studiously minimizes what might be viewed as stereotypically fearful behavior on the part of the focal characters, the couple which occupies the apartment below the haunted flat. It is also interesting to note that the ghost is a woman from the Phillipines, who finally achieves her revenge on the still-living husband who wronged her. Even those who fear her, exhibit compassion for her plight.

1927 was a banner year for Spence in terms of awards. In the third annual *Opportunity* contest (which followed the same basic format as *The Cri-*

sis contest), she won second prize in the play division for *The Hunch,* a comedy in which a rejected suitor wins back his fiancee by proving that her present fiance is a bigamist; she tied another playwright for third prize in the same contest with another one-act comedy, *The Starter.* Locke selected *The Starter* for publication in *Plays of Negro Life.* It is representative Spence—a gentle comedy built on the relationship of a strong, but not domineering woman and a weaker man. Spence's characters were often lonely people either looking for or fearing meaningful attachment. The two central characters in *The Starter* are T. J. Kelly, an elevator starter (a sort of dispatcher for elevator operators) and Georgia, a dress finisher in Manhattan's garment district. At one point Georgia comments on the fatefulness of a starter and a finisher being brought together. T. J. and Georgia occupy a bench in a Harlem park and are two street-wise characters who speak in urban dialect:

> T. J. KELLY: Say, Georgia, we'd make a good team—we would. (He gives her a tight hug)
>
> GEORGIA: (Pleased) Quit yuh kiddin'.
>
> T. J. KELLY: No kiddin.' Y'know, kid, I bin thinkin'—Say, why don't we get married? Huh? . . .
>
> GEORGIA: (Slowly) Has yuh got any money, T. J.?
>
> T. J.KELLY: (With an injured air) Money! Say! Have a heart! That's a fine question.
>
> (Locke 211)

T. J. vacillates several times during his proposal to Georgia, and by the end of the play, the question is still not settled, but the couple remains nestled on the bench.

Spence's best known play *Fool's Errand* became the one which won publication by Samuel French. The Krigwa Players entered this play in the fifth annual Little Theatre Tournament, a national competition in which any participation by African-Americans was rare. Typically DuBois took the challenge of presenting his company there, to prove itself in open competition. The choice of *Fool's Errand* as the Krigwa Players' entry might be viewed as unusual, not, however, given the view of DuBois, that the thrust of black drama should be a direct attack against racism. *Fool's Errand* gently satirizes hypocrisy in a church community—a theme which occurs in several folk plays of the era. In a later interview Spence commented that she and DuBois clashed openly:

> He didn't like anyone who disagreed with him. . . . He had hoped that this group would continue to go on to provide the nucleus . . . Of what you call the angry, explosive things we've seen in the last ten years [1960's-1970's] . . . A play should never be for propaganda.
>
> (Spence interview)

Fool's Errand made the contest finals, which were held for one week in a Broadway playhouse, the Frolic. *Fool's Errand* played twice and was reviewed by a substantial number of daily newspapers, as well as the theatrical paper, *Variety.* Though only for two nights, with an amateur production, Eulalie Spence became the first and only African-American female whose work would be seen on Broadway until Lorraine Hansberry's success with *A Raisin in the Sun* in 1959.

Fool's Errand is usually described as a comedy, but this folk play contains many elements of domestic melodrama and serio-comic satire. Though she had never visited the South (Spence interview), Spence set the play there in a rural "unprogressive Negro settlement" in the cabin home of Doug, his wife, Mom, and their teenage daughter, Maza. Maza has been the object of gossip among the church council, which is concerned that the community's youth is "getting out of hand":

> CASSIE (spitefully): It's mah 'pinion dey's bin outer han' a mighty long time. What wid de way dey cuts off de little hair Gawd gives 'em an den spends all dey' got tuh straighten it out—flyin' in de face uh Gawd, Ah calls it! . . .
>
> SISTER WILLIAMS: Ef such doins keeps on, reckon our young people'll be jes' as brazen's white folks.

Maza is later accused of concealing an illegitimate pregnancy, but it turns out, to the council's embarrassment, that it is Mom who is pregnant. The council, fueled by gossip and innuendo, has come on a fool's errand. (Perkins 119-131)

Some white critics were distracted by the color of the actors and failed to see any deviation from the norm in the portrayal of black characters:

> The hit of the evening with a cast of fourteen, varying from ace of spades black to straight haired near whites. They acted as white folks think negroes ought to act, providing amusement with prayer, song and a comedy of sex that did not violate any section of Harlem's or City Hall's penal codes.
>
> ("First Round" 28)

Others were much more favorably impressed:

> . . . Dealing with materials essentially their own, which Miss Spence had arranged with understanding of dramatic technique and effectiveness, the colored cast was uniform in excellence.
>
> ("Harlemites" 9)

Oddly enough, Spence's theatre activity tapered off after her most productive year. This may have been due partially to the breakup of the Krigwa Players, or to the fact that she had taken a teaching position at Eastern District High School in Brooklyn, which she retained until her retirement in 1958 (Perkins 105). Joseph Papp, the late founding producer of the New York Shakespeare Festival and the Public Theatre, who had once been one of her students, remembered her fondly as one who encouraged his interest in the theatre, but he never knew of her playwriting career. (Papp interview)

Spence did write some startlingly frank urban melodramas during her active writing period, the 1920's. The central character of *Hot Stuff* is a woman who will do anything, including prostitute herself, for material gain; *Undertow* is based in a love triangle which culminates in a crime of passion. Spence's only known full-length play, *The Whipping,* was optioned by Paramount Pictures in 1933, but was never produced; her body of work is estimated at fourteen plays, six of which were published. (Perkins 106)

The debates over the nature and configuration of a Black aesthetic and the African-American dramatic traditions which developed into two major strains as a result[2] did not begin or end with the Harlem Renaissance. The drama produced during that era, like most African-American authored drama produced before 1959, has been almost totally overlooked by the arbiters of the American dramatic canon, yet, it offers a revealing picture of the artistic priorities of its time, a time when black and white American playwrights were searching for the definitive indigenous American drama and mining the black American experience in that search. Willis Richardson and Eulalie Spence stand out as pioneers in their attempts to reconcile disparate critical theories by projecting, as truthfully as they could, the actions and sounds of African-American onto the stage. Simply doing so proved to be a political act; whether acknowledged as such or not, they helped to engender the developments in African-American drama and theatre which followed. In this, Richardson and Spence were successful.

Notes

1. In his essay, Rhett S. Jones explains that theatre produced in the Euro-American literary tradition has proved unappealing to the mass of AfricanAmericans, who prefer the culturally attuned theatrical rituals of the Black church and the psychologically satisfying rituals of organized sports.
2. Samuel A. Hay provides an extensive explanation of the development of two major schools of African-American drama, the Black Experience School and the Black Arts School.

Works Cited

"Colored Factor in Theatres Sharply Brought Out In Broadway." *Variety,* 10 May 1923, 23.

DuBois, W. E. B. "Krigwa Players Little Negro Theatre." *The Crisis* 32 (July 1926): 134-136.

"The First Round." *New York Sun,* 3 May 1927, 28.

Hamalian, Leo, and James V. Hatch, eds. *The Roots of African-American Drama; an Anthology of Early Plays, 1858-1938.* Detroit: Wayne State UP, 1991.

"Harlemites Score as Tourney Opens." *New York Telegram,* 3 May 1927, 9.

Hay, Samuel A. *African-American Theatre: an Historical and Critical Analysis.* New York: Cambridge UP, 1994.

Hughes, Langston. "The Negro Artist and the Racial Mountain." *The Nation* 122 (1926): 692-694.

Johnson, James Weldon. "The Dilemma of the Negro Artist." *American Mercury* 15 (Dec. 1928): 477-481.

Jones, Rhett S. "Orderly and Disorderly Structures: Why Church and Sports Appeal to Black Americans and Theatre Does Not." *Black American Literature Forum* 25.1 (Spring 1991): 43-52.

Locke, Alain, and Montgomery Gregory, eds. *Plays of Negro Life.* New York: Harper, 1927.

Locke, Alain, ed. *The New Negro.* Salem, New Hampshire: Ayer Company, 1986. Rpt. 1925 ed.

Neal, Larry. "The Black Arts Movement." *The Drama Review* 12 (Summer 1968): 29-39.

Papp, Joseph. 1988. Interview by author, 21 Nov. New York.

Perkins, Kathy, ed. *Black Female Playwrights: An Anthology of Plays Before 1950.* Bloomington: Indiana UP, 1989.

Peterson, Bernard L. Jr. "Willis Richardson: Pioneer Playwright." *The Theater of Black Americans.* Vol. I. Errol Hill, ed. Englewood Cliffs: Prentice-Hall, 1980.

Richardson, Willis. "The Hope of a Negro Drama." *The Crisis* 19 (Nov. 1919): 338-339.

———. "The Negro and the Stage." *Opportunity* 2 (Oct. 1924): 310.

———. 1974. Interview audiotaped 21 July. Hatch-Billops Archives, New York.

Schuyler, George S. "The Negro Art Hokum." *The Nation* 122 (1926): 662-663.

Spence, Eulalie. "A Criticism of the Negro Drama." *Opportunity* 6 (June 1928): 180.

———. 1973. Interview audiotaped 22 August. Hatch-Billops Archives, New York.

"Wonderful Portrayal of Wilde's Drama by Colored Artists at the Lafayette." *Amsterdam News,* 25 April 1923, 5.

Woollcott, Alexander. "Shouts and Murmers." *New York Herald,* 9 May 1923, 12.

CHRISTINE RAUCHFUSS GRAY (ESSAY DATE 1999)

SOURCE: Gray, Christine Rauchfuss. "The Education of African Americans: Willis Richardson's Approach to Drama." In *Willis Richardson: Forgotten Pioneer of African-American Drama,* pp. 55-68. Westport, Conn.: Greenwood Press, 1999.

In the following essay, Gray examines Richardson's view of Black theater as a vehicle for education.

> That the productions of [Negro] writers should have been something of a guide in their daily living is a matter which never seems to have been raised seriously.
>
> —Richard Wright

In his 1937 essay "Blueprint for Negro Writing," Richard Wright discusses black writers who "dressed in the knee-pants of servility" as they went "abegging to white America" for approval. He notes that "Negro writing was something external to the lives of educated Negroes themselves" (394-95). Nearly twenty years earlier, Richardson was working to make "Negro writing" relevant to the lives of African Americans through his plays. In 1926, DuBois wrote passionately about the stage in his call for black drama that would be "for us, by us, about us, and near us." Although he never identified whom his broad use of "us" represented, it is safe to assume that DuBois was referring to those who found little to which they could relate in nearly any dramatic production at that time. Although Georgia Johnson, May Miller, and other black dramatists heeded DuBois's call in most respects in their plays, Richardson followed a very different direction regarding "about us." In other plays of the 1920s, the "about us" aspect of African-American plays could actually be read as "about us and whites." White characters, it seems, were a necessary element in most early African-American plays. Richardson avoided relying on white characters in his plays, which may partly explain today's neglect of his work. That is, because his plays do not deal with racial strife, they seem not to have stirred interest among those researching African-American drama of the early twentieth century.

Although other black playwrights of the period wrote on topics pertinent to black life, few playwrights aside from Richardson sought material for their plays from within the black community and addressed the situations found there. In focusing on topics about and relevant to African Americans, the playwright had, by 1919, both addressed Wright's remarks in that Richardson's plays did not go "abegging to white America" for approval, and followed DuBois's prescribed features for African-American drama.

Through this shift from the usual black-white tension, Richardson avoided the image of blacks as victimized by whites; consequently, white characters and white culture do not control his stage. In their reliance on whites as antagonists, his contemporaries, by continually giving power to white characters, acknowledged the control whites had over blacks, which resulted in the simplistic situation of "white is bad" and "black is good." The predictability of the outcome for a black character in a black-white conflict lessened the play's impact and its drama, for if white characters were present, a black spectator knew that the black characters were going to suffer at the hands of the whites. The results of Richardson's creating, instead, black-black tensions and conflicts, are rounded, three-dimensional characters, a feature rarely seen in African-American drama during its formative years.

Although *Rachel* had given him the impetus to write for the stage, "Miss Grimké's *Rachel,*" he wrote, was "still not the thing [he] meant," for it "shows the manner in which Negroes are treated by white people in the United States" (**"Hope of a Negro Drama"** 338). The choices and decisions made on Richardson's stage are created and controlled by his black characters. By exploring situations and conditions within the black community, Richardson hoped to show his audiences that many of their problems and difficulties did not necessarily spring from encounters with whites, as Grimké's *Rachel* and plays by many of Richardson's contemporaries imply.

The difference between Richardson's works and plays by most of his contemporaries is evident when one considers other African-American plays written in the 1920s. Plays written by black women in the first decades of the century are, for example, frequently similar to one another. Although they implicitly attacked such stereotypical stage props as banjos and watermelons, they unwittingly created new stereotypes. Many of the folk plays written before 1930—especially those by women—feature the long-suffering, indigent black woman, the beleaguered African-American family, or the young black man about to be hanged. Churches and modest homes replace graveyards and plantations as a new cliché. Conflicts are frequently created around the impending lynching of a father or son or the encroachment of whites on the security of the black community. Georgia Johnson's *A Sunday Morning in the South* (1925) and *Safe* (1929), Mary Burrill's *Aftermath* (1919), and Myrtle Livingston Smith's *For Unborn Children* (1926), as examples, are strikingly similar in these respects.[1] Plays of this sort were no doubt the ones that Locke had in mind when he wrote about the "numerous Negro writers of amateur plays where [the] chief dramatic intention has been . . . moral allegories, rhetorical melodramas, and dramatic antidotes for race prejudice." Of Mary Burrill's play, for example, Locke wrote, "*They That Sit in the Dark* [*sic*] is written too obviously to point to a moral" (Drama Notes). The plots continually go beyond the black community in relying on whites as antagonists. In many of these plays, it seems that tensions among African Americans come about only when white characters are in the vicinity. Nearly always condemned for their victimization of blacks, whites are held responsible for the problems of the black community.[2]

Another common feature in the early black plays are the poverty-stricken characters. Because they are such a usual feature in these plays, they too create almost a stereotype of blacks. It is not that they are poor, however; instead, it is that they are spared feelings of malice or ill will. They are depicted, as Richardson wrote, as "angels," perhaps because they haven't been tainted by wealth, material goods, or life in the North. Presented as victims of circumstance, black characters are frequently predictable and, consequently, two-dimensional, nearly stock characters. This underprivileged class, the blacks, is often victimized by whites in power or with money. These plays are, for the most part, formulaic: a poor black family is preyed upon by cruel and selfish whites; the family suffers at the hands of whites; an African American is killed or dies because of whites. If these plays were designed to teach, one can only wonder what the lesson might have been. Such plays could only, one might surmise, increase tension between the races.

Richardson's plays reveal his belief that an individual sense of identity and self-worth must accompany any social reform. Attacks on white power meant that whites had a psychic and emotional hold or control over blacks. Placing whites as pivotal characters acknowledged their power, while deflecting attention from the strength and intelligence of blacks. In differentiating the black stage from the white stage, Carlton and Barbara Molette point to "purpose" as being an integral aspect of black drama:

> The African (and Afro-American) concept of art is that art is inextricably connected to life. Art is supposed to be useful to society in contrast to the Eurocentric elitist art-for-art's sake tradition. . . . A black playwright [should] intentionally disseminate information that helps black people control their own lives, for their own betterment, on their own terms.
>
> (*Black Theater* [*:Premise and Presentation,* 1985] 38)

Protest plays, such as those written by Richardson's colleagues, validated the structures of oppression. In Richardson's plays, the tension springs from the family and displays the effect on the black community when blacks themselves do not work together. Rather than attacking the white power structure, his plays have characters who deal with their own weaknesses and look to themselves as sources of strength. The white community is nearly absolved of its responsibility. His plays portray the essence of black experience in America by examining tensions between men and women, young and old, rich and poor, all set against the backdrop of urban life, rural settings, migrating north, and the church. Although the plays by women addressed matters of real concern to black Americans, these concerns become trivial through the plays' predictable reliance on melodrama. In emigrating from the South, blacks left behind their spiritual homes and entered a foreign land, a world unfamiliar and strange and one that they were often ill-equipped to handle socially, spiritually, or emotionally. By avoiding these extremes—the martyrs in plays by blacks and the exotic, dangerous or childlike in plays by whites—and by including "unpleasant endings," Richardson shifted his concerns to domestic situations, which he believed were more immediate and pressing to African Americans as they adapted to urban life.

In focusing on black-on-black relations, Richardson put at the core of his plays characters entangled in conflicts with members of their community or family. Parents, aunts, cousins, visiting relatives, aging neighbors, grandparents, adopted children, boarders, and lovers fill his stage in plots circling on tensions or rivalries between pairs: brother against brother, boarder against landlord, parent against child, and husband against wife, as he depicted the harm done to the black community by its own members. Without the drama inherent in lynching and the complications of mixed blood, Richardson's plots concern fairly mundane events. Furniture is borrowed against or repossessed, or a woman marries an older man for his relative wealth. Frequently, landlords gossip about the marital status and complexion of boarders. An indigent family in Georgia saves to make the journey north only to have one of its members steal the savings. A real-estate agent bilks a client with an ailing wife out of $500; a thief, struck with paralysis, refuses to ask for God's forgiveness before his death. Such are the problems and situations that the characters face on Richardson's stage.

In his six essays on African-American drama and in several interviews, Richardson commented on the necessity of black drama to have a purpose. To him, much of the value of drama lay in its possibilities for education. The stage was, he held, a teaching space, a platform for education. The African-American playwright had an obligation to instruct the audience on a variety of topics. The audience, more than likely, had moved from the South, leaving behind families and familiar ways of life. In adapting to urban life, they may have found themselves discriminated against in ways that were unfamiliar to them, not only by whites but also by other blacks. Perhaps those in his audiences had to deal with greedy landlords or with suspicious boarders. All in the audience were, more than likely, well aware of the white world that hovered outside of their neighborhoods. African-American plays informed their audiences of social and political conditions affecting them. The plays provided this information indirectly in the form of staged stories. In his 1924 essay, **"Propaganda in the Theater,"** Richardson wrote that although blacks had "worked upon the public opinion with nearly every available method from the prayer meeting to the indignation meeting," the stage, in his opinion, was "one medium which has not been used to any extent" (353). Richardson elaborated on his perception of the stage as being not only able but obliged to "disseminate information" for teaching purposes: "A propaganda play is a play written for the purpose of waging war against certain evils existing among the [black] people in order to gain the sympathy of those people who have seldom, or never, thought upon the subject" (353). He noted that Shaw, Brieux, and Gorki used the stage for "waging war," pointing out that African American playwrights had a similar mission. He did not believe, however, that those changes could come from whites. Instead, he thought that blacks were the chief source of problems that beset the race and should, therefore, address their problems themselves. Believing that "wonders may be done for the cause of the Negro" through propaganda plays written by blacks, Richardson urged that "teaching plays" should "cause those people who are in sympathy with the play's purpose to be up and doing" (**"Propaganda"** 353). Richardson believed that through his plays he could encourage black people to heed "our duty to strengthen the weak link [the lower-class Negro] rather than to be ashamed of it" (**"Characters"** 183). Indeed, his comment on the weak link contains the essence of Richardson's intention for his plays: to create via the stage an awareness among African Americans of the necessity for the race to work together.

In urging the use of the stage as an educational medium, DuBois played an ever-present and crucial role in Richardson's development as a playwright. In his autobiography, Richardson called the black leader his "guide," and, indeed, DuBois had encouraged Richardson when he began writing for the stage: Richardson's plays in *The Brownies' Book,* his play ***The Deacon's Awakening,*** and several of his essays on drama had all been published through DuBois's editorship at *Crisis.* In his role as mentor, spiritual or actual, DuBois had shaped Richardson's ideas for the stage. Both men believed that through drama, education, whether through plays on black history or in urging mutual support, could most readily and effectively take hold. Because the stage made the abstract visible, concrete, because witnessing a play was a communal event, and because understanding a play did not require literacy, it was the ideal medium to reach many people. In their attempts to educate an audience, both men agreed that the stage should portray aspects of black life relevant to the audience and its values. Following his mentor, Richardson saw the stage as "one of the very best means of getting an idea before the public." Its purpose was neither to pass the time nor to entertain:

> When the theatre is placed in a category where it really belongs, and intelligently considered as an educational institution along with the school, we can easily see that there should be some more important reason than [entertainment] for visiting such a place.
>
> (**"The Negro and the Stage"** 310)

Instead, his plays consider the difficulties that arise from issues of age, class, and gender. Blacks who have, for example, succeeded financially, disdain those who haven't fared well. Some of his antagonists, embarrassed by folk ways, abandon or renounce a past rooted in the South, while others turn against the less educated of the race, mocking them for their jobs or living conditions. To Richardson, the weaknesses in the black community often led to the dissolution of the family or neighborhood. We see the damage done in his plays when, for example, black landlords frequently gouge their tenants with high rents, or when black businessmen prey on the gullibility, desperation, and naiveté of the lower classes by luring them into shady deals. Black parents attempt to exert unreasonable control over their grown children or a husband dominates his wife. Lack of support, infidelity, theft, or greed among African Americans are the causes and, at times, the consequences of a tear in the fabric in families and communities. No doubt, Richardson's belief in upholding the community—its necessity for the survival of the black race—goes toward explaining why Richardson, following DuBois, believed that these plays should be performed in black churches, lodges, schools, and libraries—gathering sites for those who had a common culture. As Richardson pointed out, "***The Chip Woman's Fortune*** was about ordinary Black people. In commercial theater ordinary Black plays were not well received. Commercial [white] theater wanted plays about prostitutes, dope handlers, thieves or criminals. . . . They wanted stereotypes" (Willis). Perhaps because Richardson's plots had such mundane characters and plausible events, they portrayed life among African Americans more accurately than did other plays of the decade.

Richardson's plays are further distinguished from those of his contemporaries by the characters he created, especially those of humble means. In his plays, the characters either live in the rural South or are the offspring of parents who have made the trek to the North. His characters have moved from a world where livestock must be fed, where weather controls activities and profits, and where firewood waits to be chopped to one of crime. Accompanying these blacks in their migration to the North's industrial cities were dialect, folk beliefs, and faith in God. The blacks in Richardson's plays are kith and kin to those described by August Wilson in his prefatory remarks to his play *Joe Turner's Come and Gone* (1988):

> From the deep South the sons and daughters of newly freed African slaves wander into the city. Isolated, cut off from memory, [f]oreigners in a strange land, they carry as part and parcel of their baggage a long line of separation and dispersement which informs their sensibilities and marks their conduct as they search for ways to reconnect, to reassemble. . . .
>
> ("The Play" [*Joe Turner's Come and Gone,* 1988])

In his urban plays, Richardson portrays these citizens and their progeny, some middle class, some poor, whose lives he examines within the black community as they adapt to urban ways. Now dispersed in, yet disenchanted with, the "Promised Land" of the North, Richardson's characters must find a community in which they feel secure.

Richardson saw "the folk" as having "the soul of a people," writing that "the soul of [African-American] people is truly worth showing" (**"Hope"** 338). Like white playwright Ridgely Torrence, Richardson realized that the Irish National Theater might serve as a model of what could be achieved if African Americans developed their own theater, one based on their own experiences in America. Both cultures, after all, had been oppressed, and both had a rich folk heritage on which to build a literature. By drawing on African-American folk culture, Richardson believed, a writer could find authentic materials. He supported his belief in this stratum of society by creating powerful and memorable working-class characters: Jane Lee, Aunt Nancy, Emma Turner, Hoggy Wells, Steve Hardy. In fact, his most important plays are his folk plays: ***The Flight of the Natives, Compromise, The Broken Banjo, The Hope of the Lowly, The Chip Woman's Fortune, The Deacon's Awakening, Mortgaged, Curse of the Shell-Road Witch, Pillar of the Church***—all contain characters who exemplify his faith in the folk while revealing their weaknesses and occasionally petty ways.

To Richardson, dialect characterized this "distinctly Negro type" (Garvin). In his introduction to ***Plays and Pageants from the Life of the Negro*** (1930), Richardson wrote that he had purposely omitted plays written in dialect from this collection. Because these plays were intended for school and church productions, he thought that dialect might continue the stereotypes of blacks as uneducated. Nevertheless, he defended its use in his other plays, pointing out that "the dialect of the slave days is still the mother tongue of the American Negro" (**"Propaganda"** 354).

Richardson's own rural upbringing may explain his affinity to folk culture. As a bricklayer, his father labored manually as did his mother who took in laundry. Several of his folk plays recognize this group and, in some plays, grant working-class African Americans a dignity not ordinarily accorded them either on stage or off. Many (though by no means all) of his folk characters are proud, resourceful, and kind. Rowena Jelliffe of Cleveland's Karamu House read several of Richardson's folk plays and praised his characters for their "dignity [because] that's what [black characters] didn't have back then" (Garvin).

Richardson's lack of both a college degree and social connections seem to have shut him out of the upper stratum of black society in Washington, D.C., which may explain his frequent criticism of successful blacks. Unable to attend college—and obviously capable of and interested in going—Richardson often castigates blacks who have achieved that status. Influenced by either their careers, education, or family ties, these characters frequently abandon less fortunate blacks. The college-educated blacks in his plays tend to be pretentious, smug, and arrogant social climbers.[3] Characters who have gained standing in the community employ chauffeurs, own businesses, hold real estate, play tennis, and, in one play, have children attending Harvard and Smith colleges. However, these same characters ignore or abuse those who are financially or socially weaker.

Richardson could be considered among the first African-American feminist playwrights, for women, his most fully developed characters, hold the most powerful roles in most of his plays. In fact, in nearly all of his plays the women are rarely victims; they frequently control the situation or rescue the family from despair or tragedy.[4] The women in Richardson's plays have a texture and substance rare on the black stage at this time or preceding it. Characters modeled on those in the genteel tradition, such as Grimké's heroine Rachel, are flat characters when compared to Richardson's Jane Lee or Emma Turner. The women in his plays defend their families, stand up for women's rights, care for relatives, financially support husbands who may be involved in unscrupulous activities, and generally keep the family intact. As will be discussed, these female characters play an array of roles: Martha Jones, along with her daughter, is a champion for women's suffrage; Ruth Martin, in contrast to her lazy husband, launders for neighbors and cooks for her family and four boarders; the elderly Aunt Nancy tends to her ailing landlady and gives her landlord her meager savings; Jane Lee attempts to have the man who murdered her husband and son pay for the education of her other children; and Emma Turner uses her savings to help her husband escape. Indeed, it is generally the females in his plays who are the protagonists, the role models for others, and those who come to the aid of the community.

Richardson's female characters are often, however, quite human. In several plays, they complain about the ways and habits of their husbands, or they want money to climb the social ladder, goading their husbands to work harder to keep up the image of success, even if the money is gotten through dishonest methods. They gossip, misjudge, and attempt to play matchmaker. They complain about their maids, their husbands, and their neighbors. They frequently interfere in their children's lives. In considering the plight of the black woman, Richardson's plays frequently look at the various means they use to survive, whatever their situations. The relationships between husbands and wives are often part of Richardson's dramas. Richardson's fiancés and husbands often play minor roles; if they are present, they tend to be ineffectual, lazy, domineering, and blustering. His female characters rarely depend upon men; those who rely on their husbands must cater to their moods or whims because the women are often powerless either to change them or to leave them. Although few of his female characters are submissive, they often go to great lengths to keep peace in the home, realizing that occasionally giving in makes life smoother for all involved.

Because few of his characters are poverty stricken, the possibility of melodrama is further avoided. The plays are thus freed from maudlin episodes and thereby become more realistic. His plays gingerly take the middle course, reflecting black life "as it is" among African Americans (Garvin). The depiction of blacks as suffering "angels" was one of two criticisms directed against the work of black playwrights by several black critics at the time. At the other extreme was the complaint that in plays by whites, African Americans were, as Richardson pointed out, frequently portrayed as "pimps, drug dealers, or thieves." In *The Negro in the Making of America* (1964), Benjamin Quarles identified the very qualities that set Richardson's plays apart from other early African-American plays:

> In drama . . . the American public was slow to show any interest in the serious portrayal of Negro Life. Budding Negro dramatists like Willis Richardson faced not only white indifference but also the artistic limitations imposed by Negro audiences, who as a rule, did not like dialect, did not like unpleasant endings, and who insisted that all Negro characters be fine, upstanding persons, barely a cut below the angels.
>
> ([*The Negro in the Making of America,* 1964] 201)

In an interview, Richardson made comments in a similar vein:

> Before ***The Chip Woman's Fortune,*** most of the plays and players were put on stage just to be laughed at, never serious. [They] didn't have a Black man on stage as a serious character. Even the names of plays, Wilson's *Meek Mose* [for example],

> would show that they weren't too serious. When I started writing I made up my mind that I would be serious about it.
>
> (Garvin [Recorded interview with Larry Garvin, 27 July 1974.])

In general, Richardson's characters, rich or poor, are not predictable or cardboard. An audience often sees the same flaws and vices in the lower class as in the upper, with neither group idealized. Along with their good qualities, his African-American characters can be cruel, jealous, vindictive, greedy, petty, conniving, and dishonest. The primitive or childlike innocent "negro folk" seen in the plays of Paul Green and Dubose Heyward, both white, and those characters that are nearly sanctified in works by many of Richardson's African-American contemporaries, are absent.

Believing that the "peasant class of the Negro group has strength for material in plays," Richardson wrote:

> It is not necessary for your leading character to be a criminal, but it is very necessary for him to be interesting and distinctly a Negro type . . . distinctly different from the white man. The cultured Negro is so much like the cultured white man that he is seldom interestingly different enough to be typical of the whole Negro race. So to write a play about cultured Negroes is to very nearly write a play about cultured white people.
>
> (**"Negro Character"** 183)[5]

Prejudice is acknowledged as a fact of life—why deal with it on stage? he seems to ask. Instead, Richardson's work moves on to other topics: How does the race confront discrimination among blacks? How does one deal with African Americans who stand in the way of the progress of others of the race? How does prejudice based on the shade of one's complexion hold back the black community? What responsibility do blacks have toward one another? What are the consequences of the members of the race discriminating against one another? Urging African Americans to take responsibility for their plight, Richardson wraps his tales around "real black lives." Their commonplace occupations lend his characters credibility: porters, deacons, real-estate agents, laundresses, boot-blacks, preachers, sharecroppers, and bootleggers move into his one-act plays with their problems, chicanery, and anxieties.[6]

In Richardson's plays, the abuse of one character by another does not necessarily supply the story line. Instead, the lead characters often bring about their own demise or failure through their own choices or agency. They are frequently their own enemies, caught in webs of greed, misjudgment, and ambition.

Many of his plays seem to allow an audience to see the damage blacks inflict on other blacks through their lack of support, especially by those who are successful. According to Richardson, a play should provide glimpses of life within the African-American community where such support was not present. Instead of putting his characters in emotional or tragic situations, Richardson placed them in realistic, often mundane, scenarios. Complications arising from miscegenation and passing, for example, are rarely factors in his plays. His play ***Compromise*** (1926) is one of his very few to depend on a white antagonist.

Richardson's plays are further distinguished from those by other African Americans of the 1920s for their frequent lack of resolution. Dramas by his contemporaries have a conclusion, a traditional and expected denouement; by the final scene, the story has ended and questions have been answered. Usually this resolution comes about through death by lynching or illness. Richardson's plays offer a slice of life; although the curtain may have fallen, the central conflict has not necessarily been settled. An audience member might leave a Richardson play with the sense that the characters still have much to resolve and that their futures may not be favorable. In this non-resolution, or lack of usual closure, the curtain seems to drop *in medias res.* The action, it might be said, seems to continue with the unresolved situations only blocked from the audience's view.

In considering his reliance on black characters and situations, on working-class people, and the lack of a comfortable, or predictable, closing, one might divide Richardson's plays into two groups: those drawn from the folk culture, most often in rural Georgia or South Carolina, and those set in a city and centering on the friction between bourgeois and working-class African Americans. His folk characters are the uneducated, the underclass, those who live on the margin of a white world but do not cross that border. His indigent urban dwellers frequently remain linked to their folk past in the South through dialect, the use of roots and herbs, a reliance on the black community, and a faith in God. Those drawn from the middle-class are usually educated, arrogant, self-satisfied, and judgmental. Perhaps this was his judgment of the Talented Tenth, a group that never seemed to accept him. For the most part, this elevated group, once they have succeeded, seems to want little contact with those who are less fortunate. . . .the characters who have left behind—whether literally or emotionally—their folk past and embraced the city are the very ones who seem to turn their backs on the black community and who fail to respond to its needs, to the detriment of themselves, their families, and, by extension, the black race.

Notes

1. For a defense of the plays written by 1930 by black women, see the first chapter of Elizabeth Brown-Guillory, *Their Place on the Stage: Black Women Playwrights in America.* New York: Praeger, 1988. Nellie McKay suggests, albeit unwittingly, that there are similarities among many of the plays written by African-American women during the 1920s. See "What Were They Saying?: Black Women Playwrights of the Harlem Renaissance." In Victor A. Kramer, ed. *The Harlem Renaissance Re-examined.* New York: AMS Press, 1987: 129-47. All plays by women discussed here are located in *Black Theater, U.S.A.: Forty-Five Plays by Black Americans: 1847-1974.* James V. Hatch and Ted Shine, eds. (New York: Free Press, 1974.)

2. According to Arthur Davis and Michael Peplow, 3,052 lynchings took place in the United States between 1885 and 1919, which makes obvious the social, indeed the humane, purpose behind anti-lynching plays. See *The New Negro Renaissance.* Arthur P. Davis and Michael Peplow, eds. (New York: Holt, Winston and Rinehart, 1975: 21).

3. Langston Hughes, whom Richardson had met through Carter Woodson, also criticized the upper stratum of African Americans in Washington, D.C. See Langston Hughes, "Our Wonderful Society: Washington" *Opportunity* 5 (1927): 226-27.

4. His reliance on strong female roles may have been influenced by the number of females in his household; with him lived his wife, his three daughters, possibly his mother, and an occasional elderly aunt.

5. Richardson wrote that critic George Jean Nathan, in an essay on African-American dramatists, "spoils the chapter" by labeling blacks as "coons" and as being "porters, waiters and cooks." See George Jean Nathan. "The Black Art." In *Mr. George Jean Nathan Presents* (New York: Knopf, 1917: 115-21).

6. In a 1972 interview, Richardson commented that his play *The Chip Woman's Fortune* was "about ordinary Black people." He recounted going to the Howard Theater to see the effect of the plays on the audience:

   > One night I was standing in the right wing among the stage hands looking at a performance of *The Chip Woman's Fortune* when I heard one of the stage hands say, "ain't that just like life." I felt at that time and still feel that his simple statement was one of the finest compliments I have ever received.
   > ("Youth" [*From Youth to Age.* Autobiography. Typescript.])

FURTHER READING

Bibliography

Hatch, James V. and Abdulla, Omanii, eds. "Willis Richardson." In *Black Playwrights, 1823-1977: An Annotated Bibliography of Plays,* pp. 190–94. New York and London: R. R. Bowker Company, 1977.

Provides a complete chronological catalogue with a brief synopsis of Richardson's plays.

Criticism

Peterson, Bernard L., Jr. "Willis Richardson: Pioneer Playwright." In *The Theater of Black Americans, Volume I,* edited by Errol Hill, pp. 113-25. Englewood Cliffs, N.J.: Prentice-Hall, Inc., 1975.

Surveys the career of Richardson, discussing him as a pioneering African American dramatist and calling for a revival of interest in his work.

OTHER SOURCES FROM GALE:

Additional coverage of Richardson's life and career is contained in the following sources published by the Gale Group: *Black Writers,* Ed. 1; *Contemporary Authors,* Vol. 124; *Dictionary of Literary Biography,* Vol. 51; and *Something about the Author,* Vol. 60.

GEORGE SAMUEL SCHUYLER

(1895 - 1977)

(Also wrote under the pseudonyms Samuel I. Brooks and Rachel Call) American novelist, journalist, essayist, and critic.

One of the luminaries of the "New Negro Movement" of the 1920s, Schuyler is best known for his *Black No More* (1931), a semi-science fiction novel satirizing American racial attitudes and those who profit from perpetuating them. *Slaves Today* (1931), his novel based on his research in Liberia exposing Black enslavement in twentieth-century Africa, challenged the optimism and ideology of Marcus Garvey's Back to Africa movement and reinforced Schuyler's own lifelong commitment to the abolition of doctrines of racial superiority or separation. He also wrote *The Black Internationale* (1936-37) and *Black Empire* (1937-38), Black nationalist adventure/detective fantasy novels of Black world domination. For nearly half a century Schuyler was a widely read newspaperman: his columns and essays on race issues and the foibles of humanity appeared in *The Messenger, The Nation, American Mercury, The Pittsburgh Courier,* and *The Manchester* (New Hampshire) *Union Leader.*

BIOGRAPHICAL INFORMATION

Schuyler was born on February 25, 1895, in Providence, Rhode Island, into a prosperous northern family whose ancestry had been free at least since the time of the American Revolutionary War. His father, who died when Schuyler was three, was a chef; later, Schuyler's stepfather maintained a comfortable income, stressing to his stepson the importance of the Protestant work ethic. His mother was of a racially diverse family; she imparted to Schuyler her own love of books and learning. Schuyler grew up in Syracuse, New York. Believing that completing his schooling would not advance him in the world because of his race, he left school in 1912 and joined the army, where he began to write for army newspapers and was commissioned a first lieutenant in 1918. That year, angered by a bootblack's refusal to give him a shoeshine, he deserted, traveled across the United States, and eventually turned himself in in California. Sentenced to five years imprisonment, Schuyler served nine months and was released for good behavior. He was then discharged from the army. From 1919 to 1920 he lived in New York among gamblers, prostitutes, thieves, and homeless people, working as a building laborer, stevedore, house cleaner, and dishwasher. In 1921 he went back home to Syracuse, worked at less taxing jobs, and read voraciously in the public library. That same year Schuyler joined the town's Socialist Party. In 1923 he returned to New York, lived for a while as a hobo, but also moved among the cultural and literary figures of the Harlem Renaissance, writing for A. Philip Randolph's Black, socialist publication, *The Messenger;*

for *The Crisis,* the newspaper of the National Association for the Advancement of Colored People; and for the National Urban League's *Opportunity.* Schuyler was not, however, a dedicated socialist. According to Randolph, he was more interested in intellectual debate than ideology, and "made fun of everything—including socialism." In 1925 he joined the *Pittsburgh Courier,* where he worked as a columnist, an international correspondent, and an editorial writer; he served as its New York editor from 1944 to 1960. Despite his belief that inherent racial attributes do not exist and that art cannot be racially determined and does not reflect racial characteristics—as he argued in a 1926 article entitled "The Negro-Art Hokum"—he was concerned about the economic plight of Blacks and the cultural integrity of Africa. He wrote against the Italian assault upon Ethiopia and against the "Aryan lunacy of the Nazis," but even in 1940 he argued in the *Courier* that "our war is not against Hitler in Europe, but against Hitler in America. Our war is not to defend democracy, but to get a democracy we never had." A belief, too, that the Communist Party was using African Americans to advance its own totalitarian agenda lay at the heart of his intense rejection of communism. In 1928 Schuyler married Josephine Cogdell, a white Texas heiress and former model who also wrote for socialist papers. They had a daughter, Philippa, in 1931. Josephine was killed in Vietnam during the war while working as a newspaper reporter. Beginning in 1949 Schuyler became moderator of *The Negro World,* a radio program broadcast over WLIB in New York City. A socialist in his youth, by the end of the 1940s, with the publication of *The Communist Conspiracy against the Negro* (1947), Schuyler had declared himself a strong anti-Communist. By the 1960s he was a member of the ultra-conservative John Birch Society and wrote for its journal, *American Opinion.* He was a supporter of Barry Goldwater in 1964 and unsuccessfully ran for Congress in New York City on the Conservative Party ticket against Adam Clayton Powell. He was an opponent of Martin Luther King, Malcolm X, and the civil rights, Black Power, and Black Nationalist movements. By the 1960s Schuyler was out of favor with nearly the entire African American community and deemed irrelevant by whites for his stand against the civil rights movement.

MAJOR WORKS

Schuyler's major accomplishment is the accumulation of his daily columns over a span of nearly fifty years, rather than his few novels and essay collections. Repeatedly Schuyler attempted—through satire, invective, or fantasy—to break down the stereotypical images of Black people which he felt dominated the consciousness of both whites and African Americans. In his writings he lambasted whites who proclaimed the superiority of one skin color or hair texture over another, and then lampooned Blacks who lightened their skin and straightened their hair. In one of his columns in the *Pittsburgh Courier* in 1930, writing of the popularity of *Amos and Andy* among Blacks, he argued, "the average Negro has the same attitude toward everything, including the Negro, that the average Klansman has." Schuyler seemed always on guard in his writing that a detestation of white racism ought not to lead to a reactive Black racial mythology. Perhaps this is most clearly expressed in "The Negro-Art Hokum" and in his reporting from Liberia about Black enslavement of Blacks. In his Ethiopian novels, written under several pen names, he explored the possibility of Black heroes and adventurers, tough and savvy, with the license and mobility of privileged whites. A satire on racism, *Black No More* involves a scientist's discovery of a method of turning Black people into caucasians. In the novel, the African American Max Disher becomes the white Matthew Fischer, who comes to work for Reverend Givens and his Klan-like organization. In the course of the novel, Schuyler spared neither white racism nor Black responses to it, and exposed the folly and greed of both parties. Despite its serious message, the novel for the most part retains a light, humorous tone tempered by the political ideas Schulyer conveyed.

CRITICAL RECEPTION

In his youth Schuyler was admired by writers and readers across racial boundaries. W. E. B. Du Bois, satirized by Schuyler in *Black No More,* enjoyed the joke. H. L. Mencken befriended him, guided him, and published his works. Schuyler's work appeared in numerous publications, both African American and white. Schuyler's column ran in the *Pittsburgh Courier* for nearly fifty years, and his serialized Ethiopian stories were a boon to its circulation. When his political position veered so strongly to the right that his old publishers no longer welcomed him, others of his persuasion, like the editor of the *Manchester Union Leader,* were ready to accommodate him. Near the very end of his life, he became bigger than his politics, a figure whose life had encompassed a vast track not only of Black, but of American history and culture, and he was appreciated, in Ishmael Reed's words, for his "spunk and bluntness." Henry Louis Gates Jr. describes Schuyler as a man whose work offers a "complicated response to the pressures of ideological conformity among blacks—and [shows] the failure of most received ideological stances or political programs to account for this complexity."

PRINCIPAL WORKS

"The Negro-Art Hokum" (essay) 1926

Racial Intermarriage in the United States (nonfiction) 1929

Black No More: Being an Account of the Strange and Wonderful Workings of Science in the Land of the Free, A.D. 1933-1940 (novel) 1931

Slaves Today: A Story of Liberia (novel) 1931

The Black Internationale [as Samuel I. Brooks] (serial novel) 1936-37; published in the journal *The Courier* (Pittsburgh)

Black Empire [as Samuel I. Brooks] (serial novel) 1937-38; published in the journal *The Courier* (Pittsburgh)

The Communist Conspiracy against the Negro (nonfiction) 1947

Black and Conservative: The Autobiography of George S. Schuyler (autobiography) 1966

GENERAL COMMENTARY

ANN RAYSON (ESSAY DATE 1978)

SOURCE: Rayson, Ann. "George Schuyler: Paradox among 'Assimilationist' Writers." *Black American Literature Forum* 12, no. 3 (autumn, 1978): 102-06.

In the following essay, Rayson considers some inherent contradictions in Schuyler's attitude toward race and politics.

George S. Schuyler, often called the H. L. Mencken of Negro journalism, is the black writer who, more than any other, denied the importance of race as a factor in his life and work. Because of his stance he has generally been labeled an "assimilationist" by critics like Robert Bone, who tend to classify black writers as either "assimilationists" or "black nationalists." "A tendency toward assimilationism," says Bone, "is at bottom a matter of changing one's reference group, an attempt to abandon ethnic ties and identify with the dominant majority."[1] But using Bone's definition as a point of reference, one must conclude, after examining the evidence, that Schuyler, certainly not a black nationalist, is anything but an assimilationist. He immerses himself so completely in just one element of the dominant white culture that he ends up a member of another minority—the American right-wing, socio-political conservative.

Schuyler's ideologies concerning politics, economics, and race underwent major changes during the 1920s and '30s, and by 1940 he had firmly established himself in a classic reactionary position. A socialist during the twenties, when he wrote columns for the black socialist journal the *Messenger,* Schuyler began to develop politically into an ardent anti-communist in 1933 when the International Labor Defense tried to make the Scottsboro case into a class issue. This was the turning point in his thinking and the beginning of Schuyler's "Red Scare" paranoia and eventual political and social conservativism. His conservative views were so insistent that in 1964 he supported Barry Goldwater for President despite what most blacks regarded as a racist Republican Party platform. Throughout the 1960s, moreover, he castigated the methods, efforts, and gains of the civil rights movement. He vehemently protested Martin Luther King's being chosen to receive the Nobel Prize, arguing in terms so strong that his own paper, *The Pittsburgh Courier,* refused to print his editorial.[2] In a 1967 syndicated article, Schuyler blamed the then current race riots on the entire Negro leadership: "The agitators gather crowds by blaming the white man for all the Negroes' ills, while the responsible Negro leadership either defends this falsehood, cravenly remains silent, or whimpers, 'We didn't really mean it' after the cities have burned to ashes."[3]

As one would expect, Schuyler's views have alienated members of his own race and have been frequently attacked by other black writers. The editor of *The Crisis,* for example, said of him in 1965, concerning his anti-civil rights campaign:

> No white reader should be misled by the Schuyler tirade because, happily, he does not speak for the majority of Negro citizens of any persuasion or class. His is distinctly a minority opinion, practically a one-man minority. Moreover, Mr. Schuyler does not even comprehend the depth and fury of the Negro's resentment against the restrictions imposed upon him solely because of his race. All his years, Mr. Schuyler has been too busy breaking idols to learn this lesson.[4]

Finally, as if his alien views and activities were not enough to make his point, Schuyler became an active member of the John Birch Society, the most prominent arch-conservative organization in the country and, as such, one not representative of the "dominant majority" in American politics or racial structure. Thus, while we may legitimately attempt to label some black writers as assimilationists, we cannot put George Schuyler into this group. Clearly an iconoclast, he stands alone and, in doing so, presents us with a critical problem of classification, a paradox that requires examination.

This examination must above all concern itself with Schuyler's autobiography ***Black and Conservative.*** Then there are some records of what fellow writers and literary critics have said about him, although there is not a wealth of such secondary material. Finally, there are other important sources, such as the many articles and editorials Schuyler wrote for magazines and newspapers, and his two novels, ***Black No More*** and ***Slaves Today,*** both published in 1931. The autobiography remains important, as it is the author's self-presentation. Published in 1966 when Schuyler was seventy-one, ***Black and Conservative,*** while not itself a product of the Harlem Renaissance, does record some of that important period in Schuyler's career and reflects the political and philosophical changes that he underwent after 1923, the year he began his editorial career.

Schuyler's autobiography is as different from the generic norm as one might expect from such an author. The nature of autobiography is such that the genre lends itself to a natural degree of authorial posing and unreliability. By its very nature, being the coherent narrative of a person's life as told to the world by oneself, it is bound to be selective and biased, whether consciously or unconsciously. Yet, even if autobiographies are partially untrue or necessarily embellished, one may still, Roy Pascal has argued, use what autobiographers write as "true evidence of their personality."[5] Rather than by a presentation of direct and historical knowledge, autobiography ordinarily wins its readers by its admission to intimacy. Schuyler does not work in this direction, however. As Carleton L. Lee, who reviewed ***Black and Conservative*** for *Negro History Bulletin,* says, the book is "not conventional autobiography"; it lacks the "substance" of autobiography, and is impersonal.[6] Schuyler, in his autobiography, does not admit the reader to that intimacy that the genre customarily promises. Although there are valuable insights to be gleaned from this record, what he ends by presenting to the reader is largely a political and particularly an anti-communist tract.

One might write off Schuyler's autobiography as an aging man's attempt to justify his ultimate conservativism; yet to get an accurate picture of George Schuyler the man, one has to balance facts with authorial stances, to compare what Schuyler said and did against what he says he said. Taking the autobiography in isolation, any reader would conclude that he is either a "raceless" writer or one who is so concerned with race that he goes to an extreme to assure white readers that he is anything but a champion of black causes. Strong denial of race may be the flip side of black chauvinism. Perhaps Schuyler protests too much with his bizarre political identifications. The question remains—how do we reconcile Schuyler's history with the statements he makes, or fails to make, about race in his autobiography?

Black and Conservative has little in common with the classic confessional autobiography that many black writers like Richard Wright, J. Saunders Redding, Malcolm X, Claude Brown, Maya Angelou, and others take for a form, yet it does contain many of the crucial themes in black autobiography. For instance, Schuyler begins his first chapter with the same emphasis on race that haunts, to one degree or another, most black writers: "A black person learns very early that color is a disadvantage in a world of white folk." But in contrast to the more militant black autobiographers, Schuyler, having admitted this fact, proceeds to minimize its adverse implications: "One also learns very early to make the best of it," he says. "So the lifetime endeavor of the intelligent Negro is now to be reasonably happy though colored" (p. 1). Schuyler believes his own lifetime denies the racial factor.

Born in Providence, Rhode Island, in 1895, Schuyler grew up in Syracuse, New York, the well-adjusted son of a comfortable, even "upper-class" black family. In this area his past proves the exception to the rule, as he apparently knew little of racial prejudice. His father, the head chef in a local hotel, "was an aristocrat in the colored community, . . . affected baronial living, insisted on a good table, and dressed well" (p. 8). Although he died, leaving the family without a provider, they resiliently took domestic jobs. Apparently this did not hurt the family pride, and Schuyler seems to have accepted these changing fortunes with an objectivity and equanimity we may find peculiar. Bred black aristocrats, in the relative context within the class structure of the black community that Schuyler uses the term, the Schuylers attended the Episcopal Church ("The better class attended it" [p. 14]), and they once had been Catholics. Religious affiliation served as an external symbol of the family's social standing. As he admits, the Episcopalians looked down upon the "small" Negro Baptist and Methodist churches. Other black autobiographers have commented upon such division. H. Rap Brown in *Die Nigger Die,* for instance, says:

> Dr. So-and-So goes to the Episcopal Church, the Presbyterian or the Catholic Church. The brother on the block goes to the Baptist, the Holy Rollers or the Sanctified Church. And the Methodist Church is in between the two. It ain't as niggerish as the Baptist Church, but it's not as high class as the Episcopal Church. As negroes become more "white-educated," the tradition in religion begins.[7]

Where Brown denigrates the conventional valuations of religious affiliations, Schuyler does not. Schuyler prefers to base his political and social theories on economic class rather than on race, so that even when the two are virtually inseparable, he generally chooses to ignore the connection.

Schuyler's interpretations of lessons from his childhood and youth illustrate the economic thesis he pursues even when reporting extraordinarily personal events. His account of this period covers only thirty-two pages of his autobiography, the bulk of which describes his adult achievements, acquaintances, experiences in the publicized world, and attacks on communism. But there is one noteworthy incident from his childhood, one that is quite typical of black autobiography, the ritual scene of color recognition. He is six:

> On the opening day of the term I registered three firsts: I was called "nigger," which had never happened to me before; I had a fight with the offender, a pugnacious little Italian boy; and during the fisticuffs I had my nose bloodied. Being called "nigger" hurt me worst of all. I don't think I had ever heard the taunt before, and when I went home and asked my stepfather, he took me to the mirror and explained as well as he could. . . . I don't think it had occurred to me that there was this uncomplimentary slang synonym for colored.
>
> (Pp. 17-18)

But Schuyler is different from most black autobiographers, who see racist issues in such scenes. He must have understood the taunt; otherwise he would have had no reason to fight. Yet in the autobiography, the report of this incident triggers another kind of protest on the character of the racial problem:

> While aware that I was physically different in appearance from my white neighbors, I have never felt inferior. Indeed, I strongly question the view of many psychologists and sociologists that most colored people regard themselves as inferior. They simply are aware that their socio-economic position is inferior, which is a different thing.
>
> (P. 18)

Schuyler concludes his brief reminiscence of his formative childhood years with an account of his joining the Army in 1912 at age seventeen. He seems either not to have felt or to have been immune to the Jim Crowism of the United States Army at that time. Seeing no better job alternatives than red capping, portering, or working on the railroads, he chose to join the Army, and later reenlisted. To him the cause of the sorry employment situation for blacks prior to World War I was failure in economic competition, not racism.

Back in Syracuse later and then in New York City, Schuyler became a budding journalist. A distinct split characterizes his report and the apparent actual facts concerning events during these years. He rented a room in New York from the Universal Negro Improvement Association headed by Marcus Garvey. In his autobiography, however, he declares Garvey to be a prototype of Hitler who hypnotized the masses "with his bull voice and his cry of Africa for the Africans at a time when the independence of the Dark Continent was the sheerest wishful thinking of a few racist zealots" (p. 120). Schuyler here takes an assimilationist stance: he does not make political or moral distinctions on the basis of color. On the other hand, he had evinced black nationalist views in his editorials of the period. In 1935 during the Italo-Ethiopian crisis, "Schuyler lambasted Afro-Americans for their lack of 'solidarity with their brothers across the sea.'"[8] In 1930 he said, "The Aframerican is just a lampblacked Anglo-Saxon, with a society which in every detail is a replica of the white society surrounding it,"[9] thus prompting Arthur P. Davis to label him an assimilationist in racial matters, yet in 1940 he "proudly reported to his readers the findings of the chauvinistic black historian, Joel A. Rogers: 'The Negro is not only the primary human stock, but the most virile. . . . He originated art, religion and science. Every one of the major religions were [*sic*] started by black men.'"[10] In his autobiography Schuyler expresses the attitude of Booker T. Washington:

"My feeling was then, and it is stronger now," he says, "that Negroes have the best chance here in the United States if they will avail themselves of the numerous opportunities they have" (p. 121). Yet he had stated in a 1939 article: "Most Negroes, generations after Emancipation, enjoy today less economic, social, and political rights than the Russian *moujiks* under Nicholas II. Still subjected to systematized economic spoilation and race discrimination, there is bitterness in their hearts."[11] Despite his excursion with the socialists in the 1920s and his continuing insistence on economic collectivization, he nevertheless affirms the benefits of capitalism, as a rule.

Critics of Schuyler have been divided almost as much as the man. While some claim that Schuyler is consistent, others argue for his ambivalence as evinced in his writings. Arthur P. Davis says: "Whatever else he has been, George Schuyler has been consistent, and he has defended this position stoutly in hundreds of newspaper columns, editorials, and volumes. The assumption of the Negro's essential American-ness undergirds all of his published works."[12] In contrast, James O. Young in *Black Writers of the Thirties* contends that "it is not so easy to categorize the thought of George S. Schuyler." During the 1930s, as a columnist, he was "habitually inconsistent"; his "columns were replete with lapses of memory and self-contradictions." Young does see certain patterns emerging, but only in Schuyler's general transition from a "one-time self-proclaimed radical" to a clarion for the far-right. Young adds: "Throughout the decade he consciously argued against any form of race separatism or chauvinism. In fact, he saw the ultimate solution to the race problem in the amalgamation of the races. And yet, almost simultaneously with his outbursts against chauvinism and separatism he would make appeals for blacks to be more race conscious."[13]

A brief examination of a few of Schuyler's other writings may further explain the paradox of his career. In his novel ***Slaves Today,*** Schuyler exposes the exploitation of native labor in Liberia and is strongly propagandistic. Hugh Gloster describes the novel as one which "ranks as another manifestation of the growing concern of the American Negro for the welfare of colored people in other parts of the world."[14] On the other hand, blacks exploit fellow blacks in ***Slaves Today,*** a circumstance which, when Schuyler visited Liberia in 1931, "strengthened his conviction about the incidental importance of color,"[15] according to Henry F. Winslow. Ironically, Schuyler could not, twenty years later, go to Liberia "because of a law specifically barring him."[16] More comfortable with satire than with sentiment, Schuyler, in ***Black No More,*** the novel for which he is widely known, makes hilarious sport of the racial attitudes of both races, as he attacks the NAACP and the KKK equally. In a 1932 *Pittsburgh Courier* editorial Schuyler, growing increasingly pessimistic and critical of the left, was to reemphasize the cynicism of this novel, while publicly answering a communist friend who had accused him of being a tired radical:

> I AM a tired radical. I am tired of the cant, ignorance, blindness and lack of humor of most of the radicals, especially the extreme radicals. I am tired of a diet of slogans and catch-phrases that mean nothing. I am tired of these so-called radicals' assumption of omniscience. Indeed, I have about come to the conclusion that most of them are not radicals at all, but are maladjusted sentimentalists. It is not surprising that they have been able to corral a whole lot of Negroes, including many of our so-called intelligentsia.[17]

This period marks the beginning of Schuyler's virulent anti-communism, while at the same time it demonstrates the fact that Schuyler was less interested in consistency of position than he was in stirring up arguments. He made sure that he maintained his reputation as the most controversial columnist on the scene in black journalism. Says Melvin Tolson:

> He stimulated more differences of opinion than any other Negro writer. His column, "Views and Reviews," published in the Pittsburgh *Courier,* is the most discussed column in Negro America. I have heard his opinions attacked and defended in barbershops, Jim Crow cars, pool rooms, classrooms, churches, and drawing-rooms. Criticisms of him have run from the sublime to the ridiculous. He gets a big kick out of reading the adverse ones.[18]

Other aspects of Schuyler's life make the critic's task no easier. One manifestation of his antiracist philosophy is evident in his marriage to a white woman. Black psychologists may argue, of course, that it is an indication of conflict. In his autobiography, Schuyler says of his wife, "She was blonde and shapely. Daughter of a Texas rancher and banker in the Fort Worth area, she was liberal on the race question without being mawkish and mushy. She saw Negroes as I saw Whites, as individuals" (p. 163). Thus he wed one who in appearance, if not in attitude, was the archetypal Southern white woman. Perhaps the marriage was meant to demonstrate the depth of his commitment to his theory that miscegenation would solve racism, as he proclaimed repeatedly in editorials, however pessimistic he was about this actually happening. In an article of 1930, **"A Negro Looks Ahead,"** Schuyler stated: "Thus, on the whole, and in spite of everything, I think it is fair to say that the present strained relations between the races are likely to be transitory."[19] And Mrs. Schuyler is quoted in an *Our World* feature as saying that race mixture had a lot to do with the prodigious talents of their daughter Phillipa.[20] Consistent in his inconsistency, Schuyler stated in 1956 that "the idealists' vision of an ultimate racial Melting Pot is, to say the least, dim and remote."[21] In most areas of his life, whatever nuances of interpretation we add, Schuyler persistently ignored or suppressed his racial identity, once again deviating from the pattern of most black autobiographers.

Yet Schuyler seemed not so much to dislike blacks and like whites or love America, as he did fear communism. Everything leads back to this as the motivating factor for his reactionary position. At first he feared the Party, as he saw it, because it could manipulate blacks to its own ends. Afro-Americans became pawns. But more than this, he became disillusioned with liberal and socialist politics, not economics. Throughout the 1930s he advocated economic socialism and supported W. E. B. Du Bois's proposals, while politically he became an isolationist, bitterly opposing Roosevelt's policies, particularly those concerning foreign affairs.

George Schuyler became an arch-reactionary at a time—the 1930s—when most of his friends and associates were moving in the opposite direction. There are several possible explanations for his motives, the main one resulting from his reaction to the Scottsboro trial, at which the International Labor Defense of the Communist Party rushed to defend the nine blacks as victims of class war rather than of racism. Wrote Schuyler:

> It was most faulty tactics for the International Labor Defense to inject the issue of "the class war" into the case. Anybody who is at all familiar with the Southern psychology knows that no class issues are involved save of the most remote and inconsequential kind. It is a race issue pure and simple. On this question, the entire South, capitalist and proletarian, is united. Wherever and whenever the Negro is involved the Southern white bum and banker are as one in the cry for blood.[22]

In an *American Mercury* article of 1939, he reiterated: "It was the ILD's mishandling of the Scottsboro case that did most to discredit the communists among Negroes."[23] As a result of this kind of exploitation, Schuyler began to declare war on the communists and developed his anti-communist theme repeatedly in his columns and editorials during the thirties and after. As the decade drew to a close, Schuyler became increasingly irascible and lost much of his sense of humor.

Yet Schuyler's disillusionment with the Communist Party for trying to turn a race issue into a class issue was not isolated. Many black intellectuals felt used by the Party, although these sentiments did not surface until the forties. The theme recurs in black fiction. Ellison's Invisible Man finally discovers that his function has been that of the sambo puppet made to dance to the strings of the Brotherhood. Also, Ellison satirizes the Communist Party's use of white women to lure naïve blacks into the fold—another argument of Schuyler's in several editorials, one example being that of 1938:

> Being basically yokel-minded, they [young Negroes] were ready to be "sold" anything that promised everything for nothing, so they "joined the party." In many instances this decision was hastened by the white comrades' judicious use of flat-heeled, leather-coated lady Reds willing to sacrifice their All for the Cause.
>
> Today they are the most disillusioned people in the country.[24]

Even Richard Wright in *Native Son* has Max declare that he would not defend Bigger Thomas if the Communist Party had not been dragged into the case, and Max attempts to defend him on the issue of the Marxist class struggle. Schuyler, in this sense, anticipates the general black rejection of the Communist Party in the 1940s and '50s, although he is more extreme in his reaction than is any other writer, and it is this that sets him apart.

Later in life, having grown progressively paranoid over "big government," Schuyler crowned his political and journalistic career by supporting Senator Goldwater in the 1964 election. Concerning a radio interview in which he declared his loyalty, he says: "My reply stirred up a storm since all the civil rights organizations were openly fighting Goldwater because of his opposition to the Civil Rights Act which he regarded as unconstitutional" (***Black and Conservative,*** p. 349). Schuyler's political message is radically and, among blacks, uniquely conservative:

> There are forces in the world that want us to fail, and conspire toward that failure, which means disunity and destruction. We are here blessed with the right of mobility, the right of ownership, the privilege of privacy and development of personality, and the precious machinery of peaceful

> change. These gifts and gains it is the purpose of the conservative to defend and extend, lest we perish in the fell clutch of collectivism. These gifts and gains I have been trying in my small way to preserve.
>
> (P. 352)

No other black autobiographer has written, "At best, race is a superstition" (p. 352).

While Schuyler's psychological attitude is deceptively simple, and congenial to some white readers, beneath this objective, unemotional, and unreasonably extroverted self-portrayal certainly exists a divided self. Although Schuyler's publications of the twenties and thirties indicate a man split over the race issue, he refuses, in his autobiography, to admit that he ever questioned his own identity as a black writer and the affiliations he necessarily developed as a result of his color, preferring instead to cling to the unwavering authoritativeness of the "white" American way.

Over the years Schuyler went further than merely to accept white America; he wholeheartedly embraced its most conservative elements, while attacking black leaders and avoiding any connection with black political and social movements. As a result, he forfeited the good will of fellow blacks, while being much sought after as a speaker by white conservative organizations. Schuyler seems a unique example of the black intellectual who struggled with the race issue for years only to emerge as a reactionary who refused to recognize race as an issue. In the vehemence of his protest, then, he is not so much an assimilationist, in Bone's sense, as he appears to be a raging, incomprehensible individualist.

Notes

1. *The Negro Novel in America,* rev. ed. (New Haven: Yale Univ. Press, 1965), p. 5.
2. George S. Schuyler, *Black and Conservative* (New Rochelle, NY: Arlington House, 1966), p. 350. Future references to this book will occur parenthetically in the text.
3. Cited in "Blame for the Riots as a Negro Writer Sees It," *U.S. News and World Report,* 63 (14 Aug. 1967), 10.
4. "George S. Schuyler, Iconoclast," *The Crisis,* 72 (Oct. 1965), 485.
5. *Design and Truth in Autobiography* (Cambridge, MA: Harvard Univ. Press, 1960), p. 1.
6. 30 (Jan. 1967), 22.
7. (New York: Dial Press, 1969), p. 8.
8. James O. Young, *Black Writers of the Thirties* (Baton Rouge: Louisiana State Univ. Press, 1973), p. 90.
9. *American Mercury,* 19 (Feb. 1930), 217.
10. Young, p. 91.
11. "Negroes Reject Communism," *American Mercury,* 48 (June 1939), 176.
12. *From the Dark Tower* (Washington, DC: Howard Univ. Press, 1974), pp. 43-44.
13. Young, pp. 84, 89.
14. *Negro Voices in American Fiction* (Chapel Hill: Univ. of North Carolina Press, 1948), p. 157.
15. "George S. Schuyler: Fainting Traveler," *Midwest Journal,* 5 (Summer 1953), 30.
16. "Meet the George Schuylers: America's Strangest Family," *Our World,* 6 (Apr. 1951), 25.
17. "Views and Reviews," *The Pittsburgh Courier,* 10 Dec. 1932, Sec. 1, p. 10.
18. "George S. Schuyler," *American Mercury,* 28 (Mar. 1933), 373.
19. *American Mercury,* 19 (Feb. 1930), 218.
20. "Meet the George Schuylers," p. 25.
21. "Do Negroes Want to Be White?" *American Mercury,* 82 (June 1956), 60.
22. "Views and Reviews," *The Pittsburgh Courier,* 22 Apr. 1933, Sec. 1, p. 10.
23. "Negroes Reject Communism," 48 (June 1939), 179.
24. "Views and Reviews," *The Pittsburgh Courier,* 2 Apr. 1938, Sec. 1, p. 10.

MICHAEL W. PEPLOW (ESSAY DATE 1980)

SOURCE: Peplow, Michael W. "The Race Problem: Schuyler's Major Essays." In *George S. Schuyler,* pp. 40-47. Boston: Twayne Publishers, 1980.

In the following excerpt, Peplow examines the themes of some of Schuyler's major essays and traces the development of his views regarding race relations.

While much has been made of Schuyler's supposed assimilationism in **"The Negro-Art Hokum,"** little has been said about his race essays, which began appearing about the same time. Yet they represent some of Schuyler's best analyses of the race problem in the United States. They further reveal that Schuyler was very much a 1920s race militant.

Of the dozens of articles Schuyler wrote on the race question, I have selected seven that are considered his best efforts. **"The Negro and Nordic Civilization"** (1925), **"Blessed Are the Sons of Ham"** (1927), **"Our White Folks"** (1927), **"Our Greatest Gift to America"** (1927), and **"The Caucasian Problem"** (1944) contain some of his best satire. **"A Negro Looks Ahead"** (1930) and **"Do Negroes Want to be White?"** (1956) are essentially nonsatiric. Two of the seven essays appeared after the "literary years" and are discussed here because they show Schuyler's progression from youthful idealism about a "permanent solution" (interracial marriage) to despair over America's inability to solve the race problem. Read in order, the seven essays provide an important backdrop against which to consider ***Black No More.***

I. Schuyler's Satiric Essays

"The Negro and Nordic Civilization" appeared in *The Messenger* two years after Schuyler began his professional career. The essay shows Schuyler attempting to develop a persona or narrator and a tone of sustained irony. The persona begins by making what appears to be a concession about the "superiority" of Nordic civilization:

> I feel that we must admit in the face of a mountain of evidence that the modern civilization of the Caucasian far excels anything developed by the Negro in Africa or elsewhere. . . . True, we have our gangsters, politicians, editorial writers and drug addicts, but these are largely due to an infusion of white blood . . . and the compelling force of environment.[1]

Perhaps with some luck Aframericans "may in another half century reach the Nordic level" (198); in the meantime they must "admit" their backwardness and earnestly endeavor to appreciate the benefits [they] are undoubtedly deriving from [their] association with the supermen" (199).

This rather heavy-handed irony evidences some race pride. In discussing black contributions to civilization, the persona makes another interesting "concession":

> I am willing to concede . . . that the Negroes . . . contributed the foundations upon which Nordic civilization rests: the level, the wheel, the cam, the pulley, mathematics, paper, iron smelting, and, to go from the sublime to the ridiculous, much of what is known as Christianity. . . . I am even charitable enough to grant the Negroes such men as Antar, Pushkin, Dumas, . . . Toussaint L'Ouverture, Booker T. Washington and Henry O. Tanner. But who are such fellows . . . ? Surely we have never reached the level of Warren G. Harding!
>
> (201)

A somewhat more subtle piece, **"Blessed Are the Sons of Ham,"** was Schuyler's second contribution to *The Nation* (**"The Negro-Art Hokum"** had appeared one year earlier). Again Schuyler employs a persona whose satiric premise is that whites "have looked upon the black citizen as a tragic figure . . . a helpless transplanted child of the jungle caught in the cruel meshes of machine civilization" (the "noble savage" theory in short) and hence "feel sorry" for the Negro who must daily face Jim Crow laws and racist slurs.[2] Actually, we are gravely informed, Negroes find white racism "continuously entertaining," (313). Entertaining? The narrator describes some of these "entertaining" incidents (drawn from Schuyler's own experiences) that "prove" how "blessed" the "sons of Ham" really are. For example, the narrator once tried to cash a check in a Paris, Texas, hotel. The white clerk insulted him in as many ways as possible, at first refused to cash his check and then wearily did so after the narrator made a "pest" of himself (314). That the clerk is forced to do anything for a "nigger" is so "amusing" that the narrator leaves the hotel laughing at the ways of white folks. The clerk's "discomfiture amused me" and gave "me a thrill and a laugh to help me on my journey" (314).

The response of the narrator, so reminiscent of Schuyler's own response during the Seattle bar incident (see Chapter 1), is partly the "laughing to keep from crying" response that blacks have had to develop. It is also Schuyler's way of thumbing his nose at white racists.

As long as the incidents in this essay are "amusing" (i.e., light enough so that the reader laughs with the narrator), **"Blessed Are the Sons of Ham"** is effective irony. Unfortunately, the still youthful Schuyler becomes carried away toward the end of his essay with indignation at white racism and provides examples that are not "amusing." He describes several incidents that evoke rage or fear instead of laughter (314-315). The inclusion of these incidents violates the unity of tone set at the beginning of the essay. In other words, the persona drops his ironic mask and lashes out directly at white racism.[3] It is a literary flaw that Schuyler learned to avoid in his mature pieces.

The lead article in the December 1927 *American Mercury*, **"Our White Folks,"** was Schuyler's first piece for that famous publication. It was solicited by H. L. Mencken who, Schuyler told me in 1975, was not only *the* mentor of the era but a personal friend for many years.

In this essay, Schuyler employs a pattern he would use again and again: he first attacks white racists, then crosses over and attacks the black mentality which accepts the "White is Right" philosophy.[4] "To judge an individual solely on the basis of his skin color and hair texture is so obviously nonsensical that it seems not unreasonable to equate the bulk of Nordics with the *inmates of an insane asylum*" (my italics).[5] Indeed, "the Negro is a sort of black *Gulliver* chained by white *Lillipu-*

tians, a prisoner in the jail of color prejudice" (385; my italics). After dissecting white prejudice, Schuyler focuses on blacks who have sold out by accepting the "White is Right" attitude. Specifically, he attacks skin whiteners and hair straighteners (as he does time and again in his columns, essays, and ***Black No More***), while pointing to the proven abilities and rich history of black Americans. The Aframerican, he says, has had to be "more alert, more diplomatic, and a more skillful tactician than his white brothers" (387). He has always had a strong "pioneering spirit" as well as "energy and originality" (387). Indeed, the proud Aframerican can "put . . . the history of the blacks down through the ages alongside that of the whites and . . . not [be] ashamed":

> He knows that there is as much evidence that black men founded human civilization as there is that white men did, and he doubts whether the occidental society of today is superior to the monarcho-communist society developed in Africa. . . . The average Negro is more alert, more resourceful, more intelligent, and hence more interesting than the average Nordic. Certainly if the best measure of intelligence is ability to survive in a changing or hostile environment, and if one considers that the Negro is not only surviving but improving all the time in health, wealth, and culture, one must agree that he possesses a high degree of intelligence.
>
> (390)

This statement could hardly emanate from a man possessed by "the urge to whiteness." Neither could this graceful statement on the beauty of blackness:

> Negroes possess within their group the most handsome people in the United States, with the greatest variety of color, hair and features. Here is the real melting pot, and a glorious sight to see. . . . The percentage of beautiful is unquestionably larger than among the ofay brethren.
>
> (391)

Elsewhere the narrator amplifies: "Black? Well, yes, but how beautiful! How well it blends with almost every color! How smooth the skin; how soft and rounded the features. . . . Here in Aframerica one finds such an array of beauty that it even attracts Anglo-Saxons, despite their alleged color aversion" (392).

Published in *Ebony and Topaz* in 1927 and reprinted in V. F. Calverton's *Anthology of American Negro Literature* in 1929, **"Our Greatest Gift to America"** is probably Schuyler's most famous satiric essay.[6] The premise is deceptively simple—namely, that the "gift" is the mere *presence* of Negro Americans in the United States. Without blacks, the narrator informs us, white America would have no one to discriminate against. Further, blacks make the "gift" even more valuable by imitating whites (e.g., by trying to become as light as possible).

The narrator begins by poking fun at the Negro "intellectuals" who talk a lot but do nothing. He mocks "notable Aframerican speakers" in faddish Harlem Renaissance salons, men such as Professor Hambone of Moronia Institute and Dr. Lampblack of the Federal Society for the Exploitation of Lynching, who "eloquently hold forth for the better part of an hour on the blackamoor's gifts to the Great Republic" and completely miss the "greatest gift" (123). Such "Negro leaders" are accompanied by a New Negro poet who "recite[s] one of his inspiring verses anent a ragged black prostitute gnawing out her soul in the dismal shadows of Hog Maw Alley" (123). The irony is stinging, the references are clear: Professor Hambone is almost certainly one of Schuyler's old enemies, Robert Russa Moton of Tuskegee; the young poet must be Claude McKay, author of the poem "Young Prostitute."

Proceeding to the average black American, the persona attacks those "smokes" who quite literally destroy their bodies (and souls) by trying to be white; they try to act "just like white folks" and scorn a fellow black man by saying that he acts "just like a nigger" (123).

Then Schuyler attacks the white mentality that feeds off the presence of an "inferior" people. One of his best portraits is of Dorothy Dunce, a "demure . . . packer in a spaghetti factory" whose "indulgent parents used to scare her by issuing a solemn warning that a big black nigger would kidnap her if she wasn't a good little girl" (123):

> She naturally believes . . . that every big, burly black nigger she meets on a dark street is ready to relieve her by force of what remains of her virtue. A value is placed upon her that she would not have in Roumania, Scotland, Denmark, or Montenegro. She is now a member of that exalted aggregation known as pure, white womanhood. She is also confident of her general superiority because education has taught her that Negroes are inferior, immoral, diseased, lazy, unprogressive, ugly, odiferous, and should be kept firmly in their place. . . . Quite naturally she swells with race pride, for no matter how low she falls, she will always be a white woman . . . .
>
> (124)

Hence, "our presence . . . has been of incalculable value," for whites like Dorothy Dunce "have been buoyed up and greatly exalted by being constantly assured of their superiority . . ." (124). The Aframerican is America's "mudsill upon which all white people alike can stand and reach towards the stars" (124).

The irony in **"Our Greatest Gift to America"** is savage, specific, and well sustained. It is Schuyler at his best, and it moved Melvin Tolson, the respected black poet, to praise it as "the greatest satire on the race problem in this country that has ever been written. . . . It is Swift in one of his supreme moments."[7]

Significant as the articles already discussed are, it is only fair to Schuyler critics (and to Schuyler himself) to take notice of an optimistic piece called **"A Negro Looks Ahead."** In this essay, Schuyler unhesitatingly dismisses several current "solutions" to the race problem (return to Africa; physical separatism within the United States; separate economic development) and argues that the only logical solution is eventual "amalgamation with the Nordic population."[8] Indeed, someday current antimiscegenation laws will have been revoked, and blacks and whites will intermarry. By 2000 A.D. "a full-blooded American Negro may be rare enough to get a job in a museum"; a century hence "our American social leaders may be tanned naturally as they are now striving to become artificially" (219). In short, Schuyler bases his hopes on the melting pot theory.

Though such arguments may seem reasonable to some, for black American nationalists the article is an apparent sellout. Schuyler compounds the crime by insisting, as he had earlier in **"The Negro-Art Hokum,"** that "the Aframerican is just a lampblacked Anglo-Saxon" (220).

Schuyler's theory of amalgamation, so idealistic in the 1920s, did not remain intact as racial problems in the United States grew worse during the 1930s and 1940s. Two essays that appeared after the 1923-1933 years show Schuyler moving toward a more despairing view of the situation. **"The Caucasian Problem,"** published in Rayford Logan's *What the Negro Wants,* contains a hint of the despair to come. **"Do Negroes Want to be White?"**, which appeared in *The American Mercury* in 1956, serves as a prophetic—and despairing—warning to the citizens of the United States.

II. Schuyler's Non-Satiric Essays

"The Caucasian Problem" is significant because, although Schuyler again urges racial amalgamation, his tone is considerably less sure than it had been in the past. "By a peculiar logical inversion," begins Schuyler, "the Anglo-Saxon ruling class, its imitators, accomplices and victims have come to believe in a Negro problem."[9] Such "propaganda" is "a great testimonial to the ingenuity of exploiters with a bad conscience; for while there is actually no Negro problem, there is definitely a Caucasian problem" (282). Ranging far both geographically and historically, Schuyler lays the blame at the feet of "the international capitalists who control the lives of over a billion colored people" (283); these capitalists are "practically all white," as are "the technicians, brokers, lawyers, generals, admirals, artists and writers who serve them" and have served them since the time of slavery, through colonialism, to the present. They have established "a vicious color caste system which makes [this] world a cultured hell" (284).[10]

Pointing out that terms like "Negro" and "Caucasian" are meaningless and that the myth of white superiority totally "ignores the findings of advanced sociologists and ethnologists," Schuyler continues:

> the point is that these general terms . . . are convenient propaganda devices to emphasize the great gulf which we are taught to believe exists between these groups of people. It is significant that these divisions very conveniently follow the line of colonial subjugation and exploitation, with the Asiatics and Africans lumped together smugly as "backward peoples," "savages," "barbarians" or "primitives;" i.e., fair prey for fleecing and enslavement under the camouflage of "civilization."
>
> (287)

Warning that centuries of propaganda have to be undone, Schuyler argues with typical bluntness that "in the early days there was fraternization, intermixture and intermarriage between the masses of Negroes, whites and Indians in all the colonies;" had this been allowed to continue, he says, "there would now be no Caucasian problem" (288). What we need is to "re-condition colored and white people everywhere," to establish immediately "a revolutionary program of re-education calling not only for wholesale destruction of the accumulated mass of racialistic propaganda in books, magazines, newspapers, motion pictures and all the present [Jim Crow] laws . . . [but] a complete reorganization of our social system" (290):

> It would have to include the complete abolition of Jim Crow laws and institutions; the rescinding of all racial pollution laws barring marriage because of so-called race; a complete enforcement of the letter and spirit of the federal constitution,

and the ending of every vestige of the color bar in industry, commerce and the professions. The words "Negro," "white," "Caucasian," "Nordic" and "Aryan" would have to be permanently taken out of circulation . . . .

(293)

It is "extremely doubtful," Schuyler concludes, "that the colored people here or anywhere else will accept anything less than this" (296). The only alternative, he warns, "is to drift toward an international war" (297).

Schuyler tries to end his essay on a positive note, but he is well aware that "conflict and chaos" will probably polarize blacks and whites the world over:

there is still time to make a new world where tolerance, understanding, mutual respect and justice will prevail. . . . True, this means a complete about face on the part of the white world, but this is only right since the race problem is of its own making. The alternative here and abroad is conflict and chaos. We shall have to make a choice very soon.

(297-98)

Twelve years after the appearance of **"The Caucasian Problem,"** Schuyler realized that "the choice" had still not been made. In **"Do Negroes Want to be White?"** he again describes various aspects of "this cultured hell," then notes that black Americans have no desire to be white: "The goal is not to be white but to be free in a white world," to gain "full and immediate citizenship rights under the Constitution."[11] White America is worried, he says, about "brown-skin militancy and solidarity . . . a solidarity transcending petty divisions and appealing to pride of race" (57). Yet America is responsible for this militancy. Then Schuyler delivers the punchline in a passage that anticipates the Kerner Commission Report[12] by twelve years:

For better or for worse, two distinct, centripetal and endogamous societies have evolved in America. They seem to be as mutually exclusive as the Walloons and Flemings in Belgium. . . .

Both now have a vested interest in their integrity. Few whites want to be black and few Negroes yearn to be white. There will always be a necessary measure of cooperation and liaison between them for the common good of all, but the idealists' vision [Schuyler's?] of an ultimate racial Melting Pot is, to say the least, dim and remote.

(58-9)

The young idealist of **"A Negro Looks Ahead"** has resigned himself to the reality of the American "insane asylum." America's absurd colorphobia has won out, the melting pot solution has become a "dim and remote" possibility. By 1956 the lonely iconoclast saw that America was "beyond cure." As we shall see in Chapter 5, Schuyler the satirist demonstrated this bitterness in ***Black No More*** twenty-six years before Schuyler the essayist admitted to despair in **"Do Negroes Want to be White?"**

Notes

1. "The Negro and Nordic Civilization," *The Messenger,* 7 (May 1925), p. 198. Further references will be given in the text.
2. "Blessed Are the Sons of Ham," *The Nation,* 124 (March 23, 1927), p. 313. Further references will be given in the text.
3. H. L. Mencken wrote Schuyler about another piece and warned him not to overdue the attack: "Here again, it seems to me, you spoil a good story by showing too much indignation. . . . Thus the general effect of the article is considerably diminished. . . . In such writing . . . the really effective weapon is irony. The moment you begin to show indignation you weaken your whole case." Guy J. Forgue, ed., *Letters of H. L. Mencken* (New York, 1961), p. 349.

   Schuyler and Mencken became friends in 1927 and corresponded through 1939. Many critics have noted that Schuyler's style was Menckenesque; indeed, their philosophies were similar on a number of issues, for both of them were iconoclasts (see Chapter 8). Mencken once wrote the NAACP's Walter White to tell him to listen more carefully to what Schuyler had to say on a given issue (Forgue, pp. 478-79). And he wrote Blanche Knopf in 1937 to tell her that "there is an excellent book in George S. Schuyler . . . the best writer the Negroes have ever produced, and . . . he is a highly intelligent man. . . . He loves to tell the truth" (Forgue, p. 419).
4. See W. E. B. Du Bois, "The Browsing Reader," *The Crisis,* 39 (March 1931), p. 100, where the editor says that *Black No More* "carries not only scathing criticism of Negro leaders, but of the mass of Negroes, and then it passes over and slaps the white people just as hard and unflinchingly straight in the face." Schuyler's habit of attacking the weaknesses of one race, then crossing over and attacking the weaknesses of the other race, was established early in his career.
5. "Our White Folks," *The American Mercury,* 12 (December 1927), p. 385. Further references will be given in the text. The italicized passages show that Schuyler was still convinced that we are living in an "insane asylum," a typical satiric premise that Schuyler might have inherited from Jonathan Swift, whom he greatly admired.
6. "Our Greatest Gift to America," in Charles S. Johnson, ed., *Ebony and Topaz: A Collectanea* (New York, 1927), p. 122. Further references will be given in the text.
7. Melvin B. Tolson, "George S. Schuyler," *The American Mercury,* 28 (March 1933), pp. 373-74.
8. "A Negro Looks Ahead," *The American Mercury,* 19 (February 1930), p. 212. Further references will be given in the text. Mencken had written to Schuyler in 1929 that "the plain fact is that neither the whites nor the blacks know where they are heading. . . . I can never formulate a plausible picture of the relation of

the races . . . fifty years from now. If you care to deal with the subject realistically, I'll certainly be delighted to do the article" (Forgue, p. 313).

9. "The Caucasion Problem," in Rayford Logan, ed., *What The Negro Wants* (Chapel Hill, 1944), p. 281. Further references will be given in the text.

10. The "cultured hell" reference recalls Claude McKay's poem, "America."

11. "Do Negroes Want to be White?" *The American Mercury,* 82 (June 1956), p. 56. Further reference will be given in the text.

12. "Our nation is moving toward two societies, one black, one white—separate and unequal. . . . Discrimination and segregation have long permeated much of American life; they now threaten the future of every American. This deepening racial division is not inevitable. The movement apart can be reversed. Choice is still possible. Our principal task is to define that choice and to press for a national resolution. To pursue our present course will involve the continuing polarization of the American community and, ultimately, the destruction of basic democratic values. . . ." "Summary," *Report of the National Advisory Commission on Civil Disorders* (New York, 1968), p. 1.

HENRY LOUIS GATES, JR. (ESSAY DATE 1992)

SOURCE: Gates, Henry Louis, Jr. "A Fragmented Man: George Schuyler and the Claims of Race." *The New York Times Book Review* (20 September 1992): 31, 42-43.

In the following essay, Gates argues that Schuyler's was a personality fragmented by the dual options of racial assimilation and African American nationalism.

Black Americans, W. E. B. Du Bois believed, were haunted by a split identity, a peculiar form of psychological and political "double-consciousness." "One ever feels his two-ness—an American, a Negro; two souls, two thoughts, two unreconciled strivings, two warring ideals in one dark body," Du Bois wrote in *The Souls of Black Folk.* Expressions of this duality have long been a characteristic of black letters, but few people have embodied that division more than George Samuel Schuyler (1895-1977), one of America's boldest and most controversial journalists, essayists and satirists.

Schuyler also was a novelist who published two books in 1931. The first, ***Black No More: Being an Account of the Strange and Wonderful Workings of Science in the Land of the Free. A.D. 1933-1940,*** is a wickedly satirical fantasy in which racism is thrown a curve when a mad scientist invents an anti-melanin device. The second, ***Slaves Today: A Story of Liberia,*** is an indictment of the corruption and oppression of blacks by blacks in Liberia, which has prophetic overtones today. Neither novel, however, is as powerful as two pulp science-fiction serials, ***The Black Internationale*** and ***Black Empire,*** which Schuyler wrote under the pseudonym Samuel I. Brooks for *The Pittsburgh Courier* between 1936 and 1938.

These texts were lost from literary view until their rediscovery by Robert A. Hill, an associate professor of history at the University of California, Los Angeles, and editor-in-chief of "The Marcus Garvey Papers," and R. Kent Rasmussen, an associate editor of the Garvey papers. They made both serials available for the first time in a painstakingly detailed and annotated edition entitled ***Black Empire,*** published last year by Northeastern University Press as part of the important Northeastern Library of Black Literature series, which has pioneered in republishing out-of-print black books. Among its many virtues, ***Black Empire*** will acquaint younger Americans with George Schuyler's struggle with Du Bois's dualism, a struggle that is among the most fascinating episodes in American letters.

If these Americans know Schuyler at all, it is in his later role as a militant anti-Communist and archconservative who became a contributor to both the John Birch Society's *Review of the News* and William Loeb's *Manchester Union Leader.* It was this Schuyler who would oppose the awarding of the Nobel Peace Prize to the Rev. Dr. Martin Luther King Jr. because "neither directly nor indirectly has Dr. King made any contribution to world (or even domestic) peace. . . . Dr. King's principal contribution to world peace has been to roam the country like some sable Typhoid Mary, infecting the mentally disturbed with perversion of Christian doctrine and grabbing fat lecture fees from the shallow-pated."

. . . . .

And it was this Schuyler who said of Malcolm X in 1973: "It is not hard to imagine the ultimate fate of a society in which a pixilated criminal like Malcolm X is almost universally praised, and has hospitals, schools and highways named in his memory! . . . We might as well call out the schoolchildren to celebrate the birthday of Benedict Arnold. Or to raise a monument to Alger Hiss."

But the later Schuyler is not the socialist civil rights activist of the 1920's and 30's. And his career was not a simple drift from left to right but a complicated, painful journey filled with the sort of "double-consciousness" that continues to raise disturbing questions about what racism does to people in America.

George Schuyler was born in Providence, R.I., in 1895, into a family that had always, as he was fond of saying, been free. His stepfather's occupations as a cook and a porter made the family firmly middle class, certainly by "colored" standards at the turn of the century; their 14-room house included a library, small but canonical, where his mother taught him to read. Dropping out of school to enlist in the Army in 1912, Schuyler was eventually posted to Hawaii, where he also began his career as a journalist, contributing to local papers and even publishing his own until he was discharged as a first lieutenant in 1919. Two years later, he joined the Socialist Party of America, and soon became a stalwart of the Friends of Negro Freedom, a socialist organization founded by A. Philip Randolph and Chandler Owen.

In 1923, Schuyler became a staff member of Randolph's journal, *The Messenger,* where his monthly column, *Shafts and Darts: A Page of Calumning and Satire,* quickly became the newspaper's most popular—and controversial—feature. A year later, he began to write an additional column for *The Pittsburgh Courier,* one of the nation's largest black weeklies, an association he maintained without a break until 1965. During a professional career that spanned half a century, Schuyler would write for a wide variety of publications, including H. L. Mencken's *American Mercury, The Nation, The New York Evening Post, The Washington Post, The Philadelphia Ledger, The Crisis* and *The African,* becoming one of America's most influential black journalists. No black American, before or since, has written for such an ideologically disparate array of publications in both the black and the white press, or embodied more contradictory ideological positions.

Schuyler was a prolific writer; in addition to his columns, he wrote editorials, he was a foreign correspondent and he was a first-rate investigative reporter. His series **"Aframerica Today,"** which explored race relations in Mississippi in 1925, **"The Truth About Harlem," "Slavery in Liberia," "Racial Democracy in Latin America"** (based on his own reporting in 10 countries) and **"What's Good About the South"** can be read with profit today.

Between 1934 and 1944 Schuyler would remain an active member of the N.A.A.C.P. and write articles like **"Scripture for Lynchers," "Reflections on Negro Leadership," "Battering Down the Barriers of Prejudice"** and a widely quoted review of Margaret Mitchell, **"*Not* Gone With the Wind."** In a 1944 article, **"The Caucasian Problem,"** Schuyler called for a complete reorganization of our social system that "would have to include the complete abolition of Jim Crow laws and institutions; the rescinding of all racial 'pollution' laws barring marriage because of so-called race; a complete enforcement of the letter and spirit of the Federal Constitution, and the ending of every vestige of the color bar in industry, commerce and the professions. The words 'Negro,' 'white,' 'Caucasian,' 'Nordic' and 'Aryan' would have to be permanently taken out of circulation. . . . Unless we do so," Schuyler warned, America would "drift toward an international war."

"There is still time to make a new world where tolerance, understanding, mutual respect and justice will prevail," he said. "True, this means a complete about-face on the part of the white world, but this is only right since the race problem is of its own making. The alternative here and abroad is conflict and chaos. We shall have to make a choice very soon."

It was Schuyler's gift for satire and his caustic wit that distinguished his writings and led to his nickname, the Black Mencken. Indeed, H. L. Mencken himself called him "unquestionably the most competent Negro journalist ever heard of," and published many of his essays in *The American Mercury*. The comparison with Mencken was apt: Schuyler early on had become black America's principal debunker, emerging by 1926 as one of the first critics of the Harlem Renaissance and its belief in a black esthetic, which he called—in a heated and oft-quoted exchange with Langston Hughes in *The Nation*—**"The Negro-Art Hokum."**

Schuyler believed that "Aframerican" art should not be considered separate and distinct from American art, that there was no need to appeal to the masses and that proponents of a Negro literature were playing into the hands of a white power structure. That power structure, he maintained, wanted to limit black writing, insisting that it be "bizarre, fantastical and outlandish with a suggestion of the jungle, the plantation or the slum." Hughes's rebuttal, "The Negro Artist and the Racial Mountain," maintained that black art is inspired by the black masses and is created for the black masses.

Schuyler's position in the black intellectual community was one of critic from within. Schuyler construed his intellectual role as that of a dissident, reserving his primary animus for his fellow black intellectuals and cultivating critical skepticism as his special calling. Thus, while opposed to white racism and segregation throughout his long career, Schuyler also chastised excesses of black nationalism, from Marcus Garvey's Back to Africa movement and black on black oppression in Liberia; and his famous satirical novel about the self-consciousness of the Harlem Renaissance, ***Black No More,*** is a work that many of us still teach today.

In 1934, Schuyler attacked "the advocates of racial separation . . . the professional negrophiles, the ballyhooers of the boycott, the diligent defenders of Jim Crowism," who rationalize separatism as "a pragmatic raciology." "Negro segregation in any form is a menace to the colored folk of this country," he maintained, challenging "the so-called cultural value of voluntary segregation." It was partly in this context that Schuyler assailed Garvey and his movement. To Schuyler, Garvey's was a "comic opera movement," Garvey "the best-known of all the Negro hustlers," a "Master Megalomaniac." He parodied Garvey in ***Black No More*** as the character Santop Licorice.

Garvey, of course, fought back, engaging in several exchanges with Schuyler. Schuyler's exposé of slavery in Liberia led a Garvey spokesman to complain that Schuyler was as African "as a WHITE man." Nevertheless, almost at the same time, Schuyler was trying to organize the Young Negroes' Cooperative League, a consumer-controlled co-op designed to lead to black economic self-sufficiency.

And it is important to remember that it was George Schuyler, in the grim days of the rise of fascism and the worsening Depression, who would write that "colored people all over the world have something in common in these days of white military, economic and financial domination." "The true enemy," he concluded in 1937, was "white imperialism and [economic] exploitation." In 1936, Schuyler, the man who would later become an apologist for imperialist forces in Africa, called George Padmore's "How Britain Rules Africa" a "tour de force, a masterpiece."

But the contradictions in Schuyler's constitution led to a stranger and more intriguing rupture. We now know that Schuyler had already begun to create powerful fictions more compelling in their nationalist mythologies than anything Marcus Garvey or Elijah Mohammed ever dreamed of. For Schuyler had matched his growing conservative and anti-nationalist public persona with an underground alter ego whom Garvey would have found to be as "black" as Schuyler was "white." His vehicle would be a form he both enjoyed and disdained—pulp fiction. His audience would be one he often condescended to—the black masses. And his agent would be Samuel I. Brooks.

FROM THE AUTHOR

GENERALIZATIONS OF NEGRO ART

[American black folk art, such as spirituals and the blues, are the expression of] a caste in a certain section of the country. . . . They are no more expressive or characteristic of the Negro race than the music and dancing of the Appalachian highlanders . . . are expressive or characteristic of the Caucasian race.

SOURCE: George Samuel Schuyler, excerpt from "The Negro-Art Hokum," in the *Nation* 122, June 16, 1926.

Schuyler had invented Samuel I. Brooks in 1928, announcing a "Newly Discovered Race Writer" in the International Features Section, a magazine insert appearing in 40 Negro weeklies, which Schuyler had begun to edit in 1928, a month after *The Messenger* closed. In 1929, Schuyler used the Brooks byline on a six-part analysis of Marcus Garvey and his movement.

By 1936, in the aftermath of Italy's invasion of Ethiopia, the fall of Addis Ababa and Max Schmeling's knockout of Joe Louis, Schuyler would employ Samuel I. Brooks to raise *The Courier*'s weekly circulation with a serial destined to become the ultimate depiction of black nationalism. The first installment appeared on Nov. 21, 1936. Advertised as a fiction about "Negroes everywhere, united by a common bond of hatred of white exploitation, persecution and ostracism," the serial ***The Black Internationale*** lifted sales dramatically. It was followed by ***Black Empire.*** All together George Schuyler, writing as Samuel I. Brooks, would file 62 weekly installments until the series ended in 1938.

In this way Schuyler would play out his ambivalent feelings about the "responsible" politics for black America by literalizing Du Bois's famous metaphor of black double-consciousness and dividing himself into two: conservative, colored G. S. Schuyler and militant, black Samuel I. Brooks. He even had occasion to comment on his other self, calling Brooks's stories "hokum and hack work in the purest vein" and saying of the enthusiastic response to them, "the result vindicates my low opinion of the human race."

The Black Internationale and ***Black Empire*** are black utopian fantasies, combining devices from science fiction and the detective novel to chart the brilliant and successful campaign of Dr. Henry Belsidus to liberate all of Africa and all people of African descent throughout the world from the colonial domination of white Europe and America. Belsidus is a genius's genius: "determined, educated, suave, immaculate, cruel, immoral," as a *Courier* ad claimed. Imagine W. E. B. Du Bois, Booker T. Washington. George Washington Carver and Marcus Garvey rolled into one fascist superman, and there you have Dr. Henry Belsidus.

In ***The Black Internationale,*** Belsidus grows extraordinarily wealthy performing abortions for a white clientele. With this wealth, supplemented by money earned through an elaborate crime ring, Belsidus organizes the elite of black cultures everywhere into a powerful "internationale" dedicated to overthrowing white supremacists all over the world and restoring black rule to Africa. Equipped with a fleet of ships, a squadron of airplanes, the latest scientific technology, endless supplies of money and a neo-Dionysian black religion—and aided by covert white (or "passing") allies who sow disarray among the European and American powers—Belsidus and his Internationale liberate the entire continent of Africa, but not before assassinating the Prime Minister of England and all the members of the Chamber of Deputies in France! The sequel, ***Black Empire,*** depicts the formation and life of the Black Empire in Africa, and Belsidus's magnificent triumph over a United European invasion.

If Schuyler was outspokenly and famously anti-Garvey, Schuyler writing as Brooks carried Garveyism to an extreme. Belsidus espouses Garvey's ideals, and he wins where Garvey loses because he could provide tactical brilliance, organization and unity. Schuyler could write that "all Garvey ever freed Negroes from was their hard-earned cash." But Schuyler writing as Brooks could conclude, "Marcus Garvey has a vision. He sees plainly that everywhere in the Western and Eastern hemispheres the Negro, regardless of his religion or nationality, is being crushed under the heel of white imperialism and exploitation. Rapidly the population of the world is being aligned in two rival camps: white and black. The whites have arms, power, organization, wealth; the blacks have only their intelligence and their potential power. If they are to be saved, they must be organized so they can present united opposition to those who seek to continue their enslavement."

The Black Internationale and ***Black Empire,*** which, in the manner of the pulp science fiction of its day, combine action-packed adventure with futuristic technology, are an Afrocentrist's dream, and ought to enjoy a large readership among those in search of a black utopia. But they are particularly important for what they teach us about Schuyler's complicated response to the pressures of ideological conformity among blacks—and the failure of most received ideological stances or political programs to account for this complexity. As Toni Morrison wrote recently in *Playing in the Dark,* a collection of essays, "The trauma of racism is for the . . . victim, the severe fragmentation of the self." Nowhere is this trauma more clearly revealed than in the writings of George Schuyler.

In the end, what defeated Schuyler's grand promise as an intellectual was his failure to negotiate between these two antipodal personas, between the sanguinary nationalism of Samuel I. Brooks and the reactionary venom of his own later writings. Instead, the creative decline of Schuyler's later years was matched by a growing extremism in his political views. It made him oblivious to what was most valuable about the civil rights struggles of the 50's and 60's, and aligned him with forces that were frankly inimical to black advancement. Gone was the bracing skeptic of the Harlem Renaissance, as the master parodist became a parody of himself. The man who sought to challenge all regnant orthodoxies now found himself mired in one, a gadfly trapped in amber.

But if the elder Schuyler failed his own luminous vision of intellectual independence, he may have felt that black America failed him, too. And his contrarian role in America's racial drama, so similar in many respects to that of his fellow conservative Zora Neale Hurston, may well strike a resonant chord among a new generation of black intellectuals who are more likely than their forebears to recognize in the productive clash and contest of perspectives a source of strength.

In George C. Wolfe's musical *Jelly's Last Jam,* Chimney Man, a Mephistophelean character, judges Jelly Roll Morton's life on the basis of whether he "betrayed his race," his ethnic heritage. The conceit, effective theatrically, evokes an archetype that still haunts the lives of African-

American intellectuals and public figures. Schuyler's notion of "race loyalty"—an attribute he always claimed—was predicated on the belief that skepticism, independent critical thinking and iconoclasm were part and parcel of the intellectual's calling, and that "race loyalty" depended on just these qualities of mind. If George Schuyler's place as a major figure in black letters has not been fully acknowledged, it is in part because his conception of the intellectual's role has never fully been appreciated.

Writing in 1853, a columnist in Frederick Douglass's Paper who used the pseudonym Dion observed that much of the best in black literature was being published in newspapers, "ephemeral caskets, whose destruction entails the destruction of the gems which they contain." There are thousands of works of fiction that remain buried in black newspapers and magazines. Robert A. Hill and R. Kent Rasmussen have performed a great service by resurrecting George Schuyler's texts. Given that most of his writings remain unexhumed from their "ephemeral caskets," only scholarship such as theirs will permit a re-evaluation of his place in American intellectual and cultural history.

TITLE COMMENTARY

Black No More

JANE KUENZ (ESSAY DATE 1997)

SOURCE: Kuenz, Jane. "American Radical Discourse, 1900-1930: Schuyler's *Black No More.*" *Novel* 30, no. 2 (winter 1997): 170-92.

In the following essay, Kuenz explores Schuyler's satiric novel Black No More *in light of the early-twentieth-century debate about whether race is essential or socially-constructed.*

When George Schuyler's ***Black No More*** appeared early in 1931, it entered a culture primed for its reception by more than three decades of apprehensive and contradictory public fulmination, posing as and often passing for reasoned debate, on the subject of racial essences and their relation to national character. In his spoof of Harlem's Talented Tenth; of the stock themes, incidents, and characters peopling their work;[1] of W. E. B. Du Bois (Dr. Shakespeare Agamemnon Beard, later Dr. Karl von Beerde, editor of *The Dilemma*) and the NAACP (The National Social Equality League, later the Down-With-White-Prejudice-League); of the Virginia aristocracy (the Anglo-Saxon Association) and the Ku Klux Klan (The Knights of Nordica with their Grand Exalted Giraw); of Marcus Garvey (Santop Licorice) and Mme. C. J. Walker, hair goddess (the bankrupt Mme. Sisseretta Blandish reincarnated as Mrs. Sari Blandine, purveyor of "Egyptienne Stain"); of Protestant clergymen preaching the efficacy of lynching (Rev. McPhule) and ignorant statesmen from the rough and gentle classes (Senator Kretin and candidate Arthur Snobbcraft); of earnest anthropologists and scientists for the race—all those self-designated protectors of the national bloodlines and birthrates (Dr. Samuel Buggery); in short, in his spoof of all the "gruesome, absurd, and tedious manifestations of American racism" and racialist thinking to date, Schuyler, the "black Mencken," suggested that there was, perhaps, enough of both to go around (Lewis 252).

His plot is fairly simple, even obvious in the context of 1931, if ominous in the context of what would shortly follow in Europe. The story follows the ups and downs of picaro-cum-trickster Max Disher in profiting from the work of Dr. Junius Crookman, lately of Germany. Crookman's efforts have resulted in a treatment which lightens dark skin permanently—no bleaches or creams here; this process is "glandular" and "electrical" (Schuyler, ***Black*** 27)[2]—effectively transforming Negro into Caucasian and creating, as it were, the assimilated American population simultaneously feared and anxiously awaited by commentators on the national scene. As might be expected, however, the happy amalgamation of the country's different peoples never happens. To a black public wild to have it, Crookman's "Black-No-More" makes them not just white, but whiter than white, too white apparently for regular white folks determined to be distinguished as such. As Crookman later naively reports, Black-No-More makes one a shade paler than garden-variety whites who reason with consequent enlightenment that "if it were true that extreme whiteness was evidence of the possession of Negro blood . . . then surely it were well not to be so white" (219). Even though a secret research project reveals against the hopes of its sponsors that over 50% of the "white" American population has "tainted blood"—leading one "Nordic" to admit that "we're all niggers now" (193)—a subsequent reversal and redrawing of racial boundaries ensues, made complete and authoritative with the help of churches, courts, schools, labor unions, newspapers and magazines, social and biological sciences, political and cultural organs, and all the other ideological state apparatuses integral in the erection and maintenance of a really effective oppressive system.

This is the kind of satire for which Schuyler was justly famous, and his and the book's popularity among an African-American audience at the time of its publication signals the extent to which he and they were attuned to the contradictory claims made about race and culture in the U.S. and to the ways in which those claims highlighted and distorted other social contradictions, particularly contradictions in the articulation of working class identity.[3] ***Black No More*** is especially valuable now not just for its comic and astute critique of the "race hysteria" among white historians, anthropologists, and politicians, but for the way it links that hysteria with the parallel essentialist and primitivist rhetoric that emerged among Harlem Renaissance artists and intellectuals at the same time, though for quite different reasons. What saves ***Black No More*** from being merely the latest broadside from a writer well on his way to becoming one of America's most colorful black conservatives is the novel's broader critique of capitalism, what Du Bois calls "the whole system of exploitation" that ultimately organized and gave meaning to the racial "essences" espoused and debated by black and white race theorists (Du Bois and Stoddard 8). By recoding racial markers as class signs and showing throughout the novel their structural instability *as* signs, Schuyler situates both "blackness" and "whiteness" in relation to an industrial and market economy increasingly willing and able to manipulate and finally obliterate any semblance of culture, tradition, and individual identity, racial or otherwise, among the people it needs to keep itself going.

Unfortunately, Schuyler's later reputation as a conservative has skewed readings of ***Black No More*** in ways his contemporaries would not have understood and which now must be reexamined. If this reexamination has been a long time coming, it is because Schuyler's later views do appear so extreme. Ann Rayson argues creatively that Schuyler can't even be called an assimilationist because by the late 1960s the world he wants to be a part of is farther to the right than the majority culture in the U.S.[4] Though his public writing career began at the socialist *Messenger,* after World War II, Schuyler's became a frequent and vociferous voice against communism at home and abroad and against the civil rights movement of the 50s and 60s (Kellner 319). Rayson dates Schuyler's turn to the right a decade earlier with the Scottsboro trial and what he and many others thought was the International Labor Defense's mishandling of the defense. In his regular **"Views and Reviews"** column for *The Pittsburgh Courier* in April, 1933, Schuyler derided the defense's "faulty tactics," chief among which was its attempt to present the issues of the case in class rather than racial terms. According to Schuyler, "Anybody who is at all familiar with the Southern psychology knows that no class issues are involved save of the most remote and inconsequential kind. It is a race issue pure and simple" (qtd. in Rayson 105). If Schuyler's writing seems poised consistently to cause as much consternation among black readers as possible, even if that required what looked like inconsistencies in his own opinions, those apparent inconsistencies highlight what for him were more important underlying consistencies. Rather than as proof of his contempt for socialism and a precursor to a hard shift to the right, Schuyler's critique of the Scottsboro defense should be read alongside Du Bois's opposition to unions: both separated their support for economic socialism from the political groups espousing them. Furthermore, the terms of Schuyler's criticism of the Communist Party predate similar criticism in Wright's *Native Son* and Ellison's *Invisible Man.* Similarly, although he was a self-designated critic of New Negro excesses and of Marcus Garvey's African nationalism in particular—his novel ***Slaves Today,*** also 1931, is a thinly veiled documentary illustrating how black rule in Liberia is no better and possibly worse than white rule had been—Schuyler also published serially (and under a pseudonym) the socialist ***The Black Internationale*** and nationalist ***Black Empire.***

Perhaps understandably, critical attention has often responded solely to the conservative crank rather than the complicated and contradictory social satirist. Rayson's argument answers the charge of assimilationism from critics like Robert Bone who read Schuyler's later conservative beliefs back onto his earlier work and then cite what appears to be the latter's hypocrisy. Though in a *Messenger* column Schuyler "vehemently attacks 'the lie that Negroes wish to be white,'" says Bone, it is "this very conception" that undergirds and provides most of the humor for ***Black No More.*** This may be essentially correct, but when he continues by attacking Schuyler's anti-nationalism and "growing alienation from the realities of race"—otherwise known as "his basic assimilationist impulse"—Bone overreaches. He flattens out the novel's context by placing it in his own and loses in the process much of its cultural resonance beyond the specific immediate reference to Harlem (91). If ***Black No More*** plays on the perception that some African Americans "wish to be white," Schuyler would hardly have been the first to think so (though it does not follow, as Bone apparently assumes it does, that depicting such wishes necessarily means sharing them), just as he would have been one of many for whom "wishing to be white" might signify several, perhaps mutually-exclusive desires. Here, for example, is Schuyler's description of the heady days of scrimping and saving the money necessary for a Crookman makeover:

> Gone was the almost European atmosphere of every Negro ghetto: the music, laughter, gaiety, jesting and abandon. . . . The happy-go-lucky Negro of song and story was gone forever and in his stead was a nervous, money-grubbing black, stuffing away coins in socks, impatiently awaiting a sufficient sum to pay Dr. Crookman's fee.
>
> (87)

"The almost European atmosphere of every Negro ghetto" is the first clue here, the aside that reverses the polarity of "white" and "black" and thus confirms the suspicion that they are interchangeable: as goes the "Negro of song and story," so goes the "European atmosphere" of their community. With this, Schuyler aligns "European" with "black" and sets both off from "American," presumably "white" and clearly capitalist or, at least, "money-grubbing." It is a subtle move, one that plays on Europe's status as a kind of floating signifier in American racial taxonomies. Though it certainly had its share of non-white people in 1931, in the great morass of national discourse—including that of a lot of African Americans—"Europe" clearly signified "whiteness," particularly as it was manifested as "culture," "civilization," or their idiot cousin, "our heritage." Europe was also, ten years after the war, as it had been before, openly regarded and publicly described as a positive alternative for African Americans to Jim Crow America. "I've met a lot of Americans over here," wrote Jessie Fauset to Harold Jackman in 1924, "and believe me I sit with them whenever I'm invited" (qtd. in Sylvander 68).[5] The unnamed protagonist of James Weldon Johnson's *The Autobiography of an Ex-Coloured Man* also discovers this freedom from United States color prejudice as does *Home to Harlem*'s Jake, whose reluctant relinquishing of a favorite English suit for a "nigger-brown" one is one of the novel's signs of Jake's reinscription into American racial signifying systems. Europe is significant in these instances not because different races don't exist there, but because in comparison to the United States, difference doesn't seem to matter. Schuyler's play on Europe accounts for both significations, for "European atmosphere" specifically denotes a cultural, not racial or national, connection to black communities in the United States. In both there is the kind of freedom from self-consciousness, discrimination, and prejudice one enjoys among like-minded folks—the thing that encourages one to be "happy-go-lucky" and which here is implicitly equated with European "civilization" and presumably the unacknowledged "heritage" of all those white Americans still gloating in the post-*Plessy* days of "separate but equal."

Schuyler's elision of European and Negro is made doubly potent by the modification of the latter. In 1931, the "happy-go-lucky Negro of song and story" is an intentionally open-ended description. Is this Negro disappearing as a consequence of Crookman's Black-No-More the ubiquitous "happy darky" of racist caricature or the authentic folk creator of African-American music and literature? I would not assume that it necessarily refers exclusively to either one or the other, or that it does so in any obvious way, or that it does only that. Schuyler may, for example, be referencing and parodying Langston Hughes's "The Negro Artist and the Racial Mountain," published five years earlier in response to Schuyler's own **"The Negro-Art Hokum."** In his essay, Schuyler attacks the notion that art has an essential racial quality, calling it so much "hokum," and argues that because African Americans are "merely . . . lampblacked Anglo-Saxon[s]," they should—and in fact do—create art in the European and American traditions in which their consciousnesses are primarily shaped (**"Hokum"** 662). Schuyler was angry with *The Nation*'s editors for lining up Hughes as a critic of his piece before it had even appeared, and his satiric language in ***Black No More*** echoes Hughes's more famous formulation of the object of New Negro aesthetics as Hughes understood them:

> But then there are the low-down folks, the so-called common element, and they are the majority—may the Lord be praised. The people who have their nip of gin on Saturday nights and are not too important to themselves or the community, or too well fed, or too learned to watch the lazy world go round. They live on Seventh Street in Washington or State Street in Chicago and they do not particularly care whether they are like white folks or anybody else. Their joy runs, bang! into ecstasy. Their religion soars to a shout. Work a little today, rest a little tomorrow. Play awhile. Sing awhile. O, let's dance!
>
> (527)

Of course, African Americans are not "merely lampblacked Anglo-Saxons," nor is it fair to say, as Schuyler does, that "the literature, painting, and sculpture of Aframericans—such as there is . . . is identical in kind with the literature, painting, and sculpture of white Americans" or that "any group under similar circumstances would have produced something similar" to the spirituals of the black south. Although Schuyler attempts to historicize African American folk culture, he makes the typical conservative mistake of going only half-way: he emphasizes the primacy of environment and history over "the 'peculiar' psychology of the Negro" in the creation and elaboration of aesthetic traditions (662), but his conception of history does not allow for the possibility that aesthetic traditions found in the cultures of Africa not only continued in the New World among free and enslaved diasporic peoples, but that these traditions actively influenced and transformed the cultures they encountered here.[6]

Though he overstates his own case—and has seen his essay paired negatively with Hughes's ever since—Schuyler's concerns are real. Hughes wants people to be "Negro enough to be different," to recognize and use "racial culture"—"the eternal tom-tom beating in the Negro soul"—and give to their creations "racial individuality"—their "heritage of rhythm and warmth." Though he denies it as a specific intention, the artist Hughes envisions is able to apply that rhythm and warmth to the African American masses in such a way that they are reenvisioned for a white and black American audience historically able to see them only through the lens of racial stereotype or fear. Hughes locates the "racial mountain" obstructing this not in white prejudice and discrimination *per se,* but in the attitudes of middle- and upper-class African Americans, what he calls "the urge within the race toward whiteness" (526).

For Schuyler, however, rhetoric that speaks of "urges toward whiteness" and their attendant denials of blackness not only misses his point, but confuses the categories of race and culture he will put into play in ***Black No More.*** He is skeptical of those in Greenwich Village and Harlem "whose hobby is taking races, nations, peoples, and movements under their wing" and who, in doing so, are prepared to insist that African Americans are "living in a different world," that there are, in the words of "sainted Harding," "'fundamental, eternal, and inescapable differences' between white and black America" (662, 663). The joy-into-ecstasy prevalent among Hughes's "low-down folks" and the necessary ingredient of the "Negro art" he envisions may be real enough, but, for Schuyler, it is not authentic in any biological sense (it is "almost European" in fact) and certainly not permanent or immutable. Later he insisted that he was not denying the existence of African-American traditions—he praises Hurston, for example, as "one of the soundest writers of the Harlem Renaissance"—only the insinuations of inferiority he felt were implied by public declarations of difference (qtd. in Peplow 122 n13).[7] Taking Hughes to task for assuming the progressive quality of the working-class and folk culture he valorized in his poetry and in "The Negro Artist," Schuyler points out that by and large "it is the Aframerican masses who consume hair-straightener and skin-whitener" (qtd. in Huggins 205).[8] He concludes archly that "your American Negro," on Seventh Street or anywhere else, "is just plain American" (662).

This is a familiar debate now as it was at the time,[9] and like many, probably the majority, of his contemporaries in the twenties Schuyler worries as Du Bois did that Hughes's thinking is naive and politically dangerous. He is particularly disinclined to indulge in racial romanticism of any kind. Though he mocks the end-product, Schuyler's joke is that it is the becoming rather than the being that really renders one "white," that "whiteness"—and its corollary "race"—are not physical attributes at all; for finally it is not Dr. Crookman's process, but their own efforts and desire to be white that account for the changes in Schuyler's characters. At no time are the novel's "blacks" as "white" as they are before their actual physical transformation: secreting away nickels and dimes, they become "nervous," "money-grubbing," and "impatient"—people rather like the "hard, materialistic, grasping, inbred society of the whites" Max later encounters in Atlanta (63). In short, before they have even availed themselves of Crookman's "Black-No-More," they are already the overcivilized, uptight white people of popular imagination,[10] and their premature transformation suggests what Schuyler may have discerned in 1926: that wanting to be white is a really white thing to do.

Certainly it was for a lot of white people, and certainly this would have been clear to anyone roaming around in U.S. public culture with any degree of awareness. It would be difficult to overestimate the extent of the concern expressed in the first three decades of this century for securing "whiteness" as a personal and national trait. The national context for Schuyler's novel is one Richard Hofstadter describes as "surprisingly nervous and defensive" over the prospect that "Anglo-Saxondom," of which the U.S. was the last, best hope, was losing ground to other races, particularly, or so the imperial logic went, to Asians (185). That the "Yellow Peril" would be conjured as a threat at the moment of American imperial ventures in Asia is testament to the manipulation of racial discourse in response to the need to legitimate the accelerated and more brutal domination of subordinated peoples.[11] Locally the need during this period to reinvent whiteness and reassert its possession corresponds in this country to the great migration north of African Americans from roughly 1880-1920 and to the economic and social upheavals that movement caused in both the north and the south, to the increased radicalization made possible by that movement and by African American participation in the war, and to the influx of foreign immigrants during the same period.

The "race suicide" ostensibly sweeping the country as a proximate or direct consequence of these changes was said to be due to the U.S.'s own growing effeteness and "racial degeneracy," both products of the twin sins of modern life: "the dread incubus of miscegenation" (and its sequel "the lawless policies of hyphenism") as it was put in one context (Burr 155, 10) and the "curse" of "willful sterility" as former President Theodore Roosevelt put it in another (763). By "willful sterility" in marriage—"the cardinal sin against the race"—Roosevelt means couples with fewer than four children (763). Several solutions to the problem had been offered earlier. In an invitation to empire, Brooks Adams suggested in *The Law of Civilization and Decay* (1896) that what was needed to enervate the "exhausted" and "inert" white race was "fresh energetic material [supplied] by the infusion of barbarian blood" (qtd. in Hofstadter 187). Adams is building on the work of Arthur de Gobineau who had argued at mid-century in *The Inequality of Human Races* that "civilizations rise and flourish while they have a balance of racial intermixture" (qtd. in Gossett 344; Banton 19-60). Adams's reworking of Gobineau's conservative thesis was not, however, a particularly popular answer to the problem at hand, playing as it does on the familiar tropes of the national body and blood, but suggesting, at the height of the "one-drop rule," that racial mixing might be a pretty healthy thing. According to the "one-drop" rule, informally invoked until legally sanctioned by cases like the 1896 *Plessy vs. Ferguson,* "blackness," in Eric Sundquist's words, "outvoted whiteness in the blood" in all the ways it did not in the courts and in voting booths. Plessy lost because he was 1/16th black which was quite enough for the court and much more than the "one-drop" of black "blood" said in popular mythology to determine the racial identity and moral and intellectual capacities of individual people. The effect of "one-drop" ideology was to polarize the racial categories many people had until that time understood very well to be more fluid. It "drove mulattoes toward blacks—or, in the case of those who were light enough to pass, toward a masked existence among whites" (Sundquist 245). Similarly, though it had distinguished variations among black and white in earlier countings, by 1920, the U.S. Census dropped the category "mulatto" from its forms altogether.[12]

Roosevelt, however, is less concerned about the general population than about the unwillingness of some middle- and upper-class white married couples to produce enough fit babies, and his concern for the "American race"—his preferred term for white people who vote—indicates the increasing tendency among U.S. citizens to think of themselves as a discrete "racial stock," both inheritors of the best in western countries and a distinct improvement over them. The burgeoning field of eugenics in the first quarter of this century is a testament to both these beliefs: that the white U.S. population was simultaneously the strongest, most adept for modern life and the one most threatened by unsupervised reproduction. Groups like the American Eugenics Society, the Population Association of America, and the American Sociological Society worked hard to pass mandatory sterilization laws, first in Indiana in 1907 and then by 1915 in twelve other states as well. In 1914, the National Conference on Race Betterment met to discuss ways to implement the "eugenic ideal" in the fields of medicine, law, and social work, and in the distribution of charity monies and services (Hofstadter 164-65). These efforts were aided in 1916 by the fine-tuning of the Stanford-Binet intelligence scales, which were routinely used to "prove" the relative intelligence of entire races and nationalities and which haunt us still in the form of IQ scores.[13] Racist arguments in favor of eugenics were also strengthened by the Alpha Army Tests conducted at the beginning of the war, the results of which, as Horace Bond argued at the time, were made in the post-war years to serve as "reservoirs of information" from which could be drawn data, "accurate or not," to be used to prove almost any conclusion about the relative intellectual and creative skills of the "races" and the relative support the country should offer in the cultivation of each (454-55).

By the time Albert Wiggam's *The Fruit of the Family Tree* appeared in 1924, eugenics and the desirability of "an ordered evolution" (Josey 215) were no longer the sole concern of anthropologists and social scientists, but a national battle fought on personal fronts. Dedicated "to the health, intelligence and beauty of the unborn," Wiggam's book advises readers that they too have a role in race betterment. "Can We Make Motherhood Fashionable?" asks one chapter, picking up Roosevelt's theme regarding "willful sterility," while another, "What You Can Do to Improve the Human Race," offers counsel individually tailored to doctors, clergymen, lawyers, teachers, businessmen, editors, legislators, young men and women, and fathers and mothers. Though his major point is that intelligent people should not marry "idiots," Wiggam concludes his book by advising communities to form local eugenics societies in order to augment the native stock and help slow "the rising tide of color," as Lothrop Stoddard's famous title termed it, sweeping up from the South and across the ocean from southern and eastern Europe. The 1924 Immigration Act reiterated these efforts by further limiting the number and kind of people who could enter the country legally. The "national origins quota" of the 1921 immigration act had allowed up to three percent of the U.S. population of any one national group to enter the country. In 1924 this number was reduced in real terms by shifting the standard of measure from the 1910 to the 1890 census, that is, to a time immediately before the greatest levels of immigration from those same unfavored countries. The effect was to contain these populations as much as possible while allowing in a greater relative number of people from other national groups which already had a strong presence in the U.S. before 1890.

While both the eugenics movement and the more rigid national origins quota for immigration suggest a certain consistency of purpose in the mainstream mind, locally that mind was actually very confused about what it thought about the domestic black population and its relation to maintaining the racial integrity of whites. Most everyone, black and white, decided racial mixing was undesirable, though few could agree on why that should be so and, in some cases, what actually was meant by it. Though many African Americans like Du Bois argued now as they had in the previous century against anti-miscegenation laws because of the implication of inferiority and the need to protect African American women (though he also claimed that interracial marriage was unlikely to become much of a fad),[14] many also decried it either out of political expediency or personal distaste. Although one unstated justification for anti-miscegenation law concerned money—marriage would legally transfer property from whites to blacks—among the country's white population, the varying needs of racist discourse dictated whether the offspring of a white and black parent had been afflicted or improved by the union. Such children—the "white Negroes" or "Negro Saxons"—could be either or both better and worse than the offspring of two parents of the same race: for example, the presence of "white blood" in "black veins" could be said to account for greater grace and wisdom, but could also cause confusion and sterility.[15] Seth K. Humphrey, author of "Mankind," opined in 1919 that "the Negro-white . . . is a living protest. He is not the protest of a Negro—no Negro protests his race. It is the cry of the forceful Aryan in soul entanglement with an utterly strange being" (qtd. in Burr 295 n125). The charge of sterility (the analogy was mules) obtained in spite of the fact that non-whites—a category those in soul entanglement always found themselves—were routinely described as a more "vital" or "vigorous" than their white counterparts, whose very effeteness was a sign of both their incapacity for manual labor in factories or hot countries and their singular ability to meet the demands of democratic life. "Nordics," says Madison Grant, "grow listless and cease to breed" in tropical climates. In addition, "the cramped factory and crowded city quickly weed [the Nordic] out, while the little brunett Mediterranean can work a spindle, set type, sell ribbons or push a clerk's pen far better" (qtd. in Gossett 359). The question of whether "Nordics" would be able to deal with hot climates was taken up in national discussions of imperial endeavors; the heroic and self-sacrificing experience of the British and French in Africa and India were cited as examples for predicting probable success.

If the logic is circular, then it resembles that of a lot of thinking on race in the period. In *Democracy and Race Friction,* for example, John Moffatt Mecklin praises the "higher democracy of the spirit" described by Du Bois in *The Souls of Black Folk.* Mecklin regrets, however, that Du Bois will forever be excluded from this "higher democracy" because "the fundamental importance of race traits" pose a "disability." More specifically, "natural antipathy" between races—"prompted," he says, "by laudable instincts of group self-preservation"—prevents "social assimilation and, therefore, [the] complete social solidarity" that leads to that "higher democracy of the spirit." The only way to overcome natural antipathies is through social integration and intermarriage, which, of course, are impossible because of the natural antipathy between the races (104, 146, 172).

What requires special attention, however, is the belief that the blood of the "Anglo-Saxon"—or the more sweeping "Nordic," later just "white"—augurs a peculiar orientation toward democratic principles and the talent for successfully implementing them in public life. Reginald Horsman has traced this "secular myth of the free nature of Anglo-Saxon political institutions" in England and the United States from the sixteenth through the nineteenth centuries, noting that along the way, and in the mid-nineteenth-century U.S. particularly, the alleged source of this distinctive ability shifts from the institutions of democratic government as they were developed in England (and more broadly in the Germanic law preceding it) to the race of the people themselves. By the teens and twenties, this focus is exclusive. In the work of Burr, for example, one finds the common claim that "the nation's character . . . is indubitably linked with its past racial existence" (Burr 12). Speculating at one point that "Germanic invaders probably introduced the Italian renascence in North Italy" (184),[16] Burr asks his readers to consider the possibility that it might "be better for us to relegate the Negroes to reservations" and stop the flow of immigration of people who were unassimilable not because of race *per se,* but because their race or nationality made them incapable of understanding and appreciating "freedom" and the democratic institutions that give it form (Burr 153). African Americans, for example, were said to lack the love of "freedom" that distinguished "Anglo-Saxons," proof of which lay in the fact that blacks had once had the bad form to be enslaved. Even if doing so contradicts the very principles of equality ostensibly being praised and protected, sequestering African Americans and halting immigration would be prudent moves because "the undiluted purity of the white race is far more important than all the doctrines of liberty and democracy ever promulgated, for after all the latter are essentially the natural outcome of race homogeneity" (160). Posing a causal relation between "undiluted" whiteness and democratic government, Burr essentially announces that being black effectively removed one from the category "American." Calvin Coolidge reiterated this sentiment two years later when he argued that "America must be kept American," by which he meant English-speaking and white (qtd. in Gossett 407). Though Dred Scott encountered a similar barrier in 1857, the Thirteenth through Fifteenth Amendments forced a shift in public discourse about citizenship from the language of property and rights in law to the rhetoric of race in nature.

This later move to define national identity and the capacity for democratic government in explicitly racial terms—to construct race, as Etienne Balibar says, as a kind of "super-nationality" (285)—assumes the invisibility of whiteness as a privileged term in the construction of national unity. As the form of the universal, the "subject without properties" (Lloyd 64), this invisibility saves Coolidge's seemingly nonsensical statement from becoming the tautology it otherwise appears to be. Nevertheless, the mission of establishing nationality through race "purity" would have been seen by most African Americans as self-evidently absurd; the personal history of many was testimony enough to the impossibility of securing any such thing. What these people, including Schuyler, may have recognized is that rather than an achievable goal of national policy, racial or cultural "purity" is instead the name for the desire for it, the sign of white obsession, pure quest (Balibar 285). Although R. R. Wright, Jr.'s plea for "a *democracy* not a whiteocracy" (94) is made in recognition of just this problem—that national participation was possible only in terms unavailable to many and meaningless to all—H. H. Bancroft was having none of it. It was one thing for the Negro to labor among and for us, he said, but "as an American citizen, he is a monstrosity" (qtd. in Mecklin 75).

It should not be surprising, then, that if they were argued to be monstrously incompatible with American citizenship, George Schuyler might be wary of the peculiar, the racial, and the different in African-American life and art. Nor should it come as a surprise that his criticism of Hughes's emphasis on "racial art"—though not, it should be said, of Hughes's art itself[17]—was less popular among the majority white population than were Hughes's pronouncements, which could be and often were simply ignored or taken as further evidence of the essential differences among the races and black acceptance of that fact. Living proof of Fanon's warning that "the intellectual often runs the risk of being out of date" (180), Schuyler's too-casual "lampblacked Anglo-

Saxons" would have gotten him attacked from all sides. A decade earlier Mecklin had fretted about "the impatient, all but militant and antisocial attitude of an influential section of the Negro press"—he cites the *New York Age* and an editorial in *The Crisis* conveniently titled "Anarchism"—whose language "implies that the Negro is only an Anglo-Saxon who is so unfortunate as to have black skin" (Mecklin 46). This would clearly not do for Mecklin, as it would not for Madison Grant, author of the hugely famous bestseller *The Passing of the Great Race* (1916) and the man whose "race ecstasy" prompted the London *Athenaeum* to wonder aloud if something "passing strange" were not happening in "democratic America" (qtd. in Gossett 363). More blunt than Mecklin, Grant observed that "it has taken us fifty years to learn that speaking English, wearing good clothes, and going to church and to school, does [sic] not transform a Negro into a white man" (16).

That Schuyler is well aware of this background for his debate with Hughes is clear at the end of his essay when he argues that it is "'scientists' like Madison Grant and Lothrop Stoddard," along with the "scions of slaveholders," and "the patriots who flood the treasury of the Ku Klux Klan," who "broadcast all over the world . . . the baseless premise, so flattering to the white mob, that the black-amoor is inferior and fundamentally different." And it is on this premise, Schuyler continues, that is "erected the postulate that [the Negro] must needs be peculiar, and when he attempts to portray life through the medium of art, it must of necessity be peculiar" as well (**"Hokum"** 663). Schuyler knows that though such declarations of difference were the dogma of a good portion of Harlem Renaissance aesthetics, they were also frequently forthcoming from white speakers where they were often prefaced by concerns for preserving the racial integrity of white America, by which is meant its economic and social privilege. Lothrop Stoddard had argued explicitly along these lines only two years before the publication of ***Black No More.*** Advocating to a predominantly black audience the pursuit of "cultural recognition" rather than "social equality," and particularly opposed to the Harlem Renaissance project linking the two, Stoddard declared in his 1929 Chicago Forum debate with Du Bois that "Keeping white America unimpaired . . . is not fundamentally a matter of superiority or inferiority *per se;* it is a matter of racial difference" (Du Bois and Stoddard 13). Stoddard is more tactful here than usual; with his political opportunism posing as respect for African-American music and literature—though rather than actually praising this work, he merely notes that sales and reviews indicate that other white people seem to enjoy it—he argues to the amusement of his audience that "bi-racialism," including Jim Crow laws, is not a "caste" system because it "does not imply relative questions of superiority or inferiority, but is based upon the self-evident fact of difference" (Du Bois and Stoddard 15).[18] Self-consciously playing on rhetoric like Hughes's in "The Negro Artist and the Racial Mountain" and even like Du Bois's in the same debate,[19] Stoddard attempts to keep the discussion focused on questions of distinctive racial traits rather than on what Du Bois had posed as a focus in his opening statement: the fact that "the whole system of exploitation" of colored labor the world over is "the kernel of the organization of modern life" and "modern white civilization" in particular (Du Bois and Stoddard 8-9).

The "whole system of exploitation" is the focus of much of ***Black No More*** as well. As James A. Miller points out in the Foreword to the 1989 reprint, "Schuyler's attack on 'Negro Art' was . . . consistent with his socialist beliefs" (4-5), and, true to form, a large part of ***Black No More*** is devoted to critiquing the kinds of economic motivations and prerogatives fueling "race ecstasy" of all stripes in the U.S. Crookman's name is instructive, but the novel as a whole suggests repeatedly that what makes American racism peculiarly virulent and absurd is its relationship to the brand of capitalism developing here. Included in this condemnation is the uplift work of Harlem's Talented Tenth and the poems and novels of its more creative types which together do little to sever that relationship and may, like Stoddard's praise of difference, actually strengthen it. Besides the parody of the themes and conventions of "Negro Art," the narrator notes in passing that its success is dependent in part on the support of such notable people as Hank Johnson, an ex-convict turned wealthy numbers man, who gives "a couple of thousand dollars to advance" the cause of Negro culture before making millions by investing in the product that ensures its demise (52). Moreover, while the entire economic and social structure of the white South reels in confusion as newly-minted whites attain leadership roles in the Knights of Nordica and black babies are born to what appear to be white parents, in northern urban centers the initial consequence of the marketing of Black-No-More is the collapse of the race industry in the U.S. Black-only banks and real estate agencies fold; Harlem stores and beauty parlors go bankrupt; and all those "race men" for whom the fight against white discrimination has been a steady source of income and publicity are left with nothing to do except strategize about how to avoid the "grave crisis" threatening to extinguish the Negro race and their livelihood in particular.

This is biting satire, not entirely fair, and particularly galling to black real estate agencies that specialized in the segregated housing market because they were prevented by law or custom from doing otherwise. Because they are more readily identifiable as actual people and groups, Schuyler's satire of black leaders and communities seems harsher than his other attacks. It pales, however, in comparison to his more sweeping indictment of the "systematically distorted rationality" governing the relation of capitalist growth to racial divisiveness.[20] In the South, for example, economic losses are "considerable" because the disappearance of black people has made it impossible for businesses and state and local governments to discriminate in the quality of goods and services they provide:

> Hundreds of wooden railroad coaches, long since condemned as death traps in all other parts of the country, had to be scrapped by the railroads when there were no longer any Negroes to jim crow. Thousands of railroad waiting rooms remained unused because, having been set aside for the use of Negroes, they were generally too dingy and unattractive for white folk or were no longer necessary. Thousands of miles of streets located in the former Black Belts, and thus without sewers or pavement, were having to be improved at the insistent behest of the rapidly increased white population, real and imitation. Real estate owners who had never dreamed of making repairs on their tumble-down property when it was occupied by the docile Negroes, were having to tear down, rebuild and alter to suit white tenants. Shacks and drygoods boxes that had once sufficed as schools for Negro children, had now to be condemned and abandoned as unsuitable for occupation by white youth. Whereas thousands of school teachers had received thirty and forty dollars a month because of their Negro ancestry, the various cities and countries of the Southland were now forced to pay the standard salaries prevailing elsewhere.
>
> (133-34)

Even more pointed, Schuyler devotes several lengthy scenes to detailing the interrelation between racism and anti-unionism or, more precisely, between racial categorizing and exploiting the working class. The loss of black folks is as disconcerting to southern business leaders as it is to race leaders in the North because in the past the South's "'peculiar institutions' . . . made the worker race conscious instead of class conscious" (110). Max is particularly in tune with the logic that seeks to keep labor disorganized by distracting their attention to matters of race.

> [He] recalled what a Negro street speaker had said one night on the corner of 138th Street and Seventh Avenue in New York: that unorganized labor meant cheap labor; that the guarantee of cheap labor was an effective means of luring new industries into the South; that so long as the ignorant white masses could be kept thinking of the menace of the Negro to Caucasian race purity and political control, they would give little thought to labor organization. It suddenly dawned upon Matthew Fisher that this Black-No-More treatment was more of a menace to white business than to white labor.
>
> (64-65)

Max's success in Atlanta and as an "anthropologist" for the Knights of Nordica is directly due to exploiting the self-interest of factory owners and by bilking white workers whose unthinking racism consistently blinds them to their own best interests. He tells an assembled crowd that "Black-No-More was subsidized by the Russian Bolsheviks" (108) and foils workers' attempts to unionize by spreading innuendo about who may or may not have been previously black. Max thus assumes and plays off Du Bois's thesis that whiteness and the cultural privileges therein augment insufficient wages and make bearable the alienating class relations in which these people otherwise live. He also shows, as David Roediger has shown elsewhere, the construction of whiteness against blackness within the context of labor. Max does not merely manipulate the white working class into racism, but, in Roediger's words, he teaches that class "to think of itself and its interests as white" even when, as in Schuyler's novel, many of the people in that group are actually "black" (12).[21] As in the description of the pre-transformation Harlem, it is at moments like these that one can fully register the irony of Madison Grant's confidence that imitating the dress and manners of white people will not make a black man white. As Schuyler repeatedly suggests, imitation does exactly that largely because the supposedly natural signs of race are themselves already forms of imitation and role-playing.

This, anyway, is the white America to which African Americans like Max seek access. As I suggested earlier, criticism of Schuyler for depicting a world where African Americans want to be white is meaningless in the absence of an analysis of what whiteness means in the text, particularly in this text where depictions of whiteness and black desires for it take place in the context of a broad critique of the culture which motivate them and give them meaning. It is clear at the novel's opening, for example, that Max associates being white with sexual access to white women, a desire made literal in his approach of and rejection by Helen, a "tall, slim, titian-haired girl" from Atlanta who later marries him unaware that he has undergone "the process" just to do so (20). Schuyler is playing on the familiar refrain of white commentators that, regardless of all the talk about civil rights, the *real* goal of African-American agitation is the right to marry white men and especially women. But because Max and Helen genuinely love each other, Schuyler is also suggesting that Max's desire to be white has to do with wanting the right to pursue and marry whomever he wants. Schuyler balances Max's choice by offering alongside it the experience of Bunny Brown, Max's partner in crime, who flees the country with him, Helen, and the "sweet Georgia brown"—"probably the last black gal in the country"—Bunny has kept waiting in the wings. Asked why she never turned white, Bunny responds proudly, "She's a race patriot. She's funny that way" (195).

Besides allowing him to marry Helen, Max associates becoming white with a level and kind of economic opportunity currently unavailable to him. More generally, the desire for whiteness is made analogous to the hope for the kind of participation in the cultural, economic, and political affairs of the nation denied by definition in the racial discourse of the period; in short, wanting to be white means wanting to be a free and democratic citizen of the nation, to be included in the conceptual realm of "America," access to which in the novel's present is seemingly, and in many ways practically, limited to whites alone. This kind of access was precisely what drew African Americans to northern urban centers and midwest small towns and away from southern rural areas where it was violently denied. In his analysis of both the economic devastation wreaked on the South and the gradual loss in the North of those cultural elements that together produced the "European atmosphere" of black communities, Schuyler implicitly compares the cause and effects of Crookman's "process" to that "huge, leaderless exodus" (Hartt 102)—the mass migration of African Americans to northern urban and industralized centers where those communities and traditions were permanently transformed.

That for our hero, Max, inclusion in the space of "America" amounts to more and better ways to con others, especially white politicians and business leaders even more unscrupulous than he, suggests that Schuyler is not the naive assimilationist of critical repute.[22] While it opens certain doors and makes the bounty of the nation available, becoming white is also depicted in the novel as the violent interpellation of subjects into a brutal and faceless economic system. The underbelly of Du Bois and Roediger's analysis is the revelation of whiteness as an essentially empty thing, its distinctive value rendered meaningless by "the process," the relative economic security of its attainment easily overshadowed by the erasure necessary to secure it. Crookman's machine is an electric chair from which, as Max says, "there was no retreat. It was either the beginning or the end" (34). What begins here is a life of anonymity and standardization in an economy oblivious to individual suffering and dependent on general selfishness and ignorance. Worried that the appearance of his photograph in the local paper will expose him as really black, Max is reassured by a reporter: "'Don't worry about that,' comforted Miss Smith. 'Nobody'll recognize you. There are thousands of white people, yes millions, that look like you do" (39). Nobody recognizes him at home, either; he's become just another white guy slinking around Harlem. Mme. Blandish has a similar moment of insight when she contemplates turning white: "She had seen too many elderly, white-haired Caucasian females scrubbing floors and toiling in sculleries not to know what being just another white woman meant" (61-62). Meanwhile, "the colored folk, in straining every nerve to get the Black-No-More treatment, had forgotten all loyalties, affiliations and responsibilities" to each other and themselves (85). They bicker and riot; they hang around outside Crookman's labs like vultures or would-be millionaries around "a new oil district or before a gold rush": "excited," "wild," "strained" (87).

These are not comments about the loss of a distinctive racial culture; in Blandish's statement particularly it is easy to see that what is feared is becoming "just another white woman" like those she sees around her in New York whose lives are routine drudgery and whose deaths are unremarked. Though plenty of black people lead similarly hard-working lives and endure similarly unacclaimed deaths, their experience of capital and racism's daily effects before the appearance of Black-No-More is remembered by Max as qualitatively different: they suffered more from both firsthand, but they also enjoyed "the good breeding, sophistication, refinement and gentle cynicism" (64) that comes from consideration for and loyalty to each other and to their own better inclinations, the ability to "share . . . their troubles which they seemed always to bear with a lightness that was yet not indifference" (46). The tinge of racial romanticism here, of which there was plenty during the period, about the supposed simple pleasures and stoic fortitude of poor or colonized peoples, some of whom live in New York yet remain, somehow, outside of capital, is qualified in the novel by the fact that the entrance of several million African Americans into the daily mainstream of white America fails to produce any kind of transformative or ennobling effects therein. Consistent with Schuyler's earlier claims in **"The Negro-Art Hokum,"** most of these people are either not that different in the first place—quite possibly because they already constitute a hefty chunk of the daily mainstream of "white America"—and those that are easily absorbed in the worst sense of the term, even if, sometime later, they regret the kind of people they've become. In a gruesome scene involving the dismemberment and burning of the novel's chief villains, several whitened African Americans participate reluctantly and then only out of fear of exposure.

Occasionally, moments of regret and nostalgia surface only to be buried. Max finds the all-white cabarets "pretty dull" places where "joy and abandon" are "obviously forced" and where patrons go "to extremes to show each other they [are] having a wonderful time. . . . The Negroes, it seemed to him, were much gayer, enjoyed themselves more deeply and yet they were more restrained, actually more refined" (40). Later in Atlanta, he admits that "he found [white people] little different from the Negroes, except that they were uniformly less courteous and less interesting" (63). Though "sometimes a slight feeling of regret" comes over him "that he had left his people forever . . . but it fled before the painful memories of past experiences in this, his home town" (63). Max's nostalgia for the "courtesy" of black communities is not just for the continued love and companionship of the friends and family he's left behind, or for the beauty of black skin he occasionally praises, but for the time before his entrance into white Atlanta and the mercilessly exploitative and vicious culture he encounters there.

That in spite of this nostalgia Max nevertheless proves himself adept in his new environment confirms Bernard Bell's observation that the plot of ***Black No More*** and Max's triumph in particular illustrate Schuyler's ambivalent admiration for the "successful manipulation of color prejudice and capitalism" on the part of the novel's heroes, white and black (144). It is very clear who Schuyler's favorites are: Max, Bunny, Blandish, and Helen's father, the wily Knights leader and Democratic presidential candidate Reverend Givens—a mixed bag of hucksters and con artists of various degrees of respectability though all familiar faces in the African-American vernacular tradition of the trickster working within and outside dominant culture. What they have in common is precisely their ability to signify and, more specifically, to manipulate for their own gain the system of color prejudice and the exploitation it engenders. Even Givens, who we are told really believes the racist precepts he stupidly espouses, is recuperated in the novel by virtue of the fact that, like Max, his primary interest in the Knights of Nordica has always been the easy access he's enjoyed to its treasury. In this he is made roughly parallel to the race leaders who, in their meeting at Beard's offices, are also described as a varied cast of swindlers working the race game from their own end. But while some, like Mme. Blandish with her "Egyptienne Stain" and "Zulu Tan," prepare to hustle the country again as it becomes "definitely, enthusiastically mulatto-minded" (222), others—Max and Helen, Bunny and his Georgia Brown, and Givens himself—escape the political and social chaos Black-No-More has made of the United States. They are able to do so not just because of the money Max has swindled, but because in getting it, he has not forgotten that time before his inscription into "white America" when he was more free, more "European," and more "black." Now, he wants out. To Bunny's observation that "sometimes I forget who we are," Max responds promptly, "Well, I don't. I know I'm a darky and I'm always on the alert" (138).

With the possible exception of Max, whose self-knowledge is the measure of his refusal to be completely co-opted into the culture he understands and exploits, Schuyler's depiction of the U.S., black and white, is uniformly bleak: a world in which everyone is subject to and motivated by the same ruthless social and economic forces and out of which select winners emerge by dint of their own corresponding ruthlessness. Regardless of whatever he advocated later in life, it underestimates Schuyler's argument in ***Black No More*** to call it assimilationist. Making assimilationist arguments already presumes distinct categories of color and culture, but this would be difficult for Schuyler to do since he believed that "at best, race is a superstition" (***Conservative*** [***Black and Conservative***] 352). Certainly color is meaningless to Schuyler except as a social category, and though many of us might take that as a crucial exception, Schuyler's entire novel is devoted to mocking the notion that it could be anything else. Furthermore, any culture that might be related to race exists only as the historical fallout of several, mainly economic factors. As Ann Rayson says, "Schuyler prefers to base his political and social theories on economic class rather than on race, so that even when the two are virtually inseparable, he generally chooses to ignore the connection" (103).

This preference and Schuyler's consequent refusal to see "the connection" between class and race results in their condition in ***Black No More*** as an identity in which likeness attempts to mask and make up for the difference said no longer to be there, but which nevertheless will not go quite away. As he consistently did elsewhere, Schuyler translates the categories of racial difference current in Harlem Renaissance and white racist discourse into economic categories where they are no longer signs of racial essences but of whether you've been conscripted into the service of U.S. capitalism where these same discourses work against the interests of the people they ostensibly protect. The only New Negroes being produced in this Harlem are the whitened blacks gradually abandoning it and finding, on the other side, a parallel system of color prejudice working against them there, too. In other words, while Schuyler's novel seems to erase race by redefining it as a version of class, it ends up only highlighting the non-identity of those terms: in the world of ***Black No More,*** "blackness" can always reemerge within class in the form of the threat of alienated labor or as the comforts unavailable in this alienated world. It is in this world that "Negro ghetto" can be mistaken for "Europe": in both, "laughter" and "abandon" are found in quantities directly proportional to their distance from Black-No-More, Inc. which, as we finally discern, is synonymous with the United States itself.

As Schuyler no doubt understood and consequently feared, in the U.S. more than anywhere, "wanting to be white" was all about wanting to secure this life and the national and bodily borders on which its maintenance depends, and its corollary, being "Negro enough to be different," did not contradict that formulation so much as rephrase it. His knack in ***Black No More*** for occupying both sides of his argument with Hughes—on the one hand representing race as a cultural construction while on the other showing the progressive loss of something looking very much like "black authenticity"—is enabled by just this elision of whiteness in the United States with the United States itself. While this is the same conclusion reached by much white racist discourse and an ironic one for the writer whose work consistently assumes "the Negro's essential American-ness" (Davis 104), Schuyler reproduces it in ***Black No More*** only to empty it of any necessary racial meaning: it is not color, but the particular culture developing here—"hard, materialist, grasping, [and] in-bred"—that highlights the similarities between "European" and "Negro," makes "whiteness" visible, and in the process renders "blackness" and "Americanness" mutually exclusive.

Notes

1. Peplow isolates several literary tropes or conventions parodied by Schuyler: discussions of skin color and ranking of women accordingly (e.g., Wallace Thurman's *The Blacker the Berry* and numerous shorter set pieces); cabaret scenes with wild dancing and an obligatory brawl (Carl Van Vechten's *Nigger Heaven* and Claude McKay's *Home to Harlem*); and the ubiquitous passing literature still (even more) popular throughout the teens and twenties (James Weldon Johnson's *The Autobiography of an Ex-Coloured Man,* Nella Larsen's *Passing,* Jessie Fauset's *Plum Bun,* and Walter White's *Flight*) (58, 124 n7-9). Schuyler had already lampooned McKay's "Harlem Shadows" in his earlier satiric essay "Our Greatest Gift to America" (1927), the title itself a riff on Du Bois's 1924 *The Gift of Black Folk.* At the "literary afternoons," writes Schuyler, of such organizations as the

   > Tired Society Women's Club of Keokuk, Iowa, or the Delicatessen Proprietors' Chamber of Commerce . . . there will usually be a soulful rendition by the Charcoal Singers of their selected repertoire of genuine spirituals, and then, mayhap one of the younger Negro poets will recite one of his inspiring verses anent a ragged black prostitute gnawing out her soul in the dismal shadows of Hog Maw Alley.
   >
   > (Davis and Peplow 62)

2. Apparently Schuyler was working from earlier accounts of just such a process. On 2 November 1929, *The Pittsburgh Courier* reported that Dr. Yusaburo Noguchi claimed he could change black people into white using "sun rays, ultraviolet rays, special diets and glandular treatments." "Racial Metamorphosis Claimed by Scientist: Japanese Says He can Change Black Skin into White" (qtd. in Peplow 57, 123-24 n6). In the 1931 Preface to *Black No More* reprinted in the 1989 edition, Schuyler references this article as well as other attempts to market devices or solutions that would alter racial characteristics (13-14).

3. *Black No More* was popular at the time of its publication even among those lampooned in its pages. Du Bois called it "an extremely significant work," "a rollicking, keen, good-natured criticism of the Negro problem in the United States" (100); Rudolph Fisher found it "commendable . . . suggestive . . . swift and direct" (5); Locke added his own curious metaphorics, saying that with *Black No More* "one of the great veins of Negro fiction has been opened—may its tribe increase!" (212). Miller reports in the Foreword to the 1989 reprint that "former NAACP director Henry Lee

Moon recalled the reserved and venerable W. E. B. Du Bois laughing at his portrayal in the novel" even, apparently, at Schuyler's parody of Du Bois's sometimes florid prose (8).

4. *Black and Conservative* is the apt title of Schuyler's 1966 autobiography and a testament to the man's lifelong attempt to designate himself the race's chief iconoclast and intellectual crank. Among other things, Schuyler supported Goldwater in 1964, protested King's Nobel Prize in an editorial so extreme his home paper refused to publish it, blamed the 1967 urban uprisings on black civil rights leaders, and finally joined the John Birch Society. For these and other details of Schuyler's conservatism see Peplow 100-13 and Gates's review of the reprints of *Black Empire* and *The Black Internationale.*

5. Though many people assume that it was only artists and performers who spent time in Europe, this was not the case. 1928 was a record year for African American travel to the continent, though it is also—a year before the stock market crash—the beginning of the end of the relative freedom enjoyed there. See Lewis's account of discrimination against African Americans in what had been open establishments, including Paul and Essie Robeson's disillusionment at the Grill Room of the Savoy House (254-55). In his Columbia Oral History Reminiscences, Du Bois would remember Fauset as saying "It's so nice to start out in Paris and not have to think where you're going to get lunch" (qtd. in Sylvander 82).

6. In a detailed treatment of the relation between African and African-American vernacular and literary traditions, Gates examines this process of continuation and transformation of aesthetic traditions in the context of the trickster, Esu-Elegbara, and the Signifying Monkey. Others have traced the development of language, religious beliefs and practices, music, and visual aesthetic to African sources (see the collection of essays in Holloway). Mercer and Gilroy have argued convincingly in other contexts in favor of models of cultural analysis that allow for the complexity of the give and take—Gilroy's term is "cultural syncretism"—of the cultural production in societies and among aesthetic traditions as racially and culturally hybridized as those of Great Britain and especially the United States.

7. Schuyler's later self-defense and recriminations sound like disingenuous rationalizing after the fact; "such as there is" is an unnecessary and ignorant slight. It should be noted that some of Schuyler's unpopular views were shared by Hurston, the period's other great iconoclast. Both questioned the efficacy and point of school integration, finding it an insult to African-American teachers, and both grounded their reasoning in a perhaps too-pure logic of racial pride: any suggestion of difference among the races or efforts to offset presumed difference were taken as signs of either or both a black inferiority complex or white racism. Schuyler defended what to some looked like inconsistencies by grounding his opinions in this equation of difference with inferiority. In *Black and Conservative,* he says "I have never felt inferior." Rather than feeling inferior by virtue of race, "most colored people . . . simply are aware that their socio-economic position is inferior, which is a different thing" (18). See also Hemenway's elaboration of Hurston's views (328-37), as well as Sollors's discussion of Hurston's anti-desegregation editorial in the *Orlando Sentinel.* In the course of outlining shifts in the focus and concerns of American Studies, Sollors explicitly addresses the danger of projecting current political stances and debates into earlier, quite possibly very different historical contexts (167-90).

8. Peplow details at length Schuyler's commitment to remarking and condemning creams and devices concocted to "improve" the hair or skin of black African Americans (40-45, 123 n5). *Black No More*'s parody of Mme. Walker, the hair-straightening products that made her fortune, and her heiress daughter, the beturbanned L'Alelia who inherited the lot, is pointed and damning: "Because of her prominence as the proprietor of a successful enterprise engaged in making Negroes appear as much like white folks as possible, she had recently been elected for the fourth time a Vice-President of the American Race Pride League" (59). As she watches her clientele gradually whiten and lose the need of her services, Mme. Blandish remarks "I always said niggers didn't really have any race pride" (47).

9. Hall, for example, has recently made similar arguments: "Once it is fixed, we are tempted to use 'black' as sufficient in itself to guarantee the progressive character of the politics we fight under the banner—as if we don't have any other politics to argue about except whether something's black or not. . . . Moreover, we tend to privilege experience itself, as if black life is lived experience outside of representation. We have only, as it were, to express what we already know we are" (30). Later in the same essay, Hall notes that "the invocation of a guaranteed black experience behind it will not produce [the] politics" we need to address institutional racism in the 1990s, that, in effect, now is the "end of the innocent notion of an essential black subject" (32).

10. According to Hughes, the white world is "a world of subway trains, and work, work, work" (529). In "Jazz at Home," his contribution to *The New Negro,* Rogers discusses ragtime, jazz, and the blues as "a balm for modern ennui . . . a safety valve for modern machine-ridden and convention-bound society" which is, for him, implicitly "white" (217). Later in the same essay, he writes about a religious revival where "Negro women had the perfect jazz abandon, while the white ones moved lamely and woodenly." When he continues by saying "this same lack of spontaneity is evident to a degree in the cultivated and inhibited Negro" (220), Rogers complicates his racialist delineation in predictable ways: his unintentional confusion of the categories "race" and "culture" is the same one Schuyler relies on for comic effect in *Black No More.*

11. Michaels has argued that the rhetoric of U.S. anti-imperialists as much as the imperialists themselves "embodied the complete coincidence of racial identity with national identity" ("Souls" 188). More recently, Michaels has extended this argument to claim that there emerged in the twenties "a new cultural Americanism," an early manifestation of "what we might today call multiculturalism" ("Race" 366-67).

12. Sundquist situates the *Plessy* arguments and opinion in relation to the "second slavery" of Jim Crow America as it appears in works like Mark Twain's *Pudd'nhead Wilson* and Charles Chesnutt's *The Mar-*

row of Tradition. The irony of *Plessy,* according to Sundquist is that it is simultaneously "a mockery of law and an enactment of its rigid adherence to divided, dual realities" (237).

13. Originally used in French courts to determine competency, Binet's scales were "refined" by Lewis Madison Terman who in *The Measurement of Intelligence* (1916), proposed tests for determining intelligence on a scale from infancy to "genius." See Bond 452-59 for an early critique of Terman's methods and of his conclusion that "children along the lower slopes of the intelligence curve were usually Mexican or Negro children" (qtd. in Bond 454).

14. In his 1929 Chicago Forum debate with Stoddard, Du Bois mocks the former's fears of amalgamation. Pointing out that the people "responsible for more intermixture of races than any other people, ancient and modern," are the same ones crying "You shall not marry our daughters!" Du Bois answers, "Who in Hell asked to marry your daughters? If this race problem must be reduced to a matter of sex, what we demand is the right to protect the decency of our own daughters" (Du Bois and Stoddard 6).

15. According to Williamson, whatever privileges enjoyed by the "white Negroes" by virtue of light skin (e.g., access to jobs and public facilities, the perception that they were smarter and more attractive) were offset by the prejudice suffered from both white and black people. Citing the research of Carter G. Woodson, Williamson says that much popular opinion held that "social pressures restricted miscegenation 'to the weaker types of both races.' There emerged a popular persistent, and grossly unfair idea that the offspring of such unions were marked by special colors. Often they were designated as 'yellow niggers'" (116-18). Lighter African Americans were also associated in some black circles with the drinking, prostitution, and potential violence of chorus lines and cabaret life.

16. Though visibly white, northern Italians and the French were routinely sequestered by writers like Burr into their own lesser white camp, the "Alpines," thus allowing commentators to appropriate from those cultures at will, while relieving them of the necessity of explaining the continued unregenerate aspects of French culture.

17. He praised Hughes's 1930 *Not Without Laughter* as "*the* novel of Negro life." "More than a novel," he wrote, "it is a social document, an epic on the sable lowly that white America looks down upon. . . . *I know* the people in this novel, every one of them. They are in a hundred little ghettos. . . . The *people* are *real* and their impact is *real*" (qtd. in Peplow 34).

18. In the guise of pragmatism, Stoddard condemns the New Negro emphasis on the cultural work of art:

> If it be cultural recognition and appreciation that the cultured Negroes really want, let them get after their insurgent intelligentsia who are today seeking to use their art as a battering ram to smash the color line. For art was intended for no such purpose, and if it is used in that way most of this rapidly budding Negro talent today will be blighted and perverted into propaganda and vain bitterness in the attempt.
>
> (Du Bois and Stoddard 14)

19. Near the beginning of his talk, Du Bois claims that "by equality, I do not mean absolute identity or similarity of gift, but gifts of essentially equal value to human culture" (Du Bois and Stoddard 3).

20. This is Appiah's designation for institutional forms of racism (8). Compare it to Du Bois's remark to Stoddard, "You have made it almost impossible for America to think logically" (Du Bois and Stoddard 7) and Walter Hines Page's observation that "the Negro-in-America . . . is a form of insanity that overtakes white men" (qtd. in Frazier 54).

21. Roediger quotes Du Bois's *Black Reconstruction* (13). Wynter provides a Deleuzian analysis of a similar phenomenon: "Thus the value of white being needs to be constantly realized, recognized, attained by the social act of exchange with the relative non-value of black being, a non-value represented by the Symbolic Negro/Sambo. It is this social act of exchange that communicates to the white about his own autonomy, an autonomy which as in the case of white workers . . . the white does not *experience* in other aspects of his life" (153).

22. Arguing that "color has no reality [in *Black No More*] apart from the socially created one," Reilly reaches a similar conclusion in his brief discussion of *Black No More* as an anti-utopian novel. "Every white person in the book is an ass; every institution created by whites is debased. Schuyler's novel may represent racial assimilation as an ideal, but it does not provide an image of white society which would encourage those assimilationist goals" (107-08).

Works Cited

Appiah, Kwame Anthony. "Racisms." Goldberg 3-17.

Aptheker, Herbert, ed. *The Documentary History of the Negro People in the United States, 1910-1932.* Secaucus, NJ: Citadel, 1973.

Balibar, Etienne. "Paradoxes of University." Trans. Michael Edwards. Goldberg 283-94.

Banton, Michael. *Racial Theories.* Cambridge: Cambridge UP, 1987.

Bell, Bernard. *The Afro-American Novel and Its Tradition.* Amherst: U of Massachusetts P, 1987.

Bond, Horace Mann. "Intelligence Tests and Propaganda." Aptheker 452-59.

Bone, Robert. *The Negro Novel in America.* New Haven: Yale UP, 1965.

Burr, Clinton Stoddard. *America's Race Heritage.* New York: National Historical Society, 1922.

Davis, Arthur P. *From the Dark Tower: Afro-American Writers, 1900-1960.* Washington: Howard UP, 1974.

Davis, Arthur P., and Michael W. Peplow, eds. *The New Negro Renaissance: An Anthology.* New York: Holt, 1975.

Du Bois, W. E. B. "The Browsing Reader." *The Crisis* 39 (March 1931): 100.

Du Bois, W. E. B., and Lothrop Stoddard. "Shall the Negro Be Encouraged to Seek Cultural Equality?" Report of Debate Conducted by the Chicago Forum. Chicago: Chicago Forum Council, 1929.

Fanon, Franz. "On National Culture." *The Wretched of the Earth.* Hamondsworth: Penguin, 1969.

Fisher, Rudolph. Rev. of *Black No More. Books* Feb. 1937: 44-57.

Frazier, E. Franklin. "The Pathology of Race Prejudice." Davis and Peplow 54-61.

Gates, Henry Louis, Jr. "A Fragmented Man—George Schuyler and the Claims of Race." *The New York Times Book Review* 20 Sept. 1992: 31, 42-43.

———. *The Signifying Monkey: A Theory of Afro-American Literary Criticism.* New York: Oxford UP, 1988.

Gilroy, Paul. *There Ain't No Black in the Union Jack.* London: Hutchinson, 1987.

Goldberg, David Theo, ed. *Anatomy of Racism.* Minneapolis: U of Minnesota P, 1990.

Grant, Madison. *The Passing of the Great Race.* 1916. New York: Scribners, 1918.

Gossett, Thomas F. *Race: The History of an Idea in America.* Dallas: Southern Methodist UP, 1963.

Hall, Stuart. "What is This 'Black' in Black Popular Culture?" *Black Popular Culture.* Ed. Gina Dent. Seattle: Bay, 1992. 21-33.

Hartt, Rollin Lynde. "The New Negro." Johnsen 102-05.

Hemenway, Robert E. *Zora Neale Hurston: A Literary Biography.* Urbana: U of Illinois P, 1977.

Hofstadter, Richard. *Social Darwinism in American Thought.* Rev. ed. Boston: Beacon, 1955.

Holloway, Joseph E., ed. *Africanisms in American Culture.* Bloomington: Indiana UP, 1990.

Horsman, Reginald. *Race and Manifest Destiny: The Origins of American Racial Anglo-Saxonism.* Cambridge: Harvard UP, 1981.

Huggins, Nathan. *Harlem Renaissance.* New York: Oxford UP, 1971.

Hughes, Langston. "The Negro Artist and the Racial Mountain." Aptheker 525-30.

Johnsen, Julia E., ed. *Selected Articles on the Negro Problem.* New York: Wilson, 1921.

Josey, Charles Conant. *Race and National Solidarity.* New York: Scribner's, 1923.

Kellner, Bruce. *The Harlem Renaissance: A Historical Dictionary for the Era.* New York: Methuen, 1987.

Lewis, David Levering. *When Harlem Was in Vogue.* New York: Knopf, 1981.

Lloyd, David. "Race Under Representation." *Oxford Literary Review* 13.1-2 (1991): 62-94.

Locke, Alain. "We Turn to Prose: A Retrospective Review of the Literature of the Negro for 1931." *The Critical Temper of Alain Locke: A Selection of His Essays on Art and Culture.* Ed. Jeffrey C. Stewart. New York: Garland, 1983. 209-13.

Mecklin, John Moffatt. *Democracy and Race Friction: A Study in Social Ethics.* New York: Macmillan, 1914.

Mercer, Kobena. "Black Hair/Style Politics." *New Formations* 3 (1987): 33-54. Rpt. in *Welcome to the Jungle: New Positions in Black Cultural Studies.* Ed. Mercer. (New York: Routledge, 1994. 97-128.

Michaels, Walter Benn. "Race into Culture: A Critical Genealogy of a Cultural Identity." *Cultures of United States Imperialism.* Ed. Amy Kaplan and Donald E. Pease. Durham, Duke UP, 1993. 365-91.

———. "The Souls of White Folk." *Literature and the Body: Essays on Populations and Persons.* Ed. Elaine Scarry. Baltimore: Johns Hopkins UP, 1988. 185-209.

Miller, James A. Forward. *Black No More.* By George Schuyler. Boston: Northeastern UP, 1-12.

Peplow, Michael W. *George S. Schuyler.* Boston: Twayne, 1980.

Rayson, Ann. "George Schuyler: Paradox Among 'Assimilationist' Writers." *Black American Literature Forum* 12 (1978): 102-06.

Reilly, John M. "The Black Anti-Utopia." *Black American Literature Forum* 12 (1978): 107-09.

Roediger, David. *The Wages of Whiteness: Race and the Making of the American Working Class.* London: Verso, 1991.

Rogers, J. A. "Jazz at Home." *The New Negro.* Ed. Alain Locke. New York: Atheneum, 1992. 216-24.

Roosevelt, Theodore. "Race Decadence." *New Outlook* 8 Apr. 1911: 763-69.

Schuyler, George. *Black and Conservative: The Autobiography of George S. Schuyler.* New Rochelle, NY: Arlington, 1966.

———. *Black No More: Being an Account of the Strange and Wonderful Workings of Science in the Land of the Free, A.D. 1933-1940.* Boston: Northeastern UP, 1989.

———. "The Negro-Art Hokum." *The Nation* 16 June 1926: 662-63.

Sollors, Werner. "Of Mules and Mares in a Land of Difference; or, Quadrupeds All?" *American Quarterly* 42.2 (1990): 167-90.

Stoddard, Lothrop. *The Rising Tide of Color Against White Supremacy.* New York: Scribner's, 1920.

Sundquist, Eric J. *To Wake the Nations: Race in the Making of American Literature.* Cambridge: Harvard UP, 1993.

Sylvander, Carolyn Wedin. *Jessie Redmon Fauset, Black American Writer.* Troy, NY: Whitston, 1981.

Wiggam, Albert. *The Fruit of the Family Tree.* Indianapolis: Bobbs-Merrill, 1924.

Williamson, Joel. *New People: Miscegenation and Mulattoes in the United States.* New York: Free, 1980.

Wright, R. R. Jr., "What Does the Negro Want in Our Democracy?" Johnsen 94-101.

Wynter, Sylvia. "Sambos and Minstrels." *Social Text* 1 (1979): 149-56.

FURTHER READING

Criticism

Davis, Arthur P. "George S. Schuyler." In *From the Dark Tower: Afro-American Writers 1900 to 1960,* pp. 104-08. Washington, D.C.: Howard University Press, 1974.

Offers a brief survey of Schuyler's career and opinions.

Favor, J. Martin. "Color, Culture, and the Nature of Race: George S. Schuyler's *Black No More.*" In *Authentic Blackness: The Folk in the New Negro Renaissance,* pp. 111-36. Durham, N.C.: Duke University Press, 1999.

Discusses Schuyler's novel in the context of "the critical discourse of literary blackness."

Leak, Jeffrey B., ed. *Rac[e]ing to the Right: Selected Essays of George S. Schuyler.* Knoxville: The University of Tennessee Press, 2001, 174 p.

A copious collection of Schuyler's essays, including the transcript of a panel discussion with James Baldwin and Malcolm X, and an introduction examining Schuyler's life, career, and opinions.

Long, Richard A. "An Interview with George S. Schuyler." *Black World* 25, no. 4 (february 1976): 68-78

Interview with Schuyler.

Reilly, John M. "The Black Anti-Utopia." *Black American Literature Forum* 12, no.3 (autumn 1978): 107-09.

Examines Black No More *as an example of an anti-utopian novel and compares it to William Melvin Kelly's* A Different Drummer.

OTHER SOURCES FROM GALE:

Additional coverage of Schuyler's life and career is contained in the following sources published by the Gale Group: *Black Writers,* Ed. 2; *Contemporary Authors,* Vols. 81-84; *Contemporary Authors New Revision Series,* Vol. 42; *Contemporary Authors - Obituary,* Vols. 73-76; *Dictionary of Literary Biography,* Vols. 29, 51.

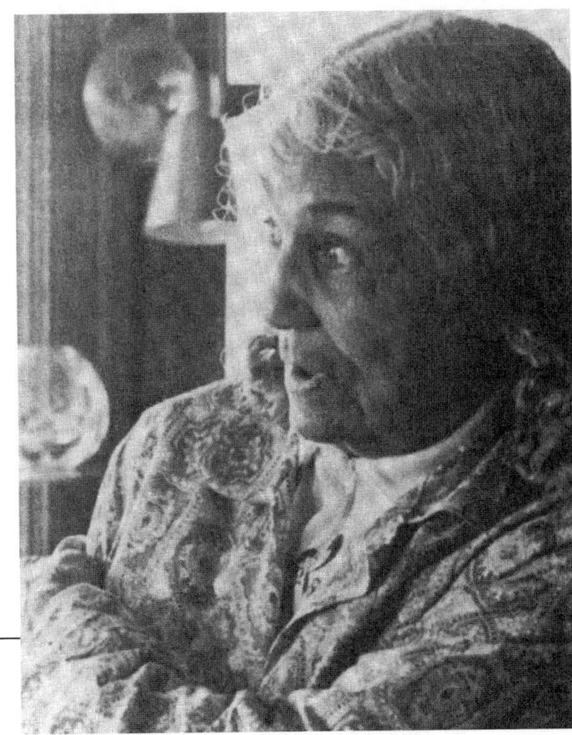

ANNE SPENCER

(1882 - 1975)

(Full name Annie Bethel Scales Bannister Spencer) American poet.

Though she rarely left her home in Lynchburg, Virginia, Spencer is remembered by critics as one of the most talented and unique poets of the Harlem Renaissance. She was somewhat older than the younger, bolder poets associated with the movement; not until she met James Weldon Johnson did she begin to publish the poetry she had been writing on scraps of paper for decades. Once she entered the public sphere, she met and entertained several important figures of the Harlem Renaissance and early civil rights movement, including W. E. B. Du Bois, Paul Robeson, and Langston Hughes. Her poetry appeared in several important collections of the 1920s, including Johnson's *Book of American Negro Poetry* (1922), Charles S. Johnson's *Ebony and Topaz* (1927), and Countee Cullen's *Caroling Dusk* (1927).

BIOGRAPHICAL INFORMATION

Spencer was born on February 6, 1882, in Henry County, Virginia. Her parents, Sarah Louise and Joel Cephus Bannister, had a tempestuous relationship, and eventually Anne and Sarah left for Bramwell, West Virginia, where Anne and her mother lived with the Dixie family. In 1893 Anne returned to Virginia to enroll at the Virginia Seminary, a boarding school for Blacks. At the Seminary she met Edward Spencer, and after her graduation as valedictorian in 1899 and after two years spent teaching in Bramwell, the two married and returned to Lynchburg. The couple had three children—Bethel, Alroy, and Chauncey—and after the birth of the third, Spencer resumed her teaching career with a short stint at her alma mater, the Virginia Seminary. In 1906 they moved into the home where Spencer would live the rest of her life: 1313 Pierce Street, now listed on the National Register of Historic Places. The couple cultivated a garden together, and Edward built a cottage they called "Edankrall," where Anne did most of her writing. In contrast to the strained relationship of her parents, Spencer maintained a close friendship and long-standing romance with her husband, who supported her love of reading, writing, and gardening by making sure family or hired help were available to manage the house and children. Spencer was active in social causes and in 1918 worked to help establish a Lynchburg chapter of the NAACP. Through this work she met James Weldon Johnson, who stayed with the Spencers as a field representative. Johnson happened upon her poems by chance and asked if he could show them to H. L. Mencken, who thought the poems quite good. Mencken, however, suggested a revision that Spencer refused, resulting in Spencer withdrawing her poems from his consideration. In February 1920 she published her first poem, "Before the Feast at Sushan," in the journal *Crisis*. *Crisis* was later the only journal she could find willing to publish her 1923 poem "White Things," one of her few poems to directly address racial conflicts. Spencer maintained a life-long affection for Johnson, for whom she wrote the tribute poem "For Jim, Easter Eve" after his death in 1938. After the loss of her patron and friend, Spencer left the public eye, working as a librarian until her retirement in 1945 and continuing to cultivate her garden with Edward. When Edward died in 1964, she gave up her garden as well. By 1970, she began writing seriously again, hoping to publish a collection. She became interested in historical leaders including the abolitionist John Brown, about whom she planned a lengthy poem that she hoped would be her masterpiece. By 1974 however, she was too ill to work. She wrote her last poem in June 1974, calling it "1975" and intending it as her final work. She died in July, 1975, in Lynchburg, Virginia.

MAJOR WORKS

Spencer's first published poem, "Before the Feast at Shushan," appeared in both *Crisis* and James Weldon Johnson's anthology *The Book of American Negro Poetry*. Johnson's poetry collection includes five of Spencer's poems—"Shushan," "At the Carnival," "The Wife-Woman," "Translation," and "Dunbar" ("Dunbar" was also published in the November 1920 issue of *Crisis*). Critics estimate that "At the Carnival" was actually written around 1910 or earlier, making it possibly one of her earliest works. Some of these poems reflect on the relationship between men and women: "Shushan" and "At the Carnival" address gender inequality, but poems such as "The Wife-Woman" and "Translation" also allow for the kind of supportive, positive relationship Spencer shared with her own husband. "Translation" also expresses the theme of friendship between lovers, a theme repeated in the poem "I Have a Friend," which was published in Cullen's *Caroling Dusk* of 1927. Other poems published in that collection are "Substitution" (reportedly one of Spencer's favorites), "Innocence," "Questing," "Life-Long, Poor Browning," and "Creed." Like the earlier poem "Dunbar," the poems "Life-Long, Poor Browning" and "Substitution" address Spencer's love of poetry. In "Substitution," Spencer explains that imagination and poetry can lift the mind out of the ugliness of reality—in the poem, that ugliness is the murder trial of a Black preacher. "White Things" is one of the few poems of racial protest that Spencer wrote; widely anthologized, it is also considered one of her best. After 1927, Spencer slowed her publishing rate. Her most significant poems following the heyday of the Harlem Renaissance are "For Jim, Easter Eve" and "1975." The former, her tribute poem to Johnson, draws together some of the major themes of her writing: the garden, spirituality, and friendship. The latter she wrote to sum up her life and works, again using imagery of the garden—clods of dirt, worms, rocks—and expressing her debt to the simplest forms of nature for revealing insights into poetry and human existence.

CRITICAL RECEPTION

Little of note was written about Spencer before 1990; her death sparked a flurry of interest, but more commonly Spencer has been mentioned in passing as one of a number of women poets of the Harlem Renaissance. For most of her life Spencer showed little interest in publishing her own poetry, allowing Johnson to help her works find an audience. She published almost nothing after Johnson died, and by the time she decided, in her nineties, that she was interested in publishing a collection, it was too late: poor health prevented her from putting together a volume herself, and after her death unknowing relatives discarded most of her writings. As a result, Spencer's poetry, though considered among the best of her era, has not generally been considered on its own. Spencer's major modern critic has been J. Lee Greene, who wrote her biography with an appendix collecting her poems. Greene's work on Spencer has emphasized the significant relationships in her life, particularly with Johnson and her husband, Edward, and her great love of nature and her garden. Though Spencer was not a topical or "protest" poet, some scholars, including Greene and Charita Ford, have noted her feminist leanings and her subtle way of addressing racial issues.

PRINCIPAL WORKS

"At the Carnival" (poem) 1910?

"Before the Feast at Shushan" (poem) 1920

"White Things" (poem) 1923

"For Jim, Easter Eve" (poem) 1938

"1975" (poem) 1974

Time's Unfading Garden: Anne Spencer's Life and Poetry (poetry) 1977

PRIMARY SOURCES

ANNE SPENCER (POEM DATE 1923)

SOURCE: Spencer, Anne. "White Things." *The Crisis.* (March 1923).

In this poem, Spencer employs descriptive language and the metaphor of colors to examine the differences between white and Black cultures.

"WHITE THINGS"

Most things are colorful things—the sky, earth, and sea.
Black men are most men; but the white are free!
White things are rare things; so rare, so rare
They stole from out a silvered world—somewhere.
Finding earth-plains fair plains, save greenly grassed,
They strewed white feathers of cowardice, as they passed;
The golden stars with lances fine,
The hills all red and darkened pine,
They blanched with their want of power;
And turned the blood in a ruby rose
To a poor white poppy-flower.

They pyred a race of black, black men,
And burned them to ashes white; then,
Laughing, a young one claimed a skull,
For the skull of a black is white, not dull,
But a glistening awful thing
Made, it seems, for this ghoul to swing
In the face of God with all his might,
And swear by the hell that sired him:
"Man-maker, make white!"

GENERAL COMMENTARY

J. LEE GREENE (ESSAY DATE 1977)

SOURCE: Greene, J. Lee. "The Poetry: Aestheticism." In *Time's Unfading Garden: Anne Spencer's Life and Poetry,* pp. 99-127. Baton Rouge: Louisiana State University Press, 1977.

In this essay, Greene reviews the major themes and images of Spencer's poetry, particularly her depiction of nature and gardens. Greene maintains that Spencer's work is infused with a spirituality that moves between a traditional Christian sensibility and a nature-centered mysticism.

"1975"

Turn an earth clod
Peel a shaley rock
In fondness molest a curly worm
Whose *familiar* is everywhere
Kneel
And the curly worm sentient *now*
Will *light* the word that tells the poet what a poem is

Anne Spencer wrote this poem in June, 1974. Stating then that it might be her last poem, she said that **"1975"** could be considered a comment on her life and writings. It was largely from the daily activities of her life that she found the settings, moods, themes, motifs, and images for her poetry. In her poetry are frequent references (though sometimes veiled) to her family, friends, and associates. A love for natural scenery in general, and especially for her garden, provided a metaphorical setting for many of her poems. From her readings in history, literature, and current events she found the germinal ideas for several of her topical poems. The statement that the "*familiar* is everywhere" when applied to her poetry borders on the mystical, for the sophisticated manner in which she approached these familiar observations of her environment allowed her to explore their meanings in uncommon depth.

At times cryptic, at other times deceptively simple,[1] her poems tell much about the inner and outer selves of the poet. A mystic she might not have been, but Anne Spencer was a visionary of sorts. Speaking of the theme in her sonnet **"Substitution,"** she said that one must substitute reality to get reality; that unless we have ideas, reality is too stark. **"Substitution,"** one of her favorite poems, is a good schematic example of the plan and themes of her poetry, as well as a partial explanation of why she wrote poetry. It begins with questioning:

> Is Life itself but many ways of thought,
> How real the tropic storm or lambent breeze
> Within the slightest convolution wrought
> Our mantled world and men-freighted seas?
> God thinks . . . and being comes to ardent things:

These opening lines deal with the power of creativity associated with God. Posing a question in the first four lines, the speaker in line five is brought to the vast and magnificent power of the Supreme Creator, who creates the world of reality in a single thought. He forms "Within [His] slightest convolution . . . / Our mantled world" and thus gives "being . . . to ardent things." He creates "The splendor of the day-spent sun, love's birth,— / Or dreams a little, while creation swings / The circle of His mind and Time's full girth." In the octave, then, the poet draws a parallel between the creative powers of God and the poet. The poet as imitator and creator substitutes for "Our mantled world" of reality his own thinking, or dreams and thus gives "being" to "ardent things." Yet in his substitution the poet also creates other mantled worlds. God creates "The splendor of the day-spent sun"; the poet assigns the birth of love to the setting sun and, in one sense, gives it human meaning. The speaker holds that anyone can create in his own mind, that creation is not limited to God and poets. The poem answers the question posed in the first line in the affirmative: life itself is but many ways of thought. The speaker whose "thought leans forward" is then quickly "lifted clear / Of brick and frame," the real world, and creates for himself a world of "moonlit garden bloom."

In 1974 Anne Spencer revised the first five lines of **"Substitution"** as they originally were published:

> Is Life itself but many ways of thought,
> Does *thinking* furl the poets' pleiades,
> Is in His slightest convolution wrought
> These mantled worlds and their men-freighted
>   seas?
> He thinks—and being comes to ardent things:

Mrs. Spencer explained that she never meant to capitalize *His* in line three, and that so doing "ruined the whole poem." She revised these lines in order to improve the diction (to delete *pleiades*) and to polish the ambiguity by deleting some references to God and the poet. With *His* in the lower case, the poem as originally published would concern primarily the poet and the speaker as creators. This capitalization "error" (but one should compare *His* in line eight, as well as *poets'* instead of *poet's* in line two) shows a blending of the human and the divine as creators, an association which is characteristic of several of her poems, and which seems to work well throughout this sonnet. The grammatical and visual relationship between *poets'* and *His* creates a kind of ambiguity or double meaning which is sustained in the poem. But Mrs. Spencer believed the ambiguity in the original version hindered more than it helped. The revision may, however, make the reader work harder to glean the meaning of these lines. It also deletes in the octave the idea that the poet shares a power of creation with God, an idea which remains in the sestet. In the original version the octave asks not one question, but poses a series of at least three different yet interrelated questions about life, creation and creators, appearance and reality.

"Substitution" conveys a desire to change this world of cold, stark reality for one of beauty and love; the sestet affirms the capacity of any person to do this. And whether in her own garden or in the garden as symbol of a perfect world in her poetry, through the creative, life-giving process Anne Spencer managed to substitute a more perfect world to compensate for the imperfect society in which she lived. This was her motivation for writing poetry.

The sestet of **"Substitution"** begins with a topical allusion—an example of how well she veils the subjective and topical to achieve the objective and universal. The lines "As here within this noisy peopled room / My thought leans forward," said Mrs. Spencer, refer to a courtroom scene where she witnessed the trial of a black preacher accused of murder. The man was possessed more by lust than love for a young girl, whom he murdered out of passion. This particular idea also is recorded in her ***Notebooks***: "The test by which we can *know* we have reached the high point in human Love is not only what I will do for it, but what I absolutely refuse to do against it." On the same topic she wrote at another time: "There is always this test: The grave, even supernatural difference between love and lust is that the loving heart desires to *do* everything for its object, and nothing against it." To escape the farcical trial, to escape the unpleasant proceedings of southern justice (or injustice), the poet-speaker could and did mentally leave this world of ugliness, impurity, and hate, and substituted a visionary world of pure love and beauty. Thematically, in a large group of her poems she envisions life as a journey through a human world of suffering and pain in quest of a spiritual world of infinite peace and harmony. **"1975"** informs us that gleaning intimations from the familiar was the approach she took to her poetry; **"Substitution"** tells us how and why she wrote poetry. What follows in this chapter is a discussion of part of what she wrote.

Using **"At the Carnival"** and **"Questing"** as thematically representative poems, I can see a large group of Anne Spencer's poems forming an aesthetic or poetic *Pilgrim's Progress*. Within the group there is a rejection of a degenerate world (**"At the Carnival"**) in quest of one of supernal beauty (**"Questing"**), in quest of the Celestial City which in her poetry is symbolized by the garden setting.

In her poems she seldom mentions from whence man comes before his life's quest. Her attention is focused on what in **"Translation"** she calls the "far country" at the end of life's journey. By focusing on this idealistic "far country" for which man quests, she necessarily draws attention to this world of reality in which we now live. The road of life is filled with ugliness, with "anvil and strife," with pain and suffering, with sorrow, with all the conditions which make the speakers of her poems strive to attain that "far country." But everything on the road of life is not negative, for there are glimmers of beauty which show us how perfect life must be in the "far country," but which make the journey through this life even more difficult because the knowledge of that ideal world reveals the imperfection of this one and fills us with yearning. The motif implies a fated philosophy: man is placed on the road of life and destined "To grope, eyes shut, and fingers touching space" (**"Questing"**) for that almost unattainable world of pure beauty.

"At the Carnival" is one of her few poems which deals specifically with this world of reality in which we live—this "sordid life," this "unlovely thing" which practically overwhelms the glimmers of beauty. In this poem the world of reality is seen metaphorically as a carnival peopled primarily by grotesque figures and blind crowds. Those at the carnival of life, whether as participants or observers, can recognize in such fragile symbols as the diving-tank girl our hopes for redemption from this world of Vanity Fair. And though the poem concentrates on negativism, on the carnival of life, it ultimately moves to a conclusive statement of hope and affirmation (though expressed somewhat despairingly): "I implore Neptune to claim his child today!"

Anne Spencer said that she wrote **"At the Carnival"** long before she wrote **"Before the Feast at Shushan,"** her first poem to be published. So **"At the Carnival"** probably was written shortly after 1910 or possibly as early as the turn of the century. During the early decades of this century carnivals and fairs were common throughout the South. Once Ed and Anne went to a carnival located just a few blocks from their home. Anne had been "out-of-sorts" for a few days prior to this, and Ed urged her to go with him, thinking that the carnival would provide some diversion and maybe relax her mind. She agreed, and shortly afterwards recorded the event:

> I came incuriously—
> Set on no diversion save that my mind
> Might safely nurse its brood of misdeeds
> In the presence of a blind crowd.
> The color of life was gray.
> Everywhere the setting seemed right
> For my mood!

The carnival mirrored her unsettled state of mind; it also probably mirrored the causes of her disturbance. A microcosm of this imperfect world after Eden, the carnival is filled with the bizarre, the ugly, the grotesque; it is full of fate and chance:

> Here the sausage and garlic booth
> Sent unholy incense skyward;
> There a quivering female-thing
> Gestured assignations, and lied
> To call it dancing;
> There, too, were games of chance
> With chances for none;

Walking through the carnival and absently gazing at all the grotesque figures "amid the malodorous / Mechanics of this unlovely thing," the speaker's attention is suddenly caught by a gleam of beauty among all this ugliness. She notices the "Gay little Girl-of-the-Diving-Tank" amid this "sordid life" and her spirits are lifted. She sees in this "darling of spirit and form" a beauty which reflects her own heart: a heart which yearns for beauty in a world which has become ugly; a heart which invariably searches for some vestige of Eden in a world of grotesques.

The world indeed has changed since Eden. The speaker, nursing her "brood of misdeeds," initially feels a sort of kinship with the "blind crowd," that crowd which is so fascinated by the grotesques of life, the freaks of nature, that it is oblivious to the "form divine." But unlike the "blind crowd," the freaks themselves can make the contrast between their own fallen state and the innocent beauty of the "Girl-of-the-Diving-Tank":

> My Limousine-Lady knows you, or
> Why does the slant-envy of her eye mark
> Your straight air and radiant inclusive smile?
> Guilt pins a fig-leaf; Innocence is its own adorning,
> The bull-necked man knows you—this first time
> His itching flesh sees form divine and vibrant health,
> And thinks not of his avocation.

After the Fall, man's destiny is to die. Through his sins he has forfeited perpetual life, "form divine," and "vibrant health" on this earth. To redeem himself and be assured of eternal life in another form, man must embrace the divine form of beauty here symbolized in the diving girl. By embracing her one can embrace the representative of God; the girl is goodness personified, "and / Whatever is good is God."

"At the Carnival" is singular among Anne Spencer's poems in that it concentrates on the evils and ugliness of a world for which the speakers of her various poems want to substitute a more perfect world. **"Substitution"** states that poetry will be the vehicle by which the poet will escape from a world morally and spiritually gone awry. The poem attests to the powers of the imagination, to the fortitude of a creative mind in search of beauty. Such an attempt to escape the sorrows of the world gives birth to poetry: "Art—a substitute for natural living—can be born either of joy

FROM THE AUTHOR

"LETTER TO MY SISTER"

It is dangerous for a woman to defy the gods;
To taunt them with the tongue's thin tip,
Or strut in the weakness of mere humanity,
Or draw a line daring them to cross.

SOURCE: Anne Spencer, from "Letter to My Sister," in *Ebony and Topaz: A Collectanea,* edited by Charles S. Johnson, National Urban League, 1927, p. 94.

or sorrow; as mother the former is very unlikely" (***Notebooks***). Practically all of the personae of her poems are pilgrims questing for a better life. Defying earthly and mortal obstacles placed in their paths, they tread relentlessly through this world of Vanity Fair as they seek the prize of knowledge and spiritual contentment in the Celestial City. It is her poem **"Questing"** which appropriately conveys this theme. **"Questing"** relates the urgency, the symbolic objective, the motivation, and the difficulty for the pilgrim poet:

Let me learn now where Beauty is;
My day is spent too far toward night
To wander aimlessly and miss her place;
To grope, eyes shut, and fingers touching space.

The thematic frame for the discussion of the poems which follow will be the poetic contrast between the degeneracy of this present world and the idealism of the world and life hereafter.

The simplicity of **"Rime for the Christmas Baby"** may cause the reader to dismiss it as a trivial occasional poem; yet it fits well into this schematic treatment of Anne Spencer's poetry. The poem is cast in the form of a letter to a friend (Bess Alexander) celebrating the birth of her baby on Christmas Day. The birth of the baby is his entry upon the journey to that "far country." His progress through this life may be hampered by mortal and non-spiritual obstacles; he may even be enticed by the false, superficial, and transient symbols of a perfect life—material possessions: "He'll have rings and linen things, / And others made of silk." But these things are transitory and unimportant when compared to what awaits him at the end of this life's journey. However, all the material and mortal possessions of this world are not negative, for "True, some sort of merit in a mart / Where goods are sold for money, / But packed with comfort is the heart / That shares with you what's funny."

We can reconcile ourselves to the "things" of this life, the superficial or even ugly things, just as the grotesques in **"At the Carnival"** resign themselves to what this life holds for them. Yet we understand that there is beauty in this world and something even better awaiting us, in the same way that the Limousine-Lady, the bull-necked man, and the speaker in **"At the Carnival"** can understand the beauty of the diving-tank girl. But there are those who cannot accept the conventionalities of life, such as the speaker in **"The Wife-Woman"** or the sister in **"Letter to My Sister."** As does the wife-woman, we might long for that "far country"; but we *must* wait, since Fate decrees it, just as it decrees that we must make this journey through life. We must, the speaker of **"Rime for the Christmas Baby"** says, resign ourselves to it: "So please kiss him when he's very bad / And laugh with him in gladness." It matters not how much we fret and pray; we have no control over our plight. There are forces greater than we who have fated us to make this journey: "Life is too long a way to go, / And age will bring him sadness." And though we pray for relief through death (a pervasive theme in her poetry), we must wait our fate. Life is hard, but one can earn salvation and achieve immortality in "Time's unfading garden."

Fate and chance are motifs which recur in Anne Spencer's poetry. But, although one must wait for that spiritual and physical salvation from this life, one must not be idle; one must struggle to attain that place, must be active and defiant of the earthly forces which retard progress. On one level, **"Letter to My Sister"** (first published in a slightly different version as **"Sybil Warns Her Sister"**) conveys the same theme. Speaking of the poem, Anne Spencer said that although she never had a congenital sister, she had close friendships with women who came near to being congenital sisters and thus were spiritual sisters. This poem is a letter to her sisters of the world. Speaking of a major idea in the poem, Mrs. Spencer said, "You don't ever get clear of problems." Often in her poems she blends or contrasts pagan and orthodox religious motifs. Here the forces of the world which one must fight against are characterized as pagan deities. "It is dangerous for a woman to defy the gods; / To taunt them with the tongue's thin tip," for the gods are very powerful. But "worse still if you mince timidly— / Dodge this way or that, or kneel or pray." Though "the gods are Juggernaut,"

> This you may do:
> Lock your heart, then, quietly,
> And lest they peer within,
> Light no lamp when dark comes down
> Raise no shade for sun;
> Breathless must your breath come through
> If you'd die and dare deny
> The gods their god-like fun.

The poem recalls a major thematic statement in Paul Laurence Dunbar's novel *The Sport of the Gods*: whom the gods wish to destroy, they first make mad.[2] It suggests Fate operating in this world (if not a tinge of fatalism), a kind of naturalistic approach to life. Naturalistic and fatalistic overtones are to be found in a poem like **"At the Carnival,"** but the thrust of Anne Spencer's poetry is her belief in the world that beauty gives us inklings of—intimations which we must cultivate like a garden. Thus her poetry and her garden are manifestations of the same principle of creativity.

Anne Spencer's garden was central to her life; it is of primary importance in her poetry. People who knew her almost always knew of her garden; frequently they knew of the garden before they knew her. When at home as a "housewife" and after coming home from her job as Dunbar High School's librarian, she would spend most of her waking hours during the week in this garden. It was not unusual for her "to plant the thorn and kiss the rose" (**"Any Wife to Any Husband"**) until she could no longer see how to work; then, if there was no light from the moon, she would use candles or other artificial light. When not tending the plants and flowers, many times she would retire to the garden house and absorb herself in reading and writing. It is in this setting that she composed many of her poems, taking much of her imagery and many of her metaphors directly from that garden world. The garden house not only held tools for gardening, but contained a library for her reading and writing and served as a second storehouse for her papers and literary materials. It follows, then, that many times she would collect her thoughts in the peaceful, harmonious atmosphere of the garden grounds ("Peace is here and in every season / a quiet beauty" [**"For Jim, Easter Eve"**]) and work on her poetry in the seclusion of the garden house. Since cultivating her garden was a major part of her day-to-day activities, it is understandable that this garden functions frequently as image, metaphor, and symbol in her poems. A short poem from her ***Notebooks*** expresses the sanctity of a garden world and man's violation of it:

> Sunday 22—'28
> God never planted a garden
> But He placed a keeper there;
> And the keeper ever razed the ground
> And built a city where
> God cannot walk at the eve of day,
> Nor take the morning air.

For a woman whose mental and spiritual selves were not in harmony with her human environment, her garden was a palliative haven. In Lynchburg it became her "last comfort in Gethsemane" as she sought spiritual shelter from the town's hostile society. Not only was it a welcome retreat from the repressive town, but the garden also allowed her to get out of the house. Such a withdrawal was not so much to escape her family, but when she retired to the garden house she was freed from living daily the traditionally exact roles of mother and wife. She needed and desired a certain spiritual nourishment which her family and friends could not provide her, and which she found in her garden world of nature.

As in her life the garden was to her an otherworldly realm of innocence, beauty, goodness, and purity, so it comes to represent Eden and the ideal realm in her poems. The contrast of the "anvil and strife" of the real world and "Time's unfading garden" is at the heart of her poetry. The garden may also be a Gethsemane, a place of grief, as in **"For Jim, Easter Eve"** where the very beauty and perfection of the place weigh upon the poet a sense of loss; but in most of the poems the garden conveys ideals, such as love, beauty, immortality.

"Before the Feast at Shushan" praises the beauty of the Garden of Shushan which reflects the Garden of Eden. Natural scenery in total—grass, flowers, birds, the landscape—becomes in her poetry an expression of beauty, whether such a natural scene is artificially tamed (such as the Garden of Shushan or her own garden) or wildly ordered (such as the Garden of Eden or the Virginia countryside in **"Life-Long, Poor Browning"**). Garden scenery thus becomes linked with the divine, with tinges of both pantheism and mysticism. As Eden was a creation of God, so natural scenery is a manifestation of God's creative powers, evidence of a divine and spiritual force in this human world. In **"Substitution"** we see the poet and God as creators, and the garden as symbolic of their creative powers. Suggested here is the idea that within the human species there is parcel of divinity, of the spiritual, which ultimately suggests (in the thematic scheme of her poetry, at least) that the human is capable of achieving immortality and sharing divinity. The human poet shares with God the power of creation. In **"At the Carnival"** if we can see the "plodder" as another creator, one who works laboriously to create what is good and beautiful, then the gardener as "plodder" has a link with the divine. The speaker in **"At the Carnival"** states: "I am swift to feel that what makes / The plodder glad is good; and / Whatever is good is God." The garden, then, the landscape, is a manifestation of beauty and of whatever is good. The garden is also used as a setting for lovers. The garden at 1313 Pierce Street remained a relic of the love bond between Anne and Edward. Edward built the garden for her and helped her cultivate it, and the two traveled many miles to acquire exotic plants for the garden. Edward also built havens for animals who were housed in the garden: bird houses (for which he gained local popularity) as homes for both special and ordinary birds and a pond for fish and frogs and any other animal that could survive there. In a quiet lyric Anne Spencer expresses Edward's attitude toward his wife and her garden:

HE SAID:
"Your garden at dusk
Is the soul of love
Blurred in its beauty
And softly caressing;
I, gently daring
This sweetest confessing,
Say your garden at dusk
Is your soul, My Love."

Moreover, the garden becomes a sanctuary of complete bliss for all lovers for all times. The theme of immortality, of transcending the world of stark reality, is central to the conclusion of **"Substitution"** where the speaker and her lover enjoy a binding love relationship that is sacred because it is not of the flesh, not of this world, but is in that world of "moonlit garden bloom." (The phrase perhaps derives from the fact that Anne and Edward often planted their garden by moonlight, or spent much time there in the quiet night of the full moon.) The same poetic function of this garden scene is evident in the two poems she wrote related to her favorite poet, Robert Browning. Both poems deal with immortality and suggest the garden scene as a sacred haven for immortal lovers. In **"Life-Long, Poor Browning"** Anne Spencer comments on the relationship between the mortal and the divine, the earthly and the heavenly.

The poem is filled with natural imagery which builds to the "immortal completeness." Garden scenery pervades the entire poem as a comparative portrait of the wild garden scenery of the Virginia countryside, English gardens, and, metaphorically, what must be heaven. The first two stanzas describe the lush countryside of Virginia as superior to that of English gardens. The third and fourth stanzas picture the Virginia landscape as rivaling heaven. Inverting the metaphor in the middle of the poem, the poet blends the heavenly and the earthly as she praises her home state. She achieves a kind of ambiguity by describing heaven in terms of the Virginia countryside, and the garden imagery which may have both heaven and Virginia as its referent expands the original metaphor. Though the closing couplet emphasizes just where "Here" is—in heaven—the metaphor still lingers and underscores again the comparison of heaven and Virginia.

The poem laments that since "Life-long, poor Browning never knew Virginia," he perhaps never knew the beauty of heaven. But "Dead, now, dear Browning lives on in heaven." He has achieved in death what this life could not give him. Browning, as poet and creator, possessed a link with the divine and thus was entitled to immortality. But the beauty of heaven itself is not sufficient, this poem says, for Browning to enjoy a full life of immortality. Differing somewhat from the usual structure of an Anne Spencer poem (which begins with doubting or questioning and moves to an affirmation), this poem ends with a question. The question is not whether Browning is enjoying immortality (affirmed at the beginning of stanza three), but whether "Shade that was Elizabeth" is there to complete his immortal life. Pondering this particular idea at one time, she recorded in her ***Notebooks***: "To meet again in another world is, I believe, so rare it must be one of the great accidents of the universe."

The closing question repeats somewhat differently an idea expressed near the end of **"Substitution"** and in other of her poems: immortal completeness implies retaining something earthly. **"Substitution"** assumes that both lovers will transcend this world. But **"Life-Long, Poor Browning"** brings this point into question and states that without reunion of man and wife (lovers) after this world, immortality would be incomplete.

"Life-Long, Poor Browning" alludes to Browning's "Home-Thoughts, From Abroad." Her second Browning poem, **"Any Wife to Any Husband: A Derived Poem,"** based on Browning's "Any Wife to Any Husband" ("This poem sounds plagiarized to me," she said), begins: "This small garden is half my world." This opening line likely refers to her physical world in Lynchburg, for there her garden indeed was a significant part of her total world. Yet the line could refer also to something larger when read in the context of the entire poem. Judging from the canon of her poetry, one may surmise that "my world" refers to time on earth and time spent in immortality. An entry in her ***Notebooks*** perhaps provides an additional gloss on the idea: "Life, death. Apart they are half; together they are one. The mystic half of what is self. The other half death makes is lovely whole and full promise." The poem ends with a similar notion to that of **"Life-Long, Poor Browning."** After the speaker is dead and the husband remarries, she wishes her husband much joy in this mortal life with his new wife, but hopes that their physical joys will not lure him from a pursuit of eternal bliss.

In **"Lines to a Nasturtium (A Lover Muses)"** again garden scenery is indicative of the love between two people. But there is a twist here. The beauty of the woman is compared to the beauty of the nasturtium, not in metaphysical but in physical terms. Unfortunately, mere physical attraction is transitory and ultimately destructive if one fails to see the inherent spirituality behind it. In this case, that beauty which attracts—which should be a gleam of the spiritual and the eternal—destroys.

"No one could be more critical than I of my proneness to [see?] Love and the obvious in what I write," she recorded in her ***Notebooks.*** Love was sacred to Anne Spencer, and that kind of love of which she wrote—love distinguished by an eternal bond between two people—is a relationship "Less as flesh unto flesh, more as heart unto heart" (**"Creed"**). Another entry in her ***Notebooks*** further characterizes her attitude toward love and writers' treatment of the subject: "Women in my day (IMD) wrote weakly of love—because of excess, pardon, expatiation on the subject. They kept love in a state of infancy—and they stayed there with it." When writing about feminine love, poets seldom, said Mrs. Spencer, write about a woman who loves her mate more than she loves (or to the exclusion of) her children, though such a situation is not uncommon in life. This is the point of view she takes in **"The Wife-Woman."**

It was perhaps about 1918 or 1919 that she wrote **"The Wife-Woman."** She said that about World War I she was reading in the newspapers about a soldier who had been killed in battle, leaving at home a widow and seven children. She wondered then how the widow felt, and there began the seed for the poem. But it was not composed immediately; it was another process of her reading which gave the poem a more definite shape. She explained: "How I make a poem. I start with a word or two and begin associating." In this case she said that she was reading a passage about the Pleiades in *Crowell's Handbook for Readers and Writers.*[3] In reference to some unfinished poems and pieces of prose on which she was working, she showed me how she derived ideas for her writings from entries in this handbook. She began associating the Pleiades and their reference to sailors with the image in her mind of the wife-woman. The idea occurred to her that many people are superstitious, and that everybody needs something to which he can pray. After this, the images, metaphors, and language for the poem concretized. Using the dominant theme of a never-dying wifely love, Anne Spencer interweaves the motifs of death, transcendence, and religion (superstition) in **"The Wife-Woman"** to express convincingly "such / Love as culture fears":

> Maker-of-Sevens in the scheme of things
> From earth to star;
> Thy cycle holds whatever is fate, and
> Over the border the bar.
> Though rank and fierce the mariner
> Sailing the seven seas,
> He prays, as he holds his glass to his eyes,
> Coaxing the Pleiades.
>
> I cannot love them; and I feel your glad
> Chiding from the grave,
> That my all was only worth at all, what
> Joy to you it gave,
> These seven links the *Law* compelled
> For the human chain—
> I cannot love *them;* and *you,* oh,
> Seven-fold months in Flanders slain!
>
> A jungle there, a cave here, bred six
> And a million years,
> Sure and strong, mate for mate, such
> Love as culture fears;
> I gave you clear the oil and wine;
> You saved me your hob and hearth—

See how *even* life may be ere the
Sickle comes and leaves a swath.

But I can wait the seven of moons,
Or years I spare,
Hoarding the heart's plenty, nor spend
A drop, nor share—
So long but outlives a smile and
A silken gown;
Then gayly reach up from my shroud,
And you, glory-clad, reach down.

In her monologue the widowed wife-woman laments the death of her soldier husband, and cannot console herself with the fact that part of her dead mate survives in their children. A superstitious woman, she is—as are most of Anne Spencer's feminine personae—defiant of cultural mores and societal laws. Shifting from a kind of paganism in the first stanza of the poem to an orthodox religious expression in the poem's conclusion, the wife-woman begins her monologue by praying to the "Maker-of-Sevens." The superstitious wife-woman defines her life in terms of seven—chance and fate—and underscores the idea that most people have the need to pray to some spiritual power. The first line, "Maker-of-Sevens in the scheme of things," may apply to both the wife-woman and the power to which she prays. The wife-woman, as does the "rank and fierce" mariner "Sailing the seven seas," prays to a spiritual force (perhaps the same) which controls the universe—"the scheme of things / From earth to star"—which controls "fate" in this "cycle" of life.

The reference to the "rank and fierce" mariner praying to the Pleiades becomes a more obvious analogy for the entire poem when in the second stanza the wife-woman begins her dramatic prayer for reunion with her dead husband (the motif culminates with the poem's conclusion). She is just as distraught about the loss of her husband as the mariner is about being lost at sea. The central theme of the poem is introduced clearly in the first line of stanza two: the wife-woman's unwillingness and inability to divide her capacity to love into wifely love and motherly love. She cannot love her children ("them") and thus feels her husband's "glad / Chiding from the grave." She still will defy cultural mores and give her all to her mate. She rejects "the *Law*" of nature (biblical doctrine) according to man that says go forth and multiply, the law which "compelled" the "seven links" for the perpetuation of the "human chain" of being. It is a similar cultural tradition of man which was responsible for her husband's military death in Flanders seven months before.

The continuity between the second and third stanzas becomes very intricate as the poem progresses. Moving from pure superstition or paganism in the first stanza to civilization in the second stanza, the poem shows that it is not a pagan but a Christian culture which has created the speaker's problems. Christian civilization and culture "compelled" the "seven links" and thus threatened or took something away from the couple's mate-to-mate love bond. It is also not paganism, but civilization—war—which has deprived the wife-woman of her mate. Stanza three alludes again to the pagan and stresses a positive contrast with the very remote past, before culture or civilization as we now know it. "A jungle there, a cave here" perhaps refers first to the jungle nature of war, the savagery, in modern terms, which has taken her husband's life and left her in despair. "A jungle there, a cave here, bred six / And a million years" in terms of sexual imagery underscores the intensity of the woman's love for her mate. She loved as a savage woman, "Sure and strong, mate for mate," the kind of love thought barbarian by modern civilization for it is "such / Love as culture fears." In the second half of stanza three, Anne Spencer returns to biblical imagery, for the most part, to express again the intensity of wifely love: "I gave you clear the oil and wine." The line suggests if not the Bible, at least that period in history usually associated with it: life at the dawn of western civilization as we know it where the woman's role was to cater to the needs and desires of her husband. The sixth line of this stanza in its language and image provides an imagistic balance between past and present expressions of this kind of wifely love: "You saved me your hob and hearth" (fire-places, symbols of western civilization's cultural domesticity and felicity). The two lines which close the stanza continue the technique of comparison-contrast. Though the lines allude to several of the poem's different motifs, their main emphasis is on the duality of a domestic love relationship, the sharing of love between wife and husband, "mate for mate," to the exclusion of all others.

The fourth and last stanza reiterates the wife-woman's unwavering position and states that her love is an undying love (what culture may even call selfish). She will "hoard" all her love and wait until the two shall meet again. A poem which began with pagan allusions and overtones now ends with a particularly Christian (or biblical) motif: she will wait until death, "Then gayly reach up from my shroud, / And you, glory-clad, reach down."

It is such an unconventional approach as this in **"The Wife-Woman"** to what otherwise would be a typical treatment of traditional themes which adds to the interest of Anne Spencer as a poet. Indeed, some of her poems follow so closely traditional techniques and themes that they do little to distinguish her as a poet who had promise or as one of achievement. **"The Wife-Woman,"** I believe, is one of her better achievements. Consistently Anne Spencer has balanced opposites: the pagan and the orthodox religions; the cultural and the uncivilized; wifely love and motherly love. The first half of the poem is contrasted and balanced with the second half; stanza with stanza; line with line. Even the alternating rhyme of the poem does not call attention to itself and functions well in the poem.

Anne Spencer was quick to point out that she was not the wife-woman. She said that members of her family had read relatively few of her poems, but that of those they had read they at times misinterpreted what seemed to be very personal allusions. **"The Wife-Woman,"** some members of her family thought, described Mrs. Spencer's feelings toward her husband and children. This is far from the case. "The wife-woman is not me," she maintained, "she is a poetic character."

At the end of **"The Wife-Woman"** the speaker looks forward to that death which will reunite her spiritually with her husband. Death was a recurrent theme in Anne Spencer's life and is quite prominent in her writings. In the early part of this chapter I stated that a large portion of the canon of her poetry can be viewed as forming a poetic *Pilgrim's Progress* which concentrates on the quest to escape this world of Vanity Fair and reach an ideal and visionary world of supernal beauty, peace, and harmony. Death is the means by which one achieves this spiritual quest, for one must die a human death and be reborn into a spiritual life (in spite of worldly obstacles) in order to reach the Celestial City of "immortal completeness." Therefore, the desire to transcend this human world of stark reality, sin, and evil and to reach that world of spiritual perfection is what one may arbitrarily term a pursuit of death, a term which I think succinctly describes important overtones in her life and a dominant theme in her writings. The pursuit of death is closely linked with a quest for immortality, and it is these two themes that I will use to divide the following discussion of the remaining poems in that group which coalesce to form a poetic *Pilgrim's Progress.*

Anne Spencer was ill on many occasions during her ninety-three years, and there were times that it seemed she was at the point of death. She probably never feared death, for death was just a means of entering a more beautiful life. Her daughter Bethel told a humorous anecdote about one of her mother's "close calls" with death. There were times when Anne Spencer just wanted to be alone, not to be bothered by human contact. Bethel remembered one occasion long ago—probably not the only one—when Mrs. Spencer was thought seriously ill. She took to her bed, thinking that now she would be left alone. Neighbors and friends sincerely concerned with her health flocked to her bedside. Looking at her lying there so helplessly in the bed, they offered phrases of pity, and Anne Spencer put on an act to feed this pity. While they were looking at or sitting with her—probably not with her permission—she would clutch at the covers as if she were taking her last breath. This frightened the onlookers, and they feared that Mrs. Spencer would not be with them long. After she had rested as long as she desired and had had the solitude she wished, she emerged from the sick bed a well woman. Some years later she evidently told how some of her "attacks" of serious illness were just excuses to be left alone.

Though she feigned serious illness perhaps more than once to gain her seclusion, there were times when she actually was ill and thought she was going to die. Though her life was relatively free of *extended* physical infirmities before 1973, periodically she was seriously ill and often anticipated death. This is evident in her writings as well as in her letters to various people. In several letters to James Weldon Johnson between 1919 and 1937, she often spoke of imminent death. In 1920, for example, about a year after first meeting Johnson, she wrote about an operation she was to undergo, and concluded: "Hold my hands. We who are about to die salute you! . . . I have been ill in bed these last three weeks, and ill out of bed more of them. . . . If Ed sends you my Bible that I've read since I was a girl, it shall mean that you are not to sorrow as one having no hope."[4] Other members of the family seem also to have been plagued by serious illness during this time. In the same letter she wrote: "For some reason my family history of last winter desires to repeat itself." This was perhaps during the winter of 1919 when Edward was very ill with pneumonia.

The subjects of pain, suffering, and death that touched her personal life also are treated in her poetry. She found much beauty amid the "strife" of this human life, but she longed for that peace and joy that would come after death. Life's pains, sufferings, and trials, whether physical, social, or psychological, ultimately were to Anne Spencer kinds of intimations of immortality. In 1924 she wrote to Johnson:

> I have not written before because, lately, all my stars surely combined to make me immensely unhappy. . . . I speak this little Jeremiad to you before you come and have done with all lamenting:
>
> Lord, still I am too strong;
> All Thy buffets fail,
> But if I abstain long,
> Willst Thou make me frail?
>
> If I love but lose,
> If I laugh . . . but cry
> Full my deeper cruse,
> Willst Thou let me die?[5]

The poem is a death plea in which the speaker laments that she, though ill, is still physically too strong to die. (Mrs. Spencer said that when she wrote this poem she did not literally want to die, or want anyone else to die. As late as July, 1974, she revised the poem in order to delete this direct reference to death.) The speaker asks that if she pretends to want to live, will the Lord then grant the opposite of her wish and allow her to die. The second stanza uses the mask motif, often found in black literature—especially in poetry—with a slight variation. Anne Spencer said that in writing the second stanza she was reminded of a time when she was on her way to work and passed a group of black men doing some menial job characteristic of the low place they had been assigned in society. Yet these men were not openly distressed about their state. One passing by would even think them happy about their lot in life. "A white man passing would look and say, 'ain't niggers jolly,'" Mrs. Spencer said. The men were laughing and joking to keep from crying, she said. In other words, these black men were wearing the psychological racial mask: openly pretending to be one thing when actually they were another. Using a variation of this idea, the speaker of the poem asks the Lord that if she "love but lose" (pretends to accept what she actually rejects), if she "laugh . . . but cry / Full my deeper cruse" (pretends to be happy in this unhappy life), will the Lord then grant her death.

The racial implication which underlies the second stanza of this poem is not readily apparent without Anne Spencer's specific remark that there is such an allusion; but the poem does not depend on this reference for its meaning. Among her papers this is one in a group of three poems titled **"Lord Songs,"** which she later titled **"Earth Songs."** In the other two poems one can see even larger racial implications. The five-line poem titled **"Liability"** is the second of the group and has suffering rather than death as its major theme:

> Lord, Thy stripes for me,
> For him the smoothéd pillow;
> My eyes were clear
> To see Thy golden stair,—
> Be mine the willow.

To force a racial connotation on the poem might be to misjudge it. But few of Anne Spencer's poems are overtly about race. And those several poems which can be interpreted as such have a much larger range of meaning: the suffering of a generation, small group, or individual is expanded to include the suffering of a people.

The third poem in the group, **"Failure,"** like the first one, more personally expresses the pursuit of death. Yet its meaning, too, can apply to a larger constituency:

> Master, the harp is broken,
> Let me die;
> Broken on a sobbing chord,
> Riven by a single word,
> Word by angels never spoken—
> Master, let me die.

The harp in the poem symbolizes beauty and harmony, and its broken state leads the speaker to desire to leave this world of pain, sorrow, and chaos for the world of peace and harmony to which death will take her. The harp is also a symbol of the poet, whose job it is to bring beauty and harmony into this world. Could it be that this poem was written at a time when Anne Spencer felt her poetic efforts were fruitless, such a time as she would write that all her muses were dead? If so, it may well be an expression of her failure to achieve in her poetry that beauty which she so desired to create in a world of ugliness, a plea to the "Master" to quell that desire which she could not articulate poetically.

The poet's role as a harbinger of spiritual beauty in a carnival wasteland is arduous because in this human world ugliness dims even further the fragile glimmers of beauty; the human overshadows the divine. If we can read **"Failure"** as an expression of the inability of the poet to create supernal beauty in this world and thus a desire to die into that life where perfect beauty reigns, then the title of the poem seems significant indeed. It is a thwarted quest for beauty and a pursuit of death. The poem **"Questing"** emphasizes this idea more thoroughly:

Let me learn now where Beauty is;
My day is spent too far toward night
To wander aimlessly and miss her place;
To grope, eyes shut, and fingers touching space.

In these opening lines the speaker states what the quest is. The symbols of beauty are here on this earth, but the complete and perfect beauty is in a world elsewhere. The poet-speaker has seen the symbols of beauty, the "handmaidens to the Queen," but wants to see the "Queen" herself. As a poet in pursuit of beauty, the speaker is little more than one of the handmaidens. She must continue the quest, though it is probable that in a human life she never can attain that queenly perfection of beauty:

But let me learn now where Beauty is;
I was born to know her mysteries,
And needing wisdom I must go in vain:
Being sworn bring to some hither land,
Leaf from her brow, light from her torchéd hand.

As a poet in this world the speaker must strive, "Being sworn," to illuminate the attributes of beauty (the "Leaf" and "light"), but only in death and immortality can this perfect beauty be comprehended.

"Questing" exhibits at least a tinge of anxiety, perhaps a result of the anxiety Anne Spencer felt from the incident which occasioned the poem's composition: her son's elopement and marriage to a lady whom Mrs. Spencer did not like. The poem is in no obvious way about that marriage, but it does attest to what Mrs. Spencer referred to as her method of composition. Often the germinal idea for a poem would be in her mind for days or as long as years before some incident, at times seemingly unrelated to the finished poem, would occur to concretize and give poetic form to the thought. Such was the case with the composition of **"Questing."**

The general background of the poem involves Anne Spencer's view of the world as a wasteland in which one easily can be enticed from a pursuit of the beautiful. It is not that she desired to infringe upon her son's freedom to determine his personal life (individual freedom was too precious to Anne Spencer for that kind of reaction), or that her reaction was based merely on her dislike for the young lady, but in this particular relationship she sensed a pursuit of the not-beautiful, another of those superficial and fleeting human obstacles placed in the path of one's quest for spiritual perfection. She sensed something not quite sacred in the relationship, and within a few years the marriage ended in divorce. "As soon as I heard Chauncey had eloped with that girl, **'Questing'** wrote itself," Mrs. Spencer recalled. She wrote to Johnson a few years after **"Questing"** was published that it was "praps using to point out D-O-N-T"; that is, don't be too easily entrapped by fake glimmers of beauty and of perfection in a relationship.

The yearning for beauty and perfection through a pursuit of death evolves into a poetic quest for immortality. A firm believer in immortality, Anne Spencer voices this death-to-immortality motif in at least two different ways in her poetry. The first and most obvious expression of this is in **"Requiem,"** where the poet seems to embrace a pantheistic philosophy in which "The grave restores what finds its bed." The poem parallels an idea in Emerson's "Hamatreya," that one cannot own the land but instead is consumed by it. Death in **"Requiem"** is seen as a natural process of nature where nothing is destroyed but is recycled.

The poem is stated somewhat matter-of-factly in terms of landscape imagery, which carries the same meaning as this imagery does in her other poems. That "far country" of immortality is more than just a beautiful, harmonious place, for there true love reigns eternally. That the objective of true love is "immortal completeness" is the motif which ends **"Life-Long, Poor Browning," "Substitution,"** and **"The Wife-Woman";** the same idea is present in other of her poems. Such a poetic attitude toward love for the most part derived from the very special and sacred relationship Mrs. Spencer had with her husband and with a few lifelong friends. After she passed ninety years of age she frequently stated that "a hundred years is long enough to live," and she yearned for death to reunite her with Edward, though she felt that his spiritual influence was ever present at 1313 Pierce Street.

Anne Spencer said that her husband Edward was father, husband, lover, and, most of all, friend. An influential force in her life, he appears often in her poetry. In her poems one sees fathers; more frequently one sees husbands, lovers, and friends, and at times the three are not differentiated. In **"Translation"** the journey of the two people into the "far country" is the journey of "My friend and I." In the middle of the poem we see the "wooing Kestrel" who "mutes his mating note" and the reference to love and lovers begins to emerge. By the end of the poem the friend merges with the lover. At this point the couple have reached the zenith of their relationship, and in this eternal "far country" the spirit of the divine hovers over them and brings them peace from the "anvil and strife" characteristic of the world they left: "And the air fleeced its particles for a coverlet; / When star after star came out / To guard their lovers in oblivion." That this "far country" is a spiritual place of divine qualities, that the entire poem recalls again Anne Spencer's recurring themes of the pursuit of death and the quest for immortality is suggested in the middle of the poem with the notation of the *time* of this journey—"at day's end."

Many of the "friends" in Anne Spencer's poems are references to people other than Edward Spencer. Commenting on the sacredness of friendship, she said, "There are two things that happen to *real* friends. Of a *real* friend you don't ask a lot of questions. And if he dies, you still have that friend's influence on you." The comments were made in reference to the second half of her poem **"I Have a Friend"**:

> He does not ask me how beloved
> Are my husband and children,
> Nor ever do I require
> Details of life and love
> In the grave—his home,—
> We are such friends.

"Translation" contains a similar idea: "Our deeper content was never spoken, / But each knew all the other said." Mrs. Spencer explained that she used the present tense "have" because once one has a friend, that friend remains throughout eternity. Of the several entries in her ***Notebooks*** concerning friendship, one notation in particular perhaps states concisely her attitude toward the subject: "Friendship is such a tenuous thing it must be strong and deathless to exist at all." Friendship is not one of the weaknesses of "mere humanity" (**"Letter to My Sister"**), but is spiritual and lasts forever. This kind of friendship describes her association with James Weldon Johnson, and if **"I Have a Friend"** had been written after Johnson's death, one would tend to think that the poem was a reference to him. The husband-lover-friend in her poems is often associated with the symbol of perfection, spiritual beauty, and all that is sacred: the garden. In this connection her poem to Johnson, **"For Jim, Easter Eve,"** comes to the forefront. That she held Johnson in this light was clear not only in her conversations about him but also in her letters to him where she frequently addressed him as "Gem."

Mrs. Spencer said that she had met but few people in her life whom she would classify with "Gem." Elsie Brown, her childhood playmate in Bramwell, West Virginia, her husband Edward, Bernice Lomax Hill, and possibly Langston Hughes are among the few. Her special meaning of friendship implies a spiritual communion and is different from, though not necessarily superior or inferior to, the love one has for one's family and acquaintances. She loved people in general, and said that she would have had little trouble getting along with her enemies or with those who might have hated her. Her special friends were few, and she met few people in her life whom she thoroughly detested. An interesting notation on the subject in her ***Notebooks*** reads: "Small wonder we hate our enemies. If we could bring loved ones back to life, we'd kill 'em, completely, two or three times a year." Her basic attitude toward friendship is typified by the following entry from her ***Notebooks***:

> Worthwhile things not only must have a standard measurement while we live, but the [trial] of their truth is found in death. Considering—taking for instance the first worthwhile unit, Time conservation—we find the arresting thought that we *spend* time to buy *eternity*. Surely a thought readily understood in so commercial a generation as our own. We must spend time in solving the human equation—with our ears close to the heart of life, listening and eager to serve; in advocating a new day in service to one another—the existence of a normality so fine that "Serve Ye, one another" shall be the very correct paraphrase for "Love Ye," that our bit may be done to widen the narrow perspectives of the server and the served. Wightman's lines entitled servants are expressive. Again, we should spend our time for friendship; not to seek friends, nor cajole them nor try to hold them lest they run away—such methods dishonor friendship.

When the major themes of her poems coalesce—a rejection of deceptive earthly symbols of perfection and beauty, a rejection of sin and evil, a pursuit of death, and a quest for immortality—it follows that the pilgrimage, a journey as well as a quest, would emerge as a recurrent motif. The personae of her poems often are presented as pilgrims rejecting this fleeting life in search of the Celestial City of infinite beauty and good, both thematically and dramatically.

This interpretation of a large group of her poems as forming a poetic or aesthetic *Pilgrim's Progress* is arbitrary, for it is doubtful that Anne Spencer consciously intended a particular thematic or philosophical design for her poems as a whole. If such an interpretation is plausible, what it shows, then, is that indeed Anne Spencer was that "private poet" which she had been called; that this design flowed naturally from her pen; and that her poetry, a private record of her attitude toward life, mirrors in poetic form the ideas and themes which shaped her life and personality. Moreover, since her poetry may not adhere absolutely to this analogous interpretation, what it shows, then, is that not only did Anne Spencer not consciously design her poems to fit such a philosophic scheme, but that since this was private poetry, she was not concerned to any large degree with the publication of her poems.

Notes

1. As Sterling Brown observes in *Negro Poetry and Drama* (Washington, D.C.: The Associates in Negro Folk Education, 1937), 66.
2. Paul Laurence Dunbar, *The Sport of the Gods* (New York: Dodd, Mead and Co., 1902), 88.
3. Mrs. Spencer said that she often had gleaned ideas for poems from reading certain entries in this handbook. But for "The Wife-Woman" she could have been mistaken, for the particular edition of *Crowell's Handbook* which I saw in her house was published in 1925, two years after the publication of "The Wife-Woman." It is possible that she was reading about the Pleiades in another book.
4. Anne Spencer to James Weldon Johnson, January 19, 1920, in James Weldon Johnson Memorial Collection of Negro Arts and Letters, Collection of American Literature, Beinecke Rare Book and Manuscript Library, Yale University.
5. Anne Spencer to James Weldon Johnson, May 8, 1924. The poem was later revised; the revised version is included in the Appendix.

J. LEE GREENE (ESSAY DATE 1978)

SOURCE: Greene, J. Lee. "Anne Spencer of Lynchburg." *Virginia Cavalcade* 27 (1978): 178-85.

In this essay, Greene offers a sketch of Spencer that focuses on her life-long connection to Virginia. Greene notes that while Spencer's somewhat retiring temperament kept her at home in Lynchburg (and therefore away from the physical center of the Harlem Renaissance), the connections she made through her friendship with James Weldon Johnson eventually brought such notable figures as Paul Robeson, George Washington Carver, W. E. B. Du Bois, Langston Hughes, and Georgia Douglas Johnson to her home.

One of the most important consequences of the migration of blacks to the urban north between 1910 and 1920 was that a large number of black intellectuals and artists converged in Harlem and brought about a movement in the creative arts during the 1920s known as the Harlem Renaissance. Harlem became identified with and symbolic of the increased artistic and literary productivity of blacks throughout the country during this decade. The literary component of the Harlem Renaissance in particular included several writers who neither lived in Harlem nor spent much of their time there. One such writer whose literary career is considered a part of the Harlem Renaissance is the Virginia poet Anne Spencer.

She was born Annie Bethel Bannister on a farm in Henry County, Virginia, on February 8, 1882, the only child of Sarah Louise and Joel Cephus Bannister. From the beginning, her parents' marriage was a discordant one of clashing personalities. Sarah, the illegitimate child of a former slave woman and a wealthy Virginia aristocrat, was always prissy, too much concerned with manners and morals. She was proud of her ancestry and maintained an aristocratic attitude all her life. Joel, of black and Seminole ancestry, was a very stern and grave man. He lived and worked to provide and to secure economic independence for his family. The saloon he opened in Martinsville, Virginia, shortly after his marriage effected this security but also precipitated the family's dissolution.

"My parents, like many unlike coupled people, used me in a doting way as their warm war coldly pursued on their personal battleground," Anne Spencer wrote. Joel often took young Annie with him to his saloon. A precocious as well as a very beautiful child, Annie, at Joel's urgings, would parade up and down the bar of the saloon and entertain the customers (all men) with her wit, intelligence, and beauty. Sarah vigorously protested. She believed the saloon an unfit environment for her child. Joel adamantly disagreed. About 1887 their frequent disagreements became irreconcilable, so Sarah left him and took Annie with her to Bramwell, West Virginia. To support herself and her child she secured a job as head cook in a local restaurant. She placed Annie with foster parents, Mr. and Mrs. William Dixie.

Anne Spencer remembered that Bramwell was a beautiful small town in the 1880s. But from the beginning Bramwell was a lonely place for her. There were only a few black children in the town and very few children at all near Annie's age. Shortly after coming to Bramwell, Annie became friends with a young white girl, Elsie Brown, and they developed a friendship that lasted until both left the area for good. Elsie was a few years older than Annie, but the two had much in common and were together so frequently that the townspeople came to accept their relationship. The absence of racial or social restrictions on her life taught her never to love or hate according to color, a philosophy she always maintained.

The influence of the six years spent in Bramwell was evident in Anne Spencer's adult life. It was in Bramwell that she acquired a love of nature that is reflected in her poetry. Living a relatively free and easy life, Annie was alone much of the time and would roam through the woods and fields. She soon grew into quite a tomboy, which irritated her mother, for Sarah spent lavishly on clothes and trinkets to make Annie a model young lady. But even as a young girl, Annie, like both her parents, was strong willed; she would not become a parlor princess.

It was also in Bramwell that she developed an insatiable interest in books. Mr. Dixie often brought home from his barbershop books and magazines he kept for his customers. Annie saw Mrs. Dixie reading the materials, and on many occasions Mrs. Dixie would read stories to her children and to Annie. When she was about eight or nine years old, Annie's determination to read the stories for herself (supported by her own rather extensive vocabulary and with Mrs. Dixie's assistance) enabled her to follow the storyline in the simpler narratives. Her mother read poorly, but she aided and encouraged her daughter's reading. By the time Annie was ten years old, she was so absorbed in observing nature and reading that she spent most of her time alone.

Precocity, a good memory, and a large vocabulary were admirable in a child of nine or ten, but these could not compensate for a lack of more formal training. Annie could have attended the free school for blacks located on the outskirts of Bramwell, but Sarah shunned the school because its pupils were children of the mineworkers. As Annie grew older she obviously needed and desired teaching beyond what she could receive at home. Sarah wrote to Joel and mentioned the problem. Joel was upset that Annie was eleven years old and not enrolled in school; he pressed Sarah to enroll her immediately. But Sarah maintained her stance that Annie would never go to school in a mining town. Joel then issued an ultimatum: Annie must be enrolled in school or he would come and take her to live with him.

Anne Spencer later remarked, "I was the battleground on which they continued to fight out their distaste for each other." A solution to the problem was soon found. Sarah learned of a boarding school for blacks in Lynchburg, Virginia, and Joel agreed to pay for Annie's schooling. In September 1893 Sarah and Annie took the train to Lynchburg, where after some difficulty Annie was enrolled in Virginia Seminary as its youngest student; she was eleven and the school's policy was to enroll only students at least twelve years old. Sarah had reassumed her maiden name after leaving Joel, so she registered her daughter as Annie Bethel Scales.

Though the seminary had been struggling to meet its financial obligations and to improve its facilities since it opened in 1890, when Annie enrolled in 1893 the school had an excellent faculty, many of whom were graduates of prestigious northern universities. Virginia Seminary provided its students with a quality education far exceeding its limited physical resources.

When she entered the seminary, she possessed only rudimentary skills in reading and writing. Annie had some difficulty at first. Yet, motivated by an inquisitive mind and sustained by a high native intelligence, she quickly learned to read well and excelled in the humanities. Before she was graduated in 1899 as valedictorian, Annie had become the favorite student of several teachers. Her abilities caught the attention of Professor Gregory Hayes, president of the seminary during Annie's matriculation, who, Anne Spencer said, was the first to teach her to look at literature as life. Throughout the rest of her life Anne Spencer loved "to talk life," as she put it, even though she was never eager to talk about her own life. She could hold the interest of others for hours, her conversations encompassing many people, places, and topics and revealing not only an alert mind but also an uncommon depth of knowledge and wisdom. When talking with her, one would never guess that her formal education had been limited to six years, but those were years of intensive and highly sophisticated learning.

It was at the seminary that she met Edward Spencer, a young man she recruited to tutor her in mathematics in exchange for her assistance in Latin. Their friendship developed into love, and in 1901 they were married in Bramwell. Immediately after their marriage the young couple moved to Lynchburg, where they remained for the rest of their lives. By 1906 they were comfortably settled into the house at 1313 Pierce Street that Edward had built and were the busy parents of two daughters, Bethel and Alroy, and one son, Chauncey.

By providing physical comfort, spiritual support, and, most importantly, love, Edward Spencer freed his wife from the traditionally exacting roles of housewife and mother and allowed her to live a life commensurate with her temperament. Even before her mother came to live with the family in the early 1920s and took over management of the household, someone was always there to take care of the three children, to do the house cleaning, to wash, to iron, and to cook. The Spencers frequently employed two or more people at one time. Anne Spencer spent her time reading, writing, and cultivating her garden.

A lover of nature since her childhood, Anne Spencer shared with Edward this love for natural things. Shortly after their marriage he developed a garden for her in their backyard where the two spent many moonlit nights planting and tending the plants and flowers. A few years after he completed the garden, Edward built Edankraal, the one-room cottage at the edge of the garden in which Anne Spencer wrote much of her poetry. In a quiet, beautiful lyric she expressed the sacredness of the garden world Edward had created for her:

> HE SAID:
> "Your garden at dusk
> Is the soul of love
> Blurred in its beauty
> And softly caressing;
> I, gently daring
> This sweetest confessing,
> Say your garden at dusk
> Is your soul, My Love."

On those infrequent occasions when she talked of her writings, Anne Spencer almost always spoke of herself as "a scrap paper scribbler in pencil." She wrote her first poem when she was fourteen, beginning a lifelong "habit of jotting down things here, there, and everywhere." As she grew into adulthood, writing became for her a means of both expressing her innermost thoughts and yet retaining the privacy of those thoughts, for she never wrote with the intention of having her works published. On paper bags, in the margins and flyleaves of books, on envelops, in tablets, on the backs of checks, or on practically any writing surface, lines for a poem, a revision of a line, an entire poem, data about her life, or just "thoughts" would appear. She said that she "wrote to keep the mortal soul alive." What survives of her "scribblings" (more properly termed her ***Notebooks***) form a fascinating record of the mind and life of this unusual woman.

Anne Spencer's verse tells much about her. She drew her aesthetic, poetic, and moral strength from the earth itself, as she expressed in a poem composed near the end of her life:

> Earth, I thank you
> for the pleasure of your language
> You've had a hard time
> bringing it to me
> from the ground
> to grunt thru the noun
> To all the way
> feeling seeing smelling touching
> —awareness
> I am here!

In her garden and through her poetry she sought to escape any limitations on her personal freedom, whether those limitations concerned her manner of dress, her civil liberties, or her rights to opinions. She said she was incapable of writing about life in its negative moments. Only on rare occasions did she write controversial or topical poems, but some of these are among her best. Regardless of their subject matter, one distinct feature of her poems is that they are invariably optimistic.

Few of her poems express the intensity of the public side of her life in Lynchburg. Anne Spencer always was active and outspoken in community affairs. She forever championed the cause of the underdog and was acutely disturbed by the arbitrary social and racial restrictions the time and place imposed. Yet Anne Spencer stood firm in the face of all opposition, even suffering at times personal derision. She initiated or promoted several community projects including library classes for black youths in order to enhance the quality of life for her neighbors and for Lynchburg citizens. In December 1923, giving up her leisurely life she walked (she would not use Jim Crow facilities) two miles to the Jones Memorial Library seeking a position as a librarian. She had no experience, but she could prove that she was a published poet, and this influenced the library board to employ her as the librarian for its branch then being established at the black Dunbar High School. This was the first lending library for blacks in Lynchburg. Though she detested being a part of segregated practices, she remained at Dunbar for longer than twenty years, and through her efforts many black readers were given access to books that they could not have obtained easily elsewhere. The public citizen and the private poet were contrasting sides of her personality.

Her initiative in community affairs and her willingness to aid the Virginia Seminary brought her into contact with James Weldon Johnson, an occasion which she often termed "an act of God." The seminary invited Johnson, then field secretary for the National Association for the Advancement of Colored People, to come to Lynchburg during the 1917-18 school term to establish a local chapter of the organization. Because the seminary's facilities for guests were limited, the Spencers consented to house the visitor, unaware at the time exactly who this Mr. Johnson was. Following Johnson's trip, Anne Spencer became active in establishing a chapter of the NAACP in Lynchburg.

Johnson's first visit to 1313 Pierce Street was one of the most significant events in Anne Spencer's life. She had been writing poetry for over twenty years before she met Johnson, but her poems and other writings remained her private and thus unpublished thoughts. While in the Spencer home, Johnson accidentally saw some of her poems and was impressed with their quality. He asked to take copies of them to show to his friends, and Anne consented. Johnson showed the poems to H. L. Mencken, a leading editor, critic, and writer, who thought they merited publication. Anne Spencer, however, refused to accept Mencken's suggestions for revising one of the poems for publication, and consequently, none of her poems was published under his auspices.

Johnson, nonetheless, encouraged her poetic talents and independence and arranged to have **"Before the Feast at Shushan"** published in the *Crisis* in 1920, her first poem to appear in print. She was thirty-eight years old. During the 1920s he assisted in having other of her poems published, many in the *Crisis,* an organ of the NAACP. By the end of the decade, seventeen of her other poems had been published in various magazines and journals such as *Opportunity, Survey Graphic,* and *Palms,* and in anthologies, including James Weldon Johnson's *The Book of American Negro Poetry* (1922), Robert Kerlin's *Negro Poets and Their Poems* (1923), and Countee Cullen's *Caroling Dusk* (1927). She won praise for the sophistication of her technique and the freshness of her perspective. Editors and anthologists made frequent requests during and after the 1920s for more of her poetry, and she was continually urged to produce prose pieces for publication. But Anne Spencer (the name under which she was published) seldom granted these requests. As she was then, she remained throughout her life very modest about her talents, and only once did she herself submit a poem for publication; all of her works were published through the initiative of her literary friends. She never published a collection of her poetry.

Since the 1920s her poems have been reprinted in practically all major anthologies that include the literature of the Harlem Renaissance, the period to which she belongs historically if not thematically. Yet her appeal has not been confined to this particular literary period, and her poems have been included in Louis Untermeyer's *American Poetry Since 1900* (1923), Francis Coleman Rosenberger's *Virginia Reader* (1948), and in the 1973 edition of *The Norton Anthology of Modern Poetry.* While Anne Spencer usually accommodated editors who wanted to reprint her poems, after 1938 she usually refused to allow a new poem to be printed.

"Gem," the name she often used for Johnson, helped move her life into the sun, Anne Spencer said. As a result of her friendship with Johnson, she and her family came to know some of the leading twentieth-century intellectuals and artists in the country. This not only allowed her opportunities to commune with minds akin to her own but allowed the entire Spencer family to extend their social and cultural contacts outside Virginia. As a result, the Spencers frequently visited Washington, D.C., New York, and other large cities in the eastern United States, where their social and cultural outlets were broadened.

During the first half of this century Lynchburg was a strategic stopover between Washington, D.C., and points north, and Nashville, Atlanta, and other points south. The people whom the Spencers came to know after 1920 frequently used their home as a restful and intellectually stimulating place to stop when traveling. Many notable persons, black and white, who stopped in Lynchburg were often guests at 1313 Pierce Street. Doctors, lawyers, singers, entertainers, college presidents, politicians, scientists, sociologists, writers, statesmen, and artists were represented among the many guests over the years. Paul Robeson, Roland Hayes, Walter White, Charles S. Johnson, George Washington Carver, Adam Clayton Powell, Jr., W. E. B. Du Bois, Langston Hughes, and Georgia Douglas Johnson were among the many who visited. And they still come to 1313 Pierce Street. Such nationally known persons as Gwendolyn Brooks and Lady Bird Johnson recently visited there. Yet visitors to the house have not been and still are not confined to the famous or familiar; as in the past, Anne Spencer's home continues to attract visitors from all walks of life.

In 1977 the house was officially declared a Virginia Historic Landmark and listed on the National Register of Historic Places. In the same year the house and grounds were designated a historic landmark by the Association for the Study of Afro-American Life and History in association with the Amoco Foundation, Incorporated. Such distinctions not only honor Anne Spencer the poet, but also testify to the historical significance of 1313 Pierce Street in the cultural life of twentieth-century America.

The garden cottage, Edankraal, recently restored, is a major attraction of the site. Its walls are lined with pictures and mementos. Its shelves are filled with artifacts and books. Its furnishings, modest and inviting, characterize the warm, tender, and creative world of Anne Spencer. The desk where she wrote so often (and where some of her literary friends wrote) still sits by the window that allows a full view of the garden; it was from the garden that she found inspiration for many of the images and references in her poems. Indeed, her garden was central to her life and to her poetry. The setting seems readily conducive to many lines she penned, such as those from **"For Jim, Easter Eve"**:

> Peace is here and in every season
> a quiet beauty.
> The sky falling about me
> evenly to the compass . . .
> What is sorrow but tenderness now
> in this earth-close frame of land and sky
> falling constantly into horizons
> of east and west, north and south;
> what is pain but happiness here
> amid these green and wordless patterns,—
> indefinite texture of blade and leaf

Whether in her garden or in the Virginia countryside, Anne Spencer's mystic attraction to nature was ever-present. She said in **"Life-Long, Poor Browning,"** a poem that praises the natural beauty of the Virginia landscape, that "Heaven's Virginia when the year's at its Spring":

> Here canopied reaches of dogwood and hazel,
> Beech tree and redbud fine-laced in vines,
> Fleet clapping rills by lush fern and basil,
> Drain blue hills to lowlands scented with
> pines . . .

James Weldon Johnson's introduction of Annie Scales Spencer to the reading public in 1920 under the name Anne Spencer brought a remarkable change in her life. When in 1938 Johnson was killed in an automobile accident, Anne Spencer withdrew from public literary activities and allowed only one additional poem of hers to be published. This was **"For Jim, Easter Eve,"** a poem in tribute to him.

By 1945, when she retired from Dunbar High School, where for more than twenty years she had worked as librarian, she had sharply decreased her public and community activities. During the next twenty years she and Edward devoted most of their time to their home and garden, and only on a few occasions did she venture to participate in public activities. When in May 1964 Edward Spencer died at the age of eighty-eight, Anne in effect completely retired from public life. Weeds overtook her garden within a few seasons, and she spent most of her waking hours absorbed in reading and writing, a daily pattern she maintained until her death.

On May 8, 1975, the Virginia Seminary and College in Lynchburg honored the seventy-fourth anniversary of her graduation by conferring upon her an honorary doctor of letters degree, but Anne Spencer was too ill to attend the ceremonies. A year earlier she had undergone surgery; several months after the surgery (from which she recovered remarkably), she was weakened by a cancerous growth in her mouth. Between 1973 and 1975, for the first time in her life, she suffered from extended illness. Having devoted so much time to reading and writing after her husband's death, she had so severely weakened her eyesight that by 1973 she could barely see. Yet she continued to read and write and produced several long prose pieces. Her most ambitious project, though, was to revise a poem she had begun fifty years before about the illustrious John Brown. Physically agile until the last few months before her death (she lived alone from 1965 until 1972) and always mentally alert, Anne Spencer worked unceasingly on the John Brown poem between the summers of 1973 and 1974. Then her eyesight became so impaired that she no longer could see the page on which she wrote. She reluctantly laid the John Brown poem aside, having completed several hundred lines (with notes) of the seven cantos planned.

In June 1974 she wrote her last complete poem and entitled it **"1975."** Though she worked intermittently on **"John Brown"** and other poems after the summer of 1974, she said then that **"1975"** (commenting on the significance of its title) would be her last poem and should be read as a gloss on her poetic career. At times she spoke of the poem as "Antaeus," indicating that all her life her strength had come from contact with the earth. She died on July 27, 1975, convinced that she, always a firm believer in immortality, would be reunited with her husband in the most perfect of worlds.

> **"1975"**
> Turn an earth clod
> Peel a shaley rock
> In fondness molest a curly worm
> Whose *familiar* is everywhere

Kneel and the curly worm sentinent *now*
Will *light* the word that tells the poet what a
poem is

J. LEE GREENE (ESSAY DATE 1987)

SOURCE: Greene, J. Lee. "Anne Spencer." In *Dictionary of Literary Biography,* Vol. 51: *Afro-American Writers from the Harlem Renaissance to 1940,* pp. 252-59. Detroit, Mich.: Gale Research, 1987.

In this essay, Greene focuses on Spencer's role in the Harlem Renaissance, discussing her work with the NAACP, her relationship with James Weldon Johnson, and the poems she published in Opportunity *and* Crisis. *Greene also reprints the poem "White Things"—one of Spencer's few poems to address racial issues directly—calling it one of the finest poems of racial protest written in the twentieth century.*

Anne Spencer is not widely known to readers of the present generation, perhaps because she published few of her poems during her life and never published a volume of her poetry or other writings. Nevertheless, the quality of the poetry she produced, the cultural and social circumstances under which she wrote, and her association with and influence on writers and others of the Harlem Renaissance period give her an important place in the literary, social, and cultural history of twentieth-century black America.

Anne Spencer was the name under which her poems were published and by which the public knew her after the early 1920s. She was born Annie Bethel Scales Bannister on 6 February 1882 on a farm in Henry County, Virginia. An only child, she spent the first few years of her childhood in Henry County with her parents, Sarah Louise and Joel Cephus Bannister. Sarah and Joel, who had barely escaped chattel slavery, struggled against the restraints of the time and the place to establish the life they desired for themselves and for their daughter. They also struggled against each other. Joel believed that the best way to achieve the life they desired was to acquire material assets by any means available. Sarah, who had grown up in the shadow of Virginia's plantation aristocracy (she was the daughter of a wealthy former slaveholder and his former slave mistress), also yearned for material prosperity, but the life she envisioned was one modeled as closely as possible on the tastes and attitudes of the white aristocracy. To her, form was primary.

Joel and Sarah were optimistic and resourceful. Each was strong-willed, independent, and unbending, characteristics which they passed on to their daughter. Joel demanded, in most instances, that Sarah adhere to the contemporary societal expectations for women and wives; she vehemently objected. Their divergent views and backgrounds and their opposing personalities occasioned frequent arguments. Anne often witnessed these arguments and they had a lasting impact on her. As a child and as an adult she was deeply concerned that while her parents loved each other, they never were friends. Friendship was important in her life and became a major theme of her writings.

The discord between her parents surfaced shortly after their marriage and intensified to the point that they separated about 1887. Sarah and her daughter moved to Bramwell, West Virginia, while Joel remained in Henry County. Anne was placed in the foster care of William Dixie and his wife in Bramwell while Sarah worked as a cook in the restaurant of a local inn. There were very few blacks in Bramwell and no black children in Anne's age group. Consequently, she was alone most of the time. With the exception of the Dixies' children, who were much younger than she, Anne's only childhood friend during the years she lived in Bramwell was a young white girl who lived in the town. Her relative isolation as a child helped produce and certainly nourished the contemplative side of her character. She was allowed to wander freely about the town and its immediate environs and early developed a love for nature, especially for plant life.

During the first eleven years of her life, Anne's contact with others was almost solely limited to adults, which in part accounts for her childhood and adolescent precociousness. By the time she was seven or eight years old she had acquired a functioning adult vocabulary. She also was pretending to read, initially motivated to imitate Mrs. Dixie, who read often. By the time she was ten years old she could read only the simplest materials, but her interest in learning to read had intensified. At eleven years old she was only marginally literate. Her increasing desire for education surpassed what Sarah (who was barely literate) or what Mrs. Dixie could teach her. Sarah wanted her daughter to be educated, yet she refused to enroll her in a nearby school for blacks whose students were children of coal miners; she did not want her daughter to associate with anyone from a lower social or economic class. Joel, who had kept in touch with Sarah and Anne, insisted that Anne receive a formal education and threatened to take his child to live with him unless Sarah enrolled her in school. In 1893 Sarah enrolled Anne in Virginia Seminary, a boarding school for blacks in Lynchburg, Virginia.

Anne excelled at the seminary. By the end of her first school term her academic standing was among the best for her class, and she had demonstrated exceptional aptitude for courses in the humanities. With a first-rate faculty and highly motivated and intelligent students, the seminary's environment brought quite a positive change to Anne's life, although she never lost the rather reserved and contemplative sides of her character which had been forming since early childhood.

When she entered the seminary she was the youngest student there. This sudden change in her social and intellectual environment created enormous frustrations for her. By then she was almost a teenager, and she needed and longed for peer friendships. Precocious, witty, even aggressive in academic situations with other students, she nevertheless was too shy to interact personally with the students. She began to turn inward to deal with problems typical of her age group, problems exacerbated in her case by the isolation of her childhood. She spent most of her free time alone, contemplating nature and studying. Yet she related well to her teachers and was one of their favorite students. By the beginning of her second year in school she had developed a cordial relationship with Gregory Hayes, the school's president. Hayes was instrumental in teaching her the close affinity between literature and life. Yet her comfortable interaction with adults could not substitute for those peer relationships which would have provided her an outlet for dealing with her more personal concerns.

When she was fourteen years old she turned to writing as a means of coping with the frustrations produced by her adolescence and by the newness of the intellectually stimulating environment. She wrote a poem, **"The Skeptic,"** which concerned the conflicts between her view of life and the views expressed by others. She knew very little about poetry at the time, but from this poem she developed her lifelong habit of writing to express the more private side of her character.

Using writing as an outlet for her emotions allowed her to interact more freely with other students and produced a surge in her academic progress. In 1899 she graduated from Virginia Seminary at the top of her class. She then returned to Bramwell and taught public school in the area for two years. On 15 May 1901 she married her seminary schoolmate Edward Alexander Spencer, and the couple moved to Lynchburg, Edward's home. Three children were born to them during the first decade of their marriage, two daughters and a son. After the birth of her son, Anne Spencer taught for a while at Virginia Seminary in order to supplement the school's teaching staff during a period when the school was having financial problems.

Edward Spencer was economically secure and understood the emotional needs of his wife. Shortly after their marriage, he hired housekeepers and in other ways released her from living the traditional role of housewife and mother. He knew that she loved nature and that she had an insatiable desire to read and to write. He built her a garden at the back of their house and constructed a one-room cottage at the edge of the garden. In the privacy of the cottage Spencer did most of her reading and writing.

During the first twenty years of her marriage she wrote numerous poems. Her habit during the day was to write down thoughts as they came to her—on paper bags, on scrap paper, in the margins of books, newspapers, and magazines, or on whatever writing surface was immediately available. In the contemplative quiet of the cottage during the evenings she transformed these thoughts into poems. By the time she was thirty-eight, the age at which she first published a poem, she had written hundreds of them. Even her family and friends were unaware of her imaginative writings before her first poem appeared in print.

From the early years of her marriage she was active in community affairs in Lynchburg. In 1918 she was a member of a committee which arranged for the national office of the National Association for the Advancement of Colored People to send a representative to Lynchburg to help establish a local chapter. James Weldon Johnson was the representative and was a houseguest of the Spencers during his stay. Johnson accidentally saw some of her poems and insisted that she allow him to show some of them to his literary friends. Shortly thereafter he began to urge her to publish her poems and offered to help arrange for their publication. She reluctantly agreed, and in 1920 her poem **"Before the Feast of Shushan"** appeared in the February issue of the *Crisis*.

In 1922 Johnson included five of her poems in his anthology *The Book of American Negro Poetry*. Four of the poems, including **"Shushan,"** thematically focus on the position of women in the larger society and on male-female love bonds. The poems echo the principles and practices of Spencer's life. Without being polemical, the poems assert that women often are the victims of an unsympathetic male-dominated society (**"At the Carnival"**), that women should not be subordinated to men (**"Before the Feast of**

Shushan"), that a woman should, if she chooses, reject societal proscriptions and be free to determine the nature of her role in a male-female love bond (**"The Wife-Woman"**), and that friendship is just as important as love in a relationship between two people (**"Translation"**). In the fifth poem, a quatrain titled **"Dunbar,"** the poet-speaker laments the untimely death of Dunbar, Chatterton, Shelley, and Keats but finds comfort in the knowledge that while poets are mortal their poems are immortal:

Ah, how poets sing and die!
Make one song and Heaven takes it;
Have one heart and Beauty breaks it;
Chatterton, Shelley, Keats and I—
Ah, how poets sing and die!

Johnson's anthology was well received and reviewers and critics cited Spencer as a fresh and invigorating new voice among black poets. Anthologists and editors began to request her permission to include her poems in their publications. Robert Kerlin (*Negro Poets and Their Poems*) and Louis Untermeyer (*American Poetry Since 1900*) included her in anthologies they published in 1923. Within a few years her poems had appeared in *Crisis, Opportunity, Survey Graphic, Palms,* and other publications. Among those who expressed interest in her writings and in helping her to get published were Alain Locke and H. L. Mencken, both of whom were influential in advancing the publishing careers of poets during the period and thus to some extent in shaping the literary tastes of the time. Locke and Mencken were willing to assist Spencer in becoming more widely published, but only if she were willing to follow their suggestions about the kind of poetry she should write for publication. She was unwilling to conform to their suggestions and thus forfeited their assistance.

One of the poems about which she and editors disagreed was **"White Things,"** a poem which she had written in the late teens. Editors considered the poem too unorthodox in its overt treatment of racial conflict. She refused to revise the poem to conform more to the racial romanticism and subtle treatment of racial themes popular during the period. However, the *Crisis* published **"White Things"** in March 1923. It was one of the very few "protest" poems she ever wrote and one of her finest poems. In fact, **"White Things"** belongs with the best poems of racial protest published in twentieth-century America. Although her poetry was widely anthologized and reprinted during the 1920s and after, **"White Things"** was never reprinted during her life.

"WHITE THINGS"

Most things are colorful things—the sky, earth, and
sea.
Black men are most men; but the white are
free!
White things are rare things; so rare, so rare
They stole from out a silvered world—somewhere.
Finding earth-plains fair plains, save greenly grassed,
They strewed white feathers of cowardice, as they
passed;
The golden stars with lances fine
The hills all red and darkened pine,
They blanched with their wand of power;
And turned the blood in a ruby rose
To a poor white poppy-flower.

They pyred a race of black, black men,
And burned them to ashes white; then,
Laughing, a young one claimed a skull,
For the skull of a black is white, not dull,
But a glistening awful thing;
Made, it seems, for this ghoul to
swing
In the face of God with all his might,
And swear by the hell that sired him:
"Man-maker, make white!"

By 1923 Lynchburg citizens were well aware that a newly published and highly praised poet lived among them. Spencer's outspoken criticism of racial stratification, her stand on other political and social issues, and her blatant defiance of any attempts to restrict her personal freedom had helped estrange her from many of the townspeople during the previous twenty years. The national attention she received as a published poet in the early 1920s somewhat mitigated hostility toward her and allowed her to interact more harmoniously with whites and blacks in the town. Still, on several occasions she was the victim of verbal abuse from whites she encountered in public sectors of the town. Yet Spencer never tempered her stance against racism. After she became known as a published poet, her detractors often dismissed her challenges of the status quo as merely the eccentric behavior of a poet.

Before the 1920s blacks in Lychburg did not have access to a library, a situation Spencer sought to correct. In December 1923 she applied for a job as librarian with the private, all-white Jones Memorial Library in Lynchburg. Lacking formal training or experience as a librarian, she used her publications and her wide knowledge of books as credentials to recommend her for the job. In January 1924, the board of trustees of Jones hired her to head a branch library to be housed in the all-black Dunbar High School. During the twenty years she remained at Dunbar she had a considerable influence on the intellectual and cultural life of the black community in Lynchburg. She encouraged students and others to read more widely and more critically; she motivated many of Dunbar's students to continue their education after high school and in general to improve their lot in life.

While working at Dunbar she continued to write and occsionally agreed to submit her poems for publication. In 1927 Countee Cullen's anthology *Caroling Dusk* included the largest collection of Spencer's poems to appear in print during her life. Seven of her ten poems in *Caroling Dusk* had been previously unpublished. The major themes of her pieces in this collection were friendship, human relations, and the personal rights of women. Images of her garden or of nature were predominant. Two of the poems concerned poets and poetry: **"Life-Long, Poor Browning"** was inspired by the personal and poetic affinity she felt for her favorite poet, Robert Browning; **"Substitution"** spoke of the function of poetry and of the creative imagination in her own life.

The 1920s was the most active and perhaps the most invigorating decade of her life. She loved her job at Dunbar, tended her garden meticulously, read and wrote constantly, entertained lavishly, traveled frequently, corresponded with leading artists and thinkers, and worked actively to break down racial barriers in Lynchburg. Some of those who resented her personal and open defiance of racial discrimination occasionally circulated rumors (from the 1930s into the 1950s) that her association with persons politically controversial, including artists and entertainers, was proof sufficient that her political sympathies were with Communists or Communist supporters. Ostensibly the rumors were a means of discrediting her, but they neither tempered her activities with civil rights organizations nor caused her to sever ties with persons alleged to have Communist links.

After the 1920s Spencer's acquaintance with nationally known persons was substantial. W. E. B. Du Bois, Paul Robeson, Langston Hughes, and numerous other artists, political activists, entertainers, and other professionals were often guests at the Spencers' home. In turn, she and Edward traveled widely, and their trips to Washington, D.C., and to New York, among other cities where aspiring and established black artists, intellectuals, and socialites gathered, were routine. She had established friendships with Du Bois and Sterling Brown through their association with Virginia Seminary and College. Through Du Bois, Brown, Johnson, Hughes, and Georgia Douglas Johnson she met a variety of people, blacks and whites, in the 1920s and after and thus rapidly expanded her contacts outside her hometown.

Lynchburg was strategically located between the major cities of the Northeast and metropolitan and educational centers of the South. In the early 1920s the Spencers' home assumed an integral place in a network blacks had established years before to compensate for their exclusion from public accommodations when traveling. Middle- and upper-class blacks of various professions who traveled across the Mason-Dixon line used the homes of other well-to-do blacks as convenient places to stop over. A mutual acquaintance usually was all that was necessary to assure that food and lodging would be available to those whose social, economic, or professional status allowed them entrance into this network. The Spencers loved to entertain and their home quickly became popular on the circuit, especially among writers, entertainers, and civil rights advocates. By the mid 1920s Hughes, James Weldon Johnson, Du Bois, and others visited Spencer in order to benefit from an intellectual exchange with her on literary, political, and social issues. Often a writer visited to seek her advice about a particular writing project on which she or he was working. At other times groups of writers gathered at her home to discuss the state of the arts. A consequence of this exchange was that she had a significant impact on the works of several imaginative writers and social critics identified with the Harlem Renaissance.

Anne Spencer attributed the expansion of her intellectual and creative worlds primarily to her association with James Weldon Johnson and thus considered her friendship with him as one of the most important events in her life. Thematically several of her poems about friendship derive from the special nature of her friendship with Johnson. He helped her gain entry into the Harlem Renaissance movement and brought her into contact with minds akin to her own. After his death in an automobile accident in 1938 she allowed only one additional poem of hers to be published during her life, **"For Jim, Easter Eve,"** a poem in tribute to Johnson. Using her garden as the central metaphor, she expressed in the poem the impact Johnson and her garden had had on her life. Within a few years after his death she had withdrawn almost completely from public life.

Spencer's garden was central to her poetry and to her life. In most of her poems images of her garden or of natural scenery suggest an Edenic setting where man is in harmony with his environment. These poems usually begin with a speaker troubled with doubts and uncertainties or with one who feels dejected. Coming into contact with and contemplating the spiritual forces manifested in nature, the speaker soon rejects the doubts and uncertainties and the tone of the poem changes from one of dejection to one of hope and affirmation. In general, this is the case in **"Life-Long, Poor Browning"** or in **"For Jim, Easter Eve,"** poems in which the garden setting provides solace for the speaker. From her garden Spencer extracted metaphors for human life. She saw in the activities of a bee, a spider, a bird, or another insect or animal metaphors for the fragility and strength of man, metaphors which she incorporated into her poems. When discouraged by the conflicts of her interaction with others, she turned to her garden as a spiritual refuge. The integral place her garden held in her life and in her poetry is expressed in lines from **"For Jim, Easter Eve"**:

Peace is here and in every season
a quiet beauty.
The sky falling about me
evenly to the compass . . .
What is sorrow but tenderness now
in this earth-close frame of land and sky
falling constantly into horizons
of east and west, north and south;
what is pain but happiness here
amid these green and wordless patterns,—
indefinite texture of blade and leaf.

After her husband died in 1964, the upkeep of her once immaculate garden sharply declined and she became a virtual recluse. She spent her time reading, especially history, and concentrated on writing prose instead of poetry. When she first began to publish her poems in the 1920s, her literary friends urged her to write prose fiction. At one time she did begin a novel, but apparently she never completed it. In the 1930s and 1940s she wrote a series of essays critically examining various American social and political institutions; these essays were intended for publication but never submitted. Her rejuvenated interest in writing prose in the mid 1960s was stimulated by her obsession with reading American history. By about 1969 she had drafted several essays but began to concentrate again on writing poetry. People and events in American history remained her primary subjects during this period and she planned and began to work on a series of poems about persons whom she considered generals, persons such as Hannibal, Douglas MacArthur, John Brown, and LeRoi Jones.

Many years before she had thought about using the abolitionist John Brown as the subject for one of her writings. From 1969 to 1971 she spent an enormous amount of time reading background materials for a long, complex poem which would use Brown as the central figure in the history of man from his beginning to the mid nineteenth century. She wrote intently to complete **"A Dream of John Brown,"** but her health, in general, began to fail and the enormous amount of time she spent reading and writing severely impaired her eyesight. She intended **"A Dream of John Brown"** to be her greatest poetic achievement and continued to work sporadically on the poem until 1974, when a serious illness forced her to halt her work after having completed several manuscript pages.

From 1971 to 1974 she also revised some of her earlier poems and wrote new ones in preparation for an anticipated collection of her poetry. At ninety years of age she was writing with the explicit intent to have her works published. Prior to this she had taken the initiative only once during her life to have any of her poems published; she always had written for her own enjoyment but had allowed Johnson and others to arrange for the publication of some of her poems. She wrote constantly during the early 1970s, following her lifelong habit of composing her poems in bits and pieces and on scraps of paper scattered here and there in her house. When in 1975 her health deteriorated to the point that she was hospitalized, friends and neighbors visiting her home evidently assumed the countless pieces of paper on which she had written lines of poetry were useless, and they innocently discarded them. Thus, most of the work she had completed during the preceding four or five years was lost. Among the manuscripts not discarded was a short poem written in June 1974 and titled **"1975,"** obviously intended as a final comment on her life and writings:

Turn an earth clod
Peel a shaley rock
In fondness molest a curly worm
Whose *familiar* is everywhere
Kneel
And the curly worm sentient *now*
Will *light* the word that tells the poet what a
poem
is

Spencer died on 27 July 1975 in Lynchburg, Virginia.

FURTHER READING

Bibliography

Johnston, Sarah Andrews. "Anne Spencer." In *American Woman Writers, 1900-1945: A Bio-Bibliographical Critical Sourcebook,* edited by Laurie Champion, pp. 312-17. Westport, Conn.: Greenwood Press, 2000.

Provides a brief biography in addition to a bibliography of sources on Spencer.

Biography

Anne Spencer Memorial Foundation. *Echoes from the Garden: The Anne Spencer Story* [documentary film]. Lynchburg, Va.: Anne Spencer Memorial Foundation/Byron Studios, 1980.

Reviews Spencer's biography, with a focus on her life in Virginia.

Criticism

Ford, Charita. "Flowering a Feminist Garden: The Writings and Poetry of Anne Spencer." *SAGE: A Scholarly Journal on Black Women* 5, no. 1 (1988): 7-14.

Considers Spencer an early feminist among the poets of the Harlem Renaissance.

Greene, J. Lee. *Time's Unfolding Garden: Anne Spencer's Life and Poetry*. Baton Rouge: Louisiana State University Press, 1977, 204 p.

Emphasizes Spencer's life in literature, analyzes several poems, and discusses her literary relationships.

Hull, Gloria T. "Black Women Poets from Wheatley to Walker." In *Sturdy Black Bridges: Visions of Black Women in Literature,* edited by Roseann P. Bell, Bettye J. Parker, and Beverly Guy-Sheftall, pp. 69-86. New York: Anchor Books, 1979.

Surveys the development of Black women's poetry, placing Spencer among the most talented and unique of those who published during the Harlem Renaissance.

Stetson, Erlene. "Anne Spencer." *College Language Association Journal* 21 (1978): 400-09.

General overview of Spencer's life and career.

OTHER SOURCES FROM GALE:

Additional coverage of Spencer's life and career is contained in the following sources published by the Gale Group: *Black Writers,* Ed. 2; *Contemporary Authors,* Vol. 161; and *Dictionary of Literary Biography,* Vols. 51, 54.

WALLACE THURMAN

(1902 - 1934)

(Full name Wallace Henry Thurman. Also wrote under the pseudonyms Patrick Casey and Ethel Belle Mandrake) American novelist, playwright, screenwriter, editor, and critic.

While he is now considered a lesser figure of the Harlem Renaissance, during the height of the movement Thurman was regarded as an important fiction writer, social commentator, and critic of Black literature. His most significant contribution was the novel *The Blacker the Berry: A Novel of Negro Life* (1929), the first novel to openly explore prejudice within the Black community. In this and other novels, Thurman also satirized the themes and the characters of the Harlem Renaissance, and in his essays he criticized the movement for what he viewed as its pandering to a white audience and for measuring the achievements of Black writers according to lower standards than their white counterparts. Thurman also criticized some figures associated with the Harlem Renaissance for, in his perception, their "decadent" lifestyle, which he claimed prevented them from making any significant contribution to American literature. Langston Hughes called Thurman "a strangely brilliant black boy, who had read everything, and whose critical mind could find something wrong with everything he read," and modern scholars have also emphasized his precocity, criticism of other writers, and satirical skills. Despite his condemnation of the movement, Thurman, in his capacity as the editor of various periodicals, did a great deal to promote works by aspiring Black writers.

BIOGRAPHICAL INFORMATION

Thurman was born in Salt Lake City in 1902. He attended the University of Utah for a year before transferring to the University of Southern California in 1922. In Los Angeles, Thurman wrote a newspaper column, "Inklings," and founded a periodical, *Outlet,* to try to promote Black writing. The magazine lasted only six months, and soon after, in 1925, Thurman moved to Harlem. The following year, he became the editor of the *Messenger* and then collaborated as editor of the literary magazine *Fire!!* with other Harlem Renaissance authors, including Zora Neale Hurston and Langston Hughes. *Fire!!* put out only a single issue, and afterward Thurman worked as a journalist, publishers' reader and editor, and a ghostwriter to earn a living. In 1928, Thurman began publishing another literary magazine, *Harlem: A Forum of Negro Life,* but it, too, folded after only one issue. In 1929, *Harlem: A Melodrama of Negro Life in Harlem,* written with William Jourdan Rapp, debuted on Broadway. The same year Thurman's novel *The Blacker the Berry* also appeared. Unable to support himself solely through his literary efforts, Thurman joined the editorial staff of McFadden Publications and worked as a reader at Macaulay Publishing, where he became editor-in-chief in 1930. While living in New York, he wrote two more novels, began a number of plays, and continued to work as a ghostwriter. He also became known for his hard-living lifestyle, frequently attending clubs and parties and drinking heavily. In 1934, Thurman moved to Hollywood, where he wrote two screenplays that garnered little attention. After two months, he returned to New York. Years of heavy drinking and neglect of his health began to take their toll, and after a drinking binge he was hospitalized and diagnosed with tuberculosis. He died six months later, on December 22, 1934.

MAJOR WORKS

While Thurman's reputation today rests on his novels, during his lifetime he was better known as an editor and critic. Although a number of the periodicals with which he was associated were short-lived, his skill as an editor was renowned. During his time as managing editor for the *Messenger,* for example, he published works by Langston Hughes and Zora Neale Hurston. Thurman was always critical of efforts by even the best writers of the Harlem Renaissance, and he claimed he published their work not because they were good but because they were the best available. Thurman's first significant literary effort was *Harlem,* a play about a Black family that moves from the South to New York City, where they are faced with unemployment and other difficulties of urban existence. The work also depicts the seamier aspects of city life, including sexual promiscuity, wild parties, and gambling. In *The Blacker the Berry,* Thurman takes a hard look at intraracial prejudice. The novel chronicles the life of a young woman, Emma Lou, whose dark complexion is a source of sorrow and humiliation not only to herself but to her lighter-skinned family and friends. She travels from Boise, Idaho, to New York's Harlem, hoping to find a safe haven in the "Black Mecca" of the 1920s. In 1932, Thurman published the novel *Infants of the Spring,* which portrays a serious young Black author who is trying to write a novel while living in a boardinghouse with others who have only pretenses to genuine literary achievement. The novel satirizes the themes and major figures of the Harlem Renaissance, and the characters are based on writers such as Hughes, Hurston, Countee Cullen, and Alain Locke. Thurman's third novel, *The Interne* (1932), co-authored with A. L. Furman, relates the experiences of the title character of the book—a white doctor in an urban hospital.

CRITICAL RECEPTION

During his life, Thurman was as well known for his drinking and his attendance at parties as he was for his literary activities. Because of his fame as an editor, he was asked by Hughes and other writers to edit *Fire!!,* but the magazine did not survive long enough to publish a second issue. Thurman also enjoyed a successful, if short, career in publishing. The critical reception of his first full-length work, the play *Harlem,* was mixed. Some found the play entertaining and realistic, but others, including many Black writers, found it exploitive and objected to the negative stereotypes of African Americans and the unflattering portrayal of their "seedy" inner-city lives. *The Blacker the Berry* also received mixed reviews, with some critics admiring Thurman's handling of the theme of Black racism and others faulting what they considered the frigidly objective tone of the narrative and its apparently slapdash structure. *Infants of the Spring,* while viewed by some as an overly ambitious and ultimately unsuccessful attempt to deal with its complex subject matter, was nonetheless praised for Thurman's depiction of Black literary society. The novel *The Interne* was dismissed by most critics as being unrealistic and uninteresting. Today, Thurman does not enjoy wide readership, and scholarly interest in his work focuses for the most part on *The Blacker the Berry* and *Infants of the Spring.* Both works, critics generally contend, retain at the very least a historical interest for the insights they provide into the Harlem Renaissance and also for the occasional touches of brilliance in Thurman's satire of Black life of the period. Some scholars have also discussed Thurman's supposed homosexuality and the homoerotic elements in his fiction.

PRINCIPAL WORKS

The Blacker the Berry: A Novel of Negro Life (novel) 1929

Harlem: A Melodrama of Negro Life in Harlem [with William Jourdan Rapp] (drama) 1929

Infants of the Spring (novel) 1932

The Interne [with A. L. Furman] (novel) 1932

Tomorrow's Children (screenplay) 1934

High School Girl (screenplay) 1935

PRIMARY SOURCES

WALLACE THURMAN (ESSAY DATE 1928)

SOURCE: Thurman, Wallace. "Night Life in Harlem." In his *Negro Life in New York's Harlem,* pp. 24-34. Girard, Kan.: Haldeman-Julius Publications, 1928.

In this excerpt, Thurman offers his perspective on Harlem nightlife, affirming that an after-hours visit to Harlem was a rite of passage for anyone wishing to label himself or herself a "New Yorker."

Much has been written and said about night life in Harlem. It has become the *leit motif* of sophisticated conversation and shop girl intimacies. To call yourself a New Yorker you must have been to Harlem at least once. Every up-to-date person knows Harlem, and knowing Harlem generally means that one has visited a night club or two. These night clubs are now enjoying much publicity along with the New Negro and Negro art. They are the shrines to which white sophisticates, Greenwich Village artists, Broadway revellers and provincial commuters make eager pilgrimage. In fact, the white patronage is so profitable and abundant that Negroes find themselves crowded out and even segregated in their own places of jazz.

There are, at the present time, about one dozen of these night clubs in Harlem—Bamville, Connie's Inn, Baron Wilkins, The Nest, Small's Paradise, The Capitol, The Cotton Club, The Green Cat, The Sugar Cane Club, Happy Rhones, The Hoofers Club and the Little Savoy. Most of these generally have from two to ten white persons for every black one. Only The Hoofers, The Little Savoy, and The Sugar Cane Club seem to cater almost exclusively to Negro trade.

At the Bamville and at Small's Paradise, one finds smart white patrons, the type that reads the ultrasophisticated *New Yorker.* Indeed, that journal says in its catalogue of places to go—"Small's and Bamville are the show places of Harlem for downtowners on their first excursion. Go late. Better not to dress." And so the younger generation of Broadway, Park Avenue, Riverside Drive, Third Avenue and the Bronx go late, take their own gin, applaud the raucous vulgarity of the entertainers, dance with abandon and go home with a headache. They have seen Harlem.

The Cotton Club and Connie's Inn make a bid for theatrical performers and well-to-do folk around town. The Nest and Happy Rhones attract traveling salesmen, store clerks and commuters from Jersey and Yonkers. The Green Cat has a large Latin clientele. Baron Wilkins draws glittering ladies from Broadway to their sleek gentlemen friends. Because of these conditions of invasion, Harlem's famed night clubs have become merely side shows staged for sensation-seeking whites. Nevertheless, they are still an egregious something to experience. Their smoking cavernous depths are eerie and ecstatic. Patrons enter, shiver involuntarily, then settle down to be shoved about and scared by the intangible rhythms that surge all around them. White night clubs are noisy. White night clubs effect weird music, soft light, Negro entertainers and dancing waiters, but, even with all these contributing elements, they cannot approximate the infectious rhythm and joy always found in a Negro cabaret.

Take the Sugar Cane Club on Fifth Avenue near 135th Street, located on the border of the most "low-down" section of Harlem. This place is visited by few whites or few "dicty" Negroes. Its customers are the rough-and-ready, happy-go-lucky more primitive type—street walkers, petty gamblers and pimps, with an occasional adventurer from other strata of society.

The Sugar Cane Club is a narrow subterranean passageway about twenty-five feet wide and 125 feet long. Rough wooden tables, surrounded by rough wooden chairs, and the orchestra stands, jammed into the right wall center, use up about three-quarters of the space. The remaining rectangular area is bared for dancing. With a capacity for seating about one hundred people, it usually finds room on gala nights for twice that many. The orchestra weeps and moans and groans as only an unsophisticated Negro Jazz orchestra can. A blues singer croons vulgar ditties over the tables to individual parties or else wah-wahs husky syncopated blues songs from the center of the floor. Her act over, the white lights are extinguished, red and blue spot lights are centered on the diminutive dancing space, couples push back their chairs, squeeze out from behind the tables and from against the wall, then finding one another's bodies, sweat gloriously together, with shoulders hunched, limbs obscenely intertwined and hips wiggling; animal beings urged on by liquor and music and physical contact.

Small's Paradise, on Seventh Avenue near 135th Street, is just the opposite of the Sugar Cane Club. It caters almost exclusively to white trade with just enough Negroes present to give the necessary atmosphere and "difference." Yet even in Small's with its symphonic orchestra, full-dress appearance and dignified onlookers, there is a great deal of that unexplainable, intangible rhythmic presence so characteristic of a Negro cabaret.

In addition to the well-known cabarets, which are largely show places to curious whites, there are innumerable places—really speak-easies—which are open only to the initiate. The places are far more colorful and more full of spontaneous joy than the larger places to which one has ready access. They also furnish more thrills to the spectator. This is possible because the crowd is more select, the liquor more fiery, the atmosphere more intimate and the activities of the patrons not subject to be watched by open-mouthed white people from downtown and the Bronx.

One particular place known as the Glory Hole is hidden in a musty damp basement behind an express and trucking office. It is a single room about ten feet square and remains an unembellished basement except for a planed down plank floor, a piano, three chairs and library table. The Glory Hole is typical of its class. It is a social club, commonly called dive, convenient for the high times of a certain group. The men are unskilled laborers during the day, and in the evenings they round up their girls or else meet them at the rendezvous in order to have what they consider and enjoy as a good time. The women, like the men, swear, drink and dance as much and as vulgarly as they please. Yet they do not strike the observer as being vulgar. They are merely being and doing what their environment and their desire for pleasure suggest.

Such places as the Glory Hole can be found all over the so-called "bad lands" of Harlem. They are not always confined to basement rooms. They can be found in apartment flats, in the rear of barber shops, lunch counters, pool halls, and other such conveniently blind places. Each one has its regular quota of customers with just enough new patrons introduced from time to time to keep the place alive and prosperous. These intimate, lowdown civic centers are occasionally misjudged. Social service reports damn them with the phrase "breeding places of vice and crime." They may be. They are also good training grounds for prospective pugilists. Fights are staged with regularity and with vigor. And most of the regular customers have some mark on their faces or bodies that can be displayed as having received during a battle in one of the glory holes.

The other extreme of amusement places in Harlem is exemplified by the Bamboo Inn, a Chinese-American restaurant that features Oriental cuisine, a jazz band and dancing. It is the place for select Negro Harlem's night life, the place where debutantes have the coming out parties, where college lads take their co-eds and society sweethearts and dignified matrons entertain. It is a beautifully decorated establishment, glorified by a balcony with booths, and a large gyroflector, suspended from the center of the ceiling, on which colored spotlights play, flecting the room with triangular bits of varicolored light. The Bamboo Inn is *the* place to see "high Harlem," just like the Glory Hole is *the* place to see "low Harlem." Well-dressed men escorting expensively garbed women and girls; models from Vanity Fair with brown, yellow and black skins. Doctors and lawyers, Babbitts and their ladies with fine manners (not necessarily learned through Emily Post), fine clothes and fine homes to return to when the night's fun has ended.

The music plays. The gyroflector revolves. The wellbred, polite dancers mingle on the dance floor. There are a few silver hip flasks. There is an occasional burst of too spontaneous-for-the-environment laughter. The Chinese waiters slip around, quiet and bored. A big black-face bouncer, arrayed in tuxedo, watches eagerly for some too boisterous, too unconventional person to put out. The Bamboo Inn has only one blemishing feature. It is also the rendezvous for a set of oriental men who favor white women, and who, with their pale face partners, mingle with Harlem's four hundred.

When Harlem people wish to dance, without attending a cabaret, they go to the Renaissance Casino or to the Savoy, Harlem's two most famous public dance halls. The Savoy is the pioneer in the field of giving dance-loving Harlemites some place to gather nightly. It is an elaborate ensemble with a Chinese garden (Negroes seem to have a penchant for Chinese food—there are innumerable Chinese restaurants all over Harlem), two orchestras that work in relays, and hostesses provided at twenty-five cents per dance for partnerless young men. The Savoy opens at three in the afternoon and closes at three in the morning. One can spend twelve hours in this jazz palace for sixty-five cents, and the price of a dinner or an occasional sustaining sandwich and drink. The music is good, the dancers are gay, and setting is conducive to joy.

LANGSTON HUGHES (AUTOBIOGRAPHY DATE 1940)

SOURCE: Hughes, Langston. "Harlem Literati." In *The Big Sea*, pp. 233-41. New York: Hill and Wang, 1940.

In this excerpt from his autobiography, Hughes offers a brief character sketch of Thurman, providing an appraisal of his writing skills and an overview of some of the author's works.

Thurman had recently come from California to New York. He was a strangely brilliant black boy, who had read everything, and whose critical mind could find something wrong with everything he read. I have no critical mind, so I usually either like a book or don't. But I am not capable of liking a book and then finding a million things wrong with it, too—as Thurman was capable of doing.

Thurman had read so many books because he could read eleven lines at a time: He would get from the library a great pile of volumes that would have taken me a year to read. But he would go through them in less than a week, and be able to discuss each one at great length with any body. . . .

Wallace Thurman wanted to be a great writer, but none of his own work ever made him happy. ***The Blacker the Berry,*** his first book, was an important novel, on a subject little dwelt upon in Negro fiction—the plight of the very dark Negro woman, who encounters in some communities a double wall of color prejudice within and without the race. His play, ***Harlem,*** considerably distorted for box office purposes, was, nevertheless, a compelling study—and the only one in the theater—of the impact of Harlem on a Negro family fresh from the South. And his ***Infants of the Spring,*** a superb and bitter study of the bohemian fringe of Harlem's literary and *artistic* life, is a compelling book.

But none of these things pleased Wallace Thurman. He wanted to be a *very* great writer, like Gorki or Thomas Mann, and he felt that he was merely a journalistic writer. His critical mind, comparing his pages to the thousands of other pages he had read, by Proust, Melville, Tolstoy, Galsworthy, Dostoyevski, Henry James, Sainte-Beauve, Taine, Anatole France, found his own pages vastly wanting. So he contented himself by writing a great deal for money, laughing bitterly at his fabulously concocted "true stories," creating two bad motion pictures of the "Adults Only" type for Hollywood; drinking more and more gin, and then threatening to jump out of windows at people's parties and kill himself.

GENERAL COMMENTARY

GERALD HASLAM (ESSAY DATE 1971)

SOURCE: Haslam, Gerald. "Wallace Thurman: A Western Renaissance Man." *Western American Literature* 6 (spring 1971): 53-9.

In the following essay, Haslam offers an overview of Thurman's life, career, and literary reputation with particular attention paid to the writer's Western roots.

Western writers—from Cooper to Waters—have long bemoaned the loss of rural, natural values and warned of the dangers of city life. And city life has pretty well managed to live up to most of the dire predictions.

Still, for Afro-Americans—"the immigrants within," as Bernard Weisenberger has termed them[1]—the city offered special hopes, and their migration from the rural South to the urban North was to produce many remarkable literary figures, most notably Langston Hughes and Richard Wright.

The "flight to the city," as the more dramatic historians have called it, has conceived diverse literary progeny, from the naturalism of Stephen Crane and Theodore Drieser, through the wild exotocism of the so-called Harlem Renaissance of the 1920's, counter-urban to the free form "hippy" writers of our own day such as Richard Brautigan and Gary Snyder.

One young man, Wallace Thurman, traveled from the Inter-mountain West, to the urban West, finally to the evil East itself, and became a luminary in the Harlem Renaissance, yet he remains an enigma. Described by Hughes as "a strangely brillant black boy, who had read everything, and whose critical mind could find something wrong with everything he read,"[2] Thurman was a Westerner not only by birth and education, but also in terms of his candor, his egalitarianism, and his ultimate rejection of the hollow aspects of urbanization. Yet he was no great admirer of the West's treatment of Negroes either.

Born and educated in Salt Lake City, the black-skinned Thurman was conspicious indeed. His own experience parallels that of one of his characters who "not only was . . . the only dark-skinned person on the platform, . . . (but) also the only Negro pupil in . . . school."[3] He enrolled in the University of Southern California following high school, but was generally disappointed with his treatment in Los Angeles, especially his treatment by social-climbing Negroes.

Like other young black intellectuals, Thurman made the pilgrimage to Harlem during the 1920's; almost immediately he thrust himself into the midst of what Alain Locke called the New Negro Movement.[4] A man of many talents, who tried "to be some modern representative of the true Renaissance Man,"[5] he soon embarked upon a journalistic career by serving as an editor of *The Messenger,* an influental Negro magazine. He worked alongside A. Phillip Randolph, and became a close associate and friend of George Schuyler, considered by some the H. L. Mencken of Negro journalism and a pioneering satirical novelist.

In 1926 he joined Hughes, Gwendolyn Bennet, Zora Neal Hurston, John P. Davis, Aaron Douglas, and Bruce Nugent in founding the short-lived, brillant journal, *Fire,* which was intended "to burn up a lot of the old, dead, conventional Negro-white ideas of the past."[6] Thurman's articles in *The New Republic, The World Tomorrow, The Independent,* and *The Bookman,* among other periodicals, soon made him a principal spokesman for that remarkable period of intellectual change and growing pride that laid the groundwork for much of the outstanding Afro-American art that followed.

Hughes and Thurman seem to have enjoyed a particularly candid relationship. Thurman once told the young poet, for example, that *The Messenger* reflected the policy of whoever paid best; buying what were to be Hughes's first published short stories for that journal, he told him that they were bad, but not as bad as others submitted. In *The Big Sea* Hughes discussed another aspect of Thurman's career:

> . . . Thurman became a ghost writer for *True Story* and other publications, writing under all sorts of fantastic names, like Ethel Belle Mandrake or Patrick Casey. He did Irish and Jewish and Catholic "true confessions." . . . Later he ghosted books. In fact, this quite dark young Negro is said to have written *Men, Women, and Checks.*[7]

Thurman made no secret of his ghost writing, and apparently thought the episode hilarious, if economically necessary. He had absorbed more than a little of Mencken's scorn for the American public's foolish gullibility.

In 1929, Thurman collaborated with white playwright William Jordan Rapp and produced ***Harlem,*** a play blending melodrama with ghetto exoticism; it ran for 93 performances, becoming "the first *successful* play written entirely or in part by a Negro to appear on Broadway."[8]

During that same year, Thurman produced his most memorable novel, ***The Blacker the Berry,*** a book that evidences more than a hint of the author's Western background, as well as his understanding of black society. The novel tells the story of Emma Lou, a Negro girl born and raised in Boise, Idaho, of a mulatto mother and black father. Emma Lou, much to her family's regret, favors her father for she is clearly Negroid in her features, and it quickly becomes "an acquired family characteristic, . . . moaning and grieving over the color of her skin."[9] Her grandmother is a social leader among the mulatto "blue-veins" of Boise, and the dark young granddaughter is clearly an embarrassment. The motto of the "blue-veins" is "Whiter and whiter every generation,"[10] so the "tragedy of her life was that she was too black."[11] Indeed, the author early states that "Emma Lou had always been the alien member of the family."[12]

To intensify Emma Lou's problems, her mother remarries, choosing an embittered, red-haired, blue-eyed mulatto son of an important Irishman. Emma Lou's step-father's "only satisfaction in life was the pleasure he derived from insulting and ignoring the real blacks."[13] Assured by an Uncle that the people in Boise—people both black and white—are fifty years behind the times, Emma Lou enrolls in the University of Southern California, looking forward to the more sophisticated atmosphere of Los Angles. Social ostracism characterizes her experiences in California, again caused by the darkness of her skin.

Like Thurman himself, Emma Lou finally travels to Harlem, only to find conditions little different there. She suffers job discrimination, is exploited by a light-skinned lover, and thoroughly disillusioned. As Robert Bone points out, "Emma Lou's real tragedy is that she accepts the values of the system which torments her."[14] Thurman is, of course, preaching self-acceptance, the credo of the New Negroes. It was Hughes who said it without metaphors: "We younger Negro artists who create now intend to express our individual dark-skinned selves without fear or shame."[15] But Thurman accomplished a bit more than a mere affirmation of New Negro principles in this novel.

For one thing, he broke with an unwritten but strong proscription against revealing intraracial discrimination; he showed both blacks and whites practicing racism against Negroes. As Therman B. O'Daniel aptly phrases it, "this book gives us a double dose of the color bias."[16] Having been raised in a Western town with few Negroes, Thurman sensed the castes within Afro-American society in high relief, and he did not forget them; throughout ***The Blacker the Berry,*** Emma Lou contrasts and compares her treatment in Los Angeles and New York with that which she received in Boise.

Preferring the razor-edge of satire to the hacking blade of overt protest, Thurman shows Emma Lou's own prejudice when he introduces a Negro girl from Texas, Hazel Mason, who says such things as "Is you . . . ," and dresses in bright colors, and talks too loud. Emma Lou fully expected the girl to be named "Hyacinth or Geranium." "No wonder," Emma Lou thought disdainfully, "the people in Boise spoke as they did about Southern Negroes . . ."[17] And, of course, Emma Lou is doubly embarrassed because Hazel commits such gaucheries in front of white folks.

While city life—particularly Harlem life—offers certain advantages over the relative isolation of Idaho, it is a long way from perfect. Despite a liberal draught of cabaret life, of frenzied gaiety, of Harlem local color generally, there is an underlying sense of the city's shallowness.

Emma Lou's affair with and exploitation by a Fillipino-mulatto symbolizes the harsh reality of Harlem life so few whites saw or imagined when they were slumming. The city—not even America's principal Negro city—of itself, offers no easily obtainable comfort for the black girl. If the caste distinctions she had sensed in the restricted society of Boise are rendered more subtly midst the masses of Harlem, they are nonetheless everpresent and oppressive. But Boise offers nothing better; she is not fool enough to think a return to the West will offer anything but a change of problems; for a black girl, the West is not the land of dreams. With her life swirling into an unbearable knot, Emma Lou is tempted to wire Boise for money and to return but "she immediately saw that going home would mean beginning her life all over again, mean flying from one degree of unhappiness to another."[18] Mere geographical flight, she decides, offers no hope; she must come to terms with herself. A verse from the novel:

> A yaller gal rides in a limousine
> A brown-skin does the same;
> A black gal rides in a rickety Ford,
> But she gets there, yes my Lord.[19]

Emma Lou determines to get there.

Thurman produced two more novels before his untimely death in 1934. ***Infants of Spring*** (1932), deeply satiric, reflected the author's pessimism about the future of Negro literature; again to quote Hughes, "He thought the Negro vogue had . . . spoiled us . . . With his bitter sense of humor, he called the Harlem literati, the 'niggerati.'"[20] He brought to this novel a Westerner's dislike of sham, "a keen sense of the phony."[21] The book broods over the failure of the New Negro Movement to accomplish more. It is set in "Niggerati Manor," and attacks the Bohemianism of the New Negro artists, with many characters no more than thinly disguised portraits of actual figures. ***Interne*** (1932), written in collaboration with Abraham L. Furman, is a story of a sensitive young man's disillusionment as he seeks to become a surgeon.

Only in ***The Blacker the Berry*** did Wallace Thurman's Western roots obviously expose themselves. The book is strongly autobiographical in a metaphoric sense, leading Bone to speculate that Thurman was the victim of self-hatred caused by his dark complexion.[22] There is, perhaps, evidence to validate Bones' speculation. Note first how the following observation from *Black Rage* seems to fit Emma Lou: "The Negro woman's black face, African features, and kinky hair are physical attributes which place her far from the American ideal of beauty . . ."[23] Add to this Arthur P. Davis' revelation that Thurman's parties always seemed to include "a disproportionate number of white girls"[24] and questions are raised concerning whether Thurman himself shared some Negroes' "desperate bread of blackness," which William Grier and Price Cobbs claim originates in "their own unreasoning self-hate and their pitiful wish to be white."[25] Withal, Thurman certainly speaks directly in favor of self-acceptance and New Negro nationalism in his novels. Perhaps the fact that he openly discussed tabooed problems of color made it inevitable that some critics would read psychopathological reversals into his motives.

But other critics have found diverse qualities and motives in Thurman's work. Hoyt Fuller praised him because he "sought to emphasize the nobility and the humanity of the ordinary Negro."[26] David Littlejohn referred to ***The Blacker the Berry*** as *"the* novel of intraracial color mania . . ."[27] In *The Negro Caravan* Thurman is called "a caustic satirist, lampooning intraracial color snobbishness . . . a clear-eyed observer, but a careless novelist."[28] Blanche Ferguson, on the other hand, thought Thurman a brilliant novelist, and also remarked that he was "the greatest dissenter in the Renaissance movement."[29]

Although he was to become pretentious and waspish, his early innocent aggressiveness and ironic humor during the years right after he went East allowed him to produce a novel that broke traditional barriers regarding candor, while at the same time he was, along with Schuyler, one of the first Afro-American authors to employ satire effectively. He was a black Westerner who made urban Negroes squirm at their own pretentiousness and take greater pride in their heritage. Black readers tended to respond with discomfort to ***The Blacker the Berry;*** "their curiosity would not let them resist it, even though they read it with resentment."[30]

The real tragedy is that this gifted young man did not live long enough to fulfill his considerable artistic promise. He had served an effective apprenticeship, reading and writing constantly, and his goal was "to be a *very* great writer, like Gorki or Thomas Mann, and he felt he was merely a journalistic Writer."[31] Although he did become the first black editor-in-chief of a major publishing house (Macaulay), he was denied his ultimate goal: literary greatness. He died—32 years old—of tuberculosis in December of 1934, ironically, just after having flown back to New York from a last visit West.

Notes

1. Bernard A. Weisenberger, "The Immigrant Within," *American Heritage,* Vol. XXII, No. 1 (Dec., 1970), pp. 32-39, 104.
2. Langston Hughes, *The Big Sea,* (New York: Alfred A. Knopf, 1940), p. 234.
3. Wallace Thurman, *The Blacker the Berry* (New York: The MacMillan Company, 1970), p. 5.
4. See Alain Locke (ed.), *The New Negro* (New York: Boni, 1925), pp. 3-16.
5. Therman B. O'Daniel, "Introduction," *The Blacker the Berry,* op cit, pp. xii-xiii.
6. Hughes, p. 236.
7. O'Daniel, p. xv.
8. Hughes, p. 234.
9. Thurman, pp. 3-4.
10. *Ibid.,* p. 12.
11. *Ibid.,* p. 5.
12. *Ibid.,* p. 15.
13. *Ibid.,* p. 17.
14. Robert Bone, *The Negro in America,* (New Haven: Yale University Press, 1965), p. 92.
15. Hughes, "The Negro Artist and the Racial Mountain." *The Nation,* Vol. 122, No. 3181 (June 23, 1926), p. 694.
16. O'Daniel, p. x.
17. Thurman, p. 25.
18. *Ibid.,* p. 225.
19. *Ibid.,* p. 224.
20. Hughes, p. 238.
21. Arthur P. Davis, "Growing Up In The New Negro Renaissance: 1920-1935," *Negro American Literature Forum,* Vol. 3, No. 2 (Fall, 1968), p. 55.
22. Bone, p. 93.
23. William H. Grier and Price M. Cobbs, *Black Rage,* (New York: Bantam Books, 1968), p. 42.
24. Davis, p. 55.
25. Grier and Cobbs, p. 67.
26. Hoyt W. Fuller, "Contemporary Negro Fiction," *The Black American Writer* (Deland, Fla.: Everett/Edwards, Inc., 1969), edited by C. W. E. Bigsby, p. 234.
27. David Littlejohn, *Black On White,* (New York: The Viking Press, 1966), p. 50.
28. Sterling A. Borwn, Arthur P. Davis, and Ulysses Lee, "The Novel," *The Negro Caravan* (New York: Arno Press, 1970), p. 143.
29. Blanche E. Ferguson, *Countee Cullen and the Negra Renaissance* (New York: Dodd, Mead and Co., 1966), p. 140.
30. O'Daniel, p. ix.
31. Hughes, p. 235.

MAE GWENDOLYN HENDERSON (ESSAY DATE 1972)

SOURCE: Henderson, Mae Gwendolyn. "Portrait of Wallace Thurman." In *The Harlem Renaissance Remembered,* edited by Arna Bontemps, pp. 147-70. New York: Dodd, Mead & Company, 1972.

In the following essay, Henderson discusses Thurman's life and his role in the Harlem Renaissance, which she claims is far greater than his literary contributions would indicate.

Wallace Thurman arrived in New York on Labor Day in 1925 during the peak of the Harlem Renaissance. In less than a decade—nine years later—he died of consumption on Welfare Island in the charity ward of City Hospital. Before his death at the young age of thirty-two, Thurman became one of the central personalities of the Renaissance. Among his friends he was known as a *bon vivant* and bohemian.[1] It was perhaps his "erotic, bohemian" life-style, as Thurman himself described it, as much as his literary creations that made him one of the most fascinating and seductive of the Renaissance figures. During his last years, which he spent in New York, Thurman achieved his greatest successes and perhaps suffered his greatest disappointments. In many ways the course of his life parallels the brief, but colorful and intensely creative, period of the Renaissance itself. As Arna Bontemps described him, "he was like a flame which burned so intensely, it could not last for long, but quickly consumed itself." Indeed, his mind was ever alert and active, his life constantly hectic and searching. It was Thurman's way to plunge himself completely into whatever he became interested in. Writing to a friend, he once said, "I have always gone in for things until I exhausted myself then dropped them."[2] But for a brief period, no personality among the "New Negroes" shone so brilliantly as that of Wallace Thurman, who found himself on a floodtide of success with the publication of his first novel in 1929, and his well-known play, ***Harlem,*** later that same year. Although he published two novels afterward, Thurman's life, like the flow of the Renaissance, had already receded into an ebbtide.

There had always been an element of tragedy about this "strangely brilliant black boy," as Langston Hughes once described him.[3] Another friend, Harlem theater critic Theophilus Lewis, said it a different way, "Thurman's nature was rich in what I might call, for want of a better name, the Shelleyean essence," wrote Lewis.[4] Probably better than he realized, Lewis had succeeded in capturing the substance of that tragic shadow that seemed to hang so vaguely around Thurman. It was perhaps the consciousness of a failure that had as much to do with his personal life as with his artistic aspirations that gave him a constant expression of melancholy, tempered only by his own self-derision and cynicism. That Thurman recognized his failure as an artist—at least by his own standards—is apparent in his letter to a close friend. "I suddenly had . . . a vision of all artists as Matthew Arnold said of Shelley—futilely beating their wings in the luminous void. If *real* artists do that—how awful," wrote Thurman "must be the fate of folk like myself not exactly burned by the magic fire of genius, but nevertheless scorched."[5]

Thurman is described by one who knew him as a slender young man, dark skinned, "with hands and eyes that are never at rest."[6] His body was always rather fragile, probably due to his tubercular condition as well as a heavy addiction to alcohol. Many of those acquanited with him were struck with his "deep and resonant voice" and "rich, infectious laughter." Dorothy West, another friend, wrote that Thurman's voice was "the most remarkable thing about him, welling up out of his too frail body and wasting its richness in unprintable recountings."[7]

He was born in 1902 in Salt Lake City, Utah, and spent two years studying at the University of Utah. He probably left the Mormon state after having a nervous breakdown, hoping to restore his failing health in California. Although initially interested in medicine, at the University of Southern California Thurman rediscovered an earlier enthusiasm for writing and literature. Writing in the third person in his unpublished ***Notes of a Stepchild,*** Thurman said of his early interest in writing:

> At the age of ten he wrote his first novel. Three sheets of foolscap covered with childish scribbling. The plot centered around a stereoptican movie he had seen of Dante's *Inferno.* It concerned the agony of a certain blonde woman. At the age of twelve, being a rabid movie fan, he began to rewrite the contemporary serial thrillers, and was more prodigious with death defying escapades for his heroes and heroines, than the fertile Hollywood scenarists. On entering high school he immediately lost all interest in writing, and did not regain it until his last two years in college, when he spent many hours composing poems about gypsies, hell, heaven, love and suicide.[8]

In Los Angeles he wrote a column called "Inklings" for a local black newspaper. During this period he began to read about the "New Negro" movement in New York and made the acquaintance of Arna Bontemps, who was himself to become a participant in the new Renaissance movement. In an effort to establish a similar movement on the Coast, Thurman began to publish his own magazine, *The Outlet.* Unfortunately, the publication lasted only six months and Thurman gave up ideas of starting a New Negro movement in California. He came to New York where his friend, Arna Bontemps, had arrived some time earlier. At the Gurdjieff meetings in Harlem, Thurman soon met Jean Toomer, Dorothy Peterson, Eric Walrond, Langston Hughes, Dorothy West, Countee Cullen, Aaron Douglas, and other eager and talented young black artists like himself.

He found his first editorial job in New York through Theophilus Lewis on the staff of another short-lived publication, *The Looking Glass.* His job as "reporter, editorial writer, assistant make-up man, and errand boy" came to an abrupt end when the newspaper went bankrupt.[9] Thurman did not realize it then, but he had not yet seen his last unsuccessful venture in the magazine business. Several years later, he told his friend Lewis that his ambition was to become editor of a financially secure magazine.

Although he remained out of work for a while, Thurman soon obtained another editorial position, again through Lewis, who was at the time drama critic for the leftist-oriented *Messenger,* published by A. Phillip Randolph and Chandler Owen. When George Schuyler, then managing editor of *The Messenger,* went on a leave of absence from the magazine, Thurman was appointed acting editor. Although outwardly cynical about his work at *The Messenger,* which he described as a magazine "reflecting the policy of whoever paid off best at the time," a friend speaks of Thurman as "secretly elated to be doing the kind of work he had dreamed of doing."[10] As editor, he began publishing not only his own work, but that of other nascent Renaissance talent, particularly the poetry of Langston Hughes and Arna Bontemps as well as a series of sketches by Zora Neal Hurston and a short story by Dorothy West. His own contributions included a modest poem, a short story, several book reviews, and an occasional nonfiction article.

Upon Schuyler's return later that year, in the fall of 1926, Thurman left the magazine. He went to *The World Tomorrow,* a white publication, and became circulation manager. His job at *The World Tomorrow* brought Thurman into contact with many leading and influential people in the literary and publishing world. Probably he made connections there which would later prove useful.

Meanwhile, in the summer of 1926, a group of young black artists and writers—Zora Neale Hurston, Aaron Douglas, John P. Davis, Bruce Nugent, Gwendolyn Bennett, Langston Hughes, and Wallace Thurman—launched "a new experimental quarterly devoted to . . . younger Negro artists," as its editor, Thurman, described the first and only issue to appear of *Fire.*[11] Its enthusiastic young publishers named it *Fire* because, as Hughes said, "the idea [was] that it would burn up a lot of the old, dead conventional Negro-white ideas of the past, *épater le bourgeoisie* into a realization of the existence of the younger Negro writers and artists . . ."[12] Thurman and his friends were interested in a magazine that would give younger artists a chance to publish their works which was not offered elsewhere. Other black magazines of the period—*The Crisis, Opportunity,* and *The Messenger*—were all primarily political organs published by racial uplift organizations. *Fire,* on the other hand, was not concerned with "sociological problems or propaganda." Thurman regarded it as "purely artistic in intent and conception." He later wrote of the magazine:

> . . . hoping to introduce a truly Negroid note into American literature, its contributors had gone to the proletariat rather than to the bourgeoisie for characters and material, had gone to people who still retained some individual race qualities and who were not totally white American in every respect save color of skin.[13]

These last remarks, of course, constituted an oblique attack on the older, more traditional, black writer of the period. Thurman felt that the black writer was doing a disservice to himself as an artist by constantly dwelling on the theme of racial struggle between whites and blacks. Such writers, he thought, tended to view their own people "as sociological problems rather than human beings."[14]

In an article published the following year in *The New Republic,* Thurman wrote that "the American Negro feels that he has been misinterpreted and caricatured so long by insincere artists that once a Negro gains the ear of the public he should expend his spiritual energy feeding the public honeyed manna on a silver spoon." The traditional black artist tried to suppress any aspects of the seamy or sordid side of life or the "low-down," common, everyday, black lifestyle, such as writers like Langston Hughes and Claude McKay wrote about in their works. Most blacks felt that they must always appear "butter side up" in public, and consequently, in literature. "Negroes in America," Thurman continued, ". . . feel they must always exhibit specimens from the college rather than from the kindergarten, specimens from the parlor rather than from the pantry. They are in the process of being assimilated and those elements within the race which are still too potent for easy assimilation must be hidden until they no longer exist."[15] Thurman felt that such writers limited themselves and "left a great deal of fresh vital material untouched." He reserved his praise for such black writers as Jean Toomer, Eric Walrond, Rudolph Fisher, and Langston Hughes, as well as such white writers as DuBose Heyward and Eugene O'Neill. He wanted the black author to "introduce a Negro note into American literature . . . by writing of certain race characteristics and institutions."

In *Fire,* Thurman hoped to establish sound artistic judgment and criticism for the literature of the Renaissance. While admitting that the Renaissance had given expression to "more articulate and more coherent cries for social justice," Thurman was more skeptical of its achievements in the arts. "[S]peaking purely of the arts," wrote Thurman, "the results of the renaissance have been sad rather than satisfactory, in that critical standards have been ignored, and the measure of achievement has been racial rather than literary." White critics had been so astonished at the phenomenon of blacks' writing that they had neglected traditional literary and critical standards in their often unqualified and unmerited praise of mediocre and ephemeral works. In an article published in *The Independent,* Thurman wrote:

> A man's complexion has little to do with his talent. He either has it or has it not, despite the dictates of spiritually starved white sophisticates, genius does not automatically descend upon one because one's grandmother happened to [be] sold down the river "befo' de wah" . . .[16]

In *The New Republic* he wrote:

> Genius is a rare quality in this world, and there is no reason why it should be more ubiquitous among Blacks than Whites.[17]

But Thurman's aspirations to promote a new Negroid note in American literature and to restore standards of artistic achievement were not to be achieved through *Fire.* Like its ill-fated predecessors, *Fire* proved to be a financial failure. The publication of a single issue had cost Thurman and his friends nearly a thousand dollars. Thurman spent his next three or four years paying the printer for the magazine.

It is worth noting that many of the older writers and critics of the period, including W. E. B. Du Bois, were harshly critical of the new magazine. The black press was just as uncomplimentary in their criticisms. Benjamin Brawley, black literary critic of the Renaissance, wrote of the magazine that "Its flame was so intense that it burned itself up immediately."[18]

Thurman had put everything into *Fire.* Long nights he stayed up getting the final drafts ready for the printer. He himself made all the arrangements for publication. The job of finding patrons and sponsors for the magazine also fell to him. He found himself constantly broke, despite his job at *The World Tomorrow.* At one point the editors at *The World* gave him a special check to purchase a new overcoat, so tattered and frayed had his old one become. During this period he wrote to Hughes, "*Fire* is certainly burning me."

But he was not yet disheartened, even after the failure of *Fire.* When he again found himself jobless, there were times when he was so broke, he could not even afford to pay for his room or purchase food. Not only was he out of work, but *Fire* had left him harassed with debt. Then he suddenly became ill. Boils, a swollen thyroid gland, and infected tonsils sent him to the hospital for an operation. "Truly I am akin to Lazarus," he wrote to Hughes.[19] Even so, all was not hopeless; at least he was writing. In 1927 he had several articles accepted by *The New Republic, The Independent,* and *The World Tomorrow.* It was largely as a result of these articles, as well as his editorship of *Fire,* that Thurman found himself a spokesman for the younger group of black Renaissance writers. In these articles, some of which have already been quoted, Thurman manifested that same skepticism which had shown itself in the pages of *The Messenger* and even earlier in his review of Alain Locke's *The New Negro* in *The Looking Glass.* "In it [*The New Negro*]," Thurman wrote, "are exemplified all the virtues and all the faults of this new movement, even to a hint of its speciousness. Many have wondered what this Negro literary renaissance has accomplished other than providing white publishers with a new source of revenue, affording the white intellectuals with a 'different' fad and bringing a half dozen Negro artists out of obscurity."[20]

In the following year, 1928, Thurman wrote articles for *The Bookman* and *Dance Magazine.* Meanwhile he also began his first novel, ***The Blacker the Berry.*** But his real desire was still to become editor of his own magazine. Two years after the extinction of *Fire,* he published another magazine. *Harlem, A Forum of Negro Life* lasted little longer than had its predecessor. *Harlem,* however, appealed to a wider audience and at twenty-five cents a copy, it was much cheaper than the earlier magazine, which had sold for one dollar. But again expenses and lack of funds prevented Thurman from realizing his dream. *Harlem* folded after just two issues. Significantly, a critic later wrote of both *Fire* and *Harlem,* "It was a lack of money not a dearth of merit which caused [these] two magazines to disappear."[21]

Meanwhile Thurman found a job on the editorial staff of MacFadden Publications and published his first novel. Although ***The Blacker the Berry*** was acclaimed by the critics, Thurman himself remained dissatisfied with the novel. The title, used by Thurman ironically, is borowed from an old black folk saying, "The blacker the berry, the sweeter the juice." The novel is a protest against forms of prejudice found within the black community. It deals with the problems of a dark-skinned girl, Emma Lou, among her own people of lighter skin. Like Thurman, Emma Lou came from a middle-class family in a small Midwestern town. Again recalling the author's own experiences, Emma Lou leaves the Midwest, going first to Los Angeles, then to New York's Harlem in a vain effort to escape the scorn and discrimination she has suffered among her own people because of her dark skin. Thurman himself hated small-town provinciality, which he thought bred petty prejudices. He once told a friend that he "hat[ed] every damned spot in these United States outside

Manhattan Island."[22] He had Emma Lou's uncle express it this way: "People in large cities . . . are broad. They do not have time to think of petty things."[23] Both Emma Lou and to some extent Thurman were disappointed to discover even in the city what Thurman once described as "interracial schisms, caused by differences in skin color."[24] In his article "Harlem Facets," published in *The World Tomorrow,* Thurman had written of the prejudice against foreigners, particularly West Indians, that existed in the Harlem community. In another article, "Negro Life in New York's Harlem," Thurman wrote, "All people seem subject to prejudice, even those who suffer from it most. . ."[25]

On another level, Thurman attempted to deal with the phenomenon of race consciousness and self-hatred. Emma Lou, who used skin bleachers and hair straighteners, had unconsciously accepted the values of those who made her suffer so unjustly. Ultimately she is made to realize that part of the difficulty lay in herself and that she herself was to blame for much of her unhappiness:

> Although this had been suggested to her by others, she had been too obtuse to accept it. She had ever been eager to shift the blame on others when no doubt she herself was the major criminal . . . What she needed to do now was to accept her black skin as being real and unchangeable, to realize that certain things were, had been, and would be, and with this in mind begin life anew, always fighting, not so much for acceptance by other people, but for acceptance of herself by herself.[26]

It is apparent, of course, that Thurman is trying to resolve some of his own problems concerning art and race and race consciousness in ***The Blacker the Berry.*** He had earlier expressed his disdain for so-called "progaganda literature" and wanted to free his own art "from all traces of interracial progaganda." In his novel he expressed a philosophy based on salvation for the individual. If an artist were talented and skillful enough, he could transcend racial barriers and limitations. But the desire to avoid propaganda did not mean that he must not write about blacks. He was not like those artists who thought they could produce better literature by writing about whites. These were artists who, like Emma Lou, were "trying to escape from a condition their own mental attitudes made more harrowing." Such artists "were inclined to forget that every facet of life could be found among their own people, and that Negroes, being human beings . . . had all the natural emotions and psychological reactions of other human beings." Continuing, he defines the role of the black artist:

> . . . if art is universal expression in terms of the particular he believed there was, if he had the talent, just as much chance for the Negro author to produce great literature by writing of his own people as if he were to write about Chinese or Laplanders. He would be labeled a *Negro* artist, with the emphasis on the Negro rather than on the artist, only as he failed to rise above the province of petty propaganda or failed to find an efficacious means of escape from the stupefying *coup d'états* of certain forces in his environment.[27]

But Thurman had not lived up to his own expectations; he had been disappointed to find that "after all his novel had been scorched with propaganda." It was true that he had avoided all interracial experiences between blacks and whites and attempted to deal only with "Negroes among their own kind." But in his effort to "interpret some of the internal phenomena of Negro life in America," he had blamed the existence of these conditions on race prejudice. To Thurman, such a manifestation "hung like a localised cloud over his whole work."[28] It is for this reason that he himself often deprecated the novel, while others, including the critics, acclaimed it. In one of his reviews, Lewis wrote that Thurman had written a novel, ***The Blacker the Berry,*** "of which he ought to be proud, but isn't."[29]

Meanwhile Thurman had become rather infamous among the more conservative circles of the Harlem literati, but quite a popular figure among the younger, more bohemian crowd. On his part, Thurman expressed only scorn and contempt for "society Negroes" and an outright rejection of established customs and traditional values. This rejection was expressed in his erotic, bohemian life-style and the group of eccentric companions with whom he chose to spend his time.

These were the days when downtown white artists, intellectuals, and thrill-seekers came to Harlem to drink bootleg liquor, eat fried fish, and pigs feet, and learn to do a dance called the "black bottom" at Saturday night rent parties and cabarets. Nightspots like the famed *Savoy* and *Cotton Club* catered especially to patrons from downtown who came seeking the primitive, the exotic, and the unusual in Harlem's night life. On Saturday nights, nearly everyone either gave parties or went to parties, including Thurman and the other members of the Harlem literati. Langston Hughes wrote in *The Big Sea* that "at Wallace Thurman's you met the bohemians of both Harlem and the Village."[30]

Downtown whites eagerly sought admission to these parties and cabarets. In fact, Thurman himself would frequently oblige those whites who were willing to make his efforts remunerative, and most of them did. He was known to escort these groups of pleasure-seekers and bohemians on frequent night excursions to Harlem's carbarets, parties, and bars. At these parties, he would often drink gin until he "pass[ed] out" and would have to "be carried bodily from a party."[31] Frequently he indulged in all-night drinking bouts with other young bohemians, would-be artists and artists who, like himself, had little regard for custom or convention. This was the period that he would later write about in his autobiographical novel, ***Infants of the Spring.*** In this second novel, a bitter and pessimistic satire, the Harlem literati, which he often found spurious in their pretensions and second rate in their productions, was renamed "Niggerati." His own house was christened "Niggerati Manor." Recalling those days, Lewis wrote several years later:

> Those were the days when Niggerati Manor was the talk of the town. The story got out that the bathtubs in the house were always packed with sour mash, while gin flowed from all the water taps and the flush boxes were filled with needle beer. It was said that the inmates of the house spent wild nights in tuft hunting and in the diversions of the cities of the plains and delirious days fleeing from pink elephants.

In a note of mild skepticism, Lewis continued:

> Needless to say, the rumors were not wholly groundless. Where there is smoke there must be fire. In the case of Niggerati Manor, a great deal more smoke came out of the windows than was warranted by the size of the fire in the house.[32]

Despite his growing popularity and his ever-widening circle of friends, however, Thurman could not escape a persistent feeling of barrenness in his life. Even the publication of his first novel and the approaching production of his play could not fill the void. There were times when Harlem living would get too hectic for him and he would seek the rest and quiet of the country where he could go for long walks in the woods, read prodigiously, and spend time writing. Occasionally he would go home to Salt Lake City, where his grandmother lived, and try to restore his failing health. At other times he would visit the homes of a couple of close friends just outside the city. Perhaps these were some of the feelings that led to Thurman's marriage to a young schoolteacher shortly after the publication of ***The Blacker the Berry.*** Unfortunately, the marriage was a failure, lasting only six months. Thurman went back to bohemia, and the schoolteacher later became active in the Communist party. The divorce and alimony payments left Thurman, who was already heavily in debt, in an even worse financial situation. And the tensions of a divorce, added to recurring health problems due to his tubercular condition, increased the strain.

When his marriage dissolved so quickly, it was rumored by some that Thurman "was not the marrying [kind]." "Scandalous things were said about the disunion," wrote Dorothy West, who herself denies any such allegations concerning Thurman. Even Miss West, however, allows that Thurman "surround[ed] himself with a queer assortment" of friends.[33] While there were a few women in Thurman's life, there can be little doubt that he had homosexual tendencies and that these inclinations contributed to his feelings of personal failure and inadequacy. The theme of homosexuality occurs repeatedly in his works and personal letters. In his autobiographical novel, ***Infants of the Spring,*** the hero, Raymond [Thurman], develops a relationship with a friend which has strong homosexual overtones. Perhaps most revealing is the letter Thurman wrote to a friend in which he tells how he found himself in a rather unusual situation involving overtures made toward him by a homosexual shortly after his arrival in New York. Another letter suggests that one of his friends living outside the city was, in fact, an intimate companion. Writing to a friend about his "disappearing act," Thurman explains:

> There are a number of good reasons for my keeping my whereabouts a secret—even from you, *pour le present.* More reasons than the obvious one that I like mysteries to crop up about myself. Some day when the censor (Freud's censor) is at ease I'll tell you . . .[34]

It would appear that Thurman saw his homosexuality as creating social as well as psychological difficulties.

In February 1929 the play, ***Harlem,*** opened at the Apollo on Broadway and skyrocketed its author to overnight fame. ***Harlem*** was an immediate hit, the most successful play of the period written by a black playwright. The critics acclaimed it as a realistic presentation of the lives and problems of blacks in Harlem. Although a white writer, William Jourdan Rapp, collaborated on the play, the plot and dialogue were written by Thurman. Rapp, who was a professional writer as well as a personal friend of Thurman's, helped to make revisions and adapt the play to a form suitable for stage production.

The play is based upon a short story entitled **"Cordelia the Crude,"** which Thurman had published in *Fire.* It is a highly melodramatic story of a Harlem family who migrated from the South to Harlem, expecting to find an escape from the poverty, hardship, and bigotry of life in the South. They seek a "city of *refuge*" which becomes, instead, a "city of *refuse*." In Harlem, the family must take in boarders in an already overcrowded apartment and give Saturday night rent parties in order to provide enough income to support itself. Most of the action centers on the older daughter, Cordelia, who leaves Basil, her West Indian lover, and gets involved with Roy Crow, an underworld character in the numbers racket. Roy is later murdered by his own partner, Kid Vamp, who accuses him of betrayal. The Kid then seduces Cordelia, who leaves with him, as Basil is left to take the blame for the murder. The play concludes as the Kid himself is approached by a rival band of white gangsters. Cordelia departs despite the pleas of her mother, who exclaims, "Lawd! Lawd! Tell me! Tell me! Dis ain't the City of Refuge."[35]

The play ran for over ninety performances and even went on the road to Los Angeles and Chicago, where it was also received warmly. As Langston Hughes commented, the play was "considerably distorted for box office purposes," although it remained "a compelling study—and the only one in the theater—of the impact of Harlem on a Negro family fresh from the South."[36] Again Thurman produced a work which focused on black life and society. Despite the rather overwhelming sensationalism of the production, he succeeded in dealing with a number of problems which were very realistic in the Harlem community—intraracial prejudice against West Indians, black migration from the South to the North, exploitation of the ghetto by black and white underworld racketeering, and lack of employment and decent housing conditions in the black community.

Describing the years between his "hectic hegira to Harlem" and the production of ***Harlem,*** Thurman had this to say:

> Three years have seen me become a New Negro (for no reason at all and without my consent), a poet (having had 2 poems published by generous editors), an editor (with a penchant for financially unsound publications), an erotic (see articles on Negro life and literature [in] *The Bookman, New Republic, Independent, World Tomorrow,* etc.), an actor (I was denizen of Cat Fish Row in *Porgy*), a husband (having been married all of six months), a novelist (viz: ***The Blacker the Berry.*** Macauley's, Feb. 1, 1929: $2.50), a playwright (being co-author of ***Black Belt***). Now—what more could one do?
>
> (Author's note: ***Black Belt*** was later renamed ***Harlem.***)[37]

Indeed, in the months and years that followed, Thurman discovered that there was much more to do, although he could not have known at the time that there remained for him but five short years.

After the production of ***Harlem,*** Thurman continued to write prolifically, sometimes ghost-writing books of the "true confessions" category. Later he wrote scripts for two lurid and second-rate movies. The pressure of his personal life and self-disillusionment as an artist had a debilitating effect on Thurman. His ailing health and his despair led him increasingly to gin, although the doctors advised against it. Finally, he determined that he would leave the city, go some place where he could exercise, read, write a little, and take a long rest. He went to Utah, then to Florida, Jamaica, and later to California, where he attempted to negotiate movie contracts for his works. Meanwhile he was also helping a young lady, who later became Rapp's wife, to write a novel based on his play, ***Harlem.***

Most of his energies during the next two years were spent writing his second novel, ***Infants of the Spring.*** But he was not happy. The writing of this novel became a strain for him. It left him "depressed and enfeebled both mentally and physically." Written from his personal experiences and attitudes toward the Renaissance, the novel led its author into a journey of introspection that was often unpleasant or disturbing. Comparing his experiences with the new novel with those of the French novelist, Proust, in *Remembrance of Things Past,* Thurman wrote of his depression and illness:

> The diagnosis is of course: too much introspection. Continual mulling over the past, berating self for innate lack of will and self-control, consciously unreeling the past to do in my new novel what Proust succeeded in doing in his volumes.

Away from New York Thurman was lonely. He yearned for the busy social life he had led there. "I was never created to forego companionship," Thurman wrote in one of his letters. Finding few friends or diversions outside of the city, Thurman continued:

> I miss New York. I miss the chats I used to have with certain kindred spirits. I miss the occasional mad nights experienced in Harlem. And yet I know should I be in New York no work would be done.[38]

Trying to impose self-discipline, he determined to stay away from the city until he had completed more writing. Thurman finished the draft of his second novel in 1929, while in Salt Lake City. Upon the completion, he wrote to his friend Rapp:

> I finished the first draft of my novel about five A.M., yesterday morning. Writing it has been an adventure. I stood as one apart and watched it issuing forth from Wallace Thurman. It is the first thing I have ever let write itself, playing amanuensis to some inner urge . . .[39]

Most of Thurman's energies during the next couple of years were spent on ***Infants of the Spring.*** A white patron, Elizabeth Marbury, assisted him financially in the completion of his second novel. It appears that about this same time Thurman went through a series of personal changes in his attitude toward his life, although he himself doubted the permanence of this new "state of mind." Disclaiming "any great reformation," he does seem to manifest the beginnings of a new maturity and awareness. He is able to express a disinterest in the pursuits which used to occupy his time. "I have more or less outgrown them," wrote Thurman. He even tried to give up gin, restricting himself to what he called "civilized tippling." Looking back on his former life, he comments sardonically:

> Perhaps, after all, these past four hectic years in Harlem have not left me in a rut. I may still have my former capacity for experiencing sea changes. In which case, there is no telling what might happen next. Howbeit, Harlem holds no more charms for me.[40]

Thurman did not publish his novel until 1932. ***Infants of the Spring*** is an autobiographical statement of his disillusionment with the outcome of the Renaissance, as well as his own personal failure as an artist. His earlier skepticism toward the New Negro movement had now turned into bitter disappointment, and his own aspirations to become a great novelist had remained unfulfilled. Thurman had read all the great writers, including Proust, Melville, Tolstoy, Dostoyevski, Henry James, and others. Hughes wrote that "Thurman had read so many books because he could read eleven lines at a time."[41]

Comparing the literature of the Renaissance with the works of great writers made Thurman a severe critic, particularly of his own works. He puzzled over the reasons for what he considered to be the lack of productivity and creativity among the Renaissance artists. In his novel, he asked whether the failure was the result of "some deep-rooted complex [racial]" or an "indication of a lack of talent."[42] In most instances Thurman thought the black artist was hindered by a preoccupation with his racial identity. Thurman had grappled with this problem when writing his earlier novel, ***The Blacker the Berry.*** Earlier, in his ***Notes of a Stepchild,*** he had written of himself: "He tried hard not to let the fact that he had pigmented skin influence his literary or mental development."

FROM THE AUTHOR

INFANTS OF THE SPRING

Being a Negro writer these days is a racket and I'm going to make the most of it while it lasts. About twice a year I sell a story. It is acclaimed. I am a genius in the making. Thank God for this Negro literary renaissance. Long may it flourish!

SOURCE: Wallace Thurman, excerpt featuring Sweetie May, a character Thurman based on Zora Neale Hurston, from *Infants of the Spring,* Macauley, 1932.

There were two ways in which he felt the major black writers dealt with the fact of race identity in their works. In ***Infants of the Spring,*** Raymond [Thurman] rejects on the one hand those writers "who had nothing to say, and who only wrote because they were literate and felt they should appraise white humanity of the better classes among Negroes." Most of the early writers of the period fell under this condemnation. Those were the writers whom Thurman called the "propagandists" and whose contribution to the Renaissance he had earlier described as "sociological rather than literary." Another group of black writers was composed of those who wanted to escape their racial identity through a denial of everything black. Again speaking as Raymond, Thurman wrote: "He had no sympathy whatsoever with Negroes . . . who contended that should their art be Negroid, they, the artist, must be considered inferior."[43] Such artists "did not realize by adhering to such a belief" they were, in effect, "subscribing to the theory of Nordic superiority."[44]

The title of the novel comes from a verse in Shakespeare's *Hamlet* which Thurman quotes in the Preface:

> The canker galls the infants of the spring
> Too oft before their buttons be disclosed
> And in the morn an liquid dew of youth
> Contagious blastments are most imminent.

It was the canker and race consciousness which they could not resolve which destroyed the young writers ["infants"] of the Renaissance ["spring"].

The weakness of the Renaissance was that all traits of individuality had been destroyed by the canker of a destructive race complex. That Thurman was only vaguely aware of his own preoccupation with race is indicated by his constant disavowals of such influences and his deliberate efforts to transcend the self-imposed limitations of race consciousness. He discovered the resolution through a philosophy of individuality. Raymond, the hero of his second novel, comments:

> Negroes are a slave race and a slave race they'll remain until assimilated. Individuals will arise and escape on the ascending ladder of their individuality.[45]

Such a statement, however, reveals the degree to which Thurman is a victim of his own self-hatred arising from his racial identity. In ***The Blacker the Berry*** he resolved this dilemma of race consciousness and individuality through an acceptance of oneself and racial identity. In this, his second novel, the answer seems to be a rejection of one's racial identity through a doctrine of what he once described as Nietzschean individuality.

Niggerati Manor is the home of a group of young bohemian artists and would-be artists who live in a state of decadence and debauchery. Most of them spend their time attempting to justify their lack of creativity. Thurman sums up his attitude toward the Renaissance in a bitter passage which describes a rent party given by the inhabitants of Niggerati Manor:

> The lights in the basements had been dimmed, and the reveling dancers cast grotesque shadows on the tapestried walls. Color lines had been completely eradicated. Whites and blacks clung passionately together as if trying to effect a permanent merger. Liquor, jazz music, and close physical contact had achieved what decades of propaganda had advocated with little success. . . . Tomorrow all of them will have an emotional hangover. They will fear for their sanity, for at last they have had a chance to do openly what they only dared do clandestinely before. This, he kept repeating to himself, is the Negro Renaissance, and this is about all the whole damn thing is going to amount to.[46]

The novel ends as Paul, one of the artists who had lived with Raymond at Niggerati Manor, commits suicide. He leaves behind his masterpiece, hoping that the publicity of his death would result in a successful posthumous publication of his novel. The fate of Paul, "a colorful, inanimate corpse," symbolized the ultimate doom of the Renaissance writers who would succeed in destroying themselves through voguish sensationalism. The endurance of their works, however, would be as ephemeral as Paul's, which had been rendered illegible by the overflow of water from the bathtub in which he drowned himself. Only the title sheet remained legible, where Paul had "drawn a distorted inky black skyscraper, modeled after Niggerati Manor."

> The foundation of this building was composed of crumbling stone. At first glance it could be ascertained that the skyscraper would soon crumble and fall, leaving the dominating white lights in full possession of the sky.[47]

The Renaissance, represented by the destruction of Niggerati Manor, was inevitably doomed because it lacked the foundation to make it "something truly epochal." The pessimistic portrait of the Renaissance in this bitter satire was Thurman's final legacy to the New Negro movement.

His last novel, ***The Interne,*** written in collaboration with Abraham L. Furman, was also published that same year. ***The Interne*** is a muckraking novel which exposes, in a rather sensational way, the corrupt and abusive conditions at the City Hospital in New York. His last work symbolizes Thurman's final break and departure from the Renaissance. The story centers on the experiences of a young, white intern at the City Hospital. It was his only work which did not deal with black life and society.

Both of these novels were published by Macaulay, where Thurman became editor-in-chief in 1932. Two years later Thurman negotiated a contract with Foy Productions Ltd, to do the scenarios for two films, ***High School Girl*** and ***Tomorrow's Children,*** a film on sterilization which was censored in New York.

For a while he was content. He was making contacts, earning good money, and had a "very swank" office at the studio. But the strain and intensity of such a life was altogether too much for Thurman. Hollywood was hectic and mad. Thurman wrote to a friend, "Don't ever be lured into the studio except as a visitor. Am going thru the most insane experience of my life in this studio."[48] Finally he became nervous and started to lose weight. By the following summer his physical condition was getting dangerously worse. In May he returned to New York, where he proceeded to go on a drinking binge which lasted until he finally passed out. Ironically he was taken to the City Hospital, the institution which he had written of in ***The Interne.*** Thurman remained a patient in the hospital in the incurable ward for six long months. He made no effort to fight his condition. He died on Welfare Island on December 22, 1934. Lewis wrote, "To the very end (for he accepted it as the end when he was borne to the hospital), he was the *bon vivant,* the bohemian to the last."[49]

In terms of his literary contributions, Wallace Thurman has been regarded as one of the minor figures of the Renaissance. His significance, however, far exceeds the work he left behind. Not only was he tremendously influential upon the younger and perhaps more successful writers of the period, but his life itself became a symbol of the New Negro movement. Thurman had made his entrance into the Renaissance at the height of the movement. His life, brilliant and turbulent as it had been, ended after the Renaissance came to a close.

Notes

1. Theophilus Lewis, "Harlem Sketchbook," New York *Amsterdam News* (January 5, 1935). Yale University, James Weldon Johnson Collection, Wallace Thurman Folder. (Hereafter referred to as Thurman Folder.)
2. Letter to Harold Jackman from Wallace Thurman, August 1930. Thurman Folder.
3. Langston Hughes, *The Big Sea* (New York: 1940), p. 234.
4. Lewis, "Harlem Sketchbook."
5. Letter to Jackman from Thurman, May 1928. Thurman Folder.
6. Richard De Roachement, "Harlem a Fraction of a Mirror," New York *Sun* (March 4, 1929).
7. Dorothy West, "Elephant's Dance," *Black World,* Vol. XX, No. 1 (November 1970), p. 77.
8. Thurman, *Notes of a Stepchild,* unpublished manuscript. Thurman Folder.
9. Lewis, "Harlem Sketchbook."
10. Hughes, pp. 233-34; Letter from Arna Bontemps to Jackman on Thurman, (March 25, 1942). Thurman Folder.
11. Thurman (ed.), *Fire.* Thurman Folder.
12. Hughes, p. 235.
13. Thurman, "Negro Artists and the Negro," *The New Republic,* Vol. LII (August 31, 1927), p. 297.
14. Thurman, "Nephews of Uncle Remus," *The Independent,* Vol. CXIX (Sept. 24, 1967), p. 39.
15. Thurman, "Negro Artists and the Negro," p. 38.
16. Thurman, "Nephews of Uncle Remus," p. 298.
17. Thurman, "Negro Artists and the Negro," p. 39.
18. Benjamin G. Brawley, *The Negro Genius.*
19. Letter to Langston Hughes from Wallace Thurman, December 8, 1927. Thurman Folder.
20. West, pp. 78-9.
21. Theophilus Lewis, "Wallace Thurman is a Model Harlemite," New York *Amsterdam News,* no date. Thurman Folder.
22. Lewis, "Wallace Thurman is a Model Harlemite."
23. Wallace Thurman, *The Blacker the Berry* (New York: Collier Books Edition, 1970).
24. Wallace Thurman, *Notes of a Stepchild.* Thurman Folder.
25. Wallace Thurman, "Negro Life in New York's Harlem," *Little Blue Book,* No. 494, edited by E. Haldeman-Julius. Thurman Folder.
26. Thurman, *The Blacker the Berry,* pp. 226-7.
27. Thurman, *Notes of a Stepchild.* Thurman Folder.
28. *Ibid.*
29. Lewis, "Wallace Thurman is a Model Harlemite."
30. Hughes, *The Big Sea,* p. 234.
31. West, p. 80.
32. Lewis, "Harlem Sketchbook."
33. West, p. 80.
34. Letter to Jackman from Thurman, May 1928. Thurman Folder.
35. Doris E. Abramson, *Negro Playwrights in the American Theatre 1928-1929* (New York, 1969), p. 37.
36. Hughes, *The Big Sea,* p. 235.
37. Abramson, p. 33.
38. Letter to William Jourdan Rapp from Wallace Thurman, no date. Thurman Folder.
39. Letter to Rapp from Thurman, 1929. Thurman Folder.
40. Letter from Thurman to Jackman, August 1930. Thurman Folder.
41. Hughes, p. 234.
42. Thurman, *Infants of the Spring* (New York, 1932), p. 62.
43. *Ibid.,* p. 91.
44. *Ibid.,* pp. 108-09.
45. *Ibid.,* pp. 141-2.
46. *Ibid.,* p. 187.
47. *Ibid.,* p. 284.
48. Letter to Jackman from Thurman, March 13, 1934. Thurman Folder.
49. Lewis, "Death Claims Noted Writer," New York, *Amsterdam News,* (December 29, 1934). Thurman Folder.

Bibliography

Books and Articles

Abramson, Doris E., *Negro Playwrights in the American Theatre, 1925-1959* (New York & London: Columbia University Press, 1969).

Black World, November 1970.

Bone, Robert A., *The Negro Novel in America,* rev. ed., (New Haven & London: Yale University Press). 1965.

Fullinwider, S. P., *The Mind and Mood of Black America. 20th Century Thought* (Homewood, Illinois. The Dorsey Press, 1969).

Hughes, Langston, *The Big Sea. An Autobiography* (New York: Hill & Wang, American Century Series, 1963).

Thurman, Wallace, *The Blacker the Berry* (New York: Collier Books Edition, 1970).

———, *Infants of the Spring* (New York: The Macaulay Company, 1932).

———, *The Interne* (New York: The Macaulay Company, 1932).

The New Republic, August 31, 1927.

The Independent, September 24, 1927.

Unpublished Materials

Yale University, James Weldon Johnson Collection, Wallace Thurman Folder.

HUEL D. PERKINS (ESSAY DATE 1976)

SOURCE: Perkins, Huel D. "Renaissance 'Renegade'? Wallace Thurman." *Black World* 25, no. 4 (February 1976): 29-35.

In the following essay, Perkins considers whether, because of his sometimes harsh criticism, Thurman should be viewed as an adversary of the Harlem Renaissance or simply as a critic who expected nothing short of excellence from other Black writers.

"Genius is a rare quality in this world, and there is no reason why it should be more ubiquitous among blacks than whites," wrote Wallace Thurman in his article, **"New Artists and the Negro,"** which appeared in the August 31, 1927, volume of *The New Republic.* In another article, entitled, **"Nephews of Uncle Remus,"** he began by saying, "Too bad that the ballyhoo brigade which fosters the so-called Negro art 'renaissance' has chosen to cheer and encourage indiscriminately anything which claims a negroid ancestry or kinship. For as the overfed child gags when forced to swallow an extra spoonful of halfsour milk, so will the gullible American public gag when too much of this fervid fetish known as Negro art is shoveled into its gaping mind and mouths . . ." (*The Independent,* Vol. CXIX, September 27, 1927). And in Chapter XX of his novel, ***Infants of the Spring,*** Thurman writes: "A few years ago it was the thing for all Negroes who could get an education to be professional men, doctors, lawyers, dentists, *et cetera.* Now, they are all trying to be artists. Negroes love to talk, love to tell the stories of their lives. They all feel that they are so different from the rest of humanity, so besieged by problems peculiar only to themselves. And since it is the fashion now to be articulate either in words, music or paint brush, every Negro, literate or otherwise, confesses and is tempted to act according to the current fad."

In the foregoing quotes, is Wallace Thurman putting down Black people? Is he lampooning the Harlem Renaissance—considered by many cultural historians to be the most significant epoch in the creative life of Black people in America? Is he a deserter, a turncoat, a traitor to the cause? Is he a renegade?

Wallace Thurman came to New York City in 1925 at the peak of the Harlem Renaissance. He was drawn to Harlem as so many others of literary talent and interests were during the 1920's: Arna Bontemps, Langston Hughes, Claude McKay, Zora Neale Hurston—all came from places other than New York City to join Countee Cullen, one of the few natives, in participating in this stirring and creative movement. To Harlem, Thurman brought some extraordinary gifts. He had a brilliant mind, read prolifically, possessed uncommon literary talent, and, more significantly, he brought to the Harlem Renaissance his capacity for acrimonious criticism. His was a mind not content to accept anything on face value or to settle for "things as they are." About this facet of his genius, Langston Hughes wrote that he was a "strangely brilliant Black boy, who had read everything, and whose critical mind could find something wrong with everything he read."[1] As one looks more closely at Wallace Thurman, the man, some light may be shed upon the reasons why Wallace Thurman and the Harlem Renaissance seemed to have been at odds—why his view of the movement is sometimes interpreted as "anti"—and why he is in some ways regarded as a renegade of the period.

Thurman was born in 1902 in Salt Lake City, Utah. His family circumstances, by prevailing standards, were considered middle-class. His college education had been gained at two reputable institutions—the University of Utah and the University of Southern California. But the call to New York City and to the intermingling of kindred spirits was too great for him to resist. From 1925 until his death in 1934, New York City became his literary home. The fact that the end came from tuberculosis at the early age of 32, in a charity ward of the City Hospital, bespoke a careless abandon which seemed to have pervaded his entire existence.

Thurman was a caustic critic, as can be concluded from some of his reviews of the books of the period. Below is an excerpt from a review of Walter White's novel, *Flight,* which was published in 1926. (Walter White was Executive Secretary of the National Association for the Advancement of Colored People at the time and had received a lucrative fellowship to complete the writing of the novel).

> I do not know which is considered the greater literary criminal, he who writes or rather tries to write without first having suitable material or he who has the suitable material and fails to do it justice . . . All art no doubt is propaganda, but all propaganda is most certainly not art. And a novel must, to earn the name, be more than a mere social service report, more than a thinly disguished dissertation on racial relationships and racial maladjustments.[2]

Again, was Mr. Thurman putting down Black writers? It may be observed that his same vitriolic pen was also used to attack a white writer, as this excerpt from his review of the novel *Black Harvest,* by I. A. R. Wylie, will attest:

> It takes a brave writer indeed in this day and time to attempt to write about any race save the one to which he belongs, and that writer who will not only write contemporaneously about some other race, but will also write speculatively about the future of that race deserves a croix-deguerre for braving fire, for to fire he will most certainly be subjected. . . . Yet this novel is far from satisfying or complete. As entertainment or as controversial stimuli it is indeed good, but one expects a little more from a volume so ambitious in theme and so bristling with positive character electrons. Thus *Black Harvest* remains one of those books that everyone should read, speculate upon, discuss, and then forget.[3]

Centuries ago, Roman philosopher Seneca, the Younger, writing in his *De Tranquillitate Amini,* suggested that there is no genius without a mixture of madness. This seems to be apropos when speaking of Wallace Thurman. He tried his talents at journalism, fiction, drama, editing, ghost writing, scenario writing, poetry, criticism, and was eminently successful in all these pursuits. But he was in a constant state of melancholy and remorse—always unhappy, ill and self-deriding. In compensation, he developed a penchant for gin and the bohemian lifestyle which only served to hasten his early death. Never satisfied, always questing, always criticizing—even his own efforts—he nevertheless emerged as one of the brilliant lights of the movement. Some indication of the recognition of his ability can be seen by tracing the positions held with various publications with which he was associated, beginning with his first job as an editorial assistant with *The Looking Glass,* through his work with *The Messenger,* to the position with *The World Tomorrow,* and finally with his appointment as editor-in-chief of Macauley Publishing Co., where he became the first Black to be so employed, as earlier he had become the first Black to be employed as a reader with a predominantly white publishing company.

His versatility is further documented in his own words. Writing about himself after three years in Harlem, he had this to say:

> Three years have seen me become a New Negro (for no reason at all and without my consent), a poet (having had two poems published by generous editors), an editor (with a penchant for financially unsound publications), an erotic (see articles on Negro life and literature in *The Bookman, New Republic, Independent, World Tomorrow,* etc.), an actor (I was denizen of Cat Fish Row in *Porgy*), a husband (having been married all of six months), a novelist (viz: ***The Blacker the Berry.*** Macauley's Feb. 1, 1929—$2.50), a playwright (being coauthor of ***Black Belt***). Now—what more can one do?"[4]

Yet, incessant critic he remained. It was his dissatisfaction with the extant literary magazines which led him to venture into the publishing business through the route of his own journals.

The central undertaking in Thurman's life and the one which reveals his posture in terms of the Harlem Renaissance perhaps more than any other work was the publication of the magazine *Fire.* In *Fire,* Thurman hoped to arrive at some sort of sound artistic judgement and criticism for the literature of the movement. He launched the magazine because he was convinced that the results of the movement had been more racial than literary and that critical standards had been ignored in an attempt by white sympathizers to herald to the world that Black people were capable of putting sentences together and writing poetry. It is reasonable to expect that a man who had read Proust, Mann, Tolstoy, and every great writer of the past would have some serious misgivings concerning the literary merits of some of the efforts of Harlem Renaissance writers. Beyond this consideration was the fact that the main publications of the period were limited to sociological and uplift magazines which served as organs for organizations and did not concentrate upon literary talent, *per se.*[5] Unmerited praise of mediocre works was not to be accepted by Wallace Thurman—and so *Fire* came into existence.

The first and only issue of *Fire* was published in November 1926. By its masthead, it was devoted to younger Negro artists. It encountered financial difficulties from its inception. The opening inscription clearly indicates that this was to be a spurious venture:

> Being a non-commercial product interested only in the arts, it is necessary that we make some appeal for aid from interested friends. For the second issue of *Fire* we would appreciate having fifty people subscribe ten dollars each, and fifty more to subscribe five dollars each.
>
> We make no eloquent or rhetorical plea. *Fire* speaks for itself.[6]

(Patrons for the first issue were: Maurine Boie, Minneapolis, Minn.; Nellie R. Bright, Philadelphia, Pa.; Arthur Huff Fauset, Philadelphia, Pa.; Dorothy Hunt Harris, New York City; Dorothy R. Peterson, Brooklyn, New York; Mr. and Mrs. John Peterson, New York City; E. B. Taylor, Baltimore, Md.; and Carl Van Vechten, New York City.)

In an attempt to rise above the many problems attendant to an embryonic publishing venture, Thurman gave his entire life to the project. Thoroughly convinced that his efforts would somehow ensure the fact that the works of Black writers were not to be judged by double standards, he virtually gave his blood to the editorship of *Fire*. Nonetheless, *Fire's* only issue cost Thurman and his backers nearly one thousand dollars. Much of his income in subsequent years was used to retire this debt.

What did *Fire* contain? It intended to assemble, under one cover, the best artistic and literary talent available at that time. While Thurman served as editor, those associated with him read like a Who's Who of the Harlem Renaissance: Langston Hughes, Gwendolyn Bennett, Richard Bruce, Zora Neale Hurston, Aaron Douglas, and John Davis. In addition, it included works by Countee Cullen, Edward Silvera, Arna Bontemps, Waring Cuney, Helene Johnson, and Arthur Huff Fauset.

What was Thurman attempting to do through this publication? It is apparent that he was not trying to denigrate Black creative talent. Rather, an honest effort was made to include the best Black talent extant. In that this magazine would be free of editorial policy dictated by ends other than those artistic, the magazine would be able to present to the reading public the best of the race. The disappointment must have been intense when Thurman learned that Black people were not ready to receive such efforts with enthusiasm. Many older writers were extremely critical of the magazine. Jokes began to abound when the plates of the magazine were indeed destroyed by fire. Was $1.00 per copy too exorbitant a price to pay for a Black-owned, Black-controlled literary magazine? Or were the consumers of the literature of the Renaissance only ready to accept works which had the approval of the white press and therefore put money in their tills?

With the demise of *Fire* in 1926 and following a brief excursion into the publication field two years hence (he tried his hand at another journal, entitled *Harlem, A Forum of Negro Life,* which folded after two issues), Wallace Thurman turned to novel writing. While his medium was to change, the scathingly critical nature of Thurman's work remained the same.

The Blacker the Berry, Thurman's first novel, published in 1929, is a caustic criticism of the kind of color discrimination Blacks practice among ourselves. Thurman, through the use of irony, delineates how cruelly inhuman the perpetrators of intra-racial prejudice can become. Emma Lou, the heroine, after having completely degraded herself in accepting jobs beneath her ability, engaging in affairs with men who had no love or respect for her, finally comes to the conclusion that she must "accept her black skin as being real and unchangeable, [and] realize that certain things were, had been, and would be, and with this in mind begin life anew, always fighting, not so much for acceptance by other people, but for acceptance of herself by herself." While he places these words in the mouth of his heroine, it is apparent that Thurman was trying to solve some of his own problems concerning race, the individual, society, the artist and other ills which beset this mad genius. Though the novel was critically acclaimed, Thurman was not quite satisfied with it—unrelenting critic that he was.

His second novel, ***Infants of the Spring*** (1932), coming at the end of the Harlem Renaissance, distinctly looks back in anger, bitterness and pessimism at the movement. The title, taken from a passage of Shakespeare's *Hamlet,* compares the infants to the Black writers and the spring to the Renaissance. ("The canker galls the infants of the spring / Too oft before their buttons be disclosed, / And in the morn and liquid dew of youth / Contagious blastments are most imminent.") Here again his critical faculty surfaces, and he laments the fact that the movement was one of pretentiousness and shams in which unmerited acclaim outdistanced unquestioned artistry. Some critics have regarded this novel as an autobiographical statement of Thurman's disillusionment with the outcome of the Renaissance as well as his own personal failure as an artist. The character within the novel who seems to speak Thurman's view of himself is Raymond Taylor, a young, sensitive, intelligent writer. In a conversation with his friend Steve, a white man, Raymond says:

> It sounds romantic, but I suppose I'm bound to thrive on antagonism. I'd be bored to death otherwise. I'll probably spend my life doing things just to make people angry. I don't expect to be a great writer. I don't think the Negro race can produce one now, any more than can America. I know of only one Negro who has the elements of greatness, and that's Jean Toomer. The rest of us are merely journeymen, planting seeds for someone else to harvest. We all get sidetracked sooner or later. The older ones become warped by propaganda. We younger ones are mired in decadence.

Here Thurman is admitting that he was born to criticize and be dissatisfied with mediocrity, near-art, propaganda and charlatanism. Yet, Wallace Thurman was like a mirror, holding up to artists and would-be artists alike the image of themselves as it appeared then and how posterity might assess it in the future. Renegade? No. Significant critic? Yes. He was a man so committed to universal standards of excellence that he himself encountered difficulty in attaining them. He was good for the Renaissance and he was good for Black people. History will accord him a more favorable position when the Harlem Renaissance is reassessed in terms of its full impact on Black arts and letters. All he seemed to be trying to say is summed up in the last paragraph of his article **"Nephews of Uncle Remus"**:

> If the negro writer is to make any appreciable contribution to American literature it is necessary that he be considered a sincere artist trying to do dignified work rather than a highly trained dog doing trick dances in a public square. He is, after all, motivated and controlled by the same forces which motivate and control a white writer, and like him he will be mediocre or good, success or fail as *ability* deserves. [Italics mine.] A man's complexion has little to do with his talent. He either has it or has it not, and despite the dictates of spiritually starved white sophisticates, genius does not automatically descend upon one because one's grandmother happened to be sold down the river "befo' de wah."[7]

Notes

1. *The Big Sea* (New York, 1940), p. 234.
2. *The Messenger,* Vol. VIII, No. 5 (May 1926), p. 154.
3. *The Messenger,* Vol. VIII, No. 5 (May, 1926), p. 154.
4. Doris E. Abramson, *New Playwrights in the American Theater,* 1928-1929. (New York, 1969), p. 37. (The title of *Black Belt* changed to *Harlem.*)
5. Examples: *Crisis* of the NAACP, *Opportunity* of the National Urban League and *The Messenger.*
6. *Fire,* edited by Wallace Thurman, Vol. 1, No. 1, frontispiece.
7. *The Independent,* Vol. CXIX, (September 27, 1927), p. 216.

DANIEL WALDEN (ESSAY DATE 1987)

SOURCE: Walden, Daniel. "'The Canker Galls . . . ,' or, the Short Promising Life of Wallace Thurman." In *The Harlem Renaissance Re-Examined,* edited by Victor A. Kramer, pp. 201-11. New York: AMS Press, 1987.

In the following essay, Walden traces Thurman's short life and career, focusing on the author's self-hatred and insecurity about his writing.

Although New York City in the 1920s was for most whites a joyous, expanding metropolis, for many blacks, Wallace Thurman among them, it was a city of refuse, not a city of refuge. Growing up at a time when many Americans—after World War I—were eager to get back to what Warren Harding would call "normalcy," Thurman reached Harlem at the moment when white Americans looked to black America, north of 110th Street and along Lexington and Convent Avenues, as the bastion of primitivism and earthiness. Some whites came to gape, some to laugh, but many came to seek exuberant escape in the so-called exotic primitivism of Negro cabaret life. As Langston Hughes exclaimed in *The Big Sea,* "thousands of whites came to Harlem night after night, thinking the Negroes loved to have them there, and firmly believing that all Harlemites left their houses at sundown to sing and dance in cabarets, because most of the whites saw nothing but the cabarets, not the houses."

During these years, nearly all the black writers and artists drifted to New York. As might be expected most were drawn by the promise of New York City as a center where art and literature would flourish. In Hughes' contemporary opinion, what was important was that black writers spoke their own words, their own truths, no matter whether blacks, or whites, were pleased or offended. For in this decade, publishers opened their doors to black authors and poets and artists. What was significant was that in New York City the NAACP, *The Crisis, Opportunity,* and several black newspapers flourished. As early as 1920, W. E. B. Du Bois pointed out, Claude McKay, Langston Hughes, Jean Toomer, Countee Cullen, Anne Spencer, Abram Harris and Jessie Fauset had already been published in *The Crisis.*

Of the whites drawn to Harlem and to black life, only a minority were interested in the discovery and development of black talent. For black writers and artists the 1920s represented an era of opportunities and hopes. It was the decade in which the writers replaced apologetics and militancy and racial propaganda with their own voices as their *raison d'être.* True, Walter White's *Fire in the Flint* (1924), W. E. B. Du Bois' *Dark Princess* (1928), and George Schuyler's *Slaves Today* (1931) maintained an offensive, anti-racist posture. But most writers tried to be writers; following the advice of Henry James (whether they had read him or not), they let their stories unfold and their characters evolve out of their stories. In some cases, the psychology of caste and the racial experience, echoing Charles Chesnutt's early models, became dominant aspects; for Rudolph Fisher, the everyday life of blacks in Harlem, linked to the trauma of Southern exposure to Northern urbanism, was played out much as everyday life was depicted by other authors. And, in Carl Van Vechten's *Nigger Heaven* (1926), a white novelist so successfully portrayed blacks in urban New York that he called up the most violent pros and cons of the period, and to a certain extent set out the parameters within which all black novelists would be judged. A "blow in the face" to Du Bois, *Nigger Heaven* was "an absorbing story" to James Weldon Johnson; Gwendolyn Bennett coined "Van Vechtenizing around," to describe the ways in which tourists saw Harlem. As Hugh Gloster put it, no matter the negative criticism, the pull of the exotic exerted an influence hard to deny. It is in the grip of all these forces that Wallace Thurman, with William Jordan Rapp, produced ***Harlem*** (1929), a play dealing with life in the ghetto; ***The Blacker the Berry*** (1929), and ***Infants of the Spring*** (1932).

Wallace Thurman, "the most symbolic figure of the Literary Renaissance in Harlem," brilliant, consumptive, desperate, was the focal point for black Bohemia in the late 1920s.[1] The inner circle included Rudolph Fisher, M.D., writer, Langston Hughes, poet, and Zora Neale Hurston, novelist. They knew the great ones, W. E. B. Du Bois, James Weldon Johnson, Carl Van Vechten; and they knew the other Renaissance writers and critics, George Schuyler, Countee Cullen, Jean Toomer, Arna Bontemps, Alain Locke, Benjamin Brawley, and Charles S. Johnson. It was Du Bois, Locke and Brawley who contended that a true renaissance in black literature was in the making.[2] The inner circle wished it were true but had their doubts. Of them all, Thurman's desire to become "a *very* great writer like Gorki or Thomas Mann," said Langston Hughes, stuck out like a sore thumb. Unfortunately, the strong feeling that he was "merely a journalistic writer" made him melancholy, suicide-prone, and disillusioned;[3] his self-hatred engendered by his dark complexion, and his reliance on bad gin, were by-products of the despair which marked his decline and early death after a brilliant and promising career.[4]

Wallace Thurman was born in Salt Lake City, Utah in 1902. His very dark skin defined him as a black though he had an Indian grandmother who married a Jewish peddler. His friends describe him as his pictures present him—a dark-skinned man. After high school he attended the University of Utah for two terms (1919 to 1920) as a pre-medical student, and then the University of Southern California. After his years in California he arrived in New York City in 1925, at the inception of what Locke called "The New Negro" Movement. During his years in Los Angeles in the early 1920s he apparently read about Harlem, and even promoted it in his own magazine, *The Outlet.* In New York Thurman worked briefly for *The Looking-Glass* and then in 1926 became managing editor of *The Messenger,* a radical monthly, the voice of A. Philip Randolph and black socialism. Also in 1926 he helped found the short-lived little magazine, *Fire.*[5] In 1929 his first novel, ***The Blacker the Berry,*** came out; in 1929 he co-authored the play, ***Harlem,*** with William Rapp, editor of *True Story* magazine, and he also took on a job as a reader at Macauley's. Thurman also began publishing fiction and ghostwriting stories for *True Story.* In 1932 he became editor-in-chief at Macauley's, published his second novel, ***Infants in the Spring,*** and co-authored his third and last novel, ***The Interns,*** with Abraham L. Furman. He wrote articles for the *Independent, Bookman* and *The New Republic.* On December 11, 1934, he died of tuberculosis in a hospital ward, in Bellevue Hospital, according to one account, on Welfare Island, according to another.[6]

There is general consensus that it was Thurman's ability to read exceptionally fast as well as his perceptive critical abilities that led to his being hired at *The Messenger* in 1926 (and subsequently by Macauley's in 1929). That summer, with Hughes, Hurston, John P. Davis, Gwendolyn Bennett and the painter Aaron Douglas, he founded *Fire,* "a new experimental quarterly devoted to and published by younger Negro artists."[7] The magazine's overpowering drive, Hughes wrote in *The Big Sea,* was "to burn up a lot of the old, dead conventional Negro-white ideas of the past, *épater le bourgeois* into a realization of the existence of the younger Negro writers and artists, and provide us with an outlet for publication not available in the limited pages of the small Negro magazines then existing."[8]

Fire was a one-issue publication however. In it appeared Cullen's "From the Dark Tower," a story by Bruce Nugent that Hughes called "a green and purple story," and Thurman's **"Cordelia the Crude,"** a story of a young woman who "had not yet realized the moral import of her wanton promiscuity nor become mercenary," a girl of sixteen who by the end of the story was working, dancing, and drinking in a well-known whorehouse on 134th Street near Lenox Avenue. Benjamin Brawley said that *Fire's* "flame was so intense that it burnt itself up immediately;" after Du Bois and other writers in the black press castigated the journal it expired.[9] Unfortunately, Thurman, who had advanced most of the money for its publication, had to spend the next few years paying off the debt. Another short-lived journal that he founded two years later, *Harlem, a Forum of Negro Life,* also folded, after only two issues.[10]

These were turbulent years in Harlem. Locke's *The New Negro* brought together the talents of many of the writers. But Carl Van Vechten's *Nigger Heaven* reflected the context in which almost all these writers worked. In her column in *Opportunity,* Gwendolyn Bennett noted that by October, two months after publication, white sightseers, visitors and other strangers were said to be "Van Vechtenizing" in Harlem. "Intrigued by the primitivistic portrayal of the Negro in the book, whites from downtown and elsewhere temporarily neglected Greenwich Village to explore Harlem and enjoy the Negro." In fact, among the good reviews were those by Thurman, in the *Messenger,* September, 1926; Charles S. Johnson, in the *Pittsburgh Courier,* September 4, 1926; James Weldon Johnson, in *Opportunity,* October, 1926; and George Schuyler, also in the *Pittsburgh Courier,* November 6, 1926. Among the many dissenting views, Du Bois's argument is persuasive, according to which *Nigger Heaven* is "a blow in the face . . . an affront to the hospitality of black folk and to the intelligence of white," a caricature, a mass of half-truths, and "a hodgepodge of laboriously stated facts, quotations and expressions, illuminated here and there with something that comes near to being nothing but cheap melodrama."[11]

Although Van Vechten's emphasis on jazz, sex, atavism and primitivism was rejected in many quarters, his influence was profound. It is in this context that Wallace Thurman in 1929 published ***The Blacker the Berry,*** a study of interracial color prejudice operating upon Emma Lou Morgan, black daughter of a light-skinned mother whose family motto was "whiter and whiter every generation" until their grandchildren would be able to pass and race would no longer be a problem. Feeling the burden of blackness, as Wallace Thurman did, his character Emma Lou is further depressed when she learns that it was her color that forced the estrangement of her mother from her second husband. Leaving Boise, Idaho, as close as Thurman apparently could get in urban tone to Salt Lake City, Emma Lou attends the University of Southern California (also paralleling Thurman's career), and tries to get a job in Harlem. Denied employment because she is so dark, she falls in love with a mulatto-Filipino, Alva, but her obsession with color drives him off. After finishing college at the City College of New York she tries again to help Alva, who is now an alcoholic and burdened by an idiot child, and is again rejected. Emma Lou, seemingly an ordinary, normal person in every way, is apparently the victim of color prejudice, in both white *and* black America.[12]

Thurman, probably influenced by *Nigger Heaven* or by the prevailing disposition to portray Harlem in its most vivid colors, describes Harlem's cabaret life, the rent parties, speakeasies (this was during Prohibition), vaudeville shows and ballroom dances as they were. But his emphasis on sex, alcohol, dancing, and gambling makes the balance disappear. Even serious fictionalized discussions with Langston Hughes (Tony Crews) and Zora Neale Hurston (Cora Thurston) turn into reinforcements of the author's already apparently set opinions. During a discussion with Campbell Kitchen (clearly modeled on Carl Van Vechten), we read that it was Van Vechten who "first began the agitation in the higher places of journalism which gave impetus to the spiritual craze . . . It was he who sponsored most of the younger Negro writers, personally carrying their work to publishers and editors." In spite of Thurman's disinclination to give Du Bois, Locke, and Johnson credit for *their* pioneering work, it is true that Van Vechten can be credited with earnest spadework. Significantly, in his novel Thurman was most angry at those blacks who perpetuated discrimination against blacks, especially black women. The doggerel verse he quotes is eloquent testimony to that: "Yaller gal rides in a limousine; / Brownskin gal rides the train. / Black gal rides in an ol' oxcart, / But she gits there jes' the same."[13]

Thurman, contrary to the emerging literary style, made a dark-skinned girl his protagonist. Black, except for the followers of Marcus Garvey, did not become fashionable or popular until the 1960s. On the other hand in all fairness it has to be said that Thurman's point was that prejudice and racism existed within the black community, not that there was an inherent advantage in blackness. Given the growing belief that "white was right," as Mrs. Morgan put it, it was not surprising that Emma Lou's color led to her mother's rejection; in turn, following the practice of many dark-skinned women (and some men), Emma Lou used skin whiteners and hair straighteners and preferred light-skinned men. At the end, if one accepts the proviso that experience is the best teacher, Emma Lou has come to terms with her identity and her color.

Unfortunately, the title, taken from an old Negro folk saying, "The blacker the berry, the sweeter the juice," has to be taken ironically, bitterly. For the point has to be made, Emma Lou was too black, too conscious of her blackness; it had to dawn on her, as it did on Thurman eventually, that the fault lay only partially in her color. As Thurman put it, "what she needed to do now was to accept her black skin as being real and unchangeable, to realize that certain things were, and would be, and with this in mind, begin life anew, always fighting, not so much for acceptance by other people but for acceptance of herself." But this also seems to mean that ***The Blacker the Berry,*** while inspired by a man's talent and commitment, failed because it lacked subtlety and complexity.[14]

In his second novel, ***Infants in the Spring,*** the focus is on Niggeratti ("Nigger" plus "literati") Manor, a huge residence cut up into studios for black artists and writers. Actually both blacks and whites live there, most of them unproductive, along with their retinues. Raymond Taylor, a talented writer hampered by his excessive race consciousness, Samuel Carter, a white militant desiring martyrdom, Eustace Savoy, a black singer hesitant about singing Negro spirituals, Pelham Gaylord, a painter and poet of little talent, Paul Arbian, a black, dissipated, homosexual painter, and Stephen Jorgenson, a white obsessed with, then repelled by, black women and primitivistic Harlem, make up the cast. Unfortunately, as Thurman's Taylor puts it, except for Jean Toomer, "the average Negro intellectual and artist has no goal, no standards, no elasticity, no pregnant germ plasm."[15] On the other hand, when the avowed brains and talent of the Negro Renaissance are brought together, their substantive essence is lost in the heat of a socio-political debate over Pan-Africanism, activism or personal self-expression. In common with Langston Hughes's words in "The Negro Artist and the Racial Mountain," whose views he would surely have known, Thurman opted for individuality. "Let each seek his own salvation." Similarly, in accord with Shakespeare's *Hamlet,* that "The canker galls the infants of the spring / Too oft before their buttons be disclosed," Thurman castigated Renaissance artists' and writers' exploitation of the whites from downtown who supported the Renaissance so long as it could remain Niggeratti Manor. In the most sarcastic tones, one of his black characters says, "Being a Negro writer in these days is a racket and I'm going to make the most of it while it lasts."[16]

Thurman was one of the fledgeling writers of the Renaissance. As a character like Raymond Taylor he could imaginatively interact with, and comment on, the personalities integral to the times. Knowing that "The American Negro . . . was entering a new phase in his development," that he "was about to become an important factor in the artistic life of the United States," Raymond still clung to the belief that unless he, or Paul, or others "began to do something worth while, there would be little chance of their being permanently established." The point is that among the emotional arguments, in the midst of the calls for a turn or return to "pagan inheritance," or "Marxism," it is Thurman's balanced view that we admire today. Answering Dr. Parkes (who reflects Alain Locke), the noted college professor who calls for a return to Africa to resurrect "our pagan heritage," as well as Fenderson, who complains about everything, and Madison, who uses Lenin as his role-model, Cedric (Eric Walrond), backed up by Raymond (Thurman), heatedly comments: "Well . . . why not let each young hopeful choose his own path? Only in that way will anything at all be achieved?"[17]

Thurman, brooding and magnetic, to a significant degree ridiculed the Renaissance of which he was part. While he was at the center of this movement, he denounced the quality of the literature because it laid at best a shaky foundation for the future. He looked for reasons within himself and the race. "That ninety-nine and ninety-nine hundredths per cent of the Negro race is patently possessed and motivated by an inferiority complex," he wrote, is a central cause. That he had the talent but not the greatness of theme and expression so needed was another. Given such rationales, not trying was an escape. Yet, as he expressed it in ***The Blacker the Berry,*** he also wrote it in ***Infants in the Spring,*** and this must be accepted as vintage Thurman: "Individuality is what we strive for. Let each seek his own salvation."[18]

In Thurman's vision the Renaissance was doomed to fail. "At first glance," it is affirmed at the end of ***Infants,*** "it could be ascertained that the skyscraper [Niggeratti Manor] would soon crumble and fall, leaving the dominating white lights in full possession of the sky." Given this assumption, Thurman felt that black writers should not be propagandists but writers, that they should not be race writers. It is not surprising that his persona, Raymond, is told that "race to you means nothing. You stand on a peak. . . . Propaganda you despise. Illusions about Negroes you have none." Nor is it surprising that shortly after ***Infants*** was published, Thurman, emancipated from everything but himself, liquor, T.B., and despair, died.[19]

Thurman's inclinations were correct. It was important to foster good writing, to reward excellence and talent. His major fault flowed from his intense self-hatred, self-doubt, and a penchant for criticism above fiction. He knew that, in the 1920s, to be successful he would have to patronize the white audience that bought the books and trekked uptown; he also knew that he wanted to write honestly, as Rudolph Fisher had done, of black Harlem as a black man, because he was black, and for blacks. In **"Cordelia the Crude"** he drew a character who represented an honest portrayal of Negro life; at the same time he undoubtedly recognized the difficulties he faced in hanging the dirty wash out to dry, for all to see. "It makes no difference if this element of their life is of incontestable value to the sincere artist. It is also available and of incontestable value to the insincere artists and prejudiced white critics."[20]

Thurman, Robert Bone has written, was the aspiring undertaker of the Negro Renaissance. Consistent with Countee Cullen's advice that the job of the Negro writer was "to create types that are truly representative of us as a people," he tried to remain true to himself; but he misused satire, he paraded his pet hates and he was, finally, too heavy-handed in his writing. On the other side, driven by his anger, his sense of rejection, his consciousness of color, and the realization that there was no resolution in sight, he ended ***Infants*** on a positive note. Although Paul slashed his wrists with a Chinese dirk, Thurman's forced ending concluded that art would be produced by individuals of talent who were willing to work hard with the self-consciousness that defied crippling doubt.[21]

Thurman undeniably was a writer of power and talent. An insider in the Harlem literary circles, he was even referred to as one of the central pivots of the Harlem Renaissance. Yet when Thurman is weighed as a writer, it is certain that he will be found wanting. Unable to control the rich literary material with which he worked, he consistently imposed a morbid look on his characters and developed stories and novels so atomized that he ultimately wound up at cross purposes with himself. His irony was well placed, whether in **"Cordelia the Crude"** in *Fire,* 1 (November 1926), or in ***Harlem*** (1929). In the latter work, a simple Southern mother seeing her family torn apart by the vagaries of Harlem, by the "sweetback" of the "hot-stuff man," by lotteries and vice, by the necessity of having rent parties, is helpless to intervene; religion and family are her refuge of last resort. Cordelia, caught up in the wild life of the city, is almost destroyed by poverty and the city. It was a startlingly realistic drama. It was also a very successful, overly melodramatic play about the harshness of life and black disillusionment. In Edith Isaacs's opinion, "Violent and undisciplined as the play was, it left a sense of photographic reality."[22]

In the same way, Thurman's talent burst out in ***The Blacker the Berry*** and ***Infants of the Spring.*** In debunking the "Negro Renaissance," in parading his pessimism, Thurman exemplified how strongly he felt about the enduring quality of the literature of the Harlem writers. He believed, as one of his characters phrased it in ***Infants of the Spring,*** "Being a Negro writer in these days is a racket, and I'm going to make the most of it while it lasts." No wonder Langston Hughes described him as having a prodigious capacity for gin, though he detested it; no wonder Hughes wrote that Thurman liked being a Negro but thought it a great handicap.[23] Most significantly, as a very dark-skinned black man who met discrimination everywhere, he set out to record honestly and realistically black life in Harlem, but wound up compromising his principles. As Margaret Perry says, "he usually settled for capitalizing on its exotic-erotic elements in order to succeed." Unhappy when forced to be with blacks, rejected so often when with whites, he wrote "I was fighting hard to refrain from regarding myself as martyr and an outcast." Yet it was both the martyr and outcast that dominated the content and the style of his writing. In the end he exhausted himself trying to please the public while at the same time trying to write with a New Negro honesty. It is entirely appropriate that ***Infants,*** a neurotic novel in which he brooded introspectively on the "failure" of the Harlem Renaissance, derives its title and theme from Laertes' advice to Ophelia:

> The canker galls the infants of the spring
> Too oft before their buttons be disclosed,
> And in the morn and liquid dew of youth
> Contagious blastments are most imminent.

Thurman's pessimism dominates his satire. The cancer that gnawed at his vitals, the cancer of Bohemianism, was a combination of color, caste and dilettantism. If he had the talent, his heavy-handedness, mixed with equal parts of disillusion and despair, of himself and the alleged achievements of the 1920s, overcame his native ability. "The most self-conscious of the New Negroes," writes Robert Bone, "he ultimately turned his critical insight against himself and the wider movement with which he identified."[24] Wanting to be a very great writer, he seems to have known he was merely a journalist. Melancholy, suicide-prone, he tried to say but ended up shouting that phoniness in the Harlem Renaissance was rampant even as he insisted, with Emersonian firmness, that capitulation to badges and names, to large societies, and dead institutions must give way to the free and individual spirit. Where he meant to write fiction, he wrote criticism; he wrote didactically. He failed, but he failed magnificently.

In December 1934, both Rudolph Fisher and Wallace Thurman died. In Dorothy West's eyes, years after the event, Thurman's death "was the first break in the ranks of the New Negro." Ironically, Thurman, who liked to drink gin, but *didn't* like to drink gin, died of T.B. in the charity ward of City Hospital, Welfare Island, New York. He would like to have believed, as he put it in ***The Blacker the Berry,*** that everyone must find salvation within one's self, that no one in life need be a total misfit, but he could not totally break with his sense of gloom and despair and rejection and self-abnegation. In terms of his literary contributions, he was one of the significant but less than major figures of the Renaissance. However, to quote Mae Gwendolyn Henderson, "His significance, . . . far exceeds the work he left behind. Not only was he tremendously influential upon the younger and perhaps more successful writers of the period, but his life itself became a symbol of the New Negro Movement."[25]

Notes

1. Dorothy West, "Elephant's Dance," *Black World,* 20 (December, 1970), 85.
2. S. P. Fullinwider, *The Mind and Mood of Black America* (Homewood, Illinois: Dorsey, 1969), 132-133.
3. Arthur P. Davis, *From the Dark Tower* (Howard University Press, 1974), 109; also see Fullinwider, 154-155, and letters from Thurman to Jordan Rapp, 1929, in James Weldon Johnson Collection, Yale University.
4. Robert Bone, *The Negro Novel in America* (Yale University Press, 1958), 92-93.
5. Ernest Boynton, Jr., "Wallace Thurman," in Rayford Logan, ed., *Dictionary of American Negro Biography* (New York: Norton, 1982), 590-592.
6. Boynton; also see Davis, 109.
7. Wallace Thurman, "Negro Artists and the Negro," *New Republic* 31 (August 31, 1927), 37-39.
8. Quoted in Hugh M. Gloster, *Negro Voices in American Fiction* (New York: Russell and Russell, 1965), 114.
9. *Fire,* 1 (December, 1926); Benjamin Brawley, *The Negro Genius* (New York: Dodd, Mead, 1937), 135.
10. Boynton, 591.
11. Gloster, 160; W. E. B. Du Bois, "Criteria of Negro Art," *Crisis,* 33 (October, 1926), 290-297.
12. *The Blacker the Berry* ([1929] New York: Collier, 1970), 12, 21; Gloster, 168-169.
13. *Blacker the Berry,* 192, 179.
14. Fullinwider, 156; *Blacker the Berry,* 256-257, 221, 226.
15. *Infants in the Spring* (New York: Macaulay, 1932), 221, 144; Gloster, 170.
16. Gloster, 171; *Infants,* 240, 230.
17. *Infants,* 61-62, 236-240.
18. *Infants,* 140, 240; Thurman to Jordan Rapp, August 1, 1929, Johnson Papers.
19. *Infants,* 284, 143.
20. Doris Abramson, *Negro Playwrights in the American Theatre 1925-1959* (New York: Columbia University, 1969), 41.
21. Bone, 93; Countee Cullen, "The Negro in Art," *Crisis,* 32 (August, 1926), 193; Margaret Perry, *Silence to the Drums* (Westport, Conn.; Greenwood, 1976), 92-93; Nathan Huggins, *Harlem Renaissance* (New York: Oxford University Press, 1973), 243.
22. Edith Isaacs, *The Negro in the American Theatre* (New York: Theatre Arts, 1947), 86.
23. Thurman, *Infants,* 230; also see Langston Hughes, *The Big Sea* (New York: Knopf, 1940), 235-239.
24. Bone, *The Negro Novel,* 94
25. West, "Elephant's Dance," 85.

DANIEL E. WALKER (ESSAY DATE 1998)

SOURCE: Walker, Daniel E. "Exploding the Canon: A Re-examination of Wallace Thurman's Assault on the Harlem Renaissance." *Western Journal of Black Studies* 22, no. 3 (1998): 153-58.

In the following essay, Walker argues that Thurman's role as the ideological leader of the younger set of Harlem Renaissance artists has been overlooked.

Many scholars misconstrue Thurman and his contributions to the Harlem Renaissance because they concentrate their inquiries on his characterization in Langston Hughes' autobiography *The Big Sea.* Hughes described Thurman as a "strangely brilliant black boy" who "wanted to be a great writer, but none of his own work ever made him happy" (234). To deal with his own shortcomings and depression Thurman, in Hughes view, "contented himself by writing a great deal for money . . . drinking more and more gin, and then threatening to jump out of windows at people's parties and kill himself" (235). When coupled with ***Interne*** and ***Infants of the Spring,*** Thurman's two depressing last novels, Hughes' depiction highlights the cynicism and despair which were so much a part of the young genius' last years. But, if one looks closely at Wallace Thurman's creative production of the 1920's, the heart of the Harlem Renaissance, another image presents itself.

Prior to his arrival in New York, Thurman wrote a column called "Inklings" in a local Los Angeles newspaper. In an effort to jump start a Negro Renaissance on the West Coast he even published and personally financed a magazine, *The Outlet,* for almost half a year (Henderson 149). At this point in his life, he was not the depressed cynic so often alluded to in historical interpretations. Rather, he was a young man who was so impressed by Jean Toomer's *Cane* and the literary ferment of Harlem, that he dedicated his life to fulfilling the promise which these opportunities engendered. Simply hearing that H. L. Mencken, Fannie Hurst, and Carl Van Vechten were discussing literature with Black artists no older than himself caused him to get excited and "to feel inspired" (West 77-78).

Thurman came to Harlem on Labor Day 1925 in hopes of finding the "New Negro" (Henderson 147). Commenting on his arrival, he explained, "I lived out in Los Angeles . . . and I heard about the 'new negro' but I didn't see any signs of him on the Pacific Coast. I tried to be a movement all by myself . . . Then I began to think about Harlem for that seemed to be the home of this 'new negro' and soon after I graduated from the University of Southern California I came here" (Hicks 10). During his initial years in Harlem, Thurman was the epitome of youthful exuberance and idealism. His demeanor was that of an individual who felt an extreme level of optimism towards the opportunities and responsibilities which the Harlem Renaissance presented for young Black artists. As his good friend Dorothy West noted, "he wanted to get in on the ground floor and not get off the crowded lift until it banged the roof off and skyrocketed him . . . to the stars" (77).

When Thurman did not find the creative space he had envisioned in Harlem, his idealism drove him to create it. On one side, he confronted a White literary community so consumed with sycophantic praise that it could neither distinguish quality art, nor adequately promote it. On the other, he faced a Black establishment which he saw as overly sensitive, elitist, and mired in the maintenance of a social hierarchy based on skin color. Given this context, a person exhibiting the pessimism and defeatism normally associated with Thurman would have simply packed his bags and gone back to his Post Office job in California. Having exposed Harlem's facade, he would have confirmed his cynical view of the world and could have lived out the rest of his life spouting sarcastic anecdotal remembrances about "the real" New Negro. Instead, Thurman attempted to recreate the world in his own image. Even though he was only twenty-five when he arrived in Harlem, Thurman accepted the mantle of leadership which he felt W. E. B. DuBois and Alain Locke, part of the Renaissance's old guard, had been ill-equipped to handle. When asked to speak to the role of the Black establishment in the movement he replied, "We laugh at them. They don't help us very much and we feel we've done more in five or six years than they have accomplished in a generation" (Hicks 10). This type of bravado exemplified the Thurman that Hughes, Zora Neale Hurston, and others gravitated towards. As West once said, "his sycophants were legion" (West 77).

Primary to Thurman's attempt to create his ideal space was an attack on the forces he believed were limiting it. In one editorial after another, he lashed out at both the Black and White literary communities. This venom was not, as many have characterized it, the product of unbridled pessimism. Instead Thurman's words were meant to inspire these communities to advocate higher standards for themselves and the younger Black artists who looked to them for guidance. He argued that it was:

> Too bad that the ballyhoo brigade which fostered the so-called negro art 'renaissance' has chosen to cheer and encourage indiscriminately anything which claims a negroid ancestry or kinship . . . Speaking purely of the arts the results have been

> sad rather than satisfactory, in that critical standards have been ignored and that the measure of achievement has been racial rather than literary . . . the negro will not be benefited by mediocre and ephemeral works, even if they are hailed by well meaning, but for the moment, simple-minded, white critics as works of genius.
>
> (**"Nephews,"** 296)

Thurman was one of the only figures of the Harlem Renaissance who argued that Black art should always exhibit a universal obligation to high standards. To him it was not enough just to be a Black artist—one had to be a competent Black artist. He asserted that his group, which included the likes of Hughes, Hurston, Aaron Douglas and Countee Cullen, did not "want to be recognized by faddist just because we are negroes. We want to do solid work and we're ready to wait until we're able to create something of value" (Hicks 10).

Thurman's insistence on quality was not just dogma, but a critical standard which he applied to all literary works. It is in his critiques that some of the most evenhanded evaluations of Harlem Renaissance literature come forth. They are not jaded by the "feel good" spirit of the period, nor are they obscured by historical reflections of a cherished, yet bygone era. Thurman believed that Claude McKay really had "something to say," but that "his message was too alive and too big for the form he chose" (**"Negro Poets"** 559). In Cullen he saw an "extraordinary ear for music, a most extensive and dexterous knowledge of words and their values, and an enviable understanding of conventional poetic forms" (**"Negro Poets"** 559). What Cullen lacked, in Thurman's view, was "originality of theme and treatment, and the contact with life necessary to have had actual, rather than vicarious, emotional experiences" (**"Nephews"** 298). While Thurman hailed Hughes' works for their depictions of common subjects, he also felt that he had "written too much" and seemed to lack "that discriminating sense of selection which makes the complete artist as critical as he is creative" (**"Nephews"** 297).

Thurman always believed that artistic concerns outweighed those of the political, social, or personal nature. This posture put him at odds with Harlem's old guard, most notably DuBois and Locke, but also Charles S. Johnson, the editor of the Urban League's *Opportunity* magazine. These individuals envisioned an artistic movement which gave credence to their social agenda. They wanted to prove to White society that they were equal by exhibiting equality in the field of Arts and Letters. In reality, they often praised mediocre works based on the images they presented, instead of on the manner in which they presented these images. Within this context, DuBois and Locke debated the utility of artistic expression and began to solidify the canonical walls which Thurman worked so hard to break down.

In his initial review of *The New Negro,* DuBois provided the counter argument to Locke's classic proposition that beauty should be the motivating factor behind all artistic endeavors (1926, "Our Book Shelf" 140-141). Locke asserted that by favoring propaganda, which was DuBois' focus, Blacks accepted the inferior status accorded to them by Whites because their efforts continually made mention of their need to be freed from second-class status (Art or Propaganda 312-313). He reasoned that a movement free of propaganda was the more mature way for those concerned with race relations to proceed. DuBois, on the other hand, cringed at the mere thought of anyone seeking to present art devoid of its social or political realities. He argued that "all art is propaganda" and that he "did not care a damn for any art that is not used for propaganda" (Criteria 296).

Although Locke did not advocate an overtly political brand of art, he did want the products of the Renaissance to transcend the boundaries of the humanities. Instead of championing "art for art's sake," he sought art which served as White America's bridge into the Negro world. It was not art devoid of race. On the contrary, Locke's vision of art attempted to define exactly what racial art, in this case Negro art, was.[1] Thurman saw neither of these views as appropriate in an era supposedly characterized by the Negro's "new" approach to art. In many respects Locke and DuBois helped to create the Wallace Thurman who repeatedly characterized himself as their antithesis.

While Thurman held true disgust for the promotion of art as propaganda, he also did not believe in the categorization of art as a racial production. He believed that native creative expression, even that which focused solely on Blacks, was still an American expression. Thurman insisted that Black production "in the field of letters must be listed as American literature, just as the works of the Scotchman Burns or the Irishman Synge are listed as English literature" (**"Nephews"** 297). While he did not believe that Black art should be judged by a separate criteria than that of Whites, he did posit that, due to different historical experiences, "there is bound to be a negro note but not a negro art" (Hicks 11). Thus Blacks could write or paint about different subjects, but the presentation of these subjects was still specifically American.

Thurman's insistence that the artistic works of Blacks be characterized as American Art should not be misconstrued. He was not one of those artists which Hughes complained about in his Renaissance manifesto "The Negro Artist and the Racial Mountain." Instead of clamoring "I want to be a poet—not a Negro poet" (Hughes, Negro Artist 305), Thurman sought to "break down the desire, which seems to be growing within the race, not to be a negro" (Hicks 11). He encouraged Black writers to explore more deeply the myriad of artistic resources available to them in their own culture. He argued that "there is, if he has the talent, just as much a chance for the negro author to produce great literature by writing of his own people" (**"Nephews"** 297). Within Black America, Thurman asserted that the experiences and expressions of common people held more artistic value than those of middle class society. In **"Harlem Facets,"** a 1927 editorial, he harangued the Black establishment for its imposed prohibitions on the traditional church. He lamented that:

> The old frame structures in which the sisters and brothers would moan and shout with the spirit while ministerial emotionalists would shake the house with sermons on Heaven, Hell, salvation and eternal damnation have given way to stately ecclesiastical edifices in which pentacostalism is frowned upon, and . . . Sister Susan Brown from Shiloh Baptist Church in Birmingham is now admonished . . . to keep quiet during the services . . . her 'amens' and 'preach it brothers' disturb those around her.
>
> (467)

Thurman's contempt for Negro high society was legendary. West put it more bluntly when she asserted, "he hated Negro society, and since dark skins were never the fashion among Negro upper classes, this feeling was occasionally mutual" (79). This contempt formed the basis of many of Thurman's analysis, but, in itself, it does not lead automatically to the consistent portrayal of Thurman as an individual consumed by this vision of reality. Just as DuBois and Marcus Garvey held dissimilar, yet highly critical, views of specific segments of the Black population, these interpretations did not mean that their entire worldview was defined by them. Like Garvey and DuBois, Thurman could write about a subject extensively and yet also see beyond his own specific circumstance. His most famous work, ***The Blacker the Berry,*** epitomizes this ability.

Although ***The Blacker the Berry*** is often read as Thurman's autobiographical treatise on intra-racial prejudice, which part of it is, it is also an indictment of Negro society and a specific analysis of the unique position, or lack thereof, of the dark-skinned Black woman within that society. Throughout the work, the protagonist, Emma Lou, is subjected to countless abuses because of her rather dark complexion. In efforts to free herself from this torture, she often resorts to drastic means, even chewing arsenic wafers, in an attempt to lighten her skin. While most scholars have been able to recognize ***The Blacker the Berry***'s overt plot designs, Emma Lou's rather numerous expressions of class-based prejudice often go overlooked. She always desires "those people who really mattered, northerners like herself or superior southerners . . . who were different from whites only so far as their skin color was concerned" (36). No matter where she establishes herself, she continually searches for the "right sort of people" (126). Thus Thurman is not only expressing his disgust with the pigmentocracy which characterized the period, but also the elitism and social posturing that goes along with any form of social hierarchy.

Although Thurman was concerned with color prejudice in general, his decision to make ***The Blacker the Berry***'s protagonist a female exposed the little mentioned, but rather obvious, exclusion of dark-skinned women from middle class society and correspondingly the Harlem Renaissance. It must be noted that throughout Thurman's work there is a constant admonishment that if Emma Lou had been a boy, "then color of skin wouldn't have mattered" (4). This difference in opportunity, predicated on sexual difference, spoke to Thurman's reality. Although he was very dark, and suffered his share of insults and innuendos, his position as a male in a sexist society offered him considerably more advantages than a dark-skinned woman. He had graduated from a prestigious private university, been accepted by Harlem's best young minds, and would later become the first Black editor of a major publishing house. Unlike many of his Renaissance counterparts, he was rarely unemployed and in a very short period of time published three separate magazines, became the first African American to pen a Broadway hit, and succeeded in having two screenplays made into Hollywood movies. Moreover, he could look to the likes of Rudolph Fisher, Claude McKay, and Aaron Douglass, who were all very successful dark-skinned men, and realize that the pigmentocracy's blade had a much sharper edge when it came to gender.

Thurman did not create Emma Lou simply to blast Negro society for its ill treatment of him.[2] He wrote ***The Blacker the Berry*** to illustrate the segment most forgotten in Black America's coming of age, the dark-skinned black woman. Scouring the pages of the extensive literary output of the period, one is hard-pressed to find a positive portrayal of a woman who shared Thurman's skin tone. Throughout the literature there exists a preoccupation with light-skinned women and the issue of passing. The darkest women are always some man's last choice for a mate or the embodiment of loose morals, most exemplified in the characterization of the Blues singer. This characterization was the logical outgrowth of a social system that placed a premium on light skin. It was the artistic expression of what was at the time a social reality.

Even after Thurman brought the question of intraracial color prejudice to the fore, critics sought to diffuse the potency of ***The Blacker the Berry*** by either indicting the author or by finding fault in Emma Lou. DuBois even accused Thurman of hating his own race. He argued that the author who could effectively analyze this issue "must believe in black folk, and in the beauty of black as a color of human skin" and that it "does not seem . . . that this is true of Wallace Thurman" (1929, "Our Book Shelf" 248-50). Other treatments of ***The Blacker the Berry*** likewise characterize Emma Lou as the epitome of a woman who hates herself because she is Black. Both of these interpretations divert attention away from an examination of the Renaissance's social hierarchy. In reality it was Negro society and its disdain for dark skin, especially when it donned the face of a woman, which forced Thurman to create Emma Lou. She was the victim of a system which hated Black skin. She was not the pigmentocracy's creator, nor was she or Thurman in a position to gain from its continuance. As Gerald Haslam writes, "perhaps the fact that he [Thurman] openly discussed tabooed problems of color made it inevitable that some critics would read psychopathological reversals into his motives" (58). Because of this misreading, ***The Blacker the Berry*** still has yet to be utilized as a tool to seriously analyze the peculiar position of dark-skinned women in the Harlem Renaissance.

Like ***The Blacker the Berry,*** all of Thurman's early works sought to infuse the New Negro movement with artistic integrity and purpose. The journal *Fire!!* epitomized this endeavor, while also underscoring Thurman's early idealism and resolve. One must remember that *Fire!!* was not Thurman's first or last attempt at self publication. Before *Fire!!* Thurman published *The Outlet* in Los Angeles and after it *Harlem, A Journal of Negro Life.* These continued attempts at independent publishing are another facet of Thurman's life that do not fit his characterization as an individual fraught with depression and cynicism. Skeptics do not continually engage in risk-taking behavior. If they do, failure at that attempt usually precludes a successive try. In the case of Thurman, at least in the 1920's, it seems as though he never stayed mired in his defeat long because some new challenge was always on the horizon. When asked specifically about *The Outlet,* he replied, "of course, it failed up, but I had a lot of fun doing it" (Hicks 10).

Even though *Fire!!* was overwhelmed with debt, it seems that Thurman also had fun creating it. The magazine utilized the services of Harlem's talented brigade of young artists taken in by Thurman's drive and vision. His leadership of *Fire!!* was in itself a testament to his personal attraction. At the time of its development, Thurman had no real recognition as an artist. While the others associated with the magazine, including Cullen, Hughes, and even Hurston, had won *Opportunity* literary contests or published collections of their works, Thurman's accomplishments in 1926 were much more personal than public. Although he was the interim editor of the *Messenger,* his status was in no way equal to his cohorts, especially Hughes and Cullen. Undoubtedly something dynamic in Thurman's personality, coupled with the rest of the group's naivete regarding publishing, caused them to follow him into this literary inferno.

Fire!! was much more than just a futile attempt at artistic independence. It provided Thurman with the opportunity to make a decisive change in the direction of the Renaissance. As editor, he eschewed prohibitions regarding subject matter, promoted excellence, and attacked the establishment that he and the others felt was stifling their creativity. *Fire!!* contained short stories about homosexuality, prostitution, and murder. It presented images which relied on folk-culture, mythic beliefs, and a strong defense of artistic freedom. It was finally what Thurman envisioned the Renaissance to be—an uncensored forum for creative expression bounded only by a high regard for artistic excellence. He called it "a revolt against the conventional type of contemporary magazine, pulsing with propaganda but devoid of art" (Hicks 10).

In *Fire!!* each artist was allowed the creative flexibility to experiment with subject and form. Richard Bruce's "Smoke, Lilies, and Jade," defied traditional structure in portraying its protagonist's somewhat hallucinatory, bisexual love triangle (33-40). Hurston's "Sweat" broke from the genteel school of Harlem Renaissance writing by presenting Southern subjects who worked in common trades, abused their women, spoke in vulgar tones, and relied on a specifically folk sense of justice (40-44). It also provided one more experimental avenue for the mythical aesthetic that shaped her seminal work *Their Eyes Were Watching God* (1937). Thurman contributed **"Cordelia the Crude,"** the story of a corruptible Southern girl in New York City who was, by all assessments, "physically, if not mentally . . . a potential prostitute" (5). **"Cordelia"** was an extreme departure from the Black establishment's desired canon and later formed the basis of Thurman's hit musical play, ***Harlem.*** All this made *Fire!!* one of the only forums during the Harlem Renaissance which truly lived up to its professed goal, "to burn up a lot of the old, dead conventional Negro-white ideas of the past" (*The Big Sea,* 235).

Even though *Fire!!* and its successor *Harlem* were short-lived, when coupled with Thurman's other productions of the 1920's, these works speak of an individual who made a definite impression on the literary scene. His contributions broke the monopoly on creative space held by the traditional White and Black publications. They provided the younger group of artists with the experience of controlling the presentation of their literary expression. More than anything, because of Thurman's high standards and creative flexibility, these works provided the note of Black self-analysis that would be heard by generations of artists who followed. In their pages one can see the beginnings of the creative space later occupied by the likes of Toni Morrison, James Baldwin, Alice Walker, Ishmael Reed and a host of other significant authors whose works go beyond affirming Black America's desire to present itself, in Thurman's words, "butter side up" to the outside world (Negro Artists 38).

Wallace Thurman's contributions to the Harlem Renaissance are much greater than his role as the period's ultimate tragedy. During his creative explosion of the twenties, Harlem's best made him their center of attention. Dorothy West believed that "perhaps if Harlem had produced a dozen contemporary minds as keen as his . . . something better might have come out of that period than the hysterical hosannas that faded on the subsequently silly night" (77). Arna Bontemps contended that Thurman was "a flame which burned so intensely, it could not last for long" (Henderson 147). Given the high regard with which his contemporaries held him, present-day scholars should begin to recast Wallace Thurman in a light equal to that which he gave to the Harlem Renaissance.

Notes

1. Locke's "Review of The Weary Blues, By Langston Hughes." (*Palms.* Oct. 1926: 24-26.) and "Sterling Brown: The New Negro-Folk-Poet." (*Voices of the Harlem Renaissance.* Ed. Nathan Huggins. New York: Oxford University Press, 1976. 251-255.). are better examples of his practical treatment of art than are his idealistic editorials.
2. Lewis states emphatically that "Emma Lou was Wallace Thurman" (237).

References

Bruce, Richard. (1926). "Smoke, Lilies, and Jade." *Fire!!.* 1:33-40.

DuBois, W. E. B. (1926). "Criteria of Negro Art." *Crisis.* 296.

———. (1926). "Our Book Shelf." *Crisis.* 140-141.

———. (1926). "Our Book Shelf." *Crisis.* 248-50.

Haslam, Gerald. (1968). "Wallace Thurman: A Western Renaissance Man." *Western American Literature.* 6:58.

Henderson, Mae Gwendolyn. (1970). "Portrait of Wallace Thurman." *The Harlem Renaissance Remembered.* (Ed.) Arna Bontemps. New York: Dodd, Mead and Company, 147-170.

Hicks, Granville. (1927). "The New Negro: An Interview with Wallace Thurman." *The Churchman.* 30:10-11.

Hughes, Langston. (1940). *The Big Sea.* New York: Alfred A. Knopf.

———. (1976). "The Negro Artist and the Racial Mountain." *Voices of the Harlem Renaissance.* (Ed.) Nathan Huggins. New York: Oxford University Press, 305-309.

Hurston, Zora Neale. (1926). "Sweat." *Fire!!.* 1:40-44.

———. (1937). *Their Eyes Were Watching God.* Philadelphia: Lippincott.

Locke, Alain. (1976). "Art or Propaganda." *Voices of the Harlem Renaissance.* (Ed.) Nathan Huggins. New York: Oxford University Press, 312.

Thurman, Wallace. (1970). *The Blacker the Berry.* 2nd ed. New York: McMillan Publishing.

———. (1926). Cordelia the Crude. *Fire!!.* 1:5-7.

———. (1927). "Harlem Facets." *World Tomorrow.* 465-467.

———. (1932). *Infants of the Spring.* New York: Macaulay.

———. (1932). *Interne.* With A. L. Furman. New York: Macaulay.

———. (1928). "Negro Poets and Their Poetry." *Bookman.* 67:559.

———. (1927). "Nephews of Uncle Remus." *Independent.* 24:296.

Toomer, Jean. (1923). *Cane.* New York: Boni & Liveright.

West, Dorothy. (1970). "Elephant's Dance: A Memoir of Wallace Thurman." *Black World.* 77-85.

TITLE COMMENTARY

The Blacker the Berry

THE NEW YORK TIMES (REVIEW DATE 1929)

SOURCE: "Latest Works of Fiction: *The Blacker the Berry.*" *The New York Times* (17 March 1929): 6.

In the following review, the critic finds Thurman's novel to be little more than a competent effort.

This novel of Harlem [***The Blacker the Berry***] and the problem of color distinctions within the black world derives its chief interest from the fact that Mr. Thurman is a negro. Better novels of negro life have been written before, and written, ironically enough, by white people. If one excludes the question of authorship, ***The Blacker the Berry*** stands out as a merely competent, somewhat amorphous story. For rhythm and pungency, Claude McKay's *Home to Harlem*—the work of a West Indian negro—still remains at the crest.

There are no passages in ***The Blacker the Berry*** to indicate that Mr. Thurman is out to astound people. He makes no effort to display the swiftly acquired erudition of a [Carl] Van Vechten, but sticks to his main thesis. That thesis is the conflict a "coal-black nigger" is subjected to now that color prejudice has crossed the line into the black belts. . . .

Mr. Thurman takes [the main character, Emma Lou,] through three unhappy years of college in Los Angeles, where she was looked upon askance by the light-hued negroes of the Greek letter society. . . . He takes her to Harlem, where she shows a deplorable lack of will and a deplorable amount of self-commiseration. Sensitive beyond the point of other coal-blacks, she lets every reference to color scrape her nerves. . . .

[This] might have made a poignant story. As it is, Mr. Thurman writes prose in imitation of the white "genteel" tradition without ever making you certain that he is composing his novel from within the vantage point of Emma Lou's "genteel" brain. He gives the effect of objectivity where subjectivity is demanded, chiefly because he reports where he should be dramatizing the world as it appeared to Emma Lou.

KASSAHUN CHECOLE (REVIEW DATE 1981)

SOURCE: Checole, Kassahun. Review of *The Blacker the Berry. Journal of Black Studies* 12, no. 1 (September 1981): 117-20.

In the following review, Checole finds that Thurman's rendering of his protagonist's life in The Blacker the Berry, *provides insights that continue to have relevance.*

Wallace Thurman's novel, ***The Blacker the Berry*** . . . , is now in its second edition with Collier Books, a subsidiary of the Macmillan Company. However, the publishers have seen no reason for changing their original sales pitch. ***The Blacker the Berry*** . . . is characterized as a lost classic in the annals of American Negro literature, a fictional work that "vividly exemplies the Negro self-hate."

That Thurman's seminal work can continue to be described as such indicates perhaps the laxity of American sociology in its failure to deal concretely with the social implications of the dynamics of the race/class question or race relations, improperly so-called.

The Blacker the Berry . . . is an exciting, frank, and timeless novel about the social-psychological framework of the Black community in the 1920s. It says much about the self-hate of "Negroes," but self-hate is not Thurman's sole preoccupation. In fact, novelist Thurman functions as an astute sociologist and provides us with a clear picture of the socioeconomic basis of oppression, as well as the ideological, psychological, and political mystifications that shroud it. The novel presents a view of the American socialization process, which results in the internalization of the perspectives of the oppressors by the oppressed.

Thurman, a writer of the Harlem renaissance period, who died in 1934, was himself a product of this same socialization process. He was born in 1902, a historical juncture in the history of the African-American migrational episode to the urban South and the North. In ***The Blacker the Berry*** . . . , the migration of large numbers of African-Americans into Northern urban centers in search of better conditions of life, freedom from the burden of the slave past and Jim Crow, and a quest for equality and "manhood," is woven around the life and times of one young woman, Emma Lou Morgan.

Thurman could not have chosen and constructed a better subject. As the story unfolds, we learn that Emma Lou is representative of the troubled but aspiring "negro." And unlike the dejected, helpless, hopeless, wondering Negro often portrayed in white literary works, Emma Lou was a power tower of ambition, hope, and purpose.

She was born in Boise, Idaho, where her parents had built a home for themselves as far away as possible from the slave-belt South. Their desire, as was that of many of their contemporaries, was to keep this distance from their slave past permanent. This literally entailed an attempt at changing the total personification of the slave self, the negative self.

As a result, Emma Lou's grandparents were protective of their blue-vein family, a breed of people "blessed" with their lighter (less of the African, more of the European in their blood) skin complexion. Emma Lou, however, was a product of a forbidden marriage between her mother and Jim Morgan, a man who, we are told, originated "from one of the few families originally from African who could not boast of having been seduced by some member of southern aristocracy, or befriended by some member of a strolling band of Indians."

Unfortunately for Emma Lou, she took after her father, and her "luscious black complexion" became a liability and a curse. To be sure, Emma Lou was no exception; but her blue-vein protectionist family considered her birth and intrusion upon their ascending social fortunes as a "black" mark. As she grew older, Emma Lou, too, began to understand this obsessive concern with complexion and its social significance.

In fact, Emma Lou internalized this value system so well that she made it her life mission to amend this fateful error committed upon herself and family by associating with the "right sort of people." By this she meant her desire to associate or marry into "the doctors, the lawyers, the dentists, the more monied pullman porters, hotel waiters, bank janitors and majordomos, in fact all of the Negro leaders and members of the Negro upper class, [who] were either light skinned themselves or else had light skinned wives." Emma Lou's desire to restore the faith was actively supported by her mother, who also strove to send her to the right school.

FROM THE AUTHOR

THE FAD OF HARLEM

The Negro and all things negroid had become a fad, and Harlem had become a shrine to which feverish pilgrimages were in order . . . Seventh Avenue was the gorge into which Harlem cliff dwellers crowded to promenade.

SOURCE: Wallace Thurman, excerpt from *The Blacker the Berry: A Novel of Negro Life,* Macauley, 1929.

It was while studying at the University of Southern California that Emma Lou learned that the task of attaining her life's goal was not going to be easy. Her "blackness" became a reason for her exclusion both from the white students and her fellow Negro students, who made fun of her attempts to lighten her complexion with the help of various bleaching aids. In her brief tenure in college, Emma Lou learned, to her disappointment, that only the "high yaller" types can associate with her. Dejected and disappointed with the low manners of the Negro students in college, she decided to move East.

Harlem was to be her destination, where, as Thurman tells us, she hoped to be a secretary "to some well-groomed Negro business man. There had not been many such in the West, and she was eager to know and admire one. There would be other girls in the office too, girls who, like herself, were college trained and reared in cultural homes, and through these fellow workers she would meet still other girls and men, get in with the right sort of people."

Harlem was also a disappointment to Emma Lou. There were no jobs for her kind of "college-trained colored girls." The employment agencies and their rude interviews made her realize her "place." Emma Lou had to come to grips with the shattering bitterness of reality, and accepted a job as a maid-in-waiting to a white actress imitating black dancers. It was not a bad job; it taught her the seedy sort of life of the white liberal, Bohemian, semiintellectual and their "concern" for and enchantment with color and "colored" people.

Emma Lou's Harlem also had its pleasant side, although it was not to last. She met and fell in love with Alva. To be sure, there were other men: John, Jasper, and Benson, but none of them could equal Alva in Emma's eyes. Alva was a charmer, and had a light complexion and soft hair. What Emma Lou did not know was that Alva made his living by retaining many "paying-off" girlfriends. It is Alva who introduces Emma Lou to the seedy part of life in Harlem; Alva who breaks her heart by first refusing to live with her, and later by living with Geraldine, one of his paying-off girlfriends who bore him a deformed child. Finally, it is also Alva who abandons her to his drunken life and womanizing, after she had returned to him in his dark days, ill and abandoned by Geraldine. Her experience with Alva taught her the bitter lesson that her obsession with color and her attempts to transcend it was the basis for her troubled life.

Thurman's rendering of the fictional life of Emma Lou provides insights that are still relevant today. The American social structure's measurement of "manhood" and beauty is still disastrously impacting upon the troubled lives of the African-American youth. The return to straightened hair, powdered faces, and so on and the sheer obsession with "personal beauty" à la *Glamour, Essence,* and *Redbook* has its basis on the notion of the negative personality imposed upon African-American consciousness by the slave past and by a socioeconomic system rooted in racial discrimination.

Thurman's book is worth reading and rereading, and it should be used again in classrooms in such a way as to counterpose the self-hate and self-blame perpetrated on African-American youth in particular and the black community in general. African-American youth must be taught to understand the deeper meaning of Thurman's argument, "the blacker the berry, the sweeter the juice . . . ," and made to realize the necessity for rejecting in strong terms the falsification and inferiorizing indoctrination peddled each day by the dominant system. The notions of color, inferiority/superiority, and the concepts of race are, after all, mere instrumentalities of both the oppressed and the oppressor. Such instrumentalities either perpetuate themselves in an atmosphere of subjugation or are bound to lead, when positive consciousness develops, to an explosion of long-repressed fury that will perhaps make the impact of the rebellions of the sixties look like a child's game.

In its sociological bent, ***The Blacker the Berry*** . . . was a good precursor to Frazier's *Black Bourgeoisie* and Nathan Hare's *Black Anglo-Saxons.* The latter, however, do not match up to or follow the ideological/political clarity and mood set by Thurman.

Infants of the Spring

THE NEW YORK TIMES (REVIEW DATE 1932)

SOURCE: "Harlem's Bohemia." *The New York Times* (29 February 1932): 22.

In the following review, the critic finds Infants of the Spring *to be unfocused, lacking in life, and pretentious.*

Infants of the Spring is a pretty inept book. It is clumsily written. Its dialogue, which ranges from elephantine witticisms to ponderous philosophizing, is often incredibly bad. Its characters, men and women who rotate giddily and senselessly through the mazes of Harlem's Bohemia, are ciphers. For all its earnestness and its obvious sincerity, the book is merely a tedious dramatization of various phases of the Negro problem, full of endless arguments endlessly prolonged.

These arguments occur chiefly in Niggeratti Manor—the name ironically given to their boarding house by a group of artists and writers who have banded together under one roof. . . . Unproductive artistically, frustrated and warped in one way or another by their race consciousness, these tormented Bohemians reel from one gain party to another in search of a workable solution which they never quite find. Only Raymond, the strongest and most intelligent of the lot, has any real prospect of ever achieving fulfillment.

This, then, is the general theme of the novel. It is not, to be sure, wholly without merit. Some of the discussions are challenging. Some of the scenes—such as that of the orgy at which blacks and whites mingle, and of the attempted "salon"—are shrewdly observed. On the whole, however, it lacks life and fails to awake in the reader the necessary emotional response. It is a more pretentious but less successful book than Mr. Thurman's earlier novel, ***The Blacker the Berry.***

FURTHER READING

Criticism

Blackmore, David. "'Something . . . Too Preposterous and Complex to Be Recognized or Considered': Same Sex Desire and Race in *Infants of the Spring.*" *Soundings: An Interdisciplinary Journal* 80, no. 2 (winter 1997): 519-29.

Discusses the treatment of male homosexuality and race in Infants of the Spring.

Carter, Linda M. "Wallace Thurman (1902-1934)." In *African American Authors, 1745-1945: A Bio-Bibliographical Critical Sourcebook,* edited by Emmanuel S. Nelson, pp. 387-95. Westport, Conn.: Greenwood Publishing, 2000.

Overview of Thurman's life and works, along with primary and secondary bibliographies.

Dickson-Carr, Darryl. "Signs of Adolescence: Problems of Group Identity in Wallace Thurman's *Infants of the Spring.*" *Studies in Contemporary Satire* 20 (1996): 145-59.

Argues that Infants of the Spring *reveals Thurman's frustration with the inability of both Blacks and whites to recognize the delimiting system of racial inequality in the United States.*

Ferguson, SallyAnn H. "Dorothy West and Helene Johnson in *Infants of the Spring.*" *The Langston Hughes Review* 2, no. 2 (fall 1983): 22-4.

Sees Infants of the Spring *as a roman à clef and compares the novel's characters Doris Westmore and Hazel Jamison to their real-life counterparts, Dorothy West and Helene Johnson.*

Gaither, Renoir W. "The Moment of Revision: A Reappraisal of Wallace Thurman's Aesthetics in *The Blacker the Berry* and *Infants of the Spring.*" *College Language Association Journal* 37, no. 1 (September 1993): 81-93.

Examines Thurman's treatment of social values in his novels.

Giles, Freda Scott. "Glitter, Glitz, and Race: The Production of *Harlem.*" *Journal of American Drama and Theatre* 7, no. 3 (fall 1995): 1-12.

Shows how the composition and production of Harlem gained Thurman positive and negative notoriety, dashed his hopes for financial stability, and strained his health to the breaking point.

Herring, Terrell Scott. "The Negro Artist and Racial Manor: *Infants of the Spring* and the Conundrum of Publicity." *African American Review* 35, no. 4 (winter 2001): 581-98.

Discusses Thurman's treatment of publicity, privacy, and the New Negro artist in Infants of the Spring.

Kelley, James. "Blossoming in Strange New Forms: Male Homosexuality and the Harlem Renaissance." *Soundings* 80, no. 4 (winter 1997): 499-517.

Discusses the role of homosexuality, primitivism, and decadence in Infants of the Spring *as well as in works by Countee Cullen, W. E. B. Du Bois, and Alain Locke.*

Klotman, Phyllis. "The Black Writer in Hollywood, Circa 1930: The Case of Wallace Thurman." In *Black American Cinema,* edited by Diawara Manthia, pp. 80-92. London: Routledge, 1993.

Examines Thurman's career as a screenwriter.

Scruggs, Charles. "'All Dressed Up But No Place To Go': The Black Writer and His Audience During the Harlem Renaissance." In *American Literature* 48, no. 4 (January 1977): 559-62.

Sketch of Thurman's life and works.

Silberman, Seth Clark. "Looking for Richard Bruce Nugent and Wallace Henry Thurman: Reclaiming Black Male Same Sexualities in the New Negro Movement." In *Process: A Graduate Student Journal of African American and African Diasporan Literature and Culture* 1 (fall 1996): 53-73.

Compares the treatment of homosexuality in Thurman's The Blacker the Berry *and* Infants of the Spring *to that in Bruce Nugent's short story "Smoke, Lillies and Jade."*

Skinner. R. Dana. "The Play: *Harlem.*" *Commonweal* (6 March 1929): 514.

Faults the play for its negative portrayal of African American life.

West, Dorothy. "Elephant's Dance: A Memoir of Wallace Thurman." *Black World* 20, no. 1 (1970): 77-85.

Presents a personal appraisal of Thurman's life and writing.

OTHER SOURCES FROM GALE:

Additional coverage of Thurman's life and career is contained in the following sources published by the Gale Group: *Black Literature Criticism,* Vol. 3; *Black Writers,* Eds. 1, 3; *Contemporary Authors,* Vol. 124; *Contemporary Authors - Brief Entry,* Vol. 104; *Contemporary Authors New Revision Series,* Vol. 81; *Dictionary of Literary Biography,* Vol. 51; *DISCovering Authors Modules: Multicultural Authors;* and *Twentieth-Century Literary Criticism,* Vol. 6.

JEAN TOOMER

(1894 - 1967)

(Born Nathan Eugene Toomer; also known as Eugene Pinchback) American poet, prose writer, essayist, and playwright.

Although he was not actively associated with other Black creative artists who had moved to New York in the 1910s and 1920s, Toomer was seen by many of them as ushering in the Harlem Renaissance with the publication of his masterwork, *Cane* (1923). The work consists of stories, poetry, sketches, and drama that depict African American culture in the rural South and urban North. Because of its portrayal of the beauty of African American culture, it affirms the cultural assumptions of the Harlem Renaissance. However, Toomer's attitudes toward race were complex; he was light-skinned and "passed" for white, and later in life he rejected the label of a Black man. His most pressing concern was a search for spiritual wholeness and meaning, although he did also write works on racial questions. Toomer's promise as the most gifted writer of his generation bore little fruit after *Cane,* and he wrote little else of any significance. This has been blamed on his embracing the philosophy of the Russian mystic Georgi Ivanovich Gurdjieff as well as his ambivalence toward his race. Toomer was all but forgotten by the late 1920s. When *Cane* was republished in 1951, interest in the writer was renewed, and by the 1960s he was hailed as one of the greatest African American writers of all time.

BIOGRAPHICAL INFORMATION

Toomer was born in Washington, D.C., in December 1894 to Nathan Toomer, a Georgia farmer, and Nina Pinchback, the daughter of a prominent Louisiana politician. Although both his parents had "Black blood," they were fair skinned, as was their son. Toomer's parents divorced when he was two, and his mother took him to live with her parents in an upper-middle-class white neighborhood. Toomer grew up surrounded by affluence, was waited upon by Black servants, and took little interest in matters of race. In 1904 Toomer's grandfather lost his estate because of gambling debts. A year later Toomer's mother remarried, and the whole family moved to Brooklyn to live with her new husband. She died four years later, and Toomer and his grandparents moved back to Washington, D.C., where they lived in an African American neighborhood. He graduated from an elite all-Black high school and then briefly attended six different colleges but never earned a degree. During this time he began writing, and he moved to Greenwich Village, where he met other writers and intellectuals, including the photographer Alfred Steiglitz, the poet Hart Crane, and the critic Waldo Frank. Frank was particularly influential and would later help Toomer get his work published. In 1920 Toomer denied his Black heritage, declaring that he was simply an "American" and refused to be categorized by what he considered simplistic racial labels. A year later he accepted a temporary job as a principal in the town of Sparta in rural Georgia. His experience in the South apparently stimulated his consciousness of his heritage and prompted him to write *Cane,* an innovative work blending poetry, prose, and drama. Around 1924 Toomer began studying the idealism of the spiritual leader Gurdjieff, and in 1924, 1926, and 1927 he attended the Gurdjieff Institute for Harmonious Development in France. He taught the Gurdjieffian gospel of higher consciousness and spiritual self-development in Harlem, then moved downtown into the white community and eventually to Chicago to create a new branch of followers. During this time he continued to write and was married twice (both times to white women, which brought him considerable publicity). In 1935 Toomer formally disassociated himself from Gurdjieff. The following year he moved to Doylestown, Pennsylvania, and in 1940 he became a member of the Society of Friends. Although he continued to write until 1950, he had difficulty getting his work published, and he eventually withdrew from public life. He continued to be interested in Gurdjieff's teaching and conducted workshops on higher consciousness in Doylestown in the 1950s. His health declined after 1957, and following several years in and out of nursing homes, he died in Doylestown in 1967.

MAJOR WORKS

Cane is considered Toomer's most important contribution to American literature. The book, which has been called a novel by some, is divided into three sections. The first is made up of six stories interwoven with twelve poems to create portraits of six southern women. "Karintha," "Becky," "Carma," and "Fern" show the richness of life's continuation, while "Esther" and "Blood-Burning Moon" depict the fading of life. The seven prose sketches and five poems of the second section are set in Chicago and Washington, D.C., where survivors of the Black South and their descendents seek a new life and hope in the urban North. The third and the longest section of the novel, entitled "Kabnis," fuses the themes of the first two sections. It has elements of autobiography, as it portrays an educated but confused Black man who travels to the South to work as a teacher. *Cane* is a lyrical, complex work that repeats images from one section to the next to create a mosaic of African American life. The life of poor Blacks in Georgia is lovingly depicted, as Toomer shows how the soil, the scent of cane, and the Georgia dusk nurture the souls of African Americans, despite their lack of material possessions. In his depiction of urban life, Toomer echoes the sentiments of such modernist writers as T. S. Eliot and Gertrude Stein, who depict the modern world as a wasteland.

Toomer wrote a few other works on racial themes, including the short story "Withered Skin of Berries" (c. 1923), the plays *Natalie Mann* (c. 1923) and *Balo* (1923), and poems such as "Gum" (1923), "Banking Coal" (1922), and others. In 1931 Toomer produced *Essentials,* a book of aphorisms, and in 1936 he published his long poem "The Blue Meridian," about the fusion of people of all colors into a new creation, the blue man. The work reflects the idealism of the Gurdjieffian philosophy in a lyrical, artistic manner and also addresses the issue of racial categorization.

CRITICAL RECEPTION

The publication of *Cane* in 1923 caused a stir in New York literary circles, and Toomer was immediately identified as one of the most significant writers of his generation. But he did not come close in the rest of his years to matching his early success. Although Toomer was admired for the beautiful lyricism of his poetry and prose, many Black writers of his day were less than enthusiastic about his ambivalence toward his racial identity and his refusal to be classified as an African American. Toomer also associated primarily with white writers and intellectuals, even though during the Harlem Renaissance he did come to know prominent Black writers as well. After the 1930s Toomer devoted his life to spiritual and religious ideas, and his works received little critical notice—if they were published at all. Toomer faded from view until the 1950s, when *Cane* was republished. Since then, numerous works have been written about Toomer's life, philosophy, and writings. Most criticism has focused on *Cane,* and has analyzed, for example, the work's structure, repeated imagery, biblical allusions, autobiographical content, use of African American music, and spiritualism. Full-length analyses of Toomer's life and relationship with Gurdjieff have also appeared, as have discussions of his racial attitudes and search for identity. Despite his unusual views on race during the years of the Harlem Renaissance, Toomer is now considered to be, along with Langston Hughes and Claude McKay, one of the three most important writers of the movement.

PRINCIPAL WORKS

**Balo: A One Act Sketch of Negro Life* (play) 1923

Cane (poetry and prose) 1923

Natalie Mann (play) c. 1923

"Withered Skin of Berries" (short story) c. 1923

Essentials: A Philosophy of Life in Three Hundred Definitions and Aphorisms (aphorisms and apothegms) 1931

"The Blue Meridian" [published in the anthology *The New Caravan,* edited by Alfred Kreymborg, Lewis Mumford, and Paul Rosenfeld] (poetry) 1936

An Interpretation of Friends Worship (pamphlet) 1947

The Flavor of Man (pamphlet) 1949

†*The Wayward and the Seeking: A Collection of Writings by Jean Toomer* [edited by Darwin Turner] (poetry, prose, essays, and plays) 1980

The Collected Poems of Jean Toomer [edited by Robert B. Jones and Margery Toomer Latimer] (poetry) 1988

A Jean Toomer Reader: Selected Unpublished Writings [edited by Frederik L. Rusch] (poetry, prose, essays, and letters) 1993

Jean Toomer: Selected Essays and Literary Criticism [edited by Robert B. Jones] (essays and criticism) 1996

* This work was first performed by the Howard University Players during the 1923-24 season and first published in the anthology *Plays of Negro Life,* edited by Alain Locke and Montgomery Gregory, in 1927.

† This work includes the first publication of *Natalie Mann,* "Withered Skin of Berries," *The Sacred Factory,* and other pieces.

PRIMARY SOURCES

JEAN TOOMER (POEM DATE 1922)

SOURCE: Toomer, Jean. "Harvest Song." *The Liberator* (1922).

Toomer adopts the perspective of a reaper in this poem of field work.

"HARVEST SONG"

I am a reaper whose muscles set at sundown. All
my oats are cradled.
But I am too chilled, and too fatigued to bind them.
And I hunger.

I crack a grain between my teeth. I do not taste it.
I have been in the fields all day. My throat is dry.
I hunger.

My eyes are caked with dust of oatfields at harvest-
time.
I am a blind man who stares across the hills, seeking
stack'd fields of other harvesters.

It would be good to see them . . . crook'd, split, and
iron-ring'd handles of the scythes. It would be
good to see them, dust-caked and blind. I
hunger.

(Dusk is a strange fear'd sheath their blades are dull'd
in.)
My throat is dry. And should I call, a cracked grain
like the oats . . . eoho—

I fear to call. What should they hear me, and offer
me their grain, oats, or wheat, or corn? I have
been in the fields all day. I fear I could not taste
it. I fear knowledge of my hunger.

My ears are caked with dust of oatfields at harvest-
time.
I am a deaf man who strains to hear the calls of other
harvesters whose throats are also dry.

It would be good to hear their songs . . . reapers of
the sweet-stalk'd cane, cutters of the corn . . .
even though their throats cracked and the
strangeness of their voices deafened me.

I hunger. My throat is dry. Now that the sun has
set and I am chilled, I fear to call. (Eoho, my
brothers!)

I am a reaper. (Eoho!) All my oats are cradled.
But I am too fatigued to bind them. And I
hunger.
I crack a grain. It has no taste to it.
My throat is dry . . .

O my brothers, I beat my palms, still soft, against the
stubble of my harvesting. (You beat your soft
palms, too.) My pain is sweet. Sweeter than
the oats or wheat or corn. It will not bring me
knowledge of my hunger.

JEAN TOOMER (POEMS DATE 1923)

SOURCE: Toomer, Jean. "Reapers" and "November Cotton Flower." In *Cane.* New York: Boni & Liveright, 1923.

In these two pieces from his landmark work, Toomer addresses the nature of field work.

"REAPERS"

Black reapers with the sound of steel on stones
Are sharpening scythes. I see them place the hones

In their hip-pockets as a thing that's done,
And start their silent swinging, one by one.
Black horses drive a mower through the weeds,
And there, a field rat, startled, squealing bleeds,
His belly close to ground. I see the blade,
Blood-stained, continue cutting weeds and
shade.

"NOVEMBER COTTON FLOWER"

Boll-weevil's coming, and the winter's cold,
Made cotton-stalks look rusty, seasons old,
And cotton, scarce as any southern snow,
Was vanishing; the branch, so pinched and slow,
Failed in its function as the autumn rake;
Drouth fighting soil had caused the soil to take
All water from the streams; dead birds were
found
In wells a hundred feet below the ground—
Such was the season when the flower bloomed.
Old folks were startled, and it soon assumed
Significance. Superstition saw
Something it had never seen before:
Brown eyes that loved without a trace of fear,
Beauty so sudden for that time of year.

GENERAL COMMENTARY

S. P. FULLINWIDER (ESSAY DATE 1966)

SOURCE: Fullinwider, S. P. "Jean Toomer: Lost Generation or Negro Renaissance?" In *Analysis and Assessment, 1940-1979,* edited by Cary D. Wintz, pp. 454-61. New York: Garland Publishing, Inc., 1996.

In the following essay, originally published in Phylon *in 1966 and the first article on Toomer to appear in a scholarly journal, Fullinwider explores Toomer's thematic concerns and attempts to assess where the author stands in the African American literary tradition.*

Now that the Jean Toomer papers have found a home at the Fisk University library it is no longer necessary to speculate as to why Toomer ceased to write after he published ***Cane*** in 1923. In fact, he did not cease to write. He continued to write, and write voluminously; but to no avail—he could find no publisher. The story of Toomer's literary efforts after 1923 is a story of frustration, despair and failure—this after what was surely one of the most promising beginnings in the history of American literature. Toomer's story is one of a young man caught up in the tangled skein of race relations in America. But it goes beyond even that. For a time, at least, it was the story of modern man; the story of a search for identity—for an absolute in a world that had dissolved into flux. It is a story of success—at the age of thirty-one his search for an identity-giving absolute was over. It is a story of tragedy. As long as he was searching he was a fine creative artist; when the search ended, so did his creative powers. So long as he was searching, his work was the cry of one caught in the modern human condition; it expressed modern man's lostness, his isolation. Once Toomer found an identity-giving absolute, his voice ceased to be the cry of modern man and became the voice of the schoolmaster complacently pointing out the way—his way. It now seems possible to take a few hesitant steps toward a closer understanding of the Negro American literary tradition by asking the question: "Who was Jean Toomer?"

Toomer's overriding concern for the human condition grew out of an early lack of self-esteem, a concomitant tendency towards introspection and soul-searching, and a loss of his childhood absolutes. His problem with self-esteem was a product of his early family life, particularly, his relationship with an imperious grandfather, P. B. S. Pinchback. The former Reconstruction lieutenant governor of Louisiana had suffered political and financial reverses when the Republicans lost power in the South, and had removed to an imposing house on Washington's Bacon Street, an all white neighborhood. There Pinchback lived a high life—the life of a social lion—while his prestige lasted. But a politician out of office quickly loses status and influence. As his fortunes declined, Pinchback became increasingly autocratic toward his daughter Nina and his sons. The beautiful Nina married twice, first to a young Southern planter who disappeared after a year, and then to a ne'er-do-well who misrepresented his wealth. The second marriage, with its drudgery and lack of love, killed her. So Jean, a product of the first match, led a troubled young life with his grandfather.[1]

As Jean Toomer grew in childhood he turned in upon himself, away from the tyrannical grandfather, away from his unhappy mother. Slowly he created a rich inner life, but it was a life almost totally disassociated from the outside world.[2] Pinchback's fortunes continued to decline. One day he moved the family from Bacon Street with its white neighborhood to a house on Florida Avenue, the heart of the Negro upper-class world. Looking back, Toomer wrote, "With this world—an aristocracy—such as never existed before and perhaps will never exist again in America—mid-way between the white and Negro worlds. For the first time I lived in a colored world." Toomer liked his new life. He felt that he found here, "more emotion, more rhythm, more color, more gaiety,"[3] than he had met in the chilling atmosphere of white society. But this was a time, too, of morbid introspection. Now fourteen, he became a nuisance in the classroom, an inveterate troublemaker. He became the victim of overpowering sex impulses, and seems to have concluded that these impulses were destroying his health. He turned to barbells and special diets. By then the Pinchbacks were on the verge of poverty and family relations were deteriorating. A three-year period of revolt and wandering began for the boy. His revolt first took him to the University of Wisconsin to study agriculture (this lasted a semester), then back to Washington to endure hard looks of reproach. He was assailed by self-doubt. He tried the Massachusetts College of Agriculture for almost a week, then a physical training college in Chicago. There he paid more attention to lectures at the Loop than to physical education. Men like Clarence Darrow held forth there on exciting subjects like Darwinism and the ideas of Haeckel—and atheism. Toomer felt his intellectual world collapse. His belief in God, he thought, evaporated. He felt "condemned and betrayed." "In truth," he later wrote, "I did not want to live."[4] His old absolutes were gone; he began a desperate search for new ones. For a time socialism seemed to serve the need.

> I had been, I suppose, unconsciously seeking—as man must ever seek—an intelligible scheme of things, a sort of whole into which everything fit . . . it was the *body,* the *scheme,* the order and inclusion. These evoked and promised to satisfy all in me that had been groping for order from amid the disorder and chaos of my personal experiences.[5]

After Chicago there were further wanderings, further soulsearchings. A reading of Lester F. Ward's *Dynamic Sociology* led to a short fraternization with that subject at New York University. But he found a history course at City College more attractive. Then history became a bore and psychology took its place. World War I came to America and he was rejected by the draft. He tried odd jobs for a year: he sold Fords in Chicago, taught physical education in Milwaukee, and did a ten-day stint as a ship-fitter in a New Jersey shipyard. His contact with the construction workers there caused him to lose interest in socialism. In 1920, Toomer returned, defeated, to his grandfather in Washington. It was not a cheerful reunion. In a mood of bitterness and an atmosphere of rejection he turned to reading literature—Robert Frost, Sherwood Anderson, the imagists. He wrote incessantly, hour upon hour for month after month, tearing up what he wrote. He learned to handle words, learned their symbolic potential. He became an artist.[6]

Toomer learned as he handled words that they had no meaning beyond what he gave them arbitrarily. He began to see that words are mere symbols of things and not the things themselves.[7] He was traveling the road to nominalism, and as he traveled that road he felt the concrete world begin to dissolve about him. He was entering the world of modern alienated man. Apparently it was during this period that he began to experience the severing of his intellect from his emotions—the seemingly peculiar phenomenon of the modern mind that has been described as the "frigidization of the self." The phenomenon has been described as an overwhelming sense of self-consciousness—a standing outside oneself, as it were; an objectification of the self. The intellect seems to overpower the emotions, making it impossible to have effective emotional relations with other people. One finds an impenetrable wall standing between oneself and those one would love.[8] Toomer made the solution of this problem—this "frigidization of the self"—his major intellectual theme. Again and again in his later writings he reverted to his argument that the intellect must somehow be fused with the emotions: "Themosense (thought *and* emotion *and* sensing) is the inner synthesis of functions, which represents the entire individual and gives rise to complete action."[9] Of course, in Toomer's case much of this "frigidization of the self" can be traced to his deliberate retreat from an outside world (his family life) that was too threatening—a retreat into the isolation of subjectivity. In one place he tells of wrongs being inflicted upon him in such profusion that "Finally we reached the stage where we vowed to suffer no more. Of people, of life, of the world we said, 'Don't touch me.' We resolved that no one ever would."[10] It was while in this mood that he accepted an offer in 1921 to act as temporary superintendent of a small Negro industrial school in rural Georgia.

Georgia was for Toomer a small shack in the hills. It was the whispering pines. It was the folk-singing that drifted over in the evenings from the Negro dwellings. Most of all, it was the Southern Negro spirit—a spirit with which he developed a deep feeling of kinship. ***Cane*** was at once the joy of discovering this folk-spirit and the sadness of the realization that it was a passing thing.

He wrote of the spirituals, "But I learned

> that the Negroes of the town objected to them. They called them 'shouting.' They had victrolas and player-pianos. So, I realized with deep regret, that the spirituals, meeting ridicule, would be certain to die out. With Negroes also the trend was towards the small town and towards the city—

> and industry and commerce and the machines. The folk-spirit was walking in to die on the modern desert. That spirit was so beautiful. Its death was so tragic."[11]

Toomer, suffering intensely from "frigidization of the self," appears to have entertained the idea that in the Southern Negro folk-spirit he might find emotional release—that in this spirit he might find not only his own salvation but salvation for the modern industrial world. This, at least, is the message of **"Box Seat,"** one of the more substantial of ***Cane***'s prose-pictures. In it appears Dan, a Southern Negro with a redemptive mission. The setting of **"Box Seat"** is Washington, D.C., or, in other words, the large city. There one is crushed and shorn of spirit by the heavy hand of civilization.

> Houses are shy girls whose eyes shine reticently upon the dusk body of the street. Upon the gleaming limbs and asphalt torso of a dreaming nigger. Shake your curled wool-blossoms, nigger. Open your liver lips to the lean white spring. Stir the root-life of a withered people. Call them from their houses, and teach them to dream.

Dan, hot-blooded and virile, is up from the primitive regions of the South to restore vigor and passion to a jaded, over-civilized people—people conquered by "zoo-restrictions and keeper-taboos." "I am Dan More," he says, "I was born in a cane-field. The hands of Jesus touched me. I am come to a sick world to heal it."[12]

To Toomer's mind the plight of modern man is that industrial civilization has shorn him of emotional spontaneity—has made him the passive mechanical pawn of social forces. While living in the hills of Georgia, Toomer could almost believe the answer lay with Dan. During those months Toomer must have felt a closer identification with the Negro race than he had ever felt before, or was to feel thereafter. A year later, in mid-1922, he wrote of his feelings to the editor of the *Liberator*: "Within the last two or three years, however, my growing need for artistic expression has pulled me deeper and deeper into the Negro group. . . . I found myself loving it in a way that I could never love the other."[13] There is every reason to believe that this was a sincere statement; Toomer, after all, had been searching for an identity throughout most of his life. But there is good evidence that Toomer was not secure in his new-found faith, even while in the midst of composing ***Cane.*** In **"Kabnis,"** the final and most compelling sketch of the book, he put on record his doubts concerning the Negro race in America. Kabnis, a product of white men's Christianity, a slave religion, is portrayed as a weak and groveling character who projects his self-hatred outward against an ex-slave, blind and deaf from years of toil. In Kabnis' eyes the old man is a servile product of the Christian religion—an Uncle Tom. A much stronger character in the sketch, Lewis, saw in the old man something much different. He saw strength growing out of hardship and pain. Thus, Toomer had two points of view towards Negroes: one expressing his doubts, one expressing his hope; one repelling him, the other attracting him. The significant point is that neither point of view gained the ascendancy in **"Kabnis."**

Thus, for a period of perhaps a year or two, the period during which he composed ***Cane,*** Toomer found a new identity-giving absolute in the Negro folk-spirit. But the absolute had, at best, a tenuous hold on the poet. It proved no more enduring than those that had gone before. Shortly after the publication of ***Cane,*** Toomer again felt himself immersed in chaos and doubt: "Everything was in chaos. I saw this chaos clearly, I could and did describe and analyze its factors so well that I got a reputation for being a sort of genius of chaos."[14]

What happened to Toomer in the years between 1923 and 1925 is described by Gorham Munson, who knew him well at the time. Toomer continued his quest for what Munson calls "unity," or "personal wholeness," first by training his "conscious control of the body," and then by spending the summer of 1924 at the Gurdjieff Institute, Fontainebleau, France.[15] Toomer found what he was looking for in Gurdjieff's philosophy—an interesting blend of Freudian categories and religion—became a disciple and spent many of his summers in Fontainebleau, returning each fall to organize psychological experiments in the United States. But the crucial moment for Toomer came one summer evening in 1926. It happened at the end of one of those humdrum days of no special significance. Toomer was waiting on an El platform in New York City, when suddenly, as he says, he transcended himself: "I was born above the body into a world of psychological reality. . . . In my private language I shall call this experience the Second Conception."[16]

That was it for Toomer; he had his absolute; his search was over. From that time he began to proselytize in the age-old tradition of missionaries. He wrote novels, he wrote philosophic works, he wrote descriptions of psychological experiments,[17] and he wrote volumes of material that is unclassifiable—all with the purpose of persuasion. The publishers were not buying; his literary life after 1926 became a dreary round of rejection slips. The fault was not his nor his publishers'. He had come up with an answer to the troubles that plagued the age. He had an answer for Van Wyck Brook's cry of "externalization"; for Waldo Frank's plight of being "objectified." He had found an answer for modern man's agonizing sense of incompleteness. His answer was couched disconcertingly in half-psychological, half-mystical language ("Our center of gravity is displaced. Our essence is passive; and we lack essential self-activating energies. . . . We have no being-aims and purposes."),[18] but what he was doing, in essence, was putting into his own symbols the age-old experience of religious conversion. Following willy-nilly behind Gurdjieff, he had got himself completely at cross-purposes with the whole thrust of American intelligence of the 1920's. Van Wyck Brooks, Charles S. Johnson, Alain Locke—all were asking that man, through his creative art, turn to experience. The answer found by these modern critics lay in creating beauty and meaning out of the living contact with the world of reality. Toomer was saying just the opposite: turn for beauty and meaning to your inner essence. "An artist," he wrote, "is able, by effort to contact his own essence, wherein exist common universal symbols."[19] Toomer was asking his age to adopt another absolute. The age was not buying.

Toomer's artistic expression lost something once he had found his answer—it became didactic, it became unconvincing. His unpublished novel, ***Eight-Day World*** (c. 1932) is a case in point. It pictures a group of people aboard a transatlantic liner escaping from their unsatisfactory lives in America. The critique of life in America was the one expressed by a hundred writers in the 1920's. Life had become materialistic, commercial, and unfulfilling. The group escaping from this life aboard the liner was no sooner at sea than in-fighting and back-biting began. The people felt inadequate to themselves, and yet strove for independence from others. It was Toomer's early experience being retold. Hugh was the one man of the story who understood something of what was going on, but he was in the same predicament as the others, trying to break down the barriers his own inadequacy built up between him and them, trying, without success, to find fulfillment. Finally, Hugh found his fulfillment in the beautiful Vera, and at the same time crystallized a philosophy of it all. He had come to understand that each person must attain a satisfying independence and yet give of self. That is the goal. But in order to achieve it, one must transcend oneself: "This means," said Hugh, "that we must recapture our full *being. Being* is the base of everything."[20]

Eight-Day World ended as Toomer had ended, with all problems solved, with everyone satisfied. The artist could no longer express modern man's restlessness and lostness. His work had become smug—and dead. Toomer had been modern in ***Cane.*** There the author had confronted his readers with the pain of reality unmitigated by the pleasant knowledge of having in hand The Answer. After writing ***Cane,*** Toomer fled from reality, found his absolute and clung to it. He talked about finding "being," but he would have been horrified at the modern definition of being—the "being" of Heidegger or of Sartre. He turned from experience of outward reality to an inner thing he called "essence" or "being," thinking that the thing he was camouflaging with the symbols of psychology was newly discovered. By 1940 he realized it was not new. He requested admittance to the Society of Friends, saying: "For some time we have shared the fundamental faith of the Friends. . . ."[21] His "essence" had been none other than the Quakers' "inner light"; in his 1926 experience of "Second Conception" had been the experience of religious conversion. Toomer had gone full cycle from his childhood faith in God, through total rejection in ***Cane,*** and then back again to God.

What, then, shall we say about Jean Toomer? Does he stand within the Negro American literary tradition? The question is not an easy one, and the answer must be a much more arbitrary one than has always been assumed. In none of his literary efforts subsequent to ***Cane*** did he make race a central or even important issue. Beyond that, he made some positive efforts to disassociate his name from Negro literature. When, for example, James Weldon Johnson, in 1930, asked his permission to use some of the poetry from ***Cane*** in the revised edition of *The Book of American Negro Poetry,* Toomer replied in the negative, saying,

> My poems are not Negro poems, nor are they Anglo-Saxon or white or English poems. My prose likewise. They are, first, mine. And, second, in so far as general race or stock is concerned, they spring from the result of racial blending here in America which has produced a new race or stock. We may call this stock the American stock or race. . . .[22]

Evidently the division of mankind into categories of race was not one of Toomer's preoccupations after his 1926 conversion experience—he had found his identity in religion and not race. Before 1926 he had made one serious attempt to find the answer to his emotional needs through an identification with the Negro race. The result had been ***Cane.*** I suspect that ***Cane*** should be seen as the point at which the broad current represented by the aspirations and needs of the Lost Generation touched the current of Negro social protest, leaving a minor monument to both.

Notes

1. Jean Toomer, "Book of Parents" (Unpublished MS., ca. 1934), pp. 17-37. Toomer papers, Fisk University Library.
2. Jean Toomer, "Outline of Autobiography" (Unpublished MS., ca. 1934), p. 2. Toomer papers, Fisk University Library.
3. *Ibid.,* p. 8.
4. *Ibid.,* p. 26.
5. *Ibid.,* handwritten note on reverse of p. 25.
6. *Ibid.,* pp. 27-55.
7. Jean Toomer, "Essentials: Prose and Poems" (Unpublished MS., 1930), pp. 70, 112-18. Toomer papers, Fisk University Library.
8. Walter H. Sokel, *The Writer in Extremis: Expressionism in Twentieth-Century German Literature* (Stanford, 1959), pp. 85-118.
9. Jean Toomer, *Work-Ideas I,* Mill House Pamphlets, Psychological Series, No. 2 (Doyleston, Pennsylvania, 1937), p. 13.
10. Jean Toomer, *Living is Developing,* Mill House Pamphlets, Psychological Series, No. 1 (Doyleston, Pennsylvania, 1937), p. 14.
11. Toomer, "Autobiography," *op. cit.,* pp. 58-59.
12. Jean Toomer, "Box Seat," *Cane* (New York, 1923), pp. 104-29.
13. Jean Toomer to editor of *Liberator,* August 19, 1922. Toomer papers, Fisk University Library.
14. Toomer, "Autobiography," *op. cit.,* p. 63.
15. Gorham B. Munson, "The Significance of Jean Toomer," *Opportunity,* III (September, 1925), 262-63.
16. Jean Toomer, "From Exile into Being" (Unpublished MS., 1938), p. 1 of Prescript. Toomer papers, Fisk University Library.
17. See, for example, Jean Toomer (Unpublished MSS. of novels: "The Gallonwerps," ca: 1927; "York Beach," ca. 1928; "Transatlantic Crossing," ca. 1930; "Eight-Day World," ca. 1932; Unpublished MS of a philosophic work, "Essentials: Definitions and Aphorisms," 1931; unpublished MS. of a psychological experiment, "Portage Potential," 1931). Toomer papers, Fisk University Library.
18. Toomer, "Essentials: Prose and Poems," *op. cit.,* p. 63.
19. *Ibid.,* p. 46.
20. Toomer, "Eight-Day World," *op. cit.,* pp. 324-25.
21. Jean Toomer to Overseers, Buckingham Meeting (Lahaska, Pennsylvania, August 28, 1940). Toomer papers, Fisk University Library.
22. Jean Toomer to James Weldon Johnson, July 11, 1930. Toomer papers, Fisk University Library.

CHARLES SCRUGGS (ESSAY DATE 1975)

SOURCE: Scruggs, Charles. "Jean Toomer: Fugitive." *American Literature* 47 (1975): 84-96.

In the following essay, Scruggs discusses Toomer's conflicted identity and the tension between his "real self" and the "idealized self" projected in Cane.

I

As a young boy, Jean Toomer attended a dinner party during which someone asked his famous grandfather, P. B. S. Pinchback, if he indeed had "colored" blood. The light-skinned former lieutenant governor of Louisiana answered enigmatically, "That is what I have claimed." According to Toomer in his unpublished autobiography, Pinchback never cleared up the matter for his grandson.[1] Toomer insisted that he never knew for sure whether or not he was part Negro.

If Toomer's racial identity was a puzzle to himself, his attitudes toward himself as Negro have also puzzled his critics. Before the publication of ***Cane*** (1923), he seemed to advertise his dark blood. After 1923 he ambiguously referred to himself as "an American, simply an American"; and around 1930 he refused to be included in several Negro anthologies.[2] In the same year he let it be known that he was actually "white," blaming the confusion on Waldo Frank, who had given the impression in his introduction to ***Cane*** that Toomer was a Negro.[3] What mystifies everyone, as Darwin Turner pointed out, is why in the summer of 1923 Toomer rejected "a racial identification which a few months earlier he had accepted as a matter of slight importance."[4]

Explanations have been offered for Toomer's apparent apostasy during and after 1923.[5] I argue that there was in fact neither a sudden apostasy in 1923 nor a significant change in outlook thereafter. Whatever did happen to Jean Toomer happened in the two or three years before March of that year. Specifically, he developed a self-image which precluded the possibility of defining himself as Negro or Negro writer. The two critical events in this development were his reading of *Jean-Christophe,* a ten-volume French novel written by Romain Rolland (1903-1912), and his encounter with Waldo Frank. In March, 1923, referring to the question of his negritude on which he had spent much thought as a boy, he wrote the editor of *Prairie:* ". . . now I'm done with it. My concern is with the art of literature."[6]

But the question wasn't done with him. It was to haunt him: the feeling that would dominate his consciousness, unhappily, was not the liberation

Jean Toomer with his wife, Marjory Latimer.

he claimed in his letter to the editor of *Prairie* but an ominous awareness, as he later recognized in his autobiography, that "I was marked and that life was shooting at me."[7]

Exactly when Toomer read *Jean-Christophe* cannot be said. But in July, 1922, he wrote Mae Wright, the sixteen-year-old girl he fell in love with at Harpers Ferry, and recommended the novel; and a month later he told her that many of Jean-Christophe's "trials and problems are mine."[8] He probably read the book around 1920 when he decided to replace his first name "Nathan" with the French "Jean."[9] Popular in America before World War I, *Jean-Christophe* belonged to a tradition of Romantic literature which recorded the struggles of the artist with society and himself. Rolland's novel painted the portrait of an artist, a musical composer, as *übermensch.* It no doubt had a special appeal for young Toomer, who in 1920-21 was also studying to be a composer.

Born into a family of musicians in a small German town, Jean-Christophe Krafft rebelled against the town's provincial culture at an early age. He came to identify with his uncle, Gottfried, called a Wandering Jew for his aimless travels about the countryside telling stories to the peasants.[10] The young boy thought Gottfried a fool; but after his uncle's death Jean-Christophe discovered that the "fool's" tales had brought joy into homes throughout the province—homes he could never hope to share. Standing over Gottfried's grave, Jean-Christophe prayed that the spirit of the wandering storyteller would enter into him (I, 560). And it did. Jean-Christophe became an artist without a country, a condition which allowed him to create a universal music.

Jean-Christophe fled Germany after killing a soldier in a tavern brawl. He went to France and fought to become accepted as a composer. Eventually his music was appreciated, but he remained a fugitive (III, 242). Though he suffered greatly, his outlaw status nourished Christophe's growth. For the author, Rolland, the artist did not exist in a static relationship to art or society; his soul constantly renewed itself. Christophe was always several steps ahead of his critics. When they finally came to understand a work, it would be representative of a self he had cast off. His new music would baffle them. Such continuous transformation forced Christophe outside the pale of society, for society was static and wished to bind both musician and man to its standards. Only by freeing himself from its restrictions would the artist be able to give it new vitality. Jean-Christophe died alone, only partially understood, deliriously striving to find the perfect music; but he had not squandered or compromised his creative energy.

Such a sketchy summary of *Jean-Christophe* does injustice to the novel's complicated structure, but it serves to point out what Jean Toomer found compelling in its protagonist. To say that his idealized self was created immediately after reading the novel would be an oversimplification, but there was a striking resemblance between Jean-Christophe and what Jean Toomer was to make of himself. He would become the fugitive as hero, not victim. This role would enable him to come to terms with the "Cain" in himself.[11]

Jean-Christophe may have been an outcast, but his status as pariah gave him a privileged view, one which escaped the nets of provincialism. So it was with Toomer. He saw himself as a person whose bloodlines—French, Dutch, Welsh, German, Jewish, Indian, and Negro—represented a new harmony which transcended the nets of race. On June 30, 1922, he wrote to John McClure, editor of *Double Dealer,* that his seven bloodlines got along "quite amicably." Their fusion allowed him to take the color of whatever group he was "sojourning in." Toomer's idealized self would be this "sojourner"; he was the artist as citizen of the world who wrote about black life but had other worlds to conquer.[12]

Being a fugitive had other advantages for the artist. It meant that his work would be in the forefront of aesthetic expression; it might, eventually, enliven a dead culture. Toomer came to see himself as a heroic fighter for a new American literature. In his autobiography he said that he identified with another fugitive, Melville's Ishmael. Ishmael lived "in spiritual . . . opposition to his surroundings."[13] He also lived to be a storyteller.

Toomer's idealized self—heroic fugitive, citizen of the world, artist as superman—emerged fully developed by 1922.[14] ***Natalie Mann,*** an unpublished play he completed in February, imaginatively embodied this new image. It was one of several pieces written around this time for which the themes were Jean Toomer, *übermensch.* Influenced by Shaw, especially *Man and Superman,* ***Natalie Mann*** celebrated Nathan Merilh's triumph over stuffy, middle-class black society in Washington. Nathan was a writer who wished, through his art, to liberate black people to a heightened awareness of themselves—beyond pity, beyond propaganda. He created a new art form, using Negro folk songs in the plays he had written, and it was rejected. Natalie Mann was the girl he loved but would not have until she freed herself from the values of the black bourgeoisie. In a leap of faith she fled with Nathan to New York. There Nathan pursued his art; a picture of Tolstoy and a picture of a powerful black man whose "forehead is massive like Tolstoy's" hung above his study desk. It was obvious that Nathan identified with both, symbolizing the merger of African culture and Western civilization which would achieve its richest expression in Nathan's plays.

Toomer was never again to express his black blood with so much assurance. Only a year later he would wear the mask of heroic fugitive in ***Cane*** with much less ease. Six years later he would publish **"Mr. Costyve Duditch"** in the *Dial,* a short story which displayed his anxiety about his identity in all its nakedness.

II

Although Toomer had met Waldo Frank in the spring of 1920, their intense friendship did not begin until March, 1922, a month after Toomer finished ***Natalie Mann.*** Where *Jean-Christophe* had made it possible for Toomer to see himself as a fugitive-hero, Frank made Toomer see that he could be a fugitive with roots in a new American Dream—the dream of creating an American literary Renaissance. Again, Toomer's black blood would serve him in good stead.

Frank had been arguing for a new American literature long before he came to know Toomer. A novelist, author of *Our America* (1919), associate editor of the defunct *Seven Arts* (1916-1917), Frank had established himself as a major critic of American life. He had used *Seven Arts* as a vehicle for attacking lingering Puritanism in America but, more importantly, as a platform for expounding a specific critical position. America had its tale to tell, Frank, Van Wyck Brooks, and others kept repeating, if only America could extricate itself from its oppressive parochialism. What was needed was a genuine American culture where artists could flourish, instead of suffocate or flee to Europe in desperation. Their criticism of America, they thought, would sweep away the rubbish that had collected in this country since its foundation.

That accomplished, an atmosphere congenial to the artist would come into being.

Following the tradition set by *Seven Arts* and Brooks's *America's Coming of Age* (1915), Frank wrote *Our America,* Toomer's favorite book by Frank, attacking Puritan America from a Freudian point of view. The early Puritans had expended their energies outwardly; they had a wilderness to conquer. What had been neglected in this direction of efforts toward empire building was the spiritual side of man—his sense of beauty. Now that the frontier no longer existed, this side of man's nature, long oppressed, would assert itself and create a garden in America's emotional desert. The artist, the dreamer, the lover—those whom "America has immemorially denied"—would lead a vanguard to restore America to the community of nations. "This then is our task," the book ended courageously: "We must begin to generate within ourselves the energy which is love of life. For that energy . . . is religious. Its act is creation. And in a dying world, creation is revolution."[15]

The prophetic, heroic tone of the book must have impressed Toomer greatly, but not until March 24, 1922, did he write Frank to express his admiration. The first letter indirectly explains why the two men would become friends and collaborators. As much as he enjoyed *Our America,* Toomer said, "I missed your not including the Negro. I have often wondered about it." He then went on to describe his own racial makeup:

> My grandfather, owing to his emphasis upon a fraction of Negro blood in his veins, attained prominence in Reconstruction politics. And the family, for the most part, ever since, has lived between the two worlds, now dipping into the Negro, now into the white. Some few are definitely white: others definitely colored. I alone have stood for a synthesis in the mind and spirit analogous, perhaps, to the actual fact of at least six blood minglings. The history . . . of five of these are available in some approximation to the truth. Of the Negro, what facts are known have too often been perverted for the purposes of propaganda. . . . It has been necessary, therefore, that I spend a disproportionate time in Negro study. Recently, facts and possibilities discovered have led to an interest mainly artistic and interpretive. . . . No picture of a southern person is complete without its bit of Negro-determined psychology.[16]

Toomer ended the letter by asking Frank if he would like to read some of his work.

It is easy to understand why Frank responded to Toomer's letter. He had discussed the plight of the Mexican, Indian, and Jew in *Our America,* but not the Negro. Here was an opportunity to meet a young Negro artist and discover his America. Toomer had gone to Sparta, Georgia, in the fall of 1921 to take a job as principal of a grammar school. Thus he was not only a black American, but he knew the South. What he found in Georgia provided the impetus for ***Cane.*** He would also discover, after he finally wrote ***Cane,*** that the book had become a *cul-de-sac* for his idealized self. Even as early as his letter to Frank he was complaining of having spent "a disproportionate time in Negro study."

But Frank chose not to hear those words. They met in Central Park and talked for an hour. It was an hour that changed Toomer's life. Frank did more than encourage Toomer the Negro artist. He convinced him that his artistic treatment of Negro life would play a part in the creation of an authentic American literature. On April 26, 1922, he wrote Frank enthusiastically: "What shall I say to you, dear friend? You have definitely linked me to the purpose and vision of what is best in creative America."[17]

Frank and Toomer were soon addressing each other as "brother" and "friend." They planned a trip south, Frank for the express purpose of writing a novel (*Holiday*) and Toomer for the opportunity of gaining fresh material. On July 25, 1922, he told Frank that his last trip to Georgia and the writing of ***Cane*** marked a period in his life and that he hoped something would come of their trip to Spartanburg, South Carolina, that fall. In another letter he said he must go south as a Negro if he were to get the most from the experience. Frank's reply was naive:

> If you go as a Negro, cant I also? What is a Negro? Doubtless, if the Southerner could see in my heart my feeling for "the Negro," my love of his great qualities, my profound sympathy for his trials and respect for the great way he bears them, that southerner would say "why you're worse than a nigger!" . . . so if you go as a Negro so go I![18]

Frank's attitude—one need only to choose Negro to be Negro—indicates that he was incapable of understanding Toomer's agony. Going south as a Negro was not a game for Toomer; it meant confronting that blank spot in his identity. Some indication of the pain he felt is suggested by remarks he made later about the writing of ***Cane.*** Most people assume, he said, that the lyricism of ***Cane*** mirrored the unruffled emotional state of the author. Nothing could be further from the truth. "***Cane*** was born in the agony of internal tightness, conflict and chaos." When people asked him why he did not remain close to the

FROM THE AUTHOR

TOOMER'S INSPIRATION

A visit to Georgia last fall was the starting point of almost everything of worth that I have done. I saw the rich dusk beauty. . . . And a deep part of my nature, a part that I had repressed, sprang suddenly to life and responded to them.

SOURCE: Jean Toomer, from an article in the *Liberator,* 1922.

conditions of life that produced ***Cane,*** he denied them: "Never again in my life do I want those conditions. . . . ***Cane*** is a swan-song."[19]

Frank outwardly sympathized with Toomer's wish not to be pigeonholed as a Negro writer. Sherwood Anderson, Toomer complained, restricted him "to Negro" in the letters they had exchanged. Frank responded: ". . . the day you write as a Negro, or as an American, or as anything but a human part of *life* your work will lose a dimension." He intended to emphasize in his introduction to ***Cane*** that "you do not write as a Negro . . . that you take your race or your races naturally, as the white man takes his."[20] Yet for all his affection for Toomer, Frank ignored Toomer's special notion of himself. His introduction to ***Cane*** did underscore Toomer's Negro blood, if in a rather oblique way. Frank insisted that Toomer was to be judged not as a Negro but as an artist. Here was a book which illustrated that the Negro artist had come of age. Though Frank supposedly put the emphasis upon "artist," "Negro" was the second half of the formula. Indeed, the whole thrust of Frank's relationship with Toomer was to push him toward expression as a Negro writer.

In December, 1922, Frank brought ***Cane*** to Horace Liveright to read. After Liveright agreed to publish it, both he and Frank put pressure on Toomer to feature "Negro" in the advertisements for the novel.[21] Excited by the idea of being published and recognized as an apostle for the revitalization of American literature, Toomer wrote his own advertisement for *Holiday* and ***Cane*** called **"The South in Literature."** Toomer perceptively saw the South as presenting to the artist a fertile area, unexplored, for great regional art. He pointed to "its peasantry, its complex life above the agricultural communities, the stark theme of the black and white races, and the sweep of its great passions." Although admired by Liveright, the essay was never published.[22] What is especially interesting about **"The South in Literature"** is the candor with which Toomer, after all, referred to himself as being "of Negro descent." Rarely in the past had he made such an outright admission. He was ordinarily consistent in discussing the advantages his multi-racial makeup gave him. The mask of Jean-Christophe may have been perilously held, but he rarely let it slip. Under Frank's influence, the idealized self which Toomer had cultivated began to blur.

Though Toomer eventually broke ties with the Waldo Frank who wanted him to become a Negro writer,[23] Frank the critic of American life helped him to refine his image of himself as citizen of the world. In his own eyes he became the American artist as prophet, the man whose racial composite stood for a synthesis of the country's diverse elements. He was filled with purpose: either everything coalesced in Jean Toomer or he was nothing.

III

Throughout the 1920's and early 1930's Toomer insisted that he stood for a new breed of American, but he occasionally caught a glimpse of the reality that this idea existed mainly in his imagination. Writing ***Cane*** showed Toomer the bone beneath the skin and the sight frightened him. He saw that the world he had created in ***Cane*** held no place for him. He was not a Negro peasant, even though he celebrated that world in **"Song of the Son."** He remained on the outside, as the narrator of **"Fern"** clearly indicates. Besides, he believed that the passing of this peasant world was inevitable; it would soon merge, he told Frank, into the "general outlines of American culture."

Neither was he a New Negro. He told Frank that the urban rhythm of **"Seventh Street"** and **"Theatre"** was not peculiarly Negro but modern, "in its healthy freedom, American."[24] Although the subject matter of both pieces was clearly Negro, and although members of the Harlem Renaissance would soon exploit their common theme of urban primitivism, Toomer was determined to see his own work as an expression of his idealized self.

Much of the success of ***Cane*** arises from a tension between Toomer's real self—outcast—and his idealized self—the son who returned to the

South to capture his racial heritage in song. Kabnis was the artist *manqué*, the "son" who returned to find that he had roots in neither black nor white world. In the small Georgia town where he taught school, he existed in spiritual limbo. Lewis, on the other hand, represented Toomer's alter ego. He was a stronger Kabnis, the artist on contract with himself to make sense out of reality no matter what the price. Toomer told Lola Ridge that both Lewis and Kabnis had their sources in himself but that he pushed Lewis into the background because he only wanted a hint of Kabnis's possibilities.[25] The explanation was more rational than true. Lewis remained a shadowy figure because Kabnis's spiritual anguish was more immediate to Toomer than Lewis's strength.

The agony Toomer felt in creating Kabnis was felt again when he wrote **"Box Seat"** and **"Bona and Paul."** He told Frank that there were two versions of **"Box Seat,"** one in which Dan Moore was "sensitive and weak" and another wherein Dan's character expanded and took on new energy.[26] In the second version, as it appeared in ***Cane,*** Dan's exit after purging himself of violent emotion was a triumph over his environment. He no longer felt compromised by Muriel and her narrow middle-class world. His symbolic embrace of Mr. Barry, the bloody dwarf, was like Carrie K's actual embrace of Father John in **"Kabnis,"** but this time the "Lewis" side of Toomer won.

In **"Bona and Paul"** victory is not so easy to discern. Paul's vision of wholeness—the merger of his dark self with the white Bona—was destroyed by his compulsion to rationally dissect what he felt. No wonder, then, that Toomer did not wish to write any more books like ***Cane.*** At one time he did outline for Margaret Naumberg an epic project which would consist of a series of novels dealing with the white and brown worlds.[27] It was a dream never fulfilled because he knew that once again he would have to face that no-man's-land in himself. That is why Toomer went to France in 1924 to find the truth in Gurdjieff's cosmic consciousness. That is why Toomer increasingly referred to himself as an "American" after 1923. Concentrating on self-awareness and the abstract concept "American," he found Negro blood not an issue. These ideas provided Toomer an opportunity for living out his dream of being Jean-Christophe.

The autobiographical **"Transatlantic"** is a case in point. Based on his sea voyage to France in 1924, the unpublished manuscript was first written in 1929 and turned into a novel, also unpublished, called **"Eight Day World,"** in 1933. In this work, life aboard ship was the world in microcosm. Personalities clashed; ideological tensions occurred; but an idealized Toomer stood for harmony amid the general dissonance. He was the vortex toward which all of the ship's energies were drawn. His unique racial makeup had given him a vision of life universal, cosmopolitan. He had traveled America from north to south, from east to west. Each place had become a part of him: "red earth, cane and cotton fields. The white South. The black South . . . the old South and the new South."[28] He clearly represented a new species of American, one whom the Founding Fathers had hoped would occupy the New World. Other idealized portraits of himself appeared in ***The Gallonwerps,*** an unpublished novel written in 1927, and the published ***York Beach*** (1929). Both works revealed the author's need to see himself as a man who transcended the limitations of circumstance through psychological insight and an act of will.

Although Toomer thought he had found a self beyond the question of race, his old fears crept into his fiction. The unpublished novel ***Caromb,*** written in 1932, was intended to document his development to psychological wholeness. What ***Caromb*** really showed was that he was still searching for internal harmony as a result of the racial hostility he felt in America. Toomer had married the white novelist Margery Latimer, and the two had participated in a Gurdjieffian experiment at Portage, Wisconsin. Jean and Margery Toomer are fictionalized as John and Marian Andrews, who fled to Caromb (Carmel, California) to escape the sensationalized publicity following a communal experience in Paula (Portage). Their reputation pursued them, especially the rumor of miscegenation. The town, the gothic landscape, the local reporter who visited them, all frightened Marian. People who break taboos, she told John, come to tragic ends. And so it seemed. Strange creatures gathered on the beach at night and uttered threatening chants. The very universe appeared to be against them. In the midst of this crisis Toomer has his hero come to an epiphany—the real danger was fear itself. Thus the novel ends happily, but the reader has the distinct impression of fear and insecurity lying just beneath the surface of apparent victory.

Perhaps the best expression of Toomer's real self occurs in a short story he wrote for the *Dial* (December, 1928) called **"Mr. Costyve Duditch."** Intended as a satirical portrait of modern man, the story presented an unconscious parody of Toomer's idealized self. Duditch had leased an apartment in Chicago but rarely stayed there, believing that a true citizen of the world is always on the move. He planned to write a book entitled "How Travel Grooms the Person." Duditch was happy when he was leaving some place, on a train, or on a ship, but never at his destination. The story deals with his arrival back in Chicago and sudden exit.

An acquaintance recognized him on the street and invited him to a tea party the next day. That morning Duditch rushed to the commercial hub of Chicago, something he felt compelled to do in every city, and in a department store he accidentally broke a bowl. He had a sudden impulse to leave Chicago immediately. He went to the party, however, and enjoyed having people ask him about his travels. Carelessly, he mentioned death: to a man who makes the world his home it did not matter where he died. "It is all earth, is it not?" he asked. The party's gaiety ended. Duditch felt as if he had again broken something. He ran from the party in panic, went to his hotel, and packed to leave, with "no wish save to see no human being on earth." Duditch was a pariah with none of the glory Toomer attached to the fugitive role. While Duditch desperately needed the human community, he was unable to live in it. His contacts took the pathetic form of recognition from bellhops in faraway cities. More intimate communication frightened him into travel. More than an angst-ridden figure, he was a muted Ishmael with no tale to tell and no audience.

This brilliant little story makes one wonder why Toomer did not use the pariah theme after ***Cane*** to express black life. Duditch was certainly as "invisible" as Ellison's "invisible" protagonist, and as much an underground figure as Wright's in "The Man Who Lived Underground." It is too easy to say that Toomer, in 1928, wished to write as a white and so created an imitation J. Alfred Prufrock as the antihero in his story. The answer lies in Toomer's ambiguous feelings about himself. Duditch was an apparition—the self behind the mask of Jean-Christophe.

On June 17, 1937, Toomer told an editor of a newspaper in Santa Fe, New Mexico, that he was using his full name, Nathan Jean Toomer, to distinguish his present writings from his earlier work.[29] This decision suggests that his illusions failed him—he no longer believed in himself as Jean-Christophe. It is difficult to say whether Toomer's masks prevented him from writing great literature about black life. It is even more difficult to say if he ever came to terms with Kabnis. Most of his work remained unpublished, and the little that was published avoided those questions about his existence which troubled him most.

Notes

1. Toomer Collection, Fisk University Library, Box 16, Folder 1. Referred to below as TC.
2. On July 11, 1930, he wrote James Weldon Johnson that he did not wish to be a part of anything which emphasized "racial or cultural divisions." His creative work was not of Negro origin but sprang "from the result of racial blendings here in America which have produced a new race or stock . . . the American race or stock." Johnson had asked Toomer if he might include him in his revision of *The Book of American Negro Poetry*. TC, Box 4, Folder 11. Other examples appear in TC, Box 7, Folder 16, and Box 1, Folder 12.
3. On August 30, 1930, Toomer's friend, H. W. Whitaker, wrote Suzanne LaFollette, editor of *Freeman,* and complained that her magazine had made a mistake about the author in a recent review of *Cane.* He was not a Negro: "Frank's introduction had pernicious influence for it created this myth." Toomer read the letter and sent it to Miss LaFollette on September 1. TC, Box 10, Folder 9.
4. Darwin Turner, *In a Minor Chord* (Carbondale, Ill., 1971), p. 35.
5. For example, Arna Bontemps argues that Toomer followed the pattern of many black writers in America. Encouraged by the critical acclaim *Cane* received, Toomer no longer wanted to be just another Negro writer; he wanted to be an American writer. Being an American writer meant writing about white people. See Herbert Hill, ed., *Anger and Beyond* (New York, 1966), p. 32.
6. TC, Box 8, Folder 5.
7. TC, Box 16, Folder 1.
8. Toomer to Mae Wright, July 27, 1922, and August 21, 1922. TC, Box 10, Folder 10.
9. "Jean" is also a bastardized version of Toomer's middle name "Eugene."
10. Romain Rolland, *Jean-Christophe* (New York, 1910), trans. Gilbert Cannan, I, 557. Cannan's translation is the one Toomer read. It was published in three volumes: *Jean-Christophe, Jean-Christophe in Paris, Journey's End* (1910-1913).
11. This subject is treated in my earlier article, "The Mark of Cain and the Redemption of Art: A Study in Theme and Structure of Jean Toomer's *Cane," American Literature.* XLIV (May, 1972), 276-291.
12. TC, Box 7, Folder 5.
13. TC, Box 16, Folder 1.
14. In "Withered Skin of Berries," an unpublished story written in 1922, Art Bond and David Teyy (each an idealized Jean Toomer) tried to pump life into Vera, a beautiful light-skinned black girl who had "withered" in her association with white people. Both symbolized vitality and power; both threatened the pallid black middle-class and white societies. TC, Box 52, Folder 13. For *Natalie Mann,* see TC, Box 49, Folder 9.
15. Waldo Frank, *Our America* (New York, 1919), p. 232.

16. Waldo Frank-Jean Toomer Correspondence, Charles Patterson Van Pelt Library, University of Pennsylvania. Referred to below as WF-JT Correspondence.

17. WF-JT Correspondence.

18. TC, Box 3, Folders 6 and 7. Also, see WF-JT Correspondence.

19. TC, Box 23, Folder 6.

20. TC, Box 3, Folder 7.

21. It is important to note that Horace Liveright at this time was eager to find Negro writers. But when Liveright accused Toomer of "dodging" his colored blood, Toomer replied angrily (September 5, 1923) that "if my relationship with you is to be what I'd like it to be, I must insist that you never use such a word . . . again." TC, Box 1, Folder 5.

22. TC, Box 26, Folder 41.

23. Toomer complained that Frank could only express America but never himself. TC, Box 29, Folder 10. On December 17, 1933, he wrote to Alfred Stieglitz that Frank had become too "Jewish" in his reaction to Hitler: "What has happened to the man who wrote *Our America*? What has happened to the man who formulated the doctrine of the *whole*?" Alfred Stieglitz Archive, Beinecke Library, Yale University.

24. TC, Box 3, Folder 7.

25. TC, Box 8, Folder 8.

26. WF-JT Correspondence.

27. Undated letter (circa 1922). TC, Box 7, Folder 17.

28. TC, Box 16, Folder 3.

29. TC, Box 7, Folder 1.

ROBERT B. JONES (ESSAY DATE 1987)

SOURCE: Jones, Robert B. "Jean Toomer as Poet: A Phenomenology of the Spirit." *Black American Literature Forum* 21, no. 3 (fall 1987): 253-73.

In the following essay, Jones discusses representative poems from over the course of Toomer's career and contends that together they constitute a "direct dramatization of consciousness."

I

Jean Toomer's popularity as a writer derives almost exclusively from his lyrical narrative ***Cane.*** He shows himself there to be a poet, but few are aware of the extensive and impressive corpus of his other poems. His poetic canon may be classified into three categories: the individually published poems, the poems first published in ***Cane,*** and the mass of over 100 unpublished poems.[1] To date, however, there has been no attempt to assemble a standard edition of Toomer's poetical works, nor has there been any comprehensive study of his poems.[2] Yet it is, perhaps, through the lens of his poetry that we are provided the most revealing commentaries on Toomer as artist and philosopher.

Toomer's poetry spans more than three decades and evolves in four distinct periods: the Aesthetic Period (1919-August 1921), marked by Imagism, improvisation, and experimentation; the Ancestral Consciousness Period (September 1921-1923), characterized by forms of racial consciousness and Afro-American mysticism; the Objective Consciousness Period (1924-1939), defined by Gurdjieffian idealism and "being consciousness"; and the Religious Period (1940-1955), distinguished by Christian Existentialism, owing to an espousal of Quaker religious philosophy. His poetic canon, then, constitutes a direct dramatization of consciousness, a veritable phenomenology of the spirit.

Toomer's career as a poet began long before the publication of ***Cane.*** Between 1919 and 1921 he experimented with several forms of poetry, including haiku, lyrical impressionism, and "sound poetry." The major influences on his artistic and philosophical development during this period were Orientalism, French and American Symbolism, and Imagism. Orientalism provided the basis for the idealist philosophy evident in all stages of Toomer's intellectual development. As he describes it, "Buddhist philosophy, the Eastern teachings, occultism, theosophy. . . . These ideas challenged and stimulated me. Despite my literary purpose, I was compelled to know something more about them. So for a long time I turned my back on literature and plunged into this kind of reading. I read far and wide, for more than eight months" (**"Outline of an Autobiography"** in Turner 119). In a specifically literary context, Orientalism was also the basis for his fascination with Symbolism and Imagism. Of the French Symbolists, his literary mentor was Charles Baudelaire, whose *Les Petits Poèmes en prose* inspired many of the poems written during this period and later provided models for the prose poems and lyrical sketches in ***Cane.*** To an even greater degree, Toomer was impressed by the poetry and aesthetics of the Imagists: "Their insistence on fresh vision and on the perfect clean economical line was just what I had been looking for. I began feeling that I had in my hands the tools for my own creation" (Turner 120).

The best examples of the Imagist poetry from this period are **"And Pass," "Storm Ending," "Her Lips Are Copper Wire,"** and **"Five Vignettes."** A sustained impressionistic portrait of twilight fading into darkness, **"And Pass"** images a picturesque sea setting in two brief movements, each introduced by "When." The poem concludes in a moment of visionary awareness, as the poet's imagination is suddenly arrested by the passing clouds, the fleeting and majestic "proud shadows." Concomitant with the poet's sense of exaltation comes a sense of his own loneliness and mortality, as "night envelops / empty seas / and fading dreamships."

Also richly impressionistic in design, **"Storm Ending"** unfolds as an implied comparison between two natural phenomena, thunder and flowers, although imagery remains the crucial vehicle of meaning:

> Thunder blossoms gorgeously above our heads,
> Great, hollow, bell-like flowers,
> Ambling in the wind,
> Stretching clappers to strike our ears . . .
> Full-lipped flowers
> Bitten by the sun
> Bleeding rain
> Dripping rain like golden honey—
> And the sweet earth flying from the thunder.

This scene captures the momentous return of sunshine and tranquility to nature following a tempest, as the sound of thunder fades into the distance.

In **"Her Lips Are Copper Wire"** desire generated by a kiss is compared to electrical energy conducted between copper wires, here imaged as lips. The evocative and sensuous opening lines, addressed to an imaginary lover, well illustrate Pound's Doctrine of the Image:

> Whisper of yellow globes
> gleaming on lamp-posts that sway
> like bootleg licker drinkers in the fog
>
> and let your breath be moist against me
> like bright heads on yellow globes . . .

Toomer's **"Five Vignettes"** is a series of imagistic sketches modeled after Japanese haiku poetry. The first is a seascape portrait of "red-tiled ships" shimmering iridescently upon the water. The ships are "nervous," under the threat of clouds eclipsing their watery reflections:

> The red-tiled ships you see reflected,
> Are nervous,
> And afraid of clouds.

The second vignette images a dynamic tension between stasis and motion:

> There, on the clothes-line
> Still as she pinned them,
> Pieces now the wind may wear.

The third vignette images an old man of ninety, still living courageously, "eating peaches," and unafraid of the "worms" which threaten his very existence. The fourth is reminiscent of an Oriental proverb, especially in its idea that suffering teaches wisdom; and the fifth images a Chinese infant, as well as our common humanity:

> In Y. Den's laundry
> A Chinese baby fell
> And cried as any other.

Vignettes four and five are as "moral" as they are imagistic, each in its own way commenting on the universal human condition. As we shall see, these "message-oriented" lyrics signal a subtle shift in Toomer's pre-***Cane*** aesthetic which is more conspicuously apparent in the poems **"Banking Coal"** and **"Gum."** The basis for this shift from an imitative toward an affective theory of art is most clearly articulated in Toomer's 1921 review of Richard Aldington's essay on Imagism, "The Art of Poetry."[3]

Several of the poetic sketches recall the linguistic impressionism of Gertrude Stein's *Tender Buttons,* especially **"Face"** and the quartet **"Air," "Earth," "Fire,"** and **"Water."** In *Tender Buttons,* Stein attempted to defamiliarize our automatized linguistic perceptions by creating a noun headnote without naming it, as she illustrates in "A Carafe, That Is a Blind Glass":

> A kind in glass and a cousin, a spectacle and
> nothing strange
> A single hurt color and an arrangement in a
> system to pointing
> All this and not ordinary, not unordered in not
> resembling.
> The difference is spreading.
>
> (Stein 461)

This lyrical sketch is reminiscent of a riddle: "What is made of glass (and its 'cousin') but is different from a drinking glass in the way it spreads (bulbously) at the bottom?" The answer would be a carafe. Like Stein, Toomer attempted to register precise nuances of perception and name them with a unique word or phrase. Here he renders an image of the noun headnote **"Face"**:

> Hair—
> silver-gray,
> like streams of stars
> Brows—
> recurved canoes
> quivered by the ripples blown by pain,
> Her eyes—
> mists of tears
> condensing on the flesh below

Toomer's quartet ensemble also demonstrates precisely how linguistic impressionism serves as a poetic medium for communicating both the uniqueness and universality of our common perceptions of the cosmic order, as in **"Fire"**:

Flickers, flames, burns.
Burns into a thing—depth, profundity
"Hot after something,"
Sparking, flowing, "in a fever"
Always stewing smoking panting
Flashy

Yet another form of linguistic impressionism is revealed in **"Sound Poem"** (I), **"Sound Poem"** (II), and **"Poem in C,"** all of which represent adaptations of French Symbolist aesthetics. The French Symbolists maintained that the purpose of language is to evoke a reality beyond the senses, rather than to state plainly or to inform. In their attempts to describe the *essence* of an object and not the object itself, they sought to produce the effects of music, thinking of images as having abstract values like musical notes and chords. Sounds and associations, then, perform the act of communication, while meaning is eclipsed, as in **"Sound Poem"** (I):

Mon sa me el kirimoor,
Ve dice kor, korrand ve deer,
Leet vire or sand vite,
Re sive tas tor;
Tu tas tire or re sim bire,
Rozan dire ras to por tantor,
Dorozire, soron,
Bas ber vind can sor, gosham,
Mon sa me el, a som on oor.

Here Toomer uses sounds and words from several languages, such as French ("mon sa me" ["mon sommeil"], "vite," "tas," "bas"), Latin ("kor" and "soron"), Spanish ("me," "el," "dice," "tu," "por"), and Japanese ("kirimoor"), as well as English, to open poetic avenues to thought, in the tradition of Rimbaud, Baudelaire, and Laforgue. An exercise in formalism and a lesson in the mystical powers of language, this sound poem also employs "-or" end rhymes, "-ire" internal rhymes, repetition ("Mon sa me el"), parallelism ("Leet vire or sand vite" and "Tu tas tire or re sim bire"), and linguistic cognates to create the illusion of meaning, while sounds guide us through the process of poetry.

II

In the months between September of 1921 and December of 1922, Toomer wrote the poems in ***Cane,*** evocative of an empathetic union between the spirit of the artist and the spirit of Afro-American mysticism. Indeed, in describing the formal design in ***Cane,*** what he termed "the spiritual entity behind the work," Toomer indicated that he viewed the book, at least retrospectively, as a mandala: "From the point of view of the spiritual entity behind the work, the curve really starts with **'Bona and Paul'** (awakening), plunges into **'Kabnis,'** emerges in **'Karintha,'** etc. swings upward into **'Theater'** and **'Box Seat,'** and ends (pauses) in **'Harvest Song.'**"[4] The mandala, a symbol of integration and transmutation of the self in Buddhist philosophy, is an arrangement of images from the unconscious to form a constellation. Usually a formalized, circular design containing or contained by a figure of five points of emphasis, each representing the chief objects of psychic interest for the maker, a mandala functions to unite the conscious intellectual perceptions of its creator with his or her unconscious psychic drives and intuitions. A mandala, then, is both an instrument of the self's awakening and a chart of its spiritual evolution. In accordance with Toomer's spiritual design, the poems which begin this mandalic cycle—**"Reapers," "November Cotton Flower," "Cotton Song," "Song of the Son," "Georgia Dusk," "Nullo," "Conversion,"** and **"Portrait in Georgia"**—represent celebrations of ancestral consciousness, whereas the ones which end the cycle—**"Beehive," "Prayer,"** and **"Harvest Song"**—chronicle the poet's loss of empathetic union with Afro-American consciousness.

The poems which begin the cycle celebrate Afro-American culture and lament its disappearance. Written in iambic pentameter couplets, **"Reapers"** depicts black workers in a rural field setting. The first half of the poem describes "the sound of steel on stone" as the reapers "start their silent swinging, one by one." The second half contrasts this human activity with the sharp efficiency of a mechanical mower, which kills a field rat with machine-like precision and continues on its way. The contrast between the human and the mechanical emphasizes not only the displacement of black workers by machines, but also the passing of an era. The poem ends with a lament for the destruction of nature by the machine: "I see the blade, / Blood-stained, continue cutting weeds and shade."

Also written in iambic pentameter couplets, **"November Cotton Flower"** is a variation of the Italian sonnet. The octave images a late autumn setting, the end of the cotton season. Drought ravages the land as birds seek water in wells a hundred feet below the ground. The sestet describes the blooming of a November cotton flower amid this arid and barren scene, an event perceived to be supernatural by the local inhabitants: "Superstition saw / Something it had never seen before." The concluding couplet reveals the poem to be an extended metaphor, completing the analogy of the flower's mystery and sudden beauty in terms of a beautiful and spontaneous brown-eyed woman: "Brown eyes that loved without a trace of fear / Beauty so sudden for that time of year." Like the November cotton flower, the woman is an anomaly within her depressed and rustic environment.

"Cotton Song" belongs to a subgenre of Afro-American folk songs which captures the agony and essence of slavery. The poet uses music—the work song itself—to symbolize the medium by which slaves transcended the vicissitudes of slavery. Moreover, it is precisely spiritual freedom which engenders thoughts of political freedom:

> Cotton bales are the fleecy way
> Weary sinners bare feet trod,
> Softly, softly to the throne of God,
> We ain't agwine t wait until th Judgement Day!

"Song of the Son" and **"Georgia Dusk"** are swan songs for the passing Afro-American folk spirit. **"Song of the Son"** develops in two movements, with images of sight, sound, and smell. The first movement invokes images of smoke and music. Once stately Georgia pines have been reduced to smouldering sawdust piles; smoke spiraling toward heaven is the by-product of their former grandeur. Similarly, the "parting soul" of the Black American folk experience has been reduced to an evening song which, like the smoke, carries throughout the valley of cane. The poet is imaged as the prodigal son, returning "just before an epoch's sun declines" to capture in art the fleeting legacy of a "song-lit race of slaves." The second movement develops as an extended metaphor of slaves as "deep purple ripened plums, / Squeezed, and bursting in the pine-wood air." The imagery recalls the cloying state of fruit as it passes into the oblivion of the post-harvest. Yet the spectatorial poet is able to preserve "one plum" and "one seed" to immortalize both the past and the passing order in art.

In **"Georgia Dusk"** the sky relents to the setting sun and night, in a "lengthened tournament for flashing gold." In this nocturnal setting, "moon and men and barking hounds" are engaged in "making folk-songs from soul sounds." As in **"Song of the Son,"** wraiths of smoke from a "pyramidal sawdust pile" symbolize the passing of an era supplanted by industry, ". . . only chips and stumps are left to show / The solid proof of former domicile." With the advent of dusk, however, comes a heightened sense of the black man's union with the spiritual world, "with vestiges of pomp, / Race memories of king, and caravan, / High-priests, and ostrich, and a ju-ju man." These mystical moments inspire the people to sing, their voices resonating and passing throughout the piny woods and the valley of cane. The poet concludes with an invocation to the singers: "Give virgin lips to cornfield concubines, / Bring dreams of Christ to dusky cane-lipped throngs." The juxtaposition of secular and religious imagery symbolizes the mystical power of Afro-American folk music to harmonize the earthly (the "cornfield concubines" and "dusky cane-lipped throngs") and the heavenly ("sacred whispers," "virgin lips," and "dreams of Christ").

"Nullo," "Conversion," and **"Portrait in Georgia"** are Imagist in form and design. **"Nullo"** captures the fiery, iridescent beauty of golden, sun-drenched pine needles' falling upon a cowpath in a forest at sunset. The poet effectively arrests the stillness and solitude of the moment: "Rabbits knew not of their falling, / Nor did the forest catch aflame." **"Conversion"** images the spirit of Afro-American culture—the "African Guardian of souls"—as compromised and debased by Western influences, "drunk with rum, / Feasting on a strange cassava, / yielding to new words and a weak palabra / of a white-faced sardonic god." **"Portrait in Georgia"** is reminiscent of **"Face,"** in which Toomer attempts to render a vision of the poem's title. This Georgian portrait, however, is one of a lynched and burned black woman:

> Breath—the last sweet scent of cane,
> And her slim body, white as the ash
> of black flesh after flame.

The sonnet **"Beehive"** discloses a shift in the poet's consciousness from spiritual identification to spiritual alienation. This lyric develops in two movements as an extended metaphor of the poet as exile in Eden. The first movement depicts the world as a black beehive, buzzing with activity on a moonlit, silvery night. The second movement, however, describes the spectatorial poet's estrangement, when he characterizes himself as an unproductive and exploitative "drone, / Lipping honey, / Getting drunk with silver honey." Although he has tasted the "silver honey" of Afro-American culture, he is nevertheless unable to bridge the gap between himself and his fellow workers, unable to "fly out past the moon / and curl forever in some far-off farmyard flower."

"Prayer" describes a waning of the spirit, and of the creative powers, which results from a dissociation of inner and outer, soul and body: "My body is opaque to the soul. / Driven of the spirit, long have I sought to temper it unto the spirit's longing, / But my mind, too, is opaque to the soul." This failure of the spirit, and of its creative powers, is reflected metapoetically in the lines "I am weak with much giving. / I am weak with the desire to give more."[5]

Completing the mandalic or spiritual design, **"Harvest Song"** dramatizes the poet's loss of empathetic union with the essence of Afro-American culture and consciousness. Ironically titled, **"Harvest Song"** describes an artist's inability to become one with the subjects of his art, as well as his inability to transform the raw materials of his labor into art. Reminiscent of Robert Frost's "After Apple-Picking," **"Harvest Song"** develops as an extended portrait of the poet as reaper. Although the poet/reaper has successfully cradled the fruits of his labor, when he cracks a grain from the store of his oats, he cannot taste its inner essence. In vain, he attempts to stare through time and space to understand the sources of his inspiration; he also tries to make up the physical distance by straining to hear the calls of other reapers and their songs. But his dust-caked senses preclude any meaningful or helpful intervention. The "knowledge of hunger" he fears is the failure of consciousness and of the creative impulse. Thus, he is reluctant to call other reapers for fear they will share their truly inspiring grains, grains he is unable to assimilate. "It would be good to hear their songs . . . reapers of the sweet-stalk'd / cane, cutters of the corn . . . even though their throats / cracked and the strangeness of their voices deafened me." Still, he beats his soft, sensitive palms against the stubble of the fields of labor, and his pain is sweeter and more rewarding than the harvest itself. He is then comforted by the pains of his struggles, although they will not bring him knowledge of his hunger.

A major unpublished poem that is also a product of this period is the mystical and evocative **"Tell Me,"** which contains nature imagery evocative of the local-color poems in ***Cane,*** although it was inspired by the majestic mountains and the scenic Shenandoah River near Harpers Ferry. Written in three four-line stanzas of rhymed iambic pentameter, this poem unfolds with a series of apostrophes to the "dear beauty of the dusk," as the poet implores the spirit of nature to share with him its dark and mysterious essence.

III

Shortly after the publication of ***Cane*** in October of 1923, Toomer began studying the austere idealism of the Greek-Armenian mystic Georges Gurdjieff, and in 1924 he attended the Gurdjieff Institute for the Harmonious Development of Man at the Ch teau de Prieuré in Fontainebleau, France. Toomer sailed back to America after two months, but returned to the Gurdjieff Institute in 1926, 1927, and 1929. Yet despite the rigorous demands engendered by his devotion to Gurdjieff, Toomer continued writing and assembling his poetry.[6] Indeed, as we shall see, poetry provided an artful medium for imaging his ideas on the phenomenology of "Objective Consciousness." While Gurdjieffian philosophy is arcane and obscure, we need not concern ourselves with its esoterica in order to formulate its major tenets as they relate to Toomer.[7] For purposes of examining the poetry written during this period, three issues must be addressed: the concept of the Absolute, the nature of consciousness, and the function of art.

Gurdjieff's concept of the Absolute is set forth in his Ray of Creation theory of the universe, which he uses to illustrate what he terms the Two Great Cosmic Laws of the universe, the Law of Three and the Law of Seven. According to Gurdjieff, the individual is a small model of the universe, made of the same materials and governed by the same rules. His Law of Three states that all phenomena, from the subatomic to the cosmic, result from the interaction of three principles or forces: two opposing forces, and a third which effects synthesis. Within the Absolute, however, these forces are supremely regulated and harmonized by Will, Full Consciousness, and Understanding. It is this supreme force which is responsible for the creation of the universe. The Law of Seven, like the Law of Three, describes the universe in terms of an immense network of energy radiations or vibrations. In accordance with the Law of Seven, the Ray of Creation was a "descending octave," much like the Great Chain of Being, with "intervals" which must be bridged if the continuous flow of energy radiations is to be maintained.

In terms of the nature of consciousness, the "ordinary man," Gurdjieff tells us, "is a three-brained being," his ontological status shared among three autonomous centers: physical, emotional, and intellectual. In some people the center of gravity is located in the moving center; in others, in the intellectual or emotional center. Beyond these centers, however, there exist higher levels of "objective consciousness," which Gurdjieff calls the "higher emotional center" and the "higher thinking center." On these levels of mystical awareness, the self is the recipient of a miraculous "energy" from a non-material source, in direct communion with the supernatural. In religious philosophy, this state of consciousness is called "illumination," "enlightenment," or "epiphany." In the words of Richard Gregg, "There is a blending of subject and object, a mutual absorption, a forgetting of everything else; there is often delight, and exaltation, an enthusiasm, a rapture, a deep and abiding joy. . . . It is not knowing from without; it is a knowing from within. It is not knowing about; it is unitive knowledge. Unitive knowledge is much more complete and deeper than knowing about" (cited in Walker 49-50). Within this realm of unitive knowledge, one is impressed not by the diversity of experience, but by its unity. Thus the closer a person gets to pure, objective consciousness, the more one finds oneself absorbed into a nameless entity immeasurably greater than the self. In this way, Gurdjieffian idealism posits the self as undifferentiated consciousness, energized by the Ray of Creation.

Finally, it is important to understand Gurdjieff's conception of art, particularly in the light of an affective aesthetic which generally characterizes the poetry Toomer wrote during this period. Gurdjieff's art aesthetic is perhaps most clearly revealed in his theory of "Objective Art":

> I measure the merit of art by its consciousness, you by its unconsciousness. A work of objective art is a book which transmits the artist's ideas not directly through words or signs or hieroglyphics but through feelings which he evokes in the beholder consciously and with full knowledge of what he is doing and why he is doing it.
>
> (cited in Walker 116)

In view of this aesthetic and its influence on Toomer, it would be appropriate to surmise that the poetry of this period was written to inspire higher consciousness. Yet we must also keep in mind that Toomer had already declared his preference for affective over emotive art as early as 1921, in his review of "The Art of Poetry."

Toomer's "Objective Consciousness" poetry may be grouped into three categories: poems on being consciousness and self-integration, such as **"The Lost Dancer," "Unsuspecting,"** and **"White Arrow"**; poems revealing mysticism (**"At Sea"** and **"The Gods Are Here"**) and **"New American"** consciousness (**"The Blue Meridian"**); poems on consciousness of the self that is the cosmos, as represented by **"Peers"** and **"Living Earth"**; and poems on consciousness of the self that is humanity, as represented by **"Men"** and **"People."**

"The Lost Dancer" expresses the poet's quest for unity of being and self-integration in terms of the failure of idealism. The dancer/artist figure is "lost" because he is unable to discover a "source of magic" whereby he can transcend the rigorous imperatives of subject/object dualism—inner and outer, essence and personality, self and world, art and life—, here symbolized by the metaphysical "vibrations of the dance" and the physical "feet dancing on earth of sand":

> Spatial depths of being survive
> The birth to death recurrences
> Of feet dancing on earth of sand;
> Vibrations of the dance survive
> The sand; the sand, elect, survives
> The dancer. He can find no source
> Of magic adequate to bind
> The sand upon his feet, his feet
> Upon his dance, his dance upon
> The diamond body of his being.

Unity of being, then, follows when the dancer is able to synthesize "the birth to death recurrences / Of feet dancing on earth of sand" (object) with "the diamond body of his being," the prismatic brilliance of inner essence (subject), to form a unified complex, the transcendental self.

"Unsuspecting" utilizes imagery borrowed from horticulture ("culls," "trims," and "prunes"), as well as reflexive rhyme ("mind" and "rind"), to suggest that refined, cultivated intellect without corresponding inner development is naïve and superficial[8]:

> There is a natty kind of mind
> That slicks its thoughts,
> Culls its oughts,
> Trims its views,
> Prunes its trues,
> And never suspects it is a rind.

Composed in iambic pentameter, **"White Arrow"** sketches the poet's Lawrentian notion of female self-actualization in contrasting images of sleeping or existing and waking or being, images drawn from the language of Gurdjieff's system. The poem unfolds as an affectionate admonition to an unnamed individual to liberate herself from the "sleep and fear" induced by the authority of gender socialization: "In faith and reason you were swift and free, / White arrow, as you were, awake and be!"

Both **"At Sea"** and **"The Gods Are Here"** offer expressions of mystical experiences. **"At Sea"** dramatizes an ephemeral and fleeting moment during which the poet is transfixed by the awesome power and beauty of the sea. During this mystical state of consciousness, he experiences a "pang of transience," when the spirit of the universe briefly reveals itself in the life and order of the cosmos:

Once I saw large waves
Crested with white-caps;
A driving wind
Transformed the caps
Into scalding spray—
"Swift souls," I addressed them—
They turned towards me
Startled
Sea-descending faces;
But I, not they,
Felt the pang of transience.

"The Gods Are Here" develops as an extended contrast between two forms of asceticism, both of which release the soul from bondage and permit its union with the divine: There is the hermit on a mountain among the wilds of nature and the poet within the domestic environment of society:

This is no mountain
But a house
No rock of solitude
But a family chair,
No wilds
But life appearing
As life anywhere domesticated,
Yet I know the gods are here,
And that if I touch them
I will arise
And take majesty into the kitchen.

A minor classic in American literature, **"The Blue Meridian"** is a Whitmanian affirmation of democratic idealism, a poetics for democracy.[9] In describing the original text of this poem, Toomer reveals his "New American" or millennial consciousness: "I wrote a poem called **'The First American,'** the idea of which was that here in America we are in the process of forming a new race, that I was one of the first conscious members of this race" (Turner 120-21). Toomer believed that his own blend of ethnic strains, like America's melting pot itself, conferred upon him a mystical selfhood and a transcendental vision of America. Like Walt Whitman, he believed that there is a central identity of self which is the foundation of freedom, that each individual is unique and yet identical with all, and that democracy is the surest guarantee of individual values. And, like Whitman, he attempted to resolve the conflict between individual and society at the transpersonal level by positing his own self, "the first American," as the self of all beings. Toomer's Adamic conception of himself as one of the first conscious members of a united human race is, then, the very cornerstone of his "First American" or "New American" consciousness. Such an exalted mind, carrying with it the conviction of absolute novelty, recalls the "Cosmic Consciousness" of Canadian psychologist R. M. Bucke. "Along with the consciousness of the cosmos," writes Bucke, "there occurs an intellectual enlightenment which alone would place the individual on a new plane of existence—would make him almost a member of a new species" (38). Having formulated an identity, Toomer, as the new American Adam, proceeds to become the maker of his own conditions by projecting a model society. According to R. W. B. Lewis, the American Adam "*projects* a world of order and meaning and identity into either a chaos or a vacuum; he does not *discover* it" (51). This is precisely what Toomer does in ***The Blue Meridian and Other Poems***:

When the spirit of mankind conceived
A new world in America, and dreamed
The human structure rising from this base,
The land was a vacant house to new inhabitants,
A vacuum compelled by nature to be filled
Spirit could not wait to time select,
Weighing in wisdom each piece,
Fitting each right thing into each right place
But had to act, trusting the vision of the possible.

"Peers" opens with an apostrophe to nature, here symbolized by a rock. For the poet, however, the mutual existence of man and nature confirms their ontological status as peers:

Some day I will see again
Your substance in the sacred flame
And meet you undisguised
In the root of all that lives.

Similarly, Toomer compares the life and order of the universe with the life and order of man in **"Living Earth"**:

Is not Earth, Being,
Is it not a core of life,
Has it not organisms with spine,
Glands, entrails, and a sage navel?
Is it not a field of Force,
Force and field living?

Rejecting the idea that the Earth is ruled by fate, blind force, and accident, the poet avers that the only conceivable accident is for mankind to attribute to the universe the blindness that is fixed within man himself. The poem ends on a note of questioning the nature of consciousness in nature, as a first step in understanding the nature of consciousness in man:

Separate in bodies
Many in desires
One in ultimate reality
Strangers on the earth

Prisoners in this world
Natives of deity.

In like manner, **"People"** asserts the unity of humanity and the belief that individuals must use their inner eyes if they are to see beings instead of races:

What odd passions,
What queer beliefs
That men who believe in sights
Disbelieve in seers.

In addition to the Objective Consciousness poetry composed during this period, Toomer also wrote poems inspired by the landscape and culture of the American Southwest, particularly New Mexico. **"Imprint for Rio Grande," "I Sit in My Room," "Rolling, Rolling,"** and **"It is Everywhere"** represent a previously unrevealed dimension of Toomer as local colorist, depicting the natural beauty of the American Southwest and, as in **"It is Everywhere,"** a kaleidoscopic panorama of the American landscape.[10]

IV

In the summer of 1938 Toomer moved to Bucks County, Pennsylvania, where he was almost immediately attracted to Quakerism. During his apprenticeship with the Society of Friends, he immersed himself in Quaker religious philosophy and wrote numerous essays on George Fox and Quakerism. In 1940, he joined the Society of Friends.[11] His interest in Quaker religious philosophy sprang from his own idea that the Society of Friends provided a radical venture beyond Objective Consciousness to a vital and transforming religious faith:

> Quakers assembled, I had been told, for silent worship and waited for the spirit to move them. This appealed to me because I had practiced meditation. Years before I had read a brief account of George Fox that impressed me. I had heard of the Quaker reputation for practicing what they preached. . . . Prior to coming into contact with Friends I had been convinced that God is both immanent and transcendent, and that the purpose of life is to grow up to God; that within man there is a wonderful power that can transform him, lift him into new birth; that we have it in us to rise to a life wherein brotherhood is manifest and war impossible.[12]

In order to define the poetry of this period as Christian Existential, two factors must be considered. In the first place, Toomer envisioned Quaker religious philosophy as a bridge between two (Kierkegaardian) levels of consciousness, the ethical or social concerns of Objective Consciousness and the religious or theistic concerns of Christianity. Indeed, in 1938 he sought to reconcile Gurdjieffian idealism with Quakerism by organizing a cooperative of both Quakers and lay individuals called Friends of Being. As we shall see, the ostensible conflict remains as the basis for a pervasive Christian Existentialism. In the second place, in contrast with Gurdjieffian idealism, Quakerism and Christian Existentialism comprise fundamentally the same religious philosophy.[13] In temperament and philosophy, Toomer's consciousness is perhaps best described as Christian Existential. And it is precisely this consciousness which is the genesis of his spiritual odyssey as a Quaker poet.

The meditative verses and confessional lyrics from this period render a vision of man as alone, estranged from society, the universe, and God. Reflecting an evolution in the poet's spiritual consciousness, these poems fall into several categories: confessional lyrics manifesting subtle tensions between Being Consciousness and Quaker Consciousness, as in **"Desire"**; meditations regarding mediation between the self and God, such as **"The Chase"** and **"Cloud"**; confessional lyrics on asceticism, such as **"Motion and Rest"**; and lyrical verses of orthodox Quakerism, such as **"To Gurdjieff Dying," "The Promise,"** and **"They Are Not Missed."**

In **"Desire,"** conflicting claims of consciousness are imaged as two types and levels of love. The poem opens with religious allusions to "suffering" and "the opened heart," symbolic of the Sacred Heart. The imagery then shifts to reflect the poet's Being Consciousness: "I seek the universal love of beings; / May I be made one with that love / And extend to everything I turn towards that love." The conflict between the "ethical" exigencies of agapé and the "moral" concerns of Logos are conditionally reconciled in favor of the latter in the closing lines of this poem:

In this new season of a forgotten life
I move towards the heart of love
  Of all that breathes;
I would enter that radiant center
  and from that center live.

The image of white birds in flight dramatizes the poet's quest for spiritual mediation in **"The Chase,"**

As the white bird leaves the dirty nest,
Flashes in the dangling sky,
And merges in the blue up there,
May my spirit quit me,
And fly the beam straight
Into thy power and thy glory.

"Cloud" employs a variation of the five-line tanka to speculate on the "livid cloud" which separates man from the "salient light" of Quaker religious faith.

"Motion and Rest" images white birds coming to rest in rendering a tranquil portrait of asceticism:

> I have watched white birds alight
> On a barn roof
> And come to rest, instantly still,
> Effortlessly relaxed and poised,
> In them no trace of former motion.
> So would I come to rest
> So should we come to rest
> At quiet time.

Within the Society of Friends, "Quietism" refers to a mystical state of consciousness wherein one experiences annihilation of the will and passive absorption in the Inner Light. The metaphor of motion and rest thus effectively dramatizes two contrasting states of consciousness: the realm of the world, with its emphasis on social engagement, and the realm of the spirit, which emphasizes quietistic contemplation.

"To Gurdjieff Dying" is a carefully crafted Italian sonnet, with variations in rhyme scheme. The poem employs end rhymes in the opening and closing lines of both the octave and the sestet, with intermediate iterating end rhymes, while retaining the conventions of iambic pentameter. A profound repudiation of Gurdjieff, this sonnet demonstrates the poet's devout acceptance of Quaker religious faith. The octave disparages Gurdjieff for "Knowing the Buddhic law but to pervert / Its power of peace into dissevering fire." He is also described as a seducer "coiled as serpent round the Phallic Tau / And sacramental loaf" and as a false prophet, "Son of the Elder Liar." The sestet further reproves Gurdjieff for having "deformed the birth-bringings of light / Into lust-brats of black imaginings, / Spilling Pan-passions in the incarnate round / Of hell and earth." The concluding lines invoke the "Lords of the Shining Rings / Skilled in White Magic," the authority of religion itself, to "Save even Gurdjieff from his hell forthright." Light and dark imagery here effectively contrasts the "black imaginings" of Gurdjieffian idealism and the "white magic" of religious faith.

"The Promise" reveals an acceptance of the paradox of religious faith in contrasting images of spring in nature and "new birth" in man. Whereas during the years of his earlier idealism Toomer had sought to spread the gospel of pantheism and cosmic consciousness, here there is manifested an essential disharmony between man and nature, and between man and God. That is, although "the cycles of the soul are sure as those of sap," in nature seasonal cycles ensure the eternal return of spring, whereas in man there is no such guarantee, for he possesses the will to seek union with God within. "It is not guaranteed that God, / Coming from the south with light and love / Will touch the seed, melt our crusts / And bestir Himself in us / When earth moves from cold to warmth." Rather, in man the spirit must "break free," in a Kierkegaardian leap of faith, before "Winter shall give way to spring within."

"They Are Not Missed" images God, time, and eternity in the context of Old Testament religious faith. The poem opens with a series of metaphors, suggesting that much in the way that old paths "forget the bruised feet," ancestral trees forget "their fallen leaves," and old houses forget "the births and deaths that echo in / Their rooms," God is similarly indifferent to "the souls who shared his glory once, long ago." That is, God, here described as "the ancient one," teleologically suspends the temporal in favor of the eternal. Like Abraham in Kierkegaard's famous parable of the conflict between the claims of man and the claims of God, man must acquiesce to God's prudent and omniscient management of the universe. Indeed, in this poem there exists no tension between the ethical and the religious; instead, there is complete acceptance of man's responsibility to "seek or sink . . . Till past and present meet, and time ends."

V

Toomer's poetic canon constitutes a study in the phenomena of the spirit, not only in its revelations of spiritualist philosophies—Orientalism, Afro-American Mysticism, Gurdjieffian Idealism, and Quakerism—but in its formal expression of the poet's highest goals—to essentialize and spiritualize experience. "I am not a romanticist," wrote Toomer, "I am not a classicist nor a realist, in the usual sense of these terms. I am an essentialist. Or, to put it in other words, I am a spiritualizer, a poetic realist. This means two things. I try to lift facts, things, happenings to the planes of rhythm, feeling, and significance. I try to clothe and give body to potentialities" (**"Reflections of an Earth-Being"** in Turner 20). He describes the mystical ecstasy of poetic creation in terms of an epiphanical experience: "A flash bridges the gap between inner and outer, causing a momentary fusion and wholeness. Thus poetry starts, at least to me." Yet, in the end, he viewed poetry not as sheer aesthetic pleasure, but as a means of enlarging one's heart and consciousness. In his own words, "Poems are Offerings. Gifts to me I give to you."[14]

Notes

1. The individually published poems are "Banking Coal," "Song of the Son," "Georgia Dusk," "Harvest Song," "Gum," "White Arrow," "Brown River, Smile," "The Blue Meridian," "See the Heart," "Five Vignettes," "The Lost Dancer," "At Sea," "And Pass," "Angelic Eve," "Honey of Being," "Sing Yes," "Men," "Peers," "Mended," "One Within," and "Imprint for Rio Grande." "Reapers," "Cotton Song," "Nullo," "Conversion," "Portrait in Georgia," and "Beehive" were initially published in *Cane.* The unpublished poems, including an untitled 1931 collection, a 1934 volume entitled *The Blue Meridian and Other Poems,* and the most comprehensive of the volumes, *The Wayward and the Seeking* (circa 1940), are located in Box 50 of the Jean Toomer Collection, housed in the Beinecke Library at Yale University.

2. Bernard Bell explores thematic relationships in "A Key to the Poems in *Cane*"; also, Carolyn Taylor discusses the Mill House poems (1936-1941) in the light of Gurdjieffian philosophy in her dissertation. Some of Taylor's research misrepresents the poems, for she fails to consider the complex intersection of Gurdjieffian idealism and Quakerism during this transitional stage in Toomer's development.

3. See Aldington 167-80. In his review, Toomer extols the formal and technical precision of Imagist poetry before arguing philosophically that poetry should be "moral" as well as imitative. He takes exception to Aldington's assertion that "the old cant of a poet's 'message' is completely discredited," arguing eloquently that poets and readers of the Western world are more inspired by what he terms "the mighty voices of the past" than mere pictorial beauty. Toomer then chides those poets "whose eyes are so charmed and fascinated by the gem, by its outward appearance, by its external form, that the spirit behind the gem is not perceived." Thus, while he adopts the formalism inherent in Pound's Doctrine of the Image, he rejects the Imagist prohibition against "message" as an integral part of the poem. Toomer's review may be located in the Jean Toomer Collection, Box 55, Folder 6.

4. Jean Toomer, Letter to Waldo Frank, 12 Dec. 1922, Jean Toomer Collection, Box 3, Folder 6. Retrospectively, Toomer viewed *Cane* as a "spiritual fusion" of his inner and his outer selves: "While my native instinct to dreams and reading built up that inner life by means of which the outer is transformed into works of art, by means of which the outer gets its deeper meaning, it must not be thought, however, that these two loves existed, as it were, side by side in a mutual and sustaining contract. For a long while just the opposite was true. Which ever was for the time being dominant would try to deny and cut off the other. And from this conflict a most distressing friction arose. In fact, only a year or so ago did they creatively come together. *Cane* is the first evidence of this fusion" (Jean Toomer Collection, Box 64, Folder 15).

5. In a letter to Waldo Frank, dated July 25, 1922, Toomer confesses, "Your letters, together with a bit of analysis on my part, have convinced me that the impulse which sprang from Sparta, Georgia last fall has just about fulfilled and spent itself" (Jean Toomer Collection, Box 3, Folder 6).

6. In 1931, Toomer assembled his poems in a loosely bound, untitled collection, divided into three parts: the extended prose poem "Sing Yes," twenty-eight lyric poems, and "The Blue Meridian." During the next three years, he added eleven poems to his collection, deleted others, and rearranged the titles, retaining the overall tripartite structure. In 1934, he personally copyrighted the volume and entitled it *The Blue Meridian and Other Poems.* Toomer projected two other volumes, both undated: *Day Will Come* (also entitled *Rise*) and *As Hands Unturned.* But by far the most complete and comprehensive of his projected volumes is *The Wayward and the Seeking,* which contains seventy poems, including fifty that do not appear in either of the earlier collections.

7. The most comprehensive studies of Gurdjieff's philosophy are those by Walker, Waldberg, King, and Ouspensky. In this context, see also Jean Toomer, "Why I Entered the Gurdjieff Work," Jean Toomer Collection, Box 66, Folder 8.

8. Toomer studied agricultural science at the University of Wisconsin (1914) and at the Massachusetts College of Agriculture (1916). His own belief in the unity of man and nature is the basis for much of the mysticism in *Cane,* as well as for the Wordsworthian pantheism that characterizes the Objective Consciousness Period.

9. Between the summer of 1920 and the fall of 1921, Toomer read Whitman's *The Complete Writings* as well as the available secondary criticism, chiefly on *Leaves of Grass.* It was during this period that he wrote drafts for "The First American," later revised as "Brown River, Smile" (1931) and finally revised as "The Blue Meridian" (1936). For discussion of "The Blue Meridian," see Wagner 272-81 and Bell's "Jean Toomer's 'Blue Meridian'" 77-80.

10. In 1925 Mabel Dodge Luhan invited Toomer to visit Taos, New Mexico, and lecture on Gurdjieff's philosophy of harmonious development. Several years later, in 1934, he and Marjorie Content lived in Taos for several weeks following their marriage. In 1939, the Toomers drove from San Francisco to Santa Fe after returning from India. In the context of Toomer's writings, see Quirk and Fleming 524-32.

11. During his apprenticeship with the Society of Friends, Toomer read voraciously—George Fox's *Journal,* Fox's epistles entitled *A Day Book of Counsel and Comfort,* Robert Barclay's *An Apology for the True Christian Divinity,* William Penn's *Rise and Progress of the People Called Quakers* and *No Cross, No Crown,* Issac Pennington's *Letters,* John Woolman's *Journal,* and Rufus Jones's multi-volume edition of the Quaker History Series.

12. Jean Toomer, "Why I Joined the Society of Friends," Jean Toomer Collection, Box 28, Folder 19.

13. See West 25. According to West, "No quotations are necessary to show that there are likenesses between Quaker and existential thought. Quakers are Existential Christians, and Fox, though he had not the philosophical equipment of Sören Kierkegaard, attacked in his life the illusion against which Kierkegaard preached: 'the illusion that there is such a "thing" as Christianity, or that any "thing," be it creed, history, code or organization, can be Christian. Only the

subjective individual can be a Christian.' Thus Richard Niebuhr describes Kierkegaard, and with the same words he might as truly have spoken of Fox. . . . Kierkegaard was in many respects waging Fox's battle two hundred years after Fox." Also, see Brinton 29.

14. Jean Toomer, "Poetry and Spiritual Rebirth," Jean Toomer Collection, Box 25, Folder 20. In a 1970 interview with Ann Shockley, Marjorie Content Toomer noted that Toomer abandoned his career as a writer in 1955. My own research corroborates Mrs. Toomer's assertion. Jean Toomer died on March 30, 1967.

Works Cited

Aldington, Richard. "The Art of Poetry." *Dial* 69 (1920): 167-80.

Bell, Bernard. "A Key to the Poems in *Cane*." *CLA Journal* 14 (1971): 251-58.

———. "Jean Toomer's 'Blue Meridian': The Poet as Prophet of a New Order of Man." *Black American Literature Forum* 14 (1980): 77-80.

Brinton, Howard. *The Religious Philosophy of Quakerism*. Wallingford: Pendle Hill, 1973.

Bucke, Richard M. *Cosmic Consciousness: A Study in the Evolution of the Human Mind*. New York: Dutton, 1923.

King, Daly. *The Oragean Version*. New York: Privately printed, 1951.

Lewis, R. W. B. *The American Adam*. Chicago: U of Chicago P, 1955.

Oupensky, P. D. *In Search of the Miraculous*. New York: Harcourt, 1949.

Quirk, Tom, and Robert Fleming. "Jean Toomer's Contributions to the *New Mexico Sentinel*." *CLA Journal* 19 (1976): 524-32.

Shockley, Ann. Oral History Interview with Marjorie Content Toomer. 24 Oct. 1970.

Stein, Gertrude. *Selected Writings*. Ed. Carl Van Vechten. New York: Vintage, 1962.

Taylor, Susan. "'Blend Us with Thy Being': Jean Toomer's Mill House Poems." Diss. Boston C, 1977.

Toomer, Jean. *Cane*. New York: Boni, 1923.

Turner, Darwin, ed. *The Wayward and the Seeking*. Washington: Howard UP, 1980.

Wagner, Jean. *Black Poets of the United States*. Trans. Kenneth Douglas. Urbana: U of Illinois P, 1973.

Waldberg, Michel. *Gurdjieff: An Approach to His Ideas*. Trans. Steve Cox. London: Routledge, 1981.

Walker, Kenneth. *A Study of Gurdjieff's Teachings*. London: Jonathan Cape, 1957.

West, Jessamyn. *The Quaker Reader*. New York: Viking, 1962.

NELLIE MCKAY (ESSAY DATE 1988)

SOURCE: McKay, Nellie. "Jean Toomer in His Time: An Introduction." In *Jean Toomer: A Critical Evaluation*, edited by Therman B. O'Daniel, pp. 179-93. Washington, D.C.: Howard University Press, 1988.

In the following essay, McKay examines Toomer's life and the beginnings of his literary career, arguing that the writer did not achieve popular success because he refused to compromise his ideals.

"When America was in winter I was born the day after Christmas 1894,"[1] begins Jean Toomer's **"Outline of an Autobiography."** Although no record of the event exists, there is no reason to doubt the accuracy of this date. Named Nathan Eugene, he was the son of Nathan Toomer and the former Nina Pinchback. They were married in March 1894 in Washington, D.C., where their son was born. But Nathan Toomer deserted his family some months after Jean's birth. Having no independent means of support, Nina Pinchback Toomer was forced to return to her father's house. In 1896 she secured a divorce from Toomer, after which she resumed use of her maiden name. Jean Toomer was called Eugene Pinchback for several years.

Toomer's seventeen years in Washington were largely influenced by the dominant personality of his grandfather, P. B. S. Pinchback, and his own sensitive awareness of the world around him. Pinchback, a charismatic figure sufficiently light-skinned to have been taken for a white man, chose to claim African heritage, and as a black man, he gained political eminence in Louisiana during Reconstruction. In the aftermath of the Democratic rise to power in the South during the latter part of the nineteenth century, he moved his family to Washington in the early 1890s, and from his grandson's account, ruled his household in the manner of a benevolent despot.

Toomer wrote of Bacon Street in Washington as a "glorious playground." The neighborhood was almost rural, with fields of weeds, wildflowers, and insects all around, and a farm nearby. It was a delightful blend of city and country, of the urban and rural, of civilization and nature. He loved all the natural things, and although he was acutely aware of the buildings going up around him, he felt no hostility toward the changing landscape. The buildings were paralleling his own growth. "While I myself [was] growing," he later wrote, "I had pictures of constructive activity, the symbol of building, impressed upon me."[2]

The families living in this area were predominantly white middle-and upper-class, and in his words, he was surrounded by "a tone of fineness and refinement." Against this background, Pinchback, a hearty and outgoing man of wide and varied contacts and who enjoyed having people around him, entertained and associated with men of all colors. He insisted, however, that his young grandson attend a Negro school, although this meant Toomer would be away from his neighborhood friends for several hours each day. It was important to Pinchback that even at that age

Toomer should have personal, direct, and concrete links to the black community, while at home he experienced an atmosphere of racial tolerance. Later, when Pinchback suffered financial losses, they moved into other, less affluent areas of the city where more black people lived.

In 1907 Nina Pinchback remarried and moved with her husband and son, first to Brooklyn, New York, and then to New Rochelle, New York. Toomer was acutely aware of the differences between his new and old environments. In Brooklyn he had his first contact with the indifference and hostility of the city, with commercial development and industry, with apartment living in contrast to living in a house, and with "tough boys." He did not like the city, but he made friends and found it stimulating. In New Rochelle he had only a few friends but enjoyed bicycling, swimming, fishing, and sailing his own boat along Long Island Sound. He discovered the public library and read intensively while in New Rochelle; earlier, in Washington, an uncle had introduced him to literature. This reading stimulated his imagination, and he began to create an inner life for himself.

In 1909 Toomer's mother died, and in 1910 he returned to his grandparents' home. The death of his mother, the financial decline of his grandparents, and the direct consequences of these events on his living arrangements contributed to insecurities and emotional problems that plagued Toomer for many years.

Between 1914 and 1919 Toomer attended a half dozen colleges and universities but remained in no place long enough to earn a degree. After many ponderings in philosophy, history, sociology, and literature, in a time of conflicts with his grandfather over money, and after an intensive internal struggle to determine what his life's work should be, in 1919 he decided to become a writer. Once the decision was made, he settled down, as he had not done before, to learn the writer's craft.

The years of his apprenticeship were difficult. He read a great deal of Shakespeare, Shaw, Dickens, Flaubert, Goethe, Dostoyevsky, the Bible, and Eastern philosophy, particularly Buddhist writings, to name a few. American writers who inspired him included Waldo Frank, who became his mentor, Walt Whitman, and Sherwood Anderson, with whom Toomer shared a warm friendship between 1922 and 1923. Although Toomer claims that he also read some literature by or about blacks in America, all of which he dismissed as nonsense, no record of what these were exists. In like manner, although by his own account, before ***Cane*** was conceived, he had a trunkful of manuscripts, none of his earliest writings are extant. In the beginning writing was difficult for him, and he was dissatisfied with his efforts. The excellence to which he aspired eluded him. Furthermore, he was convinced that he would be able to write successfully only if he were able to achieve a state of personal harmony between the physical, emotional, and intellectual parts of himself.

This was not a new idea for Toomer. As early as 1912, while he was still in high school and enduring in solitude the physical and mental strains of early manhood, he was concerned with the problems of harmony between his body and his mind. At one point in this period he thought he had found a suitable system by which he could achieve it in the works of Bernarr MacFadden, one that would help him to gain control over himself.[3] But the achievement of internal harmony eluded him. Despite many years of body building and attempts to control his mind and emotions, the problem remained, and between 1919 and 1921 he felt that it was an ever-present hindrance to his ability to learn to write. Nor was this his only concern. In the middle of 1920 he moved from New York City, where he had been living for almost two years, back to his grandparents' home in Washington. The move was prompted by his need for money and because the Pinchbacks, who were growing feeble, needed care and attention. He agreed to stay with them and to take over the household duties in return for a weekly allowance of five dollars.

This arrangement had obvious drawbacks. However, Toomer had decided on it not only for the security of a place to live and the small monetary reward but more so because of his love for his grandparents. They had been more parental to him than his parents, and their needy condition touched him deeply. But the duties he undertook seriously curtailed the time needed to explore ideas which suggested new approaches to literary materials and personal development. He felt that he had a great deal to say and that he was full of it and under pressure to get it out, but that his life experiences exceeded his ability to write them down. Furthermore, he felt disorganized, and he despaired of achieving organization. Nevertheless, he remained in Washington from the middle of 1920 until the fall of 1921. In September 1921 he received an offer to teach in a rural Georgia school for a short time. He accepted it without hesitation and with feelings of having been rescued from a quagmire. In October of that year he arrived in Sparta, Georgia, for his first experience among rural, poor black people.

Subsequent events in Toomer's life have led to a great deal of interest in, and many speculations about, his feelings about race. The meaning of race in America was an issue that he encountered early in his life. At age six he was sent to a Negro school outside of his almost all-white neighborhood, and even then he was aware of the racial differences in the two communities. As he grew up, he heard many conversations at home about the race problem in America. When he returned to Washington from New Rochelle in 1910, the Pinchbacks were living in a predominantly black area of the city, and he attended a high school for young black people. On the other hand, his grandfather, no matter what his claims of African blood, looked like a white man, his grandmother like a white woman, and for most of their lives they had lived in a manner characteristic of the white American middle class. As a result of this combination of factors, he had gained an awareness of the implications of race while he was still a child, even though his early years had not been assaulted by racial discrimination or limited by the economic deprivation that a large number of black Americans experience. As a teenager, he lived in both worlds and saw their problems from the inside. In New Rochelle he lived in an all-white world; in Washington he lived first in a mostly white world and later in an almost all-black world.

Toomer's awareness of racial differences was heightened in 1914, as he contemplated the choice of a college to attend. At this time the matter of his racial identity seemed to him a problem. He feared the reception he would receive in an all-white college when it became known that he had attended a Negro high school. He felt vulnerable on this account and decided to adopt a nonracial identity. Later, he insisted that in repudiating racial designation at that time, he was making an effort to encompass and conduct his life as close as possible to the truth of his biological heritage. He noted that many bloodlines ran in his veins (French, English, Dutch, African, Jewish, and Indian, it was said), that he wanted to deny none of them, and that he was, above all, an American. His contention was that most people in America were of mixed racial strain. The only reasonable alternative, he argued, was to adopt the notion of an American race. He also felt that in time this idea would become socially acceptable to all Americans.

Although the question of Toomer's race surfaced at least once while he was at the University of Wisconsin, there is no reason to believe it was ever a critical issue during his college years. His failure to settle down for more than a semester in any one place was a result of his ambivalence toward his personal goals and his inability to tolerate the idea of failure or defeat in anything he did. As a result, he flirted for brief periods with a variety of career ideas but gave each one up in turn at the merest suggestion of a difficulty. His determination to be a writer was the one idea of his young life in which he persisted, in spite of the frustrations he experienced from 1919 to 1921.

The impact of the 1921 Georgia experience on Jean Toomer was enormous. From **"Outline of an Autobiography"** we know that the folk culture affected him as nothing else had done before and that he immediately set out to record the feelings that were awakened in his soul.

> No plot of ground had been like this or so moved me. Here the earth seemed part of the people, and the people part of the earth, and they worked upon each other and upon me, so that my earth-life was liberated from the rest of myself. The roots of my earth-life went down and found hold in this red soil and the soil became a shining ground.
>
> I had seen and met people of all kinds. I had never before met with a folk. I had never before lived in the midst of a people gathered together by a group spirit. Here they were. They worked and lived close to the earth, close to each other. They worked and sang as part of living. They worked and loved and hated and got into trouble and felt a great weight on them. . . . And what I saw and felt and shared entered me, so that my people-life was uncased from the rest of myself. The roots of my people-life went out to those folk, and found purchase in them, and the people became people of beauty and sorrow.

And further, he wrote:

> My seed was planted in the cane-and-cotton fields in the souls of the black and white people in the small southern town. My seed was planted in myself down there.[4]

In addition to the positive rhythms of black life, he also observed and was touched by the tensions that surrounded that life—the bitterness, strain, and violence of the southern racial situation.

Toomer spent two months in Georgia and returned to Washington in November of 1921. But before he left the South he sent a poem, **"Georgia Dusk,"** to *The Liberator,* and on the train north he began to write the sketches that appeared in the first section of ***Cane.*** By the end of the year, they were completed. The southern experience had inspired him to a lyrical interpretation of the harshness, cruelty, strength, and beauty of black American reality. ***Cane*** was *his* song of celebration to the elements of the Afro-American experience, but it was not the only result of his cultural exposure. During the winter of 1921 to 1922 he wrote two plays as well: ***Balo,*** a folk play which was presented by the Howard University Repertory Company during its 1923 to 1924 season, and ***Natalie Mann,*** an expressionistic drama that satirizes middle-class black people in Washington. His discovery of poetic elements within the black experience in America provided him with the source of his first full-blown literary expression.

Nineteen twenty-two was the year of Jean Toomer's high watermark. Early in that year he returned to New York, where he renewed old friendships and made new ones within the circle of the city's literati. His social group included Kenneth Burke, Hart Crane, Van Wyck Brooks and Waldo Frank—men who perceived themselves as being in the vanguard of American letters and who respected him as a new writer. During this year he wrote with enthusiasm, and his work began to appear in literary journals and received favorable criticism. He was sought out by Sherwood Anderson, and both men corresponded for a while. After years of ambivalence and abortive attempts to find his place in the world, he was coming into his own.

Although there is only very little to link Toomer with the literary and artistic stirrings that were beginning to take place in Harlem in 1921 and 1922, there is evidence to show that during that period of his life he was not antagonistic toward blackness. His friends were white, but on the street where he lived in New York most of the families were black.[5] He made no secret of his relationship to Pinchback and discussed his racial background with a number of people. In a letter to Waldo Frank, in March 1922, Toomer noted that there were six bloodlines in his family, that the culture, history, and traditions of five of them were fairly well known and discussed with an "approximation of the truth," but that the "Negro" line had been subject to perversion for "purposes of propaganda." He was determined, he said, that in his life and work he would symbolize "a synthesis in the matters of the mind and spirit analogous, perhaps, to the actual fact of . . . the blood minglings."[6] In another letter to Frank in which he discussed some of his ideas in ***Cane,*** in his reference to **"Kabnis"** he states: "And Kabnis is Me."[7]

Waldo Frank was not the only person with whom Toomer shared the facts of his racial heritage. In letters to Sherwood Anderson he acknowledged his mixed ancestry and pointed out that he hoped his art would help to "give the Negro back to himself." He even championed the cause of black writers as a means of "building . . . Negro consciousness."[8] In addition, during this period, he was in love with Mae Wright, a young black woman from Baltimore, Maryland, who had close relatives in Washington, D.C. She was several years younger than he, but he felt deeply about her and discussed his ideas on race very freely with her. It was with her that he noted the "tyranny of the Anglo-Saxon Ideal," an ideal which expressed only the beauty of white people. He insisted that black people needed to be awakened to the significance of their lives and the sensitivity of their beauty. The goals to which he aspired in writing were to educate white people about black people and to inspire black people to the value of their lives.[9]

However, it is doubtful that Toomer saw himself as a black man at this or at any other time in his life, even if he never considered himself to be a white man either. His emphasis on blackness was on its artistic qualities. Yet, in his concentration on the aesthetic merits of black culture, he made no efforts to connect himself to a black tradition in letters, and his interactions with contemporary black artists were, at best, minimal and individualized. He acknowledged no black writers as having had an impact on him, and no one black read, criticized, or made suggestions about ***Cane*** while it was in progress. Nevertheless, Toomer admitted to Frank that his "need for artistic expression [had] pulled [him] deeper . . . into the Negro group . . . and as [his] powers of receptivity increased, [he] found [himself] loving [it] in a way [he] could never love the other."[10] He noted that after he heard the folk songs from the "lips of Negro peasants" and had seen their "rich, dusk beauty," all of his previous skepticism, which was based on what he had heard of the folk culture, vanished, and a "deep part of [his] nature, a part that [he] had long repressed sprang suddenly into life and responded to them."[11] But these feelings were never superimposed on his idea of his Americanness or, by extension, his separateness from blackness. In time, Jean Toomer would assert that the Negro blood in his veins was no more than a fiction created by Pinchback for his own political ambitions.

Toomer saw ***Cane*** as the beginning of his life as a creative writer. Confident that the South would be the center for the new American literary renaissance, he joined the Poetry Society of South Carolina as a nonresident member, an action that proved embarrassing for the society, which had never anticipated that nonwhite persons would seek membership. He was excited in his expectations of the fulfillments of the literary life. ***Cane*** was only the beginning, he thought. Still maintaining close associations with his white friends, he had some contacts with black writers. He knew and admired Alain Locke and Charles Johnson, and he had warm correspondence with Countee Cullen and Claude McKay. He even agreed to submit his work to Claude Barnett of the Associated Negro Press for publication in black newspapers and went as far as to suggest to Sherwood Anderson the need for a black arts journal.[12]

In 1922 Toomer was happy. ***Cane*** was completed and had been accepted for publication by Boni and Liveright, which had taken an option on his next two books. Frank was writing the introduction to this first work. Toomer wrote, in wonder, "My words had become a book . . . I had actually finished something."[13] He was exhilarated and felt he was part of a living world of promise. He felt united to others and wrote: "I lived in life, in love . . . I found new life . . . in a deep rich being."[14]

But before the book was published in 1923, Toomer's hopeful anticipation of pursuing a literary career collapsed. The story is well known. He was distressed that Frank, in his introduction to the book, and the publisher, in promoting it, had made an issue of his racial background. He was particularly upset with Frank, to whom he had explained his racial vision in great detail, with the assumption that Frank had understood how he felt and would respect those feelings. Thus, he turned away from Frank and withdrew from the literary world. The reasons for his rejection of a racial label may never be fully known, but to dismiss them as only the manifestation of his deep racial trauma is to do injustice to the complications of the human mind. Toomer went on to spend his life asking the most fundamental questions about human existence and to reach outward in his search for answers. He was never indifferent to the concerns of racial groups, as later papers in his collection prove, but he thought of racial issues as detrimental to the development of the human race as a whole. To be labeled a Negro writer imposed restrictions on him that he could not tolerate; thus, he ceased to create literary art.

Toomer's break with the world that he had pursued for almost four years was on one level a break with Frank, the man who had been his mentor and his model. At the same time, Frank's inability to understand his friend's sensitivity to racial designations was more than an individual's failing; it was the failure of a system, and Toomer turned away from it also. Shortly after, he met Georges Gurdjieff and became a disciple of the Eastern mystic for a number of years.

FROM THE AUTHOR

THE ADDICTION OF CREATIVITY

Once a man has tasted creative action, then thereafter, no matter how safely he schools himself in patience, he is restive, acutely dissatisfied with anything else. He becomes as a lover to whom abstinence is intolerable.

SOURCE: Jean Toomer, quoted in *The Lives of Jean Toomer: A Hunger for Wholeness,* by Cynthia Kerman and Richard Eldridge, Louisiana State University Press, 1987.

While Toomer struggled with the problems of his development and the ramifications of societal limitations on the writer, ***Cane*** took on a life of its own. Although the sales were low, the book was hailed as a masterpiece by black and white writers: Allen Tate, Lola Ridge, Sherwood Anderson, Countee Cullen, W. E. B. Du Bois, William Stanley Braithwaite, and Langston Hughes were among those who paid tribute to the writer and his work.

In 1966 Arna Bontemps, writing of the impact of ***Cane*** in its time in "The Negro Renaissance and the Writers of the 1920's," noted that black writers of the early part of that decade who were aware of the book "went quietly mad." Contemporary reviews of ***Cane*** reveal that these writers were enormously affected by the work. Among other things it opened up new possibilities in writing for them. For the first time in America there was a black writer in the forefront of the literary movement, participating on equal terms with white writers in the creation of new forms and trends. The most persistent emphasis in the analyses of ***Cane*** during the 1920s, on the part of black writers at least, is on the inherent "self-revelation" in the work. Toomer had faced the black experience in America without shame or abasement and had spun, from what others might have seen only as broken threads, a magnificent tapestry of words. He had avoided propaganda and polemic and given a moving description, through words that held color and mood, of what it meant to be black in America. He had, more than any other black writer until then, liberated black creative writing from narrow and parochial boundaries and set it on its journey toward genuine art and self-affirmation through exploration of the past. Later critics, black and white, have acknowledged Toomer's achievement and have unanimously accorded him a place of honor in the annals of the Harlem Renaissance and black creative writing.

After his disappearance from the literary horizon, for black writers Toomer represented the sphinx of their age. Nevertheless, they understood that his problem was also their own and that the black artist is vulnerable to the constant buffetings of negative social focus. Until ***Cane*** was published, Afro-American literature and black writers were always a step behind their white contemporaries; now, for the first time, there was a black writer whose work had placed him in the forefront of the literary movement. But more important, Toomer had looked at the folk culture and had seen in it beauty, strength, and value, as well as pain, suffering, and emptiness. He had not hesitated to examine the persistent despair and sterility of black urban life, but he had not omitted its dynamic energy. He had liberated the would-be black artist through his own journey toward genuine art and through his search into the past for an affirming self. And although no school of writers bearing his name sprang up after ***Cane*** was published, the later writings of the renaissance reveal a greater concern for the past, a more complete acceptance of the self, and a greater willingness to experiment with style and form than had ever before been seen in black writing.

But while Toomer no longer paid homage to the muse of artistic literature after 1923, he never gave up the idea of writing as a vocation. After ***Cane*** he continued to explore themes that had interested him even before he decided to become a writer. The form and manner of his writings changed after 1923, but his philosophic concern with the human condition never altered. His rejection of art as a goal in writing led to changes in his style that raised questions regarding the literary merits of his work. However, the wide neglect of his post-1923 writings, which lasted until the 1960s, inhibited the flow of information that was vital to determining his rightful place in the world of letters.

When Toomer rejected the label of "Negro writer," one of his motives was to transcend the limits of that identity, but the attitudes of the world would not allow him to so do in a graceful fashion. He wanted to accomplish what James Weldon Johnson once defined as the responsibility of the black artist: "to fashion something that rises above race and reaches out to the universal in truth and beauty."[15] When he felt compelled to turn aside from art, it was a great loss for American literature, and the decision altered the course of his life. In his time Jean Toomer was a powerful symbol: a rising star that fell in its ascendancy because he refused to accept the status quo.

Notes

1. Jean Toomer, "Earth-Being," Jean Toomer Collection, Fisk University Archives, Nashville, Tennessee, Box 19, Folder 3, p. 1. Subsequent material from the collection will be designated "J.T.C." "Earth-Being" is also reprinted in part in *The Wayward and the Seeking: A Collection of Writings by Jean Toomer,* ed. Darwin Turner (Washington, D.C.: Howard Univesity Press, 1980), pp. 15-27.
2. *Ibid.*
3. Bernarr MacFadden, *The Virile Powers of Supreme Manhood* (New York: Physical Culture Publishing Company, 1900).
4. Toomer, "Why I Entered the Gurdjieff Work," J.T.C., Box 14, Folder 1, p. 26.
5. Gorham Munson, interview with India M. Watterson, The Wellington Hotel, New York City 27-28 June 1969, The Amistad Collection, Dillard University, New Orleans.
6. Toomer to Waldo Frank, 24 March 1922, J.T.C., Box 1, Folder 3.
7. Toomer to Frank, ca. May 1922, J.T.C., Box 1, Folder 3.
8. Toomer to Sherwood Anderson, 1922, J.T.C., Box 1, Folder 1.
9. Toomer to Mae Wright, August 1922, J.T.C., Box 1, Folder 10.
10. Toomer to Frank, March 1922, J.T.C., Box 1, Folder 3.
11. *Ibid.*
12. Toomer to Anderson, 1922, J.T.C., Box 1, Folder 1.
13. Toomer, "Why I Joined the Gurdjieff Work," J.T.C., Box 66, Folder 8, p. 29.
14. *Ibid.*
15. James Weldon Johnson, "The Dilemma of the Negro Author," *American Mercury* 28 (December 1928): 481.

RUDOLPH P. BYRD (ESSAY DATE 1989)

SOURCE: Byrd, Rudolph P. "Jean Toomer and the Writers of the Harlem Renaissance: Was He There with Them?" In *The Harlem Renaissance: Revaluations,* edited by Amritjit Singh, William S. Shiver, and Stanley Brodwin, pp. 209-18. New York: Garland Publishing, Inc., 1989.

In the following essay, Byrd claims that Toomer was not a member of the Harlem Renaissance but rather an "ancestor" of the movement.

Like poets, critics are, for good or ill, image-makers. The medium for both is language and it is through language, sustained by some compelling purpose, that each seeks to impose an intelligible and meaningful order not only upon the page, but upon life itself. Of course, the task of the poet is different from that of the critic. The poet, seemingly with the blessing of the muse, uses language as a means to reveal some fundamental truth. The task of the critic, on the other hand, is to interpret, to evaluate, and finally to judge. The critic does not receive his inspiration from the muse, or at least he does not claim to, but from the scholarly tradition out of which he emerges and from the poet himself.

But the poet and the critic, in spite of the functional differences I have identified and others I have not, are essentially image-makers; that is to say, they are painters of verbal portraits that influence and carry meaning. The irony, however, is that the critic, in this important matter of image-making, is the more powerful, for his pronouncements to a very large extent determine the perception of a poet by both the contemporary reading public and posterity.

A critic's peculiar emphasis upon a particular feature of a poet's work—I am thinking, for example, of William Dean Howells's insistence that Paul Laurence Dunbar's greatest talent lay in writing dialect poetry—may have terrible consequences for the poet. In Dunbar's case, this public pronouncement rapidly became a public truth, which is why so many of his contemporaries were amazed to discover that he wrote sonnets. But if an undue emphasis can produce such regrettable effects, the damage that can be done to a poet's career as a consequence of a critic's distortion, purposeful or otherwise, is incalculable. I am thinking now of Jean Toomer and his fateful collision with Alain Locke.

When Toomer met Locke in the summer of 1923, ***Cane*** had not only been published, but Toomer had just returned from a two-month sojourn at the George I. Gurdjieff Institute for the Harmonious Development of Man in Fontainebleau, France. For some time, Toomer had been searching for what he called an "intelligible scheme" and he was certain that he had finally found it in Gurdjieff's psychological system. Gurdjieff was an enormously important figure in Toomer's life, and for a period it seemed that his involvement in the Gurdjieff work would eclipse his interest in literature and writing altogether. Recalling the force and effect of his duties as a Gurdjieff lecturer, Toomer wrote:

> These groups and the life that grew out of them became my life. I was worlds removed from the literary set. I knew little or nothing of what was happening in it. That I had once written a book called ***Cain*** [sic] seemed remote. What had happened to it I neither knew nor cared. . . .
>
> Gradually, however, I began making other contacts, I began awakening with interest to the wide activities of that time. Then I discovered, among other things, that a ferment was in the Negro world also, a literary ferment, and that it was producing a new literature. I was sufficiently moved to write an article. After this I viewed the movement as a splendid thing but something that had no special meaning for me.[1]

These are strange words from a writer whose first book is widely considered, as Robert Bone tells us, "the most impressive product of the Negro Renaissance."[2] Plainly, Toomer had no feeling left for the book that, in the words of Arna Bontemps, "heralded an awakening of artistic expression by Negroes that brought to light in less than a decade a surprising array of talents."[3] Nor apparently did Toomer have much feeling for the arts movement known as the Harlem Renaissance, an arts movement that Sterling Brown has labeled the New Negro Movement, since the former term confines what was really a national event not only to a portion of Manhattan, but to a particular region. In view of his unmistakable indifference to ***Cane,*** and his distance from the arts movement with which he is usually identified, how do we explain the perception, shared by students and teachers of American literature, that Toomer was an integral part of Harlem's literary scene? We return now to the notion of images and image-making, for the basis of this perception is in the pages of Locke's *The New Negro,* an anthology whose purpose was to initiate the uninitiated into the circle of concerns and interests of black American artists of the 1920s.

In his essay "Negro Youth Speaks," one of four essays by Locke in his anthology of verse, fiction, and cultural criticism, we are given a strong, promising, and oracular image of the new generation of Afro-American artists. The opening paragraph reads as follows:

> The younger generation comes, bringing its gifts. They are the first fruits of the Negro Renaissance. Youth speaks, and the voice of the New Negro is heard. What stirs inarticulately in the masses is already vocal upon the lips of the talented few, and the future listens, however the present may strain its ears. Here we have Negro youth, with arresting visions and vibrant prophecies; forecasting in the mirror of art what we must see and recognize in the streets of reality tomorrow, foretelling in new notes and accents the maturing speech of full racial utterance.[4]

In language that is lyrical and evocative, Locke conjures for us an image of a new generation of writers who are not only literate and articulate, but whose lives are joined together by one transcendent purpose: "full racial utterance." In phrases that are as subtle as Aaron Douglas's manipulation of lines and forms in *Building More Stately Mansions,* Locke suggests that the writers of the younger generation have all arrived together, and that they all stand together for the same ideals. There is also, and this is even more subtle, the implication that there is a sense of unity and coherence within this group that is not only a function of age and talent, but of an intimacy born of a shared vision and collaborative acts. The image, then, is both powerful and impressive. The words that support it are more than adequate to Locke's purpose, which is to place and explain the achievement of a group of writers of diverse interests and backgrounds. Locke cannot be faulted for his impulse to identify artistic patterns, but, as we shall see, there is a certain danger in such critical enterprises, for not every writer may conform to the pattern.

After identifying members of the older generation of writers—Charles Waddell Chesnutt, W. E. B. DuBois, Angela Grimke, and James Weldon Johnson, he proudly lists some members of the younger generation along with their preferred genre(s):

> Then rich in this legacy [the legacy of the previous generation of talent], but rather richer still, I think, in their own endowment of talent, comes the youngest generation of our Afro-American culture: in music Diton, Dett, Grant Still, and Roland Hayes; in fiction, Jessie Fauset, Walter White, Claude McKay . . . ; in drama, Willis Richardson; in the field of the short story, Jean Toomer, Eric Walrond, Rudolph Fisher; and finally a vivid galaxy of young Negro poets, McKay, Jean Toomer, Langston Hughes, and Countee Cullen.[5]

Toomer's name appears twice in this paragraph, as well as in other places in the essay, but it is one that does not fit so easily, for several reasons, into Locke's pattern.

First, when this new generation of writers began producing books—for example, Cullen's first volume of verse appeared two years after ***Cane*** and Hughes's followed it by three—Toomer had been immersed in the Gurdjieff work for at least three years, and would be leaving New York City in 1927 to lecture and establish study groups in Chicago. Thus, at the very moment when the Renaissance had found its voice, Toomer was not only in a different cultural orbit due to his duties in the Gurdjieff work, but he was out of town. Even during the period when Toomer was a resident of Manhattan, he was not uptown in Harlem with Zora Neale Hurston, Langston Hughes, and Countee Cullen, but downtown in Greenwhich Village with Waldo Frank and others. Recalling the excitement and pleasure of those early years, Toomer wrote:

> In New York, I stepped into the literary world. Frank, Gorham Munson, Kenneth Burke, Hart Crane, Matthew Josephson, Malcolm Cowley, Paul Rosenfield, Van Wyck Brooks, Robert Littell—*Broom,* the *Dial,* the *New Republic* and many more. I lived on Gay Street and entered into the swing of it. It was an extraordinary summer.[6]

Thus, Frank, Brooks, and others were Toomer's comrades in literature, and not Walrond or Fisher, as Locke suggests. Plainly, Toomer had very little contact with the writers of the Renaissance and when he did, as Hughes notes in *The Big Sea,* it was briefly and not as the author of ***Cane,*** but as a Gurdjieff lecturer.[7]

There is also a second reason why Toomer does not fit so neatly into Locke's generational scheme, and it is in many ways an extension of the first. Toomer did not identify with the writers of the Renaissance, or with their work. As we may recall, the list of writers who comprised New York City's literary scene for Toomer did not include any of the writers of the Renaissance, and it certainly did not include any of the writers to which Locke goes to great pains to link him.

Prior to Gurdjieff, the most potent figure in Toomer's imagination was Waldo Frank, who persuaded Horace Liveright to publish ***Cane.*** After Toomer's break with Frank (he made the unforgivable mistake of falling in love with Frank's wife), he continued to share and discuss his own work with Munson, who was also active in the Gurdjieff work, with Paul Rosenfield, and also with Hart Crane. Although Toomer's poem **"Song of the Son"** had appeared in *The Crisis,* an important organ for the Renaissance writers, prior to and after the publication of ***Cane*** his work appeared in *Broom, The Little Review, Double Dealer,* and *S4N.* These journals were a forum for an extremely self-conscious group of writers now remembered for their experiments in the new American idiom. Plainly, Toomer was a member of this literary cadre not only by virtue of friendship and professional ties, but because of obvious textual allegiances. In *Destinations,* Munson, under his rubric of the "Younger Writers," a later mutation of Locke's "younger generation," correctly links Toomer with such writers as Kenneth Burke and Hart Crane, and describes Toomer as a "living symbol of a really serious search for values."[8] Munson's placement of Toomer with these writers is plainly more accurate, but Locke, as we shall see, had his own reason for identifying Toomer as a New Negro.

To me, the third and final reason why Toomer does not conform to Locke's deceptively coherent pattern is Toomer's reluctance or refusal to define himself as "Negro." Toomer called himself an American, an American who was "neither black nor white."[9] He insisted upon calling himself an American not out of the need, as many have suspected, to avoid the label of Afro-American author, but out of a knowledge of his ancestry and a desire to define himself in his own terms. Toomer writes that in his body were many bloods: French, Dutch, Welsh, Negro, German, Jewish, and Indian. He was keenly aware of the strangeness and even the danger of his racial position in a nation preoccupied with racial purity, but he strove "for a spiritual fusion analogous to the fact of racial intermingling. Without denying a single element," he sought to "let them function as complements."[10] But Locke could not accept Toomer's self-definition and labeled him Negro. Locke, however, was not the only member of Toomer's generation whose traditional view of race made it impossible for him to accept any other. Waldo Frank was another, for in his foreword to ***Cane*** he identifies Toomer as Negro; this he did in spite of Toomer's several attempts to clarify his racial background and position.

On this important matter of race and self-definition, Toomer, who could have easily passed for white but did not, was generations ahead of his own generation. However, Nellie Y. McKay, in her recent book *Jean Toomer, Artist,* writes that Toomer was "hindered from developing relationships [with the writers of the Renaissance] because of his racial ambivalence."[11] I am not convinced that Toomer was ambivalent about race. Plainly, he saw race in all its baffling complexity. If he were ambivalent, he certainly would not have identified the darker strains in his ancestry as Negro. No, Toomer was not "hindered" from developing relationships with the writers of the Renaissance because of his alleged "racial ambivalence." On the contrary, he simply knew, in terms of his own artistic development, that his teachers and peers were not McKay and Hughes, but Frank and Crane.

In "The World and the Jug," in a stinging reply to public statements made by Irving Howe concerning his own literary influences, Ralph Ellison has perhaps given us the most useful framework to examine the issues surrounding a writer's place within a particular literary canon.[12] For Ellison there are "relatives," that is to say, writers who help another writer determine his growth, and "ancestors," or writers whose work becomes the standard by which a writer judges his own. If we apply Ellison's construct to Toomer's situation, we discover that Crane and Frank (and if we look backward to the previous century to Walt Whitman) were, just to name three, Toomer's "ancestors"; Hughes and Cullen, if they meant anything to him at all, were "relatives." But in tracing the development of Hughes and Cullen and their achievements as writers, we learn that Toomer was, to them, not a "relative" but an "ancestor."

Locke's placement of Toomer with the writers of the Renaissance—his artful image-making—becomes even more questionable and suspicious when we remember that the poems and stories from ***Cane*** (**"Georgia Dusk," "Song of the Son," "Carma,"** and **"Fern"**) that appeared in *The New Negro* were published there without Toomer's permission. In one of his several autobiographies, Toomer recalls his meeting with Locke and his response to the appearance of his materials in Locke's anthology:

> Locke said he was getting together a book of Negro materials and wanted something I had written, preferably a new story or a story from ***Cain*** [*sic*]. I replied that I had written no new stories of that kind and did not want ***Cain*** [*sic*] dismembered. He pressed. I thought of the article. I offered it to him. It turned out he did not want it. My expressed attitude was—the article or nothing. I concluded that the matter was finished. . . .
>
> But when Locke's book *The New Negro,* came out . . . there was a story from ***Cane,*** and there in the introduction, were words about me which have caused me as much or more misunderstanding than Waldo Frank's.
>
> However, there was and is, among other things, this great difference between Frank and Locke. Frank helped me at a time when I most needed help. . . . Locke tricked and misused me.
>
> For a short time after the appearance of Locke's book I was furious—. . . . Well, I shrugged and let it drop—but not without a pretty sharp sense of the irony of the situation.[13]

The article to which Toomer refers in these passages is one that contains his meditations on the rising prominence of black writers during the 1920s. This article was never published and is probably lost, as it seems not to be part of the Toomer Archives at Fisk University. The mention of Frank is an allusion to his foreword to ***Cane*** where he describes Toomer as Negro. As Toomer's remembrance of this event makes plain, he was quite angry with Locke, not only because he had reprinted excerpts from ***Cane*** without permission, but also because Locke had, in language that was suggestive, misleading, and, as Toomer himself points out, ironic, linked him to a group of writers with whom he did not feel the slightest connection.

Locke, however, had his own reason for appropriating Toomer's materials, and for promoting the image of Toomer as an important figure in his New Negro Movement. Since the critical acclaim of ***Cane*** had made Toomer an important literary success, Locke was extremely anxious to place him with his younger generation of black writers. In his search for shining and brilliant examples of the New Negro, Locke linked Toomer to Hughes and others because of the prestige that Toomer would bring to his efforts to increase national interest in what was then a burgeoning arts movement. If ***Cane*** had been published in 1913 or 1933, that is to say, ten years before or after its original publication date, Toomer's real relationship to the writers of the Renaissance would be astoundingly clear. In view of his involvement with the Gurdjieff work, his friendships and collaborations with Frank, Crane, Munson, and others, and his racial position, which prevented him from identifying with any group or movement that emphasized race, it is in many ways a historical accident that Toomer is grouped with the writers of the Renaissance at all.

Was Toomer then, as Locke's image of him in *The New Negro* suggests, a member of the Harlem Renaissance? Was he there with Hughes, Cullen, and the rest? Plainly, the answer is no. The facts of the relationship do not support the traditional view, and we are, therefore, moved to very different conclusions. All we can actually say about Toomer's relationship to the writers of the Renaissance is this: he was a member of this literary group to the extent that these writers read, admired, studied, and emulated his work—that is all. For these writers, Toomer was, to return to Ellison's construct, an "ancestor," not a "relative" or fellow participant, and it is in this manner that we must view him. Toomer was important to the Renaissance because he demonstrated to its writers that there was another way to see and treat Afro-American materials, and in the process he created a standard by which their work would be and has been judged. Of course, we should forgive Locke his manipulations and critical shortsightedness—his careless image-making—and hope that other critics will exercise more precision, judgment, and insight in their placement of writers.

Notes

1. Jean Toomer, *The Wayward and the Seeking,* ed. Darwin Turner (Washington, D.C.: Howard University Press, 1980), pp. 131-132.
2. Robert Bone, *The Negro Novel in America* (New Haven: Yale University Press, 1958), p. 81.
3. Arna Bontemps, "The Negro Renaissance: Jean Toomer and the Harlem Writers of the 1920s," in *Anger and Beyond,* ed. Herbert Hill (New York: Harper & Row, 1966), p. 27.
4. Alain Locke, *The New Negro* (New York: Albert and Charles Boni, 1925), p. 47.
5. Ibid., p. 49.
6. Toomer, *Wayward,* p. 126.
7. Langston Hughes, *The Big Sea* (New York: Hill & Wang, 1940), pp. 241-243.
8. Gorham Munson, *Destinations* (New York: J. H. Sears & Co., 1928), pp. 9-10.
9. Toomer, *Wayward,* p. 126.
10. Letter from Toomer to McKay, 9 August 1922. Quoted in the 1969 introduction by Arna Bontemps in Jean Toomer, *Cane* (1923; New York: Harper & Row, 1969).
11. Nellie Y. McKay, *Jean Toomer, Artist* (Chapel Hill: The University of North Carolina Press, 1984), p. 58.
12. Ralph Ellison, *Shadow and Act* (New York: Vintage Books, 1953).
13. Toomer, *Wayward,* pp. 132-133.

TITLE COMMENTARY

Cane

ROBERT BONE (ESSAY DATE 1958)

SOURCE: Bone, Robert. "The Harlem School: Jean Toomer." In *The Negro Novel in America,* revised edition, pp. 80-9. New Haven, Conn.: Yale University Press, 1965.

In the following excerpt from a work originally published in 1958, Bone considers Cane *"the most impressive product" of the Harlem Renaissance and provides the first detailed study of Toomer's hitherto neglected work.*

The writers of the Lost Generation, as John Aldridge has observed, "were engaged in a revolution designed to purge language of the old restraints of the previous century and to fit it to the demands of a younger, more realistic time."[1] Stein and Hemingway in prose, Pound and Eliot in poetry, were threshing and winnowing, testing and experimenting with words, stretching them and refocusing them, until they became the pliant instruments of a new idiom. The only Negro writer of the 1920's who participated on equal terms in the creation of the modern idiom was a young poet-novelist named Jean Toomer.

Jean Toomer's ***Cane*** (1923) is an important American novel. By far the most impressive product of the Negro Renaissance, it ranks with Richard Wright's *Native Son* and Ralph Ellison's *Invisible Man* as a measure of the Negro novelist's highest achievement. Jean Toomer belongs to that first rank of writers who use words almost as a plastic medium, shaping new meanings from an original and highly personal style. Since stylistic innovation requires great technical dexterity, Toomer displays a concern for technique which is fully two decades in advance of the period. While his contemporaries of the Harlem School were still experimenting with a crude literary realism, Toomer had progressed beyond the naturalistic novel to "the higher realism of the emotions," to symbol, and to myth.

Jean Toomer (1894-) was born in Washington, D.C., where his parents, who were cultivated Negroes of Creole stock, had moved in order to educate their children. Toomer's maternal grandfather, P. B. S. Pinchback, had been acting governor of Louisiana during Reconstruction days, so that tales of slavery and Reconstruction were a household tradition. Toomer was educated for the law at the University of Wisconsin and at the City College of New York, but literature soon became his first love. An avant-garde poet and short-story writer, he contributed regularly to such little magazines as *Broom, Secession, Double Dealer, Dial,* and *Little Review.* After a brief literary apprenticeship in cosmopolitan New York, he visited rural Georgia as a country schoolteacher—an experience which directly inspired the production of ***Cane.***

During his formative period Toomer was a member of a semi-mystical literary group which included Hart Crane, Waldo Frank, Gorham Munson, and Kenneth Burke. Influenced philosophically by Ouspensky's *Tertium Organum,* they formed a bloc called Art as Vision—some of their catchwords being "the new slope of consciousness," "the superior logic of metaphor," and "noumenal knowledge." The group eventually split over the writings of Gurdjieff, the Russian mystic. So far did Toomer succumb to Gurdjieff's spell that he spent the summer of 1926 at the Gurdjieff Institute in Fontainebleau, France, returning to America to proselytize actively for his mystical philosophy.

In spite of his wide and perhaps primary association with white intellectuals, as an artist Toomer never underestimated the importance of his Negro identity. He attained a universal vision not by ignoring race as a local truth, but by coming face to face with his particular tradition. His pilgrimage to Georgia was a conscious attempt to make contact with his hereditary roots in the Southland. Of Georgia, Toomer wrote: "There one finds soil in the sense that the Russians know it—the soil every art and literature that is to live must be embedded in."[2] This sense of soil is central to ***Cane*** and to Toomer's artistic vision. "When one is on the soil of one's ancestors," his narrator remarks, "most anything can come to one."

What comes to Toomer, in the first section of ***Cane,*** is a vision of the parting soul of slavery:

> . . . for though the sun is setting on
> A song-lit race of slaves, it has not set;
> Though late, O soil, it is not too late yet
> To catch thy plaintive soul, leaving, soon gone.[3]

The soul of slavery persists in the "supper-getting-ready songs" of the black women who live on the Dixie Pike—a road which "has grown from a goat path in Africa." It persists in "the soft, listless cadence of Georgia's South," in the hovering spirit of a comforting Jesus, and in the sudden violence of the Georgia moon. It persists above all in the people, white and black, who have become Andersonian "grotesques" by virtue of their slave inheritance. Part I of ***Cane*** is in fact a kind of Southern *Winesburg, Ohio.* It consists of the portraits of six women—all primitives—in which an Andersonian narrator mediates between the reader and the author's vision of life on the Dixie Pike.

There is Karintha, "she who carries beauty" like a pregnancy, until her perfect beauty and the impatience of young men beget a fatherless child. Burying her child in a sawdust pile, she takes her revenge by becoming a prostitute; "the soul of her was a growing thing ripened too soon."

In **"Becky"** Toomer dramatizes the South's conspiracy to ignore miscegenation. Becky is a white woman with two Negro sons. After the birth of the first, she symbolically disappears from sight into a cabin constructed by community guilt. After the birth of the second, she is simply regarded as dead, and no one is surprised when the chimney of her cabin falls in and buries her. Toward Becky there is no charity from white or black, but only furtive attempts to conceal her existence.

Carma's tale, "which is the crudest melodrama," hinges not so much on marital infidelity as on a childish deception. Accused by her husband of having other men ("No one blames her for that") she becomes hysterical, and running into a canebrake, pretends to shoot herself. "Twice deceived, and the one deception proved the other." Her husband goes berserk, slashes a neighbor, and is sent to the chain gang. The tone of the episode is set by the ironic contrast between Carma's apparent strength ("strong as any man") and her childish behavior.

Fern, whose full name is Fernie May Rosen, combines the suffering of her Jewish father and her Negro mother: "at first sight of her I felt as if I heard a Jewish cantor sing. . . . As if his singing rose above the unheard chorus of a folksong." Unable to find fulfillment, left vacant by the bestowal of men's bodies, Fern sits listlessly on her porch near the Dixie Pike. Her eyes desire nothing that man can give her; the Georgia countryside flows into them, along with something that Toomer's narrator calls God.

"Esther" is a study in sexual repression. The protagonist is a near-white girl whose father is the richest colored man in town. Deprived of normal outlets by her social position, she develops a neurotic life of fantasy which centers upon a virile, black-skinned, itinerant preacher named King Barlo. At sixteen she imagines herself the mother of his immaculately conceived child. At twenty-seven she tries to translate fantasy into reality by offering herself to Barlo. Rebuffed and humiliated, she retreats into lassitude and frigidity.

Louisa, of **"Blood-Burning Moon,"** has two lovers, one white and the other colored. Inflamed by a sexual rivalry deeper than race, they quarrel. One is slashed and the other is lynched. Unlike most Negro writers who have grappled with the subject of lynching, Toomer achieves both form and perspective. He is not primarily concerned with antilynching propaganda, but in capturing a certain atavistic quality in Southern life which defies the restraints of civilized society.

Part II of ***Cane*** is counterpoint. The scene shifts to Washington, where Seventh Street thrusts a wedge of vitality, brilliance, and movement into the stale, soggy, whitewashed wood of the city. This contrast is an aspect of Toomer's primitivism. The blacks, in his color scheme, represent a full life; the whites, a denial of it. Washington's Negroes have preserved their vitality because of their roots in the rural South, yet whiteness presses in on them from all sides. The "dickty" Negro, and especially the near-white, who are most nearly assimilated to white civilization, bear the brunt of repression and denial, vacillating constantly between two identities. Out of this general frame of reference grow the central symbols of the novel.

Toomer's symbols reflect the profound humanism which forms the base of his philosophical position. Man's essential goodness, he would contend, his sense of brotherhood, and his creative instincts have been crushed and buried by modern industrial society. Toomer's positive values, therefore, are associated with the soil, the cane, and the harvest; with Christian charity, and with giving oneself in love. On the other side of the equation is a series of burial or confinement symbols (houses, alleys, machines, theaters, nightclubs, newspapers) which limit man's growth and act as barriers to his soul. Words are useless in piercing this barrier; Toomer's intellectualizing males are tragic figures because they value talking above feeling. Songs, dreams, dancing, and love itself (being instinctive in nature) may afford access to "the simple beauty of another's soul." The eyes, in particular, are avenues through which we can discover "the truth that people bury in their hearts."

In the second section of ***Cane,*** Toomer weaves these symbols into a magnificent design, so that his meaning, elusive in any particular episode, emerges with great impact from the whole. **"Rhobert"** is an attack on the crucial bourgeois value of home ownership: "Rhobert wears a house, like a monstrous diver's helmet, on his head." Like Thoreau's farmer, who traveled through life pushing a barn and a hundred acres before him, Rhobert is a victim of his own property instinct. As he struggles with the weight of the house, he sinks deeper and deeper into the mud:

> Brother, Rhobert is sinking
> Let's open our throats, brother
> Let's sing Deep River when he goes down.

The basic metaphor in **"Avey"** compares a young girl to the trees planted in boxes along V Street, "the young trees that whinnied like colts impatient to be free." Avey's family wants her to become a school teacher, but her bovine nature causes her to prefer a somewhat older profession. Yet, ironically, it is not she but the narrator who is a failure, who is utterly inadequate in the face of Avey's womanhood.

In **"Theatre"** Toomer develops his "dickty" theme, through an incident involving a chorus girl and a theater-manager's brother. As John watches a rehearsal, he is impressed by Dorris' spontaneity, in contrast to the contrived movements of the other girls. He momentarily contemplates an affair, but reservations born of social distance prevent him from consummating his desire, except in a dream. Dorris, who hopes fleetingly for home and children from such a man, is left at the end of the episode with only the sordid reality of the theater.

"Calling Jesus" plays a more important role than its length would indicate in unifying the symbolism of the novel. It concerns a woman, urbanized and spiritually intimidated, whose "soul is like a little thrust-tailed dog that follows her, whimpering." At night, when she goes to sleep in her big house, the little dog is left to shiver in the vestibule. "Some one . . . eoho Jesus . . . soft as the bare feet of Christ moving across bales of Southern cotton, will steal in and cover it that it need not shiver, and carry it to her where she sleeps, cradled in dream-fluted cane."

In **"Box Seat"** Toomer comes closest to realizing his central theme. The episode opens with an invocation: "Houses are shy girls whose eyes shine reticently upon the dusk body of the street. Upon the gleaming limbs and asphalt torso of a dreaming nigger. Shake your curled wool-blossoms, nigger. Open your liver-lips to the lean white spring. Stir the root-life of a withered people. Call them from their houses and teach them to dream" (p. 104).

The thought is that of a young man, whose symbolic role is developed at once: "I am Dan Moore. I was born in a canefield. The hands of Jesus touched me. I am come to a sick world to heal it." Dan, moreover, comes as a representative of "powerful underground races": "The next world-savior is coming up that way. Coming up. A continent sinks down. The new-world Christ will need consummate skill to walk upon the waters where huge bubbles burst." The redemption motif is echoed in Dan's communion with the old slave: "I asked him if he knew what that rumbling is that comes up from the ground." It is picked up again through the portly Negro woman who sits beside Dan in the theater: "A soil-soaked fragrance comes from her. Through the cement floor her strong roots sink down . . . and disappear in blood-lines that waver south."

The feminine lead is played by Muriel, a school teacher inclined toward conventionality. Her landlady, Mrs. Pribby, is constantly with her, being in essence a projection of Muriel's social fears. The box seat which she occupies at the theater, where her every movement is under observation, renders her relationship to society perfectly. Her values are revealed in her query to Dan, "Why don't you get a good job and settle down?" On these terms only can she love him; meanwhile she avoids his company by going to a vaudeville performance with a girl friend.

Dan, a slave to "her still unconquered animalism," follows and watches her from the audience. The main attraction consists of a prize fight between two dwarfs for the "heavy-weight championship"; it symbolizes the ultimate degradation of which a false and shoddy culture is capable. Sparring grotesquely, pounding and bruising each other, the dwarfs suggest the traditional clown symbol of modern art. At the climax of the episode the winner presents a blood-spattered rose to Muriel, who recoils, hesitates, and finally submits. The dwarf's eyes are pleading: "Do not shrink. Do not be afraid of me." Overcome with disgust for Muriel's hypocrisy, Dan completes the dwarf's thought from the audience, rising to shout: "JESUS WAS ONCE A LEPER!" Rushing from the theater, he is free at last of his love for Muriel—free, but at the same time sterile: "He is as cool as a green stem that has just shed its flower."

Coming as an anticlimax after **"Box Seat," "Bona and Paul"** describes an abortive love affair between two Southern students at the University of Chicago—a white girl and a mulatto boy who is "passing." The main tension, reminiscent of Gertrude Stein's *Melanctha,* is between knowing and loving, set in the framework of Paul's double identity. It is not his race consciousness which terminates the relationship, as one critic has suggested, but precisely his "whiteness," his desire for knowledge, his philosophical bent. If he had been able to assert his Negro self—that which attracted Bona to him in the first place—he might have held her love.

In **"Kabnis"** rural Georgia once more provides a setting. This is the long episode which comprises the concluding section of ***Cane.*** By now the symbolic values of Toomer's main characters can be readily assessed. Ralph Kabnis, the protagonist, is a school teacher from the North who cringes in the face of his tradition. A spiritual coward, he cannot contain "the pain and beauty of the South"; cannot embrace the suffering of the past, symbolized by slavery; cannot come to terms with his own bastardy; cannot master his pathological fear of being lynched. Consumed with self-hatred and cut off from any organic connection with the past, he resembles nothing so much as a scarecrow: "Kabnis, a promise of soil-soaked beauty; uprooted, thinning out. Suspended a few feet above the soil whose touch would resurrect him."

Lewis, by way of contrast, is a Christ figure, an extension of Dan Moore. Almost a T. S. Eliot creation ("I'm on a sort of contract with myself"), his function is to shock others into moral awareness. It is Lewis who confronts Kabnis with his moral cowardice: "Can't hold them, can you? Master; slave. Soil; and the overarching heavens. Dusk; dawn. They fight and bastardize you. The sun tint of your cheeks, flame of the great season's multi-colored leaves, tarnished, burned. Split, shredded, easily burned" (p. 218).

Halsey, unlike Kabnis, has not been crushed by Southern life, but absorbed into it. Nevertheless, his spiritual degradation is equally thorough. An artisan and small shopkeeper like his father before him, he "belongs" in a sense that Kabnis does not. Yet in order to maintain his place in the community, he must submit to the indignities of Negro life in the South. Like Booker T. Washington, whose point of view he represents, Halsey has settled for something less than manhood. Restless, groping tentatively toward Lewis, he escapes from himself through his craft, and through an occasional debauch with the town prostitute, whom he loved as a youth.

Father John, the old man who lives beneath Halsey's shop, represents a link with the Negro's ancestral past. Concealed by the present generation as an unpleasant memory, the old man is thrust into a cellar which resembles the hold of a slave ship. There he sits, "A mute John the Baptist of a new religion, or a tongue-tied shadow of an old." When he finally speaks, it is to rebuke the white folks for the sin of slavery. The contrast between Lewis and Kabnis is sharpened by their respective reactions to Father John. Through the old slave, Lewis is able to "merge with his source," but Kabnis can only deny: "An' besides, he aint my past. My ancestors were Southern blue-bloods."

In terms of its dramatic movement **"Kabnis"** is a steep slope downward,[4] approximating the progressive deterioration of the protagonist. Early in the episode Kabnis is reduced to a scarecrow replica of himself by his irrational fears. His failure to stand up to Hanby, an authoritarian school principal, marks a decisive loss in his power of self-direction. Gradually he slips into a childlike dependence, first on Halsey, then on the two prostitutes, and finally on Halsey's little sister, Carrie Kate. In the course of the drunken debauch with which the novel ends, Kabnis becomes a clown, without dignity or manhood, wallowing in the mire of his own self-hatred. The stark tragedy of **"Kabnis"** is relieved only by the figure of Carrie Kate, the unspoiled child of a new generation, who may yet be redeemed through her ties with Father John.

A critical analysis of ***Cane*** is a frustrating task, for Toomer's art, in which "outlines are reduced to essences," is largely destroyed in the process of restoration. No paraphrase can properly convey the aesthetic pleasure derived from a sensitive reading of ***Cane.*** Yet in spite of Toomer's successful experiment with the modern idiom—or perhaps because of it—***Cane*** met with a cold reception from the public, hardly selling 500 copies during its first year. This poor showing must have been a great disappointment to Toomer, and undoubtedly it was a chief cause of his virtual retirement from literature. Perhaps in his heart of hearts Jean Toomer found it singularly appropriate that the modern world should bury ***Cane.*** Let us in any event delay the exhumation no longer.

Notes

1. *After the Lost Generation,* New York and London, McGraw-Hill, 1951, p. 88.
2. Quoted in Alain Locke, "Negro Youth Speaks," *The New Negro* (New York, Boni, 1925), p. 51.
3. *Cane,* p. 21 ("The Song of the Son").
4. See Gorham B. Munson, *Destinations* (New York, 1928), pp. 178-96.

CHARLES W. SCRUGGS (ESSAY DATE 1972)

SOURCE: Scruggs, Charles W. "Mark of Cain and the Redemption of Art: A Study in Theme and Structure of Jean Toomer's *Cane.*" *American Literature* 44 (1972): 276-91.

In the following essay, Scruggs discusses the intricate interrelationships within the three sections of Cane *and claims that the work suggests the biblical story of Cain and thus depicts the Black experience in mythic terms.*

Published in 1923 by Boni and Liveright, Jean Toomer's ***Cane*** was an instant failure. Although praised by the literary avant-garde of the twenties (Sherwood Anderson, Kenneth Burke, Hart Crane, Waldo Frank, Gorham Munson, to name a few), the novel sold only 500 copies in the first year. From one point of view, it is strange the novel fared so badly, for it was experimental in the manner of Sherwood Anderson's *Winesburg, Ohio,* whose influence is quite noticeable in ***Cane,***[1] and it antedates by two years the publication (also by Boni and Liveright) of Hemingway's *In Our Time,* whose form it most distinctly resembles. Also, given the emergence of "exotic Harlem" and an interest in things Negro, the public seemed ready for a novel like ***Cane,*** or at least so felt Horace Liveright.[2] Still, the novel failed, and Toomer began a slow retreat into obscurity. With the revival of interest in black literature, its reputation grew so that by 1968 Robert Bone could call ***Cane*** as good a novel as *Native Son* and *Invisible Man.*[3]

Criticism of the novel has rarely gone beyond Bone's judgment of it. ***Cane,*** as Darwin Turner says, "inspires critical rhapsodies rather than analysis."[4] The most easily recognizable pattern is its division into three sections: stories, separated by poems, of the agrarian South; stories, separated by poems and vignettes, of the urban North; and **"Kabnis,"** a story-drama involving an urban Negro living in Georgia. The themes of the novel appear to arise from the conflict between a world that is technological, culturally white and spiritually sterile, and one that is agrarian, culturally black and richly primitive.[5]

Criticism of this nature only goes halfway and by no means exhausts the intricate interrelationships within each of the sections of ***Cane.*** I base my analysis of these further relationships on my reading of the unpublished Toomer papers at Fisk University. Particularly helpful is correspondence between the writer and other literary figures of his day.

The first consideration is the pun in the title, a pun which critics have disregarded. "Cane" also means "Cain," and it is not by accident that Toomer wanted to depict the black experience in mythic terms.[6] Hart Crane, Van Wyck Brooks, Waldo Frank, and others had been urging American artists to exploit the mythic possibilities of America's past. Here specifically was one myth ready-made for black people and already a part of American folklore; the color of the black man's skin was the mark of Cain.[7]

Of course, this assertion belonged to the folklore of the dominant culture; the Negroes themselves did not always believe it. In fact, black people have tended to reverse the mark from black to white. As James Baldwin says in *The Fire Next Time*: "In the same way that we, for white people, were the descendants of Ham, and were cursed forever, white people were, for us, the descendants of Cain."[8] Toomer, on the other hand, uses the myth for aesthetic purposes while he ultimately rejects its negative implications as the lie of the white man. Like Baldwin, he suggests that the real mark may be white.

In the themes that develop from the myth of Cain, the "mark" is often distinguished from the "curse." The former can be interpreted as a badge of protection as well as shame: God "set a mark upon Cain, lest any finding him should kill him" (Genesis 4:15). It is the curse that really interests Toomer, a curse that, in American folklore, has been transferred from murderer to murdered. God tells Cain after the murder of his brother: "now art thou cursed. . . . When thou tillest the ground, it shall not henceforth yield unto thee her strength; a fugitive and a vagabond shalt thou be in the earth" (Genesis 4:11-12).

Other writers from Byron to Sartre have seen the fugitive Cain as a symbol of modern man; Toomer uses Cain as a symbol of the African in a hostile land, tilling the soil of the earth, a slave, without enjoying her fruits. Yet strangely enough, this Cain receives another kind of nourishment from the soil, spiritual nourishment, which the owners of it are denied.

Also, the Bible states that Cain's nomadic existence leads him to found a city in the land of Nod, "east of Eden" (Genesis 4:16-17). An apocryphal legend develops from this event, for he and his descendants become known as the first city-dwellers. Toomer treats this side of the myth as part of the curse. As the blacks move into northern cities "east of Eden," they are cut off from their spiritual roots in the agrarian South; their lives grow pale like the "white-washed wood of Washington" to which Toomer refers in "Seventh Street." But there is a fate worse than moving to the desolate northern cities; it is moving to those desolate cities inside your mind, as Kabnis does when he accepts the myth of the black Cain as a curse and not a badge of divine protection.

The second approach to a fuller understanding of ***Cane*** comes from Toomer's letter to Waldo Frank upon completion of the novel. Critics may be skeptical about finding any structure in the work, and certainly ***Cane*** may be appreciated without one, but Toomer himself apparently had a plan. "My brother!" he says to Frank on December 12, 1922:

> ***Cane*** is on its way to you! For two weeks I have worked steadily at it. The book is done. From three angles, ***Cane***'s design is a circle. Aesthetically, from simple forms to complex ones, and back to simple forms. Regionally, from the South up into the North, and back into the South again. Or from

> the North down into the South and then a return North. From the point of view of the spiritual entity behind the work, the curve really starts with **"Bona and Paul"** (awakening), plunges into **"Kabnis,"** emerges in **"Karintha"** etc. swings upward into **"Theatre"** and **"Box Seat,"** and ends (pauses) in **"Harvest Song."** . . . Between each of the three sections, a curve. These, to vaguely indicate the design.[9]

Toomer's outline both puzzles and informs. It puzzles because, although the novel moves from South to North to South, it does not parallel the spiritual pattern he employs. The published work begins with the **"Karintha"** section and ends with **"Kabnis."** The curves drawn on separate pages between the sections hint at a circular design, but the reader tends to associate them only with the South-North-South structural scheme.

The key, I think, lies in the word "pauses" (". . . and ends (pauses) in **'Harvest Song'**"). Toomer is describing ***Cane*** in organic terms, and therefore it never really ends. It is simply a matter of beginning all over again with **"Bona and Paul,"** the story that follows **"Harvest Song."**

Organic form interests Toomer as he reacts to the industrialization of his age. In a letter to Gorham Munson (March 19, 1923) he compares aesthetic form to a tree, with the sap as the sustenance and the arrangement of leaves as the meaning. "A machine," he says, "is all form, it has no leaves. Its very abstraction is . . . the death of it."[10] Even earlier, in a letter to Waldo Frank (July 19, 1922), he mentions plans for a collection entitled ***Cane*** with the sections "Cane stalks and choruses" (**"Kabnis"** and "K. C. A."—probably **"Karintha," "Carma,"** and **"Avey"**); "leaves and syrup songs" (the poems), and "Leaf Traceries in Washington" (the vignettes).[11]

The most meaningful statements in Toomer's December 12th letter to Frank have to do with "the spiritual entity behind the work." Words like "awakening," "plunges," "emerges," "swings upward," and "ends" suggest degrees of spiritual awareness and wholeness. It is my contention that each story or poem documents the spiritual health of its characters, their ability to accept themselves and their worlds, and it does so with important implications for the artist and his work. And the theme Toomer uses to explore the world of the soul is the myth of Cain.

Toomer labels **"Bona and Paul"** the "awakening," and to most of us this comes as a surprise; our initial reaction is probably closer to Robert Bone's, who calls the story "an anticlimax after **'Box Seat.'**"[12] But accepting Toomer's conception of structure in terms of a circle, with **"Harvest Song"** the zenith, **"Kabnis"** the nadir, it quite obviously functions as a preface to **"Kabnis,"** which it immediately precedes, and, secondly, it anticipates thematically the final fulfillment of **"Harvest Song."**

"Bona and Paul" takes place in Chicago, but Georgia mystically exerts her influence upon the northern city and the young man who does not feel at home in it. Paul, a student whose dark skin arouses the curiosity of his friends and attracts Bona, a white Southerner, is a Kabnis up North, a Kabnis before he makes his pilgrimage to Georgia:

> Gray slanting roofs of houses are tinted lavender in the setting sun. Paul follows the sun, over the stock-yards where a fresh stench is just arising, across wheat lands that are still waving above their stubble, into the sun. Paul follows the sun to a pine-matted hillock in Georgia. He sees the slanting roofs of gray unpainted cabins tinted lavender. . . . Paul follows the sun into himself in Chicago.
>
> He is Bona's window.
>
> With his own glow he looks through a dark pane.[13]

Paul feels the ancestral pull of Georgia without ever having been there because he feels out of place in Chicago. And, as the "dark pane" suggests, his estrangement is intensified by his inability to penetrate Bona's attraction to him. His isolation works on two levels: his isolation in the white man's world and his isolation from Bona.

A dream-like transformation takes place in the Crimson Gardens, a white nightclub where Paul, Bona, Art, and Helen dance one evening under "pink lights." As Paul walks into the nightclub he has a feeling of being "apart from the people around him," but the white faces take on "a glow and immediacy" (p. 145). "With his own glow, he seeks to penetrate a dark pane"—Bona (p. 147).

Driven by a mutual awareness which begins on the dance floor, they leave the nightclub to consummate their passion. The black, uniformed doorman gives them a knowing look: "Too many couples have passed out, flushed and fidgety, for him not to know." In the cold air a strange thing happens. Paul sees the gardens purple, "as if he were way off." The spell of magic broken, he rushes back to the doorman to explain the substance of his dream: "I came back to tell you . . . that you are wrong. That something beautiful is going to happen . . . that white faces are petals of roses. That dark faces are petals of dusk. That I am going out and gather petals. That I am going out and know her whom I brought here with me to these gardens which are purple like a bed of roses would be at dusk" (pp. 152-153). But this Cain has intellectualized his dream of wholeness instead of having lived it. When he returns to find Bona she is gone.

What Toomer means by calling this story the "awakening" should now be clear. Paul has had a vision of wholeness in the Gardens, but in his excitement to explain it, to understand it, he loses it. Paul's epiphany then is ironic; the purple of the Gardens at dusk suggests a fusion of the white and black worlds, specifically of Bona and Paul, but it is a fusion whose nature, like that of dusk, is only temporary. The color purple also suggests passion; Paul's passion thins out before he has a chance to experience its fullness.

Nevertheless, Paul's dream haunts Toomer. The conflict between the world of the Crimson Gardens and the world outside, like that of art and life, is a preface to the Kabnis-Cain who believes that the real Kabnis "is a dream" and that "dreams are faces with large eyes and weak chins and broad brows that get smashed by the fists of square faces. The body of the world is bull-necked. A dream is a soft face that fits uncertainly upon it . . ." (p. 158).

The myth of Cain is most relevant at the lowest point on the circle. It is crucial to the understanding of Kabnis's emotional anguish. Based upon Toomer's own experience, the story documents his spiritual conflict, for Kabnis is Toomer, or one side of Toomer, a Toomer who has yet to reach the artistic and spiritual wholeness of the singer of **"Harvest Song."**[14]

Ralph Kabnis—light-skinned, intellectual, Northern Negro—teaches school in Georgia. Like Toomer, his ancestors come from Georgia, but he has been too bleached out to accept the rich, sensual world of the South with its raw passions and racial violence. As Toomer succinctly puts it: "Things are so immediate in Georgia" (p. 164). Kabnis recoils from such immediacy, escapes at first into a world of his own dreams, and then finally clings to Halsey, the wagon-maker who has stoically survived with the help of his trade and at the expense of his soul. The story describes Kabnis's moral decline due primarily to his inability to accept himself. His spiritual despair reaches its lowest point the morning after a drunken party in Halsey's cellar. Kabnis stumbles out of bed, a ludicrous figure in a borrowed costume, a robe. He is a grim parody of a poet.

Father John, the silent old man who lives in Halsey's cellar—the "dead blind father of a muted folk" (p. 212)—utters the word "sin" and the truth about Ralph Kabnis:

> FATHER JOHN: Sin.
> KABNIS: Aw, shut up, old man.
> CARRIE K.: Leave him be. He wants t say somethin. (She turns to the old man.) What is it, Father?
> KABNIS: Whatsha talkin t that old deaf man for? Come away from him.
> CARRIE K.: What is it, Father? The old man's lips begin to work. Words are formed incoherently. Finally, he manages to articulate—
> FATHER JOHN: Th sin whats fixed . . . (Hesitates.)
> CARRIE K.: (restraining a comment from Kabnis) Go on, Father.
> FATHER JOHN: . . . upon th white folks—
> KABNIS: Suppose youre talkin about that bastard race thats roamin round th country. It looks like sin, if thats what y mean. Give us somethin new and up t date.
> FATHER JOHN: —f tellin Jesus—lies. O th sin the white folks 'mitted when they made th Bible lie.
>
> (p. 237)

Kabnis reacts to this platitude with disgust, calls Father John "You old black fakir." But he does not really hear what Father John has to say; perhaps the truth would be too awful to bear. The lie that Father John speaks of is the myth that Negroes are the descendants of Cain. Kabnis's tragedy is that he accepts the white man's lie. The curse placed upon him is not his Negro blood but his own self-hatred. He fails to realize the implications of "that bastard race thats roamin round th country."

The character Lewis—"what a stronger Kabnis might have been" (p. 189)—calls the old man "the spirit of the past" and asks Kabnis to accept him:

> KABNIS: . . . he aint my past. My ancestors were Southern blue-bloods—
> LEWIS: And black.
> KABNIS: Aint much difference between blue an black.
> LEWIS: Enough to draw a denial from you. Cant hold them, can you? Master; slave. Soil; and the overarching heavens. Dusk, dawn. They fight and bastardize you.
>
> (pp. 217-218)

Kabnis's cowardice demonstrated in denying the old man results in a denial of himself, and a denial of the richness of his past even though the past contains contradictions. The lie comes true for Kabnis in a very real sense. He has become as Cain, a cursed and alienated man.

The rejection of Father John and the blackness in himself is closely related to his failure as an artist. Like Stephen Daedalus in Joyce's *Portrait of the Artist as a Young Man,* Kabnis wants to create something beautiful but he is appalled by the actual ugliness surrounding him. He cannot reconcile the rednecks, red mud, rats, and hencoops with the beauty of the natural world: "Kabnis is about to shake his fists heavenward. He looks up, and the night's beauty strikes him dumb." In anguish, he asks God not to torture him with beauty: "Take it away. Give me an ugly world. Ha, ugly. Stinking like unwashed niggers" (p. 161). Later he gets his wish. At the drunken party he tells Lewis and Halsey that "some twisted awful thing" has taken possession of his soul and he has to feed it with words: "Not beautiful words. God almighty no. Misshapen, split-gut, tortured, twisted words. . . . White folks feed it cause their looks are words. Niggers, black niggers feed it cause theyre evil an their looks are words. Yallar niggers feed it. This whole damn bloated purple country feeds it cause its goin down t hell in a holy avalanche of words" (p. 224).

But what Kabnis is describing is the hell within himself, not out there. Unlike Yeats, Kabnis fails to realize that the source of beauty lies in the "foul rag and bone shop of the heart." He is "Kabnis, a promise of soil-soaked beauty; uprooted, thinning out. Suspended a few feet above the soil whose touch would resurrect him" (p. 191).

This failure is emphasized in a scene during which Layman, a local preacher, describes a lynching against a background of church spirituals. Suddenly, "a woman's voice swells to shouting. Kabnis hears it. His face gives way to an expression of mingled fear, contempt, and pity" (p. 175). The fear he feels recalls other fears he experiences in a world whose rawness prevents him from being a man and an artist. For the truth is, and I think Toomer is stressing this point, the shouting is beautiful though Kabnis does not respond to it as such. It is beautiful because it makes sense out of evil and suffering, such evil and suffering, for example, as the lynching. It is art because it removes experience to a realm where we can cope with it, if not understand it. This explains why Toomer has included this refrain throughout the story:

White-man's land.
Niggers, sing.
Burn, bear black children
Till poor rivers bring
Rest, and sweet glory
in Camp Ground.

To sing goes beyond resignation. It is a positive act, an artistic expression created not simply in the face of adversity, but because of it.

The mark of Cain upon Kabnis represents, as Toomer suggests in his letter to Frank, the spiritual nadir of the book. It stands thematically in direct opposition to **"Harvest Song,"** the lyric which completes the "spiritual entity" of the novel by providing an answer to Kabnis's dilemma. Also, since **"Kabnis"** concludes the novel, it forces a comparison with the lyrical opening ("emerging") story, **"Karintha."** For instance, Kabnis's spiritual alienation underscores Karintha's spiritual health. As she grows into womanhood, she transcends the moral order of men: "Even the preacher, who caught her at mischief, told himself that she was as innocently lovely as a November cotton flower" (p. 2). The bull-necked world threatens her natural beauty; men wish to "ripen a growing thing too soon" (p. 1). But it fails. Somehow her mysterious life survives the mundane fact of her illegitimate child. Like the November cotton flower to which she is compared, she blooms in a stark world: "Beauty so sudden for that time of year" (poem, **"November Cotton Flower,"** p. 7).

All the women of the opening section (with the exception of Esther[15]) are those whose natural beauty is misunderstood. They endure, but are rarely accepted. It would be foolish to insist that Karintha, Carma, Becky, Fern, and Louisa are all manifestations of Cain because of their isolation; however, the theme is significant in **"Blood-Burning Moon."** Louisa, the beautiful black woman courted by the white Bob Stone and the black Tom Burwell, cannot separate her two lovers in her mind: "for some reason, they jumbled when her eyes gazed vacantly at the rising moon" (p. 52). Their fight over Louisa, resulting in Stone's death, reenacts the first killing of brother by brother. Burwell's lynching without trial is proof of the mark placed upon him.

It is Toomer, not his characters, who bears and accepts the mark of Cain in the "emerging" section. In **"Song of the Son,"** the poem which follows **"Carma,"** Toomer sings of his need to know his heritage of slavery while there is still evidence of it:

before they stripped the old tree bare
One plum was saved for me, one seed becomes

An everlasting song, a singing tree
Caroling softly souls of slavery.
What they were, and what they are to me.
(p. 21)

This son of the fallen Adam, the one the Bible lied about, has made music of the curse. Like Carrie K. at the end of **"Kabnis,"** he has embraced Father John but unlike either of them, he will not be mute.

The spiritual quest which gains momentum in the agrarian South "swings upward" in the electric beehive of Washington. The "cane-fluted" world does not die in the North. It continues to haunt the dreams and lives of those who have strayed far from their roots to dwell in the cities. Avey, for instance, is a Fern come North where the only outlet for her natural, instinctual life is that of prostitution. The story as it progresses shifts its focus to the narrator, a wandering Cain who cannot cope with Avey for the same reason that Kabnis cannot cope with Georgia: she is too immediate. He tries to romanticize her: "I talked, beautifully I thought, about an art that would be born, an art that would open the way for women the likes of her" (p. 87). But her unresponsiveness convinces him that she is lazy, a "cow." Only at the end of the story does he understand her in a light which links their common humanity. As he watches her sleep in the city park, he sees mortality's stamp upon her face and accepts the tragic separateness of their two lives: "I saw the dawn steal over Washington. The Capitol dome looked like a grey ghost ship drifting in from sea. Avey's face was pale, and her eyes were heavy. She did not have the grey crimson-splashed beauty of the dawn. I hated to wake her. Orphan-woman . . ." (p. 88).

"Theatre," too, deals with the theme of separation. "The implication of the story," Toomer wrote Gorham Munson on October 31, 1922, "is that of a dual separation: one, false and altogether arbitrary, the other, inherent in the nature of the two beings. This coincides loosely with a conception I have of the theatre, and art in general in its relation to life."[16] The two beings are John and Dorris: one, the manager's brother, "dictie" (respectable) and the only audience at a dance rehearsal in the Howard Street theatre; the other, a chorus-girl who arouses John's passion. An emotional charge passes between them, but John's intellect short-circuits it. The social gap frightens him: "It wouldnt work. Keep her loveliness. Let her go" (p. 94). As Toomer says in the letter to Munson, "Stage-folk are not respectable; audiences are." Mame, another chorus-girl, voices the same social wisdom to Dorris, but Dorris is determined not to lose him. As Toomer tells Munson, "she uses the only art at her command: dancing." In the story he describes her dancing as singing of "canebrake loves and mangrove feastings" (p. 98). Dorris's sensuality excites John, but again his mind dilutes his passion. While she dances, he dreams, romanticizing her. Afterward she sees his face in shadow; she "seeks for her dance in it. She finds it a dead thing in the shadow which is his dream" (p. 99). She rushes from the stage in despair.

On one level, John's failure to consummate his attraction to Dorris is purely social ("false and altogether arbitrary"), but on another it raises the question of whether art is forever doomed to remain divorced from life. John, as an artist, has transmuted Dorris into a dream, and so she is both more and less real than life: more real because John sees her symbolic value as dancer (celebrator of the life force); less real because, in giving her that symbolic value, he can no longer respond to the flesh and blood. Dorris, as an artist, uses her art unsuccessfully in attempting to capture John, but in so doing she creates something beautiful. John can relate to her as an audience, but not as a lover. In other words, John's failure to approach Dorris cannot be explained simply by social fears and reservations, or by the tragic triumph of the intellect over the body.[17] The distance between the two characters measures the distance between art and life, a distance which will not be removed until **"Harvest Song."**

John dreams; Dan Moore shouts (**"Box Seat"**). Each act climaxes the character's growth.[18] In **"Box Seat"** the roles of **"Theatre"** are reversed. Muriel is "dictie" while Dan still smells of the canefield. He comes to free her from the middle-class world of Mrs. Pribby, her landlady whose "sharp-edged, massed, metallic" house closes about Muriel like a prison: "Muriel's chair is close and stiff about her. The house, the rows of houses locked about her chair" (p. 113). To avoid Dan's animal magnetism, Muriel flees to the Lincoln Theatre where Pribby's oppressive influence continues to assert itself. Each seat in the theater named for the Great Emancipator "is a bolt that shoots into a slot, and is locked there" (p. 117). And what happens on stage becomes more real than the lives of the audience.

Dan follows Muriel with bizarre visions of himself as savior come to free the world from the curse of the Pribbys, the curse of the city-dwellers choked by their houses. He dreams: "I'll show em. Grab an ax and brain em. Cut em up. Jack the Ripper. Baboon from the zoo. And then the cops come. 'No I aint a baboon. I aint Jack the Ripper. I'm a poor man out of work. Take your hands off me, you bull-necked bears. Look into my eyes. I am Dan Moore. I was born in a canefield. The hands of Jesus touched me. I am come to a sick world to heal it'" (p. 105-106). What he learns at the Lincoln Theatre is that he first must heal himself.

It is a grotesque boxing match between dwarfs by which Dan realizes himself and by which Muriel is judged. As the dwarfs battle, they soon fight in earnest and blood flows. After it ends, the champion, Mr. Barry, singles out girls in the audience, singing a love song to them, and holding a mirror "in such a way that it flashes in the face of each one" (p. 126). Dan is oblivious to what is happening until the light shines in his face. Dreaming of destroying this synthetic crystal palace like a black Sampson, he is brought back to reality by the mirror. At the next moment, the mirror and song focus on Muriel: "She shrinks away. Nausea. She clutches the brass box rail" (p. 127). The dwarf presents a horrifying sight, the blood from his lips dripping on a rose that he wishes to offer some special girl. He offers it to Muriel. Muriel flinches, terrified by both dwarf and the expectant audience. Dan looks at the dwarf, whose tortured face "grows calm and massive. It grows profound. It is a thing of wisdom and tenderness, of suffering and beauty" (p. 128). The dwarf's eyes seem to beg for acceptance. As Muriel reluctantly reaches out to touch the flower, Dan rises and shouts: "Jesus Was Once a Leper!" In rejecting the dwarf she is rejecting her black heritage—ugly, bloody, leprous—for the respectable, clean world of the audience.

It is important to notice that Dan shouts at himself as well. His recognition of the dwarf's plight means he has accepted that baboon side of himself. When he sits down, "as cool as a green stem that has just shed its flower," he has bid farewell to rage, to those apocalyptic visions in which he rides thunder in a whirlwind. As he leaves the theater, he has even forgotten about the vindictive spectator whose nose he has tweaked and whose shoes he has trampled on. He walks down the alley alone, all passion spent.

"Harvest Song" completes the cycle. The poem answers Kabnis's spiritual despair, and in its lyric simplicity it restates the thematic conclusion of **"Box Seat,"** the peace that passes understanding. In the poem, the reaper sings of his suffering. Like Cain, he tills the soil but the bread he earns by the sweat of his brow is not enough to sustain him:

> I am a reaper whose muscles set at sundown. All
> my oats are cradled.
> But I am too chilled, and too fatigued to bind
> them.
> And I hunger.
>
> I crack a grain between my teeth. I do not taste it.
> I have been in the fields all day. My throat is dry.
> I hunger.
>
> (p. 132)

His hunger is more than physical; he hungers for friendship, for spiritual understanding. Neither of these is forthcoming, yet he sings:

> O my brothers, I beat my palms, still soft, against
> the
> stubble of my harvesting. (You beat your soft
> palms, too.) My pain is sweet. Sweeter than
> the oats or wheat or corn. It will not bring me
> knowledge of my hunger.
>
> (p. 133)

A black Job, he will never understand the mysterious workings of God; he will never understand why the curse of slavery has been placed upon him.[19] Yet he sings, and his singing has transformed the pain into sweetness. As Auden expresses it best, in his elegy on Yeats: "With the farming of a verse," he has made "a vineyard of the curse."

The theme of Cain suggests even broader possibilities. Americans have tended to mythologize their experience, and they found most suitable the myth of Adam. Scholars like R. W. B. Lewis (*The American Adam*) have persuaded us that this identification was by no means accidental; it grew out of man's contact with the New World, a garden in which the vices of Europe were unknown and in which man could return to his primal innocence. For some (Thoreau, Emerson, Whitman), the world lay before this New Adam and nothing seemed impossible; for others (Hawthorne and Melville), the world constricted around his heart to remind him that evil existed even in Eden. Thus, if the dominant culture can make sense out of its experience through the myth of Adam, I would suggest that Negroes have used the myth of Cain to explain their own uprootedness, an experience antithetical to the outer culture. If America evokes the dream of Paradise regained for many white artists, so Claude McKay might see New York's fruit stands as "bringing memories" of fruit-laden trees in Africa, a paradise long since lost:

> My eyes grew dim, and I could no more gaze;
> A wave of longing through my body swept,
> And, hungry for the old familiar ways,
> I turned aside and bowed my head and wept.[20]

Langston Hughes reminds America that he too sings—"the darker brother." Cain sits in the kitchen, an outsider, growing stronger as he waits. Someday, he says, "they'll see how beautiful I am / And be ashamed,— / I, too, am America."[21]

Toomer acknowledges with some regret that "someday" might be too late. In a letter to Waldo Frank the summer of 1923, he observes that the mechanized society demands that a minority dissolve into the larger culture or get "sloughed off," and he predicts: "if anything comes up now, pure Negro, it will be a swansong. Don't let us fool ourselves, brother: the Negro of the folk-song has all but passed away: the Negro of the emotional church is fading. A hundred years from now these Negroes, if they exist at all will live in art. . . . America needs these elements. . . . Let us grab and hold them while there is still time."

He goes on to explain the role of ***Cane*** in this task: "In my own . . . pieces that come nearest to the old Negro, to the spirit saturate with folk-song: **"Karintha"** and **"Fern,"** the dominant emotion is a sadness derived from a sense of fading, from a knowledge of my futility to check solution. . . . The folk-songs themselves are of the same order: the deepest of them, 'I aint got long to stay here.'"[22]

Notes

1. Toomer admitted his indebtedness to Sherwood Anderson. In a letter to Anderson (Dec. 18, 1922), he says: "Winesburg, Ohio, and the Triumph of the Egg are elements of my growing. It is hard to think of myself as maturing without them" (Toomer papers, Fisk University Library, Box 1, Folder 1). To Gorham Munson he states that Sherwood Anderson, Waldo Frank, Robert Frost, and Carl Sandburg are the only modern writers who have immediately influenced him (ibid., Box 7, Folder 12). Later, however, he tended to denigrate Anderson's influence. He tells Gorham Munson that there is "too much Anderson" in "Fern," "too much waste." He is "through with that phase" (ibid., Box 7, Folder 12). He also complains to Waldo Frank in the summer of 1923 that Anderson sees his work only as the product of a Negro artist, that Anderson ignores dimensions "other than Negro," such as "a sense of the tragic separateness, the tragic sterility of people . . ." (ibid., Box 3, Folder 7).
2. Horace Liveright wanted to publicize *Cane* as a "Negro" novel and urged Toomer to stress his "colored blood" in an autobiographical sketch. In his reply (Sept. 5, 1923), Toomer distinguished between his racial identity and his artistic identity. He said: "feature Negro if you wish, but do not expect me to feature it in advertisements for you. For myself, I have sufficiently featured Negro in *Cane*" (ibid., Box 1, Folder 5).
3. Robert Bone, *The Negro Novel in America*, 4th ed. (New Haven, 1968), p. 81.
4. Darwin Turner, "Jean Toomer's *Cane*," *Negro Digest*, XVIII (Jan., 1969), 54.
5. Todd Lieber, "Design and Movement in *Cane*," *CLA Journal*, XIII (Sept., 1969), 38.
6. Toomer accidently wrote *Cain* for *Cane* when referring to his novel. Later he corrected his typing "error" in his own handwriting. See Toomer papers, Fisk University Library, Box 32, Folder 7.
7. See Winthrop Jordan, *White over Black: American Attitudes toward the Negro 1550-1812* (Baltimore, 1969), pp. 242, 416. Also, see Charles Nichols, *Many Thousand Gone: The Ex-Slaves' Account of their Bondage and Freedom* (Bloomington, Ind., 1969), p. 119, and James Weldon Johnson, *The Book of American Negro Poetry* (New York, 1959), p. 29.
8. James Baldwin, *The Fire Next Time* (New York, 1964), p. 59. Baldwin's assertion that black people envisioned Cain as white is reinforced by the fact that we have no way of knowing what the mark was. According to Sir James Frazer, God may have painted Cain red "like a Fijian" or white "like a Ngoni." *Folklore in the Old Testament* (New York, 1923), p. 45.
9. Toomer papers, Fisk University Library, Box 3, Folder 6.
10. Ibid., Box 7, Folder 12. Toomer's use of the organic metaphor also links him to the romantic movement in American literature. See Richard P. Adams, "Emerson and the Organic Metaphor," *PMLA*, LXIX (March, 1954), 117-130.
11. Toomer papers, Fisk University Library, Box 3, Folder 6.
12. Bone, p. 87.
13. Jean Toomer, *Cane* (New York, 1969), pp. 137-138. All subsequent references to *Cane* are to this edition, and will be found in parentheses in the text.
14. Toomer spent some time in Sparta, Georgia, in 1922. As he tells Waldo Frank (summer, 1923): "Kabnis is *Me.*" Toomer papers, Fisk University Library, Box 3, Folder 7.
15. Esther appears to be a female Kabnis, her sexual nature inhibited by her middle-class upbringing. Also, note her similarity to Alice Hindman ("Adventure") and Kate Smith ("The Teacher") in *Winesburg, Ohio.*
16. Toomer papers, Fisk University Library, Box 7, Folder 12.
17. See Bone, p. 85; Turner, p. 57; Lieber, p. 43.
18. In a letter to Gorham Munson (March 23, 1923), Toomer refers to "John's climax in dream" and "Dan Moore's in shouting." Toomer papers, Fisk University Library, Box 7, Folder 12.
19. Cf. Genesis 4:13: "And Cain said Unto the Lord, my punishment is greater than I can bear."
20. Claude McKay, "The Tropics in New York," *The New Negro*, ed. Alain Locke (New York, 1969), p. 135.
21. Langston Hughes, "I too," *The New Negro*, p. 145.
22. Toomer papers, Fisk University Library, Box 3, Folder 7.

ALAN GOLDING (ESSAY DATE 1983)

SOURCE: Golding, Alan. "Jean Toomer's *Cane*: The Search for Identity through Form." *Arizona Quarterly* 39, no. 3 (fall 1983): 197-214.

In the following essay, Golding examines the structure of polarities in Cane, *which, he states, enacts Toomer's own "struggle to reconcile the contradictory spirits of North and South and the black and white within himself."*

> Some critics have viewed the book as an experimental novel; others as a miscellany, composed of poetic, dramatic, and narrative elements; still others as a work *sui generis,* which deliberately violates the standard categories. The problem is complicated by the fact that parts of ***Cane*** were published independently as poems, sketches, and stories. This would suggest that Toomer thought of them as separate entities, whatever their subsequent function in the overall design.[1]

Thus Robert Bone summarizes the field of critical responses to ***Cane.*** Yet, in whatever way they have finally categorized Jean Toomer's collage of character vignettes, poetry, song, short story, and drama, critics have generally argued that the book exhibits various kinds of unified design. The action throughout occupies either the same setting (Parts 1 and 3 occur in Sempter, Georgia, a fictionalized Sparta) or the same *kind* of setting (Part 2 moves among various Northern cities, including Washington, D.C., and Chicago). This tripartite structure based on place provides some overall shape and readers have also noted various strains of thematic and stylistic unity in the work.[2]

If we accept that Toomer did try to shape his "separate entities" into an "overall design," then this question arises: Why? What was he after in his efforts to forge ***Cane***'s fragments into a whole? I suggest that he was striving for more than a solely esthetic unity. Toomer organizes ***Cane*** around a pattern of balanced but unresolved poles—between rural South and urban North, black emotionalism and white intellect, female sensuality and male mind. Like most such polarities these appear, from one angle, facile and rather simplistic, and it reflects negatively on Toomer that they are not post hoc critical contrivances, that they can easily be found in ***Cane.*** Yet at the same time these poles embody powerful social and personal conflicts: that of Southern, rural, black culture facing assimilation into a predominantly white, urban, Northern culture, and that of Toomer's own mixed racial identity. I shall argue that Toomer's drive to make the pieces of ***Cane*** balance or cohere enacts on the formal level his struggle to reconcile both the contradictory spirits of North and South and the black and white within himself.[3]

Toomer's search for personal and racial identity so strongly forms the basis of his art that the work after ***Cane*** disintegrates once he feels he has reached his goal of spiritual and racial harmony in discovering Gurdjieff's Unitism in 1924. He dissociated himself from racial fiction to the extent of refusing James Weldon Johnson permission to use some of the ***Cane*** poems in a revised edition of *The Book of American Negro Poetry* in 1930, on the grounds that they were neither black nor white but simply "American" poems. In fact, Toomer refused to be included in several Negro anthologies around this time, and was angry with Alain Locke for publishing parts of ***Cane*** in the Harlem Renaissance manifesto, *The New Negro.*[4] Yet asserting his black identity may have cost him the chance to publish a novel, ***Transatlantic,*** in 1929. In 1941 he gave permission for two selections from ***Cane*** to appear in an anthology of black literature, *The Negro Caravan.*[5]

Thus the evidence on whether Toomer considered himself black remains inconclusive. In an unpublished essay, **"The South in Literature,"** written partly to promote ***Cane,*** he describes himself as "of Negro descent."[6] In a 1922 letter to Sherwood Anderson he alludes to his art as having the didactic impulse to guide "the youth of the [black] race": "But I feel that in time, in its social phase, my art will aid in giving the Negro to himself. In this connection I have thought of a magazine. . . . The need is great."[7] Yet Toomer did not identify with blacks after writing ***Cane.*** The book seems to have functioned as an elegy not only for the black folk spirit but for Toomer's own blackness. As George Kent says, "Toomer may have represented the kind of racial consciousness that for a brief interval is *most* intense *precisely* because it is about to *disappear.*"[8] Toomer's temporary identification with blacks apparently released his art, as he himself admits in 1922: "Within the last two or three years, however, my growing need for artistic expression has pulled me deeper and deeper into the Negro group."[9] ***Cane*** represents what Bone calls "a momentary deviation" from a consistent, lifelong pattern of challenging racial categories.[10] Even around the time of writing ***Cane*** Toomer did little to encourage the Harlem Renaissance, and in a 1930 diary he writes "I am to decrystallize these [racial] divisions and make possible the widespread consciousness of the American race."[11]

Cane shows Toomer in 1923 intellectually an American and emotionally a black. His later writings displace this conflict from the racial to the spiritual plane and increasingly emphasize personal, spiritual integration independent of race: "Themosense (thought *and* emotion *and* sensing) is the inner synthesis of functions, which represents the entire individual and gives rise to complete action."[12] In ***Cane*** Toomer writes as a black man—but as the first black writer to attempt collapsing racial categories in literature by consistently applying white artists' formal experiments to black themes of racial disenfranchisement, oppression, and identity. Until ***Cane,*** black fiction had been represented by the straightforwardly realistic novels of Charles Chesnutt, Paul Laurence Dunbar, James Weldon Johnson, and W. E. B. DuBois. Certainly Johnson's *The Autobiography of an Ex-Coloured Man* (1912) deals with similar modes of communal black experience (oral tales, music and dance, religious oratory, lynchings) to ***Cane.*** Certainly DuBois's *The Souls of Black Folk* (1903) offers, in short sketches occasionally linked by songs, a Northerner's narrative travelogue of the rural South.[13] But ***Cane*** advanced on these works by pursuing such modernist prose techniques as the breakdown of continuous narrative into juxtaposed fragments, an emphasis on psychological over narrative realism, snatches of plot more symbolic than literal, and the elevation of governing metaphors to almost mythic status (compare Jake Barnes's groin wound or, later, Faulkner's bear to Toomer's use of cane and dusk). Clearly these techniques are not the prerogative of white writers, but they had never before appeared so sustainedly in black writing as they did in ***Cane.***

An avid reader of literary magazines, Toomer probably encountered the episodes of *Ulysses* published in the *Little Review,* and his interest in emotional realism, symbol, and myth appears to stem in part from Joyce's influence. More concretely, documented evidence shows how Sherwood Anderson influenced Toomer's style. Toomer's mentor, Waldo Frank, introduced him to Anderson's work and Toomer read *Winesburg, Ohio* just before he left for Sparta in fall 1921 for the three-month stay which gave birth to Parts 1 and 3 of ***Cane.*** He read *The Triumph of the Egg* while in Sparta. On December 18, 1922, he wrote to Anderson that "*Winesburg, Ohio* and *The Triumph of the Egg* are elements of my growing. It is hard to think of myself as maturing without them."[14] Anderson praised Toomer's lyricism and Toomer responded with similar enthusiasm to Anderson's imagery: "Your images are clean, glowing, healthy, vibrant: sunlight on forks of trees, on mellow piles of pine boards."[15]

Winesburg, Ohio is particularly apposite to the question of ***Cane***'s form. The continuity of ***Cane,*** like that of *Winesburg,* is one of tone, mood, and social setting, the form drawing on principles of mutability and process rather than of fixed linear construction. Toomer saw the making of ***Cane*** in terms of what now seems a rather conventional opposition between dead mechanical and live organic form, poles which he associated with the urban North and the rural South. Frank's position in *Our America* (1919) that "the task of the artist was to fashion counterforms, or antibodies, to the Machine"[16] encouraged him in this opposition. While writing ***Cane,*** Toomer offered Frank a metaphorical description of the work as "cane stalks and choruses," with the poems as "leaves and syrup songs" and the Northern stories as "Leaf Traceries in Washington."[17] And some months later he wrote to Gorham Munson that "a machine is all form, it has no leaves. Its very abstraction is . . . the death of it."[18]

FROM THE AUTHOR

ENOUGH

Talk about it only enough to do it. Dream about it only enough to feel it. Think about it only enough to understand it. Contemplate it only enough to be it.

SOURCE: Jean Toomer, excerpt from *Essentials,* Lakeside Press, 1931.

We often talk of "organic" form as "musical" form, and indeed ***Cane*** has been described as having a musical unity, especially in the systematic repetition and contrast of its images and themes. Munson notes that Toomer once thought of becoming a composer and discusses **"Karintha"** (p. 1) as a structural model for many of the stories.[19] This piece opens with a song, presents its theme, breaks into song once more, develops the theme further, and continues to alternate prose and "song" or poetry, with each shift qualifying the previous development. Readers have variously related ***Cane***'s repetition of images to late nineteenth-century symphonies and jazz improvisations,[20] as broad a range as one could wish for under the general rubric of "musical form." The common feature in these diverse descriptions is that which Munson proposed, an alternation between theme and refrain or variation on the theme. But one need not look as far as symphonies or jazz to find this pattern—only as far as the work song, spirituals, and call-and-response preaching which comprise much of ***Cane***'s content.

In constantly redefining its own verbal components, this cross-referential or repetitive structure also redefines the relationship between individual experience and that of the race. Thus it reflects Toomer's own vacillating sense of racial identity. The cross-referentiality occurs both within and between particular pieces. Within a piece, choric descriptive phrases such as those in **"Karintha"** or **"Blood-Burning Moon"** (p. 151) resonate with increasing richness against the main action and place the individual protagonist's experience within a broader context of racial experience. Karintha's "skin is like dusk on the eastern horizon," and the repetition of this simile accumulates to connect her awakening sexuality with that time of day when, in the world of ***Cane,*** the black soul paradoxically awakens. The ominous "blood-burning moon" in the story of that title comes to govern not only Tom Burwell's fate but that of his people, "showering the homes of folk" in the Georgia town (p. 67); its influence builds as the image is repeated.

Between pieces, Toomer mixes forms so that each piece may comment on the other. The structure of Part 1 of ***Cane*** consists of a prose piece followed by two poems which refer both backward to the preceding and forward to the following prose pieces. This poetry qualifies or provides an alternative perspective on the prose sketches. It often reminds us of hardship or pain in the midst of beauty, of suffering in acceptance, reflecting Toomer's ambivalence about his roots. In **"Reapers,"** for example, "a field rat, startled, squealing bleeds, / His belly close to ground" (p. 6), cut by a scythe. This image shows the more threatening side of the beauty-pain duality present in **"Karintha,"** where Karintha "carries beauty, perfect as dusk when the sun goes down" (p. 3) but also "stoned the cows, and beat her dog, and fought the other children" (p. 2). Then the two elements come together in **"November Cotton Flower,"** a description already attributed to Karintha: winter cold sets in, the soil fights drought, birds die, yet suddenly "the flower bloomed" (p. 7). The poems continue to reflect on the prose narratives throughout Part 1. The anonymous suffering of **"Face,"** her "Brows— / recurved canoes / quivered by the ripples blown by pain" (p. 14), generalizes the immediate, personalized pain of **"Becky"** (p. 8), and the poem's imagery is echoed later in **"Fern"**: "Face flowed into her eyes. Flowed in soft cream foam and plaintive ripples" (p. 24). This movement from particular (**"Becky"**) to general (**"Face"**) also occurs between **"Carma"** (p. 16) and **"Song of the Son"** (p. 21), and further typifies the oscillating movement of Part 1. **"Carma"** raises questions of individual freedom—"Should she not take others?" (p. 20)—which stimulate the more generalized **"Song of the Son,"** where the freedom at stake is that of a whole race.

Toomer's Georgia is saturated in song and his synesthetic metaphors aim at a Symbolist identification of image and object, of self and environment: "Pungent and composite, the smell of farmyards is the fragrance of the woman. She does not sing; her body is a song. She is in the forest, dancing" (p. 17). But most importantly for our argument, he uses musical form, actual black songs and musical imagery, to identify with the black part of himself and with the culture that ***Cane*** portrays. Thus music serves a social as well as an esthetic function for Toomer and for his black characters. In the Northern stories of Part 2, a number of characters—the jazz singers of **"Seventh Street,"** the narrator of **"Avey,"** Dan Moore, Dorris, Paul—use dance or song to release themselves from social restraints, express themselves, and assert their blackness. His Southern blacks make "folk-songs from soul sounds" and thus activate "race memories" of their African origins (p. 22). And as a phase of black culture fades ("just before an epoch's sun [p. 21]), these songs also record the meaning of that culture: "Caroling softly souls of slavery, / What they were, and what they are to me" (p. 21).

As that sun declines, then, Toomer uses musical imagery not only to celebrate an ideal but also to mourn its loss: the ideal of the black soul preserving its traditions through folk songs and spirituals. Toomer had learned in his 1922 Georgia visit that spirituals were dying, mocked even by certain of the Southern blacks themselves, and he had learned that many rural blacks cheerfully embraced urbanization:

> But I learned that the Negroes of the town objected to them [folk songs and spirituals]. They called them "shouting." They had victrolas and player-pianos. . . . With Negroes also the trend was towards the small town and then towards the city—and industry and commerce and machines. The folk-spirit was walking in to die on the modern desert. That spirit was so beautiful. Its death was so tragic.[21]

And in the withering of this folk-spirit Toomer may have sensed the withering of his own art. Only a few months after ***Cane***'s publication he summarized the spirit of his book as a spirit of fading: "a sadness derived from a sense of fading, from a knowledge of my futility to check solution. . . . The folk-songs themselves are of the same order: the deepest of them, 'I ain't got long to stay here.'"[22] ***Cane*** marked the end of a culture and of the only significant phase of Toomer's art:

> ***Cane*** was a swan-song. It was a song of an end. And why no one has seen and felt that, why people have expected me to write a second and a third and a fourth book like ***Cane,*** is one of the queer misunderstandings of my life.[23]

The music of ***Cane*** does not bring harmony; the differences between black and white culture and Toomer's ambivalent relationship to those differences remain key notes. Toomer wrote in his autobiography that the "tensions" which "arise from natural oppositions"—and which arise in human society, itself "a situation of tensions of forces," in the form of cultural conflict—"should eventuate in constructive crises."[24] **"Box Seat"** offers an integrated statement of life's source in oppositions:

> Life bends joy and pain, beauty and ugliness, in such a way that no one may isolate them. No one should want to. Perfect joy, or perfect pain, with no contrasting element to define them, would mean a monotony of consciousness, would mean death.
>
> (p. 112)

Yet just as often as they yield a vision of wholeness, Toomer's formal and psychological tensions yield crises more destructive than constructive. At the phrase and sentence level these conflicts manifest themselves in oxymorons like "do not torture me with beauty" (p. 161). At the level of the whole piece, they manifest themselves in final statements which are not borne out by the content or experience of that piece. The halting movement and tired heaviness of **"Harvest Song"** (p. 132), for example, hardly suggest that "my pain is sweet." Dan Moore's speech in **"Box Seat"** is untypical of Part 2 of ***Cane.*** More typically in Part 2, in the Northern settings where the conflicting traits of black and white culture most clearly present themselves, Toomer enacts oppositions within a character by flatly juxtaposing directly contradictory tones and feelings. In **"Theater"** the tension between the main text and parentheses embodies the speaker John's struggle between sardonically rational and yearningly physical responses to the dancers whom he is watching audition:

> Soon the director will herd you, my full-lipped, distant beauties, and tame you, and blunt your sharp thrusts in loosely suggestive movements, appropriate to Broadway. (O dance!) Soon the audience will paint your dusk faces white, and call you beautiful. (O dance!) Soon I . . . (O dance!) I'd like. . . .
>
> (pp. 92-93)

So far I have discussed how certain kinds of formal oscillation within individual pieces and within the large divisions of ***Cane*** reflect Toomer's wrestling with the future of Southern black culture and with his own racial identity. On a larger scale, contrasts between Parts 1 and 2 of ***Cane*** reflect that same wrestling. For example, Southern blacks' move from a rural past to an urban future appears through opposed geographical locations: the Georgia of Part 1, where Toomer's blacks have their roots, and the Northern cities of Part 2, where those roots are severed. To illustrate this severing of roots Toomer reverses the image patterns of Part 1 in the urban settings of Part 2. Fresh, clean pine becomes the "stale soggy wood of Washington" (p. 71). Fragrant Southern air contrasts with "smells of garbage and wet trash" or "the scent of rancid flowers" (pp. 129-30), the "smell of dry paste, and paint, and soiled clothing" (p. 100). When the Washington air is sweet, it is sweet not with cane but with "exploded gasoline" (p. 143). Vegetative imagery becomes mechanical, soft lines become hard and metallic, and the color steel blue recurs. Images of burial or confinement dominate Part 2: characters find themselves trapped in vestibules, theaters, basements, cars. Houses, narrow alleys, machines, and nightclubs all cramp movement and block communication.

A further contrast between Parts 1 and 2, between South and North, exists in Toomer's different handling of female sexuality. Part 1 shows sexuality withered (Esther), suffering (Becky), or abused because of its very fecundity (Karintha, Carma, Fern). Yet with the exception of Esther these women have an inner strength and aloof self-sufficiency which carries them beyond the pain and stress of their immediate circumstances. They rarely talk, in contrast to the constant self-justification of the Northern women. The women of Part 2, both black and white, have channeled their sexuality into social formulas. In **"Box Seat"** Muriel says to herself that "the town wont let me love you, Dan" and "I'm not strong enough to buck it" (p. 110); Bona refuses to kiss Paul because he hasn't said he loves her (p. 144).

Similarly, the free spontaneity of Southern music has been twisted in the Northern cities into music-hall parodies like **"Li'l Liza Jane."** The spiritual is now a brassy march, the music "moans," "throws a fit," and crashes (p. 120). All natural rhythms have been manipulated into social, noninstinctual forms. The city holds no roots for the black and substitutes only factory smoke for the sinuous, fetal, or animal motion of the pine smoke which "curls up and spreads" throughout Part 1. Encountering "a portly Negress" in a city theater, Dan Moore would like to believe that "Her strong roots sink down and spread under the river and disappear in blood-lines that waver south." But the woman does not conform to Dan's notions of her: "He is startled. The eyes of the woman dont belong to her. They look at him unpleasantly" (p. 119).

Toomer's Northern characters are mostly hamstrung by an overdeveloped sense of self which does not afflict the characters of Part 1: "Muriel fastens on her image" (p. 115). Accordingly the soft color tones of the South are transformed into violent colors and bright, mechanical light. In **"Theater"** a shaft of bright light serves as a metaphor for the intellectual system which creates the rift between John's mind and his body:

> John's mind coincides with the shaft of light. Thoughts rush to, and compact about it. Life of the house and of the slowly awakening stage swirls to the body of John, and thrills it. John's body is separate from the thoughts that pack his mind.
>
> (p. 92)

John, the theater manager's brother, appears, like Paul in **"Bona and Paul,"** to be a surrogate Toomer, the rift between white intellectuality and black sensuality mirroring Toomer's own experience:[25] **"Theater"** was written out of a two-week stint Toomer served as manager of Washington's Howard Theatre.

The split mind, body, and soul which dominates John, and which obsesses Dan in **"Box Seat,"** is underscored by the poem **"Prayer"**:

> My body is opaque to the soul.
> Driven of the spirit, long have I sought to
> temper it unto the spirit's longing,
> But my mind, too, is opaque to the soul.
>
> (p. 131)

Typically in Part 2 the poetry reinforces the dismal effects of long prose pieces set in painfully restrictive social situations. The sterile North bears less poetry both literally and metaphorically. Part 1 has ten poems; Part 2 has only five. The first poem of Part 2, **"Beehive,"** depicts the city of Washington; in it the brilliant moon, a bad omen in **"Blood-Burning Moon"** (p. 51) and an image of Avey's detachment in **"Avey"** (p. 76), acts as a principle of limitation beyond which the poet wants to escape: I "wish that I might fly out past the moon / And curl up forever in some far-off farmyard flower" (p. 89). The frenetic activity of **"Beehive"** anticipates the image of the broken hornets' nest in **"Kabnis,"** where the "hornets" are white lynchers (p. 172). It also recalls the "white men like ants," also lynchers, and "the taut hum of their moving" (p. 65) from **"Blood-Burning Moon,"** and the little "white-ant biddies" who enslave the black hero of Barlo's vision in **"Esther"** (p. 38). Immediately the awesome **"Storm Ending,"** in which flowers are "great, hollow, bell-like" (p. 90), undercuts the delicate flower imagery which relieves **"Beehives."** Then **"Her Lips Are Copper Wire"** (p. 101) responds to Dorris's natural beauty in **"Theater"** by couching beauty in terms of urban technology. Finally **"Harvest Song"** seals the overturning of Part 1's organic imagery. Once a time of regeneration, now "Dusk is a strange fear'd sheath their blades are dull'd in" (p. 132).

The split that many of Toomer's characters feel between mind and body, white and black experience, rural origins and an urban present only makes explicit a separateness already visible in the stance of his narrators. The narrator of Part 1 is an uprooted Northerner, mediating between the action and the reader. In **"Fern,"** for instance, he visits "the soil of . . . [his] ancestors" (p. 31) and returns north with the story of Fern, which he tells to a Northern audience "against the chance that . . . [they] might happen down that way" (p. 33). Such an outsider feels particularly transient in the South in his attempts to involve himself in a way of life of which he knows he is not ultimately part. In fact the most fully developed attitude in ***Cane*** is that of what Munson calls "the spectatorial artist."[26] This stance demands that Toomer face one central conflict of his identity and his art: how to both observe and participate in black culture? Throughout ***Cane*** a number of artist figures, Kabnis being the most notable example, fail to answer this question. In **"Avey"** the narrator expounds the values of the Harlem Renaissance by constructing an analogy between art and rebirth:

> I talked, beautifully I thought, about an art that would be born, an art that would open the way for women the likes of her. . . . I recited some of my own things to her. I sang, with a strange quiver in my voice, a promise-song.
>
> (p. 87)

Avey responds by falling asleep. John, in **"Theater,"** "reaches for a manuscript of his, and reads" (p. 99) only in dream; in reality his intellectual snobbishness keeps him from sharing himself and his work with Dorris. And in **"Box Seat"** Dan Moore's singing expresses the pain of being a feeling black artist in an unfeeling world:

> Dan sings. His voice is a little hoarse. It cracks. He strains to produce tones in keeping with the houses' loveliness. Can't be done. He whistles. His notes are shrill. They hurt him.
>
> (pp. 104-05)

Toomer sets this out-of-tune music against Dan's memories of Southern songs and the fact that he walks "southward on Thirteenth Street" (p. 104). But Muriel's capitulation to white values forces Dan to quit her company without having resurrected the black soul through his art. He ends the story "cool as a green stem that has just shed its flower" (p. 129)—free but alone.

Ralph Kabnis is ***Cane***'s central example of the spectatorial artist. Part 3, named after him, translates the imagistic, psychological, and social tensions of Parts 1 and 2 into an intellectual debate in an attempt to resolve them. It originated as one of the dramas with which Toomer experimented throughout the 1920s and in which, influenced by reading Shaw, he sought to achieve social satire in a lyric style. (One such drama is a companion piece to **"Kabnis"**: in ***Natalie Mann,*** from 1922, a racially mixed writer, Nathan Merilh, uses black folk songs in creating an art which he hopes will bring blacks to greater self-awareness.) Toomer's purpose in his plays required a technique new to American theater, flexible and nonrepresentational. **"Kabnis"** employs the expressionist technique of positing characters as human or social types. Toomer wishes to examine possible ways of being black, so the social milieu in which Kabnis moves covers a wide range: the ancient black slave John, the working craftsman Halsey, the bourgeois school supervisor Hanby with his Booker T. Washington rhetoric, the Northern black radical Lewis, the traveling minister Layman, the innocent girl Carrie, the whores Cora and Stella, the shouting church congregation. The social strata and range of attitudes scattered throughout Parts 1 and 2 are thus concentrated in one story.

Kabnis's outsider position, his failure to gain access to this society, dramatizes Toomer's final inability to reconcile the cultures of South and North. Kabnis dreams of giving words to "the face of the South" (p. 158), but short-circuits his own vision by resisting the contact with the Georgia earth that could release that vision: he listens to night winds "against his will" (p. 157) and feels himself "suspended a few feet above the soil whose touch would resurrect him" (p. 191). I have shown how Toomer denied his own racial ancestry after writing ***Cane.*** Kabnis—of whom Toomer wrote to Frank, "Kabnis is *Me*"[27]—does the same. A racially ambiguous Northern visitor in the South, he rejects the black heritage that throws him into such conflict:

> KABNIS: . . . An besides, he [Father John] aint my past. My ancestors were Southern blue-bloods—
>
> LEWIS: And black.
>
> KABNIS: Aint much difference between blue an black.
>
> LEWIS: Enough to draw a denial from you. Cant hold them, can you? Master; slave. Soil; and the overarching heavens. Dusk; dawn. They fight and bastardize you.
>
> (pp. 217-18)

Early in **"Kabnis"** the lullaby-cum-spiritual "rock a-by baby" attempts to unite Kabnis's conflicting racial roots by integrating black and white. But the song lives in a fragile condition somewhere between falling and stability and is framed by poles of peace and violence:

> The half-moon is a white child that sleeps upon the tree-tops of the forest. White winds croon its sleep-song:
>
> rock a-by baby . . .
> Black mother sways, holding a white child on her bosom.
> when the bough bends . . .
> Her breath hums through pine-cones.
> cradle will fall . . .
> Teat moon-children at your breasts,
> down will come baby . . .
> Black mother.
>
> Kabnis whirls the chicken by its neck, and throws the head away. Picks up the hopping body, warm, sticky, and hides it in a clump of bushes.
>
> (pp. 160-61)

Such violent language occurs only in **"Kabnis,"** expressing the confusion of a character who can face neither the pangs of real human and social involvement (which would mean accepting his black roots) nor the loneliness of detachment (accepting his difference from the Southern black community). Toomer wrote that "***Cane*** was born in the agony of internal tightness, conflict and chaos."[28] Nowhere does that chaos show more than in **"Kabnis,"** where Toomer most urgently tries to order it.

Kabnis personifies, then, both Toomer's own confusion about his racial identity and the cultural oppositions between Parts 1 and 2 of ***Cane.*** On the one hand "Night winds in Georgia are," like Kabnis, "vagrant poets" (p. 157); on the other, the voice of a woman shouting in church, "high-pitched and hysterical, is almost perfectly attuned to the nervous key of Kabnis" (p. 178). Houston Baker accurately observes how Kabnis "realizes that the paranoia, aggressiveness, ambivalence, and hypocrisy of the South find counterparts in his own personality"[29]—the personal and the cultural merge. As in Part 1, the experiences of pain and beauty are closely intertwined, and Kabnis's Northern detachment wins out in his struggle to live with his conflicting feelings. He uses paradox, a trope learned from his training in the white intellectual world, not to immerse himself in his heritage, as Toomer did in Part 1, but to separate himself: "Whats beauty anyway but ugliness if it hurts you?" (p. 162).

Kabnis wants "t feed the soul" (p. 224), but he has no access to the beautiful language of ***Cane***'s Part 1:

> Those words I was tellin y about, they wont fit int th mold thats branded on m soul. . . . Th form thats burned int my soul is some twisted awful thing that crept in from a dream, a godam nightmare, an wont stay still unless I feed it. An it lives on words. Not beautiful words. God Almighty no. Misshapen, split-gut, tortured, twisted words.
>
> (p. 224)

He mistakenly wants to feed the soul through limited mental consciousness and while denying the "symbol, flesh, and spirit of the [black] past" (p. 217). Of all the characters in ***Cane,*** perhaps Paul, in **"Bona and Paul,"** comes closest to resolving the differences Toomer felt between the black and white psychic and social realities. His mixed racial identity embodies ***Cane***'s recurrent tension between black emotional vitality and white intellectual knowledge. Whereas Kabnis denies his blackness, Paul perceives that he must acknowledge his blackness before he can fully love the white woman Bona and start them on the road to racial and spiritual harmony:

> I came back to tell you, brother, that white faces are petals of roses. That dark faces are petals of dusk. That I am going out and gather petals. That I am going out and know her whom I brought here with me to these Gardens which are purple like a bed of roses would be at dusk.
>
> (p. 153)

The color of the North, the garish crimson of the gardens, becomes that of the South, a soft purple. But Paul's assertion of his black self comes too late, and Bona is lost: "Paul and the black man shook hands. When he reached the spot where they had been standing, Bona was gone" (p. 153).

His final visionary tableau does suggest that Toomer saw **"Kabnis"** resolving ***Cane***'s oppositions, but it contradicts his characters' recurrent failure to bind together the fragments of their experience. The tableau almost canonizes the generational extremes of Southern black culture, its past (Father John) and its future (Carrie), and leaves us with the sun, a "gold-glowing child," rising "from its cradle in the tree-tops of the forest" and offering the town "a birth-song" (p. 239). This scene emphasizes the regenerative side of the nature that ***Cane*** celebrates. The passage is packed with the impressionistic images of Part 1: shadows of pines, dreams, music. But Kabnis's antilyrical hardness is still too much with us for this ending convincingly to effect any racial or spiritual integration. ***Cane***'s return to the geographical world of Part 1 is all the more poignant because Kabnis and Toomer himself are not part of that social world.

Cane abounds in images of a new age for blacks failing to be born. In Part 1 Becky loses her sons, the narrator loses Fern, Carma loses her husband, Esther loses Barlo, Louisa loses Tom Burwell and Bob Stone. In Part 2, John loses Dorris, Dan loses Muriel, Paul loses Bona, and Avey is an "orphan-woman" (p, 88). Finally in **"Kabnis,"** white lynchers impale a living black fetus on a tree; and Carrie, whose "nascent maternity" (p. 233) might have represented the race's future, is left alone once Lewis gives up hope of effecting change and returns North. Prose and poetry, white and black, North and South, the three parts of the book—these remain unreconciled both within Toomer and within his culture. The formal tour-de-force of ***Cane*** finally can only reflect, but not resolve, its author's conflicts.

Notes

1. Robert Bone, *Down Home: A History of Afro-American Short Fiction from Its Beginnings to the End of the Harlem Renaissance* (New York: G. P. Putnam's Sons, 1975), p. 222. The history of debate over *Cane*'s genre is also usefully summarized, although not significantly added to, by Blyden Jackson, "Jean Toomer's *Cane*: An Issue of Genre," in Warren French, ed., *The Twenties: Fiction, Poetry, Drama* (Deland, FL: Everett/Edwards, Inc., 1975), pp. 317-25; see also French's Afternote in the same essay, pp. 325-33.
2. See, for example, Todd Lieber, "Design and Movement in *Cane,*" *CLA Journal,* 13 (1969), 35-50; Bernard Bell, "A Key to the Poems in *Cane,*" *CLA Journal,* 14 (1971), 251-58; Catherine L. Innes, "The Unity of Jean Toomer's *Cane,*" *CLA Journal,* 15 (1972), 306-22; and Charles W. Scruggs, "The Mark of Cain and the Redemption of Art: A Study in Theme and Structure of Jean Toomer's *Cane,*" *American Literature,* 44 (1972), 276-91.
3. Robert H. Brinkmeyer, Jr., also argues that *Cane* illustrates Toomer's attempt to resolve these cultural, racial, and psychological tensions, in "Wasted Talent, Wasted Art: The Literary Career of Jean Toomer," *The Southern Quarterly,* 20 (Fall 1981), 75-84. He does not, however, show specifically how the book's actual *form* reflects its author's quest for resolution.
4. Toomer's refusal of Johnson, in a letter of July 11, 1930, and his rejection of the other anthologies are

documented in Scruggs, "Jean Toomer: Fugitive," *American Literature,* 47 (1975), 84. On his anger toward Locke, see Cynthia E. Kerman, "Jean Toomer?—Enigma," *Indian Journal of American Studies,* 7, No. 1 (1977), 76.

5. Robert C. Twombly, "A Disciple's Odyssey: Jean Toomer's Gurdjieffian Career," *Prospects: An Annual of American Cultural Studies,* 2 (1976), 442.

6. Jean Toomer Collection, Fisk University Library, Box 26, Folder 41.

7. Quoted in Darwin T. Turner, "An Intersection of Paths: Correspondence Between Jean Toomer and Sherwood Anderson, *CLA Journal,* 17 (1974), 460.

8. George E. Kent, *Blackness and the Adventure of Western Culture* (Chicago: Third World Press, 1972), p. 26.

9. Letter to *The Liberator,* quoted in Darwin T. Turner's introduction to the 1975 reprint of *Cane* (New York: Liveright), p. xvi.

10. Bone, pp. 206-07.

11. For this view of Toomer's relationship to the Harlem Renaissance, see Kerman, p. 76; the sentence from Toomer's diary is cited by Turner, *In a Minor Chord: Three Afro-American Writers and Their Search for Identity* (Carbondale and Edwardsville: Southern Illinois University Press, 1971), p. 35.

12. From Toomer's 1937 pamphlet *Work-Ideas I,* cited in S. P. Fullinwider, "Jean Toomer: Lost Generation, or Negro Renaissance?" *Phylon,* 27 (1966), 398.

13. For further discussion of Johnson's relation to *Cane,* see William C. Fischer, "The Aggregate Man in Jean Toomer's *Cane,*" *Studies in the Novel,* 3 (1971), 190-215; for further discussion of DuBois, see John M. Reilly, "The Search for Black Redemption: Jean Toomer's *Cane,*" *Studies in the Novel,* 2 (1970), 312-24.

14. Toomer Collection.

15. Toomer to Anderson, December 1922; quoted in Turner, "An Intersection of Paths," p. 457.

16. Bone, p. 217.

17. Toomer to Frank, 7/19/22. Toomer Collection, Box 3, Folder 6.

18. Letter dated 3/19/23. Toomer Collection, Box 7, Folder 12.

19. Gorham B. Munson, "The Significance of Jean Toomer," *Opportunity,* 3 (1925), 262-63. Page references to *Cane* are to the 1969 edition (New York: Harper & Row) and are cited parenthetically in the text.

20. On *Cane*'s supposed symphonic structure, see Innes, "The Unity of Jean Toomer's *Cane*"; on its jazz structure, see Bowie Duncan, "Jean Toomer's *Cane*: A Modern Black Oracle," *CLA Journal,* 15 (1972), 323-33.

21. Toomer, *The Wayward and the Seeking: A Collection of Writings by Jean Toomer,* ed. Darwin T. Turner (Washington, DC: Howard University Press, 1980), p. 123.

22. Letter to Frank, summer 1923. Toomer Collection, Box 3, Folder 7.

23. Toomer, *The Wayward and the Seeking,* p. 123.

24. Toomer, *The Wayward and the Seeking,* p. 20.

25. For the autobiographical element in Toomer's characters, see Turner, *In a Minor Chord,* p. 27: "[Toomer's] male figures are stereotypes, personifications, and reproductions of his satiric, self-pitying, or idealized image of himself."

26. Munson, p. 263. See also Susan L. Blake, "The Spectatorial Artist and the Structure of *Cane,*" *CLA Journal,* 17 (1974), 516-34.

27. Letter of summer 1923. Toomer Collection, Box 3, Folder 7.

28. Toomer Collection, Box 23, Folder 6.

29. Houston A. Baker, Jr., *Singers of Daybreak: Studies in Black American Literature* (Washington, DC: Howard University Press, 1974), p. 79.

FURTHER READING

Biographies

Benson, Brian Joseph and Mabel Mayle Dillard. *Jean Toomer.* Boston: Twayne, 1980, 152 p.

Traces the important events of Toomer's life, discusses his major works, and surveys contemporary Toomer criticism.

Larson, Charles R. *Invisible Darkness: Jean Toomer and Nella Larsen.* Iowa City: University of Iowa Press, 1993, 241 p.

Dual biography of two important figures of the Harlem Renaissance. In the sections on Toomer, Larson focuses on the connection between the author's life and writing and his relationship with Gurdjieff.

McKay, Nellie. *Jean Toomer: Artist: A Study of His Literary Life and Work.* Chapel Hill: University of North Carolina Press, 1984, 262 p.

Literary biography that examines Toomer's works and their intersection with his life.

Criticism

Ackley, Donald G. "Theme and Vision in Jean Toomer's *Cane.*" *Studies in Black Literature* 1 (spring 1970): 45-65.

Examines the images, symbols, and themes that pervade Cane.

Baker, Houston. "Journey Toward Black Art: Jean Toomer's *Cane.*" In *Singers of Daybreak: Studies in Black American Literature,* pp. 53-80. Washington, D.C.: Howard University Press, 1976.

Views Cane *as a protest novel, a portrait of the artist, and a reflection of African American life.*

Bell, Bernard. "Jean Toomer's 'Blue Meridian': The Poet as Prophet of a New Order of Man." *Black American Literature Forum* 14 (summer 1980): 77-80.

Views the poem "Blue Meridian" as the poetic zenith of Toomer's quest for identity.

Bontemps, Arna. "The Negro Renaissance: Jean Toomer and the Harlem Writers of the 1920's." In *Anger, and Beyond: The Negro Writer in the United States,* edited by Herbert Hill, pp. 20-36. New York: Harper & Row, 1966.

Considers Toomer the most inspiring writer of the Harlem Renaissance, attempts to understand the elusive author through a study of his writing, and discusses other critics' responses to Cane.

Brannan, Tim. "Up from the Dusk: Interpretations of Jean Toomer's 'Blood Burning Moon'." *Pembroke Magazine* 8 (1977): 167-72.

Argues that while the poem is racial in flavor, it is universal and archetypal in style, tone, and mood.

Bush, Ann Marie and Louis D. Mitchel. "Jean Toomer: A Cubist Poet." *Black American Literature Forum* 17, no. 3 (fall 1983): 106-08.

Analysis of the poems "Nullo" and "Storm Ending," claiming that these works establish Toomer as a cubist poet.

Byrd, Rudolph P. *Jean Toomer's Years with Gurdjieff: Portrait of an Artist, 1923-1936.* Athens: University of Georgia Press, 1990, 212 p.

Comprehensive analysis of the literary and philosophical influence of Gurdjieff on Toomer.

Chase, Patricia. "The Women in *Cane.*" *CLA Journal* 14 (March 1971): 259-73.

Explores Toomer's complex portrayal of women in Cane, *maintaining that his female characters are all the same archetypal woman wearing different faces.*

Clark, J. Michael. "Frustrated Redemption: Jean Toomer's Women in *Cane,* Part One." *CLA Journal* 22 (1979): 319-34.

Examination of Cane*'s portrayal of a frustrated search for redemptive knowledge through women, whom the novel's men cannot understand.*

Davis, Charles T. "Jean Toomer and the South: Region and Race as Elements within a Literary Imagination." In *The Harlem Renaissance Re-Examined,* edited by Victor A. Kramer, pp. 185-99. New York: AMS Press, 1987.

Claims that Toomer's association with the South was a form of recovery of a lost heritage.

Dorris, Ronald. *Race: Jean Toomer's Swan Song.* New Orleans: Xavier Review Press, 1997, 100 p.

Centers on Toomer's handling of the issue of race during his development as a writer, his relationship with the South, and his correspondence that discusses racial issues.

Fabre, Genevieve and Michel Feith, eds. *Jean Toomer and the Harlem Renaissance.* New Brunswick, N.J.: Rutgers University Press, 2000, 235 p.

Collection of essays by European and American scholars on a variety of subjects relating to the author.

Favor, J. Martin. "'Colored; cold. Wrong somewhere.': Jean Toomer's *Cane.*" In *Authentic Blackness: The Folk in the New Negro Renaissance,* pp. 53-80. Durham, N.C.: Duke University Press, 1999.

Considers the critical discourse on race in Toomer's novel.

Flowers, Sandra Hollin. "Solving the Critical Conundrum of Jean Toomer's 'Box Seat'." *Studies in Short Fiction* 25, no. 3 (summer 1988): 301-05.

Contends that Toomer explores 1920s class divisions among African Americans in "Box Seat."

Foley, Barbara. "Jean Toomer's Sparta." *American Literature* 67, no. 4 (December 1995): 747-75.

Locates one of the actual settings for Cane *as Sparta, Georgia, and assesses the impact of the locale on Toomer's work and life.*

———. "'In the Land of Cotton': Economics and Violence in Jean Toomer's *Cane.*" *African American Review* 32, no. 2 (summer 1998): 181-98.

Explores Toomer's treatment of economic factors and racial violence in Cane.

Gunther Kodat, Catherine. "To 'Flash White Light from Ebony': The Problem of Modernism in Jean Toomer's *Cane.*" *Twentieth-Century Literature* 46 (Spring 2000), 1-19.

Regards Cane *as a dialectical exploration of structures used to define and represent the self.*

Harmon, Charles. "*Cane,* Race, and Neither/Norism." *Southern Literary Journal* 32, no. 2 (spring 2000): 90-101.

Reviews previous criticism and discusses the place of Cane *in the African American tradition.*

Hutchinson. George. "Toomer and American Racial Discourse." *Texas Studies in Literature and Language* 35 (summer 1993): 226-50.

Contends that the predominant motif of Cane *is Toomer's exploration of his own identity.*

Jones, Robert B. *Jean Toomer and the Prison-House of Thought: A Phenomenology of the Spirit.* Amherst: University of Massachusetts Press, 1993, 191 p.

Traces Toomer's literary career from 1918 to 1955 and analyzes his work through the lens of his philosophical idealism.

Lindberg, Kathryne V. "Raising *Cane* on the Theoretical Plane: Jean Toomer's Racial Personae." In *Cultural Difference and the Literary Text: Pluralism and the Limits of Authenticity in North American Literatures,* edited by Winfried Siemerling and Katrin Schwenk, pp. 49-74. Iowa City: University of Iowa Press, 1996.

Discusses the construction of Toomer's racial personae by himself and others to show that his own blackness was at variance with that of Alain Locke's aims in The New Negro *and Waldo Frank's humanist project.*

Moore, Lewis D. "Kabnis and the Reality of Hope: Jean Toomer's *Cane.*" *North Dakota Quarterly* 54, no. 2 (spring 1986): 30-9.

Argues that the last section of Cane, *named after a male character, returns the Black man to the center of the work to resolve the dilemma of his existence in a hostile world dominated by white men.*

Munson, Gorham. "The Significance of Jean Toomer." *Opportunity* 3 (1925): 262-63.

Claims that Toomer's potential significance is greater than the actual significance of his contemporaries.

Noyes, Sylvia G. "A Particular Patriotism in Jean Toomer's 'York Beach'." *CLA Journal* 29, no. 3 (March 1986): 288-94.

Explicates the major themes of the short story "York Beach."

O'Daniel, Therman B., ed. *Jean Toomer: A Critical Evaluation.* Washington, D.C.: Howard University Press, 1988, 555 p.

Collection of forty-six critical essays by leading Toomer scholars originally published in academic journals.

Peckham, Joel B. "Jean Toomer's *Cane*: Self as Montage and the Drive toward Integration." *American Literature* 72, no. 2 (June 2000): 275-90.

Provides a stylistic analysis of Cane, *particularly focusing on the way the disparate elements of the text work together as a unified whole.*

Rand, Lizabeth A. "'I Am I': Jean Toomer's Vision beyond *Cane*." *CLA Journal* 44, no. 1 (September 2000): 43-64.

*Examines Toomer's early writings and his post-*Cane *works to understand his complex vision and voice.*

Rice, Herbert W. "Repeated Images in Part One of *Cane*." *Black American Literature Forum* 17, no. 3 (fall 1983): 100-05.

Discusses the unified image patterns in the first section of Cane.

———. "An Incomplete Circle: Repeated Images in Part Two of *Cane*." *CLA Journal* 29 (June 1986): 442-61.

Examines the connections between the images in the first two sections of Cane.

Rusch, Frederik L. "Jean Toomer's Early Identification: The Two Black Plays." *MELUS* 13, nos. 1-2 (spring-summer 1986): 115-24.

Investigates Toomer's portrayal of African American life in Balo and Natalie Mann.

———. "Form, Function, and Creative Tension in *Cane*: Jean Toomer and the Need for the Avant-Garde." *MELUS* 17, no. 4 (winter 1991-92): 15-28.

Discusses the experimental form of Cane.

Scruggs, C. W. "Textuality and Vision in Jean Toomer's *Cane*." *Journal of the Short Story in English* 10 (spring 1988): 93-114.

Discusses the influence of Sherwood Anderson and Waldo Frank on Toomer.

———. "The Reluctant Witness: What Jean Toomer Remembered from *Winesburg, Ohio*." *Studies in American Fiction* 28, no. 1 (spring 2000): 77-100.

Evaluates the influence of Sherwood Anderson's novel on Toomer's Cane.

———, and Lee Vandemarr. *Jean Toomer and the Terrors of American History*. College Park: University of Pennsylvania Press, 1998, 344 p.

Examination of Toomer's rediscovered early writings on politics and race, his extensive correspondence with Waldo Frank, and unpublished portions of his autobiographies to show how the social background of the 1920s influenced Toomer's writing and his efforts to escape the racial definitions of American society.

Taylor, Paul Beekman. *Shadows of Heaven: Gurdjieff and Toomer*. York Beach, Maine: Red Wheel/Weiser, 1998, 272 p.

Account of Toomer's personal and philosophical relationship with Gurdjieff told from the perspective of someone who grew up within the movement.

Thompson, Larry E. "Jean Toomer: As Modern Man." In *Harlem Renaissance Remembered*, edited by Arna Bontemps, pp. 51-62. New York: Dodd, Mead, 1972.

Argues that Toomer wanted to be "free of all the restrictions of modern society" and sought "singularity in himself and in mankind."

Webb, Jeff. "Literature and Lynching: Identity in Jean Toomer's *Cane*." *ELH* 67, no. 1 (spring 2000): 205-28.

Discusses Toomer's representation of race and racial consciousness in Cane.

Whyde, Janet M. "Mediating Forms: Narrating the Body in Jean Toomer's *Cane*." *Southern Literary Journal* 26, no. 1 (fall 1993): 42-53.

Investigates Toomer's narrative representation of the body in Cane.

Woodson, Jon. *To Make a New Race: Gurdjieff, Toomer, and the Harlem Renaissance*. Jackson: University Press of Mississippi, 1999, 202 p.

Discusses Gurdjieff's influence on Toomer and other writers, including Nella Larsen, George Schuyler, Wallace Thurman, Rudolph Fisher, and Zora Neale Hurston.

OTHER SOURCES FROM GALE:

Additional coverage of Toomer's life and career is contained in the following sources published by the Gale Group: *African American Writers*, Eds. 1, 2; *American Writers Supplement*, Vols. 3, 9; *Black Literature Criticism*, Vol. 3; *Black Writers*, Ed. 1; *Concise Dictionary of American Literary Biography*, 1917-1929; *Contemporary Authors*, Vols. 85-88; *Contemporary Literary Criticism*, Vols. 1, 4, 13, 22; *Dictionary of Literary Biography*, Vols. 45, 51; *DISCovering Authors Modules: Multicultural Authors*; *DISCovering Authors 3.0*; *Exploring Poetry*; *Exploring Short Stories*; *Major 20th-Century Writers*, Eds. 1, 2; *Novels for Students*, Vol. 11; *Poetry Criticism*, Vol. 7; *Reference Guide to American Literature*, Ed. 4; *Reference Guide to Short Fiction*, Ed. 2; *Short Stories for Students*, Vol. 5; *Short Story Criticism*, Vols. 1, 45; *World Literature Criticism Supplement*.

CARL VAN VECHTEN

(1880 - 1964)

American novelist, critic, and photographer.

A white midwesterner transplanted to New York, Van Vechten played an important role in the development of the Harlem Renaissance movement. As a critic, he was among the first to give serious notice to Black art forms such as jazz and blues and to acknowledge and laud the writers of the Harlem Renaissance. Van Vechten is also known for a series of novels dealing with the cultural life of New York in the 1920s and for his photographs of many of the creative people in his social circle. His most acclaimed and controversial work, the novel *Nigger Heaven* (1926), grew out of his interest in African American culture and his experience with Black artists and writers in New York.

BIOGRAPHICAL INFORMATION

Van Vechten was born in Cedar Rapids, Iowa. At an early age, he developed an interest in music and theater. In 1899, he left Iowa to attend the University of Chicago, where he studied art and music and contributed to the university's newspaper. After earning a Ph.D. in 1903, Van Vechten worked for the *Chicago American,* writing articles on a variety of topics and providing accompanying photographs. In 1906, he moved to New York City, where he was hired to be assistant music critic for the *New York Times.* He took a leave of absence from the paper in 1907 to study opera in Europe, returning to New York in 1908 and resuming work for the *New York Times.* He wrote about theater, music, and literature and was the first American critic of modern dance as well as the first to recognize jazz as a peculiarly American contribution to Western music. He left the *Times* and continued to write, publishing several collections of his essays about music and dance and, in 1922, his first novel, *Peter Whiffle: His Life and Works.* In the early 1920s, Van Vechten became interested in promoting Black artists and writers. He was an avid collector of ephemera and books pertaining to Black arts and letters, a frequent visitor to Harlem, and an advocate of social equality for African Americans. He forged relationships with such writers as Langston Hughes and James Weldon Johnson and used his connections to advance their careers. Van Vechten's experiences with writers of the Harlem Renaissance provided the inspiration for his controversial novel *Nigger Heaven.* In the early 1930s, Van Vechten turned to photography, a field in which he distinguished himself. He continued to promote African American culture by photographing Black artists and founding the James Weldon Johnson Memorial Collection of Negro Arts and Letters at the Yale University Library. Van Vechten continued his work as a photographer until his death in 1964.

MAJOR WORKS

Van Vechten produced numerous volumes of criticism and essays before he began publishing novels in his early forties. The best known of his novels are *Peter Whiffle, The Blind Bow-Boy* (1923), *The Tattooed Countess* (1924), and *Nigger Heaven.* The first two works are set in the world of New York high society, the third in the author's native Iowa, while *Nigger Heaven,* Van Vechten's most acclaimed work, takes place in the "exotic" world of Harlem's nightclubs and soirees. Van Vechten summarized the narrative of *Nigger Heaven* as follows: "A boy from a small town is bewitched, bothered, and bewildered by a big time Lady of Pleasure and is unable to meet the demands made on his character by life in the big city." While the novel was favorably received by some critics, for the most part it aroused anger and outrage for its title and its depiction of what many viewed as the depravity of Harlem cabaret life. Van Vechten wrote two more novels, *Spider Boy: A Scenario for a Motion Picture* (1928), a satire on Hollywood in the 1920s, and *Parties* (1930), about a couple who moves from party to party and keeps company with a number of colorful characters. After *Sacred and Profane Memories* (1932), a collection of autobiographical essays, Van Vechten ceased to write for publication. Several volumes of his essays, photographs, and letters have been collected by others, most of these appearing after Van Vechten's death.

CRITICAL RECEPTION

Most of Van Vechten's seven novels were comedies of manners that satirized the world of parties and indulgence that has come to be identified with the 1920s, and while they were never counted as insightful works of fiction, a few of them were warmly received and Van Vechten's talent for burlesque was praised. The novel that stirred up the greatest controversy was *Nigger Heaven.* Some readers objected to the sensationalized backdrop of the work. Many Blacks found the title, which Van Vechten intended to be ironic, to be offensive. According to the author, "nigger heaven" was slang for the topmost gallery of a theater, the only section where Blacks were permitted to sit, and the novel saw Harlem as such a gallery that looked upon the white world as "sitting down below in the good seats." Other readers simply found the work disagreeable because it was shallow. W. E. B. Du Bois, for example, said the work was neither sincere nor deep but only "bizarre." Nevertheless, another important Black writer, Van Vechten's friend James Weldon Johnson, said that it was the most revealing, significant, and powerful novel to date that was based exclusively on African American life. Certainly *Nigger Heaven* was a landmark work and a significant contribution to the Harlem Renaissance, and although it is no longer widely read, critics today see it as raising important questions that were central to the movement. Contemporary scholars have also been interested in Van Vechten's correspondence with writers such as Hughes and Gertrude Stein for the insights they provide into those authors' works. Although it was panned by critics in its own day, some scholars consider *Parties* to be Van Vechten's best work. The disconnected structure of the novel, they find, reflects the transition from the glamourous world of the 1920s to the more harsh realities that defined American life in the 1930s.

PRINCIPAL WORKS

Music After the Great War (essays) 1915

Music and Bad Manners (essays) 1916

Interpreters and Interpretations (essays) 1917; revised as *Interpreters,* 1920

The Merry-Go-Round (essays) 1918

The Music of Spain (essays) 1918

In the Garret (essays) 1920

The Tiger in the House (essays) 1920

Peter Whiffle: His Life and Works (novel) 1922

The Blind Bow-Boy (novel) 1923

The Tattooed Countess (novel) 1924

Firecrackers (novel) 1925

Red (essays) 1925

Excavations (essays) 1926

Nigger Heaven (novel) 1926

Spider Boy: A Scenario for a Motion Picture (novel) 1928

Parties (novel) 1930

Sacred and Profane Memories (essays) 1932

Fragments from an Unwritten Autobiography. 2 vols. (essays) 1955

The Dance Writings of Carl Van Vechten (essays) 1975

Portraits (photographs) 1978

"Keep A-Inchin' Along": Selected Writings of Carl Van Vechten about Black Art and Letters (criticism) 1979

The Dance Photography of Carl Van Vechten (photographs) 1981

The Letters of Gertrude Stein and Carl Van Vechten, 1913-1946 (letters) 1986

Letters of Carl Van Vechten (letters) 1987

GENERAL COMMENTARY

HUGH M. GLOSTER (ESSAY DATE 1945)

SOURCE: Gloster, Hugh M. "The Van Vechten Vogue." In *Analysis and Assessment,* edited by Gary D. Wintz, pp. 252-56. New York: Garland Publishing, 2000.

In the following essay, originally published in Negro Voices in American Fiction *in 1945, Gloster argues that Van Vechten's popularity and influence, as well as the controversy over* Nigger Heaven, *were intense but short-lived, and claims that while Van Vechten and his imitators broke away from previous stereotypes, they did not offer a realistic presentation of Harlem life.*

Perhaps the most popular novel of Negro life during the 1920's was Carl Van Vechten's ***Nigger Heaven*** (1926), a work which not only dramatized the alleged animalism and exoticism of Harlem folk but also influenced the writings of Negro Renascence authors. Appearing at the proper time, when the Negro was making considerable headway as a stellar performer in the entertainment world as well as when white Americans were inordinately curious about so-called picturesque and primitive facets of Harlem society, ***Nigger Heaven*** enjoyed widespread popularity and became a sort of guidebook for visitors who flocked uptown seeking a re-creation of the African jungle in the heart of New York City. The songs and blues selections by Langston Hughes which Van Vechten incorporated in the novel not only augmented the appeal of the book but also drew general attention to the rising young *literati* of Manhattan's black ghetto.

As a framework for his presentation of the Harlem *milieu* Van Vechten provides a slender plot tracing the rather mediocre romance of Mary Love, a respectable librarian, and Byron Kasson, an unstable and extremely race-conscious young Philadelphian who comes to New York City to seek success as a writer. Everything goes moderately well with the couple until Lasca Sartoris, "a gorgeous brown Messalina of Seventh Avenue," completely bewitches the would-be author and then deserts him for Randolph Pettijohn, the Bolito King. Rendered insanely vengeful by being jilted, Byron impulsively fires two bullets into the body of Pettijohn, who has previously been fatally wounded by a pimp called the Scarlet Creeper, and thereafter helplessly surrenders to police.

On the crowded canvas of ***Nigger Heaven*** Van Vechten presents many colorful aspects of Harlem life. He gives an account of a lavish weekend party at the Long Island estate of Adora Boniface, as ex-music hall diva who also maintains a luxurious residence on Striver's Row on West 139th Street. He essays to present *bourgeois* respectability in the life of Mary Love, who associates with young writers and other professional men, frequents dinner and bridge parties, attends plays and musical entertainments, reads the best books (including Gertrude Stein's *Three Lives,* which made a deeper impression than any of the others), and appreciates African sculpture. He describes the Charity Ball, a mammoth paid dance sponsored annually by a group of socially prominent colored women, and gives the opinions of Negroes concerning Harlem sightseers, passing, miscegenation, inter- and intra-racial color prejudice, and many other subjects.

But, with more gusto than he does anything else, Van Vechten paints Harlem cabaret life. He is particularly fascinated by the barbaric rhythms of Negro jazz, the tom-tom beat of the drum in the band, and the melting bodies of intoxicated dancers swaying to sensuous music. Contemplating the cabaret, Van Vechten surmises that Negroes are essentially primitive and atavistic. In the singing of spirituals and jazz, black folk are described as "recognizing, no doubt, in some dim, biological way, the beat of African rhythm." Even Mary Love, in spite of her respectability and horror of promiscuity, is convinced that her people are essentially savage:

> Savages! Savages at heart! And she had lost or forfeited her birthright, this primitive birthright which was so valuable and important an asset, a birthright that all the civilized race were struggling to get back to—this fact explained the art of a Picasso or a Stravinsky. To be sure, she, too, felt this African beat—it completely aroused her emotionally—but she was conscious of feeling it. This love of drums, of exciting rhythms, this naive delight in glowing colour—the colour that exists only in cloudless, tropical climes—this warm sexual emotion, all these were hers only through a mental understanding. . . .
>
> We are all savages, she repeated to herself, all apparently, but me!

Of a two-day love orgy of Byron and Lasca, Van Vechten writes:

> . . . There were rages, succeeded by tumultuous passions; there were peaceful interludes; there were hours devoted to satisfying capricious desires, rhythmical amours to music, cruel and painful pastimes.

In describing a night at the Black Venus cabaret, Van Vechten avers:

> The music shivered and broke, cracked and smashed. Jungle land. Hottentots and Bantus swaying under the amber moon. Love, sex, passion . . . hate.

Ever the painter of the exotic and fantastic, Van Vechten took particular delight in emphasizing—even in exaggerating and distorting—the primitive aspects of his *milieu.* To him the Harlem cabaret was a transplanted jungle, and Negroes were creatures of impulse and emotion, atavistically yearning for the animalistic exhibitions of Africa. This stress upon the Negro as a child of nature did at least three things: first, it increased the influx of white visitors to upper Manhattan; second, it created a furious controversy among Negro intellectuals; and, third, it made American publishers and readers eager for more works with a similar emphasis.

In the metropolitan dailies ***Nigger Heaven*** usually received favorable reviews—e.g., that of Carl Van Doren in *The New York Herald Tribune* (August 22, 1926), and that of Harry Hansen in *The New York World* (August 28, 1926)—which stimulated a wide reading of the novel and a hegira of white folk to Harlem. In "The Ebony Flute," a monthly column in *Opportunity,* Gwendolyn Bennett records, during the same year, the power of ***Nigger Heaven*** to attract outsiders to Black Manhattan. Placed on the stands in August, the book was so popular by October, as Miss Bennett notes, that sightseers, visitors and other strangers were "said to be 'van vechtening' around." Intrigued by the portrayal of the Negro in the book, whites from downtown and elsewhere temporarily neglected Greenwich Village in order to explore Harlem and enjoy the Negro. During this time the Cotton Club became one of the most celebrated night clubs in the country.

While ***Nigger Heaven*** was generally received with favor by white critics and readers, it aroused a storm of controversy among Negro intellectuals. Reviews of commendation were given by Wallace Thurman in *The Messenger* (September, 1926); by Charles S. Johnson in a letter to Van Vechten published in *The Pittsburgh Courier* (September 4, 1926); by James Weldon Johnson in *Opportunity* (October, 1926); and by George Schuyler in *The Pittsburgh Courier* (November 6, 1926). Unfavorable reactions were expressed by Hubert Harrison in *The Amsterdam News* (October 9, 1926); by Floyd Calvin in *The Pittsburgh Courier* (November 6, 1926); by Dewey R. Jones in *The Chicago Defender* (November 24, 1926); and by W. E. B. DuBois in *The Crisis* (December, 1926). Voicing nearly all of the dissenting reactions to the novel, DuBois argued that ***Nigger Heaven*** is "a blow in the face," "an affront to the hospitality of black folk and to the intelligence of white," "a caricature," "a mass of half-truths," and "an astonishing and wearisome hodgepodge of laboriously stated facts, quotations and expressions, illuminated here and there with something that comes near to being nothing but cheap melodrama." Reflecting the sentiments of Negroes who liked the novel, James Weldon Johnson insisted in his review, "Romance and Tragedy in Harlem," published in *Opportunity,* that ***Nigger Heaven*** is "an absorbing story," "comprehends nearly every phase of life from dregs to the froth," and ranks as "the most revealing, significant and powerful novel based exclusively on Negro life yet written." Johnson held that the book "is all reality" and "does not stoop to burlesque or caricature." In his opinion, Van Vechten is "the first white novelist of note to undertake a portrayal of modern American Negro life under metropolitan conditions" and "the only white novelist who has not viewed the Negro as a type, who has not treated the race as a unit, either good or bad."

The modern critic, viewing ***Nigger Heaven*** nineteen years after it was published, submits that the novel's proper evaluation is at a point somewhere between the appraisal of DuBois and that of Johnson. In stylizing the primitivism of the Negro and the jungle atmosphere of the Harlem cabaret, Van Vechten was doing no more than Langston Hughes had done a year earlier in *The Weary Blues* (1925.) In the jungle pose Langston Hughes wrote such poems as "Nude Young Dancer," "Dream Variation," "Our Land," "Lament for Dark People," "Afraid," "Poem for the Portrait of an African Boy after the Manner of Gauguin," and "Danse Africane." However, when a wealthy patron expressed dissatisfaction because he wrote "Advertisement for the Waldorf-Astoria," Hughes explained in *The Big Sea*:

> She wanted me to be primitive and know and feel the intuitions of the primitive. But unfortunately, I did not feel the rhythms of the primitive surging through me, and so I could not live and write as though I did. I was only an American Negro—who had loved the surface of Africa and the rhythms of Africa—but I was not Africa. I was Chicago and Kansas City and Broadway and Harlem.

Van Vechten, who knows or should know that the Negro is no more primitive and atavistic than any other racial group in America, was merely a literary faddist capitalizing upon a current vogue and a popular demand. In an article, **"The Negro in Art: How Shall He Be Portrayed,"** released in *The Crisis* shortly before the publication of ***Nigger Heaven,*** he expressed his interest in the literary possibilities of the wretchedness, immorality, and exoticism of Negro life:

> The squalor of Negro life, the vice of Negro life, offer a wealth of material to the artist. . . . The question is: Are Negro writers going to write about this exotic material while it is still fresh or will they continue to make a free gift of it to white authors who will exploit it until not a drop of vitality remains?

He probably did not deserve the vitriolic criticism of DuBois, for he frankly set out to exploit what he considered to be the exotic and animalistic elements in Harlem life. At the same time, however, he did not merit the high praise of Johnson, who called ***Nigger Heaven*** a mosaic of Harlem and the first work by a white novelist in which the Negro is considered as an individual rather than as a type. There were many significant phases of Harlem life which Van Vechten did not apparently know and therefore could not describe; and surely Gertrude Stein, T. S. Stribling, Waldo Frank, DuBose Heyward, and several other white predecessors of Van Vechten in the use of Negro subject-matter made departures from the stereotyped presentation of colored characters.

All these considerations notwithstanding, the Van Vechten Vogue exerted profound influence upon literature by and about American Negroes. In 1927 Countee Cullen produced *Copper Sun,* a volume of poetry which shows the imprint of the Dark Continent in its title. Partly in awareness of "the traditional jazz connotations," James Weldon Johnson called his versified sermons *God's Trombones* (1927). Wallace Thurman collaborated with William Jordon Rapp in 1929 to produce *Harlem,* a play dealing with life in the black ghetto. But the emphasis upon jazz, sex, atavism, and primitivism is much more pronounced in novels and short stories than in poetry and drama. Fictional works that stress some or all of these elements are Claude McKay's *Home to Harlem* (1928), *Banjo* (1929), and six narratives in *Gingertown* (1932); Wallace Thurman's *The Blacker the Berry* (1929) and *Infants of the Spring* (1932); and Arna Bontemps' *God Sends Sunday* (1931). All of these works, except *Banjo* and *God Sends Sunday,* are laid chiefly in New York City; but even in these two variant novels there is the same preoccupation with sensual pleasures and instinctive living. Like ***Nigger Heaven,*** the Harlem-centered works ordinarily depict cabaret scenes, interracial social gatherings, and Negro *literati.* The low-life characters of these books are primarily concerned with the pleasures of the hour—food, intoxicants, and sex. They unapologetically follow their natural impulses and have no such moral codes as those of the respectable Philadelphia *bourgeoisie* delineated by Jessie Fauset. Moreover, unlike the heroes of the propaganda novels, they do not undertake to effect racial reforms.

Being primarily a fad, the Van Vechten Vogue was doomed to fall before the first violent shock or the next new rage. The inevitable reaction came in the form of the Wall Street *debacle* of 1929 which, as Langston Hughes wittily remarks, "sent Negroes, white folks and all rolling down the hill toward the Works Progress Administration."

The fatal mistake of the Van Vechten school was to make a fetish of sex and the cabaret rather than to give a faithful, realistic presentation and interpretation of Harlem life. In spite of this error, however, the Van Vechtenites helped to break away from the taboos and stereotypes of earlier years, to make self-revelation and self-criticism more important considerations in fiction by Negroes, and to demonstrate to publishers and readers that Negro authors have an important contribution to make to the nation's cultural life.

GEORGE SCHUYLER (ESSAY DATE 1950)

SOURCE: Schuyler, George. "Phylon Profile, XXII: Carl Van Vechten." In *Remembering the Harlem Renaissance,* edited by Cary D. Wintz, pp. 154-60. New York: Garland Publishing, 1996.

In the following essay, which was originally published in Phylon *in 1950, Schuyler discusses Van Vechten's contribution to positive changes in race relations in the United States.*

A great revolution has taken place in American race relations in the past quarter century, and while this phenomenon is ascribed to many causes by various authorities on the subject, perhaps the most prepotent has been the individual effort of Carl Van Vechten.

Changes may be brought about by social forces and mass action, but all changes begin in somebody's mind and move outward like ripples in a millpond to the farthest shores, once the revolutionary idea has been accepted. Tall, white-maned Carl Van Vechten, still suave and benign at seventy, has done more than any single person in this country to create the atmosphere of acceptance of the Negro.

Styles in thinking, like styles in clothing, shoes, and house furnishings, are the creation of a few individuals. More importantly, a new style in thinking requires disciples and the speed of their own conversion depends upon the personality and reputation of the father of the idea.

Many inspired white people before Van Vechten had devoted their lives to fighting color prejudice and bettering race relations, and without them and their influence the Negro here would have been well nigh eliminated by the white Neanderthal element. They were the quintessence of the American conscience.

Unlike them, however, the Sage of Central Park West did not approach the darker brethren as a problem over which to moan and sob but as more exotic and colorful Anglo-Saxons, considerably closer to the stirring drumbeats out of the green jungles of Africa and possessed of hitherto shackeled genius, so far unhonored and unsung but eminently worthy of investigation, appreciation and acceptance.

His attitude was not that of indignant belligerence toward the Negrophobists among the civilized minority that shapes opinion the world over, but rather an attitude of pitying condescension toward those who were unaware, through ignorance or negligence, of the artistic, spiritual and cultural gifts of colored Americans.

It was one thing to utter anguished roars against the evils of peonage, discrimination, segregation and lynching but quite another to contend that these blacks were richly endowed Americans who had so much to offer spiritually and culturally to our civilization if permitted to do so.

His attack was not directed against the masses but against the upper classes who influence and direct the masses. As he said, "Break the taboo on the highest levels and finally that progress will seep down to the masses."

His attack was explosively effective because of his unprecedented technique which has been widely adopted and promoted by his disciples. As one picture is worth ten thousand words, so one association with an exceptional Negro has the impact greater than a ton of pro-Negro propaganda. Carl Van Vechten devoted himself to bringing together, physically and intellectually, the writers, actors, dancers, musicians, singers and composers of both "races" on a plane of equality.

"The more the two races get together," he held, "the better it is for race relations. Getting together should be on all levels and in all institutions." He was able to do this more effectively than others because he was already world famous as a successful critic of the ballet, of music and of the theatre, and the best-selling author of a half dozen books on music and such works as ***The Tattooed Countess, The Blind Bow Boy, Sacred and Profane Memories, Peter Whiffle, Spider Boy, The Tiger in the House, Lords of the Housetops*** and numerous light and learned essays.

The literary lights, the stars of the ballet, the kings and queens of the theater, the painters, sculptors and editors who had attained envious preeminence frequented his salons on West 55th Street and later on Central Park West; and to this company Van Vechten introduced their darker opposite numbers. Here they rubbed shoulders, sipped cocktails, nibbled hors d'oeuvres, conversed, sang and danced without self-consciousness. What was at first an innovation and a novelty soon became commonplace, an institution.

Such salons in the early twenties were rare to the point of being revolutionary. At the time it was most difficult for Negroes to purchase a ticket for an orchestra seat in a theater, even in Harlem, and it was with the greatest difficulty that a colored American in New York could get service in a downtown restaurant. Except at Coney Island, beaches were closed to Negroes and few were the other places that would tolerate their patronage. The freedom of the North was pretty much of a mockery, and this was particularly true of employment. This was the time when the production of O'Neill's *All God's Children Got Wings* was being denounced editorially in leading "liberal" newspapers, and the current Mayor of New York was refusing permission for colored and white children to appear in the first scene.

Most of the white people of Van Vechten's circle knew Negroes only as domestics and had never had them as associates. It was extremely daring for a white person to dine publicly with a Negro, and certainly to dance with one; but if those of the upper crust could be weaned over to such social acceptance, it was likely that a trend would be started which would eventually embrace the majority of those whites who shaped public opinion and set the social pace.

To this laudable endeavor Carl Van Vechten and his famous actress wife, Fania Marinoff, devoted themselves as assiduously as any sincere revolutionists could. With Machiavellian design the doyen of the dilettanti made it smart to be interracial. Once the idea took hold it spread in geometrical progression. Racial bias was eliminated on the higher levels and the Van Vechten philosophy spread like a forest fire, consuming great stands of racial snobbery along the way. Where there had been doubt and scepticism, there grew tolerance, curiosity, understanding and appreciation among both racial groups. Those who came as mere faddists left as fellow travelers of interracialism.

Indeed, it is interesting to compare the revolutionary methods of Carl Van Vechten in America with those of Willi Muenzenberg in Germany. For ten years after the Communist overthrow of the Kerensky government in Russia, the Red policy abroad was "No collaboration with the bourgeoisie," and everybody who bathed regularly, wore a white collar and did not have the palms of his hands covered with callouses was anathema to the Communists worshipping the Proletarian God. Willi Muenzenberg was the first Communist to discern that the Comrades were thus failing to utilize what could become a tremendous asset.

So Muenzenberg invented the fellow traveler. He cultivated the artistic and cultured circles, saw that they got recognition and publicity through his immense publishing facilities and influences, made it fashionable to become proletarian utopians and fight for "democracy": that is to say, totalitarianism. He believed that ten times more influential people could be made propagandists for Communism than there were card-carrying Communists, and time has confirmed him to the hilt.

With far different objectives but similar techniques, Van Vechten won over the same class in this country to acceptance of the Negro and appreciation of his potentialities and contributions. His disciples were the minority that tell the majority what to think, wear, see and hear, and they have multiplied tremendously in the past quarter century. It has now become smart to be tolerant, understanding and appreciative interracially, and if any one person can be credited with bringing about this revolution it is Carl Van Vechten. You cannot have equality unless it is desired, and it will not be desired unless the idea is first accepted, which will not happen at the bottom until it first happens at the top.

Of course, it took more than salons to do the job. After all, there is a limit to the number of people who can be invited even to Madison Square Garden. Fortunately, Carl Van Vechten had a powerful and potent pen. He had been influential in the world of opinion since he lost his first job with the Chicago *American* in 1906 for "lowering the tone of the Hearst papers." Coming from Cedar Rapids, Iowa, where his father had helped found a school for Negroes and where he had first become acquainted with Negroes through a Mr. Oliphant, he met more colored people, including a singer, Carita Day (Carrie Washington) whose talent impressed him.

When he moved to New York and became assistant music critic of the New York *Times,* he met the incomparable Bert Williams and other talented Negro artists in the course of his work. At the same time as H. L. Mencken and George Jean Nathan were first attracting widespread attention as literary and dramatic critics, Van Vechten was winning laurels for his urbane and penetrating criticism of contemporary music. He not only knew this music (he played the piano even as a boy) but was friendly with those who were composing, singing and playing it.

It was then that he inevitably became introduced to jazz, the greatest native American music, and those who sang and played it. Indeed, he was one of the pioneers in discovering the worth of this music and was certainly the first to write understandingly and enthusiastically about it in the media read by those who set the style in everything. In such de luxe publications as *Vanity Fair,* a swank, slick paper periodical avidly read by the

ABOUT THE AUTHOR

A FOND FAREWELL TO CARLO

He is gone! How strikingly strange it is to contemplate, how sad to ponder, what memories evoked!

He has gone! This unique man as symbolic of this sprawling city of his triumphs as Washington Square, Central Park, Fifth Avenue, Carnegie Hall, and the galleries of the lively arts.

SOURCE: George Samuel Schuyler, excerpt from a tribute to Carl Van Vechten upon his death, *A Fond Farewell to Carlo,* December 23, 1964.

cognoscenti of the day, he introduced Ethel Waters and the three Smith girls, Mamie, Clara and Bessie, who were packing Negro theaters to the rafters but were yet undiscovered by the "superior" race. No evidence of Negro talent in arts and letters escaped his eagle eye or his interested attention. Always a man of great enthusiasms, he plunged into this new field with a zealot's obsession. Then when he met Walter White after the publication of the latter's *Fire in the Flint,* and through him the monumental James Weldon Johnson, his enthusiastic interest became incandescent.

He attended a dance given by the National Association for the Advancement of Colored People and met the fledgling poets, Countee Cullen and Langston Hughes, and writers like Zora Neale Hurston, Eric Walrond and Rudolph Fisher who were just breaking their shells, and Jessie Fauset, whose novel *There Is Confusion* was to become a landmark of the Negro Renaissance.

Within a month Van Vechten had become a regular visitor to Harlem, knew every important Negro and a whole lot who were not. This was his first time to meet the Negro intelligentsia, the colored folk who were like the whites with whom he was wont to associate. He was fascinated by the almost Parisian sophistication of the educated Negroes, by their keen minds, by the smartness and taste of their dress and furnishings. Here were Negroes who had high standards, who were abreast of the best in literature, who were a credit to American culture, and yet who were held apart from the mainstream of national life.

How could he make the rest of America understand this sophisticated, exotic, striving microcosm of American society? How could he capture the attention of the civilized minority everywhere and make them see what he had seen and heard and felt? It was with this in mind that he went to work on a novel of Harlem life—not the Harlem of fetid slums which later writers have dwelt upon *ad nauseum,* but a civilization as unknown to white folks as some Himalayan kingdom.

The novel was published in 1926 as ***Nigger Heaven*** and attained immediate preeminence on the best-selling lists. The reaction to the book gave eloquent testimony to the contemporary status of interracialism. The whites were astonished, delighted, incredulous; some Negro critics gagged at the sardonic title while others rejoiced that at last the reading public was getting a fairly accurate portrait of Negro urban life, its polish as well as its pitfalls, its joy as well as its grief. The gulf that existed between colored and white society was revealed by the amazement of whites that such a society existed without their knowledge, and by the naive delight of Negroes in a realistic portrayal of their lives.

There is a story that one wealthy white matron in Oklahoma City asked her Negro maid: "Is it true that there are Negroes in New York who live like those described in this book?"

"Why, Madam," the maid replied, "there are Negroes in Oklahoma City who live like that!"

The Negroes who objected to ***Nigger Heaven*** were mostly those who had not read it but disliked the title. James Weldon Johnson, Alice Dunbar Nelson and the writer were the only Negro reviewers who approved it without reservation, but the novel was nevertheless widely read by colored people. James Weldon Johnson held that no other title would have been so appropriate because of its tragic irony. One of the most violent critics was Dr. W. E. B. DuBois.

The novel succeeded in getting Van Vechten a much wider audience for his viewpoint than he could ever have obtained by personal contact in his apartment between white and colored people. With the ice thus broken, many road blocks to Negro acceptance were destroyed. It is noteworthy that today there is scarcely a prominent white person in the country who does not say that he or she personally has no prejudice against Negroes.

Because he felt that a critic could not be truly objective after forty, Van Vechten stopped his musical criticism at that age after writing numerous books of penetrating observations on music and music makers. At the age of fifty he abandoned the writing of novels because he felt that he had nothing more of importance to say. But being an active person and still tremendously interested in the Negro and his acceptance by the white society, he turned to photography. After all, while most white people had heard and read about outstanding Negroes, few had seen how they looked. At that time the picture of a Negro, no matter how prominent, rarely appeared in the columns of a newspaper or magazine of general circulation.

With his usual enthusiastic concentration, Van Vechten devoted himself to photographing the outstanding Negroes of the day. He had been interested in photography since the end of the nineteenth century and by this time he was an expert. Throughout the Franklin Roosevelt and Harry Truman eras, he has given most of his attention to this task.

The result has been a tremendous volume of fine photographs of the most outstanding colored and white artists of the day in the theater, painting, sculpture, belles lettres, journalism, music and the theater. To be sure that these photographs receive wide circulation, Van Vechten has had them printed on postcards. It is not unusual to open one's mail box some morning and find a brief note from Van Vechten on the back of one of those postcards. In this way the eminent critic has reached thousands of people with wonderful photographs of Ethel Waters, Philippa Schuyler, Walter White, Marian Anderson, Avon Long and scores of others too numerous to mention.

Indeed, these photographs became so numerous that it led Van Vechten inevitably into the exhibiting of them. They have been shown almost everywhere and undoubtedly they have contributed much to breaking down barriers between the races. In these pictures of artistic and cultured Negroes he carries a message almost as effective as the essays and books he has written and the soirees he has held in his artistic, colorful and book-lined apartment on Central Park West.

Over one hundred of these photographs of outstanding Negroes were placed on exhibition at Wadleigh High School in New York City in 1949, as the Jerome Peterson Memorial Collection. He wanted to show the young people of all races how many distinguished Negroes there are in the world. He succeeded beyond all expectations.

In 1947 he presented to Howard University the Rose McClendon Memorial Collection of Photographs of Celebrated Negroes, some one hundred and seventy in all.

In 1941 he began the James Weldon Johnson Collection of Negro Arts and Letters at Yale University. It consisted of manuscripts, letters, photographs, songs and other material, and contains the major portion of James Weldon Johnson's memorabilia. Included are also many rare phonograph records.

In 1949 Fisk University was the grateful recipient of the Carl Van Vechten Gallery of Fine Arts which contained numerous books and manuscripts, the finest collection of its kind in the South. This was supplemented by the George Gershwin Collection of Music and Musical Literature to the same institution of learning. Along with this was the Florine Stettsheimer Memorial Collection of books about the fine arts. To Yale University went the Anna Marble Pollock Memorial Library on books about cats. To make sure that those who did not frequent libraries and museums would be sure to see his huge collection of photographs of notable Negroes, Mr. Van Vechten arranged an exhibition of intimate photographic studies in the windows of the Roger Kent stores in Rockefeller Plaza, in New York. Here could be seen the pictures of Marian Anderson, Leo Coleman, Joe Louis, Edward Matthews, Willard Motley, Paul Robeson, Bessie Smith, Josh White and Walter White, along with photographs of the leading white artists of stage, screen, the ballet and literature.

Many honors and testimonials have been given to the racial revolutionist of Central Park West by Negroes and whites who understand and appreciate his quiet and effective work for interracial amity. They range all the way from scrolls by Yale University to a testimonial dinner by the James Weldon Johnson Literary Guild at the Port Arthur Restaurant in Chinatown, New York City. They are just a small token of the gratitude of those who appreciate what his efforts have meant in breaking down the inhibitions, prejudices and snobbery that hampered the development of a healthy understanding and acknowledgment of the contribution of the Depressed Tenth to American culture and civilization.

Today, rich in years and knowledge, he holds open house for his friends and disciples in the vast drawing room of his colorful apartment on Central Park West, with the oil portrait of himself as a much younger man looking down benignly upon the scene. Easily he moves among his guests, replenishing glasses, conversing with this one and that, dropping a *bon mot* or a mordant observation here and there among his friends and worshippers, with an occasional aside to his petite spouse, Fania Marinoff, the perfect hostess, who has retired from the theater but will always be of it.

His great legacy to future generations is the honor of having boldly entered where lesser men feared to tread; and despite the carping criticism and sneering of the bigoted, having wrought a real revolution in white men's thinking about the Negro. His has been a labor of love and admiration, unlike the hateful efforts of more sinister propagandists proclaiming more ambitious and far-reaching goals in which they really did not believe.

His efforts have been and still are the triumph of sincerity and appreciation over bigotry and snobbery. No one today can meet and talk with him and his wonderful wife without being spiritually and intellectually enriched. No one can know of what he has accomplished in healing America's greatest wound without a feeling of deepest appreciation. For here was and is a man who, without hope or desire of mundane reward, labored in the vineyard and brought forth such bounty as men have rarely seen.

Lounging lazily on the broad settee facing his fireplace, he remarks as if to himself, that he would like to see all separation, all barriers, all handicaps removed, and all Americans regardless of color or creed, united as brothers in mutual understanding and cooperation.

"I'd like it to be," he murmurs, "—well, like my house. Colored people come in and out, play an important role in my life—but there is no problem. Just people."

MARK HELBLING (ESSAY DATE 1976)

SOURCE: Helbling, Mark. "Carl Van Vechten and the Harlem Renaissance." In *Analysis and Assessment,* edited with an introduction by Gary D. Wintz, pp. 257–59. New York: Garland Publishing, Inc., 2000.

In the following essay, which was originally published in Negro American Literature Forum *in 1976, Helbling contends that Van Vechten's publication of* Nigger Heaven *raised one of the central questions of the Harlem Renaissance—How should Blacks be portrayed in art?*

As Alain Locke began to assemble material for the proposed *New Negro,* he became increasingly anxious as to the content and ultimate form of the book. A strong beginning was important to help establish a perspective for the poetry and prose to follow. For this reason, Locke wanted something more "suggestive and concrete" than the article Albert C. Barnes had written, "Negro Art and America," which Locke had used in the Harlem issue of the *Survey Graphic.* As a consequence, Locke wrote to Carl Van Vechten and asked if he would write an article for *The New Negro* which would follow his own opening remarks and introduce Part One: "I and the publisher desirous you write an article on "The Negro and American Art' giving your notion of the promise of the present generation in the arts—emphasizing if you agree, the general cultural contribution which in process of being made. Music, drama, and poetry be highlights."[1] Van Vechten, however, pleaded lack of time because of a commitment to do an article for *Vanity Fair,* **"Prescription for the Negro Theatre: Being a Few Reasons Why the Great Colored Show Has Not Yet Been Achieved,"** which appeared in print one month before the *New Negro.*[2] Somewhat wistfuly, Locke congratulated Van Vechten on the *Vanity Fair* article and commented how much he would like to have had that particular analysis for *The New Negro.*[3]

In the same month in which Locke initially expressed regret that Van Vechten would be unavailable for *The New Negro,* Van Vechten began seriously to consider writing a novel about Harlem and its people. Three months earlier James Weldon Johnson had encouraged him to write just such a book: "You state in your very nice inscription that many of the views that you have expressed on the Negro have been considerably altered by your recent experiences. I am quite sure they have, and I am quite anxious to have you write on the subject now out of your larger experience and more intimate experience. Besides, as I once said to you, no acknowledged American novelist has yet made use of this material."[4] Now Van Vechten was ready, and he confided to Gertrude Stein, "I shall start on my Negro novel. I have passed practically my whole winter in company with Negroes and have succeeded in getting into most of the important sets. This will not be a novel about Negroes in the South or white [contacts] or lynchings. It will be about NEGROES, as they live now in the new city of Harlem (which is a part of New York). About 400,000 of them live there now, rich and poor, fast and slow, intellectual and ignorant. I hope it will be a good book."[5]

In November the first draft was begun and by March, 1926, ***Nigger Heaven*** was finished. Its publication in August brought immediate sales and immediate controversy. Both Blacks and whites attacked as well as defended Van Vechten and the novel he had written. W. E. B. DuBois was outraged, and his remarks in *The Crisis* represent the views of many who denounced ***Nigger Heaven*** both as art and as reality:

> Carl Van Vechten's ***Nigger Heaven*** is a blow in the face. It is an affront to the hospitality of black folk and to the intelligence of white. . . . The author counts among his friends numbers of Negroes of all classes. He is an authority on dives and cabarets. But he masses this knowledge without rule or reason and seeks to express all of Harlem life in its cabarets. To him the black cabaret is Harlem; around it all his characters gravitate. Here is their stage of action. Such a theory of Harlem is nonsense. The overwhelming majority of black folk there never go to cabarets. The average colored man in Harlem is an everyday laborer, attending church, lodge and movie and as conservative and conventional as ordinary working folk everywhere. . . . I cannot for the life of me see in this work either sincerity or art, deep thought, or truthful industry. It seems to me that Mr. Van Vechten tried to do something bizarre and he certainly succeeded. I read ***Nigger Heaven*** and read it through because I had to. But I advise others who are impelled by a sense of duty or curiosity to drop the book gently in the grate and try the Police Gazette.[6]

Others, however, were equally quick to praise ***Nigger Heaven*** as art and to congratulate Van Vechten for his sensitivity and perception. Both publicly and in private, Alain Locke, for example, acclaimed Van Vechten's achievement: "***Nigger Heaven,*** for me, quite the unexpected. It's art, but at the same time subcutaneous propas. I believe it will be quite effectual but really hadn't expected you to be so carefully serious and so unsatirical. But perhaps you were wise. . . . For in my [opinion] you have brought us a step nearer the flush level of Negro material in American art in this good corrective sketch for the white reader who takes Negro life underseriously and for the black reader who takes it over seriously."[7]

Whether or not ***Nigger Heaven*** is art depends to a great extent on one's definition of the term. DuBois, for example, asked questions that Locke considered irrelevant: "Does it please? Does it entertain? Is it a good and human story? In my opinion it is not; and I am one who likes stories and I do not insist that they be written solely for my point of view."[8] As a consequence, they differed drastically in their response. However, the differences they voice were only partially a matter of individual taste and understanding. For the controversy which Van Vechten ignited was itself part of a larger and more general issue—How Shall the Negro be Portrayed in Art?—that was consciously and publicly being debated for the first time.

Van Vechten's role in this debate is complex and somewhat ambiguous. But it is clear that he was more than a focus through which to judge the thought and feeling of others. Locke, as mentioned, perceived Van Vechten to be an important critical voice and solicited his opinions for *The New Negro.* Although Van Vechten was unable to fulfill Locke's request, he did accommodate Jessie Fauset who, as co-editor with DuBois, of the *Crisis,* asked that he provide a list of questions for the forthcoming series: **"The Negro in Art: How Shall He Be Portrayed?"** Under a cover letter from Miss Fauset, Van Vechten provided the following questions:[9]

1. When the artist, black or white, portrays Negro characters is he under any obligations or limitations as to the sort of character he will portray?
2. Can any author be criticized for painting the worst or the best characters of a group?
3. Can publishers be criticized for refusing to handle novels that portray Negores of education and accomplishment, on the ground that these characters are no different from white folk and therefore not interesting?
4. What are Negroes to do when they are continually painted at their worst and judged by the public as they are painted?
5. Does the situation of the educated Negro in America with its pathos, humiliation and tragedy call for artistic treatment at least as sincere and sympathetic as "Porgy" received?
6. Is not the continual portrayal of the sordid, foolish and criminal among Negroes convincing the world that this and this alone is really and essentially Negroid, and preventing white artists from knowing any other types and preventing black artists from daring to paint them?
7. Is there not a real danger that young colored writers will be tempted to follow the popular trend in portraying Negro character in the underworld rather than seeking to paint the truth about themselves and their own social class?[10]

As the interest of Locke and Fauset reveals, Van Vechten was clearly an important figure in his own right. And any assessment of his importance must include more than his controversial novel. It's ironic that he should be the author of the *Crisis* symposium, and that ***Nigger Heaven*** should be completed in the very month (March) in which his response to these questions, the first response featured, also appeared. Perhaps DuBois' indictment of ***Nigger Heaven*** as a betrayal, an act of exploitation, was not unrelated to Van Vechten's participation in the *Crisis* questionnaire. Nevertheless, the irony of this situation hints at the complexity as well as the importance of the role Van Vechten played.

In 1924 Van Vechten read Walter White's *The Fire in the Flint* and soon after was introduced to White through their common publisher, Alfred Knopf. For Van Vechten the meeting was both exhilarating and surprising. In a letter to Edna Kenton, he wrote, "Walter White, author of *Fire in the Flint,* spent two hours with me the other day. He speaks French and talks about Debussy and Proust in an off hand way. An entirely new kind of Negro to me. I shall, I hope, see something of these cultured circles."[11] Within a short time, as Van Vechten recalls, his hopes had been realized: "[In two weeks] I knew practically every famous

Negro in New York because Walter was a hustler."[12] Thus began Van Vechten's extraordinary involvement and friendship with young black writers, artists, actors, poets and singers.[13]

Through encouragement, private influence, and public endorsement, Van Vechten was of invaluable assistance in helping many Black writers to become published and recognized. Langston Hughes's commentary in *The Big Sea* could, with some modification, just as well be that of several others:

> What Carl Vechten did for me was to submit my first book of poems to Alfred A. Knopf, put me in contact with the editors of *Vanity Fair,* who bought my first poems sold to a magazine, caused me to meet many editors and writers who were friendly and helpful to me, encouraged me in my efforts to help publicize the Scottsboro case, cheered me on in the writing of my first short stories, and otherwise aided in making life for me more profitable and entertaining.
>
> Many others of the Negroes in the arts, from Paul Robeson to Ethel Waters, Walter White to Richmond Barthe, will offer the same testimony as to the interest Van Vechten has displayed toward Negro creators in the fields of writing, plastic arts, and popular entertainment.[14]

In addition, Van Vechten was a lavish entertainer who knew virtually everyone in the arts. At his parties whites and Blacks drank, sang, and conversed far into the night. The following is just a small sample of those who might find themselves together at a Van Vechten party: Bessie Smith, Somerset Maugham, Zora Neale Hurston, Sinclair Lewis, Ethel Waters, Emily Clark, Hugh Walpole, Elinor Wylie, Fannie Hurst, Waldo Frank, Louis Untermeyer, Taylor Gordon, James Weldon Johnson, Richmond Barthe, Lilyan Tashman, Salvador Dali, Theodore Dreiser, Nora Holt, Paul Robeson, H. L. Mencken, Langston Hughes and George Gershwin. Such parties served as an important place of contact not only for blacks to meet whites but also for blacks to meet one another. Zora Neale Hurston, for example, finally met Ethel Waters at a dinner party Van Vechten had arranged especially for the occasion.[15] Van Vechten, of course, relished parties and, at times, seemed to delight in them simply as a form of live art. But he also intended them to have a more serious racial and cultural significance. In 1960 he offered a retrospective interpretation as to what he had sought to achieve:

> Questioner: According to George Schuyler your combinations of Negroes and whites was instrumental in improving race relations.
>
> Van Vechten: Well, I always had something like that in mind, but I had my own pleasure too.
>
> Questioner: Was this the one "ulterior motive" you had in mind?
>
> Van Vechten: I think originally I did it because I wanted to, and I still do it for that reason, but occasionally—to help the cause along a little. I never tried to tell people what to do. I just bring them together and see what happens. I'm a catalyst, mainly.[16]

Before his meeting with Walter White, Van Vechten had had little social contact with Blacks. He had, however, taken an interest in Black arts and artists. In 1917, in an article titled **"The American Composer,"** Van Vechten criticized Americans for being imitators rather than creators of a distinctively American voice:

> The most obvious point of superiority of our ragtime composers . . . is that they are expressing the very soul of a nation and epoch, while their more serious confreres are struggling to pour into the forms of the past the thoughts of the past, rearranged, to be sure, but without notable inspiration. . . . It is only through the trenchant pens of our new composers that the complicated vigour of American life has been expressed in tone. It is the only music created in America today which is worth the paper on which it is written. It is the only American music which is enjoyed by the nation (even lovers of Mozart and Debussy prefer ragtime to the inert and saponaceous classicism of our more seriousminded composers); it is the only American music which is heard abroad, . . . and it is the only music on which the musicians of our land can build in the future.[17]

A similar enthusiasm and a similar point of view marked his writings into the early twenties. In March, 1924, in his **"Valedictory"** to music criticism, Van Vechten reminded his readers that "Jazz may not be the last hope of American music, nor yet the best hope, but at present, I am convinced, it is its only hope."[18] Thus, Van Vechten concluded a career in which he had "attended a concert or an opera or a play nearly every evening" for nearly twenty years. His interest now, his second career, was in the writing of novels. But stimulated by his recent access to Black intellectuals and his friendship with Walter White, Langston Hughes, and James Weldon Johnson, Van Vechten proceeded to write eleven articles and five book reviews on black music, literature, and theater in the two years following his farewell. Thus, he paralleled his role as a "catalyst" (one who brought people together) with the more public stance of a writer, only now Van Vechten forcefully expressed a point of view for both Blacks and whites to heed.

Although Van Vechten often referred to various forms of Black music as a source for a "modern voice," he seldom spoke of the arts and art in quite the same panegyrics as did Alain Locke. His remarks are more tempered, more hedged in irony, more concerned with the immediate problems and difficulties of creative expression. As a consequence, the enthusiasm Van Vechten voices for the Black theater, for spirituals, and for the blues is that of one who has "discovered" a form of art that commands attention solely for its intrinsic beauty, power, and originality: "The words [of the blues] in beauty and imaginative significance far transcend in their crude poetic importance the words of the religious songs. They are eloquent with rich idioms, metaphoric phrases and striking word combinations."[19] In one sense, then, Van Vechten simply sought to call attention to what heretofore had been ignored or overlooked. His praise for such individuals as Bessie Smith, Ethel Waters, Paul Robeson, Clara Smith, and the blues in general, was an attempt to awaken others to the talents of these incomparable artists.[20] But at the same time, such praise carried with it certain admonitions and counsels, for as Van Vechten saw things the problem was not simply that the American public failed to appreciate what he and a few others now championed.

In his *Vanity Fair* article **"Prescription For the Negro Theater,"** Van Vechten despaired at the corruption parading as theater on the Broadway stage. *Shuffle Along* (1920), that bright and promising beginning, had become simply a formula. Worse yet, successive revues (*Runnin' Wild*; *Dixie to Broadway*; and *The Chocolate Dandies*) continued to draw upon such minstrel traditions as the blacked faces, large carmined lips, and ghost-in-the-graveyard scenes. Thus, Van Vechten's prescription was to junk the machinery of the past and to allow Black actors and actresses the freedom to be their creative selves. This, however, was only the surface of his criticism, for the deeper problem was the fact that whites controlled the stage upon which Blacks were contracted to dance and strut: "To be perfectly fair . . . practically all the dancing and a good share of the musical rhythms now to be seen and felt on the white stage have been raped from the Negro, while [the] Negro takes over [the] stalest features of the white stage."[21] As a consequence, what was presented was a disaster. Regardless of their talent, Blacks were trapped within the imaginative limitations and the commercial considerations of others.[22]

Thus discovery was coupled with the despair that a potentially rich tradition of art and the artistic genius of Black men and women would become merely an appendage to the ambitions of others. And in the process such art and artistry would be corrupted, for as Van Vechten continued to warn, whites would not only exploit but also enfeeble. Such criticism was meant for whites, but it was also an alert to Blacks, for domination not only corrupted but was corrupting. Thus, what Van Vechten felt to be most insidious and most tragic was the complicity he perceived on the part of Blacks who were encouraged and forced to participate. At the same time, it was Van Vechten's conviction that such domination built upon and continued to perpetuate feelings of shame that blacks still felt toward a cultural tradition which had roots in a slave past: "Like the spirituals, the blues are folksongs and are conceived in the same pentatonic scale, omitting the 4 and 7 tones—and at present they are looked down upon, as the Spirituals once were, especially by the Negroes themselves. The humbleness of their origin and occasionally the frank obscenity of their sentiment are probably responsible for this condition. In this connection it may be recalled that it has taken over fifty years for the Negroes to recover from their repugnance to the Spirituals, because of the fact that they were born during slave days. . . ."[23] In literature, Van Vechten saw the same neglect and similar problems to be confronted.

In his response to the series of questions proposed in the *Crisis,* Van Vechten ventured that any restrictions placed upon the artist were inimical to art. Whether whites or Blacks chose as their subject material "the lower strata of the race" was a decision only the artist could make and others should respect. Thus, Van Vechten praised Rudolph Fisher for such stories as "Ringtail" and "High Yaller," stories which "plenty of colored folk deplored." In essence, Van Vechten's point was that the artist must not be encumbered with external considerations, whether they be political or moral. For considerations of taste and propriety were no less inhibiting and debilitating than speculation which attempted to assess whether what was said would or would not be helpful to the race. But once said, Van Vechten's advice takes a curious turn, one that has continued to raise controversy:

> You speak of "this side of the Negro's life having been overdone." That is quite true and will doubtless continue to be true for some time, for a very excellent reason. The squalor of Negro life, the vice of Negro life, offer a wealth of novel, exotic, picturesque material to the artist. On the other hand, there is very little difference if any between the life of a wealthy or cultured Negro and that of a white man of the same class. The question is: Are Negro writers going to write about this exotic material while it is still fresh or will they continue

to make a free gift of it to white authors who will exploit it until not a drop of vitality remains.[24]

Not unlike his commentary on the spirituals and the blues, Van Vechten's intent was to encourage Blacks to explore, not to ignore, the past and present realities of their cultural and social existence. Only now, however, he introduces a generalization concerning class so as to define more precisely the reality—the squalor of Negro life, the vice of Negro life—he so unreservedly urged Blacks to explore. In speaking of Black music, Van Vechten made no such distinctions and he did not justify its meaning as exotic. Perhaps he assumed this, but it is probably more accurate to say that in music he confronted a form of expression that was itself clearly central to the cultural experience of Black Americans.

The question, then, was not what should be said but learning to appreciate what was said. As for the novel, however, the emphasis was on content, not form, and the question was what should be portrayed within a form of expression that had its origins in the culture of Western Europe. The answers he gave, however, have the sense of being *the* answer rather than an answer. As a consequence, the value of his advice is ambiguous at best. The comment he makes regarding class clearly requires elaboration. As it stands it is meaningless and misleading. At the same time, given Van Vechten's frequent allusions throughout his critical writings to a racial soul and a racial experience, the notion of class nullifies, at least complicates, the former assertion. How are these two claims to be reconciled? And finally, is the implication to be drawn that Black writers are to limit themselves to the reality Van Vechten now defines as distinctive yet threatened by outside whites? Van Vechten never really attempted to deal with these questions, which is unfortunate, for they have important implications for the novel ***Nigger Heaven.*** However, before attempting to deal with this novel, it is first necessary to give attention to the novels he began to write in 1920.

Drawing upon Van Vechten's comment to a friend, Bruce Kellner has argued that Van Vechten's first four novels constitute a tetralogy: "***The Tattooed Countess*** represented aspiration; the next two, achievement (charm through ***Peter Whiffle,*** and sophistication through ***The Blind Bow-Boy***); and ***Firecrackers,*** the Gotterdammerung of the series, represented disintegration."[25] Kellner's observation is a suggestive way to read Van Vechten's work. At the same time, Van Vechten's fifth novel, ***Nigger Heaven,*** is something of a departure from the previous novels and frequently makes different demands upon the reader. Nevertheless, the spirit of Kellner's remark, I think, is more suggestive than the content. For in all of Van Vechten's novels there exist continuing thematic concerns, an ironic point of view, a manner of style of presentation, and a recurrence of characters which make neat lines of demarcation somewhat misleading. In a letter to Mabel Dodge Luhan, who appears in several novels herself as Edith Dale, Van Vechten noted, "Of course what you say about me and sex is perfectly foolish. I never invent stories. I always select a classic theme and write modern variations around it. ***Peter Whiffle*** is Electra or Hamlet; the ***Blind Bow-Boy*** is my version of the Pilgrims Progress and the ***Tattooed Countess*** is Phaedra. . . . My intention in writing is to create moods to awaken unconscious echoes of the past, to render to shadows their real importance. I don't think I ever think of sex at all. It plays around here and there, but that's not what my books are about. They seem to me to be books about a man who is alone in the world and is very sad."[26] This was written in 1924, but his comment is equally true for ***Nigger Heaven, Spider Boy,*** and ***Parties.***[27]

Although ***Nigger Heaven*** should be read in the context of his other works, the exact nature of this context must be carefully defined. For those who were repulsed by the novel the relationship seems clear enough: Once again Van Vechten, the precious dilettante with an eye and an ear for the bizarre and the exotic, has created a novel whose singular purpose is to delight the senses and arouse the emotions. Analogues, if they were sought, could easily be found. Didn't, for example, Campaspe Lorillard, in ***The Blind Bow-Boy,*** speak for Van Vechten himself: "Campaspe's philosophy was as sure at this point as at another. It was only, she frequently said, those who expected to find amusement in themselves who wandered about disconsolate and bored. Amusement was to be derived from watching others, when one permitted them to be entirely themselves. . . . A life of boredom intervened until the grave yawned, unless one surrounded oneself with people who were individual enough to comport themselves with some eccentricity, not to say perversity."[28] And wasn't the snake charmer and later movie vamp, Zimbule, the object of Campaspe's attention and delight, an early version of the seductress Lasca Sartoris in ***Nigger Heaven***: "The bed-lamp, shedding a soft amber glow, was still lighted. The floor was strewn with spangled crimson skirts, stockings the shade of blue-jay feathers, sequined caps, boots, trousers, shirts, chemises. . . . Under the sheet in Paul's superb bed, with a crest-emblazoned head-board shaped like the facade of a Dutch house and with its posts terminating in bleeding pomegranates, in this bed, which had once been the property of some Iberian grandee, lay Bunny and Zimbule, their bare arms entwined round each other's throats, their lips slightly parted, their eyes closed. They were asleep."[29] Such a response, while half right, is also more than half wrong. The ambiguity of this distinction can perhaps best be explained by giving attention to Van Vechten's first novel, ***Peter Whiffle: His Life and Work.***

The preface to ***Peter Whiffle*** is ostensibly an introduction to Van Vechten himself, the novel he is about to write, and the central character Peter Whiffle. It is not altogether clear, however, which character is which and exactly what purpose, if any, the novel is meant to have. Initially, we are informed that Peter Whiffle has recently died and in his will has requested that Van Vechten be his literary executor. Whiffle, however, has written nothing, for he ultimately came to the conclusion that art, which was definition, could only falsify the ambiguous and perpetually changing nature of reality. It seemed, then, that if his life has had any set purpose, "it [had] been not to have a purpose." It was Van Vechten's commission, however, to put his life into perspective, to detect a purpose that might lurk behind Whiffle's dedication to purposelessness. However, Van Vechten is reminded that in illuminating his subject he would soon come to understand that his subject was not Whiffle at all. If nothing else, in the search for something to write Van Vechten would, at least, be writing something. And for those who read this narrative, whatever meaning it held would ultimately depend upon their own wit, sensitivity and experience: "What is true for all books, is perhaps truest of this, that you will carry away from it only what you are able to bring to it."[30]

Peter Whiffle soon became a popular and critical success, and for many, a guessing game immediately ensued as to who Peter Whiffle really was. For some he was a real person, for others Van Vechten himself, and for still others Peter Whiffle was a blend of fact and fantasy, Van Vechten's real and imagined self. His identity is really not that important, but the guessing nicely symbolizes the problem Van Vechten presents to his readers: how much of what he writes is essentially self-indulgence, a delight both in obscurantism and the obscure.

In one sense the character Peter Whiffle is simply a device used to introduce the reader to persons; places; literary, artistic and musical interests that Van Vechten himself had experienced and loved. Thus, the reader is provided with an enchanting tour through Paris and New York; glimpses of Mabel Dodge's Villa Curonia near Florence; an evening of furious argument, gay banter, and frivolity at one of Dodge's famous 12 Fifth Avenue evenings in New York City; and a discussion of the mystical novels of Arthur Machen! And throughout, all is suffused in the special atmosphere of Van Vechten's concern for decor and detail.

> His [Whiffle's] room on East Broadway had been painted ivory-white. On the walls hung three or four pictures, one of Marsden Hartley's mountain series, Chinese juggler in water colour by Charles Demuth, a Picabia, which ostensibly represented the mechanism of a locomotive, with real convex brass piston-rods protruding from the canvas, a chocolate grinder by Marcel Duchamp, and an early Picasso, depicting a very sick-looking pale green woman, lying naked in the gutter of a dark green street. There were lovely desks and tables, Adam and Louis XIV and Francois I, a chaise lounge, banked with striated taffeta cushions, purple bowls filled with spiked, blue flowers, Bergamo and Oushak rugs, and books bound in gay Florentine wall-papers. The bed was covered with a Hungarian homespun linen spread, embroidered in gay worsteds.[31]

At the same time, however, Whiffle's unrelating concern for the art of writing, his continuing need to lift experience into art, serves to give the novel another and more complicated dimension. His quest is serious; it is also hopeless, an obsession that ultimately ends in necromancy and a disastrous explosion. Soon after, Whiffle dies of an incurable disease, but he has perceived that his previous enthusiasms were simply distractions, the frantic graspings of one who hadn't yet come to terms with himself. In their final conversation, Whiffle, who no longer coveted the idea of writing, had advice for Van Vechten who now was clearly on the threshold of a literary career:

> Try to write just as you feel and you will discover that your feeling is greater than your knowledge of it. The words that appear on the paper will at first seem strange to you, almost like hermetic symbols, and it is possible that in the course of time you will be able to say so much that you yourself will not understand what you are writing. Do not be afraid of that. Let the current flow freely when you feel that it is the true current that is flowing. . . . And if you cannot release your personality, what you write, though it be engraved in letters an inch deep on stones weighing many tons, will lie like snow in the street to be melted away by the first rain.[32]

Art was no substitute for life, and life was not art. Whatever satisfactions each held and whatever links existed between the two depended, ultimately, on the individual having the courage and the strength to be himself. As their conversation passed on to various writers, Scotch mystic Cunninghame Graham—who turned his back on civilization to write of the pampas, the arid plains of Africa, India and Spain—was discussed. As Peter ironically noted, "like all lovers of the simple life, he is very complex."[33]

Throughout Whiffle's tortuous search for an aesthetic ideal, he once contemplated a novel that had only blank pages: "And, to give this dummy over-value, to heighten its charm and its mystery, I would add an index to the blank pages, wherein one could learn that on empty page 76 hovered the spirits of Heliogabalus and Gertrude Atherton. It would further inform one that Joe Jackson, George Augustus Sala, and fireless cookers were discussed on page 129."[34] The conceit is Whiffle's; it is also Van Vechten's. The sense of the absurd becomes at times amusing absurdity with little sense. But more often, the absurd functioned as irony, Van Vechten's mockery of his own excesses and those of others. ***Peter Whiffle*** was just the beginning. In subsequent novels the tone became graver and more desperate as the various characters thrashed about seeking diversion, something to fill their boring and empty lives. ***Parties*** is the culmination, a hopeless bog of alcohol and lust. Campaspe's philosophy has now been turned inside out, for diversion only deepens the anguish and the emptiness each experiences. Resignation is all that is left. In her memoirs, *Movers and Shakers,* Mabel Dodge Luhan said of Van Vechten, "With him amusing things were essential things; whimsicality was the note they must sound to have significance. Life was perceived to be a fastidious circus, and strange conjunctions were more prized than the ordinary relationships rooted in eternity."[35] She failed to perceive, however, the fright and the alienation that lay beneath the eccentric and the exotic.

Peter Whiffle was intentionally deceptive, a game played upon the reader. For what purported to be biography was really fiction. ***Nigger Heaven,*** in contrast, was offered without trick or sleight of hand. At least, such was the intention. The title was meant to be ironic, and for fear that he might be misunderstood, Van Vechten explained the title within the text of the novel itself. A glossary of "Negro Words and Phrases" was appended to the end, and the manuscript was read prior to publication by James Weldon Johnson, Walter White, and Rudolph Fisher. In addition, much of the novel is devoted to a discussion of problems between whites and Blacks. And most importantly, Harlem is presented as a complex society fractured and united by individuals and social groups of diverse interests, talents, and values. As a consequence, for many ***Nigger Heaven*** was a triumph. Charles S. Johnson, for example, offered the following evaluation: "It is to me a new focusing, a deft orientation to artistic treasures kicked about for years. The first achievement of a novel of Negro life with a fascination springing from emotions other than patronizing sympathy—The point of beginning for a really vital novel by a Negro about his own life. . . . It has universality. Byron is symbolic to me more than you perhaps intend—he is both nebulous fringe and the disconcerting heart of young Harlem. Mary is alive with a placid intensity, and a really glowing charm."[36] Less often, but not infrequently, Lasca Sartoris drew praise as well. Nora Holt, who inspired the erotic and sadistic Lasca, wired her congratulation from Paris. And even so "respectable" a figure as Alain Locke singled out Lasca for special, though somewhat cryptic, praise: "Lasca is wonderfully drawn—I wonder if after all she isn't the crux of the whole situation—both white and black world will bite their thumbs at her—because she defies them both."[37]

Johnson's comments must have been especially appreciated by Van Vechten. In his reply to the *Crisis* questionnaire, Van Vechten had warned that unless Black writers began to treat their experience and their culture as something other than sociology and polemic, white writers would "exploit this material until not a drop of vitality remains." And to make certain his point was not missed, he included such commentary directly within his novel:

> But I find that Negroes don't write about these matters [West Indians, Abyssinian Jews, religious Negroes, pagan Negroes, Negro intellectuals, Marcus Garvey, servant-girls, etc.]; they continue to employ all the old clichés and formulas that have been worried to death by Nordic blonds who, after all, never did know anything about the subject from the inside. Well, if you young Negro intellectuals don't get busy, a new crop of Nordics is going to spring up who will take the trouble to become better informed and will exploit this material before the Negro gets around to it.[38]

Clearly, Van Vechten intended his novel to be a "new focusing" and a "point of beginning." But for many, ***Nigger Heaven*** was the exact opposite. The true irony of the novel lay not in the title but in the novel's very existence. Though the rhetoric of the novel said one thing, the form and the substance said something quite different. Thus, for W. E. B. DuBois and others, the two young intellectuals, Mary Love and Byron Kasson—their interests and their problems—were little more than the sociology and the rhetoric Van Vechten counseled others to avoid. In contrast, Lasca Sartoris, the Scarlet Creeper, and the violent, hedonistic life of the cabaret and the street, the true emotional interest of the novel, were essentially sensation. Rather than the promise of a new beginning, ***Nigger Heaven*** was insidiously bizarre, a moral and artistic dead-end.

Recently Nathan Huggins has argued that "What is missing in the novel is a clear moral or intellectual perspective that might engage the reader in the dramatic issues of Negro life."[39] Huggins' comment is important and more subtly critical than earlier opinion which too often was oriented to what others said as opposed to what the novel said. The question, then, is not subject matter per se but the over-all context of perspective within which the content of the novel is cast. Here, in Huggins' opinion, Van Vechten failed, the novel never achieved inner balance, and the reason for this failure was rooted in Van Vechten's fundamental convictions that Blacks were essentially primitives:

> Although perverted, the Creeper and Lasca are permanent, endurable, and perversely heroic because they have accepted without qualification their primitive and predatory natures—civilization, respectability, propriety, manners, and decorum are for others, for "niggers." *Try as he might to illustrate that Negroes were much like other people, Van Vechten's belief in their essential primitivism makes him prove something else. It stands to reason, after all. Had he thought Negroes were like white people, he would not have adopted Harlem the way he did.* His compulsion to be fair to the race while he exploited the exotic and decadent aspects of Harlem caused the novel to flounder.[40] [Italics added]

One can, however, make much the same criticism for all his novels, and for this reason there exists, as seen, a certain ambiguity in Van Vechten's fiction. In rationale for his work (a point of view, however, unlikely to offer a "clear moral or intellectual perspective"):

> It doesn't seem to occur to the crowd that it is possible for an author to believe that life is largely without excuse, that if there is a God he conducts the show aimlessly, if not, indeed, maliciously, that men and women run around automatically seeking escapes from their troubles and outlets for their lusts. The crowd is still more incensed when an author who believes these things refuses to write about them seriously.[41]

However, if ***Nigger Heaven*** is not fully distinguishable on this basis from his other fiction, the deeper failure, I think, is precisely the opposite of what Huggins argues. In his working notebook and journal for ***Nigger Heaven,*** Van Vechten noted:

> I am occasionally asked how it is that I know so much about Negro psychology. The secret of the writing of ***Nigger Heaven,*** if it has a secret, is that in writing about the emotions of Negroes it never occurred to me that they would behave differently than other people. *I wrote about them exactly as if they were white and there is no incident in* **Nigger Heaven** *that might not have happened on Park Ave. or somewhere else in the White Belt of Manhattan.* On the other hand, there is an enormous amount of observation of superficial characteristics, folklore, and casual habits overlaid on the incident of ***Nigger Heaven.***[42] [Italics added]

In 1925 this was an unusually advanced point of view but it is a view that exacts a price. A reading of Jean Toomer's *Cane* reveals the price that is paid. As a consequence, the ultimate irony is that ***Nigger Heaven*** is best understood not as his "Negro novel" but as one of his novels that included people called Negroes.

Not unlike Peter Whiffle, Byron seeks to be a writer. Both fail, but Whiffle's failure is a triumph, for he ultimately achieves the peace of self-understanding and an acceptance of his limitations. Byron, however, remains frustrated yet driven by his inability to resolve deep inner tensions. Unable to overcome feelings of personal inadequacy, he is consumed in self-pity and ultimately seeks escape by abandoning himself to the will and the passion of Lasca Sartoris. This, however, solves nothing and whatever self-confidence he once possessed is completely eroded. Finally, abandoned by Lasca, he seeks revenge on her new lover, Randolph Pettijohn. But even here Byron proves ineffectual. The futility of this last desperate act is fully matched by the ironic futility of the conclusion. Byron's arrest for shooting the body of a corpse.

Throughout the novel, hovering as a symbol of self-denial, is the figure of Dick Sill, who finally decides to pass as white. Although Byron never accepts this ultimate act of self-negation, we are to understand that his and Sill's problems are essentially the same—each is morally and emotionally crippled by the pressures of white racism:

> Try as he might, he could not get away from propaganda. The Negro problem seemed to hover over him and occasionally, like the great, black bird it was, claw at his heart. In his stories this influence invariably made itself felt, and it was, he was sometimes convinced, the very thing that kept him from doing better work. Wheels within wheels. A vicious circle.[43]

And yet, Sill's decision to "go white"—"I don't want to, but they make us"—to which Byron concurs has the ring of an excuse. The problems Byron articulates are real enough, but for him, as presented in the novel, they exist essentially as background. What he does and what he is made to do seem less the result of prejudice than an individual inability to accept risk and involvement. Unable to master his own emotions, he blames others and perceives in them a threat to his own strength and identity as a male. As a consequence, Mary is rejected. Although she pales in contrast to the dramatic sensuality of Lasca, she seems the greater threat: "She didn't love him at all. She just wanted to possess him, to own him, to boss him. He strode away in a renewed fit of fury and this time he did not turn back."[44] But Lasca, for all her wantonness, promises understanding, attention without commitment: "Sooner or later his thoughts obstinately reverted to Lasca. *She* had understanding. She, he felt certain, would give him sympathy. She was a real man's woman."[45] This, however, soon proved an illusion. For Lasca, too, was divided and empty, and men were simply objects to be destroyed.

Given Van Vechten's comments that his presentation of Blacks was anchored in an understanding of whites, it is difficult to understand his frequent allusions throughout the novel to primitivism and the existence of a primordial Black soul. Ostensibly Lasca most fully embodies qualities thought to be primitive. But Lasca, no less than Byron, was a figure common to Van Vechten's fiction. As Nathan Huggins has commented, "Perhaps excepting Peter Whiffle, all of Van Vechten's strong characters have been women, and emasculating women at that."[46] And the overwhelming impression she gives is one of sadness, a person driven by an inner need to wreak revenge on others.

At the same time, what is a paean to primitivism in the words of one is mindless and absurd when voiced by others. Mary, for example, is frequently self-critical and longs to regain her primitive birthright:

> How many times she had watched her friends listening listlessly or with forced affection to alien music, which said little to the Negro soul, by Schubert or Schumann, immediately after losing themselves in a burst of jazz or the glory of an evangelical Spiritual, recognizing, no doubt, in some dim, biological way, the beat of the African rhythm. Savages! Savages at heart! And she had lost or forfeited her birthright, this primitive birthright which was so valuable and important an asset, a birthright that all the civilized races were struggling to get back to—this fact explained the art of a Picasso or a Stravinsky. To be sure, she, too, felt this African beat—and it completely aroused her emotionally—but she was conscious of feeling it. This love of drums, of exciting rhythms, this naive delight in glowing in colour—the colour that exists only in cloudless, tropical climes—this warm, sexual emotion, all these were hers only through a mental understanding.[47]

But when Roy McKain and his friend Rusk Baldwin make similar comments it is made clear that they are fools confusing stereotype with reality and not to be taken seriously. Such commentary, then, is skewed and ultimately confusing. In one context, it serves to establish a moral and intellectual focus, in another it suggests insensitivity and superficiality. As a result, one is not certain that such commentary amounts to much more than the "superficial characteristics, folklore, and casual habits" Van Vechten referred to in his notes.

Van Vechten never fully thought through the problems he raised in *Crisis* magazine. As a consequence, he failed to clarify the disparate, even antithetical, elements he offered both as counsel and inspiration. In a general sense, one can, as seen, make a similar comment about all of his fiction. Perhaps for this reason, Edmund Wilson felt Van Vechten's ***Blind Bow Boy*** to be essentially prosaic: "The result, in spite of all the green orchids and the rose-jade cysts for cosmetics that the author finds in East Nineteenth Street, many come closer to the prosaic reality—or conventional reality of fiction—than Mr. Van Vechten perhaps intended."[48] But this novel and others were not consciously didactic, and the moral focus was not so much stated as created. In contrast, ***Nigger Heaven*** is structured so as to give voice to concerns and considerations that antedate, so to speak, the novel itself and that are rooted in the questions Van Vechten submitted to *Crisis* magazine. As a consequence, the sensual and the primitive are made to carry an intellectual and moral weight that is subverted by the full range of considerations he sought to dramatize. Instead of clarity there is confusion. And for this reason Van Vechten's intentions and his achievement have elicited reactions as sharply diverse as those of Charles S. Johnson and W. E. B. DuBois.

Notes

1. Alain Locke to Carl Van Vechten (5/24/1925), Yale University.
2. Carl Van Vechten to Alain Locke (6/1/1925), Yale University.
3. Alain Locke to Carl Van Vechten (10/6/1925), Yale University.

4. James Weldon Johnson to Carl Van Vechten (2/28/1925), Yale University.
5. Carl Van Vechten to Gertrude Stein (6/30/1925), Yale University.
6. W. E. B. DuBois, *Crisis,* vol. 32-33 (December, 1926), 81-82.
7. Alain Locke to Carl Van Vechten (9/2/1926), Yale University. Also, see the *Nation* (4/18/1928), p. 433.
8. W. E. B. DuBois, *Crisis,* p. 82.
9. Leon Duncan Coleman, "The Contributions of Carl Van Vechten to the Negro Renaissance 1920-1930" (unpublished dissertation, University of Minnesota), p. 165.
10. *Crisis* (2/1926).
11. Carl Van Vechten to Edna Kenton (postmark 8/28/1924), Yale University.
12. Carl Van Vechten, Columbia University Oral History, p. 20 of typescript.
13. Walter White and Carl Van Vechten were such close friends that White named his son Carl (1927) in honor of Van Vechten. And Van Vechten and James Weldon Johnson virtually shared one another's intellectual and social life. Upon Johnson's death in 1938, Van Vechten became his literary executor and later established the James Weldon Johnson Memorial Collection of Negro Arts and Letters at Yale University.
14. Langston Hughes, *The Big Sea* (New York: Hill and Wang, 1968), p. 272.
15. Zora Neale Hurston, *Dust Tracks On A Road* (New York: Arno Press and the New York Times, 1969), p. 251.
16. Carl Van Vechten, Columbia University Oral History (Columbia University, 1969), pp. 336-349 (May 18, 1960 and May 25, 1960).
17. Carl Van Vechten, *Red* (New York: Alfred A. Knopf, 1925), pp. 25-26.
18. *Ibid.,* xv.
19. Carl Van Vechten, *Vanity Fair,* "The Black Blues," 24 (8/1925), 57.
20. See "All Gods Chillun Got Songs," *Theatre Magazine,* 42 (8/1925), 24, 63. and "Negro Blues Singers," *Vanity Fair,* 26 (3/1926), 67, 106, 108.
21. Carl Van Vechten, *Vanity Fair,* 25 (10/1925), 93.
22. In "The Negro Theatre," 2/3/1919 (from his collection of essays *In the Garret,* New York: Alfred Knopf, 1920, pp. 315-19), Van Vechten had voiced a similar point of view. After reviewing the accomplishments of J. Leabrie Hill, who had put on a play of his own, "My Friend From Kentucky," Van Vechten voiced a desire to found "a real Negro theatre, in which Negroes should act in real Negro plays."
23. Carl Van Vechten, *Vanity Fair,* "The Black Blues," 24 (8/1925), 57. Also see "The Folksongs of the American Negro: The Importance of the Negro Spirituals in the Music of America," *Vanity Fair,* 24 (7/1925), pp. 52 and 92; and "Negro Blues Singers," *Vanity Fair,* 26 (34/1926), pp. 67, 106 and 108.
24. Carl Van Vechten, *Crisis,* 31 (3/1926), p. 219.
25. Bruce Kellner, *Carl Van Vechten and the Irreverent Decades* (Norman: University of Oklahoma Press, 1968), p. 166.
26. Carl Van Vechten to Mabel Dodge Luhan (10/8/1924), Yale University.
27.

Peter Whiffle	Peter Whiffle
Blind Bow-Boy	Harold Prewett
The Tatooed Countess	Gareth Johns
Firecrackers	Gunnar O'Grady
Nigger Heaven	Byron Kasson
Spider Boy	Ambrose Deacon
Parties	David Westlake

28. Carl Van Vechten, *Blind Bow-Boy* (New York: Alfred Knopf, 1923), pp. 114-115.
29. *Ibid.,* p. 90.
30. Carl Van Vechten, *Peter Whiffle* (New York: Alfred Knopf, 1922), p. 8.
31. *Ibid.,* p. 145.
32. *Ibid.,* pp. 230-31.
33. *Ibid.,* p. 231.
34. *Ibid.,* p. 186.
35. Mabel Dodge Luhan, *Movers and Shakers,* vol. 3 of *Intimate Memoirs* (New York: Harcourt, Brace and Co., 1936), p. 16.
36. Charles S. Johnson to Carl Van Vechten (9/12/1926), Yale University.
37. Alain Locke to Carl Van Vechten (8/17/1926), Berg Collection, New York Public Library.
38. Carl Van Vechten, *Nigger Heaven* (New York: Harper Colophon Books, 1971), p. 223. Byron Kasson, a young Black intellectual seeking to be a writer, was the object of this advice, for while he floundered for something to say, Roy McBain (white and in Harlem for an evening) dashed off a story that was immediately accepted for publication. Although Roy's story contrasts with Byron's failure, Van Vechten has made it clear that he had only the most superficial knowledge of what he wrote. Obviously this made little difference to publisher or public. Fiction no less than theater was a fruitful area for white enterprise and exploitation.
39. Nathan Huggins, *Harlem Renaissance* (New York and London: Oxford University Press, 1971), p. 107.
40. *Ibid.,* pp. 111-112.
41. Carl Van Vechten, *Firecrackers* (New York: Alfred Knopf, 1925), pp. 164-165.
42. Carl Van Vechten, "Notes for *Nigger Heaven,*" Yale University, p. 2.
43. Van Vechten, *Nigger Heaven,* pp. 175-76.
44. *Ibid.,* p. 206.
45. *Ibid.,* p. 201.
46. Huggins, p. 109.
47. Van Vechten, *Nigger Heaven,* pp. 89-90.

48. Edmund Wilson, "Late Violets From the Nineties," *The Shores of Light: A Literary Chronicle of the Twenties and Thirties* (New York: Random House, 1961), p. 68.

BRUCE KELLNER (ESSAY DATE 1989)

SOURCE: Kellner, Bruce. "Carl Van Vechten's Black Renaissance." In *The Harlem Renaissance: Revaluations,* edited by Amritjit Singh, William S. Shiver, and Stanley Brodwin, pp. 23-33. New York: Garland Publishing, 1989.

In the following essay, Kellner claims that of the many whites who supported and were patrons to Black artists during the Harlem Renaissance, Van Vechten had a more positive influence than most—the uneasy reputation of Nigger Heaven *notwithstanding.*

Most of the readers—black as well as white—who made Carl Van Vechten's ***Nigger Heaven*** a best-selling novel in 1926 were unaware that his involvement with the work of Afro-Americans had begun before the turn of the century. Although much of his own roaring during the twenties occurred in Harlem cabarets, he had been writing essays, reviewing plays and books, evaluating music, producing program notes and dust jacket blurbs about black artists and for black artists for over a decade, and delighting in the performances of black entertainers for over thirty years. Like the blessings of other white philanthropists, Van Vechten's were undeniably mixed. The black artist both thrived and suffered, torn between well-meaning encouragement from the white race to preserve his racial identity (usually described, though not by Van Vechten, as "primitivism") and a misguided encouragement from his own race to emulate the white one. Products designed to straighten hair and lighten skin and the regular practice of black comedians wearing blackface makeup are extreme examples at opposite ends of this appalling scale. Nevertheless, the Harlem Renaissance would not have progressed so easily beyond Harlem without the intervention and support of white patronage. That it manifested itself in action which in retrospect seems patronizing is inevitable, but to deny its positive aspects is intellectually indefensible. White patronage was merely an unavoidable element in getting from the past to the present, and the roles played by several figures made a strong supporting cast. Some were bad actors; Carl Van Vechten was a better one.

The James Weldon Johnson Memorial Collection of Negro Arts and Letters at Yale University—which Carl Van Vechten founded—gives credence to this. He began it on the basis of his own vast collection of black literature and memorabilia, continued to contribute to it both materially and financially for the rest of his life, and then specified in his will that any money ever realized from reprints of his own books and thousands of photographs be donated to the Johnson endowment fund. With the present interest in black studies, students and scholars will find themselves increasingly grateful for this legacy. It is difficult to imagine books about the Harlem Renaissance or several recent black biographies (published or about to be) without it. Moreover, Van Vechten's own writings about black arts and letters are of considerable value as well.

Still, from the vantage point of the eighties, it is difficult to embrace without reservation the naiveté and paternalism of the 1920s—Van Vechten's included—as faultless. I don't presume to undermine the zeal for an independent black consciousness, but Carl Van Vechten's assistance during the painful journey most black artists in America have had to make merits our attention. During his life, particularly at the time of their composition, most of his writings—always excepting ***Nigger Heaven***—probably had a modest impact: those who most needed to be informed of such riches awaiting discovery would not have been readily exposed to the sources in which his various papers appeared. When I gathered them together in **"Keep A-Inchin' Along"** (Greenwood, 1979) to introduce the present generation of readers to Van Vechten's legacy to the advancement of Afro-American literature, my greatest surprise came in discovering how much of his time and energy he had devoted to the subject.

His own involvement must have begun when he was about ten years old and heard Sissieretta Jones, "Black Patti" as she was called after the white opera singer Adelina Patti, when her opulent musical productions toured the country. By the turn of the century, he had encountered many other black entertainers, including Bert Williams, who left him "trembling between hysterical laughter and sudden tears," and whose ability to command simultaneously such contrary emotions explained the unique genius in black arts and letters, he often contended later.

Although Carl Van Vechten's initial exposure came through these only available sources—black performers often catering to the demands of white audiences—his private associations were deeply rooted. A black washerwoman and a black yardman were the first adults he knew outside his immediate family, and he was reared to address them as "Mrs. Sercy" and "Mr. Oliphant," with the same respect due any other adult. Such civility hardly strikes us as unusual today, but I am speaking here of the 1880s. His parents addressed these black employees formally as well. By the time Van Vechten left home in Iowa for college, he was already inoculated against racial prejudice to the extent it was possible in the turn-of-the-century climate in America. For three of his four years at the University of Chicago, he went with his fraternity's black housekeeper to the Quinn Chapel, where he played the piano for services and accompanied the singing. (The songs, of course, were more often Baptist hymns than the spirituals Van Vechten strove to popularize in later years.) From his journal entries and from his essays of the period, he seems to have adored that housekeeper, just as he had already preferred the company of older people during his childhood, and he saw these new acquaintances as "an intensely uncultured and uneducated race but just as intensely good hearted, humorous, . . . and even clever." They were "colored members of the human family," he concluded.[1] In the 1980s such observations may suggest condescension, but in a twenty-year-old in 1900 they do not, although the ignorance of innocence is invariably difficult to approximate once we have escaped it. Of greater significance—given Carl Van Vechten's extraordinary contributions to an aesthetic race consciousness—is the period of time during which his devotion developed. It refutes his critics' charges, particularly during the 1920s at the height of the notoriety of ***Nigger Heaven,*** that his interest in the race was necessarily superficial because it was so new.

Van Vechten's first professional writing devoted exclusively to the subject appeared long before the sudden craze that began with the all-black musical comedy called *Shuffle Along,* bringing in the Jazz Age. In 1913, as drama critic for the *New York Press,* he had written enthusiastically about *My Friend from Kentucky,* part of *The Darktown Follies,* at Harlem's Lafayette Theatre. That article, and a review the following season of *Granny Maumee,* a play by white writer Ridgely Torrence, with black characters performed by white actors, and its revival with black actors three years later, motivated Van Vechten's extended essay on **"The Negro Theatre,"** and it is worth noting that in 1914 he had urged the formation of a Negro theater organization, with black actors and black playwrights. Even earlier, working as a cub reporter for the *Chicago American* in 1904, he wrote about black entertainers whenever he got the chance. In the 1920s, five years after **"The Negro Theatre"** was first published,

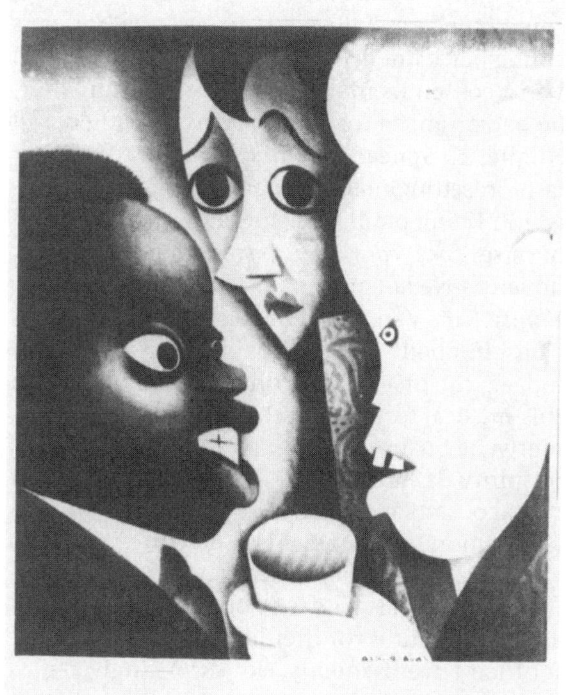

Caricature drawing, by Miguel Covarrubias, from frontpiece of *Keep a-Inchin' Along,* by Carl Van Vechten.

Van Vechten told black writer Eric Walrond he thought the essay was out of date, but Walrond contended that its ideas and points of view would still be pertinent a decade later, and he avowed that, had he not known Van Vechten, he would have thought the essay written by a black because of its racial bias.[2]

During the first half of the decade "when Harlem was in vogue,"[3] Carl Van Vechten became a popular novelist in several cheerful fictions about "the splendid drunken twenties" in New York, as he liked to call the period.[4] By the time ***Nigger Heaven*** appeared in 1926, he had become as well a self-proclaimed, unpaid press agent for Harlem's black intelligentsia, and certainly for its cabarets. He had become, he later said, "violently interested in Negroes, . . . almost an addiction."[5] His first black literary acquaintance was Walter White, whom he met through their mutual publisher Alfred A. Knopf. When White introduced Van Vechten to James Weldon Johnson, that violent interest met its catalyst. They were firm believers in the idealistic theory of the "talented tenth" and became each other's entree to each other's race, each other's literary executor, each other's best friend. Also through Walter White, Van Vechten came to know Langston Hughes and Countee Cullen, and he met Wallace Thurman and Zora

Neale Hurston—the latter responsible for having coined the term "niggerati" to describe Harlem's young black intellectuals and for having dubbed Van Vechten its first "Negrotarian." Soon after, he had arranged for some poems by Cullen and Hughes to appear in *Vanity Fair,* that popular fashion-setting magazine, and through his instigation Knopf published Hughes's first collection of verse, *The Weary Blues,* as well as books by black novelists Nella Larsen and Rudolph Fisher. For *Vanity Fair,* Van Vechten wrote several articles himself: about the spirituals; about the blues, indeed, the first serious consideration ever given this musical form; about black theater. Concurrently, he financed in large part the first programs of spirituals sung by Paul Robeson and another recital of similar materials by Taylor Gordon and J. Rosamond Johnson. Also, he contributed reviews to a number of publications, both black and white, for at least a dozen books by black writers and wrote blurbs for their dust jackets and copy for their advertisements. Not surprisingly, a gossip column in 1925 declared that he was getting a heavy tan, and, as he only appeared in public after dark, he had to be acquiring it in a taxi, bound for the nightclubs in Harlem.

In all candor, he devoted an inordinate amount of time to shabby pursuits—getting drunk in speakeasies, collecting Harlem sycophants about him, and having dates with steamy sepia courtesans or assignations with handsome black call boys—that were common knowledge. But his intellectual admiration was genuine. His response to black music and writing was firmly grounded in nearly a quarter of a century of serious, professional musical, and literary criticism. Moreover, his desire to share his discoveries resulted in a cultural exchange unique at the time. In their glamorous apartment in Manhattan, Carl Van Vechten and his wife, the actress Fania Marinoff, entertained frequently and lavishly, and always with fully integrated guest lists. The parties were eventually reported as a matter of course in some of the black newspapers of the city, and Walter White called their address "the midtown office of the NAACP."[6]

And then he wrote ***Nigger Heaven.*** In one of his *Vanity Fair* essays, just at that time, he discussed the black artist's present reluctance to develop his unique racial qualities and the danger of white artists appropriating them for their own work. A month later, in his contribution to a symposium called **"The Negro in Art: How Shall He Be Portrayed?"**—actually he had ghost-written the questions for this series of articles in *The Crisis* for Jessie Fauset—Carl Van Vechten posed a counter-question: "Are Negro writers going to write about this exotic material while it is fresh or will they continue to make a free gift of it to white authors who will exploit it until not a drop of vitality remains?"[7] Given the sensational aspects of ***Nigger Heaven*** and the controversy they aroused, the disturbing irony is either apt or cruel, and it anticipates the accusations of many who felt that ***Nigger Heaven*** encouraged the worst rather than the best efforts among young black writers who followed. Novels by Claude McKay, Wallace Thurman, and Rudolph Fisher dealt far more directly with Harlem's seamy side, for example, popularizing not an articulate and educated "talented tenth," but an "untalented ninetieth." The writers were themselves black, young, and virtually unknown both north and south of 125th Street; Carl Van Vechten's long reputation as a dandy, a dilettante, and as a writer of resolutely frivolous novels did not help. For many readers of ***Nigger Heaven,*** the black slang word for a white person—"fay" or "ofay," pig-latin for "foe"—renewed its double meaning. For blacks familiar only with the book's title, that reaction is not surprising, but Harlem knew him as a regular customer in the cabarets, jingling his bracelets when he tipped up his sterling silver hip flask; as a white judge at the black transvestite balls at the Rockland Palace Casino; as a guest in private homes and apartments; and, finally, as Nora Holt's escort and A'Lelia Walker's boon companion. In Rudolph Fisher's novel *The Walls of Jericho,* a black character at a Harlem party says to a white one obviously patterned after Van Vechten, "'You're the only fay I know that draws the color line on other fays.' 'It's natural,'" the white character replies fatuously. "'Downtown I'm only passing. These,' he waved grandiloquently, 'are my people.'"[8] It is not difficult to see here a Van Vechten perilously close to Ishmael Reed's viciously funny Hinckle Von Vampton in his novel *Mumbo Jumbo,* exaggerated perhaps, but inevitable.

Most of the negative criticism of ***Nigger Heaven*** came from reviewers who contended that Van Vechten had made use of only the "primitive" aspects of Harlem life. A surprising number of present-day critics also claim this, perhaps without having read the book themselves. By actual page count, nearly two-thirds of ***Nigger Heaven*** is given over to sociological and aesthetic discussions among black intellectuals and to a bloodless love affair between two dreary characters who control the story line and drag us through their passionless agonies. The other third—the lurid third—certainly does occur in cabarets and between the sheets. Any reader familiar with Van Vechten's earlier novels—all four of them as manicured as a Congreve comedy—would have had good reason to expect less of some pathetic little romance than of a world populated by numbers racketeers and elegant demimondaines and strutting pimps and plenty of sheiks and flappers doing the Charleston. Certainly its sensational elements helped ***Nigger Heaven*** to sell, but the same kind of elements had helped its predecessors to sell, too. ***Nigger Heaven*** was either admired or dismissed, but for the wrong reasons, for sensational is not necessarily primitive, and vice versa. "Primitivism"—a word Van Vechten never used—perhaps should not even be associated with any particular race or even any particular culture, Mark Helbling has suggested.[9] Rather, primitivism is an aesthetic point of view that concerns itself essentially with creativity. Picasso, for example, was not interested in Africans or in African "soul," but in their artifacts that could stimulate his own imagination. Van Vechten was no Picasso. His talents—and they were considerable—are simply not very well illustrated in ***Nigger Heaven.***

Photo of Cab Calloway, taken by Carl Van Vechten.

None of Van Vechten's friends seem to have misunderstood the book, and he lost no friends because of it—of either color. They were aware of his genuine concern for the race but also aware of his flamboyant behavior, and they were familiar with both sides of the paradoxical coin in his writing. His acute critical perception backed by a stubborn adherence to a highly mannered style surely deterred his ever being an entirely successful novelist. He was, on the one hand, too analytical and discursive and, on the other, too arch and ornate. For many readers not personally involved with either Van Vechten's personality or his writing, ***Nigger Heaven*** has some serious artistic troubles not remotely connected with the Harlem Renaissance. Expressions in black dialect simply jar the reader's ear as well as eye when they are followed or preceded by obsolete or fancy vocabulary lacquered into precious locutions. In another novel and quite another context, Van Vechten causes one of his characters to reflect: "A book . . . should have the swiftness of melodrama, the lightness of a farce, to be a real contribution to thought. . . . How could anything serious be hidden more successfully than in a book which pretended to be light and gay?"[10] In ***Nigger Heaven*** the minor characters might have achieved this, serving up all aspects of Harlem, for the variety is considerable and probably it does offer a better cross-section of Harlem life than any other novel of the period. But the "nice" characters predominate, as they do in no other Van Vechten novel (his nice characters are almost invariably boring), and the attempt at "a real contribution to thought" gets in the way of "real contribution to thought." Van Vechten considers it important to convey observations and reflections about Harlem's intelligentsia, but I get suspicious when a character stands stage-center and recites a canned speech. We learn more from somebody who shows us rather than tells us. The earlier novels, contrarily, were not deliberately didactic, and their moral or intellectual perspective is sufficiently veiled by their cheerful carnality and outrageous good humor. When somebody asks me, "What should I read by Carl Van Vechten?" ***Nigger Heaven*** is never the book I recommend. I don't think it is a very good novel, even though it created a large white readership for black writers and even though it popularized Harlem and brought plenty of business into the cabarets north of 125th Street. Whether those two influences are close enough in value to mention in the same sentence is open to question. Whatever ***Nigger Heaven***'s limitations, the novel strengthened Van Vechten's ties with the race and increased his loyalty. Through the rest of his long career he devoted his energies to a wider recognition of black achievements, primarily through his photography, recording nearly every celebrated Afro-American, not to add scraps to his already rich supply, but to enhance the Johnson Collection at Yale, as well as several other collections he established around the country. If the endeavor suggested sycophancy to some suspicious few who refused to be photographed, it was nevertheless as sincere as his "violent interest" was unflagging. Van Vechten easily admitted he was star-struck all his life, from the time he first knew Bert Williams in 1906, until the last summer of his own eighty-four years in 1964 when he wrote to me: "I am in my usual state of gaping enthusiasm. (Will it never end? Probably NOT.) I heard Andre Watts at the [Lewisohn] Stadium and sans doute he is the greatest living pianist. He has everything, including good taste and he will end in glory, as he has begun."[11] Bert Williams died before Van Vechten started making photographs, and he died himself before he could get to Andre Watts, but hundreds of other subjects—white as well as black—came in between. The list of black subjects is staggering, not only in quantity but in quality, especially the number of people he photographed before their talents were generally recognized, when he sensed that same "glory" he had predicted for Andre Watts: Chester Himes at 30; Shirley Verrett at 24; Leontyne Price at 23; Lena Horne at 21; and James Baldwin, LeRoi Jones, Alvin Ailey, Diahann Carroll, Harry Belafonte, and Arthur Mitchell over thirty years ago.

With the passing of time, Carl Van Vechten's significance has been down-played, on occasion, it may be, by design, and at best he has been given grudging acknowledgment. All his life Van Vechten championed the avant-garde. He wrote seriously about scores of people and movements that came into subsequent prominence, and he had the distinction of being the first person with sufficient clout to draw attention to Afro-American arts and letters at the time. By making racial integration fashionable in an attempt to introduce his own race to the pleasures he had discovered in another, he hoped to extend the possibilities implicit in that theory of the "talented tenth." Hindsight tells us that the theory was too firmly grounded in idealism ever to survive the dream. The advocates of art as well as its practitioners do not, alas, populate the "untalented ninetieth" in either race.

Nevertheless, James Weldon Johnson once wrote to Carl Van Vechten, "Has anyone ever written it down—in black and white—that you have been one of the most vital forces in bringing about the artistic emergence of the Negro in America? Well, I am glad to bear witness to the fact."[12] And George S. Schuyler, that Menckenesque editor of the *Pittsburgh Courier* who was unerringly suspicious but frequently given to overstatement, declared that "Carl Van Vechten has done more than any single person in this country to create the atmosphere of acceptance of the Negro."[13]

None of this addresses itself to the subtle distinction between "patronage" and "patronizing" to which I referred in my opening paragraph. It is doubtless easy for the one to become the other, but it may be almost as easy for the one to seem to become the other—blanket judgments are always dangerous—because of black dismay over the circumstances that led to white patronage in the first place.

Notes

1. Carl Van Vechten Collection, Manuscript and Archives Division, New York Public Library, quoted with permission of Donald Gallup, Literary Trustee to the Van Vechten Estate; hereafter referred to as CV-V.NYPL.
2. Letter to Van Vechten, circa 1925, CVV.NYPL.
3. Langston Hughes, "When Harlem Was in Vogue," *Town and Country,* 95, 49 (July 1940), 64-66.
4. Carl Van Vechten, *Fragments from an Unwritten Autobiography* (New Haven: Yale University Library, 1955), p. 3.
5. Carl Van Vechten, "A Rudimentary Narration," Columbia Oral History, Columbia University, New York City, 1963; hereafter referred to as CVV.Col.
6. CVV.Col.
7. Carl Van Vechten, "The Negro in Art: How Shall He Be Portrayed?" *Crisis,* 31 (March 1926), 129.
8. Rudolph Fisher, *The Walls of Jericho* (New York: Alfred A. Knopf, 1928), p. 117.
9. Mark Helbling, "Carl Van Vechten and the Harlem Renaissance," *Negro American Literature Forum,* 10 (July 1976), 46.
10. Carl Van Vechten, *The Blind Bow-Boy* (New York: Alfred A. Knopf, 1923), p. 163.
11. Carl Van Vechten to Bruce Kellner, 10 August 1964.
12. Quoted in Donald Gallup, *80 Writers Whose Books and Letters Have Been Given over the Past Twenty Years to the Yale University Library by Carl Van Vechten, Compiled in Honor of His 80th Birthday, 17 June 1960* (New Haven: Yale University Library, 1960), p. [12].
13. George S. Schuyler, quoted in Edward Lueders, *Carl Van Vechten* (New York: Twayne Publishers, 1965), p. 95.

TITLE COMMENTARY

Nigger Heaven

JAMES WELDON JOHNSON (ESSAY DATE 1926)

SOURCE: Johnson, James Weldon. "Romance and Tragedy in Harlem." *Opportunity* 46 (October 1926): 316-17, 330.

In the following review of Nigger Heaven, *Johnson considers it a modern novel in that it does not rely on the earlier narrative formulas for narratives about Blacks and that is presents a realistic account of social problems without moralizing or propagandizing.*

From its intriguing prologue to its tragic end, here is an absorbing story. Whether you like it or dislike it you will read it through, every chapter, every page. Mr. Van Vechten is the first white novelist of note to undertake a portrayal of modern American Negro life under metropolitan conditions. Mr. Van Vechten is also the only white novelist I can now think of who has not viewed the Negro as a type, who has not treated the race as a unit, either good or bad. In ***Nigger Heaven*** the author has chosen as his scene Harlem, where Negro life is at its highest point of urbanity and sophistication, and there the entire action of the story is played out. The economy of stage Mr. Van Vechten imposes for himself enables him to gain in dramatic intensity but it does not limit him in the scope of the action. The story comprehends nearly every phase of life in the Negro metropolis. It draws on the components of that life from the dregs to the froth.

It was inevitable that the colorful life of Harlem would sooner or later claim the pen of Carl Van Vechten. He has taken the material it offered him and achieved the most revealing, significant and powerful novel based exclusively on Negro life yet written. A Negro reviewer might pardonably express the wish that a colored novelist had been the first to take this material and write a book of equal significance and power. Mr. Van Vechten is a modernist. In literature he is the child of his age. In ***Nigger Heaven*** he has written a modern novel in every sense. He has written about the most modern aspects of Negro life, and he has done it in the most modern manner; for he has completely discarded and scrapped the old formula and machinery for a Negro novel. He has no need of a *deus ex machina* from the white world either to involve or evolve the plot. There is, of course, the pressure of the white world, but it is external. The white characters are less than incidental. The story works itself out through the clashes and reactions of Negro character upon Negro character. Its factors are the loves, the hates, the envies, the ambitions, the pride, the shamelessness, the intelligence, the ignorance, the goodness, the wickedness of Negro characters. In this the author pays colored people the rare tribute of writing about them as people rather than as puppets. This representation of Negro characters in a novel as happy or unhappy, successful or unsuccessful, great or mean, not because of the fortuitous attitudes of white characters in the book but because of the way in which they themselves meet and master their environment—a task imposed upon every group—is new, and in close accord with the present psychology of the intelligent element of the race. The only other full length novel following this scheme that I can recall at this moment is Jessie Fauset's *There Is Confusion.* It is a scheme for the interpretation of Negro life in America that opens up a new world for colored writers.

There are those who will prejudge the book unfavorably on account of the title. This was the attitude taken by many toward Sheldon's *The Nigger,* perhaps, the finest and fairest play on the race question that has yet been successfully produced in New York. This attitude is natural, but it is probable that the reaction against the title of the novel will not be so strong as it was against the title of the play which was produced sixteen years ago. Indeed, one gauge of the Negro's rise and development may be found in the degrees in which a race epithet loses its power to sting and hurt him. The title of Sheldon's play was purely ironic, and the title of ***Nigger Heaven*** is taken from the ironic use of the phrase made by the characters in the book. But whatever may be the attitudes and opinions on this point, the book and not the title is the thing. In the book Mr. Van Vechten does not stoop to burlesque or caricature. There are characters and incidents in the book that many will regard as worse than unpleasant, but always the author handles them with sincerity and fidelity. Anatoles and Rubys and Lascas and number kings and cabarets and an underworld there are as well as there are Mary Loves and Byron Kassons and Olive Hamiltons and Howard Allisons and Dr. Lancasters and Underwoods and Sumners and young intellectuals. There are, too, Dick Sills and Buda Greens, living on both sides of the line, and then passing over. It is all life. It is all reality. And Mr. Van Vechten has taken these various manifestations of life and, as a true artist, depicted them as he sees them rather than as he might wish them to be. But the author again as a true artist, deftly maintains the symmetry and proportions of his work. The scenes of gay life, of night life, the glimpses of the underworld, with all their tinsel, their licentiousness, their depravity serve actually to set off in sharper relief the decent, cultured, intellectual life of Negro Harlem. But all these phases of life, good and bad, are merely the background for the story, and the story is the love life of Byron Kasson and Mary Love.

Mary is a beautiful, golden-brown girl who works as an assistant librarian in one of the New York public libraries. She is intelligent, cultured and refined. She is sweet, pure and placid until she meets Byron; she remains sweet and pure, but her placidity is shattered, the emotions which she sometimes feared she did not possess are stirred to the depths. Byron, bronze-colored, handsome, proud, impetuous and headstrong has just been graduated from the University of Pennsylvania. At college he had made a literary reputation in the university periodicals; his professors had encouraged him; so he comes to Harlem to make writing his profession and to conquer New York. He and Mary first meet at a gay week-end house party given by a wealthy woman of the smart set at her country home on Long Island—a house party at which Mary is sadly out of place. They meet again at a dinner given by the Sumners, one of the well-to-do, cultured colored families of Harlem. Byron calls to see Mary at her home, and the beginnings of love burst into a flame. The author makes an idyl of the awakening of love in Mary's heart. Byron starts out buoyant and sanguine. He receives a small monthly allowance from his father, but he must work to supplement that sum while he makes his way as a writer. He smarts under the rebuffs he meets with in trying to find work he considers in keeping with his training. He grows bitter and cynical under failure. He finally takes a job as an elevator boy, but this job he fails to hold. In the meantime he is devoting such time as the distractions of New York leave him to irresolute efforts at his writing. But there is something wrong with his stories, he sends them out and they regularly come back. Byron begins to slip. Mary tries to give him the benefit of her intelligent opinion and her knowledge of literature but his pride will not let her. His pride also keeps him from going for assistance to the Sumners and other influential friends to whom his father had given him letters; he does not want to be "patronized" by them. Byron cannot adapt himself, he cannot bend the bars of his environment to accommodate his own needs and desires. He has already failed, but he is not yet lost. Mary's love is what he needs to keep him steady, but the very fullness of her love raises for him a wall which his rebellious nature will not permit him to get over or through. Mary's love has developed in a twofold manner, passionately and maternally; she jealously wants her handsome young lover wholly for herself, and she wants to watch over him and guide and protect him as she would a child, which in many respects he is. Byron is irritated by her jealousy and her attitude of guardianship he resents. He realizes that he is a failure compared to the young intellectuals and professional men of Mary's acquaintance and he feels that she, too, is pitying him, is patronizing him; and he will not be patronized. He begins to think of the fascinating, exotic Lasca Sartoris, whom he had met and danced with at a big charity ball. Her wit and beauty had amazed him and the talk about her purple past had stirred his imagination. He compares the tender, solicitous Mary with this superb woman, Lasca, who tramples all conventions under her shapely feet, who recognizes no limitations, who takes what she wants. Why couldn't he know intimately such a woman? That would be life—that would be inspiration.

One day Byron receives a letter from Russett Durwood, the editor of a great magazine, asking him to call regarding a story he had sent in. It is the story that carries all of Byron's hopes, his great story. He forgets all about Lasca. He rushes as fast as his feet can carry him to Mary. It is Mary to whom he wants to break the good news. He is again the buoyant, sanguine and the lovable Byron. He is sure of success now, he has regained his self-confidence and self-respect, Mary's love and solicitude are now grateful to him. The outcome of the interview is a lecture from the great editor on the defects of the story. He has sent for Byron because he is interested in Negro literature and Negro writers. He has seen from parts of Byron's story that he has talent and ability and can write. But "why in hell" doesn't he write about something he knows about? Negro life—Harlem—West Indians, Abyssinian Jews, religious Negroes, pagan Negroes, Negro intellectuals all living together in the same community. Why continue to employ the old clichés that have been worked to death by Nordics? Why not use this fresh material before a new crop of Nordics spring up and exploit it before Negro writers get around to it? Byron is stricken dumb, he can make no answer. He drags himself out of the building and makes his way to Central Park. Through whirling emotions of disappointment and heartbreak there surges a flame of fury. He will go back to the editor and tell him what he thinks of him; he will not stand to be treated as a Nigger. But he does not; instead, he sinks upon a park bench discouraged, disheartened, beaten. He hears a woman's voice calling him, he raises his head to see Lasca beckoning him from her luxurious limousine, Lasca, who takes what she wants. She takes Byron. She showers him with all the fragrance, the beauty, the wild ecstacies, the cruel-sweets of love that her perfect body and her lawless soul know. Byron, now, has not only failed, he is lost. And yet his is a fate before which self-righteousness should take no occasion to preen itself. One must, indeed, be much of a prig not to make some allowances for youth caught in the circle of the lure of Lasca, the courtesan supreme. Lasca keeps Byron for a period, then, as she had done others before, she throws him out, banishes him wholly, and takes Randolph Petijohn, the number king. From here on Byron's journey downward is steep and fast. His moral disintegration is complete. He pleads, he raves, he broods. He becomes obsessed with the desire for revenge; and he procures a revolver and haunts the cabarets, lying in wait for the two objects of his hatred. One night in the Black Venus, drunk to the point of irresponsibility, he sees the number king enter. While Byron is trying to bring together his dissolved will for the accomplishment of his purpose a shot rings out and Petijohn falls dead. The shot had been fired by Anatole, the Scarlet Creeper, who also had a grudge against the number king. Byron, playing his futile role in the drama out to the end, springs up, stands over the prostrate form and is emptying his revolver into the dead body when the law lays its hands upon him. An absorbing, a tragic, a disquieting story.

Byron is at many points a symbol of the tragic struggle of the race thrown as it is in an unsympathetic milieu and surrounded by fateful barriers. But Byron's story is especially true as an individual story. It is a true story—and an old story. It is the story of many a gifted and ambitious young colored man who has come up to New York as the field for success, and has been sucked in and down by the gay life and underworld of the great city. It is the story of talent and brilliancy without stamina and patience. The theme has been used before. Paul Dunbar used it in a measure in *The Sport of the Gods,* and I myself skirted it in a now forgotten novel. But never before has it been so well and fully used.

The book is written with Mr. Van Vechten's innate light touch and brilliancy, but there is a difference; Van Vechten, the satirist, becomes in ***Nigger Heaven*** Van Vechten, the realist. In every line of the book he shows that he is serious. But however serious Van Vechten may be, he cannot be heavy. He does not moralize, he does not overemphasize, there are no mock heroics, there are no martyrdoms. And, yet—Mr. Van Vechten would doubtless count this a defect—the book is packed full of propaganda. Every phase of the race question, from Jim Crow discriminations to miscegenation, is frankly discussed. Here the author's inside knowledge and insight are at times astonishing. But it is not the author speaking, he makes his characters do the talking, and makes each one talk in keeping with his character. If the book has a thesis it is: Negroes are people; they have the same emotions, the same passions, the same shortcomings, the same aspirations, the same graduations of social strata as other people. It will be a revelation, perhaps, a shock to those familiar only with the Negro characters of Thomas Nelson Page, Thomas Dixon and Octavius Cohen. It is the best book Mr. Van Vechten has done, and that, is saying a good deal when we remember ***Peter Whiffle.***

Nigger Heaven is a book which is bound to be widely read and one which is bound to arouse much diverse discussion. This reviewer would suggest reading the book before discussing it.

MARGO V. PERKINS (ESSAY DATE 1998)

SOURCE: Perkins, Margo V. "The Achievement and Failure of *Nigger Heaven*: Carl Van Vechten and the Harlem Renaissance." *CLA Journal* XLII, no. 1 (September 1998): 1-23.

In the following essay, Perkins offers a detailed analysis of Nigger Heaven *and its impact within the Harlem Renaissance movement.*

When Carl Van Vechten's ***Nigger Heaven*** was first published in 1926 by Alfred Knopf, the title alone created an uproar. Many African Americans were incensed, while others, whites included, were intrigued. It was a title calculated both to appeal to and to satirize the racist sensibilities of the era. Spoken by African Americans, "Nigger Heaven" was an insider's affectionate reference to Harlem as a kind of cultural Mecca or refuge in the context of a culture still virulently racist. Harlem of the 1920s was a space that African Americans could claim (at least culturally) as their own. Spoken by whites, however, "Nigger Heaven" could signify a curious place inhabited and overrun by the darker, exotic other. At the very least, Van Vechten could count on the book being noticed by both prospective audiences. The novel's first reference to the title is offered by a

Negro character,[1] Ruby Silver. In referring to the fun had by Negro Harlemites partying on the night club/cabaret circuit, Ruby confides in her companion, Anatole Longfellow (alias the Scarlet Creeper), that she "just nacherly think[s]" of Harlem as "Nigger Heaven." Much later in the novel, a more elaborate reference to the title is offered by one of the two central characters, Byron Kasson, whose lamentory tone significantly contrasts with Ruby's celebratory one. Expounding on the metaphor of New York as a theater, he cries:

> Nigger Heaven! That's what Harlem is. We sit in our places in the gallery of this New York theatre and watch the white world sitting down below in the good seats in the orchestra. Occasionally they turn their faces up towards us, their hard, cruel faces, to laugh or sneer, but they never beckon. It never seems to occur to them that Nigger Heaven is crowded, that there isn't another seat, that something has to be done. It doesn't seem to occur to them either . . . that we sit above them, that we can drop things down on them and crush them, that we can swoop down from this Nigger Heaven and take their seats. . . . Harlem! The Mecca of the New Negro! My God!
>
> (149)[2]

Byron's exposition makes it clear that Van Vechten intends the title to be ironic. On one hand Harlem is a place where black culture and social opportunities flourish. But on the other, it is a locale whose boundaries (both literal and figurative) are rigidly circumscribed by the interests and power of the dominant culture. Van Vechten reminds us that Harlem exists in part because of de facto segregation (the whites in the orchestra who do not beckon) and racist discrimination. The irony of "Nigger Heaven" is further implied by the revelation that those in heaven are not as content as the word alone would suggest. The superior positioning of black Harlem in Van Vechten's metaphorical image could be interpreted to mean that Negroes, under white oppression and domination, occupy the moral high ground. Consequently, continued white privilege is at best tenuous ("Nigger Heaven is crowded and there isn't another seat"). Van Vechten proposes change as inevitable and possibly even ominous (objects dropped from the balcony potentially "crush" those below). Although this monologue of Byron's is often cited to vindicate Van Vechten's intentions in insisting upon such a controversial title, Van Vechten himself confessed that he chose the title mainly to incite the interests of whites who might be prompted to learn more about black life in Harlem.[3] In other words, he was well aware that much of his white readership would respond favorably to a title that on the surface, at least, appeared to endorse derogatory assumptions already prevalent about Negro life. In a letter to close friend and fellow artist James Weldon Johnson, dated September 7, 1926, Van Vechten poked fun at a reviewer's apparent failure to grasp his true intentions. He wrote to Johnson: "The *New York News* (colored) says that any one who would call a book ***Nigger Heaven*** would call a Negro Nigger."[4] A more laudatory review by Eden Bliss in the (Baltimore) *Afro-American,* by contrast, maintained: "Everybody—well nearly everybody—belongs to one of two groups, those who read the book and like it, and those who haven't and don't."[5] In any event, catering to black sensitivity around the issue of the title was hardly Van Vechten's chief concern. Banking with his publisher on the sensationalism that such a title would create (a sure way to garner sales), he apparently was more willing to risk the alienation of a potential black readership.[6] In this respect, Van Vechten was hardly an exception. As African-American cultural critic Richard Long has noted:

> The white writer who wrote about black folk in the twenties, whether they were central to his fiction or merely ancillary, was writing for a white audience, both publishers and a public. He was himself part of that public.[7]

Accordingly, Van Vechten expressed concern that the (white) public be adequately prepared for the book's reception. In a letter dated December 20, 1925, to his publisher, Alfred Knopf, Van Vechten asked that the book be advertised well in advance of its publication so that prospective readers would have time to familiarize themselves with his chosen subject. In the letter, Van Vechten further stressed needing to "prepare the mind" of his readers "so that the kind of life [he was] writing about w[ould] not come as an actual shock."[8] Certainly, these last lines reveal a great deal about whom he conceived of as his primary audience. Van Vechten imagined himself disclosing the Harlem milieu not just to New Yorkers, but to a potentially vast readership beyond New York. More obvious indications of Van Vechten's targeted audience can be found in the novel's heteroglossia. Foremost, there is the "Glossary of Negro Words and Phrases," which immediately follows the novel's conclusion. In anthropological fashion, Van Vechten defines, for the benefit of outsiders, some fifty terms which appear scattered throughout the novel. The term "blue," for instance, is defined as: "a very black Negro. Not to be confused with the Blues, Negro songs of disappointment in love" (285). While an "insider" might have found such reductive treatment of black cultural and linguistic expression typically problematic and maybe even a little humorous (i.e., is the Blues really reducible to "songs of disappointment in love"?), the audience of "outsiders" to whom Van Vechten was primarily writing would likely have found such a glossary both instructive and a testament to the authenticity of the novel's representations. In general, David Lewis argues, "Whites who were sympathetic to Harlem and believed they knew something of its ways thought the novel was almost perfect."[9] An excerpt from a review by L. Kronenberger in the October 1926 *Literary Digest International Book Review* is typical of the novel's reception by the white press:

> Mr. Van Vechten has approached a field both fertile and unexplored, a field admirably suited to his talents; and if his treatment is not definitive, it is robustly and satisfyingly vivid.[10]

Of course, Kronenberger's highly subjective evaluation leads one to question: "definitive" by whose standards? And "*satisfyingly* vivid" to whom? Aside from the "Glossary," Van Vechten also anticipates his white audience by defining the context in which the term *nigger* is used. In a footnote, he explains:

> While this informal epithet is freely used by Negroes among themselves, not only as a term of opprobrium, but also actually as a term of endearment, its employment by a white person is always fiercely resented. The word Negress is forbidden under all circumstances.
>
> (26)

Ironically, the explanation also comments on the precarious position that Van Vechten himself occupies in using the term as part of the novel's title. Finally, just as the title both reinscribes and challenges racial/racist stereotypes and assumptions, so does the text it names. Where ***Nigger Heaven*** succeeds, it is a thoughtful satire on Negro life in Harlem and a scathing critique of the way racism operates (having an impact on both blacks and whites) in American culture. Where it fails, however, it is melodramatic propaganda drawing heavily on essentialist notions of race, class, and gender already prevalent in the culture.

Although Van Vechten wrote a total of seven novels over his literary career before turning, after 1930, to photography, ***Nigger Heaven*** was the first to focus on Negro subjects. In all other matters, though, the novel is said to differ very little from most of his other work. Critic Richard Kellner notes, for example, that the "scandalous drinking and sleeping around in ***Nigger Heaven*** goes on in all of Van Vechten's novels" and is thus not limited to his depiction of Negro characters.[11] Corroborating Richard Long's claim that Van Vechten wrote "quite consciously in the tradition of the 'Decadent Novel,'"[12] Peter Flora similarly maintains that all of Van Vechten's novels "were largely portraits of the exotic and decadent, and generally sought to capitalize on the fashions of the day."[13] Nevertheless, judging from a letter to Langston Hughes written in early August 1925, Van Vechten seems at least to have been self-conscious about the effects of adding race to the crucible given the potential for inadvertently defeating his own purpose. He wrote:

> I hope soon to start work on my Negro novel, but I feel rather alarmed. It would have been comparatively easy for me to write it before I knew as much as I know now, enough to know that I am thoroughly ignorant![14]

Of course, Van Vechten was neither a stranger to Negroes nor the Harlem scene prior to his writing ***Nigger Heaven.*** Born June 17, 1880, in Cedar Rapids, Iowa, Van Vechten has been described as the product of a liberal upbringing by his father, Charles Duane Van Vechten, a "Universalist," whose own values and associations encouraged his son's early acquaintance with blacks.[15] Eleanor Perényi, a longtime associate of Van Vechten, recalls that the latter maintained friendships with African Americans long before and after such intermingling of the races were fashionable. Over his lifetime, Van Vechten was known to have counted among his closest friends James Weldon Johnson, Langston Hughes, Walter White, and George Schuyler.[16] He also enjoyed mutual camaraderie with many others, some of the most prominent including Ethel Waters, Zora Neale Hurston, and Claude McKay. His enthusiastic support of black artists and art—as well as his enormous influence in determining their fate—during the period now known as the Harlem Renaissance is legendary. While his approval could easily propel young artists to public recognition, his disapproval could prove commensurately devastating. Scholars of the period, for instance, have documented Blanche Knopf's consistent (yet unofficial) reliance on Van Vechten's judgment in determining whether works by various Negro writers merited publication by Knopf, even though Van Vechten was never formally affiliated with the publishing end of the business.[17] To his credit, Van Vechten recognized the talents of many writers whose valuable contributions to American letters remain undisputed even today. However, there is no way of really knowing just how many may also have perished by the same judgment. Despite his apparent appreciation of black artistic production, Van Vechten's appraisal

ABOUT THE AUTHOR

HURSTON ON VAN VECHTEN

Go thou and buy the books and writings of certain scribes and Pharisees which I shall name unto you, and thou shalt learn everything of good and of evil. Yea, thou shalt learn everything of good and of evil. Yea, thou shalt know as much as the Chief of the Niggerati, who is called Carl Van Vechten.

SOURCE: Zora Neale Hurston, excerpt from "Book of Harlem," in *American Mercury* 45, July 1942.

of such work—consistent with attitudes of the majority of even sympathetic whites during the era—was quite often qualified. In a letter to Blanche Knopf in which he was intending to praise Langston Hughes and Ethel Waters, he indicated, for example, that he believed the two to have "more genius *than any others of their race* in this country" [emphasis mine].[18] It is this sort of ideological bent (not only is such a compliment patronizing; it is also presumptuous) that informs ***Nigger Heaven*** and, at least in retrospect, makes it a very troublesome novel.

Widely hailed as the first novel to treat the situation of the urban African American, ***Nigger Heaven*** enjoyed noteworthy commercial success, going through nine printings in just four months.[19] Its publication was thought to have an enormous impact not only in opening up an audience/market for literature addressing black subjects, but also in defining what sort of black subject matter would be acceptable/appropriate for publication in the future. Critic Amritjit Singh, author of "Black-White Symbiosis: Another Look at the Literary History of the 1920s," notes:

> Although Carl Van Vechten's ***Nigger Heaven*** (1926) was not the first or the only work by a white writer to exploit the exotic-primitive stereotype in relation to the Negro, it was certainly the most influential novel in establishing this image in the minds of the reading public in the twenties. The book ran into several editions and sold over 100,000 copies; it fanned an unprecedented nationwide interest in the Negro and clearly demonstrated the commercial value of books written in the primitivistic framework.[20]

Actualizing the situation predicted in his fictional universe of ***Nigger Heaven,*** Van Vechten embraces the challenge that Negro writers themselves apparently fail to assume. In a passage that thinly disguises his own project, Van Vechten fulfills the character Russett Derwood's prophesy as told to Byron:

> [I]f you young Negro intellectuals don't get busy, a new crop of Nordics is going to spring up who will take the trouble to become better informed and will exploit this material before the Negro gets around to it.
>
> (223)

Perényi maintains that Van Vechten "desired to be the recording angel that black society at that time lacked, and it isn't entirely certain that he failed."[21] Perényi's assessment, like Van Vechten's novel, however, fails to elaborate adequately on the problematic nature of such an enterprise. At the same time that there is throughout the novel acknowledgment of racist discrimination in the publishing industry and in the society at large, there is also an unnerving charge that Negro artists have failed to recognize and to enthusiastically explore in their own literary production the beauty and vitality (read in the parlance of the dominant culture—*exoticism*) of their own culture. Byron, the culturally alienated anti-hero of ***Nigger Heaven,*** is castigated by both his editor, Russett Derwood, and Gareth Johns (allegedly Van Vechten's fictional double[22]) for his inability to connect with and to write about the more titillating (again, read—exotic) happenings among the lower classes of his own race (the set of middle-class Negroes being but a disappointing, if not altogether boring, imitation of white middle-class culture). Gareth ventures to say to Byron:

> Well, the low life of your people is exotic. It has splendid, fantastic quality. And humour! How vital it is, how rich in idiom! Picturesque and fresh! I don't think the Negro has been touched in literature as yet.
>
> (107)

Initially, it seems that Byron's negative response to such advice (Van Vechten writes that "Byron's tone was cold" [107]) is because he is offended by Gareth's condescension. However, the narrative soon reveals that Byron's response arises out of his elitism: he does not want to be associated with the so-called "low life" of his people. Hence, the assumptions implicit in the comments expressed by Derwood and Johns essentially remain unchallenged by the narrative. That the narrative is critical of Byron (his fate is one of squandered potential; the novel's ending, in which he is upstaged by the Scarlet Creeper in his quest to get even with Randolph Pettijohn, underscores his impotence) suggests two things: (1) that Byron's downfall is because he fails to recognize the worth of his own people's culture (which is valid since Byron *is* an elitist—a situation Van Vechten intends to satirize), and (2) that portrayal of this supposedly exotic realm is the only legitimate pursuit of black writers. It is the latter assumption that is particularly disturbing. A flaw in Van Vechten's story is that even had Byron been capable of writing what he felt (the narrative reveals him to be repeatedly dishonest with regard to his own feelings), his choice of content would still have been severely circumscribed by the expectations of Derwood and others whose power alone defined what constituted appropriate literary expression by Negro artists. In reality, not only were such attempts at truthful representation being aggressively thwarted by white publishers (consider, for instance, Walter White's initial difficulty getting *The Fire in the Flint* published), but also, what was deemed beautiful and exciting about African-American culture was being defined—prescribed even—from outside the culture by the patronage and appetites of white consumers.[23] To this end, Van Vechten's remark in a letter to Alfred Knopf that "the Negro has at last learned to say what is really on his mind" is at least a little exasperating.[24] People do not have to *learn* to say what is on their minds; to the contrary, the experience of oppression makes this something that they are forced to *unlearn.* This clarification is important because it once again foregrounds the hostile context that black artists were expected to negotiate. In *Black Culture and the Harlem Renaissance,* author Cary Wintz comments on the situation faced by black writers seeking to publish during the period:

> Except for black-owned newspapers and periodicals and a few small publishing ventures usually affiliated with black newspapers or churches, this industry was exclusively white.[25]

Since African Americans as a group have been denied access to the means of cultural production and dissemination, they have had little control historically over their own images/representation. That black artists have had for reasons relating to both economics and survival (including their physical safety) to cater to the expectations and demands of the dominant culture, then, is not chiefly about their failure to recognize worth in their own culture (even though this is certainly a by-product of racist oppression and conditioning). Certainly the reality of discrimination and denied access surfaces in the novel (characters' thwarted potential is a motif throughout), but, unfortunately, the implications of this—the psychological and material impact on black artists and the kind of material they subsequently produced—are not adequately treated. To do so would likely have made even Van Vechten's novel unsuitable for publication.

In a biting and for the most part dismissive review of ***Nigger Heaven*** for *Crisis* magazine, W. E. B. Du Bois charged that the novel was "neither truthful nor artistic." He elaborated: "It is not a true picture of Harlem life, even allowing for some justifiable impressionistic exaggeration. It is a caricature."[26] Du Bois further charges Van Vechten with mistaking appearances for reality, with presuming to describe the interiority of black life from a shallow acquaintance with its exterior. Criticizing Van Vechten for reducing Harlem to the ethos of its cabarets, Du Bois wrote:

> There is laughter, color, and spontaneity at Harlem's core, but in the current cabaret, financed and supported largely by white New York, this core is so overlaid and enwrapped with cheaper stuff that no one but a fool could mistake it for the genuine exhibition of the spirit of the people.
>
> (viii)

While Du Bois' sweeping dismissal of the novel is perhaps unfair, his criticism does point to a critical shortcoming of the novel, and that is that it is plagued, like much American fiction, by white writers attempting to incorporate black subject matter and by the author's inability to decenter his own hegemonic ways of knowing. The result is that Van Vechten's characters often speak and behave improbably, i.e., like white characters in blackface. Few escape the flatness of racial stereotypes. Consistent with the dominant ideology of the period (which, interestingly, was also absorbed by several Negro writers of the period[27]), blackness is repeatedly associated with the exotic, with excess (pertaining, for example, to passion or sex), mystery, and savagery. Author Toni Morrison has aptly described this historical tendency among Euro-American writers as "American Africanism" or the "fetishizing of color, the transference to blackness of the power of illicit sexuality, chaos, madness, impropriety, anarchy, strangeness, and helpless, hapless desire."[28] In this sense, what ***Nigger Heaven*** says about the consciousness of Van Vechten is perhaps more consequential than what his characters attempt to say about the reality of Negro life in Harlem.

Repeatedly, the trope of Negro blood is used to signify passion, savagery, and excess, which stand in dialectical opposition to the supposedly

European traits of temperence, civility, and restraint.[29] The epigraph, an excerpt from Countée Cullen's poem "Heritage," that introduces the narrative is telling:

> All day long and all night through,
> One thing only I must do:
> Quench my pride and cool my blood,
> Lest I perish in the flood.

This verse from Cullen's poem captures the conscious struggle of Van Vechten's "respectable" Negro characters to continually beat back manifestations of their "essential selves." The danger (and yet, thrill) of succumbing to one's own excess emerges as a motif. The alleged passion and savagery associated with Negro-ness is revealed in Negro characters' apparent fascination with guns, knives, and razors (90). Despite the fact that Van Vechten includes in ***Nigger Heaven*** more than one tangential episode where Negro passion erupts in a confrontation between two or more unidentified characters,[30] he once confessed in a letter to Hughes that he had never in his experience of twenty-five years seen a fight in a Negro cabaret. Interestingly, he went on to say that he had never been in a white place where there was *not* one. He concludes:

> The difference, I suppose, is that white people almost invariably become quarrelsome when they are drunk, while Negroes usually become gay and are not inclined to fight unless they want to kill someone.[31]

Unlike its white counterpart, then, Negro passion is characterized by excess. Even the elite (distinct in all other matters) manifest traits in common with their lower-class brethren on account of this shared "Negro blood." The photograph of Mrs. Albright's deceased husband offers an example. As the Albrights represent the upper crust of the Negro bourgeoisie, Mary Love is surprised at what she discovers in looking at the portrait of Mrs. Albright's deceased husband: "a deep scar, almost white, extending from the left corner of his lip to his left eye" (68). Mary imagines "how Mrs. Albright must have shuddered at this squalid indignity!" Such a scar is an indignity precisely because it reveals the Negro-ness that the Albrights and others of their class are scrambling to escape.

Of course, Van Vechten's American Africanism is exposed most vividly in his descriptions of Lasca Sartoris and her milieu. Dancing at the Charity Ball with Byron, Lasca is "the most striking woman Mary had ever seen":

> A robe of turquoise-blue satin clung to her exquisite body, brought out in relief every curve. . . . Her golden-brown back was entirely nude to the waist. The dress was circled with wide bands of green and black sequins, designed to resemble the fur of the leopard. A tiara of sapphires sparkled in her hair, and a choker of these stones, around her throat.
>
> (163)

Lasca is the epitome of the exotic and the personification of Euro-American myths about the mysterious and animalistic nature of black female sexuality. The sexual world into which she introduces Byron is a mire of decadence, debauchery, and sadomasochistic cruelty. Dantéesque images of hell abound inside the Black Mass (figuratively described as a "witches sabbath"), one of the clubs she and Byron visit during a partying binge. Dancers move about the floor with zombie-like faces to the music of "demoniac saxophones wail[ing] like souls burning in an endless torment" (254). Lasca becomes the devil to whom Byron willingly surrenders.[32] The events at the Black Mass culminate eerily in a bizarre psychosexual ritual involving a young nude black woman wielding a knife. Van Vechten writes:

> She was pure black, with savage African features, thick nose, thick lips, bushy hair which hovered about her face like a lanate halo, while her eyes rolled back so far that only the whites were visible.
>
> (255)

In this passage African-ness is associated with exotic otherness as well as evil. Such stereotypes of Africa as a jungle inhabited by savages abound in ***Nigger Heaven.*** An only slightly milder version of the Black Mass, the Black Venus club is described as a "jungle land" where "Hottentots and Bantus [sway] under the amber moon" (281). Elsewhere in the narrative, Byron jestingly proclaims himself an "African cannibal" (145), while many other characters speak of latent savagery as if it were their African inheritance. Van Vechten further devotes nearly three pages to Mary's elaboration of the legend of Christophe, the nineteenth-century self-proclaimed emperor of Haiti (123-25). Though Mary's telling the story is an attempt to inspire Byron to write, the story's focus on Christophe's passion and volatility functions once again to link such traits to African blood. Even Mary's declared interest in and appreciation of African art fails to recoup Africa as more than a creation of white consciousness since her valorization of the art lies in its supposed simplicity and primitive quality; ethnocentric notions about Africa and its inhabitants are reinscribed.

If to be a Negro is to be a savage at heart—a natural pagan (59) and a slave to one's emotions/passions, then Mary Love is conscious of her own alienation from this essence. Van Vechten writes: "She admired all Negro characteristics and desired earnestly to possess them. Somehow, so many of them, through no fault of her own, eluded her" (89). Her friend Olive chides: "Everybody says you're cold, that you have no natural feeling. . . . Why don't you let yourself go once in a while?" (54) Being Negro is consequently associated with "letting one's self go." Repeatedly, Mary laments having been cheated out of her primitive birthright, which she imagines as "a love of drums, of exciting rhythms . . . [as a] naive delight in glowing colour . . ." (89). (Why this must be a "naive delight" Van Vechten does not specify. But the adjective choice has the effect of reinforcing racist notions of Negroes as children/noble savages.) Mary's alienation from her Negro-ness, her essential self, leaves her longing for the "primitive impulse" that would allow her to behave like other "daughters of her race" (134), particularly when it comes to acting on her jealousy and resentment of Lasca, in whom her own fiancé, Byron, has taken an interest.

Yet, at the same time that Van Vechten is reinscribing essentialist notions of race through Mary's longing to identify with black cultural expression, racist assumptions are also being critiqued. The text proposes and then dismisses (through Mary's own reasoning), for example, the possibility that Mary's emotional restraint has to do with her mixed-blood identity (i.e., that the presence of white blood acts as a mitigating/civilizing factor). Mary ultimately rejects this conclusion on the grounds that Olive, who is an octoroon and therefore whiter than she, after all, does not endure the same sense of cultural alienation. Other situations in the text, in which the narrative voice abruptly assumes the subjective viewpoint of a particular character, create ambiguity as to authorial intent. One such instance is Van Vechten's initial description of the crowd at the Black Venus. He writes:

> Couples were dancing in such close proximity that their bodies melted together as they swayed and rocked to the tormented howling of the brass, the barbaric beating of the drum. . . . Blues, smokes, dinges, charcoals, chocolate browns, shines, jigs.
>
> (12)

However, this description of the dancers seems meant to reflect (the character) Anatole's (subjective) gaze. A subsequent description of the crowd as representing merely a "kaleidoscope of colour" (14) signals a return to a more objective narrative voice. Since the narrator frequently appropriates language that would only be used by "insiders" (i.e., terms from the "Glossary of Negro Words and Phrases") to describe characters, scenes, and events, the question of who is telling the story at various points becomes a critical one in the sense that authorial intent is implicated. The degree of familiarity implied in Van Vechten's appropriation of black jargon is perhaps one of the reasons black critics initially found the book so objectionable.

At the same time that Van Vechten draws upon essentialist notions of black identity to delineate his Negro characters, he also endeavors to portray Negro life in some of its complexity. Included among the novel's achievements are Van Vechten's critique of intraracial class antagonisms and his attempt to portray some of the effects of white racism on black characters. The pretension exuded by the Negro elite is repeatedly satirized in ***Nigger Heaven.*** Despite the shared experience of racist oppression (Byron and Mary's respectibility, for instance, does not exempt them from being snubbed by the racist remarks of a white couple in the park,[33] nor does Byron's privileged educational background deliver him from discrimination in the workplace), there is little mingling between the different social sets. The Albrights and Orville Snodes, who eschew everything associated with their own culture in favor of European culture, are particular targets. Orville's insistence upon speaking French is clearly comical since there is no apparent reason for it; he is always in the company of native-English speakers. Mrs. Albright's and Orville's dismissal of African art as vulgar is made ironic by the enthusiastic interest that Gareth Johns, Campaspe Lorillard, and Edith Duke (who are all white) register by comparison. The latter both visit and purchase pieces from the exhibit Mary organizes at the public library (114). Van Vechten extends the same satire to the realm of letters, implying that the Negro elite are predisposed to appreciate the talents of Negro writers only *after* the latter have been recognized by the white establishment. Van Vechten writes:

> It had become, Olive observed cynically to Mary, quite the thing for these more affluent folk to take up with the young intellectuals since their work had begun to appear in the *Atlantic Monthly, Vanity Fair,* the *American Mercury,* and the *New Republic.*
>
> (42)

Byron, whom some critics have taken as the hero of ***Nigger Heaven,*** is also satirized by Van Vechten.[34] Although he fares better than the Albrights and their set, his elitism (he is initially revolted, for example, by the black laborers at the Cletheredge Building with whom he is expected to work), nevertheless, prevents him from seeing what is right before his face. While both Mary and Byron are portrayed as alienated characters (Mary, for instance, tells Byron that she learned to "speak in dialect" from *Jezebel Pettyfer* and *Porgy* [145], and Byron confesses that he learned to Charleston from a "couple of white fellows at college" [142]),[35] Byron, unlike Mary, is completely lacking in awareness of his own alienation. When, against Mary's better judgment, he submits an ill-conceived story for publication, the editor, Derwood, tells him that he should learn something about his own people. Ironically, the only praise Derwood offers is for those sections of the story dealing with white people (223), which he deems remarkably accurate. If the relationship between Mary and Byron symbolizes the ideal relationship between critic and artist[36] in that both participate in the same collective consciousness, it is thwarted by the combination of Byron's pride and his inability to embrace his own heritage. Byron is totally unreceptive to Mary's suggestion that he consider writing a different kind of story about their people. Unable to see how Negroes are fundamentally different from anybody else, he misses the more subtle implications of Mary's response. She concedes: "I suppose we are [like everybody else], only we don't eat where we want to or die where we want to" (126). Unfortunately, Van Vechten never develops this potentially radical break in the text; it is almost a call for a protest novel, for a story that would explain the myriad ways in which Negroes are prevented from being like everybody else.[37]

The novel does, however, make sundry references to the way in which Negroes are thwarted by racist assumptions and practices of the dominant culture. Howard, a law school graduate, for instance, is unemployed for two years before he is finally able to secure work in his chosen profession. Mary, though amply qualified, is denied professional mobility at the public library on account of racism. Byron, likewise, complains of the harassment he receives in his search for employment commensurate with his educational qualifications. And Adora, combining a critique of race and gender oppression, notes tongue-in-cheek that the only success for a colored woman in America is a rich husband (30). Taking his critique one step further, Van Vechten also illuminates the role of *internalized* racism in thwarting black economic advancement. Dick Sill, for instance, warns Byron that he is unlikely to garner much assistance from his own people in terms of finding employment in Harlem, as black Harlemites are more inclined to seek the services of white professionals over their own (119). When Dick goes on to speak of the survival of Negro arts as the result of white support, Olive recasts the issue in economic rather than psychological terms; that is, part of the reason Negroes do not support their own is that financially they *cannot* (120). Dick's follow-up question as to how Negroes are going to get money remains unanswered (thus creating another moment of potentially radical departure in the text). Even without exploring the issue (Van Vechten has Olive preclude further discussion by changing the subject), Van Vechten manages subtly to point to the way in which racism is implicated in American capitalism. Still other racist assumptions of the dominant culture which are challenged by the narrative include Mary's revelation that Negroes are as opposed to race-mixing as whites (47);[38] Dick's dismissal of the notion that black men sexually desire white women;[39] and Olive's revelation that *all* black people readily resort to guile to manipulate white folk when doing so appears advantageous (63). Finally, Lasca's sweeping claim that Negroes are not any worse off than anybody else is almost a trap for unsuspecting readers. She rails:

> They have the same privileges that white women had before the bloody fools got the ballot. They're considered irresponsible like children and treated with a special fondness.
>
> (235)

By associating the plight of white women with that of Negroes, Van Vechten prompts his audience to reevaluate the validity of Lasca's claim. The narrative thus satirizes rather than promotes the ideology she espouses.

Richard Long has proposed that perhaps the most significant thing about the treatment of African Americans in literature by whites of the period known as the Harlem Renaissance was that there was an apparent *increase* in such treatment.[40] Certainly, Van Vechten's ***Nigger Heaven*** did not present a revolutionary break with existing images and stereotypes about African Americans during the era. Van Vechten's inability to transcend essentialist notions of race (a fault shared by many Negro artists of the era, as well) and his immersion in American Africanism significantly compromised any serious intentions he may have entertained to educate white audiences about the richness of black Harlem life. Also, because essentialist approaches are inevitably dehumanizing, Van Vechten's project—to name the uniqueness of black culture by idealizing/valorizing specifically those aspects of it that had been degraded in the past—was necessarily a precarious one. Despite the novel's numerous shortcomings, however, ***Nigger Heaven*** was not without notable achievements. Although not unproblematic, its publishing success meant that new markets were created for the treatment of black subject matter in popular literature. Furthermore, Van Vechten's plugging within the novel the works of—then, largely unknown—black writers of both the Renaissance and earlier, including Langston Hughes, Charles Chesnutt, and James Weldon Johnson, provided valuable exposure for such artists. At one point in the novel, white characters are even satirized for their failure to appreciate the poetry and talent of Hughes. Dick Sill's patronizing friends at the Black Venus ironically accuse Hughes of failing to understand his race. Van Vechten's own known admiration of Hughes suggests that Van Vechten is ridiculing the group's ignorance (210). Elsewhere, Van Vechten attempts to educate his audience about the history of slavery, offering an explanation that, ironically, challenges reductive definitions/descriptions of Negro identity.[41] Van Vechten ventriloquizes his Biblical knowledge through Dick Sill, who reveals that Moses' wife was an Ethiopian. The revelation is intended not only to challenge religious objections to miscegenation but also situate in black Africa the lives of important Biblical figures. Finally, Van Vechten's treatment of the alienated black artist in his portrayal of Byron Kasson exposed the almost tragic predicament faced by Negro artists of the era. Given critic Bruce Kellner's assessment that "the black writer both thrived and suffered, torn between well-meant encouragement from the white race to preserve his racial identity (usually described as 'primitivism') and a misguided encouragement from his own race to emulate the white one,"[42] perhaps the most salient criticism one might offer of ***Nigger Heaven*** is that Van Vechten, in his noble insistence that the Negro writer just be himself, ultimately failed to recognize the possibility of his own complicity in delimiting what that self could be.

Notes

1. Although the term "Negro" in reference to African Americans/Blacks is outmoded in the contemporary context, I use it repeatedly herein to reflect its currency during the era.
2. Unless otherwise indicated, all textual references are to Carl Van Vechten, *Nigger Heaven* (1926; New York: Harper, 1971).
3. Peter Flora, "Carl Van Vechten, Blanche Knopf, and the Harlem Renaissance," *Library Chronicle of the University of Texas at Austin* 22.4 (1992): 72.
4. Bruce Kellner, ed., *Letters of Carl Van Vechten* (New Haven: Yale UP, 1987) 89.
5. Eden Bliss, "Harlem," editorial, *Afro-American* 2 Oct. 1926: 6.
6. Interestingly, more than one source indicates that even Van Vechten's father advised against his using such a patently offensive title.
7. Richard Long, "The Outer Reaches: The White Writer and Blacks in the Twenties," *The Harlem Renaissance Re-examined,* ed. Victor A. Kramer (New York: AMS Press, 1987) 48.
8. Kellner, *Letters of Carl Van Vechten* 86.
9. David Levering Lewis, *When Harlem Was in Vogue* (New York: Oxford UP, 1981) 187.
10. Marion A. Knight and Mertice M. James, eds., *Book Review Digest: Books of 1926,* vol. 22 (New York: H. W. Wilson, 1927) 711.
11. Bruce Kellner, "'Redefined Racism': White Patronage in the Harlem Renaissance," *The Harlem Renaissance Re-examined,* ed. Victor A. Kramer (New York: AMS Press, 1987) 104.
12. Long 48.
13. Flora 67.
14. Kellner, *Letters of Carl Van Vechten* 82.
15. Flora 66.
16. Eleanor Perényi, "Carl Van Vechten," *Yale Review* 77.4 (1988): 541. In "Carl Van Vechten, Blanche Knopf, and the Harlem Renaissance," author Peter Flora notes that Van Vechten's introduction to most of these individuals was facilitated through his friendship with Walter White, whom Van Vechten first met through the Knopfs—their mutual publisher (See Flora 71).
17. Flora 78.
18. Kellner, *Letters of Carl Van Vechten* 129. This particular letter was dated 12/14/32.
19. Lewis 185. Lewis, however, notes that critics largely ignored the fact that this subject matter (i.e., the situation of the urban Negro) had already been done, "and done well," by Paul Laurence Dunbar in *Sport of the Gods* (1902). See Lewis 182.
20. Amritjit Singh, "Black-White Symbiosis: Another Look at the Literary History of the 1920s," *The Harlem Renaissance Re-examined,* ed. Victor A. Kramer (New York: AMS Press, 1987) 34.
21. Perényi 542.
22. Lewis 185. Other real-life parallels that Lewis identifies are Lasca Sartoris as Nora Holt Ray, Mary Love as Jesse Fauset, Adora Boniface as A'Leila Walker, the Underwoods as James Weldon Johnson and Grace Johnson, and Russett Derwood as H. L. Mencken. Richard Long, on the other hand, indicates that Mary Love "could have been suggested by many serious young women in the Harlem of the twenties." He further proposes Byron Kasson as modeled on Harold Jackman, and Adora Boniface as a composite of both A'Leila Walker and an Atlantic City hostess named Rhetta Braswell. (See Long 50—footnote.)
23. Mrs. Rufus Osgood Mason, a famous patroness who preferred to be called "godmother" by the artists she supported, insisted, for instance, on several condi-

tions: the artists had to remain in Harlem, they were to focus on folk culture or primitivism in their works, and they were to conscientiously avoid overtly political themes. At various points, Mason helped finance Langston Hughes, Randolph Fisher, Zora Neale Hurston, Claude McKay, and Alain Locke, among others. See Kellner, "'Refined Racism': White Patronage in the Harlem Renaissance," in Kramer 96-97.

24. Kellner, *Letters of Carl Van Vechten* 288. The letter, dated December 19, 1962, was specifically in praise of John Oliver Killens, but also in praise of the African-American literary talent that had since emerged including James Baldwin and John A. Williams. The letter concludes on a self-congratulatory note; Van Vechten expresses pride in having, along with Knopf, "started a movement that has become so lusty."

25. Cary D. Wintz, *Black Culture and the Harlem Renaissance* (Houston: Rice UP, 1988) 155.

26. Reprinted (from the December 1926 issue of *Crisis*) in Carl Van Vechten, *Nigger Heaven* (New York: Harper, 1971).

27. For examples, see Alain Locke's acclaimed anthology, *The New Negro* (1925; New York: Atheneum, 1968).

28. Toni Morrison, *Playing in the Dark: Whiteness and the Literary Imagination* (Cambridge: Yale UP, 1992) 80.

29. Unrestrained passion is apparently shared by other non-WASPS, as well. The scene in which Byron comes across two Italians arguing is paradigmatic. When the first is unable to persuade the second to move his horse, which is grazing on the former's geraniums, the former pulls out a knife and (irrationally) stabs the animal (230).

30. On page 164, for example, Mary observes, while attending a formal ball, two unidentified women engaged in a physical confrontation over the affections of a shared lover.

31. From a letter dated May 1925. Kellner, *Letters of Carl Van Vechten* 79.

32. Van Vechten writes: "Byron offered himself freely to the conforming curves of her sensual body, delivered himself to the spell of the clouds of ever-changing colour that came up from below, of the depraved clangtints of this perverted Dies Irae that sounded from an invisible source, and of an unfamiliar, pungent aroma" (255).

33. The description of the speaker's face as "tortured" (146) seems to say something about the impact of racism on white people, as well.

34. Assuming Byron to be the novel's hero, some critics, for instance, have questioned Van Vechten's choice of ending whereby Byron faces a bleak and tragic fate, given Van Vechten's enthusiastic patronage of black writers. (See Peter Flora's essay, "Carl Van Vechten, Blanche Knopf, and the Harlem Renaissance.") Byron, whose stories are described as "spineless" (175) could hardly be expected to come to any other end. In fact, most of the narrative seems to me critical of Byron and his choices.

35. Such information both contests and reinscribes racial essentialism. On the one hand, Van Vechten is making the point that not all black people "speak in dialect" or can do the Charleston. But on the other, if Byron and Mary were not so alienated, they *would* be able to do these things.

36. Charles Scruggs, "Crab Antics and Jacob's Ladder: Aaron Douglas's Two Views of *Nigger Heaven*," *The Harlem Renaissance Re-examined*, ed. Victor A. Kramer (New York: AMS Press, 1987) 168.

37. In this sense, Van Vechten's text seems to anticipate the fiction of Richard Wright, Ann Petry, Dorothy West, and others that emerged during the late 1930s and '40s.

38. Byron concurs with Mary's sentiment: 'We don't want them. All we want is to be let alone, a chance to earn money, to be respectable" (148).

39. When asked if he prefers "pinks" in the time that he has been "passing," Dick declares: "That's the worst of it. . . I just don't. Give me blues every time" (215). While his response, unfortunately, objectifies both black and white women, it nevertheless disrupts racist assumptions about black male sexuality.

40. Long 49.

41. Van Vechten writes through Mary's consciousness, as the latter ponders the curious mixture apparent in her own father's physical features: "The old slave traders were none too particular concerning the individuals they kidnapped along the African coast.. . . Not only were the miserable human beings raped from all parts of Africa, representatives of widely differing African tribes, but also Arabs, Egyptians, Moors, and even Spaniards and Portuguese were gathered in. In America these curiously distinct races came together and bore children; further, these children were often impregnated with French, Spanish, English, and Indian blood. The result, whatever the percentage of the mixture, was known in this enlightened country as a Negro and shared all the prejudice directed towards the full-blooded African" (94).

42. Kellner, "'Refined Racism': White Patronage in the Harlem Renaissance" 93.

FURTHER READING

Bibliography

Kellner, Bruce. *A Bibliography of the Work of Carl Van Vechten.* Westport, Conn.: Greenwood Publishing, 258 p.

Comprehensive primary bibliography.

Criticism

Bernard, Emily. "What He Did for the Race: Carl Van Vechten and the Harlem Renaissance." *Soundings: An Interdisciplinary Journal* 80, no. 4 (winter 1997): 531-42.

Discusses Van Vechten's role in advancing the works of Harlem Renaissance writers.

Berry, Faith. "Did Van Vechten Make or Take Hughes' 'Blues'?" *Black World* 25, no. 4 (1976): 22-8.

Discusses Van Vechten's influence on the Harlem Renaissance and considers to what extent he helped or exploited writers such as Langston Hughes.

Coleman, Leon. "Carl Van Vechten Presents the New Negro." In *The Harlem Renaissance Re-Examined,* edited by Victor A. Kramer, pp. 107-27. New York: AMS Press, 1987.

Discusses Van Vechten's activities—such as his writing on topics of interest to Blacks and his encouragement of individual Black artists—to show that Van Vechten was the most prominent white person to help writers of the Harlem Renaissance further their careers.

———. *Carl Van Vechten and the Harlem Renaissance: A Critical Assessment.* New York: Garland Publishing, 1998.

Study of Van Vechten's role in and influence on the Harlem Renaissance.

Cooley, John. "White Writers and the Harlem Renaissance." In *The Harlem Renaissance: Revaluations,* edited by Amritjit Singh, William S. Shiver, and Stanley Brodwin, pp. 13-22. New York: Garland Publishing, 1989.

Discusses the roles of Eugene O'Neill, Waldo Frank, e. e. cummings, and Van Vechten on the Harlem Renaissance.

Flora, Peter. "Carl Van Vechten, Blanche Knopf, and the Harlem Renaissance." *Library Chronicle of the University of Texas* 22, no. 4 (1992): 64-83.

Examines Van Vechten's relationship to Knopf and his role in promoting the works of Black writers.

Kellner, Bruce. Introduction to *"Keep A-Inchin' Along": Selected Writings of Carl Van Vechten about Black Art and Letters,* edited by Bruce Kellner, pp. 3-12. Westport, Conn.: Greenwood Publishing, 1979.

Discusses Van Vechten's friendships with Black writers and his efforts to promote their works.

———. "Langston Hughes's *Nigger Heaven* Blues." *The Langston Hughes Review* 11, no. 1 (spring 1992): 21-7.

Discusses Van Vechten's relationship with Langston Hughes.

Kishimoto, Hisao. *Carl Van Vechten: The Man and His Role in the Harlem Renaissance.* Tokyo: Seibido, 1983, 148 p.

Biographical and critical study.

Larson, Charles R. "Three Harlem Novels of the Jazz Age." *Critique: Studies in Modern Fiction* 11, no. (1969): 66-78.

Compares Nigger Heaven *with works by Claude McKay and Countee Cullen.*

Lueders, Edward. *Carl Van Vechten.* New York: Twayne, 1965, 158 p.

Comprehensive study of Van Vechten's life and works.

Perenyi, Eleanor. "Carl Van Vechten." *The Yale Review* 77 (summer 1988): 537-43.

Personal reminiscence.

Scruggs, Charles. "Crab Antics and Jacob's Ladder: Aaron Douglas's Two Views of *Nigger Heaven.*" In *The Harlem Renaissance Re-Examined,* edited by Victor A. Kramer pp. 149-81. New York: AMS Press, 1987.

Offers two interpretations of Nigger Heaven *based on the perceptions of the Black artist Aaron Douglas, who was commissioned by the publisher to illustrate the advertisements for the novel.*

Worth, Robert F. "*Nigger Heaven* and the Harlem Renaissance." *African American Review* 29, no. 3 (fall 1995): 461-73.

Examines why Nigger Heaven *provoked such strong, divided reactions when it was published and asserts that the novel brought to the fore artistic, social, and political questions that were of central importance to the writers of the Harlem Renaissance.*

OTHER SOURCES FROM GALE:

Additional coverage of Van Vechten's life and career is contained in the following sources published by the Gale Group: *American Writers Supplement,* Vol. 2; *Contemporary Authors,* Vol. 183; *Contemporary Authors—Obituary,* Vols. 89-92; *Contemporary Literary Criticism,* Vol. 33; *Dictionary of Literary Biography,* Vols. 4, 9; and *Reference Guide to American Literature,* Ed. 4.

ERIC WALROND

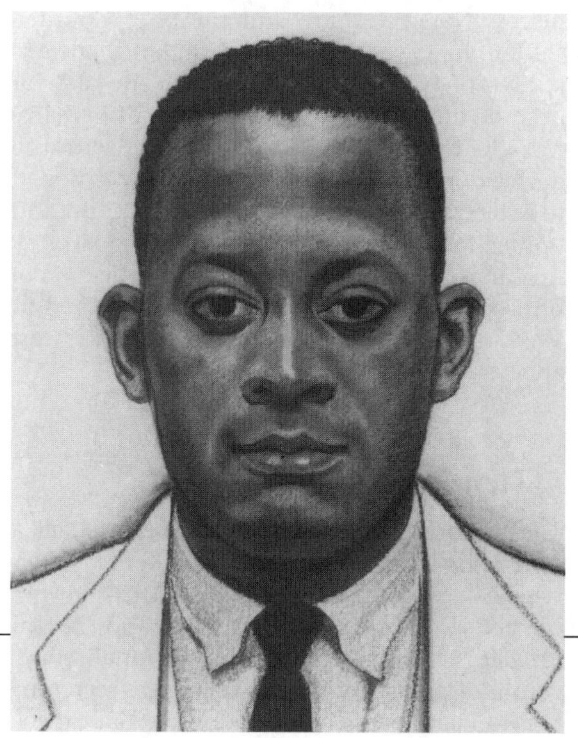

(1898 - 1966)

Guyanese short story writer, essayist, and editor.

As an editor of the National Urban League's *Opportunity* magazine and of Marcus Garvey's *Negro World,* Walrond helped create the climate and the context which fostered and inspired the writers of the Harlem Renaissance. In his essays of the early 1920s, he shaped a vision of African American identity which was expressed by the phrase "New Negro" and which differentiated the consciousness of the Black writers of his generation from that of earlier ones. In his own highly acclaimed but small body of fiction, especially in the ten lyrical stories of *Tropic Death* (1926), he revealed the psychological depths and the geographical and social circumstances of African Americans beset by the realities of economic hardship and racism.

BIOGRAPHICAL INFORMATION

Walrond was born in Georgetown, British Guiana (now Guyana), in 1898. In 1906, after his father had deserted them and after a fire had caused great destruction in Georgetown, Walrond and his mother went to live with relatives in a small village in Barbados. Walrond began attending St. Stephen's Boys' School, but around 1910 moved with his mother to Panama in search of his father. Like thousands of West Indians, Walrond's father had found work digging the Panama Canal. Walrond's parents did not reconcile, and the boy and his mother settled in Colón. Walrond became fluent in Spanish, finished secondary school, and trained as a secretary and stenographer. Upon graduation he secured a job as a clerk in the Health Department in Colón and also began working as a reporter and sportswriter for the Panama *Star-Herald.* In 1918, at the age of twenty, Walrond migrated to New York City. Unable to find work on any of the Harlem newspapers, he attended City College for three years and then Columbia University for a year, taking creative-writing courses while supporting himself as secretary to an architect and to the superintendant of a hospital. His search for a job in New York City also brought him in contact with racial discrimination of an intensity he had not experienced in the Caribbean. These experiences contributed to his belief in the importance of Marcus Garvey's quest for Black race consciousness and independence from white institutions, and they provided material for his first articles in *The New Republic* and *Opportunity*. In 1928 Walrond received a Guggenheim grant to travel and study in the West Indies and to work on a book about French involvement in the building of the Panama Canal. He moved to France in 1929 and lived there until 1932, pleased by the lack of racial discrimination, becoming familiar with French literature, and forming friendships with, among others, steamship heiress Nancy Cunard and the poet Countee Cullen. In 1932 he moved to England. Little is known of Walrond's life there, but he did not become the major writer that praise of his early work had suggested. He was unhappy with the degree of racism he found in England, continued to write essays and stories about Black culture and oppression, co-edited a collection of poetry by African Americans, and assembled a collection of photographs of African sculptures. He died in 1966, collapsing on a London street from a heart attack.

MAJOR WORKS

Walrond's first stories—"On Being Black," "On Being a Domestic," and "Miss Kenny's Marriage"—were published in the early 1920s in various periodicals including *Opportunity* and *The New Republic.* The first two stories are fictionalized accounts of the author's own experiences searching for work and being employed in menial capacities. His concerns for racial recuperation from white exploitation and for racial reconstitution are evident from his first journalistic essays such as "The New Negro Faces America" and "The Negro Exodus from the South," written in the early 1920s, through "White Man, What Now?" (1935) and "The Negro in London" (1937), to pieces in the *People's Voice* such as "West Indians Fight in Burma" (1945), "Italy Leaves Trail of Terror in Ethiopia" (1945), and "The Men of Cibao" (1945), about the U.S. occupation of Santo Domingo. *Tropic Death,* Walrond's best-known work, is a collection of ten stories drawn from African American experience, particularly Walrond's experience of growing up in the Caribbean. The stories demonstrate Walrond's concern with the subjects of Black migration, oppression, and self-development through his characteristically rich, imagistic prose, which helps to reveal depth of character, intensity of landscape, and the interplay between the two. Several gothic stories like "The Black Pin," "The Vampire Bat," and "The Voodoo's Revenge" included in the collection attest to Walrond's interest in the religious and magical culture of the Caribbean.

CRITICAL RECEPTION

In the 1920s Walrond was an important figure among African American writers and artists, who, according to Lewis Nkosi, "helped set the tone for the new writing and added a dimension of ruthless realism." His works were published in both Black and white journals, and he enjoyed status and celebrity in Paris in the early 1930s. W. E. B. Du Bois praised *Tropic Death,* while the poet Countee Cullen dedicated his famous poem about an incident of racial humiliation in Baltimore to Walrond. Some reviewers, including Waldo Frank, have chastised him for excessive sophistication in theme and language. After the 1930s, Walrond continued to write stories, essays, and pieces of journalism, but he did not produce anything like his first works, and he slipped into relative obscurity. A new collection of his works edited by Louis J. Parascandola fostered renewed critical interest in Walrond's work in the 1990s.

PRINCIPAL WORKS

Tropic Death (short stories) 1926

Black and Unknown Bards: A Collection of Negro Poetry [editor, with Rosey E. Pool] (poetry) 1958

"Winds Can Wake up the Dead": An Eric Walrond Reader (short stories, essays) 1998

GENERAL COMMENTARY

LOUIS J. PARASCANDOLA (ESSAY DATE 1998)

SOURCE: Parascandola, Louis J. Introduction. *"Winds Can Wake up the Dead": An Eric Walrond Reader,* pp. 11-42. Detroit, Mich.: Wayne State University Press, 1998.

In the following essay, Parascandola traces the major events of Walrond's life and career.

In a letter from Arna Bontemps to Langston Hughes dated September 1, 1966, Bontemps tells Hughes that Eric Walrond had died a couple of weeks earlier from "a heart attack (about his 5th) on a street in London" (474). Bontemps's casual remark is one of the few signs that anyone even noticed Walrond's passing, a sad indication of the fate that had befallen this remarkable figure. This neglect has been unfortunate. Walrond's work as an editor for Marcus Garvey's *Negro World* and Charles S. Johnson's *Opportunity* helped foster the Harlem Renaissance, and his collection ***Tropic Death*** (1926), in addition to other stories, essays, and reviews, provides great insight into that significant literary and cultural movement. He is especially important for his depiction of Black immigrant life during the 1920s, a subject that has not yet received the attention it deserves. Furthermore, the three issues that dominated his work—migration, discrimination, and racial pride—are still relevant to present-day readers, and the creative tension caused by the intersection of these issues in his literary output often results in his best writing.

Eric Derwent Walrond was born December 18, 1898, in Georgetown, British Guiana (now Guyana), to a Guyanese father and a Barbadian mother. He moved with his mother and siblings to Barbados in 1906, after a devastating fire in Georgetown in 1905. Walrond's father had gone to seek work in Panama during the building of the Canal, and Ruth Walrond, alone with her children, wanted to be near her family. Once in Barbados, Walrond was educated at St. Stephen's Boys' School, located near Black Rock (outside the capital, Bridgetown), not far from where his grandfather owned a small settlement. Gerald Bright, the young boy in the semi-autobiographical story **"Tropic Death,"** vividly describes his memories of the island in one of Walrond's typically opulent passages:

> He was back in Black Rock; a dinky backward village; . . . the crops of dry peas and cassava and tannias and eddoes, robbed, before they could feel the pulse of the sun, of their gum or juice; the goats, bred on some jealous tenant's cane shoots, or guided some silken black night down a planter's gully—and then only able to give a little bit of milk; the rain, a whimsical rarity. And then [there were] the joys, for a boy of eight—a dew-sprayed, toe-searching tramp at sunrise for "touched" fruit dropped in the night by the epicurean bats, almonds, mangoes, golden apples . . . [.]

Despite the beauty of the environment, however, these were difficult financial times for the family, a fact that is reflected in Walrond's fiction. In **"The Black Pin,"** a story from ***Tropic Death,*** the protagonist, by herself, must turn a crumbling shack inhabited by scorpions and centipedes into a suitable home for her family. These hard times are also reflected in **"Drought,"** from ***Tropic Death,*** where the family struggles to eke out a wretched existence. The glimpses in these stories mirror the harsh reality of Walrond's life. With few resources of their own and having had no word from the father for several months, the Walrond family was forced to sell their property and, in 1911, moved to Colón, in the Panama Canal Zone.

The Walronds arrived in Panama at a crucial point in its history. It had only declared its independence from Colombia in 1903 after prompting from the United States government. The area had been a magnet for Caribbean migrants since the 1880s when the French first made attempts to build a canal; however, the number of laborers increased dramatically after the United States government began overseeing the Canal Zone project in 1904. Some twenty-five to thirty thousand Caribbean people migrated to Panama between 1904 and 1914, when the Canal was completed. Life there was difficult for Black laborers since the Canal Zone was extremely segregated along color and class lines, with Blacks being paid in silver while whites received gold. It was even harder for families, such as Walrond's, headed by females (Watkins-Owens 12-17).

The move to Colón, a rapidly developing Spanish-speaking city, must have been a shock to young Walrond, a frail, overprotected anglophone child who was used to a more rural life in Barbados. The West Indian area of the city was disease-ridden, the inhabitants suffering especially from yellow fever and malaria; moreover, poverty was rampant. The tenements in which Blacks lived are described in the story **"Tropic Death"** as "a row of lecherous huts." **"Bottle Alley,"** literally paved with old wine bottles and the setting for a number of Walrond's stories, was notorious for gambling and prostitution (McCullough 147).

There was also racial bias against West Indians. In an essay, **"White Man, What Now?"** Walrond recalls that in his childhood in Panama he endured "prejudice on the basis of [his] British nationality." He was ridiculed as a "chumbo" (a Black West Indian). This race hatred often manifested itself in violence. In one story from ***Tropic Death,*** **"Subjection,"** a Black man is killed for trying to prevent the torment of another man by an American marine. The police, often of Spanish descent, are also portrayed as being brutal to West Indians in several stories. However, despite these problems, Walrond felt a fondness for Panama. In a biographical note included with his short story **"Godless City,"** Walrond said, "I am spiritually a native of Panama. I owe the sincerest kind of allegiance to it."

In Panama, Walrond became fluent in Spanish and continued his education in public and private schools and with tutors in Colón. He then accepted a position as a clerk in the Health Department of the Canal Commission in Cristobal before working as a reporter, from 1916 to 1918, for the important Latin American newspaper, *The Panama Star and Herald,* which began its run in 1849 and continues to this day. Walrond said he "used to write up brawls, murders, political scandals, voodoo rituals, labor confabs, campaigns, concerts, dramatic affairs, shipping intelligence, etc." for the paper (**"Godless City"**[1]). Unfortunately, it is difficult to evaluate the extent of Walrond's contributions to the *Star and Herald* since the paper seldom gave bylines; however, his experience with the periodical prompted him to seek new challenges. An American working for the paper gave Walrond "graphic pictures of work and opportunity 'up the States'" (**"Adventures in Misunderstanding"** *World Tomorrow* April 1926: 110). For Walrond, America "was lurking" and on June 30, 1918, he arrived in the United States, where he lived for the next ten years, a time that would constitute the most productive literary period of his life.

When Walrond arrived in New York City, the wave of West Indian immigrants was reaching its peak. Between 1900 and 1914 over 76 percent of the Black immigrants to the U.S. came from the Caribbean, largely the British West Indies (Walter 523). There were over 36,000 foreign born Blacks, mostly West Indians, in Harlem in 1920, up from 3,552 in 1900 (Holder 9). The peak years for West Indian immigration were 1911-24 (Watkins-Owens 4). The reasons these immigrants came at this time were varied. Inexpensive, regular means of transportation to America, first offered in the 1890s by the United Fruit Company, and a combination of poverty, overcrowding, and natural disasters at home all contributed to this influx (Holder 7-9). Whatever their background, West Indians saw the United States as a land of economic opportunity, and the more immigrants that came, the more those at home wanted to come, often because of the favorable reports from those who had preceded them.[2]

Although they may have come to America with great optimism, many West Indian immigrants encountered their first experience with racial prejudice once they arrived here. Jamaican W. A. Domingo wrote that "while color and caste lines tend to converge in the islands, it is nevertheless true that because of the ratio of population, historical background and tradition of rebellions before and since their emancipation, West Indians of color do not have their activities, social, occupational and otherwise, determined by their race" (650). West Indians often did not know how to respond to racial bias, and there were stories of them, when facing discrimination, crying out in anger and confusion, "I am a British subject, I will report this to my consulate" (quoted in Kasinitz 48). Walrond was shocked by the racial prejudice he experienced in New York, and he would carry its scars for the remainder of his life. In **"The Color of the Caribbean,"** he writes:

> On coming to the United States, the West Indian often finds himself out of patience with the attitude he meets here respecting the position of whites and Negroes. He is bewildered—that is, if he is not "clear" enough to pass as a Greek or Spaniard or Italian—at being shoved down certain blocks and alleys "among his own people." He is angry and amazed at the futility of seeking out certain types of employment for which he may be specially adapted. And about the cruelest injury that could be inflicted upon him is to ask him to submit to the notion that because he is black it is useless for him to aspire to be more than a trap drummer at Small's, a Red Cap in Pennsylvania Station, or a clerk in the Bowling Green Post Office.

In addition to racial prejudice, Walrond often felt bias from Blacks born in the United States. After the Civil War, but particularly after 1890, Blacks from the South had begun migrating North in large numbers. The convergence of Southern Blacks and West Indians in Harlem was not always harmonious; indeed, there were tensions between most native-born Americans and immigrants in the years shortly after World War I. West Indians, brought up to value self-respect, hard work, and thrift, were often thought to be arrogant, pushy, and miserly by many Americans. Their food, clothes, language, and culture were sometimes ridiculed as strange, but they clung to these ways, often failing (like Walrond) to become citizens. Walrond poignantly records his own feelings as an outsider in **"White Man, What Now?"**:

> I went on to New York. I settled in the Harlem Negro quarter. I found the community fairly evenly dominated by Southern Negroes and West Indian emigrants. A wide cleavage existed between the two groups. The West Indian with his Scottish, Irish or Devonshire accent, was to the native Black who has still retained a measure of his African folk-culture, uproariously funny. He was joked at on street corners, burlesqued on the stage and discriminated against in business and social life. His pride in his British heritage and lack of racial consciousness were contemptuously put down to "airs."

Despite his considerable experience as a journalist, Walrond had a difficult time finding a newspaper position, largely because of discrimination. Out of necessity, he worked as, among other occupations, a porter, a secretary, a stenographer, and a janitor. The racism he encountered in his employment experiences is described in **"On Being Black"** and **"On Being a Domes-**

tic." Eventually, he obtained work with *The Brooklyn and Long Island Informer* and Marcus Garvey's *The Weekly Review.*

Walrond won a contest sponsored by Garvey's Universal Negro Improvement Association (U.N.I.A.) for a fictional work entitled **"A Senator's Memoirs,"** published in the December 17, 1921, issue of Garvey's weekly, *Negro World.* The sketch is set in a future after Garvey's utopia of a united Africa has been achieved, with Garvey being depicted as a wise, almost godlike leader. The piece is a fantasy demonstrating Walrond's youthful adulation of Garvey. Soon after it appeared, Walrond became an assistant and then an associate editor with the periodical, between 1921 and 1923. This was Walrond's first real break in America, putting him in an important post at an early age. At its zenith in the early 1920s, *Negro World* had a circulation of 200,000 (Martin *Fundamentalism* xv) and boasted of contributors such as Claude McKay, Arthur Schomburg, Carter G. Woodson, Alain Locke, W. A. Domingo, Hubert H. Harrison, and Zora Neale Hurston. As Cary D. Wintz points out, "[t]he years of Walrond's involvement with the paper corresponded with the peak of Garvey's literary activity, some of which anticipated the developments several years later that launched the Harlem Renaissance" (148).

Initially, Walrond was attracted to his fellow West Indian's message, especially Garvey's interest in Black pride, Pan-Africanism, and his defiance of white racism. He wrote several favorable pieces about him and the U.N.I.A. In **"Marcus Garvey—A Defense,"** for instance, Walrond justifies the "czar-like methods" used by Garvey to weed out those less than 100 percent loyal to him. Walrond's essays, reviews, and sketches in the paper tended to stress racial pride, whether he was describing a visit (with Zora Neale Hurston) to bibliophile Arthur Schomburg's library or praising talented Blacks such as performer Bert Williams. Racial pride would remain a major topic for Walrond throughout his life.

Shortly after joining the paper, Walrond's views of Garvey began to change. To some scholars such as Tony Martin, Walrond's eventual rejection of the Garveyite cause made him an opportunist, or worse, a traitor (*Garveyism* 124-32). However, Walrond's shift was probably less determined by opportunistic impulses than by some genuine philosophical differences between himself and Garvey. First, the exact nature of Walrond's relationship with the U.N.I.A. is unclear. The urbane Walrond, raised by a genteel mother and largely privately educated, likely always felt some distance from the more humbly-born Garvey and his mass movement. Furthermore, Walrond in his essays and reviews consistently felt that literature should be judged for its aesthetic quality, not for its political message. As Martin says, "[f]or Walrond, propaganda tended to detract from good art" (*Garveyism* 16). This "anti-propaganda" view of literature often seemed at variance with the rest of the *Negro World* editorial staff. In addition, Walrond's own fiction contributions to *Negro World,* including a series of vignettes praising the beauty of women from a variety of racial backgrounds, were disconcerting to some staff and readers of the periodical. It should also be noted that Walrond was not the only member of Garvey's circle to question his leadership at this time. Garvey's continuing squabbles with other Black leaders, his theatrics, his fiscal troubles over U.N.I.A. funds, his disastrous meeting with members of the Ku Klux Klan in 1922, and the federal investigation of his activities (culminating in his eventual imprisonment in 1925 and deportation in 1927 on charges of mail fraud) all eroded his base of support (Lewis 40-45).

While working with *Negro World,* Walrond began to publish in several white-owned periodicals. **"On Being Black,"** a series of three vignettes portraying racial prejudice, appeared in *The New Republic.* An article praising Black authors, **"Developed and Undeveloped Negro Literature,"** was published in Henry Ford's *Dearborn Independent.* Initially, *Negro World* editors William H. Ferris and Robert L. Poston felt that Walrond's emergence in mainstream periodicals would increase the visibility of Garveyite issues. Ferris, in praising **"On Being Black,"** said that Walrond "is keen and wide-awake, has the gift of expression, and we expect great things from him in the future" (*Negro World* Nov. 18, 1922). However, the *Dearborn* article displays Walrond's increasing disenchantment with the U.N.I.A. The subtitle of the *Dearborn* essay, **"Writers Desert Great Field of Folk-Life for Propagandism,"** shows Walrond's preference for folk literature, not generally featured in *Negro World,* over literature he believed had a more overt political message.

Another essay, **"The New Negro Faces America"** (*Current History*), clearly marks Walrond's growing rift with Garveyism. Here Walrond is critical of Booker T. Washington (as represented by his successor at Tuskegee, Major Robert Moton), W. E. B. Du Bois, and Garvey. Moton is chastised for his emphasis on obtaining white acceptance and for stressing the need for learning "industrial efficiency." Du Bois is derided for being pompous and for his lack of awareness of the conditions of most Blacks; furthermore, he appears to be someone who "hates to be black." Garvey towers "head and shoulders above these two"; however, Walrond believes that Garvey does things "for theatrical effect," makes "preposterous mistakes," and is "a megalomaniac." Most important, he feels that American Blacks have no desire to return to Africa, the cornerstone of Garvey's philosophy. In rejecting all the major Black leaders, Walrond offers his own hopeful view of the New Negro, recounting the economic progress made by the race. This New Negro does not want "to be like the white man." He seeks new leadership. "He is pinning everything on the hope, illusion or not, that America will some day find its soul, forget the negro's black skin, and recognize him as one of the nation's most loyal sons and defenders." It is probably Walrond's most optimistic statement about race relations in America, an optimism that was to be short-lived. Not surprisingly, after the article appeared, Walrond's involvement with *Negro World* virtually ceased and his name was dropped from the editorial staff by August 1923.[3]

After leaving *Negro World,* Walrond reexamined his political perspectives and his literary style. As a result, he published in a variety of venues and experimented with different literary forms between 1923 and 1926. His choice of publications seems intentionally designed to make as emphatic a break from Garvey as possible. One of Walrond's earliest post-*Negro World* pieces (August 1923) was an essay on an artist known as **"El Africano"** in *Crisis,* the journal of Garvey's bitter opponent, W. E. B. Du Bois. This was the only work Walrond ever published in *Crisis* while Du Bois was the editor, not surprising considering Walrond's earlier criticism of him. Du Bois's view that "all Art is propaganda" ("Criteria" 66) was also in opposition to Walrond's theory of art. Du Bois, who believed that literature should depict the lives of the "Talented Tenth," the small group of professional Blacks who would advance the race, had many differences with Garvey, but he would agree with the *Negro World* editor that literature should portray positive images of Blacks. While Walrond was also extremely interested in "uplifting" the Black race, he felt the need to display all aspects of Black life, even unfavorable ones. His praise, for example, of Carl Van Vechten's *Nigger Heaven* (1926) and Claude McKay's *Home to Harlem* (1928) would further distance him from Du Bois and Garvey, who each wrote blistering reviews of these novels depicting the unsavory side of Harlem life.

In the early 1920s, there were also indications that Walrond was beginning to espouse an interest in socialism. This was signaled by his contributions to the leftist periodical *The Messenger,* edited by A. Philip Randolph and Chandler Owen. In **"The Black City"** Walrond forcefully speaks of the contradictions in Harlem, "a sociological *el dorado*" of vibrant creativity and crushing poverty. Walrond would later become a contributing editor of the communist journal *New Masses* from 1926 to 1930, though he never published in it. His links with radical political movements, albeit apparently without ever officially joining the socialist or communist parties, are not surprising considering his ties with the Harlem Caribbean community, where such prominent personalities as Claude McKay, Cyril Briggs, Grace Campbell, Hubert H. Harrison, Richard B. Moore, and Frank R. Crosswaith belonged to such groups. W. A. Domingo, a socialist, was on the editorial staff of *Negro World* until 1919. In fact, there was a popular notion that a Harlem radical by definition was "an over-educated West Indian without a job" (quoted in Watkins-Owens 104). Perhaps these radical tendencies hastened Walrond's break with Garvey, one West Indian leader who was generally opposed to leftist politics.

Besides his essays and reviews, Walrond tried his hand at the short story, penning **"Miss Kenny's Marriage"** for the *Smart Set,* edited by H. L. Mencken. Walrond's tale warns of the dangers of cultural assimilation as the prosperous but poorly connected Miss Kenny, newly arrived in Brooklyn, tries to marry her way into a long-established but hard up Brooklyn family. Miss Kenny's life is all show. Instead of thinking of herself as a hairdresser, she considers herself "a beauty culturist" and spices up her language with words like "trichological." She is an aspiring social climber who believes she is above most Blacks, saying "[t]here ain't none of the nigger in me." Yet despite her flaws, Miss Kenny is a likeable character. She has many friends and is beloved by her customers. When her young husband runs off with all her money, one feels some pity for her. As an outsider trying to fit into a new environment, her situation arouses our sympathy. No doubt Walrond was thinking of his own immigrant experience. Miss Kenny simply gets caught up in the trap of trying to gain happiness through money and status, ironically by selling hair relaxers and skin lighten-ers that might aid in the assimilation process. Fittingly, her shop is described as a "cobwebby parlor." Unfortunately for her, she has been caught in her own snare.

At the same time that **"Miss Kenny's Marriage"** was published, Walrond began writing for Charles S. Johnson's magazine *Opportunity,* an organ of the National Urban League. Johnson, a prominent sociologist, was national director of Research and Investigation for the Urban League and would go on to become the first Black president of Fisk University. No one was further removed from Garvey, a staunch Black separatist, than Johnson, who believed in the necessity of improving interracial relationships and felt that publishing literature displaying the intellectual capabilities of Blacks could help dispel white stereotypes. Johnson's importance to the literary movement was so strong that Langston Hughes said that he "did more to encourage and develop Negro writers during the 1920's than anyone else in America" (quoted in Lewis 125). Johnson's appreciation of literature for its aesthetic qualities appealed to Walrond, although he ultimately questioned Johnson's optimistic view of race relations.

Walrond began to hone his skills at fiction, writing six stories for *Opportunity:* four brief sketches relating encounters with racial discrimination and two pieces set in Panama that are precursors to the stories in ***Tropic Death.*** He even won a third prize in *Opportunity*'s 1925 literary contest for **"The Voodoo's Revenge."** The most intriguing of these pieces are **"Vignettes of the Dusk"** and **"The Stone Rebounds."** Walrond's work for *Opportunity,* as with other publications, often seemed contrary to the goal of the journal and the organization that supported it. His independent views would not allow him to adhere strictly to a particular party line.

"Vignettes of the Dusk" is a series of five short scenes depicting prejudice in a myriad of forms. The most full-developed of the vignettes is the first piece, set in the middle of New York's financial district. The nameless narrator has some money and seeks a more upscale eatery than is his usual wont, dreaming of mingling with the wealthy and marveling at "the beauty that is America." He is in awe of the fancy restaurant and is almost afraid to enter. When he does, he feels he does not belong and is only able to whisper his order: "Oyster salad—and vanilla temptation." The "vanilla temptation" so tentatively ordered is symbolic of the "weirdly enchanting" lure of the restaurant, and to a larger extent, white America. Oysters, often thought of as an aphrodisiac, perhaps allude to sexual stereotypes of Blacks or the narrator's own repressed desires. The waiter hands him the bag "as if its contents were leprous." The man meekly leaves, but he realizes that he's been essentially "sho[o]ed out." The message seems to be that white America wants no part of integration between the races and that if Blacks aspire to the "vanilla temptation," they will only face rejection.

Jay Berry believes that in **"The Stone Rebounds"** Walrond "assumes the persona of a white writer who has been ostracized by his colleagues for bringing a black playwright to an all-white literary gathering. Later in the story the black playwright is implicitly and indirectly criticized by his black friends for bringing the white writer into a Harlem cabaret" (298). However, the story conveys a more subtle message than mere mutual racial intolerance. Kraus, the egotistical white narrator (an attribute immediately apparent when he uses the word "I" thirty-one times in the opening paragraph), lacks any insight. He can blithely declare, "I haven't any prejudices." When Earl, his Black friend, suggests that they go to Harlem, Kraus jumps at the suggestion. He had never before visited it, but he immediately feels "[i]t is so—Bohemian." After badgering some guests with a discussion of race, there is an awkward silence while he tries "to think up clever things to say." Clearly he does not belong here, but he is too self-absorbed to realize it: "I look around. On me a houseful of eyes is cast. I do not feel out of place. I rejoice in the reaction. I know why they are staring at me. I am white." Unlike the nameless narrator in **"Vignettes of the Dusk,"** who appears ashamed of his race, Kraus exults in his whiteness.

Kraus is an armchair radical who knows little about the people or causes he purports to advance. He merely wants to be seen as avant-garde. Interestingly, the guests at the party think that he is an anthropologist, probably there to study them. They believe the only whites interested in Blacks are ones that can get something out of them. In Kraus's case, they have good reason to be suspicious. He exhibits the most superficial understanding of interracial relationships, reveling in the "exotic" differences between Blacks and whites, and ultimately he has a smug sense of superiority in being white. It is a fascinating piece, especially in a journal attempting to advance better relationships between the races. In an interview with Jacques Lebar in 1933, Walrond said he had little interest in writing about whites. This devastating critique is one of his few examinations of the white psyche.

FROM THE AUTHOR

CHARACTERISTICS OF THE NEW NEGRO

In the first place he is race conscious. He does not want to be like the white man. He is coming to realize the great possibilities within himself, and his tendency is to develop those possibilities. He is looking toward a broader leadership. . . . The new negro, who does not want to go back to Africa, is fondly cherishing an ideal—and that is, that the time will come when America will look upon the negro not as a savage with an inferior mentality, but as a civilized man. . . . He is pinning everything on the hope, illusion or not, that America will some day find its soul, forget the Negro's black skin, and recognize him as one of the nation's most loyal sons and defenders.

SOURCE: Eric Walrond, excerpt from " The New Negro Faces America," in *Current History* 17, February 1923.

Walrond's affiliation with *Opportunity* thrust him into the progressive, race-building New Negro Movement. The affable West Indian made a great hit at social events. Ethel Ray Nance, Charles S. Johnson's secretary, recalled Walrond: "He had flashing eyes; his face was very alert and very alive" (quoted in Lewis 128). He moved to Harlem (108 West 144th St.) from Brooklyn to be closer to the center of the New Negro Movement and soon became "the 'rage' of the early and mid-1920s" (Arthur P. Davis cited in Bogle 475). Through Johnson, he met and established friendships with many significant figures of the Harlem Renaissance, including Howard University professor Alain Locke and writers Gwendolyn Bennett, Countee Cullen, and Langston Hughes.[4]

Walrond's contributions to the Harlem Renaissance were significant during his time as business manager of *Opportunity* (August 1925 to February 1927). His careful monitoring of the financially fragile periodical helped assure its solvency. He was also instrumental in obtaining the support of the wealthy West Indian-born numbers banker Casper Holstein, who helped to sponsor *Opportunity*'s writing contests; Walrond would later dedicate ***Tropic Death*** to Holstein. Furthermore, Walrond helped to broaden the international scope of the journal. He was largely responsible for a special November 1926 issue focusing on the Caribbean, which included work by Holstein, McKay, and Domingo. An editorial praises Walrond's contribution: "To his thorough acquaintance with the spokesmen of the Caribbean in this country, we are indebted for the section of special articles which appear in these pages" (334).

In addition to these achievements, Walrond recommended the inclusion of many of the younger New Negro writers in *Opportunity*. A number of these authors were represented in Alain Locke's anthology *The New Negro* (1925), considered by many literary historians to be one of the most significant cultural manifestos of the Harlem Renaissance. Walrond contributed a short story, **"The Palm Porch,"** later included in ***Tropic Death.***[5] He had great respect for Locke, a very proper, highly educated man, the first Black to be awarded a Rhodes scholarship. Locke's reaction against literature "*about* the Negro rather than of him" (Foreword *The New Negro* xxv) rang true with Walrond. The Howard professor's interest in Black folklore and in the depiction of Blacks other than just the "Talented Tenth" also appealed to Walrond.

Walrond enjoyed socializing with Locke and others in the "Talented Tenth." He belonged to the very formal Harlem Eclectic Club, a "dickty" (high society) organization that was appalled when Claude McKay failed, as he said in his autobiography, to "put on a dress suit to appear before them" (114). However, Walrond's fiction rarely deals with the lives of the New Negro elite. In his earlier *Dearborn* essay, Walrond expresses his admiration for folk literature, especially singling out for praise Paul Laurence Dunbar. He expands upon this interest in the common folk in his essay, **"The Negro Literati."** Walrond, discussing depictions of upper-class Black life in fiction, argues, "if there is a society that is more stilted, more snobbish, that is harder to break into, than the Negro society these tales depict, then I've yet to hear about it." He believes that many Black authors, afraid of having whites see Blacks in a disparaging light, create an unrealistic, sterile atmosphere in their works. Instead of writing about the "Talented Tenth," as does someone like Jessie Fauset, Walrond advises the Black author to "paint pictures of people—of tantalizing black people—he knows." The authors whom he most admires, such as Dunbar, Hughes, Zora Neale Hurston, and Jean Toomer, all write in this Black folk tradition.[6] Therefore, it is not surprising that his major literary work, ***Tropic Death,*** concerns itself with the lives of ordinary folk in Barbados, Panama, and British Guiana. And, like the work of Dunbar, Hughes, Hurston, and Toomer, these stories are told in the vernacular. The title ***Tropic Death*** suggests Walrond's Caribbean: lush, beautiful, and teeming with life, but death looms behind every corner, no matter how blissful things may appear.

The ten stories in ***Tropic Death*** hold a unique place in Black literature. One of the book's most important aspects is its focus on Blacks outside the United States, displaying the Pan-African element of the Harlem Renaissance. Kenneth Ramchand calls the collection "one of the startling treasures in the lost literature of the West Indies" (67). Robert A. Hill goes further, saying it is "probably the greatest short story work in the entire body of West Indian literature" (Introduction to Garvey's *Black Man* 19). In ***Tropic Death,*** Walrond writes of the migratory nature of many Caribbean people, the oppressive colonial system which had been established in the area, the colorism that white racism had facilitated, the changes being wrought by industrialization, the beauty and harshness of the land, and the maintenance of traditional culture such as folklore, songs, and obeah (a folk belief in magic).

He is particularly concerned with the languages of the people, and he takes great pains to recreate the many dialects of the region, generally succeeding with remarkable dexterity.[7] Jamaican-born writer Michelle Cliff describes how in her writing she alternates "the King's English with *patois,* not only to show the class background of characters, but to show how Jamaicans operate within a split consciousness" (59-60). Walrond does much the same in ***Tropic Death,*** using language to probe both the European and the African aspects of Caribbean identity. Walrond, a Black immigrant living in America, often felt a duality somewhat akin to the split consciousness Du Bois ascribed to African Americans. Walrond took great pride in his heritage, celebrating his culture and language, yet he was also aware of the potential rewards (and the frequent dangers) of identifying with the language and ways of white folks. Challenging the stereotypical American view of a monolithic Caribbean, Walrond depicts a complex area rich in linguistic and cultural diversity. An examination of four representative stories in the book suggests the range of subjects Walrond explores.

"Drought," like the other stories in ***Tropic Death,*** does not present a romantic, idealized version of the Caribbean. Walrond had witnessed firsthand the devastating consequences of droughts, which periodically plagued Barbados in the early twentieth century (Richardson 15). The Barbadian peasants described in the story struggle against the forces of nature and man. The sun is seen not as a life-giving source but as an adversary, having "robbed the land of its juice, squeezed it dry." The people pray to an unfeeling God to ease the suffering caused by the drought. They are insignificant compared to the forces of nature; the protagonist, Coggins Rum, named after one of the island's major commodities, is "a black, animate dot" on the white marl road.

The harsh environment is not the only obstacle with which the natives must contend. The effects of British colonialism are also felt. Throughout the story whiteness is linked with oppression and death. The road is for the benefit of the colonizers. The road crew is led by a buckra (white) "driver" (reminiscent of the days of slavery) who has a Black mistress. However, despite the grinding poverty endured by the peasants, there is a deadly appeal in the white colonial system. The natives must wrench "themselves free of the lure of the white earth." They still follow such British rituals as having high tea at dusk, clinging "to the utmost vestiges of the Crown," but, as demonstrated in the tragic case of Coggins's six-year-old daughter Beryl, who rejects the family food and dies after stuffing herself with marl, contact with whiteness can lead to destruction. There is a suggestion, in fact, that the light-complexioned girl, with "white, shiny, appealing" eyes, "the only one of the Rum children who wasn't black as sin," may have been the result of an extramarital liaison of her mother. Ironically, the child dies at dusk, obtaining relief through death from her hard life just as the land gains relief from "the livid sun."

A frequent concern of Walrond's, as George Hutchinson remarks, is "the North American obsession with racial definability" (409). Jamaican-born Miss Buckner, in **"The Palm Porch,"** is one of Walrond's many characters with such an obsession. She is the proprietor of a bordello in Colón in which she employs her own daughters. In many ways, Miss Buckner is like her establishment. Just as the palm porch keeps "out eyes effectively," so too is Miss Buckner cloaked in secrecy. Wild rumors swirl through the city about this "half-white" woman, but no one knows the "mystical heritage" of her or her five daughters.

The palm porch is described as being "opulent" but filled with "illusion," again appropriate descriptions for Miss Buckner. She dresses in elaborate Victorian garb, but her clothing holds hidden danger, a dagger which she is not averse to using on unruly clients. After having killed one such patron with the dagger, she can calmly debate what type of dessert to have for lunch.

Miss Buckner's life is ruled by a rigid code of decorum which dictates that her daughters cannot take up with those she feels are beneath them. Obsessed with colorism, the haughty Miss Buckner (we never learn her given name) is appalled that two daughters have run off with darker complexioned men. She would much rather that they become involved with the olive-skinned Spanish captain who comes to the palm porch.

In Miss Buckner's world, one can have "manners" and display "proper" behavior despite engaging in murder and prostitution. Although Miss Buckner's actions certainly cannot be condoned, she is not without her virtues. She is an enterprising, forceful woman; in fact, she is reminiscent (with some obvious differences) of Mrs. Mooney in James Joyce's story "The Boarding House," a woman who "dealt with moral problems as a cleaver deals with meat." Again, Walrond, as an outsider, could feel some sympathy for an independent person struggling to survive in a hostile, unfamiliar environment.

In **"The Vampire Bat,"** Walrond effectively uses folklore in recounting the story of Bellon Prout, a white plantation owner who has just returned to Barbados after fighting the Boers. Prout, "a solid pillar of the Crown," refuses to take the advice of an old mulatto who warns him not to travel at night. He also dismisses the story of a frightened Black woman who tells of having seen a "man in de [sugar] canes." Continuing his journey, he sees a Black child in the burning cane fields. Prout, assuming it is an innocent victim left to die, picks up the babe; however, in the morning, Prout's bloodless body is found with a small mark on the forehead.

"The Vampire Bat" may appear to be a slight story, even if chillingly told. It is, in fact, a gothic tale, a form at which Walrond could excel. Tales of obeah, duppies (spirits), and fire hags (spirits "shedding their skins and waltzing forth at night as sheep and goats, on errands of fiery vengeance") are woven throughout the story. However, **"The Vampire Bat"** is more than just a potboiler. The story is almost allegorical in nature, amounting to a warning to the colonizers of the West Indies. Prout's destination, Mount Tabor, is "a garden of lustrous desolation," a fallen Eden, mirroring the destruction of Barbados brought on by the British as well as a harbinger of Prout's (and by extension the plantation system's) own demise. Prout's home is near Locust Hall, appropriate for the destructive nature of the colonizers; in fact, it was one of the central sugar cane factories on the island (Beckles 148). In this case, however, the British (normally the parasites) become the hosts. Prout fails to recognize the significance of the burning of the cane field, an act of rebellion against the plantocracy. He sees the child and thinks of "[a]nother of the colony's lurking evils, the desertion—often the murder of illegitimate Negro babes." Yet the plantation owner, in his arrogance, has ignored the warnings he has been given. He dismisses the customs and beliefs of the natives as mere superstition. As a result, his body is drained "utterly white and bloodless," the victim of a culture he has denigrated. It is a striking story of vengeance on those who exploit the islands of the West Indies, using the people and land for their own selfish purposes.

Walrond describes the migration of Barbadians to Panama in **"Tropic Death,"** perhaps his most autobiographical story. Walrond, like the young protagonist Gerald Bright, did emigrate from Barbados to a poor area in Panama. He, like Bright, did have a fierce love for his mother. Walrond wrote, "I owe everything to the encouragement of my mother and her determination" (note to **"Godless City"**). His mother, like the mother in the story, was a devout follower of the Plymouth Brethren, a Christian fundamentalist group Walrond describes in several stories. Walrond's family, too, went in search of a father who had gone to work in the Canal Zone. Indeed, the bond between mothers and sons, particularly when fathers are absent, is a recurrent theme in Walrond's work (Bogle 479-80).[8]

The tripartite setting of the story—in Barbados, on shipboard, and in Panama—mirrors the psychological passage of Gerald Bright from innocence to knowledge of evil and finally to forgiveness. The story is filled with religious imagery. When we first see Gerald, he is a sheltered child, one who had joyfully played in the hills of his small village in Barbados. Though poor, he has been spared the kind of existence lived by the street urchins of Bridgetown. Gerald feels veneration toward his mother for having saved him from such a life: "He wanted . . . to breathe the lovely, holy beauty of her." During the hideous Middle Passage to Panama, "[t]he sun baptized the sea."

On the crowded, fetid ship, Gerald listens to a religious zealot calling for God's forgiveness. Upon his arrival in Panama, the boy is reunited with his father, Lucian (reminiscent of the fallen angel, Lucifer), who is a womanizer and a drunkard, living in a "noisy and vulgar" place. Lucian is diseased, spiritually as well as physically, and is about to be put in a leper colony. Despite his initial anger at his father, Gerald gradually comes to love him. Although he has lost social status because of the father's desertion of the family, the boy has gained "a new resiliency, a greater maturity, and a wider experience of life" (Bone 198). It is a lesson he has learned from his mother. In contrast to her half-brother Charlie, who believes that all sinners must be condemned, Sarah maintains her belief that it is possible to obtain God's forgiveness. Despite the strictness of her religious beliefs, she shows kindness toward her husband, which prompts him to show concern, perhaps for the first time, for his family: "An' yo' mus' tek good cyah o' yo'self, heah Sarah, an' don't le' nobody tek exvantage o' yo', yo' heah, dis is a bad country—." Fittingly, this, the final story in ***Tropic Death,*** is the only piece in the collection that allows for some possibility of redemption.

Walrond's generally sympathetic portrayal of the Plymouth Brethren in the story suggests his own inner turmoil. Although Walrond enjoyed the pleasures of life too much to embrace such a harsh religion, he found it difficult to criticize the Brethren because of his feelings toward his mother. In addition, there was likely at least some appeal to Walrond in the religion, which encouraged Black leadership in the church, advocated the concerns of poorer Barbadians, and allowed the incorporation of African culture into traditional Anglican rituals (Richardson 221-23; Beckles 154).[9]

Walrond's treatment of such subjects as prostitution, colorism, poverty, crime, and vengeance in ***Tropic Death*** caused controversy. Wallace Thurman, the radical leader of the younger New Negro writers, warned that if Walrond turned his focus to America, he would "be blacklisted in polite colored circles" ("Negro Artists" 37). Indeed, as Chidi Ikonné notes, "[m]ost of the subjects treated by Walrond are matters which a large part of the black literati of the West Indies and the United States would have liked to leave unrevealed" (179). Therefore, it is not surprising that Du Bois ("Books" 152) offers a mixed evaluation of the book (although his quarrels are more with the use of dialect and the impressionistic style rather than the subject matter). Generally, however, the book was well received. Langston Hughes writes, "[t]he throbbing life and sun-bright hardness of these pages fascinate me" (9), while Benjamin Brawley believes "it is the most important contribution made by a Negro to American letters since the appearance [in 1896] of [Paul Laurence] Dunbar's 'Lyrics of Lowly Life'" (179). Even Du Bois concedes that "on the whole, it is a human document of deep significance and great promise" ("Books" 152). The favorable response of the critics prompted Walrond's publisher, Boni and Liveright, to issue a second printing and provide an advance for another book, ***The Big Ditch,*** on the building of the Panama Canal. ***Tropic Death*** secured Walrond's reputation, and many people felt he would write the great novel of the Harlem Renaissance, a pressure that would weigh heavily on him.[10]

"City Love," published in the anthology *American Caravan* (1927), added to Walrond's stature. The story is perhaps the finest literary work depicting the lives of West Indian immigrants during the Harlem Renaissance. Primus, the main character, tries to seduce a woman, Nicey, taking her to a hotel where they are rejected because they have no baggage. Primus goes home to get bags and has a row with his wife. He goes to another hotel with Nicey, but again they are refused, this time because Nicey does not have a hat. Determined to fulfill his desires, he buys a hat for her and they are finally admitted. Primus's pursuit of his mistress is filled with irony. First, we see that there is no love in this city, only lust. The lure of the city, indeed of America, for the immigrant turns out to be false. City life is sordid, squalid, and ultimately frustrating. Primus pretends to have status, but in reality, he comes from "de Back Swamp" and in New York lives in a broken-down apartment building. He is desperate to assimilate into his new surroundings, perhaps one reason why he pursues Nicey, whose speech is far less creolized than that of Tiny, his wife; in fact, the more excited he gets, the more his own accent comes out.

Primus thinks of himself as being experienced and in charge of his life; however, we see that he is a greenhorn who is powerless in his relationships with his wife, his lover, his coworkers, and the hotel workers where he brings Nicey. Instead of taking out his anger at its real sources, he rages ineffectively at his infant son. The immigrant Primus is, as Robert Bone suggests, treated as a child by the society around him and so, in frustration, he bullies his own son in a futile attempt to gain power (183). It is altogether fitting that this story, mocking a West Indian man unable to master the rules of life in the United States, was Walrond's last significant work published in America.

Walrond's success as an author may be measured by three major awards he received in 1927-28: a Harmon Award in Literature, a Zona Gale scholarship at the University of Wisconsin,[11] and a Guggenheim Award to "[t]ravel and study in the West Indies for the purpose of obtaining material for a series of novels and short stories depicting native life there" (Henry Allen Moe letter, March 13, 1928). After winning the Guggenheim award, Walrond left for Panama in September 1928, and he diligently reported his travels to Panama, Haiti, the Dominican Republic, St. Kitts, Barbados, and the Virgin Islands over the next two years to Henry Allen Moe, the secretary for the Guggenheim Foundation. He would scarcely return to America after this time. Walrond pursued many projects during his travels, perhaps being overwhelmed by possible material for study. A brief trip to Haiti, for example, caused him to consider writing a book on the country's history from 1804 to 1915 and another on the American occupation of the country beginning in 1915. These works, however, never appeared. Neither did the "series of novels" mentioned in his award, although no doubt some of his experiences became the grist for a handful of later stories. Instead, Walrond's attention turned to ***The Big Ditch,*** particularly the French involvement in the Panama Canal, and he requested permission from Guggenheim officials to continue his research and writing in France (letter to Moe, April 2, 1929).

Walrond arrived in Paris in July 1929, and he stayed in France until 1932. French interest in African culture, particularly its masks, dances, and oral literature, had been growing steadily since the turn of the century. A thriving Black community existed in France and several of Walrond's literary friends, including Countee Cullen and Gwendolyn Bennett, had spoken with him about life there. The ever-sociable Walrond easily fit into French society, and he was seen at many parties (Stovall 65, 98). He took an interest in French literature, especially the works of Gustave Flaubert and Blaise Cendrars. However, his extravagant lifestyle put him in constant need of money, and although he received a six-month extension of his Guggenheim grant, it was feared by his friends that he was quickly using up his resources.

Canadian and West Indian author John Hearne, in reflecting on Walrond, is puzzled that there is so little evidence documenting his time in France (cited in Bogle 476). There are, however, some tantalizing morsels from these years. In 1931, Walrond became part of the entourage of British steamship heiress Nancy Cunard (Crowder 132). Cunard, who shocked "polite" society with her political and social views (she was a communist and lived with Black musician Henry Crowder for several years), assembled and published a massive anthology of Black literature and culture, *Negro* (1934). Although Walrond was asked to contribute to this collection, he refused unless he received payment (Kellner 90).

Also during this period, Walrond shared an apartment for a time with Countee Cullen. The two men had long been friends, working together briefly on *Opportunity,* and Walrond had favorably reviewed Cullen's volume *Color* for the *New Republic,* writing "if there ever was a poet ordained by the stars to sing of the joys and sorrows attendant upon the experience of thwarted black folk placed in wretched juxtaposition to our Western civilization, that poet is Countee Cullen." Walrond appreciated the strength, beauty, and grace of Cullen's poetry, and Cullen returned this admiration. One of his most famous poems, "Incident," is dedicated to Walrond. Appropriately, it is perhaps Cullen's most biting racial poem, for as Blanche E. Ferguson observes, Walrond's "militant outgoing personality was a helpful contrast to Cullen's introspection" (120-21).

Walrond's writings in Europe, though not abundant, do add to our knowledge of Black expatriate life on the Continent in the 1930s and 1940s. In the early 1930s, he published several articles on Harlem and the Panama Canal for French and Spanish periodicals (Fabre 138-39). **"Harlem"** (1933) is a sketch that depicts "the Black capital" as a lively, exciting but wildly hedonistic place. Black Harlemites, like most Americans, are seen as being obsessed with making money, but because of discrimination, they can only get it through buying on credit or obtaining stolen goods. The desire for wealth led to numerous illegal activities, such as theft, prostitution, and bootlegging, frequently conducted with the tacit approval of white law officers.

The articles on the history of the Panama Canal, particularly **"Como de Hizo el Canal de Panama"** in the Madrid magazine *Ahora* (1934), are also intriguing, giving us a glimpse of ***The Big Ditch.*** Walrond continued to work on the book, and still hoped to publish it. In fact, there seemed to be enough material for two books, one "a story of the French attempt to construct a canal through Nicaragua" and another "telling the story of the American construction of the Panama Canal" (Moe to Horace Hitchcock, letter, Sept. 17, 1931).

In France, Walrond felt less of the racial discrimination he had experienced in the United States or would later encounter in England. Upon returning to America briefly in 1931, he said, "there's no particular thrill in being here again. . . . Only urgent business brought me back to this country." In commenting on his life in France, he remarked that "[n]one of the difficulties and interruptions which infest Harlem are present here" ("Eric Walrond" 11). Jacques Lebar's interview with Walrond reveals some of his feelings on the conditions for Blacks in America and France. Walrond remarks that it is easier for Blacks to assimilate in France than in America, yet one conjectures that even in the relatively benign atmosphere of France, Walrond believes that fragmentation occurs. He tells Lebar it is "your country," and he cannot remain in France any more than he could in America. He needed to come full circle. The British subject must finally venture to the "homeland."

Walrond moved to England in 1932 and, except for some years traveling, spent his remaining years there. Although Walrond's years in England remain shrouded in mystery, the following sketch may provide seeds for future research. Once in England, he was reunited with Garvey in the mid-1930s and contributed several articles to Garvey's periodical, *The Black Man.* Their reconciliation is not completely surprising. First, Garvey had never been too harsh on Walrond. His strongest words against him came in an article criticizing Claude McKay (*Negro World* Sept. 29, 1928). Walrond had been grouped with other Black writers, including Walter White and James Weldon Johnson, whom Garvey felt had been used by white publishers to cast Blacks in a disparaging light. Garvey knew that Walrond could still be useful as an author and editor in the attempt to resuscitate the flagging U.N.I.A. Walrond, in fact, published more in *The Black Man* than anyone other than Garvey himself. He was still attracted to Garvey's fighting spirit and, not finding a great deal of success in placing his works elsewhere, saw he might obtain steady employment with *The Black Man.* In addition, Walrond, soured by the racism he had encountered in America and in England, was even more receptive to Garvey's warnings about the dangers of assimilation than he had been in his younger days.[12]

Several of Walrond's *Black Man* pieces chronicle his disenchantment with the position of Blacks in England. As a youth, Walrond saw "England through a romantic and illusive veil" (**"The Negro in London"**). Upon his arrival in the "Mother Country," however, he felt alienation and discrimination because of prejudice based on race and class. This was a devastating experience for Walrond. Like many West Indians, Walrond valued many aspects of British culture, which he felt was a large part of his own identity. Encountering prejudice in Panama or America was insulting enough, but having to face it in England must have been particularly heinous for him. Perhaps this disillusionment and alienation caused the increasing militancy in these later essays. In **"The Negro before the World,"** for example, he inveighs against capitalism and imperialism, which he believes fatten off the working class only to benefit a small privileged group. In **"On England,"** Walrond attacks the rigid British class system in which "any person of gentle birth, any unborn candidate for the playing fields of Eton, any suave, gilt-edged rascal may be a gentleman." While these scamps run the government, those in the Empire are left "a crushed, unorganized and completely voiceless mass." Walrond's radical politics would continue in his articles for the *People's Voice,* edited by Harlem activist Reverend Adam Clayton Powell Jr. in the 1940s.[13]

Several of Walrond's articles in the *People's Voice* deal with the treatment of Blacks in the Royal Air Force. Walrond's anger over the lack of respect given to British soldiers in Britain is apparent in the short story **"By the River Avon,"** set in Bradford-on-Avon, in Wiltshire, where Walrond had moved in 1939. The piece, about a Black GI in England, denounces the hypocrisy of British "egalitarianism."[14]

A biographical note with **"By the River Avon"** indicated that Walrond had another collection of fiction "under his hat." Two such stories, **"Wind in the Palms"** (Sept. 1954) and **"Success Story"** (Feb.-May 1954), were published in *Roundway Review.*[15] Both pieces deal with memories from Walrond's youth in the Caribbean. The protagonist, Coolie, in **"Wind in the Palms"** is a "dougla" (a mixed race child of Black and East Indian ancestry) growing up in Colón. Although he does not know his Indian father and his name itself is a racial slur against Indians, Coolie looks down upon Blacks, vowing never to marry a woman with a wide nose. As in a number of earlier writings, Walrond is critical of the destructiveness of racism and self-loathing.

"Success Story" is, after **"Tropic Death,"** Walrond's longest published piece. Like **"Tropic Death,"** it is largely autobiographical, narrating the life of Jim Prout from his birth in British Guiana through his migrations to Barbados, Panama, and the United States. Although the story is filled with references to Walrond's own life, the process of assimilation Prout undergoes could describe any number of new immigrants to America. The story ends with Prout finally gaining employment in the shipping department of a soap company, a job Walrond himself once held.

In September 1957, Walrond returned to London. Along with Rosey E. Pool, a Dutch professor, he selected poems for a program of African American poetry presented at the Royal Court Theatre in London on October 5, 1958. The poems were published as a book entitled, like the program, *Black and Unknown Bards* by the Hand and Flower Press in 1958. The poems were selected to depict the history and conditions of Black life in America. Walrond worked diligently researching the material to be used for the recital, including spirituals, older writers such as McKay, Hughes, and Cullen, but also younger artists like Robert Hayden, Margaret Walker, and Gwendolyn Brooks. The work helped to bridge the gap between the different generations and draw attention to some poets who were not well known in England at the time.

Walrond worked on several projects for the remainder of his life. He selected photographs of African sculpture for a book on African art by Boris de Rachewiltz published in 1959. He also vowed, in a letter to Henry Allen Moe from 1960, to pursue his writing (cited in Ramchand 74-75). He sought, without success, a publisher for his book on the French involvement with the Panama Canal (entitled ***The Second Battle***). In addition, even up until his final years, Walrond resiliently explored ideas for new fiction and expressed interest in republishing ***Tropic Death*** with revisions he had made.

Despite all his plans, Walrond's literary output decreased in his later years. Perhaps a sense of self-doubt that had long plagued him stifled his genius. Walrond seems to have been driven to excel as a writer. He says, "I have got to get there—there are so many reasons why I must find my place in the sun!" (note to **"Godless City"**). His letters often speak, though, of the brooding nature that sometimes prevented him from writing. As early as 1924, he laments in several letters to Alain Locke (Moorland-Spingarn, Howard University) that he is feeling anxiety and depression that inhibit his creativity. He constantly chides himself for not fulfilling his capabilities. His letters late in life to Henry Allen Moe continue to voice this same concern. He could well have been burdened by his youthful success and his own and other people's expectations. Or perhaps he was just tired, tired of a life of constant migration and of continually fighting the prejudice he encountered wherever he went. It is this fatigue that may account for his remaining in England for over thirty years despite often feeling discrimination. In any event, Walrond was largely forgotten by the time of his death in August 1966.

Walrond's life was filled with paradox. His links at various times with different movements may seem contradictory or self-serving, but his gradual evolution reflects stages also experienced by Claude McKay. Walrond and McKay, as West Indian Blacks, never felt completely at home in the United States or Europe. Exiles, as Edward Said has indicated, often feel a strong need to belong and join organizations in an attempt to fit in their new land (150). Walrond and McKay sought a place in Garveyism, the New Negro Movement, and socialism, but none of these movements adequately addressed the authors' concerns with race and identity. Ultimately, Walrond abhorred any movement that he felt was doctrinaire, one which stressed politics over art. Inevitably, as he became more closely involved with different political, social, and literary movements, he became disenchanted with the dogma that frequently accompanied them. As the fictional Cedric Williams, a West Indian short story writer modeled after Walrond in Wallace Thurman's *roman à clef, Infants of the Spring* (1932), says, "There is ample room for everyone to follow his own individual track. . . . Only in that way will anything at all be achieved" (240). The view expressed by Williams, that the Black artist is best served by keeping an independent mind rather than slavishly following any one specific ideology, is one with which Walrond would concur.

The dominating force in Walrond's life was not so much any political or literary "movement" as actual geographic "movement." The history of the Caribbean is one built on migration, both voluntary and enforced. It is a pattern that continues to this day.[16] Walrond felt this migration in his own life, having spent considerable time in six countries, four by the time he was twenty. Not surprisingly, the movement of Blacks within and to the Caribbean, the United States, and Europe is a major focus in his work.[17] As Robert Bone states, "[h]uman transplantation is Walrond's essential theme" (177). Although shortly after leaving America he would tell people in the Virgin Islands that he felt more American than West Indian (Gereau 1), he generally identified the Caribbean as "home." Therefore, he can look at himself in the United States as a "foreigner" (a term by which he defines himself in **"Negro Literati"**). The same is true of his life in France and England. That is why his work constantly returns to the area of his youth. Like many people from the Caribbean, Walrond became a permanent migrant, always having a sense of home while simultaneously feeling the loss of it. This contradiction is what often adds power and poignancy to his work. Despite the torture of living in an American or European society in which he faced racism he could neither understand nor accept, he returned to the Caribbean only for short visits. For this reason, perhaps, his work, as critics such as Hugh Gloster (181-83) have pointed out, is detached, enabling him to write objectively about the area. Such detachment is often true for writers in exile (Said 150-51).[18]

As Guyanese-born author Jan Carew notes, "[t]he Caribbean person is subjected to successive waves of cultural alienation from birth—a process that has its origins embedded in a mosaic of cultural fragments—Amerindian, African, European, Asian" (91). Michelle Cliff echoes this sentiment when she states, "[w]e are a fragmented people . . . coming from a culture of colonialism, a culture of Black people riven from each other" (60). Walrond throughout his adult life was fragmented wherever he lived because of his position as a racial and ethnic outsider. Edward Said, citing Theodor Adorno, expresses the belief that through writing, often of their native lands, many exiles attempt to gain wholeness. They are motivated "by the belief that the only home truly available now, though fragile and vulnerable, is in writing" (150). Walrond, recognizing the fragmentation in his life, felt the need to build a home. There is often an urgency in his writing to confront his own homelessness and that of people like him. His need to document their stories, record their achievements, and pass on their heritage is, in fact, his response to the fragmentation caused by migration and the pain caused by racial and ethnic prejudice. No other element resonates more strongly in Walrond's writing than this sense of racial consciousness. In his interview with Jacques Lebar he concludes: "My duty and my *raison d'être* are to give an accurate portrayal of my race, its history, its sufferings, its hopes and its rebellions. Therein lies a rich source of emotion and pain. It is there that I draw the essence of my work, and I will dedicate my energy as a writer to serving the Black race."[19]

Rebecca Chalmers Barton believes that Walrond and McKay are writers "of local color" (108). As such, they are trying to preserve in writing a vibrant oral tradition, a history the authors feel needs to be passed on. David Anderson, in a call for papers toward a book on Claude McKay, expresses the opinion "that McKay has been unjustly ignored, partly because his multinational career does not fit the nationalist criteria used to construct African American and Caribbean literary canons and partly because his multifaceted literary output over several decades does not fit within the narrow historical and cultural boundaries accorded such literary movements as the Harlem Renaissance" (158). These words also can be aptly applied to Walrond, who has been summarily dismissed in many studies of both African American and Caribbean literature, in large part because of the difficulty in categorizing him. Margaret Perry, for example, in her survey of Harlem Renaissance literature *Silence to the Drums,* says "Eric Waldrond's [sic] best stories were uniquely West Indian; hence, they should be examined as Caribbean literature" (111). However, Walrond's work, like that of McKay and many others born outside the United States, speaks forcefully for a large segment of America's population. It represents a voice that must not be forgotten.

Notes

1. See the note to the story "Godless City," pp. 332-33 in this volume.

2. Statistics on Black immigrants are difficult to break down since no distinction tends to be made for place of origin. I have used Kasinitz's term to define West Indian: "people of African descent from the English-speaking Caribbean, including the mainland nations of Guyana and Belize, as well as their descendants from the English-speaking black diaspora communities in officially Spanish- and Dutch-speaking countries" (14).

3. Walrond criticizes Garvey more severely in "The Hebrews of the Black Race" (*International Interpreter* July 14, 1923). In this essay he condemns Garvey for stirring America's anti-West Indian sentiment. Walrond calls him "crude, blatant, egocentric, a mental lilliputian" who "by virtue of his upbringing, training, and early environment, is not representative of the best the West Indian Negroes have to offer."

   Walrond wrote one final essay on Garvey, "Imperator Africanus" (1925). There he praises Garvey for his oratorical skills and his strong resistance to white racism, but in terms of business sense, he "is a hopeless nincompoop." Still, Walrond has some sympathy for

Garvey, who remains "[un]daunted, unswerved" by the sniping of Du Bois and other Black leaders.

4. Walrond's move also marked another change in his life: his divorce from his Jamaican-born wife, Edith, with whom he had three daughters, Jean, Dorothy, and Lucille. According to Enid Bogle, Walrond remarried while in Europe (476).

5. The version of "The Palm Porch" contained in *The New Negro* seems very much like a draft. It is far less subtle in its usage of language and treatment of its subject matter than the story published a year later in *Tropic Death.* A comparison of the two pieces demonstrates Walrond's growth as a writer and also gives one an insight into Walrond's writing process.

6. Several of Walrond's letters to Countee Cullen are housed in the Countee Cullen Papers at the Amistad Research Center (Tulane University). Walrond discusses a number of his contemporaries in these missives. Particularly revealing is a letter dated October 26, 1925, in which he expresses his feelings on Fauset, Toomer, Hughes, McKay, Rudolph Fisher, and Cullen himself.

7. Linguists define a dialect as a variety of a language, characterized by a specific pronunciation, syntax, and vocabulary. However, the word "dialect" has become stigmatized in some non-linguistic quarters. I use "dialect" in the linguistic sense throughout my discussion of Walrond. For more on the subject, see Peter A. Roberts, *West Indians and Their Language.*

8. The story, however, mixes fictional elements with autobiography. Walrond, for example, emigrated to Panama when he was about thirteen, not eight, which is Gerald's age.

9. Walrond is more critical of the Plymouth Brethren in "Success Story."

10. For a list of reviews of *Tropic Death,* see John E. Bassett's *Harlem in Review: Critical Reactions to Black American Writers, 1917-1939* (Selinsgrove, Pa.: Susquehanna UP, 1992): 65-67.

11. Walrond attended Wisconsin in the spring of 1928. Earlier, he had taken courses in creative writing and literature at City College of New York (1922-24) and Columbia University (1924-26). However, he never received a degree from any of these schools.

12. There is little documentation about the relationship between the two men while they were in England. However, if Garvey's letter to his wife Amy Jacques Garvey from May 25, 1937, is any indication, the Jamaican still had some concerns about Walrond's behavior: "The fellow Walron[d] I have here seems to have been making love to all of them [Garvey's housekeepers] at one and the same time. . . . All of them had a kind of masonry and I knew nothing about it" (*Papers* 7: 743).

13. Walrond was engaged in work besides writing in the mid-'30s. He was also touring Europe with a vaudeville troupe. According to one account, he served "as publicity manager of a Negro revue" (*Daily Gleaner* Apr. 5, 1935). It was reported that the act included a number of "old West Indian melodies," an indication that Walrond's interest in preserving Black culture remained intact.

14. An article stated that Walrond had been lost in a German air raid while serving in the Royal Air Force ("Eric Waldron [*sic*], Novelist, Lost in Air Raid," *Chicago Defender* April 29, 1944). The report of his being lost was apparently unfounded (*Kaiser Index* 5: 303).

15. The *Roundway* stories are available in the Countee Cullen/Harold Jackman collection at Atlanta University. The *Review,* a monthly publication of Roundway Hospital and Old Park House in Devizes, Wiltshire, circulated beyond the immediate hospital environs, and Walrond, in addition to contributing several pieces, served as assistant editor. He was a patient, voluntarily, at Roundway, a psychiatric hospital, from 1952 to September 1957. See his correspondence with Erica Marx, editor of the Hand and Flower Press, especially his letter from May 20, 1957 (box 12, folder 6, Hoyt William Fuller Collection, Atlanta University). For information on Roundway Hospital in the 1950s, see the *Hospitals' Directory: England and Wales 1955* (London: Ministry of Health, 1956) and *The Medical Directory 1954* (London: J. A. Churchill Ltd., 1954). Thanks to Cherryl Cooper for informing me that Roundway has since changed its name to Green Lane Hospital.

16. For example, three of the five largest sources of legal immigrants to New York City between 1990 and 1994 were Caribbean nations. Walrond's birthplace, Guyana, a country of only three-quarters of a million people, was fifth on this list (Dugger, *New York Times* Jan. 9, 1997).

17. Possibly because of his own migratory experiences, Walrond had an abiding interest in the movement of American Blacks to the North. In addition to "The Negro Comes North" and "From Cotton, Cane, and Rice Fields," Walrond published two other articles on the subject: "The Negro Migration to the North" (*International Interpreter* Aug. 18, 1923) and "The Negro Exodus from the South" (*Current History* Sept. 1923). Walrond's interest in migration was no doubt stimulated by his growing involvement with sociologist Charles S. Johnson beginning in 1923. As with much of his other writing, Walrond's essays on migration emphasize the achievements of Blacks despite the obstacles they faced.

18. Said makes interesting distinctions between exiles, expatriates, émigrés, and refugees (147-48). Many West Indian writers have described themselves as exiles and written extensively on the topic (e.g., George Lamming's *The Pleasures of Exile* and V. S. Naipaul's *The Enigma of Arrival*).

19. "Mon devoir et ma raison d'être sont de peindre l'existence de ma race, son histoire, see souffrances, ses espoirs et ses révoltes. Il y a là une source féconde d'émotions et de peines. C'est là que je puise les éléments de mon oeuvre et c'est au service de la race noire que je consacrerai mon activité d'écrivain." Thanks to Shondel Nero and Pascale Lavenaire for translating from the French.

Works Cited

Anderson, David. "Claude McKay." *PMLA* 113 (1998):158.

Barton, Rebecca Chalmers. *Black Voices in American Fiction, 1900-1930.* Oakdale, N.Y.: Dowling College P, 1976.

Beckles, Hilary. *A History of Barbados: From Amerindian Settlement to Nation-State.* New York: Cambridge UP, 1990.

Berry, Jay. "Eric Walrond." *Dictionary of Literary Biography,* vol. 51: *Afro-American Writers from the Harlem Renaissance to 1940.* Ed. Trudier Harris. Detroit: Gale, 1987. 296-300.

Bogle, Enid E. "Eric Walrond." *Fifty Caribbean Writers: A Bio-Bibliographical Critical Sourcebook.* Ed. Daryl Cumber Dance. Westport, Conn.: Greenwood, 1986. 474-82.

Bone, Robert. *Down Home: Origins of the Afro-American Short Story.* New York: Columbia UP, 1975.

Bontemps, Arna, and Langston Hughes. *Arna Bontemps-Langston Hughes Letters, 1925-1967.* Ed. Charles H. Nichols. New York: Dodd, Mead & Co., 1980.

Brawley, Benjamin. "The Negro Literary Renaissance." *The Southern Workman* 56 (Apr. 1927): 177-84.

Carew, Jan. *Fulcrums of Change: Origins of Racism in the Americas and Other Essays.* Trenton, N.J.: Africa World P, 1988.

Cliff, Michelle. "A Journey into Speech." *The Graywolf Annual Five: Multicultural Literacy.* Eds. Rick Simonson and Scott Walker. Saint Paul, Minn.: Graywolf P, 1988. 57-62.

Crowder, Henry, with Hugo Speck. *As Wonderful as All That?: Henry Crowder's Memoir of His Affair with Nancy Cunard, 1928-1935.* Navarro, Calif.: Wild Trees, 1987.

Domingo, W. A. "The Tropics in New York." *Survey Graphic* (Mar. 1, 1925): 648-50.

Du Bois, W. E. B. "Criteria of Negro Art." *Within the Circle: An Anthology of African American Literary Criticism from the Harlem Renaissance to the Present.* Ed. Angelyn Mitchell. Durham: Duke UP, 1994. 60-68.

———. "Five Books." *Crisis* 33 (Jan. 1927): 152.

Dugger, Celia W. "City of Immigrants Becoming More So in 90s." *New York Times* (Jan. 9, 1997): 1+.

"Eric Waldron [*sic*], Novelist, Lost in German Aid Raid." *Chicago Defender* (April 29, 1944): 1.

"Eric Walrond, Back in City, Feels No Homecoming Thrill." *New York Amsterdam News* (Sept. 9, 1931): 11.

Fabre, Michel. *From Harlem to Paris: Black American Writers in France, 1840-1980.* Urbana: U of Illinois P, 1991.

Ferguson, Blanche E. *Countee Cullen and the Negro Renaissance.* New York: Dodd, Mead & Co., 1966.

Garvey, Marcus. *The Marcus Garvey and Universal Negro Improvement Association Papers.* 7 vols. Ed. Robert A. Hill. Berkeley: U of California P, 1983-1990.

———, ed. *Black Man: A Monthly Magazine of Negro Thought and Opinion.* Comp. and ed. Robert A. Hill. Millwood, N.J.: Kraus-Thomson, 1975.

Gereau, Adolph. "With Eric Waldron [sic] at the Eureka." *Emancipator* (St. Thomas, Virgin Islands) (Apr. 3, 1929): 1.

Gloster, Hugh. *Negro Voices in American Fiction.* Chapel Hill: U of North Carolina P, 1948.

Holder, Calvin B. "The Causes and Composition of West Indian Immigration to New York City, 1900-1952." *Afro-Americans in New York Life and History* (Jan. 1987): 7-26.

Hughes, Langston. "Marl-Dust and West Indian Sun." *New York Herald Tribune* (Dec. 5, 1926): 9.

Hutchinson, George. *The Harlem Renaissance in Black and White.* Cambridge: Harvard UP, 1995.

Ikonné, Chidi. *From Du Bois to Van Vechten: The Early New Negro Literature, 1903-1926.* Westport, Conn.: Greenwood P, 1981.

The Kaiser Index to Black Resources, 1948-1986: From the Schomburg Center for Research in Black Culture of the New York Public Library. 5 vols. Brooklyn: Carlton Pub. Co., 1992.

Kasinitz, Philip. *Caribbean New York: Black Immigrants and the Politics of Race.* Ithaca, N.Y.: Cornell UP, 1992.

Kellner, Bruce. *The Harlem Renaissance: A Historical Dictionary for the Era.* Westport, Conn.: Greenwood P, 1984.

Lewis, David Levering. *When Harlem Was in Vogue.* New York: Oxford UP, 1981.

Locke, Alain, ed. *The New Negro.* 1925; rpt. New York: Atheneum, 1992.

McCullough, David. *The Path between the Seas: The Creation of the Panama Canal, 1870-1914.* New York: Simon & Schuster, 1977.

McKay, Claude. *A Long Way from Home.* New York: Lee Furman Inc., 1937.

Martin, Tony, ed. *African Fundamentalism: A Literary and Cultural Anthology of Garvey's Harlem Renaissance.* Dover, Mass.: Majority P, 1991.

———. *Literary Garveyism: Garvey, Black Arts and the Harlem Renaissance.* Dover, Mass.: Majority P, 1983.

Perry, Margaret. *Silence to the Drums: A Survey of the Literature of the Harlem Renaissance.* Westport, Conn.: Greenwood P, 1976.

Ramchand, Kenneth. "The Writer Who Ran Away: Eric Walrond and *Tropic Death.*" *Savacou* 2 (Sept. 1970): 67-75.

Richardson, Bonham C. *Panama Money in Barbados, 1900-1920.* Knoxville: U of Tennessee P, 1985.

Roberts, Peter A. *West Indians and Their Language.* New York: Cambridge UP, 1988.

Said, Edward. "Reflections on Exile." *Inventing America: Readings in Identity and Culture.* Eds. Gabriella Ibieta and Miles Orvell. New York: St. Martin's, 1996. 147-51.

Stovall, Tyler. *Paris Noir: African Americans in the City of Light.* Boston: Houghton Mifflin, 1996.

Thurman, Wallace. *Infants of the Spring.* 1932; rpt. Boston: Northwestern UP, 1992.

———. "Negro Artists and the Negro." *New Republic* (Aug. 31, 1927): 37-39.

Walrond, Eric. "Avec . . . Eric Walrond." Interview. By Jacques Lebar. *Lectures du Soir* (Jan. 14, 1933).

Walter, John C. "The Caribbean Immigrant Impulse in American Life: 1900-1930." *Revista/Review Interamericana* 11 (1981/1982): 522-44.

Watkins-Owens, Irma. *Blood Relations: Caribbean Immigrants and the Harlem Community, 1900-1930.* Bloomington: Indiana UP, 1996.

Wintz, Cary D. *Black Culture and the Harlem Renaissance.* Houston: Rice UP, 1988.

TITLE COMMENTARY

Tropic Death

CHIDI IKONNÉ (ESSAY DATE 1981)

SOURCE: Ikonné, Chidi. "Eric Walrond." In *From Du Bois to Van Vechten: The Early New Negro Literature, 1903-1926,* pp. 175-79. Westport, Conn.: Greenwood Press, 1981.

In the following essay, Ikonné discusses the stories in Tropic Death, *praising Walrond's realistic depiction of West Indian folk life*

Eric Walrond, like Claude McKay, was not a native-born black American. Yet his creative writings, like those of Claude McKay, are among the most representative works of the Harlem Renaissance. His volume of ten short stories, ***Tropic Death*** (1926), is a mosaic of elements of the life of West Indians—their joys, their sorrows, their superstitions—artistically presented without any apparent intention on the part of the author to please or to displease anyone. In spite of the author's obvious love of adjectives, he manages to place the reader right in the middle of the action and lets him form his own opinion. No action, no belief of the ordinary West Indian is considered too sordid or too demeaning to be uncovered "to the wholesale gaze of the world at large."[1]

Set in "a backwoods village in Barbadoes" the first story, **"Drought,"** brings out the pride and love of life of peasants engulfed in a drought. The situation is so severe that:

> Turtle doves rifled the pods of green peas and purple beans and even the indigestible Brazilian *bonavis.* Potato vines, yellow as the leaves of autumn, severed from their roots by the pressure of the sun, stood on the ground, the wind's eager prey. Undug, stemless-peanuts, carrots—seeking balm, relief, the caress of a passing wind, shot dead unlustered eyes up through sun-etched cracks in the hard, brittle soil. The sugar corn went to the birds. Ripening prematurely, breadfruits fell swiftly on the hard naked earth, half ripe, good only for fritters. . . . Fell in spatters . . . and the hungry dogs, elbowing the children, lapped up the yellow-mellow fruit.
>
> [***Tropic Death***; hereafter cited as ***WTD,*** p. 18]

Yet Sissie regards as an insult to the integrity of her kitchen any attempt by her children to eat anything not cooked by her. [***WTD,*** p. 21]

Another story, **"Panama Gold,"** celebrates several aspects of folkways. Ella runs across to Lizzie's house to borrow "a pinch o' salt" with which to season the food she is cooking. The young Capadosia is punished by her mother (and promised more beating when her father returns) for turning "she back side" to Ella (when Ella asks her about her mother) "an' didn't even say ax yo' pardin." [***WTD,*** p. 37] We hear the cooing of pigeons and the folk concept of what they say "at sunrise on a soap box coop on top the latrine":

> A rooka ta coo
> A rooka ta coo
> My wife is just as good as you
> Good as you
> Good as you
>
> [***WTD,*** p. 44]

We watch Ella, the "mulatto with plenty of soft black hair," as she folksily balances a bucket of water on her head. "She didn't need a cloth twisted and plaited to form a matting for her head. . . . Her strides were typical of the West Indian peasant woman—free, loose, firm. Zim, zam, zim, zam. Her feet were made to traverse that stony gap. No stones defied her free, lithe approach. Left foot to right hand, right hand to left foot—and Ella swept down with amazing grace and ease. Her toes were broad; they encountered no obstacles. Her feet did not slip. The water did not splash. It was safe, firm, serene on top of her head." [***WTD,*** pp. 56-57]

Even the embarrassing intraracial attitudes of West Indian blacks towards skin colors are spotlighted. Ella does not repulse Missah Poyah's advances because she does not like him as a person or because he has a wooden leg. Although she is convention-conscious and must have been knocked over by what she must have considered Missah Poyah's wrong approach (she mentally advises him to "go back an' lahn, dat not de way fi' cote" [***WTD,*** p. 54], her main reason for rejecting the "wooden foot neygah man" [***WTD,*** p. 53] is the color of his skin. "Gahd, he are black in troot'," she once told herself. [***WTD,*** p. 50]

This intraracial prejudice based on the color of the skin is the leitmotiv of the third story, **"The Yellow One."** The bloody fight which results in the Yellow One's collapsing and passing out is motivated by black-skinned Hubigon's dislike for Jota Arosemena because he is yellow-skinned. *La madurita* herself—and she is the center of consciousness in most of the story—would not let black-skinned Negroes, whom she considers "ugly," come near her.

"The Wharf Rats" is a celebration of folk life. The folksiness of black diggers of the Panama Canal is highlighted when "exhausted, half-asleep, naked but for wormy singlets," they are shown humming "queer creole tunes" as they "play on guitar or piccolo, and jig to the rhythm of the *coombia*—a folk song "for *obeah*." [***WTD,*** p. 90] The description of their attachment to this folklore is worth quoting:

> Over smoking pots, on black, death-black nights legends of the bloodiest were recited till they became the essence of a sort of Negro Koran. One refuted them at the price of one's breath. And to question the verity of the *obeah,* to dismiss or reject it as the ungodly rite of some lurid, crack-brained Islander was to be accursed pale-face, dog of a white. And the *obeah* man, in a fury of rage, would throw a machette at the heretic's head or—worse—burn on his doorstep at night a pyre of Maubé bark or green Ganja weed.
>
> [***WTD,*** p. 90]

But folk life is not without its tragedies. Philip, one of the wharf rats, is seized and eaten by a shark as he entertains Europeans with the West Indian game of "cork." [***WTD,*** pp. 110-14]

"The Palm Porch," with its central black-hating character, Miss Buckner, also touches upon the anathematic subject: intraracial prejudice based on the color of the skin. "One gathered from the words which came like blazing meteors out of her mouth that Miss Buckner would have liked to be white; but, alas! she was only a mulatto." [***WTD,*** p. 125] Her reaction to her 16-year-old daughter's elopement with a black man is "It a dam pity shame"—not because the "shiny-armed black" has spent some time in a jail but because he is not light-skinned. [***WTD,*** p. 126]

The sixth story, **"Subjection,"** is a facsimile of a colonized West Indian community with all its peoples and attitudes: the docile men and women who studiously keep off "de backra dem business," prostitutes, women who must slave in order to feed their children, the baffled who find comfort only in wine and religion, the power-drunk, trigger-happy colonialist represented by the marine who slices off a boy's ear and shoots Ballet to death because he dares to speak out.

In spite of this harrowing experience, the people's nearness to their folk roots is evident not only in their idiom but also in their lifestyle. Ballet eats his *conkee* from a banana leaf. The *obeah* cult is respected and adhered to.

Adherence to *obeah* is also celebrated in **"The Black Pin."** A black pin which Zink Diggs gives to Alfie sets a house on fire because "some demon chemical, some liquid, some fire-juice, had been soaked into it originally. *Obeah* juice." [***WTD,*** p. 181] Its creator, however, is not above its power. It almost ruins Zink Diggs completely when April returns it to her by tossing it "upon a mound of fowl dung and wormy provisions scraped together in the yard" and setting it on fire. [***WTD,*** pp. 181-82]

With its focus on Seenie and her child, **"The White Sanke"** offers the reader an insight into the life-style of a lowly West Indian community. **"The Vampire Bat"** is a series of macabre episodes which, beyond the demonstration of the power of *obeah,* celebrate the triumph of the weak (blacks) over the strong (whites who exploit them economically and sexually). For example, a black woman freezes the desire of a potential rapist by plunging her umbrella into his eyes. A mulatto trader invokes the magic of *obeah* against a vessel whose master has withheld part of the goods he was supposed to deliver to him; the crew of the vessel "find a rum soaked Negro corpse doubled up in the bottom" of a cask from which they are drinking. [***WTD,*** p. 230] A white plantation owner picks up a black baby (supposedly illegitimate and abandoned) who turns into a vampire bat and kills him. The title story, **"Tropic Death,"** focuses on still seamier aspects of the black West Indian life: disease, hunger, gangsterism, together with their effects on the community.

Although Eric Walrond is in no way at his best in all the stories, he consistently captures the folk soul by making his people talk most of the time in their appropriate dialects. The following is a dialogue between Alfred and his wife, **"The Yellow One,"** who has just returned from getting water which Alfred had refused to go and get:

> Alfred was sitting up, the unpacified baby in his arms.
>
> "'Im cry all de time yo' went 'way," he said, "wha' yo' t'ink is de mattah wit' 'im, he? Yo' t'ink him tummack a hut 'im?"
>
> "Him is hungry, dat is wha' is de mattah wit' 'im! Move, man! 'Fo Ah knock you', yah! Giv' me 'im, an' get outa me way! Yo' is only a dyam noosant!"
>
> "Well, what is de mattah, now?" he cried in unfeigned surprise.
>
> "Stid o' gwine fo' de watah yo'self yo' tan' back yah an' giv' hawdahs an' worryin' wha' is de mattah wit' de picknee."
>
> "Cho, keep quiet, woman, an' le' me lie down."
>
> [***WTD,*** p. 62]

The self-confidence underneath the stories becomes significant when the assimilationist tendency of educated West Indians at that period is taken into consideration. Most of the subjects treated by Walrond are matters which a large part of the black literati of the West Indies and the United States would have liked to leave unrevealed.

Note

1. Eric Walrond, *Tropic Death* (New York: Boni & Liverighi, 1926), p. 13 (hereafter cited as *WTD*).

CARL A. WADE (ESSAY DATE 1999)

SOURCE: Wade, Carl A. "African-American Aesthetics and the Short Fiction of Eric Walrond: *Tropic Death* and the Harlem Renaissance." *CLA Journal* XLII, no. 4 (June 1999): 403-29.

In the following essay, Wade surveys the stories in Tropic Death, *showing how Walrond integrated aesthetic and political values in his works.*

Eric Derwent Walrond (1897-1967) emerged as one of the most gifted and yet enigmatic of those writers who took part in the Harlem Renaissance. His role in the great flowering of African-American writing has been extensively documented (David Levering Lewis, Robert Bone, Tony Martin). He was one of three men of West Indian origin who contributed significantly to this milestone in African-American political and cultural history, the others being Claude McKay, the poet and novelist, and, of course, the political and ideological leader, Marcus Mosiah Garvey. The publication in 1926 of Walrond's collection of short stories ***Tropic Death*** was hailed as one of the most significant literary events of that period. Nevertheless, Walrond's relationship to the Renaissance dates back to the early twenties when he was a member of the editorial staff of *Negro World,* which had been founded by Marcus Garvey in 1918. Martin credits Walrond's stewardship of this publication with providing a "potential infrastructure for the Harlem Renaissance"[1] and *Opportunity*—established in 1923 by the Urban League. It is reasonable to assume that his American experience provided for Walrond, at least for a time, a racial solidarity and a political focus in an era when opportunities for these were lacking in his own Caribbean environment,[2] and that Harlem shaped Walrond the man, and ultimately the artist, to the same extent as he may have facilitated its literary efflorescence. For many the enigma of Walrond concerns (1) an ambiguous relationship with Garveyism and his apparent ideological volteface;[3] (2) the failure after the success of ***Tropic Death*** to produce the treatise on the Panama Canal experience—tentatively titled ***The Big Ditch,***[4] which he had been commissioned to write through a Guggenheim fellowship; and (3) his obscure anonymous exile in London, where his life ended, the rich promise of ***Tropic Death*** unfulfilled. But it is Walrond's complex relationship with the Harlem movement that is the major focus of this paper. ***Tropic Death*** suggests that despite Walrond's own enthusiastic involvement with the movement's politics and its art—in many ways as a kind of early midwife to its aspiring talents—the creative outpouring of the Harlem writers of African-American descent provided his fiction with no clear and direct models, although some similarity in themes and craftsmanship between Walrond's text and the work of his African-American contemporaries is undeniable.

An understanding of the literary influences on, and models available to, Walrond is central to an appreciation of his work. When Walrond arrived in New York in 1918, he was barely in his twenties and had left behind a society that had produced very little imaginative writing or evidence of interest in literature. Ramchand's chronology[5] suggests that by 1918—the year of Walrond's departure to the US—a handful of texts mainly by white Jamaican writers such as Tom Redcam and H. G. De Lisser were the only Caribbean prose fiction works known to have appeared in print. But not only were these early Jamaican texts of limited availability (having been published locally), but their treatment of the black Caribbean reality, and of the Caribbean life as a whole, could offer little to a writer whose work would explore a wide range of social and cultural experiences from the perspective of its black characters. Ramchand puts this deficiency in its wider historical context:

> The absence of any tradition of artistic and scientific endeavor in White Creole society meant that when Emancipation came there were no models evolved in the islands to which the liberated slaves or their caretakers could either turn to, or in revolt, turn away from.[6]

It was not until 1923 that De Lisser's *Jane's Career,* the first Caribbean text known to foreground a black protagonist, was published. Walrond's work is therefore in many ways both a product and rejection of this legacy. Apart from helping to create a wider audience for Caribbean fiction, he was one of the earliest writers from the region to establish the legitimacy of peasant life as a subject for serious artistic treatment, anticipating the tradition of the fifties and the sixties, as illustrated in the work of George Lamming and Samuel Selvon, in particular.

It is against this social and literary background that Walrond's relationship with Harlem and his evolution as an imaginative writer must be appraised, and the excitement of the Caribbean writers and intellectuals at the political ferment and artistic vibrancy of the era appreciated. Harlem was an early Mecca for the Caribbean writer, as London became a Mecca for the first wave of immigrant writers such as Lamming and Selvon, if on a vastly reduced scale and in significantly different ways.

That Walrond wrote in response to social and literary imperatives different from those that inspired his African-American counterparts and had a different perspective on the relationship between artistic and social responsibilities is a reasonable conclusion to be drawn from his fiction, as well as from his critical comments as a reviewer. However enthusiastically he participated in the political and literary awakening that was the Harlem Renaissance, Eric Walrond questioned its major aesthetic, writing that "[o]ne reason why the Negro has not made any headway is due to the effects of color prejudice. It is difficult for a Negro to write stories without bringing in the race question. As soon as a writer demonstrates skill along imaginative lines he is bound to succumb to the temptation of reform and propaganda."[7] This concern with the way in which the artistic balance of African-American imaginative writing might be threatened by its social and ideological agenda is again reflected in Walrond's praise for Carl Van Vechten's *Nigger Heaven* (1926) for its "objectivity." Yet these very imperatives, in particular the notion of literature as an avenue for radical self-redefinition and self-assertion, provided the impetus for the Harlem Renaissance, complementing similar initiatives in politics and in other spheres of social and cultural activism. The African-American artists were for the most part "writing back" to literary, cinematic, and dramatic traditions to which Alain Locke alluded:

> The Old Negro . . . was a creature of moral debate and historical controversy. His has been a stock figure perpetuated as an historical fiction partly in innocent sentimentalism, partly in deliberate reactionism. The Negro himself has contributed his share to this through a sort of protective social mimicry forced upon him by the adverse circumstances of dependence. So for generations in the mind of America, the Negro has been more of a formula than a human being—a something to be argued about, condemned or defended. . . .[8]

As Amritgit Singh puts it, the Harlem Renaissance was "a logical extension in the areas of art, music, and literature of the New Negro's racial, cultural, and political thinking."[9] For Gerald Early the Renaissance "was the culmination of a series of social, political, and artistic forces which resulted in, for the first time, the articulate, self-conscious mobilization and politicization of African-American culture in the industrialized world."[10] At the core of the movement was an attraction to the social utility of art, and a desire through its manipulation to redeem the standing of the race.[11] That the objective of imaginative writing should be the creation of a "New Negro" is supported by Locke's contention that the depiction of spiritual wealth would be ample for a new judgement and a new appraisal of the race. It is consistent with the perspective of another significant figure of the times, Jessie Fauset, author of *There Is Confusion* (1924), whose literary ideas, as David Levering Lewis puts it, "hewed closely to a social code. Literary creation was both the highest measure of a race's achievement and the most effective present tactic to advance her own race."[12]

When one considers the many literary experiments of the era which challenge and transcend traditional assumptions about imaginative writing, Walrond's misgivings about the effects of propaganda on art, especially if regarded as a comment on the Harlem movement as a whole, would appear to be overstated. Jean Toomer's *Cane,* for example, as many commentators—most notably Bernard Bell—have observed, is as much an exercise in creative experimentation as it is an attempt to redefine and assert identity through imaginative writing.[13] Walrond's charges about propaganda clearly offended, alienating him from the mainstream of the movement, planting doubts about his ideological and racial loyalties, and leading to an ambiguous and uneasy relationship with his African-American and Caribbean contemporaries whose interest in the Harlem movement was more obviously ideological.[14] Walrond's skepticism about the dominant aesthetic of the era anticipates that of V. S. Naipaul, thirty years later, about the relationship between race and literature in the work of black West Indian writers:

> The involvement of the Negro with the white world is one of the limitations of West Indian writing, as it is the destruction of American Negro writing. The American Negro's subject is his blackness. This cannot be the basis of any serious literature, and it has happened again and again that once the American Negro has made his statement, his profitable protest, he has nothing to say.[15]

Yet it would be misleading, in view of the debates of the twenties about the artistic and social responsibilities of the black writer, to suggest the existence of a single aesthetic at work during this period, and to claim, as both Walrond and Naipaul do, a paramountcy of ideological and social emphases at the expense of artistic criteria in black writing. Instead, it is possible to identify a range of diverse and opposing perspectives: from Du Bois' insistence on the social utility of writing in his assertion that "all art is propaganda. I do not care a damn for art that is not propaganda";[16] to Langston Hughes' observation that "there are plenty of propagandists for the Negro, but too few artists,"[17] a position supported by

Alain Locke, whose work is recognized as a significant landmark of this epoch. As Singh writes:

> Locke . . . was suggesting a well-balanced and flexible approach to the black writer to transform the richness and diversity, the intensity and anguish of the black American experience into the stuff of art and literature. He had little sympathy for the didactic and propagandistic literature that Du Bois called for, nor did he want to inhibit the artistic depiction of the Negro by confining to a particular class, group, or region.[18]

These are but few of the several viewpoints that emerged in a movement characterized by sophisticated experimentation, whatever may have been its "dominant" aesthetic. Bell, for example, sees in the Renaissance a wide spectrum of narrative modes, including poetic realism (Toomer), historical romance (Arna Bontemps), assimilation (Fauset), and biculturalism in the work of Nella Larsen (93-149).[19] The diversity of these approaches challenges a fundamental implication of the statements of both Walrond and Naipaul: that the treatment of racial issues inevitably precludes any attention to artistic criteria. Is the exploration of racial conflict and anxieties in imaginative writing not justifiable and inevitable where these constitute a pervasive element of a writer's experience? There is in this respect a marked contrast in aesthetic orientation between the Caribbean fiction of Walrond and that of his contemporary and compatriot, Claude McKay, as illustrated by a comparative analysis of Walrond's major text and McKay's *Banana Bottom.* Despite their similarities in background and experience, there is some divergence in these writers' fictional representation of their Caribbean environment. *Banana Bottom* suggests that for McKay, as for the mainstream of the Harlem movement, literature is a strategy for self-definition; for the Walrond of ***Tropic Death*** an expression of personal, social, and even "universal" reality. Yet McKay himself would later express a skepticism similar to Walrond's about the threat to the creative process posed by overemphasis on social and ideological agenda that emerge in his disagreement with Du Bois.[20]

But Walrond's often repeated concern for the integrity of the creative process should not be interpreted as his denial of fiction's social imperatives. Tony Martin has drawn attention to an irony and even an apparent contradiction in Walrond's stance exemplified in the latter's review of Maran's *Batouala* in **"*Batouala,* Art and Propaganda"** in *Negro World,* where Walrond asserts that African-Americans will never write great literature until they can purge themselves of their emotions and "write along colorless, sectionless lines."[21] At this point black writing would be "straight from the shoulder, slashing, murdering, disemboweling."[22] This perspective is extended to his review of William Pickens' *Vengeance of the Gods,* a text he decries as an amalgam of "arguings, philosophizings, social parallels." Walrond dismisses Pickens' collection of short stories as a "sociological tract" by a writer who "forgot all about the technique of the short story."[23] But contrary to Martin's allegation, there is no contradiction in Walrond's stance, no denial of a social responsibility for the writer, least of all the black writer, nor any support for any facile notion of "art for art's sake." What Walrond implies is that "realistic" and "objective" fiction is the most powerful and effective form of social protest. Walrond's perception of the relationship of the writer to social agendas is shared by William H. Ferris, his contemporary. Ferris' favorable reading of *Batouala* was, like Walrond's, inspired by its lack of explicit propaganda, even though the text "has a powerful propaganda effect." Ferris writes, "There should be no straining for effect, no over anxiety to preach a sermon, point a moral or teach a lesson. . . . The novel, play or poem will bring its message as a novel, play, or poem."[24] Ferris expresses confidence that black writers would overcome the weight of race prejudice that bears so heavily upon them to achieve "perspective and breadth of vision."[25]

In addition to its consistency with Ferris' outlook, Walrond's aesthetic is similar to that of his white contemporary H. L. Mencken, whose publication *American Mercury* served as an additional outlook for black writing. Walrond himself makes explicit if unelaborated reference to the work of H. L. Mencken,[26] who is presented by Charles Scruggs as a "champion" of black radical writing, and an unrelenting spokesman for uncompromising realism, the sanctity of the artistic process, and for "representationality" in *all* writing.[27]

From Walrond's interrogation of one of the pervasive aesthetics of the time and from ***Tropic Death*** itself, it is possible to extrapolate a philosophy of art that is consistent with Ferris' outlook and that of H. L. Mencken, but Walrond's perspective on black writing goes beyond this: it anticipates that articulated by George Lamming almost forty years later in "The Negro Writer and His World." For Lamming, the black writer must satisfy distinct and competing, but complementary obligations to three worlds: private, social, and universal. The private and hidden self "turns quietly, sometimes turbulently, within one man, and

. . . might be only known by others after the man has spoken."[28] In Lamming's view, this is the writer's most prized possession and the basis of his work. The second world is that of the writer's immediate social context, which the writer addresses because "there is a fundamental need to present his private world in all its facets, and one of its vivid experiences will of necessity be the impact which that social world, with all its reservations and distinctions, has made on his consciousness."[29] The third world is the wider community of man to which the black writer is condemned "by the fact of his spirit in the world of men. . . . What he cannot escape is the essential need to find meaning for his destiny, and every utterance made on behalf of all men."[30] The black writer's responsibility to that other world will be judged not only by the authenticity and power with which his own private world is presented but also "by the honesty with which he interprets the world of his social relations, his country, that is, for those who have no direct experience of it, but are moved by the power of his speech, his judgement and his good faith."[31]

Although Walrond nowhere articulates such a comprehensive set of literary principles, his skepticism about the relationship between art and social responsibility helps to locate him in the continuum of Lamming's ideas. Walrond, like Lamming, appears to strive for a reconciliation of artistic imagination and vision, with social realities and universal truth, but Walrond assigns greater priority to the black writer's role as social historian than Lamming does. Far from lacking an ideological perspective of a "politically correct" nature, as some of the criticism of his statements might suggest, Walrond's major fiction probes a wide range of social issues, including some of those that proliferate in the work of the Harlem writers—such as class conflict, miscegenation, racial anxieties, and other forms of racial strife—but his examination of these themes is held in balance with the demands of other "worlds," and is influenced by a different perception of the manner in which the social utility of imaginative writing can be most powerfully effected. As we have argued, Walrond's reservations relate to the overemphasis on, or narrow treatment of, social and political issues and any consequential compromise of the imaginative writer's unique and defining qualities, and the artistic balance of his work. Such reservations may have emanated as well from the fear of distorting social reality by replacing a romantic excess by a denigrating one, a concern shared by some of Walrond's African-American contemporaries. As other Renaissance commentators see it, the use of primitivism to define identity by a writer such as McKay (in *Home to Harlem* and *Banjo*), for example, resulted not in the celebration of the uniqueness of a particular social group but in the "commodification" of their otherness. In its most extreme form this tendency constructs or panders to racist ideologies and engenders a "Negrotarian" literature characterized by "a scheduled, ritualized performance" and "racist caricature" for consumption and validation by a particular audience.[32]

Tropic Death exemplifies and extends this aesthetic that proposes that imaginative writing must respond to those competing and yet complementary "worlds." Kenneth Ramchand's tribute to Walrond as "one of the most imaginative and technically accomplished writers" to come out of the West Indies, and one whose portrait of Caribbean society "is contained within a more comprehensive vision of life"[33] may be seen as an endorsement of Walrond's success in harmonizing and keeping in balance those competing elements most clearly defined in Lamming's statement, and in reconciling the artistic and social responsibilities of the black writer. By evading some of the excesses to which his criticism alludes, Walrond transmutes personal experience into art, achieving that breadth of vision that Ferris, Lamming, and others regard as the distinguishing quality of accomplished black writing.

The imaginative force of ***Tropic Death*** derives partly from the nature and the intensity of the private and wider social experiences it encapsulates. In some ways, ***Tropic Death*** represents Walrond's own experiences of the Caribbean landscape thinly fictionalized. His personal odyssey, in the form of his own transplantation from and to unwelcoming landscapes and the predicament of the Caribbean people as a whole, is represented in these ten stories.[34]

The world that Walrond knew and presented fictionally is the Caribbean at one of the most benighted phases of its development. In documenting the social realities of Barbados at the turn of the century where Walrond spent about four years and where several of the stories in ***Tropic Death*** are wholly or partially set, Bonham C. Richardson draws attention to the abject poverty, debilitating malnutrition, disease, inhospitable climatic conditions, and generally depressing circumstances which constituted the plight of the black peasantry. He identifies some of their strategies for survival, which included migration, particularly to Panama to participate in the construction of the Canal. Richardson's portrait is generally illustrative of other Caribbean settings, as the work of several scholars attests.[35] These socioeconomic problems were exacerbated by stratification and distinctions on the basis of class and pigmentation—a problem repeatedly examined in ***Tropic Death*** and a pervasive theme in the prose fiction of later generations of Caribbean writers. In its faithful re-creation of the predicament of individual protagonists, mostly of the black peasant class, ***Tropic Death*** achieves a powerful indictment—however indirect—of the social, political, and economic arrangements under which this group subsisted. That social realism is one of Walrond's chief concerns is evidenced by the detail with which he examines those problems documented in the social histories of the period, the accuracy with which he recreates the natural and man-made landscapes and cultural pastimes, the geographical exactness of its settings—particularly its barbadian settings—and the attention paid to the speech varieties of the people, even to the extent of rendering interisland dialectal differences. In documenting the social realities of Caribbean life, ***Tropic Death*** anticipates a tradition of early West Indian prose fiction; this achievement is more valuable as the text predates the development of Caribbean scholarship in the disciplines of history and the social sciences.

Clearly modeled on a society from which its author wanted to escape, the collection occasionally celebrates the strategies for survival adopted by Caribbean man and the defeat and, occasionally, the triumph of the human spirit. Although ***Tropic Death,*** as its title implies, is a deeply pessimistic and even cynical work, its protagonists are treated compassionately and, if not romanticized, are rarely delineated with any degrading excess. Yet for all its value as a comprehensive social document of one of the most oppressive periods of Caribbean life, ***Tropic Death*** never degenerates into a simple catalogue of social injustice. Instead, Walrond uses the social circumstances of early twentieth-century Caribbean life as a context in which to explore more universal themes related to individual experience, the conflict between creative and destructive forces in life and the interconnection between social circumstances, human agency, and natural and cosmic forces. As Ramchand suggests, Walrond's portrait of Caribbean society and his concern about its social and economic problems are therefore subsumed by a larger vision of human life, by a regard for the fate of the individual, and for artistry as the definitive quality of the imaginative writer. In this way the text exemplifies those principles about imaginative writing to which Walrond appeared to subscribe, and which, as our central thesis maintains, distinguishes Walrond from many of his African-American contemporaries.

Walrond's intention in ***Tropic Death*** to give faithful expression to the realities of Caribbean life and to explore their larger, universal dimensions explains the inappropriateness to his text of the literary mode which McKay finds adequate to his own purposes in *Banana Bottom,* which invokes a pastoral element in its presentation of an idyllic Jamaican community. McKay's work, however, achieves balance through its exploration of many of the same social issues which Walrond addresses in his collection of short stories. As Sterling Brown and other early commentators have observed, naturalism pervades ***Tropic Death*** and is an appropriate literary mode in a text which has as its focus the theme of the individual in an overwhelming struggle with the forces—social, economic, human and cosmic—of existence. Maran's *Batouala* (1921), which Walrond reviewed so ecstatically for *Negro World* is a probable source of influence for ***Tropic Death.***

This naturalistic element is employed, for example, in **"Drought"** with its treatment of Nature as predator and its presentation of the individual at the mercy of natural and other forces over which he has no control. In **"Drought"** the enemy is the "roaring sun," the "livid sun," which in its "wretched fury," "had robbed the earth of its juice." Walrond's vivid descriptive powers are employed in this opening story and elsewhere in the collection to make the reader experience the physical landscape intensely and to create a view of Nature as one of the chief enemies of Caribbean man: stultifying and menacing, precipitating despair, irrationality, vagabondage, and migration to other equally hostile landscapes. Ultimately, the sun is more than Walrond's pervasive image of the Caribbean experience; it comes to personify his concept of an indifferent and implacable deity. Similar perspectives on nature, in particular of the sun, which proliferate throughout the collection and are plentiful even in the more "optimistic" tales such as **"Tropic Death,"** constitute an integral element of Walrond's larger vision, even as they suggest his intensely felt experience of Caribbean life.

In **"Drought"** Walrond's theme is the individual's response to these forces of stultification and depersonalization. Rejecting the notion of art as propaganda, Walrond is careful to present rounded characters rather than social abstractions, no matter how historically accurate his depiction of the life of that period, or how urgent his social observations. In this story Coggins Rum—his first name may be symbolic of his insignificance in the larger scheme of life—is only a "black animate dot" stumbling over life's obstacles, with an acceptance and a resignation which Walrond ridicules slightly, but ultimately celebrates. The symbolism is unobtrusive: from Coggins' name to the jagged rocks he stumbles over, to the description that prefigures his daughter's demise, inviting the reader to image her in death, Walrond describes the "black wood, expertly shellacked and laid out in the sun to dry." Nature is also victim: the earth deprived of its vitality by the sun and other natural forces come to represent Coggins' dying daughter, and the prospect of life and vitality in a larger sense. In Walrond's despairing vision, Nature turns on itself, and against itself. Deranged by prolonged unbearable hunger, Beryl turns to dust in more than one sense. In **"Drought"** there is no sense of a benevolent deity in a universe that targets the youngest, the most innocent, and most defenseless. Yet the most profound "death" is that of those like Sissie, Beryl's mother, who, unlike Coggins, loses her intuitive sympathies and her sense of life's possibilities.

Walrond maintains some narrative distance through a gentle ridicule of Coggins' naiveté in the matter of his daughter's paternity and of the genteel pretensions of the destitute peasant class. His presentation of the social and economic realities never threatens the artistic balance of the story, which makes very subtle reference to racial anxieties as well as to social inequity. There is an important but understated contrast, for example, between the material possessions and social amenities of the more aristocratic minor and incidental figures and those of the peasants; in addition, the reality of racial inequality is understood through the contrasting relationships of the protagonist and the plantation overseer with the black females. Walrond's use of ironic understatement, particularly at the end of the tale, lends a pathos and a poignancy to the story.

Walrond's ironic yet compassionate vision is extended in **"Panama Gold,"**[36] which also explores the theme of the individual in conflict with natural, human, and social forces. Here Walrond's extensive and vivid descriptions of the landscape contribute to the ironic structure of the story. This accounts for its unusually euphoric opening, its rhapsodic description of Nature in harmony with individual enterprise, represented by the achievement of the protagonist, Ella. Apart from their suggestion of unbridled optimism, these descriptions, plentiful at the beginning of the story, symbolize Ella's sexual promise: "It [the wind] shook buds and blossoms on the ground—moist, unforked ground—on Ella Heath's lap, in her black plenteous hair, in the water she was drawing from the well" (38).[37] Although Walrond gently satirizes Poyer's defiance of the depersonalizing and exploitative colonial powers, his treatment of this character at the outset of the tale functions to complement the optimism and sense of life's possibilities created through the description of Ella's achievement and of a benevolent, natural environment, and also in the prospect of a sexual (and economic) union between the two protagonists. Walrond reveals some social realities of West Indian life both in his exploration of the separate dilemmas of the protagonists and of the conflict that arises as a result of their encounter. Ella, although less economically secure than Poyer, is hesitant about a closer relationship with the shopkeeper, not simply because of her apparent self-sufficiency but, more importantly, as a result of her lighter complexion. Walrond's optimism is qualified in yet another way: Poyer's economic enfranchisement is achieved at the expense of his physical maiming. But it is in his exploration of Poyer's predicament that Walrond's ironic vision is most apparent. For having conquered these forces, the shopkeeper becomes the victim of the random design in the universe, losing his life, his money, and his property in a fire accidentally set by the village idiot. This catastrophe destroys the possibility of further achievement for both Ella and Poyer in the promise of a sexual and economic union. Walrond reveals his careful attention to the structure and symmetry of his story even when suggesting the random, inexplicable processes of existence, by bringing together all the strands of the plot at the story's climax. Descriptions of Nature and the landscape are used in **"Panama Gold"** to signal this change of mood and tone as well as to prefigure the actual catastrophe:

> The Western sky of Barbados was ablaze. A mixture of fire and gold, it burned, and burned—into one sulphurous mass. It burned the houses, the trees, the windowpanes. . . . It flung on the corn and the peas and the star apples a lavender glow. . . . It withered the petals of rose or sweet pea or morning glory. Its flame upon the earth was mighty.
>
> (46)

Walrond's descriptions of the sun's effects highlights its creative and destructive energies and symbolizes the inevitable links between advancement and decline, and between success and failure that is Walrond's view of Poyer's experience and of human experience itself. The sun "burns" (burnishes and enriches), but it also "burns" (consumes and "withers"); it is associated with both the "lavender glow" and the "sulphurous mass," calling to mind both Poyer's material success and his fiery fate.

For all his compassionate treatment of his main characters, Walrond's depiction of black Caribbean life is often disquieting, exceeding the gentle satire necessary for narrative distance. At times, his obsession with ethnicity and fine shades of pigmentation suggests that he was very much a man of his times and shared its racial anxieties, as some critics, notably Robert Bone, have maintained.[38] This is true of the opening paragraphs of **"The Wharf Rats,"** where the narrator makes reference to the "smelting cabins" which "harbored the inky ones and their pickaninnies" (68). Yet **"The Wharf Rats,"** like the **"Yellow One,"** remains one of those stories in which social and racial considerations, however implicit in the story, arouse those elemental passions which are integral to its central conflicts. In **"The Wharf Rats,"** for David Levering Lewis a "gem of the genre,"[39] these social problems are handled with characteristic understatement, no matter how explicit the initial narration. Although Walrond identifies each character by race and color, there is no detailed treatment of those racial anxieties that underpin the misunderstanding and fatal self-deception which form the major themes. His attitude toward other social conditions is implicit in his treatment of the tourist "attractions" that precipitate the tragic climax, in the form of two brothers' destruction by sharks. Walrond uses this confederacy of human agency—social and racial problems, and natural forces—to explore misguided but well-intentioned action, alienation, misunderstanding, and self-deception, keeping the larger themes and more restricted concerns of his tale in balance. It is more difficult to separate the destructive and creative forces in a story in which young people's relationships, distorted and corrupted by racial animosities, generate malevolence and insensitivity. Philip, one of the two main protagonists, although well-meaning, is hardly innocent, given his ill-advised actions protecting the sensitivities of his friend, Maura, and the conflict these engender. Although Ernest—who, like his brother Philip, perishes in the shark attack—is unaware of the tensions among his friends, he is far from being a fully realized character and therefore makes few claims on the reader's compassion. It is Maffi—the "black ominous" domestic helper, whose romantic interest in Philip is unperceived, not explicitly rejected as she thinks—in whom the destructive energies of the tale, in the form of consuming self-hatred and a malevolence that finds expression in her recourse to supernatural elements, are most fully concentrated. **"The Wharf Rats"** provides a further example of the author's tendency to locate the destablizing elements of human life in the interaction between human and external forces. The symmetrical structure of the story is more than the technical harmonizing of its various strands in the conclusion; it confirms Walrond's view of life as an intricate and complex pattern in which human agency, social phenomena, and cosmic and natural forces are inextricably intertwined.

Robert Bone interprets **"The Yellow One"**—Walrond's widely anthologized story about the fate of a woman of mixed ancestry on board a migrant ship repatriating Caribbean people to Jamaica and other ports—as a more explicit exploration of the racial tensions that have historically beleaguered Caribbean society:

> When La Madurita goes below, she is descending into the Caribbean past, into the cauldron of hatreds which are the chief legacy of white colonialism. The brawl that she unwittingly provokes is rendered in images that stress the atavistic tendencies of Caribbean life.
>
> (199-200)

Racial strife is an obvious theme in the story; the yellow one is implicated in the major incident by the fact of her ethnicity, her racial similarity to, and her involvement with, one of the participants in the climactic brawl. Despite the relevance and accuracy of Bone's interpretation, as is typical for Walrond, the story functions on several levels simultaneously. For all the ideological imperatives of the story, the racial anxieties remain a single, although a dominant, aspect of the protagonist's dilemma. The yellow one is also female in conflict with male importunity, irresponsibility, and an unsympathetic universe. She also stands for the life-giving creative forces in conflict with the destructive social elements personified by her migrant companions, the malevolent universe, and her husband, whose life-denying actions are illustrated in his treatment of his child.

On the other hand, Walrond uses the mother-child relationship to associate the protagonist with constructive energies. Here Walrond employs limited-viewpoint narration to create through the protagonist's eyes an impression of intense alienation and vulnerability; it is a narrative strategy enhanced by symbols drawn from nature to describe the malevolent universe. The description of the sea—". . . calm, gulls scuttled low, seizing and ecstatically devouring some reckless, sky drunk sprat" (56)—points to both her oppression by natural elements as well as by the social world of the ship, as the protagonist perceives it. This perception of the other as predator is introduced by the symbolism of the very first line of the story—"Once catching a glimpse of her, they swooped down like a brood of starving hawks"—and reinforced by a similar use of language at the conclusion. In **"The Yellow One"** Walrond's concern with structure is evident: the initial incidents, suspended as other lines of the story develop, are worked into its climax. As is the case of **"The Wharf Rats"** and to some extent **"Panama Gold,"** the random, pointless fate of the individual is not developed at the expense of symmetry and neatness in the structure of the story itself. In **"The Yellow One"** Walrond rises above the narrow focus on racial differences to achieve a sensitive and imaginative depiction of life as seen through the perspective of a protagonist who experiences many kinds of alienation and susceptibility.

In **"Subjection"** Walrond sacrifices fullness and realism in characterization for the sake of ideology in his most direct statement of protest on race relations and social injustice in the Canal Zone. This is the one tale in the collection where artistic effect is threatened by an overemphasis on racial and social themes. Both oppressor and oppressed are caricatured in this vitriolic story of gratuitous violence that recalls some of Richard Wright's work. Ballet—the black water-carrier—and the white lieutenant who hounds him down and shoots him are both dehumanized by racial conflict and social oppression in a story which employs exaggerated naturalism in the service of propaganda. The narrator's anger is scarcely restrained in the caustic irony at the end of the story when the black water-carrier finally falls victim to the white man's hurt racial pride: "In the Canal Zone, the Q.M. at Toro Point took occasion to extol the virtues of the Department which kept the number of casualties in the recent native labor uprising down to one" (122). These racial themes are treated more deftly in **"The Palm Porch,"** a satirical tale about social pretensions and corruption at all levels. Walrond handles the plot with characteristic innuendo, ironic understatement, and indirectness. But it is the undermining of the protagonist, Miss Buckner, through physical description and dialogue that accounts for the humor and interest of the tale.

Walrond's experiment with Gothic—**"The White Snake," "The Black Pin,"** and **"The Vampire Bat"**—to intensify his infernal vision of Caribbean life is further evidence of his attention to craftsmanship. Gothic is used in ***Tropic Death*** not to impart a sensational, exotic, or primitivistic flavor to the tales, but to deepen the impression of a world in which even supernatural forces conspire against individual well-being, and in which those elements are inextricably intertwined with social phenomena and human agency. Undoubtedly influenced by Walrond's own migration from British Guyana to Barbados, **"The Black Pin"** extends the portrait of Caribbean society in its exploration of alienation and conflict among the Caribbean peasantry, who compete for scarce living resources in an inhospitable natural and social environment. It is remarkable, too, for its detailed re-creation of the natural and man-made landscapes, both urban and rural, in the early years of this century. But Walrond's principal theme remains the conflict between constructive and destructive forces represented by the two female characters and illustrated by their contrasting relationships with Nature. While April, the Guyanese migrant and protagonist (modeled on Walrond's mother), works in harmony with Nature, the antagonist, Zink Diggs, the Barbadian neighbor, destroys the promise of life and fertility, invoking the anti-Nature forces in actions which ironically result in her own demise. Walrond examines the extent to which the severe climatic and economic conditions generate unwholesome and malevolent energies that are partly supernatural in character. **"Vampire Bat"** is a darker story in which social and racial anxieties—subtly, and not so subtly, delineated in the story—become entangled with supernatural elements. In this story—the only one in the collection with a white protagonist, Bello Prout, who is returning from military service to the Empire in the Boer War (ironically, given his attitude toward the native blacks) to resuscitate his own sugar empire, badly damaged by a hurricane—natural and supernatural forces operate in concert with human malevolence. Walrond does not distinguish between constructive or creative forces here; the protagonist's preoccupation with ethnic differences and his insensitivity to others contribute to the racial tension that is the subtext of the tale. In some ways this is a moral fable about the consequences of racial pride and blindness, and almost hubristic contempt for the complex, mysterious, and intricate pattern of existence. If, as Bone and others argue, Walrond's use of the Gothic owes much to the work of Pierre Loti and Lafcadio Hearn, whose texts presumably came to him by way of his American experience, this is another example of some of the unusual and indirect ways in which he benefited from his sojourn in Harlem—in the form of more extensive exposure to alternative literary modes. In any event, the naturalistic and the Gothic elements are complementary in Walrond's vision of human existence.

Gerald Bright's journey from Barbados to Panama in search of an errant father in the title story is closely modeled on Eric Walrond's own journey with his mother to the Canal Zone around 1910. Although **"Tropic Death"** represents Walrond's vision and imaginative powers at their most compelling, it is no less comprehensive a record of Caribbean life than other stories in the collection; it deepens the impression of social and economic depression and severe climatic conditions, as encapsulated in one of the most strikingly naturalistic passages to be found in the text:

> . . . a dinky backward village; the gap rocky and grassy, the roads dusty and green-splashed; the marl, in the dry season, whirling blindly at you, the sickly fowls dying of the pip and the yaws; the dogs, a rowing impotent lot; the crops of dry peas and cassava and tannia and eddoes, robbed before they could feel the pulse of the sun, of their gum or juice.
>
> (167)

This portrait is extended through Walrond's characteristic use of animal images to underline the antagonistic quality of human interrelationships and of the individual relationships with social and universal agents:

> Fish, lured onto the glimmering ends of loaded lines, raged in fruitless fury; tore, snarled gutturally, for release; bloodied patches of the hard blue sea; left crescents of gills on green and silvery hooks. Some, big and fat as young oxen, raved for miles on the shining blue sea, snapping and snarling acrobatically. For a stretch of days, the *Wellington* left behind a scarlet trail.
>
> (166-67)

But neither in his treatment of Barbados and of Panama, where most of the plot unfolds, is Walrond's primary interest the social realities of these settings. Instead, his larger theme is Gerald's awakening to the social realities of Caribbean life through the Barbados episodes and, more importantly—in the Panama sections—the growth of his moral consciousness, his loss of innocence, and his painful awareness of the complexities of adult relationships, the struggle of (black) women, and male irresponsibility. The religious symbolism of the garden ("It recaptured the essence of that first jungle scene. Upward, on one of the roof's hills spread the leaves of banyan tree. Fruit—mellow, hanging, tempting—peeped from between the foliage . . ."), the "serpents" that Gerald witnesses his father applying to his own body, an obvious image of self-destruction, and the sirens whose sensuality is emphasized through physical description are used by Walrond to deepen this image of Panama as Hell and symbolic adult experience. Images of death and decadence drawn from nature represent this world, in the face of which the religious initiatives of the women are ineffectual. By contrast, Gerald's celebratory and romantic reminiscences of island life and his nostalgic reflections on its simple traditions and its customs evoke the semi-idyllic world of innocence that is supplanted by the moral cesspool of Panama. Narrative intrusion is kept to a minimum in both the presentation of social realities and the more universal themes such as loss of childhood innocence. Walrond suggests Gerald's innocence and youthfulness through his use of physical description (161) and by the nature of the boy's perceptions, especially on the journey. In Panama, where "Gerald was to take on the color of life" (177), the author hints at an incipient sexual curiosity (188), a cynicism about religion (189), and about life ("He began to feel things ever so keenly. His vision, too, grew less dim. But a pallor fell on things" [188]) as indications of his protagonist's maturing. Gerald's growth results from adult conflict he witnesses and from his own sordid encounters with those of his own age who exemplify the corruption and cynicism of the adult world, in contrast to the prankishness associated with the youth in the island setting. But more than anything, the indifference, objectivity, and disgust with which the boy had formerly contemplated his errant father are replaced by compassion, an understanding of his plight, and by love.

The favorable descriptions of Barbadian life and the re-creation of its simple pleasures do more than establish the impression of the lost green world of innocence to which Panama offers a stark and marked contrast; they balance the more negative portrait of island life that is painted in other stories and in the title story itself. Beyond this they make the tale one of the most optimistic in the collection. Through these images, and in Sara Bright's resilience and unshakeable faith, and in Gerald's growth towards compassion and love, Walrond suggests some of the more fulfilling possibilities of Caribbean—and human—life.

The Harlem Renaissance provided Eric Walrond an outlet for his political and creative energies and contributed significantly to his development in these areas; however, his fictional work indicates substantial divergence from the movement on the question of the role of the black writer in society. It would appear that for Walrond and some of his contemporaries, as later for George Lamming, the most accomplished black writing reconciles the demands of the private world with those of the immediate social context, and of the wider community of man. The writer must be allowed the free use of his imaginative and creative gifts, his vision, to explore social phenomena and life in general; the integrity of the creative process must remain inviolate. In some ways Walrond oversimplified the nature of the Harlem movement, perhaps underestimating the dynamic and critically sophisticated process that it was. His own aesthetic, as far as it may be extrapolated from his critical statements and from his fiction itself, incorporates a commitment to technical artistry and personal vision, an emphasis on the illumination of social realities, and a concern for the representation of universal aspects of personal and social experiences. The black writer as artist, as social historian, and as poet singing to all men about their common humanity—this is Walrond's achievement in ***Tropic Death*** and the vision that he brought to the Harlem Renaissance.

Notes

1. Tony Martin, *Literary Garveyism: Garvey, Black Arts and the Harlem Renaissance* (Dover, MA: Majority Press, 1983) 156.
2. For an account of some of the political, intellectual obstacles faced by this generation of Caribbean radicals, see Rupert Lewis, *Marcus Garvey: Anti-Colonial Champion* (London: Karia Press, 1987) 17-53, and Judith Stein, *The World of Marcus Garvey: Race and Class in Modern Society* (Baton Rouge: Louisiana State UP, 1986) 24-37.
3. Martin 124-38.
4. Walrond, it seems, never gave up hope of completing this text on Panama. As recently as 1960 he wrote to the Secretary of the Guggenheim Foundation that he was "still endeavoring to adhere to the project," and expressed the desire to "try somehow to get on with some of my own, long-neglected work . . . in spite of age and years of silence I have not lost sight of my objectives, or the high aims with which I set out as a Guggenheim Fellow such a long time ago" (quoted in Kenneth Ramchand, "The Writer Who Ran Away: Eric Walrond and *Tropic Death*," *Savacou* 2 [1970]: 74-75).
5. Kenneth Ramchand, *The West Indian Novel and Its Background* (London: Faber, 1970) 282-86.
6. Ramchand 37.
7. Quoted in Martin 16.
8. Alain Locke, "The New Negro" [1925], *Voices from the Harlem Renaissance,* ed. Nathan Irvin Huggins (New York: Oxford UP 1995) 47.
9. Amritjit Singh, *The Novels of the Harlem Renaissance: Twelve Black Writers, 1923-1933* (University Park: Pennsylvania State University, 1976) 13.
10. Gerald Early, "Three Notes Toward a Cultural Definition of the Harlem Renaissance," *Callaloo* 14 (1991): 142.
11. David Levering Lewis, *When Harlem Was in Vogue* (New York: Vintage, 1982) 90.
12. Lewis 123.
13. "The meaning of the book is implicit in the arabesque pattern, the subtle movement of symbolic actions and objects, the shifting rhythm of syntax and diction . . ." (Bernard W. Bell, *The Afro-American Novel and Its Tradition* [Amherst: U of Massachusetts P, 1987] 98). Bell identifies pastoral, allegory, impressionism, and music as a structural device in some of the elements with which Toomer experiments in *Cane.*
14. Martin 124-28.
15. V. S. Naipaul, *The Middle Passage: Impressions of Five Societies—British, French and Dutch—in the West Indies and South America* (London: Andre Deutsch, 1962) 69.
16. Quoted in Arnold Rampersad, *The Art and Imagination of W. E. B. Du Bois* (Cambridge: Harvard UP, 1976) 184. For some commentators, most notably Rampersad, Du Bois' perspective on the relationship between artistic and social responsibilities has been oversimplified and virtually misrepresented. See Rampersad 194-201.
17. Quoted in Clare Bloodgood Crane, "Alain Locke and the Negro Renaissance," diss., University of California, San Diego, 1971, 94.
18. Singh 18.
19. Bell 93-149.
20. Rampersad 190-91.
21. Eric Walrond, "*Batouala,* Art and Propaganda" [1922], *African Fundamentalism: A Literary and Cultural Anthology of Garvey's Harlem Renaissance,* ed. and comp. Tony Martin (Dover, MA: Majority Press, 1991) 31.
22. In Martin, *African Fundamentalism* 32.
23. Eric Walrond, rev. of *Vengeance of the Gods* [1922], in Martin, *African Fundamentalism* 127.
24. William H. Ferris, "The Significance of Rene Maran" [1922], in Martin, *African Fundamentalism* (1991) 34.
25. William H. Ferris, "World's Ten Greatest Novels: Why Rene Maran's *Batouala* Won Goncourt Prize; Novels for Propaganda" [1922], in Martin, *African Fundamentalism* 39-40.
26. Martin, *African Fundamentalism* 32.
27. See Charles Scruggs, *The Sage in Harlem: H. L. Mencken and the Black Writers of the 1920s* (Baltimore: Johns Hopkins University, 1984).

28. George Lamming, "The Negro Writer and His World," *Caribbean Quarterly* 5 (1958): 112.

29. Lamming 115.

30. Lamming 115.

31. Lamming 115.

32. Chip Rhodes, "Writing up the New Negro: The Construction of Consumer Desire in the Twenties," *Journal of American Studies* 28 (1990): 196. For Rhodes, the most representative example of this kind of writing is Du Bose Heywood's *Porgy;* Nella Larsen's *Quicksand,* on the other hand, subverts this tradition.

33. Ramchand, "Eric Walrond" 70.

34. The primary source used for the stories is Eric Walrond, *Tropic Death* (1926; New York: Collier Books, 1972). Hereafter cited parenthetically in the text and notes.

35. See Franklin W. Knight, *The Caribbean: The Genesis of a Fragmented Nationalism* (New York: Oxford UP, 1978), and Velma Newton, *The Silver Men: West Indian Labour Migration to Panama, 1850-1914* (Kingston, Jamaica: Institute of Social and Economic Research, University of the West Indies, 1984) 3-27.

36. The very title "Panama Gold" reinforces the many layers of irony in this tale. As a West Indian black laborer in the Zone, Poyer could aspire to no higher status than "Silverman." In the economic caste system that operated then, as Newton points out, "Segregation was institutionalized by the use of the terms "gold" (white American) and "silver" (European white or Negro), rather than "black" and "white"" (131), Newton adds that "whatever the rationale for paying employees in gold and silver currency, the Commission's reasons for extending the terms "gold" and "silver" to other areas of life on the Canal Zone was clear. The purpose was to establish a system of racial segregation under which "gold" hospitals, villages . . . were provided for white Americans, and similar but inferior services labelled "silver" for European and dark-skinned workers" (Newton 132), Poyer's achievement of the ultimate "gole" status deepens the tragic irony of the story, underlining the extent of his loss.

37. At times Walrond's descriptions of the landscape rise to the lyrical intensity and exuberance of Toomer's *Cane.*

38. Robert Bone, *Down Home: A History of Afro-American Short Fiction from Its Beginnings to the End of the Harlem Renaissance* (New York: Putnam, 1975) 203-04.

39. David Lewis 190.

FURTHER READING

Criticism

Bone, Robert. "Eric Walrond." In *Down Home: A History of Afro-American Short Fiction from Its Beginnings to the End of the Harlem Renaissance,* pp. 171-203. New York: G. P. Putnam's Sons, 1975.

Discusses Walrond's life and works, focusing on what Bone terms his "gothic" style and the themes of identity and transplantation in his works.

Gloster, Hugh M. "Fiction of the Negro Renaissance: West Indian Realism." In *Negro Voices in American Fiction,* pp. 180-84. 1948. Reprint. New York: Russell & Russell Inc., 1965.

Praises Tropic Death *for its "dispassionate and realistic treatment "of the life of Blacks outside the United States.*

Nkosi, Lewis. "An UnAmerican in New York." *London Review of Books* 22, no. 16 (24 August, 2000): 30-32.

Explores the richness of Walrond's prose style in Tropic Death *and several other pieces, noting his overall contribution to the literature of the Harlem Renaissance.*

OTHER SOURCES FROM GALE:

Additional coverage of Walrond's life and career is contained in the following sources published by the Gale Group: *Black Writers,* Ed. 1; *Contemporary Authors,* Vol. 125; and *Dictionary of Literary Biography,* Vol. 51.

DOROTHY WEST

(1907 - 1998)

(Also wrote under the pseudonyms Mary Christopher and Jane Isaac) American novelist and short story writer.

The youngest member of the Harlem Renaissance, West rubbed shoulders with some of the greatest Black writers of the 1920s, although her own literary contribution during that decade was slight. A few of her stories about middle-class themes were published in periodicals, but she produced no book-length work until the novel *The Living Is Easy* in 1948. West's career enjoyed a revival in the mid-1990s when Jacqueline Onassis encouraged her to complete her long-neglected novel, *The Wedding* (1995). As in her other works, the novel explores questions about race, color, class, and gender against the backdrop of the middle-class Black experience.

BIOGRAPHICAL INFORMATION

West was born in 1907, the daughter of an emancipated slave who built a prosperous fruit business in Boston. She grew up in an upper-middle-class environment, and her family summered on Martha's Vineyard. West decided when she was seven that she wanted to be a writer, and by fourteen she was submitting her stories to local papers. At seventeen she and her cousin Helene Johnson were invited to an awards banquet in New York after entering a national writing contest. West took second place, sharing a prize with Zora Neale Hurston. Shortly after, West and Johnson moved to Harlem, where West joined a group of writers known as the New Negro movement, which became a driving force in establishing the Harlem Renaissance. She associated with many of the movement's most important figures, including Hurston, James Weldon Johnson, and Wallace Thurman, with whom she became good friends. West, however, published little, although she wrote a good deal.

In 1932 West traveled with other Black writers, including Langston Hughes, to Russia to take part in a film produced by the Communist Party about racial discrimination in the United States. She returned to the United States one year later after hearing of her father's death, and found that the Harlem Renaissance had come to a close. With the Depression, many of her fellow writers were no longer able to survive in New York and had moved west to find work. West stayed in New York and founded *Challenge* and then *New Challenge,* literary magazines devoted to creative writing and social activism, neither of which was successful. She also worked as a welfare relief social investigator and became involved in the Works Progress Administration Writer's Project. In 1940 she took a job writing short stories for the *New York Daily News.* By 1943, West had moved to Oak Bluffs on Martha's Vineyard.

Her first book, *The Living Is Easy,* was published in 1948, and although it received a fair amount of praise, West faded into oblivion. After many years, she became closely acquainted with one of her neighbors on Martha's Vineyard, Jacqueline Onassis, who was working as an editor for Doubleday. Onassis read West's short pieces in the *Vineyard Gazette* and began visiting her weekly. She encouraged West to finish the novel she had begun many years before, *The Wedding,* which was published in 1995. At almost ninety years old, she enjoyed a revival of interest in her work. Shortly thereafter, West put together a compilation of short stories, *The Richer, the Poorer: Stories, Sketches, and Reminiscences* (1995). West died in 1998, the last surviving member of the Harlem Renaissance.

MAJOR WORKS

West's first critical success was her story "The Typewriter," which garnered second place in the writing contest sponsored by the Urban League's *Opportunity* magazine and earned the approval of other Black writers. When she moved to New York and became a part of the Harlem Renaissance, she was only a teenager, but her talent, vivaciousness, and confidence made her a valuable member of the movement. In the 1920s and 1930s she published several stories in the *New York Daily News* and other periodicals, which were subsequently published in her 1995 collection, *The Richer, the Poorer.* In some of her stories, West does not indicate whether her characters are Black or white, but rather deals with the rites of passage in people's lives, with obstacles they overcome, and with their desires, dreams, failures, and successes. West said she wrote stories without racial conflict to accommodate her white editors and publishers, but in other stories West explores intragroup issues relating to class and color. These also are West's main concerns in *The Living Is Easy,* about an upper-middle-class, light-skinned Black woman, Cleo, who seduces her sisters' husbands. *The Wedding,* which takes place on Martha's Vineyard, explores similar themes. The novel's protagonist, also a light-skinned Black woman, is about to marry a white jazz musician, whom everyone in her family (except her white grandmother) finds unacceptable, not only because of his color, but because of his socioeconomic status and his vocation. This work, like West's other fiction, satirizes middle-class values and explores the complexities of race, gender, color, and class.

CRITICAL RECEPTION

During the 1920s and 1930s, when she was associated with the Harlem Renaissance movement, West thought of herself as "the best-known unknown writer of the time." She wrote short stories and essays and associated with other important writers, but few of her pieces were published. When it appeared in 1948, *The Living Is Easy* received generally good reviews. Most critics were impressed with the skillfulness of West's characterization and the depiction of the middle-class Black experience. Robert Bone addresses the novel's satirical style in his review. However, despite the novel's success, West faded from view for close to forty years. When *The Living Is Easy* was reissued in 1982, the author enjoyed a brief revival. She did so again with the 1995 publication of *The Wedding.* She had begun writing the novel many years before, but stopped working on it during the 1960s, fearing that other Blacks would criticize its middle-class subject matter. *The Wedding* received good reviews, although some criticized its weak ending, and it was made into a television miniseries. West's short story collection of the same year was almost unanimously praised for its skillful use of irony and the author's special ability to depict how children think and feel.

PRINCIPAL WORKS

The Living Is Easy (novel) 1948; re-issued 1982

"Elephant's Dance: A Memoir of Wallace Thurman" (essay) 1970

The Richer, The Poorer: Stories, Sketches, and Reminiscences (short stories) 1995

The Wedding (novel) 1995

GENERAL COMMENTARY

HENRY LOUIS GATES, JR. (ESSAY DATE 1998)

SOURCE: Gates, Henry Louis, Jr. "Beyond the Color Line." *The New Yorker* 74, no. 26 (27 September, 1998): 82.

In this, his obituary of West, Gates pays tribute to her portrayal of the diversity of Black life in the United States.

One recent Saturday morning, several hundred people gathered at that sacred meeting ground the Union Chapel, in Oak Bluffs, to bid farewell to one of the oldest and most celebrated citizens of Martha's Vineyard. Dorothy West, ninety-one when she died, was a novelist, short-story writer, and longtime columnist for the *Vineyard Gazette,* and the last surviving member of the nineteen-twenties literary movement known as the Harlem Renaissance. In those days, her writer friends called her "the kid from Boston." The kid from Boston got around: she once roomed with Zora Neale Hurston, was proposed to by Countee Cullen (she declined), and travelled to Soviet Russia with Langston Hughes. She had seen the revolution there, observed its failings, and couldn't be much impressed by the revolutionary posturing of the Black Power era. "Colored people," she defiantly maintained, was the aptest term for people of African descent in the United States, and, as if to testify to her good sense, the faces in attendance at the chapel were of every hue—not just the expected ebony and ivory but siennas, velvety ochres, pinks, and ambers.

Among those present were the performance artist Anna Deavere Smith, the law professor Lani Guinier, and the First Friend, Vernon Jordan. A dozen or so members of the Cottagettes Choir (the Cottagers being a sorority of black women who own homes in Oak Bluffs) delivered a spirited rendition of "I Believe I Can Fly." To its refrain, the congregants waved one arm side to side over their heads in the manner of Holy Ghost sisters in storefront evangelical churches.

"Color is not important—class is what matters," West was fond of repeating. By "class" she meant those brute inequities that color could so cunningly conceal—but also an old-fashioned sense of decorum, style, and politesse. Her Boston upbringing called for refinement in manner and dress, and a conviction "that propriety was more important than blood," as her cousin Abigail McGrath put it. One of West's abiding beliefs, McGrath recalled, was that one should "not stay too long at parties, so as to give the impression that you had a better place to go."

McGrath's first marriage helped inspire the plot of West's most successful book, ***The Wedding,*** published in 1995. It tells the story of a daughter of the Vineyard's black élite—*la crème de la crème brulé*—who scandalizes her family when she decides to marry a penniless white jazz musician. (Oprah Winfrey made it into a two-part movie for television, which was aired in February 1998.)

It took West almost five decades to complete ***The Wedding.*** She had stopped working on the novel at the height of the Black Power movement, in the late sixties, fearing that her views on race would meet a hostile reception from black militants. At the Union Chapel memorial service, the trial lawyer and Harvard Law professor Charles Ogletree recalled asking her why she was afraid of them. "Well," she said, "you know I live alone."

Who could have predicted that the book would have so much resonance in a multicultural America at the end of the century? Part of West's appeal was that she represented a felicitous combination of opposites, as you might expect from a genuine cosmopolitan who made her home on a small island and, in the last half century, seldom left it. Her writing offers both an airy lyricism and a devilish sense of humor. Whether she was working on a short story about a Harlem welfare investigator or a dispatch for the *Vineyard Gazette* about somebody's tea party, she wanted, above all, to get it *right.* To her death, she maintained that the only truthful way to write about black America was as a diversity of colors, of classes, and of sensibilities—united only by a common history and, at times, a common enemy. As a twentieth-century writer, she knew that depicting the lives of colored people with unsparing intimacy, and without ideology or argument, might just be the most revolutionary thing she could do.

DIANE CARDWELL (ESSAY DATE 1999)

SOURCE: Cardwell, Diane. "The Lives They Lived: Dorothy West, Last Leaf on the Tree." *New York Times* (3 January, 1999): 47.

In the following essay, Cardwell presents a sketch of West's life and notes the values and sense of possibility in her work.

"As a child, I decided I never wanted to be the last leaf on the tree," she told a reporter in 1995, "and now here I am, the last leaf. I was a member of the Harlem Renaissance, you know, and the youngest person is the one who lives the longest." A chatty, nut-brown woman barely big enough to see over a steering wheel, Dorothy West—accustomed to being the youngest, the first, the only—was almost congenitally predisposed to think of herself as special.

Her father, born a slave, built a prosperous wholesale fruit business in the shadow of Fanueil Hall, becoming known as Boston's Black Banana King. Her mother, a spirited beauty from a huge family, worked hard to instill pride in her Dot—even trying to keep from her news of the lynchings then plaguing the South, lest she develop an inferiority complex. Solid members of an exclusive black Yankee middle class, the Wests lived graciously in predominantly white Brookline and were among the first blacks to summer on Martha's Vineyard. West excelled in academics, starting at the elite Girls' Latin School at the precocious age of 10. Moved to tears reading Dostoevsky at 14, she decided to become a writer and began submitting stories to *The Boston Post.* At 17, West and her cousin Helene Johnson entered a national writing contest and were both invited to the awards dinner in New York.

When the two arrived at 125th Street in Harlem, West said, they were delighted to see "all these colored people" and, unable to imagine another reason for such a gathering, asked, "When is the parade?" That night, West shared second place with Zora Neale Hurston, then 25. Captivated by the heady atmosphere, she and Johnson moved to the city. West was quickly sucked into the bohemian vortex of speak-easies, "stand up" parties and long nights at the Savoy Ballroom dancing or just listening to Ella Fitzgerald. Years later, West remembered, laughing, "I mean, we didn't think of her as important at all. We were the ones who were going to be the important ones, you know."

As the Renaissance fizzled after the Crash, West decided that she and her young friends had been wasting their potential in a sea of bootleg gin. In 1932, she traveled to Moscow to be in a Communist propaganda film about the shabby treatment of blacks in America. Sent word of her father's death a year later, West returned to Harlem and tried founding two literary journals, but they failed. After working as a welfare investigator and for the Federal Writers Project, in the early 40's she went back to her mother and to the place she had always loved best, Martha's Vineyard.

The move became permanent, and it was there, in her family's weathered gray A-frame cottage, that she finished her first novel, ***The Living Is Easy,*** published in 1948. With it, West introduced a new sort of black literary heroine. Light-skinned, middle class and beautiful, modeled partly on West's mother, Cleo Judson was neither passive nor tragic, like those who had come before her, but domineering and conniving. "Cleo uses all these traits that make us hate her for a very positive end," West said in 1984, "to make conditions better for future generations."

West wouldn't publish her second novel, ***The Wedding,*** for nearly half a century, in part because she believed her sensibility—establishment, integrationist, intellectual—went out of fashion in the Black Power 60's. Through that tectonic upheaval, her basic values never changed. West's privileged upbringing, talents and single-minded ambition imbued her, just one generation out of slavery, with an exhilarating sense of possibility, with the conviction that spiritual and social uplift could be attained through sheer force of will. It was what sustained her to the end, pecking away at her old manual typewriter, late into the night.

A. YEMISI JIMOH (ESSAY DATE 1999)

SOURCE: Jimoh, A. Yemisi. "Dorothy West (1907-1998)." In *Contemporary African American Novelists: A Bio-Bibliographical Critical Sourcebook,* edited by Emmanuel S. Nelson, pp. 475-81. Westport, Conn.: Greenwood Press, 1999.

In this essay, Jimoh presents a biography of West before discussing her major works, including individual short stories, and surveys how critics have viewed her writing.

Biography

Dorothy West was born into the successful household of Isaac Christopher West and Rachel Pease Benson West in Boston. West was an only child whose extended family shared the Wests' large home in Boston. Virginia-born Isaac West owned a wholesale fruit business in the Boston Market. Rachel West was from Camden, South Carolina; she made a place for her family among Boston's small circle of successful, black, upper-middle-class families and provided her daughter with the fuel for an ironic literary approach to the issues of gender, race, class, and color consciousness, which inform much of Dorothy West's writing.

By the time West was seven, she knew that she wanted a literary career—after her father showed pride in her writing (McDowell 266-68). She attended the Girls' Latin School in Boston and, later, Boston University as well as the Columbia University School of Journalism. Dorothy West entered the second annual *Opportunity* magazine literary contest. Her entry, **"The Typewriter,"** shared second prize with Zora Neale Hurston's story "Muttsy." This literary accomplishment drew West—who was just seventeen—to New York for the *Opportunity* magazine awards banquet, which exposed her to the burgeoning Harlem Renaissance circle of writers and artists.

Dorothy West lived a writer's life for more than seventy years. During this time she published some of her writing under the pseudonyms Mary Christopher and Jane Isaac (Dalsgard 42). West's literary life included membership in the 1920s in the Boston African American writers' group the Saturday Evening Quill Club—some of her stories were published in its magazine, *The Saturday Evening Quill;* she had a brief stint with the Works Progress Administration—Federal Writers' Project in the 1930s; as founder of the literary magazines *Challenge* and *New Challenge,* West sought to nurture new, post-Renaissance literary talent, notably, Margaret Walker and Ralph Ellison; for more than two decades—1940s-1960s—she wrote short stories for the *New York Daily News;* and she contributed intermittently to the *Vineyard Gazette* from the 1960s until early in the 1990s, including a weekly column on the social activities around Oak Bluffs.

Dorothy West's father was among the first African Americans to purchase a vacation home in Oak Bluffs on Martha's Vineyard. West returned to her family's vacation home in the 1940s and lived year-round on the island until her death. While living on Martha's Vineyard, she published two novels, ***The Living Is Easy*** (1948) and ***The Wedding*** (1995) as well as a collection of short stories, sketches, and memoirs titled ***The Richer, the Poorer*** (1995). With a grant from the Mary Roberts Rinehart foundation in the 1940s, West began writing ***The Wedding.*** She also wrote two other pieces of long fiction that were never published: **"Where the Wild Grape Grows"** (McDowell 277) and **"The White Tribe of Indians"** (281), which is about the web of denials concerning ancestry among some African Americans.

In the mid-1990s, she was hailed as the last living Harlem Renaissance writer, and there was an upsurge of interest in Dorothy West as a writer and as a participant in the Harlem Renaissance. Projects such as the PBS film *As I Remember It: A Portrait of Dorothy West* (Clark, "Rediscovering" 47) and a 1998 film (Steinberg 34) based on her last novel all attest to the growing interest in recovering the literary career of Dorothy West. Into her ninth decade of life, West continued to plan new writing projects. Her latest was a historical book on Oak Bluffs.

Major Works and Themes

For Dorothy West, short stories "are the most perfect literary form" (McDowell 281). West's first published story was **"Promise and Fulfillment"** (Ferguson, *Dictionary* 188). In **"The Typewriter,"** her story for the *Opportunity* contest, a janitor dictates fictional letters to his daughter. He feels important and successful during these contrived business sessions, so he creates a fictional persona and begins to live in a fantasy world in which he is a successful businessman. This world crashes for the janitor after he reads in the newspaper that J. P. Morgan—with whom the janitor has had his most intense fantasy correspondence—has gone bankrupt. This story, among others, demonstrates West's inclination toward irony in her writing.

Seventeen of Dorothy West's stories are collected in ***The Richer, the Poorer.*** In stories such as **"The Five Dollar Bill," "Funeral," "The Bird like No Other," "The Penny,"** and others she convincingly presents a child's perspective. Frequently, West's stories, written from the perspective of innocence, are moralistic yet engaging. Through the eyes of a child, West returns to adults the contradictions that children learn from adult examples. In **"The Five Dollar Bill,"** a little girl named Judy—a name that recurs in West's stories with intelligent girl characters—witnesses and is affected deeply by her mother's duplicity.

West frequently writes about middle-class characters, yet not all of her short stories are set in a middle-class environment. When West does write about the African American middle class, she often uses irony to present a critique of their "counterfeit bourgeois" (Rodgers 161) attitudes and their "color foolishness" (Dalsgard 32). In stories such as **"Jack in the Pot,"** however, West situates poverty and its effects on one's character in the foreground. **"Jack in the Pot"** is the story of Mrs. Edmunds, a woman who wins money—jack—after she has suffered through hunger and while she is on welfare. She and her husband have lost their middle-class lifestyle because hard times caused her husband to close his business. West says that this story is her "statement on poverty" (Dalsgard 43). When West writes about poverty, she does not sentimentalize the poor. She, in fact, depicts the emotional and psychological impact of poverty. Most of West's characters, though, are successful or are from the struggling working class that made up much of the African American middle class in its nascent stages.

In a number of West's stories, especially those that she wrote for the *New York Daily News,* the author does not describe her characters in ways that would indicate whether they are black people. In other stories—**"Odyssey of an Egg"** and **"About a Woman Named Nancy"**—she pushes the boundaries of characterization and setting by eliminating references to skin color. Further, in **"Jack in the Pot"** West's references to color are so subtle as to be nearly incidental to the overall story. In West's story **"The Richer, the**

Poorer," she writes about two sisters who take opposite paths in life. Bess lives in the moment, while Lottie is cautious and industrious. In this story, West emphasizes the poverty of Lottie's miserly "life never lived" (56) and the wealth in Bess' active life, but little in this story indicates that the characters are modeled after black women West knew. During an interview with Katrine Dalsgard, West comments on the colorlessness in some of her writing. When she began to write two short stories monthly for the *Daily News,* there was a tacit agreement between West and the publishers: "For their sake, and for my sake because I had to eat, I never mentioned the word 'black'" (37). West's own personal survival and the racial politics of publishing explain her silence on color in **"The Richer, the Poorer," "The Maple Tree,"** and other stories. As a writer, West often has had to strike a delicate balance between the demands of publishing and her desire to write from her experiences.

In many of Dorothy West's short stories, she presents in condensed form several of the issues and themes that are found in her novels. West's literary corpus demonstrates that she actively engages vernacular qualities such as the black sermonic tradition and music, both of which have informed African American literature; more specifically, though, West is concerned with intragroup issues relating to class and color. These vernacular qualities as well as class and color concerns in her writing are clearly illustrated in **"An Unimportant Man," "Mammy," "Prologue to a Life,"** and **"Hannah Byde."** A compelling issue in Dorothy West's writing, however, is gender. A persistent motif in her fiction centers on the repressed female who dreams of, or connives, a position of power for herself. This quite frequently is a Pyrrhic victory for West's female characters.

Cleo, the main character in ***The Living Is Easy,*** is just such a woman. West takes her title for this novel from the song "Summertime," which is from DuBose Heyward's Broadway play *Porgy.* This novel is set in Boston from July 1914 through April 1919. Cleo Jericho Judson is southern and beautiful. At nineteen, Cleo marries a significantly older, hardworking businessman from the South named Bart Judson. West prepares readers for Cleo's manipulations of her husband and her sisters as well as for her resistance to proscribed gender roles through flashbacks to Cleo's Southern childhood. An independently minded child, Cleo fights and beats a little boy who taunts her; then she wonders, "What was there to being a boy? What was there to being a man? Men just worked. That was easier than what women did" (21). As a married woman, Cleo wants to create her own domain over which she can rule. In fact, "It had never occurred to her in the ten years of her marriage that she might be his helpmate. She thought that was the same thing as being a man's slave" (71). In the summer of 1914, Cleo brings her sisters and their children to her home in Boston for a visit, and she effectively manipulates and deceives them until they are living with her and are estranged from their husbands. The Jericho sisters all illustrate the variety of ways that gender and power operate. Lily accepts dependence; she wants to "please" Bart; she will stay quiet to keep his protection (233). Charity feels empty without her husband and substitutes food. Serena wants her own independence—even from her sister Cleo—as well as love. Cleo wants a female domain. Bart, Cleo's husband, is the means through which she reproduces herself as well as her source of financial support. Judy, Cleo's only child, observes her mother and resists her control. Judy realizes that Cleo "was the boss of nothing but the young, the weak, the frightened. She ruled a pygmy kingdom" (308). Through Cleo, West complicates two prevalent images of black women. The author revises established representations of black, middle-class, female characters by refusing to create tragic sympathy for her near-white characters. Dorothy West also transforms the concept of the black woman as the enduring, loving matriarch.

Cleo's world disintegrates after Bart's business fails, in the same way as other black-owned businesses in the novel that did not respond effectively to the forces of modernity. While West illustrates in ***The Living Is Easy*** the small space that black, middle-class women occupy, she also delineates the weakly derivative and obsessively color-conscious base on which her black middle-class characters rest. This small, exclusive group consists in the struggling descendants of tailors and stable owners who prefer light skin color and avoid acknowledging anything as ugly as lynching. Throughout ***The Living Is Easy*** West illustrates her ironic stance toward middle-class color consciousness and imitative behavior with poignant narrative commentary. When, for example, a black man "failed in business, and blew his brains out just like a white man, [e]verybody was a little proud of his suicide" (112).

Cleo Judson's actions in this novel are misguided, but her motive is to situate her vision of the lifestyle and cultural base of the African

American South within the economic base of middle-class Boston and to define a space for female power. Cleo is defeated by the broader economic and gender issues of her time as well as by her own overreaching. Cleo wonders if her sisters—because they are manless—are less like the image of their mother that Cleo remembers. She remembers the face of her mother when their father "was no where in her thinking" (284). Cleo's dream of a female utopia has become strangely dystopic without Bart's support. West's novel demonstrates the power of the dominant discourse on race and gender.

Forty-seven years after the publication of Dorothy West's first novel, she returns readers—in her second novel, ***The Wedding***—to the complexities of a class- and color-conscious environment in an exclusive circle of African Americans. The immediate action of the novel occurs in 1953 on Martha's Vineyard in the Oval, a fictional neighborhood on the island of Oak Bluffs. West's narrator, however, supplies readers with more than 100 years of history through flashbacks. The new guard in the Oval has moved away from the entrenched cultural rules. Previously, marrying light-skinned—not white—and marrying well had been the rule. Between them, Shelby Coles and her sister Liz have broken all the rules. Liz's husband is a dark-skinned physician whose occupation saves him from complete déclassé status in the Oval. Liz and Clark Coles—the sisters' father—unlike their mother and neighbors, are concerned that Shelby is rejecting black men out of fear. Shelby, notwithstanding everyone's restrained distress, is planning to marry a white jazz musician. Meade, her fiancé, is not a light-skinned black man; he is not a member of the right socioeconomic class; and his career is unsuitable for a resident of the Oval. Clark is worried about Shelby's marriage to Meade, because "I've never seen you give your respect to a colored man and I can't help but think that maybe that's some warped extension of this family's social snobbery" (201). The only member of the Coles family who has no reservations about Shelby's marriage is Gram, Shelby's white great-grandmother who dreams of regenerating the white branch of her family, which was cut off when her daughter Josephine married Hannibal, the son of a woman who was formerly enslaved at Xanadu, the family's plantation.

With this novel, Dorothy West again interrogates issues of class, color, and, to a lesser extent, gender. She demonstrates the complexities of these issues through a story that illuminates the social construction of desire and race. She further shows the numerous moral and psychological convolutions in behavior and thought that restrictive color/class practices engender.

Critical Reception

Dorothy West's novel ***The Living Is Easy*** was reviewed widely when it was first published. These reviews were, for the most part, favorable. Most of the reviewers locate West's strength in her ability to present unforgettable characters, especially Cleo. Too often, though, these early reviews were concerned with the ways in which Cleo's actions affected Bart's male identity. West occasionally has been critiqued—rightly—for her weak ending of this novel. This same, very right complaint has been leveled against West's second novel, ***The Wedding.*** Most agree, however, that Dorothy West's weak endings do not nullify the value of her novels.

To date, the bulk of scholarship on Dorothy West focuses on ***The Living Is Easy.*** In Philip Butcher's 1948 essay, he presents West as one of the then-current "raceless writers." For Butcher, "The trend toward raceless authorship seems a loss to the Negro and to American literature" (15). In 1982 the Feminist Press reissued ***The Living Is Easy*** with an afterword by Adelaide Cromwell. Cromwell discusses the ways in which West's novel transforms literary representations of black women as well as the literary image of the lives of black people in the United States. Edward Clark's 1985 essay "Boston Black and White" is concerned with Cleo's failed desire to "be both Southern and Bostonian" (85). Lawrence Rodgers presents one of the most intriguing readings of ***The Living Is Easy.*** He does not believe this novel is compromised by the dominant society's middle-class values. For him, West "mocks these values" (161). Rodgers reads Cleo as "a complex archetypal trickster whose resistance to the binary is rooted in the folk tradition" (165) of black people in the South.

Mary Helen Washington initiates scholarly focus on gender in this novel. West, according to Washington, writes a novel that is "in contradiction with itself" because there is a "sisterly community which has deposed the powerful mother" Cleo (350-51). Gloria Wade-Gayles (1984) argues that African American mother-daughter relationships in literature are different from their European American counterparts because the socialization process among black women is rooted in gender and racial struggles. Eva Rueschmann investigates the importance of sister bonds, which allow black women a mirror that reflects a model for "identity formation," which is lacking in the dominant society. For Rueschmann, West's ***The Living Is Easy*** "comment[s] ironically on women's pre-scripted fantasies about their own development and underline[s] how standards for white women have shaped black women's self-perceptions and expectations" (130). Cleo, then, tries to find in her sisters just such a mirror of their mother and herself.

Works Cited

Works by Dorothy West

"Hannah Byde." *The Messenger* 8 (July 1926): 197-199.

"Prologue to a Life." 1928. *The Sleeper Wakes: Harlem Renaissance Stories by Women.* Ed. Marcy Knopf. New Brunswick, NJ: Rutgers University Press, 1993. 84-94.

The Living Is Easy. 1948. Old Westbury, NY: Feminist Press, 1982.

The Richer, the Poorer: Stories, Sketches, and Reminiscences. New York: Doubleday, 1995a.

The Wedding. New York: Doubleday, 1995b.

Studies of Dorothy West

Butcher, Philip. "Our Raceless Writers." *Opportunity* 26 (summer 1948): 113-115.

Clark, Dorothy A. "Rediscovering Dorothy West." *American Visions* 8 (1993): 46-47.

Clark, Edward. "Boston Black and White: The Voice of Fiction." *Black American Literature Forum* 19 (1985): 83-89.

Cromwell, Adelaide. Afterword. *The Living Is Easy.* By Dorothy West. Old Westbury, NY: Feminist Press, 1982. 349-362.

Dalsgard, Katrine. "Alive and Well and Living on the Island of Martha's Vineyard: An Interview with Dorothy West, October 29, 1988." *The Langston Hughes Review* 12 (1993): 28-44.

Daniel, Walter C. "*Challenge Magazine:* An Experiment That Failed." *CLAJ* 26 (June 1976): 494-503.

Ferguson, Sally Ann. "Dorothy West and Helene Johnson in *Infants of the Spring.*" *Langston Hughes Review* 2.2 (1983): 22-24.

———. "Dorothy West." *Dictionary of Literary Biography.* Vol. 76. Ed. Trudier Harris. Detroit: Gale, 1988. 187-195.

McDowell, Deborah E. "Conversation with Dorothy West." *The Harlem Renaissance Re-Examined.* Ed. Victor A. Kramer. New York: AMS Press, 1987. 265-282.

Rodgers, Lawrence R. "Dorothy West's *The Living Is Easy* and the Ideal of Southern Folk Community." *AAR* 26 (1992): 161-172.

Roses, Lorraine Elena. "Interviews with Black Women Writers: Dorothy West at Oak Bluffs, Massachusetts July, 1984." *Sage* 2.1 (1985): 47-49.

Rueschmann, Eva. "Sister Bonds: Intersections of Family and Race in Jessie Redmon Fauset's *Plum Bun* and Dorothy West's *The Living Is Easy.*" *The Significance of Sibling Relationships in Literature.* Ed. JoAnna Stephens Mink and Janet Doubler Ward. Bowling Green, OH: Bowling Green State University Popular Press, 1993. 120-132.

Steinberg, Sybil. "Dorothy West: Her Own Renaissance." *Publishers Weekly* 242 (3 July 1995): 34-35.

Wade-Gayles, Gloria. "The Truths of Our Mothers' Lives: Mother-Daughter Relationships in Black Women's Fiction." *Sage* 1.2 (1984): 8-12.

Washington, Mary Helen. "I Sign My Mother's Name: Maternal Power in Dorothy West's Novel, *The Living Is Easy.*" *Invented Lives: Narratives of Black Women 1860-1960.* Garden City, NY: Anchor Press, 1987. 344-353.

LAURIE CHAMPION (ESSAY DATE 2000)

SOURCE: Champion, Laurie. "Dorothy West (1907-1998)." In *American Women Writers, 1900-1945: A Bio-Bibliographical Critical Sourcebook,* edited by Laurie Champion, pp. 357-62. Westport, Conn.: Greenwood Publishing, 2000.

In the following essay, Champion provides an overview of West, including a biography and a discussion of her major works and reputation.

Biography

Dorothy West was born the only child to Rachel Pease Benson and Isaac Christopher West on June 2, 1907, in Boston, Massachusetts. Her father, freed from slavery at age seven, later settled in Boston, where he profited from a wholesale fruit company and was known as the "Black Banana King" of Boston. Her mother, who came from a large family, was born in South Carolina and later moved to Springfield, Massachusetts, where she met West's father. The Wests were among the first black bourgeoisie to reside in the Oak Bluffs section of Martha's Vineyard. West was given private tutoring when she was a toddler, entered public school at age four, transferred when she was ten to a private girl's school, and later studied at Columbia University.

West's first publication, the short story **"Promise and Fulfillment,"** appeared in the *Boston Post* when she was only fourteen. In 1926, shortly before she turned eighteen, West's story **"The Typewriter"** shared *Opportunity* magazine's second prize with Zora Neale Hurston's story "Muttsy." After her initial visit to New York to receive her award, West returned to Boston, where she attended Boston University for a short time before returning to New York to participate in the Harlem Renaissance. She became friends with prominent intellectuals and writers such as

Zora Neale Hurston, Countee Cullen, Wallace Thurman, Arna Bontemps, Langston Hughes, and Nella Larsen.

During this time, West wrote mostly short stories, which appeared in magazines such as *Saturday Evening Quill.* In 1927, she performed in the original stage production of *Porgy* and also traveled to London in the summer of 1929 to perform in the play. In 1932, West went to Russia with Langston Hughes and twenty other African Americans to film *Black and White,* a documentary about American racism. The film was never produced because of political controversy, but West remained in Russia with Langston Hughes for a year. West proposed marriage to Hughes, but his exact response is not known. In her many generous interviews, West remained reluctant to discuss her relationship with Hughes.

In 1933, when West returned to the United States from Russia, most of the major members of the Harlem Renaissance were no longer living in New York. Attempting to recognize prominent African American writers, in 1934, West funded and edited the literary magazine *Challenge,* which folded in 1937 for lack of funding. Soon afterward, West launched the literary magazine *New Challenge,* which she edited with Marian Minus and Richard Wright. Appearing in the only issue of *New Challenge* was Wright's famous essay "Blueprint for Negro Writing" and works by notable authors such as Margaret Walker and Ralph Ellison.

After *New Challenge* folded, West worked for eighteen months as a welfare investigator, then joined the Federal Writers' Project. In 1943, West left New York to return to Oak Bluffs. She contributed regularly to the *New York Daily News* and completed her novel ***The Living Is Easy,*** which was published in 1948. West soon began another novel, tentatively entitled ***Where the Wild Grape Grows.*** She sent samples of this work in progress to potential publishers, but it was not well received because it concerned the black middle class. She incorporated most of ***Where the Wild Grape Grows*** into a new novel, ***The Wedding*** (1995). During the 1960s and 1970s, West held various jobs such as a clerk for the *Vineyard Gazette* and as a cashier for a restaurant, while continuing to write ***The Wedding.*** She also wrote columns for *Vineyard Gazette* such as **"The Cottager's Corner,"** about blacks on the island.

Like ***The Living Is Easy, The Wedding*** portrayed elite African Americans; but with the rise of the Black Arts movement, West feared that ***The Wedding*** would be rejected by African Americans for its portrayal of elitist blacks, who were considered Uncle Toms during the time. She was also aware that the novel would not be accepted by white readers because it defied stereotypes of African Americans, so rather than risk rejection from both black and white audiences, West ceased to work on the novel.

After many years of obscurity as a writer, in 1982, when the Feminist Press reprinted ***The Living Is Easy,*** West received renewed critical acclaim. She engaged in public speeches, performed book signings, generously granted interviews, and was noted as the only living participant of the Harlem Renaissance. After Doubleday editor Jacqueline Kennedy Onassis encouraged West to finish ***The Wedding,*** it appeared in 1995, forty years since West began writing it. That same year, shortly after the publication of ***The Wedding, The Richer, the Poorer*** was published by Doubleday. It consists of seventeen short stories and thirteen reminiscent personal essays, most of which originally appeared in publications between the 1920s and 1940s. Recently, the much celebrated ***The Wedding*** was adapted into an Oprah Winfrey miniseries, and *As I Remember It: A Portrait of Dorothy West* appeared as a PBS film. After many years of remaining unrecognized for her skills as a writer, West has finally begun to gain long overdue acclaim. In Boston, on August 16, 1998, West's death marked the end of the last living member of the Harlem Renaissance.

FROM THE AUTHOR

A SELF-FULFILLING PROPHECY

When I was a child of 4 or 5, listening to the conversation of my mother and her sisters, I would sometimes intrude on their territory with a solemnly stated opinion that would jerk their heads in my direction, then send them into roars of uncontrollable laughter. I do not now remember anything I said. But the first adult who caught her breath would speak for them all and say, "That's no child. That's a little sawed-off woman." That was to become a self-fulfilling prophecy.

SOURCE: Dorothy West, excerpt from an article in *Essence,* August 1995.

Major Works and Themes

Dorothy West's novels, ***The Living Is Easy*** and ***The Wedding,*** are part of a long tradition of novels by black women that began in the late nineteenth century with Frances Harper's *Iola Leroy,* continued through the Harlem Renaissance with novels such as Nella Larsen's *Quicksand* and Jessie Fauset's *The Chinaberry Tree* and *There Is Confusion,* and is represented more recently in works such as Andrea Lee's *Sarah Phillips* and Gloria Naylor's *Linden Hill.* Like these authors who illustrate upper-middle-class African Americans, West shows pretentiousness of the socially elite, such as the Bostonians in ***The Living Is Easy*** who avoid association with members of the lower classes and obsess over "which parties and churches to attend and which to avoid" (Cromwell 358).

The Living Is Easy and ***The Wedding*** concern important gender, race, and class issues. ***The Living Is Easy*** portrays light-skinned protagonist Cleo Jericho, who marries an older businessman, Bart Judson, in order to secure status among prestigious black elites of Boston. She invites her three sisters to live with her. Through portrayals of Cleo's childhood and her three sisters' attitudes, West explores gender roles and demonstrates that superficial middle-class values do not lead to self-fulfillment. Similarly, ***The Wedding*** satirizes middle-class values. The novel, set on Martha's Vineyard, depicts young Shelby Coles, who plans to marry a white jazz musician. With the exception of her grandmother, her family disapproves of her plans. Another central conflict in ***The Wedding*** involves Lute McNeil, a black man who tries to persuade Shelby to marry him instead of her white fiancé. The novel traces five generations and shows both personal and historical background for the context of the lives of the Coles. In both ***The Wedding*** and ***The Living Is Easy,*** West portrays blacks and women who defy stereotypes and challenges readers to consider complex dilemmas that deal with power and economics.

West's novels are important contributions to African American literature, but she excels in the short-story genre. As she says, "I think of myself first as a short story writer" (McDowell 281). Although most of West's short stories and essays originally appeared in journals and magazines between the 1920s and the 1940s, they remained uncollected until the 1995 publication of ***The Richer, the Poorer: Stories, Sketches, and Reminiscences.*** Unlike her novels, West's short stories show the despair of the lower class, such as the degraded janitor in **"Jack in the Pot"** who cannot afford a funeral for his daughter. Throughout the collection, the plight of the economically disadvantaged is frequently revealed through West's use of dualisms, which are most blatantly revealed in the title story **"The Richer, the Poorer"** and in **"The Happiest Year, the Saddest Year."** In **"The Richer, the Poorer,"** Bess marries a musician immediately after high school, while her sister, Lottie, works and saves money. Later in life Lottie realizes she has experienced a shallow life and vows to adopt a lifestyle similar to Bess's. West supports Bess's philosophy, one that advocates that life's joys are found not in material wealth but in strong personal relationships. Also representative of economic matters, two stories in the collection express denominations of money as titles: **"The Five-Dollar Bill"** and **"The Penny."** In general, these stories show ironic results of economic concerns. For example, personal triumphs are reduced in the lives of the middle class because they focus on social status and material gain at the expense of cultural, personal, and internal rewards.

West's stories also explore gender and race issues. For example, **"Hannah Byde"** exposes ways that striving for social prestige relates to women. Hannah is an unfulfilled, frustrated housewife, expected to be a model wife to her financially secure husband. Unlike some of the wives of socially prominent men in ***The Living Is Easy*** and ***The Wedding,*** who seem oblivious that they encourage the very values that demean them as women, Hannah understands her predicament. Striving for social status at the expense of racial and cultural concerns is the prevalent theme in **"An Unimportant Man."** The story concerns Zeb, who dreams of becoming "a Darrow for his race, eloquently pleading a black man's cause" (139). Because his wife is concerned with social prestige, Zeb eventually encourages his daughter to forfeit her dreams of becoming a dancer because he presumes that he is helping his race by seeking middle-class values like those expressed by his friend Parker, who does not celebrate his African American identity. Unfortunately, like the professionals in ***The Living Is Easy,*** Parker has become part of an insular, segregated subsociety striving for social status but never gaining acceptance from the larger society.

Although West's writings do not represent the degree of race consciousness found in many works by black writers who during the first half of the century expressed anger toward racial oppression that included rejecting whites, her writings reveal the need for social change based on race, class, and gender equality. A powerful writer, Dorothy West represents well the Harlem Renaissance.

Critical Reception

When it originally appeared, West's ***The Living Is Easy*** was reviewed widely and received mixed reviews. While critics pointed out West's strong characterization of Cleo, some also noted its flawed ending. Since ***The Living Is Easy*** was West's only full-length publication for over forty years, until very recently it has received the most critical attention. One recent essay, Lawrence R. Rodgers's "Dorothy West's ***The Living Is Easy*** and the Ideal of Southern Folk Community," focuses exclusively on ***The Living Is Easy*** and suggests that the novel "uses satire to revise the (male) Great Migration novel" (161).

Reviewers in general celebrated the 1995 publication of ***The Wedding,*** although some noted the flawed ending; however, apparently some reviewers received preview copies of the novel in which Doubleday's ghostwriters had tacked on an ending unapproved by West. Eventually, with the help of noted black scholar Henry Louis Gates, Jr., West was given the opportunity to complete her novel, and other reviewers were able to read the definitive text. Praise for ***The Wedding*** is exemplified in Susan Kenney's review for *New York Times Book Review:* "It's as though we've been invited not so much to a wedding as to a full-scale opera, only to find that one great artist is belting out all the parts. She brings down the house" (12). ***The Richer, the Poorer*** was published the same year as ***The Wedding*** and received overwhelmingly favorable reviews. Jack Moore, writing for *Studies in Short Fiction,* praised West's ability to depict honestly the feelings and thoughts of children and says the book represents West's artistic gifts to her readers. Since the publication of ***The Wedding*** and ***The Richer, the Poorer*** West has received renewed critical attention. Currently in press is guest editor Sharon Jones's issue of *Langston Hughes Review,* which will focus on Dorothy West.

Works Cited

Works by Dorothy West

"Hannah Byde." *Messenger* July 1926: 197-99.

"Prologue to a Life." *Saturday Evening Quill* Apr. 1929: 5-10.

"The Black Dress." *Opportunity* 12 (1934): 140, 158.

"Dear Reader [from *Challenge*]." 1934. *Voices from the Harlem Renaissance.* Ed. Nathan Irvin Huggins. New York: Oxford University Press, 1976. 391-93.

"Editorial [from *New Challenge*]." 1937. *Voices from the Harlem Renaissance.* Ed. Nathan Irvin Huggins. New York: Oxford University Press, 1976. 393-94.

The Living Is Easy. Boston: Houghton, 1948.

The Richer, the Poorer: Stories, Sketches, and Reminiscences. New York: Doubleday, 1995.

The Wedding. New York: Doubleday, 1995.

Studies of Dorothy West

Bontemps, Arna. "In Boston." Rev. of *The Living Is Easy,* by Dorothy West. *New York Herald Tribune Weekly Book Review* 13 June 1948: 16.

Champion, Laurie. "Social Class Distinctions in Dorothy West's *The Richer, the Poorer.*" *Langston Hughes Review.* Forthcoming.

Clark, Dorothy A. "Rediscovering Dorothy West." *American Visions* 8 (1993): 46-47.

Clark, Edie. "Dorothy West, Novelist: Weaver of Possibilities." Rev. of *The Wedding,* by Dorothy West. *Yankee* 59 (1995): 83-85.

Cromwell, Adelaide M. Afterword. *The Living Is Easy.* 1948. Old Westbury, NY: Feminist Press, 1982. 349-64.

Dalsgard, Katrine. "Alive and Well and Living on the Island of Martha's Vineyard: An Interview with Dorothy West, October 29, 1988." *Langston Hughes Review* 12.2 (1993): 28-44.

Daniel, Walter C. "*Challenge Magazine:* An Experiment That Failed." *CLA Journal* 19 (1976): 494-503.

Ferguson, Sally Ann H. "Dorothy West." *Afro-American Writers, 1940-1955.* Ed. Trudier Harris and Thadious M. Davis. Detroit: Gale, 1988. Vol. 76 of *Dictionary of Literary Biography.* 187-95.

———. "Dorothy West and Helene Johnson in *Infants of the Spring.*" *Langston Hughes Review* 2.2 (1983): 22-24.

Gates, Henry Louis, Jr. "Beyond the Color Line." *New Yorker* 7 Sept. 1998: 82-83.

Jimoh, A. Yemisi. "Dorothy West." *Contemporary African American Novelists.* Ed. Emmanuel S. Nelson. Westport, CT: Greenwood, 1999. 475-81.

Kenney, Susan. "Shades of Difference." Rev. of *The Wedding,* by Dorothy West. *New York Times Book Review* 12 Feb. 1995: 11-12.

Krim, Seymour. "Boston Black Belt." Rev. of *The Living Is Easy,* by Dorothy West. *New York Times Book Review* 16 May 1948: 5.

McDowell, Deborah E. "Conversations with Dorothy West." *The Harlem Renaissance Re-Examined.* Georgia State Literary Studies Ser. 2. Ed. Victor A. Kramer. New York: AMS Press, 1987. 265-82.

Moore, Jack B. Rev. of *The Richer, the Poorer: Stories, Sketches and Reminiscences,* by Dorothy West. *Studies in Short Fiction* 33 (1996): 593-95.

Newson, Adele S. "An Interview with Dorothy West." *Zora Neale Hurston Forum* 2 (1987): 19-24.

Parker, Gwendolyn M. "Echoes from the Harlem Renaissance." Rev. of *The Richer, the Poorer,* by Dorothy West. *New York Times Book Review* 6 Aug. 1995: 12.

Rodgers, Lawrence R. "Dorothy West's *The Living Is Easy* and the Ideal of Southern Folk Community." *African American Review* 26 (1992): 161-72.

Rueschmann, Eva. "Sister Bonds: Intersections of Family and Race in Jessie Redmon Fauset's *Plum Bun* and Dorothy West's *The Living Is Easy.*" *The Significance of Sibling Relationships in Literature.* Ed. JoAnna Stephens Mink and Janet Doubler Ward. Bowling Green, OH: Bowling Green State University Popular Press, 1993. 120-32.

Skow, John. "The Second Time Around." Rev. of *The Wedding,* by Dorothy West. *Time* 24 July 1995: 67.

Steinberg, Sybil. "Dorothy West: Her Own Renaissance." *Publishers Weekly* 3 July 1995: 34-35.

Washington, Mary Helen. "I Sign My Mother's Name: Alice Walker, Dorothy West, Paule Marshall." *Mothering the Mind: Twelve Studies of Writers and Their Silent Partners.* Ed. Ruth Perry and Martine Watson Brownley. New York: Holmes, 1984. 142-63.

"West, Dorothy." *Current Biography Yearbook.* Vol. 58. Ed. Elizabeth A. Schick. New York: Wilson, 1997. 604-8.

TITLE COMMENTARY

The Living Is Easy

ROBERT BONE (ESSAY DATE 1965)

SOURCE: Bone, Robert. Review of *The Living is Easy.* In *The Negro Novel in America.* Rev. ed., pp. 187-91. New Haven, Conn.: Yale University Press, 1965.

In the following excerpt, Bone emphasizes the biting satire of The Living is Easy *while pointing to some flaws in West's narrative structure.*

The Living Is Easy (1948), by Dorothy West, is a bitingly ironic novel which deals with the ruthless success drive of the Negro middle class and its staggering toll in ruined personalities. Boston's "counterfeit Brahmins" are the objects of Miss West's satire, and she belabors them with an enthusiasm born of personal rebellion. Yet in presenting her indictment, she never subordinates psychological interest to social criticism. Such is her gift for characterization that even her minor figures come alive, while Cleo, the protagonist of the novel, is unforgettable. Manipulative, domineering, unscrupulous, and yet in her selfish way, loving, this castrating female is the most striking personality in recent Negro fiction.

Dorothy West's literary career spans three decades in the history of the Negro novel. A native Bostonian, she was educated at Boston University and the Columbia School of Journalism. She began to write during the mid-1920s, publishing short stories in *Opportunity,* the *Boston Post,* and *The Saturday Evening Quill* (literary organ of the local "New Negro" group). During the 1930s, as editor of *Challenge* and *New Challenge,* she helped keep alive the idea of a distinctive Negro art. A depression job as relief investigator in the Harlem tenements introduced a sociological note into her work; eighteen months on the Federal Writers' Project and personal contact with Richard Wright drew her briefly into the orbit of the Communist party. During the forties, she contributed short stories regularly to a news syndicate, while completing work on her first full-length novel.

The Living Is Easy reflects most of this background. From the Renaissance period comes a touch of primitivism, a Freudian approach to personality, a positive attitude toward Negro folk culture and a negative attitude toward the Negro middle class. From the author's depression experience comes an ability to root her characters solidly in their social milieu. Hers, however, is a primarily Renaissance consciousness. The very title of the novel, though ironic, helps to define its essential spirit through association with Catfish Row. The novel, in fact, seems to have had its inception in a short story which appeared originally in *The Saturday Evening Quill.* **"Prologue to a Life"** (April 1929) contains the prototypes of Cleo and Bart, the central figures of the novel. Their names are changed in the later work, but the essential circumstances of their lives remain unaltered.

Cleo is an ambitious parvenu from "down home" who sacrifices the happiness of herself and her family for the sake of admission to the ranks of the Boston élite. In a flashback to her Southern childhood, Cleo's dominant personality traits are revealed. Her tremendous vitality, wildness, and daring are displayed in the episode of the roaring stallion; her masculine protest, in her fight with a boy whom she defeats by butting him in the groin. Her warped values are anticipated by a querulous remark to her father: "I don't want a kiss, I want a copper." Proud and despotic, she tyrannizes over her weaker sisters, blackmailing them out of their share of penny candy without scruple or remorse. Her deepest motives, however, spring from her relationship to her mother. The dethroned eldest child, she wants desperately to be loved best, and this neurotic need sets the pattern of her adult personality.

As the present action commences, Cleo is well on the way to social success. Having left the South with no assets but a fair complexion, she enters a loveless marriage with Bart Judson, "the Black Banana King." In an unguarded moment she admits her husband to her bedroom; the result is

Judy, a disappointing dark child who takes after her father. In spite of this setback, Cleo resolves to raise her daughter as a proper little Bostonian. She steals from her husband, lies to her friends, and deprives Judy of her childhood in order to accomplish this objective. In her treachery and deceit, her willfulness and ambition, her fierce self-containment and her infinite capacity for rationalization, Cleo's literary archetype is Iago. What makes her a more successful character is her humanity, her capacity for suffering as well as inflicting pain.

Cleo's inner conflict is developed along typical Renaissance lines: "You really had to love Bostonians to like them. And the part of Cleo that did like them was continually at war with the part of her that preferred the salt flavor of lusty laughter" (p. 44). In color, in social position, in personality Cleo hovers between two worlds. In order to enjoy the best of both, she gathers her sisters around her, destroying their marriages in the process. But the climax of the novel occurs when Cleo symbolically turns her back on the Negro struggle in the South. This is the final price of acceptance by a group whose "lives were narrowly confined to a desperate effort to ignore their racial heritage." Nemesis arrives in the form of the first World War, which ruins her husband's wholesale banana business. Cleo's power was her husband's money; now she can rule only "the young, the weak, and the frightened." Gradually she is deserted by her sisters, her daughter, and at last her husband.

Cleo mutilates her "Rabelaisian soul" in order to become a Bostonian. Similar mutilations in other characters serve to broaden the theme. There is the Duchess, who buries her Catholic heart in an unsanctioned marriage, in order to pour tea for Boston ladies who have scorned her mother. There is the Duchess' husband, Simeon, who relinquishes the editorship of a militant Negro newspaper, in order to secure his sister's social position. There is a young doctor, interested in cancer research, who turns to the abortion trade as a source of ready cash. All, like Cleo, have paid too high a price for belonging; their Spartan discipline in the face of personal tragedy is described in one of Miss West's early stories: "The race was too young, its achievements too few, for whimsical indulgence. It must not matter whom you loved; it must not matter what you desired; it must not matter that it broke your heart, if sacrifice meant a step forward toward the freedom of our people."[1]

Out of the dramatic structure of the novel comes a persistent thematic idea: "there can be no interlocking of separated worlds." The immediate reference is to the secular and religious worlds of Simeon and the Duchess, but the concept is universal in application. The clashing worlds of past and present, of child and adult, of male and female, of white and colored, of South Carolina and Boston fall within its scope. Cleo's tragic error is her determination to unite these worlds by sheer force of will. The result is universal misery. The novel thus becomes a plea to respect individual differences; an admonition against "easy" solutions which involve self-mutilation of any kind.

The most characteristic feature of Miss West's style is her use of verbal irony. The ironist is ultimately concerned with values, and in this instance her shafts are aimed at the specious values of the Negro middle class: "Mr. Hartnett failed in business and blew his brains out just like a white man. Everybody was a little proud of his suicide." The tone flows spontaneously from the nature of her material. Miss West writes of a time when "a tailor and a stable-owner were the leaders of colored society." A Negro élite whose economic base is so inadequate to its social aspirations invites ironic treatment. Only once, and at her peril, does the author abandon this steady perspective. In handling the subject of Southern injustice, she drops her ironic tone and immediately lapses into the wildest melodrama.

The Living Is Easy, in spite of occasional brilliance, is a diamond in the rough. There is little to distinguish its style, other than a certain neatness and economy. Serious difficulties on the narrative level prevent the novel from realizing its full potential. The plot falters more than once, as the author's inventiveness fails to keep pace with Cleo capacity for bitchery. Perhaps most damaging is the novel's lack of proportion. The formal division into Part I (280 pages) and Part II (67 pages) is indicative of the problem. Part II is in fact an epilogue which ties up the loose ends of the plot on an incredibly eventful day some years after the main action. Somewhere in the course of the busy day the conflicts initiated in Part I are hastily resolved. What can be said in extenuation of such formlessness? Only the trenchancy of its satire and the vividness of its characterization save the novel from oblivion.

Note

1. "An Unimportant Man," *Saturday Evening Quill* (June 1928): 21-32.

The Wedding

ELIZABETH MUTHER (ESSAY DATE 1999)

SOURCE: Muther, Elizabeth. "The Racial Subject of Suspense in Dorothy West's *The Wedding*." *Narrative* 7, no. 2 (May 1999): 194-212.

In the following essay, Muther presents a detailed analysis of The Wedding, *arguing that the narrative structure of this genealogical novel follows from the work's central idea about race and heritage.*

Dorothy West begins her late-career novel ***The Wedding*** (1995)[1] by establishing time and place, but with a curious ironic embodiment: "On a morning in late August, the morning before the wedding, the sun rising out of the quiet sea stirred the Oval from its shapeless sleep and gave dimension and design to the ring of summer cottages" (1). The first character to be introduced, "the Oval," is indeed not a human character at all, but a neighborhood or, better, a social place and mentality, which comes to consciousness in the novel's opening sentence. The Oval is in fact a palpable consciousness, and Dorothy West's discursive project in ***The Wedding*** is to place and examine her human cast of characters against the historical coercions and entanglements of class and color held in the numbing and hierarchical mind of the Oval. These are the summer houses of the old guard, the elite and exclusionary upper reaches of the African American middle class on Martha's Vineyard. The time is 1953.

Shelby Coles is at the focal point of the Oval's pernicious mentality, this being the eve of her wedding. For Shelby to wrest her life away from the Oval's control and to define her freedom will require a remapping of the racist episteme and a reauthoring of her identity. The narrative form of this genealogical novel, with its powerful analepses,[2] follows from West's engagement with the problem of color. Shelby faces the threat that a "colorist"[3] reification of human value—and the inevitable distortions of relationship that follow from it—will erupt once again in the Coles family. Her parents' relationship is dead. Her love, too, is placed in mortal danger on the day prior to her wedding. It is apparent that she will not be able to act rightly and to love well if she is subverted or waylaid by color-coded judgments. The novel's driving suspense, therefore, is in excess of what it would be if Shelby's story merely involved the playing out of a love plot. Shelby is endangered—not by the person of Lute McNeil who tries to abort her marriage—but by the threat of the recurrence of the defining pathologies of her family's history. West maps the genealogical structure of the novel to expose both the shadow of racism and the heritage of love in Shelby's own family's stories.

The marriage plot is virtually complete for Shelby at the opening of the novel, as the Oval awakens on the day before her wedding. The entire present action of the novel occurs within a little more than twenty-four hours from that moment, though the genealogical flashbacks in the text traverse almost a century. Shelby's story, though she cannot know it, is woven out of the lives of four generations, some beyond the reach of memory.

Shelby Coles, in the dangerous hours prior to her wedding, is drawn in West's novel from the certainty of her singular love for Meade, her fiancé, a white jazz musician. While off-stage for the entire novel, Meade makes a credible and desirable mate for her. Every shred of internal evidence makes Lute McNeil, who West's readers can see is pathologically abusive to women, a supremely unworthy rival to Meade. Even what Shelby can see—that he has three children by three marriages, that he is an overt social climber, and that he is barely literate—would eliminate him definitively. Lute's only qualifying attributes are that he is black and physically attractive.

In ***The Wedding,*** analepsis becomes genealogy.[4] West's narrator often moves precipitously into the lives of Shelby's forebears, both maternal and paternal, into parts of her story that are in some cases beyond the horizon of memory. The narrator is historian, naming and reclaiming the characters whose love has created the novel's converging lineages. These lives are mapped on the family tree that stands before Chapter One with Shelby's name—a visual emblem of the novel's suspense—linked tentatively within the tree to Meade's, "Meade engaged to Shelby," but also attached by a suggestive dotted line to Lute McNeil's.

The tension inherent in the conventional love plot—will Shelby marry the right man?—is compounded by the numerous distortions of expectation created by the presence of racial signs and markers. Shelby's freedom of judgment is endangered by the projections of others: she is mapped as a black body moving under the laws of the racist episteme. Others try to make her body and her behavior conform to the rules of the racial order.

She cannot love freely under such constraints. And yet, beyond the reach of her memory, her own family's heritage authorizes her strong love across racial boundaries. Shelby lives under a double inheritance, the effects of which she can only understand in part. In the concatenation of generations in her family—each of which only receives a partial measure of the wisdom of the previous—there is a persistent drive to preserve and to love children. Her paternal grandfather leaves his parents at age eleven to travel north for an education. The Preacher takes his son to the station, and Isaac feels the pressure of his father's hand upon his shoulder for the rest of his life. The treacherous part of Shelby's heritage is registered in skin color, which carries its own semiotic agendas, wrought out of the conflict between colorist values within black culture and the binary formalism of white supremacy.

Marie-Laure Ryan argues that "the narrative effect we call suspense derives from the confrontation of characters, whose foresight is limited, with a reader who anticipates—correctly or not—the situations into which they should run" (330-31). In ***The Wedding,*** Shelby is caught between foresight and hindsight, and the two are of the same teleology. She is vulnerable, liable to fall into the trap that is set for her, because she does not have adequate hindsight. She cannot see clearly the positive heritage behind her, though she is defined and has been strengthened by it. She cannot feel, three generations removed, the pressure of the Preacher's hand on Isaac's shoulder—or if she can feel it she cannot be confident of what it is telling her. She cannot know that if one of her paternal great-great-grandfathers (a slave owner, the Preacher's real father) raped her great-great-grandmother as a prerogative of ownership, that her other paternal great-great-grandfather (also a slave owner) loved the Ebony Woman across the color line, outside of social law, with such abiding and equalizing love that he refused to live on beyond her death—and died lying on her grave.

With analepses, West displaces the drive of the prosaic suspense structure of the novel's love plot and substitutes for it the infinitely more profound and disquieting history of Shelby's family on both the maternal and paternal sides. The inset stories—accessed through convergences, syllogisms, superimpositions and other such foregrounded interventions—become one story, a family's story. As a composite, they refigure Shelby's defiant innocence. She has hope, on the one hand, of troping on the love beyond color in her own family's intimate history. She is, on the other hand, at risk of revisiting the negative history of her family's acts of capitulation to the gods of skin colorism.

Even as the weight of the conservative, classist consciousness of the Oval becomes palpable in the early moments of West's novel, the spry and rigorous energy of West's ironic narrator is no less fully engaged in the opening pages of the book.[5] West seems, in fact, to bring the crackling electrical humor of her narrative spokesperson to the highest voltage while she is caricaturing the collective mentality of the Oval. The Coles' home, which stands as the "prize piece" of the bulwark of houses comprising the Oval, dominates the scene, and yet, through the layered irony of the opening pages, the house connotes death. The family, by inference, is perhaps entombed in its immensity—even as Shelby, lovelier than even her lovely sister, Liz, prepares for her imminent wedding. West's narrator moves in for a close-up of the house, complete with wide "glassed-in porches," against which, she notes, "many birds had dashed themselves to death." The ballroom, in poised readiness for the wedding, is prepared with its own "little gilt chairs" and "the undertaker's chairs in sober alignment." The mansion is set on wide expanses of lawn "that kept the lesser cottages at a feudal distance" (2-3).

The house represents the body of death because it is the outward showcase of a relationship—that of Shelby's parents, Clark and Corinne—which never had a living center or truth. They chose each other for color and class, and their house, despite its rich history, represents a deathly embodiment of that falseness. Their desire for each other was only about acquisition—and hence their kinship with Lute—and their house is evidence of their material achievement. Both conceal beneath the surface of their showcase marriage the black body of their desire. Both have dark-skinned lovers—Clark just one, Corinne many—who are hidden from view behind the loveless facade of their marriage.

The house contains ghosts, however: Clark's own family history resides within the walls of the mansion. He did not realize until after he had purchased it, virtually unseen, that his own father, Isaac, had spent numerous summers as a boy and adolescent in the very same house, with Amy Norton Norton, the white schoolteacher who had brought him north for his education. West writes as if out of the frame of Isaac's consciousness, regretting that Amy Norton Norton has been forgotten: "She was the hand of God who had plucked him out of the Jim-Crow-riddled South and into a new life" (194).

The early part of ***The Wedding*** develops around two sincere if supremely dangerous prayers, which also figure suspense. Both represent embedded expectations for the direction of narrative: one of the prayers is tragic; the other remains unfulfilled. The first is framed out of deep desire by Tina, Lute McNeil's middle daughter of three. She falls victim to Lute's machinations concerning Shelby when he tells his children his plan to marry the "beautiful lady" who lives in the "beautiful house." He gives imaginative form to Tina's intense desire for a mother, telling them that she "would take care of you and be your new mother" (26). The other children, Barby and Muffin, do not want a mother. Both have acute knowledge of the domestic violence at the center of Lute's marriages; for Muffin, "Women were all the same, even when they were housekeepers. Sooner or later they cried, and Daddy hit them" (27). But Tina desires: she longs for a mother, like the mother who has lived next door in the Oval and shown her deep affection through the summer. Lute's words bring her to a moment of prayer that structures the tragic subplot of the novel and prefigures her death: "Please, gentle Jesus, let her be next door's mother. Let me stay in the Oval my whole life forever. Amen" (27). Lute's promises are pernicious because they have the full authority of parental law behind them, even as they are rapacious and acquisitive. The full sickness of Lute's displacements is clear here: Lute desires to do everything he can for Tina, but he cannot act except through his drive to sexual conquest, which doubles for material acquisition. Maternal love itself—which he was denied—is sought in a displaced form, where it can never be found.

The other prayer—singular, importunate, and in earnest—is Shelby's maternal great-grandmother Gram's. Gram, who is white, smells death in the Oval on the wings of Tina's prayer, perhaps, which concludes the previous chapter. "Our Father, who art in heaven," she begins, and she prays first not to die. Then she pleads to God to act through Shelby: "Make my great-granddaughter Your instrument. She's marrying a man true white. Put it in her listening mind to live like white" (30). By the end of the next chapter, that petition has transformed itself into a desire to be gathered up into what she sees as Shelby's commission: "Gram picked up her cane and started that long, long walk to Shelby's room, on her way back to living true white, her cane and her trembling old hand along the wall giving what little help they could" (49).

Shelby's love looks like Gram's fixation. It is not. For a life-endangering moment, however, her family casts a shadow of doubt across the field of Shelby's self knowledge. Shelby cannot sustain the illusion of living with an original or authentic identity, or an uncorrupted love, outside of the damaging work, the "addling" that color has done, in West's terms, "since Moses married the Ethiopian woman and God made leprous the skin of the sneering man who challenged His right to move Moses to love" (82). And yet West makes clear that Shelby has arrived at her defiant love for Meade precisely as she has dropped her childlike conviction that color is the bond of belonging. Shelby loves Meade despite the world of people around her who "wished," for largely racist reasons, that "she loved him less" (82). Still, over the course of the novel, even that defiant confidence is put to the most extreme test. Her father and her sister both prey on her knowledge of her own motives. Could her love, she begins to wonder after Clark's distraught intrusion into her bedroom, be predicated—though she does not believe it to be—on color, or on some fear-driven response to the color-plot she knows has defined her parents' relationship?

Each transitional vehicle in West provides an interpretive map—a miniature subtext, which for its vigor and directedness, enforces connections that become as imperative as the forward drive of the novel's strong suspense itself. They function as ironic subtexts to the narrative, as substitute vehicles for temporality itself.[6] Foregrounded, dizzying, and ingenious, these devices invite history. They make possible precipitous scene changes. They erase sequence in favor of overlay, juxtaposition, and argument by parallelism, though they are finally woven back together by the very generative authority they possess. The space between Chapter One—which is inhabited by the mind of the Oval, given in parodic lucidity by West's caustic narrator—and Chapter Two—which introduces Lute and his daughters—is traversed, for example, by Lute McNeil's check for the rental of Addie Bannister's cottage. Addie accepts the check at the end of Chapter One; Chapter Two begins with a zoom focus on Lute's signature upon it. The check, which Addie accepts transgressively, out of a need so great that she does not care whose signature is upon it, represents the reification of social relations, the very materiality of social law.[7] Lute's signature, which does for others signify greatly, authorizes his presence in the story: he is written into the social arena of the Oval by the desperate actions of the impecunious Addie, against "the code," the classist and racist strictures of the Oval.

Lute's presence in the Oval, therefore, is strictly an error. Every other cottage is "part of the preparations" (7) for the wedding. But Lute is engaged in the parallel project of endeavoring to write himself into, to sign his name upon, the world of the Oval. If he cannot secure an invitation to the wedding—and this goads him—then he will secure the bride for himself, and all the material and social benefits that would accrue from that union. Lute's plot, therefore, is on one level a class-based revenge story. Shelby and the Coles, in their almost but not quite the "real thing" status at the pinnacle of black middle-class society, sit too high. Lute, in the heat of misogynist and class-linked anger, endeavors to author a counter-narrative, to script an alternative ending with his signature, to Shelby Coles's personal tale.

Cleo Jericho Judson, the female protagonist of West's satiric first novel, ***The Living is Easy*** (1948), manages to ruin the lives of all of her sisters by endeavoring to create a position for her family in the suffocatingly narrow social spaces of Boston's black elite in the early decades of the century. West reembodies the type of the arch manipulator in a male character in ***The Wedding,*** published a full 47 years later, in the person of Lute McNeil, whose malignancy again works through sheer calculated class aspiration. Like Cleo, Lute's values are derived—if sharpened and further pathologized—from the structural, historical weaknesses of the black middle class. Both Cleo and Lute are on the margins of the elite, and both not only desire to enter in but both are also willing to wreck lives to accomplish their aims. Both are sexual terrorists: Lute in violent conquest and abuse of his wives, three in succession; Cleo in a calculated and prideful marital frigidity.

The suspense structure of West's novel, therefore, is not predicated on a merely circumstantial threat to Shelby's love; Lute is not there as a mere plot device, a haphazard circumstance thrown across Shelby's pathway to love. Lute is an emblem: he stands for and articulates Shelby's vulnerability. He operates outside of the social sphere of the Coles until, that is, Adelaide Bannister's lapse in allowing him to rent her cottage in the Oval. His presence there, however, is no assurance of future association and acceptance, quite the contrary in fact. Lute nonetheless embodies the falsity of striving for love, or rather for sexual conquest and material acquisition, on the grounds of color and class. These preoccupations, received out of history, have been Shelby's family's besetting sins, as well: hence Shelby's actual vulnerability to Lute, which makes no sense otherwise.

Lute's own story of origin is a blank: his mother abandoned him before he can remember, and he enacts revenge against her—and against his disrupted story—through scripted cross-racial conquest and abuse of the three women who bear him children. West's narrator provides full access to the story, which of course is unknown to Shelby, in a long flashback from a moment of morning play with his three children. Out of these recollections, she also affirms Lute's immeasurable love, nonetheless, for Tina. This knowledge is critical to the suspense involved in his attempts to seduce Shelby and abort her wedding.

From Tina's point of view, Lute is truth: "From their Lilliputian perspective Lute stood giant size astride the world he had made for them" (10). He has three daughters by three different white women whom he has serially hated and rejected. Lute loves all three of his children, but not impartially. He loves one the most: that is Tina, the middle daughter, the one of the three who longs for a mother. Tina is the locus of wanting among the children. West gives us unequal access to her perspective on things. Of the three girls, hers is the consciousness most often registered and given authority in the narrative.

Lute's drive to acquire Shelby actually has its roots in his desire to please Tina. She has been happier than ever before in her life in the Oval, where maternal energy and love seem almost coincident with place. Mothers there are available to ponder and to borrow: "She loved the maternal eye of the Oval, where all the children were partly owned by all the watchful mothers, not knowing she played in the park on sufferance, or that her summer was almost over" (25). The Oval itself, therefore, becomes the real object of Lute's sexual acquisitiveness. Lute wants the Oval to accept him. In a perverse displacement, class striving doubles for the pursuit of mother's love, which Lute experiences vicariously through Tina.

Lute is a character always driven to move beyond the immediate object of sexual conquest towards some other embodiment of whiteness. Once he has acquired what he has sought, he does not desire it any longer, for it was never more than a reification of color. The "she" of his desiring—since he is pathologically drawn to women—does not exist except in her objectness. The white racist imaginary is in Lute seated in the black body. Lute, whose viciously angry love turns repeatedly to violence, enacts a role historically scripted for him as sexual terrorist, even as he embodies the self-hatred of the black middle class. Hegemony here works through the racist hierarchy: white makes right. The internalization of the binary law of white supremacy is manifest in the desire, on the part of the aspiring and accommodationist class, to draw ever closer to white. The relationships born under this ideology cannot be about tenderness or reciprocity. Lute's "love" relationships come to double for class aspirations, because the engine of his "love" is acquiring. Since desire is literally objectified as color, it doubles for material acquisition. He desires Shelby in part because of the historical pathology of the color complex, and he shares with Shelby's parents the material desire to acquire what is closest to white.

In Della, his third wife, he acquired a wealthy white woman, but even then her social sphere was ultimately out of reach for him. He is a voyeur: the black subject wedded to the white female, but prevented by racial law from fully possessing what she has. She flaunts her status and wealth; he can never fully command them. She has married him, West writes, because she "carried within her the seed of self-destruction" (20). Their marriage is a secret because its exposure would result in her being disinherited: the denial of her marriage to Lute, a black man, is the prerequisite to her being able to hold onto her birthright—her material wealth. With Della, he has acquired the white object, but cannot fully possess it.

With Shelby, Lute sees that conquest—the doubling of sexual and material possession—could be complete. Shelby, who is black, but in appearance whiter than white, lives at the pinnacle of the African American social hierarchy. In the dissembling game of class aspiration by the black middle class—a game of imitation, snobbish pretension and exclusionary privilege—the Coles are perhaps, West suggests, closest to the imitative object of their quest: "The Clark Coleses," West's narrator suggests with ironic inflection, "came closest to being as real as their counterparts" (3). Shelby, ironically, is first described as the image of her great-grandmother, who is white: "the image of Gram in that tinted picture of Gram as a girl, with rose-pink skin, golden hair, and dusk-blue eyes" (3-4). With Shelby, Lute's acquiring gaze sees the possibility of arriving at the highest point of status, with full rights of possession, that could be allowed within the binary racial universe they inhabit in 1953. He will never cross over into Della's space; even once her inheritance has been secured, he can never fully acquire what she has. Della knows this and plays off of it. With Shelby, Lute would reach the apex, the highest point of achievable status and completeness, where color and wealth coincide. Lute is a crude mercenary, but he is playing in a crasser form the same game that has been played by Corinne and Clark—and that is embodied in the Oval. These are the forces against which Shelby must defend her love.

West provides the clearest intimations of who Shelby's off-stage fiancé, Meade, might be through Shelby's mother's negative responses to him. Corinne doesn't object to his whiteness; it may appeal to her. What she cannot fathom is his work. Meade is an artist, a jazz pianist, with a singular commitment to his music. Corinne is a shallow character in many ways; she is the least developed, and in some sense the least appealing, member of the inner circle of the Coles family. She does not have the depth that Clark has, but she is also the product, as West shows in a flashback, of a profoundly disturbing interracial relationship: a marriage which does not survive emotionally beyond its earliest hours. Corinne's mother, Josephine, lived in an all-absorbing racist abhorrence of the act she committed in marrying Corinne's father, Hannibal. The fissure for Corinne between black—what she desires, what structures her affairs—and white—whose values she imitatively subscribes to, having been brought up by Gram—is so deep that she cannot see who Meade is: "Her lust for dark black men under cover of the night mirrored her repulsion during the day, and perhaps it was jazz's open, even cerebral flirtation with the dark side, its willingness to let go and improvise with mind as well as body, that explained it, when for Corinne the two had always been sundered by a divide too vast to bridge" (216). The resistance Corinne feels to the hybridity of jazz, its openness and its defiance of binaryness, gives Meade credibility, even in his absence from the action.

Shelby loves Meade. She knows him, and with him she has theoretically and effectively demolished the exclusionary, deadening laws of color. Her supposed innocence, however, is a goad to everyone within the novel and, perhaps, without. The structuring, bourgeois exactitude of Shelby's innocence—as it is dangerously figured across the fraught, almost unspeakable text of interracial marriage—is more than can be borne.

In Joseph Boone's terms, West's readers are perhaps keyed by tradition, and by the power of counter-plot, to be alert to a more disorderly kind of resolution.[8] Shelby's appearance alone implicates her in an implacable social text. Despite her resoluteness, her convincing self-knowing, she lives and will live with her life complicated at the very least by the laws of the racist episteme. Will she pass? Liz asks not so obliquely. Shelby's historical problem has not been a desire to pass, but rather living in a body which is coded white. Others cannot see her as black out of context. Marrying white, she will have to exercise additional conscious will to resignify her body, to retain the critical connectedness she needs to her own heritage.

Shelby has to answer back to her father, then, after he stumbles into her bedroom on the eve of her wedding, fresh from the ultimate rebuff of his life. Clark has just received a letter from his beloved, Rachel, informing him that she has married someone else. Clark's love for Rachel—over 20 years—has been the secret of his life, known of course through slips and intimations to his family, but excluded from the text of his public existence. He has planned to divorce Corinne for Rachel after Shelby's wedding, but Rachel preempts that belated fulfillment of their love, in revenge against him perhaps for what she describes in the letter as her unconceived children.

Shelby faces Clark, therefore, on the eve of her wedding as he attempts to enter into a critique of her sexual judgments. In this invasive action, Clark revisits his own mistakes and questions the integrity of Shelby's love, objectifying color as the ground for desire. Clark erred profoundly—and as it turns out irredeemably—in marrying Corinne for her color and her class: "She was everything his Brookline background demanded—she was fair, she would give him fair children, and her father was near the top of an honorable profession" (196). He questions Shelby out of his own shock and despair to make sure she is not marrying for color, for Meade's whiteness. But he seems not to have derived fully from his relationship with Rachel the insight that love is colorless, that his mistake was not in marrying light instead of dark, but in marrying against love and desire.

Shelby's father therefore invades her life and goes too intimately into the question of her sexual desire, asking her on the night before her wedding to a white man if she is sure that she is not afraid to love black bodies. Clark makes her vulnerable in that action, by going too close to the ground of her independent love, to the ground of her desire and judgment, and planting seeds of doubt there. He authorizes the return, with these belated and grotesquely inappropriate questions, of the text, the terms and the power of the mediating color plot: that corrupt motive frame that has broken his life and could, if not contested, ruin Shelby's as well. That plot, as dependent on the brutal and political objectification of color, can privilege either black or white skin as reified objects. In effect, it privileges both, but only in their dissociated objectness, as mirror opposites dependent on each other for definition.[9] Shelby's parents privilege both—the one for love, the other for status—but in so doing deny the possibility of honest relational justice. Clark and Corinne both marry light and love dark.

When Shelby's sister, Liz, plays broker for Lute a few chapters later, bringing Shelby the letter that has been passed from Lute's housekeeper to the Coles', she is also playing a dangerous game. Shelby has had her worse fears stirred up by her father's visit, and Liz's gleeful and teasing involvement in Lute's master plot constitutes an unintentional act of conspiracy to undermine Shelby's marriage. West finds a way for Liz to be a facilitator here, without placing full moral responsibility upon her or turning her into an evil figure. Liz, of course, like Shelby, has no idea how demonic Lute in fact can be. They see him in the flesh, in full self-possession, wearing masculine beauty as coded black. Liz truly does like Meade, but she imagines that by humoring Lute for this moment she will be allowing Shelby to confront her fears: "Liz knew that whatever spell he had her in would burst like a soap bubble upon close inspection, but unless Shelby faced Lute, confronted him, saw him for what he was, then it would be too late. She would be married, and a nagging cloud of doubt would never entirely leave her" (213).

Meade's rival, therefore, is not really Lute himself, but rather the mediating presence of the color plot within Shelby's own family. Lute operates through the binary power of the racist imaginary. He knows the moves perfectly, and in his rescripting of Meade's and Shelby's relationship, both partners play standard roles—the white male sexual aggressor, the exploited black female object: "Oh, he's hot for you now, but once he has had his fill of your hot black blood he'll cool, all right. You'll see. Mr. Charlie's been doing it to our women since slave days—what's different now?" (223) Shelby resists the paradigm, but Lute has seconded the doubt her much more powerful father and sister have already planted in her mind. Her vulnerability is a measure of the precariousness of unmediated innocence. She cannot remain innocent of what she embodies.

The name Shelby had belonged to her slave-owning great-great-grandfather, Gram's father, the master of Xanadu, the plantation which has grown ever more fantastical in Gram's imaginative life. Gram herself, an exile in black culture, has prayed that Shelby's engagement might be a chance to propel the family—or Shelby's redeemable branch of it—towards "true white." Shelby is, furthermore, the child of a union formed only because of class and color, a materialist, class-based privileging of light skin over dark. She is the image of Gram's tinted photograph, "with rose-pink skin, golden hair, and dusk-blue eyes." To say that she is in danger of being appropriated by the machine of colorist body commodification would be an understatement. And she is doubly endangered: on the one hand, she must free herself from the bind of Gram's drive to whiteness—and the echoes of that in her parents' personal histories and in the imitative colorism of the Oval, which does not approve of white, but sanctions light; on the other hand, she must free herself from the inverse, the erotic drive towards darkness as an end in itself that has been the hidden subtext of her parents' relationships.

When Gram peers down from her upstairs window in the Coles house on the present action of the novel, she does so bearing the weight of ninety-eight years of "her trouble on this earth." She mutters "her displeasure" at what she sees: Lute and his children, "the dark man and his golden dark daughters" (28). Gram's gaze propels the story backwards in time; it opens the way for the arc of family history. Lute's children—measurably lighter in skin tone than their father—are evidence of more co-mingling of the races, the chief source of Gram's dissatisfaction with "all that has come to pass" in her ninety-eight years. Gram, the matriarch who nurtured Corinne from babyhood, lives and suffers in exile from white culture. All her kin "since the South's beginning" had been white until, in hunger and desperation, her daughter Josephine "crossed her true white blood, her blue blood, with colored, and broke Gram's heart" (28). Gram, white supremacist, gazes upon Lute and the spectacle of his family, even as Lute is maneuvering to entrap her great-granddaughter.

In prelude to Gram's story, West's ever morally animated, versatile and here finally deeply sympathetic narrator presents Gram's two problems. The first is that no one in the Oval cares about her story and that in fact most do not even know it. Even though the map of the memory of the Coles family extends barely one generation back, the urgency of that memory is written into the design of West's novel. Analepses speak to the very blindnesses that endanger Shelby as she is acted upon by her family members and by a sexual predator in the person of Lute. Gram's other problem is related to the first: her kin—and this is for Gram a problem to be measured against the end of time itself—are all black. Her alienation from her own descendants, inscribed in acrid ink by West's ironic narrator, is so complete, that although she loves them, she despairs that her distinction from them will not be measured when the last trump sounds: "And Gram, the born aristocrat, lived surrounded by descendants of slaves, with nowhere to die but among them, no grave to claim her but the one they put her in, and nothing to mark her bones from theirs on Judgment Day when heaven rolled back to receive those born to sit or serve at God's table" (29).

West's narrator, however, expends less spite in characterizing Gram, for all of her alienating worshipfulness of the Shelby blood that still pumps slowly through her heart, than she does on the middle-class mind of the Oval with its reified and dissembling judgments and its colorist codifications. Gram lives in ever deepening fantasies of her youthful home at Xanadu, a huge plantation "that took up half a county, a mansion that must have had fifty rooms, and slaves enough to make a small army, every one of them willing to lay down his life for Marse Lance, and accepting freedom only because it was forced on them" (29). And yet at least Gram loves. If her ideological roots in the slave south are never destroyed, she becomes an agent for the survival of her descendants, albeit in her view from the wrong side of the color line.

In Gram's story, she ends an era when she lies to her neighbors, the genteel impoverished, who are dissembling as much as she is and barely surviving in the post-bellum south. Gram lies to account for her daughter Josephine's absence after she precipitously goes north to marry a black man, Hannibal, not for love or mutual recognition, not in defiance of the laws of white supremacy, but simply to survive. Gram goes north, too, because her strength of survival breaks through her racist torment and the imaginings she has of her monstrous "mongrel grandchild" before she even knows it has been conceived. When Josephine writes that she is in fact "with child" and dying of it, Gram's "frozen heart was freed to fill with yearning." West writes, "The longing to see Josephine, who was her child, and was with child, and dying of it, was stronger than her shame" (44). Gram goes north, and her going tropes on the mythic, migratory journeys northward made by innumerable African Americans across the decades: Gram goes north to meet her black family. The story she would have had to tell of it could not have been comprehended or withstood by her friends. It remains unnarrated and unimagined altogether by white culture: "The truth about Josephine would have knocked them down like ninepins. They, like herself, had too little left in their lives to have their faith in their divinity destroyed by Josephine's apostasy" (45). Gram leaves and crosses a line, enters a story that cannot be understood by her own culture. She passes without passing. She enters black culture as her kin become black.

It is not as if Gram ever embraces the change, but what she does do ultimately is embrace her grandchild—her "mongrel grandchild," Corinne, who is lovely—and her almost white and lovely great-grandchildren, Shelby and Liz, and finally, before the novel is over, her beautifully dark great-great-granddaughter, Laurie. Gram, a white supremacist in heart and soul, a narrator of the living myth of antebellum civilization, never forgets her roots, but embraces the destiny of many southern migrants. Trains on the north-south axis are a destiny for black culture, from the underground railroad to Plessy v. Ferguson—and this train ride, Gram's journey north, is mythic in proportions. Gram is not black, but she is becoming so. Her flesh, her only descendants, are from Josephine's transgression—this moment forth—all black. Gram, having already lived one lifetime and invested it utterly in an expired civilization, goes north to begin another, to bear witness to the generations coming. She is, with her lies and contrivances, the cover story no one has the energy to contest, caught by circumstance in that arresting moment when white culture encounters its own blackness: its children or grandchildren, as blood commingles, instantly becoming black.

West's narrator, who with such a delicate hand slides in and out of the consciousness of her characters, is not ironic here. Gram is a racist beyond redemption. Gram boards a train heading north within twenty-four hours of receiving Josephine's letter, and yet the severance of ties—not just with region, past or personal history, but with a defining world view, the religion of white supremacy—is brutal: "she who had never surrendered to the North, uprooted at a time of life when the roots have grown too deep and spread too far for a spade to search them out. The impatient ax must finish the job, and the severing is like blood soaking into the earth. The whole is never whole again, for a whole is the sum of all its parts" (45). The narrator renders Gram's story through pathos, not irony, however, because Gram, despite her complete and uncompromising subscription to the laws of the south, finds the strength to walk across a cultural chasm of unanswerable depth. Gram finds within her the capacity, the necessity and the will to love the baby, her granddaughter Corinne, and to be her buttress against the world: the baby whom neither parent can touch, her mother out of horror, her father out of fear.

The heady transitions that structure West's novel provide markers of the emotional design of the text. Analepses, including Gram's long story, are always motivated by a need for illumination, for light to be shed on the narrative drive toward Shelby's wedding. When Shelby gets lost at age six and leaves the safety of her family's colored universe—the "order and homogeneity" of a world that identifies "color as the core of character" (82)—flashback becomes figure and ground for understanding her desire to love authentically outside of the strictures of color. The catharsis of Shelby's return to the Oval after she is found opens for her an awareness of the codes and mysteries of color. "Oh, Gram," she says, "I'm so glad we're all colored. A lady told me I was white" (80). "Love and likeness," West says, become one for Shelby in this "first embrace of belonging" (82). But, even as Shelby reads Gram, who of course is white, wrong here, Shelby's life journey takes another turn. Measuring self against others, she gradually learns to read into the text of character, beyond the measure of color alone. That is, as she grows she tries on "bits and pieces" of other people, gradually seeing through their inadequacies into her own way: "Then slowly, at snail's pace, and with a snail's patience, she would thread her frailties and fears, her courage and strength, her hopes and doubts, into the warp and woof that would cloak her naked innocence into a soul of her own" (81).

When Shelby gets lost, she is effectively erased from social existence for a day. She wanders the island, talking with people, but she is not recognizable. The islanders have no category for her: a "colored" child who looks white. She is outside of the margins of their binary conceptions of black identity, and she is not equipped at age six to reconstruct a workable semiotics of skin color for herself. She is interviewed, admired, and sent along her way, "not knowing that the distance she had come was the infinite distance between two worlds and two concepts of color" (61). The island is abuzz, but Shelby is not able to be found. They are looking for a black child: "A snowballing word of mouth, a genuinely sympathetic mouth, had needlessly falsified the child's description by its thoughtless indulgence in that strange habit of whites of prefacing any and all mention of colored people with the identifying label of race" (62-63). Shelby's identity itself can seemingly not be sustained without the buttressing modalities of power that uphold the fiction of binary racial difference. She is unseen. Even as her hair is tugged at the end of the episode and is determined to be "real gold," even as her shirt is pulled up to reveal a tan line at the elastic—"a sharp barrier of crimson between dry rust and creamy white" (71)—and even as she is interviewed on her race, and cannot answer definitively, the white adults who find her remain beyond perplexed.

Shelby cannot be processed: there is no constitutive "outside" or "other" marked by her appearance. She cannot reconfirm the identity and meaning of whiteness by her difference. Shelby does not match the word-of-mouth identity she has acquired over the course of the day of her absence—and that identity, which owes itself to the political inventedness of race, has far more authority for her unintentional rescuers than does the very appearance of the child before them, even once they know her name. West compounds the critical powerlessness of childhood in this chapter with the defining circumstances of Shelby's experience: that she does not look to type, that the semiotics of race that are in play around her cannot account for her. When she is lost, she is erased, placed outside of the register of social meaning. Relieved finally at her return, the Ovalites take turns, as West puts it, "at the dead horse," joking despairingly about white culture: "Those of us with light-skinned children should put a tag on them, 'Please return to the colored race'" (75).

Shelby, the child who was erased from social existence for a day, is still enormously at risk, as Lute intimates, of erasure again, as an adult. She is still one with that child in her invisibility—her almost whiteness—upon which worlds of meaning, not of her own authoring or desiring, can be constructed. Her vulnerability lies both in her unawareness of how she is read and in the seductive allure of color, which others intrusively inject into her self-imaginings on the night before her wedding.

Shelby's childhood misadventure lays bare the grief that community, even across racial bounds in some abstract imaginary, shares with parents in the loss of a child. West touches those emotional registers in the anxieties of those who wait—Corinne collapses, her face rushing to meet the floor—and those who bear witness, if across the alien reaches of racial difference. The story of the lost child, of Shelby outside of the "concentric circles of her special world," is echoed in Tina's story. Tina, the child who was "dreamwashed with love for next door's mother," really is lost in the novel, destroyed with all the innocence of her hopes, killed by her father's car as he careens out of the Oval, attempting to get his battered third wife out of his life so that he can complete his seduction/assault of Shelby and stop her marriage. Tina is six, as Shelby was six in the critical flashback where she gets lost and can "not find her way back to the road that separated the races" (81). Shelby's father also careens through the Oval, driving recklessly back to the house after receiving Rachel's letter and compulsively entering Shelby's room to interrogate her on the grounds for her love. All the prefigurations—Lute's kiss that draws blood from Tina's lip, her prayerful petition to remain always in the Oval—compound the drive towards fatal closure. Shelby is spared, but Tina's story articulates with overdetermined power the fatality of the colorist, acquisitive love plot. Though Lute loves Tina with an immeasurable intensity, his drive to acquire status and position for her at all costs ultimately negates her desire for a mother's love. Tina had wanted a real mother, not a showcase mother, someone else's mother, or a purchased mother.

"The morning of the wedding broke cool and clear" (230), West writes, but Lute speaks again his fatal promise to Tina. "You're going to have," he says, "a new mother soon to take care of you, and to make sure you grow up right" (232). The arrival of Della, Lute's third wife, whom he has not yet divorced, represents a grim, momentary fulfillment of Lute's promise. Tina witnesses the violence of their already doomed union and, in their interracial economy of abuse, the moment when Della spits, "Let go of me, *nigger*" (235), and Lute slaps and then beats her into quiescence. When Tina escapes to find refuge in the next door mother's house, the mother has just discovered that the dress she had bought six months earlier for the wedding does not fit. West's barbed narrator returns: "in her understandable agony she was totally unable to take time with a child who did not know what real agony felt like" (237). Tina, rejected, goes outside, throws a rock at her dog, regrets it, tries to run after him, and collides with Lute's car. And so Tina dies, hit by her father's car as he careens out of the Oval to get Della back to the airport. Tina had tried to love well. Her desire, with all its primacy—her need for a mother—provides the critical emotional subtext of the novel.

Tina and Shelby are both literally bound in the grips of Lute's manipulations. Both characters want to love outside of what has been plotted for them. Shelby, despite Liz's glib assumption that she will see through Lute right away, is on treacherous ground. Her own father has opened a wound that is not only his but that is also a manifestation of a deep historical pathology, borne out of slavery itself. He has exposed the rent that divides the American psyche: the failure to see the image of oneself in the other, to see the commingling of black and white across history. And while Shelby escapes, Tina does not. That is the shock of the novel. The suspense of the story was not directed to a resolution of Shelby's fate alone: that is achieved. Shelby's wedding will happen after the action of the novel. But while there is redemption in the novel—Shelby sees her own, and claims her love—it comes at so great a cost that it almost cannot be borne. Tina dies in the playing out of precisely the drama that was conceived to draw Shelby into the prison house of race. West will not let this resolution come cheaply. Tina's death is not gratuitous. Its shock value—while sensational—is grounded in the deepest moral perceptions of the novel. Color is false; love is not.

Lute is a lost child as well, one who embodies evil but who is not entirely defined by it. Lute was driven, for all his abusive misjudgment, by a certain love for his children, especially Tina. It is within the frame of his world that Tina's loss is felt. In Oprah Winfrey's made-for-TV movie version of ***The Wedding,*** Tina does get hit by Lute's car and is rushed off to the hospital. It later turns out that she is okay. In the revised and inverted plot line of the TV version, for all the power of Charles Burnett's directing, it would be incoherent for Tina to die: colorism is not the defining issue in the TV text.[10] Shelby, played by Halle Berry, is no longer light enough to pass—which is not in itself a problem, since Shelby in the novel never considered passing and definitely rejects Liz's query about her intentions in this regard. It does, however, radically change the racial semiotics of the story. Lute's racist violence is absent from the movie; he is arguably more sexually attractive than is Meade—and would finally seem to be a viable alternative (until Della arrives at least) if Shelby had not finally decided for no reason other than the arbitrariness of soap operatic assignment of desire and choices to go ahead and marry Meade, supposedly for love, but without any emotional scaffolding to suggest what love in fact might be. The radical biological binary, which West's novel ultimately unseats, remains intact and in fact is celebrated, even as Shelby and Meade embark on the mock-heroic civil rights project of overcoming together the world's patent racism. The TV version arguably finally participates in that racism by signaling their difference from each other, not by cultural heritage and background, not by their historical assignment to different sides of the color line despite their similar racial appearance, but by classical skin color differences—which others can easily read.

Tina could not die in the made-for-TV version of ***The Wedding*** because it would be impossible to stage a full-blown wedding on screen after a child's death, and because it would not be clear what she has to die for. In West's novel, Tina dies because Lute has made her a fatal promise: he has said that she will have a new mother. But Lute can only conceive of acquiring such a mother through a terrorist and materialist assault on Shelby—turning her into a racial object—and endeavoring to acquire her for her family's real estate. Tina dies because adults betray her: even next door's mother fails her when she most needs her love.

In the novel, West's readers grieve with Lute, who had been the antagonist, the master manipulator. To the very degree that Lute was not a circumstantial adversary—that he was an emblem of Shelby's vulnerability, that he redoubled her own family's colorist and materialist values—Lute is not dismissible as a mere agent within the machine of plot. Lute's suffering is indigenous to his revengeful pursuit of social station. It is a register of the consequences of the social machinations—and denials—of the aspiring black middle class.

Suspense in ***The Wedding*** could not anticipate Tina's death: "Tina died in the nest of next door's mother's arms, too numb with pain to feel it or know she was dying, she who did not even know that children could die before they grew up to be like real people" (238). There is a consummation, however, in Tina's death, of the novel's intimations of danger, its warning signals, its manipulations of expectation.

When Shelby sees the family tableaux—Della in the car, Lute with his daughters, "two alive and one dead"—West writes, "A roiling fireball of rage and grief engulfed her" (239). She comprehends at once, though Tina did not have to die for Lute's plot to be exposed. Della's presence alone would have betrayed his lies. Tina dies because Lute's obsession, his lies and deceptions, his slurs and digs, his materialist plot to own Shelby's body—and all the accouterments of privilege associated with it—is costly. It is patterned out of the very pathologies that have obscured memory and have threatened to reduce love and sacrifice to the materialist and cautionary class pretensions of the Oval. West does not recuperate Lute, but she does not objectify him as raw evil either. West's readers grieve with Lute because he is a motherless child even as Tina is a motherless child. They grieve with Tina's sister, Barby, because she wants to stop Tina from dying, and she knows that Tina has died because Lute does not like mothers: "You don't like mothers. You make them die. All Tina wanted was a mother and you made her die to make her stop saying it" (239).

Lute stands accused, though he did try—through his own understanding—to get Tina a mother. Lute's grief, therefore, echoes a broader cultural grief for children lost to the fatal misunderstandings of adults: for children without mothers, for children disinherited, for children alienated from their own kin. In the end, Liz stands next to Gram, with Laurie in her arms, on the porch of the Coles' house, watching the crowds that gathered around the accident begin to disperse. Laurie begins to cry, "softly at first but then loudly" (240). Her tears are not tears of grief; babies do not grieve. Laurie has not understood what has been witnessed by the others. But she has, perhaps, felt it, and her mother cannot comfort her. Laurie's crying, perhaps, gives form to that broader cultural sorrowing, even as she moves the story out of it. The baby does not know what has happened, but Gram—who would not touch her dark great-great-grandchild—responds to the tears, crosses over again, and reenters love: "She felt the baby grow quiet in her arms, and she thought of Josephine, whom she had held the same way so many years before" (240). Gram embraces her great-great-granddaughter, the flesh of her flesh, and loves beyond her color aversions, beyond the dead-lock grip of white supremacy.

Karla F. C. Holloway discusses "recursive structures" in African American women's fiction that defy the linearity of historical memory for a kind of translucence, where texts become "emblematic of the culture they describe as well as interpretive of this culture" (55). She is describing multi-layered texts—where narrative temporality figures displacement and "narrative structures . . . force the words within the texts to represent (re)memories in/of events and ideas that revise and multiply meanings" (56). West's novel brings to memory what has been forgotten, even as it exposes the forces that have suppressed memory. Stories are forgotten in part because children cannot take the full measure of their parents' loving and cannot know what it cost to survive. The stories that remain untold are stories that parents do not tell to children, experiences that are too strong or too painful to transmit.

Each generation, in West, finds its own way of loving. What Shelby cannot know, because these stories have slipped away beyond reaching, is what West's narrator lays bare: that men and women loved in her family's past both violently and rapaciously and with singular passion and tenderness across racial boundaries. The reclamation of the past, the reaffirmation of what has been forgotten out of the lived experience of African American history, within families in acts of love and resistance: this is the power of West's storytelling.

Robert Gooding-Williams proposes in framing a model of ideology critique to undertake the "genealogical exposure of racial representations." His approach involves reading the exposed representations as "socio-political allegories" and then demythifying that allegorical content. The theoretical purpose of his project is to "disclose the interpretive origins of those representations" (160). West's fictional genealogies in some sense also literally expose the "interpretive origins" of racial representations: the blinding pathologies of colorist and binaryist body objectification, the false values that could undermine Shelby's efforts to act rightly and to love well. West's genealogies also reestablish common memory: accounts of black and white cultural intersections, of acts of engendering love across the color line. West reaffirms the possibility of familial love that acts against racial exclusions. Shelby has a double heritage: on the one hand, a history of color obsessions—the stuff of destroyed lives and false reckonings; on the other, a history of strength and survival.

The hypothetical cast of one of West's genealogical flashbacks only underscores the power of the story that will be narrated:

> If in Gram's distorted eye Liz's baby Laurie was a carbon copy of Hannibal, if in Liz's biased eye Laurie was the wonder child of the world, an impartial eye presented with an album of Laurie's ancestors might have lingered longest on a tintype of a preacher, Preacher Coles, born a slave around the time that Gram was born the daughter of blue-

blooded slave owners, living and dying without ever knowing that Gram existed, but cofounder of the same family nonetheless.

(114)

Laurie—the youngest in the family line, the first of the next generation—is the axis around whom this transition turns. The pathology of what Gram makes of Laurie will be expelled from the present tense of the novel. The love that Liz bestows upon Laurie will engender the future. Most significantly, though, West's narrator looks toward a picture album that does not exist—toward a tintype of one of Laurie's ancestors, who while outside the memory of his descendants, leaves them with a heritage worth fulfilling. Its very fictionality, the hypothetical "might" quality of what this "impartial eye" would do if it could, only reaffirms the importance of what West accomplishes in ***The Wedding.*** She must tell the stories: the picture album is not there, and others have forgotten. Her very engendering of the word, the reclamation of the stories forgotten, reconstructs the terms for an acceptance of Shelby's singular love. Dorothy West brings back into memory in ***The Wedding*** the terms of narrative freedom: Shelby Coles will write her own story across the fictive boundary line between black and white.

Notes

1. West dedicates *The Wedding* to Jacqueline Kennedy Onassis: "Though there was never such a mismatched pair in appearance, we were perfect partners" (iii). Onassis, who was an editor at Doubleday, is credited with having convinced West to resume work on the novel: "The most famous resident of Martha's Vineyard, Onassis had read West's column in the *Gazette* and learned that she was sitting on a long-unfinished novel. Onassis secured a contract for West with Doubleday, and reportedly visited the writer every Monday during the summers of 1992 and 1993 to encourage West to finish it" (Schick 607). Onassis died before the book was published. David Streitfeld reports that Doubleday initially released advance copies of *The Wedding* in bound galleys to reviewers—with a ghostwritten conclusion! Doubleday was ultimately compelled to hold the book for a month while West completed the last chapter. Streitfeld provides a full account of the controversy, including the conflicting subsequent explanations of it (*Washington Post* 6 July 1995).

2. Gérard Genette defines "analepsis" as "any evocation after the fact of an event that took place earlier than the point in the story where we are at any given moment" (40). I am following Genette and others in using the term "analepsis" to neutralize the possible cinematic or psychological connotations of the terms "flashback" or "retrospection."

3. Alice Walker apparently coined the term "colorism" (and by implication, the adjective, "colorist")—which is now in broad usage—for intraracial preoccupations with skin color in an essay entitled, "Embracing the Dark and the Light," in *Essence* in July, 1982. See also Russell, Wilson, and Hall, *The Color Complex.*

4. In Genette's terms, genealogical analepses in West might be considered both homodiegetic and heterodiegetic: on the one hand, they follow the descent of characters within the same family; on the other, the characters in the first narrative have little access to or knowledge of these stories about their forebears, even from the immediately preceding generation. Between the two, arguably, lie the pathos and the suspense of the novel. See *Narrative Discourse* (48-67).

5. Linda Hutcheon establishes that irony, like other communication acts, is "always culture-specific relying on the presence of a common memory shared by addresser and addressee" (98). Hutcheon suggests, however, that this common memory may be inferred from the very text of the ironist. Chapter One of West's novel, much of which is given as if narrated out of the mind of the Oval, presupposes the addressee's awareness of irony's play—of the self-incriminating quality of the Oval's narrowness of collective mind.

6. In Michael Riffaterre's terms, these devices are "fictional indices that have both a diegetic and a logical function" (52).

7. For perspective on Addie Bannister, see Kevin Gaines on the "dissembling" poverty of parts of the historical black elite: "Thus, in light of their tragic plight within a racist social formation, it is more accurate to say that many blacks, or whites, for that matter, were not middle class in any truly material or economic sense, but rather, represented themselves as such, in a complex variety of ways" (17).

8. Joseph Boone suggests in *Tradition Counter Tradition* that there is "a long chapter, if not an entire book, that remains to be written on the problematic relation of black fiction to the middle-class marriage tradition" (23). Ann duCille responds by applying—with qualifications—Boone's model of counter-traditional protest against the "hegemony of the marriage tradition" within the Anglo-American novel to the African American tradition in *The Coupling Convention* (16-17).

9. Stuart Hall's discussion of identities as "constituted within, not outside, representation" (4) seems essential to a consideration of this problem. Hall writes, "representation is always constructed across a 'lack', across a division, from the place of the Other, and thus can never be adequate—identical—to the subject processes which are invested in them" (6).

10. *The Wedding* appeared forty-seven years after the publication of West's first novel, *The Living is Easy.* West has indicated to numerous interviewers that she began work on *The Wedding* decades ago, but that she had never finished it, fearing at certain periods what kind of reception it might meet. "It coincided with the Black Revolution, when many Blacks believed that middle-class blacks were Uncle Toms. . . . I feared that some black reviewer would give *The Wedding* a bad review, because it was a book about Black professional people" (McDowell 278). Lawrence R. Rodgers offers a valuable discussion of West's career and the problem of "productive communities" (162). See also Dalsgard, De Veaux, and Streitfeld. By 1995, such specific concerns had abated, but Oprah Win-

frey's made-for-TV version of the story, with its erasures and revisions, does suggest that what is most challenging about the novel may still be uncomfortable for broad receptive communities.

Works Cited

Boone, Joseph. *Tradition Counter Tradition: Love and the Form of Fiction.* Chicago: Univ. of Chicago Press, 1987.

Dalsgard, Katrine. "Alive and Well and Living on the Island of Martha's Vineyard: An Interview with Dorothy West, October 29, 1988." *Langston Hughes Review* 12 (1993): 28-44.

De Veaux, Alexis. "Bold Type: Renaissance Woman." *Ms.* 5 (May-June 1995): 73.

duCille, Ann. *The Coupling Convention: Sex, Text, and Tradition in Black Women's Fiction.* New York: Oxford Univ. Press, 1993.

Gaines, Kevin. *Uplifting the Race: Black Leadership, Politics, and Culture in the Twentieth Century.* Chapel Hill, N.C.: Univ. of North Carolina Press, 1996.

Genette, Gérard. *Narrative Discourse: An Essay in Method.* Translated by Jane E. Lewin. Ithaca, N.Y.: Cornell Univ. Press, 1980.

Gooding-Williams, Robert. "'Look a Negro!'" In *Reading Rodney King: Reading Urban Uprising,* edited by Robert Gooding-Williams, 157-77. New York: Routledge, 1993.

Hall, Stuart. "Introduction: Who Needs 'Identity'?" In *Questions of Cultural Identity,* edited by Stuart Hall and Paul du Gay, 1-17. London: Sage, 1996.

Holloway, Karla F. C. *Moorings & Metaphors: Figures of Culture and Gender in Black Women's Literature.* New Brunswick, N.J.: Rutgers Univ. Press, 1992.

Hutcheon, Linda. *Irony's Edge: The Theory and Politics of Irony.* New York: Routledge, 1994.

McDowell, Deborah. "Conversations With Dorothy West." In *The Harlem Renaissance Re-examined,* edited by Victor A. Kramer. New York: Ames Press, 1987.

Oprah Winfrey Presents: "The Wedding." Directed by Charles Burnett. ABC, 1998.

Riffaterre, Michael. *Fictional Truth.* Baltimore: Johns Hopkins Univ. Press, 1990.

Rodgers, Lawrence. "Dorothy West's *The Living is Easy* and the Ideal of Southern Folk Community." *African American Review* 26 (1992): 161-72.

Ryan, Marie-Laure. "Embedded Narratives and Tellability." *Style* 20 (1986): 319-33.

Schick, Elizabeth A., ed. "West, Dorothy." In *Current Biography Yearbook,* 1997, 604-608. New York: H. W. Wilson Company, 1997.

Streitfeld, David. "Dorothy West: Renaissance Woman." *Washington Post,* 6 July 1995.

Walker, Alice. "Embracing the Dark and the Light." *Essence* 13 (July 1982): 67.

West, Dorothy. *The Living is Easy.* 1948. Old Westbury, N.Y.: Feminist Press, 1982.

———. *The Wedding.* New York: Doubleday, 1995.

FURTHER READING

Bibliography

Harrison, Naomi. "Dorothy West: A Bibliography." *Bulletin of Bibliography* 56, no. 4 (1999): 181-87.

Comprehensive bibliography that includes details of West's early periodical publications.

Criticism

Butcher, Philip. "Our Raceless Writers." *Opportunity* 26 (summer 1948): 113-15.

Examines the trend toward "raceless" writing that West viewed as a loss to African American literature.

Codman, Florence. Review of *The Living Is Easy. Commonweal* (25 June 1948) 264-65.

Favorable review praising West's graceful style and able characterization.

Dalsgard, Katrine. "Alive and Well and Living on the Island of Martha's Vineyard: An Interview with Dorothy West, October 29, 1988." *The Langston Hughes Review* 12, no. 2 (fall 1993): 28-44.

Interview in which West discusses her association with the Harlem Renaissance.

Ferguson, SallyAnn H. "Dorothy West and Helene Johnson in *Infants of the Spring.*" *The Langston Hughes Review* 2, no. 2 (fall 1983): 22-24.

Compares the characters Doris Westmore and Hazel Jamison in Wallace Thurman's novel to Dorothy West and Helene Johnson.

Guinier, Genii. *Black Women Oral History Project Interview with Dorothy West, May 6, 1978,* pp. 1-75. Cambridge: Schlesinger Library, Radcliffe College, 1981.

Interview with West.

Jones, Sharon L. "Reclaiming a Legacy: The Dialectic of Race, Class, and Gender in Jessie Fauset, Zora Neale Hurston, and Dorothy West." *Hecate* 24, no. 1 (1998): 155-65.

Discusses how these three writers broke through the categories of "folk," "bourgeois," and "proletarian" assigned to their fiction.

McDowell, Deborah E. "Conversations with Dorothy West." In *The Harlem Renaissance Re-Examined,* edited by Victor A. Kramer, pp. 265-82. New York: AMS, 1987.

West's reminiscences on the Harlem Renaissance.

Moore, Jack B. Review of *The Richer, the Poorer: Stories, Sketches, Reminiscences. Studies in Short Fiction* 33, no. 4 (fall 1996): 593-96.

Favorable review citing West's exceptional skill at depicting the thoughts and emotions of sensitive children.

Peters, Pearlie. "The Resurgence of Dorothy West as Short Story Writer." *Abafazi: The Simmons College Review of Women of African Decent* 8, no. 1 (fall/winter 1997): 16-21.

Interview with the author after the publication of The Richer, the Poorer.

Rodgers, Lawrence R. "Dorothy West's *The Living Is Easy* and the Ideal of the Southern Folk Community." *African American Review* 26, no. 1 (spring 1992): 161-72.

Attempts to deconstruct the image of West's novel as outside the mainstream of twentieth-century American literature, placing it within the context of southern Afrocentric values.

Roses, Lorraine Elena. "Interviews with Black Women Writers: Dorothy West at Oak Bluffs, Massachusetts, July, 1984." *SAGE: A Scholarly Journal on Black Women* 2, no. 1 (spring 1985): 47-49.

Brief interview in which West discusses her early works.

Rueschmann, Eva. "Sister Bonds: Intersections of Family and Race in Jessie Redmon Fauset's *Plum Bun* and Dorothy West's *The Living Is Easy.*" In *The Significance of Sibling Relationships in Literature,* edited by JoAnna Stephens Mink and Janet Doubler Ward, pp. 120-31. Bowling Green, Ohio: Bowling Green State University Popular Press, 1992.

Argues that understanding the relationships Cleo forges with her sisters is central to understanding her complex character.

St. Andrews, B. A. Review of *The Wedding. World Literature Today* 69 (autumn 1995): 799.

Favorable review of West's portrayal of the complexities an American family faces involving ancestry, economics, and race.

Schraufnagel, Noel. "The Revolt against Wright." In *From Apology to Protest: The Black American Novel,* pp. 51, 61-63. New York: Everett/Edwards, 1973.

Claims that The Living Is Easy *is "accommodationist" and illustrates attempts by African Americans to adjust to white society.*

Skow, John. "The Second Time Around." *Time* (24 July 1995): 67.

Discusses West's revived literary fame in the mid-1990s.

Steinberg, Sybil. "Dorothy West: Her Own Renaissance." *Publishers Weekly* (3 July 1995): 34-35.

Based on an interview in which West says that class, not color, is important for success in the United States.

Wade Gayles, Gloria. "The Truths of Our Mothers' Lives: Mother-Daughter Relationships in Black Women's Fiction." *SAGE: A Scholarly Journal on Black Women* 1, no. 2 (fall 1984): 8-12.

Compares the treatment of mother-daughter relations in West's The Living Is Easy, *Paule Marshall's* Brown Girl, Brownstone, *and Toni Morrison's "The Bluest Eye."*

Washington, Mary Helen. "I Sign My Mother's Name: Alice Walker, Dorothy West, Paule Marshall." In *Mothering the Mind: Twelve Studies of Writers and Their Silent Partners,* edited by Ruth Perry and Martine Watson Brownley, pp. 142-63. New York: Holmes & Meier, 1984.

Compares the writers and their relationships to their mothers.

OTHER SOURCES FROM GALE:

Additional coverage of West's life and career is contained in the following sources published by the Gale Group: *Black Writers,* Ed. 2; *Contemporary Authors,* Vol. 143; *Contemporary Authors - Obituary,* Vol. 169; *Dictionary of Literary Biography,* Vol. 76; and *Twentieth-Century Literary Criticism,* Vol. 108.

WALTER WHITE

(1893 - 1955)

American novelist, journalist, and essayist.

White spent his entire life fighting for racial equality in the United States and used his talents as a novelist, journalist, and leader of the National Association for the Advancement of Colored People (NAACP) to champion the cause of Black Americans. Because of his connections in the publishing world, White served as a literary guide to many younger writers of the Harlem Renaissance. His own novels *The Fire in the Flint* (1924) and *Flight* (1926) examine various aspects of race relations in the United States, and his nonfiction work explores the sociology and psychology of racism and, in particular, the phenomenon of lynching. Because White was fair-skinned and blue-eyed (according to his *New York Times* obituary "only five-thirty-seconds of his ancestry was Negro"), he could "pass" for white. He did so to report eyewitness accounts of lynchings and other racial incidents in his native Atlanta and elsewhere. His fiction also explores the notion of "passing" and the idea of color consciousness.

BIOGRAPHICAL INFORMATION

White was born in 1893 in Atlanta, Georgia. When he was twelve he witnessed a violent race riot in his hometown and thereafter committed himself to the cause of civil rights. In 1916 White graduated from Atlanta University and went to work for the Standard Life Insurance Company. When the Atlanta Board of Education ended public schooling for Blacks after the sixth grade, he became active in efforts to form an Atlanta branch of the NAACP. This impressed James Weldon Johnson, the organization's field secretary, and in 1918 White was invited to join the national organization in New York as assistant secretary. White's early duties included investigating race riots and lynchings, for which he exploited his ability to pass as a white man.

While in New York, White became acquainted with many of the best Black writers of the day. Because of his contacts with the NAACP, he was able to help many writers have their work published. In 1922 White married Gladys Powell, and their apartment was known as "The House of Harlem" because of the prominent figures who were guests there. Like his mentor, Johnson, White believed that art—writing in particular—had a crucial role to play in mending the racial divide in the United States, and he actively promoted the work of other writers. On the urging of editor and satirist H. L. Mencken, White wrote his first novel, *The Fire in the Flint,* about the "Negro experience" in the United States. A second novel was followed by a Guggenheim Fellowship to Paris, where in 1929 he wrote *Rope and Faggot,* a study of the phenomenon of lynching. White did not return to fiction writing, but continued to work tirelessly for civil rights (including testifying before Congress on behalf of the Federal Anti-Lynching Bill and campaigning for integration in public schools) and produced books and articles on racial themes.

White also traveled to Europe during World War II to investigate discrimination against Blacks in the armed forces, was instrumental in the formation of the Joint Committee on National Recovery to fight discrimination in New Deal programs, advised President Franklin Delano Roosevelt on the executive order for Fair Employment Practices during World War II, and forged a relationship with labor unions. In 1945 and 1948, White served as a consultant to the U.S. delegations to the newly formed United Nations. In 1949 he divorced his first wife and married a white woman, Poppy Cannon. The couple lived together until White's death in 1955.

MAJOR WORKS

Between 1924 and 1929 White produced his three most important works. His novel *The Fire in the Flint* is the story of a white doctor who tries to fight for racial tolerance and friendship in a town in the American South. A second novel on race relations, *Flight,* is about a light-skinned Black girl; with this work White attempted to explore questions about "passing," about being of mixed race, and about Black identity. Although White intended his third book to be a novel, *Rope and Faggot* is an analysis of the sociology, psychology, and economics of lynching. In 1945 White published *A Rising Wind: A Report on the Negro Soldier in the European Theatre of War,* a study of his findings after his European visit. Three years later he published his autobiography, *A Man Called White* (1948), in which he discussed racial oppression from a personal and political point of view.

CRITICAL RECEPTION

Athough White did not produce a large body of work, he was considered a major player in the Harlem Renaissance because of his support and mentoring of other writers. White's first novel, *The Fire in the Flint,* was a popular success from the outset: it went through three printings, was also published in England, and was translated into five foreign languages. While Charles S. Johnson praised White's realism in the work, other critics asserted that it was melodramatic propaganda.*Flight* also received mixed reviews, with many faulting the poor structure of the work. On the other hand, White received almost universal praise for *Rope and Faggot,* which became required reading at several colleges and universities, but Melvin Herskovits comments that White's analytical approach detracts from the passionate subject of the work.

After White gave up his literary career and interest in the Harlem Renaissance in the early 1930s, his work continued to reach a wide audience because of his association with the NAACP. His novels are, unfortunately, of little interest today except to literary scholars; even his autobiography and other nonfiction, while providing interesting insights into the sociology and politics of race relations, are not widely read. White's enduring legacy is his work on behalf of the Civil Rights Movement and, to a lesser degree, his influence on up-and-coming Black writers during his association with the Harlem Renaissance.

PRINCIPAL WORKS

The Fire in the Flint (novel) 1924

Flight (novel) 1926

The American Negro and His Problems (nonfiction) 1927

The Negro's Contribution to American Culture (nonfiction) 1927

Rope and Faggot: A Biography of Judge Lynch (social history) 1929

What Caused the Detroit Riot? [with Thurgood Marshall] (nonfiction) 1943

A Rising Wind: A Report on the Negro Soldier in the European Theatre of War (nonfiction) 1945

A Man Called White: The Autobiography of Walter White (autobiography) 1948

How Far the Promised Land? (nonfiction) 1955

PRIMARY SOURCES

WALTER WHITE (ESSAY DATE 1925)

SOURCE: White, Walter. "Color Lines." *The Survey Graphic* 6, no. 6 (march 1925): 680-82.

In the following essay, White addresses the issue of color lines—the concept of Black/white segregation—in both literal and figurative practice.

The hushed tenseness within the theatre was broken only by the excited chattering between the scenes which served as oases of relief. One reassured himself by touching his neighbor or gripping the edge of the bench as a magnificently proportioned Negro on the tiny Provincetoun Theatre stage, with a voice of marvelous power and with a finished artistry enacted Eugene O'Neill's epic of human terror, *The Emperor Jones.* For years I had nourished the conceit that nothing in or of the theatre could thrill me—I was sure my years of theatre-going had made me immune to the tricks and the trappings which managers and actors use to get their tears and smiles and laughs. A few seasons ago my shell of conceit was cracked a little—in that third act of Karel Capek's *R. U. R.* when Rossum's automatons swarmed over the parapet to wipe out the last human being. But the chills that chased each other up and down my spine then were only pleasurable tingles compared to the sympathetic terror evoked by Paul Robeson as he fled blindly through the impenetrable forest of the "West Indian island not yet self-determined by white marines."

Nor was I alone. When, after remaining in darkness from the second through the eighth and final scene, the house was flooded with light a concerted sigh of relief welled up from all over the theatre. With real joy we heard the reassuring roar of taxicabs and muffled street noises of Greenwich Village and knew we were safe in New York. Wave after wave of applause, almost hysterical with relief, brought Paul Robeson time and time again before the curtain to receive the acclaim his art had merited. Almost shyly he bowed again and again as the storm of handclapping and bravos surged and broke upon the tiny stage. His color—his race—all, all were forgotten by those he had stirred so deeply with his art.

Outside in narrow, noisy Macdougal Street the four of us stood. Mrs. Robeson, alert, intelligent, merry, an expert chemist for years in one of New York's leading hospitals; Paul Robeson, clad now in conventional tweeds in place of the ornate, gold-laced trappings of the Emperor Jones; my wife and I. We wanted supper and a place to talk. All about us blinked invitingly the lights of restaurants and inns of New York's Bohemia. Place after place was suggested and discarded. Here a colored man and his companion had been made to wait interminably until, disgusted, they had left. There a party of four colored people, all university graduates, had been told flatly by the proprietress, late of North Carolina, she did not serve "niggers." At another, other colored people had been stared at so rudely they had bolted their food and left in confusion. The Civil Rights Act of New York would have protected us—but we were too much under the spell of the theatre we had just quitted to insist on the rights the law gave us. So we mounted a bus and rode seven miles or more to colored Harlem where we could be served with food without fear of insult or contumely. The man whose art had brought homage to his feet from sophisticated New York could not enter even the cheapest of the eating places of lower New York with the assurance that some unpleasantness might not come to him before he left.

What does race prejudice do to the inner man of him who is the victim of that prejudice? What is the feeling within the breast of the Paul Robesons, the Roland Hayes's, the Harry Burleighs, as they listen to the applause of those whose kind receive them as artists but refuse to accept them as men? It is of this inner conflict of the black man in America—or, more specifically in New York City, I shall try to speak.

I approach my task with reluctance—it is no easy matter to picture that effect which race or color prejudice has on the Negro of fineness of soul who is its victim. Of wounds to the flesh it is easy to speak. It is not difficult to tell of lynchings and injustices and race proscription. Of wounds to the spirit which are a thousand times more deadly and cruel it is impossible to tell in entirety. On the one hand lies the Scylla of bathos and on the other the Charybdis of insensitivity to subtler shadings of the spirit. If I can evoke in your mind a picture of what results proscription has brought, I am content.

With its population made up of peoples from every corner of the earth, New York City is, without doubt, more free from ordinary manifestations of prejudice than any other city in the United States. Its Jewish, Italian, German, French, Greek, Czechoslovakian, Irish, Hungarian quarters with their teeming thousands and hundreds of thousands form so great a percentage that "white, Gentile, Protestant" Nordics have but little opportunity to develop their prejudices as they do, for example, in Mississippi or the District of Columbia. It was no idle joke when some forgotten wit remarked, "The Jews own New York, the Irish run it and the Negroes enjoy it."

New York's polyglot population which causes such distress to the Lothrop Stoddards and the Madison Grants, by a curious anomaly, has created more nearly than any other section that democracy which is the proud boast but rarely practiced accomplishment of these United States. The Ku Klux Klan has made but little headway in New York City for the very simple reason that the proscribed outnumber the proscribers. Thus race prejudice cannot work its will upon Jew or Catholic—or Negro, as in other more genuinely American centers. This combined with the fact that most people in New York are so busy they haven't time to spend in hating other people, makes New York as nearly ideal a place for colored people as exists in America.

Despite these alleviating causes, however, New York is in the United States where prejudice appears to be indigenous. Its population includes many Southern whites who have brought North with them their hatreds. There are here many whites who are not Southern but whose minds have indelibly fixed upon them the stereotype of a Negro who is either a buffoon or a degenerate beast or a subservient lackey. From these the Negro knows he is ever in danger of insult or injury. This situation creates various attitudes of mind among those who are its victims. Upon most the acquisition of education and culture, of wealth and sensitiveness causes a figurative and literal withdrawal, as far as is humanly possible or as necessity permits, from all contacts with the outside world where unpleasant situations may arise. This naturally means the development of an intensive Negro culture and a definitely bounded city within a city. Doubtless there are some advantages, but it is certain that such voluntary segregation works a greater loss upon those within and those without the circle.

Upon those within, it cuts off to a large extent the world of music, of the theatre, of most of those contacts which mean growth and development and which denied, mean stagnation and spiritual atrophy. It develops as well a tendency towards self-pity, towards a fatal conviction that they of all peoples are most oppressed. The harmful effects of such reactions are too obvious to need elaboration.

Upon those without, the results are equally mischievous. First there is the loss of that deep spirituality, that gift of song and art, that indefinable thing which perhaps can best be termed the over-soul of the Negro, which has given America the only genuinely artistic things which the world recognizes as distinctive American contributions to the arts.

More conventional notions as Thomas Dixon and Octavus Roy Cohen and Irvin Cobb have falsely painted them, of what the Negro is and does and thinks continue to persist, while those who represent more truly the real Negro avoid all contact with other races.

There are, however, many other ways of avoidance of proscription and prejudice. Of these one of no small importance is that popularly known as "passing," that is, those whose skin is of such color that they can pass as white may do so. This is not difficult; there are so many swarthy races represented in New York's population that even colored people who could easily be distinguished by their own race as Negroes, pass as French or Spanish or Cuban with ease. Of these there are two classes. First are those who for various reasons disappear entirely and go over the line to become white in business, social and all other relationships. The number of these is very large—much larger than is commonly suspected. To my personal knowledge one of the prominent surgeons of New York City who has an elaborately furnished suite of offices in an exclusive neighborhood, whose fees run often into four figures, who moves with his family in society of such standing that the names of its members appear frequently in the society columns of the metropolitan press, is a colored man from a Southern city. There he grew tired of the proscribed life he was forced to lead, decided to move North and forget he was a colored man. He met with success, married well and he and his wife and their children form as happy a family circle as one could hope to see. O'Neill's *All God's Chillun Got Wings* to the contrary, his wife loves him but the more for his courage in telling her of his race when first they met and loved.

This doctor's case is not an exception. Colored people know many of their own who have done likewise. In New York there is at least one man high in the field of journalism, a certain famous singer, several prominent figures of the stage, in fact, in almost any field that could be mentioned there are those who are colored but who have left their race for wider opportunity and for freedom from race prejudice. Just a few days before this article is being written I received a note from a woman whose name is far from being obscure in the world of the arts. The night before, she wrote me, there had been a party at her studio. Among the guests were three Southern whites who, in a confidential mood, had told her of a plan the Ku Klux Klan was devising for capitalizing in New York prejudice against the Negro. When I asked her why she had given me the information she told me her father, resident at the time of her birth in a Southern state, was a Negro.

The other group is made up of the many others who "pass" only occasionally. Some of these do so for business reasons, others when they go out to dine or to the theatre.

If a personal reference may be forgiven; I have had the unique experience within the past seven years of investigating some thirty-seven lynchings and eight race riots by the simple method of *not* telling those whom I was investigating of the Negro blood within my veins.

Large as is the number of those who have crossed the line, they form but a small percentage of those who might follow such an example but who do not. The constant hammering of three hundred years of oppression has resulted in a race consciousness among the Negroes of the United States which is amazing to those who know how powerful it is. In America, as is well known, all persons with any discernible percentage of Negro blood are classed as Negroes, subject therefore to all of the manifestations of prejudice. They are never allowed to forget their race. By prejudice ranging from the more violent forms like lynching and other forms of physical violence down to more subtle but none the less effective methods, Negroes of the United States have been welded into a homogeneity of thought and a commonness of purpose in combatting a common foe. These external and internal forces have gradually created a state of mind among Negroes which is rapidly becoming more pronounced where they realize that just so long as one Negro can be made the victim of prejudice because he *is* a Negro, no other Negro is safe from that same oppression. This applies geographically, as is seen in the support given by colored people in cities like Boston, New York and Chicago to those who oppose lynching of Negroes in the South, and it applies to that large element of colored people whose skins are lighter who realize that their cause is common with that of all Negroes regardless of color.

Unfortunately, however, color prejudice creates certain attitudes of mind on the part of some colored people which form color lines within the color line. Living in an atmosphere where swarthiness of skin brings, almost automatically, denial of opportunity, it is as inevitable as it is regrettable that there should grow up among Negroes themselves distinctions based on skin color and hair texture. There are many places where this pernicious custom is more powerful than in New York—for example, there are cities where only mulattoes attend certain churches while those whose skins are dark brown or black attend others. Marriages between colored men and women whose skins differ markedly in color, and indeed, less intimate relations are frowned upon. Since those of lighter color could more often secure the better jobs an even wider chasm has come between them, as those with economic and cultural opportunity have progressed more rapidly than those whose skin denied them opportunity.

Thus, even among intelligent Negroes there has come into being the fallacious belief that black Negroes are less able to achieve success. Naturally such a condition had led to jealousy and suspicion on the part of darker Negroes, chafing at their bonds and resentful of the patronizing attitude of those of lighter color.

In New York City this feeling between black and mulatto has been accentuated by the presence of some 40,000 Negroes from the West Indies, and particularly by the propaganda of Marcus Garvey and his Universal Negro Improvement Association. In contrast to the division between white and colored peoples in the United States, there is in the West Indies, as has been pointed out by Josiah Royce and others, a tri-partite problem of race relations with whites, blacks and mulattoes. The latter mingle freely with whites in business and other relations and even socially. But neither white nor mulatto has any extensive contact on an equal plane with the blacks. It is this system which has enabled the English whites in the islands to rule and exploit though they as rulers are vastly inferior numerically to blacks and mulattoes.

The psychology thus created is visible among many of the West Indian Negroes in New York. It was the same background of the English brand of race prejudice which actuated Garvey in preaching that only those who were of unmixed Negro blood were Negroes. It is true beyond doubt that such a doctrine created for a time greater antagonisms among colored people, but an inevitable reaction has set in which, in time, will probably bring about a greater unity than before among Negroes in the United States.

We have therefore in Harlem this strange mixture of reaction not only to prejudice from without but to equally potent prejudices from within. Many are the comedies and many are the tragedies which these artificial lines of demarcation have created. Yet with all these forces and counter forces at work, there can be seen emerging some definite and hopeful signs of racial unity. Though it hearkens back to the middle ages, this is essential in the creation of a united front against that race and color prejudice with which the Negro, educated or illiterate, rich or poor, native or foreign-born, mulatto, octaroon, quadroon, or black, must strive continuously.

GENERAL COMMENTARY

GLOSTER B. CURRENT (ESSAY DATE 1969)

SOURCE: Current, Gloster B. "Walter White and the Fight for Freedom." *Crisis* 76, no. 3 (march 1969): 113-19, 134.

In the following essay, Current offers a brief history of White's exploits and his efforts to advance civil rights for African Americans.

The National Association for the Advancement of Colored People and its leaders appear to be the principal casualities in the efforts of some "historians" to rewrite the story of the Negro in America. Save for W. E. B. DuBois and, to a lesser extent, James Weldon Johnson, the historic exploits of NAACP leaders who gave dedicated and effective service to the advancement of black folk in our country are seldom mentioned.

Because of solid achievements, Walter White, who died 14 years ago on March 21, 1955, will survive any attempt to read him out of the history of the Negro to which he contributed immeasurably. Fair-skinned, blue-eyed and blond, he could well have concealed his remote African ancestry and crossed over the color bar into the white world. He was a Negro by choice and that choice was made irrevocably on a warm September afternoon in 1906 when, at 13 years of age, he stood, rifle in hand, with his father to protect their Atlanta homestead from a mob of whites who had invaded their neighborhood in search of "nigger" blood.

After the mob was dispersed without young Walter having to fire a single shot, he fully realized on which side of the color bar he belonged. Later he wrote: "I knew then who I was. I was a Negro, a human being with an invisible pigmentation which marked me a person to be hunted, hanged, abused, discriminated against, kept in poverty and ignorance, in order that those whose skin was white would have readily at hand a proof of their superiority, a proof patent and inclusive, accessible to the moron and the idiot as well as to the wise man and the genius."

White became interested in the NAACP as a result of a school bond fight in Atlanta in 1917. The local school board announced a bond issue to build a new white high school. To help finance this proposal, the board planned to eliminate the seventh grade of the colored grammar school. In similar action two years previously, the board had eliminated the eighth grade without protest from the Negro community.

The Negro leaders of the business community banded together to oppose this betrayal. Harry Pace, president of Standard Life, suggested writing for advice to the then young National Association for the Advancement of Colored People in New York. James Weldon Johnson, recently appointed NAACP field secretary, was dispatched to Atlanta to assist the new branch.

Johnson spoke to an overflow audience urging, with irrefutable logic, a protest vote against the bond issue. Called upon unexpectedly, White appealed for memberships in the new branch and urged support of the campaign to defeat the bond issue. His speech so impressed Johnson that, upon his return to New York, he recommended the employment of the dynamic young Atlantan as assistant secretary.

Entering upon his new duties, February 1, 1918, Walter White immediately embarked upon the most daring phase of his brilliant career—one which was to project him into the forefront of the civil rights struggle—on-the-spot investigation of lynchings. At his request he was sent to Estill Springs, Tenn., to get the full story of the gruesome lynching of Jim McIlherron, a Negro sharecropper, who was burned to death at the stake by a howling mob of sadistic whites. His crime? Resisting assault by his employer.

Posing as a prospective land buyer, White, whose racial identity was unsuspected, mingled with the townsfolk and learned many facts about lynchings which stood him in good stead later. Johnson, who had been leading the NAACP anti-lynching crusade, asked his assistant to accompany him to Washington where he reported his findings to sympathetic congressmen. Thereafter, White investigated more than 40 lynchings and was awarded the Spingarn Medal in 1937 for his outstanding achievement in this field. He became the most effective leader of the crusade to rid the nation of this bestial crime.

His investigation of lynchings in the South prepared him for later action in connection with race riots in the North which erupted following World War I in such cities as Chicago, Philadelphia, Washington, Omaha and others. The experience in France of Negro war veterans embittered them against Jim Crow practices in the United States. Meanwhile, hundreds of thousands of Negroes in search of jobs, better education for their children, and freedom, migrated, in a vast hegira, from the South. The result was overcrowding, conflict and competition.

He was sent to investigate the six-day riot in Chicago which broke out in August, 1919, and cost the lives of 38 persons—23 Negroes and 15 whites. The evidence and findings which White uncovered were turned over to "Big Bill" Thompson, then Mayor of Chicago. The NAACP investigator reported that Negroes were being victimized by sharp real estate practices, required to pay high rents for slum quarters, denied opportunity to obtain decent housing outside the ghetto except at exorbitant prices. This economic squeeze, he reported, spawned social disorders—crime, juvenile delinquency and disease.

White also discovered that his fair skin could be a handicap within Negro neighborhoods in time of stress. During the Chicago turmoil, he was shot at by a Negro gunman. Later, he recalled: "I ducked as a bullet whanged into the side of the building exactly where my head had been a fraction of a second before. With most undignified speed, I gained the magnificent shelter of the bank (Binga State Bank) and thereafter made sure to have as a companion a Negro who was distinctly a Negro whenever I had business on the South Side."

Once, during the "Red Summer" of 1919, he was almost lynched while investigating violence in Phillips County, Ark., where organized Negro sharecroppers shot back at a white mob attacking Negroes assembled in a small church. A white man was killed in that exchange of shots. Subsequently, some 200 Negro men, women and children were hunted and many shot down in cold blood by white killers.

A self-appointed "Committee of Seven" conducted a kangaroo court to pass on the "good" and "bad niggers," the chief test being whether they had joined or disapproved of the tenant farmers union, which was seeking a fair return for crops the members raised.

Seventy-nine refused to yield to intimidation and were indicted for murder, insurrection and other crimes. Twelve were found guilty and sentenced to death, 67 others were given prison terms ranging from 20 years to life. The trials were held within five days.

White covered the trial as a reporter for the *Chicago Daily News.* Informed by a Negro that the whites were planning to get him, the NAACP investigator caught the next train out of Helena. The conductor said: "But you're leaving, mister, just when the fun is going to start." Asked what fun, the conductor replied, "There's a damned yellow nigger down here passing for white and the boys are going to get him." "What'll they do with him?" White asked. "When they get through with him he won't pass for white no more!" the conductor replied. When White reached Memphis, the news had been circulated that he had been lynched in Arkansas that afternoon.

NAACP lawyers won a reversal of the convictions in the United States Supreme Court after six years of legal jousting. The case of *Moore v. Dempsey* upheld the principle that a courtroom must be free of intimidation and bias.

During James Weldon Johnson's leave of absence to work with the Garland Fund, a philanthropic enterprise designed to help various Negro civil rights causes, including such organizations as the NAACP, Walter White was named acting secretary. At the end of his leave in 1931, Johnson resigned and later became professor of creative writing at Fisk University. The young Atlantan succeeded him.

Walter White became the Association's image and also its chief lobbyist. For many years the primary goal of the Association's legislative program was a Federal law to punish the lynchers. The long-range objective was and is full equality. White pursued these goals relentlessly. He was widely regarded as the foremost spokesman for Negroes who generally backed him up when he threatened politicians with Negro voter reprisal while simultaneously working to build up Negro voter strength throughout the country.

Johnson had utilized the pamphlet, "Thirty Years of Lynching," to highlight the problem and to support his lobby for passage of the Dyer antilynching bill. White kept the national spotlight focused on America's most heinous crime through his on-the-spot investigations of numerous lynchings; appearances before congressional committees; books such as the novels ***Fire in the Flint,*** 1924, and ***Flight,*** 1926, and his study, ***Rope and Faggot—A Biography of Judge Lynch,*** 1929.

The NAACP-sponsored campaigns placed this crime on the nation's conscience. Lynchings declined steadily under this assault. Several antilynching measures were passed in the House only to be killed by filibuster in the Senate. In later years, White and the Association turned their attention to changing the rules of the Senate to permit cloture by a majority vote, a fight still going on today under the leadership of Roy Wilkins and the Leadership Conference on Civil Rights.

It was while he was serving as acting secretary in 1931 that White achieved another great triumph of his dramatic career, namely, the rejection of President Hoover's nominee for associate justice of the United States Supreme Court. The President had submitted to the Senate for confirmation the name of Judge John J. Parker of North Carolina. In 1920 when he was the Republican candidate for governor of North Carolina, Judge Parker had approved a proposal to restrict Negro voting. "The participation of the Negro in politics is a source of evil and danger to both races and is not desired by the wise men in either race or by the Republican party of North Carolina," he said at that time.

The NAACP urged the President to withdraw the nomination. When he failed to do so, the Association mounted a national campaign to get the Senate to withhold confirmation. Parker failed of confirmation by a vote of 41-39. Thereafter, Walter White conducted a campaign to defeat those senators who supported the Parker nomination. Roscoe C. McCulloch of Ohio and Henry J. Allen of Kansas were defeated in the next election. These defeats, spearheaded by colored voters acting under direction of the NAACP, marked the coming of age politically of the Negro in America. In subsequent elections other Parker supporters were defeated. This successful campaign remains a classic in lobbying and voter reprisal.

As war clouds gathered in Europe, the nation entered a period of stepped-up production in defense plants, assuming the role of Arsenal of Democracy. The NAACP was determined that Negro workers would be employed in these new industries and colored servicemen trained and utilized in every branch of the armed services.

Secretary White investigated employment conditions in aircraft factories of California, Washington, Maryland and Michigan. Branches were urged to survey local defense plants and picket those which were practicing discrimination in employment and upgrading.

The Selective Service Act, signed September 14, 1940, contained a non-discrimination clause, yet the War Department, on October 9, reaffirmed its segregation policy:

> The policy of the War Department is not to intermingle colored and white enlisted personnel in the same regimental organizations. This policy has been proved satisfactory over a long period of years and to make changes would produce situations destructive to morale and detrimental to preparations for national defense.

President Roosevelt, at the request of Walter White, received a delegation, September 27, 1940, consisting of White, A. Philip Randolph, president of the Brotherhood of Sleeping Car Porters, and T. Arnold Hill of the National Urban League to discuss employment discrimination in the armed services and defense industries.

A memorandum, prepared in the office of the Washington Bureau, was left with the President in order that there would be no misunderstanding of the position of the conferees. Roosevelt was asked to abolish racial discrimination and segregation in the armed services. The President promised to talk with his Cabinet. On October 9, the White House issued a statement declaring that the traditional policy of segregation would be continued. Stephen Early, White House press secretary, inferred to the press that Randolph, White and Hill had agreed with this policy. Denying this assertion, White released the text of the memorandum left with the President.

Northern Democrats were furious at Early for this blunder. White informed the press that the only way the damage could be repaired would be for the President to end discrimination in the armed services and industry.

Largely as a result of the NAACP protests, Judge William H. Hastie was appointed Civilian Aide to the Secretary of War, Colonel Benjamin O. Davis, the highest ranking Negro officer in the Army, was promoted to Brigadier General. Colonel Campbell Johnson was appointed Special Aide to the Director of Selective Service. These token appointments did not satisfy White.

Although A. Phillip Randolph conceived the March on Washington Movement and has been generally credited with obtaining issuance of the anti-discrimination Executive Order 8802, he early enlisted the support of Walter White who gave invaluable assistance to this enterprise.

Roosevelt, informed of Randolph's threat, used New York City Mayor Fiorello LaGuardia and Mrs. Roosevelt in an attempt to get the March called off. On June 18, 1941, the President summoned Randolph and White to a conference at the White House where they talked with the President, Secretary of War, Navy, and other officials. The President, skeptical of Randolph's claim that 100,000 would march, asked White "How many will march, Walter?" Without batting an eye, White replied: "No less than 100,000."

On June 25, the President issued Executive Order 8802, creating the wartime FEPC banning discrimination in defense industries.

White was involved in labor's drive to organize the Ford workers. The United Automobile Workers-CIO struck the Ford plant in 1941. Negro workers, particularly those in the foundry, resisted organization. Ford's policies of fair employment, hospitalization and vocational training were the most progressive of any local auto industry. Negro ministers of the three largest churches had served as volunteer employment agencies.

Invited by Dr. J. J. McClendon, president of the Detroit Branch, White flew to Detroit and urged support of the strike. Hiring a sound truck, White, McClendon and the Rev. Horace White, militant pastor of Plymouth Congregational Church, circled the Ford plant, successfully urging Negro workers to join the strike.

In order to examine critically the role and treatment of Negro servicemen abroad, White made an extensive tour of European and Mediterranean Theaters of Operation as a correspondent for the *New York Post.* Upon his return, he submitted a memorandum to the War Department with 14 recommendations "ranging from the initiation of non-segregated bomber crews to the creation of a special Board of Review for court-martial cases." He made a similar tour of the Pacific Ocean area later that year. In his book, ***A Rising Wind: Report of Negro Troops in the ETO,*** 1945, White reported on this visit with the servicemen.

As in World War I, Negro veterans of World War II were abused, humiliated, denied employment and otherwise mistreated. And there was violence.

Among the incidents of violence which upset Negro Americans were these:

The blinding in 1946 of a veteran, Isaac Woodard, on a bus by Batesburg, S. C., Police Chief Linwood Shull who was acquitted; the lynching of four veterans in Walton County, Georgia, because they sought to register and vote; the brutal blowtorch lynching in Minden, Louisiana, of ex-Corporal John Jones accused of "loitering"; the escape of his cousin, Albert Harris, who later told the story to officials of the Justice Department, helping to obtain indictments against the lynchers who were subsequently acquitted.

White helped form a National Emergency Committee against Mob Violence, August, 1946. On September 19, he visited President Truman to demand Federal remedial action. In the delegation were James Carey, CIO secretary, Boris Shiskin, AFL, Dr. Channing H. Tobias of the Phelps-Stokes Fund and Leslie Perry, NAACP Washington Bureau. As spokesman, White related stories of rising violence and urged Presidential action. Out of this meeting came the suggestion by Presidential Assistant David K. Niles for the appointment of a Presidential Committee to investigate the entire subject of violation of civil liberties and to recommend corrective action.

Responding to the skepticism voiced by White, Tobias and others that such a committee should not be used to postpone action, the President agreed to create the Committee by Executive Order, financed from contingency funds.

The Civil Rights Committee, thus created, headed by Charles E. Wilson of General Motors, reported its findings in 1947, on lynching, police brutality, administration of justice, involuntary servitude, wartime evacuation of Japanese; denial of citizenship rights, including the right to vote and the poll tax; discrimination in the armed services, civil service, employment, education, housing, health services, public services and accommodations; and segregation as national policy. The hard-hitting report pointed up the responsibility of government and shook up the country with its declaration: "*the time for action is now.*" Practically all of its principal recommendations have since been achieved.

Walter White was an internationalist and attended numerous meetings in foreign countries. He attended the Pan African Conference in 1921, a conference sponsored by the NAACP under the leadership of Dr. W. E. B. DuBois. This Conference met in England, Belgium and France to seek better treatment of African colonials.

White, DuBois and Mrs. Mary McLeod Bethune, represented the Association as consultants to the American delegation at the founding of the United Nations in San Francisco, in 1945. The NAACP representatives proposed that the colonial system be abolished, that equality of races be recognized and a bill of rights for all peoples be adopted; that an international agency be established to replace the colonial system. Many of these recommendations have since been adopted by the UN.

Viewers of today's television specials, commercials, popular serials such as *Julia* starring Diahann Carroll and films starring Sidney Poitier, Ossie Davis, Harry Belafonte, Lena Horne, Sammy Davis, Jr., and other Negro performers are largely unaware of the contributions of the NAACP to these advances. Little remembered are the menial roles Negro actors and actresses were restricted to and the difficulty these performers, as well as writers, encountered in efforts to break into the communications, motion picture and entertainment fields.

White sought to establish a Hollywood Bureau, continually importuned the motion picture industry for better roles for Negroes, often incurring the outspoken animosity of Negro performers who understandably regarded their menial roles as a source of income and were, at that time, unconvinced that better roles were obtainable.

He successfuly enlisted the aid of Wendell Willkie, defeated Republican Presidential candidate, who had been made counsel to the motion-picture industry. Through Willkie, White was able to appeal to Walter Wanger and Darryl Zanuck of Twentieth Century-Fox for more representative roles for Negroes in films. In 1942, Willkie spoke at the NAACP Convention in Los Angeles. During sessions of the conference, White again spoke with Wanger and others about better roles for Negroes. White and Willkie discussed setting up a Hollywood Bureau of the NAACP to advise producers, but Willkie's untimely death ended that hope.

After the election of President Eisenhower in 1952, White, along with Arthur Spingarn, Theodore Spaulding, and Dr. Channing H. Tobias, called on the newly elected President to present civil rights proposals, urging that he use his executive powers to eliminate discrimination and segregation in Federal installations.

During White's helmsmanship, the NAACP fought and won for the Negro the right to vote in the South; opposed the poll tax and other devices inhibiting Negro voting; forged an alliance with industrial trade unions; knocked the props out from legally protected residential segregation; killed the Southern white primary; opened the doors to undergraduate and graduate collegiate institutions; and equalized teachers' salaries. The legal assault upon Jim Crow during this period was initiated by Charles H. Houston and carried out by Thurgood Marshall, culminating in the Supreme Court's historic decision banning segregation in public education, May 17, 1954, nine months before White's death.

Walter White was truly a great warrior and hero in the fight for equal justice. In a foreword to White's posthumously published book, ***How Far the Promised Land?,*** 1955, his good friend, Dr. Ralph J. Bunche, wrote this fitting epitaph:

> One so seldom meets a truly dedicated person, and when such a one is also keenly intelligent, vibrant, engaging, and warmly human—and this was Walter White—his going leaves a sorrowful void.

CHARLES F. COONEY (ESSAY DATE 1972)

SOURCE: Cooney, Charles F. "Walter White and the Harlem Renaissance." *Journal of Negro History* 57, no. 3 (1972): 231-40.

In the following essay, Cooney examines White's role in the Harlem Renaissance, showing how he helped other African American writers get their work published, and concludes that it was partly through White's efforts that the flowering of the Renaissance occurred.

The aesthetic limitations of Walter White's two novels, ***The Fire in the Flint*** (New York, Alfred A. Knopf, 1924), and ***Flight*** (New York, Alfred A. Knopf, 1926), have precluded any serious attempt to define his role in the Harlem Renaissance.[1] That role derives its significance not from the novels he wrote, but from the part he played in bringing the works of more talented black writers to the attention of publishers and editors. Even though White responded to the same stimuli that had moved an older generation of black writers, he welcomed rather than resented the "New Negro."[2]

When the first vague stirrings of interest in the Negro arose among white intellectuals, Walter White was in a particularly advantageous position to exploit their interest on behalf of black writers. As Assistant Secretary of the NAACP since 1918, White was beginning to achieve a degree of prominence through his well publicized lynching investigations. In addition, he was closely associated with James Weldon Johnson. Through Johnson, White secured introductions to numerous figures prominent in publishing and critical circles. Frederick Lewis Allen, Alfred and Blanche Knopf, H. L. Mencken, and Carl and Irita Van Doren were among those with whom he could claim acquaintance.[3]

In the increasing interest in the Negro, White perceived the opportunities both to enhance his own reputation and, by helping other black writers as well, to begin the process of breaking down the complacently held stereotypes of Negroes cherished by most whites. When it was suggested that he seek a Negro publisher for his own novel, he replied:

> Colored people know everything in my book—they live and suffer the same things every day of their lives. It is not the colored reader at whom I am shooting but the white man and woman . . . who has never suspected there are men like Kenneth Harper [the protagonist in ***The Fire in the Flint***], who believes that every lynching is for rape, who believes the ex-confederates are right when they use every means, fair or foul, "to keep the nigger in his place."[4]

Doubtless, this same attitude underlay his extensive efforts to be of service to black writers who, in one way or another, sought to diminish the influence of a hundred years of stereotyped black characters.

Walter White's efforts to further the careers of black writers began as early as 1920, when he sent some stories by Harry H. Pace to H. L. Mencken for consideration. Mencken found the stories wanting, and therefore rejected them, but felt that Pace showed promise and encouraged him. White continued to exploit his friendship with Mencken, but on his own behalf. Between 1922 and 1924, White wrote and published ***The Fire in the Flint*** with substantial assistance from Mencken in both phases of the project.[5]

During the time he was involved with his own novel, White did not have much time to devote to other writers. He did correspond briefly with Jean Toomer, and advised Toomer to contact Joel Spingarn regarding "developments which may be of advantage to you."[6] When the publication of his own novel was assured, however, White again began to promote the careers of aspiring black authors.

On April 14, 1924, White wrote a brief note to Countee Cullen stating that he wanted to talk with Cullen and look over some of Cullen's best poetry. He added that "something worth while may come of it because of a statement made to me last night by a certain publisher." Cullen hastened to take advantage of the opportunity and took his poems to White. After looking the poems over, White decided to seek an outside opinion. White wrote to Carl Van Doren and asked him to read the poems and give his opinion on the advisability of finding a publisher for them. He explained that Cullen was seeking a Rhodes scholarship and felt it essential to gain some literary distinction since he had no athletic prowess. White then added that Horace Liveright had expressed an interest in Cullen's work and had asked him to look over the poetry, but that he felt he didn't know enough about poetry and was therefore seeking Van Doren's opinion.[7]

Several days later, Van Doren gave his opinion. He felt that Cullen did not have enough poetry for a volume that would be "worthy of him." He stressed that he would be more encouraging if he could, but that he was too interested in Cullen's future to counsel premature publication unless it would help obtain the scholarship. He also added that he would like to see the best of Cullen's unpublished poems and consider them for *The Century Magazine*.[8]

Despite Carl Van Doren's unencouraging opinion, White decided to try to induce Horace Liveright to publish a volume of Cullen's poetry. On April 25, he wrote Liveright that he had gone over Cullen's poems and felt that there were about thirty of them which were "well worth publication." He noted that a volume about the size of Edna St. Vincent Millay's *A Few Figs From Thistles* could perhaps be brought out, and added that Witter Bynner had agreed to do an introduction. From a commercial point of view, White felt that Cullen had a "considerable reputation for a young man and many friends who would help push the book," and that it could be made worth while to bring out a volume of Cullen's verses. On the same day, White wrote to Cullen and advised him of the steps he had taken. He also cautioned Cullen that when he and Liveright met, Cullen was to be "sublimely innocent of my connection in any way." Cullen wrote back that he was "deeply grateful" for what he had done for him.[9]

Cullen sent his poems to the Liveright firm, and waited anxiously for a decision. The decision was transmitted first to Walter White. On May 2, Liveright wrote to White and told him that he was going to return the manuscript. He stated that both of his poetry readers liked the book, but thought it wasn't "distinctly big" and felt that it didn't have any chance for a sale. It had, he said, an individual poetic note that he would like to recognize, but that his organization "kicks at me continually for putting books on the list that tremendously increase their work and on which I expect some returns. . . ." He might put it out if Cullen guaranteed a sale of 500 copies, even though he disliked financed books.

On the following day, White sent Cullen a copy of Liveright's letter. He was sorry at the outcome, but conceded that perhaps "it would be wisest for you to give up the idea of publication until you have done some more of the work of which you are capable." He did not want Cullen to "run the risk of being labeled as anything less than a poet of the first class." He reiterated his willingness to help Cullen in any way he could, and admonished him not to forget to send some poems to Carl Van Doren.[10] On May 6, Cullen replied:

> You may be sure I am quite sorry that things turned out as they have, and I am sure you have done your utmost for me, for which I am sincerely grateful to you. I have not yet heard from Mr. Liveright, but his letter to you seemed quite definite.
>
> Of course I haven't the funds to finance a book, nor should I do so were I able. Just a matter of pride.

I am not in the least discouraged, however, as better poets have waited longer for publication.

Yet Cullen did not have much longer to wait for publication. Less than a year later, in March, 1925, the staid firm of Harpers accepted a volume of Cullen's verse. Again, Walter White played a significant role. He did not figure quite so prominently as in the effort to persuade Liveright to publish Cullen, but he was sought out by Eugene Saxton of Harpers and asked for his opinion. White counseled Saxton in much the same terms he had advised Horace Liveright; he noted Cullen's high reputation for a young man, and stressed that Cullen had a large number of influential friends who would "do all in their power to see that the book is circulated."[11]

On March 6, 1925, again preceding official notification by the publishing firm, White wrote to Cullen and, this time, congratulated him on the acceptance of his book of poems. He also promised Cullen, as he had previously promised Frederick Lewis Allen and Eugene Saxton of Harpers, his assistance in promoting the book. In the efforts to promote the book, White expended considerable effort. He wrote the biographical sketch, made a list of individuals to whom complimentary copies might be sent, spread news of the book among his friends, and even read some of the poetry over the radio. In later years, Cullen and White retained their friendship. White wrote an introduction to a special issue of *Palms* (October, 1926) devoted to Negro poetry and edited by Cullen, advised him on the selections for *Caroling Dusk* (New York, Harper and Bros., 1927), and extended his assistance to Cullen whenever asked.[12]

At the same time Walter White was seeking publication for Countee Cullen, he was also acting as an informal agent for Claude McKay. During the years McKay was abroad, White was one of his principal links to the United States, and one of his chief sources for news of stateside activities. The fruitful relationship between the two began in January, 1924, when White sent McKay $100.00 in response to a plea McKay had written, and that found its way to White.[13]

On August 15, 1924, White wrote to McKay of the publication of ***The Fire in the Flint,*** and inquired about McKay's progress on the novel he had mentioned briefly when he had thanked White for the hundred dollars. As the months passed, White became increasingly interested in McKay's novel, and in October and November, 1924, he capitalized on a recently cultivated friendship with Sinclair Lewis in order to benefit McKay. On November 6, 1924, White wrote McKay and urged him to see Lewis when the latter was in Paris. He told McKay that he and Lewis had gone "over page by page, line by line, parts of ***The Fire in the Flint*** and I learned more about the things that I must correct in my style than from all of the treatises that have been written on the novel." White also inquired into McKay's finances and offered to do anything he could to help, even though it might not be much.

A month later, McKay wrote to White and described his meeting with Lewis:

Day before yesterday I met Sinclair Lewis and wife. He's a good chap. I had dinner with him again yesterday and we were out drinking all night at the N. Y. Bar. I have given him my book to read as I am sure he can give me some good tips for publishers.[14]

Years later, in his autobiography, *A Long Way From Home* (1937; reprint New York, Harcourt Brace and World, 1970, p. 259), McKay acknowledged that Lewis had provided him with "a few cardinal and practical points about the writing of a novel. I remembered them so well that some critics saw the influence of Sinclair Lewis in my novel."

In a few months, McKay felt that the novel was sufficiently near completion to warrant looking for a publisher. Since he was unable to leave Paris, he entrusted the task to Walter White and Arthur Schomburg.[15] These two began the search for a publisher, and after a few months White received an interested response from George Oppenheimer of the Viking Press. McKay, however, expressed a preference for a more established firm when he wrote to White in response to the news. Nevertheless, White continued to keep Viking informed, and pursued contacts with other publishing firms as well.[16]

As the summer drew to a close, McKay's novel had not been placed, and he began to give evidence of some concern. He was financially pressed, and worried on that account, but was also concerned, as he informed White, because "I . . . hear in a roundabout way that your friend Carl Van Vechten is doing a novel on Harlem Negro life and I don't want him to get in ahead of me."[17] Unfortunately, White and Schomburg met with no further success although they continued their quest for a publisher for McKay's book.

In order to relieve his ever present financial difficulties, McKay began to write stories and poems and sent them out while revising his novel. Again he called on White for help. Although he initially submitted his poems and stories to magazines himself, he asked editors to send them to Walter White if they were not suitable. Occasionally, he sent material directly to White.[18] White felt that much of the material McKay sent was "distinctly third rate,"[19] but he tried to place it. Sometimes he succeeded; more often he failed.

In 1926, Carl Van Vechten published his novel of Harlem life, *Nigger Heaven* (New York, Alfred A. Knopf, 1926), and in 1927, McKay finished his revisions of *Home to Harlem.* In 1928 McKay's novel was published by the established firm of Harpers, but Walter White could claim no credit for its placement. In 1927, White had left for France on a Guggenheim fellowship and was there when McKay's novel was published.

Another participant in the Harlem Renaissance to whom White extended a helping hand was Rudolph Fisher. On February 3, 1925, White wrote to Fisher and told him that Robert Bagnall, Field Secretary of the NAACP, had brought Fisher's name to his attention. He confessed that he did not know Fisher's writings, but was interested, and would be glad to "be of any help to you if by chance there is anything at all that I can do?" Fisher responded to White's letter, "losing no time in seizing the opportunity it proffers." Enclosed in the letter was a short story, "High Yaller," which Robert Bagnall had suggested White might be willing to send to H. L. Mencken. He also excused White's ignorance of his work because his first published story was just then coming out in the February *Atlantic Monthly.*[20]

On February 6, White wrote Fisher and assured him that he would send "High Yaller" to Mencken. He added the cautionary note that he had recently spoken with Mencken who had told him that he had accepted a great deal of material by and about Negroes. In the event of its rejection, White suggested that he would be glad to send the story to Carl Van Doren of *The Century.* In a postscript he told Fisher that he had read "The City of Refuge," in the *Atlantic Monthly* and was most enthusiastic about the ability it demonstrated. He promised to call the attention of Carl Van Vechten, Zona Gale, Sinclair Lewis, and others to Fisher's story.

True to his word, White sent "High Yaller" to Mencken, and in a covering letter praised Fisher highly. On the same day he wrote to Carl Van Vechten about Fisher.[21] Unfortunately, Mencken was unable to use the story and returned it to Fisher. He felt that Fisher showed promise, however, and asked if he would write an article about the Negro physician.[22] Undaunted, Fisher sent the story to Thomas Wells of *Harper's* and wrote to White, asking if he would put in a good word with Frederick Lewis Allen in order to strengthen its chances of acceptance. White readily agreed to speak to Allen.[23]

During the time *Harper's* was considering Fisher's story, he and White corresponded and discussed trends in the literary market place. Fisher was somewhat discouraged that there was a greater market for expository prose than for fiction, as Mencken's suggestion of an "article" implied. White tried to renew his flagging enthusiasm by pointing out that while there were signs of limitations in the writing of fiction, those who were writing about the Negro were tapping a largely untouched vein. He stated that in a recent talk with two publishers, they had expressed the opinion that the interest in the Negro as an artist was a "movement that was destined to develop and flower." He added that he had called the attention of the two publishers to Fisher and his work.[24]

While Fisher and White were thus loftily engaged, *Harper's* rejected Fisher's story. Somewhat chagrined, Fisher once more sent the manuscript to White. He asked White if it would be convenient for him to show the story to Carl Van Doren of *The Century,* as he had promised he would do. White again sent the story out with a letter praising Fisher's ability. Ironically, Van Doren was unable to accept the story largely because they had just published an article entitled "White but Black" by Walter White. Van Doren sent the manuscript back to Fisher. White then suggested that Fisher try to place the story in *Scribner's,* though he added that he knew no one there, and that the chances were that they would not accept it.[25] In October, 1925, "High Yaller" finally surfaced as the Amy Spingarn Award first prize story in *The Crisis* (Volume 30 No. 6, pages 281 to 288 and Volume 31 No. 1, pages 33 to 38 October-November 1925).

Though White had been unable to place "High Yaller" for Fisher in the *American Mercury, Harper's* or *The Century,* he had certainly introduced Fisher's name and work to a great many people who, in the years to come, could be of great benefit to him.

Walter White did not limit his assistance to the writers of the "Harlem School"; he also gave assistance to several writers who belonged, along with White, to that group of black writers of the 20's which Robert Bone has designated "The Rear Guard." The best of the writers in that group was

Nella Larsen (Imes). In 1926, she sent to White the manuscript of her novel *Quicksand.* Unfortunately, most of her dealings with White were in person rather than through correspondence. The extant correspondence between them indicates only that White read the manuscript and suggested some minor changes. Later, he persuaded his secretary, Carrie Overton, to type the manuscript for Mrs. Imes. When Mrs. Imes was probably seeking a publisher for her novel, White was in France on his fellowship.[26]

The record of White's efforts on behalf of Georgia Douglas Johnson's book, *An Autumn Love Cycle,* is more complete. On August 1, 1926, Mrs. Johnson wrote to White and told him that she was about to leave for the South in connection with her work, but wished to have her volume of poems into the hands of a publisher, or into the hands of some one who would deal with publishers on her behalf, before she left. She asked if White would be willing to try and place the book for her, for pay. White replied:

> Under no circumstances would I want any pay for helping to get your manuscript published. I make no promises and do not know how successful I will be, but if you will send the manuscript to me at my home . . . I will see what can be done.[27]

Mrs. Johnson sent the manuscript and advised White that she had already tried Boni and Liveright, and Alfred A. Knopf as possible publishers.[28]

In the following weeks, White submitted *An Autumn Love Cycle* to several prominent publishers, but each time it was rejected. On September 24, he wrote to Mrs. Johnson and told her the negative results of his efforts. He told her that while most of the publishers thought her poems good, they also felt that too many other poets had written equally good poetry dealing with the same themes and emotions. It was with regret that he sent the manuscript. Mrs. Johnson thanked him for his efforts and said that she realized that her poetry was not "modern." Eventually, in 1928, Mrs. Johnson succeeded in finding a publisher for her book.[29]

Shortly before White's efforts on behalf of Negro writers came to a temporary halt due to his departure for France on the Guggenheim writing fellowship, he tried to place some poems of Langston Hughes' in *Harper's.* As early as 1925, White had confided to Hughes that he was well acquainted with a number of critics, and expressed his willingness to try and turn his acquaintanceships to Hughes' advantage.[30] Hughes did not often take advantage of White's offer, however, until he resumed his academic career. While a student at Lincoln University in Pennsylvania, he was able to visit New York only on week ends,[31] and thus decided to let White try to place some poems for him.

In February, 1927, Hughes left some poems at the offices of the NAACP for White to try and place. White wrote to Hughes and told him that he would try either *Harper's* or *The Century.*[32] On February 17, he sent Hughes' poems to Frederick Lewis Allen for consideration by *Harper's.* Allen seems to have preferred the more classical cadences of Countee Cullen's poetry, however, for he rejected Hughes' poems. Hughes was nonetheless grateful for White's efforts.[33] A few months later, White left for France.

Upon his return from France he found an altered situation in the offices of the NAACP. James Weldon Johnson's health was suffering, and an increased share of the work of the association was placed on White's shoulders. Shortly afterwards, in 1929, Johnson received a Rosenwald fellowship and White became acting Secretary of the Association.[34] Clearly, he had far less time to devote to literary activities. He did, however, continue to read manuscripts sent to him by unknown but aspiring black writers.

Reviewing Walter White's activities as a literary entrepreneur, it would appear that he failed far more often than he succeeded. It should be remembered, though, that from 1924 to 1927, the Harlem Renaissance was yet in a nascent stage.[35] It was through the efforts of Walter White, and the similar efforts of Carl Van Vechten, Alain Locke, and Charles S. Johnson, that the flowering of the Renaissance occurred.

By the end of 1930, the Negro had become one of the casualties of the stock market crash, and the Harlem Renaissance a vestige of the past. To be sure, black writers continued to write, and Walter White continued to lend them assistance when he could,[36] but that an era had ended was only too clear.

Notes

1. See Robert Bone's comments in *The Negro Novel in America* (New Haven, Yale University Press, rev. ed., 1965) pp. 99-100. Hugh Gloster, *Negro Voices in American Fiction* (Chapel Hill, University of North Carolina Press, 1948) pp. 147-151, evaluates *The Fire in the Flint* as a work of propaganda. In Edward Margolie's *Native Sons* (Philadelphia, J. B. Lippincott, 1969), David Littlejohn's *Black on White: A Critical Survey of Writings by American Negroes* (New York, Viking Press, 1966), and Nathan I. Huggins' *The Harlem Renaissance* (New York, Oxford University Press, 1971), White is conspicuous by his almost complete absence.

2. An example of the resentment towards the "New Negro" is Benjamin Brawley, *The Negro Genius* (New York, Dodd, Mead & Co., 1937) esp. pp. 235-268.

3. Walter White, *A Man Called White* (New York, The Viking Press, 1948), p. 43.

4. Walter White to H. L. Mencken, October 17, 1923, NAACP Papers, MSS Div., L.C. Through a filing quirk, almost all of White's correspondence with Mencken is in a single folder filed under Mencken's name in the files for 1942. See also: Walter White "The Negro in Contemporary Literature," ca. 1928, typescript article, NAACP Paper, Administrative File: Speeches and Articles. At this time I wish to thank the NAACP for their permission to consult these records.

5. White to Mencken, October 6, 1920, and Mencken to White, October 7, 1920; Mencken's role in the writing and publication of *The Fire in the Flint* is described in detail in Charles F. Cooney, "Mencken's Midwifery: A Case Study," *Menckeniana* [1972].

6. White to Jean Toomer, November 16, 1923, NAACP Papers, Administrative File; Personal Papers, Walter White, MSS Div. L.C. All letters cited are from this file unless otherwise noted.

7. White to Carl Van Doren, April 18, 1924.

8. Carl Van Doren to White, April 22, 1924.

9. White to Cullen, April 25, 1924; Cullen to White, April 28, 1924.

10. White to Countee Cullen, May 3, 1924.

11. White to Eugene Saxton, February 13, 1925.

12. Cullen to White, January 16, 1926, for introduction to *Palms:* White to Cullen, June 14, 1927, for *Caroling Dusk.*

13. White to Claude McKay, January 26, 1924.

14. McKay to White, December 4, 1924. See also White to Sinclair Lewis, October 15, 1924; and Lewis to White, November 12, 1924.

15. McKay to White, March 14, 1925.

16. George Oppenheimer to Walter White, May 25, 1925; McKay to White, July 6, 1925; White to Oppenheimer, August 26, 1925.

17. McKay to White, August 4, 1925.

18. Several groups of material in the NAACP files document McKay's habits. EG: Filed under the date of October 27, 1925, are a letter from McKay to Mencken which reads, in part: "Perhaps you may find one or both of these poems suitable for the *Mercury* . . . If you do not I should be grateful if you would have them sent to Walter White," two poems, "America in Retrospect," and "My House," and a letter from Charles Angoff of *The American Mercury* forwarding the poems to White. Similar groups of material can be found filed under the date November 9, 1925, and a letter from McKay to White dated October 11, 1925, asks White to place a short story.

19. White to Langston Hughes, December 18, 1925.

20. Rudolph Fisher to White, February 5, 1925.

21. White to Mencken, February 10, 1925 (see footnote 4); and White to Carl Van Vechten, February 10, 1925.

22. Mencken to White, February 23, 1925 (see footnote 4).

23. Fisher to White, February 15, 1925; and White to Fisher, February 17, 1925.

24. Fisher to White, February 25, 1925; and White to Fisher, March 12, 1925.

25. Fisher to White, March 10, 1925; White to Fisher, March 12, 1925; White to Carl Van Doren, March 12, 1925; Van Doren to White, March 13, 1925; and White to Fisher, March 16, 1925.

26. White to Nella L. Imes, October 1, 1926; Nella Imes to White (ND, but ca. November, 1926); and White to Nella Imes, November 16, 1926.

27. White to Georgia Douglas Johnson, August 3, 1926.

28. Mrs. Johnson to White, August 5, 1925.

29. Mrs. Johnson to White, October 18, 1926.

30. White to Langston Hughes, June 2, 1925.

31. Langston Hughes, *The Big Sea,* (1940; rpt., 1963, New York, Hill and Wang), p. 278.

32. Hughes to White, February 5, 1925; White to Hughes, February 11, 1927.

33. White to Hughes, April 13, 1927; and Hughes to White, May 10, 1927.

34. James Weldon Johnson, *Along This Way* (1933; rpt. 1968, The Viking Press, New York), pp. 382 and 393; White, *A Man Called White,* p. 103-104.

35. Between 1924 and 1927, only three novels written by Negroes associated with the "Harlem Renaissance" were published; in the year 1928 alone, five such novels were published.

36. For example, in April, 1930, White acted as an intermediary on behalf of Arna Bontemps.

EDWARD E. WALDRON (ESSAY DATE 1973)

SOURCE: Waldron, Edward E. "Walter White and the Harlem Renaissance: Letters from 1924-1927." *College Language Association Journal* 16, no. 4 (June 1973): 438-57.

In the following essay, Waldron examines White's letters to show his influence on the major writers of the Harlem Renaissance, including Langston Hughes, Claude McKay, Countee Cullen, and Alain Locke.

In his capacity as Assistant Secretary of the National Association for the Advancement of Colored People, Walter White played many important roles which helped the then struggling organization become a major influence in the Black community in America. Much is known about his activities as an investigator of lynchings and his involvement in such historic cases as Scottsboro and the Sweet case in Detroit, but almost nothing has been said about the tremendous influence he had on the flowering of literary production that has been named the Harlem Renais-

FROM THE AUTHOR

WHITE ON THE UNIFYING POWER OF ART

It has long been my feeling that the greatest aid towards solution of problems of race and color is to be gained through the art approach, and by the very excellence of each race's and each individual's gifts will come lessening of hatred and distrust and cruelty of race to race. Harry Burleigh, Roland Hayes, Paul Robeson, Countee Cullen, Dr. Du Bois and other artists in their various fields are, I feel, tearing down barriers of all sorts.

SOURCE: Walter White, quoted in *Dictionary of Literary Biography* 51: *Afro-American Writers from the Harlem Renaissance to 1940,* Gale Research, 1987, p. 302.

sance. Both because of his office and because of his own personal charm and strength, White was able to help many of the young Black writers—Fisher, Hughes, McKay, Cullen, and others—get published; his contacts with editors like Carl Van Doren and publishers like Alfred Knopf enabled him to bring the attention of these men to the burgeoning poets and novelists of the nineteen-twenties. The NAACP Executive Correspondence files in the Manuscript Room of the Library of Congress contain a wealth of information, in the form of letters to and from White, concerning his role as literary entrepeneur.[1]

Walter White was as aware as any one of the awakening of interest in the Negro American in the nineteen-twenties. On January 28, 1924, he wrote to Alain Locke: "I am glad you emphasize so splendidly the interest in Negro art which is being manifested in Europe. I, myself, have been tremendously pleased during the past few days by similar indications both in Europe and in America." At this time, too, White, Locke, and others were trying to establish a "Negro Foreign Fellowship Fund" through the aid of the American Fund for Public Service, Inc. Although they were subsequently turned down by the Fund, they had seen their proposed foundation as a source where young Negro artists could receive funds for study abroad where, in Locke's words, they might gain "a wider social vision and contact with progressive movements such as is almost impossible for them to obtain under present conditions in America."[2]

At the same time White was encouraging the young writers with the news of this awakened interest, he was also expressing his elation over the changes this interest brought about in prospects for artistic productions by and about Negroes. His letter to Claude McKay (then in France) on August 15, 1924, expressed this optimistic view:

> I know you will be delighted to hear of the many changes that have come in America since you left. The marvelous success of Roland Hayes and of Paul Robeson in *The Emperor Jones* and *All God's Chillun Got Wings,* coupled with the various novels, poems and other signs of an awakening artistic sense and articulacy on the part of the Negro have caused what seems to be a new day to set in.

A few months later he wrote to Mordecai Johnson concerning the widening opportunities for Negro writers, as well as the small successes already achieved:

> As never before in the history of the Negro is there opportunity today for him to have his say. Within the last few months, I have been asked by five publishers, every one of them of the first rank, to keep my eye open for any promising writer among us. I was glad indeed to be of a little help recently in getting a volume of verse by Countee Cullen [*Color*] accepted by Harpers and I was much elated recently in coming upon a young doctor now at Freedman's Hospital in Washington who shows very decided genius. His name is Rudolph Fisher and he had a story, "The City of Refuge", in the February *Atlantic Monthly.*[3]

Through out this period White was constantly praising one or the other of the young men whose work he was helping get recognized; often his letters of praise sound more like the work of a proud father than of a "detached" third party.

During this period of artistic explosion from the Black community, there was much controversy within that community regarding the "proper study" of Black artists. Claude McKay's realistic approach to the "low-life" of Harlem was bitterly opposed by writers like Jessie Fauset who sought to present only the "good" side of Negro life, i.e. the side that conformed to the prevailing white standards. White seemed caught in the middle. On the one hand, he did not approve of the stereotyped portrayal of the Negro as either a buffoon or an animal; on the other hand, he did not agree that Negro writers should ignore the racial problems they all knew so well. These two views were expressed in two letters written only four months apart. On December 8, 1924, White wrote to Florence Mills, congratulating her on the success of *Dixie to Broadway* and objecting to certain "low" elements in the play. One of his strongest objections was to some of the "vulgar" songs sung by Cora Green and to lines spoken by Miss Green in a "Harlem bedroom scene": "I am not a prude but I think one of the most magnificent things about the colored shows on Broadway is that most of them have depended on clean humor and have set a high standard which has had its effect on other shows." Another aspect of the show that upset him concerned the set. He specifically objected to the curtain which, he noted, "on one side represents two cornfield Negroes shooting dice and on the other side two others chasing a chicken." He went on to make his objection clear: "The proverbial chicken-stealing, dice-shooting, watermelon-eating, and razor-carrying Negro has been so long stereotyped that whatever humorous effects it might have had seem to me have long since passed away." He thought that the curtain was out of place with the "high type" characters of the performance and added: "Looking at it not from the racial but from the artistic standpoint, it jars the senses miserably." No indication is given about the impact of White's criticism on the production, but at least his sentiments were clearly presented here.

While White did agree with the "best-foot-forward" school of thought concerning the use of stereotyped characters, he did not agree with their inclination to ignore or to soft-sell the problems of racism in America. In a letter to Professor Edgar H. Webster of Atlanta University dated April 14, 1925, White responded to a charge by Webster that White's ***The Fire in the Flint*** was mere propaganda:

> There are some people who say that in writing about the Negro one should leave out the racial and interracial conflict. I most passionately do not believe in that school of thought. If one is going to write realistically about the Negro or Negro characters, he cannot leave out this phase of the Negro's life in America for no Negro, intelligent or non-intelligent, illiterate or educated, rich or poor, ever passes a day but that, directly or indirectly, this thing called the race problem creeps into his life. Thus I feel sure that no writer who is honest with himself can ever ignore so important a factor as this and, if he is honest about it, he is going to present it exactly as his characters would see the situation. If by so doing I am to bear the label of "propagandist", I shall do so cheerfully and with a light heart.

And, of course, White spent his entire adult life, in literature and out of it, making people aware of "this thing called the race problem."

This does not mean, however, that Walter White viewed literature as a sociological tool. Indeed, many of his letters of criticism to writers who sent him their work for evaluation centered on the fact that the writer was more concerned with social theories than with art. His letter to James L. Dameron of February 27, 1926, summarized his position well: "All fiction more or less contains convictions of one sort or another whether sociological or economic. But there is a rather definite dividing line between a novel as a work of art and a sociological treatise. Any novel which demands attention as a work of art cannot therefore be overly burdened with theories." This statement might have been violated in fact by his own two novels, but White obviously did not view literature produced to espouse social theory as theoretically sound. Yet he did view art as a possible aid to bettering race relations, not as propaganda, but as evidence of the Negro's abilities and sensitivities. He wrote several letters in which he expressed this view; the one he wrote to Louis Marshall on May 5, 1925, presents his point well:

> It has long been my feeling that the greatest aid towards solution of problems of race and color is to be gained through the art approach, and by the very excellence of each race's and each individual's gifts will come lessening of hatred and distrust and cruelty of race to race. Harry Burleigh, Roland Hayes, Paul Robeson, Countee Cullen, Dr. DuBois, and other artists in their various fields are, I feel, tearing down barriers of all sorts. . . .

White felt very keenly, then, the good that excellent art from the Black community could do, not only for the Black man, but for the whole country. Perhaps this is why he devoted so much of his energy to helping Black artists become known.

Although most of White's energies directed toward the arts were expended in helping writers, he also extended his aid to artists from other fields. One man in particular he was helping at this time was Jules Bledsoe, a baritone whom White considered to have great potential. White wrote many letters to Mr. Judd and others at the Boston Symphony Hall trying to arrange concert appearances for Bledsoe; he also hosted several social hours to which he invited influential critics so that they might hear Bledsoe perform. When Carl Van Vechten told White of a sensational singing group in Richmond called the Sabbath Glee Club, White tried several times to set up dates with representatives from the Victor Talking Machine Company to listen to the group. And, when an editor at Harper and Brothers wanted a singing group to appear on a radio show (which was to feature Countee Cullen's poetry, among other things), White suggested "a young musician in Harlem . . . training a double quartette which sings spirituals very well." That young musician was Hall Johnson. Later, White also tried to secure a recording contract for J. Rosamond Johnson and Taylor Gordon.

The real thrust of Walter White's endeavors, however, went toward the aid of young writers. One such writer was Rudolph Fisher. White first corresponded with Fisher on February 3, 1925, when he wrote: "Mr. Bagnall has told me of some of the very interesting things you have written. I blush to confess that I did not know of your work but I am tremendously interested. I am looking forward to reading your article in the Harlam [*sic*] number of *The Survey*." He offered his help and asked if Fisher would "care to let me see some of the work you have done." An eager young Fisher responded immediately, saying how much he appreciated White's "generous spirit" in his letter, adding:

> It's not very surprising that you knew nothing of my work, since my first story, "The City of Refuge," tho accepted fully a year ago, has only just come out in the February *Atlantic Monthly*. I should be glad, if you find time, to get your reaction to it.[4]

With the letter Fisher enclosed a story manuscript and asked White if he could present it to H. L. Mencken at the *American Mercury*, ". . . only if [he] felt that the story was really worth the effort." The story was entitled "High Yaller."

In reply, White expressed his tremendous enthusiasm for Fisher's talent. He read both of the stories and said "they are both gorgeous pieces of work. You have very real ability as a writer, you handle your situation splendidly, and you have not only the ability to express what you see but, what is more important, you have eyes that [can] and do see." Earlier in the letter White expressed his special interest in literature and offered some encouragement for the young writer:

> I am tremendously glad to know of your work because I am so deeply interested in literature and particularly things that you and I and the rest of us can do now and will do in the future. To me, there is no more absorbing or worthwhile way to which to devote one's every effort. . . .[5]

In addition to these words of encouragement, White said that he had sent Mencken "High Yaller" and that he had mentioned Fisher's story in the *Atlantic Monthly* to Carl Van Vechten, Carl Van Doren, Sinclair Lewis, Zona Gale, and others.

Fisher's inclination to press on with his work as a doctor and, more specifically, with his specialty of "X-ray work," made him hesitate about any firm commitment to writing, and this was not helped any by Mencken's (and later Van Doren's) rejection of "High Yaller." Mencken thought the story was too long for the *Mercury*, and Van Doren did not want to publish it so soon after White's own article, "White But Black," adding: "Moreover, I think it's a little unorganized." White never quit, though, and he was always praising Fisher's craft in letters.

Of course, Fisher was very thankful for White's help, and he expressed his gratitude many times. On February 11, 1925, he wrote White: "Because I place high value upon your opinion, I am very much pleased with what you say about my two stories. Thank you for your interest and help and for the contacts which you allow me to anticipate." White responded on February 14 and expressed his philosophy of helping others:

> You owe me no thanks for any interest that I may show or help that I may give. As I see it, there is such a tremendous field open to those of us who have the urge to write that any of us who refused to do anything he could to help the other would be a small person indeed.

In the same letter, White encouraged Fisher to come to New York, which he described as a Mecca for writers:

> To me, there is but one place in America for a writer to live and that is Manhattan—that is if he can adjust to the hectic life here and keep out of his life all the external things which prevent one from doing his work . . . in New York the contacts which are possible so far as I know only here of all places in America, keep one keyed up to such a point that no matter how much work he may do, nevertheless he feels like a loafer when almost every day he meets someone who is doing two or three times as much as he.

It is very difficult to imagine anyone doing "two or three times" as much work as Walter White; yet he tried to instill into others his enthusiasm for work and development.

The correspondence between Fisher and White tapered off after this initial burst in 1925, but picked up again later, in the thirties. Nonetheless, White obviously played a major role in getting the rather reluctant Fisher to work on his writing as well as his medical pursuits. White's keen reading eye had quickly discovered Fisher's talent, and he was determined in his attempts to get Fisher's writing career moving.

Another young Negro writer whose career was just beginning to unfold in the mid-twenties was the poet Langston Hughes. The first reference to Hughes in White's correspondence in the NAACP files was in a letter from White to Mrs. Blanche Knopf, written on January 4, 1925, in which White thanked Mrs. Knopf for sending him the proofs of *The Weary Blues,* which he planned to review. He added "I have followed Mr. Hughes' writing since he was first published in *The Crisis* and I look forward eagerly to reading these poems."

The direct correspondence of White and Hughes began with a congratulatory letter from White (May 19, 1925) on Hughes' *The Weary Blues.* In the letter White told Hughes that he had sent out a press notice on the book and offered to help in any way he could, promising to contact "Mrs. Knopf about the book and find out in what way I can help." A brief reply followed from Hughes, thanking White for his letter and asking advice for "a budding writer." White answered, rather modestly: "I don't know of any suggestion right now which I could make you and I am always reluctant to offer advice." He did advise Hughes, however, to read his poems to "women's clubs and other meetings," emphasizing that "personal contact" was the best way to interest people in a book.[6] After a letter from Hughes on June 13, in which he thanked White for his suggestions and his offer to call the attention of several critics to Hughes' book, and a reply from White dated June 17, in which he again pledged to aid the sale of the book as much as he could, the letters dropped off for a few months.

On October 29, 1925, Hughes wrote his "dear friend" about his efforts to gain enough money to enroll at Lincoln University in February. He had applied to James Weldon Johnson to see "if he and The Garland Fund can't help me . . . Some big hearted person ought to be interested enough in the development of talent to grant me a loan." *The Weary Blues* had gone to press, and Hughes stated that he was at work on a "book of prose which will perhaps be called *Scarlet Flowers: The Autobiography of a Young Colored Poet.* You think that's a good title?" White's answer was delayed because of his involvement with the Sweet case in Detroit, but when it came, it had White's gentle but sarcastic touch: "I am mighty glad to know you are at work on a book of prose. Frankly, the title, *Scarlet Flowers: The Autobiography of a Young Poet* doesn't exactly hit me between the eyes. Somehow or other it sounds like Louisa M. Alcott."[7] Almost immediately Hughes responded (December 17, 1925) and agreed that the title did "sound sort of Louisa Alcottish"; then he complained of not being able to work as much as he liked on writing, since his work at a hotel wore him out.

White's paternal concern for the young writer is brought out well in his letter of December 18, 1925:

> There are lots of things I want to talk over with you, especially in regards to your forthcoming volume of verse and your prose volume. Don't worry about a title for the latter. I am not saying that *Scarlet Flowers* is not a good one—it just doesn't strike me smack between the eyes. If you like it, disregard utterly any opinion that I or any other person may have. I know the difficulties you are undergoing in writing it.

This same gentle guiding and directing is reflected in White's other letters of criticism to writers who sought his advice; he always was ready to react to the works sent to him, but he never demanded that his reactions be accepted as anything final.

The last significant correspondence between White and Hughes during this period centered on Hughes' second collection of poems, *Fine Clothes to the Jew,* published in early 1927. In the typescript of his review of *Fine Clothes to the Jew* dated February 1, 1927, and sent to Harry Hanson of the New York *World,* White took a great deal of space apologizing for the poetic limitations of the blues form that Hughes made use of so extensively in that collection. In one spot White said: "Inevitably the repetition of a single emotion in time grows monotonous and often triteness cannot be avoided because there are few changes to be rung on the blues theme." He suggested that the reader listen to Bessie or Clara Smith in order to gain familiarity with the form as it is used vocally. He was concerned, however, that Hughes might be limiting himself too much with the blues poems, as this section of the review indicates:

> Out of the blues form it is possible and probable that a more inclusive poetic form may develop but that form would not be blues as the term is now interpreted. It will be interesting to watch these changes as they are developed by Mr. Hughes . . . Mr. Hughes' friends and admirers may perhaps have some apprehension that too diligent working of this vein may cramp him or lessen the fine, flowing, ecstatic sense of rhythm which he so undoubtedly possesses.

The review then praised some of the non-blues poetry in which Hughes "evokes magnificently stirring emotions from the life of Negro porters and prostitutes and others of humble estate." After quoting "Brass Spittoons" and "Mulatto," a poem which "brought tears to the eyes of

Carl Van Vechten and Clarence Darrow," White concluded with praise for the book as "one that will grow upon its readers in its evocation of beauty and rhythm and color and warmth."

A day after this piece was composed, White wrote Hughes to thank him for an inscribed copy of *Fine Clothes to the Jew* and indicated that he had not had time to read the collection thoroughly (after he had written the review!). He did say he liked what he had read, and he called the book "even a finer piece of work than *The Weary Blues.*" The remainder of their correspondence in 1927 dealt mainly with White's efforts to place more of Hughes' poetry in various magazines.

White's real attitude toward Hughes is difficult to uncover. He undoubtedly liked Hughes' work, at least part of it, but his enthusiasm for Hughes' poetry, in this period at least, was not nearly so emphatic as was his enthusiasm for Cullen's poetry or Fisher's prose. In a letter to Frederick Allen of *Harper's* on March 4, 1927, White wrote: "There is a sharp division of opinion as to the relative merits of Cullen and Hughes as poets. A number of people whose opinion I respect think Hughes is a better poet, while the majority favor Cullen." Perhaps this was diplomatic hedging on his part, because White was probably including himself in "the majority."

If White's attitude toward Hughes is unclear, his attitude toward Claude McKay is truly confusing. By 1924, McKay had already established himself as a poet, having published three volumes of poetry. At this time, he was living in France, apparently in almost destitute circumstances. On January 26, 1924, White wrote McKay and sent him one hundred dollars that he had raised in response to a plea from McKay for funds. Tactfully, White added in his letter: "I need hardly say that, knowing your sensitiveness, I approached only those who knew you well that there be no thought of anything other than joy in coming to your aid on the part of those approached." Not quite so tactfully, White included an itemized list of the amounts contributed by each person; Arthur Spingarn contributed fifty dollars, while the others contributed one or five dollars. This listing was characteristic of White, though, as his background as accountant and insurance man always showed in his meticulous concern for exactness in money matters.

The letter McKay wrote pleading for help was addressed to Grace Campbell, who forwarded it to White. McKay's tone is typical of the frequent letters he wrote in these years: pleading, yet tinged with an air of aloof pride and an expectation of service. In asking for money to be raised "to tide me over these bad times," McKay added:

> You might show them that I have been working here—not idling and that so far it was impossible for me to sell anything to the bourgeois papers . . . My life here is unsatisfactory for a propagandist—cadging a meal off people who are not at all sympathetic to my social ideas. There is so much work to be done if I am helped a little, but no one can work against such odds single handed, especially when he is not even guaranteed a little food and a bed!

Several times during their correspondence of these years McKay was to plead his destitute condition to White. His proud begging for assistance becomes rather ironic in light of a poem he wrote in 1925 entitled "We Who Revolt" and dedicated to Max Eastman. In the second stanza of the poem McKay asserted: "Reckless we live, careless of clothes or victuals, / And all the things that tend to blind and bind." Apparently McKay suffered the revolutionist's predicament of needing physically what he tried to reject theoretically.

While much of Claude McKay's correspondence with Walter White dealt with his own problems, he often included his observations about other Negro writers and the problems of the Negro artist in America. In a letter to White dated December 4, 1924, McKay had this to say about Alain Locke:

> It's so hard to pin down what he's driving at. It's a fault of many colored writers. I don't know if it can be traced to the long years the black race has lived in America without being allowed to express its own thoughts and feeling . . . He could really do wonderful things if he would be simple and clear and not confuse the reality of Negro life in the purple patches of mysticism.

When White wrote later of the successes being made in America by young writers like Cullen and Hughes, McKay responded: "I was interested to hear of Cullen's work—I don't care for what I have seen of his poetry but Langston Hughes is a real poet strikingly original if he will only work hard and take his work seriously . . . We correspond with each other."[8]

McKay was also worried that Negro writers would take advantage of the new interest in their work and fail to meet genuine artistic standards. In the same letter in which he commented on Locke's writing, McKay had this to say about Negro artists and criticism:

> If we're going to do anything in literature and art we've got to stand good straight-out criticism and not allow ourselves to be patronized as Negro artists of America. Another thing that might hurt

> Negro writers is too much indiscriminating praise from Negro Journals. Braithwaite's "scholarly" article some time back could not have been worse. He is a nice man, appreciates literature, but as a critic of high discriminating taste he is futile and hopeless.

In the June 15, 1925, letter referred to earlier he expressed his happiness in the "aroused interest" in Negro art and added his hope that the artists would "discipline themselves and do work that will hold ground besides the very highest white standard. Nothing less will help Negro art forward. . . ." The reason for his push for the highest artistic standards is given in his apprehension concerning the stability of this new interest: ". . . a boom is a splendid thing but if the works are not up to the standard people turn aside from them after the novelty has worn off." His fears appear to have been well founded, since after the Renaissance, the fickle white reading public seemed to forget most of those artistic productions until only recently.

At this same time McKay was at work on his first novel, *Home to Harlem,* getting it into final shape and trying to line up a publisher. White and others in the States were doing their best in attempting to place the manuscript. Among other things White sent McKay a city map of New York and two hymnals—one A. M. E. and one from a "colored Baptist church"—which McKay needed for some details in his novel. McKay did not particularly want to submit his novel to Harcourt, Brace & Company, who published *Harlem Shadows* for him; his letters to White never mention why. White, meanwhile, tried to convince McKay to submit his work to a new firm, Viking Press, for reasons he elaborated in a letter written July 8, 1925: "The advantage of a firm just starting out is that they of necessity, for reasons of finance and of reputation, must push every book on their list," whereas older firms might not be able to afford to push every work as hard. Finally, however, after Knopf refused the manuscript because "the element of prudery or candid references appear too strong for publication,"[9] the novel was accepted for publication by Harper and Brothers.

Between the initial search for a publisher and the final acceptance McKay went through considerable anguish regarding his novel. For one thing,, McKay had heard "by a roundabout way" that Carl Van Vechten was planning a novel "on Harlem Negro life" and he was afraid Van Vechten's work would hurt the sales of his own book, since Van Vechten was "a white man and a popular novelist known to all the gaudy crop of bleating reviewers. . . ."[10] In the same letter he continued his objection to white critics and their reactions to Negro art:

> If people who can stomach Mrs. Warren's profession . . . can't stand *Color Scheme* [original title for *Home to Harlem?*] it would only demonstrate that the white literate cannot stand for a black author laughing at white folks foibles. That would be at the bottom of any objection to the theme of the book. I hope that such a supposition has no validity that, benighted as America is with all its Great White Ways, there is yet a silver stream of intelligence that remains unpolluted.

McKay's contempt for the fear of rejection by white critics that hampered many "minority" writers was made clear in a letter to White on September 7, 1925, in which he declared: "We are made impotent by the fears and misgivings of minorities and by the harsh judgment of majority opinion, and thus we become emasculated in ideas and the expression of them."

McKay's rejection of "majority opinion" did not, however, prevent his trying to make his novel as "presentable" as possible. On August 4, 1925, he wrote:

> I'm all willing to take out anything illegal that might involve me with the Laws of the Land. In reality I tried hard to avoid anything of that sort but something *may* have slipped up . . . I should not like harmless innuendoes and jokes that flavor the narrative to be touched at all.

Later, on October 15, he wrote to White that Max Eastman, who had been helping him survive in France, had read the novel and had "put his finger (from his long experience as an editor) on every point that he thought objectionable and impossible for the American market—and there were many!" Unfortunately, McKay never mentioned any specific changes he might have made in the novel, so there is no way to know, through this correspondence, how much or how little he sacrificed in order to get his novel published.

In the course of his correspondence with White, McKay espoused many of his views on the nature and function of art; one comment he made in a letter written September 7, 1925, concerned art as propaganda and has particular significance to the idea of a Black aesthetic today:

> Every work of art is in reality personal propaganda. It is the way in which the artist sees life and wants to present it but there is a vast chasm between the artist's personal expression of himself and his making himself the instrument of a group or a body of opinion. The first is art the last is

> prostitution and that is the sole difference between art and propaganda whether the field be that of conservative or radical politics, national or racial questions!

Whatever the new Black critics might think of McKay's work, and it *was* extremely revolutionary in its time and still bears the mark of a rigid individualist who was against the system, they will undoubtedly object to his assessment of art and propaganda. For all his outward protestations, McKay was writing from a personal, not a class position.

There was a considerable gap in the correspondence between McKay and White after late 1925, although White kept busy trying to place some of McKay's poems in spite of his feeling, as expressed to Langston Hughes, that the poems were "uniformly third rate."[11] Included in these poems was one then titled "Desolate," which was later changed to "The Desolate City" and published in 1953 in McKay's *Selected Poems.* This poem, and another titled "The Shadow-Ring," were both labeled "In Hospital" and dated 1923; they both reflect his depression as he was recovering from a paralytic stroke, and, as might be expected, both project a gloomy, deathly aura. Also included in these poems was "We Who Revolt," referred to earlier, and two poems that dealt with subjects McKay had treated before. "America in Retrospect" is a sonnet reminiscent of his "America," and "My House" seems to be a logical reversal of "The White House," as this poem deals with the "particular tint" that paints the poet's house; both poems were dated 1925. Judging from White's comment to Hughes quoted above, one might assume that White thought McKay a somewhat lesser talent than his favorite, Countee Cullen, but, again, White tirelessly gave McKay all the help he could.

That Walter White held Countee Cullen in the highest esteem is evident in all phases of their correspondence. In April of 1924, White, attempting to get Cullen's poetry published, sought the help of some of his friends. In a letter to Carl Van Doren on April 26, White indicated that he was sending some of Cullen's poems for his assessment; he also indicated that he had talked to Horace Liveright about publishing Cullen's poetry in a volume, adding: "Two things cause me to go slow: one is that I don't know enough about poetry, and the other is, I am so fond of much that Cullen has done that my judgement, such as it is, is biased in his favor." Later, when Cullen was negotiating with Harper and Brothers about *Color,* White wrote to Eugene Saxton concerning Cullen:

> I for one have great admiration for him not only because of the excellent technique of his poetry but because he to me seems to have that indefinable thing which stamps him as a poet of very considerable gifts.[12]

And in a typescript copy of a Pittsburgh *Courier* column (undated), White had nothing but praise for Cullen's *Color.* In the concluding lines of the column he stated: "Perhaps you have gained the impression that I am enthusiastic about Countee Cullen's verse. If so, you are wholly right. His achievements must inevitably be of magnificent encouragement to other Negro poets, who, dismissing racial barriers, or using those barriers as foot stools, has sung and made the world listen to those songs."

White's efforts to get Cullen published in book form began with a rather secretive note from White to Cullen on April 14, 1924: "I want to have a talk with you soon; I want to look over some of your poetry that you like best. Something worth while may come of it because of a statement made to me last night by a certain publisher." The "certain publisher" turned out to be Horace Liveright, and on April 25, White wrote Liveright and said that about thirty of Cullen's poems seemed "to be well worth publication." He added that Cullen had "a considerable reputation for a young man and many friends who would help push the book." The same day he wrote to Cullen, enclosing a copy of his letter to Liveright and advising Cullen: "Remember my word of caution. You are to know nothing of my conversation with Mr. Liveright. In talking with him, be sublimely innocent of my connection with it in any way." Liveright responded to White on May 2 that his poetry readers liked Cullen's work but felt that he did not have enough poems of merit for a collection. White answered that he was in agreement with Liveright, and on May 3 he wrote Cullen: "While you have done some poems which are of the first rank, I do not feel that you have enough to your credit as yet to run risk of being labeled as anything less than a poet of the first class." Disappointed but undaunted, Cullen responded on May 6: "I am not in the least discouraged . . . as better poets have waited far longer for publication."

White was always on the alert to make people aware of Cullen, as is evident in two letters written months apart. On December 23, 1924, White wrote to a Mrs. Mary A. Trafton who had given a talk on Negro writers and had omitted Cullen:

> Countee Cullen who had poems in the November *American Mercury, Harpers,* and *The Bookman* and in the December *Harpers,* is beyond doubt one of

the most talented of the Negro poets. Though he has not as yet published anything in book form, Negro poetry could hardly be considered adequately with his name omitted.

Several months later White responded to an inquiry from Miss Ruth W. Thompson of the Mentor Personal Service Department concerning information about Negro poets. After referring Miss Thompson to James Weldon Johnson's *The Book of American Negro Poetry* as a good source, White added: "There are two Negro poets of real merit who have come to the fore since Mr. Johnson's book was published. One of these is Countee Cullen whose first volume, *Color,* will be published next month by Harper . . . The other poet is Langston Hughes. . . ."[13] While, as this last reference shows, White was ever ready to keep the young writers' names in peoples' minds, he clearly illustrated a fondness for Cullen that was not present in his comments on the other writers.

In a letter to Cullen dated January 4, 1926, White made a rather cynical comment on some of the people to whom he was making his pitch for Cullen:

> I spoke at The Plaza last Wednesday and devoted a good deal of time to you, reading a number of your poems. A number of the smug, fur-coated, well-fed ladies wrote down the title. I hope they spend some of their money for copies.

Even though White was most ingratiating in all his correspondence and was ever the Southern gentleman in direct correspondence, his cynical attitude toward many of the people with whom he had contact often crept through in letters like this one, addressed to third parties.

Cullen was, of course, very grateful for all the aid White was giving him. After *Color* was published, White pushed it hard, in press releases through the Association's network and at the NAACP's national convention. On June 20, 1925, Cullen wrote White: "I think Harper and Bros. or I ought to pay you. If the book has any sale at all, much of it will surely be due to the fine spirit of cooperation you have shown in the matter." In the same month White sent some of Cullen's poems to Irita Van Doren of the *Tribune*'s book section; she chose to publish three of the poems: "Black Magdalens," "More than a Fool's Song," and "Atlantic City Waiter." In gratitude Cullen wrote White July 20, 1925, thanking him for his "kind service and all you are doing for me." He continued: "Irita Van Doren wrote me telling me she had taken three poems, all to be published sometime this summer. She was quite sure, as she was due to be, that she had you to thank for getting them."

When *Color* was published in the fall of 1925, White went busily to work, bringing it to the attention of as many people as he could. He wrote Carl Sandburg, then at the Chicago *Daily News:*

> You probably know of the work of Countee Cullen, the young poet who has achieved such unusual fame during the past two or three years . . . I am very much interested in him and his progress and I am taking the liberty of sending you a copy of his book which I hope you will enjoy reading. If you should like it, I wish that you would use whatever efforts you may choose to help secure for Mr. Cullen's first book the recognition I feel it so richly merits.

He also supplied Harper and Brothers with an extensive list of the names of people he felt could "do the book some good," for which he was thanked by Ruth Raphael on December 31, 1925: "I am gratified to tell you that *Color* is enjoying a very good sale . . . the book is in demand from coast to coast . . . it is selling very much better than the average book of poetry. We are certainly grateful to you for your splendid help."

White's association with Cullen was more than just that of writer and agent, though. In January of 1926 White wrote an introduction for a Negro poetry issue of *Palms,* a Mexican literary publication, which Cullen was editing. The idea for Cullen's anthology of Negro verse, *Caroling Dusk,* undoubtedly sprang from this project, and in June of 1927, White offered some suggestions on that collection. Cullen had given White the manuscript for the book, and White, in a letter dated June 14, gave Cullen his reactions to the poems in the proposed anthology, which White said could "stand a good deal of pruning." Two of White's favorite Cullen poems, "For a Lady I Know," and "Incident" were not included, and White also missed Hughes' "Mulatto" and "Brass Spittoons." In the rather lengthy letter, White went through each of the poets included in the anthology and gave his views of their works. His final comment expressed a concern for the possible abuse of the current popularity being enjoyed by Negro writers:

> You have material for a magnificent anthology if it is thoroughly weeded. A hostile critic could take three or four poems of the present collection and print them as samples and damn the book. Negro poetry has reached the stage where a poem has no distinction simply because it has been written by a Negro.

This kind of frank criticism was typical of the reaction White offered, not only to Cullen, but to all who wrote seeking his advice.

White's true affection and admiration for Cullen's work is probably best summarized in the "blurb" White wrote for Harpers to use in promoting *Color:*

> Countee Cullen belongs to that company of lyricists of which A. E. Housman and Edna St. Vincent Millay are the bright stars. He is no mere versifier, no simple matcher of words that rhyme without meaning or feeling, no trite measurer of lines. His verse has an emotional depth which is extraordinary in one of Mr. Cullen's years, he makes his words hum and sing with none of the triteness and verbosity usual in a beginner. He etches his emotions and pictures with acid clearness, while underneath lies a genuine and sympathetic understanding of the joys and sorrows of life itself. All this he does with a magnificent imagery that seldom permits anything he writes to savor of the commonplace. Countee Cullen is a real poet.[14]

Walter White did not limit his aid to these emerging literary powers of the Harlem Renaissance. Through just this brief period of three years, he was helping numbers of people with his advice, criticism, and influence in the publishing world. He frequently corresponded with Georgia Douglas Johnson, Nella Larsen Imes, Anne Spencer, and others; and, his correspondence was certainly not limited to Black writers. Over the years he developed a friendship with Sinclair Lewis, who helped White with criticism of ***The Fire in the Flint*** and ***Flight.*** Although James Weldon Johnson certainly needed no outside help in his work, White wrote the Pulitzer Prize Committee on July 11, 1927, recommending Johnson's *God's Trombones* for the Pulitzer Prize in poetry, "to call attention to this valuable source of beauty, strength and rythmic [*sic*] power which has sprung from American soil."

Even when White was in the midst of writing his own two novels and a play based on ***The Fire in the Flint*** (which, incidently, was rather a disappointment to White and everyone else), he found time in his already exhausting schedule to help others. In his autobiography White mentioned almost nothing of this phase of his career; yet he devoted almost as much of his energy to freeing the Black man in the arts as he did to freeing him from the fear and tyranny of the lynch-mob violence racking the country in the turbulent twenties. While credit for the Harlem Renaissance is usually equally divided between the emergence of real creative freedom (and the artists to use that freedom) within the Black community and the "open-door" policy of American publishers at that time, Walter White's combined efforts as friendly critic, fatherly advisor, and concerned publicity agent certainly had their effect on the successful meeting of the two factors. He was one important catalyst who helped make the Harlem Renaissance possible.

Notes

1. The dates 1924-1927 are set as boundaries for this paper for a number of reasons: (1) 1924 is an excellent starting date for examining the beginnings of the Harlem Renaissance; (2) the Walter White correspondence files begin January, 1924; and, (3) 1927 is the year that White went to France under a Guggenheim grant and, therefore, his correspondence as available in the files is negligible.
2. Letter from Alain Locke to White, April 14, 1924.
3. March 10, 1925.
4. February 5, 1925.
5. February 6, 1925.
6. May 27, 1925.
7. December 15, 1925.
8. June 15, 1925.
9. Letter from Arthur Schomberg to White, July 24, 1925.
10. August 4, 1925.
11. December 18, 1925.
12. February 13, 1925.
13. September 28, 1925.
14. Typescript copy, undated, but probably written August 21, 1925. (Signed by White)

THOMAS HACHEY (ESSAY DATE 1998)

SOURCE: Hachey, Thomas. "Walter White and the American Negro Soldier in World War II: A Diplomatic Dilemma for Britain." In *Race and U.S. Foreign Policy from 1900 through World War II,* edited by Michael L. Krenn, pp. 333-41. New York: Garland Publishing, Inc., 1998.

In the following essay, Hachey discusses how White's travels to Europe to investigate discrimination against Blacks were viewed by the British government, revealing that the government took pains to ensure that White's findings would not embarrass them.

World War II is more frequently viewed by the Western World as a struggle which liberated millions from fascist or Nazi tyranny than as a war which hastened the emancipation of the colored races from the oppression of a Caucasian-dominated world. Since that emancipation has been an evolving consequence of the Second World War rather than one of the principal Allied objectives, the real significance of that epic conflict for the nonwhites of the world was not immediately apparent in the post-war years. In retrospect, it can be seen that the callous or indifferent attitudes of American and British authorities, both military and political, further exacerbated frictions in the multi-racial societies and in the territories governed by a white, imperialist elite. The plight which black Americans shared with colored peoples in other parts of the globe was typified by the indignities suffered by Negroes serving in the United States Army during World War II. The arrival of black American troops in England during 1942 produced problems which were invariably the result of racial bigotry on the part of white officers and soldiers, principally from the American armed forces, against blacks in their own army. British government and military authorities supplemented the overtly prejudicial policies of the United States Army with a more covert bias and attitude of condescension toward Negro American troops.[1] When, in 1943, Walter White, the vocal and militant Executive Secretary of the National Association for the Advancement of Colored People (NAACP), announced his intention to investigate the treatment accorded Negroes serving with U.S. armed forces in England, and to visit other war theatres, including British colonial territories in Africa and Asia, he caused reverberations in London which were felt in nearly every office in Whitehall.[2]

British authorities were well aware that Walter White was not to be dismissed as a person of little consequence. It was this same man who, together with A. Philip Randolph, had organized a march on Washington to protest discrimination in war industries. President Roosevelt succeeded in prevailing upon the Negro leaders to cancel their march, but only after promising to issue an executive order against job discrimination. The story of how White did indeed visit the war fronts in Europe and the Far East to investigate cases of discrimination against black soldiers, as well as foreign victims of racial prejudice, is best recalled in his 1948 autobiography ***A Man Called White.***[3] What remained unknown until recently, however, is the degree to which his travels concerned the British Government, and the confidential precautions which were undertaken, some of them in conjunction with American authorities, to insure that White's travels and investigations would not embarrass or prove troublesome to either Ally. The telegrams, dispatches and memoranda of the London war-time ministries provide that account. Documents such as these would have remained closed to public view for many more years had it not been for the reduced restrictions of the Public Records Act of 1967 and a subsequent parliamentary ruling in 1971 which authorized the opening of government archives through the year 1945.[4] These heretofore unavailable archival sources were accordingly declassified, arranged by subject headings, and made available at the London Public Record Office for the first time in 1972.[5] The value of these documents for those interested in the black American experience, apart from their significance for students of Anglo-American relations, lies in the unique perspective which they render, as the confidential observations of professionally skilled foreign observers, on Mr. White's historic journey.

Since succeeding James Weldon Johnson as Executive Secretary of the NAACP in 1929, Walter White had taken an activist role. His determination to redress the injustices suffered by black Americans was extended overseas when the military demands of the Second World War resulted in the assignment of tens of thousands of blacks to foreign posts.[6] Despite the war-time censorship in the United States, there were occasional cryptic press reports from abroad of clashes between white and Negro American soldiers as early as 1942. It was primarily for the purpose of investigating these stories that Walter White applied to the War Department for permission to travel overseas.

He was also interested in gathering material for a book on "Global War in Terms of Race-Relations," however, and it was this latter quest and his expressed desire to visit military theatres in Asia and Africa which caused the London Government rather considerable concern. When the Foreign Office received a communication from Ambassador Halifax in Washington outlining the projected travel plans as White had represented them at the Embassy, London responded with an urgent telegram reflecting His Majesty's Government's grave misgivings over specific parts of White's proposal. The Foreign Office told Halifax that it had no objection to the first part of White's itinerary, in which he planned to visit United States armed forces stationed in England. But his proposal to visit India and to meet with nationalist leaders Mohandas Gandhi and Jawaharlal Nehru was quite another matter since both men had been interned by British authorities for seditious activities which were not without racial overtones. Moreover, the Foreign Office reasoned, Wendell Willkie had been denied access to those same leaders when he had undertaken a similar world tour in 1941-42 and any special consideration for White might be viewed as discrimina-

NAACP anti-lynching poster. Walter White reported on lynching and other racial disturbances.

tory by Willkie. The Foreign Office instructed Ambassador Halifax to determine whether President Franklin Roosevelt supported White's request to visit India and remarked that Secretary for India Leopold Amery would be glad to see him but that he should be under no illusion as to the prospects of being permitted to see Gandhi.[7]

Doubtlessly preoccupied with many other urgencies of the moment, the British Embassy in Washington failed to inform London of White's departure for England on January 3, 1944. Nevile Butler of the Foreign Office received a telephone call on January 11 from an irate Robin Cruikshank of the Ministry of Information, the man whose responsibility it was to deal with foreign correspondents, demanding to know why the Embassy had not alerted anyone to White's arrival. Since Viscount Halifax had known that the NAACP leader's trip was imminent, Cruikshank thought the Embassy should be reproached for its negligence. He reminded the Foreign Office that the Colonial Office was anxious "to deflect" Mr. White from some of his intended plans, but added that Amery would be happy to receive the visitor. Cruikshank also cited Herbert Agar[8] as his source in describing Walter White's status as that of a war correspondent attached to several publications, including the *Saturday Evening Post, Time,* and *Fortune,* and whose expenses were being funded by the NAACP.[9]

Butler promised to give the matter his immediate attention and, a few days later, sent a memorandum to both the Colonial Office and the India Office in which he represented White as war correspondent for *Life* magazine "whose London bureau are said to be not too pleased at his coming." White was also described as being potentially troublesome and, as evidence of this, Butler cited an article from the *Chicago Defender,* a Negro newspaper, in which White had described the moderates in India, saying, "It appears that Negroes are not the only ones who are cursed with Uncle Toms."[10]

If White's arrival in England seemed to catch British officials by surprise, the American Embassy and military authorities in London appeared to be fully informed. In his autobiography, White conjectured that it probably had been the War Department in Washington which had sent word of his coming and had warned that he be "handled carefully." He sensed that American military officers were making elaborate efforts to prevent him from visiting certain areas and troops. But he also found Major General John C. H. Lee to be exceptionally candid and cooperative. At a dinner hosted by General Lee, the NAACP leader was introduced to the top-ranking officers of the Service of Supply. Lee conceded to White that frictions between Negro and white American soldiers were creating problems for the United States Army both in its relations with the British and in its preparations for the invasion of France. The General then assigned one of his officers to act as White's guide, and provided him with a staff car and chauffeur. He also directed commanding officers of areas and base sections to permit White to see whatever he wished under any circumstances of his choosing. White was also pleased to find at General Lee's dinner party, "my old friend Jock Lawrence, whom I had known in Hollywood, who had just been made Chief of Army Public Relations."[11]

It would seem that the Americans, at least up to this point, kept the London Government better informed on Mr. White's whereabouts and activities than did the British Embassy in Washington. On January 24, a Foreign Office official wrote a minute for that ministry's internal circulation which read in part: "Herbert Agar and Jock Lawrence (P.R.O. to Eisenhower) think they can keep WW in order, according to Lawrence—they are going to see everything he writes. . . ." It went on to state that Lawrence was in favor of letting White go to India and had told his British colleagues that White had a personal letter from FDR to Stalin. The minute concludes: "With the Negro and liberal vote so important in the [upcoming 1944 presidential] election this solicitude for WW is not surprising."[12]

At the Ministry of Information on Mallet Street in London, Robin Cruikshank was by this time in close contact with White and the latter's activities were reported to the Foreign Office in some detail. Since Cruikshank's letter of January 18, 1944 to his colleagues at the Foreign Office reveals at least as much about official British attitudes toward the visiting American journalist as it does about Walter White himself, the letter is included here in its entirety:

> Walter White, the Negro secretary of the National Association for the Advancement of the Coloured People, has gone on a fortnight's tour of U.S. Army camps in this country.
>
> He came to see me again on Saturday and told me that General Lee and his staff entertained him to dinner to discuss the position of the coloured troops, and that Mr. [John G.] Winant [United States Ambassador to Britain] had also had a long talk with him.
>
> White went on to say that he hoped to see Mr. [Anthony] Eden [Foreign Secretary], the Prime

> Minister [Winston Churchill] and Mr. [Leopold] Amery. He described several conversations he had had with Lord Halifax. He has an introduction to [British Ambassador to Moscow] Sir Stafford and Lady Cripps from Madame Chiang and the Generalissimo [Chiang Kai-shek] promised to see him in Chunking.
>
> White's two preoccupations are "the resentment of the coloured troops at race discrimination" and the position of India. He has some interesting stories to tell of the way in which Berlin and Tokio radio play on the race theme.
>
> One small but significant touch. Since he has been in London White has heard two Air Raid alerts, accompanied by a very moderate amount of gun fire, but this has impressed him quite beyond expectation. "Ah", said he, shaking his silver head, "that brings home the terrible reality of war in a way you could never know in New York." I think there is a key to the solving of the White problem here: he is an imaginative and impressionable character, and if our people can show him stirring and remarkable things when he goes about the Empire it will do much more good than arguing over his race theories. We have a hard nut to crack, but he is well worth taking a lot of trouble over, for by so doing we may be able to soften some of the preconceptions which are going to subserve that famous book on "Global War in Terms of Race". I did my best with him, and he is going to call on me again when he comes back to town.
>
> By the way I don't know if I explained that he is as white as his name, and does not appear to possess a chemical trace of coloured blood. His accent is only very faintly Southern American. (He was born in Georgia). He is a cultured and intelligent man; has great charm of manner; and it is difficult to believe that he is as inflexible in his outlook as he really is.
>
> Yours ever, R. J. Cruikshank[13]

Ambassador Halifax sent a telegram to the London Foreign Office on January 22 in reply to a telegram received by the British Embassy in Washington from that Ministry only a few days before. London had instructed its Ambassador to ascertain whether or not the United States Government would take the initiative in preventing Walter White from journeying to other war theatres following his visit in England. Halifax could only respond that the War Department, which had accredited White as a war correspondent to the British Isles only, was disinclined to accredit him to any other theatre. But the Ambassador thought that the United States Government probably would be unwilling to prevent White's journeying elsewhere because of the bad publicity it would engender amongst the black community in America. "If we want to keep him out of India or the Colonies," continued the Ambassador, "we shall have to do so ourselves by refusing him a visa." Halifax thought that it might be best to tell White that London was prepared to let him go anywhere the United States War Department agreed to accredit him. "This would place the onus of opposition on the United States authorities."[14]

Meanwhile, White undertook a tour of American military bases throughout England during which he interviewed Negro soldiers about their treatment by the United States Army. Commanding officers, White recalls, were often less than cooperative until he insisted upon the prerogatives promised him by General Lee. Thereafter, he was usually able to speak with the black troops in mess halls, or in barracks, and without the intimidating presence of their superiors. White deemed this experience to be "no credit to America." An appalling number of men put their prejudices above their patriotism and actively conspired to make the lot of the Negro soldiers as unpleasant as possible. The same tactics were also employed against white officers and enlisted men who had the temerity to oppose such mistreatment and humiliation. Furthermore, there were innumerable instances where Negro soldiers were court-martialed, convicted, and sentenced to long terms for minor offenses while white soldiers who had committed far more grievous crimes were either acquitted or punished lightly.[15] Upon returning from his investigative trip, White ensconced himself at the Cumberland Hotel on the outskirts of London and immediately began to write a report on his findings.

On January 28, Nevile Butler sent a confidential letter to Robin Cruikshank at the Ministry of Information thanking him for keeping the Foreign Office apprised of Walter White's plans and movements. Inasmuch as White, through Cruikshank, had requested an interview with Secretary for India Lepold Amery, Foreign Secretary Anthony Eden, and Prime Minister Winston Churchill, Butler advised the Ministry of Information that so far as the Prime Minister was concerned, apart from the heavy demands on his time, such an exclusive interview would inevitably create unhappiness among other American journalists who were not accorded the same courtesy. There was, however, no political objection to White's visiting with the Foreign Secretary; but such arrangements normally were made through the American Ambassador to the Court of St. James. Moreover, George Hall, the parliamentary undersecretary of state for foreign affairs, had expressed a strong interest in meeting White and the Foreign Office was equally anxious that he should see Amery at the India Office. The latter wished to impress upon White the fact that he would not be permitted to see interned Indian politicians should he choose to visit that country.[16]

Following Walter White's return to London, he conferred with Robin Cruikshank and informed the latter that he had abandoned his plan of going to Russia and India. He still hoped, however, to visit Africa and said that the United States Army had promised him transportation to that Continent. With an evident sense of relief, Cruikshank reported this latest disclosure to the Foreign Office saying: "His grandiose plans of travelling are gradually diminishing and I am hopeful that he will not cause us as many problems as one time seemed likely."[17] On the following day, February 11, Cruikshank wrote to Angus Malcolm at the Foreign Office subsequent to another visit with White. Cruikshank advised that ministry of White's intention to submit copies of his elaborate report on the treatment of Negro troops in Britain to Generals Dwight D. Eisenhower and John C. H. Lee, as well as to American Ambassador John Winant. Perhaps of greater interest to the Foreign Office was Robin Cruikshank's disclosure that one of the outstanding features of White's document would be a tribute to the kindly way in which the British public had received "the coloured soldiers." It was also noted that Walter White intended to be very condemnatory of certain United States Army officers for their complicity in or indifference toward blatant practices of racial discrimination on bases under their command in England.[18]

White left the United Kingdom for Africa on March 8, 1944, and the London Foreign Office alerted its representatives in Algiers, Casablanca, Brazzaville, Lagos, Accra, Monrovia and Dakar, of his imminent arrival in those cities. The communication read in part:

> He [White] is primarily interested in condition of United States negro troops but is also gathering material for a book on "Global War in terms of Race-Relations." Though strongly anti-imperialist he is personally cultured and agreeable and has been much impressed by things here. Please show him any courtesy that you can.[19]

In his memoirs, White described American Ambassador Winant and Generals Eisenhower and Lee as having been gravely disturbed by the report which he had submitted to them. The NAACP leader remembered Winant actually having requested material which could be used by the Joint Anglo-American Board, of which he was a member, which largely determined both civilian and military life in England. Indeed, White was aware of how various civil and military British agencies had actively and sometimes belligerently resisted, at the outset of the United States' entry into the war, the demands made by some Americans that a rigid color line, which had not existed before the war, be established. He also knew that various and inexorable pressures had changed this initial attitude considerably, especially with respect to contacts between British civilians and Negro American soldiers.[20] Recently released secret British War Cabinet minutes confirm White's suspicions beyond any shadow of a doubt and show him to have been remarkably accurate in his assessment of Anglo-American collusion in the treatment accorded blacks throughout the United Kingdom during World War II.[21]

With unmistakable ebullience, the London Foreign Office's Nevile Butler wrote Sir Ronald Campbell, a subordinate to Ambassador Halifax in Washington, on March 14, 1944:

> He [White] has come and gone. . . . What he did not succeed in doing was in getting interviews with the Secretary of State, the Prime Minister or (he even suggested it!) The King. It was felt here that the way in which our public have received the coloured troops has not altogether pleased our Southern friends who think it may lead to trouble for them after the war, and therefore that we might be sticking our necks out rather far if we asked the Secretary of State to see him on his own request alone. It was noted that the President's [Roosevelt's] recommendation was the mildest possible and we therefore asked that his request should be sponsored by [Ambassador] Winant in the proper way. Winant was unwilling, but White was keen. There followed a period of scuffling during which Herbert Agar tried to shoo White away from Winant; the Ambassador stood his ground and, in the end, White went away. He was rather disgruntled, we gather, with Winant and Agar but not, it seems, with us—which is a pleasant surprise. . . .[22]

Before departing England on the global trip which he so ably chronicled in his autobiography, White gave General Eisenhower, as promised, the substance of his findings, together with recommendations. The latter included the establishment of an impartial and biracial board to review the court-martial records of blacks serving in the United States Army; the assignment of white and Negro military police to work in mixed pairs in all areas where troops of both races were garrisoned adjacent to one another; and the termination of discriminatory practices which allowed for "white only" units, such as the medical corps, air and naval units, and the relegating of Negro troops to service and supply branches rather than combat units from which they were totally excluded.[23]

Perhaps there is no real way to determine the measure of influence, if any, which Walter White had upon the plight of colored peoples in other lands either during or following the Second World War. But his achievements in the fight which he waged on behalf of the rights and dignity of black Americans constitute an enduring legacy of considerable significance. Although bigotry and prejudice still contribute occasionally to racial disharmony in the American armed forces, Walter White and the NAACP can claim much of the credit for President Truman's decision to desegregate all branches of the United States military in 1948 which, at the very least, terminated once and for all the disgraceful practice of officially sanctioned discrimination.

Notes

1. See Thomas E. Hachey, "Jim Crow with a British Accent: Attitudes of London Government Officials Toward American Negro Soldiers in England During World War II," *The Journal of Negro History,* XLIX (January, 1974), 65-77.
2. In addition to the telegrams, dispatches and letters, to and from the London Foreign Office, regarding Walter White and his intention to tour different parts of Europe, Africa and Asia, there exist a substantial number of Foreign Office minutes, as well as communications to and from other ministries in the British Government which provide still further evidence [not cited herein] of the importance which English officials attached to the journey of the NAACP leader. See the entire volume in F.O. 371/38609.
3. Walter White, *A Man Called White* (New York, 1948). Aside from his autobiography, White's other publications include: *Fire in the Flint* (New York, 1924); *Flight* (New York, 1926); *Rope and Faggot* (New York, 1929); *Rising Wind* (New York, 1945), and a book which was published posthumously entitled *How Far the Promised Land* (New York, 1955).
4. Access to British Government archives is presently governed by the Public Records Act of 1967, which introduced from January 1, 1968 a "thirty year rule," opening the records then to the end of 1937 and making provision thereafter for the annual advancement of the open date on January 1 of each year. A few papers are closed for fifty years by virtue of the Lord Chancellor's instruments under Section 5 (i) of the 1958 Public Records Act.
5. The suspension of the 1967 Public Records Act was intended to assist scholars engaged in studies which extend over the entire period of World War II. Other than this specific exception, so generously authorized by Parliament, the "thirty year rule" is still in force.
6. An informative contemporary study of American Negroes in the military is L. D. Reddick, "The Negro Policy of the American Army," *Journal of Negro History,* XXXIV (January, 1949), 9-29.
7. *Telegram* No. 8207, London Foreign Office to the British Embassy, 27 November, 1943. F.O. 371/38609.
8. After having edited the *Louisville Courier-Journal* from 1940 to 1942, Herbert Agar, the distinguished author, editor and publisher had settled in England where he was a frequent consultant to both the American Embassy and the British Foreign Office.
9. Foreign Office *Minute,* January 11, 1944. F.O. 371/38609.
10. Foreign Office *Memorandum,* January 14, 1944. F.O. 371/38609.
11. White, *A Man Called White,* pp. 242-43.
12. Foreign Office *Minute,* January 42, 1944. F.O. 371/38609.
13. *Letter,* Robin Cruikshank, Ministry of Information, to Nevile Butler, Foreign Office, January 18, 1944. F.O. 371/38609.
14. *Telegram* No. 318, British Embassy, Washington, to the London Foreign Office, January 22, 1944. F.O. 371/38609.
15. White, *A Man Called White,* pp. 243-45.
16. *Letter,* Nevile Butler, Foreign Office, to Robin Cruikshank, Ministry of Information, January 28, 1944. F.O. 371/38609.
17. *Letter,* Robin Cruikshank, Ministry of Information, to Nevile Butler, Foreign Office, February 10, 1944. F.O. 371/38609.
18. *Letter,* Robin Cruikshank, Ministry of Information, to Angus Malcom, Foreign Office, February 11, 1944. F.O. 371/38609.
19. *Telegram* No. 235, London Foreign Office to British Ambassador, Algiers (repeated to Casablanca, Brazzaville, Monrovia, and Dakar), March 8, 1944. F.O. 371/38609.
20. White, *A Man Called White,* p. 247.
21. See, for example, *Memorandum* by the Lord Privy Seal on United States Troops in the United Kingdom to the War Cabinet, 17 October 1942. Cab. 66/30.
22. *Letter,* Nevile Butler, Foreign Office, to Sir Ronald Campbell, British Embassy, Washington, March 14, 1944. F.O. 371/38609.
23. White, *A Man Called White,* pp. 247-48.

TITLE COMMENTARY

The Fire in the Flint

KENNETH R. JANKEN (ESSAY DATE 1996)

SOURCE: Janken, Kenneth R. "Civil Rights and Socializing in the Harlem Renaissance: Walter White and the Fictionalization of the 'New Negro' in Georgia." *Georgia Historical Quarterly* 80, no. 4 (winter 1996): 817-34.

In the following essay, Janken shows how White drew upon his extensive knowledge of southern Georgia to write The Fire in the Flint, *claiming that his depictions of places and events is authentic.*

"I wrote feverishly and incessantly for twelve days and parts of twelve nights, stopping only when complete fatigue made it physically and mentally impossible to write another word," described Walter White of the creative process that resulted in the manuscript of ***The Fire in the Flint,*** his first novel about race relations, racial violence, and a nascent black consciousness in south Georgia. The book completed, he "dropped on a near-by couch" at "Riverbank," Mary White Ovington's cottage where it was born, and slept for hours.[1] Refreshed, the NAACP assistant secretary and Harlem Renaissance socialite set off with the breathlessness that characterized his prose (and everything he did) to elbow his way onto the literary palisades. This famous son of Atlanta succeeded in several respects. ***The Fire in the Flint*** created quite a stir in the months before and after its appearance in 1924; its portrayal of white depravity and the ineffectuality of the few well-meaning southern whites was too strong for the George H. Doran Company, which rejected it before Knopf issued it. Further, the book's profile was raised considerably by the calumny heaped upon it by substantial portions of the southern press. But despite these rejections—perhaps even because of them—his efforts paid off as White earned the respect, friendship, and assistance of many literary elites and helped to publicize both the New Negro movement and the fight for civil rights.

The Fire in the Flint's straightforward plot moves at an energetic clip. Kenneth Harper, an Atlanta University graduate, talented northern-trained physician, and World War I veteran, returns from service in France to his home in fictional Central City in real south Georgia, to start up a medical practice. He is determined to establish himself in short order not simply as a competent Negro doctor but as a surgeon and owner of a state-of-the-art clinic to serve the entire region of the state. Although he has lived in the relative freedom of the North and Europe (the latter especially was the stuff of contemporary mythology), Harper is determined not to buck Jim Crow. When his younger brother Bob, who withdrew from Atlanta University and returned to Central City to shoulder family obligations after their father's death, despairs of the increasingly antagonistic postwar race relations, Kenneth denies there are significant obstacles. "I'm going to solve my own problem, do as much good as I can, make as much money as I can! If every Negro in America did the same thing, there wouldn't be any 'race problem.'"[2] He would be like his father, a small construction contractor, who had accumulated enough wealth to provide for his family's comfortable existence. "Hope you ain't got none of them No'then ideas 'bout social equality while you was up there," one of the town's most prominent whites told Kenneth. "Jus' do like your daddy did, and you'll do a lot to keep the white folks' friendship" (p. 53). Kenneth escaped the pressures of caste by reading, and although W. E. B. Du Bois was the author he most admired, he hewed most closely to the Booker Washington nostrum that racism was something to be lived down, not talked down (p. 46).

Despite his best efforts, Kenneth is drawn inexorably into the web of racial conflict. When his sister Mamie is subjected to the importuning of some young rednecks on the town's main street, Bob is incensed and wants to act, but Kenneth demurs, preferring to speak in confidence with Roy Ewing, a representative of the "better class of whites." Ewing, while sympathetic to Mamie's plight, refuses to try to reign in the white boys, fearing that his actions would be detrimental to his business. Thus begins the erosion of Kenneth's faith in accommodationism. It is further eroded in a series of instances in which Kenneth provokes the whites' hostility by correctly diagnosing patients and countermanding treatment prescribed by Central City's white Dr. Bennett.

White belligerence toward Kenneth increases as he reluctantly champions the cause of the area's black sharecroppers. The previous incidents had opened Kenneth's mind to the futility of accommodationism. But it was his awkward love for Jane Phillips, a handsome woman possessed of refinement, intelligence, and a keen racial consciousness that moved him to put his oratorical and organizational skills behind the formation of the National Negro Farmers' Co-Operative and Protective League and help sharecroppers escape the crop-lien system. His involvement in this organization leads the Ku Klux Klan to watch him closely and causes most of the good will he had inherited from his father to vanish, while Kenneth tries—once again abortively—to enlist the aid of white liberals.

The last shred of Kenneth's faith in the better class of whites vaporizes when his sister Mamie is raped by the same gang of whites. Brother Bob grabs a pistol, storms up Lee Street, kills two of the offending whites, escapes out of town, but then kills himself when capture by the pursuing mob is imminent. Cheated out of torturing and lynching him, the vigilantes nevertheless riddle Bob's corpse with bullets, drag him back to town, and set him afire next to the Confederate memorial; children dash into the dying embers to retrieve charred bones to display on their mantles.

In the final chapters, Kenneth's rage bursts like a ruptured appendix. "If by raising one finger I could save the whole white race from destruction," he told a white woman who pleaded with him to save her daughter's life, "and by not raising it could send them all straight down to hell, I'd die before I raised it! You've murdered my brother, my sister's body, my mother's mind, and my very soul!" (p. 279) Still, he relents and agrees to treat the girl at her home. On the way home from this midnight emergency, the Klan, which had been planning to attack Kenneth, seized the surprise opportunity of his leaving a white woman's house at night and lynches him, but not before he kept his oath that "before I go I'm going to take a few along with me!" (p. 295)

Walter White drew upon an extensive knowledge of south Georgia to produce this novel: "I was born in the South at Atlanta and lived there until six years ago," he wrote to Will W. Alexander of the genesis of the book. "During my college work at Atlanta University and after graduation I spent considerable time in small Georgia towns as an agent of the Standard Life Insurance Company."[3] When critics assailed the truthfulness of the portrait of the South, White insisted he was not only accurate but understated. Among his significant early duties with the NAACP was the investigation of racial violence. By his own reckoning in late 1923, White had probed eight lynchings, including, at great personal risk, the one in Elaine, Arkansas in 1919. Kenneth Harper was based upon his close friend and personal physician, Dr. Louis T. Wright, who became treasurer of the Atlanta branch of the NAACP at the same time that White became its secretary. (In 1935, Wright, who fled the South for New York City in 1919, became the national chairman of the association, a position he occupied until his death in 1952.)[4]

In large, ***The Fire in the Flint*** is accurate. Central City appears to be a composite picture of small-town southwest Georgia, as Lee Formwalt has recently described it in the *The New Georgia Guide.*[5] Yet in his rendering of Central City, White likely drew literary inspiration from W. E. B. Du Bois's observations of Albany. Central City's pace of life, "Drowsy, indolent during the first six days of the week" (p. 32)—and its strict segregation of comparably debased white mill hands of "Factoryville" and residents of "Darktown" resemble nothing so much as W. E. B. Du Bois's commentary in *The Souls of Black Folk:* "Albany is to-day a wide-streeted, placid, Southern town, . . . whites usually to the north, and blacks to the south. Six days in the week the town looks decidedly too small for itself, and takes frequent and prolonged naps. But on Saturday suddenly the whole county disgorges itself upon the place, and a perfect flood of black peasantry pours through the streets."[6] Likewise, the sharecroppers' conditions, which White adumbrated as he tracked Kenneth Harper's racial awakening, recall Du Bois's chronicle of the misfortunes and resilience of blacks in Dougherty County.[7]

Besides the local color, the major incidents that lead to Bob's immolation and Kenneth's shooting ring authentic. Central City's volatile racial climate, to which Kenneth returned, had been ratcheted up several notches by the return of black soldiers from World War I. In the North and in the urban South, racial friction was compounded by competition for jobs and housing resulting in periodic bursts of mob violence, as in the Red Summer of 1919. In south Georgia, as in other parts of the cotton South, where the economy was founded upon a dependent labor force, whites feared, rightly, that black veterans would take seriously the propaganda that the war was fought for democracy. Throughout ***The Fire in the Flint*** Kenneth Harper's tormenters grumble about "those niggers who went over to France" or had lived in the North (p. 53). Among the most prominent targets for white attempts to prevent agitation for equality were blacks in uniform. Many African Americans, infused with the spirit of the New Negro, engaged in retaliatory violence. But Kenneth Harper's desire to dodge trouble at all costs was not uncommon; while he was extreme in his efforts to hold on to his Panglossian views, others, such as the Kentucky educator Rufus Atwood, simply jettisoned both the uniform and any semblance of New Negro assertiveness.[8]

White tapped into a significant source of racial animus when he explored white resentment over the Harpers' relative affluence that stoked the drive to lynch Bob and Kenneth. Their father, Joe Harper, had started out as a carpenter and slowly expanded his work to the point where he was a prosperous builder, having constructed most of the two-story buildings in Central City's business district. He prospered because he was honest and efficient, because he kept scrupulous books, and, most likely, because he had whites of some standing vouch for him. As soon as he died, however, the town's leading businessmen set to cheating his estate out of thousands of dollars. "Just yesterday," Bob complained to Kenneth, "Old Man Myggat down to the bank got mad and told me I was an 'impudent young nigger that needed to be taught my place' because I called his hand on a note he claimed papa owed the bank. He knew I knew he was lying, and that's what made him so mad. They're already saying I'm not a 'good nigger' like papa was" (pp. 25-26).

That thriving blacks were special targets of mob violence was a fact known to Walter White personally. His family occupied one of the more comfortable homes in black Atlanta, on the perimeter of a white neighborhood. During the 1906 Atlanta riot, a large mob formed and marched down Houston Street, stopping in front of his house; one of the leaders yelled, "Let's burn him out—he's got too nice a house for a nigger to live in!"[9] As an adult, his years spent investigating lynching for the NAACP taught him that his experience was not unique. In his classic study, ***Rope and Faggot,*** White demonstrated that increases in African-American wealth and concomitant growth in economic independence were significant factors that stoked white rage.[10] Neil McMillen, in his exhaustive study of Jim Crow in Mississippi, reinforces this when he points out that blacks who enjoyed material comfort were frequent targets of one or another variety of coercion. *Goin'back to T-town,* the documentary film about Tulsa, Oklahoma's black community, shows that a salient cause of the racial violence there in 1921 that destroyed more than a million dollars in property was white resentment of black prosperity.[11]

White also got right one of the more controversial scenes in ***The Fire in the Flint,*** the rape of Mamie Harper, who was assaulted just past downtown, right after she exited the dry goods store. Claude McKay doubted this scene. "You make your rape take place right in the heart of a pretty populous city. . . . If you had sent her out walking on the Central City country road, brooding over her unhappy state in Georgia, have her wandering home through a field and then the attack—I think your case would have been far more effective. For if these things happen as you must and as I am bound to believe the world should see them in the true light—not in a melodramatic fashion."[12]

In a letter to McKay, White wrote that he had been engaged in a spirited debate with Carl Van Vechten and Sinclair Lewis on just this point. White conceded McKay's argument to a point. A sexual assault in a very public area would be unlikely, he wrote, if it was carried out by one man. "I quite agree that except a woman is drugged or beaten into unconsciousness, I don't believe that rape by one man is possible." But with more than one perpetrator, it is quite conceivable. Mamie's ordeal was not melodrama, but an accurate reflection of reality. Yet in an important sense McKay's reservations about the location of the rape was beside the point. White's statement that assaults on African-American women were "so common, yet so carefully concealed" indicates his understanding that rape was not primarily a crime of opportunity but of power, that white rapists would violate black women wherever they wanted so long as they could assure themselves that there would be no reprisal.[13]

It was this last point, not the number of rapists or the site, that was the principal reason for White including Mamie's rape. In White's opinion, an attack on a black woman was one of the few things that would propel a black man to use retaliatory force; in ***The Fire in the Flint,*** Bob reacts to Mamie's distress by killing two of the perpetrators. It was a situation that recalled the rape of John Jones's little sister in Du Bois's "Of the Coming of John."[14] How common this response was is not known; while lynchings of blacks for supposed assaults on white women were publicized in banner headlines, stories of black men defending black women against whites were routinely suppressed. Walter White believed this to be not unusual, and he recorded cases of this in ***Rope and Faggot.*** Likewise, John Dittmer, in his study of African Americans in Progressive-era Georgia, documented incidents of this type.[15]

While Claude McKay doubted the authenticity of the rape scene, several well-meaning whites questioned whether ***The Fire in the Flint*** overstated its case. Here White saw an opportunity to engage whites who were sympathetic to the cause of black advancement in a dialog. A typical letter came from Jacob Billikopf, the lawyer and civic reformer. "I am familiar with life in the South and your pictures of the various characters are absolutely true to life. I am just wondering whether the activities against the negro [sic] are not a bit overdrawn. I do not want some folk to come back at you with that accusation." White firmly but politely dissented from this future NAACP board member, pointing to a legion of examples of the barbarous treatment of African Americans.[16]

More skeptical was A. S. Frissell, a founder and official of the National Urban League. Frissell had registered a complaint with Alfred Knopf. The book was "untimely," he wrote. Although he conceded that "it is possible that there are individual cases similar to it," he believed "that the statistics show that the lynchings are decreasing throughout the country. I do not think this book will help it."[17] White replied, tactfully, that Frissell was deluded about the race problem.

> If I may be permitted to say so, your letter proves exactly the tragedy of the whole race problem in America—that one like yourself who has contributed so generously of his time to work for the Negro should feel that the story is overdrawn. My dear Mr. Frissell, I could furnish you with hundreds, even thousands, of cases far more terrible than anything that is pictured in my novel and the pitiable thing to me is that with your intimate knowledge of the whole question, you should be unaware of the fact that these things are so common.[18]

White was more direct in his criticism of Frissell to an official at Knopf, calling his comments stupid and identifying him as "a man who is an ardent believer in 'sweetness and light,' believing that the only way to cure a cancer is by smearing vaseline on it." So he was delighted and surprised when Frissell recanted: "I was at a meeting of the officers of the National Urban League recently and I spoke about your book. Nearly every one there and perhaps all of them approved of it. Therefore, I think I was wrong—as I usually am—in the position I took in my note to Mr. Knopf. What more can I say?"[19]

Annie Bridgman, a leading colleague of White's older brother George in the American Missionary Association, expressed pleasure with the novel, and, perhaps because she had heard about him from George, commented that his cheerful demeanor gave her hope about the race problem. In this respect, she continued, he was not at all like W. E. B. Du Bois, whose comments about whites in an article in the *American Mercury* as "damned fools" almost caused her to stop being friendly to African Americans. Du Bois was "too apt to tell only a half truth." Accepting her congratulations on his novel, he then empathized with her discomfort at reading Du Bois's words and acknowledged that many whites thought Du Bois bitter. But, he went on, wondering "what peculiar factor there is in the makeup of the Negro which prevents him from being ten thousand times as bitter as he is."[20]

In the correspondence with Billikopf, Frissell, and Bridgman, one can see that Walter White conceived of his role as a novelist essentially as complementary to his duties in the NAACP as an investigator and reporter of racial violence. Whether he corrected, chastised or sympathized with the contradictory feelings of white progressives, White the novelist and White the NAACP functionary sought simultaneously to expose injustice and narrow the chasm between the races.

Members of the African-American elite shared this orientation and believed that ***The Fire in the Flint*** went a long way toward achieving it. Two of the leading black newspapers wanted to serialize the novel; White refused the 1925 request of the *Baltimore Afro-American,* saying that it would cut into sales but relented to the request by the *Pittsburgh Courier* the next year. W. E. B. Du Bois, reviewing the novel in *The Crisis,* called it a "stirring story and a strong bit of propaganda against the white Klansman and the black pussyfoot." Charles S. Johnson, writing in the Urban League's *Opportunity,* compared it favorably with *Uncle Tom's Cabin* and *The Jungle.*[21]

Both Du Bois and Johnson commented on White's lack of subtlety in character development, an opinion seconded by friendly white writers. Joel Spingarn, the NAACP treasurer, patron of the Harlem Renaissance, and distinguished literary critic, thought ***The Fire in the Flint*** an "overwhelming story." But the novel's characters were wooden: "They simply do not live; and incident without character is melodrama, not drama."[22] Sinclair Lewis praised the book in a publicity blurb, predicting that it and E. M. Forster's *A Passage to India* "will prove much the most important books of this autumn." Privately, however, he offered White a passel of advice, mainly on character development. (Lewis's reading of White's book began a long friendship between the two men.)[23] Eugene Saxton and John Farrar, both fixtures at Doran Company, liked the novel enough to publish it; they were overruled by George Doran, who balked at issuing a book that might hurt company sales in the South. H. G. Wells was the least ambivalent; he declined to endorse the novel, saying that "it is a good second rate novel."[24] To these critiques, White was uncharacteristically modest. He acknowledged freely and with only a trace of defensiveness his rookie errors.

Critical press reviews were another matter, and some southern papers and writers, though not all, protested ***The Fire in the Flint***'s appearance—loudly. The *Savannah Press* printed an editorial that branded the novel "unfair, unjust, and thoroughly reprehensible." A. S. Bernd, who self-consciously styled himself after H. L. Mencken and whose iconoclastic column appeared under the pseudonym Coleman Hill in the *Macon Tele-*

graph, reported favorably on White's novel. But the paper was besieged with letters from irate readers, and subscribers stopped taking it. When Lawrence Stallings, a Macon native who expatriated himself to New York, where he was an editor at the *New York World,* favorably reviewed the book, the *Telegraph* pilloried him, warning him not to return home and to drop the claim that he was a "home boy." (On the other hand, Josephus Daniels, Jr., the son of the publisher of the *Raleigh News & Observer,* wrote an evenhanded review.)[25]

Although White answered some of his critics, he was not terribly bothered by the bad reviews, especially those from the South. There was no such thing as a bad review; he welcomed anything that created publicity. "You need have no more fears about my getting too much praise on ***The Fire in the Flint,***" he wrote to Sinclair Lewis. "In the last few days, I have been getting editorials from southern newspapers and I am delighted at the denunciation which is coming to me."[26]

White discerned that what counted most at this early stage of the Harlem Renaissance was simply the existence of published black authors. Once blacks established a presence in the world of culture, issues of quality would become more pronounced. His sense of the way forward left him remarkably flexible and unruffled in the face of both friendly and hostile criticism, something that is apparent in the publishing history of his novel.

According to White, he showed the manuscript to John Farrar, who submitted it to George Doran Company without his knowledge; Doran initially was enthusiastic, then expressed reservations, and finally asked for significant changes. "I felt, however," he wrote to one correspondent, "that I had told the truth as I saw it and I informed them that I would destroy the manuscript before I would submit to emasculation which would kill the effectiveness of the novel. I withdrew the novel from that firm though they were willing to go ahead with their agreement." He then submitted it to Knopf, who was delighted to have it in its catalog.[27]

In fact, White was far more accommodating than he let on. He of course would not concede the authenticity of his story when Doran raised objections. But he did not refuse to budge either, and he looked for any number of ways to come to an agreement with Doran. Among his suggestions were asking Joel Spingarn and his brother Arthur, Will Alexander, and others to intercede in his behalf, suggesting publication of the book with prefatory material that would explain Doran's objections to the characterization of the white South.[28] His efforts failed to convince Doran to publish the novel and contrary to White's assertions, it was the company that finally and unambiguously rejected it.[29]

In his pleading, Walter White appeared to be something like the character in the Beatles' song "Paperback Writer." His flexibility is not hard to understand for he not only sensed that the immediate task in the Harlem Renaissance was to get black authors published, he also had an extraordinary knack for promotion, and he had a passionate desire to be included in the ranks of published novelists. He begged Doran to change its mind because

> there is no firm that I want as publishers as much as I do Doran. As I said to you, Boni and Liveright will bring out in the spring a novel by Miss Jessie Fauset [*There is Confusion* (1924)]. *The first novel in the field giving the reactions of the educated Negro is going to have a tremendous advantage. That is why I want Doran to publish the novel prior to any other of its kind.* Will you not, therefore, tell me specifically the things in the novel to which you object and also the things that you feel ought to be added?[30]

With Doran's rejection, though, White seems not to have missed a step. Within ten days he delivered the manuscript to Knopf and outlined for Blanche Knopf his plan to use the NAACP branches to promote the book, and he spent a generous amount of time constructing a distribution network within the black community.[31] When Knopf accepted ***The Fire in the Flint*** for publication in December 1923, White's stock immediately soared in the literary world. He accepted congratulations from literary leaders such as Eugene O'Neill, who wanted to turn the novel into a play, Konrad Bercovici, and Carl Van Doren, who commented shrewdly, "I am pleased to death at the news about your novel. You see not all publishers are idiots. If ***The Fire in the Flint*** sells well I shall decide that the public isn't all idiots either."[32]

With the appearance of his novel, Walter White became a fashionable conduit between the white producers of culture and their African-American counterparts, and he and his wife Gladys frequently hosted interracial gatherings for those elites who wanted to have fun. His social calendar for 1925 was especially busy. At one party, he told Roland Hayes, were Jule Bledsoe, Paul Robeson, James Weldon and Grace Johnson, Carl Van Vechten and Fania Marinoff, the caricaturist Miguel Covarrubius, and George Gershwin.

"We had a gorgeous time and the only thing lacking was your presence. The affair being exceedingly informal, I believe you would have enjoyed it."[33] He fretted that he could not pull together a party for Grace Lewis, Sinclair's wife, when she was in town: "Gladys has been trying her best to get hold of some people for the evening when Gracie is to be in town but, unfortunately, we have had no success as yet. Larry Brown [Paul Robeson's accompanist] has gone South with William Lawrence [Roland Hayes's accompanist] to gather new Spirituals and work songs; Paul Robeson is in London; Roland Hayes is in Germany, and Julius Bledsoe is hard at work preparing for his recital at Town Hall on the 17th. By the way, he is a great artist and a chap you would adore."[34] The year ended with the Whites making a sweep of New Year's Eve parties; he had to miss the costume ball hosted by Aline and Arthur Garfield Hays because he had stayed at Alfred and Blanche Knopf's until three in the morning, but mostly because "we hadn't been able to decide on costumes or to fix them up."[35]

When White wasn't entertaining at their Harlem apartment at 90 Edgecombe Avenue, he was showing whites the sites of Harlem. He took Konrad Bercovici, who wrote a favorable review of ***The Fire in the Flint,*** to see the musical *Runnin' Wild.* At first White was reluctant to initiate him in this manner, fearing that he was a thrill-seeker, but he was pleasantly surprised at Bercovici's seriousness. Later, he took Bercovici and Rebecca West, the British novelist, to Abyssinian Baptist Church and then out visiting; another time the three were joined by Heywood Broun.[36] He even piqued the interest of Oswald Garrison Villard, who, after being unable to arrange an outing, chastised White, writing, "what a miserable foreflusher, liar, and falsifier you are in the matter of your conducting me into the evil ways of Harlem night life!"[37]

White used his status to advantage in promoting ***The Fire in the Flint.*** He worked exceedingly hard adapting it for the theater—and telling (confidentially, of course) all who would listen that Paul Robeson was slated to play Kenneth Harper and Charles Gilpin would likely appear in another role. Ultimately both Eugene O'Neill and Courtney Lemon of the Theatre Guild declined to mount productions. From this distance it is unclear how real a possibility a stage version was; it may be that White's enthusiasm was part wish and part hype.

Still, he did not reserve his abundant energy for himself alone. As he grabbed his place among the literary notables and socially conscious socialites, he put his unconcealed zeal, which rivaled that of a Madison Avenue advertising executive, to work for emerging black cultural figures. He shopped manuscripts to major publishing houses and literary magazines for Langston Hughes, Countee Cullen, Nella Larsen, and Rudolph Fisher, among others. He helped boost the concert careers of Jule Bledsoe and Roland Hayes, and he took credit for steering Paul Robeson away from a career in law. He tried earnestly to sell paintings for Hale Woodruff.

Seventy years after its publication, ***The Fire in the Flint*** is still a crisp read, which, in Du Bois's review of it, "is the first business of a story." If its literary qualities were not unalloyed, it was nevertheless an unqualified success. In clearing a path for White's celebrity, it also opened up possibilities for other African Americans who wanted through cultural means to make a claim for the race's humanity and civil rights; the publication of White's novel helped to create an appetite among white audiences for such work. A brisk seller (in French, German, Japanese, Russian, as well as in English), it brought to a large number of white readers the horrors of lynching and Jim Crow codes in the South, winning converts to at least some of the views of the NAACP. And if Walter White the author went head-first through the Harlem Renaissance having a jam of a time, Walter White the assistant secretary of the NAACP approached race advancement seriously but with the same abandon.

Notes

1. Walter White, *A Man Called White* (New York, 1948), 66. See also Walter White to Claude McKay, August 15, 1924, Papers of the National Association for the Advancement of Colored People (Bethesda, Md., 1993), pt. 2, reel 7, frame 721, microfilm (hereinafter cited as NAACP/mf, followed by a part, reel, and frame number). The author would like to thank Reg Hildebrand for his comments and suggestions.

2. Walter White, *The Fire in the Flint* (1924; rpt., Athens: University of Georgia Press, Brown Thrasher Books, 1996), 28; subsequent references to this book will appear in the text.

3. White to Will W. Alexander, September 11, 1923, NAACP/mf p2 r7 f426.

4. White to Eugene Saxton, August 23, 1923, NAACP/mf, p2 r7 f406; Rayford W. Logan, "Wright, Louis Tompkins," in *Dictionary of American Negro Biography* (New York, 1982).

5. Lee W. Formwalt, "Southwest Georgia: A Garden of Irony and Diversity," *The New Georgia Guide* (Athens, Ga., 1996), 497-536, esp. 506-508.

6. W. E. B. Du Bois, *The Souls of Black Folk,* in Eric J. Sundquist, ed., *The Oxford W. E. B. Du Bois Reader* (New York, 1996), 158.

7. *Ibid.,* chaps. 7-8. For a photographic record of Du Bois's journey, see Lee W. Formwalt, "'Corner-Stone of the Cotton Kingdom': W. E. B. Du Bois's 1898 View of Dougherty County," *Georgia Historical Quarterly* 71 (Winter 1987): 693-700.

8. John Dittmer, *Black Georgia in the Progressive Era, 1900-1920* (Urbana, Ill., 1977), 203-204; Gerald L. Smith, *A Black Educator in the Segregated South: Kentucky's Rufus B. Atwood* (Lexington, Ky., 1994), 25.

9. White to William Aspinwall Bradley, February 2, 1927, NAACP/mf p2 r10 f559; see also White, *A Man Called White,* 11.

10. Walter White, *Rope and Faggot: A Biography of Judge Lynch* (1929; rpt., New York, 1969), 102-105.

11. Neil R. McMillen, *Dark Journey: Black Mississippians in the Age of Jim Crow* (Urbana, Ill., 1990), 192-93; W. Fitzhugh Brundage, *Lynching in the New South: Georgia and Virginia, 1880-1930* (Urbana, Ill., 1993), 108-120; *Goin' back to T-town* (Alexandria, Va.: PBS Video, 1992). See White's report of his investigation of the 1921 Tulsa riot, Board of Directors Minutes, June 13, 1921, NAACP/mf p1 r1 f837. The danger posed to White by his investigative work was cause for worry by the NAACP board, which passed a resolution forbidding him from engaging in this type of activity.

12. McKay to White, December 15, 1924, NAACP/mf p2 r8 f355.

13. White to McKay, November 6, 1924, NAACP/mf p2 r8 f230.

14. Du Bois, *Souls of Black Folk,* in *The Oxford W. E. B. Du Bois Reader,* 219-30, esp. 228-30.

15. White, *Rope and Faggot,* 78-79; Dittmer, *Black Georgia in the Progressive Era,* 136-37.

16. Jacob Billikopf to White, September 25, 1924, NAACP/mf p2 r8 f115; White to Billikopf, September 26, 1924, NAACP/mf p2 r8 f114. White wrote a less cordial missive to the *Boston Independent,* which, in a book review, charged him with the same sin. See White to the *Boston Independent,* September 26, 1924, NAACP mf p2 r8 f113.

17. A. S. Frissell to Alfred Knopf, September 17, 1924, NAACP mf p2 r8 f80.

18. White to Frissell, September 20, 1924, *ibid.*

19. White to George S. Oppenheimer, September 20, 1924, NAACP/mf p2 r8 f87; Frissell to White, September 29, 1924, NAACP/mf p2 r8 f134. White was gracious in receiving this admission; see White to Frissell, October 6, 1924, *ibid.*

20. Annie Bridgman to White, November 5, 1924, NAACP/mf p2 r8 f237; White to Bridgman, November 8, 1924, NAACP/mf p2 r8 f236.

21. White to Blanche Knopf, March 17, 1925, NAACP/mf p2 r8 f641; Edward E. Waldron, *Walter White and the Harlem Renaissance* (Port Washington, N.Y., 1978), 76-77; W. E. B. Du Bois, review of *The Fire in the Flint, The Crisis* 29 (November 1924): 25; Charles S. Johnson, review of *The Fire in the Flint, Opportunity* 2 (November 1924): 344-45.

22. Joel E. Spingarn to White, October 2, 1923, NAACP/mf p2 r7 f442.

23. Sinclair Lewis to Spingarn, September 6, 1924, NAACP/mf p2 r8 f46; Charles F. Cooney, "Walter White and Sinclair Lewis: The History of a Literary Friendship," *Prospects* 1 (1975): 63-75.

24. H. G. Wells to White, July 3, 1924, NAACP/mf p2 r7 f560.

25. *Savannah Press* and *Macon Telegraph* quoted in "Southerners at Odds over *The Fire in the Flint,*" press release, November 28, 1924, NAACP/mf p2 r8 f299. Josephus Daniels, Jr., review of *The Fire in the Flint, Raleigh News and Observer,* October 10, 1924.

26. White to Lewis, October 15, 1924, NAACP/mf p2 r8 f168.

27. White to Robert T. Kerlin, December 26, 1923, NAACP/mf p2 r7 f463; see also White to McKay, August 15, 1924, NAACP/mf p2 r7 f721, and White, *A Man Called White,* 65-67. The publishing history of *The Fire in the Flint* with Doran can be traced in the following correspondence: White to Saxton, July 17, 1923, NAACP/mf p2 r7 f396; White to Saxton, August 23, 1923, NAACP/mf p2 r7 f406; White to Saxton, August 29, 1923, NAACP/mf p2 r7 f412; White to Saxton, August 23, 1923, NAACP/mf p2 r7 f416; Saxton to White, June 8, 1923, NAACP/mf p2 r7 f374; Saxton to White, July 23, 1923, NAACP/mf p2 r7 f401; Saxton to White, August 16, 1923, NAACP/mf p2 r7 f411; Saxton to White, August 21, 1923, NAACP/mf p2 r7 f416; Saxton to Alexander, August 30, 1923, NAACP/mf p2 r7 f426; Saxton to White, October 8, 1923, NAACP/mf p2 r7 f444. See also Walrond, *Walter White and the Harlem Renaissance,* 47-55; Charles W. Scruggs, "Alain Locke and Walter White: Their Struggle for Control of the Harlem Renaissance," *Black American Literature Forum* 14 (Fall 1980): 91-99, esp. 92; and David Levering Lewis, *When Harlem Was in Vogue* (New York, 1982), 132-36.

28. White to Arthur Spingarn, August 22, 1923, NAACP/mf p2 r7 f421; White to Joel Spingarn, August 22, 1923, NAACP/mf p2 r7 f422; Saxton to Alexander, August 30, 1923, NAACP/mf p2 r7 f426; Alexander to White, October 1, 1923, NAACP/mf p2 r7 f438; White to Saxton, August 23, 1923, NAACP/mf p2 r7 f416.

29. Saxton to White, October 8, 1923, NAACP/mf p2 r7 f444.

30. White to Saxton, August 23, 1923, NAACP/mf p2 r7 f406, emphasis added.

31. White to Alfred A. Knopf, October 17, 1923, NAACP/mf p2 r7 f454; White to Blanche Knopf, December 18, 1923, NAACP/mf p2 r7 f478; White to Blanche Knopf, April 21, 1924, NAACP/mf p2 r7 f597. For two among a large number of examples of White's distribution work, see White to E. R. Merrick, May 8, 1924, NAACP/mf p2 r7 f621, and Bishop John Hurst to White, September 5, 1924, NAACP/mf p2 r8 f20.

32. Eugene O'Neill to White, October 12, 1924, NAACP/mf p2 r8 f368; O'Neill to White, October 24, 1924, NAACP/mf pr 28 f367; Konrad Bercovici to White, February 28, 1924, NAACP/mf p2 r7 f553; Carl Van Doren to White, December 24, 1923, NAACP/mf p2 r7 f477.

33. White to Roland Hayes, January 5, 1925, NAACP/mf p2 r8 f421.

34. White to Lewis, October 8, 1925, NAACP/mf p2 r9 f234.

35. White to Aline and Arthur Garfield Hays, January 2, 1926, NAACP/mf p2 r9 f392.

36. White to Van Doren, January 26, 1924, NAACP/mf p2 r9 f478; White to Alain Locke, January 28, 1924, NAACP/mf p2 r7 f525; Bercovici to White, January 28, 1924, NAACP/mf p2 r7 f531.

37. Oswald Garrison Villard to White, October 28, 1925, NAACP/mf p2 r9 f297.

Flight

NEIL BROOKS (ESSAY DATE 1998)

SOURCE: Brooks, Neil. "We Are Not Free! Free! Free!: *Flight* and the Unmapping of American Literary Studies." *College Language Association Journal* 41, no. 4 (June 1998): 371-86.

In the following essay, Brooks examines the concept of "remapping" American culture and racial identity, or revising the treatment of race in literary studies, using the example of White and his novel Flight.

In her essay "Interrogating 'Whiteness,' Complicating 'Blackness': Remapping American Culture," Shelley Fisher Fishkin observes that "if we apply to our culture the 'one drop' rule that in the United States has long classified anyone with one drop of black blood as black, then all of American culture is black."[1] Fishkin's call to "remap American culture" in order to recognize the long neglected contributions of African-American heritage at first seems particularly appropriate and appealing since hers is the concluding essay of a volume entitled *Criticism and the Color Line: Desegregating American Literary Studies.* Yet the very deliberate act of remapping can itself rehierarchize literature or literary standards in ways which dangerously reinscribe racial coding. Fishkin quotes Henry Louis Gates's important observation that "whatever the outcome of the culture wars in the academy, the world we live in is multicultural already. Mixing and hybridity are the rule not the exception" (275); however, her remapping does not recognize her own historical horizon and does not accommodate the ways in which "hybridization and mixing" yield outcomes that often cannot be mapped because of the changes introduced by each new generation. I wish to interrogate this concept of remapping with reference to a novel of the Harlem Renaissance largely left off the established maps of American literary studies drawn by both black and white critics, which nonetheless directly addresses the issue of racial coding and is by an author who was a very prominent African-American voice in the first half of this century. Walter White's 1926 novel ***Flight*** illuminates the impossibility of mapping the American racial or cultural landscape in anything but the most provisional manner.

The above criticism of Fishkin's mapping metaphor should not impugn in any way her motivations, nor negate the importance of her call for scholars "to revise the stories we tell about who we are to reflect what we've learned about where we've been" (276). What I do question is her optimism (shared by many of the other authors in *Criticism and the Color Line*) that recent studies "mark the 1990's as a defining moment in the study of American culture" (251) and that the "new vision of our culture will be truer than any we've had before—and more interesting. It will also be a healthier base on which to build our society's future" (276). Fishkin's suggestion that we as scholars now have access to a transcendent "truth" that in posterity will be looked on any differently than that espoused by earlier generations seems self-justifying and may even reify new critical and social orthodoxies which future generations may have to battle equally hard to overcome. Awareness of how "power relations built on antiquated, discredited assumptions of racial difference sustain and perpetuate themselves" (276) does not necessarily result in the ability to objectively see beyond and to overcome those power relations. Rather, we must if anything "unmap" American culture in order to facilitate the new understandings that might bring the racial justice which current American social narratives fall so spectacularly short of achieving.

Of course, Fishkin herself gave us what is by many considered one of the most significant revisions of American literary history in her provocatively titled *Was Huck Black? Mark Twain and African-American Voices.* Before the book was even published, Fishkin's thesis had been analyzed in the *New York Times,* the *Chronicle of Higher Education, Newsweek,* and many other widely circulated periodicals giving her an audience far wider than that accorded virtually any other academic publication of the 1990s. Fishkin had the temerity to suggest that "black speakers and oral traditions played an absolutely central role in the genesis of *Huckleberry Finn.* Twain couldn't have *written* the book without them."[2] The heated response to Fishkin's assertion, as she herself anticipated, often did not address her evidence but rather her natural conclusion that American culture could not be separated into that which was clearly white and that which was not. Critics in euphemistic or cloaked tones assessed how one drop of African-American blood might alter our understanding of Twain's masterpiece. Living in an academic culture where such a claim as "Twain was influenced by African American culture" could generate such controversy, is itself compelling evidence that whiteness does continue to require "interrogating" and that blackness does demand further "complicating"; still, drawing a fixed map of our conclusions is at best premature and is probably counter to the very project of allowing new stories to enrich our understanding of our social and cultural landscape.

Walter White clearly understood the inadequacy of American narratives of race to capture many American individuals' experience of race. His 1948 autobiography, ***A Man Called White,*** provides a neat counter-balance to Fishkin's *Was Huck Black?* White confronts his provocative title in his opening sentences: "I am a Negro. My skin is white, my eyes are blue, my hair is blond. The traits of my race are nowhere visible upon me."[3] White goes on in the same vein, commenting on all those who cannot comprehend his "decision" to assert a black identity with "There is no mistake. I am a Negro. There can be no doubt" (4). This assertion of racial pride, of an apparently hidden but empowering racial identity, fuels much of White's prose until the final chapter, where he seemingly contradictorily contends that "one of the most absurd fallacies in all thought [is] the belief that there is a difference between a Negro and a White man" (364). Clearly, White is not seeking to solve the paradoxes his life presents; rather, he is foregrounding the irresolvable contradictions. He is not rending the veil that Du Bois argues enshrouds black consciousness, but asserting that the veil itself needs to be understood as part of his identity.

In his autobiography, White seems skeptical of the influence that literature can have in leading to a new racial understanding. ***Flight*** is conspicuous in being almost entirely absent from White's recollection of his achievements. His only mention of his novel is the terse dismissal "because the story it told was less melodramatic and because it was not as bitterly attacked as my first novel, its sales were small and it was soon forgotten" (80). The dismissal, of course, is not directly of the book, but of the way in which fiction that takes complex attitudes towards race is (mis)understood. The circulation of ***Flight*** was limited although it did receive a great deal of attention in the black press, garnering largely negative reviews by Wallace Thurman in *The Messenger* and Frank Horne in *Opportunity.* These reviews led to "a lively rebuttal . . . by White's protege Nella Larsen Imes,"[4] who herself would go on to write *Passing* and *Quicksand,* which also were "forgotten" but in the last twenty years have received a great critical resurgence.[5]

One could certainly argue that ***Flight,*** despite White's own comment, suffers from no lack of melodrama, since the heroine, Mimi Daquin, experiences tragedy after tragedy, humiliation after humiliation until she is eventually forced to abandon her race and "pass" as white.[6] Still, Mimi's story, like White's own, shows the inadequacy of trying to theorize the hybridization of American racial culture in any systematic way. Some may question pairing White's own life story with that of the protagonist of his second novel—she abandons her race and passes for white, and only in the final chapter does she attempt to return to black society; he, on the other hand, becomes a tireless worker for black rights, serving for many years as secretary of the National Association for the Advancement of Colored People. Yet, clearly Mimi's race consciousness was modelled on White's own. White writes in his autobiography of his experiences during the Atlanta riots of 1906:

> I am a Negro. There can be no doubt. I know the night when in terror and bitterness of soul, I discovered that I was set apart by the pigmentation of my skin (invisible though it was in my case) (4). . . . In the flickering light the mob swayed, paused, and began to flow toward us. In that instant there opened up within me a great awareness; I knew then who I was.
>
> (12)

Mimi also has her epiphany of identity during the Atlanta riots of 1906:

> To her before that dread day, race had been a relative matter, something that did exist but of which one was not conscious except when it was impressed upon one. The death before her very eyes of that unknown man shook from her all the apathy of the past. There flashed through her mind in letters that seared her brain with words, "I too am a Negro" (74). . . . Mimi dated thereafter the consciousness of being colored from September, nineteen hundred and six.[7]

Although White published the books more than twenty years apart, he gives further details and descriptions of the incident that are remarkably similar in the memoir and the novel. White, then, has created in Mimi a character who could easily have grown up to be Walter White, but instead often quietly suffers many of the indignities that White devoted his life to combatting. The fundamental difference between their stories comes at the intersection between race and gender. The novel's exploration of gender restrictions in relation to arbitrary social constructs of race renders ***Flight*** a novel which, despite its melodrama,[8] is worthy of revisiting. White's own positioning in the text is illustrative of the instability of demarcations concerning race and identity and of those concerning fiction and reality.

White makes explicit the connection between race and gender in relaying Mimi's experiences as a dispossessed single mother in Philadelphia:

> Life for any woman who was unprotected and who sought to live up to certain ideals was hard. But when that woman was colored she was more than ever at the mercy of those who were her constant pursuers. She found her old race-consciousness surging up again.
>
> (169)

The clichéd tone of a "woman unprotected" does not suggest that in marriage or dependence Mimi will find life easier; rather, Mimi is able to overcome the obstacles precisely by asserting herself against those who sought to protect her. For example, her father, Jean, and lover, Carl, both try to encourage her to think and act independently and give her many books to read, but both, with "elaborate indirection" (172), keep the writings of Walt Whitman from her. Later, when poverty-stricken and in despair Mimi indulges in a copy of *Leaves of Grass,* "the words gave her a comforting sense of direction" (173), presumably because Whitman sings of the autonomy of the individual. Similarly, when Mimi finds herself pregnant, everyone she speaks to insists that she must be married; Mimi's steadfast refusal leads her to many hardships, but it also allows her to develop an independent sense of self. Indeed, after leaving Atlanta pregnant and alone, she realizes that "[g]one was a sense of being a depraved, a disgrace, a low creature. . . . She was free! Free! Free!" (158). Although this sense of absolute freedom ultimately proves falsely conceived, Mimi still does escape some of the societal constraints which prevent her from asserting any individuality. One way in which she protects this freedom is, ironically, by buying herself a wedding ring in a pawnshop. The ring allows her to avoid the questions and prohibitions which would limit her freedom; thus, she creatively uses patriarchal assumptions to resist restrictions of her patriarchal society.

White inverts traditional imagery of freedom most obviously when Mimi's "old race-consciousness surges up" (169) in the novel. Her black self, far from being associated with an enslaved, downtrodden people, is, in fact, what allows her to overcome the restrictions she faces. Early in the novel, before Mimi has developed her own race consciousness, her father describes her black ancestry, asserting, "I'm telling you, for when you run up against hard situations later on in life—and we all do—the knowledge of what's back of you will give you strength and courage" (38). When Mimi hears jazz music at a nightclub, Mimi understands that the notes reflect "a freedom from inhibition" (97). All of these assertions of the authenticity of black culture and the strength and pride available to those who embrace their black heritage would seem to place ***Flight*** within a category—identified by Judith Berzon—of black-authored novels about passing which offer "the lesson that happiness is the reward of those mulattoes who remain within or return to the Negro group."[9] But ***Flight*** denies the reader that comfortably righteous position because Mimi passes not to find freedom as a white woman, but to escape persecution from the black community. When her life is destabilized in New York City after a visitor from Atlanta rejects her as a single mother of questionable moral character, she feels that passing as white (or, more accurately, passing over to a white identity) is her only alternative. She does so with great resentment, because, unlike other passers who deny their black heritage, Mimi takes enormous pride in hers and "her passing from the race seemed to Mimi persecution greater than any white people had ever visited upon coloured people—the very intolerance of her own people had driven her from them" (212).

This is not the first time a self-righteous black bourgeoisie receives harsh censure in the novel. Mimi's shallow and self-righteous stepmother belongs to the Fleur-de-Lis social club, "where none of the women have a complexion darker than a light brown" (48). Earlier Jean had expressed his dissatisfaction with Atlanta's black middle class, decrying, "Here are these coloured people with the gifts from God of laughter and song and creative instincts . . . and what are they doing with it? They are aping the white man—becoming a race of money-grubbers with ledgers and money tills for brains and Shylock hearts" (54). Jean's own essentialism and conflicted attitudes towards race contribute to Mimi's confusion. During her early reflections about race, she ponders with bewilderment "sharp, unchanging lines which seemed to matter with extraordinary power" (54) drawn by white and, more disturbingly, black society. As the narrator observes, "She was too young and inexperienced to realize that these people were in a large part the victims of a system which made colour and hair texture and race a fetish" (55). This fetishization of physical characteristics is shown as a way of reducing the individual to merely an exemplum, and ultimately this tendency is the primary object of White's critique in ***Flight.*** That the African American can be treated as an "exemplum of the subhuman" is the most extreme consequence of a dehumanizing modern society, but in the biracial Mimi we are shown how these attitudes can destroy both the black and the white individual.

Throughout the novel, two principal image patterns recur. From the beginning an authentic engagement with the organic world is contrasted with the mechanistic existence of American capitalistic pursuits. Secondly, Mimi's response to the dehumanizing environment is to fictionalize her life, to imagine she is writing a novel or watching a film. She reduces momentous events in her life to mere chapters in a book. Further, she often avoids confronting that which is unpleasant by taking "flight" from the vital and taking the position of observer of her own unfolding drama. White develops neither the imagery of mechanization nor that of flight from a disturbing reality in a particularly subtle way. However, taken together, these images do further evidence the text's rather subversive attitude towards race. Early in the novel, Jean observes for Mimi that

> the world's gone mad over power and wealth. The strongest man wins, not the most decent or the most intelligent or the best. All the old virtues of comradeship and art and literature and philosophy, in short, all the refinements of life are being swallowed up in this monster, the Machine, we are creating which is slowly but surely making us mere automatons, dancing like marionettes when the machine pulls strings and bids us dance.
>
> (54)

Jean concludes that someday Mimi, after his death, may think back to the day and concur with his assessment. White, then, repeats the imagery throughout the novel, but only in the final chapters while Mimi is married to the blantantly racist Jimmie Forrester does she start to share her father's views on a conscious level.

The connections between Jean's pronouncements and both Marxist thought and Naturalist writing are rather self-evident, but White makes the connections even more clear by having Jimmie tell Mimi that her pessimism comes from "reading these stories by fellows like Dreiser and Sinclair Lewis—I told you they'd make you unhappy . . . they're always picking flaws in the best civilization the world's seen" (265). Jimmie instead recommends Lothrop Stoddard[10] and defends his civilization's defenders such as the Ku Klux Klan.

Since Mimi cannot alter Jimmie's attitudes and cannot reconcile being his wife with her now hidden but still strongly felt black identity, she retreats to her habit of viewing her life as if she were a detached observer. This is a common trope in "passing" literature, where the passer must bury her/his own individuality so deeply that she/he feels uninvolved in her/his own existence; for example, James Weldon Johnson's unnamed narrator in *The Autobiography of an Ex-Coloured Man* asserts from a detached distance that his life is "a curious study to me" and confesses to a "sort of savage and diabolical desire to gather up all the little tragedies of my life, and turn them into a practical joke on society."[11] Similarly, Mimi repeatedly reflects on her life as if it is a film she is watching or a book she is reading, not realizing that this too strips her of her humanity. She sympathizes with the factory worker turned into the "mere tender of a dehumanizing machine" (269) and is appalled by how Jimmie and his uppercrust friends have become so caught up in social roles that they become "cogs in a machine . . . a machine of which they are intensely proud of which they think they are masters. Instead, ironically enough, the machine has mastered them and they must do its bidding" (268). Nonetheless, Mimi herself lives such a circumscribed life that she too is left bereft of human desire or emotion. After she starts passing we are told that "she has been tempted—sorely tempted—'to yield to one hour of glorious strife'—to find relief in some folly, some wild breaking of the bands which bound her with terrific solidity" (237), but Mimi never gives in to these temptations. Even when she marries Jimmie she retains tight control over her emotions and over how her story will be understood by those with whom she comes in contact.

In the concluding chapter, Mimi leaves Jimmie and returns to the black community and her own black identity. The authenticity of this community, compared with Jimmie's capitalism, has been established through contrasting scenes of characters responding to music. At a "very smart and very expensive nightclub," she watches her high-society friends as they "grimly went about the task of acquiring pleasure, their faces set in hard, nervous lines" (267). She tells Jimmie that they dance "as though they were saying: This night is costing me a couple of hundred dollars and I *will* get a couple of hundred dollars' worth of fun out of it" (267). This, of course, contrasts with the "freedom from inhibition" that she had earlier observed in the disreputable jazz nightclub and, more directly, with the epiphanic scene in the book's climax, where she listens to a singer (clearly modelled after Paul Robeson) at Carnegie Hall who sings "songs of his own people," and the notes are "soothing, comforting, they brought peace and rest and happiness" (297). This concert leads Mimi to realize that she must leave Jimmie and return to the authentic life of her own people.

But here again White refuses to let the clichés he has so carefully explored (white industrial culture equals dehumanization; black folk culture equals authenticity) be accepted simplistically. Mimi's final "flight" away from Jimmie is not clearly different from her early flights away from difficulties. Once again she is removing herself from the vital sphere into an aesthetic world of self-fictionalization, where the real-world narratives of race and gender no longer restrict her. As she listens to the soothing, comforting sounds, she feels "all worries, all lines of sex and class and race melting the heterogeneous throng into a perfect unity" (297).[12] She then has thoughts of her African ancestry and her slave heritage, and realizes that "whatever other faults they might possess her own people had not been deadened and dehumanized by bitter hatred of their fellowmen" (299). In returning to "her own people," Mimi is undoubtedly choosing the better path, but she does not necessarily move to the sort of complete happiness and autonomy that she imagines when in the final paragraph she again cries "Free! Free!" (300). Those words are a refrain that has occurred throughout the book and each time Mimi's sense of utter freedom has proven false.

Mimi can never be completely free because she remains both black and white in a society that insists she must be one or the other. Her story concludes in sharp contrast to that of the protagonist of Johnson's *The Autobiography of an Ex-Coloured Man.* He ends within white society feeling that he "[has] sold [his] birthright for a mess of pottage";[13] Mimi reclaims her birthright but at the expense of living in an idealized fictional world where she must deny a part of her identity and, moreover, willfully remain oblivious to that denial. What can one make of the imagery in the novel's final sentence?

> "*Petit Jean*[14]—my own people—and happiness!" was the song in her heart as she happily strode through the dawn, the rays of the morning sun dancing lightly upon the more brillant gold of her hair. . . .
>
> (300)

The language too closely reflects other occasions of Mimi's self-delusion, and the novel owes too much to the earlier-alluded-to Dreiser and Lewis to accept this utopian ending uncritically. By stressing the often fetishized "brilliant gold of her hair" in the final phrase, White is perhaps again drawing attention to the instability of societal structures of race. Undoubtedly, Mimi has embarked on a course that will allow her better opportunity for genuine self-expression, but her society will never allow her the perfect freedom she finds only by removing herself from her life through music or by relating to her own life as a work of art. White's choosing to conclude with an ellipsis perhaps best illustrates my assertion that Mimi's story will not fit into any of the maps of race (or literary studies) we have thus far developed. Rather, the story must continue to be told, rearticulated—but never concluded. In ***A Man Called White,*** White began assertively "I am a Negro"; yet that book concludes:

> I am white and I am black, and know that there is no difference. Each casts a shadow and all shadows are dark.
>
> (366)

Like the ellipsis, the shadow conceals, but in concealing makes a claim that there is more that remains unseen or unspoken, and ultimately unmappable.

The foregoing reading of ***Flight*** would be impossible if it were not informed by the critical discourse that Shelly Fisher Fishkin catalogues in "Interrogating 'Whiteness,' Complicating 'Blackness': Remapping American Culture," a discourse to which she has made valuable contributions. But it remains a discourse generated within an America where discussions about race remain shadowed by unexamined assumptions, some almost certainly so deeply ingrained that we still fail to recognize them. Passing literature offers a particularly fruitful site for examination of those assumptions by foregrounding the impossibility of any definitive determinations of race. Perhaps we are moving to a time when the question "Was Huck black?" will not generate such heated debate, because when the question is understood to mean "Was the development of Huck fundamentally influenced by African-American culture?" the answer would have to be "Of course, Huck is black and Hester and Ishmael, and Gatsby, and Scarlett, and Bigger, and Slothrop, and Beloved are also black." As Fishkin's work makes clear, literary criticism which remains bound by the same binary oppositions of race as the society which produces them will fail to advance our understanding of the complexity of racial experience in America.

This is not to suggest that studies, programs, and departments in African-American culture are not in themselves extremely important. They have been and will continue to be absolutely essential in developing the perspectives that move American Studies forward. Further, those of us fortunate enough to be able to teach courses in African-American literature have had the opportunity to develop our and our students' understanding through works unavailable to scholars even a generation ago. Similarly, American literature courses have been enriched immeasurably by the new texts available to us and the new ways of understanding those texts, which critics continue to develop. But the shadows remain. Our criticism must, as Fishkin asserts, "examine how an unequal distribution not of talent, but of power allowed a patently false monocultural myth to mask and distort a multicultural reality" (276). But we do come with perspectives, maps, which to some extent predetermine our conclusions. Only if we acknowledge that our vision too remains in the shadow, that any maps we draw will inevitably be dismissed by later cultural cartographers, will we avoid becoming like Mimi Daquin, optimistically deluding ourselves that we are "Free! Free! Free!" as we move towards a future that remains uncertain and threatening.

Notes

1. Shelley Fisher Fishkin, "Interrogating 'Whiteness,' Complicating 'Blackness': Remapping American Culture," *Criticism and the Color Line: Desegregating American Literary Studies,* ed. Henry B. Wonham (New Brunswick, New Jersey: Rutgers UP, 1996) 275. Hereafter cited parenthetically in the text.
2. Shelley Fisher Fishkin, *Was Huck Black?: Mark Twain and African-American Voices* (New York: Oxford UP, 1993) 251.
3. Walter White, *A Man Called White* (New York: Viking, 1948) 3. Hereafter cited parenthetically in the text.
4. David Lewis Levering, *When Harlem Was in Vogue* (New York: Knopf, 1981) 143.
5. The resurgence of interest in Larsen evidences renewed critical attention paid both to the writings of the Harlem Renaissance and to the genre of "passing" literature; however, *Flight* still remains largely ignored. See Jacquelyn McLendon's *The Politics of Color in the Fiction of Jessie Fausset and Nella Larsen* for a good bibliography of writings about Larsen.
6. To briefly summarize some important details of the plot of *Flight:* Mimi Daquin is a Creole born in New Orleans to light-skinned black parents. When the novel opens, the thirteen-year-old Mimi's mother has died and Mimi and her father, Jean, are arriving in Atlanta with Mimi's stepmother to start a new life. The novel follows through Mimi's adolescence until soon after she finishes high school. Her father dies and Mimi finds herself unmarried and pregnant. Refusing to get married, Mimi travels to Philadelphia alone and struggles to raise her child alone. Eventually, she accepts that she must temporarily put the baby in an orphanage and moves to New York, where she is introduced to black society by Jean's sister, Aunt Sophie. However, when a woman from Atlanta sees Mimi and spreads rumors about her past, Mimi feels outcast in black society and passes as white, eventually becoming an extremely successful dressmaker. Years later, she marries Jimmie Forrester, who turns out to be a blatant racist, and as the novel concludes, she is leaving Jimmie to return to "her own people" in the black community.
7. Walter White, *Flight* (New York: Knopf, 1926) 77. Hereafter cited parenthetically in the text.
8. A colleague has pointed out to me that my own dismissal of melodrama judges in precisely the manner that this paper argues critics must vigilantly examine. Literary criticism's aversion to melodrama is itself an expression of our hierarchical construction of standards of value.
9. Judith Berzon, *Neither White Nor Black: The Mulatto Character in American Fiction* (New York: New York UP, 1978) 159.
10. Stoddard is the same racist pseudoscientist whose *The Rise of the Colored Empires* Tom Buchanan quotes (misremembering the name of Goddard) in *The Great Gatsby.*
11. James Weldon Johnson, *The Autobiography of an Ex-Coloured Man,* in *Three Negro Classics,* introd. John Hope Franklin (New York: Avon, 1965) 393.
12. These aesthetic moments of complete harmony seem similar to the moments of perfect order found in the contemporaneous modernist works of authors such as Virginia Woolf and James Joyce.
13. Johnson 511.
14. "Petit Jean" is Mimi's child, whom she had to give up in order to pass as white. Given my comparatively narrow focus, I have ignored Mimi's relationship with her son, but any thorough study of the novel would have to explore the ways in which Mimi is positioned as "mother" in the text. Both in the black and white communities, Mimi must "pass" as a woman with no children, and this denial is certainly as painful as any of the other denials she must make about herself.

Rope and Faggot

MELVIN J. HERSKOVITS (ESSAY DATE 1929)

SOURCE: Herskovits, Melvin J. "Lynching, an American Pastime." *The Nation* CXXVIII (15 May 1929): 588.

In the following excerpt, Herskovits argues that the restrained analytical approach and use of scientific evidence employed by White in Rope and Faggot *is inappropriate to the passionate subject of the work.*

[We] wonder if Mr. White's restrained treatment of his theme meets the purpose of his book [***Rope and Faggot***].

Certainly no one is more competent than Mr. White to tell of the phenomenon of lynching, especially when it has to do with Negroes. . . . In his reports and in one of his novels he has given the theme the stark treatment it deserves, making his reader blaze with indignation at the sheer barbarity he describes. But in this book there is relatively little of the passionate protest for which we hope. There is, rather, a calm, measured analysis which, while convincing, is obviously not Mr. White's forte. And the book he has produced suffers because of his academic approach. I realize that had Mr. White written with the feeling of which he is capable he would be condemned by some for not being sufficiently dispassionate. Yet Judge Lynch is a ruffian, and is not to be handled with kid gloves.

The book, therefore, must be discussed as an analytical treatment of lynching rather than as an emotional protest against it. And as such it has many excellent pages. The second chapter, which treats of the extent to which lynching occurs, is most revealing and cites several striking cases. Taken in connection with the statistical appendix it affords a mine of factual material for those who wish to know the facts. The consideration of the relation between lynching and its economic background is a demonstration of the grasp of the subject which Mr. White possesses. The chapter entitled "The Price of Lynching" is another of the brilliant sections which this work contains. And the digest of what has been done to stem the tide of lynching through legal enactment is readable and useful. Nor does Mr. White end on a false note of optimism. He is, above all, a realist, and he is sufficiently tough-minded to face the situation in all its grayness of outlook.

Some of the reasoning in other chapters, I must confess, I cannot follow. I do not believe that a statement such as this can be substantiated: "It is exceedingly doubtful lynching could possibly exist under any other religion than Christianity." If this hypothesis can be maintained it should hold true at least for all Christian sects, and not only for the Baptists and Methodists, as Mr. White claims. This statement, the thesis of an entire chapter, seems to me to be too simplistic to be acceptable, and to this extent it weakens the general argument of the book. In a similar way the chapter in which Judge Lynch is psychoanalyzed seems to me to contain a theoretical approach which pushed much farther than our present knowledge allows. That there is a sex element present in the sadistic performances with which those who have gone into the account of lynchings are familiar, must be admitted; but to make this a basic cause throws the picture out of focus.

The chapter which is entitled "Science, Nordicism, and Lynching," I think is ill-advised For one thing, too much old material is rehandled. Must one read again of Bean's study of brain-weight of Negroes and whites and Mall's refutation of it? Must the army psychological tests once more be refuted? These have been discussed so often that I do not see that they need be repeated here, where they are literally brought in by main force and where they have little to do with the main subject of the book. If Mr. White wished to discuss theories of racial inferiority and superiority, he should have found at least some of the fresh work that has recently been done. Instead, he has relied on frayed secondary sources and, as a result, gives us only these well-worn accounts.

However, Mr. White does not claim to be an expert in the fields of religious psychology, psychoanalysis, or comparative anatomy. He has fought too courageously and too intelligently against Judge Lynch for us to carp at him for these chapters in his book. There is in it much considered presentation of the highest order; there are many facts which we all should know; and there is a point of view that is healthy, sane, and desirable.

A Rising Wind

JOHN DESMOND (REVIEW DATE 1945)

SOURCE: Desmond, John. "Reporting on Our Negro Troops Overseas." *The New York Times Book Review* (4 March 1945): 3.

In the following excerpt, Desmond discusses the findings of White's study A Rising Wind.

At the last counting there were 701,678 Negroes in the United States Army. Of these 411,368 were overseas; the rest were scattered at various stations in the United States. Only a few of the troops overseas had seen active combat duty. Those who had—like the Ninety-ninth Pursuit Squadron of the MAAF of the Ninety-second Infantry in Italy—had made combat records comparable to their white fellow-soldiers. But in the Negroes' eyes these had been few in proportion to the number of Negroes in uniform. This "discrimination" has been the subject of study by numerous observers. . . .

One such study is offered in [***A Rising Wind,***] Walter White's survey of the conditions of Negro troops in England, Africa and Italy. Mr. White went overseas with the consent and active cooperation of the American High Command. He had an excellent opportunity to observe the relations between Negroes and whites in their billets and, in England at least, the relations between Negroes and the native white population. This book is a report on those observations. For the most part it is a pulling together and an elucidation of information that has trickled back to this country in the form of newspaper accounts and letters from soldiers.

In brief it adds up to this: that much of the racial discrimination that is an unfortunate part of American life has been exported to England and other war theaters; that many white Americans, despite the many changes that war has brought them, have not altered greatly in their racial thinking; and that, in a more hopeful vein, there has been, particularly among enlisted men, a noticeable letting down of racial bars.

In evaluating these observations Mr. White discouragingly points out that the first two represent conditions that are fairly constant, while the third exists chiefly in combat areas where men are drawn into close interdependence by the presence of danger. They prompted him to plead the more fervently with American military authorities to assign greater numbers of Negroes to first-line divisions. In this quest, he gratefully comments, he found many Army officers, from General Eisenhower down, sympathetic and helpful.

Mr. White concedes that it is too late in this war to change the patterns of the Army and Navy in such a way as to hasten a solution of the post-war problem. But he reminds us that Negro soldiers and sailors who have served in the uniforms of the United States in the various war theatres will not be content to return to the old way of life in the post-war era. . . .

How white America meets this challenge, Mr. White implies, may well determine the stability and durability of the peace. He points out, as have many other commentators, that the Negro problem is no longer exclusively American. In a world in which the so-called "white races" are in the minority, Mr. White reminds us, the non-whites will regard our relations among fellow-Americans as an earnest of our intentions toward the people of China, India and Africa. It is a challenge that cannot be sidestepped. Mr. White's reasoned and reserved contribution to it deserves to be read by all. . . .

A Man Called White

ANNE L. GOODMAN (ESSAY DATE 1948)

SOURCE: Goodman, Anne L. "Blockade Runner." *The New Republic* 119, no. 16 (18 October 1948): 23-4.

In the following excerpt, Goodman praises A Man Called White, *citing its vivid insight into the problem of American racial oppression.*

[***A Man Called White***] is both autobiography and a study of the Negro problem in America written from a peculiar vantage point. Walter White, as he makes clear in his opening paragraph, could pass anywhere for a white man.

At the same time, and despite the ugly experience in his youth that first forced the fact of his race upon him, he has, it seems obvious, been spared some of the worst humiliations of the Negro—the slights from casually encountered strangers, the omnipresent fact of a black skin and the awareness of it everywhere: in a store, restaurant, theatre, subway. White has moved between two worlds, consciously a member of the one but able to pass at will into the other without the constant, choking resentment of the unmistakable Negro, to whom no choice is offered.

The advantages of this have been a self-confidence, apparent in his writing, and a perspective that enables him to see the attitude of the white man to the Negro as well as the reverse, and the wider problem of prejudice . . . .

White relates his experiences in an easy and readable manner, but his facts, not his writing, give the book its force. However familiar the details of American race prejudice during the last thirty years may be, this factual, personal recapitulation of them comes with a new shock. That the struggle White describes is one of the most important parts of the most important struggle in America today—the struggle to realize as well as to preserve the democracy we boast of—seems self-evident . . . .

Perhaps the most shocking evidence in White's book appears in the later chapters which recount the postwar maimings and lynchings of Negro veterans. We have read of them before, but seldom in such detail and without other distracting news of the cold war and the rising cost of living, which has helped to hide their real significance

In conclusion, White lists recent advances on behalf of the Negro, achievements which "would have seemed to most Negroes only a dream of the millennium even twenty-five years ago." If they seem pitifully weak when weighed against the evidence on the other side, they still cannot be overlooked . . . . The NAACP's battle is far from won, but White seems to suggest, there are signs that we approach the turning point.

FURTHER READING

Biographies

Cannon, Poppy. *A Gentle Knight, My Husband Walter White.* New York: Rinehart, 1956, 337 p.

Reflections by White's second wife about her husband and interracial marriage.

Fraser, Jane. *Walter White.* New York: Chelsea House, 1991, 111 p.

Detailed biography of White written for young adults emphasizing his role as a civil rights leader; includes photographs and a bibliography.

Nelson, Emmanuel S. "Walter White (1893-1955)." In *African American Authors, 1745-1945: A Bio-Bibliographical Critical Sourcebook,* edited by Emmanuel S. Nelson, pp. 469-73. Westport, Conn.: Greenwood Publishing, 2000.

Presents a biography and brief overview of White's works and reputation.

Salters, George K. R. "Walter White." *Crisis* 96, no. 1 (January 1989): 53.

Profile of White in his role as executive secretary of the NAACP from 1931 to 1955.

Waldron, Edward E. *Walter White and the Harlem Renaissance.* Port Washington, N.Y.: Kennikat Press, 1978, 185 p.

Biography and study of individual works supporting White's position as a central figure in the Harlem Renaissance.

Criticism

Cooney, Charles F. "Walter White and Sinclair Lewis: The History of a Literary Friendship." *Prospects: Annual of American Cultural Studies* 1 (1975): 63-79.

Discusses the relationship between White and Lewis, which lasted for nearly a quarter of a century and was reflected in Lewis's work.

Montagu, M. F. Ashley. Review of *A Rising Wind. Psychiatry* 8 (November 1996): 8.

Favorable review stating that White's calm tone adds force to his message.

Scruggs, Charles W. "Alain Locke and Walter White: Their Struggle for Control of the Harlem Renaissance." *Black American Literature Forum* 14 (1980): 91-9.

Argues that White and Locke challenged one another for leadership of the Harlem Renaissance and shows that the system of patronage and the publishing environment for black writers were more complicated than previously thought.

Suggs, Jon Christian. "'Blackjack': Walter White and Modernism in an Unknown Boxing Novel." *Michigan Quarterly Review* 38, no. 4 (1999): 515-40.

Examines the manuscript of White's unpublished novel about a black boxer.

OTHER SOURCES FROM GALE:

Additional coverage of White's life and career is contained in the following sources published by the Gale Group: *Black Literature Criticism,* Vol. 3; *Black Writers,* Ed. 1; *Contemporary Authors,* Vol. 124; *Contemporary Authors - Brief Entry,* Vol. 115; *Dictionary of Literary Biography,* Vol. 51; *DISCovering Authors Modules: Multicultural Authors*; and *Twentieth-Century Literary Criticism,* Vol. 15.

INDEXES

The main reference

Hughes, (James) Langston (1902-1967) **1:** 24, 82, 87, 91-92, 94, 124, 176, 191, 215, 253, 257, 279, 281-282, 284-285, 288, 307, 321-325, 348-363, 438-443, 442-443; **2:** 69, 171, 373, 413, **595-646,** 652; **3:** 5, 39, 144, 199, 281, 282, 290, 296, 299, 315, 347-348, 390-391, 413, 482, 593-594

lists the featured author's entry in either volume 2 or 3 of Harlem Renaissance; *it also lists commentary on the featured author in other author entries and in volume 1, which includes topics associated with the Harlem Renaissance. Page references to substantial discussions of the author appear in boldface.*

The cross-references

See also AAYA 12; AFAW 1, 2; AMWR 1; AMWS 1; BLC 2; BW 1, 3; CA 1-4R; 25-28R; CANR 1, 34, 82; CDALB 1929-1941; CLC 1, 5, 10, 15, 35, 44, 108; CLR 17; DA; DA3; DAB; DAC; DAM DRAM, MST, MULT, POET; DC 3; DLB 4, 7, 48, 51, 86, 228; EXPP; EXPS; JRDA; LAIT 3; MAICYA 1, 2; MTCW 1, 2; PAB; PC 1; PFS 1, 3, 6, 10; RGAL 4; RGSF 2; SATA 4, 33; SSC 6; SSFS 4, 7; WCH; WLC; WP; YAW

list entries on the author in the following Gale biographical and literary sources:

AAL: Asian American Literature
AAYA: Authors & Artists for Young Adults
AFAW: African American Writers
AFW: African Writers
AITN: Authors in the News
AMW: American Writers
AMWR: American Writers Retrospective Supplement
AMWS: American Writers Supplement
ANW: American Nature Writers
AW: Ancient Writers
BEST: Bestsellers (quarterly, citations appear as Year: Issue number)
BLC: Black Literature Criticism
BLCS: Black Literature Criticism Supplement
BPFB: Beacham's Encyclopedia of Popular Fiction: Biography and Resources
BRW: British Writers
BRWS: British Writers Supplement
BW: Black Writers
BYA: Beacham's Guide to Literature for Young Adults
CA: Contemporary Authors
CAAS: Contemporary Authors Autobiography Series
CABS: Contemporary Authors Bibliographical Series
CAD: Contemporary American Dramatists
CANR: Contemporary Authors New Revision Series
CAP: Contemporary Authors Permanent Series
CBD: Contemporary British Dramatists
CCA: Contemporary Canadian Authors
CD: Contemporary Dramatists
CDALB: Concise Dictionary of American Literary Biography
CDALBS: Concise Dictionary of American Literary Biography Supplement
CDBLB: Concise Dictionary of British Literary Biography
CLC: Contemporary Literary Criticism
CLR: Children's Literature Review
CMLC: Classical and Medieval Literature Criticism
CMW: St. James Guide to Crime & Mystery Writers
CN: Contemporary Novelists
CP: Contemporary Poets
CPW: Contemporary Popular Writers
CSW: Contemporary Southern Writers
CWD: Contemporary Women Dramatists
CWP: Contemporary Women Poets
CWRI: St. James Guide to Children's Writers
CWW: Contemporary World Writers
DA: DISCovering Authors
DA3: DISCovering Authors 3.0
DAB: DISCovering Authors: British Edition
DAC: DISCovering Authors: Canadian Edition
DAM: DISCovering Authors: Modules
  DRAM: Dramatists Module; *MST:* Most-Studied Authors Module;
  MULT: Multicultural Authors Module; *NOV:* Novelists Module;
  POET: Poets Module; *POP:* Popular Fiction and Genre Authors Module
DC: Drama Criticism
DFS: Drama for Students
DLB: Dictionary of Literary Biography
DLBD: Dictionary of Literary Biography Documentary Series
DLBY: Dictionary of Literary Biography Yearbook
DNFS: Literature of Developing Nations for Students
EFS: Epics for Students
EXPN: Exploring Novels

EXPP: Exploring Poetry
EXPS: Exploring Short Stories
EW: European Writers
FANT: St. James Guide to Fantasy Writers
FW: Feminist Writers
GFL: Guide to French Literature, Beginnings to 1789, 1798 to the Present
GLL: Gay and Lesbian Literature
HGG: St. James Guide to Horror, Ghost & Gothic Writers
HLC: Hispanic Literature Criticism
HLCS: Hispanic Literature Criticism Supplement
HW: Hispanic Writers
IDFW: International Dictionary of Films and Filmmakers: Writers and Production Artists
IDTP: International Dictionary of Theatre: Playwrights
LAIT: Literature and Its Times
LAW: Latin American Writers
JRDA: Junior DISCovering Authors
LC: Literature Criticism from 1400 to 1800
MAICYA: Major Authors and Illustrators for Children and Young Adults
MAICYA: Major Authors and Illustrators for Children and Young Adults Supplement
MAWW: Modern American Women Writers
MJW: Modern Japanese Writers
MTCW: Major 20th-Century Writers
NCFS: Nonfiction Classics for Students
NCLC: Nineteenth-Century Literature Criticism
NFS: Novels for Students
NNAL: Native North American Literature
PAB: Poets: American and British
PC: Poetry Criticism
PFS: Poetry for Students
RGAL: Reference Guide to American Literature
RGEL: Reference Guide to English Literature
RGSF: Reference Guide to Short Fiction
RGWL: Reference Guide to World Literature
RHW: Twentieth-Century Romance and Historical Writers
SAAS: Something about the Author Autobiography Series
SATA: Something about the Author
SFW: St. James Guide to Science Fiction Writers
SSC: Short Story Criticism
SSFS: Short Stories for Students
TCLC: Twentieth-Century Literary Criticism
TCWW: Twentieth-Century Western Writers
WCH: Writers for Children
WLC: World Literature Criticism, 1500 to the Present
WLCS: World Literature Criticism Supplement
WLIT: World Literature and Its Times
WP: World Poets
YABC: Yesterday's Authors of Books for Children
YAW: St. James Guide to Young Adult Writers

AUTHOR INDEX

The Author Index lists all of the authors featured in the Harlem Renaissance *set. It includes references to the main author entries in volumes 2 and 3; it also lists commentary on the featured author in other author entries and in volume 1, which includes topics associated with the Harlem Renaissance. Page references to author entries appear in boldface. The Author Index also includes birth and death dates, cross references between pseudonyms or name variants and actual names, and cross references to other Gale series in which the authors have appeared. A complete list of these sources is found facing the first page of the Author Index.*

B

Bennett, Gwendolyn B. (1902-1981) **1:** 86, 262, 324; **2: 1–34; 3:** 7, 160
See also BW 1; CA 125; DLB 51; WP

Bonner, Marita (1898-1971) **1:** 122–125, 391–392; **2: 35–59**
See also BW 2; CA 142; DFS 13; DLB 51, 228

Bontemps, Arna(ud Wendell) (1902-1973) **1:** 254, 312; **2: 61–103,** 222, 613–614; **3:** 395
See also BLC 1; BW 1; CA 1-4R; 41-44R; CANR 4, 35; CLC 1, 18; CLR 6; CWRI 5; DA3; DAM MULT, NOV, POET; DLB 48, 51; JRDA; MAICYA 1, 2; MTCW 1, 2; SATA 2, 44; SATA-Obit 24; WCH; WP

Braithwaite, William Stanley (Beaumont) (1878-1962) **1:** 293; **2: 105–143; 3:** 26, 47, 49, 133–137, 187–191
See also BLC 1; BW 1; CA 125; DAM MULT; DLB 50, 54

Brown, Sterling Allen (1901-1989) **1:** 84, 85, 87, 125–126, 214; **2: 145–203; 3:** 161–162, 291
See also AFAW 1, 2; BLC 1; BW 1, 3; CA 85-88; 127; CANR 26; CLC 1, 23, 59; DA3; DAM MULT, POET; DLB 48, 51, 63; MTCW 1, 2; RGAL 4; WP

Bruce, Richard
See Nugent, Richard Bruce

C

Casey, Patrick
See Thurman, Wallace

Christopher, Mary
See West, Dorothy

Cullen, Countee (1903-1946) **1:** 67, 77–78, 258, 276–278, 280, 295–297, 321, 324; **2:** 25, **205–258,** 589–590, 612, 633–634; **3:** 4–5, 130–133, 528, 585–586, 596–598
See also AFAW 2; AMWS 4; BLC 1; BW 1; CA 108; 124; CDALB 1917-1929; DA; DA3; DAC; DAM MST, MULT, POET; DLB 4, 48, 51; EXPP; MTCW 1, 2; PC 20; PFS 3; RGAL 4; SATA 18; TCLC 4, 37; WLCS; WP

D

Du Bois, W(illiam) E(dward) B(urghardt) (1868-1963) **1:** 22, 45, 67–68, 119, 157–158, 163, 182, 192, 220, 236–239, 249–252, 305, 316–318, 319, 324, 330–334, 335-336, 337, 388–392, 456–459, 489–490, 518–519, 545–546, 552; **2:** 83, 84–85, 132–133, 238, **259–321,** 444–445, 445, 472–473, 609; **3:** 4, 19, 26, 38, 254, 315, 322, 324, 341–345, 409, 414, 482, 488, 509, 522
See also AAYA 40; AFAW 1, 2; AMWS 2; BLC 1; BW 1, 3; CA 85-88; CANR 34, 82; CDALB 1865-1917; CLC 1, 2, 13, 64, 96; DA; DA3; DAC; DAM MST, MULT, NOV; DLB 47, 50, 91,

N

O

P

R

S

T

V

W

TITLE INDEX

The Title Index alphabetically lists the titles of works written by the authors featured in volumes 2 and 3 of Harlem Renaissance *and provides page numbers or page ranges where commentary on these titles can be found. English translations of foreign titles and variations of titles are cross referenced to the title under which a work was originally published. Titles of novels, dramas, nonfiction books, and poetry, short story, or essay collections are printed in italics; individual poems, short stories, and essays are printed in body type within quotation marks.*

A

B

C

D

E

F

G

H

I

O

P

Q

R

S

T

U

V

W

Y

SUBJECT INDEX

The Subject Index includes the authors and titles that appear in the Author Index and the Title Index as well as the names of other authors and figures that are discussed in the Harlem Renaissance *set. The Subject Index also lists literary terms and topics covered in the criticism. The index provides page numbers or page ranges where subjects are discussed and is fully cross referenced. Page references to significant discussions of authors, titles, or subjects appear in boldface; page references to illustrations appear in italic.*

A

B

C

D

E

F

G

SUBJECT INDEX

H

I

J

K

L

M

SUBJECT INDEX

N

O

P

Q

R

S

T

U

V

W

Y

Z

GERMANNA COMM COLLEGE LOCUST GROVE VA
3 7218 000 174 917